Handbook of
SOCIOLOGY

Handbook of
SOCIOLOGY

Neil J. Smelser
EDITOR

SAGE PUBLICATIONS
THE PUBLISHERS OF PROFESSIONAL SOCIAL SCIENCE
Newbury Park   Beverly Hills   London   New Delhi

For information address:

SAGE Publications, Inc.
2111 West Hillcrest Drive
Newbury Park, California 91320

SAGE Publications Inc.
275 South Beverly Drive
Beverly Hills
California 90212

SAGE Publications Ltd.
28 Banner Street
London EC1Y 8QE
England

SAGE PUBLICATIONS India Pvt. Ltd.
M-32 Market
Greater Kailash I
New Delhi 110 048 India

Library of Congress Cataloging-in-Publication Data

The Handbook of sociology / edited by Neil J. Smelser
    p.   cm.
    Bibliography: p.
    Includes index.
    ISBN 0-8039-2665-0
    1. Sociology. I. Smelser, Neil J.
HM51.H249 1988   87-36762
301—dc19   CIP

FIRST PRINTING 1988
PRINTED IN THE UNITED STATES OF AMERICA

Book Design by Sidney Solomon

Contents

Acknowledgments   7

Introduction   9
    NEIL J. SMELSER

I.
THEORETICAL
AND METHODOLOGICAL ISSUES

1. Toward a Disciplinary Matrix in Sociology   23
    WALTER L. WALLACE

2. The New Theoretical Movement   77
    JEFFREY C. ALEXANDER

3. Social Structure   103
    NEIL J. SMELSER

4. On Sociological Data   131
    PETER H. ROSSI

5. Causal Inference for Sociological Data   155
    RICHARD A. BERK

II.
BASES OF INEQUALITY
IN SOCIETY

6. Inequality and Labor Processes   175
    MARK GRANOVETTER △ CHARLES TILLY

7. Race and Ethnicity   223
    KATHERINE O'SULLIVAN SEE △ WILLIAM J. WILSON

8. Sociology of Age   243
    MATILDA WHITE RILEY △ ANNE FONER △ JOAN WARING

9. Gender and Sex Roles   291
    JANET Z. GIELE

III.
MAJOR INSTITUTIONAL
AND ORGANIZATIONAL SETTINGS

10. *Jobs and Work*   327
    JOANNE MILLER

11. *Environments and Organizations*   361
    HOWARD E. ALDRICH △ PETER V. MARSDEN

12. *Political Sociology*   393
    ANTHONY M. ORUM

13. *Trends in Family Sociology*   425
    JOAN HUBER △ GLENNA SPITZE

14. *The Sociology of Education*   449
    CHARLES E. BIDWELL △ NOAH E. FRIEDKIN

15. *Sociology of Religion*   473
    ROBERT J. WUTHNOW

16. *The Sociology of Science*   511
    HARRIET ZUCKERMAN

17. *Medical Sociology*   575
    WILLIAM C. COCKERHAM

18. *Mass Media Institutions*   601
    GAYE TUCHMAN

IV.
SOCIAL PROCESS AND CHANGE

19. *Spatial Processes*   629
    W. PARKER FRISBIE △ JOHN D. KASARDA

20. *Deviance and Social Control*   667
    ANDREW T. SCULL

21. *Social Movements*   695
    DOUG McADAM △ JOHN D. McCARTHY △ MAYER N. ZALD

22. *Development and the World Economy*   739
    PETER B. EVANS △ JOHN D. STEPHENS

SUBJECT INDEX   775

NAME INDEX   792

ABOUT THE AUTHORS   820

Acknowledgments

The introductory chapter contains a background statement and an explanation of the organization of this handbook, and the individual chapters contain its substance. It remains only to extend a few acknowledgments.

When this project was launched it was under the coeditorship of Ronald Burt of Columbia University and myself. Together we planned the organization, designated the chapters, selected the authors, and twisted their arms. We also carried out a preliminary plan for coauthoring what is now Chapter 3 (''Social Structure'') and exchanged some outlines and draft material. And we devised a division of labor for monitoring and, if necessary, leaning on individual authors. At a certain moment, Ron was forced to conclude that he could not complete the necessary work for this in the necessary time, because of the crunch of numerous commitments to complete other research and writing projects, teaching assignments, and administrative obligations. He asked me to bring the project to a close on my own. So, although his name does not appear officially either as coauthor or coeditor, I would like to take the opportunity to record his substantial contribution and to extend my thanks to him.

The idea of launching the handbook project was, I believe, the brainchild of Al Goodyear.

When he approached me to undertake the editorship along with Ron Burt, I had no hesitation, largely because I felt the idea was sound and because I had such a rewarding past relationship with Al. While he sought other pastures before the project was under way, I would like to record my appreciation to him for his initiative.

Mitch Allen has been our man at Sage. He helped to keep things moving, and he handled with skill and tact those few delicate situations that inevitably arise in such a project. And in my periodic meetings with Mitch, he proved to be an informed, stimulating, and respected intellectual companion. Toward the end of the project he married one of my favorite officemates at the Institute of International Studies on the Berkeley campus, Vida Prater; this event also added to my sense of solidarity.

Finally, I would like to thank my assistant of many years, Christine Egan. She managed the mountain of correspondence involved efficiently, steered the several drafts of Chapter 3 and the Introduction through the word processor, and helped me hold Mitch Allen at bay when he was pressing for deadlines.

—*Neil J. Smelser*

Introduction

NEIL J. SMELSER

It has been two and a half decades since a general handbook of sociology has appeared on the scene. That predecessor to this one is titled *Handbook of Modern Sociology*, which was edited by Robert E. Lee Faris of the University of Washington (Faris, 1964). The volume was a remarkable one, drawing on the very best sociological talent of the day, and giving a faithful, accurate, and sophisticated representation of the discipline as it had developed to that time. My modest hope is that this volume, which is in many respects historically overdue, will measure up to that one in scientific and scholarly quality.

It was also about three decades ago—1959—when Talcott Parsons, regarded at that time as the preeminent sociological theorist of his age, prepared a statement on the problems confronting sociology as a profession, and delivered this statement as a background for a general session of the annual meetings of the American Sociological Association in September of that year. Even before he delivered the paper it was published in the *American Sociological Review* (Parsons, 1959). The editor, probably under the influence of Parsons's coaching, described it as "a preliminary formulation." On reading the report, however, it constitutes a remarkably comprehensive statement; furthermore, it raised many issues I want to address in this introduction to the handbook. To telegraph my message, I note that my descriptions and conclusions about the field will differ substantially from those of Parsons. This statement should not come as a surprise, however, for I have had the benefit of 30 years of history that have transpired since Parsons's statement, years that inform my views on retrospect and prospect in sociology.

Parsons's report, written at the acme of perhaps the greatest single period of growth, enthusiasm, and effort to integrate in the history of the social sciences, is understandably sanguine in many respects:

• While Parsons saw the development of sociology as a distinct discipline "recent, incomplete, and unstable" (1959, p. 548), he portrayed it as having achieved a distinct level of differentiation from "social philosophy" and "social problems" on the one hand, and from the other behavioral and social sciences on the other. By "social philosophy" he no doubt referred to sociology's European origins, which included not only philosophy but historical, classical, and legal studies as well; by "social problems" he referred to its American origins in the social gospel and progressive movements but also in the early scholarly preoccupations with social problems in the "Chicago School"; and by the other behavioral and social sciences I believe he referred mainly to economics and psychology, which were established in the American university system before sociology made its appearance, and which were some of sociology's main institutional reference groups in its early history.

• He saw great strides in the discipline's institutionalization; "for the first time, sociology has come to be recognized as one of the regular disciplines in every major university in the United States" (1959, p. 552).

• He noted the "far deeper and broader battery of research technology" as well as "the output of superior research results" and the improvement of their quality (1959, p. 558).

• Largely as a result of these three trends, he described sociology as having achieved a notable increase in status—"from being the least respectable social science discipline to being the most controversial" (1959, p. 553).

• He suggested the emergence of a "sociological ideology"—superseding the economic and psychological emphases of earlier decades—that focused on the problem of conformity, or "the problem of constraints on individual freedom" (1959, p. 554). (Psychology and economics, it might be observed, have traditionally shared a more individualistic approach than sociology, but the latter is certainly not free from that approach.)

• He observed that after a period of "rather sharp withdrawal [from an interest in social problems] in favor of building up the central academic core of the discipline," sociologists were now returning to applied interests "over a far broader front than before," mainly in applied professional schools, such as medicine (1959, p. 555).

With respect to "serious difficulties and dangers" facing the profession, Parsons mentioned the need to maintain interdisciplinary contacts (associated with the differentiation *away* from the other disciplines), the looming ethical problems associated with applied activities (associated with the increasing salience of those activities), and the danger that increased involvement in ideological controversy (no doubt associated with the emergence of a sociological "ideology") could divert attention from the central task of "the development of [the profession's] discipline and the training of its successors in carrying out that function (1959, p. 559). Notably absent in his entire essay, however, is any mention of possible *stagnation* or *contraction* of the resource base for the discipline, and any mention of *internal* differentiation, fragmentation, and conflict. These themes must be at the center of any discussion of sociology since Parsons wrote.

The Status of Sociology as a Discipline

Even though we may be tempted to look back —whether wistfully or in anger—to earlier historical periods and find moments of consensus, in fact there have never existed such moments in the brief history of sociology. The seminars, annual meetings, and learned journals have forever echoed and re-echoed with debates over the basic definition of the field as well as its academic and practical priorities. Nevertheless, it is possible to speak of periods of *relative* dominance of certain paradigms, perspectives, and methodological emphases in different periods (for example, the evolutionary perspective in the last decades of the nineteenth century, the positivist stress of the early part of the twentieth century).

The 1950s constituted such a period of relative dominance. At the risk of oversimplifying, one might suggest that at that moment the Durkheimian vision of sociology had risen to prominence—again, in relative degree—over competing alternatives in three respects. The first was that sociology is the study of observable and objective *facts* in the social world—not speculative philosophy, not moral inquiry (Durkheim, 1958). This positivistic perspective had been developed by William Fielding Ogburn and others from the 1920s (Ogburn, 1930), and while it had come under criticism from a variety of sources (Ellwood, 1933; Lynd, 1939) in the 1930s, it persisted in good health, and was given added strength by the development of a vast array of techniques of measurement and analysis after World War II. The second respect was the Durkheimian insistence that sociological investigation lies at an analytically distinct *social*—not psychological or biological —level, and that society constitutes an independent level of reality (Durkheim, 1958). While Durkheim's particular definition of social facts had perhaps been superseded, the dominant stress still was on the study of social structures and social systems. And the third element, also inherited from Durkheim, was that with regard to the understanding of social systems, greatest stress was given to the functional coherence and integration of their component parts (Durkheim, 1947).

As I indicated, this dominance must be regarded as relative, and signs of vigorous internal dissent and reformulation were already in evidence in the 1950s: for example, Lewis Coser attacked those sociologists who overstressed consensus and ignored conflict as a source of cohesion, and while his reformulation retained a functionalist flavor, it constitutes a significant critique (Coser, 1956). But during the 1960s and 1970s, these lines of dissent reached a crescendo, and new, competing theoretical positions came to be consolidated. To say "new," of course, is to mislead; most of these positions were revitalizations and elaborations of themes that had been in existence for a long time. In particular, the Marxian and Weberian perspectives enjoyed a resurgence, and a number of social-psychological positions rose in salience. Regarding those two decades generally, however, the paradigmatic turbulence can be regarded as a complicated mosaic of criticizing, moving away from, and consolidating new positions in relating to the three "Durkheimian" elements that constituted the dominant cluster in the 1950s. The following paragraphs will illustrate this point.

First, a number of attacks were launched as explicit or implicit critiques of sociological positivism. The symbolic interactionist perspective has always had this as one of its ingredients: for example, the methodological critique of "objective" measures such as responses to questionnaire items on surveys, because they miss the reality of interpretative mental and interactive processes. Ethnomethodologists developed essentially the same critique when they stressed that "social facts" are not given but are continuously generated and reproduced through personal interaction and that many such facts are not simply recorded passively by observing social scientists and their subjects. Other phenomenologists in Europe developed similar lines of criticism. Neo-Marxist critics came at positivism from a different source, arguing that positive social science—with its morally neutral pretensions and empiricism—is far from being an objective set of procedures developed to understand the social world; it is rather part of the ideological complex that serves to buttress and reproduce the institutions of capitalist or postindustrial society. In my estimation these attacks on sociological empiricism have not been very successful; the vast majority of those engaged in actual sociological research—those in the trenches, as it were—still adhere to a kind of theoretically eclectic empiricist perspective. And when phenomenological and Marxist critics conduct empirical research themselves and are called upon to defend the result of that research, they inevitably face some of the same issues of measurement and analysis faced by positivistically inclined social scientists, and adopt some of their methods.

Second, the focus on social structure and social systems either as the proper focus of inquiry or as a source of explanations was challenged in a variety of ways, and a variety of alternatives were proposed. This might be called the "microscopic revolution." In 1961 Dennis Wrong warned against an "oversocialized" view of human nature, chastised systems theorists for propounding this view, and put forth an alternative psychological view, using psychoanalytic and other perspectives (Wrong, 1961). That is also the thrust of the several phenomenological perspectives, the major focuses of which are on individual and interactive monitoring of meanings; they tend to regard society as constructed of and sustained by these activities (Blumer, 1969; Garfinkel, 1967). Utilizing an entirely different kind of psychology—social behaviorism —as his vehicle, George Homans nevertheless agreed with these critics that the individual in his or her matrix of social rewards is the fundamental unit of analysis, and that social regularities and institutional behavior are in effect derivable from individual actions. That is certainly what "bringing men back in" meant (Homans, 1964). Finally, a new debate on biological determinism was occasioned mainly by the work of E. O. Wilson, whose position called for a shift from the social to the organismic—indeed, genetic—level as the basic source of determination of social behavior (Wilson, 1975).

Third, and perhaps most familiar, is the development of a variety of perspectives stressing domination, oppression, and conflict as the central organizing basis and explanation in social life. Beginning with the Simmel-inspired critique by Coser, the Marxian critique by Mills (1956), and the Weberian critique by Dahrendorf (1958) in the 1950s, the conflict perspective burgeoned into dozens of avenues and affected subfield after subfield of sociology, including sociological theory (Habermas, 1973, 1975; Marcuse, 1964), industrial sociology (Braverman, 1974), the sociology of gender (Hartmann, 1981), the sociology of education (Bowles and Gintis, 1976), and deviance (Taylor, Walter, and Young, 1973). And at the societal level, dependency and world-system theories, both neo-Marxist in character, moved in as challenges and alternatives to modernization theory.

The intellectual pattern created by these tendencies is very complex, partly because of the different permutations and combinations of the reactions and new formulations. Collins embraced the idea of a positive science warmly, but stressed the conflict perspective (Collins, 1975); symbolic interactionism rejected the social-structural level but stressed meshing of meaning-systems and "joint actions," eschewing a special stress on conflict; the neo-Marxist approaches rejected the perspective of consensus and solidarity but retained the social-system perspective.

Despite all the complexities, these debates displayed a common thread: They were struggles in which adherents attempt simultaneously to "deobjectify" the perspectives of competing approaches, to "objectify" or perhaps "reobjectify" a preferred alternative, and perhaps to claim a gain for some theoretical or ideological position implied by the preferred perspective. To illustrate this dynamic, the rise of "labeling theory" in the study of deviance was an effort to render unimportant (and perhaps unreal) psychological tendencies to deviance, and to locate the more important (and perhaps more real) power of agents of social control who apply designations of deviance on less powerful victims, thereby changing the apparent psychological causes to by-products of the more fundamental social processes of labeling. The neo-Marxist "new criminology" revealed the same thread, arguing, however, that the most fundamental causes that lead agents of social control to "create" deviance are to be found in the contradictions of capitalist society and its efforts to deal with those contradictions.

To add one more set of themes to this apparent cacophony, I call attention to the proliferation of many specialized substantive subfields during the past several decades. The sociology of education and the sociology of medicine, for example, are specialties of very recent vintage; so are the sociology of gender, the sociology of leisure, and the sociology of age stratification. As each of these subspecialties arises, moreover, positions within them begin to precipitate out, and to correspond to some degree to the alternative perspectives mentioned; thus it is possible to identify fairly clearly a functionalist, a conflict, and an interactionist perspective in the areas of medicine, education, and gender. Study of almost all of the substantive chapters in this handbook—for example, "Gender and Sex Roles," "Political Sociology," "Sociology of Science," and "Spatial Processes"—will show this progressive rise of new or revised perspectives in all of them, making for both greater richness and less unity.

To summarize thus far, it is apparent that even in the 1950s Parsons's stress on "a new level of maturity" and "[relative differentiation] from the philosophical matrix" (1959, p. 551)

exaggerated the internal unity of the discipline; such descriptions, if applied today, would appear almost ludicrous. Rather, the themes have been and are increased specialization of inquiry, diversification of both perspectives and subject matter studied, and considerable fragmentation and conflict. There appears to be no present evidence of an overarching effort at theoretical synthesis of the sort that Parsons sought to effect, and little reason to believe that such an effort is on the horizon. The more likely prospect is for rather more specific kinds of middle-range syntheses and generalizations. I have in mind as examples the explanation of a range of economic, organizational, and laboratory behavior under a common model of risk-taking under conditions of uncertainty; the synthesis of heretofore unconnected ranges of economic behavior under a model of the family life cycle or the invention and application of broadly explanatory epidemiological, stochastic, and other mathematical models. These kinds of examples certainly do not constitute a theoretical synthesis of an entire discipline, as Parsons envisioned, but perhaps we have by now gone too far down the road of specialization and diversification to expect such a result.

A Few Glances Forward

There is nothing easier—and perhaps nothing so perilous—than to predict that things will stay much the same as they are. But in one respect, at least, one must do this. That has to do with the specialization, knowledge explosion, fragmentation, and competition among perspectives in the field. The reason I make this prediction is that the causes of these phenomena show little signs of change. New subfields will come up as new social problems come up; we chase the world, and just as the sociology of gender and the sociology of the environment appeared as offspring of social concerns and social movements, we may expect more of the same in the future. The various specialties and perspectives I described in the first part of this essay have become somewhat institutionalized in departmental appointments, journals, and special semiprofessional societies and associations; one by-product of this institutionalization is for the associated groups to see to it that their interest is perpetuated. And we have the eternal generational problem, which assures that the coming generation differentiates itself from—and perhaps rejects—the generation that went before it, and this too leads to more diversity and conflict.

This pattern of flux will no doubt continue to complicate the organizational life of the profession. At the level of the academic department, competition among representatives of different specialties and perspectives over curriculum, personnel, and other departmental resources will continue to be brisk, and the goal of departmental "comprehensiveness" and "balance" will prove even more elusive than it is now. There will also be competition in the American Sociological Association for journal space, special sections, representation on the program of the annual meetings, offices, and any other resources that might lend increased symbolic legitimacy and jurisdiction to a given specialty or perspective. And while there are obvious occupational career reasons for individuals who have been trained as sociologists to continue to call themselves sociologists, the likelihood that that name will be denotative of an identifiable field will be diminished; it is likely that commitment to the discipline in general will diminish, and that smaller groups will seek their interaction and identification in suborganizations that are inside (for example, special sections) or outside (for instance, a society for public choice) the American Sociological Association.

But we must not stop at this point of chaos. Earlier in my remarks I indicated that the diversification, if not fragmentation, of sociology is not simply a random babble. It is in large part a systematic dialogue with the past. Furthermore, to speak of many voices in the discipline does not imply that some voices are not stronger or more influential than others. Some are, and the strength of the stronger ones determines in part the content of the message of the weaker ones. With these points in mind, let me return to the idea of the model of sociology as a science, and build from that to a scenario that I have been contemplating for some time.

I mentioned the notion of sociology as an empirical, if not positive, science earlier, and stressed how dominant this view had become in the first third of the twentieth century and how it continued despite critiques and laments. What were the origins of dominance? The answer to this question is by no means final, but I can supply two plausible suggestions.

First, from the beginning sociology has been a field struggling to gain legitimacy as an academic discipline in a university system that was, to be sure, dominated for centuries by the classical humanistic tradition, but has been recently infused with a stress on natural science and practical subjects associated with the expansion of state universities under the Morrell Act of 1862. As indicated, psychology and economics had begun to work their ways successfully into the universities' departmental structures and curricula as legitimate branches of learning in the late nineteenth century, and sociology was just beginning to make such a move in the early twentieth. It is plausible to assert that American sociology was recapitulating Durkheim's great "public relations" effort of the late nineteenth century, in which he argued passionately for the independent status of sociology as a science (with one eye on its university status, no doubt), and, in a savage polemic, attempted to differentiate it from scientific psychology. Sociology—and, to a degree, the other social sciences—chose the route to intellectual legitimacy by modeling itself on the established sciences and insisting that it too was a positive science. This impulse, encouraged by the continuing pecking order of universities—with the natural sciences remaining consistently near or at the top—continues to the present day, and constitutes a continuing model for academic sociology to sustain itself as a fully accepted citizen in the academy.

(This point is underscored by a comparison. The history of European sociology is conditioned by the fact that it had a different range of dominant reference groups before it. These were the great traditions of classical learning, history, philosophy, and law. They were and continue to be in some degree the main models, and sociology on that continent has sought legitimacy in the mode of critical reflection about the nature of society and the state and about the meaning of human civilization. American sociology, while strongly influenced by these traditions from time to time, has been relatively more timid as it has devoted more of its energy to establishing itself as a science.)

Second, the state has played a role. The 1920s, in particular, epitomized by the presidency of Herbert Hoover, the engineer, marked an era of businesslike, practical, and scientific approach to the solution of social problems on "facts." And later, while New Deal leaders abandoned this everyday, businesslike approach in favor of a style of political heroics, they nevertheless ushered in a great array of social programs, generating in their own turn great public bureaucracies, which developed a way of justifying their intended programs and rationalizing their ongoing programs by reciting evidence in the form of "facts." This stress has grown steadily, with the growth of government, and in my reading of the politics of the early 1980s, the massive Reagan-Stockman effort to hack away at governmental support of the behavioral and social sciences was undermined most successfully by the argument that the governmental enterprise itself is dependent on these sciences for the supply of objective and useful facts on which its policies must be based.

An additional line of support of sociology—and the other behavioral and social sciences—to posture themselves as scientific comes from the more recently developed system of federal support for research. I will concentrate on the National Science Foundation, which is the largest single source of funds, and which is a kind of "model" agency because of its commitment to the support of basic science.

Organizationally, the behavioral and social sciences are a part of the National Science Foundation, and are supported by the same general budget that is appropriated for the foundation annually by Congress. Yet it is apparent that these disciplines occupy a minor place in that agency; the Science Board (its policymaking board of trustees) has virtually no behavioral or social sciences as a subpart of a division known as the Biological, Behavioral, and Social Sciences, the director of which is invariably a biological scientist. Furthermore, the sums available to the behavioral and social sciences within the foundation are minuscule in comparison with the total budget. Perhaps most decisive, however, and perhaps the ultimate reason for all of the above, is the fact that much of the "hard science" leadership of the National Science Foundation and the science establishment in Washington—while they grant a place for the behavioral and social sciences—still regard these enterprises as basically "soft" and not really "scientific."

The other important point to mention about the National Science Foundation—and all other government granting agencies—is that they are publicly visible, and come under annual review at budget time by the Office of Budget and Management in the executive branch and both Houses of Congress. The view of the behavioral and social sciences in the halls of government, moreover, is fraught with ambivalence. On the one hand, government officials are forever faced with and must deal with pressing social problems of poverty, unemployment, crime, mental health, economic instability, and so on, all of which are most directly related to and informed by behavioral and social science research. This concern tends to generate a positive attitude toward the behavioral and social sciences, and to incline governmental officials to support research in those areas out of the conviction that increased knowledge about those problems will

be enlightening and will lead to more effective attacks on them.

On the other hand, there are pockets of hostility toward the behavioral and social sciences on the part of government officials, and while these vary in importance and salience over time, they are identifiable and take the following forms:

• Research in the behavioral and social sciences produces trivial, obvious, and unimportant results, and expenditures on that kind of research are wasteful of public funds. This attitude is symbolized in the annual "Golden Fleece" awards named by Senator William Proxmire, the intent of which is to show that the federal government has been fleeced of its gold by studies funded to study the sex life of goats, the sociology of love, and other such subjects.

• Research in the behavioral and social sciences is of no use to the government, and therefore should not be funded; this opinion is associated with public statements by David Stockman, President Reagan's former budget adviser, made during congressional budgetary hearings in the early 1980s.

• Research in the behavioral and social sciences is basically unscientific—according to the canons of hard science, and is therefore undeserving of study. This is a kind of spillover of the above-mentioned attitude on the part of many physical and life scientists.

• Research in some branches of the behavioral and social sciences (such as the study of race relations, fundamentalist religious beliefs, family life, and other areas) is basically dangerous ideologically, because it is likely to generate criticism of institutions and practices that are either considered sacred or uneasily taken for granted, and to suggest changes in such areas. This kind of hostility is difficult to document, because it is often shrouded in one of the less frank forms just listed; nevertheless, it exists, and reflects both right-wing political sentiments and the fact that social scientists themselves are more politically liberal and critical than other groups in the political spectrum.

It is difficult to conceive how the behavioral and social sciences could be simultaneously trivial, useless, unscientific, and threatening. Be that as it may, these attacks surface from time to time, and as such they constitute a source of embarrassment and difficulty for the leadership of the National Science Foundation and other funding agencies. To them the behavioral and social sciences appear as a minor part of their operation from an organizational and budgetary point of view, but as a major source of criticism and trouble from those quarters that matter.

It follows from this account that the main temptations generated by these pressures on the behavioral and social sciences are two: first, to maintain as low a profile as possible, to avoid political notice and thereby survive; and second, to present themselves as respectably and undangerously as possible and thereby to curry political and budgetary support. The main response to these temptations, according to my observations, is for the spokespersons of the behavioral and social sciences to represent themselves as adhering to the model of positive science, as methodologically sound, and as therefore supportable on the grounds that they are legitimately scientific. This strategy emerges —whether it is, in the end, effective or self-defeating—as the one that is most likely to blunt criticism both within the donor agencies and on the part of other government officials. In the end, of course, this response emerges as a victory of the positive-science emphasis, and as a kind of marriage of convenience between the behavioral and social scientific investigators in the academy on the one hand and the Washington social-science establishment on the other —a marriage that encourages those in the academy to support so-called hard behavioral and social scientific investigators because such a policy encourages funding agencies to give research grants to such investigators because it provides evidence that their own standards are strictly "scientific."

This "sociology-of-knowledge" diagnosis has perhaps gone on too long, but its implications are clear. Unless we witness major changes in the structure and prestige systems of universities, and/or major changes in the politics affecting the behavioral and social sciences, the model of the social sciences—including, of course, sociology—as sciences will be the dominant voice of the future. Empirical science models of social study and explanation will be center stage, and will call the tune, as it were, for those voices that will continue to reassert the concern with philosophical, moral, and social problems that has occupied a salient past in sociology, and from which Parsons mistakenly thought that sociology had differentiated itself. The content and tone of the dominant voice in counterpoint with subordinate protesting voices will change with changing times, but I would predict that it will be the main melody of the future.

National and International Sociology

It should be remarked that every author represented in this handbook is American. Some of these authors, of course, take serious note of past and present sociological theory and research in Western Europe and in other parts of the world. The volume is, however, predominantly a book on sociology as it stands in the United States. The only justification for this is that sociology has been and remains a subject dominated by this country, if numbers of professionals, resources available, and degree of institutionalization in the academy are used as measures. At the same time, sociology has an international dimension as well. There have been areas of theoretical ferment in Europe during the past two decades—as represented by names such as Jurgen Habermas, Niklas Luhmann, Alain Touraine, Pierre Bourdieu, and Anthony Giddens—that arguably have been more influential than American theoretical writers during the same period. Furthermore, in one way or another sociology is institutionalized in every country in the world that has institutionalized a system of higher education. And government after government has discovered that, despite active or lingering ideological ambivalence toward the field, sociological research into the conditions of their societies is a requisite part of effective policymaking and governance. These circumstances call for a few comments on the subject of the national and international dimensions of the discipline.

The ideal for sociology—as with all bodies of knowledge that characterize themselves as science—would appear to have a body of theory and a body of methodology for the conduct of empirical research that have a universal quality, crosscutting national and cultural boundaries. This ideal derives from the situation that characterizes other bodies of knowledge, such as mathematics, physics, chemistry, and the life sciences. (Exceptions in these areas occur, however, as the history of scientific-religious controversies over cosmology and more recent debates such as the Mendelian-Lamarckian controversy in genetics attest.) In some respects sociology measures up to this ideal. Sociologists the world over call themselves by the same name, recognize the same people as the giants of their traditions, share certain methodological canons for empirical research, and make use of common research techniques, such as the sample survey and ethnographic observation. At the same time it is the case that national and cultural differences in the field exist, and it is also the case that there exist a number of intellectual and social-structural forces that work toward the persistence of these differences, despite the thrust toward the internationalization of sociological knowledge. I would like to comment on these forces.

Beginning with the intellectual forces, it is possible to argue that the discipline has developed, if not "matured," more in some societies than others, and this makes for a different substance and flavor of knowledge in different societies. An example from economic sociology will illustrate this point. Several decades ago economic sociology in the United States was dominated by what was called industrial sociology, and that field was in turn dominated by a perspective that has been called "managerial" in character—that is, stressing productivity and worker morale, as well as ways of augmenting both of these in the interests of economic efficiency. In recent decades the American concern with the economic life of workers has moved away from this limited perspective, and brought other perspectives, such as work careers, contract arrangements, patterns of domination, and the structure of the labor market to bear on the study of jobs and occupations. The literature of some other countries, however, still manifests an overriding preoccupation with the "applied" or "social problem" aspects of labor, such as absenteeism, morale, alcoholism, motivation to change jobs or residence, and the like. These differences in emphases, all embedded in the economic and historical situations of the countries in question, make for differences in conceptual approaches and types of empirical research and, derivatively, difficulties in scientific communications among scholars from the different societies.

A second intellectual force, if we may call it that—perhaps ideological would be a better word—is the subordination of the scientific impulse in sociology and the other social sciences to nationalistic sentiments. Somehow there persists, unhelpful as this may be, a sense that there is such an entity as "North American Sociology," "Western European Sociology," "Socialist Sociology," "Third World Sociology," or, even more, a sociology associated with a specific country, such as France, Italy, or Israel. Certainly there are sociological problems or issues that are peculiar to those regions or countries of the world. But one wonders whether there is a sociology that should be identified in those terms. Be that as it may, the nationalistic mentality survives, and in some respects is a

competitor with the internationalization of our discipline.

A third factor should be mentioned. That is the difference among nations with respect to those domestic political conditions that are encouraging or discouraging to the establishment of sociology as a science that is autonomously institutionalized and relatively free from the intrusion of political authorities, the press, or public opinion generally with respect to its own freedom to develop in the directions in which it chooses to develop. Sociology has never been a politically or ideologically neutral field. Its subject matter touches issues that are forever sensitive—equality and inequality, religion, family, morality—about which regimes and peoples have strong feelings. Insofar as those feeling inhibit or otherwise impinge upon the field through political repression, budgetary punishment, or bad press, it constitutes a pressure against the true internationalization of the field, because it diverts its attention to peculiarly domestic concerns.

Turning to social structural forces, it should be mentioned first that while national governments, as mentioned, find much of value in the kind of information and thinking that sociology and the other social sciences produce, their interest tends to be parochial more often than not. Governments and other social agencies fund social science research, but as a rule that funding is driven by a concern with domestic social and political problems, and with the setting of problems in accordance with domestic national needs. There is, I believe, no country in which this principle does not hold in some degree.

In addition, it remains the case that nation-based university systems are the principal career paths for scholars, and these systems are the center of the reward system for them. The international science is virtually devoid of career rewards for social scientists. The one exception to this is the recognition and reward for gaining an "international reputation" through publications. In many countries, particularly those with minor languages, scholars sense the desirability, if not necessity, to write and publish their works in the English language, and this makes for additional possibilities for dissemination.

Sociology, like virtually all of its sister disciplines, has an association that is internationally based, the International Sociological Association (ISA). Many research committees, dedicated to subfields and themes of sociology, have grown up within the ISA, and tend to dominate the programs at its meetings. Some of these committees have proven to be extremely valuable vehicles for international collaboration and the exchange of knowledge and expertise. Yet as an international enterprise the ISA cannot be regarded as very effective. It meets only every four years; it is a poverty-stricken organization from the standpoint of financial support. And its "United Nations" principle of representation —with the same number of delegates from every member country as members of a somewhat unwieldy council—has contributed to the development of nationally and regionally based politics within the association, politics that do not particularly help the advancement of sociological knowledge.

International collaborative scholarship, of course, is one of the principal avenues to the development of international sociology—that is, when scholars from different countries come together to work on a common research problem. There have been a number of examples of this kind of scholarship within organizations such as the ISA and Organization for Economic Cooperation and Development, and private foundations have provided considerable support for international scholarship and exchange. Governmental funding policies, however, whether direct or through government-sponsored Social Science Research Councils, tend to discourage international collaboration, for example, giving it generally low priority or by adhering to policies that prohibit the funding of foreign scholars.

From this brief excursion we may conclude that the internationalization of sociology and sociological knowledge is—as it is in many fields—a constant and unresolved struggle between the ideals of science and scholarship on the one hand, and the national, political, and ideological obstacles to realizing these ideas on the other.

The Plan for This Handbook

The ideal handbook, I believe, is a massive undertaking that makes an effort to come as close as possible to covering a field comprehensively and in a catholic, balanced manner. Its contributing authors cannot be expected to cover everything—indeed, it is probably the case that there could be a full handbook on virtually ever chapter in this one—but they make as objective an effort as possible to select out the most important theoretical themes and empirical research in their purview. Finally, a handbook should be a blend of discussing problems and issues that have persisted in the field (and its

subfields) over the generations on the one hand, and bringing the reader right up to date on recent trends in empirical research on the other.

This ideal was kept in mind in designing this handbook, but in at least two respects it deviates from it. First, it was impossible to include topics that many would argue should be in the book. Social psychology—itself a topic deserving a handbook (Rosenberg and Turner, 1981)—is slighted, even though discussions of the social psychological literature appear in different chapters, such as Chapter 10 (Jobs and Work) and in Chapter 3 (Social Structure). Other significant omissions might also be mentioned— sociology of law, policy applications of sociology, economic sociology (see, however, Chapter 6, Inequality and Labor Processes; Chapter 10, Jobs and Work; and Chapter 11, Environments and Organizations); the sociology of the state (see, however, Chapter 12, Political Sociology, and Chapter 22, Development and the World Economy), sociology of art and literature, demography, and no doubt others. In the mind of the editor these kinds of omissions are regrettable but inevitable as strategic decisions had to be made about representing a field so comprehensive and differentiated as sociology.

Second, it was felt that an overemphasis on inclusiveness, balance, and catholicity would make for a certain blandness of tone in the chapters. Accordingly, each author was asked at the outset to strike some sort of balance between dispassionate and exhaustive coverage on the one hand, and selectivity and representation of his or her personal assessment and intellectual position on the other. How to strike this balance was left up to each author, and the judgment as to how well this balance was struck is left up to the reader.

Each individual chapter is self-contained and speaks well for itself, so it seems unnecessary to represent any kind of running summary. It remains only to indicate how the handbook is organized. Part I deals with theoretical and methodological issues. Walter Wallace's statement (Chapter 1) and that of Jeffrey Alexander (Chapter 2) present two distinct and in many respects opposed representations of the knowledge in sociology as a social science. My own chapter (3) extracts what is arguably the most central organizing concept in sociology—social structure—and traces the vicissitudes of that concept as it has been employed at both macroscopic and microscopic levels of analysis. The chapters by Peter Rossi and Richard Berk (4 and 5) discuss the methodological status of data and its measurement and the problem of inferring causal relationships, respectively, which are the two major methodological pillars on which sociological analysis stands.

Part II focuses on inequality, another central organizing conceptual framework in sociology. It is organized according to the major bases of inequality in society—economic (Chapter 6, by Mark Granovetter and Charles Tilly); racial and ethnic (Chapter 7, by William Wilson and Katherine See); age (Chapter 8, by Matilda Riley, Anne Foner, and Joan Waring), and gender and sex (Chapter 9, by Janet Z. Giele).The major institutions of society constitute the focus of Part III. That section begins with political and economic institutions (Chapter 10, by Joanne Miller, Chapter 11, by Howard Aldrich and Peter Marsden, and Chapter 12, by Anthony Orum). The next focus is on institutions that have a primacy emphasis on socialization—family (Chapter 13, by Joan Huber and Glenna Spitze) and education (Chapter 14, by Charles Bidwell and Noah Freidkin). The latter provides a bridge to four chapters that are concerned with institutions that deal with culture (Chapter 15, by Robert Wuthnow and Chapter 18, by Gaye Tuchman) and with knowledge and its applications (Chapter 16, on science, by Harriet Zuckerman, and Chapter 17, on medicine, by William Cockerham).

Finally, Part IV contains four chapters that are best categorized as dealing with social processes and social change. Chapter 19, by Parker Frisbie and John Kasarda, deals with the organization of social processes around the dimension of space. Chapter 20, by Andrew Scull, reviews recent developments in the familiar sociological subfield of deviance and social control. Moving more toward macroscopic processes, Chapter 21, by Doug McAdam, John McCarthy, and Mayer Zald, deals with the dynamics of social movements. The book concludes with the most macroscopic topic of all, international economic arrangements and their impact on developmental processes within nations (Chapter 22, by Peter Evans and John Stevens).

Virtually every chapter in the book reveals the interesting dynamic discussed earlier in this introductory chapter, namely the "invasion" of all subfields of sociology by the different and competing perspectives and paradigms that characterize the field as a whole. This makes for two effects: the increased diversity and richness of interpretative frameworks within each subfield, and a lesser degree of consensus about what is the central organizing basis for knowledge generated in that subfield.

REFERENCES

Blumer, Herbert. 1969. *Symbolic Interactionism: Perspective and Method*. Englewood Cliffs, NJ: Prentice-Hall.

Bowles, Samuel and Herbert Gintis. 1976. *Schooling in Capitalist America: Educational Reform and the Contradictions of Economic Life*. New York: Basic Books.

Braverman, Harry. 1974. *Labour and Monopoly Capital: The Degradation of Labour in the Twentieth Century*. New York: Monthly Review Press.

Collins, Randall. 1975. *Conflict Sociology: Toward an Explanatory Science*. New York: Academic Press.

Coser, Lewis. 1956. *The Functions of Social Conflict*. Glencoe, IL: Free Press.

Dahrehdorf, Ralf. 1958. "Out of Utopia: Toward a Reorientation of Sociological Analysis." *American Journal of Sociology* 64:115-124.

Durkheim, Emile. 1947. *The Elementary Forms of the Religious Life*, translated by Joseph Ward Swain. Glencoe, IL: Free Press.

———— 1958. *The Rules of Sociological Method*, edited by George E.G. Catlin, translated by Sarah A. Solovay and John H. Mueller. Glencoe, IL: Free Press.

Ellwood, Charles A. 1933. *Methods in Sociology: A Critical Study*. Durham, NC: Duke University Press.

Faris, Robert E.L., ed. 1964. *Handbook of Modern Sociology*. Chicago: Rand McNally.

Garfinkel, Harold. 1967. *Studies in Ethnomethodology*. Englewood Cliffs, NJ: Prentice-Hall.

Habermas, Jurgen. 1973. Theory and Practice. Boston: Beacon Press.

———— 1975. *Legitimation Crisis*. Boston: Beacon Press.

Hartmann, Heidi. 1981. "The Family as Locus of Gender, Class, and Political Struggle. The Example of Housework." *Signs* 6:366-394.

Homans, George. 1964. "Bringing Men Back In." *American Sociological Review* 29:809-818.

Lynd, Robert S. 1939. *Knowledge for What? The Place of Social Science in American Culture*. Princeton, NJ: Princeton University Press.

Marcuse, Herbert. 1964. *One Dimensional Man*. Boston: Beacon Press.

Mills, C. Wright. 1956. *The Power Elite*. New York: Oxford University Press.

Ogburn, William F. 1930. "Presidential Address: 'The Folkways of a Scientific Sociology.' " In *Studies in Quantitative and Cultural Sociology*. Chicago: University of Chicago Press.

Parsons, Talcott. 1959. "Some Problems Confronting Sociology as a Profession." *American Sociological Review* 29:547-559.

Rosenberg, Morris and Ralph H. Turner, eds. 1981.

Social Psychology: Sociological Perspectives. New York: Basic Books.

Taylor, I., P. Walton, and J. Young. 1973. *The New Criminology: For a Theory of Social Deviance*. New York: Harper & Row.

Wilson, Edmund O. 1975. *Sociology: The New Synthesis*. Cambridge, MA: Harvard University Press.

Wrong, Dennis H. 1961. "The Oversocialized Conception of Man in Modern Sociology." *American Sociological Review* 26:183-193.

Part I

THEORETICAL AND METHODOLOGICAL ISSUES

1

Toward a Disciplinary Matrix in Sociology

WALTER L. WALLACE

This chapter sets forth a matrix of concepts aimed at making the essential constituents of all orientations, paradigms, theories, propositions, hypotheses, and findings (indeed, all empirical statements of any kind) that have ever been current, or that are likely soon to become current, in sociology plainer and more systematically useful for understanding, constructing, criticizing, and testing theory, and research—both pure and applied.[1]

The contents of this matrix—consisting of a set of descriptive variables, a set of explanatory-predictive variables, and a set of causal images for linking variables in the first two sets together—are in no sense original with the author but are, rather, the collective products of our discipline as a whole across the 150 years of its international history. Because this claim is a major justification for calling the matrix "disciplinary," a wide variety of quotations (and critical interpretations of them) here will try to document it and thereby demonstrate the nearly universal extent to which we already implicitly

I owe thanks to Russell Sage Foundation and to the Center for Advanced Study in the Behavioral Sciences for time and space, some years ago, to work out many of the ideas here, and more recently to Neil Smelser, and also to Sarane Boocock, Samir Khalaf, John Kitsuse, Robert Liebman, Clifford Nass, Michael Simpson, Robert Wuthnow, and graduate students in recent seminars on sociological theory at Princeton University, for useful comments on early drafts of this manuscript.

share the matrix. It remains only to make that sharing explicit.

A Natural Science

The premise that sociology rightfully belongs to the natural sciences rather than to the humanities—is crucial to the matrix proposed here because every natural science depends, above all, on its practitioners adhering to some set of empirically based terms as representing their discipline's standard (but, of course, not fixed) matrix of ideas.[2] The appalling fact, however, is that even now, after many decades of research and teaching, virtually *none* of the key substantive terms in sociology has acquired an explicitly standard meaning to any large majority of sociologists. For one cardinal example, the authoritative *Encyclopedia of the Social Sciences* declares, in all seriousness, that "the concept 'social structure' is . . . so fundamental to social science as to render its uncontested definition virtually impossible" (Udy, 1968, p. 489); 13 years later, the astonishing judgment is repeated: "Of all the problematic terms in the sociological lexicon, 'social structure' is perhaps the most troublesome. There is little agreement on its empirical referents" (Warriner, 1981, p. 179); and, still closer to the present time, one reads yet again that "despite sociologists' frequent use of the term social structure, its meaning remains unclear'' (Turner, 1986, p. 407, italics removed). Indeed, it is perhaps just this frequency with which we blithely go on using a term so utterly fundamental to our discipline without making a concerted effort to standardize its meaning that comes closest to justifying the charge that, scientifically speaking, we sociologists simply do not know (and may not care) what we are talking about. And never having established a common definition of ''social structure'' (and many other terms of similar centrality, including ''culture,'' ''status,'' ''role,'' ''value,'' ''norm,'' and most important of all, the term ''social phenomenon'' itself) *it is no wonder* that the catalog of sociological natural laws remains so empty.[3]

As Blumer (skeptical though he is that the situation can be remedied in sociology) puts it, ''Generic variables are essential . . . to an empirical science—they become the key points of its analytical structure. Without generic variables, variable analysis [and let us add, *any* analysis—*WLW*] yields only separate and disconnected findings'' (1956, p. 684). Thus although the premise that sociology is and should be a natural science is certainly not the only reason for establishing a disciplinary matrix there (anyone who is interested, for *whatever* reason, in improving communication among sociologists should favor it), that premise makes the need for an immediate, concerted, and determined effort to agree on such a matrix in sociology—whether it be the one proposed here or not—obvious and undeniable.[4]

Control Over Social Phenomena

But why *should* we pursue sociology as a natural science? There seem to be two answers to this question. The first is that no matter how imperfect natural science is and must always remain, it is by far the most reliable known strategy for *doing* something about the world— that is, for purposefully changing it, or for keeping it the same when we want it that way—and, potentially, thereby improving the quality of human life.[5] There is considerable classical precedent for this view in sociology: Weber, noting that ''science contributes to the technology of controlling life,'' says, ''One does [science] first, for purely *practical*, in the broader sense of the word, for technical purposes: in order to be able to orient our practical activities to the expectations that scientific experience places at our disposal'' (1958a, pp. 150, 138;

italics added). Similarly, Comte says, ''All positive speculations owe their first origin to the occupations of *practical* life'' (1975, p. 321, italics added). Freud says, ''It is not to be supposed that men were inspired to create their first system of the universe by pure speculative curiosity. The practical need for *controlling* the world around them must have played its part'' (1950, p. 78, italics added; see also 1961, p. 22). Durkheim says, ''The reason to which I make my appeal is reason applying itself to a given matter in order to understand the nature of past and present morality, and which draws from this theoretical study its *practical* consequences'' (1974, pp. 66-67, italics added; see also 1984, p. 278). Marx and Engels say, ''[W]here would natural science be without industry and commerce? Even this 'pure' natural science is provided with an aim . . . through the sensuous *activity* of men'' (1969, Vol. I, pp. 28-29, italics added). Mead says human society ''has gradually become aware of the method of meeting its problems. . . . The method is that of experimental science, by means of which men *change* the environment within which society exists, and the forms and institutions of society itself'' (1938, p. 508, italics added; see also p. 511). Mannheim says, ''In modern times much more depends on the correct thinking through of a situation than was the case in earlier societies. The significance of social knowledge grows proportionally with the increasing necessity of regulating *intervention* in the social process'' (1955, p. 2, italics added).[6]

Of course, science is not without rivals in human efforts to change the world, but two of these rivals (magic and sorcery) are notoriously unreliable, and the third (random trial-and-error) immediately turns into science as soon as it becomes intersubjective and deductively selective—that is, as soon as replications of the same trial by different observers lead to predictions of future trial outcomes (i.e., hypotheses), which then influence judgments about which trials should actually be run.

Therefore, if one happens to be dissatisfied with some aspect of human social life (whatever it may be), and if one wants to improve that aspect (no matter how one defines ''improve''), then science is unquestionably the best choice.[7] Indeed, once we set aside those who believe the world is either fated or divinely directed in every last detail and cannot or should not be improved—and also set aside, of course, the proponents of magic, sorcery, and random trial and error—we seem forced to conclude that, of the remainder, only those who are satisfied with the world as it is and do not want it to be improved can rationally oppose others' efforts to apply scientific methods to the world—including, now more than ever, its human social aspects. (We must say "others' " efforts because it is one thing to direct *one's own* efforts, for any number of personal reasons, toward something other than the application of natural science to the world but it is quite another thing to argue that *no one* should work toward this end.)

Once science's uniquely reliable ability to exert human control over the world is granted, one asks What feature of science makes this ability possible? Comte's aphorism, "From science comes prevision; from prevision comes action" (1975, p. 88)—as well as Weber's stress on "the expectations that scientific experience places at our disposal" (quoted above), and Simmel's claim that "every single step of our life is determined and rendered possible by the fact that we perceive [sic] its consequences, and likewise because we perceive them only up to a certain point" (1971, p. 354)—identifies that feature as science's ability to make reliable predictions, and such predictions (again, never perfect but always of greater reliability than those produced by other means) seem classifiable into the following five types.[8],[9]

Predicting the Target Before Intervention

The first type of prediction addresses the fact that any purposive intervention in the world has to be launched ahead of the time we want it to take effect, so that, like a football thrown to a running receiver, the intervention and its target will reach the same place at the same time. We are thus compelled to base all our efforts to control targeted aspects of the world on predictions of where those aspects (and our efforts) will be at specific future times. Only such predictions can enable us to take accurate aim by giving the target an appropriate "lead."

Predicting the Target After Intervention

But even when it is accurately aimed, a given kind and amount of intervention may not always bring about the same change in its target. For example, raising the temperature of water at sea level by one degree will have quite different effects if the water is initially at 0 °C, 50 °C, or 99 °C, and all these effects may be changed if the water is in a different environment—say, ap-

preciably above or below sea level. For another and more sociological example, Durkheim predicts that social interaction that is too intense ("altruism"), and normative controls that are too strong ("fatalism"), will have the same socially disruptive effects (i.e., high suicide rates) as when the one is too diffuse ("egoism") or the other too weak ("anomie") (see 1951, p. 276, note 25)—so that, below a certain ideally moderate threshold (Durkheim says, "Health consists in a moderate degree of activity" [1984, p. 183]), one unit further strengthening of social interaction or of normative controls will have an integrative effect, but above that threshold the same amount of additional strengthening will have a disintegrative effect. It follows that if we want to bring about a *particular* change, and not just *any* change, in some targeted aspect of the world, we need a second type of prediction —one that specifies the likely course of that aspect *after* a given human intervention.

Predicting Points Susceptible to Intervention, and Predicting Effective Intervention

The third and fourth types of prediction recognize that in the indefinitely large web of causal relations of which any targeted aspect of the world is a part, some variables and relations are "softer"—that is, more susceptible to a given kind of intervention—than others. Thus, if we want to change a given process efficiently, we need to predict which point in it will prove most susceptible to a given intervention, and we need to predict the kind of intervention that will most affect such a point. These two predictions —jointly of susceptibility and effectiveness— are what Weber refers to when he says

> The question of the appropriateness of the means for achieving a given end is undoubtedly accessible to scientific analysis [inasmuch] as we are able to determine (within the present limits of our knowledge) which means for the achievement of a proposed end are appropriate or inappropriate [1949, p. 52].

Predicting Secondary Effects

The fifth predictive contribution of science to human control over the world recognizes that any manipulation of one part of the world is likely to have ramifications (side effects and long-run effects) on other parts of the world, and these ramifications may or may not be desirable from the standpoint of the manipulator. Thus, as Weber says,

> [W]hen the possibility of attaining a proposed end appears to exist, [science] can determine (naturally within the limits of our existing knowledge) the consequences which the application of the means to be used will produce in addition to the eventual attainment of the proposed end as a result of the interdependence of all events. We can then prepare the acting person with the ability to weigh and compare the undesirable as over against the desirable consequences of his action [1949, p. 53].

Note that not only do these five types of predictions provide the planning bases for *initiating* a given effort to control the world, but subsequently updated versions of these same types of predictions (collectively referred to as empirical "evaluations" and pursued in a formal manner by "evaluation research" and by monitoring social and cultural "indicators") enable us to decide whether or not that effort is succeeding, and therefore whether to continue, change, satisfiedly terminate, or disappointedly abandon the effort.

It would be difficult, however, to miss the fact that the sciences have not all made equally large contributions to human efforts to control the world. Indeed, the most fateful crises of our time seem traceable in large part to an explosively widening gap between the predictive capabilities of the physical and biological sciences and those of the social sciences. Myrdal notes precisely this: "It is their [i.e., the 'natural' sciences'] discoveries and inventions which are compelling radical changes in society, while ours [i.e., the social sciences'], up till now, have been very much less consequential. There is spreading a creeping anxiety about the dangerous hiatus inherent in this contrast" (quoted, with disapproval, in Giddens, 1986, p. 349). It seems clear that unless humankind is willing and able to halt the accelerating progress of the physical and biological sciences, the burden rests with the social sciences to catch up and close the gap before it is too late. At least, we must *try*—in the hope that social scientists may, through increasing the accuracy of their predictions of social phenomena, eventually come to "play the part of watchmen in what would otherwise be a pitch-black night" (Mannheim, 1955:160-161).[10] An agreed-upon disciplinary matrix in sociology would serve that hope by standardizing the basic terms of our predictions—a necessary step, because "The success of prediction in the natural sciences is bound up with the [extent to which] all states of the system [which one is predicting], past and future, can be described in the same range of concepts, as values, say, of the same variables" (Taylor, 1979, p. 69).[11]

The first reason, then, for pursuing sociology as a natural science is that with it, we humans may increase our collective *control* over social phenomena. The second, almost equally compelling reason is that through the methods of science we may increase our collective *knowledge* of social phenomena. The two, of course, are interdependent: Scientific knowledge depends on being able to control the world—most obviously in that rigorously focused kind of observation called, significantly, the "controlled experiment," but also in any systematic field observation—and scientific control depends on knowledge of the world to the extent, as we have just seen, of reliably predicting what it is going to do next. Thus, "the problem of scientific truth [and] that of . . . practical implications [are] inseparably mingled with each other" (Nakano, 1979, p. 87).[12]

But in view of the fact that natural science has at least three rivals in human efforts to acquire knowledge of the world (i.e., authority—including theism and mysticism—solipsism, and formal logic; see Wallace, 1971, pp. 11-13), let us examine the distinctive features of scientific knowledge-seeking because they have direct bearing on the matrix proposed here as disciplinary.

Knowledge of Social Phenomena

Scientific knowledge-seeking centers on its dedications to intersubjective empiricism and cognitive exhaustiveness. All other distinctive characteristics of science—including its "institutional imperatives" and "technical norms" discussed by Merton (1973, pp. 266-278; see also Mulkay, 1979, pp. 93-94), and also including its emphasis on discovering natural laws, and its employment of causality and logical induction and deduction in doing so—seem derivable from just these two.

Intersubjective Empiricism

In order to be scientific, our knowledge of the world must be both empirical and intersubjective. That is, not only must it place sensory observations in determining positions, but those observations must be replicated (or at least presumed replicable) by others. Regarding observation, Simmel says, "Only some fundamental relation to actuality can save one from sterile inquiries or from . . . haphazard formulation of scientific concepts" (1971, p. 25), and Carnap illustrates: "Consider the law: 'When iron is heated, it expands.' Another law says 'When iron is heated it contracts.'. . . The first law is accepted, rather than the second, only because it describes a regularity *observed in nature*" (1966, p. 199). Regarding intersubjectivity, Weber says, "All interpretation of meaning, like all scientific observations, strives for clarity and *verifiable* accuracy of insight and comprehension" (1978, p. 5, italics added), and Popper explicates this statement when he says:

> the *objectivity* of scientific statements lies in the fact that they can be *inter-subjectively tested*. . . . Only by such repetitions can we convince ourselves that we are not dealing with a mere isolated "coincidence," but with events which . . . are in principle intersubjectively testable [1961:44-45].

Of course, no two individuals are likely to agree at all times and places on all their observations in all detail. Many factors, including the individuals' differently trained and augmented sensory and conceptual apparatuses, and their different power and prestige, seem operative here (see Merton, 1973, pp. 439-496). In addition, of course, there is good reason to believe that the "same" object necessarily varies (however minutely) from one place to another and from one time to another in which it may be observed; that every object is in some way changed by the act of observing it; and that the magnitudes of such difference and change vary with type of object and type of observation. As a result, "The potential for true replication varies greatly among the sciences" (Zuckerman, 1977, p. 93), and therefore the tolerance limits of what is regarded as acceptable replication vary from one science to another, and from one time and place to another. The principle of replication, however (whether within narrow or broad tolerance limits, whether deliberate or not, and including replication not of every observation but only of theoretically strategic ones), remains indispensable to science because it forms "the cornerstone of [science's] system of social control" (Zuckerman, 1977, p. 92). It is this indispensability that best accounts for the universal scientific interest in regularities rather than uniquenesses. That is, to the extent that different observers occupy different spaces and times, as scientists they can be interested only

in those aspects of their observations that they agree to look upon as regular (and therefore replicable) across those spaces and times.

The entire sociocultural construction we call "science," then, depends on several kinds of empirically oriented, but always tentative and changeable, collective agreements. Such agreements, however, depend on communication, and such communication depends on the use of standard symbols bearing standard meanings —that is, on disciplinewide technical languages. Imagine what modern physics or chemistry or biology would be like without standardized symbols bearing standardized meanings (not *fixed* meanings, but meanings that at almost any given time are relatively clear and uniform across each entire discipline) being adhered to by their respective practitioners.

Cognitive Exhaustiveness

The second distinguishing feature of scientific knowledge—namely, the pursuit of cognitive exhaustiveness—has at least two manifestations in sociology. One of them impels us beyond knowledge of social actualities toward knowledge of social possibilities as well; the other impels us beyond knowledge of specifically human social phenomena toward knowledge of social phenomena among all kinds of organisms.

The first impetus means that scientists want to know not only how the world *has* been, and *is*, and *will* be. We also want to know how the world *could* be. That is, in addition to everything that historians, journalists, and forecasters want to know, scientists want to know what unrealized but realistic *possibilities* lie dormant in the world (see Weber, 1949, p. 164-186).[13] Is a world without war, poverty, ascriptive discrimination, and censorship realistically possible or is such a world only a bleeding-heart's pipe dream? Must there always be wars and rumors of wars; must the poor, the ascriptively disadvantaged, and the ignorant be with us always?

Counterfactual propositions and their evaluation play key roles in moving science in the direction of such exhaustive knowledge. Nagel says, "When planning for [i.e., seeking control over] the future or reflecting on [i.e., seeking knowledge of] the past, we frequently carry on our deliberations by making assumptions that are contrary to the known facts" (1961, p. 70). Thus,

> a physicist designing an experiment may . . . assert the counterfactual [that] "if the length of [a given] pendulum . . . were shortened

to one-fourth its present length, its period would be half its present period" . . . [and among historians] the counterfactual "If the Versailles Treaty had not imposed burdensome indemnities on Germany, Hitler would not have come to power". . . has been a controversial one [Nagel, 1961, pp. 70, 73].

But how are we to distinguish between valid and invalid counterfactuals—which is to say, between genuinely creative imagination and merely titillating fantasy? Nagel answers this question as follows: "Disputes as to whether a given counterfactual is true can be settled only when the assumptions and suppositions on which it is based are made explicit" (1961, p. 72)—but lest we think logical explication is sufficient, Carnap requires that the explicated counterfactual also be in accord with empirically supported scientific law: "It is reasonable to assert [a given] counterfactual because it is based on a genuine law" (1966, p. 210; see also Weber, 1949, pp. 174-175).

Thus, although counterfactuals pertain to that uniquely useful and intellectually fascinating concern of science with the world's still unrealized possibilities, their evaluation has the same general requirements as the evaluation of what we might call "factuals," and these requirements are logical explication and empirical support. But because there are often many alternative ways in which the same social possibility can be realized (see the discussion of equifinality, below) such explication and support may require surveying all those ways before deciding whether a given counterfactual is or is not true. The disciplinary matrix proposed here is intended to state systematically the elemental constituents of such ways.

Now inasmuch as the world appears infinite and our minds are only too obviously finite, the pursuit of exhaustiveness in our knowledge of the world also requires that that knowledge be given the simplest possible form. As a consequence, scientists always try to subsume two or more areas of inquiry under a single more general area, and with the aid of this inductive simplification, come to understand each area better. Here the second impetus of the pursuit of cognitive exhaustiveness—namely, the impetus toward understanding *all* social phenomena within the same frame of reference—shows itself. From its standpoint, if we want the fullest possible knowledge of social phenomena, we must eventually understand the overarching principles of *sociality* that underlie all the social sciences—including anthropology, economics, geography, history, political science, social psychology, sociology, and also the several fields that investigate social phenomena among nonhuman organisms (i.e., all or parts of ethology, entomology, ecology, behavior genetics, comparative psychology, primatology, microbiology, and marine biology--fields that will be referred to collectively here as "sociobiology").

The disciplinary matrix proposed here, while formally limited to sociology (solely because of limits in the author's disciplinary competence and not because of any supposed intrinsic barrier between sociology and the other social sciences) is also tentatively set forth as applicable to *all* the social sciences, and therefore as a conceptual basis for their eventual unification into a single multifaceted discipline.

Some Objections to Scientific Sociology

Now, having sketched some reasons why we should pursue sociology as a natural science, there remains the question of whether it is logically possible to do so. Let us consider some representative denials of that possibility. Winch, for one, insists that

> the central concepts which belong to our understanding of social life are incompatible with concepts central to the activity of scientific prediction. When we speak of the possibility of scientific prediction of social developments . . . we literally do not understand what we are saying . . . because it has no sense [1958, p. 94].

Why does it have no sense? In answer, Winch tells us that "sometimes even if [an observer] knows with certainty the rule which [a subject individual] is following, he cannot predict with any certainty what [that individual] will do . . . e.g. in circumstances markedly different from any in which [the rule] has previously been applied," and claims the existence of "human decisions which are *not determined by their antecedent conditions*" (1958, 92-93, italics added).[14] All this boils down to a claim that humans are intrinsically (if only "sometimes") unpredictable—a claim whose fall-back position seems expressed in Westhues's assertion that humans are intrinsically autonomous (i.e., even if humans *are* predictable, they are not predictable by natural science methods): "The laws governing how people behave do not inhere in nature but have been devised by people" (1982, p. 12).

In considering Winch's position, it seems important to bear in mind that because no prediction in *any* science can carry *absolute* certainty (and here it is just as important not to overestimate the capabilities of the physical and biological sciences as it is not to underestimate those of the social sciences), the important question is always relative: Does a given prediction carry *more* certainty than other predictions of the same event?[15] To this, it seems fair to say that, all other things being equal, an observer who knows the rule a subject is following can always predict what that subject will do with more certainty than an observer who does not know the subject's rule, no matter how "marked" the difference in circumstances. By the same token, of course, a prediction grounded in knowledge of the subject's rule *plus* knowledge of the "rules" being followed by other forces, both inside and outside the subject, that might help or hinder the subject to follow his or her rule will have still greater certainty. In general, the more rules we know, the more certain is our prediction—a principle on which the second, explanatory-predictive, part of the matrix proposed below is founded.

The human autonomy claim, though less extreme than the unpredictability claim, seems even more baffling because when Westhues says unqualifiedly "*the* laws governing how people behave . . . have been devised by people," one cannot easily believe he means *all* the laws, or even the most influential laws. If we did believe that, how should we regard the laws of human genetics (which have obviously not been devised by people but inhere in the nature of humankind's evolutionary relations to other organisms), and the laws of ecology (which inhere in the nature of matter and energy, Earth, solar system, galaxy and universe—all vastly antedating humankind's existence)?[16] It is almost inconceivable that Westhues really wants his readers to believe these laws do not *also* govern the behavior of people.

A related objection to applying scientific analysis to human social phenomena argues that because humans have the ability voluntarily to change their social phenomena, their knowledge of predictions about these phenomena may lead them consciously or unconsciously to negate, or fulfill, the predictions.[17] In this way, sociological predictions (or, more exactly, knowledge of such predictions by participants in the phenomenon being predicted) may become important factors in their own realization (see Merton, 1957, pp. 128-129, 421-436). Friedrich's claims that as a result of this possibility "the search for 'laws' of human nature and for fundamental social

processes that are in principle stable is ultimately destined to be futile" (1970, pp. 180-181) and similarly, Giddens asserts "There are no universal laws in the social sciences, and there will not be any . . . because . . . the causal conditions involved in generalizations about human social conduct are inherently unstable in respect of the very knowledge (or beliefs) that actors have about the circumstances of their own action" (1986, p. xxxii).[18]

In considering this argument, it seems useful (especially when addressing Friedrich's formulation), first, to reemphasize that purposeful change in the world (i.e., control) is one of the two paramount goals of every natural science. Therefore—because no such change can be achieved in "processes that are in principle stable"—what is, from the standpoint of science's knowledge goal, a search for stable processes is at the same time, from the standpoint of science's control goal, a search for what lies *inside* that limit—namely, processes that are in principle *unstable*—and for knowledge of such conditions and limits of that instability as would render it humanly manipulable. Second, it seems very likely that the search for "fundamental . . . processes that are in principle stable" is "ultimately destined to be futile" in *all* the sciences, and it seems both naive and facilely self-excusing to think this futility qualitatively distinguishes the social and behavioral sciences from the rest.

Finally, it appears that the stability of any given natural process can vary greatly when confronted with different destabilizing forces in different contexts (for example, that currently ultimate constant, the speed of light, is a constant only in "free space"—otherwise it varies according to the medium through which it passes). In accord with this general principle, Nicholson points out that the claim "that a prediction will sometimes affect what is predicted . . . is simply an assertion that statements . . . may have social consequences. . . . Such effects are important in some contexts, though there are still many circumstances where statements have little effect" (1983, p. 162). It seems reasonable to conclude that the social and cultural effects of prediction statements are not to be taken for granted, but are themselves appropriate subjects for scientific study—exactly as are the effects of any other kind of statement.

Closely related to Friedrich's and Giddens' objections is Taylor's: "With changes in [man's] self-definition go changes in what man is, such that he has to be understood in different terms. . . . [Frequently the changed terms] cannot be defined in relation to a common stratum of expressions. The entirely different notions of bargaining in our society and in some primitive ones provide an example'' (1979, p. 69). Having granted Taylor's point that prediction is possible only when the system being predicted is understood in terms of "the same variables" (or, as he puts it here, "a common stratum of expressions"), one must admit that whenever such a straum is absent, no natural science can exist.

But one has only to note, first, that such a stratum is often already available even though a given analyst may not be aware of it (indeed, Taylor's own example clearly, if unwittingly, rests on a commonly accepted, generic, definition of "bargaining"—otherwise he could neither use the term nor speak of "entirely" different notions of that definition), and when such a stratum is not already available, the interested natural sciences must invent one. Second, this process of concept invention yields problematic and impermanent results in *every* natural science, not just in the social sciences, but this is no reason to stop trying to improve those results. The disciplinary matrix set forth here, then, is designed as a step (inevitably flawed and impermanent) toward such improvement in sociology—a step, incidentally, that includes the explanatory-predictive variables Taylor most favors, namely, "intersubjective or common meanings" (1979, p. 54), and also permits—with two essential provisos—the use of "interpretive method" in scientific sociological analysis.[19]

To sum up the argument so far, there are good reasons for pursuing sociology as a natural science, and there seem to be no logical barriers to doing so. Several characteristics required of scientific sociology (characteristics, therefore, to be served by the disciplinary matrix proposed below) have been sketched. Scientific sociology should regard the making of reliable predictions as its prime objective; it should concern itself with regularities rather than uniquenesses; it should pursue knowledge of possibilities as well as actualities; and for all these reasons, it should rely on collectively standardized rather than personally idiosyncratic concepts, terminology, and measurement.

All these are features that sociology should have by virtue of sharing the general aims and methods of natural science. But what features should it have by virtue of taking social phenomena as its special subject matter? In order to answer this question (and before considering a formal definition of "social phenomena"), let us examine what seems to be the most distinctive single characteristic of that subject matter— namely, a very high degree of equifinality.

Equifinality in Social Phenomena

Equifinality means "There's more than one way to skin a cat"; "All rivers run to the sea"; "All roads lead to Rome"; "And how dieth the wise man? as the fool." The concept "equifinality," then, indicates that alternative processes may have the same outcome and one may differentiate degrees of equifinality (sometimes called structural "flexibility"—see Parsons, 1964, p. xlv) according to the number of such processes.[20] Von Bertalanffy identifies equifinality with open systems (which he defines as maintaining themselves "in a continuous inflow and outflow, building up and breaking down of components" [1956, p. 31]): "in open systems . . . the same final state may be reached from different initial conditions and in different ways. This is what is called equifinality" (1956, p. 4). And where von Bertalanffy explicitly points to system openness, Simon implicitly points to hierarchic structure, as possessing a high degree of equifinality—in the following sense. Defining as hierarchic "a system that is composed of interrelated sub-systems, each of the latter being, in turn, hierarchic in structure until we reach some lowest level of elementary subsystem" (1965, p. 64), Simon shows that complex systems (he uses a watch as case in point, but extends his argument to naturally evolved living organisms and to human problem-solving) may be assembled and maintained more efficiently if individual parts are joined into several subassemblies and then these subassemblies are joined into the final system, because, as Simon says, if the watchmaker has "to put down a partly assembled watch in order to answer the phone, he [would lose] only a small part of his work" (1965, p. 66).

The important thing to note here is that this special efficiency of hierarchic structure implies equifinality insofar as when one constructs stable subassemblies of a watch, an organism, a jigsaw puzzle, a mathematical proof, or whatever, one makes a particular final outcome more resistant to interruptions and other obstacles, thereby enabling that outcome to be reached despite them—which is to say, in different ways.

Thus, von Bertalanffy claims that a high degree of equifinality characterizes open systems and, by implication, Simons claims it characterizes hierarchically structured systems. It follows that insofar as social scientists universally regard social phenomena as hierarchically structured (i.e., as being divisible into micro, meso, and macro levels—see below) as well as open (i.e., having flow-throughs of individual participants and other energies), we invoke two strong reasons for presuming that any given social phenomenon may be explained-predicted in more than one way—that is, with different explanatory-predictive variables arranged in different causal relationships. Thus Weber says, "Common customs may have diverse origins"; "The same result may be reached from various starting-points" (1978, pp. 394, 454). Simmel concurs: In principle, every end can be attained by more than one means" (1955, p. 27); and "Events may be incommensurate in their intrinsic meanings but so similar in respect to the roles they play in our total existence as to be interchangeable" (1971, p. 187). Marx is much more reluctant to admit equifinality, although he does argue, at one point, that "the village commune . . . [can] take advantage of all the positive achievements of [capitalist production] without passing through all [the] dreadful vicissitudes [of that production]" (Marx and Engels, 1969, Vol. III, p. 153)—that is, the village commune can reach the same end points that capitalism reaches, but by a different route. Durkheim's analysis of four different circumstances all producing the same outcome— namely, a high suicide rate (see the earlier discussion)—is an exemplary classical investigation of equifinality in social phenomena—and this despite Durkheim's own strenuous resistance, both to the concept itself (see 1982, p. 148) and to its role in the analysis of suicide (see 1951, pp. 277-294). More recently, Merton relies on the principle of equifinality when he proposes *functional alternative* as a term denoting "possible variation in the items which can . . . subserve a [given] functional requirement" (1957, p. 52). Stinchcombe says, "Functional causal imagery is . . . indicated whenever one sees (or thinks he sees) a pattern of equifinality in social phenomena" (1968, p. 82; but see note 61 here); Moore refers to the same principle when he coins the term *structural substitutability* (1959, p. 838); and, similarly, Bourdieu and Passeron argue that "different values [may] orient similar behaviors" (1979, p. 19).

The principle of equifinality, insofar as it applies to social phenomena (and it should be emphasized that that principle seems applicable, in varying degrees, to all phenomena) warns us never to assume that any single causal model will explain or predict all the variance in a given social phenomenon, and warns us not to give exclusive allegiance to any currently available paradigm in sociology (see the related views of Blalock, 1979, p. 881; Luckmann, 1978, pp. 237-239; and Merton, 1975, pp. 28-29).[21] We should instead strive to incorporate all the essential features of such paradigms into one systematic matrix of concepts from which multiple equifinal explanations of, and equioriginal predictions from, the same social phenomenon may be constructed.[22] Such incorporation is the aim of what now follows.

Describing Social Phenomena

It is certainly no revelation to say sociology investigates social phenomena, but exactly what do we mean by social" phenomena? How are such phenomena defined generically? This is the single most crucial question for the future of sociological analysis because unless we agree on the observable signature of the phenomena at the focus of our discipline's attention, neither descriptive nor explanatory-predictive analysis in sociology can ever become rigorously comparable and cumulative.

For maximum universality within sociology, the definition should subsume all those now explicitly or implicitly present in the sociological literature, and for this, it (and, indeed, all the concepts incorporated into any disciplinary matrix) should be as simple as possible. That is, our disciplinary matrix must give up the pursuit of conceptual "richness" in favor of maximum simplicity—a simplicity, however, that like Mendeleev's systematization of chemical elements should be capable of yielding any desired amount of complexity by combining its elements in appropriate ways.

With these two criteria in mind, we arrive at the following: A social phenomenon may be generically defined as an *interorganism behavior regularity*—that is, as a nonrandom coincidence in time and/or space of two or more organisms' behaviors. Let us consider some of the most important implications of this definition.

First, it should be noted that this definition links sociology to all the other natural sciences through sharing their general format for defining any kind of phenomenon—namely, as some more or less complex "interentity behavior regularity." For example, an organism may be scientifically defined as an intercell behavior regularity; a cell as an interprotoplasm (e.g., membrane, cytoplasm, mitochondria, nucleus, chromosome) behavior regularity; any of these protoplasmic structures may be defined as an intermolecule behavior regularity; and any molecule may be defined as one or more interatom, and ultimately interparticle (i.e., lepton, quark, and/or boson), behavior regularities.

Second, the claim that the definition is

"generic" means it refers to only the most broadly inclusive category of phenomena called "social," while leaving open the specification of any number of varieties within that genus. That is to say, although individual analysts may not remove elements from the generic definition (i.e., they may not claim that nonorganisms are participants in social phenomena; or that a regularity in only one organism's behavior constitutes a social phenomenon; or that a single, unique, and incomparable coincidence of behaviors across two or more organisms constitutes a social phenomenon), they are free to add further restrictions in order to construct special definitions. Thus analysts are free to specify certain organisms and not others, certain behaviors and not others, certain regularities and not others, as constituting the particular social phenomenon in which they happen to be interested. Moreover, they are also free to specify interest in behavior regularities between *groups* of organisms—say, between organizations, communities, societies, or groups of societies (more on this, below).

Third, by virtue of the generality of the term *organism*, the definition encourages close relationships between sociology and sociobiology, including not only the recognition of conceptual isomorphisms between within-discipline studies of all-human social phenomena and all-nonhuman social phenomena, but interdisciplinary studies such as of human and pet social phenomena (see Sussman, 1985), human and laboratory-animal social phenomena (see Linden, 1986), and human and animal-in-the-wild social phenomena (see Goodall, 1986).[23]

Fourth, by referring broadly to "behavior," the definition includes literally *all* organismic behavior (whether motor, visceral, endocrine, neural, voluntary, involuntary, conscious, unconscious, intentional, unintentional, purposive, nonpurposive, or whatever—and any combination thereof) as admissible constituents of social phenomena. Choice of the specific behaviors to be included in a given description is thus left entirely up to the researcher. Here, of course, the definition encourages close relationships between sociology and the more behavior-specific social sciences like economics and political science.

Fifth, the definition refers simply to "regularity" and thus requires, at minimum, only a nonzero probability of observing one organism's behavior, given that at least one other organism's behavior is also observed. Note that by leaving "regularity" unqualified, the generic definition leaves the researcher free to focus on long-term versus short-term, ordinary versus extraordinary, revolutionary versus evolutionary (etc.) temporal regularities, and also free to focus on dense versus sparse, radial versus concentric, coastal versus inland (etc.) spatial regularities (see Bourdieu, 1977, pp. 5-9; Giddens, 1986, pp. 110-161; Wallace, 1983, pp. 133-155). Almost needless to add, by permitting both temporal and spatial regularities, the generic definition of social phenomena formulated above encourages close relationships between sociology, on the one hand, and history and geography, on the other.

Finally, special attention should be paid to the fact that as a protection against tautological explanatory propositions, the generic definition of social phenomena contains no a priori explanations or predictions of social phenomena. Such explanations and predictions are thus left open to empirically testable propositions rather than preempted by arbitrary conceptual definition. Thus one reason no mention is made of "interaction" as part of the generic definition is that it would require a priori acceptance of a particular explanation—namely, that B's behavior is causally explained by A's action on B, and that A's behavior is causally explained by B's action on A—as is explicitly the case in Homans's definition of "social behavior" as "behavior in which the action of one man is a stimulus to . . . the action of another" (1974, p. 56; see also p. 77). The other reason interaction is not required by the generic definition is in order to permit the regular action of two or more organisms not on each other but on their environments (as when different people turn their TVs on or off, or put up or down their umbrellas), and also the "one-way" action of one organism on another—including both that of the beheader on the beheaded and that of the dead on the living through the many intended and unintended bequests of the former—to come under the generic definition of social phenomena.

Here are a few of the classical and modern statements from which the definition proposed above as generic was derived.

Classical Definitions

Marx and Engels say, "By social we understand the co-operation of several individuals" (1969, Vol. I, p. 31)—although "joint activity" seems a more faithful translation of the original *Zusammenwirken* than "co-operation" because it permits competition and conflict (i.e., "struggle") also to be regarded as social. Comte joins Marx and Engels in allowing the "regularity" component of the generic definition to remain only implicit while making the "interorganism" and "behavior" components explicit: "The exercise of a general and combined activity is the essence of society" (1975, p. 20). Weber, however, is explicit about the "regularity" component: "Sociology seeks to formulate type concepts and generalized uniformities of empirical process. This distinguishes it from history, which is oriented to the causal analysis and explanation of individual actions, structures, and personalities" (1978, p. 19). In this statement, however, Weber omits reference to the "interorganism" and "behavior" components—an omission made good when he defines a "social relationship" as the "behavior of a plurality of actors." Weber then goes on, however, to require the involvement of not one but two kinds of behavior ("physical action behavior and psychical orientation" behavior) in the regularity when he says, "In its meaningful content, the action of each [actor] takes account of that of the others and is oriented in these terms" (1978, p. 26)—a requirement that must be regarded as special, optional, and therefore nongeneric. Simmel imposes another special requirement, namely, interaction: "Society merely is the name for a number of individuals, connected by interaction" (1950, p. 10). Simmel takes note (however unclearly) of variability in temporal regularities in social phenomena when he says, "Sociation ranges all the way from the momentary getting together for a walk to the founding of a family,. . . from the temporary aggregation of hotel guests to the intimate bonds of a medieval guild" (1971, p. 24; see also Weber, 1978, p. 28), and (more clearly) spatial regularities in social phenomena when he refers to the "expansion [of social relations] involving ties across great distances" (1971, p. 255; see also Weber, 1978, p. 635).

"*Social facts.*" Durkheim's discussion of "social facts" illuminates the generic definition of social phenomena in a special way. Durkheim offers two definitions, back to back: "A social fact is any way of acting, whether fixed or not, capable of exerting over the individual an external constraint; *or*: which is general over the whole of a given society whilst having an existence of its own, independent of individual manifestations" (1982, p. 59). He then unblinkingly assures us the two are equivalent: "The second definition is simply another formulation of the first one: if a mode of behaviour existing outside the consciousnesses of individuals becomes general, it can only do so by exerting pressure upon them" (Durkheim, 1982, p. 57). But obviously the two are *not*

equivalent: the "generality" stipulation is an arbitrary conceptual definition whereas the "pressure-exerting" stipulation is a hypothetical explanation of the condition specified by that definition. Moreover, the principle of equifinality (both exemplified and opposed by Durkheim, as mentioned earlier here), argues that that hypothesis will be false to the extent that a given mode of behavior can become general across a society in ways other than its exerting external pressure on individuals (i.e., if pressure from other external phenomena, and/or pressure from internal phenomena, can bring about the same generality). We must therefore reject Durkheim's equivalence claim, reject his first definition on the ground that it is really a hypothesis, and accept only his second definition (namely, "A social fact is any way of acting . . . which is general over the whole of a given society whilst having an existence of its own, independent of individual manifestations").[24] This latter definition, however, reduces to a special (societal level) case of "interorganism behavior regularity" once it is granted that with the expression "*way* of acting" (rather than simply "*act*") Durkheim implies behavior *regularity*, and that by "independent of individual manifestations" he means relatively independent of *any particular* manifestation—in just the way that an average computed over many individual values is relatively independent of any particular one of them although, of course, not independent of them all (see Durkheim's tacit admission of this: 1982, p. 55). In the final analysis, then, Durkheim's definition of social facts supports rather than challenges the definition of social phenomena being put forward here as generic.

Modern Definitions

Merton says the "object of [functional] analysis [must] represent a standardized (i.e., patterned and repetitive) item, such as social roles, institutional patterns . . . etc." (1957, p. 50, italics removed). Blau and Scott say "Social organization refers to . . . the observed regularities in the behavior of people" (1962, p. 2)—but they join Merton in neglecting to require that the regularities (or the patterning and repetitiveness) must be between the behavior of different people rather than in the behaviors of the same person (although the former seem clearly their, and Merton's, intent). A similar comment is pertinent in Homans's case when he says, "The usual description of groups consist of statements of . . . recurrences in human behavior at different places or at different intervals'' (1950, p. 28). Parsons's definition of a ''social system'' (as he himself admits) is more restrictive than those just mentioned insofar as it requires both interaction and specific kinds of participant behavior: ''Though the term social system may be used in a more elementary sense, for present purposes . . . attention [is] confined to systems of interaction of . . . individual actors oriented to a situation and where the system includes a commonly understood system of cultural symbols''(1951, p. 5).[25]

Thus, it seems fair to say that all these leading modern as well as classical definitions of human social phenomena are subsumed as special cases of the definition proposed here as generic.

Descriptive Variables

Given these elaborations and brief supporting citations, we are now in position to suggest how the generic *definition* of social phenomena yields the three most important distinctions that sociologists (and all other social scientists) draw in *describing* these phenomena, namely, (1) the distinction between human social phenomena and social phenomena among other organisms, (2) the distinction between social structure and cultural structure, and (3) the distinction between the spatial dimension and the temporal dimension of both social structure and cultural structure. To this end, consider Figure 1.1 and its set of eight elemental types of variables employed in the descriptive analysis of social phenomena.

In cell a we have descriptions of social phenomena in which interhuman *physical* (skeletomuscular and visceral) behavior regularities in space are of primary interest—for example, descriptions of voting patterns in Maine. In cell b we have descriptions of social phenomena in which interhuman *psychical* (neuroendocrine) behavior regularities in *space* are of primary interest—for example, descriptions of political beliefs in Maine.[26] In cell c we have descriptions of social phenomena in which interhuman *physical* behavior regularities in *time* are of primary interest—for example, descriptions of voting patterns during the twentieth century. In cell d we have descriptions of social phenomena in which interhuman *psychical* behavior regularities in *time* are of primary interest—for example, descriptions of political beliefs during the twentieth century. Cells e, f, g, and h, of course, refer to descriptions paralleling those in cells a, b, c, and d—except that the participants in the former are nonhuman (i.e., plant, animal, and, potentially, artificial) organisms.

Almost needless to add, any two or more of the variables shown in Figure 1.1 may be combined—either into more complex variables, or into propositions—when describing a given social phenomenon. For example, a description of pet ownership among human residents of New York City in the late twentieth century might implicate at least cells a, b, c, d, e, and g—and perhaps also f and h. Note, also, that neither Figure 1.1 nor the other two figures offered in this chapter purport to be either maximally detailed or logically exhaustive.[27] It follows that the disciplinary matrix set forth here remains open to, and solicitous of, further internal specification and external broadening of

	Human Organisms		Nonhuman Organisms	
	Physical behavior	Psychical behavior	Physical behavior	Psychical behavior
Spatial regularity	a	b	e	f
Temporal regularity	c	d	g	h

FIGURE 1.1
Matrix of Variables Describing Social Phenomena

scope. Although it is systematic, the matrix is by no means rigid or fixed.

At the same time, however, a strong empirical claim can be made for Figure 1.1—namely, that it systematically subsumes all descriptions of social phenomena to be found in the sociological literature—which is to say, every such description is classifiable either within some single cell, or some combination of cells, shown in Figure 1.1.

Social Structure and Cultural Structure;
Their Spatial and Temporal Dimensions

Focusing on the "human" side of Figure 1.1 (similar claims hold for its "nonhuman" side), cells a and c are what we mean by "social structure"—things given people *do* together (whether constructive, destructive, or transportational things; whether to themselves, each other, or to nonpeople objects in their environments; and whether in unison, conflict, cooperation, or competition, with each other) regularly in space and/or time. Cells b and d are what we mean by "cultural structure"—things given people *think-feel* together (whether cognitive, cathectic, or conative things; whether consciously or unconsciously; whether about themselves, each other, or nonpeople objects in their environments; and whether in consensus, complementarity, or dissensus with each other) regularly in space and/or time.[28,29] Cells a and b are what we mean by the spatial dimension of social structure and cultural structure— roughly speaking, the *places and distances* over which given people regularly do and/or think-feel things together—while cells c and d are what we mean by the temporal dimension of social structure and cultural structure—roughly speaking, the *times and durations* over which given people regularly do and/or think-feel things together.

At this point, an explicit DANGER sign must be posted over the unfortunately long-standing ambiguity that tradition in sociology has assigned to the term *social*. That is, social has both a generic meaning (as in "social phenomena," including *all* cells of Figure 1.1), and a specific meaning (as in "social structure," including only the *physical* behavior cells a, c, e, and g of Figure 1.1). Weber adds still another confusion when he defines the "*social order*" as "the sphere of the distribution of *honor*" (1978, p. 938; italics added)—that is, as comprising

shared evaluative *psychical* behaviors—a phenomenon that Figure 1.1 (and Weber himself, elsewhere), calls "cultural."[30] Some of the misapprehensions that result when the first two, not to mention all three, meanings are not kept carefully separated may be illustrated by the following remarks made by one writer in the same analysis: (1) "The social-system focus is on . . . the interaction of actual human individuals. . . . [whereas the] cultural-system focus . . . is on 'patterns' of meaning, e.g., of values, of norms, of organized knowledge and beliefs, of expressive 'form'"; and (2) "the structure of social systems *consists* in institutionalized patterns of normative culture" (Parsons, 1961, pp. 34, 36). If we assume (as we must, because Parsons does not tell us to do otherwise) that the word "social" has the same meaning in both statements, then the statements contradict each other: the first statement implies that the social system and the cultural system have their own distinct structures (i.e., patterns of physical "interaction," and " 'patterns' of [psychical] meaning," respectively), but the second implies the social system has *no* structure of its own; its structure is that of the *cultural* system! If we conjecture, however, that the first statement's "social" is really intended to have the specific (social structure) meaning, while the second statement's "social" has the generic (social phenomenon) meaning, the contradiction disappears—provided also that the second statement is interpreted not as a description of what the social system's structure *consists in* but as a causally explanatory (specifically, cultural structural—see below) hypothesis of where that structure *comes* from (i.e., from the cultural system's causal regulation, through its norms, of the interactions of which the social system's structure is composed). The moral is this: Different usages of the same key term, *social*, can lead us unknowingly into self-contradiction or tautology unless we sustain a deliberate, careful, and unrelenting effort to keep them separate.[31]

Wuthnow et al. rightly deplore another far-reaching difference in usage: "Theorists of culture remain sorely divided on how best to define culture" (1984, p. 3). In setting forth their own "provisional" definition, the authors present two main objections to other definitions, and these objections cast important light on the definition proposed in this chapter. Their first objection is to definitions claiming that "culture consists primarily of thoughts, moods, feelings, beliefs, and values" (Wuthnow et al., 1984, p. 3) on the ground that all such phenomena are *"invisible"* and *"unobservable"* (in contrast with the supposed visibility and observability of physical behaviors and therefore social structure—see 1984, pp. 4-5), and that "It would scarcely do (for building an empirical science) to explain the observable activities of human actors in terms of unobservable cultural predispositions" (1984, p. 5).[32]

This objection should be rejected on the ground that not only "thoughts, moods, feelings, beliefs, and values" are invisible and unobservable; strictly speaking, no phenomena outside the observer are directly observable; we perceive not *things* but their presumed *indicators* (more precisely still, we can directly observe only our own sensory organs' responses—responses *presumably* to these indicators, but we can be—and often are—fooled). Thus to say we observe someone physically walking is to say that we believe we perceive phenomena (a certain moving pattern of light, correlated changes in sound, changes in air pressure, and so on) that we habitually—but certainly not infallibly—accept as indicators of "someone walking."[33] Similarly, in order to observe someone thinking-feeling, we must also look to external, physical, indicators—that is, we read (critically and often suspiciously) what that someone writes; we listen closely to what he or she says; "we take notice of slight, evanescent tones of his voice, expressions of his face, movements of his hands, ways of carrying his body" (Homans, 1950, p. 39); or we watch physical changes in EEG, polygraph, skin conductance, and other meters. Thus although observing a person's psychical behavior usually requires one more inference (i.e., from the person's—or a meter's—physical behavior to the person's psychical behavior) than does observing the same person's physical behavior, *both* kinds of observations depend on highly problematic subjective inferences; *neither* is directly "visible," "observable," or unambiguously "objective," and in both cases the observer's problem is the same—to select, evaluate, and integrate optimally reliable and valid indicators.

There is, then, no unique methodological reason conceptually to reduce cultural structure to social structure (or vice-versa), and because avoidance of that reduction enables us to make room in the proposed disciplinary matrix for the many well-established hypotheses that causally explain the one kind of observation with the other (see the discussion below of cultural structural and social structural explanatory-predictive variables), it seems essential to reject the behavioristic reduction of cultural structure to social structure, and to reflect the conceptual separation of these variables operationally by simply identifying and clearly labeling the physical indicators chosen for each of them, just as we must do for any other phenomena.[34] In this way, let us bring *mind* back into the study of culture (that is, explicitly back; implicitly, of course, it never left).

Whereas the first objection raised by Wuthnow et al. is therefore rejected here, their second objection—namely, to definitions based on "the assumption that only individuals have culture" (1984, p. 6)—is more consistently adopted here than in their own discussion. Thus the present definition explicitly makes cultural structure, like social structure, not an intra-individual behavior regularity, but an inter-individual behavior regularity—thereby putting the two structures on equal conceptual footings. Contrary, then, to the concession that "at one level it makes sense, of course, to limit culture to individuals" (Wuthnow et al., 1984, p. 6), the present definition asserts that although psychical behavior seems properly defined as limited to individuals, culture (i.e., inter-organism psychical behavior regularity) is an exclusively social phenomenon. According to this definition, then, at *no* level does it make sense to limit culture to individuals.

Finally in reference to Figure 1.1 (and as just mentioned), note that social structure and cultural structure are here construed as logically independent dimensions of social phenomena. That is to say, the principle of equifinality assures us that in any given set of organisms, physical behavior regularities may logically exist, and may logically vary, independently of psychical behavior regularities, and vice-versa. It follows that the question of whether *both* social structures and cultural structures exist in a given social phenomenon is not to be taken for granted but can only be settled by empirical research.[35] Similarly, the exact characteristics of these two structures (and whether they are similar to each other, complement each other, conflict with each other, or are irrelevant to each other) when both *are* observed in a given social phenomenon, can only be settled by empirical research.[36] It also follows that in making and reporting such observations, their physical and psychical behavior elements (and for the same general reasons, their spatial and temporal regularity, and their human and nonhuman organism, elements) should be *separately* identified before being brought together into a comprehensive description of the phenomenon as a whole. Such separate identification is required for keeping track of how different kinds of social structure and cultural structure do or do not combine, and for comparing different descriptions, explanations, and predictions of each.[37]

Whenever we bypass the standardizing descriptive procedure just outlined (or one like it) and employ only a terminology specific to the particular social phenomenon we happen to be studying, we fail to meet our analytical responsibility as scientists and deeply undermine comparability and cumulativeness in sociology—exactly as any chemist who might bypass that discipline's standard "H_2O" designation in devising only case specific descriptions of, say, rainwater, seawater, tap water, ice, snow, and steam would undermine those goals in chemistry.

Micro, Meso, and Macro
Social Phenomena

Now let us consider the following descriptive claims: Blumberg says, "All societies have a minimum of two . . . 'nesting' levels: the *household* level . . . and the level of the *community* or local group"; and adds that "in class-stratified and politically centralized societies, a minimum of two more levels must be taken into account: that of the *class* and that of the larger *society*" (1984, p. 48). To this, Wallerstein adds the level of "world-systems. . . . [which] contain within them a multiplicity of cultures" (1974:348), and Bergesen tops it off: "There is only *one* world economy, *one* social formation, and, most important, *one* world or global mode of production. . . . [having within it only] the global class relation of core ownership and control over peripheral production" (1984, p. 370). In brief, we have descriptions here that look upon social phenomena as hierarchically ordered, such that the most elemental social phenomena are aggregated, and then these aggregates are aggregated, and so on up, from micro through ever more macro levels. How do such descriptions come under the generic definition of social phenomena as interorganism behavior regularities?

According to the generic definition, all social "collectivities"—of whatever inclusiveness—can be composed only of individual organisms behaving regularly (no matter how simply or complicatedly) with respect to one another, and we describe one collectivity as distinguished from another by pointing to differences in their rosters of participating *organisms* alone, regardless of what their behaviors and regularities may be. But this is only one of the macro descriptions subsumed by the generic definition. We also describe one social or cultural "system" or "subsystem" as distinguished from another by pointing to differences in their constituent *be-haviors* (e.g., economic, political, educational, religious), regardless of which collectivities (whether overlapping in membership or not) manifest them and regardless of which regularities characterize them. Finally, we describe one social "location" or social "timing" (e.g., apartment or block, European or American, daily or yearly, nineteenth or twentieth century) as being different from another by pointing to differences in the spatial and/or temporal *regularities* that correlate behaviors across participants, regardless of which groups and/or behaviors are characterized by these regularities.

Thus although "microsociology" is said to specialize in analyzing social structures where the organisms are few *and* their interorganism behaviors are of few types *and* their regularities are of small extension (e.g., "conversations," "face-to-face interaction"), whereas the opposite is said to describe "macrosociology," these become only two of many possible descriptive combinations when we (1) add "meso" levels to the oversimplified micro-macro dichotomy and (2) apply the idea of such levels to each component of the generic definition (i.e., organisms, behavior, and regularity) separately.[38,39] With these steps, we free ourselves to describe not only the polar and homogeneous (i.e., all-micro and all-macro) types, but also variably mixed types such as those where the organisms are few but the behaviors of interest have moderate, or great, variety and the regularities have moderate, or great, extension (e.g., intercontinentally mobile and/or long-lived members of a single household having widely different occupations), and those where the organisms are many but the behaviors of interest are of small or large variety, and their regularities have short, or moderate, extension (e.g., the audience of a particular TV show, commuters crowding into a subway, national elections, fans at a soccer game).[40]

Now the following question arises: What are the empirical limits on where lines between levels may be drawn? The generally (if only implicitly) agreed-upon answer seems to be that we recognize a substantively significant discontinuity (and therefore draw a line) between levels in either the organisms, behavior, or regularity hierarchy when we find it is correlated with discontinuities in the remaining two hierarchies. For example, Simmel associates the membership difference between collectivities having two, and three, participants with behavior differences: "Precisely the fact that each of the two knows that he can depend only upon the other and on nobody else, gives the dyad a special consecration . . . [but] among three elements, each one operates as an intermediary between the other two'' (1950, p. 135). And, Simmel adds (so that we will not underestimate the significance of this correlation), ''[T]he further expansion to four or more by no means correspondingly modifies the group any further'' (1950, p. 138). In much the same way, Berger and Luckmann associate the difference between a childless married couple and the same couple when they have a child with a behavioral difference that reflects a perceived temporal regularity difference: ''The habitualizations and typifications undertaken in the common life of A and B . . . now become historical institutions. . . . This means that the institutions that have now been crystallized are experienced as existing over and beyond the individuals who 'happen to' embody them at the moment'' (1967, p. 58).

Thus, because the descriptive analysis of hierarchical structure in social phenomena requires us to look for discontinuities that are correlated across all three constituents of social phenomena, that analysis focuses on the following kinds of questions. (1) What are the behavior and regularity properties of different levels of collectivities (dyads, triads, and up)? Simmel's, and Berger and Luckmann's, observations—cited above—address this question. (2) What are the collectivity and regularity properties of different levels of behavior (subsystem, system, and higher)? Here we want to know whether certain levels of social, and cultural, structural complexity are found only in collectivities at certain levels of complexity and whether these structures manifest distinctively complex spatial and/or temporal regularities. (3) What are the behavior and collectivity properties of different levels of regularities? Here we want to know, for simplest example, whether small or large geographical spaces, and short or long durations, are associated with certain levels of behavior, and collectivity, complexity.

Whenever such interlocking descriptive analyses reveal correlated discontinuities, we are apt to ask ''why?'' and ''so what?''—thereby moving the analysis into its next, explanatory-predictive, phase. Here we search for ''a kind of 'causal decoupling' between different organizational levels [in contrast to causal coupling within such levels—*WLW*] as one moves from the microcosm to the macrocosm'' (Pagels, 1986, p. 161, italics added)—thereby testing the sciencewide proposition that at least some of the causal relations holding on one side of the discontinuity do not hold (or hold in some significantly different way) on the other side.[41] Such decoupling seems clearly what Giesen has

in mind when he refers to a '' 'falling out' of the micro and macro levels'' and calls it ''a well-known experience of everyday life . . . [where] the macrostructural properties of a social system no longer correspond to the internalized rules and intentions of the individual actors'' (1987, p. 338).

And having passed from problems of the descriptive analysis of hierarchical structure in social phenomena to problems of its explanatory-predictive analysis, we reserve further discussion (specifically, of how different levels are produced in the first place, how they are held together internally afterwards, and how they are terminated) for a later section here on causal images.

Explaining and Predicting Social Phenomena

The first part of the disciplinary matrix proposed here for sociology is (as we have just seen) devoted to systematizing conceptual elements used in the description of social phenomena. Obviously, specifying the nature of such elements is indispensable to our discipline not only because it tells what sociology is ''about'' in a general way but, more important, because descriptive analysis specifically sets the stage for explanatory and predictive analysis.[42]

Such stage setting (or, more exactly, target identification) is necessitated by the fact that, as Weber points out, every ''concrete phenomenon'' is ''infinitely complex'' and ''every single perception [of such a phenomenon] discloses on closer examination an infinite number of constituent perceptions.'' It follows, Weber says, that ''an *exhaustive* causal investigation of any concrete phenomenon in its full reality is not only practically impossible—it is simply nonsense.'' We finite humans can investigate and explain ''Only *certain sides* of the infinitely complex concrete phenomenon''—sides that we select as being, for one reason or another, ''worthwhile knowing'' (1949, p. 78, italics changed; see also p. 169). The act of selecting these sides, and communicating that selection, is called ''description'' and Hempel's portrayal of its indispensable role in identifying the target of explanation is succinct: ''[R]equests for an explanation . . . have a clear meaning only if it is understood [via a description] what aspects of the phenomenon in question are to be explained'' (1965, p. 334). Let us consider, then, the explanatory-predictive target that is implied by defining and describing social phenomena in the manner set forth above.

The key point is that in order fully to explain or predict a given social phenomenon, we must explain or predict the behavior of *one participating organism at a time*.[43] To see why this is so, imagine two organisms (the minimum required for a social phenomenon), each existing anywhere, anytime. One of them, say organism A, may behave freely—that is, with any (or no) regularity whatever. B, however, must behave regularly with respect to A's behavior if they are to be considered participants in the same social phenomenon. Even if A's behavior is irregular in itself, the regular coincidence of B's behavior with A's irregular behavior constitutes an inter-organism behavior regularity (e.g., *milling* and collective *excitement*, to use the social structural and cultural structural terms found in the literature on crowds). It is therefore the constraining of organism B's behavior into regularity with A's behavior—whatever the latter may be—that we have to explain or predict.

The same principle applies to all more complicated situations, such as when we want to explain or predict social phenomena involving more than two organisms, or involving behavioral reciprocation between organisms: In principle, we have to explain or predict the behavior of one organism at a time.[44] This enables us to acknowledge the equifinality discussed above (i.e., the likelihood that different instances of the same social phenomenon may be explained or predicted in different ways) by taking into account the likelihood that different social participants may do, or think-feel, the same things for different reasons—and different things for the same reasons.

It is essential to add, however, that reducing the explanation-prediction of social phenomena, in principle, to that of one participating organism's behavior at a time does not mean that we may not construct *typical* (modal) explanations-predictions across the relevant behavior of as many such organisms as we like—thereby explaining-predicting social phenomena of any group or subgroup, system or subsystem, we see fit.[45] Typical explanations-predictions, indeed, have been the social scientist's stock-in-trade so far. We should not forget, however, that they are *only* typical—that is, only estimated central tendencies that ignore the range of other explanations-predictions that may very well accompany them (and so often *do* accompany them, judging from the large amounts of unaccounted for variance with which nearly all sociological analyses are left).[46]

Explanatory and Predictive Variables

Having ascertained that regardless of the methodological shortcuts we may find practical in a given research, the full explanation-prediction of any social phenomenon logically requires the explanation-prediction of each individual participant's contributed behavior taken separately, we may now ask what kinds of variables can impinge on (and can be impinged on by) that behavior. A combination of six dimensions seems to encompass the essential elements of all such variables so far employed in the scientific analysis of social phenomena—whether human or nonhuman.[47]

The dimensions in question may be described most simply in terms of the following dichotomies: First, an individual's behavior can be constrained mainly from inside or mainly from outside that individual. Second, if from inside, the constraints can be exerted mainly by the individual's own skeletal-muscular-visceral system ("body"), or mainly by the individual's own neuroendocrine system ("mind"). Third, if from outside, the constraints can be exerted mainly by people (more inclusively for sociobiological purposes, conspecifics), or mainly by "things" (nonconspecifics), in the individual's environment. Fourth, the external constraints that emanate from people can be exerted mainly by the bodies of such people, or mainly by the minds of such people. Fifth, the external constraints that emanate from the nonpeople ("thing") environment can be exerted mainly by living, or mainly by nonliving, entities and forces. The sixth and final dimension intersects with all five others, dividing each of them into a socially generated component and an unsocially generated, existentially given, component.[48]

Combining these dimensions yields the set of 12 elemental types of sociological explanatory-predictive variables shown in Figure 1.2. The same kind of empirical claim may be made for this figure as for Figure 1.1, namely, that it systematically subsumes all the explanatory-predictive variables to be found in the sociological literature—which is to say, every such variable is classifiable either within some single cell, or some combination of cells, shown in Figure 2.1.[49]

It is essential to bear in mind that Figure 1.2 *makes no claims whatever regarding the empirical validity of locating a given observation in this or that category or combination of categories*. The way analysts have categorized their observations is the only concern of this chapter; no judgment is passed here on the (sometimes hotly contested) past, present, future, or possible *accuracy* of these categorizations. Similarly, no claim is made here regarding the explanatory-predictive weight that any given type of variable may be expected to carry —which is another way of saying the discussion is intended to be strictly nonpartisan toward (though cognizant of) all the "isms" (e.g., functionalism, materialism, symbolic interactionism) now current in our discipline. In a word, the analysis in this chapter comments exclusively on the *literature* regarding social phenomena; it does not comment on those phenomena themselves, or on the degree of congruence between the literature and them.

With those necessary disclaimers, let us now survey the types of variables shown in Figure 1.2, beginning with those pertaining to the nature of the participant himself or herself, moving next to those pertaining to the people in the participant's environment, and closing with those pertaining to the nonpeople things in that environment.[50]

Internal Variables

When drawn together, the remarks of four writers offer useful introduction to the double roles of internal variables in sociological explanations and predictions. (1) Weber emphasizes the role of internal mind variables as *originators* of influence on participants' behaviors: "We understand in terms of motive the meaning an actor attaches [to his action] . . . in that we

Origin of Causal Influence

	Existentially Given (Not In Prior Social Phenomena)	Socially Generated (In Prior Social Phenomena)
Location of Causal Influence		
In the participant's own:		
Mind	Instinct	Enculture
Body	Physiology	Nurture
In the participant's environing people:		
Their minds	Psychical contagion	Cultural structure
Their bodies	Demography	Social structure
In the participant's environing "things":		
Living	$Ecology_L$	$Technology_L$
Nonliving	$Ecology_{NL}$	$Technology_{NL}$

FIGURE 1.2
Matrix of Variables Explaining-Predicting Social Phenomena

understand [thereby] what makes him do this at precisely this moment and in these circumstances" (1978, p. 8, italics removed). (2) Marx emphasizes a similarly originating role for internal body variables: "[M]an produces universally. . . . [M]an produces even when he is free from physical need and only truly produces in freedom therefrom" (1977, p. 68). (3) Mead stresses the way internal mind variables act as filters or *gatekeepers*, determining which of the influences that originate outside the participants actually affect those participants:

> Our whole intelligent process seems to lie in the attention which is selective of certain types of stimuli. Other stimuli which are bombarding the system are in some fashion shunted off. . . . Here we have the organism as acting and determining its environment. It is not simply a set of passive senses played upon by the stimuli that come from without [1934, p. 25].

(4) Watkins implies the same gatekeeper role for internal body variables: "Speaking loosely, one can say that . . . alcohol causes road accidents. But speaking strictly, one should say that alcohol induces changes in people who drink it . . . it is the behavior of alcohol-affected people, rather than alcohol itself, which results in road accidents" (1973, p. 179)—that is, it is only because people possess a certain kind of physical constitution that alcohol can induce the changes in them that it does.

The entire class of internal mind, and body, variables depicted by Figure 1.2—all of which can play roles both as originators and as gatekeepers—is divided into four types: instinctual, physiological, encultural, and nurtural.

INSTINCT

Instinctual variables refer to existentially given behavioral aspects of the participant's own neuroendocrine unconsciousness-consciousness systems, or "mind." Although one of the first criticisms a sociologist may make of sociobiological analyses of human social phenomena pertains to the sociobiologist's frequently heavy explanatory-predictive reliance on instinctual variables, such variables appear more often than one might think in sociological analyses—though usually without being so labeled. Some of these variables are said to vary from one individual to the next: "Do not the individual's [mental] capacities depend to more than a trivial degree upon the genetic material with which he enters the social contest . . . ?" (Eckland, 1967,

p. 194). Others have been said to characterize genetically circumscribed categories (e.g., sex, age, or race) of individuals. Thus Maccoby and Jacklin argue that four, presumably innate, psychical sex differences are "fairly well established": "girls have greater verbal ability," "boys excel in visual-spatial ability," "boys excel in mathematical ability," and "males are more aggressive" (1974, pp. 351-352; for a related but different list, see Rossi, 1980, pp. 12-14). Moore claims that "when different age groups are compared at a given time, total intelligence test scores reach a peak in the late teens or early 20s and then decline with age" (1968, p. 255; compare Riley, 1987, pp. 7-8). Jensen asserts that "there seems to be little question that racial differences in genetically conditioned behavioral characteristics, such as mental abilities, should exist" (1969, p. 80; compare, among others, Eckland, 1967, pp. 190-191; Hirsch, 1967, pp. 431-434; and Taylor, 1980).

Still other instinctual variables, of course, are said to be universally human. Here we include Simmel's declaration that "there must be . . . a moral instinct" (1971, p. 164); Freud's claim that "the evolution of civilization . . . [consists of] the struggle between . . . the instinct of life and the instinct of destruction" (1962, p. 69); Homans's claims that "a tendency to imitate others is genetically inherited" and that "men could hardly have maintained pack behavior if they did not find social life as such innately rewarding" (1974, pp. 24, 27); Tiger's claim that "humans must have hope. There must . . . be a program for hope springing eternally in our innards" (1979, p. 21); and perhaps also Goffman's more noncommittal claim that "whatever it is that generates the human want for social contact and for companionship, . . . [that want includes] a need for an audience . . . and a need for teammates" (1959, p. 206; see also p. 253). Here, too, we find the several "pattern variables," "interpretive procedures," and "accounting practices"—all of which are posited by their originators as psychical techniques used by social participants for constructing and communicating interpretations of the social phenomena they experience. Such techniques, though never explicitly named "instinctual" by those using them, seem clearly so conceptualized— as the following brief comments try to document.

Parsons and Shils implicate instinctuality as essential to the pattern variables when they claim some of these variables are "determined by . . . interests *inherently* differentiated within the system of [the actor's] value-orientation itself," and others are "determined by . . .

the alternatives which are *inherent* [i.e., inherently perceived by the actor to be] in the structure of the object system" (1951, p. 84, italics added). Note that although the particular *choices* that given actors make are, in Parsons's view, socially generated, the *alternatives* themselves are "inherent"—that is, existentially given—in the actor. Cicourel implies a similar instinctuality when he claims the "interpretive procedures . . . emerge *developmentally* [in the individual]" (1974, p. 30, italics added). Garfinkel is harder to pin down on this question, but when Sacks and he refer to the "*unavoidable* and *irremediable*" practice of social participants "demonstrating the rational accountability of everyday activities" (1970, p. 339, italics added; see also Garfinkel, 1967, p. 34), he strongly implies that a drive toward rationality (and toward acquiring the "social support" attendant on its display [see Garfinkel, 1967, p. 281]) is innately human.[51]

Note that the concepts called pattern variables, interpretive procedures, and accounting practices seem to share not only the same instinctuality hypothesis but also the same specific explanatory-predictive problem—namely, how social participants manage to assign generalized meaning to particular situations that they have not experienced before and that, like all situations, are intrinsically ambiguous.[52] Thus, Parsons and Shils say, "The objects of the situation do not interact with the cognizing and cathecting organism in such a fashion as to determine automatically the meaning of the situation. Rather, the actor must make a series of choices before the situation will have a determinate meaning" (1951, p. 76). Similarly, Cicourel is dissatisfied that most sociological models of the actor lack "explicit statements about how the actor recognizes relevant stimuli and manages to . . . locate the stimuli in a socially meaningful context" (1974, p. 27); and Garfinkel asserts that "recognizable sense, or fact, or methodic character, or impersonality, or objectivity of accounts are not independent of the socially organized occasions of their use [i.e., they are not inherent in the accounts as such, but are]. . . . an ongoing, practical accomplishment [of the actors, on those occasions]" (1967, pp. 3-4). It seems noteworthy that such ongoing practical accomplishment is exactly the kind of problem for whose solution students of nonhuman social phenomena have most frequently turned to instinctual (e.g., "innate releasing mechanism") variables (see, among others, Bonner, 1980, pp. 37-38; Etkin, 1964, pp. 177-180; Lorenz, 1970, Vol. I, pp. 103-108).

PHYSIOLOGY

Such variables refer to existentially given (genetically inherited) behavioral aspects of the participant's own skeletal-muscular-visceral systems, or "body." Such variables stress the sociological explanatory-predictive power of innate bodily abilities like breathing, drinking, eating, vocalizing, manipulating (Mead says, "Speech and the hand go along together in the development of the social human being" [1934, p. 237]), bipedal walking and running ("the advantages of freeing the hands from full-time locomotion [are] great. Not only could food and tools be carried, but the hand could evolve as a precision organ" [Campbell, 1985, p. 28]), coitus (on which, until recently, the biological reproduction of all mammals has depended), sitting (consider all the social phenomena that depend on the human organism's ability to sit for long periods of time [see Hediger, 1961, pp. 36-38]), and so forth.

Marx and Engels's analytical reliance on physiological variables emphasizes production capabilities: "[Human beings] begin to distinguish themselves from animals as soon as they begin to produce their means of subsistence, a step which is conditioned by their physical organization," and "an animal produces only under the domination of immediate physical needs, whilst man produces even when he is free from physical need and only truly produces in freedom therefrom" (1969, Book I, p. 20, italics removed; 1977, p. 76; see also Simmel, 1971, p. 49). But where Marx and Engels see human individuals as innately all-producing, Durkheim sees them as innately all-consuming: "[H]ow determine the quantity of well-being, comfort, or luxury legitimately to be craved by a human being? Nothing appears in man's organic nor in his psychological constitution which sets a limit to such tendencies. . . . [O]ur needs," says Durkheim, "are unlimited so far as they depend on the individual alone" (1951, p. 247).

As in the case of instinctual variables, certain physiological variables have been regarded as universally human. Thus Berger and Luckmann claim, "Human being is impossible in a closed sphere of quiescent interiority. Human being must ongoingly externalize itself in activity. This anthropological necessity is grounded in man's biological equipment. . . . [T]he necessity for social order as such stems from [this] biological equipment" (1967, p. 52). Certain other physiological variables have been regarded as individually variable (e.g., sex, handedness), and still others have been regarded as sex-linked, age-linked, or race-linked: Rossi argues that the "reproductive and endocrine systems that underlie childbearing and lactation are functioning systems within the female throughout her life cycle, and to deny their significance to female psychology or to the organization of family systems is to devalue a central fact of human species survival" (1977, p. 9; see also Blumberg, 1984, pp. 33, 68; Freud, 1961, p. 24; Weber, 1978, p. 357). Moore says, "Psychologists and scholars in various fields have observed pronounced changes in the behavior of the aging organism. Among these are deficits in sensation and perception, in muscular strength, in the ability to react quickly to stimuli and to respond by means of complex sensorimotor coordination" (1968, p. 241). Spuhler and Lindzey argue that "albinism is regularly associated with distinctive behavior in certain environments; and there is no doubt that there are racial differences in the frequency of the gene for albinism" (1967, pp. 373, 390). And Bang, arguing that sickle-cell anemia "has a genetic basis" and that the disease's "highest prevalence is in West Africa" and among American Blacks, also notes that the same alleles that cause red blood cell sickling and death when homozygotic are "associated with resistance to malaria" (1969, pp. 10-11) when heterozygotic—thereby influencing social phenomena in two opposite ways.

ENCULTURE

Encultural variables include the same kinds of "mind" variables discussed under "instinct," but here their socially generated (i.e., "socialized") aspects are of primary interest. The encultural variables to be examined here all derive from the more inclusive concept called "norm" (and, when shared, "cultural norm")—defined as a highly plastic and even decomposable (see Swidler, 1986), associatively addressed (see Powers, 1973, pp. 212-213), chain of four socially learned types of expectation components. Such a chain provides that certain broadly or narrowly designated (1) *actors* (some of which designations include the individual himself or herself, while some do not—for example, "human being," "adult," "registered voter," "optometrist," "Ronald so-and-so"), when confronted by certain broadly or narrowly designated (2) *situations*, will (3) *respond* (physically and/or psychically) in certain broadly or narrowly designated ways, and that these responses will have certain broadly or narrowly designated (4) *consequences* invested with variable affective weights (thereby becoming "values"). In short, a norm tells social partici-

pants who (and what) should be expected to do and/or think-feel what, under which circumstances, with what looked-for effects (see Wallace, 1983, pp. 97-121). The expectation that individuals designated as "drivers" will "stop their cars" "at red lights," thereby avoiding "collisions" with other cars and pedestrians (and "tickets" from police officers) and arriving at their destinations safely, cheaply, and quickly, is an example.[53] Every such norm, no matter how stereotyped and automatic, requires some interpretation, some " 'art' of the necessary improvisation" (Bourdieu, 1977, p. 8, italics removed)—such that individuals who comply with the norm they have learned generally do so intelligently, sensitively, and not as "judgmental dopes" (Garfinkel, 1967, p. 67)—and such that interaction, even between individuals who hold the "same" norm, always involves some interpretive negotiation (see especially Goffman, 1967, and see the discussion of symbolic interactionism below).[54]

In the following discussion, then, the encultural variable called "self" is regarded as a major subdivision within the "actor" component of norms; "institution" is a major subdivision within the "situation" component; "role-expectation" is a major subdivision within the "response" component; and "conscience" is a major subdivision within the "consequence" component.

Self. Giddens says, "Theorizing [about] the self means formulating a conception of motivation . . . and relating motivation to the connections between unconscious and conscious qualities of the agent," and defines the self as "the sum of those forms of recall whereby the agent reflexively characterizes 'what' is at the origin of his or her action. The self is the agent as characterized by the agent" (1986, pp. 36, 51). On the whole, Mead emphasizes the *qualities* of the other people in the agent's environment, whereas Simmel emphasizes their *quantities*, in generating that agent's self. Thus, Mead says, "The individual . . . becomes an object to himself only by taking the attitudes of other individuals toward himself within a social environment" (1934, p. 138), but Simmel focuses on the "forms of individualism which are nourished by the quantitative relationships in the metropolis" (1971, p. 338; see also pp. 291-292). Stryker links the self to role expectations (see below) when he refers to "an image of the person as a structure of positions and roles which, internalized, is the self," and notes Manford Kuhn's summary claim that "a core self is both the product of the expectations of groups in which the person interacts and a shaper of [that] interaction" (1980, pp. 79, 102). Smelser examines another feature of the socially generated self—namely, defense mechanisms—by arguing that on the one hand society—or more accurately, culture—selects out and defines specific types of action and symbols "as [psychologically] threatening," and on the other, "society and culture are provenders of preferred psychological defenses against many threats" (1987, p. 282). Based on Freud's conceptualizations, Smelser offers a classification of such defenses (see 1987, pp. 271-281).[55]

Institutions. The "self" is the participant's image of himself or herself as a social and cultural participant, but "institutions" (here used loosely to include organizations, mass movements, class, ethnic, gender, age, and racial groups, nations and groups of nations, and other meso and macro social phenomena), constitute one central feature of the participant's image of his or her environing social situation. Regarding this image, Berger and Luckmann argue that "the objectivity of the institutional world, however massive it may appear to the individual, is a humanly produced, constructed, objectivity" (1967, p. 60)—constructed, that is, by the individual having learned to make certain cognitive generalizations (Berger and Luckmann call them "typifications") across multiple microevents. This seems to be what Collins means when he says, "Social patterns, institutions, and organizations are only abstractions from the behavior of individuals . . . if [these abstractions] seem to indicate a continuous reality it is because the individuals that make them up repeat their micro behaviors many times" (1981, p. 989).[56]

Role expectations. A role expectation may be regarded as a collection of more or less specific response rules held in the individual social participant's mind and accepted by that participant as referring directly to his or her own (and others') behavior in relation to one or more objects. Thus Goode defines a role expectation as "an organization of norms, that is, a connection among several norms" (1960, p. 251, italics removed); Scott says a "role" (i.e., role expectation) is a "collection of norms delimited by what a single actor may be expected to perform" (1971, p. 85); and Turner (also using "role" as shorthand for role expectation) claims "there is not just one role which enables an individual to interact in what is adjudged a consistent way with a given other-role. Roles are often comprehensive alternative ways of dealing with a

given other-role" (1962, p. 29). Taken all together, an individual's role expectations (pertaining to himself or herself and others) constitute a route-marked mental map of the social structural and cultural structural terrain he or she inhabits.

Conscience. Weber argues that the Puritan "acted in business with the best possible conscience" (1978, p. 616) and claims this conscience as a major explanation of the rise of modern Western capitalism. Freud argues that in order to enable individuals to participate in society, "Civilization . . . obtains mastery over the individual's dangerous desire for aggression . . . by setting up an agency within him to watch over it, like a garrison in a conquered city" (1962, pp. 70-71). This agency, Freud says, is conscience (the "essence" of which is " 'social anxiety' " [1959a, p. 7]), and its punishing instrumentality is guilt (see 1962, p. 70, and 1960, pp. 40-41). More recently, Scott defines conscience as a "dutiful condition or . . . the more general one of obligation," and guilt as that "aspect of conscience" which is "the expectation of punishment when the individual is aware that he has violated a . . . norm to which he has a learned commitment" (1971, pp. 124-125; see also Simmel, 1971, p. 313 for a similar view of shame). In short, it is claimed that through our socially generated consciences we anticipate others' positive and negative sanctions as being among the likely consequences of our responses; we sanction ourselves in anticipation of those sanctions, and then steer our social participation accordingly.

NURTURE

Nurtural variables refer to socially modified aspects of physiological (body) variables—modified, that is, through social structural access and cultural structural conventions of diet, exercise, medicines, surgery (and also deprivations, poisons, imprisonments, tortures). Complementing Freud's stress on the social modification of instinctual variables (id) into encultural ones (ego and super-ego; see 1960, pp. 9-29), Engels stresses the social modification of physiological variables into nurtural ones:

> The human hand . . . has been highly perfected by hundreds of thousands of years of labour. . . . Thus the hand is not only the organ of labour, it is also the product of labour. . . . First labour, after it and then with it, speech—these were the two most essential stimuli under the influence of

which the brain of the ape gradually changed into that of man [Marx and Engels, 1969, Vol. III, pp. 67-69].

More recent references to nurtural variables include Mechanic's claim that "although death is a biological [i.e., physiological] process, how and when it occurs are conditioned by sociocultural . . . factors" (1978, p. 179). "Innumerable studies," says Mechanic, "indicate that . . . the poor have a greater prevalence of illness, disability, and restriction of activity because of health problems" (1978, p. 198). Suchman, too, argues that "social class or family eating patterns will affect the amount and types of foods offered the child. This will influence his resistance to disease-causing agents or his interest in exploring his environment, which, in turn, will affect his physical, social, and mental development" (1968, p. 62; see also Levitsky and Stupp, 1985, p. 358). And Nriagu, defending the "hypothesis that the Roman Empire declined as a result of plumbism [lead poisoning from their use of this metal and its compounds in food, drink, cosmetics, and medicines] among members of the aristocratic oligarchy," says such poisoning "can be seen to have affected the vitality of Roman culture in two fundamental ways: It ruined the reproductive capacity of the ruling class, and it macerated their ability to govern effectively" (1983, pp. viii, 407).

Now, as we turn from internal variables to external ones, the complementarity between Mead's, and Watkins's, view of internal variables as gatekeepers that determine external variables' social influence (quoted at the beginning of this section) and Simmel's emphasis on the converse—namely, external variables as determining internal variables' social influence —can serve as transition:

A man, taken as a whole, is, so to speak, a somewhat unformed complex of contents, powers, potentialities; only according to . . . a changing existence is he articulated into a differentiated, defined structure. As an economic and political agent, as a member of a family or of a profession, he is, so to speak, an *ad hoc* construction [1971, p. 131].

External People Variables

If we ask what aspects of the people in the participant's environment can influence his or her social participation, the answer implicates all the internal variables again, but with a dif-

ferent locus. Now they refer not to the participant himself or herself but to the people (conspecifics) environing that participant. And insofar as such people may manifest one or more interorganism behavior regularities among themselves, we also meet social and cultural structures again, but this time as variables causally explanatory and predictive of subsequent social phenomena rather than as variables descriptive of such phenomena.

PSYCHICAL CONTAGION

Psychical contagion variables explain-predict an individual's social participation by referring to genetically given features of the minds of people who are in that individual's environment.[57] Blumer, for example, claims that among "cattle in a state of alarm, [the] expression of fear through bellowing, breathing, and movements of the body, induces the same feeling in the case of other cattle" (1946, p. 170), and that the same process occurs among humans—producing —"social unrest." The latter, in turn, is "the crucible out of which emerge new forms of organized activity—such as social movements, reforms, revolutions, religious cults, spiritual awakenings, and new moral orders" (Blumer, 1946, p. 173).

LeBon is classic here ("In a crowd every sentiment and act is contagious" [1960, p. 30]), as are Marx ("social contact begets in most industries an emulation and a stimulation of the animal spirits that heighten the efficiency of each individual workman" [1967, Vol. I, p. 326]), Weber (in his discussions of "affectual" orientation and "charismatic authority"—see 1978, pp. 25, 241-245, 1111-1157), Simmel ("the individual [in a crowd] feels himself carried by the mood" of the mass . . . [but actually] the individual, by being carried away, carries away" [1950, p. 35]), and Durkheim:

When [members of aboriginal societies] are once come together, a sort of electricity is formed by their collecting which quickly transports them to an extraordinary degree of exaltation. . . .[E]ach [member] re-echoes the others and is re-echoed by the others. The initial impulse thus proceeds, growing as it goes, as an avalanche grows in its advance [1965, p. 247].

More recently, Clynes explicates such variables by claiming that

the [human] nervous system appears to be programmed in such a way as to be able to both produce and recognize [certain ways of expressing particular emotions] precisely. They thus represent windows across the separation between individuals and allow contagion of emotion to take place, and they provide emotional understanding of one another [1980, p. 273].

Plutchik, noting that "the *expression* of emotions and the *recognition* of emotions are two different processes," concludes, regarding the first process, that research now supports the view that "certain basic emotional expressions are unlearned and reflect basic neuromuscular, genetically determined programs," and, regarding the second process, quotes Ekman and Friesen to the effect that "particular [perceived] facial expressions are universally associated with particular emotions"(1980, pp. 263, 259, 256). Implicitly, Bourdieu identifies psychical contagion as a major explanatory-predictive variable in the arts: "The work of art always contains something ineffable . . . something which communicates, so to speak, from body to body, i.e. on the hither side of words or concepts, and which pleases (or displeases) without concepts" (1977, p. 2).

DEMOGRAPHY

Demographic explanatory-predictive propositions claim that a human individual's participation in a social phenomenon (and therefore that phenomenon itself) will be influenced by the absolute number of people in his or her environment, and by the naturally given reproduction, production, consumption, migration, morbidity, and mortality propensities of those people. It follows that from the standpoint of sociology the key demographic variables are population size, age distribution, sex ratio, and replacement (i.e., migration and natural increase) rates.

Population Size. Davis refers to the effect of population size on ecological and artifactual (see below) resources for human life, and thereby indirectly on human social phenomena, when he says, "Human increase may be retarding the rise in level of living or thwarting it altogether," and such increase has brought "most underdeveloped countries . . . dangerously close to making genuine economic development impossible for themselves" (1976, p. 273). Simmel, however, employs population size as a direct influence on social phenomena when he says, "Where three elements, A, B, C, constitute a group, there is, in addition to the [immediate] relationship between A and B, for instance, their [mediated] one, which is derived from their common relation to C" (1950, p.

135), as does Blau: "The larger the difference in size between two groups, the greater is the discrepancy in the rates of intergroup associations between them" (1977, p. 23).

Age Distribution. Waring argues that "Cohorts which are too large . . . create a 'people jam' at the entrances to the successive age grades they seek to occupy. Without intervention only some members of the cohort can experience the promised succession. The others risk role disenfranchisement" (1976, p. 108). Davis makes the closely related claim that in order to absorb a suddenly increased number of youths, "an economy must expand rapidly. If it falters, large numbers become unemployed. If they attend school, they become a class of 'educated unemployed.' With youthful energy and idealism but no stake in the existing society, they are politically explosive" (1976, p. 277).

Sex Ratio. Individuals environed by populations having different sex ratios are apt to be differently influenced to the extent that males and females are innately capable of doing different things—especially with respect to the production and early sustenance of infant recruits to that population. In addition, there may be strong causal interaction between the individual's own sex and the sex ratio in its environment—as Guttentag and Secord suggest: "The individual member whose own sex is in short supply has a stronger position and is less dependent on the partner because of the large number of alternative relationships available to him or her" (1983, p. 23).

Replacement Rates. Davis points out that "in the process of development, agrarian countries face a movement of something like sixty percent of their people from the country to the cities," and adds that although

urban populations of the past usually failed to replace themselves because their deaths far exceeded their births . . .today . . . the cities of the Third World . . . are growing rapidly by their own excess of births over deaths. This means that they cannot absorb migrants as fast as the industrializing cities of the past could . . . [and in these] cities, rapid growth and poverty are creating history [1976, pp. 278, 279-280].

CULTURAL STRUCTURE
AND SOCIAL STRUCTURE

Cultural structure variables explain and predict an individual's social participation (and therefore the social phenomenon in which he or she participates) by socially generated interorganism *mind* behavior regularities among the people in the participant's environment, while social structure variables explain and predict it by socially generated interorganism *body* behavior regularities among those people. The debate between proponents of these two kinds of variables is undoubtedly the most famous controversy in the history of sociological theory. On the side of social structure, Marx and Engels claim that "morality, religion, metaphysics, all the rest of ideology and their corresponding forms of consciousness . . . have no history, no development . . . [independently of] material production and . . . material intercourse" (1969, Vol. I, p. 25). On the side of cultural structure, Weber claims that "the magical and religious forces, and the ethical ideas of duty based upon them have . . . always been among the most important formative influences on conduct" (1958b, p. 27). Bourdieu and Passeron combine both kinds of variables in an interaction causal image (see below). Thus when they claim that

the [pedagogic action] whose arbitrary power to impose a cultural arbitrary rests . . . on the power relations between the groups or classes making up the social formation in which it is carried on . . . contributes, by reproducing the cultural arbitrary which it inculcates, toward reproducing the power relations which are the basis of its power of arbitrary imposition [Bourdieu and Passeron, 1977, p. 10],

they are hypothesizing that a particular social structure produces a particular cultural structure, which then reproduces the original social structure, which in turn reproduces the original cultural structure.

It will be efficient to examine cultural structural and social structural explanatory-predictive variables jointly here because there are four main subtypes of each (plus one attempted integration of each set of subtypes) that are often employed in pairs (though not only in the conveniently simple ones discussed here).

In the first such pair (consensus cultural structure with unison social structure), the people in the participant's environment are thinking-feeling, and doing, the *same* things together and these things are logically and situationally *compatible* (i.e., they occur without interfering with each other). In the second pair (complementarity cultural structure with exchange social structure), they are thinking-feeling, and doing, *different* and *compatible* things together. In the third pair (dissensus cultural structure with conflict social structure), they are thinking-feeling, and doing, *incompatible* things together such that some participants must lose whenever others gain. In the fourth pair (plural cultural structure with segregation social structure), they are thinking-feeling, and doing, things in such spatial and/or temporal *insulation* from one another that their compatibility or incompatibility does not matter causally.

Consensus Cultural Structure and Unison Social Structure. Durkheim is classic here when he claims that "segmentary" (unison) social structure ("made up of similar segments, and these in turn comprise only homogeneous elements" [1984, p. 128]) generates "mechanical solidarity" (consensus cultural structure), which is "a solidarity deriving from resemblances . . . which arises because a certain number of states of consciousness are common to all the members of the same society" (1984, pp. 61, 64)—and when he claims that these variables together explain preindustrial society (see 1984, pp. 83-86). More recently, Asch (1958) identifies conditions under which subjects yield to consensus cultural structure (Asch calls it "group pressure") and join a unison social structure by giving the same verbal expressions as do others in their environment—even when they do not join the consensus cultural structure itself (also see Simmel, 1971, p. 262).

Parsons and Shils argue that consensus cultural structure must underlie whatever complementarity cultural structure sustains social structural differentiation (and exchange) among participants: "It is [the] integration of common values . . . which characterizes the partial or total integrations of social systems" (1951, p. 203; see the earlier discussion of Parsons and the two meanings of "social").

Complementarity Cultural Structure and Exchange Social Structure. Durkheim is classic here, too, when he claims "organized" (exchange) social structure ("a system of different organs, each of which has a special role, and which themselves are formed from differentiated parts" [1984, p. 132]) generates "organic solidarity" (i.e., a "collective consciousness" or cultural structure which "assumes that [individuals] are different from [and complement] one another" [1984, p. 851])—and that these two variables together explain modern industrialized society (see 1984, pp. 83-86).

More recently, although Schegloff is ambiguous when he calls the "turn-taking organization for [sic] conversation" a "coherent set of practices *or* rules'' (1987, pp. 210, 208, italics added), his actual discussion seems clearly an analysis of practices (exchange social structure) *and* rules (complementary cultural structure). Gouldner argues for a similar pairing of variables when he says, ''Reciprocity is a . . . [social structural] pattern of exchanging goods and services,'' whereas ''the [cultural structural] *norm* of reciprocity holds that people should help those who help them and, therefore, those who you have helped have an obligation to help you'' (1960, pp. 170, 173). Gouldner stresses the explanatory-predictive power of the latter, complementarity cultural structural, variable but Homans stresses the power of the exchange social structural variable. Thus defining ''social behavior as an exchange of activity, tangible or intangible, and more or less rewarding or costly, between at least two persons'' (1961, p. 12), Homans argues that ''stable and differentiated social structure in . . . social group[s] . . . arise[s] out of a process of exchange between members'' (1958, p. 604). Note, however, that Homans declares himself ''anxious to get motive into the system'' (1961, p. 13), and thus relies heavily on complementarity cultural structure insofar as in his image of exchange one person's psychically defined ''reward'' is complemented by the other's psychically defined ''cost,'' and vice-versa. Blau, too, makes exchange social structure more explicit and central to his theory than complementarity cultural structure:

> To be sure, each individual's behavior is reinforced by the rewards it brings, but the psychological process of reinforcement does not suffice to explain the exchange relation that develops. This social relation is the joint product of the actions of both individuals, with the actions of each being dependent on those of the other [1964, p. 4].

Bourdieu proposes certain distinctions among social structural exchanges that depend on the complementarity (and consensual) cultural structures that he believes invariably accompany them:

> In every society it may be observed that, if it is not to constitute [i.e., be consensually defined as] an insult, the counter-gift must be *deferred* and *different* because the immediate return of an exactly identical object clearly amounts to [i.e., is likely to be consensually interpreted as] a refusal ([that is,] the return of the same object). This gift exchange is opposed on the one hand to *swapping*, which, like the theoretical model of the cycle of reciprocity, telescopes gift and counter-gift into the same instant, and on

the other hand, to *lending* [where literally the same object is returned] [1977, p. 5].[58]

Dissensus Cultural Structure and Conflict Social Structure. Marx and Engels pair these two kinds of variables when expressing their desire ''to instill into the working class the clearest possible recognition [cultural structure] of the hostile antagonism between bourgeoisie and proletariat, in order that . . . the fight [social structure] against the bourgeoisie itself may immediately begin'' (1969, Vol. I, p. 137). Dahrendorf also pairs these variables when he says, ''The great creative force that carries along change in the model I am trying to describe is [social structural] conflict'' and in that model, the ''characteristic values'' (cultural structure) of a society are ''ruling rather than common, enforced rather than accepted'' (1958, pp. 126, 127). Coser acknowledges the distinction drawn here between conflict social structure and dissensus cultural structure when he says, ''Social conflict always denotes social interaction, whereas [hostile or antagonistic] attitudes or sentiments are predispositions to engage in action'' and notes that the latter ''do not necessarily eventuate in conflict'' and the former ''need not be accompanied by hostility and aggressiveness'' (1956, pp. 38, 59). Collins, too, combines conflict social structure and dissensus cultural structure when he insists that ''the only viable path to a comprehensive explanatory sociology is a conflict [social structure] perspective,'' and calls for the recognition of ''competing interests [cultural structure] as a matter of *fact*'' (1975, p. 21).

Plural Cultural Structure and Segregation Social Structure. Kuper refers to a plural cultural structure as ''a medley of peoples, for they mix but do not combine. Each group holds by its own religion, its own culture and language, its own ideas and ways'' (1969, pp. 10-11); Durkheim describes each segment in ''segmentary'' social structure (see above) as being segregated from the others insofar as it ''has its own organs that are, so to speak, protected and kept at a distance from similar organs by the partitions separating the different segments'' (1984, p. 211); Fanon says the social structure of ''the colonial world'' is ''divided into compartments. . . .The zone where the natives live'' and ''the zone inhabited by the settlers'' (1963, pp. 31-32)—each possessing its own cultural structure; Carmichael and Hamilton, rejecting the immediate integration and acculturation of Blacks into the predominantly White cultural and social structures of the United States, argue that ''the goal [should be] to build and strengthen the black community . . . [which] must win its freedom while preserving its cultural integrity" (1967, pp. 54-55); and Dahrendorf combines the concepts of plural cultural structure and segregation social structure in his discussion of what he calls simply "pluralism" in relations between "the state, industry, and the church" (see 1959, pp. 213-218), as does Blau's discussion of "segregation" and "consolidated nominal parameters" (see 1977, pp. 83-93).

Now let us briefly survey the leading attempts to integrate consensus, complementarity, dissensus, and plural cultural structure, on the one hand, and unison, exchange, conflict, and segregation social structure, on the other.

Symbolic Interactionism and Structural Functionalism. The essential claim of symbolic interactionism is that social phenomena are explainable and predictable by the socially acquired psychical interpretations that participants reciprocally assign to their physical behaviors:

> Human beings interpret or "define" each other's actions instead of merely reacting to each other's actions. Their "response" is . . . based on the meaning they attach to such actions. Thus, human interaction is mediated by the use of symbols, by interpretation, or by ascertaining the meaning of one another's action [Blumer, 1962, p. 180].

Bourdieu's quotation from Leibniz outlines alternative mechanisms whereby consensus about such meaning may be (equifinally) reached:

> "Imagine," Leibniz suggests, "two clocks or watches in perfect agreement as to the time. This may occur in one of three ways. The first consists in mutual influence; the second is to appoint a skillful workman to correct them and synchronize them at all times; the third is to construct these clocks with such art and precision that one can be assured of their subsequent agreement" [1977, p. 80].

Symbolic interactionists—as one might guess from their name—emphasize "interaction" (i.e., reciprocal psychical influence mediated by physical signs or symbols) as the mechanism that determines the origin and development of "agreement" among social participants.[59] Thus Stryker says symbolic interactionists look upon social behavior as "developing through a tentative, sometimes extremely subtle, probing interchange among actors that can reshape the form and the content of the interaction" (1980,

p. 55). Similarly, Blumer says "many . . . situations may not be defined in a single way by the participating people. In this event . . . [i]nterpretations have to be developed and effective accommodations of the participants to one another have to be worked out" (1962, p. 188). That such "accommodations" (i.e., outcomes of interactive negotiation) may include cultural structural consensus, complementarity, dissensus, and/or plurality between negotiators is epitomized by Goffman's analysis of "performances," "audiences," "teams," and "regions" in what he terms "the presentation of self in everyday life" (1959); and by Becker's examination of "the drama of moral rhetoric and action in which imputations of deviance are made, accepted, rejected, and fought over" (1973, p. 186).

Symbolic interactionism claims that the *reciprocation of psychical interpretations* between participants explains and predicts social phenomena; the correlative claim of structural functionalism is that the *reciprocation of physical contributions* explains and predicts such phenomena. (The reciprocation involved in both cases justifies references to symbolic "interactions" and functional "systems"—see the discussion of causal images below.) Thus structural functionalism combines two logically independent propositions: (1) any social phenomenon (structure), when looked upon as a whole (a system of parts), may be explained and predicted by the contributions (functions) that its parts make to it (parts → whole); (2) any social phenomenon, when looked upon as a part of some larger whole, may be explained and predicted by the contributions that whole makes to it (whole → parts).[60]

Expressing the parts → whole proposition, Radcliffe-Brown says, "The continuity of [social] structure is maintained by the . . . activities and interactions of the individual human beings and of the organised groups into which they are united" (1965, p. 180). But what kinds of activities and interactions are required for this? The several lists of functional "prerequisites," "requisites," and "imperatives" (defined broadly as "things that *must be done* in any society if it is to continue as a going concern" [Aberle et al., 1950, p. 100, italics added; see also Levy, 1952, p. 62; Malinowski, 1944, p. 125; Merton, 1976, pp. 92-95; Parsons and Smelser, 1956, pp. 16-18] have been proposed as answers to this question—answers with which it is claimed the social structure of all societies can be explained in broad outline. Parsons and Smelser, for example, claim that "societies tend to differentiate into sub-systems (social structures) which are specialized in each of . . . four primary functions" (1956, p. 47).

Functionalists tend to take the reciprocal of the parts → whole proposition—namely, whole → parts—for granted (Gouldner says the "concept of reciprocity [is] apparently smuggled into the basic but *unstated* postulates of functional analysis" [1960, p. 163, italics added]). It is, nevertheless, often clearly discernible—as when Davis claims functionalism sees "one part as 'performing a function for'. . . the whole society" (a statement exemplifying the parts → whole proposition), and then, without acknowledging having changed perspectives, goes on to claim that functional analysis relies on "the interpretation of [social] phenomena in terms of their connection with societies as going concerns" (1959, pp. 758, 760)—a statement that, even allowing for the ambiguity of "interpretation" and "connection," seems to express the whole → parts proposition. Merton's reliance on the latter proposition is still less explicit than Davis's: "the central orientation of functionalism [is] expressed in the practice of interpreting data by establishing their consequences for larger structures in which they are implicated" (1957, pp. 46-47). But assuming Merton really wants to say the social structures described by data have (causal) consequences for the social structures of which they (the social structures, not the data describing them) are parts, then the idea of parts being "implicated in" a whole suggests the latter has consequences for the former (whole → parts), just as the former have consequences for the latter (parts → whole). In other words, as Merton also says, functional analysis "involves the notion of 'interdependence,' 'reciprocal relation,' or 'mutually dependent relations' " (1957, p. 21), where (Merton does not say this) the phenomena participating in these relations are described as hierarchically related—that is, as parts, on the one hand, and the whole they constitute, on the other.

In any case, both the parts → whole proposition and the whole → parts proposition are required by the functionalist claim that a given social structure (part) can be explained by what it does for its social system (whole), insofar as that claim assumes the system reciprocates by doing things for the structure. As Gouldner puts it, "The demonstration that A is functional for B can help to account for A's persistence only if the functional theorist tacitly assumes some principle of reciprocity" (1960, p. 163).[61]

That relations between whole and part may take the form of unison, exchange, conflict, and/or segregation social structures is nearly ex-

plicit in Merton's call for "a concept of multiple consequences and a net balance of an aggregate of consequences" that one social phenomenon (whether whole or part) may have for another, and his claim that the separate consequences entering into such an aggregate may include "functions," "dysfunctions," and "nonfunctional consequences" (1957, p. 51).[62] One needs only add "nonconsequences" (i.e., actions by one social structure that have *no* observed consequences for some other such structure by virtue of their isolation from one another) to include the segregation case.[63]

Finally, let us add to the above-mentioned complementarities between symbolic interactionism and structural functionalism a substantive interpenetration that strengthens the grounds for their eventual integration: In symbolic interactionism, social structures—consisting of verbal and nonverbal bodily gestures—play key roles in negotiating cultural structural meanings among participants (see, for example, Mead, 1934, pp. 13-18, 42-51, 68-75); in structural functionalism, cultural structures—consisting of values, norms, and role-expectations—play key roles in creating social structures (whether functional, dysfunctional, nonfunctional, or nonconsequential) among participants (see, for example, Parsons, 1951, pp. 24-45).[64]

External Thing Variables

The third and final subset of sociological explanatory-predictive variables focuses on nonpeople (again, more broadly, nonconspecific) "things" in the participant's environment. Living and nonliving categories of such things (subscripted L and NL, respectively, in Figure 1.2) will be examined together here for the sake of brevity.

ECOLOGY

Ecological variables refer to those aspects of the participant's nonconspecific environment that the analyst regards as given in nature. For example, Hawley argues that

> space in which to carry on necessary activities, and food with which to maintain vital processes . . .[are the] elemental requirements [that] cause life to be irrevocably implicated in the physical world. . . . [Moreover,] the adaptive efforts of individuals culminate in a community of interorganic relationships. . . .That the community is the essential adaptive mechanism may be taken as the distinctive hypothesis of ecology [1950, pp. 12, 31].

Weber claims "the boiling heat of modern capitalistic culture is connected with heedless consumption of natural resources, for which there are no substitutes," and explains the difference between the "rural social structure" of western and southern Germany, on the one hand, and that of eastern Germany, on the other, by arguing that "in the west and south, bottoms, river valleys, and plateaux, are intermingled" and therefore the people there produce and exchange different goods, while "In the east . . . the neighboring towns have much more frequently nothing to exchange with each other . . . [because they have] the same geographical situation [and] produce the same goods" (1958a, pp. 366, 377-378). Complementing these invocations of the explanatory-predictive power of naturally given spatial regularities in the inanimate environment, Hawley invokes the power of naturally given temporal regularities in that environment: "Two natural recurrences—the diurnal cycle and the lunar phase—serve as universal time units. . . . It is the variation of light and darkness and the concomitant alternation of waking and sleeping that supply the fundamental rhythm of community life" (1950, p. 296).[65]

Note that ecological variables are specified here as existentially given—that is, independent of human social influence. It follows that the architectural or otherwise humanly constructed distributions of space in a city, factory, apartment house, classroom, and so on, are not ecological but artifactual variables (see below), although they are often called the former. For the same reason, the division of time into days and nights, lunar months, seasons, and years should be regarded as accomplished ecologically, but its division into seconds, minutes, and hours is accomplished only through artifacts.

The whole of modern cosmology, biology, and human prehistory and history bears testimony to the power of ecological factors to originate, sustain, change, and terminate individual organisms and the social phenomena in which they participate. For example, Campbell says, "The creative process of natural selection is driven by the environment; ultimately by the climatic changes which inevitably occur, and by the immense variety of different environments which the planet Earth carries" (1985, p. 5). It is no accident, says Campbell, that

> Human colonization of the world began . . . in the tropics and subtropics, where there are abundant and varied plants. Only in relatively recent times did it reach the arctic, where humans are dependent upon other predators for food (bears, seals, etc.).

> . . . [T]he densest human populations in the world today are in those tropical areas where there is primary dependence on plant resources. . . . [D]espite astounding technological advances, [humans] are still part of the natural world [1985, pp. 7, 8, 17].

And specifically regarding the termination of social phenomena, Mead notes that "the geological forces, the so-called 'acts of God'. . . . [can] come in and wipe out what man has created. Changes in the solar system can simply annihilate the planet on which we live" (1934, p. 250); Zinnser says, "Civilizations have retreated from the plasmodium of malaria, and armies have crumpled into rabbles under the onslaught of cholera spirilla, or of dysentery and typhoid bacilli" (1967, p. 6); and Campbell anticipates a potentially disastrous interaction among ecological, demographic, artifactual, social structural, and cultural structural variables:

> [F]resh water presents a growing problem: 148 of the largest water basins in the world are controlled by only two countries and 52 more by ten other nations. Population projections imply that water requirements in the year 2000 could be double what they were in 1971 and more will be required if living standards are improved. Competition for control of limited water resources could easily exacerbate international tension [1985, p. 186].

ARTIFACTS

Because "technology" often includes physical techniques and psychical knowledge as well as physical artifacts, the latter term is used here in order to restrict attention to the nonpeople *things* (including tools, weapons, instruments, machines, shelter, clothing, domesticated plants and animals, pollutants, sound waves, radio waves, etc.) that are the intended and unintended, life supporting and life destroying, transitory and long lasting, physical effects of human social phenomena on the Earth and the universe at large as explanatory-predictive variables in sociology.[66] Techniques and knowledge (social structural and cultural structural variables, respectively) must be analytically separated from such artifacts in order to acknowledge (1) the latter's causal potential independently of the techniques and knowledge (or lack thereof) that gave rise to them (radioactive fallout from atomic bomb explosions, and the surviving pyramids of ancient Egypt, are cases in point), and (2) that different techniques and knowledge can be applied to the same artifacts with different consequences for social phenomena (as witness the widely varying uses of explosives).[67]

Freud mentions a type of *living* artifact (i.e., domesticated animals, including cattle) as having helped terminate an early stage in the development of religious cultural structure: "The domestication of animals and the introduction of cattle-breeding seems everywhere to have brought to an end the strict and unadulterated totemism of primaeval days" (1950, pp. 136-137).[68] Weber complements this picture by citing a type of *nonliving* artifact (i.e., housing) as having helped initiate a later stage in the same cultural structural development:

> The product of the potter, weaver, turner and carpenter is much less affected by unpredictable natural events [than is that of agricultural workers]. . . . The resulting rationalization and intellectualization [among the former occurs] because the work is done largely within the house. . . . The forces of nature become an intellectual problem as soon as they are no longer part of the immediate environment. This provokes the rationalist quest for the transcendental meaning of existence, a search that always leads to religious speculation [1978, p. 1178].

Indeed, although artifacts are certainly not the explanatory-predictive mainstays of his theory, Weber calls on them again and again: "A certain degree of development of the means of communication . . . is one of the most important prerequisites for the possibility of bureaucratic administration"; "War in our time is a war of machines, and this makes central provisioning necessary, just as the dominance of the machine in industry promotes the concentration of the means of production and management"; "By contrast [with the Orient], all . . . city unions of the Occident . . . were coalitions of *armed* strata of the cities. This was the decisive difference" (1978, pp. 973, 981, 1262); and "To maintain a dominion by force, certain material goods are required, just as with an economic organization" (1958a, p. 81). In similar fashion, Comte says, "Language gives the name of 'capital' to every permanent aggregate of material products, and thus indicates its fundamental importance to the sum of human existence" (1975, p. 403); Simmel claims that "if all the watches in Berlin suddenly went wrong in different ways even only as much as an hour, its entire economic and commercial life would be derailed" (1971, p. 328); and Durkheim notes that "material things . . . play an essential role in the common life. . . . [For example,] avenues of communication which have

been constructed before our time give a definite direction to our lives, depending on whether they connect us with one or another country" (1951, p. 314; see also p. 292).

Despite the frequent appearance of artifact explanatory-predictive variables in the works of these and other theorists, however, Marx and Engels remain the outstanding classical proponents of such variables, and although their attention focuses on instruments ("means") of economic production (see especially Marx's explications of "capital," 1967, Vol. I, pp. 177-185, 371-386), they do not overlook instruments of idea production ("The class which has the means of material production at its disposal, has control at the same time over the means of mental production" [1969, Vol. I, p. 47]); instruments of exchange, and of individual nourishment ("Money is the procurer between man's need and the object, between his life and his means of life" [1977, p. 120, italics removed]); and instruments of destruction ("With the invention of a new instrument of warfare, firearms, the whole internal organization of the army necessarily changed . . . and the relations of different armies to one another also changed" [1969, Vol. I, p. 159]).[69] Most important of all, Marx, alone among classical theorists in sociology, foresaw robotics ("an automatic system of machinery . . . set in motion by an automaton, a moving power that moves itself; this automaton consisting of numerous mechanical and intellectual organs" [1973, p. 692, italics removed]). Fittingly, Weber, alone among classical theorists in sociology, *almost* foresaw artificial intelligence:[70]

> Bureaucracy . . . [and] the factory . . . both determine the character of the present age and of the foreseeable future. . . . The fully developed bureaucratic apparatus compares with other forms of organizations exactly as does the machine with the non-mechanical modes of production. . . . An inanimate machine is mind objectified. . . . [just as is] that animated machine, the bureaucratic organization [1978, pp. 1400-1401, 973, 1402; see Inbar, 1979, for a more explicit and detailed prediction—and advocacy—of "computerized bureaucracies"].

Finally in this section, we should overlook neither Ogburn's claim that because "six others invented the steamboat at about the same time [as Robert Fulton, the] . . . invention of the steamboat might well be better attributed to the steam engine than to a great man, in much the same way as the discovery of America was due to a new means of navigation rather than to a particular individual'' (1957, p. 17), nor Ong's reminder that writing is ''a matter of tools outside us'' (1978, p. 6), and that

> Many of the features we have taken for granted in thought and expression in literature, philosophy and science, and even in oral discourse among literates . . . have come into being because of the resources which the technology of writing makes available to human consciousness [1982, p. 1; see also Bourdieu, 1977, pp. 186-187; Gouldner, 1976; Marx, 1973, p. 111; Postman, 1982; and Simmel, 1971, p. 273].

Now, having completed this overview of the kinds of *variables*—both descriptive and explanatory-predictive—that comprise the subject matter of sociology, let us with equal speed survey one set of conceptual instruments for constructing testable hypotheses, theories, paradigms, and so on from such variables. There are actually three sets of such instruments: images of causation, rules of logical induction, and rules of logical deduction.[71] For lack of space, the following discussion is confined to the first, although the second and third are of no less importance.

Causal Images

Despite the presence of certain ''reductionisms'' (Homans calls himself a ''psychological reductionist'' [1974, p. 12]) and what might be called ''essentialisms'' in sociology (Smelser insists that unless we ''endow [historical] facts with special meaning for the historical actors involved . . . we do not have an explanation'' [1980, p. 28, italics removed]), there seem to be no serious *single*-variable explanations or predictions (i.e., those having only one cause variable or one effect variable) in sociology.[72] We almost always link several variables together—either in explanation-prediction, description, or both. The question we turn to now is, What basic images are used in constructing such linkages?[73]

In seeking an answer to this question, one notes that the direction of causation between any two variables may be regarded as one-way (such that the net influences between them favors *one* variable as cause of the other), or two-way (such that *both* variables are equally causes, and effects, of each other)—or, of course, noway (such that *neither* variable is cause, or effect, of the other). The first two possibilities appear in the horizontal dimension of Figure 1.3. The vertical dimension of that figure acknowledges that any final effect that a given image is called upon to explain or predict may be re-

garded as developing discontinuously or stepwise from the image's operation, or it may be regarded as evolving continuously, or it may be regarded as maintained in a steady state (rather than being developed at all), by that operation.

Before examining types of images that result from cross-classifying these two dimensions, let us fix in mind their simplest forms—namely, action, and interaction—because all the other images represent compounds of these elements (action, of course, is the simplest form of all insofar as interaction is a compound of reciprocal actions).

Action

The elemental one-way causal image portrays the action of one variable on another variable—an image that may be extended into a sequence or ''chain'' of any number of variables leading (in explanatory analysis) to, or (in predictive analysis) from, the phenomenon of interest. For example, Weber proposes a three-step sequence (i.e., politics → prophecy → pariah situation): ''Except for the world politics of the great powers which threatened their homeland . . . the [ancient Israelite] prophets could not have emerged,'' and ''Without the promises of prophecy an increasingly 'civic' religious community [of Jews] would never voluntarily have taken to . . . a pariah situation'' (Weber, 1952, pp. 268, 364). Douglas proposes a five-step sequence founded on the instinctualist hypothesis that it is ''part of our human condition to long for hard lines and clear concepts.'' This longing, she claims, produces ''ideas about separating, purifying, demarcating and punishing transgressions; these ideas produce their ''external signs,'' including ''rituals''; these, in turn, produce ''the necessary sentiments . . . to hold men to their roles''; and the final outcome is society, a sociocultural structure of matching role-performances and role-expectations (Douglas, 1969, pp. 162, 4, 62, 65, 3).

Note that different steps in any such causal sequence may be assigned different probabilities, and if the difference between two adjacent probabilities is deemed great enough, the sequence is said to contain one or more ''bottlenecks'' or ''thresholds,'' with the accompanying possibilities of ''blockages'' and ''breakthroughs.''

Interaction

The simplest two-way image portrays only two variables, each of which is directly and simultaneously (or alternately) cause and effect of the other.[74] Kleck relies on such causal interdependence when referring to "a deadly circularity of gun ownership and homicide, homicide pushing up gun ownership and gun ownership at the same time pushing up homicide. . . . [C]rime is a cause of gun ownership just as gun ownership is a cause of crime" (1979, p. 908). Such an image may be made more complex by inserting, between the original variables, others that slow down, speed up, attenuate, intensify, or otherwise mediate the impact of one or both original variables on each other. Spencer, for example, argues that "in both individual and social organisms, after the inner and outer systems have been marked off from one another, there begins to arise a third system, lying between the two and facilitating their cooperation" (1896, Vol. I, p. 494), and Simmel, after asserting that "the numerically simplest structures which can still be designated as social interactions occur between two elements," adds that a "third element . . . often has the function of holding the whole together" (1950, pp. 118, 146). In a more recent invocation of the mediated interaction image, Wallerstein argues that

> the world-economy . . . without a semiperiphery . . . would be far less politically stable, for it would mean a polarized world-system. The existence of the third [semiperiphery] category means precisely that the upper stratum is not faced with the unified opposition of all the others because the middle stratum is both exploited and exploiter [1979, p. 23].

Now let us examine the 12 elaborations on action and interaction that are shown in Figure 1.3. Note that each elaboration is either paired with its complement—whose causal outcome develops in the opposite direction (e.g., convergence is paired with divergence)—or incorporates such a complementarity within itself (i.e., as we shall see, the dialectical image incorporates alternating fusion and fission phases as well as fusion and fission alternative outcomes; and the cybernetic image incorporates amplifying and damping phases).

Development of Effect	Directionality of Causation	
	One-Way (Action)	Two-Way (Interaction)
Stepwise	Value-added, and "Value-subtracted"	Dialectic
Continuous	Convergence, and Divergence	Amplification, and Damping
	Fusion, and Fission	
Steady State	Cross-pressure, and Tension	Cybernetic

FIGURE 1.3
Matrix of causal images explaining-predicting social phenomena.

One-Way (Action) Images

VALUE-ADDED, AND "VALUE-SUBTRACTED"

Here, two or more one-way, nonreciprocal, causal sequences interweave—such that a particular sequence of effects is brought about by a particular sequence of causes. In the value-added image, the final effect is constructed, assembled, or built up in discrete, fixed-order steps; in the "value-subtracted" image, that build up is reversed (again, in discrete, fixed-order steps) and the final effect is reached by stripping down, disassembling, or reducing whatever is initially given to one of its more primitive states.

Smelser, explicitly applying the value-added image to the analysis of collective behavior, says

Each stage "adds its value" to the final . . . finished product. The key element . . . is that the earlier stages must combine *according to a certain pattern* before the next stage can contribute its particular value to the finished product. . . .The sufficient condition for final production . . . is the combination of *every* [such stage] according to a definite pattern [1962, pp. 13-14; see also LeBon, 1960, p. 80].

Becker offers an implicitly value-added image of deviant careers:

In accounting for an individual's use of marihuana . . . we must deal with a sequence of steps. . . .Each step requires explanation, and what may operate as a cause at one step in the sequence may be of negligible importance at another step. . . .The variable which disposes a person to take a particular step may not operate because he has not yet reached the stage in the process where it is possible to take that step. . . .[N]o one could become a confirmed marihuana user without going through each step [1973, p. 23].

Examples of what are here called "value-subtracted" images (enclosed in quotation marks because from the standpoint of economics, the discipline in which they originated—see Smelser, 1962, p. 13—these are only other value-*added* images) include Berger's statement that "secularization manifests itself in evacuation of the Christian churches of areas previously under their control or influence—as in the separation of church and state" (1969, p. 107), and Goffman's statement that "the [mental] hospital prepatient starts out with at least a por-

tion of the rights, liberties, and satisfactions of the civilian and ends up on a psychiatric ward stripped of almost everything" (1961, p. 140).

CONVERGENCE, AND DIVERGENCE

These images (equifinal and equioriginal, respectively) portray two or more *alternative* causal sequences leading to, or from, the social phenomenon of interest. Inkeles employs both, in his claim that "Convergence [among different industrialized societies] is most dramatically and unambiguously illustrated by birth and fertility rates . . . converging on a condition of zero population growth," while "Divergence is most dramatically illustrated in the realm of production and the generation of physical wealth" (1981, pp. 14, 23). In addition, Merton's concept of "functional alternatives" (as has already been mentioned) exemplifies alternative causal sequences converging on a common outcome, while Blau and Blau's image (derived from Coser; see 1956, pp. 48-55) of two alternative "reactions of the underprivileged" (one being "to organize collective violence to overthrow the existing order and redistribute resources," and the other being to engage in "diffuse aggression" and "criminal violence" [1982, p. 119]) exemplifies causal divergence from a common origin (namely, socioeconomic inequality).

FUSION, AND FISSION

These images are similar to the two just mentioned, except the causal sequences here are coalescing, and radiating, respectively—thus *additive* rather than alternative.[75] Using the fusion image, Durkheim argues that the "different social causes of suicide . . . [may] impose their combined effects" (1951, p. 145); and Hart says, "Every invention consists of a new combination of old elements. For example, an airplane is a combination of a box-kite, a windmill, a gasoline engine, a pilot, and the atmosphere" (1957, p. 48). Using the fission image, Durkheim says the division of labor "consists in the sharing out of functions that up till then were common to all" (1984, p. 218); Ogburn says,

The influence of an invention does not always end with its first derivative effects. . . . Thus the loss of passengers on railroads because of the use of automobiles may lead to a reorganization of a railroad, and abandonment of short-haul tracks off the main line, or a modernization of equipment—all second derivatives of the invention of the automobile [1957, p. 20];

and Parsons cites "the emergence of both the modern family household and the modern employing organization from the . . . peasant family household" (1971, p. 26).[76]

CROSS-PRESSURE, AND TENSION

In these images, the phenomenon of interest is regarded as subjected to simultaneous, roughly equal, and opposite pushes or pulls that add up to a steady (but unstable) state in that phenomenon.[77,78,79] Mannheim is classical here when he describes members of the "socially unattached intelligentsia" as "determined in their outlooks by [an] intellectual medium which contains all [the] contradictory points of view" characterizing their society. Intellectuals, Mannheim says, because they are subject to such multiple cross-pressures or tensions, are able to achieve "an intimate grasp of the total situation" and can produce a "dynamic synthesis," a "total perspective" (1955, pp. 157, 160), for the society as a whole.[80] Consistent with this view of cross-pressured participants as potential inventors of new stabilities, Berelson, Lazarsfeld, and McPhee argue that "it is the people with 'cross-pressured' opinions on the issue or candidates or parties—that is, opinions or views simultaneously supporting different sides—who are more likely to be unstable in their voting position during the campaign" (1954, p. 19). Simmel employs a similar causal image when he says,

> We are constantly orienting ourselves . . . to an "over us" and an "under us," to a right and a left, to a more or less, a tighter or looser, a better or worse. The boundary, above and below, is our means for finding direction in the infinite space of our worlds [1971, p. 353].

"Life," Simmel concludes, is "formed about midpoints" (1971, p. 363). Similarly, Weber says, "The action of individuals can well be subjectively oriented toward *several* orders, whose meaning . . . 'contradict' each other" (1981, p. 162), and Merton calls attention to "socially prescribed ambivalence . . . in the therapist role of the physician which calls for *both* a degree of affective detachment from the patient and a degree of compassionate concern about him" (1976, p. 8).[81]

Two-Way (Interaction) Images

Before turning to the particular images cited as two-way in Figure 1.3, it should be noted that the presence of interaction between physical elements (or the presence of logical interdependence between symbolic elements) is the defining feature of all "systems"—including social and cultural structural ones. Thus von Bertalanffy refers to physical systems as "complexes of elements standing in interaction" (1956, p. 2); Hall and Fagen describe "abstract or conceptual systems" as complexes of concepts standing in interdependences resulting from the inclusion of constants and simultaneities (see 1956, p. 19); and Parsons says, "The concept of social systems . . . [refers to the] *inter*action of individual actors," including both social structure "action systems," and cultural structure "symbolic systems" (1951, p. 3, 11; see also Nakano, 1979, p. 87; and Giddens, 1986, p. 28). Not every element of a system need be regarded as interacting directly with all others, however—some may be regarded as standing in no causal relation at all, or in only a one-way relation, to other elements. One-way relations may thus be parts of larger systems, and "open" systems are always parts of larger one-way and/or two-way relations (see Hall and Fagen, 1956, pp. 21-22).

DIALECTIC

The Marxian version of this image contains two alternative (equioriginal, divergent; see above), discontinuous or stepwise, causal paths. The first depicts interaction between opposing variables (called "thesis" and "antithesis") developing to the point of their *fusion* into a new variable ("synthesis") at a hierarchically higher level—a variable that then fissions into a new pair of conflicting variables (a new thesis and antithesis), whereupon the process repeats itself at the new level to which it has been promoted (see Engels, 1939, pp. 148-156; Marx, 1955, pp. 92, 94, 106-107). The second alternative depicts interaction developing to the point of both interacting variables *fissioning* and thereby demoting the system to a hierarchically lower level. Thus:

> The history of all hitherto existing society is the history of class struggles. . . .[Here,] oppressor and oppressed stood in constant opposition to one another [and] carried on . . . a fight that each time ended, either in a revolutionary re-constitution of society at large, or in the common ruin of the contending classes [Marx and Engels, 1969, Vol. I, pp. 108-109].

In what seems classifiable as another version of the dialectical image (one that seems applicable only to variables representing ideas—being, in this substantive sense, closer to Hegel's original version—and that does not specify alternative paths of development), the opposing variables are neither destroyed by fission nor fused together into a new synthesis but continue their separate existences after a new idea (represented by a new variable) is produced by the minds in which the first two ideas occur—an idea that subsumes both of these ideas, thereby reconciling them and ending their opposition. Thus Berger and Luckmann argue that "legitimation produces new meanings that serve to integrate the meanings already attached to disparate institutional processes" (1967, p. 92); after that, two or more disparate "new meanings" become integrated by newer and still more inclusive meanings—and so on up the hierarchical scale, until

> the reflective integration of discrete institutional processes reaches its ultimate fulfillment. A whole world is created. All the lesser legitimating theories are viewed as special perspectives on phenomena that are aspects of this world [1967, p. 96].[82]

AMPLIFICATION, AND DAMPING

The amplification (in the extreme case, "explosion" or "boom") image of interaction between two variables portrays an increase in one of them being caused by an increase in the other—and so on, smoothly back and forth; similarly, the damping (in the extreme case, "crash" or "bust") image portrays a decrease in one variable being caused by a decrease in the other. Both relationships, therefore, depend on continuous positive feedback and both are subsumed in the idea of a "vicious circle" or what Blumer calls "circular reaction"—that is, "a type of interstimulation wherein the response of one individual reproduces the stimulation that has come from another individual and in being reflected back to this individual reinforces the stimulation" (1946, p. 170)—although, in his next sentence ("Thus the interstimulation assumes a circular form in which individuals . . . *intensify* [each other's] feeling" [italics added]), Blumer focuses entirely on amplification, ignoring the fact that "circular reaction" can as easily diminish feelings as intensify them. Simmel, too, limits himself to amplification when he claims "Human crowds . . . are characterized by casual stimuli making for enormous effects, by the avalanche-like growth of the most negligible impulses of love and hate. . . .[In this growth,] the individual, by being carried away,

carries away" (1950, p. 35). Penrose, however, links amplification and damping images together sequentially: "The course of a craze is marked by certain phases. . . .[including] the phase during which . . . the idea spreads rapidly . . . [followed by phases during which] the velocity of the wave . . . begins to slacken . . . [and finally becomes] stagnant" (quoted in Smelser, 1962, p. 210).

CYBERNETIC

In this image, the influences between the interacting variables are such that one variable is confined to certain limits (and, in contrast with the cross-pressure and tension images, the steadiness here is stable) despite exogenous influences tending to force it outside those limits. In order to achieve this constancy, the interaction in question must be capable of being sometimes amplifying and sometimes damping (thereby counterbalancing the sometimes negative, sometimes positive, potential effects of exogenous influences) and for this, the second variable must sometimes feedback *negatively* to the first variable—raising it when it has been driven too low and lowering it when it has been driven too high (see Wiener, 1954, pp. 15-27; Stinchcombe, 1968, pp. 87-91).

Thus, Merton, sketching the constant articulation and rearticulation of role expectations within the individual's "role-set," argues that "inadequate articulation of [different] role-expectations tends to call one or more social mechanisms into play, which operate to reduce the amount of patterned role-conflict" (1957, p. 380)—reducing it, presumably, to some constant, acceptable level. Bales relies on a similarly cybernetic image in analyzing the social structure of small groups when he claims steadiness there is recurrently lost and gained by the process of role differentiation and interaction *between* participants:

> the stable structure is never . . . a "simply organized" one. It is rather one in which differentiated roles have appeared, in which one specialist "undoes" the disturbance to the equilibrium created by another, and in turn is dependent upon another to remove the strains he himself creates—the total constellation of specialists being one which [maintains the equilibrium of] the system [1953, pp. 148-149].

And to this, Parsons adds that equilibrium in such groups is also maintained by differentiation and interaction, *within* each participant, between motivations calling for deviance and motivations calling for control of deviance (see 1951, pp. 250, 207).

Emergence (Integration), Contextuality, and Disintegration

Finally, three causal images already represented in Figure 1.3 deserve further attention because they permit us systematically to address the problems, mentioned earlier here and postponed till now, of how different micro and macro levels of social phenomena originate, hold themselves together, and terminate. All three images derive from the sciencewide principle of hierarchic structure—namely, that everything is presumed to be composed of parts, and that everything is presumed to be part of some more inclusive whole. In the first image, emergence, a particular set of micro-level variables later defined as "parts" combines or integrates into a more macro level, "whole," variable. In the second, contextuality, a particular macro-level, "whole," variable maintains itself by constraining its micro-level "parts" to operate in ways they would not outside that whole. In the third image, disintegration, a "whole" variable breaks up and its parts scatter on their own, now independent, causal trajectories. Contextuality is why "the whole is greater than the sum of its parts"; emergence is why "synthesis is creation"; disintegration is how "time . . . hath an art to make dust of all things."

Durkheim is classical on emergence: "Whenever elements of any kind combine, by virtue of this combination they give rise to new phenomena. . . . It is not the non-living particles of the cell which feed themselves and reproduce —in a word, which live; it is the cell itself and it alone" (1982, p. 39).[83] Simmel is classical on contextuality: "The group interest . . . entitles, or even obliges, the individual to commit acts for which, *as* an individual, he does not care to be responsible" (1950, p. 134). Among recent writers, Blau says "the division of labor in a community . . . is an emergent property of communities that has no counterpart in a corresponding property of individuals" (although one wonders how to think of the locomotive function of legs, the information-processing function of brain, and so on, if not as constituting a structural division of labor within the individual), and says, "Emergent properties are essentially relationships between elements in a structure" (1964, p. 3)—assuming the "relationships" he has in mind are causal rather than, say, spatial or temporal. Lenski provides an empirical example of emergence when, after defin-

ing "status crystallization" as individuals' "degree of consistency of . . . positions in several vertical hierarchies," he claims that "individuals characterized by a low degree of status crystallization differ significantly in their political attitudes and behavior from individuals characterized by a high degree of status crystallization" (1954, pp. 405-406). Sherif offers experimental evidence of contextuality in small groups:

> When the individual, in whom a [perceptual] range and a norm within that range are first developed in the individual situation, is put into a group situation, together with other individuals who also come into the situation with their own ranges and norms established in their own individual sessions, the ranges and norms tend to converge. But the convergence is not so close as when they first work in the group situation, having less opportunity to set up stable individual norms [1936, p. 104].

Combining emergence and contextuality images, Laumann and Pappi argue that "the hallmark of a network analysis . . . is to explain, at least in part, the behavior of network elements [contextuality] . . . and of the system as a whole [emergence] by appealing to specific features of the interconnections among the elements" (1976, p. 20); and Coleman says, "The central theoretical problems [are]: how the purposive actions of the actors combine to bring about system-level behavior [emergence], and how these purposive actions are in turn shaped by constraints that result from the behavior of the system [contextuality]" (1986, p. 1312).

Marx and Engels, Durkheim, and Simmel are all classic on disintegration (which we may also call, for symmetry with emergence, "submergence"). As we have already seen, Marx and Engels claim that the class struggle has sometimes ended in "the common ruin of the contending classes," and Marx's discussion of "estrangement" emphasizes the tendencies toward social disintegration between worker and entrepreneur (see 1977, pp. 70-71). Durkheim says, "If normally the division of labor produces social solidarity, it can happen, however, that it has entirely different or even opposite results" (1984, p. 291). Simmel argues that "the self-preservation of very young associations requires the establishment of strict boundaries and a centripetal unity. . . . [But to] the extent that the group grows . . . to the same degree the group's direct, inner unity loosens, and the rigidity of the original demarcation against others is softened. . . . At the same time, the individual gains freedom of movement, far beyond the first jealous limitation" (1950, pp. 416-417). More recently, Eisenstadt claims disintegration is latent in all contextuality ("organization not only fails to solve the problems of potential social disorder but also in a sense exacerbates them by . . . [making] them into foci of conscious concern" [1978, p. 20]), but it also seems possible that further emergence is also latent there (i.e., organization may facilitate the realization not only of social disorder, but of still greater social order).

In light of these (and other) examples, it seems fair to say that emergence is specifically represented by the fusion image in Figure 1.3 (where multiple variables are integrated into a new variable), contextuality is specifically represented by the cybernetic image (where variables interact with, and thereby constrain, one another), and disintegration is specifically represented by the complement of fusion—namely, fission.[84] More generally, however, the principles of equifinality and equioriginality suggest that three of the one-way images may be implicated in emergence (such that different variables may approach the point of combination via value-added, and/or convergent, and/or cross-pressure paths) while the other three one-way paths ("value-subtracted," divergence, and tension) may be implicated in disintegration, and all of the two-way images may be implicated in the mutual constraining of variables (such that that constraining may be dialectic, and/or amplification, and/or damping). Thus when Coleman rejects (without defining) "*simple* aggregation" (1987, p. 157, italics added) as a model for "the micro-macro transition" (1987, p. 157), Figure 1.3 and the above discussion offer several non-simple images for analyzing not only this transition, but the macro-micro transition, and macro maintenance, as well.

In closing, it seems reasonable to make the same kind of claim for Figure 1.3 as was made for Figures 1.1 and 1.2, namely, that it systematically subsumes all causal images to be found in the sociological literature—which is to say, every such image is classifiable either within some single cell, or some combination of cells, shown in Figure 1.3.And it follows, at last, that to the extent to which all existing and foreseeably future empirical sociological statements consist entirely of some combination of the descriptive variables, explanatory-predictive variables, and causal images represented in Figures 1.1, 1.2, and 1.3 (plus logical induction and deduction), the stated aim of this chapter has now been achieved. In closing, let us briefly consider what difference disciplinewide consensus on a matrix like this can make.

Conclusions

From the standpoint of this chapter, the entire history of substantive work in sociology so far represents nothing more than the discipline's childhood, and at the end of any childhood there is often a disconcerting pause while the juvenile's strategy becomes reorganized toward coping with the exigencies of adulthood. Thus if there is an "interregnum," a "theoretical lull" (Wiley, 1985, p. 180) in sociology, "if there is a rather widespread feeling that sociology in recent years has been in a depression . . . [accompanied by] boredom [and] the feeling that our work is going nowhere" (Collins, 1986, pp. 1336, 1342; see also Alexander, 1982, p. xiii; Gans, 1986, p. 1), one likely reason is not that we are stalled in the middle of an era, but that we have successfully completed an era and have not yet begun the next. That is, any malaise we feel may be the temporary result of what this chapter has tried to make explicit, namely, awareness that all the "big" ideas of our disciplinary matrix have now been created and there is simply no more work of this kind to be done—unless we are willing to scrap these ideas and start all over with some new matrix whose dimensions are different (a step that, considering the histories of the other natural sciences, seems not unlikely in the long run). Having come to the end of our discipline's grandly inventive, exuberantly contentious, but inevitably simplistic childhood, then, we pause to pull ourselves together before taking off on the next, more comprehensive (and much more difficult) phase.

That such a phase should eventually come to pass in sociology seems clearly implied by even the most passionately tendentious of classical theorists. Engels, for one, says, "Marx and I . . . had to emphasize the main principle vis-a-vis our adversaries, who denied it, and we had not always the time, the place or the opportunity to allow the other elements involved . . . to come into their rights" (1969, Vol. III, p. 488). Freud says: "If psycho-analysis is compelled—and is, indeed, in duty bound—to lay all the emphasis upon one particular source [of religion], that does not mean it is claiming either that that source is the only one or that it occupies first place among the numerous contributory factors" (1950, p. 100; see also 1960, p. 1). And Weber, while propounding his own view of sociology as "a science concerning itself with the interpretive understanding of social action," feels compelled to add that "sociology, it goes without saying, is by no means confined to the study of social action . . . [nor does a focus on social action] imply any judgment on the comparative importance of this and other factors'' (1978, p. 24).

This chapter claims, and has cited a variety of evidence to demonstrate, that sociology (and all the other social sciences) at last possesses the conceptual materials capable of realizing the comprehensiveness foreshadowed by the remarks just quoted, and capable of giving detailed and systematic meaning to what has recently (and vaguely) been called ''multidimensionality'' in sociology. As a result, it may be possible now, for the first time, to reach a clear and disciplinewide consensus on a single conceptual matrix and general nomenclature.

What will such consensus do for us? Most important of all, it should result in improving the quality and practical usefulness of our predictions. It has been tellingly observed that ''social scientists are happy enough when they have gotten hold of one paradigm or line of causation . . . [but] their guesses are often further off the mark than those of the experienced politician whose intuition is more likely to take a variety of forces into account'' (Hirschman, 1979, p. 177).[85] But with agreement on a matrix that includes, and systematizes, all the elements (and perhaps more besides) from which the experienced politician fashions his or her comprehensive but jealously *private* predictions of social phenomena, we will increasingly augment and eventually, in some realms, supersede those predictions with more reliable, precise, and maximally *public* ones—thereby further enlightening the electorate and further democratizing the process of deciding whether and how control over such phenomena will be sought.

Second, by recognizing the many ways that hitherto disparate theoretical positions relate to and *need* one another, the consensus in question should help us achieve an informed allegiance to a common cause, and that allegiance, in turn, should help heal our many disciplinary fractures. One recent president of the American Sociological Association describes that organization as ''paralyzed intellectually'' by the ''diversity of viewpoints among our members and accompanying pluralism of substantive and professional paradigms'' (Rossi, 1980, p. 7). Consensus on a disciplinary matrix of universal scope as well as systematic discriminative power can be the crucial step in breaking the paralysis without either fragmenting or homogenizing the discipline. And, almost needless to add, the same matrix consensus, once achieved within one social science, may well become a significant step toward the much wider consensus required for that eventual unification of all the social sciences mentioned early in this chapter.

Third, consensus on a disciplinary matrix within sociology should make it unthinkable to teach, study, or create sociological theory, methodology, or empirical research without making explicit reference to that matrix.[86] Thus, although every sociologist must always be free to combine elements of the matrix in new ways, free to coin new names for such combinations (and free, of course, to seek converts to his or her own idiosyncratic matrix), once we have achieved our first matrix consensus every sociologist should come under professional obligation to explicate the relations of such new combinations, names, and matrices to the consensually disciplinary matrix—giving special attention, of course, to relations that call for modification or replacement of that matrix. Needless to add, past (and especially ''classical'') sociological work should be similarly explicated, with the net result of enhancing communicative exactness and comparability across the entire sociological literature.

Finally, note that although consensus on a disciplinary matrix may, at casual first glance, seem likely to stifle or regiment scientific controversy, this is not the case. Controversies thrive only when grounded in consensus regarding the key terms employed in them; otherwise the participants talk abrasively past each other, generate heat rather than light, and end up merely strutting and shrieking. Consensus on a disciplinary matrix, which explicitly leaves up to each individual analyst the way these concepts are further specified in order to correspond to the actual observations at hand, the way they are combined into complex variables or hypotheses, and the importance assigned to each of them in such variables and hypotheses (and leaving the validity of all these judgments up to disciplinewide agreement on the results and interpretations of empirical comparisons), should greatly improve the quality and productivity of controversies in sociology by strengthening confidence that all parties to such controversies share the same understanding of the same basic nouns and verbs. Blalock is most persuasive here:

> We can ill afford to go off in our own directions, continuing to proliferate fields of specialization, changing our vocabulary whenever we see fit, or merely hoping that somehow or other the products of miscellaneous studies will add up. . . .[A] sustained effort to clarify our theoretical constructs and self-consciously to ask ourselves how different strategies of conceptualization relate to problems of data collection and measurement . . . will better enable us to

comprehend what each of us is trying to say and to appreciate more fully the complexity of the theories and analyses needed to understand a very complex reality [1979, p. 893].

And speaking of measurement, one last point: It is of the utmost importance not to forget the general priority that qualitative rigor holds over quantification in natural science. Kuhn, for example, observes that "much qualitative research, both empirical and theoretical, is normally prerequisite to fruitful quantification of a given research field" (1977, p. 213). Thus "Before [quantitative work on magnetism] could be done, a better qualitative understanding of attraction, repulsion, conduction, and other such phenomena was needed. The instruments which provided a lasting quantification had then to be designed with these initially qualitative concepts in mind" (Kuhn, 1977, p. 217; Weber, too, notes that "the exact natural sciences do not proceed without qualitative categories" [1949, p. 74]). Kuhn also emphasizes that the reverse sequence, namely, quantification prior to establishing a rigorous and consistent qualitative base, is very likely to be futile: "In the absence of . . . prior [qualitative] work, the methodological directive, 'Go ye forth and measure,' may well prove only an invitation to waste time" (1977, p. 213), and Campbell adds the familiar fact that "without competence at the qualitative level, one's [quantitative] computer printout is misleading or meaningless" [1984, p. 34])—all of which is to say: *garbage in, garbage out*. It therefore seems fair to conclude that such conceptual rigor as may be engendered by diligent application of the disciplinary matrix set forth here (or some other) is indispensable rather than in any way secondary or antithetical to powerful quantitative (and, of course, qualitative) empirical research, as well as theorizing, in sociology.[87]

NOTES

1. Kuhn says a disciplinary matrix is " 'disciplinary' because it refers to the common possession of the practitioners of a particular discipline; 'matrix' because it is composed of ordered elements of various sorts [including symbolic generalizations, models, values, and paradigms]," and adds that "all or most of the objects of group commitment that my original text makes paradigms, parts of paradigms, or paradigmatic are constituents of the disciplinary matrix" (1970, p. 182; see also 1974, p. 471, note 16). The issues are complex here, but the only important point for present purposes is that Kuhn envisions each disciplinary matrix, while it exists, as including the elements from which many different paradigms—and therefore theories, propositions, and findings—are constructed. The same intention motivates the present chapter.

2. The distinction between the natural sciences and the humanities is essential: Whereas the humanities are devoted to creating values—that is, conceptions of the ultimately good, true, and/or beautiful—the natural sciences are entirely incapable of such creation. As Weber says, "An empirical science cannot tell anyone what he *should* do—but rather what he *can* do—and under certain circumstances—what he wishes to do" (1949, p. 54), and "Natural science gives us an answer to what we must do *if* we want to master life technically. It leaves quite aside, or assumes for its purposes, whether we *should* . . . wish to master life technically" (1958a, p. 144, italics added). Similarly, Einstein: "Objective knowledge provides us with powerful instruments for the achievement of certain ends, but the ultimate goal itself and the longing to reach it must come from another source. . . . [K]nowledge of truth . . . cannot prove even the justification and the value of the aspiration towards that very knowledge of truth" (1950, p. 22). Mead makes explicit reference to sociology in this regard: "Historical criticism, psychology, and sociology can in a manner explain the changes which have taken place in [our] values . . . but no one of them . . . is competent to determine for us what traits of people and things *should* attract our interest, nor what reshaping of goods *should* take place" (1938, p. 502, italics added). Incidentally, the term *natural science* in this chapter is meant to include the usual three divisions: physical, biological, and social. The social sciences are regarded here as presently comprising a subdivision of the biological (just as the biological is a subdivision of the physical), but with the increasing production of artificial organisms—including "partly human" ones—as participants in social phenomena, the social sciences will come to be regarded as a bridge between, and an integration of, the physical and biological sciences.

3. Although not much space can be given to the matter here, it should at least be mentioned that *ambiguity* of meaning (1) does not exclude standardization of meaning (one has only to standardize the limits of the ambiguity—and ambiguity must have limits, otherwise it degenerates into meaninglessness), (2) has some positive functions in every natural science, and (3) is, in any case, unavoidable. Levine says: "[B]y enhancing adaptiveness to change, by facilitating negotiation, by mobilizing constituencies [etc.]—ambiguous talk makes modern politics [and, let us emphatically add, modern natural science—*WLW*] possible" (1985, p. 43). But on the other hand, Levine argues, "Univocal discourse" also has positive functions. It "advances our capabilities for gaining cognitive mastery of the world, both by the determinateness that it lends to the representation of external phenomena and the control over internal sentiments by which it disciplines verbal communications. . . .[It facilitates] the precise designation of

specific rights and responsibilities and [constitutes] . . . unequivocally understood tokens and measures that are available to a wide public" (1985, pp. 39-40). However, the distinction between ambiguity and univocality seems dangerously misconstrued when presented as such a discrete one as this last sentence implies, and also when identified with the distinction between "theological and metaphysical thinking," on the one hand, and "positive science," on the other (see Levine, 1985, p. 40). It seems more accurate to regard *every* discourse, in all disciplines and all subject matter areas, as univocal in some respects (and to some degree) and ambiguous in others, and to identify the natural sciences never with the full *achievement* of univocality but with the collective, self-conscious, and unrelenting *striving* in that direction.

4. See Crosland (1962) for the history of the achievement of a disciplinary vocabulary in chemistry.

5. Contrast this view with Collins's emphasis on the pursuit of personal publicity and prestige for their own sakes, independent of any practical and collective concerns: "The aim of intellectual life, above all, is to be heard, to publicize one's views, and to receive recognition for them" (1986, p. 1337).

6. Giddens, too, says he believes "social theory" has to do with "grasping the *practical* connotations of social analysis" (1986, p. xvii, italics added), but his subsequent claim that "the task of constructing stably established generalizations . . . is not an ambition of much relevance to social science" (1986, p. ix) renders such grasp impossible insofar as generalizations about the past that permit us to infer predictions about the future are essential to the practical connotations of any theory—as is suggested below.

7. Regarding the inability of science to define "improve," see note 2.

8. Compare Gibbs's claim that "predictions are made only for the purpose of assessing . . . theory" (1972, p. 65). In the present view, predictions are made primarily to enable control over the world, and reliable predictions would be valuable to us even if they were based upon, and bore upon, no theory at all.

9. Note the emphasis here on relative reliability. Scientific predictions often have less *precision* than the other kinds (magical or sorcerous divination, and random guessing), and no human prediction whatever—whether scientific or not—can be *absolutely* reliable (see note 15). Obviously, predictive precision varies with the phenomenon being predicted and with the development of the science doing the predicting (see the impact on prediction in particle physics of the Heisenberg uncertainty principle as discussed in Davies, 1984, pp. 27-49).

10. Mannheim's use of the term *watchmen* rather than, say, *oarsmen*, or *captains* helps clarify the sharp contrast between Wallerstein's opinion that sociology should only be pursued "in conjunction with praxis" (1984, p. 114) and the same Wallerstein's later and more welcome opinion that "the task before us [sociologists] is to . . . illuminate the historical choices rather than presume to make them" (1986, pp. 1307-1308).

11. For reasons discussed later here, however, Taylor does not think such standard variables are possible in sociology.

12. For a systematic picture of that "inseparable mingling," see Wallace, (1983, pp. 355-388). In this connection, we should not overlook the abundant evidence from experimental psychology that an individual's sense of control over, and knowledge of, the world help determine that individual's physical and psychical well-being. Glass and Singer, for example, conclude that "behavioral impairments are an immediate consequence of unpredictable and uncontrollable aversive events" (1972, p. 139), and Weidner and Matthews add that "unpredictable and uncontrollable events are associated with such negative states in humans as depression . . . self-reported tension and distress . . . and accidental injuries . . . as well as major illnesses such as coronary heart disease" (1978, p. 1213). The two phases (pure and applied) of natural science, then, appear to serve fundamental (instinctual?) human needs at the individual as well as collective level.

13. The conservation laws (e.g., of energy, of momentum), and the limiting parameters (e.g., the speed of light, entropy) in physics are of such fundamental importance to our knowledge and control of physical phenomena because they specify what we believe to be the limits of possibility in such phenomena. The several lists of functional and structural "requisites," "imperatives," and so on (see below) have been proposed as similar specifications for social phenomena.

14. Winch says, "I am not denying that it is *sometimes* possible to predict decisions" (1958, p. 93, italics added)—leaving us to wonder what differentiates the times when it is possible from those when it is not. Winch equivocates in a similar way when he argues that "a given set of 'calculations' [by a given human subject] may lead to any one of a *set* of different outcomes"—thereby admitting that other "sets" of outcomes may be ruled *out* by the "calculations" in question, an admission reinforced by his remark that the given set of calculations "does limit the range of possible alternatives" (1958, p. 91, italics added; p. 92). Again, we are left to wonder what prevents predicting at least that limited range of possible alternatives, and if that range, why not (by adding variables other than the subject's calculations) a still more limited range within it, and, in principle, so on toward absolute determinacy—exactly as in all the other natural sciences—of course, without ever reaching that absolute in any natural science. Popper indicates this when he says, "Measurement should be described [as observing]. . . that the pointer of our measuring apparatus lies *between* two gradations on the scale. . . .Thus, an interval, a range, always remains" (1961, p. 125).

15. It seems abundantly clear that no explanation

or prediction of *anything* can be made with absolute certainty without explaining or predicting *everything* with absolute certainty, and insofar as such perfect knowledge is impossible for manifestly imperfect beings such as we, it becomes self-evident that, in Popper's words, "every scientific statement must remain *tentative for ever*" (1961, p. 280). Although the social sciences have not yet discovered the "uncertainty principle" that will formulate the limits of their predictive accuracy, we can be sure of two things even without it: (1) such limits exist, and (2) we have not reached them yet.

16. More precisely, of course, all these laws inhere in *human perceptions* of the nature of these phenomena, but that applies to the nature of "people" and their laws, as well.

17. No one, to my knowledge, denies the applicability of scientific analysis to social phenomena among nonhuman organisms—which raises the question of where those who deny its applicability to human social phenomena would draw the nonhuman-human line in the paleontological record of primate evolution. Again to my knowledge, no one asserting that denial has offered an answer to this question, which is, of course, highly relevant to the study of human social prehistory.

18. It seems especially noteworthy that Giddens includes "the *validity of the propositional content of that knowledge*" (1986, p. 345, italics added) as influencing the instability in question—such that valid knowledge has more influence than invalid. But obviously this contradicts the claim of instability itself, for what can the (external) "validity" of a proposition mean if not its *stability* across cases other than the ones from which it was derived? Giddens's belief that "there will not be any . . . universal laws in the social sciences" seems related to a still more comprehensive and most remarkably antiquated position expressed when he declares that "life is . . . not of nature and is set off against it. Human beings emerge from the 'nothingness' of inorganic nature and disappear back into that alien state of the inorganic" (1986, p. 193). Modern natural scientists seem very nearly unanimous in holding that, far from being set off against nature, life is an intrinsic part of nature; that human beings emerge exclusively from organic and never from inorganic nature (so far, we emerge as individuals exclusively from other human beings, and we emerged as a species from closely related precursor primate species—only the very first, simplest, life forms are claimed to have emerged from inorganic nature); and that the state into which we "disappear" at death (a state that is, incidentally, usually much more organic than inorganic) is in no sense "alien" but, again, only natural. Einstein's remarks seem relevant here: "A human being is part of the whole, called by us 'Universe'; a part limited in time and space. He experiences himself, his thoughts and feelings as something separated from the rest—a kind of optical delusion of his consciousness. This delusion is a kind of prison for us" (quoted in Pagels, 1986, p. 381).

19. The two provisos are as follows. First, whereas Taylor makes much of rejecting what he calls "brute data" (i.e., "data whose validity cannot be questioned by offering another interpretation or reading, data whose credibility cannot be bounded or undermined by further reasoning" [1979, p. 30]—an altogether inexplicable description, because, as note 15 here indicates, *no* data *in any* science can ever be so regarded), the disciplinary matrix proposed here accepts any and all data so long as they are intersubjectively verifiable. This brings us to the second proviso, for whereas Taylor believes "there is no verificational procedure which we can fall back on" (1979, p. 66) (and believes there *should* be none), the disciplinary matrix proposed here is premised on the possibility and desirability of such a procedure and is aimed at strengthening it. In support of that possibility and desirability, Weber says, "Sociology must reject the assumption that 'understanding' and causal 'explanation' have no relationship to one another," and goes on to describe the relationship they should have as follows: "Explanations of concrete behavior in terms of its meaning are, even with the highest degree of self-evidence, only explanatory hypotheses for sociology. They therefore need to be empirically verified in essentially the same manner as does every hypothesis" (1981, p. 157). Thus Weber asks us to "consider the 'meaning' which 'we' could dogmatically or prescriptively ascribe to [a given social process]. Was it also the 'meaning' which each of the actual participants ascribed to it? Or did each of the participants ascribe some other 'meaning' to this process? Did they consciously ascribe any 'meaning' at all to the process?" (1977, p. 112). These are the questions that need to be empirically verified rather than left, in the event of disagreement among analysts, to an exchange of mere vanities regarding which analyst's "intuition" is the more "adequate" (see Taylor, 1979, pp. 67, 68).

20. Biologists refer to the honeybee's, and the bat's, wings as "analogous" structures because they have the same outcome (function) but different origins (genetic causal processes). The complement of equifinality (present in biologists' references to "homologous" structures—like the wing of a bat and the arm of a human—that have the same origin but different functions) has been variously called "multifinality" and "equioriginality" (see Wallace, 1983, pp. 410-413). "Turning-points," "crises," "two roads [that] diverged in a wood," and "to be, or not to be" express equioriginality. Sociological expressions of equioriginality include Weber's claim that "action that is 'identical' in its meaning relationship occasionally takes what is, in the final effect, a radically varying course" (1981, p. 156), and Eisenstadt's question of "whether social movements with seemingly similar characteristics . . . may give rise, in different societies or historical settings to different structural outcomes" (1978, p. 85).

21. One of three authors of the (at this writing) dominant theory of superconductivity claims that " 'superconductivity' may turn out to have as many

causes as the common cold" (*Time*, May 11, 1987, p. 49); Feynman diagrams describe alternative paths of a given electron from one point to another; and at a more general level of abstraction, Hempel, discussing "explanatory overdetermination" (i.e., the theoretical representation of equifinality) says "an event [of any kind] is overdetermined if two or more alternative explanations with non-equivalent explanans-sets are available for it" (1965, p. 419, italics removed).

22. Equifinality, it should be noted, always has its limits (although there may be more than one way to skin a cat, not all ways of *behaving* toward a cat, fortunately for the cat, will skin it) and these limits are, in principle, discoverable. The aims of explanatory-predictive analysis in sociology, therefore, are to separate the ways that do produce a given outcome from those that do not (recognizing, of course, that no two outcomes are ever perfectly identical; we only treat them as such for given purposes), and to sort out the ways that do according to their different variables and causal paths—and therefore their different costs and benefits to concerned parties.

23. For citations from the sociobiological literature relevant to the following discussion of definition and description, see Wallace, 1983, pp. 49-53.

24. Note that Durkheim gives the hypothesis three successive forms, silently gliding from the strong claim that social facts actually *do* exert the causal influence in question ("Here, then, is a category of facts which . . . *exercise* control over [the individual]"), to weaker ambiguity ("A social fact . . . . *exerts or is capable of exerting* [coercion] upon individuals"), and finally to the weakest possible causal claim that "a social fact is . . . . *capable* of exerting [constraint] over the individual" (1982, pp. 52, 56, 59, italics added). The first formulation is obviously untenable as a definition of social facts because of its implicit circularity: Sociologists who accept this formulation must already have carried out the research necessary to ascertain that a given way of acting does in fact exert the causal influence in question before they can permit themselves (as sociologists) to carry out that research in the first place. The third formulation is causally weakest because since Newton, and then Einstein, *any* phenomenon must be presumed *capable* of influencing all other phenomena not lying in its past. The requirement that a social phenomenon must have this capability has, therefore, to be counted so undistinguishing as to be vacuous. Why does Durkheim include these variously hypothesis-implying formulations in his definition of social facts? Perhaps he unconsciously wishes to bias explanatory hypotheses regarding such facts in favor of his prejudicial injunction that "the determining cause of a social fact must be sought among antecedent social facts and not among the states of the individual consciousness" (Durkheim, 1982, p. 134, italics removed)—an injunction that is only barely saved by the vague term "determining cause" from banning all but two (social structure and cultural structure) of the 12 types of possible causes of social phenomena cited in Figure

1.2. Durkheim, of course, is not the only theorist who would like to define social phenomena in a way that biases their explanation (see Wallace, 1983, p. 42).

25. Note that although Parsons and Shils say their theory "does not treat the *actor* as an organism" (and by this they mean their theory treats the actor only as a thinking-feeling mind), they add that "the concrete individual who behaves is, however, . . . always an organism" (1951, p. 102)—thereby foreshadowing Parsons's splitting off of the "behavioral organism" from the "personality subsystem" in his "general theory of action" (see 1959, p. 613).

26. The distinction here between physical and psychical behavior is not intended to challenge the view of psychophysiology that all psychical behavior events may be reduced to physical events (i.e., to the electrochemical behavior of cells, their physical components and physical inputs and outputs). The distinction merely acknowledges that, so far in its history, sociology has not required reduction to the level of psychophysiology (although it may require it, eventually) and continues instead to rely on Mead's rough definition of "the psychological datum" as that "which is accessible, in the experience of the individual, only to the individual himself" (1934, p. 5)—whereas the physiological datum is accessible to other, outside, observers. See note 34 for further discussion of this point.

27. To be logically exhaustive, every dimension of all three parts of the matrix would have to include a residual category, and, for simplicity, none do. The matrix, however, can be (and is claimed to be) empirically exhaustive without being logically so.

28. Contrasts that refer to social structure as simply "structure" and to cultural structure as simply "culture" (for example, Blau says, "I am a structural determinist, who believes that the structures of objective social positions among which people are distributed exert more fundamental influence on social life than do cultural values and norms" [1977, p. x; see also 1987, p. 75]) are dangerously misleading: They imply that only shared *physical* behaviors have structure and that shared *psychical* behaviors have none. But oddly, Blau defines "social position" as "any difference in attributes among people that *they* themselves take into account in their social relations" (1987, p. 76, italics added)—thereby making "social position" into exactly the kind of "subjective" variable Blau says he does not want it to be. That is, the definition makes shared psychical taking-into-account (i.e., cultural structure, whether conscious or unconscious) the criterion for "social position."

29. The social-versus-cultural distinction seems to be what Weber means when he distinguishes between "factual regularities *of* conduct ('customs')," and "rules *for* conduct ('conventions,' 'laws')" (1978, p. 332); what Marx means when he distinguishes between social "relations" and social "consciousness" (1969, Vol. I, p. 503); what Durkheim means when he distinguishes between "modes of action" and

"states of opinion" (1965, p. 51); what Kroeber and Parsons mean when they distinguish "culture . . . [i.e.,] values, ideas, and other symbolic-meaningful systems" from "society . . . [i.e.,] interaction among individuals and collectivities" (1958, p. 583); and what Merton means when he distinguishes between "cultural structure [as an] organized set of normative values . . . and social structure [as an] organized set of social relationships" (1957, p. 162)—despite the unexplicated circularity of defining "social structure" in terms of "social relationships." Incidentally, as used here, the term *structure* refers to any statistical regularity between two or more phenomena of *any* kind (see Ashby, 1968, p. 108)—"social" and "cultural" being only two kinds in a presumably infinite variety.

30. Weber says, "We are *cultural* beings endowed with the capacity and the will to take a deliberate *attitude* towards the world and to lend it significance," defines "cultural phenomena" as "all those which are *meaningful* to us" (1949, pp. 81, 70, italics changed), and defines "meaning" as an object's "relation to human action in the role either of means or of end; a relation of which the actor or actors can be said to have been *aware*" (1978, p. 7, italics added).

31. In still another usage, Luhmann says, "Social systems, according to this theory, consist of communications and nothing but communications—not of human beings, not of conscious mental states, not of roles, not even of actions" (1987, p. 113)—although when he says "persons. . . can *leave* the system" (1987, p. 114, italics added), he clearly implies that social systems do contain human beings. Moreover, it is not clear what Luhmann means by "communication"—whether the spoken, written, or printed code or the sender's and receiver's interpretations of that code—but having ruled out "conscious mental states," it is not easy to see how he can include either of the latter.

32. Oddly, Wuthnow et al. have no difficulty claiming that the reverse operation—namely, explaining the unobservable cultural predispositions of human actors in terms of observable activities—"has proved more attractive" (1984, p. 5), when an "unobservable" should prove as big a stumbling block to science when it is the dependent variable as when it is an independent variable of an explanation. Swidler agrees with Wuthnow et al. that, as she puts it, "Debate has raged for several academic generations over defining the term 'culture' " (1986, p. 273), and also seems to share their misplaced concern with observability when she defines culture as "symbolic vehicles of meaning" and includes among such vehicles "publicly available" (i.e., 'directly' observable) "ritual practices, art forms and ceremonies, . . . language, gossip, stories, and rituals of daily life" (1986, p. 273). (Inexplicably, Swidler also includes "beliefs" here, but surely beliefs cannot be called "publicly available" if they remain only beliefs and not physical expressions or meterings thereof.) It should be obvious, however, that no "practices" can justifiably be called "ritual" or "ceremonial"—

and no artifact can justifiably be called "an art form" —unless one assumes that some shared thoughts and/or feelings of the actors are represented by them; no utterances can justifiably be called "language" or "gossip" or "stories" unless one makes similar assumptions; indeed, no "vehicle" can justifiably be called "symbolic" or "meaningful" without such assumptions. Needless to add, therefore, even though she seems unaware of them, Swidler's definition of culture depends entirely on assumptions about the subjects' minds—as does Geertz's (see Wallace, 1983, p. 46).

33. Campbell quotes Rice to the effect that if a jazz concert patron visually sees a saxophone, " 'Corroboration would be required in the form of other sense impressions . . . emanating from or relating to the saxophone'" (1958, p. 16), before the patron could safely say his or her vision of a saxophone is not a hallucination.

34. Needless to add, what serves as an indicator of one phenomenon (say, cultural structure) in one analysis may well serve as an indicator of a quite different phenomenon (say, social structure) in another analysis. The issue here, however, is not the methodological one of *which* indicators to use (these will vary from analysis to analysis), but the conceptual one of whether *any* indicators can and should be used specifically for cultural structure, and if so, with what definitional justification. In this connection, note that although Wuthnow et al. reject "thoughts, moods, feelings, beliefs, and values" as referents of "culture," they claim their own definition of culture ("the symbolic-expressive aspect of human behavior"[1984, p. 3]) is "sufficiently broad to take account of the verbal utterances, gestures, ceremonial behavior, ideologies, religions, and philosophical systems that are generally associated with the term culture" (1984, p. 3). But it can hardly be doubted that every one of these indicators is conceptually identified (in the sociological, as well as other, literatures) with exactly such thoughts, moods, and so on, and it is only that identification which endows these indicators with their special sociological significance. Indeed (as in the case of Swidler—see note 32), it is only that identification that justifies Wuthnow et al. calling a particular utterance or hand movement "verbal" or "gestural" (i.e., symbolic).

35. Contrast this with Giddens's assertions (which he does not, and surely cannot, support with empirical evidence) that "structure has no existence independent of the knowledge that agents [participating in it] have about what they do," and that "generalizations in the social sciences always presuppose . . . the intentional activities of human agents" (1986, pp. 26, 141), and with Münch's and Smelser's assertion that "interaction is *always* communication, not mere exchange" (1987, p. 366, italics added).

36. The points being made here generalize on Merton's claim that "conduct may or may not conform with . . . beliefs. . . . [and] attitudes need not coincide with . . . behavior" (1976, p. 192, italics removed; but note the remark in which he inexplicably

contradicts this view: "Of course social conflict cannot occur without a clash of values, norms, or interests" [1975, p. 38]).

37. "Institutionalization," for example, is almost universally defined as a process whose outcome is such a combination (see Berger and Luckmann, 1967, p. 54; Blau, 1964, p. 25; Parsons, 1961, p. 35; Parsons and Shils, 1951, pp. 40, 191). In addition, Merton defines a "society" as a particular combination of social and cultural structure: "It is . . . only because behavior is typically oriented toward the basic values of the society that we may speak of a human aggregate as comprising a society" (1957, p. 141). The ways in which such combinations occur, however, remain key questions for systematic detailing.

38. For example, Collins says, "Microsociology is the detailed analysis of what people do, say, and think in the actual flow of momentary experience. Macrosociology is the analysis of large-scale and long-term social processes" (1981, p. 984)—although one would certainly prefer to say "what people do, say, and think *together*" (i.e., in *inter*organism behavior regularities), because otherwise, microsociology becomes individual physiology and psychology.

39. The potentially key role of meso levels of social phenomena is a theme running through much sociological theory. For example, Durkheim says, "A nation cannot be maintained unless, between the state and individuals, a whole range of secondary groups are interposed" (1984, p. liv); Gerstein notes the opposite causal direction: "States relate to individual actions exclusively through the groups that constitute them [sic]" (1987, p. 109); and Simmel discusses alternative ways in which the individual may participate in such "secondary," meso-level groups (see 1955, pp. 146-154). See also Collins ("The distinction between micro and macro levels is a continuum, not a dichotomy" [1987, p. 196]), and Schegloff (some have proposed contexts of a scope intermediate between the largest structures of a society and the details of interaction" [1987, p. 218]).

40. Compare such separate application with Collins's more indiscriminate mixing of the regularity and organisms components of the generic definition when, for example, he arbitrarily identifies a "3-10^2 sq ft" spatial level with a "small group" organisms level and calls the resultant combination of number of organisms and spatial extension simply a "*space scale*" (1981, p. 986, italics added). Separating the two components of this scale would permit "small groups" to extend over any conceivable spatial (and temporal) distance—thereby including such cases as that of astronauts standing, say, on Mars and their families back home in Indiana.

41. Pagels continues: "The details of the atomic nucleus—the quarks inside the protons and neutrons—are 'causally decoupled' from the chemical properties of the atom. . . .[T]o understand chemistry one must comprehend the rules obeyed [not in the atomic nucleus, but] by the valence electrons in the outer parts of atoms. . . .[Such] 'causal decoupling' . . . becomes reflected in the establishment of separate

scientific disciplines" (1986, p. 161; see also Wallace, 1983, p. 170-173). Simmel cites an instance of decoupling when he claims "the metropolis is indeed characterized by its essential independence even from the most eminent individual personalities" (1950, p. 419), as do Münch and Smelser when they find in Marx's discussion of "the self-alienation of the human individual in commodity production, a notion that explicitly states the independence of commodity production as a macroscopic system from individual action" (1987, p. 368). But Münch and Smelser also seem to deny decoupling when they argue that "order does not come from chaos; it always presupposes some other order" (1987, p. 365)—a claim that runs inexplicably counter to currently well-established principles of cosmology and biology (see Pagels, 1986, pp. 234-268, and Schrödinger, 1968, pp. 145-146).

42. On the vastly simplifying presumption called the " 'principle of the uniformity of nature' " (Popper, 1961, p. 252), explanations of observations that have already been made are regarded here as logically equivalent to predictions of observations that have not yet been made: "an explanation . . . is not complete unless it might as well have functioned as a prediction" (Hempel, 1965, p. 234; see also Wallace, 1983, pp. 414, 461).

43. "To explain or predict a given social phenomenon" here subsumes three partly separate analytical problems—namely, that of explaining or predicting (1) the origin, (2) the maintenance (including change), and (3) the termination of the phenomenon in question. Both Durkheim and Weber emphasize the difference between the first two problems: Durkheim says, "The utility of a fact is not what causes its existence [but] it must generally be useful to continue to survive. . . .[Therefore] when one undertakes to explain a social phenomenon the efficient cause which produces it and the function it performs must be investigated separately" (1982, p. 123, 122), and Weber says, "Once [a particular kind of politico-religious order became] established, the life conditions of [the social strata among which it became established] gave it by far the greater opportunity to survive . . . against the other, less stable political organizations. The question, however, why such an order emerged at all, was determined by quite concrete religious-historical and often highly personal circumstances and vicissitudes" (1952, p. 80). In contrast, Marx and Engels concentrate on separating the second and third problems by predicting that the conditions that will terminate capitalism will not be simply deterioration of the conditions that have maintained it (see especially 1969, Vol. I, pp. 111-119). In all three problems, however, the point characterized here as "key" remains the same.

44. Note that although describing a social phenomenon requires the analyst to observe at least *two* organisms (because it takes two to tango), explaining-predicting a social phenomenon requires the analyst, in principle, to concentrate on only *one* of these organisms at a time (because members of any given tango couple are apt to be dancing the same tango

for different reasons). This crucial distinction between descriptive and explanatory-predictive analyses in sociology seems to be what Homans has in mind when he says, "Though much emerges in social behavior . . . which goes beyond anything we can observe in the behavior of isolated individuals, yet nothing emerges that cannot be explained by propositions about the individuals as individuals" (1974, p. 12).

45. Coleman faults Weber's study of the Protestant ethic and the spirit of capitalism for not indicating how an individual's economic behavior could "help bring about capitalist economic organization in a society" (1987, p. 155). The fault, Coleman argues, lies in Weber's not differentiating among groups of individuals: "Some combination of individual actions is necessary to generate a macrosocial outcome. The orientations toward action of a worker in a capitalist enterprise are not the same as those of an entrepreneur, yet both are necessary to the enterprise. . . .[T]he aggregate value orientation of the population is not sufficient" (1987, p. 155). But note that nothing prevents an analyst from analyzing that "combination of individual actions" by aggregating observations on individuals into whatever groups, subgroups, and sub-subgroups seem appropriate and estimating the typical values on any given variable for each of them—as Weber himself does when he divides his subject population of Protestant laypersons into exactly the two groups Coleman recommends. Thus, according to Weber, the typical spirit of capitalist *entrepreneurs* is one of continual calculation: "Everything is done in terms of balances: at the beginning of the enterprise an initial balance, before every individual decision a calculation to ascertain its probable profitableness, and at the end a final balance to ascertain how much profit has been made" (Weber, 1958b, p. 18). The typical spirit of capitalist *workers*, however, is one of noncalculation: "At least during working hours, [labour must be] freed from continual calculations of how the customary wage may be earned with a maximum of comfort and a minimum of exertion. Labour must, on the contrary, be performed as if it were an absolute end in itself, a calling" (Weber, 1958b, pp. 61-62; for another statement of this entrepreneur-worker distinction, see 1968, p. 247). Thus Weber explicitly employs "the aggregate value orientation" not (as Coleman and many others think) of the undifferentiated total population of participants in capitalism, but of two different subpopulations—and he could, using the same method of subdivided aggregation, and with equal analytical sufficiency, employ the aggregate value orientations of any number of such subpopulations, sub-subpopulations, and so on, down to dyads.

46. In apparent opposition to this identification of a single target of explanation-prediction in both micro- and macrosociology, consider Coleman's opinion that "a widening gap [exists] within the discipline between theory and research: Social theory continues to be concerned with the functioning of social systems of behavior, whereas empirical research . . . is largely concerned with explaining individual

behavior" (1987, p. 153), and Blau's claim that "microsociology and macrosociology . . . explain [social life] in different terms" (1987, p. 71). This opposition, however, is not as sharp as it appears because Coleman modifies his view enough to assert that "the focus on individual behavior as the phenomenon to be explained is not completely misplaced in sociology" (1987, p. 153)—although he does not say *why* it is not misplaced. And Blau, too, qualifies his view enough to claim that "the macrosociological approach, painting a large canvas in broad strokes, cannot explain [social] processes because it does not investigate interpersonal relations in depth" (1987, p. 83)—thereby implying that macro- and microsociology do not explain social life in different terms after all, inasmuch as only the latter explains.

47. For citations from the sociobiological literature that parallel those made below from the sociological literature, see Wallace (1983, pp. 200ff).

48. Note the references, in the primary dimensions of Figure 1.2, to "putative" determinants of causal influence, and "putative" sources of causal influence. Both qualifications serve to rule out the necessity of conclusively demonstrating a particular combination of determinants and sources before conceptualizing a given explanatory-predictive variable with reference to these dimensions (see note 24). This (1) permits different sociologists to define variables to which they give the same name (e.g., "social class," "technology") in terms of different putative determinants and sources of causal influence, but calls on them to explicate and debate these differences; (2) recognizes that consensus in the natural sciences on these questions is almost never complete at any given time, and almost inevitably changes over time; and (3) points out the role—in such sociological debates and in the overall natural science consensus of which they are parts—of certain major informational dependencies of sociology on the other natural sciences, and viceversa.

49. For example, in line with Durkheim's restriction (see note 24), Blau says "both the explicandum and the explicans" of his theory "are distinctly social" (1987, p. 75), and Wippler and Lindenberg say, "The central task of sociology consists of showing how social behavior and collective phenomena . . . are socially determined" (1987, p. 135). In a restriction different from and more confusing than these, Alexander and Giesen would limit sociological theory to " 'the problem of action': Is the knowing actor rational or [sic] interpretive . . . and the problem of order [i.e., is] the ultimate [sic] source of this knowledge [sic] . . . located inside or outside the knowing individual" (1987, p. 13). "Action and order," Alexander proclaims, "represent *the true* presuppositions of sociological debate" (1982, p. 65, italics added). All such constrictions of interest and attention (assuming they can be explicated without internal inconsistencies) are freely permitted by the matrix set forth here—but only as *options* available for voluntary choice by analysts self-consciously pursuing different specializations within the discipline's overall division of labor,

not as *dogmas* to be imposed uniformly across all specializations and all analysts in the discipline.

50. The typology used by Eisenstadt (with Curelaru) when he identifies "four kinds of paradigms [for the explanation of social life]: "individualistic, sociologistic, cultural or culturalistic, and environmental" (1976, p. 85; see also pp. 59, 350-353), roughly corresponds to this classification but he does not systematically differentiate subtypes within each kind of paradigm. For trends in the prominence of some of the types of explanatory variables discussed below as they appeared in *American Sociological Review* articles from 1936 through 1978, see Wells and Picou (1981, pp. 107-113, 130-137, 143-147).

51. See Garfinkel (1967, pp. 30 and 262-283 for the several meanings he attaches to "rationality." It may be thought that Garfinkel regards these several meanings not as existentially given but as socially generated when he says "the properties of a status arrangement are determinative of the extent to which the actions of actors show the rationalities" (1967, p. 282), but note that it is only the *extent* to which actions *show* the rationalities that is specified as socially determined here—not the existence, within the actors, of the rationalities themselves. In this, Garfinkel's view seems to parallel Freud's, where the extent to which the individual's actions show the id's instinctual drives is regarded as socially determined (see 1962, pp. 70-71).

52. Similarities notwithstanding, however, there are important differences in the ways that the pattern variables, interpretive procedures, and accounting practices, respectively, propose to solve this problem—ways that seem to depend on breaking the process of assigning meaning into steps that begin with social participants perceiving and conceptualizing a situation, and end with them communicating about it. Thus, first, the pattern variables are proposed as alternative conceptions (e.g., "Universalism [or] Particularism" [Parsons and Shils, 1951, p. 77; see pp. 76-84]) with which participants in an interaction situation automatically (i.e., instinctively, by virtue of the "inherences" mentioned above) present themselves when called upon (again, instinctively) to assign meaning to that situation. Second, the interpretive procedures are proposed as rules that participants (instinctively) use when actually choosing between such kinds of alternatives (e.g., "treat a given lexical item . . . as an index of larger networks of meaning" [Cicourel, 1974, p. 35; see pp. 34-35, 85-88; also see Garfinkel, 1967, pp. 41-42, 272-276]). And third, the accounting practices are proposed as rules participants (instinctively) use when communicating to each other the assignments of meaning they have made (i.e., such practices are "members' procedures for making [everyday social] settings 'account-able' . . . [which is to say,] observable-and-reportable" [Garfinkel, 1967, p. 1]).

53. Homans comes close to this specification when he says, "A norm . . . is an idea in the minds of the members of a group . . . specifying what the members or other men should do . . . under given circum-

stances," adding that "A statement of the kind described is a norm only if any departure of real behavior from the norm is followed by some punishment," and that "some norms . . . define what a single member in a particular position is supposed to do" (1950, pp. 123, 124). When Swidler says, "Culture [is] a 'tool kit' for constructing 'strategies of action'" (1986, p. 277), the four norm components cited here (actor, situation, response, and consequence) may be regarded as the principal types of "tools" (often fashioned into "pre-fabricated links" [Swidler, 1986, p. 277]) contained therein—although Swidler unaccountably denies that values (i.e., affectively weighted expected consequences) can be part of such a kit: "Action is not determined by one's values. Rather action *and* values are organized to take advantage of cultural competences" (1986, p. 275). It would seem, however, that no "competence" can be identified without reference to some affectively weighted expected consequence as criterion (one is competent in making money, or telling jokes, or whatever), and certainly the idea of "taking advantage" of such a competence implies a valued end to which it should be put.

54. Note that although Bourdieu stresses the improvisational character of the individual's "habitus" (which he defines loosely as "a socially constructed system of cognitive and motivating structures [1977, p. 76, see also p. 72]), he nevertheless insists that such improvisation is "orchestrated" and "regulated"—albeit "without *express* regulation or an *institutionalized* call to order (1977, p. 17, italics added). More to the present point, Bourdieu claims there is "a differentiation of the domains of practice according to the degree of codification of the principles governing them [ranging from] the areas that are apparently 'freest' because given over . . . to the regulated improvisations of the habitus . . . [to] the areas most strictly regulated by customary norms and upheld by social sanctions" (1977, pp. 20-21).

55. Smelser's claim that "the ego, in dealing with external threats and deprivations, uses precisely the same repertoire of defensive modes as it does in dealing with [internal] instinctual representations and conflicts" (1987, p. 278) may be regarded as explicating two otherwise discrepant views expressed by Freud: that the ego uses defense mechanisms to "protect the id *from the dangers of the external world*" (quoted in Fodor and Gaynor, 1950, p. 33, italics added), and that defense mechanisms serve "the protection of the ego *against instinctual demands*" (Freud, 1959b, Vol. XX, p. 164, italics added).

56. "Are *perceived* to repeat" seems more accurate.

57. The term "psychical 'contagion' " is Weber's (1978, p. 17), and subsumes "emotional contagion" (Freud, 1959a, p. 16; Park, 1972, p. 20).

58. In stressing the explanatory-predictive power of "symbolic capital," Bourdieu claims that such capital is "always *credit*" (1977, p. 181)—thereby implicitly identifying the complementarity between the creditor's psychical *trust* that the debtor will pay, and the debtor's equally psychical *commitment* to

pay. But note that when it is said that trust and commitment are *given* and *accepted*, a physical exchange is indicated, involving, for example, the shaking of hands, the speaking or writing of words, and so on —behaviors that the participants may believe signify the otherwise invisible trust and commitment. Thus when Bourdieu goes on to describe credit as being granted to "those who give . . . the best material and symbolic guarantees," and says it follows that "the *exhibition* of symbolic capital . . . is one of the mechanisms which (no doubt universally) make capital go to capital" (1977, p. 181, italics changed; see also Merton's discussion of the "Matthew effect" [1973, p. 446]), he refers, albeit only implicitly, to such physical exchange. It seems important to make the reference explicit, however, in order to allow analysts to distinguish among physical exchanges that are accompanied by accurate and inaccurate psychical appraisals of "good faith" and "bad faith" on either or both sides, and among psychical trust-commitment complementarities that are accompanied by different kinds of exchanges—or by none at all.

59. Bourdieu, however, favors Leibniz's third alternative: "The objective homogenizing of group or class habitus [defined as "a socially constituted system of cognitive and motivating structures" in the mind of each social participant (1977, p. 76)] which results from the homogeneity of the conditions of existence is what enables practices to be objectively harmonized . . . and mutually adjusted *in the absence of any direct interaction*" (1977, p. 80). It is difficult, however, to believe that Bourdieu really means to exclude "direct interaction" from "conditions of existence." Indeed, when he says the habitus is "laid down in each agent by his earliest *upbringing*" (Bourdieu, 1977, p. 81, italics added), such interaction seems clearly implied.

60. The focus on endogenous causal relations between social phenomena that the analyst has described beforehand as hierarchically ordered—that is, as a whole, on the one hand, and as one or more of its parts, on the other—is a central but sometimes overlooked feature of structural functionalism (see Stinchcombe's references merely to "behavior," its "causes" and "consequences" [1968, p. 80]). Propositions that do not specify such hierarchical order, including part ⇄ part propositions, tend to fall within the provinces of unison, exchange, conflict, and segregation social structure—although Davis claims one of the things functionalism is said to do is "relate one part [of society] to another" (1959, p. 758).

61. Stinchcombe overlooks this reciprocity when he says, "Functional theories explain phenomena by their consequences. . . .By a functional explanation we mean one in which the consequences of some behavior . . . are essential elements of the causes of that behavior" (1968, pp. 98, 80, italics removed). The only thing Stinchcombe can reasonably mean here is that the consequences of some behavior are essential elements of the causes, not of that particular behavior, but of a *new* (and therefore different) instance of behavior of that *kind*—thereby making it

clear that functional theories never explain phenomena by *their own* consequences but only by the consequences of *prior* phenomena like them, and permitting functionalist explanation to come under the purview of scientific rather than mystical explanation. (Incidentally, Giddens, too, attributes reversibility to time: "the events and routines of daily life do not have a one-way flow to them. The terms 'social reproduction,' 'recursiveness' [sic] and so on indicate the repetitive character of day-to-day life" [1986, p. 35]—an assertion Heraclitus effectively challenged some time ago. See note 56 here for what may be the needed specification of Giddens's assertion.) Stinchcombe's discussion (1968, pp. 80-101), which restricts itself to the *form* or "causal imagery" of functionalist arguments (an imagery called "cybernetic" below), also overlooks the indispensable *content* of all functionalist arguments—namely, that the social phenomenon to be explained is looked upon either as a whole (which is then explained by its parts), or as a part (which is then explained by the whole to which it belongs)—a content that need not implicate either the equifinality nor the homeostasis specified by Stinchcombe.

62. Merton also distinguishes between "manifest" and "latent" functions (see 1957, p. 51)—identifying the latter as "those which are neither intended nor recognized"—and argues that "the distinctive intellectual contributions of the sociologist are found primarily in the study of unintended consequences (among which are latent functions) of social practices" (1957, pp. 51, 66). Viewed in functionalist context, then, Bourdieu and Passeron may be interpreted as contrasting this revelatory function of sociology with a presumed secretive function of formal education "because in matters of culture absolute dispossession excludes awareness of being dispossessed" (1977, p. 210).

63. Merton expresses this concept in a different context—namely, his discussion of "the mechanism of insulating role-activities from observability by members of the role-set" (1957, p. 374).

64. For what amounts to an attempt at such integration, see Parsons (1960).

65. See also Melbin's (1978) discussion of "similarities between land frontiers and time frontiers' in patterns of human settlement.

66. "Tool," "instrument," "implement," and so on are insufficiently general terms because they imply that the variable in question must be either used or designed to be used for some human purpose or in connection with some human technique. "Artifact" is meant to include these possibilities, of course, and more besides.

67. The same analytical separation contrasts, in a different way, with Campbell's inclusion, under "culture," of "knowledge, behaviour, and artefacts" —although he acknowledges that "many social anthropologists define culture only in terms of ideas and norms held by a group" (1985, pp. 8-9; see the discussion earlier here of social structure and culture structure).

68. One wonders what effects on modern religions Freud would predict for biotechnology and its present, and immediately foreseeable, ability to produce "transgenic creatures like a pig with a cow gene . . . , cows that produce medicines instead of milk, or even babies destined to have a particular height, hair color or other traits" (*The New York Times*, June 8, 1987, pp. A1, A17).

69. Weber counters this last claim with a cultural structural explanation: "The kind of weapon has been the result and not the cause of discipline. Exclusive use of the infantry tactic of close combat . . . brought about the decay of cavalry" (1958a, p. 256).

70. Whereas Marx is optimistic, even jubilant, concerning the sociocultural consequences of robotics (which he predicts will lead to "the artistic, scientific etc. development of the [human] individuals in the time set free, and with the means created, for all of them" [1973, p. 706]), Weber is adamantly pessimistic, and claims that "together with the inanimate machine," the animate machine, that is, bureaucracy, is "busy fabricating the shell of bondage which men will perhaps be forced to inhabit some day, as powerless as the fellahs of ancient Egypt" (1978, p. 1402; see also 1958b, pp. 181-182). More recently, Jastrow (1981), and Moravec (1982) have carried plausible speculation about the long-run consequences of robotics and artificial intelligence much further than either Marx or Weber.

71. Note that the entire discussion of sociological explanatory-predictive variables here has referred to *causal*, not logical (deductive), explanations and predictions. Thus although Blau argues that "heterogeneity *promotes* intergroup relations," and that "inequality *fosters* status-distant social relations" (1987, p. 80, italics added), these are deductive rather than causal claims. That is, intergroup relations *follow deductively* from heterogeneity because homogeneity, by definition (i.e., logically, not causally), excludes more than the one homogeneous group. Insofar as there can only be intergroup relations where there is more than one group, the claim that "heterogeneity promotes intergroup relations" presents this deductive explanation as though it were causal. The same argument holds for the "fostering" of status-distant social relations by inequality.

72. Along the same lines but more recently, Münch and Smelser claim that "how actors act is determined by the meaning they attribute to each others' actions" (1987, p. 366)—a view standing in some contrast with the one adopted here: "*ideas* present in the minds of men [are] *one among other* determining grounds of their actions" (Weber, 1975, p. 146, italics in original).

73. The term *image* is used here to indicate the usually verbal or diagrammatic notions of how causation works with respect to social phenomena in general, rather than those usually mathematical or computer "models" that represent its working with respect to one or another specific phenomenon (see Blalock, 1971; Brodbeck, 1959; Kaplan, 1964, pp. 264-265).

74. Homans's definition of interaction—"when an activity (or sentiment) emitted by one man is rewarded (or punished) by an activity emitted by another man . . . we say that the two have interacted" (1961, p. 35, italics removed)—is both more and less inclusive than this one. It is more inclusive insofar as it does not require the first man's activity to influence the second's; it is less inclusive insofar as it requires the second man's activity not merely to influence but to "reward" or "punish" the second's.

75. Ogburn uses "convergence" for what is here called fusion, and "dispersion" for fission (see 1957, pp. 21, 22).

76. As will be mentioned below, the fusion image is also employed in portraying emergence causal relations between levels. Parsons's use of the term *emergence* here, however, implies fission rather than fusion.

77. When they are exactly and stably equal, we speak of "deadlock" and of the phenomenon being "torn."

78. "Unstable" because any exogenous influence that augments either of the opposing pushes or pulls can upset the balance.

79. The image of "tension" proposed here differs from Moore's portrayal of tensions as "inconsistencies and strains" (1963, p. 100), and from Stinchcombe's portrayal of them as "difficulties, which tend to upset [stable relations]" (1968, p. 88). In the present view, tensions may as easily represent consistencies and strengths as inconsistencies and strains, and may as easily maintain as upset a given stability—all depending on whether the tension is balanced or unbalanced.

80. Such syntheses seem much like the "new meanings" produced by "legitimation" in Berger and Luckmann's theory (see 1967, p. 92), and also like the "attitude of the generalized other" achieved by child socializees in Mead's theory of "the game" (1934, pp. 154-156).

81. This appears to be another instance of confusion resulting from the dangerously different meanings of "social" discussed earlier here. Merton undoubtedly means "*cultural structurally prescribed*" (and perhaps also social structurally enforced)—even by his own definition of cultural structure as an "organized set of normative values . . . common to members of a designated society or group" (1957, p. 162).

82. Similarly, Parsons argues that "Weber postulates a basic 'drive' toward meaning and the resolution of . . . discrepancies" between what a normative order says ought to happen and what actually happens—a drive that leads to "continually more 'ultimate' reference points," such that "The 'explanations' [of the discrepancies] . . . must be grounded in increasingly generalized and 'fundamental' philosophical conceptions" (1964, pp. xlvii-xlviii). Contrast both these views with Kuhn's: "Though logical inclusiveness remains a permissible view of the relation between successive scientific theories, it is a historical implausibility" (1962, p. 97).

83. Similarly, Minsky employs emergence (and a distinctly sociological image that, incidentally, exemplifies the potentially wide relevance of sociological principles) in his explanation of mind: "I'll call 'Society of Mind' this scheme in which each mind is made of many smaller processes. These we'll call *agents*. Each mental agent by itself can only do some simple thing that needs no mind or thought at all. Yet when we join these agents in societies—in certain very special ways—this leads to true intelligence" (1985, p. 17).

84. See Münch and Smelser (1987, pp. 376-382) for a discussion of "modes of moving from the small to the large" (i.e., emergence), and "modes of moving" in the opposite direction (i.e., contextuality).

85. Although Weber holds that for purposes of the applied science of pedagogy, for example, "the results of [pure] experimental psychology are extremely meager," and that "From a pedagogical point of view, 'common sense' and 'practical experience' are much more significant" (1975, p. 138), he seems unwilling to concede the field of practical problem-solving to the interest-narrowed intuition of politicians (for "All party struggles are struggles for the patronage of office, as well as struggles for objective goals" [1958a, p. 87]), preferring the discipline-broadened "empathic understanding" or "interpretive method" of social scientists (see 1975, pp. 138-140). Comte is also unwilling to concede the field, but he espouses a different method and expects a longer wait before it bears fruit: "Our business, it is clear, is with theoretical researches, letting alone their practical application altogether. Though we may conceive of a course of study that should unite the generalities of speculation and application, the time is not yet come for it. . . .To say nothing of its vast extent, it would require preliminary achievements that have not yet been attempted. We must first be in possession of appropriate special conceptions, formed according to scientific theories; and for these we have yet to wait" (1975, pp. 89-90).

86. The matrix proposed here offers some goals for methodology by indicating the kinds of variables and causal connections we need to be able to measure.

87. One sociologist quaintly attributes what he regards as "the growing interest in theory" among American sociologists partly to "The bloom [being] off the rose of quantitative sociology" (Alexander, 1984, p. 410), as though theory and quantification were antithetical.

REFERENCES

Aberle, D. F., A. K. Cohen, A. K. Davis, M. J. Levy, Jr., and F. X. Sutton. 1950. "The Functional Prerequisites of a Society." *Ethics* (January): 100-111.

Alexander, Jeffrey C. 1982. *Theoretical Logic in Sociology*, Vol. I. Berkeley, CA: University of California Press.

_____ 1984. "The Parsons Revival in German Sociology." In *Sociological Theory: 1984.*, edited by Randall Collins. San Francisco: Jossey-Bass.

Alexander, Jeffrey C. and Bernhard Giesen. 1987. "From Reduction to Linkage: The Long View of the Micro-Macro Link." In *The Micro-Macro Link*, edited by Jeffrey C. Alexander et al. Berkeley: University of California Press.

Asch, S. E. 1958. "Effects of Group Pressure Upon the Modification and Distortion of Judgments." Reprinted in *Readings in Social Psychology*, edited by Eleanor E. Maccoby et al. New York: Holt, Rinehart, and Winston.

Ashby, W. Ross. 1968. "Principles of the Self-Organizing System." In *Modern Systems Research for the Behavioral Scientist*, edited by Walter Buckley. Chicago: Aldine.

Bales, Robert F. 1953. "The Equilibrium Problem In Small Groups." In *Working Papers In the Theory of Action*, edited by Talcott Parsons, Robert F. Bales, and Edward A. Shils. Glencoe, IL: Free Press.

Bang, Frederick B. 1969. "Introduction." In *Biology of Populations*, edited by Brenda K. Sladen and Frederick B. Bang. New York: Elsevier.

Becker, Howard S. 1973. *Outsiders*. New York: Free Press.

Berelson, Bernard R., Paul F. Lazarsfeld, and William N. McPhee. 1954. *Voting*. Chicago: University of Chicago Press.

Berger, Peter L. 1969. *The Sacred Canopy*. Garden City, NY: Doubleday/Anchor.

Berger, Peter L. and Thomas Luckmann. 1967. *The Social Construction of Reality*. Garden City, NY: Anchor Books.

Bergesen, Albert. 1984. "The Critique of World-System Theory: Class Relations or Division of Labor?" In *Sociological Theory: 1984*, edited by Randall Collins. San Francisco: Jossey-Bass.

Blalock, H. M., Jr. 1971. *Causal Models in the Social Sciences*. Chicago: Aldine-Atherton.

_____ 1979. "Measurement and Conceptualization Problems: The Major Obstacle To Integrating Theory and Research." *American Sociological Review* 44(6): 881-894.

Blau, Judith R. and Peter M. Blau. 1982. "The Cost of Inequality: Metropolitan Structure and Violent Crime." *American Sociological Review* 47(1):114-129.

Blau, Peter M. 1964. *Exchange and Power in Social Life*. New York: John Wiley.

_____ 1977. *Inequality and Heterogeneity*. New York: Free Press.

_____ 1987. "Contrasting Theoretical Perspectives." In *The Micro-Macro Link*, edited by Jeffrey C. Alexander et al. Berkeley: University of California Press.

_____ and W. Richard Scott. 1962. *Formal Organizations*. San Francisco: Chandler.

Blumberg, Rae Lesser. 1984. "A General Theory of Gender Stratification." In *Sociological Theory:*

1984, edited by Randall Collins. San Francisco: Jossey-Bass.

Blumer, Herbert. 1946. "Collective Behavior." In *New Outline of the Principles of Sociology*, edited by A. M. Lee. New York: Barnes & Noble.

———— 1956. "Sociological Analysis and the Variable." *American Sociological Review* 21(December):683-690.

———— 1962. "Society as Symbolic Interaction." In *Human Behavior and Social Process*, edited by Arnold M. Rose. Boston: Houghton-Miflin.

Bonner, John Tyler. 1980. *The Evolution of Culture in Animals*. Princeton, NJ: Princeton University Press.

Bourdieu, Pierre. 1977. *Outline of a Theory of Practice*. New York: Cambridge University Press.

———— and Jean-Claude Passeron. 1979. *The Inheritors*. Chicago: University of Chicago Press.

Brodbeck, May. 1959. "Models, Meaning, and Theories." In *Symposium on Sociological Theory*, edited by Llewellyn Gross. New York: Harper & Row.

Campbell, Bernard. 1985. *Human Ecology*. New York: Aldine.

Campbell, Donald T. 1958. "Common Fate, Similarity, and Other Indices of the Status of Aggregates of Persons as Social Entities." *Behavioral Science* 3(1):14-25.

———— 1984. "Can We Be Scientific in Applied Social Science?" Pp. 26-48 in *Evaluation Studies Review Annual*, Vol. 9, edited by Ross F. Conner et al. Beverley Hills, CA: Sage.

Carmichael, Stokely and Charles V. Hamilton. 1967. *Black Power*. New York: Vintage Books.

Carnap, Rudolf. 1966. *Philosophical Foundations of Physics*. New York: Basic Books.

Cicourel, Aaron. 1974. *Cognitive Sociology*. New York: Free Press.

Clynes, Manfred. 1980. "The Communication of Emotion: Theory of Sentics." In *Emotion: Theory, Research, and Experience*, edited by Robert Plutchik and Henry Kellerman. New York: Academic Press.

Coleman, James S. 1986. "Social Theory, Social Research, and a Theory of Action." *American Journal of Sociology* 91:1309-1335.

———— 1987. "Microfoundations and Macrosocial Behavior." In *The Micro-Macro Link*, edited by Jeffrey C. Alexander et al. Berkeley: University of California Press.

Collins, Randall. 1975. *Conflict Sociology*. New York: Academic Press.

———— 1981. "On the Microfoundations of Macrosociology." *American Journal of Sociology* 86: 984-1014.

———— 1986. "Is 1980's Sociology in the Doldrums?" *American Journal of Sociology* 91: 1336-1355.

———— 1987. "Interaction Ritual Chains." In *The Micro-Macro Link*, edited by Jeffrey C. Alexander et al. Berkeley: University of California

Press.

Comte, Auguste. 1975. *Auguste Comte and Positivism*, edited by Gertrud Lenzer. New York: Harper Torchbooks.

Coser, Lewis A. 1956. *The Social Functions of Conflict*. Glencoe, IL: Free Press.

Crosland, Maurice P. 1962. *Historical Studies in the Language of Chemistry*. Cambridge, MA: Harvard University Press.

Dahrendorf, Ralf. 1958. "Out of Utopia: Toward a Reorientation of Sociological Analysis." *American Journal of Sociology* 64:115-127.

———— 1959. *Class and Class Conflict in Industrial Society*. Stanford, CA: Stanford University Press.

Davies, Paul. 1984. *Superforce*. New York: Simon & Schuster.

Davis, Kingsley. 1959. "The Myth of Functional Analysis as a Special Method in Sociology and Anthropology." *American Sociological Review* 24:757-772.

———— 1976. "The World's Population Crisis." In *Contemporary Social Problems*, edited by Robert K. Merton and Robert Nisbet. New York: Harcourt Brace Jovanovich.

Douglas, Mary. 1969. *Purity and Danger*. London: Routledge & Kegan Paul.

Durkheim, Emile. 1951. *Suicide*. Glencoe, IL: Free Press.

———— 1965. *The Elementary Forms of the Religious Life*. New York: Free Press.

———— 1974. *Sociology and Philosophy*. New York: Free Press.

———— 1982. *The Rules of Sociological Method*. New York: Free Press.

———— 1984. *The Division of Labor in Society*. New York: Free Press.

Eckland, Bruce K. 1967. "Genetics and Sociology: A Reconsideration." *American Sociological Review* 32:173-194.

Einstein, Albert. 1950. *Out of My Later Years*. New York: Philosophical Library.

Eisenstadt, S. N. 1978. *Revolution and the Transformation of Societies*. New York: Free Press.

———— with M. Curelaru. 1976. *The Forms of Sociology: Paradigms and Crises*. New York: John Wiley.

Engels, Friedrich. 1939. *Herr Eugen Düring's Revolution in Science*. New York: International.

Etkin, William, ed. 1964. "Theories of Animal Socialization and Communication." In *Social Behavior and Organization Among Vertebrates*. Chicago: University of Chicago Press.

Fanon, Frantz. 1963. *The Wretched of the Earth*. New York: Grove.

Fodor, Nandor and Frank Gaynor. 1950. *Freud: Dictionary of Psychoanalysis*. New York: Philosophical Library.

Freud, Sigmund. 1950. *Totem and Taboo*. New York: Norton.

———— 1959a. *Group Psychology and the Analysis of the Ego*. New York: Norton.

———— 1959b. *The Standard Edition of the Com-*

plete Psychological Works. London: Hogarth.
_____ 1960. *The Ego and the Id*. New York: Norton.
_____ 1961. *The Future of an Illusion*. New York: Norton.
_____ 1962. *Civilization and Its Discontents*. New York: Norton.
Friedrichs, Robert W. 1970. *A Sociology of Sociology*. New York: Free Press.
Gans, Herbert J. 1986. "Sociology In America: The 1988 Theme." *Footnotes* 14:1, 4.
Garfinkel, Harold. 1967. *Studies in Ethnomethodology*. Englewood Cliffs, NJ: Prentice-Hall.
_____ and Harvey Sacks. 1970. "On Formal Structures of Practical Actions." In *Theoretical Sociology: Perspectives and Developments*, edited by John C. McKinney and Edward A. Tiryakian. New York: Appleton-Century-Crofts.
Gerstein, Dean. 1987. "To Unpack Micro and Macro." In *The Micro-Macro Link*, edited by Jeffrey C. Alexander et al. Berkeley: University of California Press.
Gibbs, Jack P. 1972. *Sociological Theory Construction*. Hinsdale, IL: Dryden.
Giddens, Anthony. 1986. *The Constitution of Society*. London: Macmillan.
Giesen, Bernhard. 1987. "Beyond Reductionism: Four Models Relating Micro and Macro Levels." In *The Micro-Macro Link*, edited by Jeffrey C. Alexander et al. Berkeley: University of California Press.
Glass, David C. and Jerome E. Singer. 1972. *Urban Stress*. New York: Academic Press.
Goffman, Erving. 1959. *The Presentation of Self in Everyday Life*. Garden City, NY: Doubleday/Anchor.
_____ 1961. *Asylums*. Garden City, NY: Doubleday/Anchor.
_____ 1967. *Interaction Ritual*. Garden City, NY: Doubleday/Anchor.
Goodall, Jane. 1986. *The Chimpanzees of Gombe*. Cambridge, MA: Belknap Press of Harvard University Press.
Goode, William J. 1960. "Norm Commitment and Conformity to Role-Status Obligations." *American Journal of Sociology* 66:246-258.
Gouldner, Alvin W. 1960. "The Norm of Reciprocity." *American Sociological Review* 25:161-178.
_____ 1976. *The Dialectic of Ideology and Technology*. New York: Seabury.
Guttentag, Marcia and Paul F. Secord. 1983. *Too Many Women?* Beverly Hills, CA: Sage.
Hall, A. D. and R. E. Fagen. 1956. "Definition of System." Pp. 18-28 in *General Systems Yearbook*, Vol. 1. Society for the Advancement of General Theory.
Hart, Hornell. 1957. "Acceleration in Social Change." In *Technology and Social Change*, edited by Francis R. Allen et al. New York: Appleton-Century-Crofts.
Hawley, Amos. 1950. *Human Ecology*. New York: Ronald Press.

Hediger, Heini P. 1961. "The Evolution of Territorial Behavior." In *Social Life of Early Man*, edited by Sherwood L. Washburn. Chicago: Aldine.
Hempel, Carl G. 1952. "Fundamentals of Concept Formation in Science." In *International Encyclopedia of Unified Science*. Chicago: University of Chicago Press.
_____ 1965. *Aspects of Scientific Explanation*. New York: Free Press.
Hirsch, Jerry, ed. 1967. "Behavior-Genetic Analysis." In *Behavior-Genetic Analysis*. New York: McGraw-Hill.
Hirschman, Albert O. 1979. "The Search For Paradigms As a Hindrance to Understanding." In *Interpretive Social Science*, edited by Paul Rabinow and William M. Sullivan. Berkeley: University of California Press.
Homans, George Caspar. 1950. *The Human Group*. New York: Harcourt Brace Jovanovich.
_____ 1958. "Social Behavior As Exchange." *American Journal of Sociology* LXIII:597-606.
_____ 1961. *Social Behavior: Its Elementary Forms*. New York: Harcourt Brace and World.
_____ 1974. *Social Behavior: Its Elementary Forms* (Revised). New York: Harcourt Brace and World.
Inbar, Michael. 1979. *The Future of Bureaucracy*. Beverly Hills, CA: Sage.
Inkeles, Alex. 1981. "Convergence and Divergence in Industrial Societies." In *Directions of Change: Modernization Theory, Research and Realities*, edited by Mustafa O. Attir, Burkart Holzner, and Zdenek Suda. Boulder, CO: Westview.
Jastrow, Robert. 1981. "The Post-Human World." *Science Digest* 89:89-91, 144.
Jensen, Arthur. 1969. "How Much Can We Boost IQ and Scholastic Achievement?" In *Environment, Heredity, and Intelligence* (compiled from the *Harvard Educational Review*). Cambridge, MA: Harvard Educational Review.
Kaplan, Abraham. 1964. *The Conduct of Inquiry*. San Francisco: Chandler.
Kleck, Gary. 1979. "Capital Punishment, Gun Ownership, and Homicide." *American Journal of Sociology* 84:882-910.
Kroeber, A. L. and Talcott Parsons. 1958. "The Concepts of Culture and Social System." *American Sociological Review* 23:582-583.
Kuhn, Thomas S. 1962. *The Structure of Scientific Revolutions*. Chicago: University of Chicago Press.
_____, ed. 1970. "Postscript—1969." In *The Structure of Scientific Revolutions*. Chicago: University of Chicago Press.
_____ 1974. "Second Thoughts on Paradigms." In *The Structure of Scientific Theories*, edited by Frederick Suppe. Urbana: University of Illinois Press.
_____ 1977. *The Essential Tension*. Chicago: University of Chicago Press.
Kuper, Leo. 1969. "Plural Societies: Perspectives and Problems." in *Pluralism in Africa*, edited by Leo

Kuper and M. G. Smith, Berkeley: University of California Press.

Laumann, Edward O. and Franz U. Pappi. 1976. *Networks of Collective Action*. New York: Academic Press.

LeBon, Gustave. 1960. *The Crowd*. New York: Viking.

Lenski, Gerhard. 1954. "Status Crystallization: A Non-Vertical Dimension of Social Status." *American Sociological Review* 19:405-413.

Levine, Donald N. 1985. *The Flight From Ambiguity*. Chicago: University of Chicago Press.

Levitsky, David A. and Barbara J. Stupp 1985. "Nutrition and the Behavior of Children." In *Nutrition in Pediatrics*, edited by W. A. Walker and J. B. Watkins. Boston: Little, Brown.

Levy, Marion J., Jr. 1952. *The Structure of Society*. Princeton: Princeton University Press.

Linden, Eugene. 1986. *Silent Partners: The Legacy of the Ape Language Experiments*. New York: New York Times Books.

Lorenz, Konrad. 1970. *Studies in Animal and Human Behaviour*. Cambridge, MA: Harvard University Press.

Luckmann, Thomas, ed. 1978. "Philosophy, Social Sciences and Everyday Life." In *Phenomenology and Sociology*. New York: Penguin Books.

Luhmann, Niklas. 1987. "The Evolutionary Differentiation Between Society and Interaction." In *The Micro-Macro Link*, edited by Jeffrey C. Alexander. Berkeley: University of California Press.

Maccoby, Eleanor Emmons and Carol Nagy Jacklin. 1974. *The Psychology of Sex Differences*. Stanford: Stanford University Press.

Malinowski, Bronislaw. 1944. *A Scientific Theory of Culture*. Chapel Hill: University of North Carolina Press.

Mannheim, Karl. 1955. *Ideology and Utopia*. New York: Harvest Books.

Marx, Karl. 1955. *The Poverty of Philosophy*. Moscow: Progress.

_____. 1967. *Capital*, Vols. 1-3. New York: International Publishers.

_____. 1973. *Grundrisse: Foundations of the Critique of Political Economy*. New York: Vintage Books.

_____. 1977. *Economic and Philosophical Manuscripts of 1844*. Moscow: Progress.

_____. and Friedrich Engels. 1969. *Selected Works*, Vols. 1-3. Moscow: Progress.

Mead, George Herbert. 1934. *Mind, Self, and Society*. Chicago: University of Chicago Press.

_____. 1938. *The Philosophy of the Act*. Chicago: University of Chicago Press.

Melbin, Murray. 1978. "Night as Frontier." *American Sociological Review* 43:3-22.

Mechanic, David. 1978. *Medical Sociology*. New York: Free Press.

Merton, Robert K. 1957. *Social Theory and Social Structure*. Glencoe, IL: Free Press.

_____. 1973. *The Sociology of Science*. Chicago: University of Chicago Press.

_____. 1975. "Structural Analysis in Sociology." In *Approaches to the Study of Social Structure*, edited by Peter M. Blau. New York: Free Press.

_____. 1976. *Sociological Ambivalence*. New York: Free Press.

Minsky, Marvin. 1985. *The Society of Mind*. New York: Simon & Schuster.

Moore, Mary E. 1968. "Behavioral Changes." In *Aging and Society*, edited by Matilda White Riley and Anne Foner. New York: Russell Sage Foundation.

Moore, Wilbert S. 1959. "Sociology and Demography." In *The Study of Population*, edited by Philip M. Hauser and Otis Dudley Duncan. Chicago: University of Chicago Press.

_____. 1963. *Social Change*. Englewood Cliffs, NJ: Prentice-Hall.

Moravec, Hans P. 1982. "The Endless Frontier and the Thinking Machine." In *The Endless Frontier*, edited by Jerry Pournelle with John F. Carr. New York: Ace Science Fiction Books.

Mulkay, Michael. 1979. *Science and the Sociology of Knowledge*. London: Allen & Unwin.

Münch, Richard and Neil Smelser. 1987. "Relating the Micro and Macro." In *The Micro-Macro Link*, edited by Jeffrey C. Alexander et al. Berkeley: University of California Press.

Nagel, Ernst. 1961. *The Structure of Science*. New York: Harcourt, Brace.

Nakano, Hideichiro. 1979. "Systems Thinking in Contemporary Sociology: An Ideological Approach." *Kwansei Gakuin University Annual Studies* 28:85-93.

Nicholson, Michael. 1983. *The Scientific Analysis of Social Behavior*. New York: St. Martin's Press.

Nriagu, Jerome D. 1983. *Lead and Lead Poisoning in Antiquity*. New York: John Wiley.

Ogburn, William F. 1957. "How Technology Causes Social Change." In *Technology and Social Change*, edited by Francis R. Allen et al. New York: Appleton-Century-Crofts.

Ong, Walter J. 1978. "Literacy and Orality in Our Times." *Association of Departments of English (ADE) Bulletin* 58:1-17.

_____. 1982. *Orality and Literacy: The Technologizing of the Word*. London: Methuen.

Pagels, Heinz R. 1986. *Perfect Symmetry*. New York: Bantam Books.

Park, Robert Ezra. 1972. *The Crowd and the Public*. Chicago: University of Chicago Press.

Parsons, Talcott. 1951. *The Social System*. Glencoe, IL: Free Press.

_____. 1959. "An Approach to Psychological Theory in Terms of the Theory of Action." In *Psychology: A Study of a Science*, edited by Sigmund Koch. New York: McGraw-Hill.

_____. 1960. "Pattern Variables Revisited: A Response to Robert Dubin." *American Sociological Review* 25:467-483.

_____. 1961. "An Outline of the Social System." In *Theories of Society*, edited by Talcott Parsons et al. New York: Free Press.

_____ 1964. "Introduction." In *The Sociology of Religion*, by Max Weber. Boston: Beacon.

_____ 1971. *The System of Modern Societies*. Englewood Cliffs, NJ: Prentice-Hall.

_____ and Edward A. Shils. 1951. "Values, Motives, and Systems of Action." In *Toward A General Theory of Action*, edited by A. Shils. New York: Harper Torchbooks.

Parsons, Talcott and Neil Smelser. 1956. *Economy and Society*. Glencoe, IL: Free Press.

Plutchik, Robert. 1980. *Emotions*. New York: Harper & Row.

Popper, Karl R. 1961. *The Logic of Scientific Discovery*. New York: Science Editions.

Postman, Neil. 1982. *The Disappearance of Childhood*. New York: Delacorte.

Powers, William T. 1973. *Behavior: The Control of Perception*. Chicago: Aldine.

Radcliffe-Brown, A. R. 1965. *Structure and Function in Primitive Society*. New York: Free Press.

Riley, Matilda White. 1987. "On the Significance of Age in Sociology." *American Sociological Review* 52:1-15.

Rossi, Alice S. 1977. "A Biosocial Perspective on Parenting." *Daedalus* 106:1-131.

Rossi, Peter H. 1980. "The President Reports." *Footnotes* 8(4):1, 7.

Schegloff, Emanuel A. 1987. "Between Micro and Macro: Contexts and Other Connections." In *The Micro-Macro Link*, edited by Jeffrey C. Alexander et al. Berkeley: University of California Press.

Schrödinger, Erwin. 1968. "Order, Disorder, and Entropy." In *Modern Systems Research for the Behavioral Scientist*, edited by Walter Buckley. Chicago: Aldine.

Scott, John Finley. 1971. *Internalization of Norms*. Englewood Cliffs, NJ: Prentice-Hall.

Sherif, Muzafer. 1936. *The Psychology of Social Norms*. New York: Harper.

Simmel, Georg. 1950. *The Sociology of Georg Simmel*. Glencoe, IL: Free Press.

_____ 1955. *Conflict and the Web of Group Affiliations*. New York: Free Press.

_____ 1971. *On Individuality and Social Forms*. Chicago: University of Chicago Press.

Simon, Herbert. 1965. "The Architecture of Complexity." *General Systems: Yearbook of the Society for General Systems Research* X:63-76.

Smelser, Neil. 1962. *Theory of Collective Behavior*. New York: Free Press.

_____ 1980. "Biography, the Structure of Explanation, and the Evaluation of Theory in Sociology." In *Sociological Theory and Research*, edited by Hubert M. Blalock, Jr. New York: Free Press.

_____ 1987. "Depth Psychology and the Social Order." In *The Micro-Macro Link*, edited by Jeffrey C. Alexander et al. Berkeley: University of California Press.

Spencer, Herbert. 1896. *The Principles of Sociology*. New York: Appleton.

Spuhler, James and Gardner Lindzey. 1967. "Racial Differences in Behavior." In *Behavior Genetic Analysis*, edited by Jerry Hirsch. New York: McGraw Hill.

Stinchcombe, Arthur L. 1968. *Constructing Social Theories*. New York: Harcourt, Brace, and World.

Stryker, Sheldon. 1980. *Symbolic Interactionism*. Menlo Park, CA: Benjamin/Cummings.

Suchman, Edward A. 1968. "Sociocultural Factors in Nutritional Studies." In *Biology and Behavior: Environmental Influences*, edited by David C. Glass. New York: Rockefeller University Press and Russell Sage Foundation.

Sussman, Marvin. 1985. *Pets and the Family*. New York: Haworth Press.

Swidler, Ann. 1986. "Culture in Action: Symbols and Strategies." *American Sociological Review* 51:273-286.

Taylor, Charles. 1979. "Interpretation and the Sciences of Man" In *Interpretive Social Science*, edited by Paul Rabinow and William M. Sullivan. Berkeley: University of California Press.

Taylor, Howard F. 1980. *The IQ Game*. New Brunswick, NJ: Rutgers University Press.

Tiger, Lionel. 1979. *Optimism: The Biology of Hope*. New York: Simon & Schuster.

Turner, Jonathan H. 1986. *The Structure of Sociological Theory*. Chicago: Dorsey Press.

Turner, Ralph H. 1962. "Role-Taking: Process Versus Conformity." In *Human Behavior and Social Processes*, edited by Arnold M. Rose. Boston: Houghton Mifflin.

Udy, Stanley H. Jr., 1968. "Social Structure: Social Structural Analysis." In *International Encyclopedia of the Social Sciences*, Vol. 14, edited by David L. Sills. New York: Free Press.

von Bertalanffy, Ludwig. 1956. "General System Theory." *General System Yearbook* I:1-10.

Wallace, Walter L. 1971. *The Logic of Science in Sociology*. Chicago: Aldine.

_____ 1983. *Principles of Scientific Sociology*. Hawthorne, NY: Aldine.

Wallerstein, Immanuel. 1974. *The Modern World-System*. New York: Academic Press.

_____ 1979. *The Capitalist World-Economy*. Cambridge: Cambridge University Press.

_____ 1984. "The Development of the Concept of Development." In *Sociological Theory: 1984*, edited by Randall Collins. San Francisco: Jossey-Bass.

_____ 1986. "Marxisms as Utopias: Evolving Ideologies." *American Journal of Sociology* 91:1295-1308.

Waring, Joan. 1976. "Social Replenishment and Social Change." In *Age in Society*, edited by Anne Foner. Beverly Hills, CA: Sage.

Warriner, Charles K. 1981. "Levels in the Study of Social Structure." In *Continuities in Structural Inquiry*, edited by Peter M. Blau and Robert K. Merton. Beverly Hills, CA: Sage.

Watkins, J.W.N. 1973. "Methodological Individualism: A Reply.'' In *Modes of Individualism and Collectivism*, edited by John O'Neill. New York: St. Martin's Press.

Weber, Max. 1949. *The Methodology of the Social Sciences*. Glencoe, IL:Free Press.

———— 1952. *Ancient Judaism*. New York: Free Press.

———— 1958a. *From Max Weber: Essays in Sociology*. New York: Oxford.

———— 1958b. *The Protestant Ethic and the Spirit of Capitalism*. New York: Scribner's.

———— 1968. *The Religion of China*. New York: Free Press.

———— 1975. *Roscher and Knies: The Logical Problems of Historical Economics*. New York: Free Press.

———— 1978. *Economy and Society*. Berkeley: University of California Press.

———— 1981. ''Some Categories of Interpretive Sociology.'' *Sociological Quarterly* 22:151-180.

Weidner, Gerdi and Karen A. Matthews. 1978. ''Reported Physical Symptoms Elicited by Unpredictable Events and the Type A Coronary-Prone Behavior Pattern.'' *Journal of Personality and Social Psychology* 36:1213-1220.

Wells, Richard H. and J. Steven Picou. 1981. *American Sociology: Theoretical and Methodological Structure*. Washington, DC: University Press.

Westhues, Kenneth. 1982. *First Sociology*. New York: McGraw-Hill.

Wiener, Norbert. 1954. *The Human Use of Human Beings (Cybernetics and Society)*. Garden City, NY: Doubleday/Anchor.

Wiley, Norbert. 1985. ''The Current Interregnum in American Sociology.'' *Social Research* 52:179-207.

Winch, Peter. 1958. *The Idea of a Social Science and Its Relation to Philosophy*. London: Routledge & Kegan Paul.

Wippler, Reinhard and Siegwart Lindenberg. 1987. ''Collective Phenomena and Rational Choice.'' In *The Micro-Macro Link*, edited by Jeffrey C. Alexander et al. Berkeley: University of California Press.

Wuthnow, Robert, James Davison Hunter, Albert Bergesen, and Edith Kurzweil. 1984. ''Introduction.'' In *Cultural Analysis*, edited by Robert Wuthnow et al. Boston: Routledge & Kegan Paul.

Zinnser, Hans. 1967. *Rats, Lice and History*. New York: Bantam Books.

Zuckerman, Harriet. 1977. ''Deviant Behavior and Social Control in Science.'' In *Deviance and Social Change*, edited by Edward Sagarin. Beverly Hills, CA: Sage.

2

The New Theoretical Movement

JEFFREY C. ALEXANDER

Sociological theory is at a turning point. The once youthful challengers to functionalist theory are becoming middle aged. Their polemical lessons have been well learned; as established traditions, however, their theoretical limitations have become increasingly apparent. Despair about the crisis of sociology marked the birth of the postfunctionalist epoch. Now, when this postfunctionalist phase is itself coming to an end, one senses not a crisis but a crossroads, a turning point eagerly anticipated.

Against the postwar domination of functionalism, two revolutions were launched. On one side, there emerged radical and provocative schools of microtheorizing, which emphasized the contingency of social order and the centrality of individual negotiation. On the other side, there developed vigorous schools of macro theorizing, which emphasized the role of coercive structures in determining collective and individual action. These movements transformed general theoretical debate and permeated empirical practice at the middle range. Even as they have triumphed, however, the self-confidence and momentum of these theoretical approaches has begun to wane.

They have become enervated because their one-sidedness has made them impossible to sustain. This, at least, will be the central claim of the essay that follows. I will demonstrate that one-sidedness has created debilitating contradictions within both the micro and macro traditions. It

has been in order to escape these difficulties, I will suggest, that a younger generation of sociological theorists has set out an agenda of an entirely different kind. Among this new generation of theorists there remain fundamental disagreements. There is one foundational principle, however, about which they agree. Neither micro nor macro theory is satisfactory. Action and structure must now be intertwined. Where even 10 years ago the air was filled with demands for radical and one-sided theoretical programs, in the contemporary period one can only hear urgent calls for theorizing of an entirely different sort. Throughout the centers of Western sociology—in Britain and France, in Germany and the United States—synthetic rather than polemical theorizing now is the order of the day.

My ambition in this essay is to provide an analytical reconstruction of this new and quite surprising shift in the progress of general theory. I must begin, however, by justifying the project of general theory itself. That theorizing at the general level—theorizing without reference to particular empirical problems or distinctive domains—is a significant, indeed, a crucial endeavor should, it seems to me, be beyond dispute. It has been general theorizing, for example, that articulated and sustained the developments I have just described. Crystallized by broad theoretical debates, moreover, these developments did not remain segregated in some abstract theoretical realm. To the contrary, they permeated every empirical subfield of sociology in turn. In American sociology, however, the significance and even the validity of general theory is subject to constant dispute. The reflection of a deeply ingrained empiricist bias, this questioning makes it more difficult to perceive broader developments and to argue about the direction of sociology in a rational and disciplined way. It seems clear that as a prelude to any substantive theoretical exercise, the project of general theory must be defended and the reasons for its unique relevance explained.

I will make this defense of general theory in the context of illuminating the special nature of a social science. I will argue that prediction and explanation are not the only goals of social science and that the more general modes of discourse that tend to characterize theoretical debates are just as significant. I will insist, moreover, that there are immanent in such discourse evaluative criteria other than empiricist ones. After making this case, I will try to articulate such truth criteria for the "presuppositional" level of discourse. Only at this point will I return to the substantive ambition that is at this essay's central core. I will reconstruct the development of the micro and macro responses to the functionalist tradition and evaluate these discourses in terms of the validity criteria I have laid out. After identifying the theoretical projects which are emerging in response to the failures of these micro and macro traditions, I will sketch the outlines of what a new synthetic model of the interrelation between action and structure might be.

Sociology as Discourse and Explanation

In order to defend the project of general theory, it must be accepted that sociological arguments need not have an immediate explanatory payoff to be scientifically significant. Whether or not social scientists can accept this statement depends, first, on whether or not they regard their discipline as a nascent form of natural science and, second, on just what they conceive natural science to be. Those who oppose generalized argument not only identify sociology with natural science but view the latter as an antiphilosophical, observational, propositional, and purely explanatory activity. However, those who wish to legitimate generalized argument in sociology may also identify with natural science; in doing so, they point to the implications of the Kuhnian revolution and argue that nonempirical and philosophical commitments inform and often decisively influence natural scientific practice. It was this approach to the defense of generalized argument that I followed in my first book, *Positivism, Presuppositions, and Current Controversies* (Alexander, 1982).

This defense against the claims of a narrowly explanatory positivism has proved to be a limited one. There is no doubt, I think, that in response to such an argument a more sophisticated understanding of science has gradually emerged among social science practitioners. As a result, there has indeed developed a greater tolerance for general theorizing within some members of the empiricist camp.[1] By stressing the personal and subjective aspects of natural science, however, the postpositivist position has failed to account for its relative objectivity and its astonishing explanatory success. This failure has cast doubt on its defense of generalized argument in social science. That natural science has its own hermeneutic cannot be doubted. If, however, this subjectivity has not prevented the construction of powerful covering laws and an overall accumulation of factual knowledge, then it would seem that even a postpositivist social science can continue to be held to these empiricist criteria alone. Yet this conclusion is not warranted. Criteria other than explanatory success are deeply implicated in social scientific debate. As compared with natural science, arguments that do not have immediate reference to factual and explanatory concerns are omnipresent. One can only conclude that the strategy of identifying social science with an interpretive natural science is misleading. The defense of generalized argument in social science, then, cannot rest entirely on the Kuhnian redefinition of natural science.[2] It must also differentiate social from natural science in decisive ways. That both activities share an interpretive epistemology is the beginning, not the end, of the argument.

It is time, then, to recognize that the scientific hermeneutic can issue in very different kinds of scientific activity. Only in this way can the massive role of generalized thinking in social, as compared to natural, science truly be understood, much less accepted as a legitimate activity in its own right. Only insofar as its significance is recognized, moreover, can the truth criteria that are implicit in such generalized argument be formalized and subject to explicit rational debate. To abandon empiricism is not, after all, to embrace relativism in an irrationalist form.[3]

That science can be understood as a hermeneutic activity does not, I am suggesting, determine the particular topics to which scientific activity is allocated in any given scientific discipline. Yet, it is precisely the allocation of such activity that is responsible for the relative empirical or theoretical "feel" of a discipline. Even outspoken postpositivists have acknowledged that modern natural science can be distinguished from other kinds of human studies by its ability to exclude from its objects of study the subjective moorings on which it stands. For example, while Holton (1973) has painstakingly demonstrated that arbitrary, supraempirical "themata" deeply affect modern physics, he insists that it has never been his intention to argue that thematic discussions should be introduced "into the practice of science itself" (1973, pp. 330-331). He suggests, indeed, that "only when such questions were ruled out of place in a laboratory did science begin to grow rapidly." Even the forthrightly idealist philosopher Collingwood (1940: 33), who insisted that scientific practice rests upon metaphysical assumptions, allowed that "the scientists's business is not to propound them but only to presuppose them."

Why, despite the subjective aspects of their knowledge, are natural scientists able to make such exclusions? The answer to this question is important, for it will tell us why social scientists cannot. It is not because natural scientists are more committed to rational norms and procedures. Rather, the allocation of scientific activity depends upon what rational practitioners consider intellectually problematic. It is because natural scientists so often agree about the generalized commitments that inform their craft that more delimited empirical questions usually receive their explicit attention. This is precisely what allows normal science, in Kuhn's sense (1970), to proceed as an activity of empirical puzzle solving and specific problem solutions. Habermas is also particularly sensitive to the relationship between this empirical specificity and generalized agreement. Taking normal science to characterize natural science as such, Habermas (1971, p. 91) writes that the "genuine achievement of modern science does not consist primarily in producing truth [but in] a method of arriving at an uncompelled and permanent consensus."

Only if there is disagreement about the background assumptions that inform a science do supraempirical issues come explicitly into the play. Kuhn calls this a paradigm crisis. It is in such crises, he believes, that there is "recourse to philosophy and to debate over fundamentals." In normal periods of science, these nonempirical dimensions are camouflaged; for this reason, it appears that speculative hypotheses can be decided by reference either to sense data that are relatively accessible or to theories whose specificity makes their relevance to such data immediately apparent. This is not the case in social science, because in its social application science produces so much more disagreement. Because persistent and widespread disagreement exists, the background assumptions that remain implicit and relatively invisible in natural science here come vividly into play. The conditions that Kuhn defines for paradigm crisis in the natural sciences are routine in the social.[4]

By stressing the significance of disagreement in social as compared to natural science, one need not embrace relativism in a radical way. There remains the possibility for rational knowledge in the social sciences even if the empiricist conception of objectivity is abandoned. Nor does this recognition necessarily deny the possibility that covering laws can be constructed for social processes or even that relatively successful predictions can be pursued.[5] It is possible to gain cumulative knowledge about the world from within different and competing points of view (compare Wagner, 1984). It is also quite possible to sustain relatively predictive covering laws from within general orientations that differ in substantial ways.

What I am suggesting, however, is that the conditions of social science make consistent agreement about the precise nature of empirical knowledge—let alone agreement about explanatory covering laws—highly unlikely. Because competition between fundamental perspectives is routine, the background assumptions of social science are routinely visible. Generalized discussion is about the sources and consequences of fundamental disagreement. Because background assumptions are so visible, then, generalized discussion becomes integral to social scientific debate, as integral as explanatory activity itself. In social science, therefore, arguments about validity cannot refer only to more empirical concerns. They cut across the full range of nonempirical commitments that sustain competing points of view.

Adherents to the positivist persuasion will respond to this argument by suggesting that, far from pervasive disagreement being the source of the difference between natural and social science, it is the result. They conclude (e.g., Wallace, 1983) that if sociologists were only more faithful to the rigor and discipline of natural science, then the generalized and speculative quality of social science discussion would abate and disagreement eventually disappear. This argument is fundamentally misconceived.

Far-reaching disagreement is inherent in social science, for cognitive and evaluative reasons.

Insofar as the objects of a science are located in the physical world outside of the human mind, its empirical referents can, in principle, more easily be verified through interpersonal communication. For social science, the objects of investigation are either mental states or conditions in which mental states are embedded. For this reason, the possibility for confusing mental states of the scientific observer with mental states of those observed is endemic. This is the social science version of the Heisenberg Uncertainty Principle.

Resistance to simple agreement on empirical referents also emerges from the distinctively evaluative nature of social science. In contrast to natural science, there is in social science a symbiotic relationship between description and evaluation. The very descriptions of the objects of investigation have ideological implications. Is society called "capitalist" or "industrial"? Has there been "proletarianization," "individuation," or "atomization"? Each characterization initiates what Giddens (1976) has called the double hermeneutic, an interpretation of reality that has the potential of entering social life and of circling back to affect the interpreter's definitions in turn. Moreover, insofar as it is difficult, for cognitive and evaluative reasons, to gain consensus about even the simple empirical referents of social science, about the abstractions from them that form the substance of social science theory there will be even less.

Finally, it is because there is endemic empirical and theoretical disagreement that social science is formed into traditions and schools. These solidary groupings are not simply manifestations of scientific disagreement, moreover, but bases upon which such disagreements are promoted and sustained. Indeed, rather than accepting disagreement and the distorted communication that goes along with it as necessary evils, many social science theorists (e.g., Ritzer, 1975) actually welcome interschool conflict as an indication of a healthy discipline.

For all of these reasons, discourse—not just explanation—becomes a major feature of the social science field. By discourse, I refer to modes of argument that are more consistently generalized and speculative than normal scientific discussion. The latter are directed in a more disciplined manner to specific pieces of empirical evidence, to inductive and deductive logics, to explanation through covering laws, and to the methods by which these laws can be verified or falsified. Discourse, by contrast, is ratiocinative. It focuses on the process of reasoning rather than

the results of immediate experience, and it becomes significant where there is no plain and evident truth. Discourse seeks persuasion through argument rather than prediction. Its persuasiveness is based on such qualities as logical coherence, expansiveness of scope, interpretive insight, value relevance, rhetorical force, beauty, and texture of argument.

Foucault (1970) identified intellectual, scientific, and political practices as "discourses" in order to deny their merely empirical, inductive status. In this way, he insists that practical activities are historically constituted and shaped by metaphysical understandings that can define an entire epoch. Sociology, too, is a discursive field. Still, one finds here little of the homogeneity that Foucault attributes to such fields; in social science, there are discourses, not a discourse. These discourses are not, moreover, closely linked to the legitimation of power, as Foucault in his later work increasingly claimed. Social scientific discourses are aimed at truth, and they are constantly subjected to rational stipulations about how truth can be arrived at and what that truth might be.

Here I draw upon Habermas' (e.g., 1984) understanding of discourse as part of an effort that speakers make to achieve undistorted communication. If Habermas underestimates the irrational qualities of communication, let alone action, he certainly has provided a way to conceptualize its rational aspirations. His systematic attempts to identify modes of argument and criteria for arriving at persuasive justification show how rational commitments and the recognition of supra-empirical arguments can be combined. Between the rationalizing discourse of Habermas and the arbitrary discourse of Foucault, this is where the actual field of social science discourse uneasily lies.

It is because of the centrality of discourse that theory in the social sciences is so multivalent and that compulsive efforts (e.g., Wallace, 1983) to follow the logic of natural science are so misguided.[6] Followers of the positivist persuasion sense the tension between such a multivalent conception and their empiricist point of view. To resolve it they try to privilege "theory" over what they pejoratively call "metatheory" (Turner, 1986); indeed, they often try to exclude theory altogether in favor of "explanation" narrowly conceived (Stinchcombe, 1968). These distinctions, however, seem more like utopian efforts to escape from social science than efforts to understand it. Generalized discourse is central, and theory is inherently multivalent. If social science could actually pursue an entirely explanatory strategy, why would an avowed empiricist like Stinchcombe feel compelled to devote himself to the task of defending empiricism through discursive argument? The substance of Stinchcombe's (1968, 1978) arguments is ratiocinative; his goal is to persuade through compulsion of generalized logic.

Overdetermination by Theory and Underdetermination by Fact

The omnipresence of discourse, and the conditions that give rise to it, make for the overdetermination of social science by theory and its underdetermination by what is taken to be fact. There is no clear, indisputable reference for the elements that compose social science—definitions, concepts, models, or "facts." Because of this, there is not neat translatability between different levels of generality. Formulations at one level do not ramify in clear-cut ways for the other levels of scientific concern. For example, while precise empirical measurements of two variable correlations can sometimes be established, it is rarely possible for such a correlation to prove or disprove a proposition about this interrelationship that is stated in more general terms. The reason is that the existence of empirical and ideological dissensus allows social scientists to operationalize propositions in a variety of different ways.[7]

Consider, for example, two of the most conscientious recent efforts to move from data to more general theory. In an attempt to test his newly developed structural theory, Blau starts with a proposition he calls the size theorem—the notion that a purely ecological variable, group size, determines outgroup relations (Blau, Blum, and Schwartz, 1982, p. 46). Drawing from a data set that establishes not only a group's size but its rate of intermarriage, he argues (p. 47) that the relationship he discovers between intermarriage rates and group size verifies the size theorem. Why? Because the data demonstrate that "group size and the proportion outmarried are inversely related." But outmarriage is a datum that does not, in fact, operationalize "outgroup relations." It is one type of outgroup relation among many others, and as Blau himself acknowledges at one point in his argument, it is a type into which factors other than group size enter. Outgroup relation, in other words, does not have a clear-cut referent. Because of this, the correlation between what is taken to be its indicator and group size cannot verify the general proposition about the relation between group size and outgroup rela-

tions. Blau's empirical data, then, are disarticulated from his theory, despite his effort to link them in a theoretically decisive way.

Similar problems emerge in Lieberson's (1980) ambitious study of black and white immigrants to the United States since 1880. Lieberson begins with the less formally stated proposition that the "heritage of slavery" is responsible for the different achievement levels of black and European immigrants. In order to operationalize this proposition, Lieberson takes two steps. First, he defines heritage in terms of "lack of opportunity" for former slaves rather than in cultural terms. Second, he identifies opportunity in terms of the data he has developed about varying rates of education and residential segregation. Both these operationalizations, however, are eminently contestable. Not only would other social scientists define the heritage of slavery in very different terms—for example, in cultural ones—but they might conceive of opportunities in ways other than education and residence. Because there is, therefore, no necessary relationship between the rates Lieberson has identified and differences in opportunities, there can be no certainty that his data demonstrate the more general proposition relating achievement and heritage. The measured correlation, of course, stands on its own as an empirical contribution. Still, the broader theoretical payoff is not there, for the correlation cannot test the theory at which it is aimed.

It is far easier to find examples of the contrasting problem, the overdetermination by theory of empirical "facts," for in virtually every broadly gauged theoretical study the sampling of empirical data is open to dispute. In *The Protestant Ethic and the Spirit of Capitalism*, for example, Weber's (1958/1904-1905) equation of the spirit of capitalism with seventeenth- and eighteenth-century English entrepreneurs has been widely disputed. If the Italian capitalists of the early modern city states are conceived of as manifesting the capitalist spirit (e.g., Trevor-Roper, 1965), then Weber's correlation between capitalists and Puritans is based on a restricted sample and fails to substantiate his theory. Insofar as this is true, Weber's empirical data was overselected by his theoretical reference to the Protestant ethic.

In Smelser's famous study, *Social Change in the Industrial Revolution* (1959), a similar distance between general theory and empirical indicator can be found. In his theory, Smelser argues that shifts in familial role divisions, not industrial upheavals per se, were responsible for the radical protest activities by English workers that developed in the 1820s. In his narrative historical account, Smelser describes fundamental shifts in family structure as having occurred in the sequence he had suggested. His more technical presentations of archival data (Smelser, 1959, pp. 188-199), however, seem to indicate that these family disturbances did not develop until one or two decades after significant industrial disputes had begun. Smelser's theoretical concern with the family overdetermined the presentation of data in his narrative history, just as his technical, archival data underdetermined his general theory in turn.[8]

In Skocpol's (1979) more recent effort at documenting a historical and comparative theory, the same kind of overdetermination is exercised by a very different theory. Skocpol (p. 18) proposes to take an "impersonal and non-subjective viewpoint" on revolutions, which gives causal significance only to "the institutionally determined situations and relations of groups." Her search is for the empirical data of revolution and the only a priori she acknowledges is her commitment to the comparative method (pp. 33-40). Skocpol acknowledges at various points, however, that local political culture and traditional rights do play a role (e.g., pp. 62, 138), and that political leadership and ideology must (however briefly) be essayed (pp. 161-173). In doing so, the theoretical overdetermination of her data becomes apparent. Her structural preoccupations have led her to leave out of her account of relevant data the entire intellectual and cultural context of revolution.[9] It is because these countertheoretical data do not exist that Skocpol can proceed to interpret the subjective factors she does briefly mention in a determinately structuralist way.

Empirical undetermination of theory and theoretical overdetermination of data go hand in hand, and they are everywhere to be found. The result is that, from the most specific factual statements up to the most abstract generalizations, social science is essentially contestable. Every empirical conclusion is open to argumentation by reference to supra-empirical considerations, and every general statement can be contested by references to unexplained "empirical facts."

In this way, every social scientific statement becomes subject to the demand for justification by reference to general principles.[10] Arguments against Blau's work need not be limited to the empirical demonstration that structural considerations are only one of several that determine outmarriage; one can, instead, demonstrate that the very stipulation of purely ecological causation rests upon presuppositions about action that are of an excessively instrumental kind. In

considering Lieberson's work one can bracket the empirical question of the relation between education and objective opportunity in a similar way. Instead, one can suggest through discursive argument that Lieberson's exclusive focus on the heritage of slavery, and the way he operationalizes it in purely structural terms, reflects not only an a priori ideological agenda but a commitment to narrowly conflictual models of society. Smelser's work can be discursively criticized by questioning its logical adequacy or by criticizing the overemphasis on the internalization of family values in early functionalist models. Skocpol's argument can also be evaluated without any reference to empirical material on revolutions. One could demonstrate, for example, that she misconstrues "voluntaristic theories of revolution"—her polemical target throughout—as individualistic theories positing rational knowledge about the consequences of action.

To make such arguments is to engage in discourse, not explanation. As Seidman (1983) has emphasized, discourse does not imply the abandonment of claims to truth. Truth claims need not be limited to the criterion of testable empirical validity. Each kind of discourse has imbedded within it distinctive criteria of truth. These criteria go beyond empirical adequacy to claims about the nature and consequences of presuppositions, the stipulation and adequacy of models, the consequences of ideologies, the metaimplications of methods, and the connotations of definitions. Insofar as these claims become explicit, they can be seen as efforts to rationalize and systematize what is usually the merely intuited complexity of social analysis and social life. Current disputes between interpretive and causal methodologies, utilitarian and normative conceptions of action, equilibrium and conflict models of societies, radical and conservative theories of change— these are discursive, not, in the first instance, explanatory disputes. They reflect efforts by sociologists to articulate criteria for evaluating the "truth" of different nonempirical domains.

It is no wonder that the discipline's response to important works bears so little resemblance to the neat and confined responses that advocates of the "logic of science" suggest. Skocpol's *States and Social Revolutions*, for example, has been evaluated at every level of the sociological continuum. The book's presuppositions, ideology, model, method, definitions, concepts, and—yes, even its facts—have been clarified, disputed, and praised in turn. At stake are the truth criteria Skocpol has employed to justify her positions at each of these levels. Very little of the disciplinary response to this work has involved controlled testing of its hypotheses or the reanalysis of its data. Decisions about the validity of Skocpol's structural approach to revolution certainly will not be decided on these terms.[11]

In the following section I will suggest that a wide swath of recent sociological history can be interpreted in terms of the perspective I have just laid out. I will try to show that the truth value of these recent developments must be considered in primarily discursive terms.

Discursive Formations in the Postwar Era

Because it is discursive, sociology can progress in a narrowly empirical sense without any clear forward movement in more general theoretical terms. Discursive arguments and the rational criteria they imply are only subjectively compelling. They are accepted for reasons that are orthogonal to conventional empirical tests. This is simply another way of saying that social science flows inside of schools and traditions. The flow resembles the movement of a conversation more than the progress of a rational proof. It moves forth and back between limited and deeply entrenched ways of seeing. It looks more like a pendulum than a line.[12]

If we reflect on sociological theory since World War II we can see just such a pendulum pattern at work. The split between action theories and structural theories that has marked (very roughly) the last 25 years did not develop in a historical vacuum. Every point on a pendulum responds to the motion that has come before.

Discourse about action versus structure emerged in reaction to Parsons's structural-functional work. Parsons had set out to end the "warring schools" once and for all. He had tried to bring idealism and materialism together in his systems theorizing, voluntaristic action and structural determination together in his thinking about the individual. Yet, while in critical respects the most sophisticated and far-reaching general theory yet conceived, Parsons's work failed to achieve its goal. In part the problem was intellectual, for Parsons did not actually pursue his synthesis in an evenhanded way (Alexander, 1983b). While acknowledging contingent action, he was in fact more interested in socialized individuality; while formally incorporating material structures, he spent vastly more time theorizing normative control. There

were social reasons for Parsons's failure as well. Indeed, like the ideas that Weber called the switchmen of history, the intellectual strains in Parsons's work provided the tracks along which the ideal and material interests of entrenched theoretical schools and traditions could run. Individualistic and structuralistic thinking are deeply entrenched in the historical development of the social sciences; it would take more than a sophisticated theoretical formulation—even one that could maintain its synthesis in a more consistent way—to knock them from their place.

Thus, even though Parsons's functionalist thinking opened up new paths of theory and research in the postwar period, the pendulum was bound to swing back. Powerful theorizing emerged to open up the black box of contingent order. Brilliant reformulations of pragmatic, economic, and phenomenological thinking emerged. The other new tendency, the macro one, opposed Parsons's idealization of action. Returning to Marx and the instrumental stream of Weberian thought, "structural" theory developed new and powerful versions of macro-sociology.

I do not wish to deny that these postfunctionalist movements often took a decidedly empirical form or that contemporaries were often convinced because of the new facts they revealed and the more powerful explanations they could provide. Symbolic interaction and ethnomethodology made breakthrough studies of deviance, collective behavior, and social roles. The methodological polemics associated with these studies, moreover, convinced many sociologists that more individualistic and naturalistic approaches allowed greater access to reality. The structural movement also made convincing empirical claims for fields like stratification, modernization, and social change, and for methodologies of a more concrete, historical, and comparative bent.

What I do wish to assert, however, is that the disciplinary success of these postfunctionalist movements was not based primarily on such empirical claims. In the first place, these claims were not in themselves simply empirical. They were embedded within, and thus were in important ways an expression of, more generalized commitments of a supra-empirical kind. These powerful theoretical commitments, moreover, were not latent but manifest; as such, they themselves became principal foci in the postfunctionalist movement. It was, in other words, not just empirical studies in which postfunctionalist challengers engaged but in myriad highly generalized theoretical disputes. These disputes were omnipresent; they entered into the most ostensibly empirical work. The post-functionalist movement, in sum, was rooted as much in discourse as in explanation; vis-a-vis Parsonian theory, and one another's as well, each position was justified through argument, not simply through the empirical procedures of verification or falsification.

In the following I will focus on what each of these perspectives presupposed about the nature of individual action and the origins of collective order. I will try to show what contemporaries found particularly attractive about these presuppositions, despite the fact that each tradition conceptualized action and order in a clearly one-sided and limiting way. Thus I will not just be examining discursive argument but engaging in it myself. I will try to demonstrate what these one-sided limitations are, and I will suggest that in a more synthetic model they might in principle be overcome.

Presuppositions and Theoretical Dilemmas

By presuppositions (Alexander 1982a, 1987b), I refer to the most general assumptions sociologists make when they encounter reality. Every social theory and every empirical work take a priori positions that allow observers to organize in the most simple categorical terms the data that enter their minds via their senses. Only on this basis can the more conscious manipulations that constitute rational or scientific thought be made. Presuppositions are subjects of discourse, and they are sometimes even discursively justified. For the most part, however, they originate in processes that precede the exercise of reason itself.

Perhaps the most obvious thing that students of social life must presuppose in their encounters with social reality is the nature of action. In the modern era, when one thinks about action, one thinks about whether it is rational or not. I do not mean to imply here that common sense equation of rational with good and smart, and nonrational with bad and stupid. Rather, in modern social science, this dichotomy refers to whether people are selfish (rational) or idealistic (nonrational), whether they are normative and moral (nonrational) or instrumental and strategic (rational), whether they act in terms of maximizing efficiency (rationally) or are governed by emotions and unconscious desires (nonrationally). In terms of empirical orientations, of course, the descriptions I have just offered—of rational action and of nonrational action—differ

from one another in specific and important ways. In terms of theoretical practice, however, these orientations have, in fact, formed two ideal types. In the history of social theory these ideal types of rational and nonrational have demarcated distinctive theoretical traditions and discursive argument of the most polemical kind.[13]

How can these traditions be defined in terms that supersede but do not violate the more finely graded distinctions upon which each is based, in such a way, for example, that moralistic theories and emotionalist theories may both be seen as part of the "nonrationalist" tradition? The answer is deceptively simple; it is to see the dichotomy as relating to the internal versus external reference of action (see Alexander, 1982a, pp. 17-79). Rationalistic or instrumental approaches portray actors as taking their bearings from forces outside of themselves, whereas nonrational approaches suggest that action is motivated from within. It is possible, in principle, to presuppose that action is both rational and nonrational, but it is surprising how rarely in the history of social theory this interpenetration has actually been made.

Yet to answer the central question about action is not enough. A second major issue needs to be presupposed as well. I refer here to the famous "problem of order," although I will define it somewhat differently than has typically been the case. Sociologists are sociologists because they believe there are patterns to society, structures somehow separate from the actors who compose it. Yet, while all sociologists believe such patterns exists, they often disagree sharply about how such an order is actually produced. Once again, I will cast these disagreements in terms of dichotomous ideal types because it is just this agglomerated antipathy that has characterized the empirical and discursive history of social thought (see Ekeh, 1974; Lewis and Smith, 1980). This dichotomy refers to the opposition between individualistic and collectivist positions.

If thinkers presuppose a collectivist position, they see social patterns as existing prior to any specific individual act, as in a sense the product of history. Social order confronts newborn individuals as an established fact outside of them. If the confusion aroused by Durkheim's (1937/1895) early formulations of this position is to be avoided, and if the necessity for "correcting" Durkheim's errors by developing equally one-sided discursive justifications on the other side is to be avoided as well, certain codas to this definition of collectivism must immediately be made.[14] If they are writing about adults, collectivists may well acknowledge that social order exists as much inside the individual as without; this is, in fact, an important qualification to which we will return. Whether it is conceptualized as inside or outside an actor, however, the collectivist position does not view order as the product of purely this-instant, this-moment considerations. According to collectivist theory every individual actor is pushed in the direction of preexisting structure; whether this direction remains only a probability or a determined fate depends on refinements in the collectivist position I will take up below.

Individualistic theories often acknowledge that there do appear to be such extraindividual structures in society, and they certainly recognize that there are intelligible patterns. They insist, however, that these patterns are the result of individual negotiation. They believe not simply that structure is "carried" by individuals but that it is actually produced by the carriers in the course of their individual interactions. The assumption is that individuals can alter the fundaments of order at each successive moment in historical time. Individuals, in this view, do not carry order inside of them. Rather, they follow or rebel against social order—even the values that they hold within themselves—according to their individual desires.

Once again, whether it is possible to combine some elements of this contingent position with a more collectivist emphasis is a matter I will take up in the following discussion. What I wish to emphasize at this point is that the problems of action and order are not optional. Every theory must take some position on both. The logical permutations among these presuppositions form the fundamental traditions of sociology. As such, they form the most important axes around which social science discourse revolves.

Presuppositions are so central to discourse because they have implications that go well beyond the explanatory concerns I have just defined. The study of society revolves around the questions of freedom and order, and every theory is pulled between these poles. Modern men and women believe that individuals have free will and that, because of this capacity, individuals can be trusted to act in responsible ways. To one degree or another, this belief has been institutionalized in Western societies. Individuals have been set apart as privileged political and cultural units. Elaborate legal efforts have been made to protect them from the group, from the state, and from other coercive organs like an established church.

Sociological theorists, whether individualist or collectivist, are likely to be as committed to the autonomy of the individual as other citizens. Indeed, sociology emerged as a discipline as a result of this differentiation of the individual in society, for it was the independence of the individual and the growth of his or her powers to think freely about society that allowed society itself to be conceived of as an independent object of study. It is the independence of the individual that makes order problematic, and it is this problematizing of order that makes sociology possible. At the same time, sociologists acknowledge that the everyday life of an individual has a patterned quality. It is this tension between freedom and order that provides the intellectual and moral rationale for sociology. Sociologists explore the nature of social order, and discursively justify the positions they adopted in regard to this question, because they are deeply concerned about its implications for individual freedom.

Individualistic theories are attractive and powerful because they preserve individual freedom in an overt, explicit, and thorough-going way. Their a priori postulates assume the integrity of the rational or moral individual, taking for granted actors' abilities to act freely against their situations, which are defined either in material or cultural terms. It is because of this natural convergence between ideological and explanatory discourse that individualism has been such a powerful strand in modern thought.

Social theory emerged out of the long process of secularization and rebellion against the hierarchical institutions of traditional society. In the Renaissance, Machiavelli emphasized the autonomy of the rational prince to remake his world. English contract theorists, like Hobbes and Locke, broke free from traditional restraints by developing a discourse claiming that social order depended on individual bargaining and, ultimately, upon a social contract. The same path was followed by some of the principal thinkers of the French Enlightenment. Each of these individualistic traditions was a strongly rationalistic one. While emphasizing different kinds of individual needs—power, happiness, pleasure, security—each portrayed society as emanating from the choices of rational actors. The crucial conceptual bridge between these traditions and contemporary theorizing in the social sciences was utilitarianism, particularly classical economics, whose theory of the invisible regulation of markets provided an elegant empirical explanation of how individual decisions can be aggregated to form societies.[15] It is from quasi-economic discourse that the central justifications for rationalistic modes of individualistic theorizing are largely drawn today.

Individualistic theories have, of course, also assumed a nonrational form. In its inversion of the Enlightenment and its revulsion against utilitarianism, romanticism inspired theories about the passionate actor (see, e.g., Abrams, 1971) from Wundt to Freud. In its hermeneutic version, which stretches from Hegel (Taylor, 1975) to Husserl and existentialism (Spiegelberg, 1971), this antirationalist tradition takes on a moral and often cognitive form.

The advantages that an individualistic position bestows, then, are very great. Still, it can be achieved only at great theoretical cost. These costs emerge because such individualistic theories begin from a wholly unrealistic perspective about voluntarism in society. By radically neglecting the power of social structure, individualistic theory in the end does freedom no real service. It encourages the illusion that individuals have no need for others or for society as a whole. It also ignores the great sustenance to freedom that social structures can provide. It is upon such costs that the discourse against individualistic theory focuses its aim.

By acknowledging that social controls exist, collectivist theory can subject them to explicit analysis. In this sense, collectivist thought represents a real gain over the individualistic position, in moral as well as theoretical terms. The question is whether this gain, in turn, has been achieved only at an unacceptable price. What does such collectivist theorizing lose? How is the collective force it postulates related to the individual will, to the possibility of preserving voluntarism and self-control? In order to answer this decisive question, it is necessary to make explicit a point that has only been implicit in my discourse thus far. Assumptions about order do not entail any particular assumptions about action. Because of this indeterminacy, there are very different kinds of collectivist theory.

Whether collective theory is worth the cost depends on whether it presupposes the possibility for moral or expressive, that is, for nonrational, action. Many collectivist theories assume that actions are motivated by narrow, technically efficient forms of rationality. If such an assumption is made, then collective structures must be portrayed as if they were external to individuals and entirely unresponsive to their will. Political or economic institutions, for example, are said to control the actors from without, whether they like it or not. They do so by arranging punitive sanctions and positive rewards for actors who are reduced—whatever the specific nature of their personal goals—to calculators of pleasure and pain. Because such actors are assumed to respond rationally to this external situation, motives are eliminated as a theoretical concern. Such theorizing assumes that the actor's response can be predicted from analysis of the external environment alone. Rational-collectivist theories, then, explain order only by sacrificing the subject. In effect, they dispense with the very notion of an autonomous self. In classical sociology, orthodox Marxism presents the most formidable example of this development, and the coercive implications that surround its discourse—as revealed, for example, in recurring references to the "dictatorship of the proletariat" and the "laws of history"—have generated intense critical response (e.g., van den Berg, in press). The same tendency to justify a discourse without a subject permeates every neoclassical theory that has collective ambitions, and Weber's sociology as well, as the controversy over the status of "domination" in the Weberian corpus demonstrates.

If, by contrast, collectivist theory allows that action may be nonrational, it perceives actors as guided by ideals and emotion. This internal realm of subjectivity is initially structured, it is true, by encounters with external objects—with parents, teachers, siblings, and books. In the process of socialization, however, such extraindividual structures become internal to the self. Only if this phenomenon of internalization is accepted can subjectivity become a topic for collectivist theory. According to this view, individual interaction becomes a negotiation between two "social selves." The dangers that such theorizing encounters are quite the opposite from collectivist theories of a more rationalistic kind. It tends to engage in moralistic rhetoric and idealistic justifications. As such, it often underestimates the ever-present tension between even the socialized individual and his or her social environment. This tension, of course, is most obvious when the theorist must consider an environment that is material in form, a possibility that cannot be conceptualized when collectivist theory is formulated in a one-sidedly normative way.

In the discussion of recent theoretical discourse that follows, I will focus on how presuppositional commitments have shaped sociological debate over the last 25 years. They have exerted their influence, of course, even if no attempt has been made discursively to justify them. The central figures in these debates, however, have sought such discursive justification. This, indeed, is what made them influential theorists. Through their discourse these theorists developed claims about the scope and implications of their theories, claims that stipulated "truth criteria" at a supra-empirical level. In the present section I have laid out my own conception of what such criteria should be. When I apply these criteria to recent theoretical debate, I will often be arguing in opposition to the truth claims of the principal participants in these debates. This, of course, is the very stuff of which social science discourse is made.

Reconsidering Micro and Macro Theory

It is perhaps because of the discipline's methodological and empirical focus that the massive renewal of individualistic theorizing in sociology has been seen as a revival of "microsociology."[16] For, strictly speaking, micro and macro are thoroughly relativistic terms, referring to part/ whole relationships at every level of social organization. In the language of recent social science, however, they have been identified with the distinction between taking individual interaction as an empirical focus, on the one hand, and taking an entire social system as one's empirical focus, on the other.

When Homans (1958, 1961) introduced exchange theory, he was renewing the very utilitarian position that had constituted the basis of Parsons's (1937) earliest and most powerful critique. Not only did Homans reject the collective tradition in classical and contemporary sociology, but the interpretive strand of individualistic theorizing as well. He insisted that the elementary forms of social life were not extraindividual elements such as symbol systems but individual actors of an exclusively rationalist bent. He focused on what he called subinstitutional behavior, the behavior of "actual individuals," which he believed to be entirely independent of socially specified norms. The procedures through which individuals make calculations occupied Homans's attention. So did the balance of supply and demand in the actor's external environment. In Homans's rationalistic perspective the social forces impinging on actors could only be conceived in an objectified and external way.

Exchange theory became enormously influential in reviving the case for microsociology. Its simple and elegant model facilitated predictions; its focus on individuals made it empirically operational. It also caught hold of a fundamental insight that Parsons and, indeed, collectivist theorists of every stripe had ignored: It is through individual actors making decisions about the costs of contingent exchange that

"objective social conditions" become articulated vis-à-vis the everyday life of individuals, institutions, and groups.[17] The price for such insights was high, however, even for theorists inside the paradigm itself. For example, Homans (1961, pp. 40, 54-55) was never able to define the "value" of a commodity in anything but a circular way; he was compelled to argue that it stemmed from reinforcing an orientation that was already in place. His conception of distributive justice showed similar strains (1961, chap. 12); he was forced to refer to "irrational" solidarity in order to decide just what the definition of an equitable "rational" exchange might be.

The other major strands of microtheorizing have taken up the interpretive side. Blumer (1969) was the general theorist most responsible for the revival of Meadian theory, although the tradition that Blumer (1937) labeled *symbolic interactionism* took up pragmatism only in its radically contingent form.[18] Blumer insisted that meaning is determined by individual negotiation—indeed, by the reaction of others to the individual's act. The actor is not seen as bringing some previously defined collective order into play. It is immediate situational relevance, not internalization, that defines attitudes. Through "self-indication" actors make objects even out of their own selves. It is the temporally rooted "I" of the actor, not the more societally focused "me," that determines the pattern of social order described in Blumer's work.

Though powerful, Blumer's most influential writing was almost entirely discursive in form; even when it was programmatic, moreover, it focused more on promoting the methodology of direct observation than on elaborating theoretical concepts. It is Goffman who must be seen as the most important empirical theorist of the symbolic interactionist movement. To most contemporaries, Goffman's work appeared merely to point interactionist theory in a more problem-specific and dramaturgic direction. Certainly his early work tends to support this reading. In contrast to the clear collectivist strains that emerged in his later theorizing, Goffman (e.g., 1959) emphasized individuals' desires to manipulate the presentation of self in opposition to socially structured roles, and he tried (1963) to explain institutional behavior as emerging from face-to-face interaction.

Ethnomethodology, and phenomenological work more generally, presents a more complicated story. Garfinkel was a student not only of Schutz but also of Parsons, and his earliest work (e.g., 1963) accepts the centrality of internalization. What Garfinkel explored in this early writing was how actors make social norms their own; he explored, that is, their "ethno" methodology. Emphasizing the constructed character of action, he described how, through cognitive techniques like "ad hocing" (Garfinkel, 1967), individuals conceived of contingent and unique events as representations, or "indexes," of socially structured rules. In the process, he showed, these rules were in actuality not simply specified but modified and changed.

As ethnomethodology became a major theoretical movement, it was forced to justify itself in general and discursive ways. In the process, its concepts became more one-sided. Presenting itself as committed to an alternative sociology, ethnomethodology emphasized "members' own practices" over and against structure. That constitutive techniques like indexicality were omnipresent, it was now argued, should be seen as evidence that order is completely emergent, and the endlessly resourceful practice of orderly activity came to be identified (Garfinkel, Lynch, and Livingston, 1981) with social order itself. That this kind of individualistic reduction is somehow inherent in a phenomenological approach is belied, however, by other strains that emerged from the ethnomethodological school. Conversational analysis (Sacks, Schegloff, and Jefferson, 1974), for example, viewed speech as subject to strong structural constraints even if it did not usually conceptualize these constraints in a systematic way.

It is certainly an ironic demonstration of the lack of linear accumulation in sociology that, concurrent with this resurgence of microtheorizing, there emerged a strong movement toward equally one-sided kinds of macro, collectivist work. This movement began when "conflict theorists" justified themselves by defining Parsonian work as "order theory." Like the new microsociologists, these theorists, too, denied the centrality of internalization and the link between action and culture that concept implies. Rather than emphasizing individual consciousness as the basis of collective order, however, conflict theorists severed the link between consciousness and structural processes altogether. Dahrendorf (1959) gave to administrative power positions the central ordering role. Rex (1961) emphasized the allocative economic processes that gave power to the ruling class.

While conflict arguments certainly provided the most powerful justifications for structural theorizing in its initial phase, it was the Marxism of Althusser and his students (Althusser and Balibar, 1970; Godelier, 1967) that formulated the most sophisticated and influential discourse in its later phase. Drawing from Spinoza and

as well as from modern linguistic and anthropological theory, this so-called structural Marxism analyzed historical developments as particular variations, transformations, and incarnations of fundamental structural principles. Rather than starting with the empirical and phenomenal diversity of social actions and lifeworlds, as contemporary micro theorists advised, these Marxist structuralists gave ontological and methodological primacy to the "totality." Although individual actions may deviate from structural imperatives, the objective consequences of these actions are determined by structures that exist beyond the actors' control.

While just as deterministic, this structural Marxism was less directly economic than other variants. It emphasized the political mediation of productive forces rather than their direct control (e.g., Poulantzas, 1972). This discourse about mediation and structural "overdetermination" set the stage for Marxist theorizing with a distinctively Weberian cast. Critical political economists like Offe (1984/1972) and O'Connor (1978) focused on the function of the state in capitalist accumulation and tried to derive social problems and crises from "inevitable" state intervention.

While the most important discursive justifications for the new structural theory have come from Europe, its influence in America has depended on a series of influential arguments at the middle range. Moore's (1966) major work on the class origins of state formations provided the major impetus for this work, though it was much more classically Marxist than the neo-Weberian structuralist work that followed in its wake. The most imposing single work that followed Moore's was Skocpol's (1979). Skocpol not only provided what appeared to be a powerful new covering law to explain revolutions but offered a widely persuasive polemic against subjective and voluntaristic theories of revolution (in the name of her structural theory). Wright's (1978) class analysis takes up the same anti-micro theme, arguing that ambiguities in a group's class consciousness come from "contradictory class locations." Treiman (1977) similarly produced what he called a "structural theory of prestige" that converted cultural into organization control and denied to subjective understandings of stratification any independent causal role. In still another influential work, Lieberson (1980) put his explanation for racial inequality in the terms of this same highly persuasive discourse. He identified "structures of opportunity" with material environment and justified this by dismissing the focus on subjective volition as conservative and idealist.

The New Theoretical Movement

The efforts to reformulate sociology as either an exclusively action- or structurally oriented discipline emerged in response to frustration with the unfulfilled promises of functionalist work and to fundamental disagreement with these promises as well. In the 1960s these challenges to functionalism created a sense of crisis in the discipline. By the late 1970s the challengers had triumphed and sociology seemed to settle down, once again, into a secure if more fragmented middle age. Marxist discourse permeated sociological writing in England and the continent. In America, a new Marxist section of the national association was formed and quickly gained more members than most of the long-established sections. New sections on political and historical and comparative sociology followed, and their largely structuralist approaches earned them a similar response. Micro theory also gained tremendous authority. When ethnomethodology first emerged, it was met with discourse that questioned its fundamental legitimacy and dismissed it as either bizarre or corrupt (e.g., Coleman, 1968; Coser, 1975; and Goldthorpe, 1973). By the late 1970s, its discursive justifications were accepted by many leading theorists (e.g., Collins, 1981; Giddens, 1976) and taken seriously by most others. Goffman's work passed even more quickly from controversy to classical status.

Yet, even as these once bumptious challengers became the new establishment, even as the "multiparadigmatic" character of sociology passed from daring prophecy (e.g., Friedrichs, 1970) to conventional wisdom (e.g., Ritzer, 1975), the vital and creative phase of these theoretical movements had come to an end. In the present decade a strikingly different phase of theoretical argument has begun to take shape. Stimulated by the premature theoretical closure of the micro and macro traditions, this phase is marked by an effort to link theorizing about action and structure once again. Such efforts have been made from within each of the newly dominant theoretical traditions, from both sides of the great micro/macro divide.

There are social and institutional as well as intellectual reasons for this new development in theoretical work. One certain factor is the changing political climate in the United States and Europe. Most radical social movements have faded away, and in the eyes of many critical intellectuals Marxism itself has been morally delegitimated. The ideological thrust that in the United States fueled post-Parsonian discourse in its micro and macro form and that justified

Marxist structuralism on the continent is spent. In America, once-fervent structuralists are now looking for ways to use cultural analysis, and former ethnomethodological sectaries are looking for ways to integrate constructivist with traditional macro theory. In Germany, England, and France, the new post-Marxist generation has been influenced by phenomenology and American microtheorizing. The migration of Parsonian ideas to Germany (Alexander, 1984), rather than renewing what is now seen as an obsolete debate, has inspired new efforts at theoretical reintegration.

There has been the passage of intellectual time as well, a passage regulated by the exigencies of theoretical rather than social logic. One-sided theories are provocative, and at certain junctures they can be highly fruitful. Once the dust of theoretical battle has settled, however, the cognitive content of their theorizing is not easy to maintain. Revisionism is the surest sign of theoretical discontent.[19] Those who seek to maintain an established tradition are particularly sensitive to its weaknesses, for it is they who must face the demands for discursive justification that gradually accumulate in its wake. In response to such immanent strains, talented students and followers introduce ad hoc revisions in the original theory and develop new and often inconsistent modes of discourse. The problem is that unless the entire tradition is overturned, such revisions end up being residual categories. The discursive arguments generated by criticism and reposte do have an unintended consequence, however. They highlight the weaknesses in the original tradition. In so doing, they make more likely openings, or crosscuttings, between what once were bolderized traditions.[20] It is by studying revisionism within the micro and macro traditions that the new theoretical movement in sociology can be revealed.

Striking developments have occurred, for example, in symbolic interactionism. Although Goffman began his career more or less within the radically contingent tradition of Blumer, in his later writings there emerged a dramatic shift toward more structural and cultural concerns. The creative strategies of actors were still Goffman's target, but he (e.g., Goffman, 1974) now referred to them as means of instantiating cultural and stratificational structures in everyday life. Similarly, whereas Becker's (1963) early impact on deviance theory derived from his emphasis on contingency and group behavior, his most recent work takes a decidedly systemic view of creativity and its effects (Becker, 1984). Indeed, a spate of efforts by symbolic interactionists to systematize the links between actors and social systems has recently appeared. Lewis and Smith (1980), for example, have challenged the fundamental discursive justifications of the tradition by arguing that Mead, allegedly the founder of the school, was actually an anti-nominalist who took a collective rather than individualist position. Stryker (1980, pp. 52-54, 57-76) has gone so far as to present interactionism as if it were basically a modification of social systems theory itself (see also Alexander and Colomy, 1985; Handel, 1979; Maines, 1977; Strauss, 1978).

Similar developments can be seen in the rational action model revived by Homans's exchange theory. Students felt pressure to demonstrate that this polemically micro approach could cope with the truth criteria generated by macrosociology. As a result, they gradually shifted the focus of analysis from individual actions to the transformations of individual actions into collective effects and, by extension, to unintended rather than purposive activity. Thus Wippler and Lindenberg (1987) and Coleman (1987a) now reject the notion that the connection between individual actions and structural phenomena can be viewed as a causal relation between discrete empirical events. Because there is, instead, empirical simultaneity, the linkage between micro and macro has to be seen as an analytical one sustained by invisible processes in the larger system. This analytical linkage is achieved by the application of "transformation rules," like voting procedures, to individual actions.

Theorists have been led by this focus on transformation to consider individual actions not as objects for analysis in their own right but as initial conditions for the operation of structural mechanisms. In this way, structural explanations—about the rules of constitutions (e.g., Coleman, 1987b), the dynamics of organizations and intergroup relations (Blau, 1977), the system of prestige allocation (Goode, 1979)—have begun to replace utility arguments within the rationalistic micro tradition. There has also emerged extensive theorizing about the unintended effects of individual actions (Boudon, 1982, 1987) and even about the genesis of collective morality (Ekeh, 1974, Kadushin, 1978, and Lindenberg, 1983).

Although Garfinkel, the founder of ethnomethodology, continues to advocate a radical micro program (Garfinkel, Lynch, and Livingston, 1981), and although the revisionist movement beyond one-sided theorizing is less developed here than within the other micro traditions, it seems impossible to deny that a similar

unease and a similar movement permeat phenomenological sociology. Cicourel, for example, certainly one of the key figures in the earlier phase, has recently pushed for a more interdependent and synthetic approach (Knorr-Cetina and Cicourel, 1981). A phenomenologically based "social studies in science" movement, while arguing for a new, much more situationally specific approach to science, refers routinely to the framing effects of social structure (Knorr-Cetina and Mulkay, 1983; Pinch and Collins, 1984). Although Smith (1984) and Molotch (Molotch and Boden, 1985) have both insisted on the indispensable autonomy of constitutive practices, they have recently produced significant studies that demonstrate how these practices are structured by organizational context and the distribution of power. These new phenomenological efforts, it should be stressed, do not simply involve revised explanatory schemes. They are deeply involved with new modes of discursive justifications, efforts that seek to incorporate the truth criteria of more structuralist work (see, e.g., Schegloff, 1987).

Similar revisionist efforts mark a new movement beyond the confines of the rational-collectivist, or structural position. There has always been an abundance of internal contradictions in such theorizing, contradictions that, if anything, have been more pronounced in the work of its leading theorists. Rex (1961, pp. 113-128), for example, argued that a truce situation would eventually develop between ruling and subject classes that would introduce a period of tranquility and the possibility for new and more integrative forms of socialization. Why this would evaporate in the face of new and "inevitable" class conflict was something Rex asserted but never successfully explained. Whenever Althusser tried to reassure his readers that vis-a-vis the relative autonomy of political and ideological systems there would always be economic determination "in the last instance" (Althusser, 1970), his usually precise theorizing became lost in a gauzy metaphysical haze. Skocpol's (1979, pp. 3-15) insistence that nonstructuralist explanations were individualistic was never discursively justified; her demotion of revolutionary ideology to conjunctural strategy rather than sociological cause (Skocpol, 1979, pp. 164-173) revealed the weaknesses in her argument even if it allowed its surface coherence to be maintained.

It is only recently, however, that these strains in theoretical logic have manifested themselves by overt revision and by efforts to incorporate manifestly different discursive modes. On the American side of the structuralist school, Moore began to write about the subjective rather than structural sources of working-class weakness (Moore, 1978) and about the proletarians' sense of injustice rather than objective injustice itself. Because the shift in the tenor of Skocpol's arguments has been more rapid and theoretically self-conscious, it illustrates the new theoretical movement in an even more suggestive way. It was in an effort to explain the Iranian revolution that Skocpol (1982) first raised the possibility that religious causes were comparable to economic and political ones. In a recent effort to justify her position vis-a-vis the discursive claims of a cultural critic (Sewell, 1985), she has given up significant discursive ground, despite her insistence (Skocpol, 1985) that cultural explanations must have a realistic and protostructural cast.

Indeed, in the last five years there has been an extraordinary cultural turn in what was until recently the securely structuralist domain of social history. Sewell and Hunt, once devoted to Tilly's version of conflict sociology, are now opponents of historical sociology in its structural form. Their writings have become major sources for an alternative, much more cultural discourse (Hunt, 1987; Sewell, 1985) and their explanations of revolutionary changes in French society directly counter structural models and causal proposals (Hunt, 1984; Sewell, 1980).[21] Darnton (1984), once a leading American exponent of Annalist "material culture," now offers interpretive criteria for historical truth and cultural reconstructions of popular myth as history. The "new social history" grew out of its association with the once new structural sociology. To many younger historians, such history now seems old and its definition of "social" much too restricted.

It is from anthropology, not sociology, that historians increasingly draw.[22] In that neighboring field, culture and meaning have assumed an increasingly central place, as the far-reaching significance of Geertz (1973), Turner (1969), and Douglas (1966) attests. Behind this shift in anthropology, of course, there stands the broad renaissance of cultural studies more generally conceived (see, for example, Alexander and Seidman, in press). This development has been sustained by the renewed interest in hermeneutic philosophy, the flowering of semiotic and poststructuralist work, and the introduction of a new version of Durkheimian sociology that is much more symbolic than before (see, for example, Alexander, 1988a; Wuthnow et al., 1984, Zelizer, 1985).

Sociology has only begun to be significantly affected by this shift in its intellectual environ-

ment. The new direction in Skocpol's work is one of the most important indications that the shift is beginning to be felt. The recent appearance of some polemically antistructural works of historical sociology (Calhoun, 1982; Prager, 1986) gives promise of a deepening of this development. At this writing, indeed, a new section on cultural sociology has been formed in the American Sociological Association and major new works of macrocultural sociology are in progress (e.g., Archer, 1987; Eisenstadt, 1986; Wuthnow, 1987). While these cultural developments in American macrosociology are not linked directly to the antimaterialist movement of Gouldner's later work, they complement it in a clear and revealing way. In the sustained attack on "objective Marxism" that Gouldner (1982) issued just before his death, he called for a renewed appreciation of the voluntaristic tradition in American sociology. Only this antistructural tradition, Gouldner believed, is capable of theorizing an autonomous civil society against state and economy.

The culturalist revolution that Meyer and Scott (1983) have begun to effect in the sociology of organizations makes an oddly similar point. In a polemic against instrumentalist theories that tightly link organizational structures to the demands of external technical requirements, they argue for the "decoupling" of administrative arrangements and actual production activities. Because organizations are infused with the same meanings as the society at large, their actions should be viewed more as ritualistic reproductions of these cultural ideals than as rational exercises in efficient intervention. From this cultural perspective, the modern Western state is hardly an iron cage crushing civil society; it must be viewed, rather, as a controlling representational system that elaborates broader themes of cultural rationality. In a recent collection devoted to this approach, which has come to be called "institutionalism," Zucker (1988, p. 24) calls formal organizations the "cultural engines of modern social systems," and DiMaggio (1988, p. 5) polemically contrasts institutional theorists with "utilitarian and conflict theorists, who have assumed that organizations and the people in them are more plastic, calculating, and manipulable than they usually are."

This uneven but persistent challenge to structuralist theorizing and explanation within American macrosociology has been more than matched by the critical discourse against structural Marxism in Europe. In "The Poverty of Theory," Thompson (1978) launched a heated polemic against Althusserianism in the name of a voluntaristic and culturally centered critical theory. Only upon this revised theoretical basis, Thompson argued, could moral responsibility for radical political behavior be sustained. This essay became a lightning rod for what has become a fundamental reversal in theoretical sensibility. For example, in his early and still most widely cited article, Michael Mann (1970) attacked Marxist and liberal versions of consensus theory as overly emphasizing ideology, and he called for a more social structural approach to the problem of working-class consent. In the writing that followed he continued to focus on organizational issues like labor markets (Mann and Blackburn, 1979) and state financing (Mann, 1979). His current work—a massive reconsideration of the origins and patterns of organized social power—marks a decided departure from this perspective. Not only does power become redefined in a pluralistic fashion, but ideological linkages play perhaps the most critical historical role. Discussing the effects of Christianity, for example, Mann (1986, p. 507) acknowledges, "I have singled out one [network] as necessary for all that followed." For Perry Anderson (1986. p. 1406), Mann's reviewer in the *Times Literary Supplement* and himself a former leader of the British structural movement, this turn toward the cultural has not been decisive enough. For Anderson's current taste, Mann still "veers close to the characteristic modern confusion that simply equates power and culture" and he recommends that culture be considered in a still more "autonomous" way. In its insistence that the autonomy of religious elites is a critical issue for comparative civilization development, Hall's *Powers and Liberties* (1985) presents yet another example of this cultural turn in recent historical sociology. As Anderson criticized Mann for not going far enough, so Hall and Mann, and, indeed, Anderson as well, have been taken to task by S. N. Eisenstadt (1987) for conceiving of religious and political institutions as "ontologically separate" entities. Eisenstadt calls for a more analytic approach, which will demonstrate that "cultural visions . . . are constitutive elements of the construction of social order and institutional dynamics."[23]

Outside of England there have been similar upheavals in the structuralist edifice. In Eastern Europe (compare Sztompka, 1974, and Sztompka, 1984, 1986, in press), Scandinavia (Eyerman, 1982, 1984), France (Tourraine, 1977), and Italy (Alberoni, 1984), theorists once sympathetic to Marxist arguments have shifted their concern away from the contradictions that limit action to the social movements that respond to them. Elster's (1985) rational choice Marxism can be seen as a similar effort to avoid determinism, but his narrowly rationalistic understanding of action has been sharply criticized (e.g., Lash and Urry, 1984; Walzer, 1986) for its inability to encompass the moral strivings of critical social movements.

This revolution against Marxism has been brought to a head by the poststructuralist movement that originated in France. While in principle as critical of symbolic structuralism as of Marxist reduction, the main impact of poststructural theorizing on the social sciences has been to reduce the influence of Marxist directions in critical thought. In Foucault's theory (e.g., 1970), discursive formations replace modes of production. In Bourdieu's (e.g., 1986), cultural capital replaces capital of a traditionally economic kind. In Lyotard's (1984), the historical contribution of cultural narratives about rationality and rebelliousness replaces explanations that assume rationality and relate rebellion to domination alone.[24]

There has, of course, been an equally important movement against Marxism from the German side, one which for the practice of sociology has had even more widely ramifying effects. I am speaking here of the drastic shift in Jurgen Habermas's theorizing away from Marxist concepts to what he calls "communicative theory." I will discuss Habermas's ideas in the broader context of shifts in general theory itself. With this discussion, my presentation of the new theoretical movement in sociology will come to an end.

General theorizing from a macro perspective has always had a special position in social science. It is this relatively abstract and often rather speculative mode that reaches into the nooks and crannies of the discipline, orienting sociology by providing it with, if not a reflection of itself, then a reflection of its aspirations. In recent years the work of the most widely discussed general theorists has evidenced a decisive shift away from a one-sidedly structural bent. Giddens's earliest work (1971) was continuous with the structuralist thrust of conflict theory and neo-Marxism, but in the later 1970s he fundamentally changed his course. Giddens became convinced of the need for a complementary theory of action. Building from the phenomenological insistence on the reflexive nature of human activity, he developed a theory of "structuration" (1985), the intention of which is to interweave contingency, material structure, and normative rules. Collins's development shows a similar trajectory. Although more interested in ethnomethodology from the beginning of his career than Giddens, in his early work Collins (1975) presented primarily a case for structuralistic conflict sociology. In recent years, by contrast, he has embraced radical microsociology, both phenomenological and Goffmanian. He has also moved toward the "late Durkheim." Collins now (e.g., 1981, 1988) argues that chains of interaction rituals mediate social structure and contingent action.

Habermas, too, began his career with a more typically macrostructuralist model of social dynamics (Habermas, 1973). Although there are clear references to moral claims and to different types of action in that early work, they remained residual to his heavily political-economic model of institutional life. In his recent work, however, Habermas (1984) explicitly and systematically develops theories about the normative and microprocesses that underlie and sometimes oppose the macrostructures of social systems. He has used individual moral and cognitive development to anchor his description of world-historical phases of "social learning," descriptions of speech acts to develop arguments about political legitimacy, and the conception of an interpersonally generated life-world to justify his empirical explanation of social resistance and strain.

What is missing from these macrotheoretical arguments is a robust conception of culture. Habermas shies away from cultural systems because the notion introduces an element of arbitrariness and irrationality into every conceivable stage of historical life. Giddens and Collins cannot embrace it because, overly influenced by microsciology, they conceptualize the actor in a highly discrete, altogether too reflexive way.[25] In contrast to these efforts, my own work began with a commitment to the macrocultural stance. I argued (Alexander, 1982b) that because Marx lacked Durkheim's insight into the structure of symbolic systems his radical theorizing had an inherently coercive cast. Weber's political sociology followed in this Marxist vein, I suggested (Alexander, 1983a), because Weber's conception of modern society denied the possibility of integrative cultural wholes. To argue for the significance of culture in this way is to recognize the central importance of Parsons's theoretical contributions, particularly his differentiation between culture, personality, and society. In this earlier work, however, I tended also to follow Parsons in his neglect of order in an individual sense. Since that time I have turned much more directly to theorizing in the micro traditions (Alexander 1985a, 1988; Alexander and Colomy, 1985; Alexander and Giesen, 1987). I have outlined a model that conceives of action as the contingent element of behavior that can be differentiated analytically from mere reproduction. This action can be conceived of as a "flow" within symbolic, social, and psychological environments. These environments interpenetrate within the concrete empirical actor, who is no longer identified with purely contingent action as he or she typically is in the traditions of micro theory.

The new theoretical movement in sociology is advancing on a number of fronts and under various names. It will continue to do so until the energy of this current movement of the disciplinary pendulum is used up. In my view, the key to making this motion intellectually progressive is a more direct recognition of the centrality of collectively structured meaning, or culture. There is a yawning gap between most of the newly synthetic thrusts in general theory, on the one hand, and the turn toward cultural theory that has characterized the new macro-theorizing in its more substantive forms, on the other. Only if general theorists are prepared to enter the thicket of "cultural studies"—with, of course, their sociological armaments well in hand—will this gap gradually be closed. This time around, however, theorizing about culture cannot be allowed to degenerate into a camouflage for idealism. Neither should it be given an aura of objectivity that preempts individual creativity and the rebellion against norms.[26] If these mistakes are avoided, the new movement in sociology will have a chance to develop a truly multidimensional theory. This will be a permanent contribution to social thought, even if it will not prevent the pendulum from eventually swinging back once again.

NOTES

1. One can observe this effect, for example, in the recent work of Kreps (e.g., 1985, 1987). Committed to the practical goal of developing lawful explanations for disaster research, he feels compelled to engage in an ambitious program of general theorizing and to make explicit his commitments at the most nonempirical, presuppositional level.

2. Kuhn (1970) himself, of course, would have been the first to insist that his redefinition of natural science did not deny to it a relatively objective and cumulative character and that social science had rarely achieved anything approaching this condition.

3. One form of irrationalism is precisely the danger in the resolutely "antifoundationalist" position that has been staked out by Richard Rorty. In *Philosophy and the Mirror of Nature* (1979), Rorty provided a sharply critical review of the history of Western philos-

ophy. He argued that because the centuries-long effort to establish epistemological foundations for objective evaluations has proved to be unsuccessful, the effort to engage in such generalized reasoning should be abandoned. From here it is but a short step to the call to abandon social scientific efforts to construct general theories, either of society or of theory as such. Thus, building on Rorty, philosophers (e.g., Rajchman, 1985) have argued for the reduction of philosophy to literary theory, sociologists (see, e g , Waldell and Turner 1986) for a turning away from general theory to moral reasoning. In an effort to create some middle ground between positivism and self-styled hermeneutics, my argument in this essay takes direct issue with such views. It is one thing to abandon the search for epistemological access to the "real" in a direct, reflective, "mirroring" sense. It is quite another to give up on the search for consensual, universal, and impersonal criteria for evaluation, that is, on the project of rationality itself. To conflate these abandonments is to put powerful exemplifications of rationality on a par with vulgar empiricism, as Sica (1986, p. 155) does when he characterizes Habermas's theorizing as "pointless rigidification in favor of the scientism he prefers." While such arguments draw inspiration from hermeneutics, an understanding truly rooted in the latter need not, in fact, abandon the effort to construct cognitive truth; it must simply give up the utopian hope that a single ahistorical standard of truth can ever be established. It is, then, the distorted self-understanding of social science that must be set aside, not the discipline of social science as such. My aim in the following is to demonstrate that this discipline—as practiced, not as conceptualized in the terminology of positivist reconstruction—is neither empiricist nor lacking in the efforts, often enormously clarifying, to establish universalistic standards for objective knowledge.

4. This is one reason so many of the early applications of Kuhnian ideas to sociology (e.g., Friedrichs, 1970) seem in retrospect hyperbolic and overblown. They proclaimed revolutionary upheavals in a discipline that had always been in a more or less continual state of sharp disagreement and theoretical upheaval.

5. In this respect Wagner and Berger (1984) and Wagner (1984) are surely correct to stress the similarities between scientific progress in the hard and soft sciences. By sharply separating explanatory research programs from what they call "orienting strategies," however, they overlook the discursive and generalized quality of social science argument and, therefore, the relativism that is inherent to all "progress" in the social sciences.

6. It is not simply that Wallace (1983)—who provides the clearest recent illustration of this viewpoint—is wrong to force social science theory into the natural science mold. It is that he mistakes a logical reconstruction of how natural science "should" proceed for a map of how good science is actually made. This strategy of reconstruction began with the philosophical ambition of the Vienna logical positivists to eliminate speculative and nonempirical ideas from

philosophical thought. Whatever its merits philosophically—and they are real if ultimately limited ones—this logic should not be conceived of as providing the grounds for the practice of science itself. Practicing scientists have never been able to understand their own work in these terms—or in Popperian ones, for that matter—and this inability has been one of the strongest motivations for the growth of postpositivist understandings of natural science. The present essay proceeds in this spirit; it is an attempt to understand what social science theory actually is, not what some of its critics think it should aim to be. Any critical agenda for sociological theory must be couched within an understanding of its distinctive character. In terms of recent debate in moral and political philosophy (e.g., Williams, 1985; Walzer, 1987), this represents an internalist position, as compared to the more abstracted, externalist position taken by sociology's empiricist, "logic of science" critics.

7. For a powerful demonstration of the inevitability of empirical underdetermination, which is tied to an historical indictment of the origins of contemporary quantitative traditions, see Turner (1987).

8. It demonstrates Smelser's conscientiousness as a historical researcher that he himself presented data that, as it were, went beyond his own theory (see Walby, 1986). This is not usually the case, for the overdetermination of data by theory usually makes countervailing data invisible, not only to social scientists themselves but often to their critics.

9. Sewell (1985) has forcefully demonstrated this gap in Skocpol's data for the French case.

10. This can be seen as the specifically social-scientific version of the thematization that, Habermas (1984) has argued, must lay beyond every effort at rational argument.

11. There are far-reaching implications of this discursive view of social science that I will not be able to take up here. One of the most important is that it helps to explains why the classics continue to be so central to the structure and arguments of social science. Discourses that are not purely factual must be adjudicated by reference to standards that are widely available throughout the discipline and that do not, as a rule, have to be articulated in a formal way. In order to meet this need disciplines make a select number of works "classical." The universe from which classical works can be chosen, however, depends on intellectual achievement. The further one moves away from natural science—the more discursive truth criteria become explicit topics of discussion—the more that decisive formulations of rational truth depend on intellectual qualities (personal genius, sensibility, etc.) that are not progressive in the empiricist sense. It is because he accepted the natural science model that Merton (1967) denied the centrality of the classics. From a discursive perspective on social science, however, his distinction between the history and systematics of sociology cannot be sustained. I have developed this discussion about the role of the classics in a companion piece to this chapter (Alex-

ander, 1987a), from which I have drawn freely in this section.

12. This metaphor of conversation has also been employed by Rorty: "If we see knowing not as having an essence, to be described by scientists or philosophers, but rather as a right, by current standards, to believe, then we are well on the way to seeing conversation as the ultimate context within which knowledge is to be understood" (1979, p. 389). It is characteristic of Rorty, however, that he uses this metaphor to deny the relevance of pursuing either empirical truth or general theory, advocating instead a kind of philosophical historiography: "Our focus shifts from the relation between human beings and the objects of their inquiry to the relation between alternative standards of justification, and from there to the actual changes in those standards which make up intellectual history" (1979, pp. 389-390).

If social science is a conversation, attention to alternative standards of justification is certainly in order. This does not necessitate, however, a diminution of interest in the empirical "objects" of social science or the adoption of a purely historical—rather than systematic and foundational—approach to considering what these standards imply. Rorty himself is ultimately ambiguous on this point, as he is on many others. In a subsequent essay (1984) he insists, against the opponents of rationalist reconstruction, that we "want to imagine conversations between ourselves . . . and the mighty dead [philosophers] in order to assure ourselves that there has been rational progress in the course of recorded history" (1984, p. 51). Vis-a-vis earlier philosophers, he here advocates "finding out how much truth they knew" and endorses "such enterprises in commensuration" even if they are historically anachronistic (p. 53). Perhaps there is not such a great gulf between postempiricism and foundational attempts to establish rational evaluations, after all. That is certainly my contention here.

13. The claim that rational and nonrational have, in fact, informed broadly distinctive traditions in the history of social thought has been advanced by a wide range of different writers, for example, Parsons (1937), Hughes (1958), and Habermas (1971).

14. It is just such an overreaction against the standard misreading of Durkheim's position that marks Giddens's position (e.g., Giddens, 1976). This overreaction has led him to an overly individualistic position on the order question.

15. In his subtle essay on the origins of modern economic theory, Hirschman (1977) has shown that contract theories that emphasized market exchanges originated as part of a struggle against the arbitrary power of despots and kings. He also suggests, however, that in its early stages—for example, in the work of Montesquieu—such contract theories had a relatively social and often normative and emotional bent, for such self-interested exchanges were supposed to civilize passionate and often destructive human instincts. The initial rationale for this prototype of individualistic and rationalistic theory, then, was clearly cultural and collective. As market theory developed, however, it became more purely materialistic in orientation, and the notion that contractual exchanges had any relationship to subjective motive dropped out. This account provides a historical documentation for the theoretical criticism I make below—namely, that the whole topic of volition and will is eliminated by rationalistic and individualistic theories.

16. For a historical perspective on shifts in theorizing the micro/macro link, as well as a more detailed and systematic account of the analytic issues involved, see Alexander and Giesen (1987). I have drawn from this essay for many of the arguments that follow.

17. In explaining the success of exchange theory one would not want to underestimate the power and bombastic eloquence of Homans's discursive justifications on its behalf. He first articulated exchange theory (Homans, 1958) in a purely discursive way, in his highly publicized presidential address to the American Sociological Association. In the major introduction to his collection of essays (Homans, 1962), he developed new modes of biographical and ideological discourse to justify exchange theorizing. His remarkable dedication to developing discursive justifications for exchange theory continues to be revealed in his recent autobiography (Homans, 1984), which, I have argued elsewhere (Alexander, 1987c), creates a series of not entirely accurate frameworks through which the exchange perspective is presented as psychologically, morally, scientifically, and historically inevitable.

18. Lewis and Smith (1980) demonstrate this point in a powerful and systematic way in their brilliant reinterpretation of the history of pragmatic social theory in America. That upon its publication this book became extraordinarily controversial points, in my view, to the danger its argument posed to the discursive justifications of symbolic interactionism in its Blumerian mode.

19. Elsewhere I have applied this conception of revisionism to the classical and Parsonian traditions (Alexander, 1982b, 1983a, 1983b) and to Kuhn's work (Alexander, 1982c). I have elaborated revisionism in contemporary theoretical traditions in much more detail in Alexander (1987b).

20. Eisenstadt (Eisenstadt and Curelaru, 1976) was one of the first sociologists to become sensitive to the possibility for such cross-cuttings. As a functionalist who was himself straining to develop new forms of theoretical discourse, he was quick to point out similar attempts that were emerging in other traditions. Because he was committed to an explanatory and basically empiricist conception of social science, however, he viewed these openings as part of the linear progress of sociology rather than as one phase in the pendulum movement of a discipline which is as discursive as it is explanatory.

21. Another revealing example of the confrontation between the new cultural history and the once-new social history can be found in the relationship between Edward Berenson's and Eugene Weber's accounts of the behavior of peasants in nineteenth-century France. Weber, long one of the major pro-

ponents of social history despite his moderate political stance, published a major work (1976) arguing that the backward and conservative mentality of French peasants had been transformed in the latter part of the nineteenth century as the result of technological and economic developments. Berenson, politically more liberal and more closely aligned with recent intellectual movements, reviewed Weber's book and criticized it for its materialism (Berenson, 1979). Berenson's own work (1984) on the origins of the revolution of 1848 emphasizes, by contrast, the peasants' critical role and how their consciousness was transformed by their participation in the radical Christian movements that enveloped much of the French countryside in the early nineteenth century.

22. This new preoccupation with anthropological theory is reflected in an entire issue the *American Historical Review* devoted to "the state of history" published by Rabb and Rotberg (1982). A major section is devoted to the relationship between anthropology—which is defined in distinctively cultural terms—and history (see the articles by Bernard S. Cohen, John N. Adams, Natalie Z. Davis, and Carlo Ginsberg, pp. 227-291). At the center of this relationship has been Clifford Geertz, whose work has had an enormous impact in America on both European and American history. Sewell spent five years at the Institute for Advanced Study, where Geertz is a dominant figure. Darnton, a member of the Princeton University history department, jointly taught seminars with Geertz for several years. A leading young historian of American history, Sean Wilentz, acknowledges the central role of Geertz in the Davis Center seminars (also at Princeton) from which he (Wilentz, 1985) drew his recent collection of historical essays about ritual and power. Geertz, of course, was trained by Parsons, and though his work has become significantly more culturalist since then, his contemporary prominence provides yet another indication that social science discourse has turned back to the synthetic concerns that Parsons so forcefully expressed.

23. Eisenstadt presents this analytical approach as prototypically Weberian, but Thompson, Hall, Mann, and Anderson have at least as much a claim to this mantle as he. Weber's own corpus, after all, is a complex jumble of institutional, ideational, and genuinely reductionistic works (Alexander, 1983a). In light of this legacy, it would be more accurate to see Eisenstadt's insistence on an analytic approach to cultural "institutionalization" as distinctively Parsonian, and the massive project of comparative civilizational history upon which he has been engaged (see, for example, Eisenstadt, 1986) as a form of neofunctionalism. This circling back to Parsons's earlier synthetic work, in terms of ambitions and sometimes also in terms of actual concepts, is a significant and visible characteristic of the new theoretical movement I am describing here (see note 25). Mann (1986), for example, makes careful reference to Parsons's antireductionist approach to organizational capacity. When in a recent work Meyer extends his institutional

theory to civilizational history and criticizes comparative research for "a kind of reductionism in which we treat the forces and relationships within the Western situation as somehow natural or universal, ignoring their sociocultural constitution," the echos of Eisenstadt's and Parsons's analytic approach to culture are very clear.

24. This postructuralist thinking has already begun to spread deeply into British sociology, as the recent writings by Thompson (1984, 1986) and Lash (1985) indicate.

25. As Archer (1985b) has observed, Giddens's exaggerated separation of individuals from their environments is the other side of his frequent overemphasis on the coercive materiality of social structure.

26. These, of course, are the very errors that Parsons made in his effort to synthesize the warring schools of sociology two generations ago. Nonetheless, it is the same type of effort—to synthesize action and structure, culture and material force—in which the younger generation of theorists is currently engaged. It should not be surprising, then, that one of guises that this new theoretical movement has taken is a broad revision and revival of Parsonian theory, which I have called neofunctionalism (see, for instance, the essays collected in Alexander, 1985b, and Alexander and Colomy, 1988). In her recent work advocating a renewed focus on culture in macrosociology, Archer (1985a) can also be seen as returning to Parsons's approach in a less orthodox way. Culture can be reinstated, she argues, only by avoiding the conflation of cultural patterning with social equilibrium. This argument is elaborated in her book, *Culture and Agency* (1988), which represents a major effort to insert culture back into general sociological theory.

Even in the more orthodox strands of this revival the impact of the new movement can be seen. Although Luhmann (1979) has raised the radically macroconcept of "systems" to a new and overbearing height, it should not be forgotten that he explains the very existence of systems by referring to fundamental microprocesses, which he identifies as the individual's existential need to reduce complexity. In his more recent work on autopoietic systems (Luhmann, 1987), moreover, he makes the dialectic of micro and macro into the very essence of modern societies. This emphasis has had a major influence on Munch's important efforts (1981-1982) to reshape Parsons's systematic theory. While he generally criticizes the radical micro traditions and in this way follows Parsons's collective emphasis, he has moved to incorporate contingency into his revised four-dimensional models in a way that Parsons never contemplated.

REFERENCES

Abrams, M. H. 1971. *Natural Supernaturalism*. New York: Norton.

Alberoni, Francesco. 1984. *Movement and Institution*. New York: Columbia University Press.

Alexander, Jeffrey C. 1982a. *Positivism, Presuppositions, and Current Controversies. Theoretical Logic in Sociology*, vol. 1. Berkeley: University of California Press.

_____ 1982b. *The Antinomies of Classical Thought: Marx and Durkheim*. Berkeley: University of California Press.

_____ 1982c. "Kuhn's Unsuccessful Revisionism: A Rejoinder to Selby." *Canadian Sociological Review* 7:66-71.

_____ 1983a. *The Classical Attempt at Synthesis: Max Weber. Theoretical Logic in Sociology*, vol. 3. Berkeley: University of California Press.

_____ 1983b. *The Modern Reconstruction of Classical Thought: Talcott Parsons. Theoretical Logic in Sociology*, vol. 4. Berkeley: University of California Press.

_____ 1984. "The Parsons Revival in German Sociology." Pp. 394-412 in *Sociological Theory*, edited by R. Collins. San Francisco: Jossey-Bass.

_____ 1985a. "The Individualist Dilemma in Phenomenology and Interaction." Pp. 25-57 in *Macrosociological Theory*, edited by S. N. Eisenstadt and D. Halle. Beverly Hills, CA: Sage.

_____, ed. 1985b. *Neofunctionalism*. Beverly Hills, CA: Sage.

_____ 1987a. "On the Centrality of the Classics." Pp. 11-57 in *Social Theory Today*, edited by Anthony Giddens and Jonathan Turner. London: Macmillan.

_____ 1987b. *Twenty Lectures: Sociological Theory Since World War II*. New York: Columbia University Press.

_____ 1987c. "Science, Sense, and Sensibility." *Theory and Society* 15:443-463.

_____, ed. 1988a. *Durkheimian Sociology: Cultural Studies*. New York: Cambridge University Press.

_____ 1988b. *Action and Its Environments: Towards a New Synthesis*. New York: Columbia University Press.

_____ and Paul Colomy. 1985. "Towards Neofunctionalism: Eisenstadt's Change Theory and Symbolic Interaction." *Sociological Theory* 3:11-32.

_____, eds. 1988. *Differentiation Theory and Social Change: Historical and Comparative Approaches*. New York: Columbia University Press.

_____ and Bernhard Giesen. 1987. "From Reduction to Linkage: The Long View of the Micro-Macro Link." Pp. 1-42 in *The Micro-Macro Link*, edited by Jeffrey Alexander et al. Berkeley: University of California Press.

_____ and Steven Seidman. eds. In press. *Culture and Society: Contemporary Debates*. New York: Cambridge University Press.

Althusser, Louis and Etienne Balibar. 1970. *Reading Capital*. London: New Left Books.

Anderson, Perry. 1986. "Those in Authority," a review of *The Origins of Social Power*, vol. I by Michael Mann. *Times Literary Supplement* (December 12): 1405-1406.

Archer, Margaret. 1985a. "The Myth of Cultural Integration." *British Journal of Sociology*. 36: 333-353.

_____ 1985b. "Structuration versus Morphogenesis." Pp. 58-88 in *Macrosociological Theory*, edited by S. N. Eisenstadt and D. Halle, Beverly Hills, CA: Sage.

_____ 1988. *Culture and Agency*. London: Cambridge University Press.

Becker, Howard. 1963. *Outsiders. Studies in the Sociology of Deviance*. Glencoe, IL: Free Press.

_____ 1984. *Art Worlds*. Berkeley: University of California Press.

Berenson, Edward. 1979. "The Modernization of Rural France." *The Journal of European Economic History*, 8(1):209-215.

_____ 1984. *Populist Religion and Left Wing Politics in France, 1830-1852*. Princeton, NJ: Princeton University Press.

Blau, Peter. 1977. *Inequality and Heterogeneity*. New York: Free Press.

_____, Terry C. Blum, and Joseph E. Schwartz. 1982. "Heterogeneity and Intermarriage." *American Sociological Review* 47:45-62.

Blumer, Herbert. 1937. "Social Psychology." Pp. 144-198 in *Man and Society*, edited by E. D. Schmidt. Englewood Cliffs, NJ: Prentice-Hall.

_____, ed. 1969. "The Methodological Position of Symbolic Interactionism." Pp. 1-60 in *Symbolic Interactionism*. Englewood Cliffs, NJ: Prentice-Hall.

Boudon, Raymond. 1982. *The Unintended Consequences of Social Action*. New York: St. Martin's.

_____ 1987. "The Individualistic Tradition in Sociology." Pp. 45-70 in *The Micro-Macro Link*, edited by Jeffrey Alexander et al. Berkeley: University of California Press.

Bourdieu, Pierre. 1986. *Distinction*. Cambridge, MA: Harvard University Press.

Calhoun, Craig. 1982. *The Question of Class Struggle: The Social Foundations of Popular Radicalism*. Chicago: University of Chicago Press.

Coleman, James. 1968. "Review Symposium on Harold Garfinkel's Studies in Ethnomethodology." *American Sociological Review* 33:126-300.

_____ 1987a. "Microfoundations and Macrosocial Behavior." Pp. 153-175 in *The Micro-Macro Link*, edited by Jeffrey Alexander et al. Berkeley: University of California Press.

_____ 1987b. "Toward a Social Theory of Constitutions." Unpublished manuscript.

Collingwood, Charles. 1940. *Metaphysics*. Oxford: Clarendon.

Collins, Randall. 1975. *Conflict Sociology*. New York: Academic Press.

_____ 1981. "On the Microfoundations of Macrosociology." *American Journal of Sociology* 86: 984-1014.

_____ 1988. "The Conflict Tradition in Durkheimian Sociology." In *Durkheimian-Sociology: Cul-

tural Studies, edited by Jeffrey C. Alexander. New York: Cambridge University Press.

Coser, Lewis. 1975. "Presidential Address: Two Methods in Search of a Substance." *American Sociological Review* 40:691-700.

Dahrendorf, Ralf. 1959. *Class and Class Conflict in Industrial Society*. Stanford, CA: Stanford University Press.

Darnton, Robert. 1984. *The Great Cat Massacre and Other Episodes in French Cultural History*. New York: Vintage.

Di Maggio, Paul. 1988. "Interest and Agency in Institutional Theory." Pp. 3-21 in Lynn G. Zucker, *Institutional Patterns and Organizations Culture and Environment*. Cambridge, MA: Ballinger.

Douglas, Mary. 1966. *Purity and Danger*. London: Penguin.

Durkheim, Emile. 1937. *The Rules of Sociological Method*. New York: Free Press. (Originally published in 1895)

Eisenstadt, S. N. 1986. "Culture and Social Structure Revisited." *International Sociology* 1(3): 297-320.

_____. 1987. "Macro-Sociology and Sociological Theory: Some New Directions" (Review Essay). *Contemporary Sociology* 16(5):602-610.

_____ and M. Curelaru. 1976. *The Forms of Sociology: Paradigms and Crises*. New York: John Wiley.

Ekeh, Peter K. 1974. *Social Exchange Theory: The Two Traditions*. Cambridge, MA: Harvard University Press.

Elster, Jan. 1985. *Making Sense of Marx*. New York: Cambridge University Press.

Eyerman, Ron. 1982. "Some Recent Studies of Class Consciousness." *Theory and Society* 11:541-553.

_____. 1984. "Social Movements and Social Theory." *Sociology* 18:71-81.

Foucault, Michel. 1970. *The Order of Things*. London: Tavistock.

Friedrichs, Robert. 1970. *A Sociology of Sociology*. New York: Free Press.

Garfinkel, Harold. 1963. "A Conception of and Experiments with Trust as a Condition of Concerted Stable Actions," Pp. 187-238 in O. J. Harvey, ed., *Motivation and Social Interaction*. New York: Ronald Press.

_____. 1967. *Studies in Ethnomethodology*. Englewood Cliffs, NJ: Prentice-Hall.

_____, Michael Lynch, and Eric Livingston. 1981. "The Work of Discovering Science Construed with Materials from the Opitically Discovered Pulsar." *Philosophy of Social Science* 11:131-158.

Geertz, Clifford. 1973. *The Interpretation of Culture*. New York: Basic Books.

Giddens, Anthony. 1971. *Capitalism and Mod·rn Social Theory*. New York: Cambridge University Press.

_____. 1976. *New Rules of Sociological Method*. New York: Basic.

_____. 1985. *The Constitution of Societies*. London: Macmillan.

Godelier, Maurice. 1967. "System, Structure, and Contradition in 'Capital.' " Pp. 91-119 in *The Socialist Register*, edited by Ralph Miliband and John Saville. New York: Monthly Review Press.

Goffman, Erving. 1959. *The Presentation of Self in Everday Life*. Garden City, New York: Doubleday.

_____. 1963. *Behavior in Public Places*. New York: Free Press.

_____. 1974. *Frame Analysis*. New York: Harper & Row.

Goldthorpe, John. 1973. "A Revolution in Sociology?" *Sociology* 7(3):449-462.

Goode, William J. 1979. *The Celebration of Heros: Prestige as a Social Control System*. Berkeley: University of California Press.

Gouldner, Alvin. 1982. *The Two Marxisms*. New York: Seabury.

Habermas, Jurgen. 1971. *Knowledge and Human Interests*. Boston: Beacon Press.

_____. 1973. *Theory and Practice*. Boston: Beacon Press.

_____. 1984. *Reason and the Rationalization of Society. The Theory of Communicative Action*, vol 1. Boston: Beacon.

Handel, J. 1979. "Normative Expectations and the Emergence of Meaning as Solutions to Problems; Convergence of Structural and Interactionist Views." *American Journal of Sociology* 84: 855-881.

Hirschman, Albert. 1977. *The Passions and the Interests*. Princeton, NJ: Princeton University Press.

Holton, Gerald. 1973. *Thematic Origins of Scientific Thought: Kepler to Einstein*. Cambridge. MA: Harvard University Press.

Homans, George. 1958. "Social Behavior as Exchange." *American Journal of Sociology* 62: 597-606.

_____. 1961. *Social Behavior: Its Elementary Forms*. New York: Harcourt, Brace and World.

_____, ed. 1962. "Introduction." In *Sentiments and Activities*. New York: Free Press.

_____. 1984. *Coming to My Senses*. New Brunswick, NJ: Transaction.

Hughes, H. Stuart. 1958. *Consciousness and Society*. New York: Random House.

Hunt, Lynn. 1984. *Politics, Culture, and Class in the French Revolution*. Berkeley: University of California Press.

_____. 1988. "The Sacred and the French Revolution." In *Durkheimian Sociology: Cultural Studies*, edited by Jeffrey C. Alexander. New York: Cambridge University Press.

Kadushin, Charles. 1978. "Cast Thy Bread Upon the Waters ..." Graduate Center, City University of New York. Unpublished manuscript.

Knorr-Cetina, Karen and Aaron Cicourel. eds. 1981. *Advances in Social Theory and Methodology: Towards an Integration of Micro and Macro*

Sociology. London: Routledge & Kegan Paul.
_____ and Michael Mulkay. eds. 1983. *Science Observed: New Perspectives on the Social Study of Science*. Beverly Hills, CA: Sage.

Kreps, Gary. 1985. "Disaster and the Social Order: Definition and Taxonomy." *Sociological Theory* 3(Spring):49-64.

_____ 1987. "Classical Themes, Structural Sociology, and Disaster Research" in *Sociology of Disasters* edited by R. R. Dynes and Carlo Pellanda. Goprizia, Italy: Franco Angell.

Kuhn, Thomas. 1970. *The Structure of Scientific Revolutions*. Chicago: University of Chicago Press.

Lash, Scott. 1985. "Postmodernity and Desire." *Theory and Society* 14:1-34.

_____ and John Urry. 1984. "The New Marxism of Collective Action: A Critical Analysis." *Sociology* 18(1):33-50.

Lewis, J. David and Richard L. Smith. 1980. *American Sociology and Pragmatism: Mead, Chicago Sociology and Symbolic Interactionism*. Chicago: University of Chicago Press.

Lieberson, Stanley. 1980. *A Piece of the Pie*. Berkeley: University of California Press.

Lindenberg, Ziegfried. 1983. "The New Political Economy: Its Potential and Limitations for the Social Sciences in General and Sociology in Particular." Pp. 7-66 in *Oknonomische Erklarung sozialen Verhalt*, edited by Wolfgang Sedsur. Duisberg, West Germany: Sozial wissen schaftlicke kooperative.

Luhmann, N. 1979. *Trust and Power*. New York: John Wiley.

_____ 1987. "The Evolutionary Differentiation Between Society and Interaction." Pp. 112-113 in *The Micro-Macro Link*, edited by Jeffrey Alexander et al. Berkeley: University of California Press.

Lyotard, Jean-Francois. 1984. *The Postmodern Condition*. Minneapolis: University of Minnesota Press.

Maines, Davis. 1977. "Social Organization and Social Structure in Symbolic Interactionist Thought." *Annual Review of Sociology* 3:235-260.

Mann, Michael. 1970. "The Social Cohesion of Liberal Democracy." *American Sociological Review* 35:423-439.

_____ 1979. "State and Society, 1730-1815: An Analysis of English State Finances." Pp. 165-208 in *Political Power and Social Theory*, vol. 1., edited by Maurice Zeitlin. Greenwich, CT: JAI Press.

_____ 1986. *The Origins of Social Power*, Vol. 1. *A History of Power From the Beginning to AD 1760*. London: Cambridge University Press.

_____ and Robin M. Blackburn. 1979. *The Working Class in the Labor Market*. London: Macmillan.

Merton, Robert K., ed. 1967. "On the History and Systematics of Sociology." Pp. 1-38 in *Social Theory and Social Structure*. New York: Free Press.

Meyer, John W. 1987. "Conceptions of Christendon: Notes on the Distinctiveness of the West." Paper presented at the Annual Meetings of the American Sociological Association, Chicago, August.

_____ and John Scott. 1983. *Organizational Environments: Ritual and Rationality*. Beverly Hills, CA: Sage.

Molotch, Harvey and Deirdre Boden. 1985. "Talking Social Structure: Discourse, Domination, and the Watergate Hearings." *American Sociological Review* 50:273-287.

Moore, Barrington. 1966. *The Social Origins of Dictatorship and Democracy*. Boston: Beacon Press.

_____ 1978. *Injustice: The Social Bases of Obedience and Revolt*. Boston: Beacon.

Munch, Richard. 1981. "Talcott Parsons and the Theory of Action, Parts I and II." *American Journal of Sociology* 86-87:709-749, 771-826.

O'Connor, James. 1978. *The Fiscal Crisis of the State*. New York: St. Martin's.

Offe, Claus. 1984. *Contradictions of the Welfare State*. Cambridge, MA: MIT Press. (Original work published in 1972)

Parsons, Talcott. 1937. *The Structure of Social Action*. New York: Free Press.

Pinch, T.J. and H. M. Collins. 1984. "Private Science and Public Knowledge." *Social Studies in Science* 14:521-546.

Poulantzas, Nicou. 1972. *Political Power and Social Classes*. London: New Left Books.

Prager, Jeffrey. 1986. *Building Democracy in Ireland: Political Order and Cultural Integration in a Newly Independent Nation*. New York: Cambridge University Press.

Rabb, Theodore K. and Robert I. Rotberg. ed. 1982. *The New History: The 1980's and Beyond*. Princeton, NJ: Princeton University Press.

Rajchman, John. 1985. "Philosophy in America." Pp. ix-xxvii in *Post-Analytic Philosophy*, edited by Rajchman and Cornell West. New York: Columbia University Press.

Rex, John. 1961. *Key Problems in Sociological Theory*. London: Routledge & Kegan Paul.

Ritzer, George. 1975. *Sociology: A Multi-Paradigm Science*. Boston: Allen & Bacon.

Rorty, Richard. 1979. *Philosophy and the Mirror of Nature*. Princeton, NJ: Princeton University Press.

_____ 1984. "The Historiography of Philosophy: Four Genres." Pp. 49-76 in *Philosophy in History*, edited by R. Rorty, J. B. Schneewind, and Quentin Skinner. New York: Cambridge University Press.

Sacks, Harvey, Emmanuel A. Schegloff, and Gail Jefferson. 1974. "A Simplest Systematics for the Organization of Turn-Taking for Conversation." *Language* 50:696-735.

Schegloff, Emmanuel. 1987. "Between Macro and Micro: Contexts and other Connections." Pp.

207-235 in *The Micro-Macro Link*, edited by Jeffrey Alexander et al. Berkeley: University of California Press.

Seidman, Steven. 1983. "Beyond Presentism and Historicism: Understanding the History of Social Science." *Sociological Inquiry* 53:79-94.

_____ "Classics and Contemporaries: The History and Systematics of Sociology Revisited." Unpublished manuscript.

Sewell, William. 1980. *Work and Revolution in France*. New York: Cambridge University Press.

_____ 1985. "Ideologies and Social Revolutions: Reflections on the French Case." *Journal of Modern History* 57:57-85.

Sica, Alan. 1986. "Hermeneutics and Axiology: The Ethical Content of Interpretation." Pp. 141-157 in *Sociological Theory in Transition*, edited by Mark L. Nardell and Stephen J. Turner, eds., *Sociological Theory in Transition*. Boston: Allen and Unwin.

Skocpol, Theda. 1979. *States and Social Revolutions*. New York: Cambridge University Press.

_____ 1982. "Rentier State and Shi'a Islam in the Iranian Revolution." *Theory and Society* 11:265-284.

_____ 1985. "Cultural Idioms and Political Ideologies in the Revolutionary Reconstruction of State Power: A Rejoinder to Sewell." *Journal of Modern History* 57:86-96.

Smelser, Neil. 1959. *Social Change in the Industrial Revolution*. Berkeley: University of California Press.

Smith, Dorothy. 1984. "Textually Mediated Social Organization." *International Social Science Journal* 36:59-75.

Spiegelberg, H. 1971. *The Phenomenological Movement: A Historical Introduction*. The Hague: Martinus Nijhoff.

Strauss, Anselm. 1978. *Negotiations: Contexts, Processes and Social Order*. San Francisco: Jossey-Bass.

Stinchcombe, Arthur. 1968. *Constructing Social Theories*. Baltimore, MD: Johns Hopkins University Press.

_____ 1978. *Theoretical Methods in Social History*. New York: Academic.

Stryker, Sheldon. 1980. *Symbolic Interactionism: A Social Structural Version*. Menlo Park, CA: Cummings.

Sztompka, Piotr. 1974. *System and Function*. New York: Academic Press.

_____ 1984. "The Global Crisis and the Reflexiveness of the Social System." *International Journal of Comparative Sociology* 25(1-2):45-58.

_____ 1986. "The Renaissance of Historical Orientation in Sociology." *International Sociology* 1:321-337.

_____ In press. "Social Movements: Structures in Statu Nascendi." *International Sociology*.

Taylor, Charles. 1975. *Hegel*. New York: Oxford University Press.

Thompson, E. P. 1978. "The Poverty of Theory of an Orrery of Errors." Pp. 1-210 in Thompson, ed., *The Poverty of Theory and Other Essays*. New York: Monthly Review Press.

Thompson, John B. 1984. *Studies in the Theory of Ideology*. Berkeley: University of California Press.

_____, ed. 1986. "Editor's Introduction." Pp. 1-27 in *The Political Forms of Modern Society: Bureaucracy, Democracy, Totalitarianism*, by Claude Lefort. Cambridge, MA: MIT Press.

Tourraine, Alain. 1977. *The Self-Production of Society*. Chicago: University of Chicago Press.

Trevor-Roper, H. R. 1965. "Religion, the Reformation and Social Change." *Historical Studies* 4:18-45.

Treiman, Don. 1977. *Occupational Prestige in Comparative Perspective*. New York: John Wiley.

Turner, Jonathan. 1986. "Review: The Theory of Structuration." *American Journal of Sociology* 91:969-977.

Turner, Stephen P. 1987. "Underdetermination and the Promise of Statistical Sociology." *Sociological Theory* 5(2):172-184.

Turner, Victor. 1969. *The Ritual Process*. Chicago: Aldine.

van den Berg, Axel. In press. *The State of Marxism*. Princeton, NJ: Princeton University Press.

Wagner, David G. 1984. *The Growth of Sociological Theories*. Beverly Hills, CA: Sage.

_____ and Joseph Berger. 1984. "Do Sociological Theories Grow?" *American Journal of Sociology* 90:697-728.

Walby, Sylvia. 1986. *Patriarchy at Work*. London: Macmillan.

Waldell, Mark L. and Stephen P. Turner. eds. 1986. *Sociological Theory in Transition*. Boston: Allen & Unwin.

Wallace, Walter. 1983. *Principles of Scientific Sociology*. Chicago: Aldine.

Walzer, Michael. 1986. "Review of Jan Elster, *Making Sense of Marx*." *New York Review of Books* 32(Nov. 21): 43-46.

_____ 1987. *Interpretation and Social Criticism*. Cambridge, MA: Harvard University Press.

Weber, Eugene. 1976. *Peasants into Frenchmen*. Stanford, CA: Stanford University Press.

Weber, Max. 1958. *The Protestant Ethic and the Spirit of Capitalism*. New York: Scribner's. (Original work published 1904-1905)

Wilentz, Sean, ed. 1985. *The Rites of Power*. Philadelphia: University of Pennsylvania Press.

Williams, Bernard. 1985. *Ethics and the Limits of Philosophy*. Cambridge, MA: Harvard University Press.

Wippler, R. and S. Lindenberg. 1987. "Collective Phenomena and Rational Choice." Pp. 135-152 in *The Micro-Macro Link*, edited by Alexander et al. Berkeley: University of California Press.

Wright, Erik Olin. 1978. *Class, Crisis, and the State*. London: New Left Books.

Wuthnow, Robert. 1987. *Meaning and Moral Order: Explorations in Cultural Analysis*. Berkeley: University of California Press.

_____ Edith Kurzweil, James Hunter, and Albert Bergesen. 1984. *Cultural Analysis*. Routledge & Kegan Paul.

Zelizer, Viviana. 1985. *Pricing the Priceless Child*. New York: Basic Books.

Zucker, Lynn G., ed. 1988. "Where Do Institutional Patterns Come From? Organizations as Actors in Social Systems," Pp. 23-49 in Zucker, ed., *Institutional Patterns and Organization: Culture and Environment*. Cambridge, MA: Ballinger.

3

Social Structure

NEIL J. SMELSER

It is difficult to conceive of any line of scientific inquiry without sooner or later invoking the notion of structure. We find it everywhere in the sciences: atomic structure, molecular structure, anatomical structure, even the structure of the universe. This statement remains true even though some scientific theories build into their first assumptions some notion of uncertainty or indeterminacy. The reason structure is so central to the scientific enterprise is because, by tradition, that enterprise is dedicated to discovering both (1) *regularities* in whatever part of nature it undertakes to investigate (and regularities mean repeated, nonrandom) and (2) *systematic relationships* among the things it studies. Both of these aims lead to and are implied by the notion of structure; correspondingly, wherever we find scientists at work we find some notion of structure, whether that is represented as found in nature or imposed upon nature by investigators as a kind of heuristic device. This characterization applies to the behavioral and social sciences as well; if we consider only the ABCs of our methodological tool bag—statistical analyses—we find that they are predominantly devoted to proving that things could not be arrayed or have happened by chance alone; that is to say, if they are not, there is some kind of pattern or structure that is observed or inferred.

In this chapter I will ask—selectively but extensively—how social structure has been diversely characterized in sociology, and what place the notion has in different kinds of sociological theory. By way of offering an introductory apology for this enterprise, it can be argued that the idea of social structure is at the very heart of sociology as a scientific enterprise. The component "social" connotes the distinctive subject matter and analytic level of the field, and the component "structure" connotes the preoccupation with regularities characteristic of any scientific enterprise. At the same time, the notion of social structure reaches toward the psychological and cultural levels as well. As we will see, those who make efforts to explain why social structures—or social order generally—are sustained or break down make appeal to psychological concepts, such as the need to control basic human selfishness or destructiveness (Thomas Hobbes, Sigmund Freud) or the natural harmony of individual interests (Adam Smith); in addition, there is a long sociological tradition of asking what the psychological or more general human consequences of incumbency in a social structure are: for example, alienation (Karl Marx), disenchantment (Max Weber), or anomie (Emile Durkheim). On the cultural side, social structures are invariably legitimized by references to values and ideologies, or, if attacked, delegitimized by the same kinds of cultural elements.

Viewed in another way, this chapter constitutes a sample of the major frameworks that are invoked selectively to explain or account for various kinds of empirical arrangements and regularities that become evident in the conduct of empirical research. In still another significant way, the chapter outlines the major bases of paradigmatic debates and conflicts in the history of sociological theorizing, debates, and conflicts that carry through up to contemporary times.

Some Generic Features of the Concept of Structure

On beginning this inquiry I did not go first to the sociological masters, but to a plainer but very helpful source, the *Oxford English Dictionary*. Under *structure* I found seven separate listings, most of them very static in nature, having to do with architecture and with things such as buildings that have been constructed (same root). Two meanings, however, seemed helpful for my purposes:

• Structure: "the coexistence of a whole of distinct parts having a definite manner of arrangements";

• Structure: "an organized body or combination of mutually connected and dependent parts or elements."

When I scanned the list of illustrative specifications of these two general meanings, I found the sociologist lurking anyway. Under each definition was a quotation from Herbert Spencer. In the same order:

• "Though structure up to a certain point [in the animal organism] is requisite for growth, structure beyond that point impedes growth."

• "The general law of organization . . . is that distinct duties entail distinct structures."

It does not seem necessary to regard either of these definitions or their corresponding sociological illustrations as the final word. Nevertheless, they provide a good starting point and from them it proved possible to elaborate the following separable ingredients of the idea of structure, which are six in number:

(1) The idea calls for the specification of basic *units of analysis* of some kind, which make up the "parts" or "elements" of what is logically implied by the concept of structure to be "multipart" or "multielemental." In much of

personality and social psychology, the basic structure studied is at the level of individual personality (or self), and the basic elements are subparts of that: needs, feelings, aptitudes, attitudes, defenses, and the like. The basic units of analysis in the sociological study of structure are two: first, certain relational characteristics that arise from the location and interaction among individual persons, as role relationships (parent-child), in the complex patterning of role relationships into institutional form (market structure, family structure, educational structure), and in stratified relations among persons along lines of wealth, power, and prestige; and, second, in relational characteristics among groups, or social associations involving common interaction, membership, feelings of belonging, and identification as such by those outside the group (Merton, 1968). Examples are relations among social cliques, political parties, voluntary associations, and social classes. In the following section I will elaborate these two different notions of structure.

(2) The notion of structure also implies that the basic units have some kind of special or nonrandom *relationship* to one another. Implied in the idea of sociometric structure, for example, is the notion that likes and dislikes are differentially and systematically distributed among members of a group. Implied in the idea of a market structure, is the notion that producers, distributors, wholesalers, retailers, and customers stand in a definite, systematic relationship with one another in the production-consumption cycle.

(3) Closely related to this is the implication that interactions among the basic elements of analysis are *repetitive* in space and time. It is difficult to conceive of the notion of structure without including this notion of repetition. In fact, it is the "dynamic" or "process" side of the more statically conceived element of "relationship." Certainly the types of social structure identified in the preceding paragraph imply repeated interactions among role incumbents and group members, as well as among groups themselves. Conceived in this way, structure and process are two expressions of the same thing: Structure is a kind of generalization based on observations of repeated processes of interaction among the basic units of analysis, and process is the behavioral manifestation and evidence for structure.

(4) Implied by the notion of a relationship repeated through processes among the basic units is that the relationships within a structure are *different from* relationships with units that are considered to lie outside the structure. The

notion of the self or the personality, for instance, while it typically allows for interaction with objects, ideas, and persons outside the self, also contains some notion of boundaries between the self and what is outside. The sociological conceptions of interaction in institutional structure, as well as group structure, carry the same implication of boundary. If there were no differences between interactions within a structure and interactions without (for example, if all these interactions were random), the concept of structure would disappear altogether, because there would be no basis for identifying it as such. The idea of a structure, in a word, implies the idea of a qualitatively different nonstructure.

(5) This notion of difference-from-outside gives rise to the further notion of *structure-in-situation* or *structure-in-environment*, as well as the notion of the degree to which the structure is closed from or open to influences or interactions with units or forces outside the structure. Taking family structure as an example, it is seen as existing in an environment that includes a system of property, a legal system, and an occupational system, of which the family is not customarily considered a part, but changes in that environment may affect family structure profoundly. It may also be asked whether the external environment *itself* has some structure—that is, is regular and repetitive in its impact on the structure in question—and, if so, what are the implications for that structure.

(6) Finally, and most tentatively—because this does not appear to be a necessary ingredient of descriptions of structure—many accounts of structure include some reference to the *reasons* for, or *causes* of structure; that is, why it hangs together and continues to differentiate itself from its environment. Ideas of adaptation, maintenance of social integration, and coercion figure prominently among these reasons or causes. We will see, as the chapter unfolds, that these accounts of the fundamental bases of social structure constitute the bases of the major theoretical differences and paradigmatic conflicts in sociology.

The Basic Units of Social Structure

Earlier I noted that, for sociologists, the units of social structure are conceived of, first, as relational characteristics that arise from interaction among persons (in which the unit of analysis is the relationship, such as role relationship or rela-

tions within and among institutions), and second, as relationships among groups (in which the unit of analysis is collectivities of individuals). In his statement on social structure, Radcliffe-Brown (1952) made this distinction explicitly. "[Direct] observation," he asserted, "[reveals] to us that human beings are connected by a complex network of social relations. I use the term 'social structure' to denote this network of actually existing relations" (p. 190). At the same time he "[includes] under social structure the differentiation of individuals and classes by their social role" (p. 191). This line of distinction is most pervasive in sociological thinking. For example, as a general rule those who have been designated as "functionalist" in orientation have tended to stress structure as relational characteristics; those who have stressed "conflict" have stressed the group-relational characteristics; some theorists (e.g., Marx), however, have made an effort to synthesize both perspectives in a single theory.

One of the universal features of both relational structures and groups is that they become the bases of inequality in society. Specific kinds of institutions (religion, the military, commerce) may be regarded as especially important in the range of society's institutions, and be therefore endowed with greater resources, respect, freedom, and privilege than others. In addition, social groups, especially classes, are the recipient of differential prestige, wealth, and power.

Some of the most interesting (and as yet incompletely answered) questions in sociology concern the *relations* between the relational perspective and the group perspective. It is clear, for example, that many groups arise from and have their relationship to other groups defined by the positions in the institutional structure: capitalists, workers, women, pensioners, engineers, students. At the same time, the degree to which identifiable groups are precipitated out from institutional structures is variable; group crystallization around occupational and class categories varies greatly, and some structural categories (for example, students on fellowships) seldom become the basis for group membership. Looking at those relations the other way around, some groups are relatively passive or ineffective in influencing the course of development of relational structures in society, but it is also true that contests among groups (reform-movement organizations, racial and ethnic groups, social classes, political parties), and their resolution in the polity have been the basis for structural innovation and the creation of new relational structures in society (for example, educational systems, legal systems for the regulation of commerce, agencies for conflict management). The stress on the active role of purposive groups (especially social movements) in creating society's structural apparatuses has been at the center of the recent "new social movements" literature in continental Europe (Klandermans, 1986; Touraine, 1981). The problematic relationship between these two main perspectives will reemerge repeatedly in the course of this chapter.

Some Macroscopic Conceptualizations of Structure[1]

STRUCTURE AS ARISING FROM CONSIDERATIONS OF SOCIETAL SURVIVAL OR THE EFFECTIVE FUNCTIONING OF SOCIETY. One recurrent tradition in sociological theorizing has been the appeal to the biological analogy: namely, that biological organisms, confronted with a variety of environmental exigencies, must function in relation to these exigencies if they are to survive, and that specialized structures (organs, systems such as the circulatory, digestive, and so on) arise as adaptive mechanisms in this struggle. Some illustrations follow:

Spencer. The biological analogy runs throughout Spencer's *Principles of Sociology* (1897). This is best observed in his empirical illustration of the major structures in a modern economy:

> The clustered citizens forming an organ which produces some commodity for national use, or that otherwise satisfies national wants, has within it subservient structures substantially like those of each other organ carrying on each other function. Be it a cotton-weaving district or a district where cutlery is made, it has a set of agencies that collect and send away the manufactured articles; it has an apparatus of major and minor channels through which the necessities of life are drafted out of the general stocks circulating through the kingdom, and brought home to the local workers and those who direct them; it has appliances, postal and other, for bringing those impulses by which the industry of the place is excited or checked; it has local controlling powers, political and ecclesiastical by which order is maintained and healthful action furthered [Spencer, 1897, Book I, p. 478].

Spencer regarded social evolution as involving, among other things, a progressive differentiation (specialization) of social structures and a corresponding mutual interdependence among them. Again, appealing to the biological analogy, "[the] mutually-dependent parts, living by and for one another, form an aggregate constituted on the same general principle as an individual organism" (Book I, p. 462).

One of the pressures imposed upon a theorist who regards structures as serving essential functions is to specify what those functions are. Spencer did not fail to do so. The first and most urgent exigency facing society has to do with its relations to its environment, especially the "offensive and defensive activities" dealing with "environing enemies and prey" (Book I, pp. 493, 547). The second exigency is "inner activities for the general sustenation," or the necessity for economic survival. The third, termed "distribution," has to do with facilitating exchange among the differentiated parts; market and credit mechanisms would be an example. And finally, as the mutual dependence of parts of a society grows, there arises a "regulating system" designed to facilitate the cooperation among the differentiated parts. This system itself is subject to further specialization, and may evolve subsystems for regulating protective and warlike activities, sustenance activities, and distributive activities (Book I, chaps. 6-9).[2]

In using this scheme for the classification of societies and their predominant types of structures, Spencer made use of only two of the major exigencies: if the "offensive and defensive activities" predominate, the result is a *militant* type of society; if sustenance activities predominate, the result is an *industrial* type of society. Each type of society is coordinated by a different principle. For the military society, the characterizing trait is that:

> its units are coerced into their various combined actions. As the soldier's will is so suspended that he becomes in everything the agent of his officer's will; so is the will of the citizen in all transactions, private and public, overruled by that of the government. The co-operation by which the military society is maintained, is a *compulsory* co-operation. The social structure adapted for dealing with surrounding hostile societies is under a central regulating system, to which all the parts are completely subject; just as in the individual organism the outer organs are completely subject; just as in the individual organism the outer organs are completely subject to the chief nervous centre [Spencer, 1897, Book I, p. 564].

The industrial type of society is

characterized throughout by that same individual freedom that every commercial transaction implies. The co-operation by which the multiform activities of the society are carried on, becomes a *voluntary* co-operation. And while the developed sustaining system, which gives to a social organism the industrial type, acquires for itself, like the developed sustaining system of an animal, a regulating apparatus of a diffused or uncentralized kind, it tends also to decentralize the primary regulating apparatus, by making it derive from more numerous classes its deputed powers [Spencer, 1897, Book I, p. 569].

Spencer viewed these two principles as "diametrically opposed . . . when . . . evolved to their extreme forms." Furthermore, he saw "the contrasts between their traits as among the most important with which sociology has to deal" (Book I, p. 574). Accordingly, Spencer described the ways in which the two different types of societies may be contrasted. These have been extracted from the chapters of the *Principles of Sociology*, and are presented in Table 3.1. In characterizing the two societies in these terms,

Spencer acknowledged that all societies display a mixture of structures for carrying on conflict and structures for dominance of each type (Book I, p. 574).

I have given some detail in presenting Spencer's view of society and its structures for several reasons:

(1) The biological analogy is especially striking in his work.

(2) His theoretical position not only gives the concept of structure a central place, but also contains the idea that any given type of society manifests a more or less coherent *system* of structures; the logic of Table 3.1 illustrates this principle of societal interconnectedness of structures.

(3) The militant and industrial societies, as described, involve contrasting models of the internal organization of societies, and as such, manifest and foreshadow the two great contrasting traditions in sociology, referred to variously as "domination versus cooperation," "conflict versus consensus," "coercion versus voluntarism," and so on, which still characterize theoretical debates in the field. It is not widely

TABLE 3.1
The Contrast Between Militant and Industrial Societies

Characteristic	Militant Society	Industrial Society
Dominant function or activity	Corporate defensive and offensive activity for preservation and aggrandizement	Peaceful, mutual rendering of individual services
Principle of social coordination	Compulsory cooperation; regimentation by enforcement of orders; both positive and negative regulation of activity	Voluntary cooperation; regulation by contract and principles of justice; only negative regulation of activity
Relations between state and individual	Individuals exist for benefit of state; restraints on liberty, property, and mobility	State exists for benefit of individuals; freedom; few restraints on property and mobility
Relations between state and other organizations	All organizations public; private organizations excluded	Private organizations encouraged
Structure of state	Centralized	Decentralized
Structure of social stratification	Fixity of rank, occupation, and locality; inheritance of positions	Plasticity and openness of rank, occupation, and locality; movement between positions
Type of economic activity	Economic autonomy and self-sufficiency; little external trade; protectionism	Loss of economic autonomy; interdependence via peaceful trade; free trade
Valued social and personal characteristics	Patriotism; courage; reverence; loyalty; obedience; faith in authority; discipline	Independence; respect for others; resistance to coercion; individual initiative; truthfulness; kindness

SOURCE: Adapted from Spencer (1897; Book I, chap. 10; Book II, chaps. 17 and 18).

recognized, furthermore, that Spencer systematically incorporated *both* these contrasting dimensions into his sociology.

(4) Spencer believed the main determinant of whether a society would manifest a militant tendency was the extent to which a society was engaged in war (in this way he posited a positive relationship between the conduct of war and the emergence of totalitarianism); most other conflict theorists tend to locate relations of domination in features of the internal organization of society.

In these ways Spencer's work contains many of the ingredients of debate among theorists of society and its structures. I now turn to the work of a few other theorists who, in one respect or another, fall in the Spencerian tradition and can be compared and contrasted with him.

Durkheim. Durkheim is often contrasted with Spencer, largely because his first great work, *The Division of Labor in Society* (1969/1893) contained a very extended critique of Spencer, a critique mainly of his utilitarian assumptions that social integration can be realized through the unregulated interaction of independent parties. It is certainly true that Durkheim's sociology gave a much greater and more independent significance to the issue of integration than did Durkheim. At the same time, when it came to the analysis of social structures, Durkheim's early work bears some similarities of that of Spencer.

The first is the persistence of the biological analogy. In *The Division of Labor*, Durkheim compared the societies with a division of labor limited to that between the sexes and among persons of different ages. Durkheim termed this a *segmental society*, and noted that it contained structurally identical kinship units, which resemble the rings of an earthworm; if some of these units are removed, they can be replaced immediately by new and identical parts. By contrast, more complex societies develop more specialized structures, progressively both more unlike one another and more dependent on one another, and thus resemble more complex organisms.

The main basis for classifying societies and tracing their evolution has to do with their degree of complexity. Spencer spoke of the movement "from small groups to larger; from simple groups to compound groups; from compound groups to doubly compound ones." In this process, "the unlikeliness of parts increase" (Spencer, 1897, Book I, p. 471). Similarly, Durkheim (1958/1895) began with the simplest

society, the hypothetical horde, which "does not include . . . within itself any other more elementary aggregate" (p. 83), and then proceeds to more complex types, such as combination of hordes or clans, "polysegmental societies simply compounded," the city-state, and so on (p. 84). Furthermore, in his monograph on the division of labor, the general principle described is the increasing differentiation of labor, increasing unlikeness of parts, and greater individuation of persons.

In the end, furthermore, increasing complexity is adaptive. In Book II of *The Division of Labor*, Durkheim undertook to explain the augmentation of the division of labor on grounds that it was, in the end, a mechanism for greater effectiveness in the struggle for survival, and that it is traceable to the increasing "moral density" of society, to which Durkheim came ultimately very close to tracing to population pressure. While this formulation has been faulted as a poor explanatory device and not consistent with Durkheim's more complete theory of differentiation (Alexander, in press; Parsons, 1937), the logic of functional adaptiveness is found in Durkheim's formulation.

Radcliffe-Brown. Often regarded as the premier functionalist in anthropology (though he denied that the term should be applied to him), Radcliffe-Brown's essays stand in the center of that tradition. Like that of Spencer and Durkheim, his work embodies the biological analogy. His central theoretical position is encapsulated as follows: "The concept of function . . . involves the notion of *structure* consisting of a *set of relations* amongst unit entities, the *continuity* of the structure being maintained by a *life-process* made up of the *activities* of the constituent units" (Radcliffe-Brown, 1952, p. 191). Three distinctive observations should be made about this formulation.

First, Radcliffe-Brown stressed the totality of society as his point of reference. The first way in which the function of any recurrent activity is to be assessed, he noted, is "the part it plays in the social life as a whole" (1952, p. 180). This meant both guaranteeing both the unity and the continuity of the larger system. Radcliffe-Brown's stress led Merton (1968, pp. 79-80) to identify Radcliffe-Brown as the main exponent of "the postulate of functional unity." Perhaps because of this singular emphasis on integration, Radcliffe-Brown never developed an explicitly detailed list of the various functions a structure might serve.

Second, he stressed continuity in general. Acknowledging that major historical events such as revolutions and military conquests might involve a certain "relative suddenness" of change, he nevertheless maintained that "even in the most revolutionary changes some continuity of structure is maintained" (1952, p. 192). Such statements stand as the main polemical target of those who argue that the structural-functional approach has a "stability" or "conservative" bias.

Third, he observed limits to the biological analogy:

> In relation to organic structures we can find strictly objective criteria by which to distinguish disease from health, pathological from normal, for disease is that which either threatens the organism with death (the dissolution of its structure) or interferes with the activities that are characteristic of the organic type. Societies do not die in the same sense that animals die and therefore we cannot define dysnomia as that which leads, if unchecked, to the death of a society. Further, a society differs from an organism in that it can change its structural type, or can be absorbed as an integral part of a larger society. (Pp. 194).

Marx. Marx's appearance under this heading is in one sense anomalous, because in the literature he is consistently listed first as opposed to the kinds of emphases that appear in the structural-functional literature. This listing is in many respects correct, as we will see as we return to Marx from time to time in the exposition. However, one part of his theory can be seen as consistent in many respects with the conceptualization of structure that is now being presented.

The continuity is this: According to a consistent Marxist emphasis, the basis for all society is the productive forces organized by it—"the basis of all their history," in Marx's terms (1973/1846). The ultimate basis for this primacy must clearly be adaptive—as are the "sustenance" activities stressed by Spencer—for they are the first essential without which both individuals and human society cannot survive. Beyond these forces are the "social relations of production," which are the interactions (for example, through employment and property arrangements) into which people enter at a given level of the development of the forces of production. Together, these two structural elements make up the distinctive mode of production of a given society. In addition, Marx also referred to "legal and political superstructure" to "social, political and intellectual life process" as ingredients of society, suggesting a range of noneconomic institu-

tions as well. It is clear, moreover, that these ingredients of society bear a systematic relationship to one another. For one thing, the super-structural ingredients are derived from and consistent with the economic structure of society at the time; furthermore, the main societal function of the superstructural elements is to secure the continuity of the economic base, and to ease the necessarily developing contradictions that are evolving within it. The points of continuity with the functionalist emphasis are the notion of a differentiated structure, the notion of systematic relationships among the elements of the structure, and the idea that each element of the society "contributes" something to its functioning.

The points of discontinuity, however, are that the noneconomic structures are not viewed as vaguely cognate with the economic structures, but dependent upon them in the last analysis; and that the forces working toward maintaining the stability of the system (feudalism, capitalism, etc.) are, in the longer run, unable to do so, as they are overwhelmed by the contradictory forces within the system and subject to cataclysmic transformation into another type of system. And, as we will see, this "functionalist" ingredient in Marxian society is only a small piece of his theory of social structure and social processes.

Talcott Parsons. Parsons is regarded as the theorist who brought the structural-functional approach to its most developed form. His early statements (1954/1945) resemble those of Radcliffe-Brown as far as definition of structure is concerned: "a set of relatively stable patterned relationships of units" (p. 230). Even in these early formulations, however, a number of new elements were to be introduced. First, under the influence mainly of Malinowski, Parsons included the exigencies of both society and its individual members as functional categories. Second, he stressed the normative element of structure—namely, the presence of "patterned expectations defining the *proper* behavior of persons playing certain roles" (p. 231; italics in original). This is an important addition, looking in the direction of culture, values, and norms, that had been conspicuously absent in earlier statements; the reference to this level meant going beyond "sets of activities" or "sets of relationships," insofar as it suggested a principle—normative expectations—by which regularities are generated. Third, Parsons looked more in the psychological direction as well, arguing that the understanding of the processes that underlie the dynamics of structural behavior are psychological in character: "the basic dynamic categories of social systems are 'psychological.' "

> The relation of psychology to the theory of social systems appears to be closely analogous to that of biochemistry to general physiology. Just as the organism is not a category of general chemistry, so social system is not one of psychology. But within the framework of the physiological conception of what a functioning organism is, the *processes* are chemical in nature. Similarly, the *process* of social behavior as of any other are psychological [Parsons, 1954/1945, pp. 234-235].

If Parsons had added "group dynamics" to "psychological dynamics," he would have moved further theoretically than he did; for the dynamics of social structure and social change cannot be understood without reference to group processes as well.

Parsons spent much energy and thought in the decade following 1945 in ascertaining exactly what the "functions" to which socially structured activities are oriented. His 1945 version included three categories: (1) situational, or the "organization of roles about aspects of the situation in which actors and social systems are placed" (p. 323); he mentioned biological relatedness and kinship as well as territoriality in this context; (2) instrumental, or oriented toward the attainment of specific goal; the institution of medicine was mentioned as an example; (3) integrative, or institutions "oriented to regulating the relations of individuals as to avoid conflict or promote positive cooperative," institutions such as stratification and authority. This scheme for categorizing social structures (most often described as institutions by Parsons) evolved through a number of phases, including a major statement in *The Social System* (Parsons, 1951), but ultimately evolved into a statement in 1956, in *Economy and Society* (Parsons and Smelser, 1956), which changed little thereafter in Parsons's theoretical writings. This statement involved four functional exigencies around which structural specializations (institutions) clustered:

(1) *Latent pattern-maintenance and tension-management.* Any given social system is characterized by a dominant cultural system (values, cosmology, ideologies) that forms the basis for legitimizing the society's structural arrangements. The main institutions specializing in this function are the family, religion, education, and science on the "pattern-maintenance" side, and the family on the "tension-management" side, which refers to the working through of motiva-

tional tensions and ambivalences on the part of individuals in relation to commitment and conformity to the cultural patterns.

(2) *Goal-attainment.* Some structured activities cluster around the mobilization of society's resources to attain collective goals that are legitimized in the name of the cultural system. At the societal level Parsons referred to the "polity" in this connection, and the main institutional structures that are involved are government at all levels.

(3) *Adaptation.* One of the features of organized social life is that the goals of the society are not realized automatically, and that the society must come to terms with its external environment in order to facilitate the attainment of goals. At the societal level the primary adaptive system is the economy, with its industrial, commercial, and market arrangements.

(4) *Integration.* Another exigency facing the social system is its own internal organization, and the society has interest in minimizing conflict among individuals and groups in it, thereby maintaining a requisite level of internal stability. Legal and other conflict-mediating institutions are the clearest example of integrative structures.

One of the advantageous features of Parsons's scheme is that it is somewhat more systematically derived than most enumerations of functional needs or exigencies; that is to say, it is derived from a view of society as a system with internal and external environments, calling for both instrumental and consummatory (expressive) activities. Parsons and Smelser argued, furthermore, that the functional exigencies are to be conceived of as analytic categories, and that the matter of institutional specialization along these lines is a matter of primacy; all institutional arrangements must deal with all exigencies in one way or another, so that the notions of functional exigency and organized structures are not reducible to one another.

There are a number of analytic or methodological criticisms that have been or might be made of the accumulated structural-functional tradition.

First, there has never been agreement on a definitive list of functional needs or exigencies at the societal level. A number of lists have appeared, and there are certain constant features of all of them—economic or sustenance activities, socialization, maintenance of social order, for example—but both substantive and semantic difficulties in achieving such agreement persist.

Second, the "functions" or "functional exigencies" have always been presented as a set of invariant conditions facing society. At the same time, structural arrangements that have been established to deal with these conditions have always been recognized as variable. It is a reasonably well-established methodological canon that it is difficult to explain the variation in variable conditions (structures) by appealing to unvarying determinants (functions). As a result, the specified functions turn out to offer few guides for explaining comparative variations in structures, beyond identifying and describing these variations as fulfilling those functions.

Third, because many different structures (religion, family, for example) can fulfill the same function (integration), and because a single structure (industrial organization) can fulfill a number of different functions (production of goods and services, socialization through training, social control; Merton, 1968), it is difficult to assign functional primacy to any given structure or set of structures, and no definitive methodological rules have been established to avoid arbitrariness in this assignment.

A Final Example: Population Ecology. One of the approaches to organizational change discussed by Aldrich and Marsden in their chapter on environments and organizations in this volume goes under the heading of "population ecology" (Hannan and Freeman, 1977). According to this line of analysis, the fate of individual organizations (birth, transformation, death) is regarded as an interactive relationship between adaptive strategies of organizations on the one hand and the constraints (mainly in the form of resource opportunities) in the environment on the other. The analogy is frankly biological—specifically Darwinian—though the logic of economic competition in the market also informs the explanatory models employed. While this kind of analysis is seldom linked with the structural-functional models discussed in this section, the logic of accounting for structure in terms of adaptation and effectiveness of functioning bears some similarity to those models.

STRUCTURE AS ARISING FROM CONSENSUS ON SOCIETAL VALUES AND NORMS. Parsons is the primary exponent of this position, though as this chapter will indicate, Parsons as well as other theorists rely on a variety of explanations of structural regularities in society. Two examples from Parsons's work will illustrate the logic of the position.

A microexample is found in Parsons's writing on the structure of medical practice (1951). The doctor-patient relationship, an authority rela-

tionship, is based on shared expectations that, when sick, the patient will be exempted from role responsibilities such as work, that being "sick" is beyond the patient's control, and that the patient will be motivated to get "well" and will seek technically competent help. There is also consensus that the physician will be affectively neutral in his or her treatment of the patient, that the physician's interest will be specifically limited to the health of the patient, and the criteria for deciding on the patient's state of health or illness will be made on universalistic grounds, without reference to any other kind of relationship the physician might have with the patient. Above all, the physician and patient are committed to the common goal of working toward restoring the patient to a state of health. It is on the basis of these understandings and shared values and norms that the patient will subordinate himself or herself to the physician's treatment and that the physician will conduct himself or herself in a properly professional manner. What is explained by this reasoning is the social structure (role relationships) of medical practice.

A macro-example is found in Parsons' last exposition of his theory of stratification (1954). The basic postulate is that a stratification system, in its valuational aspect, is "the ranking of units in a social system in accordance with the common value system" (1954, p. 388), though any empirical ranking system will deviate from this ideal ranking because of the differential power and resources that enable individuals to protect and enhance their status in society. Parsons classifies what he calls "paramount value systems" according to the importance they place on one or another of the functional exigencies outlined above: adaptation (technical efficiency); commitment to collective goals; system-integrative; and qualitative-ascriptive. In characterizing the American value system in particular, Parsons stressed the society's commitment to "universalistic-performance values" as the key to its paramount value system; presumably the major determinant in ranking social positions in society would be the degree to which they exemplify these values. In other societies, for example, Great Britain, the ranking of values would presumably be different, with hierarchy and system integration having a more prominent place. Parsons qualified his major position in a variety of ways, pointing out that other kinds of values found their place in any society's ranking system; nevertheless a primary part of the explanation of the structure of any societal stratification system rests on the assumption of a commonly held paramount value system.

Insofar as a theory traces structural regularities to commonly held values and norms, it is evident that one of the main *mechanisms* in establishing motivation to behave in accordance with these values and norms is internalization of them through a process of socialization (Parsons, 1951, p. 205). In his most elaborate statement of this position (Parsons, 1955), Parsons treated the development of the personality system as such as a progressive series of internalization of relevant social objects (parents, siblings, peers, etc.), and the role expectations associated with them.

STRUCTURE AS ARISING FROM DOMINATION AND COERCION. The theoretical positions of Hobbes, Freud, Marx, Dahrendorf, and representatives of the critical school can be subsumed under this tradition, though the paths they traversed in arriving at this explanation of social structure are very diverse.

Hobbes and Freud. Hobbes's theory of the state is a macroscopic theory in that it deals directly with the nature of large-scale political institutions. Yet the path by which he arrives at his theory of the state is from microscopic origins, namely a theory of human nature. This theory is simultaneously individualistic and pessimistic. It is individualistic because it does not conceive of any natural or prior basis for organized society; rather, it regards human life as a collection of individuals. It is pessimistic in that Hobbes regards these individuals as vain, self-seeking, inhumane, and anarchistic, to the effect that if individuals only are taken into account, human society is impossible. Hobbes resolved this problem by postulating further that by virtue of the destructive character of humans, all live in dread fear of their own destruction, and will subordinate themselves to an absolute, repressive state; thus the theoretical closure that was reached by Hobbes is found in his consistent argument that only something as radical and strong as political repression can control individual passions; it is the only way that society is possible.

Ferrarotti (in press) has vigorously criticized the Hobbesian dualism, and has cited writers as diverse as Adam Ferguson and Antonio Gramsci as muting Hobbes's view and opening up the possibility of civil society, not simply repression. Ferguson, for example, though not denying self-interest, argued that this could be muted by human involvements in conventions and traditions such as morals and laws as well as the power of social relations and mutual affection. The family in particular caught Fergu-

son's attention as an institution that cements human bonds and civilizes people. Gramsci, though taking a very different theoretical line, also identified certain mobilizing capacities of groups, that engaged individuals in constant political activity (thus renewing the state and preventing its absolutization). This stress on intermediate institutions might also be found in Tocqueville, who identified in the United States a number of laws and customs that protected society from despotism. Among the laws, he identified the principle of federal union, the institutionalization of townships (which could resist central authority), and the judicial system; among the customs, he stressed the presence of a common religion that encouraged liberty, the separation of church and state, a common language, and a high level of education. He also regarded the freedom of the press and the presence of voluntary associations as important mechanisms to forestall the development of despotism. The work of modern political theorists of civic culture (Almond and Verba, 1963), provides moderating influences on the state through political participation in voluntary associations, in a sense of political competence, and in the substitution of legitimate acceptance of the state instead of cynical submission.

To place Freud in this context perhaps appears odd, since Freud was first of all a psychologist, not a theorist of the state and society primarily. On the other hand, Freud also fashioned a view of the individual and society itself, particularly in his later writings, and some of his formulations are formally comparable with those of Hobbes. In particular, in his characterization of the id and superego, and the relations between them (which predated his official recognition of the ego), his formulations bear a striking resemblance to those of Hobbes, though at an intrapsychic rather than a sociopolitical level. The id was represented as a cauldron of instinctual representations, seeking only gratification and knowing no morality, and, if left to itself, uncontrollable. (The parallels with Hobbes's theory of human nature are evident; Hobbes's psychology can be regarded, looking backward, as a psychology of the id, which only external repression by political authorities can check.) Standing in sharp opposition to the id impulses is the superego, the ultimate function of which is to engage in a kind of surveillance operation, by which the conscience was maintained, high moral ideals held out, and impulses repressed. The superego, especially in its early formulations, was held by Freud to be as moral, strident, and punitive as the impulses were incessant and amoral. Such is the Hobbesian kind of dualism between anarchy and control that is to be found in Freud.

Subsequently, however, when Freud "discovered" and elaborated the ego as the third great establishment of the personality (around 1923), he introduced a principle of interposition and intermediation between the id, the superego, and external reality, thereby introducing into his conception of personality a principle that is functionally parallel to Ferguson's notion of institutions or civil society. That is to say, the ego was now endowed with a variety of mechanisms of defense (rather than repression) that permitted the diversion and disguised expression and gratification of instinctual demands, especially through sublimation. The introduction of the ego, in short, marked a more benign and optimistic turn in Freud's psychology, and broke through the pessimistic dualism of the impulse-repression model of the mind.

In his writings on society and civilization, however, Freud never really developed any functional equivalent of the ego, and therefore remained fundamentally Hobbesian in his formulation. In discussing the phenomenon of leadership in the group (1955/1921), he identified this phenomenon as a shared regression on the part of the followers and the introjection of the leader as their ego-ideal (superego). All members of the group are desirous of the leader's love and envy one another for that love. Since all cannot possibly gain the leader's exclusive love, however, they renounce their selfish desires and believe that the leader does love all of them equally. "No one must want to put himself forward, every one must be the same and have the same" (1955/1921, p. 120). The final result of this phenomenon is that everyone is equal except the leader, who is superior in equal degree to all the others—or, in more Hobbesian terms, the renunciation of individualistic selfishness and destructiveness through subordination to an absolute leader.

Later (1930) the Hobbesian dualism reappears, as Freud developed his notion of civilization. The main theme of *Civilization and Its Discontents* is, in the words of a subsequent editor, "the irremediable antagonism between the demands of instinct and the restrictions of civilization" (Strachey, in Freud, 1961/1930, p. 60). Freud wrote, "it is impossible to overlook the extent to which civilization is built upon a renunciation of instinct, how much it presupposes the non-satisfaction [by suppression, repression, or some other means] of powerful instincts" (1961/1930, p. 97). While in the same era Freud was developing a notion of ego

at the level of personality, he did not significantly formulate a social analogue, which would have been institutions or social organization as intervening between the irreconcilable antagonism between instinctual gratification and civilization. For, indeed, while institutions such as the law and the family have their repressive side, they mediate the gratifications of instinctual forces as well. The law, particularly in its civil aspects, is a mediator of conflict and interpersonal aggression, and mutes it through judicial procedures, which determine whose aggression is legitimate; the institutions of marriage and prostitution are both contrived, in part, to permit and channel sexual gratifications. Tournaments, athletic contests, ritual rebellions (and even war) are contrived, in part, to permit the expression of aggressive impulses. If Freud had developed some notion of institutions and organizations (social structure), in short, he would have moved in the direction of Ferguson's (and others') principle of society's mediation of both selfishness and domination.

Marx. Marx's theory of social structure and society also rests on a theory of human nature, but a very different one from Hobbes or Freud. Correspondingly, he took a very different theoretical journey in arriving at his view of that structure even though, in the end, the view is one of society based on the principles of domination and coercion. The starting point is, of course, materialist: the assumption that the foundations of all human society are based on the way in which that society has developed its relation to its mode of material production:

> Assume a particular state of development in the productive forces of man and you will get a particular form of commerce and consumption. Assume particular stages of development in production, commerce, and consumption and you will have a corresponding social order, a corresponding organization of the family and of the ranks and classes, in a word a corresponding civil society. Presuppose a particular civil society and you will get particular political conditions that are only the official expression of civil society [1973/1846, p. 3].

This particular starting point was elaborated with a further series of assumptions about human nature and society. The first was that in any confrontation with material nature, people will develop a certain division of labor, control of property, and social groupings (classes) around these social relations of production. Marx assumed further that these divisions will have an ingredient of domination (with those in control of the particular form of property characterizing a given historical period being dominant over those not in control). Finally, he assumed that people in these classes stand in necessary antagonism to other classes, and that—in the long run at least—these antagonisms will constitute their "interests" as classes, and they would behave in accordance with those interests.

The core feature of social structure, then, for Marx, is the relations of domination and subordination among classes that evolve ultimately from the mode of production of society. Several elaborations of this basic notion of economic and class structure must be made. First, note should be made that Marx supplemented this essentially dualistic view with the notion that certain arrangements and classes survive from an earlier era (in capitalism, for example, the aristocracy and peasant classes), and that the main classes are subject to certain internal differentiation (petty bourgeoisie, lumpenproletariat in capitalism, for example). All this complicates class relations in any given era.

Second, Marx took note of and analyzed various characteristics of the "superstructure," a range of political institutions (including the state and "civil society"), legal institutions, and the family, as well as cultural systems such as religion and philosophy. In principle, then, he took cognizance of that very range of institutions that Ferguson and others had interpreted as exercising a benign influence on pressures toward despotism in society. Yet in his interpretation he turned their significance around. He posited that this range of institutions fundamentally buttressed and strengthened the core structure of domination in the larger society. It must also be pointed out that in the writing of Marx and Engels there is a certain ambiguity as to how immediate and complete is the subordination of the superstructure to the production system of a society or, to put it differently, to what degree the kinds of institutions (particularly the state) can assume an autonomy of their own and possibly work at cross-purposes with the dominant economic classes. In fact, it might be argued that many of the really fundamental debates within and about Marxist sociology during the past century have had to do with this issue, the degree of economic dominance over the political, cultural, and other aspects of institutional life.

Third, this account of the main contours of social structure in Marx's thought is incomplete. For all past and present societies, the structural relations—for all the efforts on the part of dominant groups to maintain them—are basically unstable and ultimately give way to their own change and destruction by political and social revolution. The dynamics of this are found in the dynamics of exploitation, contradiction, and the class and political mobilization of the subordinated groups in society.

And, finally, it is evident that Marx's theory of structure is simultaneously both a theory of relations among different economic and other institutional activities and a theory of relations among groups. This makes Marx's theory more complex and more simple than many others: more complex because many theories give primacy to only one or the other perspective, and more simple because Marx posits a more or less direct parallelism between the relational structures (mainly the system of production) and the groups (classes) that are precipitated from them.

Dahrendorf. Dahrendorf's major theoretical statement of the late 1950s (1959/1957) was a polemic directed at two of the approaches already reviewed—that of Talcott Parsons (integration theory) and that of the Marxian tradition (coercion theory), one stressing "social structure in terms of a functionally integrated system held in equilibrium by certain patterned and recurrent processes," and one viewing "social structure as a form of organization held together by force and constraint and reaching continuously beyond itself in the sense of producing within itself the forces that maintain it in an unending process of change" (1959/1957, p. 159). And while Dahrendorf described himself as treading a supplementary and synthesizing path between these two versions of theory, his view of the "integrative tradition" was mainly a negative one—including few of its ingredients into his positive theory—and his main innovation appears to be within the coercive tradition.

Dahrendorf's positive theory began with a critical question about Marx: "Is property for Marx a special case of authority—or, vice versa, authority a special case of property?" (1959, p. 21). Marx would clearly argue the latter, but Dahrendorf took the former interpretation, thereby deserting, in large part, the materialist basis of Marxian theory and substituting a political basis for his own. Accordingly, the main question for Dahrendorf was whether people stand in a superordinate-subordinate authority relationship to one another, and that is a critical issue, no matter in what organizational context (economic, political, military, or administrative). While rejecting the specific formulations of Marx and trying to make Marx's formulations a special case of inequalities in authority, Dahrendorf nevertheless accepted the Marxian assumptions that authority differentials are "a structural determinant of conflict groups" and, more strongly, that "the distribution of authority in associations is the ultimate 'cause' of the formation of conflict groups" and that such conflicts are inevitably polarized or "dichotomous," involving two groups, the haves and have-nots in authority relationships (1959: pp. 172–73).

Like Marx, Dahrendorf also included a theory of group structure along with his structure of (authority) relations. Relational structures are the determinants of conflict groups, as in Marx, but Dahrendorf presented a somewhat more flexible account of these relations. There are latent group interests, predetermined by structural position but having no relationship to "conscious orientations." Contrasting to these are "manifest interests," which have a conscious or psychological dimension and "constitute a formulation of the issues of structurally generated group conflicts" (1959, p. 178). (Dahrendorf explicitly refers to manifest interests as being parallel to the Marxian notion of class-consciousness.) Running parallel to this distinction is that between quasi groups and "interest groups," the former being categories of persons in a structure with potential group interests, whereas the latter possess group qualities of membership, a feeling of belongingness, and a sense of purpose; they are recruited from quasi-groups, and they are the "real agents of group conflict" (1959, p. 180).

Both Marx and Dahrendorf regarded the transition from latent (false-conscious) groups to manifest "conscious" groups as inevitable, but also as subject to certain conditions. Marx mentioned the degree of homogeneity of labor and their degree of concentration in urban and factory settings as facilitating factors; but Dahrendorf's qualifications are stronger. He mentioned technical conditions of organization, citing the need for leadership and an articulated ideology; political conditions of organization, which refer mainly to the degree of permissiveness in the political environment for them to organize; social conditions of organization, which refer mainly to the degree of permissiveness in the political environment that allows them to organize; social conditions of organization, or the capacity of members of a conflict group to communicate and interact with one another; and diverse psychological conditions. In citing these conditions, Dahrendorf loosened the broader picture of a dichotomous, locked-in-conflict view of social structure, and introduced a number of features that intensify or soften the coercion-conflict model of social structure.

CRITICAL THEORISTS. Critical theory is subject to as many internal variations and nuances as any other theoretical tradition, so in the context of this essay I will give only two illustrative observations on the character of structure in capitalist (or perhaps postindustrial) society. These are the observations on Marcuse and Habermas.

Marcuse. In its most important aspect, the work of Herbert Marcuse (1964, especially) is an effort to maintain the essential domination model of society generated by Marx, but to rewrite and extend it to take into account fundamental changes that mark the differences between early and advanced industrial society. The basic continuity with Marx is the stress on the economic dimension: "[even] the most highly organized capitalism retains the social need for private appropriation and distribution of profit as the regulator of the economy . . . it continues to link the realization of the general interest to that of particular vested interests" (1964, p. 53).

The discontinuity with Marx arises in connection with the mode that domination takes. The principal characteristics of advanced industrial society, by Marcuse's account, are an enormous growth in labor productivity through technological advance, the rise in the birth rate of the population, the permanent defense economy, and the economic-political integration of the capitalist countries and their domination of the underdeveloped areas. The impact of these changes is that the satisfaction of the real needs of the population—"nourishment, clothing, lodging at the attainable level of culture"— are now capable of being met, so that the struggle in society is not at the material level. In fact, Marcuse found little overt conflict at all: "Under the conditions of a rising standard of living, non-conformity with the system itself appears to be socially useless, and the more so when it entails tangible economic and political disadvantages and threatens the smooth operation of the whole" (1964, p. 2).

But at the same time the vast majority of the population is dominated—indeed, enslaved—by the system. The main mechanism is technological and administrative manipulation of the needs of the population, partially through the sustaining power of technical culture and language, which is disseminated largely through the mass media. Marcuse regards as false needs "most of the prevailing needs to relax, to behave and consume in accordance with the advertisements, to love and hate what others love and hate" (1964, p. 5). A kind of false consciousness appears to be nearly universal, as people come to "recognize themselves in their commodities." There also exists, however, an additional category of persons outside the system—the poor, the unemployed, persecuted people of color, and inmates—which constitutes a kind of lumpenproletariat, a truly revolutionary class that defies the rules of the system, but Marcuse regarded these groups as repressed by the police arm of the state.

Under these circumstances political conflict becomes subdued. Marcuse pointed in particular to the collusion and alliance between business and organized labor, between conservative parties and working-class parties in political orientation. The most fundamental basis for conflict in Marx's account disappears. The fundamental principles of democracy—economic freedom, political freedom, intellectual freedom, and tolerance—continue to exist, but they are systematically undermined because they are no longer grow increasingly meaningless because of the technological-administrative-media apparatus that prevents their realization. Indeed, Marcuse went so far as to maintain that "democracy would appear to be the most efficient system of domination" (1964, p. 2). The political domination, moreover, is the more insidious because it is depersonalized. The technological transformation "alters the base of domination by gradually replacing personal dependence (of the slave on the master, the serf on the lord of the manor, the lord on the donor of the fief, etc.) with dependence on the 'objective order of things' (on economic laws, the market, etc.)" (1964, p. 144).

This model of domination is no doubt among the most extreme to be encountered because of the pervasiveness of the forces identified by Marcuse, as well as among the most pessimistic with respect to alternatives. The only hope held out is the stubborn defiance of the underclass outside the system, which may be a fact "that marks the beginning of the end of a period" (1964, p. 257). The critical reader may wonder, however, about the viability of a theory that rests its case almost entirely on the operation of forces scarcely visible to any members of the society, and whose characterization of a society's state of affairs is so at odds with that experienced by its population. Within his particular view of the pervasiveness if not the visibility of near-universal domination, however, Marcuse becomes able to regard phenomena that would, on the face of it, be disconfirming data—for example, the continued institutionalization of various kinds of freedom—and read them as confirming data.

Habermas. The work of Jurgen Habermas is an extraordinary complex corpus, and draws on such a diversity of traditions—Marxist, psychoanalytic, phenomenological, critical—that it defies adequate summary as a whole. In this essay I draw out only a few themes relating to Habermas's characterization of social structure.

Habermas, like Marcuse, shows a basic continuity with the Marxian mode of analysis in that he regards all societies from traditional through postcapitalist as "class societies" in their basic organization. Each of these types of societies has their distinctive principles of class organization, but for postcapitalist society the principles of class organization have evolved away from the capitalist mode analyzed by Marx in several important respects: (1) the separation of state and society, which characterized liberal capitalism, has been superseded by a remerger between the two; (2) the standard of living has risen sufficiently so that emancipation is no longer primarily an economic matter; and (3) the role of proletariat as the special agent of class revolution has been dissolved and class consciousness is not to be found in that particular group (Habermas, 1973, pp. 195-197).

With respect to the mode of domination, Habermas argues, again contrary to Marx, that in postcapitalist societies "the political system . . . assumes a superordinate position vis-a-vis the socio-cultural and economic systems" (1975, p. 5). He represented the special relationship among the three systems schematically as follows:

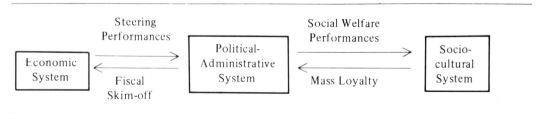

The state exists on the surplus generated by the economic system, but has involved itself deeply in the organization and manipulation of the economy through regulation and intervention—these are what Habermas refers to as "steering performances." In addition, the state directly enters the economy, in, for example, the provision of educational services and training programs, direct supervision of maintaining and constructing a material infrastructure (transportation, housing construction, etc.), and organizing arms races and space exploration. As for the populace (the sociocultural system), the state gains its loyalty (sometimes passive) by assuring the flow of consumer goods in its direction, by providing cushions against crisis through the provision of welfare, and through ultimate control of the mass media.

Of special salience in Habermas's work is the notion of the administrative system of state-economy. The dominant mode of coordination and control by that apparatus is to rely on instrumental-technical mastery, of the adaptation of knowledge to the pursuit of policy and other state and economic ends. In this regard, Habermas interprets positive science as one of the major instruments of control and domination in postcapitalist society. Sociology, in particular, with its reifications and its treatment of community and society as objective, "to a growing degree, is becoming an applied science in the service of administration. The technical translation of research results is not applied to analytic schemata, but instead to a social reality which has already been schematized" (1973, p. 208). These kinds of developments have led to a situation in modern Western societies that promotes "a distorted understanding of rationality that is fixed on cognitive-instrumental aspects and is to that extent particularistic" (1984, p. 66), and inhibits the development of alternative forms of rational discourse. Much of the dominating impulse is thus manifested in a "cultural" (i.e., scientific-technical) form.

Habermas's account of the social structure of advanced capitalist societies, then, bears some resemblance to that of Marcuse, in the sense that the principal model is one of domination, that the mode of domination is a mix of state-administrative and cultural, and that the instrumental-technological mode is one key ingredient in the pattern. Their precise formulations, however, differ considerably. The really major difference appears in their diagnoses for the prospects of breakdown and change. Marcuse's diagnosis is pessimistic in the extreme, holding out only a glimmer of hope for the disruptive potential of the outsiders and outcasts of the system. Habermas, by contrast, identified a range of crises that stand as a continuous threat to the stability of the advanced capitalist system. In particular, he identified (1) economic crises, such as inflation, financial breakdowns, and failures of productivity; (2) rationality crises, such as failures in planning and administrative paralysis and error in the face of multiple demands from multiple constituencies; (3) legitimation crises, such as the failure of the state-administrative to deliver on its promises, and its failure to manipulate the loyalties of the subordinate classes; and (4) motivation crises, or the erosion of values such as individualism and achievement, which are necessary for commitment to the working of advanced capitalist society. Any or all of these crises can lead to serious breakdowns in the system.

At another level, Habermas holds out hope for another kind of rationality in society, which he calls "communicative rationality." While this concept appears to have a residue of ambiguity, he defines it formally as

> the central experience of the unconstrained, unifying, consensus-bringing force of argumentative speech, in which different participants overcome their merely subjective views and, owing to the mutuality of rationally motivated conviction, assure themselves of both the unity of the objective world and the intersubjectivity of their lifeworld [1984, p. 10].

The "rationality" here appears to be the process of building consensus out of the free, undistorted communication of individuals, in which the claim to validity is not cognitive-rational, but in the giving of reasons, normative justifications, and ultimate validity to experience. The kind of social structure that emerges from communicative action is a kind of free community—free from the distortions of the cognitive/rational mentality—an emancipated community based on consensus and reason, a community capable of concerted group action and capable of breaking down the irrationalities of challenging and breaking down the repressive administrative/rational system of domination.

In the end, then, Habermas appears to have two theories of structure in his work, one a macro theory of domination based on the cognitive/instrumental rationality, the other a micro theory of cooperation, consensus, and normative regulation based on a rationality of free communicative communities that appears to be the mechanism that can undermine that distortion and make for a freer, unrepressive society.

Some Microscopic Conceptualizations of Structure

Earlier in the essay I identified two examples of macroscopic theories of social domination and coercion (Hobbes and Freud) that, however, rested ultimately on specifically individualist views of human nature, thereby qualifying them as partially microscopic in emphasis. Now I turn to a series of explicitly microscopic in formulation. To include these representations in a chapter on "social structure" may seem anomalous, because they sometimes take an assault on social-structural analysis as their main negative polemic, and insist that the most fundamental social reality lies at the microinteractional level. Reading these works, however, reveals that they, too, often contain an explicit or implicit transition to more macroscopic levels, and for that reason have something to say about the major sociological topic of this essay.

SOCIAL STRUCTURE AS ARISING FROM AG-GREGATED EFFECTS OF INDIVIDUAL INTERAC-TIONS. For a number of social theorists, the starting point of theorizing is the ways in which individuals interact with one another, and in this line of theory, the movement to the macro level is of two sorts: (1) aggregating the in-dividual interactions, and (2) making certain special assumptions about the larger structural environment in which they interact. To illustrate this approach, three bodies of thinking are chosen: classical economic analysis, modern ex-change theory, and contemporary network theory.

Classical Economics. The starting point of classical economics is the interactions between individual sellers of resources, products, and ser-vices, who, because of a certain differentiation of roles and interests, are assumed to be inter-ested in what the other has to offer in exchange. So the initial interest is clearly microscopic in character. To supplement this kind of starting point, classical economics rested on a series of psychological postulates that defined the reasons for and conditions governing that mutual in-terest. The first assumption is a materialist one, resting in the classical utilitarian tradition, that individual actors will behave so as to maximize their material well-being (utility) in economic transactions. It is further assumed that actors know about the availability of products, prices to be paid, opportunities for jobs, and so on, as well as about the nature of their own tastes. These assumptions unite in a further assump-tion that individuals will behave rationally—in relation to their own interests and in full knowledge of their circumstances.

Certain other assumptions are made about the institutional order within which transactions take place: It is assumed that transactions will take place in a peaceful setting, and that the main form of exchange will be exchanges of goods and services for money, not as a result of coercion or theft; a supply of money is assumed; a certain kind of property system is assumed (use, control, and disposal of one's own labor and one's own products); and, finally, it is assumed that no producer or consumer is able to influence output or prices (an assumption later to be challenged by theorists of imperfect competition).

These assumptions made, the transition from the microscopic world of thousands of individual exchanges is basically an act of aggregation. On the basis of these interactions, and the solutions to thousands of supply-demand intersections, it is possible to arrive at certain solutions at the macro level of the allocation of resources and the distribution of shares of income, as well as the structure of production and the structure of the market. The basic stability at the macro-institutional level was usually solved by some kind of "natural identity of interests" or "in-visible hand" so that by the rational exchange of interested individuals, equilibrium of the market would be assured.

Social Behaviorism and Exchange. In his later (1974/1961) work, Homans established a co-herent perspective commonly referred to as social behaviorism. This tradition drew from the classical economic tradition in that it incor-porated such familiar conceptions as maximiza-tion of utility, diminishing marginal utility, and rationality of behavior. Equally if not more im-portant, it built on the behaviorist tradition in psychology, which is based on the premise that scientific findings will be based on objective measures of objectively discernible influences from the external environment on the person (stimuli), and on objective measures of objec-tively discernible items of behavior (responses), and that stimuli and responses stand in lawful association with one another. Homans himself built his system on a number of propositions, for example, the more often an action is reward-ed, the more likely the person is to perform that act; a reinforcement principle; a frustration-aggression principle, and so on. I would like to explore the implications of this perspective with respect to both the structure of the person and social structure.

One of the central propositions put forward by Homans, the value proposition, states that the more valuable the result of an action is to an individual, the more likely he or she is to perform the action. The key term is, of course, *valuable*. Valuable for what? The term calls out for a specification of values held by the individual or needs on his or her part demanding satisfaction, or some other statement of criteria of what makes an action valuable for a person. (Classical and neoclassical economists attempted to solve this issue formally by positing "tastes" and sometimes representing them formally, but Homans made no such effort.) No kind of "inner" criterion is found in Homan's formulations, which is not surprising since it stands squarely in that positivist-behaviorist tradition that shuns the elusive internals such as motivation and seeks the measurable externals of behavior. "Valuable" thus reduces to a simple valence, positive or negative: Is the individual rewarded, or is he or she punished? This is an externally determined phenomenon. The behavior and its results are removed from any individual strivings and, therefore by definition, from any kind of structured organization of those strivings. The main "structure" that appears to be involved appears to be the regular and repeated association among stimuli and responses that express some kind of relational process linking the individual person with his or her situation.

Much the same can be said with respect to social structure. Homans himself simply asserted that he was not interested in "characteristics of communities . . . or organizations," or in the contents of norms or authority relationships (1974, p. 2)—all of which are the typical ways in which the external environment is structured to make for nonrandom and systematic influences on the individual. Rather, Homans focuses only on the "elementary forms" of behavior within these environments, and in the end those forms come down to whether the stimuli emanating from them are rewarding or punishing to the individual, again without regard to context.

It is possible to find only two hints about structure in Homans's work, and both these are weak in character. The first hint is to be found in his first two propositions, which, if taken together, indicate that behavior is likely to be repeated if it is consistently rewarded, and that similar stimuli will evoke similar kinds of behavior if the stimuli are rewarding. These propositions establish the ingredient of "regularity" or "repetition" that I identified earlier as a generic feature of structure, but that ingredient stands virtually alone because it has no particular status as an established apparatus (it would be altered or vanish if the character of the stimuli changes) and it is not represented as standing in relationship to any other kind of behavior above and beyond the stimulus. The "repetition" principle is further qualified by Homans's "deprivation-satiation" or diminishing marginal utility proposition, which states that the more often a person has received a certain reward in the recent past, the less valuable it becomes (and, by extension, the less likely to evoke repetitive behavior in its presence). Even taking this qualification into account, however, the item of behavior is related to no other contextual element than the stimulus itself.

The second hint emerges in Homans's discussion of exchange. When the stimulus-emitting object is another person, and when conditions prevail such that the behavior of that person is rewarding to the subject, and the behavior of that subject is rewarding to that person, then the conditions are set for a continuous and nonrandom relationship (exchange) between the two persons, since both are experiencing the "value-proposition" along positive, rewarding lines, and so neither party has reason to quit the exchange. The result is a relationship, a little bit of structure. The same principle can be generalized to other relations, such as authority. But in all cases this bit of structure is on the fleeting side because of its tendency to vanish if the mutual rewarding ceases.

The two main lines of criticism of Homans that have arisen add up to messages that his theory ignores structure. On the one hand, it is asserted that the associative relations between stimuli and responses are not as automatic as Homans posits, but that there is an intervening process whereby values, personal tastes, meanings, and inhibitions complicate the picture of simple responses to simple stimuli on the basis of simple reward and punishment. The second line of criticism is that within the social-behaviorist perspective, it is difficult to make the transition—including through aggregation —to the workings of social structure, and that, if such a transition is attempted, the reward-punishment scheme would make only a very limited contribution to the understanding of the persistence and change of social structures.

Network Analysis: Structure Within Structure. It is difficult to know where to place this discussion of network analysis—sometimes also referred to as "structural theory" (Burt, 1982) —because its focus is so different, as we shall see, from virtually all the other approaches to structure discussed in this chapter. Certainly it is not entirely "microscopic" in character, though one of its exponents (Granovetter, 1976) has indicated that that has been its main focus. Certainly it is not in the same camp as social exchange or social behaviorism, though it does qualify as involving "aggregated effects of individual interactions." Despite these pigeonholing difficulties, it seems essential to include a mention of the approach, precisely because it does provide a unique perspective in social structure.

Most of the theorists discussed in this volume explicitly or implicitly regard structure as that set of relationships arising from differentiated positions according to age, sex, kinship, functional specialization, class membership, ethnic membership, and so on. Structure thus defined emerges as a set of relations among different role incumbents or institutions on the one hand, or social groups on the other. This dominant conception of structure has a certain formality or perhaps even bloodlessness about it, precisely because it focuses on relations among structured activities and positions. Furthermore, most of the theorists discussed in this chapter made an effort to give an account of the reasons or causes involved in the structuring of social relations and society.

Network analysts, by contrast, generally take the system of structured positions in society as a starting point for study, and move on from there to see what kinds of structural relations among individuals actually develop in the larger context. Or, in the words of Peter Blau (1977, p. xx),

> The structure of societies and communities are delineated by parameters. Structural parameters are the axes in the multidimensional space of social positions among which population is distributed. They are attributes of people that underlie the distinctions they themselves generally make in their social relations, such as age, race, education, and socioeconomic status. . . . In short, a parameter is a variable that characterizes individuals and differentiates their relations and social positions.

This statement is a bit difficult to decipher, because the notion of "parameter" normally connotes an unvarying contextual condition that, if varied, would make a great deal of difference, but not as a "variable." This ambiguity aside, it seems fair to interpret Blau's words as implying that social structure, as generally defined in this chapter, is taken as a given.

Network analysts, as a general rule, appear to take the larger, more formal structure of society for granted, and ask what kind of interactional relations among individuals (or groups or organizations) arise within that structure. For example, in a classic study often regarded as a forerunner of network analysis, Roethlisberger and Dickson studied the emergence of friendship and clique relations within a setting of formal work relations (management, foremen, workers), and analyzed further the impact of these informal relationships on worker performance within that setting. Sometimes the formal structure is an important determinant in shaping the actual patterns of observed interactions; for example, cliques and friendship grouping in an industrial plant will develop among managers and among workers, but membership in these cliques seldom crosses over the management-worker line. Similarly, ethnic group membership strongly conditions individuals' interaction patterns.

Network analysis, then, takes as its starting point the actually observable patterns of interaction among individuals and groups. The content of the relations described "may be any kind of socially meaningful tie" (Leinhardt, 1977, p. xiii), such as friendship, advice seeking, providing assistance, influencing, or dominating. The principal interest of the student of networks is to determine "how the relations are arranged, how the behavior of individuals depends on their location in this arrangement, and how the qualities of the individuals influence the arrangement" (Leinhardt, 1977, p. xiii). Numerous typologies of networks have been put forward (e.g., Burt, 1982), and many types of relations (strong, weak, simple, multiplex) have been identified. But the key difference between "social structure" as used by network theorists and most other conceptions of social structure is that network analysts regard structure as empirically discovered regularities of interaction of various types—regularities that are taken as they exist, not regarded as rooted in some more general theory of the individual and society— and regularities that constitute an independent variable in explaining individual behavior and beliefs, as well as larger social processes.

SOCIAL STRUCTURE AS EMERGING FROM THE NOTION OF MEANINGFUL INTERACTION: WEBER. The work of Max Weber is a convenient starting point for this discussion, for clearly his theoretical starting points foreshadow more contemporary variants of the phenomenological tradition.

Weber's definitions of action and social action are clearly phenomenological in origin, since they link action to subjective meaning that the actor endows to his or her own behavior. Action is defined as such "insofar as the acting individual attaches a subject meaning to his behavior—be it overt or covert, omission or acquiescence." Action is "social" insofar as "its subjective meaning takes account of the behavior of others and is thereby oriented in its course" (1968, Book I, p. 4). This starting point led Weber to view sociocultural phenomena in a different light than it is possible to view the phenomena that are the subject matter of the natural sciences, and to dedicate a considerable amount of his methodological discussion to fathoming the ways in which these "intellectual and psychological" phenomena can be sensitively and accurately grasped through the process of *Verstehen*, or sympathetic understanding (1968, I, pp. 5-12). Even "objective" statistical series, such as crime statistics, cannot be understood only as they are taken as "manifestations of the understandable subjective meaning of a course of social action" (1968, I, p. 12).

From the standpoint of the main questions of this essay—what is the nature of social structure, what are its origins, and how is it sustained?—Weber's starting point is not a particularly auspicious one, because of its individualistic cast. It is difficult to conceive of individual actors' subjective meaning systems as other than idiosyncratic in crucial respects, and therefore not comparable with one another. How, it must be asked, can we make the transition to the notion of commonly understood social structures, to say nothing of arriving at general statements with respect to the relations of these structures to one another?

Weber's methodological solution to this issue lies in his reliance on the notion of the ideal type, which permits, at least in principle, those transitions from subjectivity of meaning to general statements. The ideal was characterized as a kind of construct or device generated in the mind of the investigator, but at the same time having a basis in the empirical world. Weber's formal definition of an ideal type is that it is "formed by the one-sided *accentuation* of one or more points of view and by the synthesis of a great many diffuse, discrete, more or less present and occasionally absent *concrete individual phenomena*, which are arranged according to those one-sidedly emphasized viewpoints into a unified *analytical* construct" (1969/1904, p. 90). Concrete examples of ideal types, as employed by Weber, are the major world religions and their internal variations, types of authority, bureaucracy, rational bourgeois capitalism. According to Weber's account, the ideal type

facilitated the comparison and measurement of reality, and permitted the investigator to arrive at general analyses of historical phenomena and their connections.

While Weber's particular version of the ideal type has been criticized on grounds that the rules for arriving at them were not adequately specified—that for that reason there is likely to be an element of arbitrariness in constructing them—and that they appear to be scattered over many different levels of generality (Smelser, 1976), it nevertheless remains the case that they constitute an avenue for moving from an extreme subjectivism to the analysis of social and cultural structures. I will now take three modern exemplifications of the phenomenological perspective, and attempt to assess how they responded to the same issue.

Symbolic Interactionism: Structure Rejected. In introducing his methodological account of symbolic interactionism, Blumer (1969) put forth a quadruple negative polemic—what symbolic interactionism is not—all facets of which are anti-structural in character:

(1) Human behavior cannot be regarded as the result of psychological factors producing it—factors such as stimuli, attitudes, conscious or unconscious motives, and so on. The rejection of both behaviorism and the psychoanalytic perspectives is virtually explicit in this statement, and the basis for both is the same: that, in attempting to gain explanatory determinacy by linking these "pushing" factors with specifics, the investigator bypasses the "meanings of things for the human beings who are acting" (Blumer, 1969, p. 50).

(2) Similarly, human behavior cannot be regarded as the product of social factors such as social position, status demands, social roles, norms and values, and the like. The reason for Blumer's objection in this case is the same: The individual is treated like a passive vessel through which forces flow, giving that individual no power to endow those forces with meaning, deflect them, influence them, and thus give a distinctive, individual, meaning-filled stamp to his or her actions.

(3) The meaning of things—even such common objects as chairs and tables—is not to be found in any objective characteristic of the thing itself. There is a distinctive human element involved in the generation of meaning. By this assertion Blumer appears to have rejected both the realistic and positivistic philosophical traditions, both of which posit that structure (and order) is found in nature.

(4) By the same token, the "meaning of things" is not to be found by referring to distinctively psychological predispositions brought to them by individuals—predispositions such as feelings, memories, motives, and attitudes. This source of structuring is also viewed by Blumer as erroneous, and in thus concluding he appears to have rejected both philosophical subjectivism and the psychoanalytic perspective.

The notion of meaning, then, is essential to the symbolic interactionist perspective. What is its source? It is found, as the title of the perspective implies, in the interactive process between people. In this process, individuals communicate with one another, create and derive meanings, and act on them accordingly. An added ingredient in this process is that the interpretative process involved in interaction has an intra-individual component, namely that an individual engages in communication with himself or herself, making the kinds of selections, corrections, indications, and conclusions that he or she makes in the interpersonal interaction setting. The processes as depicted by Blumer, following George Herbert Mead, is extremely complicated, involving reading of others' meanings, revising meanings on the basis of that reading, and guessing what readings the other might have of one's behavior, and readjusting one's behavior and anticipations in line with those guesses.

Since Blumer was so exhaustive at the outset in rejecting so many possible sources of structure in describing or explaining human behavior, one might ask where it is possible to find the idea of structure, either internal to the self or person or external in the society. In seeking an answer to this question, one comes up rather empty-handed. In all of Blumer's writings, as well as other exponents of the perspective, there is little evidence of subdivisions of the general concept of meaning that might be regarded as "parts" or "elements" of a meaning system that could serve as a basis of some kind of analysis of meaning as a system. The stress, rather, appears to be on the concept of meaning in general as a central organizing concept. There is the division the person—deriving from Cooley and Mead—as having an observing self and an objectified self, but the distinction goes no further. There are also hints that macroscopic features of social structure are determined or derived from the interactive process. There is the assertion, for example, that "culture . . . is clearly derived from what people do," and that social structure refers to relationships derived from how people act toward each other" (1969,

p. 64), but neither statement is carried further. There is the notion that society derives from the "fitting together" of meanings that come to be commonly shared and thus become the basis for institutionalized, more or less enduring interaction, and this constitutes the fabric of institutions and society. (This formulation is reminiscent of Homans's idea that exchanges form on the basis of common interests and "joint action.") But in all cases the formulations are sufficiently indeterminate that they yield such vague indication of what might drive collective or institutionalized action that they cannot be regarded as the seeds of any kind of macroscopic social theory.

If we return to the original point made in this essay—namely, that some idea of structure is essential to the enterprise of scientific explanation—then it appears reasonable to conclude that Blumer moved away from this position about as far as a theorist can move. There appears to have been no effort, as we found in Weber, to move from the subjective to the structural. He appears to have substituted unstructured process for structure more or less completely. Insofar as symbolic interactionists share this methodological position, it is not difficult to understand why they have had difficulty in making progress in empirical social-scientific research, in which investigators are more or less called upon to simplify the number of determinants they are considering, place these determinants in some kind of relationship to one another, and, on that basis, generate expectations as to some kind of behavioral outcome. Such procedures seem offensive to the methodological position espoused by Blumer. To put the matter differently, just as the behavioral perspective strives for scientific status by stripping stimuli and responses—and their associative connections—from any meaning context by considering them objective, comparable, and measurable positive factors, so the symbolic interactionist perspective denies all these possibilities—and the possibility of scientific status—by insisting that any phenomenon be interpreted in an unspecified context of individual meaning systems.

Ethnomethodology. Two of Garfinkel's targets of negative polemic that inform the starting point of his own exposition are quite similar to those put forward by Blumer:

(1) role theory , which rests on the assumption that there exists a kind of independent—if not transcendent—social reality of norms, expectations, and institutions separate from the

individual person (insofar as individuals behave in conformity with these regulating forces, then their behavior is thereby structured, and insofar as they believe in them, their attitudes and values are thereby structured); and

(2) any kind of psychological determinism that treats individual choices of action as "compelled on the grounds of psychoanalytic biography, conditioning history, and the variables of mental functioning" (Blumer, 1969, p. 12).

Such explanations, Garfinkel argued, portray the individual as a "judgmental dope," responding more or less unreflectively to fixed expectations and determinants. By contrast, the ethnomethodological perspective involves a vision of a freer, more practical, more improvising, more negotiating individual who, in the course of social interaction, has at his or her disposal a wide variety of alternative actions and "rationalities"; the task of ethnomethodology is to investigate the lines of action taken, the accounts that are given for this action, and the ways that "taken-for-granted" understandings are brought to bear and are more or less explicit. Consistent with the view of much of the phenomenological tradition, the structure of social reality is not in any sense "given," but is continuously constituted, reconstituted, reproduced, and accounted for in interaction.

Taken at this level, ethnomethodology can be regarded as a partial abandonment of structure, both external (cultural or normative determination) and internal (psychological determination), and the substitution of interaction process instead, in which a wider range of behavioral lines of action are available, and these unfold in ways that are not predictable. The stress on "accounting" for situational actions stresses the "indexical" nature of expressions, that is, their specificity to situational context. Even in situations in which actors seemingly apply general norms, they have to define their meaning in the situation of action itself. This situational richness and complexity implies, for any given event, myriad idiosyncratic associations, meanings, and psychic structures. The methodological thrust of the ethnomethodological perspective is to reduce a scientific claim to determinacy of explanation, but at the same time perhaps to increase the accuracy and richness of descriptive accounts of behavior.

One of the main ways in which Garfinkel and his associates attempted to demonstrate the power of their formulations was by what Mary Douglas (1986) has called "back-door" analysis, that is to say, by making inferences about taken-for-granted understandings and norms when they break down, or, in the case of Garfinkel's experiments, investigators make them break down. These experiments involved haggling about prices when prices were posted as fixed, cheating in games, treating intimate family members as strangers, and the like. A great deal of work has also been done about the kind of "repair work" that is done when the rules of pausing, interrupting, and turn taking break down in conversation (Schegloff, 1987). These investigations are meant to show both the problematic nature or contingency of norms, and to demonstrate the kind of negotiated processes of restoration that takes place when these norms break down.

Yet it is in these very investigations that the ethnomethodological approach appears to reintroduce the notion of structure—even cultural structure, which was the target of polemic attack at the outset. There are two reasons for assuming this. First, it is evident that unless there is some kind of structure, some kind of shared expectations, something to which people are expected to conform, it is impossible for anything like a breakdown to be recognized as such. The concept of a breakdown presupposes something structured, something unbroken to be broken down. Furthermore, the apparent desire on the part of individuals to keep these structured rules intact and not broken down is quite strong, for the breakdowns often trigger strong affects and signal the occasion to divert attention away from the ongoing flow and mobilize communicative efforts to repair the breakdown. Finally, most evidently in the case of language breakdowns, it is apparent that the target for reconstruction is not completely wide open—interacting partners do not have to invent new languages when breakdowns occur—but that there is a kind of "target" of grammar and usage rules that are learned (internalized), thereby giving structure to the range of limited alternatives available to interacting individuals. Considerations such as these suggest the partial aptness of the label *microfunctionalist* in that the main stress of that analysis is on maintenance and restoration, particularly of language systems but of other normative systems as well. The gain that the ethnomethodologists may have made is to remind us that the resources and strategies available to actors are greater than heretofore thought, and that the process of restoration is correspondingly less automatic and more contingent.

Two Microscopic Theories of Social Control and the Establishment of Structure: Parsons. Earlier we noted that Parsons, in expositing his position on consensus on values and norms as a source of structure, identified the mechanism of socialization, or the internalization of common values, norms, and social objects, with the corresponding expectation that conformity would be a matter of self-regulation. At the same time, Parsons acknowledged that "both within the individual actors as personalities and in the situation in which they act there are factors tending to upset the equilibrium" implied in a model of adequate socialization. This is when tendencies to deviance or nonconformity develop, and a separate set of mechanisms, falling under the category of social control, come into play.

Parsons's model of deviance begins on the microscopic side in that he put forth the postulate that in any interactive role situation, there are fundamental sources of ambivalence, both toward the interacting other ("a cathected other"), and on the values and normative expectations that regulate the interaction. Building on these distinctions, and noting that deviance may take either an active or passive character, Parsons developed an elaborate classification of the directions that deviant behavior may take. Among the sources of additional stress that may contribute to the genesis of deviance are the denial of gratification in some role settings (as with affectively neutral roles), indefiniteness of norms, and role conflict.

It is in the discussion of processes of social control that the question of the maintenance of the structure comes into sharp focus. That maintenance is the principal starting point is clear: "our attention will be focussed on . . . the forestalling of the kinds of deviant tendencies we have analyzed . . . and the processes by which, once under way, these processes can be counteracted and the system brought back, in the relevant respects to the old equilibrium states" (Parsons, 1951, p. 298), though he hastened to add that no system is ever perfectly equilibrated and integrated. Parsons mentioned a diversity of means or even strategies that are likely to be helpful in this process. Among the less extreme ones are the display of a certain amount of support and restricted permissiveness of deviant behavior, without at the same time reciprocating it in a positive way (the prototype of this pattern is found, for Parsons, in the institutionalization of psychotherapy). Beyond these certain institutional strategies—such as the setting of institutional priorities, scheduling of potentially conflicting activities at different times and in different places—that tend to mitigate the sources of strain, especially role conflict. The institutionalization of limited "acting-out" possibilities, as in youth culture, is another. And at the more extreme levels the strategies of insulation and isolation of deviants (hospitalization and imprisonment) are available.

In certain places, Parsons recognized that deviance involves a certain struggle over meanings. Sometimes a deviant "liberal" youth sets up his or her own values and worldview against the "fundamentalism" of the parents; and in those cases of deviance when it becomes collectivized, as in the case of a religious cult or a radical political group, an entire new set of symbols of legitimacy may be adopted and become the focus of intense identification and loyalty on the part of the deviant group, and the basis for challenging agents of social control. That this struggle may ultimately involve large-scale conflict and change was recognized by Parsons in the final point of his diagnosis of deviance: "Structured deviant behavior tendencies, which are not successfully coped with by the control mechanisms of the social system, constitute one of the principal sources of change in the structure of the social system" (1951, p. 321).

Labeling Theory. This approach to deviance, associated mainly the works of Lemert (1972), Becker (1963), and Goffman (1961, 1963), can in many respects be regarded as a polemic reaction against the tradition of social control that Parsons represents. The main points of critique and reformulation are these:

(1) Parsons, like most of those working in the field of deviance, defined deviance primarily in terms of the behavior, characteristic, or condition of the deviant. While rooted in the personal interaction, and while assessed always in terms of some understood value or normative expectation, the starting point is nevertheless with the behavior of the deviant, and the reactions of others, including agents of social control, to that behavior. While labeling theorists have been somewhat ambiguous in their statements about the relations of behavior to the phenomenon of being labeled "deviant," the key point is that the labeling of deviant is mainly determined by the power of those in positions of social control (doctors, judges, law-enforcement officials, etc.) to enforce a definition upon them. In this sense the problem of deviance is even more clearly defined as a struggle over meanings—indeed, a power struggle—with the more powerful usually able to impose their definitions, even though a variety of strategies may be employed by those labeled as deviant to subvert or manipulate those meanings.

(2) Parsons's main concern is with the consequences of deviance for the larger system: how it is disequilibrating and calls for efforts to restore equilibrium; the strategies by which this is accomplished; and, to a lesser extent, how deviance may be the basis for ultimate structural change in the system. By contrast, the focus of most labeling theorists is on the deviants themselves—how they come to be defined, both in their own and others' minds, as having committed a deviant act; how they come to be defined as a deviant person; and how they cope with the career of being deviant.

(3) From the standpoint of the maintenance of structure, the two perspectives also differ decisively. As indicated, Parsons' starting point is with the maintenance of equilibrium, so the main focus is on the phenomenon of "bringing back into line" with the dominant institutionalized role expectations. The most extreme measures of social control, insulation and isolation, appear to mark a kind of admission of defeat, as it were, as restorative efforts are given up and more extreme measures of removal take over. But the main stress is on containing and restoring, thus maintaining the dominant structures in society. Labeling theory, once again by contrast, posits a kind of tendency of relevant authorities to create *new* structures by assigning, more or less indefinitely, deviants to a kind of disadvantaged underclass, which the authorities are interested in maintaining. In this respect, deviance theory moved more in the direction of the dominance view of structural maintenance and away from the consensus view.

An Effort at Synthesis: The Social Construction of Reality. To consider the work of Berger and Luckman (1967) is perhaps a fitting way to close this exploration, since, while clearly microscopic in its theoretical starting points, it marks an ambitious attempt to make a transition from that perspective to social structure, and to indicate how social structure, once established, then becomes an independent objective reality that constitutes the basis of organized and orderly social life. The authors themselves referred to their work as an effort to understand "the dialectic of individual and society" (1967, p. 186), and explicitly mention a great diversity of sources—Marx, Parsons, symbolic interactionist —as informing their work.

The starting points borrow heavily from the symbolic interactionist perspective. The most important experience of life takes place in face-to-face interaction, which has the following central characteristics:

In the face-to-face situation the other is presented to me in a vivid present shared by both of us. I know that in the same vivid present I am presented to him. My and his "here and now" continuously impinge on each other as long as the face-to-face situation continues. As a result, there is a continuous interchange of my expressivity and his. I see him smile, then react to my frown by stopping the smile, then smiling again as I smile, and so on. Every expression of mine is oriented toward him, and vice versa, and this continuous reciprocity of expressive acts is simultaneously available to both of us [1967, p. 29-29].

At a given moment, however, Berger and Luckman introduced what proves to be the key postulate in their analysis: the need for simplification and routinization in this interaction. "The inherent instability of the human organism makes it imperative that man himself provide a stable environment for his conduct" (1967, p. 52).

This human need for habituation is inherent in interaction and is prior to institutionalization, but becomes the basis of institutionalization. As common routines and understandings are established, they come to be "externalized" insofar as they become to be represented as objective reality, most notably in their transmission through socialization to future generations. Habituation is thereby institutionalized as "the way things are." Berger and Luckman also envision the proliferation of institutionalization into many specialized spheres, as well as the creation of definite roles, but they also argue that the various institutional spheres "hang together." The reason for this is also psychological, and rooted in the need for cognitive consistency; "while performances can be segregated, meanings tend toward at least minimal consistency. As the individual reflects about the successive moments of his experience, he tries to fit their meanings into a consistent biographical framework" (1967, p. 64).

In the course of historical time, selected meanings and knowledge, largely in the form of language representation, undergo a process of "objectivated sedimentation" in the consciousness of society's members. As such, they tend toward a process of reification, or the "apprehension of human phenomena as if they were things" (Berger and Luckman, 1967, p. 87). Institutional reality is further bolstered by a wide range of legitimizations, found in language, knowledge, mythology, and theology, which establish this reality as natural and right, and provide a machinery for dealing with alternative (deviant) symbolic universes. Specialists in the maintenance of symbolic universe arise (religious leaders, legal officials) as a further way of bolstering the legitimacy of the symbolic order.

Turning to the other side of the dialectic, Berger and Luckman regarded the imposition of the now-objectified reality as progressing mainly through socialization: primary socialization, in which the fundamental rules, reality perceptions, and identifications of children are assured, and secondary socialization, which is more specialized learning and preparation for specific differentiated roles. But in addition to socialization, however, which is never complete, there is required some kind of institutionalized means for "reality-maintenance" routine, which rests mainly on conversation. "One may view the individuals's everyday life in terms of the working away of a conversational apparatus that ongoingly maintains, modifies, and reconstructions his subjective reality" (1967, p. 152). Maintenance in the face of crisis calls for more "explicit and intensive" means of social control, of which ritual has a special place. Berger and Luckman also envisaged the possibility of isolating potential through assigning him or her to a "profiled type—the cripple, the bastard, the idiot, and so on" (1967, p. 1965), but also "collectivization of deviance" through the transformation through mechanisms such as religious transformation, and the establishment of countersystems of legitimacy on the part of groups.

Enough has been sketched to indicate the degree to which Berger and Luckman have attempted to make use of many of the perspectives reviewed: symbolic interactionism, structure through value consensus and social control, labeling, and ethnomethodology. As for their own account of structure, the main critique appears to be that it is on the indeterminate side; while they speak of differentiation and specialization of roles and structures, their reference to these is only illustrative. The reason for this is that, in the last analysis, their analysis rests on only one set of structural exigencies toward which social structure (institutionalization) is directed: the exigencies of habituation, externalization, and control. Given that focus on one function, it is difficult to provide a basis for any systematic classification of structures or any statement of the systematic relationship among them; all structures are much the same in the end in their functional significance.

Concluding Remarks

The first remarks to be made in closing this chapter are to register a few qualifications about its scope, some imposed by the limitations of space and some imposed by the competence of its author. These are:

(1) The chapter could have been more inclusive of contributions and approaches to the theme of the chapter. For example, Goffman's dramaturgical approach was passed over in the critical review of phenomenological themes; the same could be said for the review of behaviorism and exchange theory, which did not include the work of Peter Blau; and almost all the traditions represented could have been broken into more variants than they were. The issue is to strive for coverage at the cost of superficiality on the one side, or more depth at the expense of scope on the other. I am certain that many readers who are also authors have experienced that dilemma themselves.

(2) As the title suggests, the chapter focused on the issue of social structure as such, and while issues of structural change emerged from time to time, this dimension was probably slighted. It is hoped that some compensation for this will appear at various places in the others chapters on the handbook.

(3) The important phenomenon of the increasing importance of the structure of relations among nations—economic, political, social, and cultural—and the interdependence between this kind of structure and the structural arrangements within societies. This is a perspective that is gaining in visibility in the social sciences, and is reflected in part in the final chapter of the volume, by Evans and Stephens.

(4) Located in the "theory and methods" part of this handbook, the chapter concentrates on theories that have taken distinct and forcefully articulated viewpoints. Most professional sociologists—both those inclined toward theory and those more interested in empirical research—probably would not subscribe, though they might lean toward one or more of these theoretical positions. Working as sociologists who come across specific and definite intellectual and scientific problems, most sociologists are driven somewhat in eclectic directions, as the complexity of their contexts and their explanations becomes evident.

These cautionary notes aside, I would like to

make a further general point about the history of theorizing and analyzing social structure in sociology and some of the other social sciences as well. It appears to me possible to identify two recurring levels of discourse. I remarked in this connection that the two main foci of this description were systematically related structures of activities (most commonly called institutions) on the one hand, identifiable collectivities (groups, parties, classes) on the other. The two most common structural patterns that have been apparently noticed are the degree of specialization of institutional activities and diversification of group life on the one hand, and the degree, kind, and extent of stratification and domination among institutional clusters and groups on the other.

It strikes me that both theorists and empirical investigators have been able to agree on the nature of these foci. Of course, there are differences in conceptualization and representation, and there are enormous methodological difficulties in generating reliable measures of specialization, integration, inequality, domination, and the rest; but it is in these descriptive areas that the observer finds more continuity in the sociology of social structure.

The second level of discourse is in the *explanation* of the origin of social structure, and the conditions underlying its maintenance and change. In this chapter I have identified, for example, some notion of survival or adaptation, some notion of functional requirements, submission out of fear of destructive impulses, economic domination, domination through authority, technological domination, social control, and the psychological need for continuity and routinization. This list could have been expanded and elaborated if the chapter had been more exhaustive.

It also strikes me that discourse at this second level has been less satisfactory. Most of the debate, conflict, and contending schools of thought have swirled around the "explanations" or "causes." One of the reasons this is so is because these are relatively invisible by comparison with the first level—difficult to observe, difficult to measure, and difficult to link definitively with their presumed structural effects (Zelditch, 1986). There does not seem to be any basis, through decisive experiment or compelling evidence, either to establish or reject any of the ever-expanding list on a definite basis. As such they constitute a kind of reservoir, a fully packed suitcase, if you will, of available preferences and theoretical positions to be

pulled out on the basis of both opportunism or on the basis of predilection; that is, when they seem to present a more plausible line of explanation with respect to some problem under question, or because they seem to mesh with the systematic preferences (scientific, methodological, aesthetic, ideological) of the investigator.

It seems, finally, that greater cognizance should be taken of the fact that there also probably is legitimately some plausible reason the various explanatory perspectives on the origins and maintenance of social structure persis—namely, that there is some kind of ingredient of validity in each of them, and that each is applicable in varying degrees of usefulness in different kinds of historical situations and historical sequences.

The constructive attack on existing limitations of accumulated thinking on social structure might take several forms. One might be the continued efforts to reach more sophisticated, accurate, and valid definitions of measures of structure itself. Another line might be theoretical in character, an effort to tighten and make more definite the precise links that might be expected to emanate from each explanatory perspective and manifest themselves empirically. Still another might be to extend our efforts to develop and execute improved designs for comparative and historical analyses of conditions of growth, conflict, stagnation, and breakdown, with an eye to assessing the relative strength or weakness of the several perspectives. And finally, some advance might be gained by a diminution of the combative and an augmentation of the synthetic impulse, as hinted by the efforts of Berger and Luckman, and as manifested by recent simultaneous theoretical trends in both Europe and North America (Alexander et al., 1987) to seek theoretical and empirical links between microscopic and macroscopic accounts of society. In all likelihood, it is essential that all these strategies be pursued simultaneously to improve our record with respect to the theory of social structure.

NOTES

1. By "macroscopic," I refer to institutional structures and social systems as units of analysis; by "microscopic," I refer to social-psychological and interpersonal-interactional processes.

2. The correspondence between some of Spencer's and Parsons's categories is evident: general sustena-

tion (adaptation); offensive and defensive activities (goal-attainment); distribution and regulation (integration). What is missing in Spencer is any reference to culture (latency).

REFERENCES

Alexander, Jeffrey. In press. "Durkheim's Problem and Differentiation Theory Today." In *Modernization and Social Change*, edited by Hans Haferkamp and Neil J. Smelser. Berkeley: University of California Press.

_____. Bernhard Giesen, Richard Munch, and Neil J. Smelser, eds. 1987. *The Micro-Macro Link*. Berkeley: University of California Press.

Almond, Gabrielle and Sidney Verba. 1963. *The Civic Culture*. Boston: Beacon Press.

Becker, Howard S. 1963. *Outsiders*. New York: Free Press.

Berger, Peter, and Thomas Luckman. 1967. *The Social Construction of Reality*. Garden City, NY: Doubleday.

Blau, Peter. 1977. "A Macrosociological Theory of Social Structure." *American Journal of Sociology* 83:26-54.

Blumer, Herbert. 1969. *Symbolic Interactionism: Perspective and Method*. Englewood Cliffs, NJ: Prentice-Hall.

Burt, Ronald S. 1982. *Toward a Structural Theory of Action: Network Models of Social Structure, Perception, and Action*. New York: Academic Press.

Dahrendorf, Ralf. 1959. *Class and Class Conflict in Industrial Society*. Stanford: Stanford University Press. (Original work published 1957)

Douglas, Mary. 1986. "Institutionalized Public Memory." Pp. 63-76 in *The Social Fabric: Dimensions and Issues*, edited by James F. Short. Beverly Hills, CA: Sage.

Durkheim, Emile. 1958. *The Rules of Sociological Method*. Glencoe, IL: Free Press. (Original work published 1893)

_____ 1969. *The Division of Labor in Society*. New York: Free Press. (Original worked published 1893)

Ferrarotti, Franco. In press. "The State and Civil Society." In *The State and Society in Contemporary European Theory*, edited by Saad Nagi. Columbus: University of Ohio Press.

Freud, Sigmund. 1955. "Group Psychology and the Analysis of the Ego," Pp. 69-143 in *The Standard Edition of the Complete Psychological Works of Sigmund Freud*, edited by James Strachey. London: Hogarth Press. (Original work published 1921)

_____ 1961. "Civilization and Its Discontents." Pp. 64-145 in *The Standard Edition of the Complete Psychological Works of Sigmund Freud*, edited by James Strachey. London: Hogarth Press. (Original work published 1930)

Garfinkel, Harold. 1967. *Studies in Ethnomethodology*. Englewood Cliffs, NJ: Prentice-Hall.

Goffman, Erving. 1961. *Asylums: Essays on the Social Situation of Mental Patients and Other Inmates*. New York: Doubleday/Anchor.

_____ 1963. *Stigma: Notes on the Management of Spoiled Identity*. Englewood Cliffs, NJ: Prentice-Hall.

Granovetter, Mark. 1976. "Network Sampling: Some First Steps." *American Journal of Sociology* 81:1078-1095.

Habermas, Jurgen. 1973. *Theory and Practice*. Boston: Beacon Press. (Original work published 1971)

_____ 1975. *Legitimation Crisis*. Boston: Beacon Press.

_____ 1984. *Theory of Communicative Action*. Boston: Beacon Press.

Hannan, Michael T., and John Freeman. 1977. "The Population Ecology of Organizations." *American Journal of Sociology* 82:929-964.

Homans, George. 1974. *Social Behavior: Its Elementary Forms* (revised edition). New York: Harcourt Brace Jovanovich. (Original work published 1961)

Klandermans, Bert. 1986. "New Social Movements and Resource Mobilization: The European and the American Approach." *International Journal of Mass Emergencies and Disasters* 4:13-37.

Leinhardt, Samuel, ed. 1977. *Social Networks: A Developing Paradigm*. New York: Academic Press.

Lemmert, Edwin M. 1972. "Social Problems and the Sociology of Deviance." Pp. 3-25 in *Human Deviance, Social Problems, and Social Control* (second edition), edited by E. Lemert. Englewood Cliffs, NJ: Prentice-Hall.

Marcuse, Herbert. 1964. *One Dimensional Man*. Boston: Beacon Press.

Marx, Karl. 1973. "Letter from Karl Marx to P.V. Annenkov." In *Karl Marx on Society and Social Change*, edited by Neil J. Smelser. Chicago: University of Chicago Press. (Original work published 1846)

Merton, Robert K. 1968. *Social Theory and Social Structure* (revised and enlarged edition). New York: Free Press.

Parsons, Talcott. 1937. *The Structure of Social Action*. New York: McGraw-Hill.

_____ 1951. *The Social System*. Glencoe, IL: Free Press.

_____ 1954. "The Present Position and Prospects of Systematic Theory in Sociology." Pp. 212-237 in *Essays in Sociological Theory* (revised edition). Glencoe, IL: Free Press.

_____ 1954. "A Revised Analytical Approach to the Theory of Stratification." Pp. 386-439 in *Essays in Sociological Theory* (revised edition). Glencoe, IL: The Free Press.

_____ 1955. *Family, Socialization and Interaction Process*. Glencoe, IL: Free Press.

_____ and Neil J. Smelser. 1956. *Economy and*

Society. Glencoe, IL: Free Press.

Radcliffe-Brown, A. R. 1952. *Structure and Function in Primitive Society*. Glencoe, IL: Free Press.

Schegloff, Emanuel A. 1987. "Between Macro and Micro: Contexts and Other Connections." In *The Micro-Macro Link*, edited by Jeffrey C. Alexander, Bernhard Giesen, Richard Munch, and Neil J. Smelser. Berkeley: University of California Press.

Smelser, Neil J. 1976. *Comparative Methods in the Social Sciences*. Englewood Cliffs, NJ: Prentice-Hall.

Spencer, Herbert. 1897. *The Principles of Sociology*. New York: D. Appleton.

Touraine, Alain. 1981. *The Voice and the Eye*. New York: Cambridge University Press.

Weber, Max. 1968. *Economy and Society*, edited by Guenther Roth and Claus Wittich. New York: Bedminster Press.

———. 1969. *The Methodology of the Social Sciences*, edited by Edward A. Shils and Henry A. Finch. New York: Free Press. (Original work published 1904)

Zelditch, Morris, Jr. 1986. "The Problem of Order." Pp. 107-114 in *The Social Fabric*, edited by James F. Short, Jr. Beverly Hills, CA: Sage Publications.

4

On Sociological Data

PETER H. ROSSI

In the design of sociological research, a critical issue arises over what kinds of observations should be made on which kinds of units. Deciding upon an appropriate unit of observation defines the scope of the research, places limits on the analyses that can be attempted upon the resulting data, and often determines the extent to which validity issues can be successfully addressed. Similarly, the proper solution to issues of measurement are often basic to many validity issues, can effect the power of a research design to provide definitive data, and affect the forms of analysis to be used.

Sociologists have many kinds of units of observation among which to choose. It must be emphasized that decisions on units of observation and on kinds of observations to be made are highly dependent on the substantive issues that drives the research effort. A research issue that involves families clearly will lead the researcher to observe different entities than research issues involving nation states or economic enterprises. As emphasized by every methodologist of any epistemological persuasion, there can be no observation without some conceptual framework to which the observations are linked. For example, absent the concept of family (or its equivalent), families cannot serve as units to be observed. This point may be painfully obvious in this instance because the concept of family'' is so firmly rooted in everyday language and in the vocabulary of social science. For other concepts of importance to social scientists—for example, economic sector, reference group, or occupation—the entities involved as units of observation need careful delineation.

The purpose of this chapter is to provide an understanding of the issues involved and knowledge from which to make more informed decisions about which units to observe and which kind of measurement is most appropriate to the research tasks at hand.

Units of Observation (UOs): Framing Observations

The concept of "units of observation" (UOs) is fundamental to the topic of this chapter. The camera provides a useful analogy: What to include within and exclude from the frame outlined in a camera's viewfinder is analogous to the decision upon a unit of observation. To decide upon the units of observation to be used in a particular research endeavor is to decide about the entities on which observations are to be made for the purposes of the research. By "entity" we mean some unit that is recognizable as distinguishable from other units or from the background in which the entity may be found. (The neutral term *entity* is deliberately employed because the UOs of social science can range widely over physical objects to persons and aggregates of persons.) By the term *recognizable* in the last sentence, we mean that any social scientist can be trained to apply simple rules in observing that will reliably identify whether or not some object—person, group, organization, physical artifact, and so on—is to be classified as a unit of observation in the study in question.

For example, a UO for some particular research may be defined as a household. The relevant rules for observers might consist of the following definition: A household is a group of adults and associated dependent children sharing the same dwelling unit as their current non-temporary address, the adults sharing some joint responsibility for household expenditures and upkeep of the dwelling unit. The group of adults in question may consist of one or more persons. These rules provide guides to observers that distinguish households as entities from nonhousehold groupings. (In actual practice, rules for determining what is a households may occupy several pages of print, as the handbooks for census enumerators and survey interviewers indicate.)

Such rules need to be stated both positively and negatively, defining respectively what entities are to be regarded as included as a unit of observation and which are *not* to be so regarded. For example, entities regarded as units of observation in a particular research may be human beings, books, administrative records, human artifacts, organizations, and so on. The rules for identifying such entities need not be formidable, but only sufficiently detailed so that a trained observer following such rules can identify units of observation with reliability (without too many errors either of inclusion or exclusion.) A rule for identifying units of observation for a survey of voting intentions in a presidential election might specify that the units of observation should be persons who are citizens of the United States, and also 18 years of age or older. Excluded from the UO definition are persons who are not U.S. citizens and who are under 18 years of age. A decision to state the rules in this fashion may be based on the broadest legal definition of who is eligible to cast votes in such elections.

In designing research, the choice of UO determines the basic form of the records and files to be assembled from the data collected and conditions the ways in which generalizations may be sustained from summarizing records. The observations made on a unit of observation constitute a record, with each record corresponding to a single UO. A set of records (or file) for a research project consists of a record for each UO containing the observations made upon each UO. Thus in a sample survey of individuals, the basic data records usually consist of filled-out interview schedules or questionnaires obtained by posing questions of the individuals who were selected as units of observation for the study. A file of records for a census of households might consist of all the observations made on each of the households studied.

Defining the units of observation also defines the relevant universe to which generalizations can be made. If the UOs are defined as adult citizens, then the study can be generalized to adults citizens generally (assuming that the sampling selection was appropriate).

Indivisibility

What should be the entity that serves as a UO for a given research project is clearly a matter mainly of the research question that drives the research. A question that is concerned with cities—for instance, "The larger the city, the more extensive its division of labor"—suggests that cities should be the units of observation, whereas a question that focuses on sequences of interpersonal behavior—"In dyadic interaction, an inquiry by ego is almost invariably followed by a declarative statement by alter"—suggests that the UO for that research might profitably be behavioral sequences in the interaction between pairs of persons. Identifying the unit of observation most appropriate to a given research project is clearly an important first step in the design of research.

Once established and used in a research, units of observation tend to become indivisible, by which we mean that the units of observation become entities that can not be further subdivided or disaggregated within that research. Hence it is important to define units of observation carefully, choosing a definition that is likely to be as fine as the proposed study's analysis may require. For example, in a study of urbanization, defining the units of observation as counties ordinarily precludes studying persons and households. Statements about the impact upon individuals and households of living in urban areas may not be possible to support because observations were made about county characteristics and not on households or individuals living within counties.

It is important not to be misled by our linguistic conventions. Some entities appear to be "naturally" indivisible primarily because conventional language regards them as such. In a personal interview survey, persons are ordinarily identified as the units of observation and it is difficult to conceive of dividing an individual person into constituent parts. However, for some purposes, it is useful to conceive of individual persons as composed of behavioral acts, for example, answers to questions, trips on public transportation, and so on. In such cases, the units of observation may be usefully defined as such acts. For example, a personal interview study may define as its UOs the answers given to questions posed to persons.

Independence

An often desired feature of collections of observations is independence. That is, the observations obtained from one UO are not in any way dependent on the observations collected in another. In "pure" random samples, the quality of independence is assured since each UO is chosen independent of whichever UO is chosen before or later. Thus an observation made on, say, the tenth UO is not dependent on the observation made on any other UO. For example, knowing the gender of any one respondent in a random survey, I cannot, on that basis predict the gender of any other respondent. In contrast, dependence is a circumstance in which the qualities of UOs are in some way linked. For example, knowing the gender of one adult person in a household, the chances are that any other adult in that household is of the opposite agenda (primarily because the typical household is two adult members who are married to each other).

Many statistical models require independence among observations in order to be employed properly. However, it often is neither possible nor desirable to obtain independent observations. "Pure" random samples of persons households or other entities are frequently neither possible nor efficient. Most sample surveys chose respondents in clusters—usually geographic but also based on membership. The clustering of UOs in space, time, or on the basis of some other types of collections is characteristic of social research.

Although as a general rule, independence among observations is usually desirable. However, it is also often difficult to live up to this standard. In addition, for some research purposes it is actually undesirable to collect independently drawn samples of UOs. For example, studies of households and families cannot avoid the fact that observations made about the members of a household are not likely to be in-

dependent since household members often share the same standard of living and mutually affect each other. Similarly, members of the same neighborhood or community may be more like each other than persons chosen randomly from among a variety of neighborhoods or communities. The answer given by a respondent to one item on a questionnaire is not likely to be independent of the answers given by the same respondent to another item. A final example illustrates how difficult it is to avoid dependence among UOs: Studies of friendship dyads clearly cannot choose friends as UOs without producing dependent data. By virtue of being mutually chosen as friends, persons who are friends are more likely to resemble each other in a variety of ways than persons randomly selected.

The fact that UOs used in social science research are often dependent on each other statistically need not be a crippling fact to the researcher. For example, it is often the case that dependence occurs if UOs have been defined in an inappropriate manner. Samples of friendship relationships can often be selected independently; however, the use of members of such pairs as samples of individuals raises the issue of lack of independence. Similarly, households may be selected independently, but the disaggregation of household samples into samples of individuals raises the same issue. In short, it is important to define a UO for a research project that minimizes as much as possible the problems brought about by dependence, except in those studies where the dependencies themselves are the objects of the research.

Furthermore, when dependence cannot be avoided for some reason, the selection of appropriate statistical models may compensate. Realizing that lack of independence among UOs is a necessary consequence of the fact that social scientists are vitally interested in precisely many of those circumstances that produce dependence, statisticians have devised statistical models that are based on dependence assumptions. For example, time-series analysis models routinely take into account the fact that observations taken over consecutive time periods are seldom independent and sampling statisticians have worked out ways of calculating reasonable estimates of the sampling errors for clustered samples that take into account the effects of clustering.

Aggregation

In some social researches, units of observation may be thought of as consisting of entities that are obviously composed of collections of entities that also might be defined as units of observation in some other study. Thus fertility may be studied either as the fertility experiences of individuals, using individual women as UOs, and querying women about the children they have ever borne. Or, fertility may be studied either approached as a study of birth events as UOs, using birth certificates on file in some vital statistics office. The kinds of research questions that can be answered by using women as UOs are different than those that can be answered using birth certificates as UOs. For example, it is obvious that using women as UOs allows one to investigate the correlates of differential fertility, while birth certificates ordinarily cannot support such research issues. Interviewing women about their fertility experiences uses women as UOs and is likely the most efficient way of collecting data. In principle, we could accomplish the same end by starting with birth certificates and linking them together through mothers' names, ending up with collections of birth certificates, each collection representing the fertility history of one woman. Setting aside the difficult technical task of record linking, this would mean considering all the birth certificates that would span the possible fertility histories of some specified cohort of women, say women currently 45 to 65—a task that would tax the patience and resources of any social researcher.

In a study of classroom behavior of students, the appropriate UOs may be alternatively defined as global ratings of the overall behavior of entire classes, or as measures characterizing sequences of interaction among two or more students or between students and teachers. Or, households may be defined as entities, but households in turn are made up of individuals, also each definable as entities.

Units of observation may be linked in some way to relate to some derivative higher order unit that is composed of the linked units. For example, the birth records relating to an individual mother may be linked to form a record of her fertility experience, or the letters written by an individual may be linked to form a record of that individual's correspondence; or the members of an organization—say, workers in a factory—may be linked to form work force aggregates. (We will have more to say about linking units of observation in a later section of this chapter.)

It should be emphasized that once observations have been made, it is usually not possible to subdivide or disaggregate units of observation. Thus once having used counties as the units to be observed, it is usually not possible to subdivide counties into households or individuals. For this reason, it is important to define units of observation as on the level of the finest subdivision that one can anticipate might be used in the analysis of resulting data. Therefore, if the aim of a research is to make statements about families, then taking observations of counties is not appropriate, even though statements could be made about average families in the county aggregate.

A detailed example may be appropriate: A study that used counties as UOs might find that average household incomes among counties in the United States is negatively related to the average per household ownership of firearms. It would be inappropriate to infer from that finding that poor households are more likely to own firearms. In fact, as other studies using households as UOs have shown, higher-income households are more likely to own firearms. Households were not the UOs used in the first study and any inferences about households cannot be legitimately made. However, it is correct to infer that among counties with relatively low household income, firearms ownership is more widespread, a finding that is legitimate because it is confined to the level of the UOs defined for that study.

A more general statement of the aggregation problem is that UOs for a research study should be chosen at the finest level of disaggregation that is most appropriate to the substantive concerns of the research.

The Significance of UOs

In the next section of this chapter, the most common among different types of units of observation that social scientists commonly use will be listed. The reader should keep in mind that the purpose of defining the units of observation in a study is to clarify for the researcher just what it is she or he is planning to observe and make measurements upon. Thus to decide that individuals are the units of observation means making plans to interview persons or to observe persons and to prepare to make records, one for each individual observed.

Defining what is to be a UO also means that the universe of potential entities to be observed has been identified. This is the first step in designing samples in which explicit rules have to be articulated about how to select, say, individual persons for interviewing, out of all the possible individuals that would qualify as subjects on which to make the relevant observations.

Depending on how such rules are formulated the researcher will end up with a set of records that will or will not support generalization to all UOs of interest.

This is not the place for an extended discussion of how full enumerations are conducted or how samples are drawn. Making an exhaustive enumeration or designing an unbiased sample are both topics that require more space than can be devoted here. However, it is important to emphasize that the first task in designing either an enumeration or a sampling strategy is to decide on what entities observations are to be made. In short, defining the units of observation helps to keep the study on the right track for arriving at its intended destination—namely the answering of the research question(s) that motivated the study in the first place.

Units of Analysis

Although units of observation simply (and importantly) define for a given research the entities that will be observed, the defined units of observation may not be the same as the units in which the data will be analyzed. For example, a study of collectivities may use individuals who make up each of the collectivities as UOs, but the analysis may center on collectivities seeking those differences that, on the average, obtain between persons belonging to one collectivity as opposed to another. The units of analysis in this case are collectivities, each being characterized by summary measures calculated by summarizing the characteristics of UOs that belong to each collectivity. Thus a study of gender differences might collect data by using men and women as units of observation, but then present the findings in terms of average differences between men and women.

A Catalogue of Units of Observation

Although the social sciences are concerned with human behavior and with the organization of human organizations and societies, the units of observation in social research need not always be individual human persons or organizations. Indeed, much of the research work of social scientists uses nonhuman entities as units of observations making observations that are related to human behavior in some way. For research on past events and past humans, it is per

force necessary to rely on documents, administrative records, ruins, archaeological artifacts, or other physical objects that can provide information on humans who lived in the historical period in question.

A list of common units of observation that have been used routinely by social scientists follows, roughly in order from least to most intrusive. That is, the UOs high on the list are ones that disturb the "normal" functioning of humans least, while those lower on the list intrude most into the lives of possible human subjects. Correspondingly, those high on the list are the most indirect indicators of human behavior, the link between the unit being observed and the human behavior that affected the unit is indirect and in some cases almost a matter of speculation.

Human Physical Traces

Humans are messy creatures: They disturb the soil, move masses of rock, produce garbage, change the ecological balances of their environment, wear pathways through the land, lay down roads, build structures, and in many other ways leave behind enduring physical traces of their presence on the earth. These traces of past human transformations of physical objects or materials or physical transformations of space and the earth can be units of observation, as in much archaeological research or in studies in human ecology.

Such human traces in the form of physical objects and their characteristics are studied because they can yield information about past human activities. Some traces are quite durable, lasting centuries, allowing the archaeologist to make inferences about what the societies and people were like who produced them. Ruins of Mayan settlements are thus meticulously studied for the information such ruins may yield about the Mayan economy, social structure, and customs.

The use of human traces as UOs is not restricted solely to the study of the past: A minor subdivision of anthropology called garbology is devoted to the analysis of contemporary garbage, reading the traces of human behavior in the physical objects discarded as garbage.

What is to be observed about human traces is not obvious. Indeed, in some cases, it may not be obvious whether some feature of the physical environment is or is not a human trace, but rather the outcome of some transformation accomplished by natural processes. Research using human traces as UOs has to be illuminated by some intelligent conception of the relationship between the traces and the human behavior that is to be inferred. For most forms of human behavior, traces are indirect indicators of the human behavior about which inferences are to be made, whose interpretation requires some theoretical framework that links human activity and the human traces in question. The theoretical framework may often come from engineering, agriculture, or some other discipline that deals with the materials under study, as well as from one or another social science.

For example, whether or not the remains of some building on an excavated site was a dwelling or a storage building depends upon knowing what the traces associated with each kind of use are, such as how buildings are constructed, how to interpret analyses of pollen grains in the soil, how to use social science knowledge concerning the typical composition of households, and how space within dwellings was used by the people who constructed the dwellings in question.

A complete listing of all the human traces that might be used as UOs would be very lengthy. Humans use many physical objects in their activities and transform the naturally occurring configurations of the landscape in so doing. Skillful observers with knowledge about how human activities affect the material environment can infer from the traces the activities that generated them.

The study of human traces is also used in ingenious ways in the study of contemporary society. Observing the patterning of house lights being turned on in winter mornings, the Lynds (Lynd and Lynd, 1929) inferred that working-class families started their waking hours at a much earlier point in the day than middle-class houses. W. H. Whyte (Whyte, 1956) observed the gradual diffusion of consumer behavior from neighbor to neighbor by observing the patterning of ownership of outside awnings on residential blocks in Philadelphia. Researchers attempting to estimate the impact of aircraft noise on neighborhoods surrounding airports may study aerial photographs to determine whether there are more or fewer physical signs of outdoor activities in neighborhoods close by as compared to those located at some distance from airports.

Garbage left for collection has been used to study dietary patterns and media reading habits. In a possibly apocryphal study, listenership of television shows was measured by observing comparatively the drops in municipal water pressure that coincided with the showing of commercials during prime time shows. Presumably, during commercials that achieved audience attention, fewer persons left their sets to relieve

themselves, thereby collectively affecting the pressure in the community water supply.

Webb and his colleagues (Webb et al., 1966) suggest quite a large number of ways in which the observations on the characteristics of material environments can be used as traces to obtain information about human behavior.

A record based on a human trace as a UO typically consists of observations taken and recorded on the trace under observation. Thus a study that uses pottery shards as UOs may consist of measurements taken of the composition of the clay used, types of manufacturing method used, colors used in decoration, patterning of decoration used, and so on. A study in human ecology in which cities are the units of observation and the measurements are concerned with the patterning of human settlement might generate records in which the diverse indicators used include street patterns, gradients of density of land use, and so forth.

Human Documents

Human documents as UOs are among the most useful. Human documents are physical objects, usually artifacts, upon which some person has placed written language. An all-inclusive list of human documents would also be extremely lengthy. Some of the more important to social researchers are as follows: autobiographies, diaries, personal or business letters, memoranda, books, administrative forms, bills of lading, invoices, loan agreements and other financial instruments, learned articles, popular magazines and other periodicals, unpublished manuscripts, appointment calendars, and graffiti. The human documents may be as contemporary as yesterday's newspaper and as remote in the past as Sumerian clay tablets recording commercial transactions that took place at the beginning of written language use.

Using human documents as UOs sometimes raises privacy and confidentiality issues. When in the public domain, human documents are ordinarily unobtrusive UOs; that is, they can be used without affecting appreciably the individuals or organizations to whom they refer. For example, public birth records can be used in research without affecting the persons involved or even their parents. Especially when the documents were generated well into the past, human documents are usually unobtrusive, since the persons involved are long deceased and beyond the reach of personal harm. But when such documents refer to persons still alive, their use in ways that reveal their specific sources may be intrusive and potentially harmful to those persons.

The possibility that the research use of human documents may be harmful has led to conventions concerning their use that attempts to preserve the privacy of the individuals involved. Some human documents (for example, the manuscript census records or income tax returns) have been declared confidential by federal statute with quite strict rules concerning their release. The use of informal human documents (for example, personal letters or diaries) are protected from public identification by professional conventions that require their specific origins to be concealed. For this reason, the ethics codes of social science professional organizations stress that whenever possible individual subjects should not be identified in a research report, unless the persons involved have been public figures.

The critical difference between human documents and human traces is that a document contains marks that can be translated into words of some known human language. In using human documents, the problem of inferring their meaning is not as great since the language of the author can often be a very direct indicator of meaning. Of course, the words of the author need to be understood according to the particular style in which it was written. An ironic comment may mean something quite opposite to its literal meaning.

The use of human documents can sometimes be made difficult because of the shifting meanings of language. It is well known that words change in their meanings over a relatively short period of time: "Prestigious" in the early nineteenth century meant false pretensions to high social status and today the same word means pertaining to high status without any suggestion of pretentiousness (Unabridged Oxford English Dictionary). A reference to some person as "prestigious" in an early nineteenth-century personal letter is likely a derogatory remark, while the same reference in a late twentieth-century letter is laudatory.

Even if one understands the language correctly, there is still the problem of how properly to generalize from the findings. Romantic short stories in popular magazines can be more credibly used to indicate what editors of the time thought might be acceptable to readers than to indicate what were common courtship practices of the time. The former interpretation of the romantic stories is more credible because it is bolstered by our knowledge of how such stories are ordinarily selected by editors to appear in the publications, whereas the second interpretation needs to be bolstered by a theory relating the editorial selection processes to common courtship practices, an endeavor likely based more on speculation than on firm knowledge.

In short, the use of human documents in social research requires a theoretical framework that links the documents in question to some social phenomenon. Such frameworks should include consideration of three issues.

(1) *How such documents originate*. This is always a crucial issue. For example, a collection of autobiographies of working-class people in nineteenth-century New England factory towns is most likely a biased collection, having been written by persons who were literate. Whether the lives depicted in those biographies can be taken as in some way representative is quite problematic. Counterbalancing this judgment is the undoubted fact that there is no way that one can get an unbiased set of autobiographies of nineteenth-century working-class persons. It is better to use such unique material (with appropriate caveats) than to ignore the biographies because of their possible selection bias.

(2) *The connection between the content of the document and the concepts of which the documents are the indicators*. If the documents are supposed to reflect the experiences of the author, then there is an issue of the extent to which the author selects among her or his experiences. If the documents are supposed to reflect, say, relations between spouses, then there is the issue of how to interpret statements made by an author as expressing such relations.

(3) A final problem concerns whether the purposes for which the documents were produced permits their use for other purposes. For example, arrest slips made out by the police are designed at least in part to justify the arresting action of the officer and may not, for that reason, represent an unbiased view of the behavior that led to the arrest. Furthermore, police have developed stylized expressions that are used to make the writing of arrest slips easier. The notation on an arrest slip, "The alleged perpetrator declined to desist, when requested, and had to persuaded" may actually represent a rough-and- tumble episode and not the well-mannered exchange the formal language appears to suggest.

A class of human documents that is especially important for the social sciences are ones that are by-products of state administrative procedures, such as birth certificates, death certificates, marriage certificates, divorce decrees, judicial court decisions, real property tax rolls, police arrest reports, income tax returns, business records, and so on. These human documents form the basic records that lie behind vital statistics, crime rates, and business condition indicators.

It is important to bear in mind that such records are not produced primarily for research purposes but for use in providing to public authorities information deemed useful for running the society. Most of the records are filled in by administrative clerks whose knowledge about what are useful and interpretable entries for research purposes often leaves much to be desired. Besides, the clerks are usually mainly concerned with filling out the documents in ways useful to state officials. Indeed, it is a tribute to the cooperation between demographers and administrative officials that birth and death certificates are filled in so consistently in our country. Nevertheless, such human documents must be used with some caution, particularly for historical periods before social scientists were able to lobby effectively for sound reporting practices.

Two technical issues confront the users of administrative documents for social research:

(1) How good is the coverage of the administrative procedures involved—that is, are all events covered that should be covered?

(2) Are the entries made consistently and with due attention to representing the "facts" accurately?

For example, it is well known (U.S. Department of Justice, n.d.) that crimes reported to the police are only some fraction of the total crimes committed in a jurisdiction since a report is only generated when a citizen—usually a victim—reports a crime to the police. Hence the coverage of crime reports as administrative records leaves much to be desired. It is also well known that the officially recorded grounds for divorces resemble only slightly what may have been the actual grounds for divorce, and are usually tailored to fit the state laws concerning divorce. For example, in jurisdictions that (historically) only accepted adultery as the basis for a divorce, adultery was the major recorded grounds for the divorce. With changes in the divorce laws to allow other grounds, the official statistics may change drastically in the distribution of grounds recorded. Still another example exists in the diagnoses submitted by medical doctors in their requests for reimbursement from government agencies or insurance companies: There is more than indirect evidence that doctors tend to favor diagnoses for which they can get reimbursement.

Human documents may be specially generated for research purposes. A favorite method employed by Znaniecki (Thomas and Znaniecki, 1918) was to advertise a contest in the popular press for the best autobiography, using all the entries submitted to the contest as data for research purposes. In studying the impact of the Great Depression on young people, Lazarsfeld and his colleagues ran a contest in local newspapers for the best essay submitted by young people on their aspirations for adulthood (Jahoda, Lazarsfeld, and Zeisel, 1971).

Despite all their possible faults, human documents are for some topics the only source of information about the past and for many topics excellent information about the present. Information about vital processes (births, deaths, marriages, divorces) in the past derives almost exclusively from such human documents. Administrative records obtained from regulatory agencies are often our best or only sources for certain types of information about business firms and other large-scale organizations, for example, financial data, civil law violations, and so on.

Political Entities

Units of observation may be political jurisdictions such as nations, provinces or states, counties, cities, towns, or any other political jurisdiction that has identifiable boundaries in space. When taken as indivisible units of observation, the observations made on such entities are of characteristics that are observable only on the unit as a whole, as, for example, governmental structure, size of area in jurisdiction, types of laws and regulations, trade balances, export statistics, and so forth. Political entities may also be characterized by measurements derived from their constituent parts—for example, population size, average age of constituent population, measures of unit gross income (e.g., Gross National Product), flows of goods, crime rates, unemployment rates, and so on—all measurements derived from summarizing over constituent parts that are contained in some way within the political entity. Hence records for political entities tend to be mixtures of observations made on the entity as such and derived measurements taken as summaries over constituent parts.

Researches that use political entities as units of observation are fairly widely found in the social sciences because so much data is summarized for political jurisdictions and because political jurisdictions are regarded as important entities for study in their own right. Nation states, regional political units, and local jurisdictions attempt through legislation, their courts, and administration to affect the behavior of individuals, organized groups, and formal organizations. Studies of the impact of public policies and of legal codes are appropriately centered on political entities as UOs, since legal codes are indivisible features of such UOs.

For example, there are several studies of the impact of gun control legislation on crime rates that use states as units of observation, correlating the stringency of criminal laws regulating the ownership and usages of guns with rates for crimes in which guns are implicated (Wright et al., 1983). Since each of the states has its own criminal code that obtains over the entire state, presumably the code that rules in a state has an impact on how guns are used and hence can be used as a measure characterizing the entire state.

Other studies have looked at the fiscal relations among nation states and attempted to test theories that claim that development in former colonial states has been retarded by the type of trade between developed and underdeveloped nations (Chase-Dunn, 1975). Here, again, nation states are appropriate UOs since the theories being tested pertain to those entities.

Geographical Units with Arbitrary Boundaries

For a variety of purposes, social scientists often use geographical units whose boundaries coincide with no existing single political jurisdiction. For example, regions of the United States are often defined as more or less arbitrary combinations of contiguous states (sometimes of contiguous counties), the resulting combinations outlining areas that are not political jurisdictions. Standard Metropolitan Statistical Areas (SMSAs) have been created by the U.S. Census, each defined as the set of urbanized counties surrounding a central city of a population of at least 50,000. SMSAs are arbitrary geographical entities in the sense that usually there are no particular political jurisdiction or other type of social unit to which they correspond.

A very popular arbitrary geographical unit is the census tract. Census tracts have been drawn by the Bureau of the Census for each of the urbanized areas in the country. Tract boundaries have remained relatively fixed from census to census (except for subdivision of tracts that have grown too large and consolidation of tracts that

were formerly populous). The actual boundaries are drawn using suggestions made by local committees recommending boundaries that enclose relatively demographically homogeneous areas. Since the census attempts to keep boundaries intact from census to census, the tracts are not as homogeneous as intended since change produces heterogeneity. Each tract has been drawn by the census to consist of a subarea of an urban place containing about 3,000-4,000 households. For each SMSA, the census publishes data summarized by tracts on a variety of topics covered in the population and housing censuses.

Census tracts have been used extensively as units of observation primarily because so many agencies have taken to using tracts as geographical units for which data are summarized and published. For example, many police departments summarize crime statistics by census tracts; health departments summarize fertility and mortality by such areas, and sometimes municipalities will also present census tract summaries of electoral behavior. Social researchers can take advantage of these published summaries to analyze the kinds of neighborhoods (i.e., census tracts) that have high or low crimes rates, mortality, or voting levels for particular candidates or parties.

Blocks in urban areas are even smaller arbitrary geographical units for which census data are routinely summarized. A block is the smallest area defined by boundaries of streets or combinations of streets and natural barriers —rivers, lakes, railroads, and so on. The published volumes of the census routinely contain statistics of housing and some population characteristics summarized by blocks within urban areas, making it possible for social scientists to combine sets of contiguous blocks to constitute larger geographical units representing neighborhoods, precincts, or some other larger unit useful to the purpose of the research in question.

There are very good social science reasons for using arbitrary geographical units of the sort discussed above as units of observation. First of all, much of human behavior is spatially patterned. Populations residing within a given area tend to be relatively homogeneous, with homogeneity increasing with smaller area. Thus the population found within a given census tract tends to be more homogeneous than persons chosen at random from the general population. In part, this homogeneity is the outcome of economic forces in which the prices of homes and the rents for dwellings are determined by locational factors, ensuring that persons residing in a tract are relatively homogeneous socioeconomically. In addition, processes of self-selection are also at work, which bring kin closer together than non-kin and hence promote ethnic homogeneity within census tracts. Processes of discrimination are also at work through which real estate and housing entrepreneurs and brokers tend to operate in a way that makes small neighborhoods racially and ethically homogeneous. Third, and perhaps most important of all, human biology with its built-in necessity for sleep requires that we all have a residence, a housing unit where we can sleep relatively safely from disturbance and harm. Given how housing is provided by the real estate market in our society, almost all persons have an address, giving the coordinates of some housing unit to which we more or less regularly return. The fact that almost all persons have such addresses makes it possible to devise relatively efficient strategies for contacting persons and obtaining measurements on those persons.

The concept of community as a social unit with which inhabitants identify plays an important role in urban sociology. A community is not exactly congruent with a local political jurisdiction, and although located in space is not easily given precise boundaries. In practice, social scientists who work with this concept in their research have had to accept working definitions that either coincide with political jurisdictions or are aggregates of arbitrarily defined geographical units. For example, a metropolitan community may be defined in principle as the population whose livelihood is largely determined by the economic activities that have their headquarters in a large urban center. This definition has much to recommend it since it seemingly is sensitive to the fact that economic activities are at the core of human settlements. However, in practice, this definition is not workable since it provides no mechanisms for identifying the boundaries of a metropolitan community. The firms with headquarters located, say, on the island of Manhattan in New York City, affect the lives of persons all over the world, as well as those who live within the geographical boundaries of New York City and surrounding satellite cities and suburbs. Because of the inherent practical difficulties of drawing boundaries that are fully meaningful, metropolitan areas are usually defined for working purposes as aggregates of political jurisdictions.

Similar problems are encountered in the use of such important social science terms as *neighborhoods* or *regions*, usually defined as geographical units whose residents are either homogeneous in socioeconomic or ethnic terms and who identify themselves as residents. Such definitions are also unworkable in practice, with researchers settling on definitions that are either political entities or arbitrary geographical entities or combinations of one or the other or both. (See Rossi, 1972, for discussion of the difficulties with definitions of community.)

As in the case of political entities, discussed above, the records generated by using arbitrary geographical units as units of observation tend to be mixtures of primary and derived observations. Thus when using census tracts as units of observation, a record may consist of measures of the location of the unit (e.g., distance from the center of the metropolitan areas, density of housing units per unit of area, etc.) and derivative measures formed by summarizing records for other units of observations (e.g., average age of the tract population, proportion of houses that are dilapidated, crime rates, fertility measures, and so on).

For example, in a study of the impact of natural hazards on "neighborhoods," Wright et al. (1979) used census tracts as units of observation, linking together primary measurements on whether or not each of some 13,000 tracts had experienced a flood, tornado, or hurricane in the period between 1960 and 1970, with derivative measures obtained from the 1960 and 1970 censuses to determine whether or not tracts that had experienced such events differed in their population and housing stock in 1970 in any way from tracts that did not have such experiences in that period.

Formal Organizations

Business firms, political parties, governmental agencies and bureaus, churches, and voluntary associations of all sorts are examples of this important type of unit of observation. Although formal organizations come in a wide variety of forms and have widely diverse central activities, it is possible to specify some characteristics that almost all have in common: First of all, a formal organization ordinarily has a "charter," usually written, consisting of sets of rules specifying how persons can be designated members, how membership can be removed, and how one may distinguish members from nonmembers (for example, a business firm can define who its employees and officers are and a voluntary organization usually has ways in which a person can become a member). Second, the charter of a formal organization ordinarily also contains definitions of the duties, responsibilities, and powers of members and officers. A third distinguishing feature of a formal organization is some recognition in law as an organizational entity along with legal definitions of the limits, powers, and responsibilities of the organization. Thus a corporation is established by a legal procedure—an act of incorporation—exists as an entity in law, and is usually empowered by the act of incorporation to engage in some activities (and by implication may not do others).

Other types of formal organizations have similar characteristics. The organization and membership of political parties is defined by statute and by the internal rules of the party. Government agencies are similarly defined. Hence it is usually possible to determine—at least in principle—who are the members of a formal organization, the individuals who are officials of the organization, and an address or location at which organization representatives may be contacted. In short, a formal organization ordinarily can be identified with sufficient precision that measurements can be taken of organizational qualities.

Voluntary associations are often more loosely organized. It is only in a very loose sense that general membership in, say, the American Red Cross, is defined: Anyone who donates funds is a member, but there are no definite duties or responsibilities involved. It is unthinkable that a member be expelled. But at the same time, the American Red Cross does have a structure, hires employees, has chapters in localities, and a structure of governance that operated under a charter granted by Congress. Other voluntary associations are so loosely defined that the definitional boundaries between some voluntary associations and collectivities (see below) are quite unclear.

Using formal organizations as units of observation leads to records that are formally similar to those described above in connection with political entities, consisting of primary measurements on indivisible characteristics of the organization—for example, its financial transactions, rules of governance, table of organization, headquarters location, primary activity as an organization, and so on—as well as derivative measurements computed as summaries of characteristics of subunits within the organization. For example, a data record for a high school might consist of the following mixture of primary and derivative measures: Primary measures might consist of curricula offered, whether it serves a single community or is a consolidated high school, how much fiscal autonomy is enjoyed by the school, the number of volumes in the school library, whether the school has microcomputers available for its students, and so on. On the same record may be placed

derivative measures consisting of the average achievement scores attained by pupils at various grade levels, the average age of teachers along with their average educational attainment, the proportion of students entering the school who complete the requirements for graduation, the socioeconomic levels of parents, and so on (Coleman et al, 1982.)

Because most formal organizations have a defined structure of authority, those members in positions of authority and responsibility within the organization are legally entitled to act in the name of the organization. They are also useful for research purposes as persons who can respond on behalf of the formal organization to inquiries concerning the organization's activities and functions. Thus a research project on the hiring practices of business firms may query the administrative officers of the firms about the practices of the firm, say, in the hiring of women for executive positions. Or the financial officer of a firm may be the best source possible for the collection of data relating to the debt structure of firms.

Collectivities

Collectivities are sets of individuals who share some distinguishing characteristic in common and, in addition, are recognized generally as groups that share common positions in either the socioeconomic structure of the society or share some ideological or structurally determined interests in the outcomes of societal policy. Collectivities are not formally organized, but exist without formal structures or rules of membership, although there may exist formal organizations that are based largely on collectivity memberships.

Examples of collectivities are ethnic groups, genders, age groups, socioeconomic groups, audiences, crowds in particular locations (e.g., persons in a public park or attending a baseball game). Examples of collectivity-based formal organizations include the National Association for the Advancement of Colored People, the National Organization for Women, the American Legion, and so on.

Although collectivities may have leaders and spokespersons, those positions are not defined formally but behaviorally. For example, the late Reverend Martin Luther King was regarded widely as a leader of American blacks but mainly because his public statements were attended to widely among both blacks and whites either as expressing the collective views of many blacks or as highly influential among members of that ethnic group. The Reverend King's formal organization, the Southern Christian Leadership Conference, certainly based much of its membership on blacks as an ethnic group but could not pretend to encompass all blacks in our society.

Similarly, men and women both constitute important collectivities, and while there are many persons who may be regarded as leaders within each collectivity, no person or set of persons can officially—by reason of office—speak for a collectivity simply because there is no office to speak from.

The lack of formal structures for collectivities presents a serious problem for social researchers since it is not easy to devise a strategy for using them as units of observation, even though collectivities are recognized as of considerable importance in our society. Hence most records that are built on the basis of using collectivities as units of observation are based upon derivative measurements. Thus studies that compare ethnic groups ordinarily use records that are summaries taken across persons who are presumably members of ethnic groups, such as average income levels, average educational attainment, regional distribution, and so on. In addition, periodicals addressed largely to ethnic groups or the statements made by ethnic group formal organizations may be used as UOs and added to the records for each ethnic group.

The problems to be encountered in the study of collectivities can be usefully illustrated by attempting to design a study that is concerned with the Right to Life movement. This collectivity may be viewed as composed in part of formal organizations that are primarily dedicated to this cause, formal organizations that have in public expressed support for the aims of the movement, and an amorphous set of persons who are not members of either formal organization but who have values and hold attitudes in sympathy with the Right to Life ideology. How to identify appropriate UOs for such a study presents a considerable puzzle: Alternative solutions might be to restrict the study to explicitly Right to Life formal organizations and their publicly published statements, to define the study as one of members of such organizations, or to define the study as persons who subscribe to the ideology of the movement (using a sample survey approach), or to define the study as combining all three approaches.

Kinship Groups

These are groups of persons who are related to each other through proximate kinship bonds. Thus a family group may be defined as consisting of all persons with the same patronym who are not more than twice removed in lineage (either by natural descent or through adoption). Under this definition a group of brothers, their children, their unmarried sisters, and the parents of the fraternal sib set may constitute a family. This definition also excludes from the concept of a family all married sisters of the fraternal unit, all married female offspring, and the spouses of the fraternal group. If one changes this definition to include kin relationships that include married sisters and spouses and/or kinship ties that are more than once removed, then the definition of family is considerably enlarged. Furthermore, all married persons belong to two kinship groupings, respectively defined by their own blood ties and those of their spouses. Indeed, the sensitivity of the definition of family to seemingly slight alterations in the terms of a definition is one of the major reasons kinship groups are so rarely used as units of observation, at least in our modern Western societies. An additional reason kinship groups are rarely used as UOs involve the fuzziness of kinship in our society. For example, the definition used above assumes patrilinearity, with women assuming their husband's patronym upon marriage, a pattern that shows some signs of no longer being universal in our society.

A more frequently used UO in contemporary social research is the household, roughly defined as consisting of the set of all the persons who share the same dwelling unit. Tying the social unit to dwelling units makes the household a much more easily employed UO than one based on kinship ties. (Households as UOs are discussed in more detail in the next subsection.)

When kinship is studied, it is most ordinarily defined as a kinship dyad, that is, as a pair of persons who are linked together by a given degree of kinship relationship. Examples of kinship dyads include the following paired relationships: husband-wife, mother-daughter, father-son, brother-brother, brother-sister, and so forth.

A record based on father-son kinship dyads might consist of measurements taken of the two persons involved (Blau and Duncan, 1967), perhaps containing such information as the ages of both, their occupational careers, levels of educational attainment, frequency of contact, and so on. Records of dyads present special opportunities (and problems) for analysis, as discussed in greater detail below.

Households

A household group consists of all the persons who claim a given dwelling unit as their address. Although what constitutes a dwelling unit is subject to some ambiguity, the overwhelming majority (more than 95%) of Americans can be allocated to a dwelling unit and hence to a household. The exceptions consist of persons who are homeless, institutionalized in hospitals or nursing homes, or living in group quarters (such as emergency shelters, school dormitories, or military barracks). Although a household may consist of one person or a very large number of persons, most households consist of a married couple, their dependent children and at most one or two persons related by kinship to one or the other spouse. Nevertheless, in the last two decades single-adult households have increased to the point that in some cities, for example, San Francisco, such households constitute a majority among all households.

Household groups are important to social scientists because members of a household ordinarily share the same socioeconomic level, the same ethnicity, more or less jointly make certain decisions concerning expenditures, savings, moving, and migration, and often are homogeneous in belief and ideology. A study concerned with patterns of medical care would be wise to use households as units of observation since most households assume jointly the financial and other burdens of medical care of individual members. (Indeed, medical care insurance policies recognize this pattern by providing family coverage policies.)

A record based on the household as a unit of observation ordinarily has a mixed character, being composed of both primary and derivative measurements. Primary observations may include household size, measures of the household's location in terms of settlement density (that is, whether rural or in urban areas of varying sizes), proximity to significant kin of certain household members, sources of household income, measures of household saving, descriptions of the dwelling occupied, and so on. Derivative measurements may be computed by considering the members of the household as a group and summarizing the group characteristics, with measures such as the average age of children or of adults, per capita income, and so on.

Individuals

For several reasons, individuals are perhaps the most commonly used units of observations. First, much of our data come from querying persons, as in census or survey operations of all sorts, and hence the basic data often can be most easily organized as relating to individuals, since census schedules and survey questionnaires are often physically related to a single person as either informant or as respondent. Second, much of the substantive concern of social scientists is with individual persons: An economist may be interested in economic decision making by individual consumers; a sociologist with how a person's collectivity memberships impact upon his or her values or attitudes, and a social psychologist with how an individual's belief structures are inter-related.

The data assembled into a record based on an individual as a unit of observation may vary across all the types of observations than can be made on an individual. Thus a record may consist of the following mixture:

(1) observations made by the researcher about the individual in question—such as skin color, apparent age, and degree of articulateness;

(2) responses made by the individual to specific questions directed at him or her, as in the typical survey;

(3) measures that describe the individual's physical or social environment—for example, ownership or rental of dwelling unit, type of neighborhood or community;

(4) scores on tests either taken from human documents or obtained by directly testing the individual; and

(5) measures that concern the relationship between a respondent and other persons, such as friends, kin, voting preferences, and so forth.

A full catalogue of all the measurements that can be meaningfully related to individual humans would be a very long document.

Beyond all doubt, persons have been (and will continue to be) the most frequently used UO in sociology. Even in studies in which the basic UO does not appear to be persons, as in studies that use published census data, the data used have been derived from individual records. Studies of organizations are often based on individuals as UOs, each individual providing information on the organization in question. Sample surveys are perhaps the most popular form of data collection for those sociologists who engage in original data collection. Indeed, there can be little doubt that the most important technical advance in social research has been the invention of the sample survey as a data collection method.

Although the adoption of the sample survey by sociologists as the major research method has been of enormous benefit to the field, it has also had some unfortunate side effects. It has deflected sociological research from a concern with social organization and social relationships to a study of individual differences, or away from studies of social organization to social psychological studies. For example, the subfield of political sociology has been more concerned with the effects of political attitudes on voting preferences—a task to which the sample survey is admirably suited—than with the effects of the structure of the state institutions on the administration of policy and programs, a task to which the sample survey is poorly suited. There are undoubtedly dozens of empirical studies of how voters form their candidate preferences, but only a few studies of how government agencies administer the laws and regulations in the implementation of programs and policies.

A similar "distortion" of emphasis occurs in the study of the family. There are few studies that examine the network of exchange relationships among kin (financial help, services, information, etc.) in comparison to the multitude of studies of marital happiness based on the compatibility or incompatibility of the personal characteristics of the two spouses.

These comments are not to be understood as stating that voting behavior or marital happiness are not legitimate topics for sociologists. The intended import of these remarks is that the ease of conducting sample surveys with individuals as UOs has led to an unfortunate slighting of studies of social organization. It should also be noted that the sample survey can be used for the study of social relationships as the next few pages will indicate. All that is necessary is that the social researcher frame questions in organizational terms and conduct sample surveys with the view of transforming individual data records based on persons as UOs into relational data records that are derivative records.

Dyadic Social Relationships

We have already discussed one form of dyadic social relationship, pairs of kin, that can serve as a unit of observation. The myriad forms of connections between pairs of individuals, however, each define additional types of dyads as units of observation. A dyad as a unit of observation consists of some form of social relationship between a pair of individuals, that is, some

regular and recurring form of interaction among members of the pair in question. Perhaps the most frequently studied dyads are those formed by the social relationships of marriage, kinship and friendship, but others frequently studied include being coworkers, or neighbors, professional relationships such as doctor-patient or teacher-student, or embodying special types of asymmetry as in leader-follower, buyer-seller, or artist-member of audience, and so on.

In principle, one might suppose that dyads ought to be the most frequently used units of observation employed by social scientists. The very definition of social scientist includes at its center a concern with social relationships or interactions among at least two individuals. Furthermore, the more complex forms of social structure can be seen as having dyads as basic building blocks. Just as we earlier built a definition of family around defining certain possible kin relationships among possible pairs of individuals, so the more complex forms could be built around similar building blocks of dyads, as for example, defining business firms as collections of coworker pairs, markets as defined by collections of buyers and sellers, and so on.

The practical obstacles to an approach to studying social structure through the collection of data on dyads lies in the complexity of patterns that characterize the higher-order relationships that are built out of dyads. For example, a factory work force consists of persons who have many dyadic relationships with each other, the total patterning of which reflects the particular process of production used in the firm, as well as the administration of personnel and payrolls. Defining each of the possible types of combinations of dyads leads to a morass of possible data that obstinately would resist reduction to patterns. Hence the study of dyads has so far been restricted to relatively simple relationships, as, for example, friendship and kinship (including marriage).

There are two alternative approaches to obtaining observations on dyads. Perhaps the most often used approach is to observe a dyad through querying one of the dyadic partners. Thus a person may be asked to designate her best friend" and then is questioned about critical characteristics of that person. The resulting record provides data on the dyad as refracted through the assessments of one of its members. This approach has economy as its major advantage but runs the risk of obtaining inaccurate data on the uninterviewed partner to the dyad. The most prominent example of this kind of dyad research is Blau and Duncan's (1967) study of occupational mobility through querying male respondents in a sample survey about their fathers' occupations. An alternative, but much more expensive, approach is to query both partners, each providing data on his or her own personal characteristics and on the relationship. Although one can be more confident about the validity of the information obtained in this second approach, it is clearly more expensive.

Dyads as units of observation result in fairly simple records on which measures relating to each member of the dyad and to the tie between them may be placed. Thus a friendship dyad may generate a record on which is placed the age, gender, ethnicity, and so forth of each member plus a measure of the degree of intimacy of the friendship, the length of time it has been in existence, and so on.

Behavior Sequences

An interesting unit of observation involves entities that consist of sequences of human behavior, in which each sequence of behavior is regarded as the object of interest. Thus an educational social psychologist might be interested in the interactions between a teacher and a student, classifying each sequence of action and then reaction as to its content, whether initiated by the student or the instructor, observing what transpires whenever a student starts some action directed toward a teacher, such as asking a question, making a request, or uttering a remark. Or, a sociologist interested in how police interact with citizens in the course of duty might take extensive notes on each encounter between a citizen and a police officer (Reiss, 1971). Or an economist might be interested in transactions between buyers and sellers on some market, using as her units of observation each sale on that market. Or, a communications expert might extract all the sentences in Soviet and American political speeches that deal with relations between the USSR and the United States in order to study the terms used by Soviet and American politicians in referring to the other country involved.

A behavior sequence as a unit of observation leads to simple records. A record generated by a police-citizen encounter might contain such information as who initiated the contact, the demeanor of both persons, the apparent age and sex of the citizen, a recording of the oral exchanges between the two, the outcomes of the exchange, and so forth. Note that it may in some instances be difficult to decide whether the unit of observation is a behavior sequence or a dyadic relationship, the major distinction being

whether or not the interest of the observed is in the relationship between the persons involved or the content of an exchange between individuals.

Modes of Observation

The selection of a UO does not necessarily determine fully how observations are to be made. For many types of UOs, the researcher has freedom to choose among several modes of observation (or data collection method), a choice that will affect to some degree the kind of data that may be collected and the efficiency of data collection (for example, the unit cost of collection). In addition, for a given purpose, some modes of observation are preferred because they are believed to yield data of greater validity than alternative modes.

An observation or data collection mode may be defined as the procedures used by which observations are made. An observation mode may be, as discussed earlier, at one extreme, highly unobtrusive or, at the other extreme, highly intrusive, depending on the extent to which the human subjects involved are aware of the data collection and the extent to which the act of data collection is itself a social relationship. Clearly, the making of measurements of any sort on human traces or the reading and coding of human documents is unobtrusive with no element of social relationship involved. This is especially the case when applied to historical artifacts and documents whose owners, originators, and/or users may safely be considered dead. It is only when human traces and documents are used as units of observation to study relatively current times that issues of intrusiveness arise.

Observation modes may be roughly classified along two dimensions: (1) the degree to which the procedure involves active or passive observation, and (2) the extent to which there is actual social interaction between the observer and the UO. An active observation procedure interrupts the sequence of "natural activity" of a unit in order to make the observation in question. Thus asking a question of an individual is an active observation procedure, while the counting of persons passing a given point on a street is relatively passive.

The second dimension involves whether measurement is taken while interacting with the unit being measured. Thus asking a question involves social interaction, while reading a document ordinarily does not.

The cross classification of these two dimensions, each viewed for present purposes as a dichotomy, yields four types of measurement procedures, as follows:

Passive Observation Without Social Interaction

The researcher simply observes the unit without interacting with it. Thus a researcher may be posted to a restaurant where he notes the apparent ages and sexes of groups who are dining with each other, using the group seated at each table as a unit of observation. Or, a researcher reads a file of newspapers in a library, copying or coding those articles that contain references to specified topics, places, or persons.

Passive observation may at first appear to be a mode that would be used frequently by social researchers. There are no issues of intrusiveness and often none of privacy. However, the types of data that can be collected using this mode are very limited. For example, the analysis of human documents appears very attractive to social researchers, except for the fact that compared to the total amount of human behavior, that which results in written documents or in human traces is very slight: We can learn much from birth certificates about fertility but very little about parenting or marriage.

Passive observation of ongoing human behavior is restricted to those places to which there is free public access and in which the act of passive observation is itself not intrusive. One can "hang around" in the lobby of a building for just so long before attracting attention. Besides, much of human and organizational behavior takes place in relatively restricted-access places, such as homes and workplaces where it is not possible to observe without permission.

Passive Observation With Social Interaction

In this mode the researcher observes UOs and at the same time interacts with the units being observed but not as an explicitly designated researcher. This is ordinarily called participant observation in which a researcher joins the unit being observed as part of the ordinary, natural social environment of the unit. Thus a researcher may join an apocalyptic religious cult as an ordinary member would, acting as an ordinary member while at the same time recording his observations of the cult. Or, a researcher joins someone drinking at a bar, strikes up a seemingly casual conversation, and later records what was said.

Passive, interactive observation is an attractive mode for many reasons: First of all, what is observed seemingly has higher validity than under circumstances where the UOs involved know that the observer is a researcher. For example, compared to using sample surveys, we would probably obtain more valid information on the ways in which real estate dealers treat persons of varying ethnic backgrounds by enlisting social researchers of varying backgrounds to act as potential home buyers, approaching real estate dealers, and observing how each simulated home buyer is treated. Second, for some topics there may be no other way that observations can be made. It probably is not possible to know what goes on within a criminal gang, or a secret society without joining the group in question as a member.

However, passive interactive observation has considerable limitations. To begin with, there is always an element of deception in passive interactive modes of observation. Although the objective of the study and of the observer may be benign, there is still the issue of fully informed consent on the part of the UO under observation. Clearly, when a UO thinks the researcher is an ordinary denizen of a bar, he has not given his consent to having his or her conversation recorded. For these reasons, passive interactive modes of observation should only be used under conditions in which the anonymity of the UO can be fully guaranteed and for projects of considerable importance in which observations could not be taken in any other manner. For example, participant observation within a Mafia group would most likely be considered unethical behavior, besides subjecting the researcher to some considerable personal risk. In contrast, there may be no better way to study variations in the definition of personal space than to observe passively how individuals react in crowded elevators to an observer standing close by.

Active Observation With Social Interaction

In this case, the researcher interacts with units in a relatively standardized way recording the reactions of the unit as observations. This mode of data collection includes all forms of interviewing, the distribution of questionnaires, or the observation of ongoing interaction in which participants understand that the observer is a researcher. Examples include the interviewing that takes place in connection with censuses or surveys, and field or laboratory experiments in which the researchers actively change the life conditions of UOs, observing the reactions of UOs to those changed conditions.

Perhaps the most intrusive of all active interactive research designs are field experiments in which persons are recruited as experimental subjects, administered some sort of experimental treatment, with their responses to the treatment being recorded extensively. For example, in Rossi, Berk, and Lenihan (1980), some 4000 persons released from the prisons of Georgia and Texas were observed for a year after release to assess the impact upon postrelease adjustment of small weekly monetary payments (simulated unemployment benefits). Released prisoners were divided randomly into an experimental group who received the benefits and a control group who did not. Both groups were followed for a year beyond release through administrative records and by personal interviews. Field experiments on this scale are among the most expensive of social researches and hence are relatively rare.

Compared to field experiments, censuses and surveys are much more frequently employed. The basic characteristic of both censuses and surveys is the active interaction of researchers (or their representatives) with humans as UOs, with the resulting behavior of the UO being the source of the observations. The interaction may be highly standardized through the use of fixed sets of questions, as in census schedules and most sample surveys, with the basic observations being the answers given by UOs in response to the questions. Other active interactive modes include semistructured interview studies in which the topics are standardized but the researcher (or representative) is given the freedom to form questions according to on-the-spot judgments about what questions are most appropriate.

The validity of active interactive observation modes rests upon the assumption that the behavior of UOs in reaction to the active observation is meaningfully related to behavior evoked in the course of ordinary, everyday events. This assumption has often been questioned, usually in the following form: "Do attitudes (as expressed, say, in the form of answers to survey questions) predict behavior?" Although this controversy has not been fully settled one way or the other, it has become increasingly clear that a complex chain of relationships connects the behavior (including verbal behavior) of UOs under active observation to the

ordinary behavior of UOs. A one-to-one correspondence of observer-evoked and "natural behavior" has been ruled out by the negative findings of scores of studies, with the latter being heavily influenced by situational elements. For example, evoked consumer buying intentions predict only modestly whether consumers will buy the products in question in the time period in question. Yet, those who indicate intentions to buy are more likely to do so than those who do not. Even more tenuous links connect, say, expressed kinship obligations and actual patterns of help given to kin, the latter being influenced strongly by the resources of the individual, distance to the kin in question, competing obligations, and so on. Proper employment of data derived from active interactive observations requires an appreciation of the indirect links between evoked verbal behavior and "natural behavior," and the measurement of more than just expressed preferences or intentions.

In addition, active interactive observation modes run the risk of producing observations that would ordinarily not appear "naturally." An interviewer asking a question on a topic with which the respondents is not familiar may get a response that is largely a function of the question asked and not characteristic of the respondent. For example, a question concerning the Soviet treatment of ethnic Tartars may elicit responses that have little to do with the respondent's assessment of either the treatment or the Tartars because the respondent has little or no knowledge of either. Furthermore, for most American respondents, there may be no occasion for "naturally occurring" behavior vis-a-vis Tartars or the USSR.

Despite the questions raised by the validity issues, active interactive observation modes are the most frequently used in social research. There are several reasons for the popularity of this mode of observation. First, the range of subject matter to which this observation mode is appropriate far exceeds that of any other. Human documents cover only a very small set of topics, with extensive coverage given to those topics over which there is some administrative concern. Passive observation modes are restricted to those situations in which it is possible to be a passive observer. In contrast, censuses and surveys can cover almost any topic ranging from sexual practices to religious beliefs and involve UOs from all segments of a society. Second, the more standardized forms of active interactive observation lend themselves to large-scale studies. There is no way a population census of a large population can be carried out without an extensive organization of enumerators, supervisors, and technicians and standardized observation instruments. Similarly, large-scale sample surveys simply cannot be carried out using either passive observation modes or unstandardized observation. Finally, active interactive observation modes are efficient, costing less per unit of information than most other modes. Passive modes in which the observer waits for "natural behavior" of the desired variety to occur are time consuming and therefore expensive.

Active Observation Without Social Interaction

In this mode of observation a researcher acts in some way toward UOs without interacting with the UOs in question. The researcher does something to the UO without the UO being aware of its source. Most of the examples of researches using this mode are field experiments in which a researcher introduces some new element into the lives of UOs as if the new element were a "naturally occurring" event. Thus in the one of earliest field experiments, Gosnell (1938) mailed leaflets before a local election to registered voters in a set of Chicago precincts urging the voters to participate in the forthcoming election. The content of the leaflets varied. One variation used a "rational" appeal, emphasizing the importance of participation to the democratic electoral process, while another version of the leaflet used an "emotional" appeal stressing the patriotic duty of citizens to vote. The relative effectiveness of the several appeals was judged by consulting official records on who among those sent leaflets actually voted.

Another example consists of the researchers altering the physical layout of streets in an urban neighborhood by designating some streets as one way, turning others into cul-de-sacs—all with the hope of altering the flow of foot and vehicular traffic through the neighborhood for the purpose of lowering the crime rate. The effect on the crime rate was measured through crimes reported to the police by neighborhood residents in the period following street pattern alterations. Market researchers have inserted trial advertisements into ongoing cable television programs to observe the effects of the trial ads on product sales in the stores.

There are many attractive features to the active, noninteractive observation mode. However, this mode is not often used because most active procedures inherently involve social interaction. In addition, this mode shares with other noninteractive modes the fact that some element

of deception, however benign, is ordinarily involved. Thus the Chicago voters who participated in Gosnell's experiment did not know the source of the leaflets they received and, of course, did not give their consent—explicitly or implied—to participate in the experiment.

Choosing a Mode of Observation

The mode of observation to be used in a planned research should be chosen both to suit the purpose of the research and to fit the resource budget allocated. Each mode of observation has some advantages and some disadvantages. Passive observation procedures have the attractive quality of disturbing units of observation least and hence neither putting a burden upon the unit nor producing behavior that may be in some way non-natural. Thus to ask a person what he or she thinks of an issue about which that person may have never before given any thought, may be to "create" an opinion that may be different from what the individuals in question may have arrived at "naturally." Or a queried person may give answers that he or she thinks will enhance the interviewer's opinions. In the passive observation modes, a person who does not have an opinion is not likely to voice one. In addition, because the observed person is not aware of being the observer's center of attention, the former may not tailor his or her remarks to enhance the observer's opinions.

The disadvantage of passive modes of observation is that they may be very inefficient. A researcher may have to listen (perhaps impatiently) to hours of natural conversation before hearing any opinions expressed on a topic of central research interest. Similarly, watching how whites react to having blacks sit next to them on public transportation may catch expressions of negative attitudes that would never be expressed under direct questioning about hypothetical situations, but the researcher may have to travel many miles on the local bus routes to obtain even a minimally adequate number of such encounters. In contrast, active measurement procedures have the advantage of being relatively efficient per unit of relevant data collected and the disadvantage of producing observations that result from non-naturally occurring circumstances and hence possibly more likely to be atypical behavior.

Observation that accompanies interaction has the disadvantage that the behavior observed may be partially determined by the interaction itself and less a function of the characteristics of the UO. Thus it has been repeatedly shown that black interviewers get different answers from both black and white people when asking questions that deal with race relations.

In the interpretation of data derived from all modes of observation, the mode itself has to be considered as potentially affecting the observations obtained. This last statement does not mean that the observation is completely determined by the data collection mode, but only that the observation might be so affected. For example, it probably makes little difference in the observation outcome whether the sex of a UO is determined by asking a question, or making inferences from observing dress, physique, and the like. In contrast, the observed sexual preferences of individuals may vary significantly according to the mode of observation used.

From Observations to Measurement

As discussed in the last section, observation may take a variety of forms, but the outcome always consists of an observer's "mark" on a UO record indicating that some value of a quality (attribute, class, variable) has been observed on the UO in question. An observer's mark may take a variety of forms. Thus a particular "mark" may consist of an arbitrary code (e.g., "M" or "F") or a written note (e.g., "John is a male"), a direct quote of a respondent's reply to a question, or a "coded" response that uses a numerical code, each number corresponding to a class of observations.

Although in many observations the researcher has some interest in the observation itself, in many others the observation is obtained because it is an indicator of some quality of the UO in question that cannot be directly observed. The distinction drawn in the last sentence is between an observation of the apparent sex of a person (UO) and an observation that a person endorses the right of persons to speak their minds on political issues. In the first case, the observation itself can be used as without further transformation, whereas in the second case the observation may be taken in order to be able to classify a person as relatively liberal or conservative on civil rights issues. In the second case, the observation is an indicator of a (presumably) generalized predisposition to endorse liberal positions on a variety of civil rights issues, a more generalized construct that includes many other political issues besides freely speaking one's mind.

Measurement is the transformation of observations into numbers in order to use the resulting numbers either directly in simple calculations or to stand for some underlying concept of which the observations are indicators. The resulting numbers can be used to summarize the data and to make description of the data easier to comprehend, and/or in more complicated form to uncover relationships and processes within UOs. Measurement is accomplished by systematically assigning numbers to observations either to (1) reflect the presence or absence of some quality in an object being measured, (2) reflect the ordering of such objects according to the magnitude of amount of some quality, or (3) reflect directly the amount of such qualities. The qualities may be directly reflected in the observations (as in the case of apparent sex, discussed above) or indirectly (as in the case of some postulated construct). At the least, measurement produces numbers that allow an ordering of UOs in terms of relative magnitudes of some quality; at the most, measurement assigns numbers that are capable of being used in arithmetic calculations.

Measurement is not the arbitrary assignment of numbers to observations. Ideally, measurement proceeds by using a device (or model) that is a set of rules for assigning numbers to observations and for combining those numbers into some composite number, the latter presumably reflecting the latent construct involved. A measurement model incorporates into its rules assumptions about the ways in which constructs and observations are related, providing a rationale for a linkage between the latent and manifest levels. A comprehensive measurement model also provides a basis for the arithmetical treatment of the composite numbers produced by the model.

Measurement may take any one of a variety of forms, discussed in the following sections.

Binary Measurement

Binary measurement is often regarded as the most primitive measurement form, simply a record of the presence or absence of some attribute or quality in the unit being measured. In number terms, the convention ordinarily followed is that a "1" is used to mark the presence of some quality in a UO and a "0" used to mark its absence. Thus a binary measurement may be used to mark whether a person UO is standing or not, appears to be white or nonwhite, or wearing glasses or not. In addition, binary measurement may be used to measure and mark two mutually exclusive qualities, for example, gender, in which being a female is marked with a "1," and apparent maleness noted with a "0."

Binary measurement is about the simplest measurement form possible. Yet despite its simplicity, it is possible to express almost every quality that can be observed in binary terms. Complex qualities, for example, marital status, can be expressed as a series of binary measurements; a person is either married or not, either single and never married or not, either formerly married or not. Or, a person may be measured as old or not old, using some threshold chronological age as the dividing point between persons marked "1" and those marked "0." (Although "1" and "0" are conventionally used, any pair of unequal numbers would serve the same purpose.)

Binary measurement is at the base of enumeration, the counting of UOs, either as such or as possessing some quality. Thus the number of persons counted in a city or county can be regarded as the outcome of summing the result of binary measurements that identified objects as persons ("1") or not-persons ("0"). The sum of all the positive judgments ("1s") is the number of persons in the city or county in question. (Obviously, the census enumerator makes a mark only when a person is encountered.)

Unordered Classification

In this type of measurement a unit is observed to belong to one of a set of mutually exclusive but unordered and unequally numbered classes. For example, a person may be classified as a member of one of the following ethnic groups: whites, blacks, Hispanics, or "others," and given the numbers 1 through 4 accordingly. Or, persons may be classified according to the state of which they are residents or in which they were born, leading to a classification into one of 51 different and mutually exclusive groups. (Note there are 51 classes in this case since an additional class of "other place" is needed besides the 50 states in order to take care of persons born outside the United States.) This kind of measurement is called "unordered classification" because there is no sensible inherent arrangement of the states or ethnic groups, such that the states or ethnic groups can be placed in the order to which they each have more or less of some "state" or "ethnic" quality.

It should be noted that unordered classifications can also be expressed as a set of mutually exclusive binary measurements and are easily transformed into binary measurements. Thus the state of residence of a person can be represented by a set of binary classes, one for each of the 50 states, with the person having a "1" marked for his or her state of residence and "0s" for the 49 other states.

When observations are turned into binary measures or given arbitrary numbers as in unordered classifications, the numbers are mainly used as simplified "shorthand" labels that serve to distinguish one qualitative observation from another. The appropriate manipulation of numerical codes consists of enumeration, the counting of how many of each numerical code can be found in a data set. Thus we may count that there are 400 UOs coded 1 (and hence males) and 600 that were coded 2 (and hence females). From enumerations of this sort, important quantitative statements may be made. For example, we may divide each of the enumerative quantities by the total number of records involved to arrive at percentages, a calculation that standardizes these enumerations that standardizes these enumerations to the base of 100. In this case, we find that 60% are females, a standardized statement that means simply that there are, on average, 60 females to be counted in each 100 records. Percentages make possible the easy comparison between record sets of different sizes.

Percentages are simply a special case of rates, numbers that express the number of cases of some particular type to be found in a given standard number of cases. Thus an annual death rate of 5.6 per 10,000 for, say, New York state indicates that of 10,000 New Yorkers alive at the beginning of a year, 5.6 will have died at the end of that year.

Enumerations are an important operation in social research. The counting of UOs showing some sort of identifiable quality produces quantities that are of interest in and of themselves and form the bases for many additional calculations that provide summary information about the UOs observed.

Ordered Classification

This type of measurement places units into groups that can be arranged in rank or size order. Thus persons may be classified as "youths," "young adults," "adults," and "old people" with each group being progressively older. Note that the difference in age between pairs of successive age groups is not uniform; The class of youths may span about four years from puberty to age 18, while young adults may span 10 years, adults 40 years, and old people may mean anyone over 65.

In the case of the example of age groups in the last paragraph, we know that the classification produced groups that were not equal distances apart in chronological age, but in the case of many social science measurements we know intuitively that we have ordered persons in some sort of rank order but we have no idea whether the groups are equal or unequal distances apart. For example, an attitude test may yield scores that we believe represent increasing degrees of punitive attitudes toward convicted felons, but we do not know whether the scores represent uniform and equal degrees of such attitudes. Thus the computed scores may range from 1 to 20 but we cannot be sure that the latter score represents someone who is 20 times more punitive than some persons who was given a score of 1.

Cardinal Measurement

This is a form of measurement in which numbers assigned to a unit may be treated as representing unit increments of some quality. Thus a cardinal measurement of attitudes toward convicted felons would produce scores of punitiveness that can be added and subtracted. A score of 20 would be regarded as marking a person who is 20 times more punitive than someone with a score of 1.

In addition, most discussions of measurement identify a fifth form in which the numbers assigned have an agreed upon zero point and in which ratios between pairs of numbers equally far apart are themselves equal. These ratio scales have important properties but are found so rarely in the social sciences that we may safely forgo discussion in this chapter.

Deciding on Measurement

Any observation may be recorded as a binary measurement, as simply the presence or absence of some quality, as observed in the unit under study. In many cases, binary measurement is all that may be called for or needed. Thus gender is often rightfully recorded as a binary measure, with the person observed being marked as either male or female. (Strictly speaking, gender calls for two binary measures, "male" or "not male" and "female" or "not female," but since there is no possibility of a person being both male and female, the two binary measures can be combined into one, since being not male implies being female and being not female implies being male.)

An unordered classification may be regarded as a set of mutually dependent binary measures, in which a unit that is classified as having one of the qualities is, by definition, classified as having none of the other qualities. Thus the unordered classification, religious affiliation as Catholic, Protestant, or Jewish can be also con ceptualized as a set of binary measures, Catholic or non-Catholic, Protestant or non-Protestant, and Jewish or non-Jewish in which a person cannot, by definition, be positive on any two or all three of the binary measures.

When the measurement implies degrees or amounts of some quality, as in ordered classification and cardinal measurement, then matters becomes somewhat more complicated. There are no absolutely clear distinctions between the two kinds of measures and in application to specific research problems the same measure may be regarded quite differently by various researchers. In some contexts, some measures are conventionally regarded as cardinal. Accordingly, we ordinarily regard chronological age as a cardinal measure equating each calendar year of age as equivalent no matter when in the life course it falls. An additional year beyond 90 is regarded the same as an additional year beyond age 10. In many contexts, this conventional usage makes little sense since there are considerable differences of an important qualitative sort between an additional year in early childhood and the same passage of time for a mature adult. Indeed, for some purposes, we may want to regard age not as a cardinal measure but as an ordered classification recognizing in our classification some set of life cycle stages.

In the final analysis, whether a measure is an ordered classification or a cardinal measure depends on what makes best sense in the context of the research problem in question. It may make a great deal of sense to regard years of seniority in a job as a cardinal measure since most employers regard it as such in endowing seniority with privileges (e.g., seniority is measured in years, with all years being regarded as equal in value). But in other contexts, years may be regarded as unequal, as in the study of child development.

Direct and Indirect Measurement

In addition, measurements may be either direct or indirect. A measure is a direct one when the resulting data do not need any further interpretation to be used. For example, the observation that a person is a male can be made directly: The definition of being a male is equivalent to the observer or researcher making a judgment to that effect. It should also be noted that several observers would ordinarily agree with considerable consistency on the measurement made. In contrast, an indirect measurement involves qualities that are not perceivable directly but must be inferred from observations that reflect or indicate the quality in question. Thus it is not possible to observe directly whether a person is a political liberal or a conservative, but one infers the subject's political stance from a wide variety of statements of a political nature made by the person or infers from answers to questions posed to the individual. Furthermore, there are a variety of ways in which such qualities as political liberalism may manifest themselves and hence there is no bounded set of statements or of answers to questions that completely exhausts the conceivable indicators of that state.

Much, if not most, of the measurements in which social scientists are interested are indirect measurements based upon sets of indicators that are more or less adequate to the task. The science of how to infer from indicators the underlying condition that generated such indicators is known as measurement theory. Although it is not possible in this chapter to go into that topic in any depth, the interested reader is referred to Duncan (1986) and Torgerson (1958) for further information.

Unit Records and Aggregated Data

The data collected concerning a unit of observation consists of the measurements made directly on that unit from observations (measurements) made and other measures that are derivative from other records. Since there are several ways in which data about a unit can be assembled to form a record, there are different kinds of records, a topic that will be discussed in this section.

A unit record is a collection of all the data that have been assembled in a research project about a unit. The actual physical form of a unit record may be a file folder in which notes are filed, a set of index cards on which measurements on a unit are recorded, a set of punched cards, or a computer tape or disk. The physical form is important only for the relative ease in which the form provides access and facilitates the analysis of data.

A unit record may be composed of either one type of record or it may be a composite of several record types. Some of the important types of records are described below.

Primitive Records (or Zero-Order Records)

These are records in which each of the component measurements are indivisible and generated from direct observation of the unit alone. Such records are called primitive not because of the crudity of the measurement but because each measurement is obtained directly from observation and is not derivative from other observations.

For example, a primitive record from a sample survey would be a record containing only the responses of a respondent to the questions included in the survey in question. A primitive record derived from a content analysis of articles appearing in popular magazines would be a record in which the only observations appearing in the record would be ones resulting from a reading and subsequent coding of an article. Another example of a primitive record would be the manuscript copies of census schedules, the direct observations of a census taker on the individuals or households covered by the census.

First-Order Derivative Record

This is a record composed of measurements that are made by combining two or more primitive records whose units are related to each other in some way. These are important types of records because for some of the units in which social scientists are interested, the units cannot be observed directly but only by creating primitive records for constituent parts.

For example, a friendship relationship can only partially be observed directly, but individuals who form a friendship pair can be observed and the resulting primitive records can be combined to form a first-order derivative record. Direct observation may include measures of the places in which the friends meet or of the content of their conversations. The first-order derivative records consist of measurements each of which relate solely to one of the individuals involved. Thus a derivative first-order record of a friendship may include such individual characteristics as the age, sex, occupation, and marital status of the individuals involved. Combining the two primitive records into a first-order derivative record makes it possible to look at the interrelationships between the ages, sexes, and occupational statuses of the pairs of individuals who are friends.

Another example of a first-order derivative record would be of sales transactions, in which the characteristics of buyers and sellers would be obtained from primitive records relating respectively to buyers and sellers and combined to form first-order derivative records.

Indeed, first-order derivative records are the basic data assembly formats for the study of all kinds of dyads, which in turn constitute the basis for the study of higher-order complex relationships, such as families, households, friendship cliques, and so on.

Second-Order Derivative Records

A second-order derivative record is formed by summary measures taken over more than two primitive records that pertain to individuals who are members of some formal group or collectivity. Second-order derivative records may be formed for such groups as households, families, kinship groups, collectivities, formal organizations, arbitrary geographical entities, and for political jurisdictions. The measurements used in second-order derivative records are some sort of summaries of characteristics shown by constituent members.

For example, a second-order derivative record for a household might consist of the average age of members, per capita income, proportion of persons in household under the age of 18, per capita number of bedrooms, and so on. These are measures of the household but derived from (at least partially) measures taken of each of the household members.

Similarly kinship groups, however defined, might best be analyzed by forming second-order derivative records from the primitive records of kinship group members, including such measures as the maximum socioeconomic distances among pairs of members, the average age of members, the proportion who have married outside the predominant ethnicity and religious denomination of the group and so on.

An important type of second-order derivative record is used in the analysis of arbitrary geographical entities. Census tracts are frequently used as units of observation in studies in which the geographical distribution and clustering of human activities is critical. Virtually all measurements available on census tracts are second-order derivative records in which summary measures of the housing and population to be found in tracts are the basic measures used. Thus a tract record—second-order derivative—might consist of the average age of dwellings in the tract, median rents for renter-occupied dwellings, average size of households, the average age of persons over the age of 16, median household income, and so on. These summary measures that constitute the second-order derivative records are obtained by summarizing information obtained from the primitive records for structures, dwelling units, households, and individuals in the tract in question.

Researches on formal organizations must also lean very heavily on second-order derivative records for the organizations being studied. Such records would consist of summaries of primitive records pertaining to members of the organization, for example, all employees, managers of an enterprise, offices of a voluntary organization, and so on. Indeed, one of the major obstacles to the full development of an empirically grounded theory of formal organizations is the great expense involved in developing second-order derivative records for a sufficient number of formal organizations. Unfortunately it takes as large a sample of any one organization to establish with precision the characteristics of organizations members as it takes to establish the characteristics of the pooled employees from a larger set of organizations. Second-order derivative records for organizations might contain such summary measures as average wages for employees on various levels, median levels of educational attainment, mean length of tenure in the organization, and so on.

Reflective Unit Records

These are records concerning a unit made up of measurements taken from the primitive records of other units. For example, a reflective record for individual A might consist of a summary of how well liked that individual was, consisting of the proportion of other persons in some organization to which A belonged who chose A as a friend. Thus the popularity of a school child might be defined as the number of her classmates who chose her as a friend. Or the prestige position of an occupation has been measured as the average rating given to the occupation by the members of the society in question.

Mixed-Character Unit Records

While the above discussion has centered on

records that are purely primitive or purely derivative in some way, actual records are often mixtures of the types discussed above. Thus a unit record might consist of some primitive measurements, some derivative measurements, and perhaps some reflective measures as well. Indeed, some of the more sophisticated studies deliberately are planned to contain mixtures of all the types discussed.

Ordinarily sociological research on any appreciable scale is carried out using modern computers as an aid in the numerical analysis of the data involved, using statistical packages on high-speed computers. Most such packages allow the researcher to assemble files that facilitate the use of records of a wide variety. Combining records obtained from various sources, or linking records according to some common identifier can be accomplished with relative ease.

Some Concluding Remarks on Sociological Data

The variety of UOs available to the sociological researcher covers a rich and extensive range. There are few sociological topics concerning our contemporary society for which it is clearly beyond our capability to collect relevant data and to analyze them appropriately. Our major limitations appear to those of the imagination and courage. Imagination is needed to conceive of the relevant observations, and courage is needed to plan the observations needed to form the appropriate measurement of our key concepts. Concerning the past, however, we are limited to the exploitation of human traces and human documents, a choice that often renders the detailed study of the past difficult if not impossible.

It cannot be overstressed that data collection is not an activity to be engaged in without considerable thought and prior planning. We cannot observe without ideas about what it is relevant to observe. There is no "raw" observation, only observation guided by a framework of concepts and theory that relates those concepts to each other. Critical first steps in planning sociological research include choosing or developing a conceptual framework and the models of how the resulting measures need to be integrated.

REFERENCES

Blau, Peter M. and Otis D. Duncan. 1967. *The American Occupational Structure*. New York. John Wiley.

Chase-Dunn, Christopher. 1975. "The Effects of Economic Dependence on Development and Inequality." *American Sociological Review* 40: 720-739.

Coleman, James S., Thomas Hoffer, and Sally Kilgore. 1982. *High School Achievement*. New York. Basic Books.

Duncan, Otis D. 1986. *Notes on Measurement*. New York. Russell Sage Foundation.

Gosnell, Harold F. 1938. *Getting Out the Vote*. Chicago: University of Chicago Press.

Jahoda, M., T. S. Lazarsfeld, and H. Zeisel. 1971. *Narienthal: The Sociography of an Unemployed Community*. Chicago: Aldine.

Lynd, Robert and Helen M. Lynd. 1929. *Middletown: A Study in American Culture*. New York: Harcourt, Brace.

Reiss, Albert J. 1971. *The Police and the Public*. New Haven: Yale University Press.

Rossi, Peter H. 1972. "Community Social Indicators." Pp. 16-42 in *The Human Meaning of Social Change*, edited by Angus Campbell and Philip Converse. New York: Russell Sage Foundation.

———— Richard A. Berk, and Kenneth Lenihan. 1980. *Money, Work, and Crime*. New York: Academic Press.

Thomas, William I. and Florian Znaniecki. 1918-1920. *The Polish Peasant: Monograph of an Immigrant Group*. Chicago: University of Chicago Press.

Torgerson, Warren F. 1958. *Theory and Methods of Scaling*. New York. John Wiley.

U.S. Department of Justice, Bureau of Justice Statistics. n.d. *Sourcebook of Criminal Justice Statistics*. Washington, DC: Government Printing Office.

Webb, Eugene J., Donald T. Campbell, Richard D. Schwartz, and Lee Sechrest. 1966. *Unobtrusive Measures*. Chicago: Rand McNally.

Whyte, William H. 1956. *Organization Man*. New York: Simon & Schuster.

Wright, James D., Peter H. Rossi, and Kathleen Daly. 1983. *Under the Gun: Weapons Crime and Violence in America*. New York. Aldine.

Wright, James D., Peter H. Rossi, Sonia R. Wright, and Eleanor Weber-Burdin. 1979. *After the Cleanup: The Long Range Effects of Natural Disaster*. Beverly Hills, CA: Sage.

5

Causal Inference
for Sociological Data

RICHARD A. BERK

Over a 10-year period, beginning around 1965, sociologists such as Hubert M. Blalock and Otis Dudley Duncan produced an accessible foundation for representing a wide variety of sociological phenomena in algebraic form. When experimental methods could not be employed, one or more of these "structural equations" were to serve as a "model" from which causal inferences could be drawn.

Despite clear cautions from many of the individuals who introduced sociologists to structural equation modeling, the new technology soon dominated empirical work found in the discipline's flagship journals.[1] With the development of structural equation models using "latent variables" (e.g., Jöreskog and Sörbom, 1979), the hegemony was near complete. While there certainly were lively debates over details (e.g., Bielby, 1986; Sobel and Borhnstedt, 1985), few within sociology questioned the fundamentals; causal inferences followed automatically from structural equation models.

Yet, as Bernert (1983, p. 230) has observed in his 70-year survey of causal terminology in American sociology, "Causality in sociology has proved to be a fragile core-concept." At the turn of the century, the prospect of applying causal concepts to social phenomena was met with "uncritical adulation." In the 1930s widespread skepticism prevailed, but by the 1960s discussions of causality had settled into a kind of "pragmatic utilization." When pushed, many sociologists acknowledged that there were difficult conceptual problems, but in an imperfect world, work had to go on.

Empirical practice was, by and large, built on the same pragmatic rationale. Structural equation models surely had their flaws, but "useful" results could nevertheless be produced. Sociologists argued that they were learning things and that substantive literatures were productively growing.

Over the past several years, however, far-reaching criticisms of structural equation models have been increasing. Most of the concerns have come from other disciplines, sometimes directed toward work done by sociologists (Freedman, 1985; Holland, 1986c) and sometimes attacking related research closer to home (e.g., Leamer, 1978, 1983). In addition, with the publication of Duncan's *Notes on Social Measurement* and Lieberson's *Making it Count*, two prominent sociologists identified with quantitative approaches unambiguously expressed their strong dissatisfaction with business as usual.[2] In short, the structural equation framework borrowed from the "-metrics" of biology, psychology, and economics is increasingly being criticized, from a variety of perspectives, as confused in concept and arrogant in execution.

Otis Dudley Duncan and Sarah Fenstermaker provided a number of helpful suggestions in response to an earlier draft of this paper.

In this context, it is very difficult to write a handbook chapter. An evenhanded reading of the critical literature on causal modeling reveals a burgeoning dissatisfaction. Moreover, many of the issues are very difficult to summarize adequately. Nevertheless, in the spirit of the methodological pragmatists, I will in the pages ahead briefly review the intellectual roots of current practice and then turn to very recent developments. This will lead to a consideration of extant practice and its difficulties. In the process, I will extract some general lessons that may prove helpful for hands-on sociological researchers.[3] However, space considerations preclude discussion of many related topics. I will be focusing on conceptions of causality and causal inference, especially when there are implications for empirical work. I will not be addressing statistical inference, measurement, or generalizability. I will also not dwell on the details of various statistical procedures, but will summarize the issues and then send the reader to far more complete sources.

Some History

While philosophical considerations of causality often begin with Aristotle's *Physics*, most of the current ferment about causal inference can be traced to the work of David Hume (1740, 1748). Hume stressed that causality could never be directly observed; causality was an *interpretation* of observables. One might determine that events A and B were contiguous in space and time. One might determine that event A preceded event B in time. One might determine that event A and event B always occurred together or never occurred together. From these three criteria causality might be *inferred*, but causality per se was unobservable. In other words, Hume argued that it is impossible to demonstrate empirically that a cause produces an effect. To this day, there is no effective rebuttal. Causal statements are always inferential statements.

Hume's three criteria for causation (spatial and temporal contiguity, time ordering, and constant conjunction) have also been influential. They anticipate more thorough procedures for inferring cause, but in so doing, also anticipate two major problems to which we will return: neither "cause" nor "effect" are clearly defined, and only deterministic relationships can be the source of casual inferences. In the first case, Hume at best provides *operational*

definitions. In the second case, there is not room for the stochastic world of today's science.

Despite Hume's enormous contributions, current empirical work of sociology rests far more on methods proposed by John Stuart Mill (1872). Like Hume, Mill required that a cause had to precede an effect. But unlike Hume, Mill provided a set of rather explicit procedures by which causes were to be identified. Cohen and Nagel (1934, p. 250) provide a good summary of Mill's approach, in which a "problem" is essentially some empirical question, a "factor" is a prospective cause, and "order" refers to some stable pattern or relationship perceived in the empirical world.

"In the first place, some selected portion of our experience is taken for further study because of its problematic character. The problem must then be formulated in terms of the situation which provokes the inquiry, and an analysis of the situation must be made into a certain number of factors, present or absent, which are believed to be relevant to the solution of the problem. Now the order for which we are in search is expressible, as we have seen, in the form: C is invariably connected with E. And this means that no factor can be regarded as a cause if it is present while the effect is absent [i.e., Method of Agreement], or if it is absent while the effect is present [i.e., Method of Difference], or if it varies in some manner while the effect does not vary in some corresponding manner [i.e., Method of Concomitant Variation]. The function of [an] experiment is to determine with regard to each of the factors entertained as a possible cause, whether it is invariably related to the effect. If C and E are the two factors or processes, there are four possible conjunctions: we may find CE, $C\bar{E}$, $\bar{C}E$, or $\bar{C}\bar{E}$, where $\bar{C}$ and $\bar{E}$ denote the absence of these factors. To show that C is invariably connected with E we must try to show that the second and third alternatives do not occur."[4]

Mill was basically trying to provide *procedures* by which, through a process of elimination, the cause of an effect could be identified. Causes and effects in turn were defined in terms of necessary and sufficient conditions. Thus, much like Hume, one is provided with no formal definition of a cause or an effect, and there is no possibility for a stochastic world. Moreover, there is no room for conditional effects (i.e., interaction effects). In short, if Mill's criteria are taken literally, no cause-and-effect relationships could be found by sociologists.[5]

It is probably fair to say, however, that despite the obvious difficulties with the way causal inference was approached by Hume and Mill, their views have dominated the ways in which empirical sociologists talk about causal inference. To be sure, allowances have been made for the "special" nature of social science (Nagel, 1961), and more precise approaches were developed with statistical technology, but the historical debts are clear (e.g., Blalock, 1968; Cook and Campbell, 1979; MacIver, 1942).

Current Controversies

Since the work of John Stuart Mill, the nature of causality and causal inference has continued to draw the attention of a diverse set of scholars. However, while some of the older controversies have been laid to rest, new ones have surfaced. Thus Bunge (1959, p. 1) begins his book on causality by addressing the "bewildering confusion prevailing in contemporary philosophic and scientific literature with regard to the meanings of the words 'causation,' 'determination,' 'causality,' and 'determinism.' " On a slightly more optimistic note, Cook and Campbell (1979, p. 10) observe that "the epistemology of causation, and the scientific method more generally, is at present in a productive state of near chaos." And focusing explicitly on how one infers that a causal relationship exists, Glymour (1986, p. 965) complains that "the philosophical community, unfortunately, has not been very energetic in addressing . . . [this] mystery."[6]

Nevertheless, on at least two issues, there seem to be significant progress, and both have important implications for sociological practice. The first issue is the role of chance and the second issue is how to think about causal effects within an experimental framework.

The Role of Chance

Recall that earlier thinkers defined causality on an all-or-nothing basis; a cause was a necessary and sufficient condition for an effect. Part of this no doubt stemmed from eighteenth-century views that relations among all empirical phenomena were fully determined. That is, with the correct understanding of the relevant natural laws and accurate measures on all the relevant factors, the future (and the past) could be predicted without error. Thus Pierre Laplace, an eighteenth-century French mathematician, "once boasted that given the position and

velocity of every particle in the universe, he could predict the future for rest of time" (Crutchfield et al., 1986, p. 46). This unbending determinism dominated the scientific world for well over a century (Ehrenberg, 1977), creating difficult problems for those interested in studying human behavior. In brief, within a deterministic world there could be no free will. And since it was difficult to dispense with free will as an essential part of human activity, social science was apparently impossible (Kaplan, 1964, p. 121; Nagel, 1961, pp. 504-509). In other words, if one accepted the possibility of free will, one seemed to be giving up the deterministic world and with that, the prospect of doing "real" science.

Two developments have led to what Ehrenberg (1977, pp. 52-69) calls the "decline and fall of physical necessity." First, beginning around the turn of the century, evidence was accumulating in particle physics that did not square with a deterministic worldview, and new theories were emerging in response (Ehrenberg, 1977; Wolf, 1981). By the 1930s the efforts of Bohr, Heisenberg, Born, and others produced the "new physics" resting on principles from quantum mechanics, in which subatomic particles were governed by relationships that were *inherently stochastic*. For example, an electron never had a specific location, but only a probability of being at a specific location. It cannot be overemphasized that the stochastic subatomic world was *not* a product of measurement error or incomplete knowledge. Indeterminacy was an essential feature of the subatomic physical world.

The practical and philosophical consequences of quantum theory are still being digested (e.g., Davies, 1983; Fetzer, 1983). However, it has been clear for decades that science can proceed with stochastic laws replacing deterministic laws. Ehrenberg (1977, p. 64) quotes Born as follows: "The motion of particles conforms to the laws of probability, but probability itself is propagated in accordance with the laws of causality." In other words, one does not have to accept a deterministic worldview to do science; indeed, a deterministic worldview is no longer tenable.

It is one thing to accept a stochastic world at the level of subatomic particles and quite another to accept it for macro phenomena. Electrons are so far removed from the world of everyday experience that the lessons they teach may not carry over. As Crutchfield and his colleagues (1986, p. 48) explain,

The sources of unpredictability on a large scale must be sought elsewhere, however.

Some large scale phenomena are predictable and others are not. The distinction has nothing to do with quantum mechanics. The trajectory of a baseball, for example, is inherently predictable; a fielder intuitively makes use of this fact every time he or she catches the ball. The trajectory of a flying balloon with air rushing out of it, in contrast, is not predictable; the balloon lurches and turns erratically at times and places that are impossible to predict.

Observations such as these have recently led to an entirely new view of uncertainty, chance, and probability under the rubric of Chaos Theory. The basic idea is that minute differences in the initial conditions of some dynamic systems rapidly produce large perturbations overwhelming the system's predictable properties. That is, "error" is quickly compounded and amplified so that "noise" soon dominates what is observable.

Consider the opening break in a game of eightball. All of the billiard balls obey the usual deterministic laws of Newtonian mechanics. However, because of the curvature of each ball, small differences in where the balls make contact with one another translate into big differences in trajectory. With each collision, the importance of earlier small differences in points of collision are amplified so that after several collisions, the trajectories are effectively unpredictable. In other words, relationships that begin as effectively deterministic become effectively random.

A growing number of natural phenomena, such as the weather or the growth of crystals, are being productively explored with Chaos Theory (e.g., Sander, 1987). For our purposes, there are three important implications. To begin, it is no longer clear what "deterministic" and "stochastic" really mean (Kolata, 1986; Jensen, 1987). When at a macro level, deterministic relationships produce what appear to be stochastic results, all conventional distinctions break down.[7] Lots of hard conceptual work lies ahead.

In addition, one must be rather more cautious about using prediction as a means of verifying causal assertions. If a system is truly chaotic, one may have the right theory and still not be able to make meaningful predictions in the usual sense. For nonchaotic systems, accurate predictions may be useful tools for empirical work. But for chaotic systems, other means must be employed. Since in sociology we have yet to begin considering Chaos Theory, we have no idea which kinds of social systems may be chaotic, or even if Chaos Theory ever applies.[8]

However, it may be useful to start examining how the concept of prediction may be altered to include the kinds of patterns that chaotic systems may produce.

Finally, it is apparent that definitions of causality and procedures for inferring cause must allow for either stochastic or chaotic relationships. Perhaps the most well-known attempts to address causality in stochastic terms have been produced by Patrick Suppes (1970, 1982). Stripped of many of the details, which are primarily of interest to philosophers, Suppes (1982, pp. 240-242) begins by requiring that causes precede effects in time. Then, a "prima facie" cause is essentially a zero-order relationship. Event C is a prima facie cause of event E if the probability of E conditioned on C is larger than the unconditional probability of E.[9] A prima facie cause becomes a spurious cause if after conditioning (partialing) on some event that precedes the prima facie cause in time, the prima facie relationship disappears. Finally, the prima facie cause C is a genuine cause of E if it is not a spurious cause. This is little more than the usual partialing strategy used by sociologists for 40 years, in which "control" variables are introduced to see if a particular association disappears. However, Suppes makes clear that the partialing strategy has reasonable (though arguable) philosophical foundations resting in a stochastic view of the world.[10]

To summarize, there seems to be widespread agreement that one must view the social world as inherently or effectively stochastic. Whether justifications rest, as discussed above, on an inherent uncertainty in all social (and physical) phenomena or practical uncertainty resulting from inevitable measurement error, causality cannot rest on deterministic relationships. Then, causality may be defined through what are basically statistical operations, from which causal inferences may be drawn. It is fair to say all causal modeling in the social sciences shares these foundations (e.g., Swamy, Conway, and Muehlen, 1985).

Experimentation and Manipulable Causes

Cook and Campbell (1979, pp. 25-28) point out that at least since the 1940s there has been a particular kind of dissatisfaction with the partialing approach to causality and causal inference. Basically, an essential ingredient has been ignored: A cause is something that is manipulated. That is, the conception of a cause is "bound up with the idea of a practical science which informs us about the consequences of performing particular acts" (Cook and Campbell, 1979, p. 26). Thus an arrest may be usefully seen as a cause of more law-abiding behavior. A water conservation program may be usefully seen as a cause of reduced water consumption. Or, smaller classes may be usefully seen as a cause of better reading skills. Arrests, conservation programs, and class sizes are manipulable, at least in principle. In contrast, race and sex cannot be treated usefully as causes of income because a person's race and sex cannot be manipulated.[11] Requiring that all causes be manipulable seems to place significant restrictions on the kinds of analyses sociologists can do and needs to be carefully examined.

Among the most recent, and certainly the most vocal, supporters of "no causation without manipulation" are statisticians Donald Rubin and Paul Holland. In a series of articles (in particular, Holland, 1986a, 1986b; Holland and Rubin, 1983; Rubin, 1977, 1978), they provide a framework for causality and causal inference using an experimental paradigm in which manipulation is a central feature.

Rubin and Holland (hereafter called R & H) begin by observing that virtually all of the earlier thinking on causation focuses on the nature of causes. An effect is typically treated as a primitive (i.e., undefined). R & H propose to focus on the nature of effects, leaving cause as a primitive. This is a strategic decision that can be evaluated only by the usefulness of the resulting framework.

The R & H definition of an effect has four components. First, the effect of a cause is *always* relative to another effect of a cause. For example, the response to a question, "What is the effect of a prison sentence on recidivism?" is "Compared to what?" Is the baseline probation, a jail sentence, a methadone treatment program, or even vocational training? In a similar fashion, the effect of divorce on a household's children is relative to the baseline chosen: the effect of a "happy home," an unhappy" but intact home, a foster home, and so on.

The relative nature of effects holds as well for nondiscrete causes. One can compare the effects for different *levels* of the cause and/or summarize the relative effects through some functional form. For example, in a linear model, an effect is proportional to a cause, with the regression coefficient the constant of proportionality. Thus one may compare the effect on income of 11 years of education versus 12 years of education and assume that identical conclusions

would be drawn for any pair of comparisons one year apart.

Second, causal effects are defined in "what if" terms for a given unit. That is, a cause of an effect compares what *would* have happened had the object in question (a person, family, organization, or whatever) been exposed to the treatment with what *would* have happened had the object in question been exposed to the control condition.[12] For example, suppose one were interested in the impact of zoning ordinances on the price of housing. The causal effect of zoning would be defined beginning with what would have happened to the price of housing in a given city if strict ordinances were in place compared to what would have happened to the price of housing in *the same city* if lax ordinances were in place. This means that each unit must be potentially exposable to the treatment and control conditions. Otherwise, the "what if" formulation is not instructive.

Third, a causal effect is defined for the given unit as the arithmetic difference between what would have happened under the treatment condition and what would have happened under the control condition. For example, if in a given city strict ordinances would have led to a median housing price of $100,000 and if in that same city lax ordinances would have led to a median housing price of $80,000, the causal effect is simply $20,000.[13]

Definitions are neither right nor wrong. The question is whether a definition is useful. R & H argue that their definition squares with common sense meanings of a causal effect, organizes a great deal of earlier writings, and leads to a number of useful insights affecting empirical practice.

To begin, the R & H definition of a causal effect helps clarify Hume's insight that causality is an inference from observable phenomena. That is, causality cannot be directly observed. R & H call this the "Fundamental Problem of Causal Inference" (Holland, 1986a, pp. 947-948). With a causal effect defined for a given unit as the difference between what would have happened under the experimental and control conditions, a causal effect can be observed directly only if that unit is exposed to the experimental and control conditions in a form that duplicates the "what if" definition of a causal effect. Exposing the unit to one condition *and then* the other condition does not qualify. The experience is not one condition *or* the other, but one condition *and* the other. Clearly, these are formally different. Likewise, exposing the unit to both conditions simultaneously is formally different. Thus causal effects must be inferred.

How then may casual effects be inferred? There are two classes of procedures, which may be combined as useful and feasible. "Scientific" approaches exploit various assumptions about the units and/or the phenomenon. For example, one might compare the outcome for one unit under the experimental condition to the outcome for another unit under the control condition, assuming that the units would have had identical responses to one another under the experimental condition and identical responses to one another under the control condition (called the "Unit Homogeneity Assumption"). Then, the difference in the outcomes is the same as the difference under the "what if" formulation; in practice, the two units are fully comparable. For example, one might be able to make the case in testing the effect of a new drug that identical twins would show the same physiological responses to both the drug and a placebo. Then, the causal effect of the drug could be obtained by giving one twin the drug and the other twin a placebo.

Alternatively, one might assume (1) that the value of the outcome under the control condition does not depend on when the outcome is measured and (2) that the value of the outcome under the experimental condition is not affected by prior exposure to the control condition. These two assumptions, called by Holland (1986a, p. 948) "Temporal Stability" and "Causal Transience," solve the Fundamental Problem of Causal Inference; causal effects may be inferred by exposing an observational unit first to the control condition and then the experimental condition. Consider the effect of turning on a light switch. If one can assume that the level of darkness before turning the switch on is constant over some reasonable period of time, and that after the switch is turned on, the brightness of the room does not depend on how dark the room was before the switch was turned on, a simple pretest/posttest design will allow one properly to infer a causal effect.

Unfortunately, scientific solutions are typically not compelling for social science problems. Hence, there is a second strategy relying on "statistical solutions." One begins with some well-defined population and the idea of an *average* causal effect. Imagine that *all* units in the population were exposed to the experimental condition and that their mean response was calculated. Also imagine that *all* units in the population were exposed to the control condition and that their mean response was calculated. The average causal effect is defined as the difference between these two means. This difference also may be expressed as the mean of the difference in response of *all* units exposed to both conditions.

In practice, we do not observe what would happen if all units were exposed to the experimental and control conditions. There are a host of problems with such pretest/posttest designs, and it is possible to do much better. What we obtain typically is the average response for units actually exposed to the treatment, which will not necessarily equal the average that would have been observed if *all* units had been exposed to the treatment. Likewise, we typically obtain the observed average response for units actually exposed to the control condition, which will not necessarily equal the average response if *all* units had been exposed to the control condition. In other words, in both cases, the *conditional* expectation observed will not necessarily (in fact, rarely) equal the *unconditional* expectation sought. Hence, there is no necessary correspondence between the average causal effect formally defined and the average causal effect obtained from the data.

For example, suppose the treatment condition is a prison term and the control condition is probation. Also suppose the response variable is arrests for new crimes. The average causal effect is defined as the difference between the expected (or mean) number of new crimes if all offenders in the population were put in prison and the expected (or mean) number of crimes if all offenders in the population were put on probation. However, the observed average causal effect must rest on the average response for offenders actually imprisoned and the average response for offenders actually put on probation. Since there is no reason to assume that these two subsets each accurately represent the response of the full population, the observed average causal effect may well be misleading. Offenders with longer prior records, for instance, may be overrepresented in the prison subset and underrepresented in the probation subset. And since prior record is often a good predictor of future crimes, the observed average causal effect will make prison look less effective than it may be.

Within this formulation, it should now be clear how the average causal effect may be more usefully constructed. If the problem lies in the unrepresentativeness of the experimental and control subsets, simple random sampling is the solution. Experimental and control units should be sampled at random from the population (without replacement). With representativeness assured (within the bounds of sampling error), the observed means for the experimentals and controls become unbiased estimates for the population as a whole, and the observed average causal effect becomes an unbiased estimate of the population average causal effect. Random sampling from a given population to construct experimental and control groups is, of course, nothing more than an experiment with random assignment.[14]

Even randomized experiments, however, depend on important assumptions. In particular, Rubin (1986, p. 961) requires the "stable-unit-treatment-value assumption" (SUTVA). Under SUTVA one asserts that the response of a unit exposed to the treatment is unaffected by (1) the mechanism by which the treatment is assigned, and (2) the treatments other units receive. If SUTVA does not hold, there are versions of the treatment that are not being captured. For example, under the "John Henry Effect," a subject receiving a less desirable treatment (or the control condition), may work extra hard to show the researcher that he or she can excel nevertheless. That is, the less desirable treatment now has two perfectly confounded parts: the original treatment content and new motivational content. What one takes to be the response to the original treatment content is actually a response to the original treatment content plus the new motivational content.

The importance of the SUTVA assumption cannot be overemphasized. It urges enormous care in the implementation of randomized experiments. At the very least, potential violations should be anticipated and documented. Proper caveats can then be included when the results are reported. For example, the process of random assignment to experimental and control conditions per se may demoralize the controls.[15] Ideally, however, the experimental setting can be constructed in a fashion that makes the SUTVA assumption plausible. For instance, it may be important not to tell experimental subjects what the controls are experiencing and vice versa.

The SUTVA assumption is just as important when random assignment is not employed. We will return to this point later when the R & H framework is generalized to observational studies. We will see that one of the reasons for limiting causal analyses to manipulable interventions is that the SUTVA assumption is likely to be more plausible.

To summarize, recent thinking on causality and causal inference has legitimized causal thinking in an effectively stochastic world and provided a particularly clear framework for addressing cause within an experimental paradigm. However, while randomized experiments are being increasingly used by social scientists to address both basic and applied problems

(Berk et al., 1985), most empirical work in sociology rests on other kinds of research designs. I will turn to these alternatives now.

Causal Inference In Observational Studies

William Cochran (1983, p. 1) defines observational studies as having two characteristics: (1) the objective of the research is to study causal effects, and (2) the investigator cannot determine how the intervention of interest is assigned. In other words, observational studies have the same goal as randomized experiments, but the assignment process is not under the control of the researcher. In practice, this means random assignment is not employed, and as we will soon see, enormous complications typically follow.[16]

The key idea in the transition from randomized experiments to observational studies is "strong ignorability" (Rosenbaum and Rubin, 1983, 1984a, 1984b; Rubin, 1977, 1986). For the mechanism by which units are assigned to treatment(s) and control conditions to be strongly ignorable, three assumptions must be met: (1) all variables related to *both* the treatment and control conditions assigned *and* the response measure are included in any statistical analysis as covariates, (2) all units have a nonzero probability of being assigned to *all* the experimental and control conditions, and (3) SUTVA holds. Under strong ignorability for the assignment mechanism, unbiased casual effects may be obtained.

The first assumption is a restatement of the of the well-known econometric result on omitted variables (e.g., Pindyck and Rubinfeld, 1981, pp. 128-130). Consider the path diagram in Figure 5.1. R is the response variable (e.g., income). T is the treatment/control variable (e.g., vocational training or not). X is a confounding covariate (or vector of confounding covariates) affecting who experiences vocational training and the response (e.g., motivation). Z is a covariate (or vector of covariates) affecting the response but nothing else (e.g., age). W is a covariate affecting the confounding covariate but nothing else. The e's represent unobservable disturbances meeting the usual (and sometimes heroic) assumptions.

Assuming that the path diagram properly represents the relationships being examined, a failure to control (partial) for X will bias any estimate of the impact of T on R. This means that X must be known and measured without error (no small feat for a variable like "motivation"). If Z is ignored, one sacrifices some statistical power, to the degree that Z by itself (i.e., after partialing) can account for variance in R, but unbiased estimates of the impact of T on R can be obtained. If W is ignored, nothing is lost, unless the impact of W on X is of interest by itself. In short, the first characteristic of strong ignorability will be met if the relationship between T and R is conditioned on X.[17]

The second assumption basically requires the presence of the disturbance e_2. In Figure 5.1, the absence of e_2 implies that X and T are indistinguishable; T is some deterministic function of X. Since the research is being undertaken to estimate the impact of T by itself, the perfect collinearity between X and T is problematic.[18]

There is, in addition, a more subtle difficulty. Suppose there were another observable variable, Q, that affected only T. There would then be no need to condition on Q as well as X, and T would no longer be perfectly collinear with X. However, depending on the joint distribution of X, T, and Q, there could well be for certain values of X situations in which only experimentals or only controls were represented. For example, suppose X was measured simply as high or low motivation. For low-motivation females, all of the units could be controls. Or, all of the units could be experimentals. In either case, how could the average causal effect be

calculated for that cell? Clearly, it cannot be unless the missing information were imputed. While there are lots of ways that imputation might be accomplished, virtually any imputation must rest on assumptions that are not fully testable.[19] And untestable assumptions of this sort preclude strong ignorability.

The third assumption (SUTVA) was discussed earlier. The main issue it raises in observational studies is how one determines the degree to which SUTVA holds. Clearly, lots of detailed data are required on the process by which the treatment and control conditions were assigned and on the study site more generally. That is, *the implementation of the intervention becomes a study in itself*. In the case of vocational training program, for example, as much effort would need to be invested in learning how people were recruited for the program, and how the program functioned, as in learning about the impact of the program on future earnings.

If strong ignorability holds, causal inference is in principle straightforward. After conditioning on X, one simply estimates the average causal effect. Then one may apply significance tests to evaluate one or more a priori hypotheses (e.g., there is no causal effect) or place confidence intervals around the estimated causal effect. It cannot be overemphasized, however, that everything depends on the accuracy of one's model, in Figure 5.1 represented as a path diagram, and the ability to control for X.

The lessons learned from Figure 5.1 generalize along the following lines. First, all of the variables in Figure 5.1 may be nominal, ordinal, or equal interval. While the way in which the variables are represented has critical consequences for statistical analysis, the implications of strong ignorability are unchanged.[20] Second, T, like X, may be a vector. This means that each variable in T plays two roles simultaneously: as a causal variable, the impact of which needs to be estimated, and as a covariate, the impact of which must be conditioned away. These two roles are neatly partitioned in common multivariate procedures such as multiple regression (Draper and Smith, 1981, pp. 196-204.) Third, one may allow for T to affect R and for R to affect T. That is, two variables may have reciprocal causal effects. The implications of strong ignorability still hold, although reciprocal effects may significantly complicate the statistical analysis (Pindyck and Rubinfeld, 1981, pp. 319-353). Finally, in principle any of the variables in Figure 5.1 may be unobservable, except indirectly through other variables serving as indicators. For example, motivation to succeed on the job cannot be directly observed, but observ-

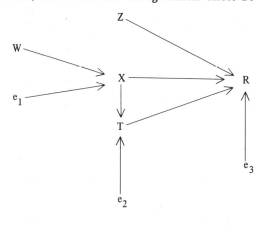

$$X = f(W, e_1)$$
$$T = f(X, e_2)$$
$$R = f(Z, X, T, e_3)$$
$$cov(e_1 e_2) = cov(e_1 e_3) = cov(e_2 e_3) = 0$$

FIGURE 5.1
An Illustrative Path Diagram

ables such as showing up to work on time, working through one's lunch hour, and working overtime may be useful indicators. Again, the implications of strong ignorability hold despite the prospect of a far more complicated statistical analysis (Fox, 1984, pp. 274-301).

Tricks of the Trade

It has long been recognized that a necessary condition for unbiased estimates of a causal effect is including all of the confounding covariates or randomizing their impact away. If random assignment is impractical, and one must rely on a partialing strategy, how can one make the case that all of the relevant covariates have been taken into account? Five kinds of strategies have been popular.

Theory and Past Research

First, and perhaps most important in principle, one tries to make the case on theoretical grounds or by citing past empirical research. This assumes, of course, that for a particular substantive problem, there exists a widely accepted and well-verified body of theory or at least a sufficient number of verified facts. In sociology, there is arguably no such material on which to draw, at least at the level of specificity required. For example, it may well be clear on theoretical and empirical grounds that education is one important cause of earnings, but an unbiased estimate of the impact of education requires that all covariates related to both education and earnings be included in the analysis.

As a fallback position, some have argued that while in the absence of randomized experiments unbiased estimates can never be obtained, the biases in practice will often be small. Some also assert that with many different investigators attacking a given substantive question from different points of view, the biases in each study will tend to cancel out. A "meta-analysis" (e.g., Hedges and Olkin, 1985) will then produce a good approximation of the truth. Unfortunately, it is difficult to find any evidence for these beliefs.

Quasi-Experimental Research Designs

When randomized experiments are impractical, one may employ quasi-experimental de-

signs. Quasi-experimental designs capitalize on different ways in which data may be collected to improve the credibility of one's causal inferences. In the language of Campbell and Stanley (1963), quasi-experiments vary in their "internal validity," and more powerful designs lead to higher internal validity. For example, longitudinal data are desirable when causal direction needs to be established.[21]

There are a large number of different quasi-experimental designs with different trade-offs (Campbell and Stanley, 1963; Cook and Campbell, 1979). In addition to the regression-discontinuity design mentioned earlier (see note 18), another powerful design is the interrupted time series (Cook and Campbell, 1979, pp. 207-232).[22] The basic idea is to collect a large number (typically over 50) of evenly spaced, longitudinal observations and then determine if there is a change in the temporal pattern around the time when an intervention was introduced. In the simplest case, the postintervention observations are on the average shifted up or down compared to the preintervention observations. While making such determinations often requires considerable statistical work (Box and Tiao, 1975), the results sometimes can be quite compelling, at least compared to weaker designs.

Consider, for instance, the impact of environmental legislation on air quality. With a simple pretest/posttest design, one might find that air quality after the legislation was better than before and be inclined to attribute the improvement to the legislation. However, an interrupted time series design might reveal that air quality had been improving for several years before the legislation was implemented and that the positive time trend simply continued after the legislation. In other words, the inferred causal impact of the legislation was spurious.

Quasi-experimental designs are terribly underutilized by sociologists despite their considerable potential. While they are certainly no substitute for random assignment, the stronger quasi-experimental designs can usually produce far more compelling causal inferences than conventional cross-sectional data sets.

Nested Significance Tests for Causal Parameters

An essential feature of the structural equation approach to causal modeling is the use of tests of statistical significance to determine which casual variables should be included. One begins with a "full" model, which includes all of one's prospective explanatory variables, and then tests whether subsets of explanatory variables may be dropped because the null hypothesis of no effect cannot be rejected. Such tests are "nested" in the sense that all of the smaller models considered are subsumed within the initial model, and the eventual product is presumably the most parsimonious version of it (Harvey, 1981, pp. 183-185).

In practice, the theory of nested tests is widely abused. For example, large numbers of ad hoc tests are routinely undertaken that capitalize on chance, and, as a logical matter, do not provide clear guidance. Perhaps the most vulgar approach is built into stepwise regression procedures, which essentially automate mindless empiricism (e.g., Berk, 1983; Leamer, 1978). It is also common to choose the level of statistical significance *after* looking at the results, or to report different levels for different findings so that a large number of findings become "statistically significant."

However, even when nested tests are properly undertaken, there are serious difficulties. Even ignoring all of the controversy among statisticians about the meaning of such procedures (Barnett, 1982), everything depends on the inclusiveness of the full model. The theory of nested testing breaks down if strong ignorability is not met initially.

Goodness-of-Fit Tests

Goodness-of-fit tests may be nested or non-nested significance tests. They compare the data on hand with what the data should be if the structural equation model in question is correct. Alternatively, they compare observed moments from the data with the moments implied by the structural equation model. A model is deemed "good" if the difference between the observed data and the derived data is small enough to have occurred easily by chance. In addition, the tests are used by some to choose between competing models. Models that fit the data better are preferred to those which fit the data worse, and sometimes a single "best" model may be selected. Goodness-of-fit tests are widely used in the analysis of contingency tables (Feinberg, 1977) and in models with latent variables (Jöreskog, 1979).

There is considerable controversy surrounding the use of goodness-of-fit tests (e.g. Sobel and Bohrnstedt, 1985). For example, with large samples, small departures in fit will be statistically significant at conventional levels. That is, what

looks to be a good fit to the eye is formally rejected. Some argue that under these circumstances the goodness-of-fit tests are misleading. However, this seems to miss the point. Goodness-of-fit tests indicate whether a model fits or not.[23] Why a model does not fit is a *substantive* question for which there are no statistical fixes.

But more important, a good fit is only that. Particularly in the case of non-nested tests, it is often not clear why a good fit is good. Consider two ways of estimating the impact of fertility counseling on birth rates. On the one hand, one might undertake a randomized experiment, which, if properly implemented, is likely to produce unbiased treatment effect estimates. On the other hand, consider the conventional cross-sectional data set in which, for reasons that would have to be determined from the data, some individuals were exposed to counseling and others were not. To analyze the data, a researcher would probably estimate the parameters of one or more structural equations. Because these models would almost certainly include a large number of variables related to birth rates, they might well pass a goodness-of-fit test. In contrast, the model used to analyze the randomized experiment might fail. However, estimates of the impact of the counseling from the cross-sectional data set would almost certainly be biased, perhaps severely. In other words, the better fit is produced by estimates with more bias. Examples with similar conclusions can be easily constructed for a wide variety of substantive problems, even when the results of a randomized experiment are not used as the benchmark (e.g, Freedman, 1985, p. 360-364; Rogosa and Willet, 1985).

Perhaps the overall message is that goodness-of-fit tests are inherently indirect. Estimates of causal effect speak to the parameters associated with one's causal variables, and it is these estimates that need to be "good" (e.g., unbiased and efficient). Unless the case can be made for a particular analysis that a better fit implies better parameter estimates for the causal variables of interest, goodness-of-fit tests are not especially helpful.[24]

Specification Tests

For the general linear model (i.e., multiple regression, analysis of variance, and analysis of covariance), it has long been recognized that some forms of bias from omitted variables (or the wrong functional form), have implications for the residuals. For example, if the residuals do not have a spherical form, the explanation may depend on one or more omitted variables. Building on this insight, statistical tests have been developed (Fromby, Hill, and Johnson, 1984, pp. 409-412), which will in principle reveal departures from assumed residual distributions. A statistically significant departure is, then, a warning that all is not well. In other words, tests on the residuals may reveal problems with one's model specification. It cannot be overemphasized, however, that these specification tests can produce false positives (or even false negatives) resulting from other complications, such as heteroskedasticity, and there is little in the test results conveying how then to proceed.[25]

Researchers have also long recognized that different kinds of structural equation models may imply the need for different statistical procedures. For conventional recursive models, for example, ordinary least squares may suffice. In contrast, for nonrecursive models, two-stage least squares or full information maximum likelihood techniques will probably be necessary (Pindyck and Rubinfeld, 1981, pp. 319-324).[26] When researchers are not sure whether simultaneous causation exists in a multiple equation system, it is common to apply both ordinary least squares and two stage least squares and compare the results. If the regression coefficients differ substantially depending upon the estimation procedure employed, the ordinary least squares results are discarded.

The seat-of-the-pants rationale is that in large samples, ordinary least squares results have less desirable statistical properties (i.e., inconsistency) than the two-stage least squares results. Hence, if the estimates for the two statistical procedures differ, the latter are superior, which implies that the nonrecursive formulation is correct. In short, a comparison of two sets of statistical results is used to assist in model specification. Of course, this only works if the *sole* problem is causal direction; other forms of specification error (e.g., omitted variables) muddy the waters.

The seat-of-the-pants rationale has been, over the past decade, formalized and generalized (Fromby, Hill, and Johnson, 1984, pp. 412-414) as the next generation of Specification Tests. The basic idea is formally to compare the regression coefficients from two competing estimation procedures. The statistical procedures are selected so that different model specifications are indirectly pitted against one another. (For a sociological application, see Berk et al., 1982). However, much like the earlier specification tests, the results may well be misleading if there

are *any* other statistical assumptions that are substantially violated; the tests are problem specific.

A Bottom Line

It should be clear that there are a large number of tools available to assist researchers trying in observational studies to meet Rubin's requirement of strong ignorability. It is equally clear that at least some of the tools can be quite helpful in principle. The question is, then, how helpful are they in practice?

To begin, one must distinguish between proper and improper practice (e.g., Cooley and LeRoy, 1981; Leamer, 1983). There is no doubt that sloth, incompetence, and perhaps even fraud can be found even in the best sociological journals. However, for our purposes, the more important issue is whether in observational studies strong ignorability is a pipe dream.

In the short term, there are ample grounds to worry. Besides the growing chorus of concern about model specification in the social sciences (cited throughout this chapter), there is some empirical evidence that when randomized experiments are pitted against observational studies, the latter are found to be deficient. Recently, Robert J. LaLonde (1986) compared results from a large randomized experiment with the results of several alternative approaches popular in the econometric literature. In particular, he compared estimates of the impact on earnings of the National Supported Work Demonstration, which used random assignment to treatment and control groups, with estimates of the impact of the program on earnings, when the comparison groups were constructed with samples drawn from other data (e.g., the Panel Study of Income Dynamics).[27] Even with state-of-the-art economic theory and econometrics, the results from the randomized experiment differed substantially from the other results. Moreover, the results from the observational data sets varied considerably among themselves, depending on the comparison group chosen. Sometimes the estimated causal effects were too high and sometimes too low. A similar experience is reported by Fraker and Maynard (1987) using comparison groups constructed from the Current Population Survey. Again, even state-of-the-art procedures failed to save the day.

These studies are troubling for sociologists in part because the job training literature in economics is at least as good as the very best literatures in sociology. Moreover, much of the very best quantitative work done by sociologists draws heavily on this tradition. Finally, these studies reveal exactly the problems cited by statisticians critical of structural equation modeling and are fully consistent with demonstrations and simulations they have reported (Holland and Rubin, 1983; Rogosa and Willett, 1985).

To summarize, there is good reason to be uneasy with the causal inferences sociologists have been drawing from observational studies. At the very least, this implies a need to upgrade current practice. But more fundamentally, and perhaps more accurately, this may well imply a need to reexamine how we do our work. For example, even the most sophisticated statistical analysis may not compensate for a weak quasi-experimental design, and sociologists may have to reassess their apparent belief that a fancy data analysis will absolve them of their data collection sins.

Does Causation Require Manipulation?

Observational studies, as defined here, require that any causal variable be subject to manipulation, at least in principle. This is, of course, fully consistent with the Rubin and Holland framework, but seems to rule out some of the most popular causal variables in sociology: race, sex, and age. How necessary, therefore, is the requirement of manipulation?

Consider an illustration recently the subject of some controversy in the *Journal of the American Statistical Association*. In an article on causal inference, Pratt and Schlaifer (1984a) considered the meaning of the following question: "Would there be more snow in Denver if the Rocky Mountains were lower?" Pratt and Schlaifer (1984a, 1984b) argued that the question is meaningful and that the height of the Rocky Mountains can be a cause of the amount of rainfall in Denver, even through the height of the Rocky Mountains is not manipulable. One can easily undertake a "conceptual manipulation," they argue, in which ceteris paribus, the height of the Rocky Mountains is varied, much as in a "real" experiment. Moreover, this mental experiment can be represented as a structural equation model from which proper causal inferences may be drawn.

Rosenbaum and Rubin (1984c) and Dawid (1984) strongly disagree. Elaborating a bit on their rationale, there seem to five major objections to the Pratt and Schlaifer position (rebuttals will follow). First, the epistemological status

of a conceptual experiment is obscure. Whatever the epistemological problems with actual experiments, there is at least extensive thinking about what can be learned from them and how such learning is accomplished. There is nothing comparable for conceptual experiments.

Second, conceptual experiments pose serious practical difficulties for the scientific community.[28] The process of undertaking a real experiment is reasonably clear and replicable and therefore accessible to different investigators. For example, there are currently six replications under way of the Minneapolis Spouse Abuse Experiment (Sherman and Berk, 1984). The replications involve random assignment to experimental and control conditions, explicit definitions of the kinds of households to be involved, common data collection instruments, comparable methods for monitoring the implementation of the experiments, comparable data coding conventions, and so on. While the new experiments could never be literal replications of the Minneapolis Experiment, the explicit nature of a real experiment makes useful approximations possible. In contrast, how does one learn about the activities necessary for a conceptual experiment, and how does one replicate them?

Third, recall that strong ignorability requires that all covariates related to both the treatment assigned and the response be included as conditioning variables. Unless one has considerable understanding of the means by which treatment assignment is actually accomplished, there is no way to determine which prospective covariates are related to treatment assignment. For the Rocky Mountain conceptual experiment, how would one know which of the variables affecting rainfall in Denver also alter (in the conceptual experiment) the mountains' height?

Fourth, as emphasized earlier, the SUTVA assumption is necessary if the impacts of manipulable treatments are to be properly interpreted. Recall that this requires a detailed consideration of *how* the units are assigned to treatment and control conditions and *how* the interventions are implemented. How does one consider such issues in a conceptual experiment?

Finally, if the point of an experiment is to learn what will happen if some variable is manipulated, then it follows that manipulating the variable is an instructive thing to do. The actions undertaken respond directly to the question being asked. In the case of Pratt and Schlaifer's Rocky Mountain experiment, there is no plan to lower the Rockies; no manipulation is being anticipated. Therefore, it is not clear what question is being answered by their conceptual experiment.

It is possible to construct four distinct rejoinders from published material (Geweke, 1984; Glymour, 1986; Granger, 1986; Pratt and Schlaifer, 1984b). First, it is one thing to say that the epistemological status of conceptual experiments may be unclear, and quite another to say that nothing can be learned from them. We seem to learn useful things in many ways that are still not well understood by philosophers (e.g., through induction). In short, epistemological clarity should be sought, but in the meantime, useful work may well be possible.

Second, there is no reason in principle why conceptual experiments cannot be made more replicable. Researchers need only provide more information about what they are assuming. For example, they may simply assume perfect implementation of the treatment and response variables measured without error. It is just these kinds of abstractions—bypassing the messy empirical world—that have proved useful in the natural sciences. However, it cannot be overemphasized that if the data do not behave as anticipated, it may not be clear whether the premise of the conceptual experiment is wrong or whether the simplifications imposed are wrong.

Third, the same arguments can be made about the SUTVA assumption. In a conceptual experiment, one can simply assume that they are met. But again, if the data do not perform as expected, it may not be clear where the problem lies.

Finally, one can achieve strong ignorability by statistical overkill. If *all* of the variables affecting the response are included as covariates, even if some are not related to treatment assignment, then among them will be all of the variables related to both treatment assignment and the response. This means that one does not need to know about the assignment process to achieve strong ignorability. However, specifying and measuring all of the variables affecting the response is hardly an easy undertaking, even if sufficient degrees of freedom exist. And one risks serious multicollinearity.

There remains, however, one problem for which not even partial rejoinders have to date been articulated. For nonmanipulable variables, the conceptual tools and language of the experimental framework do seem problematic. If the point is not to manipulate the world, why impose an experimental conception? Perhaps one answer is that it is the only apparatus we have, or at least the only one that is sufficiently developed. Yet, this seems short-sighted. For many sociological questions, our understanding may be significantly enhanced without the use of causal concepts. Much may be learned, for example, by studying joint and conditional distributions without going beyond association and possibly time ordering. "Mere" description well done is well worth doing. Indeed, many sociologists may have prematurely tried to make the leap from description to causal imputation.

Perhaps more important, for nonmanipulable variables, alternative conceptions of cause may be useful. For example, Granger (Granger and Newbold, 1986, pp. 220-223) defines causality in predictive terms using two assumptions: (1) "The future cannot cause the past. . ." and (2) "A cause contains unique information about an effect that is not available elsewhere" (Granger and Newbold, 1986, p. 220). Basically, X "Granger causes" Y if after taking into account all of the information available except X, X then adds to one's ability to predict Y in the future. As a first approximation, Granger cause can in practice be conceptualized as a nonzero partial correlation that improves one's forecasting ability. Note that there is no reference to manipulation. Rather than manipulate the world, the idea is to predict it. Thus the height of the Rocky Mountains may well Granger cause the amount of snow in Denver.

In short, it seems difficult to impose an experimental framework when one's causal variables are not manipulable. Holland and Rubin may well be essentially correct. However, one can accept the Holland and Rubin position and *not* all of the Holland and Rubin illustrations. Indeed, on close inspection, variables such as race, age, and gender may be at least in part manipulable. As noted earlier, for many sociological questions, one is not really interested in the impact of gender per se, but some *aspect* of gender that *can* be altered. The same holds for race and age. It is certainly possible to manipulate the racial composition of high schools, for example, or the apparent gender of students' essays. The point is that the impact of race, age and gender are *socially* determined. While race, age and gender cannot be directly manipulated, their social manifestations often can.

In addition, there are indirect strategies that may be used to obtain some purchase in the impact of race, age, and gender. For example, suppose one believed that women graduate students in the natural sciences are professionally disadvantaged because prospective male mentors are more likely to recruit male graduate students. If one can assign graduate students to senior faculty (within interest areas) on the basis of known covariates, such as performance on standardized tests, by grade point average, or based on the quality of written work, the assignment mechanism is ignorable. Then, if the impact of gender on some outcome, such as future publications, is truly operating through differential mentoring, an analysis of the impact of gender, holding constant the covariates, would show no gender effects.[29] This is, of course, just a generalization of a regression-discontinuity design (Trochim, 1984). The overall lesson is that one can learn a lot about the impact of variables that are not easily manipulated by research in which the effects of those variables can be made to disappear or change.

Unfortunately, there remain social processes where manipulation is not just practically difficult (which is *not* the Rubin and Holland point), but conceptually misleading (which *is* the Rubin and Holland point). Historical events are perhaps a good example. It is difficult, for instance, to conceptualize the Protestant Reformation as manipulable. Under these circumstances, sociologists have no business talking about cause and effect. Put more positively, alternative conceptions of cause and effect need to be developed coupled with a coherent set of analytic procedures. One of the strengths of the experimental framework is that along with a definition of a causal effect comes an internally consistent set of data analytic techniques. Nothing less should be expected from alternative approaches.

Conclusions

One of the major problems with popular conceptions of causality and causal inference is that little attention is directed beneath the buzz words to the types of questions that are really being asked. Rather than moving rapidly to the data analysis after asking, for example, whether education is a cause of income, it is essential to consider what the word *cause* is meant to convey.

If by cause one is interested in the possible consequences for a person's income of manipulating that person's education, for example, an experimental framework may be usefully imposed. Within that framework, all of the pieces seem to fit, at least approximately. That is, there is a coherency linking conceptions of cause, to techniques of data collection, to procedures for data analysis. One can, therefore, apply much of technology currently available for quantitative empirical work. The practical problems are extremely demanding (and usually underestimated), especially when random assignment is not employed, but there is an instructive tradition on which to draw.

For some sociological questions, however, "cause" cannot be meaningfully linked to manipulation. To wonder about the causal impact of the industrial revolution on the nature of social control (Foucault, 1977) is not to wonder what would happen if the content and/or timing of the industrial revolution were literally altered. No such action can be reasonably anticipated or envisioned. Consequently, the experimental framework that seems helpful for thinking about manipulations of the world, does not formally apply.

Under these circumstances, there seem to be three options. One can proceed within the experimental tradition despite serious epistemological, conceptual, and practical difficulties. Presumably, researchers taking this path have to assume that their activities are in fact sensible, and that eventually, philosophers and statisticians will figure out why.

Alternatively, one can be satisfied with noncausal statements about the empirical world. While this implies to some a scaling down of sociological ambitions, it may also be viewed as finally doing the kind of homework necessary for real progress in the discipline. In other words, the second option calls for a return to the basics (which will be plenty hard enough).

Finally, one may develop different conceptions of cause, perhaps requiring somewhat different statistical tools, that correspond to the questions being asked. For example, might not Granger's approach to cause be applied to Foucault's work? Efforts such as these, which begin with rather different views on what about the world is to be learned, may be where future breakthroughs will be found.

NOTES

1. For example, in the preface to *Introduction to Structural Equation Models*, Duncan (1975, p. viii) writes, "It is not my purpose to advocate or defend the use of structural equation models in sociology. Indeed, I hold a rather agnostic view about their ultimate utility and vitality in that discipline, fascinating as the models may be in purely formal terms." A bit later he stresses, "The last thing I want to do is suggest that the structural equation approach comprises a new recipe for conducting sociological research" (Duncan, 1975, p. viii).

2. Lieberson's book has been widely and properly criticized for major technical errors (Berk, 1986; Bohrnstedt and Arminger, 1987). Nevertheless, when a sociologist of Lieberson's stature disavows the very tradition he has nurtured, it's big news.

3. I will be assuming a working knowledge of the general linear model at about the level taught to first-year graduate students in sociology (Hanushek and Jackson, 1977; Pindyck and Rubinfeld, 1981).

4. Mill's Method of Residues essentially rests on results from one or more of the first three methods. In brief, once one has taken into the account of one set of causes, any remaining effects can be attributed to a second set of causes.

5. A variety of more subtle criticisms can be found in Cohen and Nagel (1934, pp. 245-272).

6. On the other hand, in the words of Arthur C. Clark (1986: 260), "No serious philosophical problem is ever settled."

7. Matters are further complicated by the fact that the "random results" described by Chaos Theory are not necessarily pure noise. That is, the noise is "patterned" so that certain outcomes are virtually precluded (Crutchfield et al., 1986). It is impossible to predict what will occur, but some specified outcomes can be accurately predicted not to occur.

8. I am skeptical about the possibility that Chaos Theory will work for social systems. The systems for which Chaos Theory seems to work are far simpler than social systems.

9. Suppes assumes that all of the relevant relationships are positive, but that seems to be primarily for convenience. By redefining the measures, positive relationships can be made negative and negative relationships can be made positive. For example, a binary variable coded "1" for male and "0" for female may be coded "0" for male and "1" for female.

10. Suppes is working with a three-variable system: one prospective cause, one prospective effect, and one prospective control variable. If more than three variables are involved, the issues are more complicated (more on that shortly), but genuine causes are still found through time order and partialing. Note also, Suppes does not concern himself with the difference between direct and indirect causes; both may be prima facie, spurious, or genuine causes.

11. Of course, *knowledge* about a person's race or sex may be manipulated. For example, one can compare differences in grades for men and women when papers are graded blind versus when each student's name is attached. Likewise, at an aggregate level, such as a classroom, race or sex *composition* may be manipulated. I will capitalize on these possibilities later. However, for all practical purposes, one cannot alter the race or sex of an individual.

12. For ease of exposition, I will use discrete causes and experimental terminology. But the arguments carry over to the more common empirical problems faced by sociologists.

13. In some applications, a ratio or log-ratio, rather than the difference, could be used. The algebraic form is not an essential part of the definition.

14. There are other more technical, but straightforward, justifications for randomization within the statistical traditions (frequentist) most sociologists employ (Box, Hunter, and Hunter, 1987, pp. 93-106). For Bayesians, rationales for random assignment are far more complicated and problematic (Kadane and Seidenfeld, 1987; Rubin, 1978). Later, I will make some indirect use of Bayesian thinking about randomization, but an explicit discussion of the issues raised by the Bayesians are well beyond the scope of this chapter.

15. I was recently involved in an evaluation of a job training program where members of the randomly selected control group (not receiving any training) often became terribly demoralized. Some saw the training program as their last hope and actually became clinically depressed when they lost out by the luck of the draw.

16. Occasionally, lotterylike devices are used in policy settings, and then de facto randomized experiments are possible. For example, between 1970 and 1972 men in the United States were drafted through a lottery that closely approximated a randomized experiment. Hearst and his colleagues (1986) used this "randomized natural experiment" to study the impact of the draft on later mortality in civilian life. They concluded that being drafted was linked to higher rates of later suicide and fatal motor vehicle accidents.

17. Another way of thinking about the role of X is that after conditioning on X, one is left with a randomized experiment in which the randomization process is represented by e_2. The conditioning may be accomplished in one of two ways. First, one may match cases on X. Then, average causal effects can be calculated for all cases that are identical on X. Matching has the advantage of assuming no functional form, but if X is several variables and/or if measured X has many values, very large samples are required to find a sufficient number of matches. (But see Rosenbaum and Rubin, 1984a, 1984b, 1984c, for a possible solution.) Second, one may undertake statistical adjustments, such as analysis of covariance, which make the experimentals and the controls *as groups* identical on the average for all included covariates. In short, matching attempts to make individual experimentals and controls identical, while statistical adjustments attempt to make the means for the experimentals and controls identical.

18. There is an important exception. Under a regression-discontinuity design, a threshold is defined on X. Units with values above (below) the threshold are assigned to the experimental group and units with values below (above) the threshold are assigned to the control group. Then, X and T are not perfectly collinear and under certain functional form assumptions (Berk and Rauma, 1983; Trochim, 1984), unbiased causal effect estimates may be obtained after conditioning on X. For a Bayesian approach to what in effect is assignment by covariates, see Kadane and Seidenfeld (1987).

19. To take a simple illustration, for the two-by-two table crossing motivation with the assigned treatment or control condition, one might simply insert a row or column mean.

20. Actually, it's not quite that simple. For statistical models that are inherently nonlinear (e.g., logistic regression), one risks heterogeneity bias even if there is no omitted variable problem. In brief, one's estimates risk being sample specific (Gail, Wieand, and Piantodosi, 1984).

21. For some important relationships in sociology, the causal direction is clear without longitudinal data. For example, retrospective data may be collected as an approximation of true longitudinal data. And sometimes, the nature of the variables makes causal directions apparent. Thus if one is prepared to accept race as a causal variable, race can affect income, but not the reverse. It is also possible to get the causal direction wrong despite having longitudinal data. The use of cross-lagged correlation" techniques is a good example (Rogosa, 1980).

22. There is some question as to whether the R & H experimental framework cna be applied to longitudinal data (Granger, 1986). If the causal variables are manipulable, there do not seem to be any conceptual problem. Recall that Holland's assumptions of Temporal Stability and Causal Transience apply to longitudinal data. However, the analysis of temporal data will often be quite different from the analysis of cross-sectional data.

23. Put another way, such tests indicate whether you have accounted for all of the systematic aspects of your data with your model.

24. There is a variant on goodness-of-fit tests based on the amount of "information" a model contains (e.g., Harvey, 1981, pp. 175-177), and the same criticisms apply. Selecting regression models based on the proportion of variance explained (adjusted for degrees of freedom) is a special case.

25. Heteroskedasticity is also a problem, but my point is that it will typically be impossible to determine if the difficulty is omitted variables or unequal disturbance variances per se.

26. For ease of exposition, I am assuming that all of the other necessary assumptions are met, and the dependent variables are equal interval and not truncated.

27. This is common practice in the job training literature. The idea is to find a comparison group as similar as possible to the experimental group and then condition on theoretically relevant covariates.

28. This is not to say that conceptual experiments are not useful for clarifying one's thinking.

29. This is because there would be no relationships between gender and mentoring after conditioning on the covariates. Of course, random assignment would be at least more statistically efficient. However, quasi-experiments using assignment by known covariates are often politically feasible when random assignment is not (Kadane and Seidenfeld, 1987).

REFERENCES

Arminger, Gehard and George W. Borhnstedt. 1987. "Making It Count Even More: A Review and Critique of Stanley Lieberson's 'Making It Count: The Improvement of Social Theory and Research.' " In *Sociological Methodology*. Edited by C. C. Clogg. Washington, D.C.: American Sociological Association.

Barnett, Vic. 1982. *Comparative Statistical Inference*. New York: John Wiley.

Berk, Richard A., D. Rauma, D. R. Loseke, and S. F. Berk. 1982. "Throwing the Cops Back Out: The Decline of a Local Program to Make the Criminal Justice System More Responsive to Incidents of Domestic Violence." *Social Science Research* 11:245-279.

———. 1986. Book Review. *American Journal of Sociology* 82(2):462-465.

———. 1987. "Causal Inference as a Prediction Problem." In *Classification and Prediction in Criminal Decisions*, edited by D. Gottfredson and W. Tonrey. Chicago: University of Chicago.

——— and Thomas F. Cooley. In press. "Errors in Forecasting Social Phenomena." In *Forecasting in the Social and Natural Sciences*, edited by S. Schneider and K. Land. New York: D. Reidel.

Bernert, Christopher. 1983. "The Career of Causal Analysis in American Sociology." *British Journal of Sociology* 34(2):230-254.

Bielby, William T. 1986. "Arbitrary Metrics in Multiple-Indicator Models of Latent Variables." *Sociological Methods & Research* 15(1-2):3-23.

Blalock, Hubert, M., Jr. 1971. *Causal Models in the Social Sciences*. Chicago: Aldine-Atherton.

——— and Ann B. Blalock. 1968. *Methodology in Social Research*. New York: McGraw-Hill.

Bunge, Mario. 1959. *Causality*. Cleveland, OH: World Publishing.

Box, George E. P., William G. Hunter, and J. Stuart Hunter. 1987. *Statistics for Experimenters*. New York: John Wiley.

Box, G.E.P. and G. C. Tiao. 1975. "Intervention Analysis with Applications to Economic and Environmental Problems." *Journal of the American Statistical Association* 70:70-79.

Campbell, Donald T. and Julian Stanley. 1963. *Experimental and Quasi-Experimental Designs for Research*. Chicago: Rand McNally.

Clarke, Arthur C. 1986. *The Songs of Distant Earth*. New York: Ballantine.

Cochran, William G. 1983. *Planning and Analysis of Observational Studies*. New York: John Wiley.

Cohen, Morris R. and Ernest Nagel. 1934. *An Introduction to Logic and Scientific Method*. New York: Harcourt, Brace.

Cook, Thomas D. and Donald T. Campbell. 1979. *Quasiexperimentation*. Chicago: Rand McNally.

Cooley, Thomas F. and Stephen F. LeRoy. 1981.

"Identification and Estimation of Money Demand." *American Economic Review* 71:825-844.

Cox, D. R. 1986. "Comment." *Journal of the American Statistical Association* 81(396):963-964.

Crutchfield, James P., J. Doyne Farmer, Norman H. Packard, and Robert S. Shaw. 1986. "Chaos." *Scientific American* (December): 46-57.

Davies, Paul. 1983. *God and the New Physics*. New York: Simon & Schuster.

Dawid, A. P. 1984. "Causal Inference from Messy Data." *Journal of the American Statistical Association* 79:22-24.

Draper, N. R. and H. Smith. 1981. *Applied Regression Analysis*. New York: John Wiley.

Duncan, O. Dudley. 1975. *Introduction to Structural Equation Models*. New York: Academic Press.

———. 1984. *Notes on Social Measurement: Historical and Critical*. New York: Russell Sage.

Ehrenberg, Werner. 1977. *Dice of the Gods*. London: University of London.

Fetzer, James H. 1983. "Probability and Objectivity in Deterministic and Indeterministic Situations." *Synthese* 57:367-386.

Feinberg, Stephen E. 1977. *The Analysis of Cross-Classified Categorical Data*. Cambridge, MA: MIT Press.

Fox, John. 1984. *Linear Statistical Models and Related Methods*. New York: John Wiley.

Foucault, Michel. 1977. *Discipline and Punishment*. New York: Vintage.

Fraker, Thomas and Rebecca Maynard. 1987. "Evaluating Comparison Group Designs with Employment-Related Programs." *Journal of Human Resources* 2:194-227.

Freedman, David A. 1985. "Statistics and the Scientific Method." Pp. 343-366 in *Cohort Analysis in Social Research*, edited by William M. Mason and Stephen E. Fienberg. New York: Springer-Verlag.

Fromby, Thomas B., R. Cater Hill, and Stanley R. Johnson. 1984. *Advanced Econometric Methods*. New York: Springer-Verlag.

Gail, M. H., S. Wieand, and S. Piantodosi. 1984. "Biased Estimates of Treatment Effect in Randomized Experiments with Nonlinear Regressions and Omitted Covariates." *Biometrika* 71:431-444.

Geweke, John. 1984. "The Indispensible Art of Econometrics." *Journal of American Statistical Association* 79:25-26.

Glymour, Clark. 1986. "Statistics and Metaphysics." *Journal of the American Statistical Association* 81:964-966.

Granger, Clive. 1986. "Comment." *Journal of the American Statistical Association* 81:967-968.

--- and Paul Newbold. 1986. *Forecasting Economic Time Series*. New York: Academic Press.

Harvey, A. C. 1981. *The econometric Analysis of Time Series*. New York: John Wiley.

Hanushek, Eric A. and John Jackson. 1977. *Statistical Methods for the Social Sciences*. New York: Academic Press.

Hearst, Norman, Thomas B. Newman, and Stephen B. Hulley. 1986. "Delayed Effects of the Military Draft on Mortality." *New England Journal of Medicine* 314:620-624.

Hedges, Larry V. and Ingram Olkin. 1985. *Statistical Methods for Meta-Analysis*. New York: Academic Press.

Holland, Paul W. 1986a. "Statistics and Causal Inference." *Journal of the American Statistical Association* 81:945-960.

———. 1986b. "Rejoinder." *Journal of the American Statistical Association* 81:968-970.

———. 1986c. "Which Comes First, Cause or Effect?" *Program in Statistics Research*. Technical Report 87-74. Princeton, NJ: Educational Testing Service.

Holland, Paul W. and Donald Rubin. 1983. "On Lord's Paradox." In *Principles of Modern Psychological Measurement*, edited by H. Wainer and D. Messick. Hillsdale, NJ: Lawrence Erlbaum.

———. 1987. "Causal Inference in Retrospective Studies." *Program in Statistics Research*. Technical Report 87-73. Princeton, NJ: Educational Testing Service.

Hume, David. 1740. *A Treatise on Human Nature*.

———. 1748. *An Inquiry Concerning Human Understanding*.

Jensen, Roderick V. 1987. "Classical Chaos." *American Scientist* 75:168-181.

Jöreskog, Karl G. and Dag Sörbom. 1979. *Advances in Factor Analysis and Structural Equation Models*. Cambridge, MA: Abt.

Kadane, Joseph and Teddy Seidenfeld. 1987. "Randomization in a Bayesian Perspective." Pittsburgh: Department of Statistics, Carnegie-Mellon University.

Kaplan, Abraham. 1964. *The Conduct of Inquiry*. San Francisco: Chandler.

Kolata, Gina. 1986. "What Does it Mean to be Random?" *Science* 231:1068-1070.

LaLonde, Robert J. 1986. "Evaluating the Econometric Evaluations of Training Programs with Experimental Data." *The American Economic Review* 76:604-620.

Leamer, Edward E. 1978. *Specification Searches*. New York: John Wiley.

———. 1983. "Let's Take the Con out of Econometrics." *American Economic Review* 73:31-43.

Lieberson, Stanley. 1985. *Making it Count*. Berkeley: University of California Press.

MacIver, R. M. 1942. *Social Causation*. Boston: Ginn.

Mill, J. Stuart. 1872. *A System of Logic*. London: Longmans, Green, Reader and Dyer.

Nagel, Ernest. 1961. *The Structure of Science*. New York: Harcourt, Brace & World.

Pindyck, Robert S. and Daniel L. Rubinfeld. 1981. *Econometric Models and Economic Forecasts*. New York: McGraw-Hill.

Pratt, J. W. and Robert Schlaifer. 1984a. "On the Nature and Discovery of Structure." *Journal of the American Statistical Association* 79:29-33.

———. 1984b. "Rejoinder." *Journal of the American Statistical Association* 79:29-33.

Rogosa, David. 1980. "A Critique of Cross-Lagged Correlation." *Psychological Bulletin* 88:245-258.

——— and John B. Willet. 1985. "Satisfying a Simplex Structure is Simpler Than It Should Be." *Journal of Educational Statistics* 10:99-107.

Rosenbaum, Paul R. 1984. "From Association to Causation in Observational Studies: The Role of Tests of Strongly Ignorable Treatment Assignment." *Journal of the American Statistical Association* 79:41-48.

——— and Donald B. Rubin. 1983. "The Central Role of the Propensity Score in Observational Studies for Causal Effects." *Biometrika* 70:41-55.

———. 1984a. "Reducing Bias in Observational Studies Using Subclassification on the Propensity Score." *Journal of the American Statistical Association* 79:516-524.

———. 1984b. "Estimating the Effects Caused by Treatments." *Journal of the American Statistical Association* 79:26-28.

———. 1984c. "Comment." *Journal of the American Statistical Association* 79:26-28.

Rubin, Donald B. 1977. "Assignment of Treatment Group on the Basis of a Covariate." *Journal of Educational Statistics* 2:1-26.

———. 1978. "Bayesian Inference for Causal Effects: The Role of Randomization." *Annals of Statistics* 6:34-58.

———. 1986. "Which Ifs Have Causal Answers." *Journal of the American Statistical Association* 81:961-962.

Sander, Leonard W. 1987. "Fractal Growth." *Scientific American* (January):94-100.

Sherman, Lawrence W. and Richard A. Berk. 1984. "The Specific Deterrent Effects of Arrest for Domestic Assault." *American Sociological Review* 49:261-271.

Sobel, Michael E. and George W. Bohrnstedt. 1985. "Use of Null Models in Evaluating the Fit of Covariance Structure Models." In *Sociological Methodology 1985*, edited by Nancy Brandon Tuma. San Francisco: Jossey-Bass.

Suppes, Patrick. 1970. *A Probabilistic Theory of Causality*. Amsterdam: North-Holland.

———. 1981. "Causal Analysis of Hidden Variables." *PSA 1980* 2:563-571.

———. 1982. "Problems of Causal Analysis in the Social Sciences." *Epistemologia* 5:239-250.

Swamy, P.A.V.B., R. K. Conway, and P. von zur Muehlen. 1985. "The Foundations of Econometrics—Are There Any?" *Economic Reviews* 4:1-61.

Trochim, William M. K. 1984. *Research Design for Program Evaluation*. Beverly Hills, CA: Sage.

Wolf, Fred Alan. 1981. *Taking the Quantum Leap*. San Francisco: Harper & Row.

Part II

BASES OF INEQUALITY
IN SOCIETY

6

Inequality and Labor Processes

MARK GRANOVETTER
CHARLES TILLY

General Introduction

Changing Views of Labor Processes and Inequality

To each generation its own intellectual agenda. Scholars—especially American—who emerged from World War II analyzed labor processes and inequality in the context of economic growth. In his lucid little *Impact of Industry*, published in 1965, Wilbert Moore summed up the dominant postwar view of the problem:

> Economic development entails a new system of social placement and differential valuation. Systems of stratification may compete for considerable periods. The point of present relevance is that the change to new economic activities almost inevitably entails

a change of most aspects of the "way of life" and the motivational rewards and penalties for the individual will necessarily include his position in the community, the esteem of his friends and acquaintances, and his expectations for himself and his children. The individualizing of incentives implicit in mobility aspirations is thus always likely to be tempered by group orientations and collective aspirations. These may be as particular as the "circle" of family and friends, as general as a social class or even the whole nation [Moore, 1965, pp. 43-44].

In treating transformations of production, Moore concentrated on the consequences of mechanization, and especially "the spatial juxtaposition of workers and fixed machines for daily or continuous operation" (Moore, 1965, p. 48). But he also emphasized the emergence of norms: functional specificity, impersonality, affective neutrality, and other criteria of "modernity" then in vogue (Moore, 1965, p. 51). On the side of inequality, Moore likewise stressed normative changes. "Industrialization," he argued, "inevitably produces a new set of social positions and new criteria of social placement and valuation. At the very least, therefore, it must result in a more complex system of social differentiation. More commonly, it gives rise to *competing systems* of stratification, since its criteria of placement and valuation contrast sharply with traditional modes of assigning

The authors are listed alphabetically. A previous version of this chapter elicited an extraordinary number of helpful comments. We are grateful to Howard Aldrich, Paul Attewell, Hal Benenson, John Bodnar, Dan Clawson, Sam Cohn, Alan Dawley, Mary Freifeld, Carmenza Gallo, David Halle, Heidi Hartmann, David Lee, Sue Model, Ewa Morawska, Chick Perrow, Michael Schwartz, Robert Thomas, Ross Thomson, Stephen Wood, and members of the New School's proseminar on inequality. The first author is grateful for the facilities and support of Stanford Business School, provided during the term of his visiting appointment in 1986-1987.

status, power, and prestige" (Moore, 1965, p. 92; emphasis in text). When it came to the relationship between inequality and the organization of production, Moore's analysis epitomized the ideas of a whole generation of scholars.

What ideas? America's postwar sociologists portrayed preindustrial society as coherent and slowly changing. They saw industrialization as a general process with its own powerful rationale. They conceived of social stratification as a comprehensive system of ranking that spanned a whole society and cut across the worlds of work, politics, and leisure. According to those views, the logic of industrialization—with its demands for individualistic competition, mobility, and general standards of evaluation—entailed a new system of stratification. The new system contradicted, challenged, and eventually displaced the old. All this happened as part of a broader, revolutionary process of modernization.

That approach had some important advantages. It lent itself to systematic comparisons of industrializing countries. It also focused attention on the interdependence of changes in production and in organized inequality. But the approach had serious drawbacks. It rested on the poorly explicated but potent assumption of a "society" held together by coherent, compelling norms. It postulated an emerging industrial society and a global process of industrialization, each of them embodying an inexorable logic. It supposed that the hierarchy of rewards within any population represented the norms and values that prevailed within that population, thus implicitly denying the importance of struggle and division.

With those postulates, analysts directed their theories and research to alterations of norms and attitudes, neglecting to examine the processes by which production and inequality actually changed. That neglect, in its turn, encouraged acceptance of what Charles Sabel and Jonathan Zeitlin call a "narrow track" interpretation of industrialization, which takes technological innovation as the driver of economic change and the large factory as the quintessence of industrial production (Sabel and Zeitlin, 1985, p. 137).

Sabel and Zeitlin typify a new scholarly generation, theorists of political economy rather than of modernization. They are more sympathetic to Marxist statements of problems (if not necessarily to conventional Marxist answers), more skeptical of the autonomous impact of technology, less convinced that "societies" are meaningful actors, more sensitive to the exercise of power and the influence of national states, more inclined to think in terms of class than of stratification, more concerned to root their analyses in history. Conflict figures much more prominently in their accounts of industrial change. For this generation, it comes naturally to ask about the connections between labor processes and inequality.

The battle between modernization theorists and analysts of political economy has, happily, faded away. These days the burning differences of opinion concern the relationship between labor processes and inequality: To what extent and how does coercion enter into the relationship? Ideology? Strategic bargaining? Economic interest, narrowly defined? Technology? Ostensibly extraneous characteristics of workers such as race and gender? How much of the inequality in income, wealth, and power that is associated with different positions in the organization of production stems directly from the logic of production itself? What independent effect, if any, has the structure of labor markets? All these questions have generated intense controversy.

The shadow of Karl Marx falls long over any discussion of connections between labor processes and inequality. Broadly speaking, Marx saw productive forces as constraining the relations of production and viewed larger social inequalities as emerging from the relations of production. But there, for students of Marx, the difficulties begin. To what extent, and how, do the forces of production determine the relations of production? What else affects the form, consciousness, and collective action of social classes? Both inside and outside Marxist analyses, technological determinism struggles with arguments that subordinate technology to organizational logics driven by the requirements of capital, labor, and command. Our own arguments generally take sides against technological determinism and for the logic of organization.

Within and outside Marxism, likewise, functionalist explanations (which assert that particular social arrangements exist because they serve some end of an overarching system) contend with assertions that social conditions prevailing at one point in time cause social arrangements that then endure and constrain subsequent social arrangements. Our own arguments generally favor this more historically oriented line.

Our Problems

Let us plunge into the questions that arise when we take labor processes and inequality as our starting points. How do the two connect? To what extent does one cause the other? And what *are* "labor processes" and "inequality"? By *labor process* we mean how labor is used in the production of goods and services. This includes the allocation of labor among different aspects of production, the technical conditions for its application, and the intensity of effort required. By *inequality* we mean the existence of regular differences in power, goods, services, and privileges among defined sets of people. We close in on inequalities in rewards to labor. To what degree, and how, do variations in the use of labor in the production of goods and services determine differences in rewards to labor? What else determines differences in those rewards?

Let us begin with a crude conception of labor: any effort that adds use value to goods or services. If the quality of the effort affects how much the producer receives for it, that quality becomes part of the explanation for differential rewards to labor. To the degree that inequalities in rewards to labor create, result from, or correspond to socially visible categories such as class, race, national origin, gender, or residence, those categories enter our area of concern. When they bear on differential rewards to labor, inequalities between those who work and those who do not—rentiers, dependent members of households, and so on—also command our attention.

A full examination of the relations between inequality and labor processes would take us through systems of feudalism, slavery, household production, corporate craft production, domestic service, intermittent wage labor, and continuous wage labor. But we will concentrate on North American and European experience over the last two centuries, and give the American experience priority. That means concentrating on industrial capitalism.

Our Argument

Our general analysis of inequality under industrial capitalism places bargaining, negotiation, and struggle over work and its rewards at the very center. For analytic purposes, we distinguish (1) processes, (2) actors, (3) strategies, (4) arenas, and (5) outcomes. We try to identify the main processes that shape the pattern of unequal rewards for labor: ranking, sorting, performance, discrimination, and bargaining. We likewise single out the actors—capitalists, workers, independent producers, and others—who have interests in this pattern, and who pursue them within the limits set by their interpersonal networks and the resources they control. We discuss the main strategies actors use to influence these processes, and the varying arenas in which they do so. We introduce a rough distinction between *intrinsic* and *extrinsic* features of labor processes, considering intrinsic only those applications of labor without which the product in question would not exist. We then inquire into the impact on inequality-producing processes of extrinsic social categories, and of those matters intrinsic to labor processes that are frequently called on to carry the main burden of explanation in studies of inequality: technology and skill.

We specify inequality in rewards to labor as outcomes of bargaining in various arenas among actors who vary in resources and strategies—bargaining over the interaction among labor processes, ranking, sorting, discrimination, and work performance. We try harder to identify the chief mechanisms linking inequality and labor processes than to arrive at a precise specification of any one of those mechanisms. We hope to gain more in scope than we lose in precision.

PROCESSES AND ARENAS

Inequality associated with labor results from the conjunction of processes that concern work positions on the one hand and persons on the other. Inequality occurs in part because work positions differ greatly with respect to the rewards available to them. We will thus be concerned with how jobs, firms, and employment statuses are created, destroyed, transformed, and ranked—a set of processes that we will call *ranking*. Individuals and groups take up a position in the structure of inequality through a process of *sorting*. If the structure of positions were absolutely fixed in its rankings and in the proportions in different ranks, the question of who is sorted into what positions would not concern the distribution of inequality but only who was assigned to what part of the structure. But in fact, sorting processes also determine the size of different categories and can affect their ranking as well. Individual *performance* can affect rewards from labor, as in the proposition from neoclassical economic theory that workers are paid their "marginal product"; but jobs differ in the extent to which this can make a significant difference. One aspect of sorting has to do with whether one ends up in a position where it can make a difference, and where one's particular talents are especially appropriate.

This formulation still reifies too much the concept of "skill" as external to the labor process (see later discussion). And the general proposition that the ranking of positions and the sorting of individuals into those ranked positions determines inequality is correct only in the absence of *discrimination*: the unequal distribution of rewards among individuals occupying identical jobs, firms, and employment statuses, where this inequality results not from performance but from categorical characteristics of individuals that are ranked outside of the labor market.

As a first approximation, then, our argument follows this line:

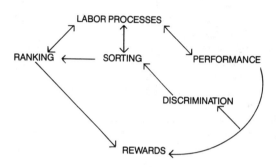

Ranking, sorting, performance, and discrimination, mediate all impacts of labor processes on rewards. Ranking, sorting, and performance all affect labor processes as well as being affected by them. And discrimination has an impact both on sorting processes and on the relationship between performance and rewards.

Sorting and ranking occur in three *arenas*: (1) among *employment statuses*—for example, the statuses of employers, independent producers, workers, and unemployed persons; (2) among *jobs and occupations*; and (3) among and within firms and industries—the level of analysis usually called the *labor market*, including both the external (between firms) and internal (within firms) labor market. Processes within all three arenas contribute significantly to differences in returns to labor. Working through established networks, employers recruit workers to particular firms and jobs, which differ with respect to the returns, present and future, on which their occupants acquire claims. We will qualify this simplification repeatedly—for example, by pointing out that "jobs" adapt to the persons who are available to work, and by recognizing that managers and owners themselves struggle over the rewards of labor, including their own. And the three arenas intersect: Many people who are now unemployed got that way by leaving or losing a job, some employers began as workers, and almost all labor markets crosscut occupations. Nevertheless, the sorting within the three arenas operates through somewhat different mechanisms, and with somewhat different effects.

The largest differences in returns to male and female labor, for example, result not from sorting within labor markets but from the fact that many women, including all housewives, receive no wages for their work. Household composition provides another example. In the contemporary United States, female-headed households live on dramatically lower incomes than those including an adult male (Corcoran, Duncan, and Hill, 1984, Duncan and Hoffman, 1985). The two events most likely to cast a household from relative prosperity into poverty are a major wage earner's loss of a job and the loss of a major wage earner through divorce, separation, or death (Duncan and Morgan, 1981, pp. 34-38). Inequality among households therefore depends strongly on their age-sex composition and on the current pattern of unemployment. Thus the model, despite its simplifications, conveniently poses some difficult questions.

THE ACTORS

Five sets of actors figure in our analysis: capitalists, workers, organized groups, households, and governments. No one ignores the first two in studies of inequality. Yet arguments that focus narrowly on the point of production, often miss the key role of the last three. Within each of the three arenas identified above, these actors contend over the allocation of returns to labor, but they do not intervene with the same vigor or effectiveness in all three. Decisions made in today's American households, for example, significantly affect employment status, have a lesser effect on the distribution of persons and rewards among firms, and make little difference to allocation within firms. Although capitalists act effectively in all three arenas, in contrast, they come closest to untrammeled control within their own firms.

Changes in the relative involvement of actors in different arenas matter a good deal. Before the late nineteenth century, households often hired themselves out as whole work teams in agriculture, manufacturing, or services, established their own divisions of labor, and allocated internally the payment the household head received for all their work; that arrangement has become rare in Western countries. Over the same period, governments increased their intervention in all three loci, but especially within firms—which had once been a zone of relatively free action for employers and workers.

Let us look more closely at the interests and activities of each major actor.

Capitalists live chiefly on income from capital they control. They differ from independent workers to the extent that the disposition of their capital, rather than their labor, determines their income. That is clearly a matter of degree; dentists, for example, charge their patients not only for the actual labor of drilling and filling, but also for the expensive education and equipment in which every dentist invests. Many economists make every individual at least a bit of a capitalist by speaking of the "human capital" that accumulates in a person's skills. Nevertheless, the differences between (a) corporate owners and rentiers, on one side, and (b) independent professionals, artisans, shopkeepers, and laborers, on the other, are clear enough to justify singling out a capitalist class.

Capitalists intervene actively in all three arenas: employment, labor markets, and jobs. We have generally paid too much attention to the influence of capitalists on jobs, and too little to their influence on the divisions among the unemployed, independent producers, employers, and workers. Not that jobs are unimportant; but a significant portion of inequality results from divisions in relations to capital, and the behavior of capitalists strongly affects those divisions.

Historically, capitalists drove the process of proletarianization; that process expanded the number of wage workers producing under direct supervision as it practically eliminated households as units producing goods and services for sale. The line between the employed and the unemployed—temporary and permanent—became a fundamental division, and lack of at least one employed member came to condemn a household to poverty. Thus proletarianization worked simultaneously to create jobs, to rank them, and to sort people into them. Capitalists made jobs salient. By continuing to make the crucial decisions concerning what jobs exist, who will have a job, and who will not, capitalists have kept jobs salient.

Workers, however, also influence the division of the world into capitalists, independent producers, workers, and unemployed persons, not to mention the operation of labor markets and job assignments. Individually, they do so by their own life courses: seeking or leaving education, migrating from one labor market to another, retiring from work, accumulating capital to enter the ranks of capitalists or (more likely) independent producers, and so on. Collectively, they do so by the forms of competition, collaboration, and collective action they create both on and off the job.

Households enter the action at its starting point: the production and reproduction of labor power. Although that way of putting it stems from Marxist theory, neoclassical economists make a similar observation in their treatment of households as loci for the creation and accumulation of human capital. To the extent that households vary in the quantity or quality of labor power they produce, they participate in the creation of inequality. Where life depends on wages and wages depend on education, households that experience high fertility and high infant mortality, or that have little time and money to invest in the average child's education, produce adults who have serious disadvantages in the labor market.

Organizations whose activities have considerable impact on inequalities in returns to labor include employers' organizations, trade unions, professional associations, and political parties. Most of them took shape in the nineteenth century, as time-disciplined wage labor outside of households became the dominant form of work. Employers' organizations and trade unions shaped each other in the course of struggles over labor processes and returns to labor; in our own time, they continue to struggle.

Employers' organizations seek a stable, docile, inexpensive but suitably skilled labor force. Trade unions organize firm by firm, often one trade at a time, and likewise agglomerate to industries. Both develop interests in monopolies over opportunities for employment. They therefore acquire grounds for bargaining with each other despite their more clearly defined antagonism with respect to wages, hours, working conditions, and power within firms. In the case of American craft labor markets before World War I, Robert Max Jackson shows how the unions

> won a collective monopoly over jobs by insisting that employers hire only union members for the tasks they claimed. They also achieved control over the allocation of jobs to individual members of the union: in the building trades business agents acquired a monopoly of the knowledge and connections necessary for employment, and in printing, foremen were required to be union members regulated by restrictive rules. The unions also won mutual control over apprenticeship with employers' associations. The unions developed each of these paths to labor market control in order to protect workers' jobs and the power of the union [Jackson, 1984, pp. 317-318].

Nevertheless, craft control did not last forever. Effective craft labor markets only persist so long as workers and their unions can keep employers from modifying labor processes in ways that make their particular skills and recruitment networks expendable.

The chief difference between craft unions and professional associations lies in the fact that unions concentrate on conditions of employment, while professional associations seek to construct monopolies over both employment and the market for their members' services (Abbott, 1986b; Collins, 1979; Larson, 1977; Starr, 1982). Both kinds of monopolies affect inequality in two distinct ways. First, they exclude some potential workers from the labor market; in so far as the principle of exclusion corresponds to categories of race, age, gender, citizenship, or national origin, it contributes to systematic inequality in that regard. Second, they affect the position of the organized industry vis-a-vis all other industries—usually by producing higher returns to labor within the monopoly than outside it, thereby compounding the effects of any categorical exclusion of potential workers.

Governments also intervene in labor markets, sometimes quite vigorously. National states often become guarantors of professional monopolies, a tendency that Adam Smith denounced more than two centuries ago, and that Mancur Olson (1982) has portrayed as contributing to the decline of nations. They do so both through solicitation by the professionals and through intervention in ongoing struggles within industries. They likewise regulate strikes and other struggles over returns to labor; the nineteenth-century legalization of strikes and of labor unions in most Western countries involved great increases in states' day-to-day monitoring and control of industrial conflict. National patterns differed as a function of national politics and the power of capitalists.

In late nineteenth- and early twentieth-century France, for example, workers typically had allies or direct representatives in the central government. They actually gained, on the average, from state intervention, and therefore adopted tactics that incited the intervention. In the United States, on the other hand, governments intervened more rarely, and workers stood to lose when they did. The Knights of Labor were the only major American labor federation deliberately to attract state intervention; they lost heavily as a consequence (Friedman, 1985).

Governments vary more generally in the extent to which they intervene in the sorting processes that produce inequality. Since World War I, all Western governments have enacted more extensive controls over the conditions of employment, work, and remuneration. The great expansion of direct government employment has increased the zone of political control over inequality; governmental bureaucracies and military forces, for example, often restrict discrimination by race, gender, and national origin, if not by age. Since governmental bureaucracies and armed forces also give exceptional weight to seniority, however, their hierarchies preserve earlier competitive differences among groups over long periods of time.

Taxation and the public distribution of services, furthermore, affect differential returns to labor significantly, if indirectly. One of the most important distinctions between capitalist and socialist states concerns the degree to which the mechanisms affecting inequality fall under central administrative control. Ivan Szelenyi (1978, 1983) has argued that where Eastern European socialist states have substituted administrative for market control, they have not so much reduced inequality as made position within the party hierarchy the prime principle of allocation. They have done so by tying housing, transportation, and many services to jobs, firms, and governmental offices in which relation to the party hierarchy weighs heavily.

In a similar vein, Michael Burawoy (1985) describes a shortage-racked, supply-driven, administratively coordinated production system in Hungary; it gives exceptional power to the small group of workers who link a plant to the party hierarchy. Again, Andrew Walder (1986) speaks of Chinese "communist neo-traditionalism" in which a household's returns to labor depend heavily on the enterprises to which they are attached; in that system, enterprises themselves divide into privileged core patron-client networks that are closely linked to the party, on one side, and a large but peripheral remainder of underprivileged workers, on the other. All three converge on a portrayal of state-socialist systems in which a ruling party provides not only a major link among units but also a strong stimulus to unequal rewards.

THE ARGUMENT SUMMARIZED

We argue that the five sets of actors just identified contend over the rewards for labor in the three arenas of employment status, jobs, and labor market and do so primarily by attempting to influence the processes of ranking and sorting. Although discrimination and estimates of likely performance play a part in sorting workers into different employment categories, jobs, and firms, performance and discrimination account for little of the variation in rewards to labor within a given arrangement of ranking and sorting. Differences in bargaining power among the actors are thus a prime subject for us to explain. To be more exact, they depend on the resources each actor brings to the bargaining and on the interpersonal networks in which the actors are embedded. Workers' success in strikes depends, for example, not only on their ability to hold out without wages, but also on their capacity to keep out strikebreakers and to enlist the support of third parties, including government officials (see Conell, 1980; Friedman, 1985; Korpi, 1983). And workers' ability to control employment depends on their ability to intervene in the networks employers use to search for new labor. Both the networks and the resources embedded in them alter through non-bargaining processes, and thereby affect the relative ability of all parties to affect bargains that establish unequal returns to labor. Thus we must pay some attention to these non-bargaining processes that indirectly determine outcomes.

In bargaining both the character of the labor process and the allocation of workers among jobs and firms are at issue; actors extrinsic to the labor process (such as governments and households) sometimes enter the bargaining, and all actors sometimes bargain for the installation into the labor process of categorical divisions logically extrinsic to it. Since the outcomes of bargaining have inertia, furthermore, inequality at a given point in time depends on the previous history of bargaining. The outcomes of bargaining by the current occupants of jobs, firms, and employment statuses affect not only the future bargaining positions of those occupants but the relative rewards and bargaining positions of future occupants of similar positions. Similarly, the outcome of current bargaining depends not only on the overall strength of employers and workers but also on the relative timing of their bargaining advantages and disadvantages.

Our model has a powerful implication for the relationship between labor processes and inequality: Whether one labor process is more advantageous to employers or workers than another depends on their previously existing social relations—especially on their relative bargaining situations. No labor process is itself inherently profitable or menacing to workers' welfare. Labor processes' impacts on inequality stem from their interaction with other decisions and struggles.

The argument thus contradicts four other prominent models of inequality: its emanation from a society's dominant value system, its direct derivation from the technology of production, its attribution to the routine operation of competitive markets, and its imputation to the straightforward designs of powerful capitalists. As we proceed, we shall try to make these contradictions explicit.

Trends

We will be concentrating our attention on inequality and labor processes in twentieth-century North America. But the conditions under which these are determined resulted from an historical process that we will first review in order to establish a context for our discussion.

In our model, changes in bargaining power and strategies of households, capitalists, workers, organizations, and governments produce reallocations of rewards to labor. They also strongly constrain both the forms of labor processes and the influence of labor processes on inequality in rewards to labor. They do so by altering the ranking, sorting, discrimination, and work performance that constitute the immediate links between unequal rewards and labor processes. The last few hundred years have brought momentous changes in the bargaining power and strategies of the major actors, and therefore transformed the prevailing patterns of inequality in Western countries. Without attempting a comprehensive history of inequality's transformation, let us recall some of the ways in which our two major elements—labor processes and inequalities in rewards—have changed in Western countries since the eighteenth century.

Proletarianization and the Growth of Manufacturing

The most important trends in labor processes include the concentration and fixing of capital, increases in the scale of producing units, mechanization, extensions of time discipline, urbanization of production sites, and the introduction of applied science to the design and execution of production processes. With regard to inequality, the last two centuries have seen the extension of wage labor, the expansion and formalization of non-wage benefits, the embedding of divisions by gender, race, national origin, and other "extrinsic" categories into positions within single firms, the decline in domestic goods such as food and housing as part of direct compensation, and increasing state intervention.

Crucial for both labor processes and inequality, the last few centuries have witnessed a vast proletarianization of labor in Europe and North America. By this we mean an increase in the proportion of all labor (1) performed for wages and (2) employing means of production owned or controlled by other people. These two components are logically independent; sometimes alienation of productive means advances without an increase in wage labor (as when petty entrepreneurs begin to own the looms worked by cottage weavers) and sometimes the opposite occurs (as when craftsmen shift from selling their products for fixed prices to producing the same items for a wage on a merchant's premises). But usually the expansion of wage labor and the alienation of productive means have proceeded together and reinforced each other.

Proletarianization has made the division between employment and unemployment sharper and more critical. For a long time, authorities in Western countries used such terms as *vagabond* and *beggar* for proletarians who were not currently receiving a wage. Yet the line between working and not working remained vague. With the nineteenth-century concentration and fixing of capital, the idea and the fact of unemployment crystallized (see Keyssar, 1986). An unemployed person came to be someone who had held a job, but lost it. During the twentieth century, states intervened increasingly in defining and regulating employment. To the extent that they adopted Keynesian conceptions and policies, states moved the definition of unemployment toward anyone who was not currently employed, but was "available" for wage work; thus some people who had never held a job counted as unemployed. The expanded definition reflects a reality: dependence on wages as a nearly universal experience, employment as a near necessity for economic survival.

Concretely, what do these trends mean? Two centuries ago, very little production took place within large, heavily capitalized organizations. Most European and American workers spent at least part of their time in agriculture. A great deal of manufacturing, furthermore, occurred in small towns, villages, and rural households (see, e.g., Gullickson, 1986). Contrary to common belief, however, most households—rural and urban alike—already drew a significant part of their income from wage labor of one kind or another. In Europe as a whole, indeed, rural areas remained the primary sites of proletarianization until well into the nineteenth century.

At the start of that century, most agricultural workers were not peasants in any strong sense of the word, but short-term tenants, servants, or day laborers. Within cities, in contrast, rentiers, clerics, artisans, masters, and merchants—none of them proletarian—remained numerous. As a result, the proletarian share of the population probably remained higher in rural areas than in cities until after 1850 (Tilly, 1984, pp. 33-36). In the United States, a higher proportion of farms ran as family affairs, but in the South the bulk of agricultural workers were slaves, then proletarians; as a result, most likely American cities as a whole, like their European counterparts, only became more proletarian than their hinterlands toward the end of the nineteenth century.

With the concentration of capital and shift toward machine production in the nineteenth century, larger firms and urban locations became more important than single-master shops and rural households. Mass production expanded more rapidly than craft production. Yet the scale of production rose only slowly; Sabel and Zeitlin point out that in the 1970s "roughly 70 percent of all production in the metalworking sector in the United States consisted of small batches" and small firms continued to thrive (Sabel and Zeitlin, 1985, p. 137; see also Granovetter, 1984).

In many respects, the fixing of capital and labor mattered more than the sheer increase in scale. Before the nineteenth century, most production of goods and services involved very little fixed capital, and only small concentrations of circulating capital. Rural textile manufacturing, organized by petty merchants but occurring within individual households, provides a typical and important example (see Berg, Hudson, and Sonenscher, 1983; Kriedte, Medick, and Schlumbohm, 1977; Tilly, 1983). Correspondingly, the labor force swarmed incessantly. Contrary to widespread impressions, even the craft shop of masters, journeymen, apprentices, and servants commonly experienced enormous turnover. In eighteenth-century Paris and Rouen, for example, Arlette Farge shows that it was rare for craftsmen to spend more than three months in a single job (Farge, 1986, p. 128). On the whole, the nineteenth-century concentration and fixing of capital led to a decline, not a rise, in labor mobility (see, e.g. Chatelain, 1976). Increasingly employers, with more fixed capital at risk, sought to stabilize and discipline their work forces—assembling them under one roof, establishing time schedules, organizing systems of payment, housing, and other returns to labor that made it costly for workers to decamp. Thus, paradoxically, the same process that turned the mass of labor power into formally free workers also fixed it into long-term jobs, and depressed its long-term mobility.

Even industry's urbanization flowed with frequent countercurrents—as, for example, urban textile entrepreneurs sought out rural locations combining water power and cheap labor (e.g., Wallace, 1978). Over the longer run, furthermore, net shifts from agriculture into services far outshadowed the growth of the industrial labor force as such.

One might imagine that the growth of manufacturing would drive the increase in urban population, and the two would therefore rise in parallel. That is not the case. Paul Bairoch estimates that while the proportions of the labor force of "developed" countries in extractive and manufacturing industry tripled between 1800 and 1980, from 10% to nearly 30%, the proportions of their populations in urban places more than sextupled, from 10% to 64% (1985, p. 591). Two facts account for most of the discrepancy between these rates: (1) during the earlier decades, a significant part of the increase in the urban industrial labor force resulted from a transfer of manufacturing and its workers out of the countryside into cities; to that extent, the urban population grew without a change in the nation's industrial labor force; (2) service industries grew disproportionately fast in cities, and thereby produced an important share of the cities' total increase.

Agriculture and Services

While manufacturing proletarianized, the agrarian sector behaved differently. In Europe, the agricultural labor force of 1800 consisted largely of wage workers, servants, serfs, and other dependent workers. During the nineteenth century, agricultural wage work expanded for a while, but then gave way as rural workers migrated to cities and to the Americas. The decline of rural industry accelerated the emigration. Since owners and long-term tenants tended to stay behind, the countryside became less proletarian. Peasant and petty-commodity production reestablished their dominance in European rural areas. Within the continental market for wheat, in fact, family farms specializing in wheat production displaced large landlords and capitalist producers (Friedmann 1978a).

In the case of wheat, the augmentation of American household production also helped transform the world market. Most likely the American rural population began the nineteenth century with a much higher proportion of owner-operators than in Europe, and proletarianized much less thoroughly and rapidly; although that is less likely to be true of the South, it is surely the case of the North and the West. By 1980, in any case, 57% of all persons working on American farms qualified as owners or managers; in contrast, only 22% of the non-farm labor force fell into the Census category "Managerial and Professional," and a number of them were actually subordinate employees (Bureau of the Census 1975, p. 139; 1985, pp. 395, 400).

The growing importance of services in American employment appears from the percentage distributions of "gainfully employed" persons in 1940 and of employed persons 16 and over in 1970 and 1983 (Bureau of the Census, 1975, I, p. 138; 1985, p. 404).

TABLE 6.1
Percentage Distribution of "Gainfully Employed" Persons in 1940 and of Employed Persons 16 and Over in 1970 and 1983, United States

Employment Categories	Percentages Employed		
	1940	1970	1983
Agriculture, forestry, fisheries	18.3	4.5	3.5
Mining	2.2	0.6	0.9
Construction	7.0	6.1	6.1
Manufacturing	23.9	26.4	19.8
Transport, communication, utilities	8.3	6.8	6.9
Wholesale and retail trade	14.4	19.1	19.8
Finance, insurance, real estate	3.1	5.0	6.5
Professional and related services	8.0	16.4	20.5
Other services	11.4	9.4	10.1
Public administration	3.4	5.7	4.7
Total	100.0	99.2	98.8
All civilian employment (thousands)	49,980	78,678	100,834

SOURCE: Bureau of the Census (1975, I, p. 138; 1985, p. 404).
NOTE: The category "public administration" appears in the 1970 and 1983 data; it is narrower than the category "government," used for the 1940 data. From another set of figures, "government" comprises 15.2% of 1970 employment, and 15.4% of 1982 (Bureau of the Census 1986, p. 405).

From the end of the Great Depression to 1983, the American economy saw a massive shift away from agriculture, mining, and manufacturing, and toward services. Except for a minor surge in mining induced by high oil prices, every industry whose share of the labor force increased from 1970 to 1983 produced services rather than goods. In that period, manufacturing dropped from a quarter to a fifth of the U.S. labor force, as agriculture continued its long decline, and as mining and construction more or less held their own. Any analysis of the relationship between labor processes and inequality in the contemporary United States obviously has to consider labor processes outside of agriculture, mining, construction, and manufacturing. Increasingly, it must consider services.

Trends in Labor Processes

From a strictly quantitative point of view, service industries have long dominated the American labor force. They are growing even more dominant. Unfortunately, scholars have accumulated much less knowledge about changing forms of production in the service sector than in agriculture and manufacturing. For that reason, let us begin with manufacturing, and then try to reason about differences between manufacturing and services.

As a crude approximation, American manufacturing since 1800 has moved through three phases: (1) the expansion of craft industries, (2) the growth of mass production, (3) and the increasing importance of continuous-process production. To be sure, all three coexisted; the phases simply mark their relative expansion and contraction. In craft industries, where a firm typically produces only one object (a building, a ship, a rocket) or a small batch at a time, hierarchies remain relatively short and either one worker makes the whole object or supervisors coordinate the work of specialists who have complementary skills. In mass production, hierarchies are long and workers produce by means of machines under close supervision, according to an organized time schedule; textiles and automobiles typify the sector. In continuous-process production (as illustrated by oil refining and soft-drink bottling), hierarchies are likewise long, but supervision is much looser (Stinchcombe, 1983, pp. 112-116; later, we will criticize this rough classification, and suggest explanations for the variations in hierarchy and supervision).

A number of other differences follow. Craft production, for example, typically involves many shops in the same industry, and those shops are often clustered in space; diamond-cutting provides a good example. Owners intervene directly and frequently in the labor process, exercising what Richard Edwards (1979,

p. 19) calls simple control. Compensation for labor commonly resembles the sale of a product: Workers receive so much per task or per piece, at a price bargained out with the whole community of employers. In such communities, workers' collective action frequently divides between pressures on other workers to maintain control of the local labor market, and pressure on employers both to maintain the labor market and to sustain the price for labor. Instead of firm-by-firm strikes as we know them today, the withdrawal of labor tends to take the form of communitywide actions. Craftsmen of nineteenth-century Europe and America, for instance, often used the turnout: Workers assembled in public space, marched from shop to shop calling for other workers to join them, gathered to deliberate a common set of demands to all the masters, then stayed away from their workshops until they had struck a bargain with the masters or lost their ability to resist.

Many features of the craft system differ significantly from the normal characteristics of mass production. Mass production ordinarily includes the relative isolation of sites in the same industry from each other, payment by the hour or the day, ineffectual control of the labor market, and firm-by-firm strikes declared within each plant. Automobile manufacturing provides the classic example. Continuous-process production, in its turn, tends to involve very large and isolated sites, salaried workers, extensive internal labor markets, and conflict through other means than strikes and turnouts. The chemical industry organizes much of its work in continuous processes.

Outside of manufacturing, however, these well-known distinctions do not work so well. In service industries such as medicine, insurance, banking, retail trade, education, and transportation, the "product" is diffuse. It often consists of a transformation of the consumer rather than anything the producer can deliver to the consumer. Unlike manufacturing, furthermore, the organization that produces a service usually delivers it directly to consumers, rather than through middlemen. For these reasons, relations between producers and consumers are generally more particular than in the case of manufacturing, and result in a more circumscribed market for each producer.

Work in service industries divides broadly into four categories: (1) production of the service, (2) maintenance of the means of production, (3) sales, and (4) supervision. Service industries differ especially with respect to the size distribution of firms, the relative magnitude of the four activities, and the extent to which the activities separate from each other. These variations significantly affect patterns of inequality in returns to labor. In very small service firms, for example, members of the same household often share the labor, and pool their returns. Very large service firms, in contrast, often form hierarchies and systems of payment that resemble those of mass-production manufacturing.

Trends in Inequality

As a first approximation, let us think of inequality as having three aspects: (1) a number of forms, (2) a set of population categories that differ with respect to those forms, and (3) a series of distributions of the various forms among individuals and categories. The forms of inequality include the various goods with respect to which categories differ. Social scientists (e.g. Lenski, 1966) commonly begin with the distinctions among power, privilege, and prestige before moving on to more refined and concrete differentiations. Although returns to labor certainly include power and prestige, they center on material varieties of privilege: cash income, other perquisites, and accumulation of capital.

Among the material privileges, trends do not always move in the same direction. In examining racial differences in the United States, Reynolds Farley shows that between 1959 and 1982 black/white disparities in education declined considerably, the gap in hourly wages declined for men and disappeared for women, but the difference in overall family incomes hardly changed at all. More precisely, black family income rose from 52% of white family income in 1959 to 64% in 1970, then dropped back to 55% in 1982; changes in employment and household composition combined to depress the position of blacks during the 1970s (Farley, 1984, p. 199). Most likely trends in wealth and in job-related perquisites would show even greater discrepancies. To have a full picture of inequality, we must look at its multiple forms.

Many, many *categories* of the population are unequal with respect to returns from labor. Observers of Western countries have called attention to inequality by region, size of place, religious affiliation, sexual preference, educational experience, household composition, family position, and many others. Which unequal categories attract attention depends largely on: (1) the extent to which other social structures, especially those affecting differential rewards, articulate with the categories in question and (2) the degree to which members of the categories

have mobilized and pressed claims on their own behalf. The categories that matter analytically are those around which people—deliberately or not—have built extensive networks, social practices, and systems of belief that in their turn promote differential returns to labor. In that perspective, any student of American social life must pay attention to inequality by race, gender, citizenship, national origin, and age, and may well want to add other categories to the list.

At the extreme, students of inequality often take individuals or households as their units of observation, only grouping them into categories after examining the unequal distribution of resources across the entire population. Thus Simon Kuznets's pioneering studies of income distribution generally estimated the shares of total income received by the top 5%, the top 20%, and the bottom 60% of all consuming units. Johan Soderberg uses similar evidence to conclude that in Sweden and Britain the eighteenth century saw declining inequality, the first half of the nineteenth a rise in inequality, and the latter half of the century another decline (Soderberg, 1985, p. 20). Jeffrey Williamson's work on Britain (1985) confirms Soderberg's timetable, but makes it clear that the early rise in inequality dwarfed the later equalization. Hartmut Kaelble concludes that despite important countercurrents, the dominant trend in the nineteenth-century distribution of income and wealth among European individuals and households "ran toward a sharpening of inequality and of separation"—separation, for example, of wage income from profit and rent (Kaelble, 1983, p. 54).

Such overall measures of inequality matter; they make broad comparisons over space and time practical, and provide a general indication of how much inequality among categories we have to explain in any particular time and place. The aggregate measurement of inequality, however, tells us little about categories as such. For that purpose we must turn to distinctions among social classes and other categories of the population.

Social classes are categories that derive directly from the logic of production. Within capitalist production, relations to capital define the fundamental distinctions among social classes. But how those distinctions work in practice depends on the combination of productive forms that prevails in a given time and place. In the case of France, Adam Przeworksi, Barnett Rubin, and Ernest Underhill point out that the petite bourgeoisie (including owner-operators in agriculture) has been declining steadily during the twentieth century as proletarianization has advanced. As a net effect of changes in agriculture, manufacturing, and service industry, plus the rise of compulsory education and retirement, wage-labor has remained constant at about 40% of the adult population. Twentieth-century French proletarianization, then, has resulted mainly from increasing alienation of the means of production rather than from the spread of wage labor (Przeworski, Rubin, Underhill, 1980, p. 750). Throughout the transformation, however, fundamental differences in income and wealth between bourgeois and proletarians have persisted.

Differences among social classes in income and wealth are sufficiently large and regular, indeed, that citizens of capitalist countries often take income and wealth to define social class. Other sets of categories than social classes, such as race and age, likewise differ dramatically with respect to income and wealth. Median household per capita income, for example, differs enormously by race, national origin, and gender of household head. In the United States as a whole from 1959 to 1975, median income per person in households headed by an American Indian or an Alaskan native ran from 26% to 30% of median income in all households headed by majority whites. Japanese-American households, on the other hand, increased their advantage over majority white households from 114% in 1959 to 141% in 1975. Clearly, we have major differences in income to explain. The differences, furthermore, reflect far more than variations in education, age distribution, and labor force participation; refined comparisons taking such obvious variations into account always leave important differences in income and wealth to be explained (e.g. Hirschman and Wong, 1984).

In any of these regards, distributions among individuals or categories are always unequal, but vary in the degree and shape of their inequality. Concentrating on overall distributions of wealth and income in the United States since 1800, Williamson and Lindert offer this summary of their findings:

It now appears that the main epoch of increasing inequality was the last four decades before the Civil War. The Civil War itself reduced inequalities within regions, but it also increased inequality between regions by opening a severe income and wealth gap between North and South. Although we can find no evidence of rising inequality across the remainder of the nineteenth century, trending inequality emerges once more between the turn of the century and World

War I. World War I administered a brief, strong dose of equality, but the effects had worn off by 1928. The Kuznets-Lampman finding of considerable equalization in income and wealth between 1929 and mid-century appears to survive all the critical adjustments one might care to perform. After World War II, there was no sharp reversion to earlier high degrees of inequality, as happened after World War I. Instead postwar distributions appear to us to exhibit a curious stability: a slight increase in pretax and pretransfer inequality has been offset by the impact of taxes and transfers such that post-fisc'' inequality has declined slightly since the Korean War [Williamson and Lindert, 1980, p. 5].

They provide evidence that numbers of poor people, absolute living standards, wage ratios among different groups of workers, and overall inequalities in wealth and income fluctuate together—in short, that their trends are not statistical artifacts. Estimates of their general-equilibrium models suggest that three main relationships underlie the trends: uneven technological development, rapid increases in the supply of unskilled labor, and accelerated capital accumulation all foster inequality of income and wealth, while their opposites foster equality. Although cast in a very different idiom, the Williamson-Lindert findings are consistent with our argument: Uneven technological development and accelerated capital accumulation indicate sharpening divisions of rewards between possessors and nonpossessors of capital as well as between persons working in capital-intensive firms and others, while increasing supplies of unskilled labor further undermine the bargaining positions of the unskilled in general.

Trends sometimes reverse. Harrison, Tilly, and Bluestone (1986) showed that wage inequality has been increasing in the United States since the mid-1970s. They suggest, but do not establish, that the upward swing of inequality results less from changes in the pay differentials of existing jobs than from changes in employment patterns—who works full time, who works at all for pay, and so on. So far, however, their analysis has not gone far enough to constitute a challenge to Williamson and Lindert's observation of relative stability since World War II.

As the cool wind of Williamson and Lindert's analysis lifts the fog, we begin to see the mountain before us. First of all, we have many kinds of inequality to consider: income, wealth, privilege, power, and much more. They need not vary together. Furthermore, inequality appears at many scales: at the point of production, at the level of the firm, within communities, among regions, nationally, and internationally; the concept has no meaning until we specify the scale of analysis and the units we are comparing.

Finally, to perceive the two-way relationship between inequality and labor processes, we must take many third factors into account. When, for example, we find persistent connections among race, job assignment, and wages, how shall we sort out what the impact would be of making job assignment independent of race (see Wilson, 1980)? An old problem, but never an easy one. Similar problems threaten our efforts to take account of gender, education, national origin, age, seniority, and many other forms or putative bases of inequality.

Where Now?

Here is the context of our analysis: a world of proletarianization in which capital-concentrated production became more and more prominent; a world in which agriculture declined as a source of employment, manufacturing held its own, and service industry greatly increased; a world in which manufacturing saw a net shift from craft industry to mass production to continuous-process production; a world in which overall inequalities of income and wealth swung decisively up and down. Within that world our analysis concentrates on commodified labor— labor treated as an object of exchange—as a locus and basis of generalized inequality. We pay attention to self-employment, household labor, and other forms of work insofar as they interact with commodified labor.

We begin our analysis with a discussion of how sorting and ranking processes take place within the three arenas we have identified, and how the five sets of actors in our story attempt to influence these processes. We next take account of the impact on inequality of ranked social categories—of sex, age, race, and ethnicity—that are logically extrinsic to labor processes but frequently play an important role in them. We then zero in on the processes of bargaining and struggle, paying special attention to how employers attempt to gain the upper hand with various techniques of control and how workers resist these attempts with formal and informal means. In this part of the analysis we also concern ourselves with the levels of division and cooperation existing within capital and labor. Next we consider the impact of the details of labor processes, and consider claims that technology and skill mainly account for the levels of inequality we observe among those who work. Throughout, we consider the causal role of

matters beyond our actors' control—population trends, the state of the labor and product markets, the level of aggregate demand—and at the end we offer general reflections on the significance of our analysis for further research.

Our story is willfully incomplete. It neglects, among a great many other things, demographic effects and educational transformations. At a general level, it says rather little about how households, capitalists, workers, organizations, and governments change. It collapses into "markets" a great many complex relationships among firms, suppliers, consumers, and other actors. Its individual episodes nevertheless take up these complexities, usually at the cost of concentrating on just one pair of actors and only one or two causal connections; most frequently the tale concerns one kind of relationship or another between capitalists and workers. The outcomes that interest us most, in any case, are ranking and sorting; together they cause the great bulk of inequality in rewards to labor.

In the present state of knowledge, to be sure, all our generalizations are historically contingent and open to empirical challenge. In the analyses that follow, they will serve as orienting hypotheses rather than dogmas. Even concerning our own time, we know surprisingly little about the causal relations among labor processes, organized inequality, and the routine operations of employing organizations. Thus our arguments do not add up to a comprehensive theory of the relations between inequality and labor processes. They do, however, point toward an account in which struggles among parties having unequal resources and conflicting interests strongly affect those relations. In that respect, at least, they follow the trend of recent work in political economy. We have examined the general history of labor processes and of inequality in order to have the context right; at the end we hope to have singled out the most important causal connections between labor processes and social inequality.

The Dynamics of Ranking and Sorting

We have distinguished between processes of ranking positions and sorting of individuals into those ranked positions, arguing that it is the conjunction of ranking and sorting that results in observed levels and forms of inequality. But now we must face a theoretical difficulty concealed in our simple formulation: These two processes go on simultaneously, sometimes involving the same actors in the same arenas, but sometimes rather separately. When people from a named group are sorted into a new, highly ranked position created as the result of bargaining, the ranking and sorting are barely distinguishable from one another; thus, when members of minority groups generate administrative positions in antipoverty programs or as affirmative action officers, ranking and sorting combine. But sharp separation in time and space is at least as common. Changes in the relative standing and reward of different jobs take place over long periods, as instanced by the history of political and cultural bargaining in the medical profession (Collins, 1979; Starr, 1982).

Most sorting processes, by contrast, occur in the short run. Still, few ranking changes are without sorting implications, as Collins emphasizes in his status competition interpretation of the rise of the medical profession in the twentieth century: He sees professionalization as a defensive impulse on the part of dominant ethnic groups against a rising tide of competition from lower-status groups, whose entry to medicine was made more difficult by the "reforms" that required more years of training and thus forgone income.

On a smaller scale, once people are sorted into positions, jockeying over the ranking of positions continues. Much workplace bargaining implicitly revolves around such ranking since it is carried out by groups and thus concerns sets of jobs that are named as certain positions, rather than the rewards of particular individuals. The changes that result from this short-term jockeying are typically minor; yet if they accumulate in the same direction for some time they produce larger-scale, visible changes in ranking—as when skilled dayworkers feel threatened by the rising position of the unskilled and semiskilled, who are paid by results. Such visible changes are usually interpreted as reflecting some coherent logic. But we believe that they often result instead from the aggregated outcomes of many separate bargains struck in separate times and places. Whether there is an overall logic to the outcome depends on whether the same causes that generate successful bargaining in one part of the economy are important in many others as well.

Ranking and Sorting Among Categories of Employment

Divisions among capitalists, independent producers, workers, and unemployed persons emerged largely as a result of capitalist action. Proletarianization transformed peasants, artisans, serfs, and servants into formally free workers—persons who labored for wages using means of production controlled by the capitalists who paid them. "Unemployment" came into being because the world split increasingly into capitalists, proletarian workers, independent producers, and households depending for their survival on the sale of labor power; bargaining between capitalists and members of households then created the distinction between those persons who worked for wages and those who did not. Governments and organized workers, to be sure, took part in the relevant decisions, excluding young children, the ill, and the aged from paid employment and setting stringent limits on the wage work of adult women.

Even there capitalists often spoke decisively. Howard Marvel (1977) shows that larger British industrial capitalists lined up in support of the restrictions on women's and children's labor in the 1833 Factory Act. The new regulations squeezed smaller competitors who maintained their position in the textile trade by employing cheap labor; the larger manufacturers, with more fixed capital at risk and wages a smaller proportion of their total production cost, could forgo cheap labor to their own advantage; that has often been the case with "protective" legislation.

Similar maneuvers occurred within firms. Nineteenth-century employers often hired young women for jobs with short learning curves such as routine clerical work, but fired them if they married, justifying the policy on moral grounds. Taking records of Britain's Post Office and Great Western Railway as his evidence, Samuel Cohn (1985) has shown that capitalists thereby saved themselves the increments that otherwise would have come to senior female employees. Over the long run, in these and other ways, the actions of capitalists dominated the process of allocation; by their investments, capitalists reproduced themselves, determined the level and incidence of employment, and set limits on opportunities for independent producers.

The four categories—capitalists, independent producers, workers, and the unemployed—differ enormously with respect to returns to labor, and with respect to their composition by age, gender, race, national origin, and citizenship. The differences in returns to labor among the four result largely from their relative proximity to capital (see Wright, 1985, chap. 6). That proximity has two aspects: (1) the amount of capital that is at risk to the individual's performance and (2) the extent to which the individual controls the returns from capital. Capitalists receive large returns to their labor (that is, for the increases in use values their efforts cause) because they deploy it in conjunction with capital; unemployed persons receive very small returns because they have no capital to deploy. Independent producers and workers stand between because they have some control over capital, at least to the extent that their action or inaction affects capitalists' own returns. Entertainers and operators of high-technology equipment often receive high rewards, despite having little control over returns from capital, because extensive capital is at risk to their performances.

Nevertheless, capitalists do not run the game alone; they feel the limits set by their own interpersonal networks, those of the people with whom they deal, and the resources deployed by each major actor. Those resources, furthermore, do not remain constant, and do not always alter in line with a single party's interests. The actual composition and identities of the major actors—capitalists, workers, households, governments, organized groups—shift in response to changes over which no one party has control. The ebb and flow of international migration, for example, has a powerful impact on American and European employers' labor policies. Changes in the population's age structure interact with swings in the economy to affect who can be capitalists, workers, independent producers, and unemployed, and with what returns to their labor (Easterlin, 1980; Preston, 1984). Although in some sense innumerable small-scale bargains underlie all such transformations of resources and identities, direct bargaining among major actors plays a fairly small part. Instead, the outcomes of such cumulative and cyclical processes set the stage for bargaining.

Bargaining enters the matching process most directly when and where people who control recruitment networks make or break connections with others who control supply networks. Henry Ford's decision, during the labor shortage of World War I, to encourage black religious leaders to recruit southern blacks to work in segregated divisions of Ford's Detroit works established a system of migration, employment, and unemployment that shaped Detroit's experience for 40 years. The consequences of such bargains often stay in place for a long time.

Given a stable matching process, bargaining also helps determine the relative returns to labor of capitalists, independent producers, workers, and unemployed persons—and therefore of categories of age, gender, race, national origin, and citizenship that distribute differently among employment statuses. The most visible arenas for such bargaining are not labor markets but governments. To the extent that tax structures redistribute income to unemployed persons, for example, they impinge on income inequality by age, gender, race, national origins, and citizenship; most of the time redistribution to the unemployed mitigates such inequalities slightly. Tax structures themselves result from bargaining—often fierce—among political authorities and organized groups. Similarly, government policies with regard to capital formation, individual or household enterprise, and unemployment or employment significantly affect the returns to labor of capitalists, independent producers, workers, and unemployed persons.

Within the arena of employment categories, then, we see multiple actors embedded in their own social networks, disposing unequally of resources, and bargaining over the creation and ranking of positions with respect to labor processes, over the sorting of individuals and groups into those positions, and over discrimination among individuals within those positions. Similar processes govern allocation within the other two arenas: jobs and labor markets. Let us take them up in turn.

Ranking and Sorting Among Jobs and Occupations

The great bulk of social-scientific work has gone into examination of inequality among jobs and among holders of similar jobs. Yet that work has produced great uncertainty and contestation about the determinants of that inequality. And we will move cautiously in extending our arguments about jobs to occupations. Most occupations are, to be sure, simple aggregations of jobs. Simple, but not innocent. One can understand social scientists' concentrating their analyses on occupations; censuses and other surveys make aggregations of job titles very convenient bases of comparison. In some cases, something we can reasonably call an occupational structure connects most of the people who do a given kind of work for a living: baseball players, schoolteachers, railroad engineers, and so on. Change and variation in distributions of occupational titles within labor forces provide useful first approximations of differences in the organization of production. But on the whole that emphasis on occupations has produced an intellectual disaster: reifying categories constructed by statisticians, presuming social structure where none exists, inferring that people experience moves from "service" to "skilled" occupations as "social mobility," facilitating the identification of the person with the category, and diverting attention from the actual processes matching persons with jobs. Thus, though we will talk about both jobs and occupations here, we must move from one to the other only with caution.

If recent studies of inequality have produced one major finding, it is this: Whatever the fundamental reasons for it, the great bulk of inequality in returns to labor among employed wage-workers in contemporary capitalist economies occurs through the assignment of different kinds of people to different jobs, within and across firms. These assignments matter because of how different jobs have come to be ranked. Compared to sorting, ranking—which occurs over a longer period—is a less visible and more diffuse object of study.

Our argument about how such ranking takes place is inconsistent with (1) the functionalist argument that positions are ranked in relation to their societal "importance" and the scarcity of available incumbents (Davis and Moore, 1945); (2) the related neoclassical assertion that positional ranks derive from supply and demand, modified only by the returns to human capital investment and by compensating differentials that raise the wages of jobs with nonpecuniary disadvantages; (3) the Marxist-functionalist deskilling argument that positions are ranked by their level of skill, which is easily manipulated by capitalists; and (4) the more complex Marxist view that the ranking of positions results from labor market segmentation generated by employers in response to problems of control (Gordon, Reich, and Edwards, 1982). We differ from all four in the central place we give to conflict among purposive networks of collective action in determining positional creation and ranking. Because the conflicts are many sided, occur in several different arenas, and are constrained by demographic and macroeconomic trends beyond the control of the most powerful individuals and groups, we are skeptical of accounts that make the outcome a simple result of societal needs or of the desires of a single important group.

The study of organized professions gives us a starting point for our theoretical account. The best exemplars of this work (e.g., Collins, 1979; Starr, 1982) stress the collective action of organized groups and networks and point out that the outcome is far from guaranteed for any particular profession and place. This literature is, however, incomplete for the purpose of getting a comprehensive picture of the creation and maintenance of labor inequalities; like other literature on the professions, it usually deals with one profession at a time. What is then missing from the picture, and begins to be filled in by Abbott's pathbreaking work (1986b), is the fact that the professions, like other kinds of work, do not evolve in isolation, but in relation to one another. Different groups compete for jurisdiction over different kinds of work, and the final outcome—our encrusted and reified sense that one task is for orderlies, another for nurses, another only for doctors—is the result of these legal, political, and economic struggles, just as are the names of the professions themselves and their associated rewards. Abbott's work is also instructive in showing how the aggregation of jobs into "occupations" is a process constantly in flux, as certain kinds of work are defined into and out of particular occupational categories as the result of the struggle over jurisdiction. What typical occupational categories of statistical analysis do is to freeze a snapshot into official definition.

Similar processes occur in work outside the professions as well, but are less visible to the extent that there are no central coordinating groups of the kind that characterize would-be professionals. So, just as doctors and nurses or lawyers and real estate agents may compete over what are allowable tasks, so do machinists and numerical control programmers, or machine-tenders, technicians, and chemists in continuous-process plants. When a previously lower-ranked position succeeds in wresting away some task from a higher one, this has several effects: (1) it closes the gap between rankings of the previously higher and lower positions; (2) it redefines the meaning of the position, sometimes resulting in a new and more impressive title. (Hence the attempt to relabel stockbrokers as "financial consultants," resulting in large part from the deregulation of financial services and the attempts to generate one-stop financial "supermarkets"); (3) it can increase the contact between the two groups, making linkage via a promotion ladder more likely.

Such linkage does not directly reduce cross-sectional labor inequality but may reduce it over the life cycle, in that one's stay in a lower-ranked position becomes only transitional. Such promotion linkages, when tasks begin to overlap, are so natural that it requires a concerted use of power and ideology to block them. Thus considering the similarity between the everyday tasks of nurses and interns, it might strike us as remarkable that no mobility route exists from the one position to the other, were we not so strongly conditioned to think of these as utterly separate professions, as organized medical associations prefer.

Ranking and Sorting in Labor Markets

EXTERNAL LABOR MARKETS

Some important part of inequality derives from how workers are sorted among firms and industries. There would be less to study if workers typically stayed in one firm during their entire career. But, though many older workers in the United States are in jobs that will last 20 years or more (Hall, 1980, 1982), the level of interfirm mobility is nevertheless very high compared to other countries (Cole, 1979). Given the large number of workers in firms too small to sustain complex internal labor markets, this should not be surprising (Granovetter, 1984).

The labor market would also lack interest if income derived entirely from workers' personal characteristics, and was not affected by the characteristics of jobs. But this occurs only in tribal economies that lack institutionalized roles, as in Melanesia (Oliver, 1955). While some self-employed individuals in our society, such as independent doctors, lawyers, and writers, resemble the Melanesian "big-men" in that their rank depends on a following, their personal characteristics are linked to rewards only by a complex institutional system (Collins, 1979; Coser, Kadushin, and Powell, 1982; Faulkner, 1983; Starr, 1984). This is all the more true when those who attract a following are employees, such as professional athletes and salespersons (otherwise Satchel Paige would have died a millionaire).

Yet, some important research traditions have slighted the impact of job characteristics on rewards—especially the "status attainment" line of research in sociology and the "human capital" tradition in economics, both of which focus on the worker or supply side of the labor market. Other traditions look mainly at the demand side—the ranking of jobs—as if personal characteristics, activities, and bargaining had no impact on rewards. Thus Davis and Moore (1945) explain inequality by an argument about why some *positions* are rewarded more than others; the deskilling literature initiated by Harry Braverman (1974) also rests on analysis of changes in jobs. We emphasize the importance of the labor market as a set of institutions that sorts individuals with different personal characteristics into positions with differing rank or potential rewards. This matching process is central in any system where the characteristics of both persons and positions affect inequality, as in all advanced industrial economies (see Granovetter, 1981).

Matching almost never occurs in the impersonal auction markets of stylized neoclassical economics (see Marsden, 1986), but results instead from the articulation of *recruitment networks* by which employers bring in new labor, and *supply networks* by which people search for opportunities to use their labor. Independent producers, for example, construct recruitment networks that bring some new people into their trades, but exclude many others. In our time, governments often attempt to construct supply networks that find jobs for the jobless. The two kinds of networks almost always connect, but are almost never identical.

The distinction between networks of recruitment and of supply matters for two important reasons. First, supply networks differ greatly in composition by age, gender, race, national origin, and citizenship; which supply networks articulate most directly with which recruitment networks therefore strongly affects the recruitment of workers to firms. Second, once established and producing satisfactory results for those who control the recruitment network, a given articulation of recruitment and supply networks tends to reproduce itself, as we have observed for the case of the networks activated by Henry Ford. Characteristics of migrant populations that observers see as transplanted ethnic traits, in fact, commonly emerge from just such joining of networks.

Employers and workers are not the only relevant actors. Governments, trade unions, and other organized groups play significant roles in allocating workers to firms, especially where hiring operates as a form of patronage; nineteenth-century urban America's political machines built their strength especially on the ability to find jobs for politically reliable workers. In our own time, governments have had more success in reducing inequalities of hiring practices of firms than they have in promoting equality at the levels of employment status and jobs.

The actors involved have unequal resources. Workers can only maintain strength within labor markets by means of shortages—absolute or induced—of qualified labor. Capitalists typically have the advantage of access to alternative technologies with different labor requirements, not to mention opportunities to move their capital elsewhere. Yet workers and capitalists do not entirely control the value of their resources; a new wave of immigration often undermines workers' existing control of their labor markets, and fluctuations in the demand for a firm's product strongly affect its vulnerability to worker action.

In late nineteenth-century Britain and the United States, independent or "inside" contractors often mobilized labor; in effect the primary employer, they supplied workers to firms and sometimes supervised their work. Such systems often established and perpetuated inequalities in access to jobs. In agriculture, mining, and some other industries small subcontractors were often household heads, and their "employees" members of their own households. Sweated industries usually organize around one kind of subcontracting or another (Schmiechen, 1984; Stansell, 1983). Subcontractors work more effectively with ready access to a flexible labor supply that he or she can discipline. From that point of view, networks of kinship, friendship, and common ethnic and/or national origin serve very well—especially if the networks include distant potential migrants who have much to gain from moving to the new jobs subcontractors control. Chain migration therefore complements subcontracting. By means of the subcontractor, networks of recruitment and supply fuse into a continuous system for the pumping of labor power.

Such contractors were frequently powerful figures, with incomes much higher than skilled workers. In nineteenth-century America, the factory foreman often filled this role; Nelson (1975) speaks of the shop floor as "the foreman's empire." This power over production is cited to explain employer attempts to replace the subcontracting system, which had all but disappeared by World War I (Clawson, 1980; Littler, 1982).

In skilled crafts such as printing and construction, unions play a role in recruitment, if not in supervision, analogous to subcontractors—supplying workers, regulating apprenticeship, and commanding more worker loyalty than firms, since movement among firms is frequent. Formal labor market institutions such as these are not given in any simple way by the technology or other details of the labor process; they emerge from a long process of negotiation and struggle between labor and capital, whose outcomes are contingent at many points on a balance of power determined far from the point of production (Jackson, 1984).

Apart from craft markets and those agencies and contractors who still supply labor, especially for the short term in cyclical and contract- or project-dependent industries, workers are typically matched to jobs through informal local institutions and networks of personal contacts (Granovetter, 1974, 1981, 1986). Contact networks are usually the largest channel of job matching and are associated with higher incomes in some occupations (Granovetter, 1974, p. 14) and greater economic gains from changing employer (Campbell and Rosenfeld, 1986). Since personal relations are typically homogeneous by class, ethnicity, and region, this mode of allocation can efficiently reproduce existing inequalities. This reproduction is robust because most employers prefer informal recruitment, a cheap way to maximize information about new employees. Impersonal computerized matching systems, proposed and attempted periodically by economists who see them as resembling the abstract auction model of competitive labor markets, fail for the same reason that computerized dating services rarely end in marriages: the quality of information each side gets about the other is too low to make a good match likely.

Employers and employees alike prefer information about the other obtained through trusted intermediaries who are familiar with both of them. This is cheaper than massive talent searches that result in information overload. The cost to intermediaries is low, since they typically know both sides from past involvement and thus have no new costs of information search. Labor-market information, costly to assemble directly, is obtained every day as a costless by-product of the social interactions that constitute economic life; the usual recruitment and job-finding strategies are built around this embeddedness of information in social structure.

Resources of the contending parties thus operate within limits set by established social networks. Robert Thomas offers a telling comparison between two large California lettuce producers: Miracle and Verde. At Miracle, the foremen control hiring; at Verde, the United Farm Workers have bargained hiring into union-controlled halls. At Miracle, according to Thomas,

Despite the fact that Miracle maintains an office at company headquarters ostensibly for the purpose of hiring and placing workers, the bulk of hiring takes place in two locations: in the field or in the company bus yard where the crews assemble each morning. The foremen are the principal conduits into a job. Foremen use a variety of networks for recruiting workers. Interviews with foremen and workers show that there are basically four ways in which workers are recruited: through friends and family of the foreman, the foreman's own kin networks; through other workers; through walk-ons, people (such as myself) who just show up looking for work; and through coyotes (smugglers), who arrange passage and employment for undocumented workers [Thomas, 1985, p. 140].

With the small exception of walk-ons, then, the foreman's personal networks define the pool of potential employees at Miracle. The existence of a hiring hall at Verde does not formalize the process but rather displaces it to the union's own networks. Both draw mainly on women and on Mexican citizens—often undocumented immigrants to California. Thomas points out that lettuce companies draw great advantages from this pattern of recruitment. The threat of deportation greatly limits the power of foreign workers, while women provide a pool of stable, low-wage labor suitable for a mechanized, capital-intensive yet seasonal agricultural labor process. In this industry, capitalists have reshaped the labor process in response to the availability of different kinds of labor at least as much as they have altered labor recruitment in response to shifts in technology.

Grace Anderson (1974) has shown the articulation of recruitment and supply networks in Toronto. Jobs that resemble each other in pay and working conditions are sometimes stepping-stones and sometimes traps. Stepping-stones are initial jobs that lead to other, better jobs; in Toronto, initial jobs in demolition and construction act as stepping-stones for Portuguese immigrants. Traps do not lead anywhere; initial jobs as janitors or bakery helpers are usually traps. Anderson studied three migration streams of similar Portuguese villagers. With the help of "occupational gatekeepers" in Toronto, some found their first jobs in traps, others in stepping-stones, still others in intermediate industries such as railways and farming. Despite similar "human capital" and initial jobs that provided almost indistinguishable rewards, the three groups ended up quite differently; at the time of Anderson's interviews, for example, men who began in traps were averaging $2.22 per hour, intermediates $2.85 per hour, and stepping-stones $3.30 per hour. Bodnar, Simon, and Weber's (1982) analysis of migrants to Pittsburgh during the early twentieth century identifies similar processes in the sorting of migrant groups into various industrial jobs.

These authors concentrate on job assignments rather than sorting into firms. Yet their evidence actually lends insights into all three arenas of inequality. For the same matching of recruitment and supply networks channels migrants—and, for that matter, nonmigrants—into different firms and employment statuses (see

Waldinger, 1986). Suzanne Model (1985a) has shown that among blacks, Italians, and Jews in New York since 1910, the availability of employment by others of the same ethnic/racial origin (net of "human capital" and ethnic/racial composition of the industry) has enhanced the success of newcomers to the labor market. Her findings suggest, furthermore, that the effects of coethnic employment compounded from one generation to the next, with ethnic firms serving as accumulators of capital that families then invested in the placement of their offspring. In New York, contrary to a common misunderstanding, blacks were not highly segregated by firm or industry; on the contrary, they spread most widely of the three groups across industries, and suffered for it. Blacks did better in those few industries, such as Pullman car portering, in which networks of recruitment and of supply fused into a near-monopoly of employment (see also Reitz, 1984).

Not that ethnic segregation guaranteed mutual aid. Ethnics often exploited their fellow ethnics, working them harder and paying them less than other workers in the same industries. Still, the worst positions, in both the long run and the short, belonged to those who occupied segregated, subordinate positions in firms and industries dominated by members of a different racial or ethnic group.

Recruitment networks, supply networks, and the junctions between them are all historical products; when and where they first form considerably affects the subsequent experience of people with them and the sequence of transformations in the networks strongly constrains possibilities for subsequent transformations. Migration, for example—from Italy, from Central and Eastern Europe, from the American South—creates a social structure and a set of relations between the migrant population and concrete opportunities for employment that in their turn make a great difference to the "success" or "failure" of what come to be defined as ethnic and racial groups.

The effectiveness of matching between networks of recruitment and of supply—from whosoever standpoint we choose to judge effectiveness—depends on the resources each actor within the networks brings to the matching process. Three factors in particular produce major group differences in access to different firms and industries: the networks of capitalists within the firms and industries, the timing of group entries into the labor market, and the relative power of the groups and their allies. The three combine to produce the queueing for desirable employment that Stanley Lieberson (1980) describes for blacks and white immigrants to the United States from 1880 to 1980.

This sort of inequality has given rise to recent theorizing about "split" or "segmented" labor markets. In favored sectors of the labor market, it is argued, employers and workers develop compacts that provide the employers with a stable, reliable labor force and the workers with superior remuneration and job security; in other sectors, competition, conflict, exploitation, and instability rule the day. In industries having large firms, such as insurance or automobile manufacturing, the favored markets appear largely within firms, in the form of career ladders, internal recruitment, seniority systems, pensions, and other guarantees of security for workers. In small-firm industries such as architecture and law, professional organizations and networks have similar effects. In the latter case, organizations of workers, of employers, and of both together play crucial roles in stabilizing the labor market. Once again, to the extent that the boundaries of such organizations correspond to well-established divisions within the population as a whole, the organizations contribute to the creation and maintenance of inequality in returns to labor.

Neither the capitalist nor any other single actor entirely controls the opportunities for employment or the resources available to any of the competitors for employment. Demand for a firm's goods is an obvious example: A declining industry provides a poor base for social mobility. Again, population processes that no single individual or group controls significantly affect the bargaining positions of different actors. A system of chain migration that breaks contact with its point of origin thereby loses one of its great advantages. Through the alteration of such resources and the transformation of relevant networks, such ostensibly external factors as commodity markets, capital markets, governmental policies, and demographic shifts impinge on inequality in returns to labor.

Capitalists, workers, and other actors bargain over the allocation of people among firms within limits set by existing resources and networks. Nevertheless, bargaining occurs. As is obvious to any union member who has seen a unionized firm undermined by a nonunion shop, capitalists and labor unions struggle continually over the sorting of workers among firms. The hiring policies of unions, furthermore, make a difference to inequality. Orley Ashenfelter (1973) has provided evidence, for instance, that on the whole unionization increases the ratio of black to white wages outside of construction, but decreases the ratio in construction; craft unions, with their greater control over networks of labor supply and recruitment, more often produce this sort of categorical inequality among workers than do industrial unions.

We have always to remind ourselves that not all inequality is the intended result of bargaining processes. Some is instead created and reproduced by behavior that rationally pursues some small-scale aim without seeing what larger effect ensues. Thus employers want new employees who are certified by current ones, believing not only that they will be competent but also that with connections to existing employees they will learn the ropes quickly. They sense that—as we discuss in detail later in our analysis of the impact of skill on inequality—what "skills" will be exercised depends in part on these social connections. The exclusion, by this practice, of those whose supply networks do not connect to the recruitment networks of the existing work force is incidental to the strategy pursued. It follows that antidiscrimination legislation may serve not only to overcome prejudice, but more important, may force employers to recruit in ways that would not ordinarily seem efficient—to hire more unknown quantities than usual. Once a core of employees is in place from some group previously unrepresented, a multiplier effect changes the situation: Each such new employee serves to recruit others from this group. The new situation may then be reproduced as efficiently as the old (see Granovetter, 1974, chap. 10).

INTERNAL LABOR MARKETS

A different aspect of sorting and ranking in labor markets has to do with how individuals *within* a particular firm are assigned to jobs and how promotion decisions are made. (See Granovetter, 1986, for a more extensive discussion of promotion systems.) Why finely graded sets of positions should exist at all is problematic, and thus presents an opportunity for functionalist arguments. In radical accounts, the problem "solved" by this grading is the threat of worker solidarity; workers are pitted against one another by a technically unnecessary elaboration of positions meant to stimulate "hierarchy fetishism." Neoclassical functionalist accounts assert instead that this elaboration makes possible a proper matching of talents to rewards, bringing wage and marginal productivity into line (Williamson, Wachter and Harris 1975). Edwards's Marxist account of "bureaucratic control" has in common with the neoclassical view that it also assumes promotions to result mainly from adherence to stated criteria of performance (1979, p. 139ff).

But even if productivity were easily measurable, other factors bear heavily on promotion, such as seniority (Abraham and Medoff, 1983), ethnic and other particularistic criteria, and one's position in workplace political coalitions (e.g, Dalton, 1959, chap. 6). The pivotal position of senior employees in workplace coalitions may explain why they are favored for promotion even in nonunion firms where there is no such contractual provision. Rosenbaum's study of promotions in a large corporation shows the importance of motivating the nonpromoted, by avoiding sharp age discontinuities in the distribution of those promoted; otherwise entire age groups would feel their prospects were dim, depressing performance (1979, p. 28).

Rates of promotion also depend heavily upon sheer availability of positions. Vacancies occur in chains (White, 1970): A retirement or newly created job attracts a new incumbent who leaves a vacancy in his previous job, which attracts a new incumbent, and so on. The chain ends when someone enters a vacancy who previously held no job or when a vacant job is abolished. Rates of retirement and labor force entry depend on general population demographics, rates of creation, and abolition of jobs on the business cycle. These four rates determine the length of "vacancy chains" and thus the number of promotion opportunities (see also Stewman and Konda, 1983).

One reason promotion is often not based on productivity is the difficulty of measuring productivity. This arises in part because supervisors cannot observe workers continuously, but instead take occasional samples. Sampling variability is higher in small samples, implying lower correspondence between promotion and productivity early in one's job tenure (March and March, 1978). Early, chance advantages snowball, leading to the "fast track." Early winners are seen as " 'high-potential' people who can do no wrong, and who are given additional opportunities and challenges while those who do not win the early competition are given little or no chance to prove themselves again" (Rosenbaum, 1981, p. 236; 1984).

Direct measurement of productivity is feasible mainly in jobs with well-defined output such as typing or piecework. But even here it is difficult to monitor maintenance of machinery, use of materials, and level of cooperation with other workers. Though output can at times be easily measured, individual productivity is inextricably intermeshed in a network of relations with other workers. Whether skills that can be learned on the job actually are learned there is determined by workers' positions in the status hierarchy of the work group, as we shall emphasize later in our discussion of skill.

Sorting and ranking in the labor market account for much of the inequality among categories of ethnicity, race, and sex. Before we discuss the details of categorical sorting and ranking, we sketch out its extent and hazard some general comments on the significance of such categories in a treatment of inequality and labor processes.

Categorical Distinctions in Labor Processes

In several contexts so far we have noticed the ways that inequality among those engaged in labor processes follows the lines of established social categories such as race, gender, national origin, and age. Such categories are logically extrinsic to labor processes. Yet, empirical differences in labor returns by category shows that they are by no means external to those processes. Among Americans with four or more years of college, median earnings in 1975 for those who had any earnings were as shown in Table 6.2 (U.S. Commission on Civil Rights 1978, p. 24).

TABLE 6.2
Median Earnings for Americans with Four Years of College, by Ethnicity and Sex, 1975

	Female	Male
Category	$	$
American Indian/ Alaska Native	10,283	11,678
Blacks	9,911	12,324
Mexican Americans	6,967	10,786
Japanese Americans	8,383	14,253
Chinese Americans	6,421	12,790
Philipino Americans	9,038	13,091
Majority	8,106	15,165

Thus college-educated black women earned more per year than similarly educated white women, while among college-educated males blacks earned about 81% of what whites did. [Differences were similar for the entire population: The hourly earning of employed black males in 1980 stood at 81% of employed white males, while differences between white and black females were negligible (Farley, 1984, p. 126).] Mexican-Americans with four or more years of college had the lowest incomes, while Japanese-Americans and the majority population had the highest. Group by group, college women earned from 50% (Chinese Americans) to 88% (American Indians and Alaska natives) of their male counterparts. Because educational levels and employment vary by category, actual income differences among these categories in the population as a whole were much larger.

Many factors besides outright wage discrimination by race or gender contribute to such differentials, but we do not attempt to decompose statistically the various sources. And we avoid what might seem to be another logical task for this chapter: determining what part of total labor inequality can be "attributed" to these differentials. We can imagine statistically partitioning total variance in labor incomes between a part "explained" by or falling between social categories, and another part lying strictly within such categories. We do not do so in part because this would require lengthy discussion of data and procedures that would go beyond the scope of this chapter. But more important, such a decomposition implies that the two kinds of inequality—that within and that between the groups we name—are independent of one another and stem from different causes.

This would be misleading. Some of the inequality that occurs *within* an ethnic group may result from its generally subordinate position and the lack of internal solidarity that can accompany such a position. Evidence of growing inequality among black workers since affirmative action initiatives began suggests that these initiatives disproportionately favor those with middle-class backgrounds and educational credentials (Wilson, 1980). In the scramble for what often turn out to be token positions, those without the cultural capital to occupy them often end up worse than before. That external pressures and exploitation may lead to internal inequality is a point familiar from dependency theories of development. It is not a large step to import such ideas to our context. Furthermore, the level of inequality within one group often has an impact on the level in others. Thus status among domestic servants has often been derived from that of their employers, inducing an isomorphism between the status structures of the groups. Thus some unknown but possibly substantial amount of "within-group" labor inequality is causally related to intergroup relations and processes.

Moreover, to divide inequality into that between and within groups reifies the group categories, even though, not excepting sex and age, their significance for inequality is socially constructed by bargaining and competition, sometimes conscious but often not. We shall try to

avoid the full force of this difficulty by repeatedly stressing the embeddedness of social categories in purposive networks of collective action that themselves create, embellish, and modify the meaning of such categories. The use of these categories in economic competition does not reflect our living in a country that is unusually oriented to race, sex, age, or ethnicity, but is instead universal in the economic life of differentiated countries.

Max Weber identified the centrality of this process:

> One frequent economic determinant is the competition for a livelihood. . . . When the number of competitors increases in relation to the profit span, the participants become interested in curbing competition. Usually one group of competitors takes some externally identifiable characteristic of another group of (actual or potential) competitors— race, language, religion, local or social origin, descent, residence, etc.—as a pretext for attempting their exclusion. It does not matter which characteristic is chosen in the individual case: whatever suggests itself most easily is seized upon [1968/1921, pp. 341-342].

Lieberson uses a similar argument in his analysis of the deteriorating economic situation of American blacks vis-a-vis European immigrants from about 1920 on. He notes that

> much of the antagonism toward Blacks was based on racial features, but one should not interpret this as the ultimate cause. Rather the racial emphasis resulted from the use of the most obvious feature(s) of the group to support the intergroup conflict generated by a fear of Blacks based on their threat as economic competitors. If this analysis is correct, it also means that were the present-day conflict between Blacks and dominant white groups to be resolved, then the race issue could rapidly disintegrate as a crucial barrier between the groups [1980, p. 383].

He supports this view by showing that before massive black immigration from the South threatened whites' economic situations, black and South and Central European immigrants' educational and occupational attainments and levels of residential segregation were not much different; but with the cutoff of European migration in 1924 and the huge black influx from the South beginning in the World War I, attitudes toward blacks hardened and their situation deteriorated.

Conversely, the Chinese and Japanese, currently much more successful economically than blacks, experienced violent prejudice when they first arrived in the United States. Because they were foreign, however, immigration could be cut off, and their total numbers kept sufficiently low that many could be absorbed into "ethnic enclaves" that kept them less visible to the majority, reduced their competitive threat, and permitted them to gather their economic resources and pass them along to their children. Once the economic threat was largely ended, the "racial" salience of Orientals was greatly attenuated (Lieberson, 1980, pp. 381-382). If the offending groups had been absolutely identical racially, but different in point of origin, we can suppose that these differences would have been magnified to the point where they became quasi-ethnic, and the focus of hostility. If, for example, World War I had seen a large influx not of blacks but of Southern whites, who are quite similar to white northern Protestants in their ethnic background, Northerners would almost surely have constructed derisive categories, or used existing ones—"crackers" or "white trash" —to help preserve their own economic position. Similarly constructed "ethnic" animus can be observed, on a smaller scale, against white "hillbillies" in Chicago or "Okies" in Los Angeles.

Notice in this discussion the crucial importance to ethnic definition and competition of the details of population flows. We could predict from neoclassical economic theory alone that a large increase in labor supply, without significant change in demand, would depress wages. But social organization explains why this depression is unlikely to occur homogeneously across all workers. People use ethnic or other markers as a convenient and emotionally effective rallying point to bring together for collective action those who can be defined as similar. Because such markers coincide with previously existing personal networks, institutions, and resources, their invocation builds on and solidifies what was only a potential for cooperation; they can be especially valuable in helping to overcome the typical jealousies and rivalries that permeate clique-ridden ethnic groups, divided as they usually are among groups from different villages or regions in the home country, or by religious differences that seem slight to outsiders but paramount to those in the know.

Nor do the markers that groups seize on to exclude other groups from economic competition have to be mainly negative in their connotation, as "ethnic" markers mainly are. Age and sex can be such markers, and then it is impractical to denounce all members of the offending group—usually women or the young; they, after all, are necessarily an integral part of all racial and ethnic groups. Instead, they can be removed from a competitive position in the labor market by a "protective" strategy: the claim that any work, or many kinds of work, would in some way be exploitative or damaging when carried out by workers too delicate or young—as we will note in our account of how women came to be relegated to housewifery. Similar arguments could be made for the proliferation of child-labor laws and the institution of mandatory schooling.

Since group markers are arbitrary, a focus on group distinctions can be misleading. Though such distinctions have a massive reality at any given time, especially for those in the disadvantaged groups, what is truly central are the processes of which group identity markers are convenient tracers. Groups that use these markers in economic conflict devote considerable resources to ossifying and reifying them. As analysts, we have the dual responsibility of explaining how the resulting hardening of distinctions affects inequality but also of not being ourselves deceived by it. This is not to say that the use of such markers is not an important process in itself, virtually universal in advanced capitalist and perhaps all industrial societies—but only that the particular configuration of such markers in use is arbitrary, and results from the details of population flows, social networks, and cultural symbols and resources available for mobilization in the effort to redefine those markers.

Now on to processes. Most of the inequality associated with labor results, we argue, from ranking of positions and sorting of individuals into those ranked positions. Group inequality by national origin, gender, age, or race emerges primarily from sorting, secondarily from ranking, and only marginally from individual discrimination and work performance. The sorting of people into jobs, firms, and employment statuses results from the shapes of interpersonal networks linking people to jobs, the resources held by different parties to the sorting process, and the bargaining that takes place within constraints set by the networks and resources.

Each of our arenas presents a somewhat different explanatory problem. Within the arena of employment, we must explain how categories of age, race, national origin, citizenship, and gender come to be distributed differently among capitalists, independent producers, workers, and the unemployed. We want to know also how these categories are sorted out with respect to jobs and occupations. And with respect to labor markets, we seek to understand why the same categories differ in their distribution across firms and the clusters of firms we call industries, and within firms as well. We search for explanations by analyzing the actors, resources, interpersonal networks, and bargaining processes that produce inequality within each arena.

Rather than a comprehensive survey we offer what we consider important illustrations of the processes that have resulted in categorical inequalities. We begin with a brief account of the creation of sex differentials by employment category. Consider households as actors. To the extent that households invest more of their resources—time, money, food—in boys than in girls, they foster differential success in the labor market. (Most likely similar discrimination occurs according to age and birth order, but that possibility has so far produced very little theory or research.) Amartya Sen (1983, 1985) suggests that in poor countries households typically give males favored access to the necessities of life, including food and health care; the discrimination results in higher life expectancy and better health for males. In rich countries, male/female differences with respect to life-sustaining goods are small, and female life expectancy is often greater than male life expectancy. In rich countries, however, households still seem to discriminate with respect to their investment in remunerative job skills (Folbre, 1986). Relatively minor household discrimination by gender then compounds the widespread discrimination by other groups to produce wide male/female gaps

Households, furthermore, generally organize their internal lives in ways that foster gender inequality in returns to labor. The most evident example is the creation of the position of housewife in Western industrial countries. Two centuries ago, few women in those countries were housewives—devoting full-time effort to unpaid household work and child care. Instead they worked, like men, in household production of goods for sale. Domestic servants, given subsistence and occasional cash payments, came closest to the work positions of today's housewives.

"Servants" once consisted of all workers who lived under an employer's roof, received subsistence as part of their wages, and had no claims on the means of production. Servants in this broad sense once performed a significant share of all agricultural labor in Western countries, and played an important part in manufacturing and services as well (see, e.g., Kussmaul, 1981). During the period of capital-concentrated industrialization, servants shrank to domestic service, feminized, and eventually

came close to disappearing (Chaplin, 1964; Engelsing, 1973, pp. 225-261). By the later stages of the shrinking process, domestic servants were usually single women. As domestic service declined, wives took over their responsibilities. Those responsibilities expanded, furthermore, as household standards of cleanliness, food preparation, and child care became more demanding. In all Western countries, housewives now constitute the largest single category of underpaid laborers.

As wage labor outside of households became more prevalent, men and boys took up that wage labor disproportionately, especially when it came to long-term, relatively secure employment. Among households in which males made a high enough wage to cover the household's cash purchases, a division commonly arose between the "real" work that brought income, and unpaid family labor, which was necessary but inglorious. A good husband came to be a man who worked steadily, brought home his whole pay envelope, and refrained from beating his wife and children. From a general survey of household divisions of labor in nineteenth-century England, Wally Seccombe (1986, p. 65) concludes that the sharp division between male breadwinners and unpaid female housekeepers arose especially in the skilled trades; those skilled trades, with their superior organization, managed to stamp the division upon much of the labor market.

As Bruce Laurie points out for nineteenth-century Philadelphia, even radical organizers promoted the idea that women's place was in the home: "Like most male workers, they decried the 'multiplying descriptions of labor for females' as a 'pecuniary injury' to men, because of job competition, and a 'moral injury' to women, because gainful employment transferred them from the protective isolation of the home to the inelegancies of the workshop, where they rubbed shoulders with crude and vulgar men and risked acquiring 'ruder habits' and 'losing all that sacred influence which it is the peculiar prerogative of woman to exercise over man'" (Laurie, 1980, p. 94, quoting documents in John R. Commons, *Documentary History of American Industrial Society*). We hear the language of skilled workers, and witness the creation of housework as a separate female sphere.

Despite the enormous increase of paid employment among women, the distinction persists today. Time-budget studies show clearly that when married women work, they essentially carry on two jobs—one at home and one outside—while their husbands participate little more in household work than do their counterparts who have full-time housewives. Among 434 Toronto couples with children that his group interviewed in 1980, William Michelson found the following mean minutes per day spent on employment, housework, and child care (Michelson 1985, p. 55):

| | Wife's Employment Status | | |
	Full Time	Part Time	Not Employed
Wives	584	482	436
Husbands	529	556	554

Thus wives with full-time jobs spent 34% more time at work (paid and unpaid) then unemployed wives, while their husbands spent 5% less time than the husbands of unemployed wives. In Toronto and elsewhere, gender inequality still prevails within households. In these and other ways, the behavior of households affects inequality in returns to labor.

At the level of occupations and jobs, an enormous amount of social scientific work has gone into examination of inequality. Yet that work has produced great uncertainty and contestation about the determinants of that inequality. Janice Fanning Madden concludes a careful review of work on male-female pay differentials by remarking that "it is disappointing to complete a review of such an extensive research literature and to realize that there is no consensus on the answers to the most important questions. The research literature truly contains something for every partisan, but no complete answers for the scholar" (Madden, 1985, p. 109). "Partisan" is, of course, the right word: Burning questions of public policy depend on the explanation of wage differentials by gender—not to mention by race, age, national origin, and citizenship.

A good deal of the controversy concerns who makes the binding decisions, and to what extent they are justified. If women end up heavily located in jobs that pay less well than men's jobs, is that because (1) employers discriminate against women or against jobs containing many women, (2) women have, on the average, poorer job qualifications or lower productivity than men, or (3) women freely choose the sorts of jobs that pay less well? If the object is to equalize the pay—or the opportunity for pay—of employed men and women, the three answers point to very different remedies. The same choices apply to all the other kinds of inequality we have been reviewing.

The analysis we have presented so far raises doubts about the value of setting up the problem in terms of such choices. For none of them takes account of the bargaining over job allocation among employers, workers, potential workers, and other actors that occurs within the limits set by existing social networks and resources, or of the ways that changes in the networks and resources alter the outcomes of bargaining. All we can do here is to suggest some ways in which bargaining processes enter into the matching of persons with jobs and into the creation of unequal returns to labor by gender, citizenship, race, national origin, and age. If recent studies of inequality have produced one major finding, it is this: Whatever the fundamental reasons for it, the great bulk of inequality in returns to labor among employed wage workers in contemporary capitalist economies occurs through the assignment of different kinds of people to different jobs, within and across firms.

Findings for race and gender are dramatic: Every analysis of the United States labor force finds substantial segregation of jobs by race and gender, with a large share of income differences attributable to the differences in jobs. (See Roos, 1985, for evidence of gender segregation in 12 industrial societies.) More controversial, however, is the extent to which the job differential itself results from women's preference for certain kinds of jobs, male resistance to female entry into predominantly male jobs, male-female differences in job-related skills and experience, differences in effort, or discrimination by employers. Using occupational data, Treiman and Hartmann (1981) find a correlation of .45 between the proportion of males in an occupation and the median annual earnings (adjusted for work time) of people in the occupation. Their analysis surely underestimates the extent of segregation and its relation to earnings. Those relationships, of course, underlie the recent debate on "comparable worth."

Bielby and Baron (1986) studied data from 290 California economic establishments between 1964 and 1979; at the level of establishment job titles, they found almost complete segregation: 96% of the female employees would have had to change job titles in order for females to approximate the male job distribution. Scrutinizing the distribution of men and women among jobs within detailed occupational categories that had from 20% to 80% male occupants, they found that women in those categories are: "most likely to be excluded from job classifications that are specialized; require heavy lifting; do not require finger dexterity, verbal aptitude, or clerical perception; or have longer training requirements. Women are also more likely to be absent from jobs that involve variable tasks, spatial skill, eye/hand/foot coordination; that are in larger establishments; or that are in enterprises with unions or formal bidding arrangements'' (Bielby and Baron 1986, p. 782).

Some authors have attributed similar observations to ''statistical discrimination''—to employers' use of categorical judgments, based on genuine experience with productivity, to assign whole groups to jobs, thus penalizing the above-average members of less favored groups and rewarding the below-average members of more favored groups. Other evidence leads Bielby and Baron to doubt that such a process explains their findings, and especially to question whether the categorizations California employers use are productively efficient. It seems more likely that employers are solving other organizational problems by creating jobs with particular pools of labor in mind. Because we have very few reliable direct studies of the process by which detailed jobs take shape and job assignments occur, we cannot be sure. But the rare direct studies confirm both the complexity of the process and the centrality of employer strategies to it.

Susan Hirsch's analysis of the Pullman Company's rich employment records from 1900 to 1969, for example, provides strong evidence of deliberate shaping of jobs to fit the available labor. Early in the century, Pullman faced a conflict between its interest in cheap, docile labor and its concern about command and succession. Clerks at Pullman, as in many other nineteenth-century concerns, had typically been boys and men in training for management. With the routinization of clerical work, however, the company starting hiring women. Nevertheless in 1902 ''the company decided not to employ women in the operating department in the future and transferred all women clericals from the central office to the auditing and manufacturing departments. President Thomas H. Wickes explained that 'we found they [women] were standing in the way of young men whom we wished to educate and promote' '' (Hirsch, 1986, p. 32).

At the start of World War II, in contrast, the company responded to the shortage of males by hiring women as clerical workers in its Richmond, California, repair shop. Despite the objections of the company union, it paid the women less than their male counterparts, and gradually replaced men with women. These and many other pieces of evidence lead Hirsch to conclude that ''at least through the 1940s, management seems to have been the primary actor in the sex-typing of jobs and the unequal pay of men and women. While the company

consciously used a racial strategy to segment the labor force, its use of the gender division was more complex. Management could use women as cheap labor and was always ready to take advantage of the lower pay rates common for women, but it maintained the sex-typing of blue-collar jobs because of deeply-held prejudices about women's skills'' (Hirsch, 1986, p. 43). Hirsch's evidence suggests that the ''deeply-held prejudices'' connected with the implicit management policy of keeping command and the work they regarded as crucial to the company's success in the hands of white males.

Hirsch's study of Pullman is exceptional both for its direct evidence on job assignments and for its long time span. Most studies of organizational contributions to categorical inequality suffer from a concentration on the short run. In the short run, we might expect employers to prefer the cheapest labor available—with ''cheapness'' taking into account the cost of finding and training the persons in question. They rarely do so, however. They commonly exclude qualified workers who are available at relatively low wages. The excluded workers, furthermore, often cluster into disfavored categories of age, gender, race, national origin, and citizenship. Most recent research on discrimination in firms and labor markets concerns precisely this process: Are the excluded workers actually less productive or more costly to recruit and train? Do workers who are already employed collude with employers to exclude cheaper rivals? If so, why don't competing firms seize the cheaper labor and undersell their discriminating competitors?

Answers: All these things happen under some conditions, but the conditions are hard to specify. When skilled male workers, for example, control a craft, they often defend themselves in ways that reinforce the sexual division of labor. Printers provide numerous instances. After 1850 American publishers tried repeatedly to train and hire women as compositors, but generally failed. They failed, among other reasons, because male printers campaigned successfully for ''equal pay for equal work'' specified as a wage adequate to support a family, and gained support of women who were already in the trade for that demand (Baron, 1982, 1986). Thus organized printers, progressive and militant in many other regards, helped maintain the inferior claims of women to employment.

Where employers face well-organized craft workers and have access to technologies that would permit the employment of cheaper labor, they often try to break worker control, encountering fierce resistance, yet they often win in the long run. The situation is different where employers have established effective coalitions with the elite among their workers—especially where considerable capital is at risk and those workers belong to the internal chain of succession and command. Then employers are much more likely to forgo cheaper labor. Employers usually gain more in control over production from their segregated labor forces than they lose by failing to employ the cheapest available labor. Or so we think; the vast literature on job segregation contains remarkably few observations on gains from internal control.

Nevertheless, down the mountain of research on discrimination in firms and labor markets there do flow some limpid streams. Work such as that by Bielby and Baron, for example, has made it clear that segregated job structures account for major inequalities among workers; neither variation in personal qualifications nor direct discrimination within jobs explains away the compelling findings in that regard. What we need now are close analyses of the strategies and struggles that create segregated job structures.

Control, Resistance, and Solidarity: The Dynamics of Bargaining and Conflict

Systems of Control: Their Cost, Distribution, and Consequences

So far we have discussed how sorting and ranking go on in various arenas, and how the interested actors typically behave in relation to these processes. We have frequently invoked the importance of conflict between labor and capital, but not focused on the details of that conflict, especially within the firm. In this section, we narrow our focus in this way, moving our analysis closer to the point of production. In doing so, we will frequently remind the reader of our view that while what happens at the point of production is a significant determinant of labor inequality, these events can be understood only in the broader context that we have laid out in earlier sections.

To that context we must add that within any firm certain market conditions, independent of the basic labor process, strongly affect the relative bargaining power of employers and workers (and therefore influence the likelihood that any particular labor process will actually materialize). This bargaining power depends in part on employers' sensitivity to changes in wage rates, indexed by the price elasticity of labor demand. Some determinants of that elasticity are summarized in labor economics by the "Hicks-Marshall laws": that the elasticity of demand for a certain category of labor is greater when (1) the price elasticity of demand for the product is high; (2) other factors of production can easily be substituted for the category of labor in question; (3) the supply curves of other factors of production are highly elastic; and (4) the cost of employing the category of labor constitutes a large share of the total cost of production (Farkas, England, and Barton 1986, p. 9; Hicks, 1963, pp. 241-247). We assume that bargaining power falls as elasticity of demand for labor rises. Thus where the demand for a firm's products is price inelastic, the kind of labor in question invulnerable to substitution, the other factors of production that might be substituted in short supply, and labor costs a relatively small part of the total cost of production, workers' bargaining strength increases.

Other circumstances clearly complement the Hicks-Marshall conditions: the unity of workers, the reserve of resources at their disposal, their support by power holders outside the firm, the extent of their control over the supply of competing labor, their ability to damage the employer's capital and impede its redeployment, the tightness of overall labor supply, and the vulnerability of employers' profits to short-run disruptions of production. These conditions determine the extent of worker success in strikes (Conell, 1980, pp. 84-158), and when employers organize or accept internal labor markets and welfare schemes. They significantly affect the nature and outcome of bargaining between employers and workers. In no sense do they reduce to straightforward consequences of labor processes. Indeed, labor processes take shape partly in response to the bargaining strength—and the actual bargaining—of workers with employers.

Since the middle of the nineteenth century, capitalists have often attempted to derail worker bargaining efforts by direct repression of worker organizations and their activists as well as by creation of counterorganizations such as company unions. These efforts typically aimed at immediately perceived threats.

In addition, employers had several day-to-day strategies available to help them control their work force and gain leverage in the bargaining process. Over a long period, many workers have opportunities to embezzle, steal, shirk, sabotage, and otherwise diminish an enterprise's profitability. Some of them take those opportunities. But most do not, at least not to a large degree. Why? Systems of control make a difference.

Systems of control fall along a dimension indexing the extent of coercion experienced by workers. Although the dimension is continuous, we might distinguish four points along it:

PAYMENT
LOYALTY   INCENTIVE   BY RESULTS   SURVEILLANCE
  I   I   I

At one extreme stands systems of *loyalty* that promote workers' commitment to the enterprise quite aside from their material interest. These shade over into (and are almost invariably paired with) *incentive systems* that promote workers' productivity and discourage stealing, shirking, and sabotage by tying their material interests to those of the firm. Some such systems build loyalty as well through their apparent generosity. For this reason we will use the term "loyalty system" loosely to mean any system that builds worker commitment to the firm by means of positive incentives as well as symbolic devices.

Schemes for promotion and seniority, for deferred payments and benefits, and for bonuses based on profit fall into this category. Wages that are higher than average for the type of work performed can elicit loyalty and productivity, as Henry Ford knew, and as labor economists have recently discovered in the literature on "efficiency wages" (Akerlof and Yellen, 1986).

Systems of *payment by results* (PBR), such as piecework and task work, also involve incentives, but generally have a more coercive edge. At the most coercive end of our continuum stands systems of *surveillance*, where the employer places little or no trust in the worker, allows the worker little or no autonomy, and drives the worker through close time-discipline.

Loyalty systems can be quite extensive, and often mix negative with positive incentives. The Amoskeag Mills of Manchester, New Hampshire, not only built company housing whose occupancy depended on employment (and therefore on the approval of supervisors) in the mill, created recreational facilities, and organized a vigorously active employee club, but also established an employment office that administered welfare benefits, hired, fired, and kept employee records that served as blacklists for "unsatisfactory" workers (Hareven, 1982, pp. 38-68).

The Ford Motor Company, in addition to its effective checking of labor unions, set up a search for workers who qualified for "American pay" of five dollars per day in wages and profit sharing; the company put its search into the hands of a "Sociological Department" charged with investigating the "manhood and thrift" of the applicants and with applying programs to promote the learning of English, the maintenance of clean dwellings, and the accumulation of savings (Zunz, 1982, pp. 310-318). (Until 1919, however, blacks could only get heavy, unskilled jobs in Detroit's manufacturing firms, including Ford; even when Ford opened up skilled and semiskilled employment to blacks, other firms followed only very slowly).

Typically, employers segregate their workers into two or three categories subject to rather different combinations of control. These divisions often appear within hierarchies of control, with supervisors integrated into loyalty systems but charged to motivate their subordinates by means of surveillance and/or payment by results. Subcontracting systems invert the order, by employing middlemen who are paid by results but build their own loyalty systems to get those results.

Employers also typically face the problems of recruiting allies and potential successors, in order to forward their plans within the enterprise. They sometimes need to maintain secrecy about their products or business dealings. For those purposes loyalty and positive incentive systems have immense advantages over systems stressing surveillance or payment by results. Those advantages increase if only the essential minimum of workers receive the major benefits built into the loyalty systems. The advantages do not, however, work instantaneously; they take a long time to pay off.

Employers' choices of control systems make a difference to inequality. A loyalty system does not necessarily build on loyalty to the firm or the employer; it sometimes depends on commitment to some larger network, such as a profession; in that case, professional ethics and monitoring provide some guarantee that a professional employee will perform reliably. Whether loyalty is internal to the firm or not, however, the system often includes orderly careers in which exemplary performance at one stage produces rewards in the next; benefits to seniority; promotion ladders; social access to superiors; visible symbols of elite position. Loyalty systems do not serve merely to provide incentives to individual employees; they operate as networks of command, patronage, information flow, and succession.

For that reason, employers frequently draw a sharp line between workers who fall inside and outside the loyalty system. Military services make the distinction between officers and enlisted men on just such grounds—even though non-commissioned officers come to occupy a separate loyalty system, play major roles in the on-the-job training of newly commissioned officers, and sometimes become commissioned officers themselves. In small firms, the line between the owner's family and everyone else often separates the loyalty system from systems of surveillance and/or payment by results.

How do employers make their decisions about control systems? The decisions depend in part on questions of recruitment. Let us reify jobs by forgetting—only temporarily—that the contours of positions within firms result from bargaining and adapt to the characteristics of available workers. In general, employers estimate a job's minimum skill requirements in terms of the capital at risk, labor productivity, suitability of the occupant for movement into linked jobs, and externalities such as the employee's contribution to the firm's overall sales or prestige. Within those requirements, they recruit the workers who will make the largest contribution to profit.

The closer the job comes to being repetitive, unskilled work for a stable market, the more likely that the workers recruited will be the cheapest labor available within the employer's immediate contact network. The closer it comes to being nonroutine skilled work for a volatile market, work whose execution sets substantial capital at risk and is critical to the firm's overall performance, the more likely that employers will recruit costly labor by means of extensive, specialized interpersonal networks, and will maintain portions of those networks within their own firms.

Since employers seek to maximize profit in the long run as well as the short, it may pay to invest in workers' stability and loyalty at the expense of short-run return. When does it pay? The greater the capital at risk per worker, the more secure the firms' market and the longer the delay in receiving profits from any particular investment, the more likely are employers to invest in stability and loyalty. Thus we expect that loyalty systems encompass higher proportions of all workers where (1) considerable capital is at risk and returns to capital have long delays; (2) labor is nonroutine, hard to supervise, not easily substitutable, and a relatively small part of the total cost of production; (3) markets are stable and secure, and (4) the firm's profitability depends on the favorability of its public image or the followings of its employees. The same conditions promote employers' reliance on ex-

tensive, well-established recruitment networks in their search for new workers. Loyalty systems within firms and extensive recruitment networks outside them articulate with and reinforce each other.

The profitability of a given arrangement differs at the scale of a day, a month, a year, a worker's lifetime or the lifetime of a firm. Loyalty systems typically bind a minority of workers to the firm in the interests of long-term profitability. Hence their importance for categorical inequality. First, it costs something to install within a firm the distinction between people in the loyalty system and others in systems of surveillance or payment by results. Recruitment of the people from distinctive social origins and categories reduces the cost, especially if the pattern of preference within the firm reproduces the one prevailing outside. (Witness the military services' recruitment of officers first from aristocrats and then from college graduates.) Here we see another way that employers' interests in reducing their own costs institutionalizes inequality among socially defined categories; this result is a by-product rather than an essential goal of their strategy.

Second, to the extent that they operate as networks of command, patronage, information flow, and succession, loyalty systems benefit from intense socialization, prior screening of their members, membership in groups outside the firm that guarantee and monitor the worker's behavior, and extensive off-the-job social relations. Thus employers have considerable incentives to homogenize new members of the loyalty system and to recruit them within the same existing social networks.

Third, for all the reasons discussed earlier, networks of recruitment and supply ordinarily form within homogeneous social categories—categories of age and sex to some extent, categories of race, national origin, and citizenship to a large degree. Coupled to contrasting systems of control within firms, essentially the same processes that sort people among firms and industries by age, gender, race, national origin, and citizenship also produce sharp differences in job assignments within firms. As one studies actual practices of hiring and supervision, it becomes less and less surprising to encounter descriptions like Ewa Morawska's of Johnstown's Cambria steel mills early in the twentieth century:

There were in the Cambria mills two "occupational circuits" based on ethnic divisions. The first, with higher wages and better working conditions in more prestigious finishing departments, employed predominantly native-born American and western European workers. The second, largely unskilled, with unhealthy and dangerous jobs in the open-hearth, blast furnace, and railroad departments, and in the foundries and coal mines, employed the immigrants [Morawska, 1985, p. 101].

Nor are we surprised to learn that the company deliberately formed work crews by nationality, practically excluded Southern and Eastern Europeans from promotion, and gave foremen great autonomy in hiring, firing, and job assignment. Such arrangements once formed the standard for large-scale American industry. In subtler forms, similar divisions in job assignments persist today, and account for much of the inequality in returns to labor by race, age, national origin, citizenship, and gender.

Nevertheless, employers do not remain entirely free to design systems of control at their own whim. The costs of control systems vary enormously. The system adopted affects the attractiveness of employment in the firm to different groups of potential workers. And other actors have interests in the character of control within firms: not only the workers in the firms and their households, but also governments and organized groups such as labor unions.

Even here bargaining enters the picture, from shop-floor fights over job assignments to union-management disputes over hiring and firing to government prosecution for discriminatory hiring. As usual, the bargaining takes place within limits set by the resources of the actors and the social networks in which they are embedded. But it deeply affects the processes by which groups of people defined by gender, age, citizenship, national origin, and race come to occupy very different jobs and to receive greatly different rewards for their labor.

We choose two topics for further exploration under the general rubric of control systems. One is the way in which incentive and surveillance systems operate in large, bureaucratic firms; the other is the operation of systems of payment by results. In both we stress that employers cannot install control systems in a costless, unilateral way, and that even in settings where the balance of power is decisively on the side of capital, costs are incurred and control systems rarely work quite as planned.

Control Systems, Hierarchy and the Size of Workplaces

One factor often alleged to affect inequality and control systems is the scale of operations in which an individual works. Certainly, the self-employed, employers, and those who work for others, for example, receive very different rewards for similar levels of effort, and face changing technologies of production in distinctive ways. Though "labor processes" suggests employer-employee relations, nearly 8 million non-agricultural workers—7.7% of the employed population—were self-employed in 1984 (*Monthly Labor Review*, December 1985, p. 60). Space limits prevent us from doing more than deploring the paucity of research on the self-employed (two rare, systematic accounts can be found in Friedman and Kuznets, 1945; Form, 1985, chap. 4).

For employed workers, an important issue is the size of their workplace. The advent of factories increased this size, but despite the location of most industrial sociology in large manufacturing plants, this is not where most workers are found. In part this is because manufacturing has declined so steeply as a proportion of the work force, and services have so greatly increased. The trend is relevant because manufacturing plants are so much larger than service establishments (Granovetter, 1984, p. 325). In the late 1970s, one in four private-sector workers were employed in establishments of less than 20 employees, half in establishments of less than 100, and more than four out of five in those of less than 1000 (Granovetter, 1984, pp. 326-327). Establishments may be part of larger firms, but even so, more than four in 10 work in a firm of less than 100 employees and more than six of 10 in firms of less than 1000 (Granovetter, 1984, pp. 328-329).

Not only has the shift to large workplaces been exaggerated, but also the significance of such workplaces for inequality and for control of workers. Dual economy arguments associate large firms with the economic "core" and small ones with the "periphery," and cite higher wages in larger firms. But this literature focuses heavily on manufacturing, a declining sector; there is almost no correlation between wages and establishment size in services (Granovetter, 1984, p. 331).

Large firms and plants typically have hierarchies that define and shape inequality among workers. Why do such hierarchies exist? Functionalist accounts abound. Economists propose that they solve problems of economic efficiency. Reinventing the Davis-Moore (1945) argument, Sherwin Rosen suggests that "it pays to assign the most talented persons to positions of greatest power and influence. . . . Large wage payments to superior managers in large firms are sustained by corresponding increments of productivity . . . " (1982, p. 321). For Oliver

Williamson the problem solved by hierarchy, which explains the rise of the factory system and of much vertical integration, is that the cost of complex transactions between independent economic units is too high, given problems of information and dishonesty; these costs are reduced by authority relations in hierarchically organized firms (1975; 1985).

Marxist functionalists (especially Marglin, 1974) argue instead that hierarchy solves the problem of tighter control over the work force, especially in conjunction with advanced technology. Edwards (1979) elaborates this argument by identifying three types of control systems: "simple control"—the personal control typical of small plants; "technical control," where technology paces the work; and most recently, and characteristic of large plants with extensive internal labor markets, "bureaucratic control," where an extensive set of rules and promotion procedures keeps workers in line.

Though Williamson attacks these Marxist accounts (1985, chap. 9), they resemble his own in asserting that hierarchy responds to and solves a problem. Both views overstate the difficulties encountered prior to the development of hierarchy and its success in solving them. Williamson exaggerates the level of disorder in dealings between independent firms as well as the level of compliance within hierarchically organized ones (Granovetter, 1985). Marxist-functionalist arguments have similar problems. Control over workers differs drastically between factories with similar technology and organization, depending on the bargaining power of workers vis-a-vis employers and on market conditions. Braverman depicts deskilling as a reaction against workers' "craft control," but greatly overstates the level of nineteenth-century craft worker autonomy (Clawson, 1980, pp. 160-166; Littler, 1982, chap. 6).

Both Marglin and Williamson cite embezzlement of materials in the putting-out system as an incentive for hierarchical factory organization. But economic historian S.R.H. Jones points out that "although manufacturers universally deprecated the practice, one can detect in many of their comments a tacit acceptance of the fact that embezzlement was, in some sense, part of the wage bargain" (1982, p. 131; compare Liebow on institutionalized on-the-job stealing in the Washington ghetto, 1967, pp. 37-38, and Ditton, 1977). Though Marglin believed that the "factory effectively put an end . . . to 'dishonesty' . . . " (1974, p. 51), this overestimates the ability and underestimates the cost to managers of monitoring materials (Jones, 1982, p. 132).

Like Braverman's account of deskilling, these writers assume that employers always get their way. This neglect of constant worker bargaining, negotiation and struggle, surprising for Marxists, results in large part from neglect of the informal level of organization highlighted by traditional industrial sociology (a point made also by Littler, 1982, p. 40, and Burawoy, 1985, pp. 36-41). Edwards's "bureaucratic control," for example, reinvents Weber's ideal type of bureaucracy, where actors proceed *sine ira ac studio*, following rules and procedures. But he undercuts his own account by noting the importance of "rulebook slowdowns" in bureaucratic firms (1979, p. 155): these would be no weapon at all if "working to rule" were the everyday norm.

Although employers (and industrial sociologists) have commonly seen workers as organizing to break rules and restrict output, workers actually vary enormously in how much they collaborate or resist. For German factory workers before World War I, Alf Ludtke describes a politically significant marking off of workers' time and space on the shop floor; workers struggled to exclude bosses from times and spaces that nominally belonged to the enterprise, insisting on their rights to wander, gather, eat, and take breaks in defiance of the regulations (Ldtke, 1985, p. 323). In an American plant, however, Michael Burawoy saw less resistance. Burawoy analyzed relations between workers and employers on the floor of the machine shop in which he worked during 10 months of 1975. Although Burawoy sometimes witnessed open struggle over returns to labor and, less often, over the structure of power, on the whole he saw workers collaborating—intentionally with each other, and unintentionally with a profit-making system that rewarded them individually for overfulfilling production quotas—but only by so much, lest the rate-fixer increase the quotas (Burawoy, 1979). Thus unauthorized shop-floor organization among the workers influenced the returns to labor, but within stringent limits set by capitalist decisions.

Informal social organization in the workplace underlies resistance to management authority, ranging from large-scale political and economic activity (Burawoy, 1985; Sabel, 1982; Sayles, 1958) to the successful organization of theft of company materials. (See Dalton, 1959, chap. 7, for a brilliant account of the latter.) It is exactly in large bureaucratic settings, with elaborate internal labor markets, that long tenures facilitate the construction of coalitions with shared assumptions and goals inimical to those of the firm. Thus just where functionalist theorists assert that bureaucratic control works best, it is most disabled by the effective bargaining and purposive action that flow out of stable, co-herent social formations. Where there is no hierarchy and thus no job ladders, tenures are typically short and turnover rates high; it is then hard to sustain organized resistance to manage-ment demands. We must avoid confusing the apparatus of control with its achievement.

The Control System of Payments by Results

The main distinction among contemporary pay systems is between payment by time ("day-work") and payment by results ("PBR," or "piecework"). In historical perspective, the distinction is inadequate. It fails to separate task work (where a worker carries out the full pro-duction of an item and essentially sells it to a merchant-employer), subcontracting (where a worker recruits, supervises, and remunerates a team that produces the work for which he or she receives a lump sum), collective production-incentive schemes, and straight piecework (see Mottez, 1966). Historically, task work often marked the early stages of capitalist production. Workers such as miners often resisted employers' efforts to transform it into daywork, which or-dinarily entailed much closer supervision and timing of their production. Nevertheless, in our own time the choice between daywork and piecework has dominated worker-management struggles over the forms of pay.

Modes of payment become a critical issue in radical accounts of piecework as an attempt to strip workers of earlier autonomy (e.g., Clawson, 1980, p. 169). Organized labor did consistent-ly oppose its introduction, with some success in crafts such as printing and construction (Jackson, 1984, p. 10). Neoclassical economic accounts omit disapproval of employers but similarly stress piecework as an attempt to "monitor" employee "shirking" (Pencavel, 1977; Goldin, 1986a). Industrial sociology has long paid more attention to workers in PBR systems than to those paid by time (Burawoy, 1979; Whyte, 1955), obscuring the fact that even in manufac-turing, no more than 30% of production workers appear ever to have been paid by results, this in the 1940s. The figure had fallen to about 20% by the late 1960s and continues to decline (International Labor Office, 1984, chap. 8). Current employment growth occurs in industries where time-rates predominate—such as the ser-vices and highly capital intensive manufactur-ing, like continuous-process industries. These trends reappear in most Western European countries (International Labour Office [ILO], 1984, pp. 124-131).

Marxists treat PBR systems as attempts to destroy worker solidarity by focusing on indi-vidual achievements. But there is little evidence that PBR ever succeeded in this. Burawoy sug-gests that Taylorism's detailed specification of work performance, far from generating em-ployer control, aroused so much resistance that it "may have undermined capitalist controls over the obscuring of surplus. . . . Insofar as Taylorism fostered antagonism between capital and labor, the coordination of interests became less feasible and the reliance on coercive meas-ures more necessary" (1985, p. 41). Most work groups developed elaborate schemes to cope with PBR, and the attainment of quotas—"making out"—introduced a gaming element to work without breaking workers' spirits (e.g., Roy, in Whyte, 1955, p. 35).

Early PBR systems were abusive in that "all earnings were variable and workers bore all the risks of fluctuating output. [But] in most coun-tries and industries the acceptability of this ap-proach has diminished greatly with time" (ILO, 1984, p. 86). Most PBR systems now include contractual minima not based on output, and piece-rates do not appear to be cut as ruthlessly as in the heyday of scientific management (e.g., Burawoy, 1979, pp. 71-72).

Historically, PBR work rates have been tight-est in slack economic periods when labor is plen-tiful and consumer demand low; when workers are scarce and consumer demand high, PBR rates have eased. Thus how successfully workers can be driven and controlled under a PBR system depends on bargaining power and the state of the labor and product market. This shows again the primacy of causal factors far removed from the point of production.

Piecework systems do affect workplace in-equality when some groups achieve high rates and consequent bonuses in relation to others; the others are sometimes dayworkers who thus cannot compete. This leads to conflict when it upsets previously established rankings, as when skilled workers demand increases to offset the erosion of differentials caused by high PBR bonuses paid to semiskilled or unskilled workers (ILO, 1984: 36), when piece-rates reverse status differences carried in from outside the plant (Whyte, 1955, chaps. 8 and 9), and when similar but not identical jobs have different rates. In the usual plant situation of interrelated work groups, such invidious comparisons may cascade and lead to persistent grievances (Whyte, 1955, p. 81). PBR systems can thus be used as one weapon by workers in the constant jockeying for position that goes on among different work groups.

Some employers have implemented PBR schemes geared to group productivity; this eliminates the problem of "rate-busters" and attempts to direct group solidarity and output norms toward increased production. Such plans have become increasingly important in the United States and other countries, resulting in part from the increasing predominance of technology that makes individual output difficult to measure (ILO, 1984, p. 136). Schemes in which the performance of the entire plant is the basis for bonuses have the greatest impact on inequality. The best-known such experiment is the Scanlon plan (ILO, 1984, chap.7; Whyte, 1955, chaps. 12-14). Such plans institutionalize participative machinery meant to draw upon workers' store of information and techniques for improving production, and remove much of the reason for rivalry between work groups. But unless the plant is small enough for personal relations between groups of managers and workers, participative machinery typically becomes unwieldy and workers see too little relation between their own efforts and bonuses (ILO, 1984, pp. 113-119). The problem of the "rate-buster" is then replaced by the opposite one of the "free-rider."

These share plans call for bonuses beyond some fixed compensation. Economist Martin Weitzman goes farther, arguing that the payment of any fixed wages is macroeconomically inefficient and should be replaced by a "share economy" where each worker is paid a share of revenue (1984). He argues that in a fixed-wage system, employers stop hiring workers when the revenue to be gained by having an additional worker is exceeded by the wage, but that if an additional worker received a share of average revenue per worker instead, firms could keep hiring. Share firms are thus always short of labor and "always on the prowl—cruising around like vacuum cleaners on wheels, searching in nooks and crannies for extra workers" (1984, pp. 98-99; depending on economies of scale, to be sure, workers currently employed in such a system would often have an incentive to resist new hires that would reduce the average share). Data are scarce on the actual number of profit-sharing plans; the few companies that currently tie a major part of wages to profits have typically instituted this plan as an extension of paternalistic, antiunion policies. As predicted by Weitzman, they do have unusually low frequency of layoffs in economic slumps (see Leib, 1986).

Though there is little systematic evidence on how group incentive schemes affect inequality, we have good reason to expect them to reduce it. The plantwide unit of account for bonuses should reduce the jockeying for position among different work groups and the advantages of seniority should be attenuated (Weitzman, 1984, p. 108). Leib points out that some labor leaders oppose profit-sharing because it forces "senior employees to give up the steady, high wages of a labor contract for something they do not really need—protection from layoffs" (1986). This configuration of interests may act as a powerful drag on the widespread adoption of group incentive or profit-sharing arrangements.

The Impact of Technology and Skill on Labor Inequality

It will by now seem eccentric to many readers that in an essay on inequality and labor processes we have said little about the actual details of labor processes at the point of production. This may seem all the more odd since so much existing literature traces inequalities directly to those details. We have already indicated our skepticism of such claims: in the "perennial friction between 'iron law' theorists and conjunctural theorists" (Littler, 1982, p. 3) we stand with the latter. To see inequality as resulting mainly from characteristics of labor processes at the point of production is myopic, reminiscent of pre-1960s organization theory, which slighted the impact of organizational environments on internal functioning. Such accounts also typically treat labor processes as if they resulted from technology or employer choice, when in fact they typically emerge from long and intricate negotiation. We will find repeatedly that what impact on inequality any particular aspect of the labor process has depends on the relative bargaining strength of employers and workers in this negotiation and on the current state of the labor and product market.

Technology and Inequality

We use "technology" and "skill" to refer to the types of capital and labor, respectively, used in the production of goods and services. We begin with separate discussions of machines and people. Later, the discussions necessarily merge.

Two streams of 1960s literature claimed that technology strongly influenced labor inequality: the "contingency theory" of organizations, originating with Joan Woodward (1970, 1980), and a series of books on high technology, the best known being those of Robert Blauner (1964) and Serge Mallet (1963). Woodward's empirical studies suggested that contrary to standard organization theory, there was no "best way" to structure an organization; the best way was contingent on a firm's technology. Successful firms were those in which the organizational form was appropriate to the technology. Woodward's widely followed typology of firms' technologies rested on the size and discreteness of products and product batches. She collapsed her 11 initial categories into three: unit and small batch production, large batch/mass production, and continuous process (as for chemicals and candy, where machines run continuously).

Woodward presented the ordering as one of "technical advance" (1980, p. 51), and found that certain organizational characteristics related to inequality—such as the length of the line of command—are empirically related to such advance. Short hierarchies in unit/small batch firms result from the constant need for production changes that a long chain of command would inhibit. Thus control is exercised mainly through personal hierarchy (1970, p. xi; see Edwards's "simple control," 1979). But in some ways small-batch and continuous-process firms are more similar to one another than to mass-production firms: in having smaller middle-management and first-line supervisor span of control, higher proportions of skilled workers, more delegation of authority, less reliance on organization charts and less stringent and elaborate supervision of work and application of sanctions (1980, p. 60ff). Stringent supervision in mass production derives from assembly line technology where small problems ramify (Stinchcombe, 1983, p. 114). Hence relations among managers and between employers and employees work better at the "extremes" of the technical scale than in the middle (Woodward, 1980, p. 80).

A second stream of theory asserted the importance of the growth of continuous-process production. In *Alienation and Freedom* (1964) Robert Blauner, like Woodward, argued that workers in such industries had an unusual amount of job satisfaction and good relations with superiors. Automated machine-tending work not only blurred the line between blue and white-collar—being clean, responsible and clerically oriented—but also allowed freedom of movement and reduced time pressures. Blauner projected from this a profound transformation of work in which class lines would blur and the factory would see a new social integration. Serge Mallet, in France, noting many of the same technical aspects of continuous process work in his *La Nouvelle Classe Ouvriére* (*The New Working Class*) (1963) came to opposite conclusions: that these new responsibilities and freedoms would create enhanced working-class consciousness and resentment of class privilege.

Empirical studies have not sustained such unconditional claims for the impact of technology. Attempts to replicate Woodward's original survey findings have often failed (see Dawson and Wedderburn, in Woodward, 1980, p. xxiii; and Pfeffer, 1982, p. 152). Sabel's finding that small-batch shops may, under some conditions, be at the cutting edge of advanced technology (1982, pp. 40, 223-226) rather than technologically primitive as implied by Woodward, points up that Woodward's taxonomy is not actually defined by technology, except for the continuous-process case. The link of large-batch/mass production to assembly line technology may be strong empirically, but is not a matter of definition. The link to technology seems especially weak for small-batch production. Though Sabel does find the short hierarchies predicted by Woodward for small-batch shops (1982, pp. 223-224), this pattern derives not from technology but from the level of continuity in product demand—a matter far removed from the point of production.

Case studies of work in continuous-process plants paint a picture quite different from that of Woodward, Blauner, and Mallet. In two oil refineries in Britain and two in France, Duncan Gallie (1978) found a quite variable level of autonomy for technologically similar work, depending on cost considerations, managerial philosophy, and differences between the countries in working-class institutions and culture. Supervision in France was much more intense and generated much more resentment than in Britain (Gallie, 1978, p. 235). Few workers in either country found the work interesting; most were indifferent and many complained about the shift work required for continuously running machines.

David Halle's seven-year study of a New Jersey chemical plant (1984) found the work not only unrewarding and dull but also dangerous. Chemicals leak and must be cleaned up; the danger of fire and explosion is always present. Like Gallie, Halle stresses the diversity of jobs in a continuous-process plant, and the distortion involved in characterizing the entire industry by the work of machine tenders, who fill only about one in five of the blue-collar jobs; these are in fact the least popular jobs within the plant, often deserted for openings in ware-housing and maintenance. There is considerable control over the organization of work, based on workers' "secrets"—special knowledge of the production process, which, despite advanced automation, has many idiosyncrasies (Halle, 1984, pp. 119-124). If there is class struggle, it is over free time: "Most men would rather play than work . . . throughout the plant men strug-gle to increase the proportion of time they can spend on social activities" (1984, p. 138). Con-versation, card games, newspapers and maga-zines, radios and TVs and cooking equipment are everywhere—all with the implicit connivance of management. Supervisors who patrol in more than the ritual and predictable way informally expected to find production in their section of the plant declining.

Thus we find neither the solidarity with management predicted by Blauner nor the com-bative class consciousness predicted by Mallet. But despite technological similarity there are variations in solidarity, ranging from fairly har-monious relations in Britain to antagonistic ones in France, with American workers mostly indif-ferent. What accounts for these variations? Gallie argues that the "coldness and distance of relations between management and workers is a problem that is likely to be found much more widely in French industry" (1978, p. 235), and asserts the importance of "the wider cul-tural and social structural patterns of specific societies for determining the nature of social in-teraction within the advanced sector" (1978, p. 295). That is, the tenor of bargaining and negotiations between workers and management is determined not mainly by technology but by the history, resources, and social structure of the two sides. In a later book, Gallie (1983) traces the greater radicalism of French workers back to their collective encounter with an uncompromis-ing government during and after World War I.

Gallie suggests that the French working class has higher aspirations and expectations for equality and standard of living than the British, yet faces a worse objective situation; they are thus more militant and dissatisfied. French managers, on the other hand, are socialized into a managerial culture different from the English, with "different normative assumptions about the importance of preserving managerial prerogative" (1978, p. 310); this may be be-cause, as one of Gallie's English informants said, French managers are drawn especially from the elite engineering schools. The lack of combative class consciousness among Halle's American chemical workers may result from their situation beyond the workplace: they do not live in dis-tinctively blue-collar neighborhoods; rather, their income allows them to "compete with many white-collar employees in the housing market, to purchase similar consumer goods, and to enjoy a comparable leisure life" (1984, p. 294).

What determines outcomes, then, are such matters as the resources, bargaining power, socialization, cultural and social structural pat-terns of negotiating groups, and the state of labor and product markets. All are given short shrift by concentration on the point of produc-tion, and are thus rarely studied systematically by those concerned with how labor processes generate inequality.

Technology and the Social Production of "Skill"

The claim for a powerful impact of technology on inequality is often framed in terms of the effects of automation on skills. Harry Braver-man's pioneering 1974 work, *Labor and Mon-opoly Capital*, awakened a long-dormant in-terest in labor processes with the claim that capital accumulation under advanced monopoly capitalism required deskilling via extensive divi-sion of labor, scientific management, and auto-mation. Upgrading that resulted from these processes would be outweighed by downgrading of skills that eventually cut out the middle.

But Braverman's conception of skill is indi-vidualistic and removed from social context. Like human capital theorists in neoclassical eco-nomics, he conceives individuals to have well-defined skills, and jobs to have quite definite skill requirements independent of incumbents. Jobs, not individuals, are "deskilled." Once the skill level of a job has been reduced, according to Braverman, the helpless worker can exercise only the skills required; other skills he may possess will fall into disuse.

In actual work situations, however, the skill requirements of jobs and the relations among technology, skill, and control are not fixed; they vary with negotiating strength and market con-ditions. Given technologies are often compati-ble with a surprisingly wide range of skills. Many machine tools can be used in radically different ways, depending on the skill of the operator. In volatile markets skilled workers are needed to execute frequent changes in product; in stable markets, unskilled workers execute rigid rou-tines. When volatile markets stabilize, firms often switch from skilled to unskilled labor, as in the American metalworking industry from 1910 to 1930 (Sabel, 1982, p. 68; see also Jones,

1982, for a similar account based on a study of numerical control equipment in Britain). Only the skill mix has changed, not technology or any worker's skills; firms have gone from unit/small batch to large batch/mass production, with the changes to be expected from Woodward's argument. But these changes derive from product market shifts, not from alterations in technology or skills.

Groups of workers that consider themselves skilled may substantially influence how machines are operated. Historical studies show that output from the same machines in different locations is inversely related to the bargaining power of workers who run them (e.g., Clawson, 1980, pp. 194-195; Stern, 1986, p. 26). At times, groups of workers with control of entry and apprenticeship have successfully bargained to be named and treated as "skilled" workers even though their work differed little from those "lower" in the skill hierarchy (Penn, 1982; More, 1982; see also Hobsbawm, 1964, on the idea of a "labor aristocracy"). Cohen (1984) shows that after technological changes in nineteenth century spinning made the work less skilled, American spinners lost control but British spinners "retained their craft control untouched" and continued to claim skilled status (1984, p. 13; see Freifeld, 1986, however, for reservations on the extent of deskilling in mule spinning). The main explanations center on bargaining power: The stronger organization of British workers before automation, and the greater unity of American employers.

The very meaning of skill is elusive. It refers both to jobs and to people (Spenner, 1983). It compounds two different elements: personal capacity and substitutability. A skilled worker is someone who, in the present organization of labor processes (1) has a personal capacity that enhances the firm's productivity, and (2) would be expensive to replace by another worker. Skill often involves subtle, "tacit knowledge" that is difficult to articulate (Jones and Wood, 1985; Kusterer, 1978). The social relations of the workplace determine to what extent such knowledge is passed along to others, and thus play a major role in determining how "skilled" one appears to be. Economists have pointed out that this occurs more readily when job security is high, as where unions enforce seniority rights (Freeman and Medoff, 1980, p. 77) and internal labor markets limit entry from outside (Thurow, 1975, p. 81).

One's purely social relations with other workers also determine whether needed assistance materializes. The worker whose status in the group is low will appear less skillful from lack of this assistance (see, e.g., Dalton's account of race relations and apparent skill, 1959, pp. 128-129). Blau (1963) stresses that experts may exchange time-consuming advice for deference and higher group status. One's appearance of skill may thus be determined in part by how much social status one is willing to trade away. Skill then results from a trade-off against other elements valued in the social situation of the workplace.

How much skill one develops also depends on what value a group attaches to skill. In some settings skill serves as a status currency. Sabel (1982, p. 84) argues that in the tightly knit world of craftsmen, social mobility is unimportant; what counts "is technical prowess, not place in an officially defined hierarchy of jobs: Titles are not important, *savoir faire* is." Thus Burawoy reports that in the machine-shop where he worked,

> Once I knew I had a chance to make out [attain the rate acceptable to the group] . . . I found myself spontaneously cooperating with management in the production of greater surplus value. Moreover it was only in this way that I could establish relationships with others on the shop floor. Until I was able to strut around the floor like an experienced operator, as if I had all the time in the world and could still make out, few but the greenest would condescend to engage me in conversation [1979, p. 64].

Automation, Skill and Inequality

Since the skill workers display is neither a well-defined trait of worker nor of job, but emerges instead from interaction and bargaining among workers, employers, and one another, technological change cannot automatically impose deskilling and employers' control. Marxist accounts of automation often suggest that this outcome occurs because the particular technology chosen is determined by the drive to maximize control of workers rather than by technical considerations (Clawson, 1980; Noble, 1977, 1984; Shaiken, 1985, p. 5). But evidence of the drive for control is usually inferential, and as Littler and Salaman point out, control of the labor process "may be achieved in ways which are not apparent at the point of production itself. This can occur through the organization of the employment relationship, for example. It can also occur through selection procedures, preparatory training and socialization" (1984, p. 64).

Even when control is the aim, new machines

and methods rarely work as well in practice as anticipated; unless production is absolutely routine, unforeseen difficulties arise that require workers' practical knowledge. As equipment ages, it develops quirks that demand extensive hands-on experience with tricks that coax it to operate as intended (see Halle, 1984, 119ff; Sabel, 1982, p. 62).

The case of automation with numerical control equipment is instructive. For Braverman it is the type-case of deskilling via separation of conception from execution, since a programmer writes a program for equipment that is then run by an unskilled worker (1974, pp. 197-206; see also Noble, 1984, and the perceptive review by Fallows, 1984). But in practice, programming and execution can often not be efficiently separated. When programmers and machinists do not know one another's skills, programs "tend to be roundabout, if they function at all" (Sabel, 1982, p. 66; see also Jones, 1982). Thus programmers and machinists must collaborate more than the design of the equipment foresees (Shaiken, 1985, p. 81).

Shaiken emphasizes that this collaboration is hampered by a perceived class difference between the two groups, and that much valuable worker knowledge does not reach the higher levels both because workers protect their secrets and because supervisors and programmers do not ask. Further study of the social insulation of these strata and the status consequences for them, within their own groups, of seeking help from the shop floor, would reveal much about the functioning of industrial settings. To the extent that supervisors and programmers consider it demeaning to seek this help, solutions may be implemented instead that do deskill machinists. But a system that prevents machinists from programming imposes a cost on managers: increased dependence on programmers (Shaiken, 1985, p. 101). This point could be made for most claims of separation of conception from execution: control gained at the point of production is often sacrificed one or two levels beyond it; narrow attention to the point of production obscures this trade-off.

Whether deskilling occurs depends not only on these social dynamics and on jockeying for position among workplace groups but also on whether automation really creates so many new jobs, as in optimistic accounts, that net upgrading occurs. Whether this occurs depends on what tasks are eliminated and newly created by automation, and which workers do the old and the new tasks. Upgrading requires that unskilled tasks be eliminated, more interesting ones substituted and assigned to workers who previously did less skilled work. If such workers are instead let go and the new tasks are parceled out to those already in skilled work, then upgrading does not occur and total inequality increases.

Sabel suggests that technical change upgrades the skills of workers "who service, repair, draw plans for and even participate in the design of new machines" (1982, p. 57), and creates new jobs that involve servicing increasingly complex machines in the course of production. Thus a machine setup man does a job formerly carried out by a craftsman, but now separated out and defined as a lower skill grade. Such jobs "tend to be held either by craftsmen no longer able to find employment for the full range of their skills or by formerly unskilled workers whose new positions of responsibility privilege them with respect to their old workmates" (Sabel, 1982, p. 58). Which is the case determines the impact on inequality: The former represents deskilling, the latter upgrading—for identical patterns of automation.

Our problem is therefore to explain which outcome occurs. One argument often made is that the widespread entry of women to an occupation occurs where automation has reduced the skills previously exercised there. Such an argument cannot apply clearly to this controversy without information about the previous work carried out by women entering the occupation. Thus Montgomery notes that during World War II, welding—previously part of machinists' training—was separated and taught to women, "most of whom had previously been garment and textile workers," so that the new job "represented a considerable improvement in their economic status" (1979, p. 118).

Such discussions are complicated by powerful images of deskilling that may be inaccurate. Cohn, for example, examines the feminization of clerical work in the nineteenth century, and asserts that the image of mechanization as deskilling is "based on an overromanticized conception of the quality of clerical life in the nineteenth century" (1985, p. 119). While some devices deskilled, others eliminated tedious and menial tasks such as licking stamps and hand-copying. Using measures of skill exercised and changes in wages he concludes that there was no obvious predominance either of upgrading or deskilling during this period.

One important reason that newly created tasks sometimes go to those previously holding less skilled positions is economic expansion. In good times there is less pressure to use automation to eliminate workers displaced by machines. Automation has never produced mass unemployment, in part, because capital infusions required for it have been available only in prosperous periods. Because labor is often scarce in such periods, upgrading existing employees whose jobs are displaced by automation is a cheaper option, when increasing production, than hunting for new ones whose skills may look better on paper but who are not known quantities. The rate of growth of the labor force affects the supply side of this discussion. Leontief and Duchin (1986) argue (contrary to earlier concerns about automation expressed by Leontief himself) that this rate will be sufficiently slow as to imply no increase in unemployment due to automation at least until the turn of the next century.

Upgrading due to automation can reduce overall labor inequalities. This may be a special case of a more general process proposed by economist Melvin Reder (1955) to explain why pay differentials between skilled and unskilled labor diminish in boom times. One might suppose that increased labor demand would put upward pressure on skilled and unskilled wages alike; Reder suggests instead that some employers in need of highly skilled workers promote from below rather than search in a tight market. If pursued vigorously this strategy leaves a shortage in the next-to-highest skill category. That shortage may be met by promotion from the group below that, and so on. When a shortage then appears in the lowest skill group, and no new labor supply is available, the wages of that group are bid up, reducing the skill differential. Thus the upgrading that results from automation may be an instance of the upgrading that always occurs in tight labor markets, and is not ultimately caused by events at the point of production.

The extent of upgrading in specific settings depends not only on the general macroeconomic situation but also on how automation affects promotion ladders. In a highly automated medical insurance claims office studied by Attewell (1985), computerization eliminated a variety of menial clerical tasks. The redundant employees were retrained as DPE (data process and entry) clerks, who entered claim information for examiners, which they perceived as upgrading. Because some examiners had poor handwriting, supervisors assigned examiners specific clerks who were used to the writing. Seeing claims from only one or two group plans, the clerks became more familiar with the plans and with some cases; they began catching examiners' coding errors, which led examiners to transfer the coding work to the clerks—a higher level of decision making than envisioned in the DPE job. This made the clerks logical candidates

for promotion to examiner, a crucial link in the job ladder since examiners can attain several higher levels in the organization.

Before automation, such workers were in classic "dead-end" jobs. Attewell reports that such promotions did take place (though not for Asian women, seen as lacking requisite language skills) (1985, pp. 23-24). Shaiken found that in shops where there is resistance to having machinists involved with numerical control programming, there is nevertheless a desire for programmers with a machining background. This dilemma "is often resolved either by making programmers out of managers who were machinists or by promoting machinists into a new position that takes them off the shop floor" (1985, p. 103).

But automation may also introduce a level of scientific abstraction into the work process that is beyond the experience of manual workers and thus breaks up previously existing promotion ladders. Halle observed a gulf between the plant chemists and the process workers or even the lab technicians, based on knowledge of the formal principles of chemistry. Without college degrees in this technically sophisticated setting, "they are unlikely to rise above second-line supervision" (1984, p. 149). Sabel reports a study by Lutz and Kammerer of the changing place of night-school engineers in the West German machine-tool industry. Often craftsmen who had upgraded their skills, they could easily cope with existing methods. "But when techniques were revolutionized by fundamental breakthroughs, only engineers and scientists recently trained at leading research centers understood the new ideas well enough to apply them practically" (Sabel, 1982, p. 87). However, Sabel also describes, in Italy, a complex conjuncture of political events, a strong economy and demand for more differentiated products that gives many small firms a foothold in high-technology manufacturing. In these small, flexible settings, craftsmen "are capable of inventiveness and sophistication that confounds middle-class expectations about the possibility of learning by doing" (1982, pp. 224-225).

Whatever we may find in a particular industry or occupation about upgrading or deskilling, the broader question must be what is the balance of occupations in each category throughout the entire economy. Aggregate analyses appear to support a picture of general upgrading rather than deskilling (Attewell, 1986, pp. 16-19; Leontief and Duchin, 1986), but this outcome may well depend on a continued strong economy. This is the most important analytical conclusion; processes at the point of production cannot explain the impact of automation on inequality. As David Lee points out, Harry Braverman has in common with Clark Kerr, John Kenneth Galbraith, and Daniel Bell the assumption that there is a straight line of causation from the technical requirements of jobs to the evolution of class structure (Lee, 1982); like Lee, we are skeptical of this neat account.

Conclusions

We have argued that inequalities associated with labor result from bargaining and conflict among workers, capitalists, households, organizations, and governments over the ranking of positions and the sorting of individuals and groups into those ranked positions, in the three arenas of employment categories, jobs, and labor markets. This conflict is carried out within the limits of the contenders' interpersonal networks and the resources found within those networks, which are in turn profoundly influenced by such demographic matters as population age structure and flows of immigration, and such macroeconomic conditions as the level of aggregate demand, the composition of demand for particular products, the looseness or tightness of the labor market, and the dispensability of particular types of labor.

Because our argument highlights the role of collective action, it draws special attention to the level of the informal organization of both workers and employers, generally neglected in economic, structural-functional and Marxist accounts, and links this level to larger outcomes. Thus informal organization strongly affects the definition and transmission of skill, as well as the functioning of technical or organizational arrangements. "Shirking," or other resistance to employers, for example, is often taken by prevailing views as the result of individual initiatives rather than of a social process, thus missing the significance of long-standing social structures for that resistance. Having identified this source of resistance we are alerted to the importance of matters we would have missed because their connection to collective action fits no neat story.

Thus the extent of long-standing informal networks in firms is greater where tenures are long and internal labor markets extensive. This is more likely in oligopolistic industries with large firms. In highly competitive industries, where workers are handicapped by the lack of organization characteristic of spot markets, small owners enter and leave business frequently, and are thus similarly handicapped in their possibilities of developing coherent purposive action.

The social organization of managers and capitalists also determines the extent to which management adopts a militant stance rather than seeking accommodation or even advice from workers. Not only profit and efficiency affect such decisions, but also social pressures within cohesive capitalist or managerial groups toward a conception of their status that requires resistance to the contamination implied by accommodating a lower group. Workers may be similarly socialized, or may be sufficiently mixed socially to lack such clear and combative consciousness.

The labor market affects inequality when existing boundaries of informal interaction in that market reproduce associated inequalities as the result of recruitment through contact networks. But contact networks can at times reduce rather than reproduce inequality. Earlier we cited Reder's (1955) argument for the compression of skill differentials in boom times by upward substitutions that generate shortages in the lowest skill category. He assumed that when skilled workers are scarce the option of substituting from the "next skill-category down" is clearly defined by the technical meaning of skill categories. But our discussions of the socially negotiated meanings of skill and of informal recruitment patterns make us doubt this. Which labor pool seems logical to upgrade depends less on skill categories than on the structure of personal communications, as for Attewell's DPE clerks who connected to a mobility ladder through their personal ties to claims processors (1985). Changes in relative wages thus occur among sets of jobs linked by a chain of upward substitutability that results from personal and occupational contact networks. The cascade of effects through such a chain is similar to that in vacancy chains among jobs (Stewman, 1986; White, 1970). These wage compressions may disorganize the labor-market segments cited by such theorists as Gordon, Edwards, and Reich (1982), since wage differentials between them would decline and individuals could cross segments by breaking out of previous dead-end jobs. So reductions in inequality may occur in economic expansions, but we can understand the extent and shape of reductions only by a close examination of the proximate causes of job matching. Neither the point of production nor the larger macroeconomic situation in isolation can be the sole focus of inquiry, but rather the ebb and flow of forces back and forth, as mediated by daily purposive action.

Our argument in this chapter is more complex and conjunctural than the main alternatives, which are (1) the sociological functionalist argument that inequality results from a society's dominant value system—that positions are ranked in relation to their societal importance, and to the scarcity of available incumbents; (2) the neoclassical economic assumption that sorting is based on acquired human capital, and ranking of positions on the supply and demand for the work done in those positions, as modified by differentials compensating for investments in human capital and nonpecuniary disadvantages of jobs; (3) the Marxist-functionalist argument that inequality results from the distribution of skill levels in the structure of jobs, which is easily manipulated by capitalists; and (4) the more complex, but still rather functionalist, Marxist view that any divisions observed in the labor market must have been installed by capitalists in their ceaseless quest for control over a restive labor force (Gordon, Edwards, and Reich, 1982).

Functionalist models endow societies and societal processes with too much coherence. "Societies" are arbitrary social constructions, consisting of some boundary that analysts, as well as citizens, put around a collection of processes not necessarily closely related to one another. We focus instead on large numbers of individuals and groups, linked by multiple ties, engaged in purposive action. To suppose that these myriad activities, and the demographic and economic processes that shape them, should all mutually reinforce one another and lead to some easily ascertained outcome is to eliminate the most interesting problems that social science must address.

In short, we veer away from the quest for One Big Equation specifying relations between labor processes and inequality, toward a series of simultaneous contingent relationships. But we believe that our position is systematic enough to avoid the perils of historicism. Everything does not depend on everything else, nor is everything possible; some causal patterns can be clearly traced.

We have pointed to many complex relationships surrounding bargaining, resources, and the means of collective action. We have taken up some—but only some—of these relationships, and call attention to the rest as challenges for theory and research. The agenda for students of inequality and labor processes that we have set is a daunting one. But its outlines are clear. Many particular problems we have discussed can be tackled with the kit of theoretical and empirical tools already available to modern social science. The links we have drawn between our arguments and some of the most vital current traditions in sociology and history—such as the study of resource mobilization, collective action, social networks, and the broad "conjunctural" view of historical development characteristic of the Annales school—holds out the promise that the study of inequality and labor processes will break out of its isolation from other sociological problems and be seen as a special case of questions we must ask in many other contexts. If we succeed in furthering that promise, our labor here will have been amply rewarded.

REFERENCES

Abbott, Andrew. 1986a. "The System of Professions." Unpublished manuscript. Department of Sociology, Rutgers University.

———. 1986b. "Jurisdictional Conflicts: A New Approach to the Development of the Legal Professions." *American Bar Foundation Research Journal* xx:187-224.

Abraham, Katherine and James Medoff. 1983. *Length of Service and the Operation of Internal Labor Markets*. Working Paper 1394-83, Sloan School of Management, Massachusetts Institute of Technology, Cambridge.

Akerlof, George and Janet Yellin. 1986. *Efficiency Wage Models of the Labor Market*. New York: Cambridge University Press.

Aldrich, Howard, John Cater, Trevor Jones, and Dave McEvoy. 1983. "From Periphery to Peripheral: The South Asian Petite Bourgeoisie in England." *Research in Sociology of Work: Peripheral Workers* 2:1-32.

Aldrich, Howard, Trevor P. Jones, and David McEvoy. 1984. "Ethnic Advantage and Minority Business Development." Pp. 189-210 in *Ethnic Communities in Business: Strategies for Economic Survival*, edited by Robin Ward and Richard Jenkins. Cambridge, England: Cambridge University Press.

Anderson, Grace M. 1974. *Networks of Contact: The Portuguese and Toronto*. Waterloo, Ontario: Wilfrid Laurier University Publications.

Anderson, Perry. 1976. *Considerations on Western Marxism*. London: NLB.

Ashenfelter, Orley. 1973. "Discrimination and Trade Unions." Pp. 88-112 in *Discrimination in Labor Markets*, edited by Orley Ashenfelter and Albert Rees. Princeton, NJ: Princeton University Press.

Attewell, Paul. 1985. "The Automated Office: A Case Study." Mimeographed. Department of Sociology, State University of New York at Stony Brook.

———. 1986. "The Deskilling Controversy." Mimeographed.

Bairoch, Paul. 1985. *De Jéricho à Mexico. Villes et économie dans l'historie*. Paris: Gallimard.

_____ and J.-M. Limbor. 1968. "Changes in the Industrial Distribution of the World Labour Force, by Region, 1880-1960." *International Labor Review* 98:311-336.

Baron, Ava. 1982. "Women and the Making of the American Working Class: A Study of the Proletarianization of Printers." *Review of Radical Political Economics* 14:23-42.

_____ In press. "Contested Terrain Revisited: Technology and Gender Definitions of Work in the Printing Industry, 1850-1920." In *Transformations: Women, Work and Technology*, edited by Barbara Wright et al. Ann Arbor: University of Michigan Press.

Baron, James N. and William T. Bielby. 1985. "Organizational Barriers to Gender Equality: Sex Segregation of Jobs and Opportunities." Pp. 233-251 in *Gender and the Life Course*, edited by Alice S. Rossi. New York: Aldine.

Bennett, Sari and Carville Earle. 1983. "Socialism in America: A Geographical Interpretation of its Failure." *Political Geography Quarterly* 2:31-55.

Berg, Maxine. 1985. *The Age of Manufactures: Industry Innovation and Work in Britain, 1700-1820*. Oxford, England: Blackwell.

_____, Pat Hudson, and Michael Sonenscher. 1983. *Manufacture in Town and Country Before the Factory*. Cambridge, England: Cambridge University Press.

Bergmann, Barbara R. 1986. *The Economic Emergence of Women*. New York: Basic Books.

Bielby, William T. and James N. Baron. 1986. "Men and Women at Work: Sex Segregation and Statistical Discrimination." *American Journal of Sociology* 91:759-799.

Blau, Francine D. and Marianne A. Ferber. 1986. *The Economics of Women, Men, and Work*. Englewood Cliffs, NJ: Prentice-Hall.

Blau, Peter. 1963. *The Dynamics of Bureaucracy*. Chicago: University of Chicago Press.

Blauner, Robert. 1964. *Alienation and Freedom: The Factory Worker and His Industry*. Chicago: University of Chicago Press.

Bodnar, John, Roger Simon, and Michael P. Weber. 1982. *Lives of Their Own. Blacks, Italians, and Poles in Pittsburgh, 1900-1960*. Urbana: University of Illinois Press.

Bottomore, Tom, ed. 1983. *A Dictionary of Marxist Thought*. Cambridge, MA: Harvard University Press.

Braverman, Harry. 1974. *Labor and Monopoly Capital. The Degradation of Work in the Twentieth Century*. New York: Monthly Review Press.

Bridges, William P. 1982. "The Sexual Segregation of Occupations: Theories of Labor Stratification in Industry." *American Journal of Sociology* 88:270-295.

Burawoy, Michael. 1979. *Manufacturing Consent. Changes in the Labor Process under Monopoly Capitalism*. Chicago: University of Chicago Press.

_____ 1985. *The Politics of Production*. London: Verso.

Bureau of the Census. 1975. *Historical Statistics of the United States, Colonial Times to 1970*. Washington, DC: Government Printing Office.

_____ 1985. *Statistical Abstract of the United States*. Washington, DC: Government Printing Office.

Campbell, Karen and Rachel Rosenfeld. 1986. "Job Search and Job Mobility: Sex and Race Differences." *Research in the Sociology of Work* 3. (Entire issue)

Chaplin, David. 1964. "Domestic Service and the Negro." In *Blue Collar World; Studies of the American Worker*, edited by Arthur B. Shostak and William Gomberg. Englewood Cliffs, NJ: Prentice-Hall.

Charlot, Bernard and Madeleine Figeat. 1985. *Histoire de la formation des ouvriers, 1789-1984*. Paris: Minerve.

Chatelain, Abel. 1976. *Le Migrants temporaires en France de 1800 à 1914* (2 vols.). Villeneuve d'Ascq: Publications d'Université de Lille.

Cheng, Lucie and Edna Bonacich, eds. 1984. *Labor Immigration under Capitalism. Asian Workers in the United States before World War II*. Berkeley: University of California Press.

Chiswick, Barry R., Carmel U. Chiswick, and Paul W. Miller. 1985. "Are Immigrants and Natives Perfect Substitutes in Production?" *International Migration Review* 19:674-685.

Clawson, Dan. 1980. *Bureaucracy and the Labor Process*. New York: Monthly Review Press.

Cohen, Isaac. 1984. "Management Control, Immigrant Labor and Strikes: British Factory Workers in Industrial America 1800-1880." Mimeograph.

_____ 1985. "Workers' Control in the Cotton Industry: A Comparative Study of British and American Mule Spinning." *Labor History* 26:53-85.

Cohn, Samuel. 1985. *The Process of Occupational Sex-Typing. The Feminization of Clerical Labor in Great Britain*. Philadelphia: Temple University Press.

Cole, Robert. 1979. *Work, Mobility and Participation: A Comparative Study of American and Japanese Industry*. Berkeley: University of California Press.

Collins, Randall. 1979. *The Credential Society. An Historical Sociology of Education and Stratification*. New York: Academic Press.

Conell, Carol. 1980. "The Value of Union Sponsorship to Strikers." Ph.D. dissertation, University of Michigan.

Corcoran, Mary, Greg J. Duncan, and Martha S. Hill. 1984. "The Economic Fortunes of Women and Children: Lessons from the Panel Study of Income Dynamics." *Signs* 10:232-248.

Coser, Lewis, Charles Kadushin, and Walter Powell. 1982. *Books: The Culture and Commerce of Publishing*. New York: Basic.

Coverman, Shelley. 1983. "Gender, Domestic Labor Time, and Wage Inequality." *American Sociological Review* 48:623-636.

Dalton, Melville. 1959. *Men Who Manage*. New York: John Wiley.

Davis, Kingsley and Wilbert Moore. 1945. "Some Principles of Stratification." *American Sociological Review* 10:242-249.

Ditton, Jason. 1977. "Perks, Pilferage and the Fiddle: The Historical Structure of Invisible Wages." *Theory and Society* Vol. 4.

Dublin, Thomas. 1979. *Women at Work. The Transformation of Work and Community in Lowell, Massachusetts, 1826-1860*. New York: Columbia University Press.

Duncan, Greg J. and Saul D. Hoffman. 1985. "A Reconsideration of the Economic Consequences of Marital Dissolution." *Demography* 22:485-498.

Duncan, Greg J. and James N. Morgan. 1981. "Persistence and Change in Economic Status and the Role of Changing Family Composition." Pp. 1-44 in *Five Thousand American Families—Patterns of Economic Progress. Volume IX: Analyses of the First Twelve Years of the Panel Study of Income Dynamics*, edited by Martha S. Hill, Daniel H. Hill, and James N. Morgan. Ann Arbor: Survey Research Center, Institute for Social Research, University of Michigan.

Easterlin, Richard A. 1980. *Birth and Fortune. The Impact of Numbers on Personal Welfare*. New York: Basic Books.

Edwards, Richard. 1979. *Contested Terrain. The Transformation of the Workplace in the Twentieth Century*. New York: Basic Books.

Eichengreen, Barry and Henry A. Gemery. 1986. "The Earnings of Skilled and Unskilled Immigrants at the End of the Nineteenth Century." *Journal of Economic History* 46:441-454.

Elster, Jon. 1985. *Making Sense of Marx*. Cambridge, England: Cambridge University Press.

Engelsing, Rolf. 1973. *Zur Sozialgeschichte deutscher Mittel- und Unterschichten*. Gottingen: Vandenhoeck and Ruprecht.

England, Paula and George Farkas. 1986. *Households, Employment, and Gender*. New York: Aldine.

Fallows, James. 1984. "A Parable of Automation." *New York Review of Books* (September 27):11-17.

Farge, Arlette. 1986. La vie fragile. Violence, pouvoirs et solidarites a Paris au XVIIIe siecle. Paris: Hachette.

Farkas, George, Paula England, and Margaret Barton. 1986. "Factor Markets, Product Markets, and Bargaining within Firms and Industries: The Economic and Social Determinants of Worker Compensation." Unpublished manuscript, University of Texas at Dallas.

Farley, Reynolds. 1980. "The Long Road: Blacks and Whites in America." *American Demographics* 2:11-17.

_____ 1984. *Blacks and Whites. Narrowing the Gap?* Cambridge, MA: Harvard University Press.

Faulkner, Robert. 1983. *Music on Demand: Composers and Careers in the Hollywood Film Industry*. New Brunswick, NJ: Transaction Books.

Folbre, Nancy. 1986. "Hearts and Spades: Paradigms of Household Economics." *World Development* 14:245-255.

Form, William. 1985. *Divided We Stand: Working-Class Stratification in America*. Urbana: University of Illinois Press.

Freeman, Richard and James Medoff. 1980. "The Two Faces of Unionism." *Public Interest* 39: 69-93.

Freifeld, Mary. 1986. "Technological Change and the 'Self-Acting' Mule: A Study of Skill and the Sexual Division of Labor." *Social History* 11:319-344.

Friedman, Gerald. 1985. "Politics and Unions. Government, Ideology, and Unionization in the United States and France, 1880-1914." Ph.D. dissertation, Harvard University.

Friedman, Milton and Simon Kuznets. 1945. *Income from Independent Professional Practice*. New York: National Bureau of Economic Research.

Friedmann, Harriet. 1978a. "World Market, State, and Family Farm: Social Bases of Household Production in the Era of Wage Labor." *Comparative Studies in Society and History* 20:545-586.

_____ 1978b. "Simple Commodity Production and Wage Labour in the American Plains." *Journal of Peasant Studies* 6:71-100.

Frisch, Michael H. and Daniel J. Walkowitz, eds. 1983. *Working-Class America: Essays on Labor, Community, and American Society*. Urbana: University of Illinois Press.

Gallie, Duncan. 1978. *In Search of the New Working Class: Automation and Social Integration Within the Capitalist Enterprise*. New York: Cambridge University Press.

_____ 1983. *Social Inequality and Class Radicalism in France and Britain*. Cambridge, England: Cambridge University Press.

Goldin, Claudia. 1983. "The Changing Economic Role of Women: A Quantitative Approach." *Journal of Interdisciplinary History* 13:707-733.

_____ 1984. "The Historical Evolution of Female Earnings Functions and Occupations." *Explorations in Economic History* 21:1-27.

_____ 1986a. "Monitoring Costs and Occupational Segregation by Sex: A Historical Analysis." *Journal of Labor Economics* 4:1-27.

_____ 1986b. "The Economic Status of Women in the Early Republic: Quantitative Evidence." *Journal of Interdisciplinary History* 16:375-404.

Gordon, David M., Richard Edwards, and Michael Reich. 1982. *Segmented Work, Divided Workers. The Historical Transformations of Labor in the United States*. New York: Cambridge University Press.

Gottfried, Heidi and David Fasenfest. 1984. "Gender and Class Formation: Female Clerical Workers." *Review of Radical Political Economics* 16:89-103.

Granovetter, Mark. 1974. *Getting a Job: A Study of Contacts and Careers*. Cambridge, MA: Harvard University Press.

———. 1981. "Toward a Sociological Theory of Income Differences." Pp. 11-47 in *Sociological Perspectives on Labor Markets* edited by Ivar Berg. New York: Academic Press.

———. 1984. "Small is Bountiful: Labor Markets and Establishment Size." *American Sociological Review* 49:323-334.

———. 1985. "Economic Action and Social Structure: The Problem of Embeddedness." *American Journal of Sociology* 91:481-510.

———. 1986. "Labor Mobility, Internal Markets and Job-Matching: A Comparison of the Sociological and the Economic Approaches." *Research in Social Stratification and Mobility* 5:3-39.

Gullickson, Gay L. 1986. *Spinners and Weavers of Auffay: Rural Industry and the Sexual Division of Labor in a French Village, 1750-1850.* Cambridge, England: Cambridge University Press.

Hall, Robert. 1980. "Employment Fluctutations and Wage Rigidity." *Brookings Papers on Economic Activity* 1:91-123.

———. 1982. "The Importance of Lifetime Jobs in the U.S. Economy." *American Economic Review* 72:716-724.

Halle, David. 1984. *America's Working Man: Work, Home and Politics Among Blue-Collar Property Owners.* Chicago: University of Chicago Press.

Handl, Johann, Karl Ulrich Mayer, Walter Muller, and Angelika Willms. 1979. "Prozesse Sozialstrukturellen Wandels am Beispiel der Entwicklung von Qualifikations—und Erwerbsstruktur der Frauen im Deutschen Reich und der Bundesrepublik Deutschland." Arbeitspapier 6, VASMA-Projekt, University of Mannheim.

Hanagan, Michael. 1980. *The Logic of Solidarity. Artisans and Industrial Workers in Three French Towns, 1871-1914.* Urbana: University of Illinois Press.

Hareven, Tamara. 1982. *Family Time and Industrial Time. The Relationship Between the Family and Work in a New England Industrial Community.* Cambridge, England: Cambridge University Press.

Harrison, Bennett, Chris Tilly, and Barry Bluestone. 1986. "Wage Inequality Takes a Great U-Turn." *Challenge* 29:26-32.

Hicks, J. R. 1963. *The Theory of Wages.* London: Macmillan.

Hirsch, Susan. 1986. "Rethinking the Sexual Division of Labor: Pullman Repair Shops, 1900-1969." *Radical History* 35:26-48.

Hirschman, Charles and Morrison G. Wong. 1984. "Socioeconomic Gains of Asian Americans, Blacks, and Hispanics: 1960-1976." *American Journal of Sociology* 90:584-607.

Hobsbawm, Eric J. 1964. *Labouring Men: Studies in the History of Labour.* New York: Basic Books.

———, ed. 1982. *The History of Marxism. Vol. 1: Marxism in Marx's Day.* Bloomington: Indiana University Press.

Horan, Patrick M. and Thomas A. Lyson. 1986. "Occupational Concentration in Work Establishments." *Sociological Forum* 1:428-449.

Hout, Michael. 1984. "Occupational Mobility of Black Men: 1962 to 1973." *American Sociological Review* 49:308-322.

Huber, Joan. 1986. "Trends in Gender Stratification, 1970-1985." *Sociological Forum* 1:476-495.

Hudson, Pat. 1986. *The Genesis of Industrial Capital: A Study of the West Riding Textile Industry, 1750-1850.* Cambridge, England: Cambridge University Press.

International Labour Office. 1984. *Payment by Results.* Geneva: Author.

Jackson, Robert Max. 1984. *The Formation of Craft Labor Markets.* New York: Academic Press.

Jacobs, David. 1985. "Unequal Organizations or Unequal Attainments? An Empirical Comparison of Sectoral and Individualistic Explanations for Aggregate Inequality." *American Sociological Review* 50:166-180.

Jones, Bryn. 1982. "Destruction or Redistribution of Engineering Skills? The Case of Numerical Control." Pp. 179-200 in *The Degradation of Work?* edited by Stephen Wood. London: Hutchinson.

——— and Stephen Wood. 1985. "Tacit Skills, Division of Labour and New Technology." Mimeographed.

Jones, S.R.H. 1982. "The Organization of Work: A Historical Dimension." *Journal of Economic Behavior and Organization* 3:117-137.

Kaelble, Hartmut. 1983. *Industrialisierung und soziale Ungleichheit.* Gottingen: Vandenhoeck and Ruprecht.

Kaufman, Robert L. 1983. "A Structural Decomposition of Black-White Earnings Differentials." *American Journal of Sociology* 89:585-611.

Kemp, Alice Abel and E. M. Beck. 1981. "Female Underemployment in Urban Labor Markets." Pp. 251-272 in *Sociological Perspectives on Labor Markets*, edited by Ivar Berg. New York: Academic Press.

Keyssar, Alexander. 1986. *Out of Work: The First Century of Unemployment in Massachusetts.* Cambridge, England: Cambridge University Press.

Korpi, Walter. 1983. *The Democratic Class Struggle.* London: Routledge & Kegan Paul.

Kriedte, Peter, Hans Medick, and Jurgen Schlumbohm. 1981. *Industrialization Before Industrialization.* Cambridge, England: Cambridge University Press.

Kussmaul, Ann. 1981. *Servants in Husbandry in Early Modern England.* Cambridge, England: Cambridge University Press.

Kusterer, Ken. 1978. *Know-How on the Job.* Boulder, CO: Westview Press.

Kuznets, Simon. 1966. *Modern Economic Growth. Rate, Structure, and Spread.* New Haven, CT: Yale University Press.

Kynch, Jocelyn, and Amartya Sen. 1983. "Indian Women: Well-Being and Survival." *Cambridge Journal of Economics* 7:363-380.

Larson, Magali Sarfatti. 1977. *The Rise of Professionalism. A Sociological Analysis.* Berkeley: University of California Press.

Laurie, Bruce. 1980. *Working People of Philadelphia, 1800-1850.* Philadelphia: Temple University Press.

Lebergott, Stanley. 1964. *Manpower in Economic Growth: The American Record since 1800.* New York: McGraw-Hill.

Lee, David. 1982. "Beyond Deskilling: Skill, Craft and Class." Pp. 146-162 in *The Degradation of Work?* edited by Stephen Wood. London: Hutchinson.

Leib, Jeffrey. 1986. "The Promise in Profit-Sharing." *The New York Times* (February 9):(business section).

Leibowitz, Arleen. 1975. "Women's Work in the Home." Pp. 223-243 in *Sex, Discrimination, and the Division of Labor,* edited by Cynthia B. Lloyd. New York: Columbia University Press.

Leontief, Wassily and Faye Duchin. 1986. *The Impact of Automation.* New York: Oxford University Press.

Lenski, Gerhard. 1966. *Power and Privilege. A Theory of Social Stratification.* New York: McGraw-Hill.

Levine, David, ed. 1984. *Proletarianization and Family History.* Orlando, FL: Academic Press.

Liebow, Elliott. 1967. *Tally's Corner.* Boston: Little, Brown.

Lieberson, Stanley. 1980. *A Piece of the Pie. Blacks and White Immigrants since 1880.* Berkeley: University of California Press.

Lis, Catharina. 1986. *Social Change and the Labouring Poor. Antwerp, 1770-1860.* New Haven, CT: Yale University Press.

Littler, Craig. 1982. *The Development of the Labour Process in Capitalist Societies: A Comparative Study of the Transformation of Work Organization in Britain, Japan and the USA.* London: Heinemann.

Littler, Craig and Graeme Salaman. 1984. *Class at Work: The Design, Allocation and Control of Jobs.* London: Batsford.

Ludtke, Alf. 1985. "Organization Order or Eigensinn? Workers' Privacy and Workers' Politics in Imperial Germany." Pp. 303-333 in *Rites of Power: Symbolism, Ritual, and Politics since the Middle Ages,* edited by Sean Wilentz. Philadelphia: Temple University Press.

Madden, Janice Fanning. 1985. "The Persistence of Pay Differentials: The Economics of Sex Discrimination." *Women and Work: An Annual Review* I:76-114.

Mallet, Sege. 1963. *La Nouvelle Classe Ouvrière.* Paris: Gallimard.

March, James C. and James G. March. 1978. "Performance Sampling in Social Matches." *Administrative Science Quarterly* 22:434-453.

Marglin, Stephen. 1974. "What Do Bosses Do?" *Review of Radical Political Economics* 6:33-60.

Marsden, David. 1986. *The End of Economic Man? Custom and Competition in Labour Markets.* New York: St. Martin's.

Marvel, Howard P. 1977. "Factory Regulation: A Reinterpretation of Early English Experience." *Journal of Law and Economics* 2:379-402.

Mayer, Karl Ulrich. 1980. "Sozialhistorische Materialien zum Verhältnis von Bildungs- und Beschäftigungssystem bie Frauen." Pp. 60-79 in *Bildungsexpansion und betriebliche Beschäftigungspolitik,* edited by Ulrich Beck et al. Frankfurt, West Germany: Campus.

Michelson, William. 1985. *From Sun to Sun. Daily Obligations and Community Structure in the Lives of Employed Women and Their Families.* Totowa, NJ: Rowman & Allenheld.

Miller, Herman P. 1971. *Rich Man, Poor Man.* New York: Crowell.

Miller, Jon. 1986. *Pathways in the Workplace. The Effects of Gender and Race on Access to Organizational Resources.* Cambridge, England: Cambridge University Press.

Mills, C. Wright. 1951. *White Collar. The American Middle Classes.* New York: Oxford University Press.

Model, Suzanne. 1984. "Competitive Individualism and the Persistence of Minority Disadvantage." Working Paper 320, Center for Research on Social Organization, University of Michigan.

——— 1985a. "The Effects of Ethnicity in the Work Place on Blacks, Italians, and Jews in 1910 New York." Working Paper 7, Center for Studies of Social Change, New School for Social Research, New York.

——— 1985b. "Ethnic Bonds in the Work Place: Blacks, Italians, and Jews in New York City." Ph.D. dissertation, University of Michigan.

——— 1985c. "A Comparative Perspective on the Ethnic Enclave: Blacks, Italians, and Jews in New York City." *International Migration Review* 19:64-81.

Montgomery, David. 1979. *Workers' Control in America: Studies in the History of Work, Technology and Labor Struggles.* New York: Cambridge University Press.

Moore, Wilbert E. 1965. *The Impact of Industry.* Englewood Cliffs, NJ: Prentice-Hall.

Morawska, Ewa. 1985a. "The Modernity of Tradition: East European Peasant-Immigrants in an American Steel Town, 1890-1940." *Peasant Studies* 12:257-278.

——— 1985b. *For Bread With Butter. Life-Worlds of East Central Europeans in Johnstown, Pennsylvania, 1890-1940.* Cambridge, England: Cambridge University Press.

More, Charles. 1982. "Skill and the Survival of Apprenticeship." Pp.109-121 in *The Degradation of Work?* edited by Stephen Wood. London: Hutchinson.

Mottez, Bernard. 1966. *Systèmes de salaire et politiques patronales. Essai sur l'évolution des pratiques et des idéologies patronales.* Paris: Editions du Centre National de la Recherche Scientifique.

Nelson, Daniel. 1975. *Managers and Workers.*

Origins of the New Factory System in the United States, 1880-1920. Madison: University of Wisconsin Press.

Nardinelli, Clark. 1980. "Child Labor and the Factory Acts." *Journal of Economic History* 40: 739-756.

Noble, David. 1977. *America By Design*. New York: Knopf.

———. 1984. *Forces of Production: A Social History of Industrial Automation*. New York: Knopf.

Oaxaca, Ronald. 1973. "Sex Discrimination in Wages." In *Discrimination in Labor Markets*, edited by Orley Ashenfelter and Albert Rees. Princeton, NJ: Princeton University Press.

Oliver, Douglas. 1955. *A Solomon Island Society*. Cambridge, MA: Harvard University Press.

Olson, Mancur. 1982. *The Rise and Decline of Nations. Economic Growth, Stagflation, and Social Rigidities*. New Haven, CT: Yale University Press.

O'Neill, June. 1985A. "Role Differentiation and the Gender Gap in Wage Rates." *Women and Work: An Annual Review* I:50-75.

———. 1985b. "The Trend in the Male-Female Wage Gap in the United States." *Journal of Labor Economics* 3(suppl.):S91-S116.

Parcel, Toby L. and Charles W. Mueller. 1983. *Ascription and Labor Markets: Race and Sex Differences in Earnings*. New York: Academic Press.

Pencavel, John 1977. "Work Effort, On-the-Job Screening and Alternative Methods of Remuneration." *Research in Labor Economics* 1:225-258.

Penn, Roger. 1982. "Skilled Manual Workers in the Labour Process, 1856-1914." Pp. 90-108 in *The Degradation of Work?* edited by Stephen Wood. London: Hutchinson.

Perrow, Charles. 1986. "Economic Theories of Organization." *Theory and Society* 15:11-46.

Pfeffer, Jeffrey. 1982. *Organizations and Organization Theory*. Boston: Pitman.

Phelps Brown, Henry. 1977. *The Inequality of Pay*. Berkeley: University of California Press.

Portes, Alejandro and Robert D. Manning. 1986. "The Immigrant Enclave: Theory and Empirical Examples." Pp. 47-68 in *Competitive Ethnic Relations*, edited by Susan Olzak and Joane Nagel. Orlando, FL: Academic Press.

Preston, Samuel H. 1984. "Children and the Elderly: Divergent Paths for America's Dependents." *Demography* 21:435-456.

Przeworksi, Adam, Barnett R. Rubin, and Ernest Underhill. 1980. "The Evolution of the Class Structure of France, 1901-1968." *Economic Development and Cultural Change* 28:725-752.

Reder, Melvin. 1955. "The Theory of Occupational Wage Differentials." *American Economic Review* 45:833-852.

Reitz, Jeffrey G. 1984. "Ethnic Group Control of Jobs." Unpublished paper, University of Toronto.

Reitz, Jeffrey G., Liviana Calzavara, and Donna Dasko. 1981. "Ethnic Inequality and Segregation in Jobs." Research Paper 123, Centre for Urban and Community Studies, University of Toronto.

Reskin, Barbara F., ed. 1984. *Sex Segregation in the Workplace. Trends, Explanations, Remedies*. Washington, DC: National Academy Press.

Reskin, Barbara F. and Heidi Hartmann, eds. 1986. *Women's Work, Men's Work. Sex Segregation on the Job*. Washington, DC: National Academy Press.

Reynolds, Lloyd G. 1951. *The Structure of Labor Markets. Wages and Labor Mobility in Theory and Practice*. New York: Harper and Brothers.

———. 1974. *Labor Economics and Labor Relations*. Englewood Cliffs, NJ: Prentice-Hall.

Robinson, Robert V. and Maurice A. Garnier. 1985. "Class Reproduction among Men and Women in France: Reproduction Theory on its Home Ground." *American Journal of Sociology* 91: 250-280.

Roos, Patricia. 1985. *Gender and Work: A Comparative Analysis of Industrial Societies*. Albany: State University of New York Press.

Rose, Sonya O. 1986. " 'Gender at Work': Sex, Class and Industrial Capitalism." *History Workshop* 21:113-131.

Rosen, Sherwin. 1982. "Authority, Control and the Distribution of Earnings." *Bell Journal of Economics* 13:311-323.

Rosenbaum, James E. 1979. "Organizational Career Mobility: Promotion Chances in a Corporation During Periods of Growth and Contraction." *American Journal of Sociology* 85:21-48.

———. 1981. "Careers in a Corporate Hierarchy." *Research in Social Stratification and Mobility*. (Entire issue)

———. 1984. *Career Mobility in a Corporate Hierarchy*. New York: Academic Press.

———. 1985. "Persistence and Change in Pay Inequalities: Implications for Job Evaluation and Comparable Worth." *Women and Work: An Annual Review* I:115-140.

Rueschemeyer, Dietrich. 1986. *Power and the Division of Labor*. Stanford, CA: Stanford University Press.

Sabel, Charles. 1982. *Work and Politics: The Division of Labor in Industry*. New York: Cambridge University Press.

Sabel, Charles and Jonathan Zeitlin. 1985. "Historical Alternatives to Mass Production: Politics, Markets and Technology in Nineteenth-Century Industrialization." *Past and Present* 108:133-176.

Salais, Robert, Nicolas Baverez, and Benedicte Reynaud. 1986. *L'Invention du chômage. Historie et transformation d'une catégorie en Frances des années 1980 aux années 1980*. Paris: Presses Universitaires de France.

Sayles, Leonard. 1958. *The Behavior of Industrial Work Groups*. New York: John Wiley.

Schmiechen, James A. 1984. *Sweated Industries and Sweated Labor. The London Clothing Trades,*

1860-1914. Urbana: University of Illinois Press.

Seccombe, Wally. 1986. "Patriarchy Stabilized: The Construction of the Male Breadwinner Wage Norm in Nineteenth-Century Britain." *Social History* 11:53-76.

Sen, Amartya. 1983. "Economics and the Family." *Asian Development Review* 1:14-26.

_____ 1985. "Women, Technology and Sexual Divisions." *Trade and Development* 6:195-223.

Shaiken, Harley. 1985. *Work Tranformed: Automation and Labor in the Computer Age*. New York: Holt, Rinehart and Winston.

Shaw, William H. 1978. *Marx's Theory of History*. Stanford, CA: Stanford University Press.

Soderberg, Johan. 1982. "Causes of Poverty in Sweden in the Nineteenth Century." *Journal of European Economic History* 11:369-402.

_____ 1985. "Trends in Inequality in Sweden, 1700-1914." In *Stagnating Metropolis: Growth Problems and Social. Inequality in Stockholm, 1760-1850*. Research Report 5, Stockholm Group for Comparative Studies in Economic History Project, Stockholm.

Sokoloff, Kenneth L. 1984. "Was the Transition from the Artisanal Shop to the Nonmechanized Factory Associated with Gains in Efficiency? Evidence from the U.S. Manufacturing Censuses of 1820 and 1850." *Explorations in Economic History* 21:351-382.

Stansell, Christine. 1983. "The Origins of the Sweatshop: Women and Early Industrialization in New York City." Pp. 78-103 in *Working-Class America: Essays on Labor, Community, and American Society*, edited by Michael H. Frisch and Daniel J. Walkowitz. Urbana: University of Illinois Press.

Starr, Paul. 1982. *The Social Transformation of American Medicine*. New York: Basic Books.

Stephens, Evelyne Huber. 1980. *The Politics of Workers' Participation. The Peruvian Approach in Comparative Perspective*. New York: Academic Press.

Stern, Marc J. 1985. "Determinants of Innovation: The American Pottery Industry, 1850-1900." Mimeographed. Department of History, State University of New York at Stony Brook.

Stewman, Shelby. 1986. "Demographic Models of Internal Labor Markets. *Administrative Science Quarterly* 31:212-247.

_____ and Suresh Konda. 1983. "Careers and Organizational Labor Markets: Demographic Models of Organizational Behavior." *American Journal of Sociology* 88:637-685.

Stinchcombe, Arthur L. 1983. *Economic Sociology*. New York: Academic Press.

Stockmann, Reinhard. 1985. "Gewerbliche Frauenarbeit in Deutschland 1875-1980. Zur Entwicklung der Beschäftigtenstruktur." *Geschichte und Gesellschaft* 11:447-475.

Szelenyi, Ivan. 1978. "Social Inequalities in State Socialist Redistributive Economies." *International Journal of Comparative Sociology* 19:63-87.

_____ 1983. *Urban Inequalities under State Socialism*. London: Oxford University Press.

Thomas, Robert J. 1985. *Citizenship, Gender, and Work. Social Organization of Industrial Agriculture*. Berkeley: University of California Press.

Thurow, Lester. 1975. *Generating Inequality*. New York: Basic Books.

Tienda, Marta and Jennifer Glass. 1985. "Household Structure and Labor Force Participation of Black, Hispanic, and White Mothers." *Demography* 22:395-414.

Tilly, Charles. 1978. "Migration in Modern European History." Pp. 48-72 in *Human Migration: Patterns, Implications, Policies*, edited by William H. McNeill and Ruth S. Adams. Bloomington: Indiana University Press.

_____ 1983. "Flows of Capital and Forms of Industry in Europe, 1500-1900." *Theory and Society* 12:123-143.

_____ 1984. "Demographic Origins of the European Proletariat." Pp. 1-85 in *Proletarianization and Family Life*, edited by David Levine. New York: Academic Press.

Tilly, Louise A. 1985. "Family, Gender and Occupation in Industrial France, Past and Present." Pp. 193-212 in *Gender and the Life Course*, edited by Alice S. Rossi. New York: Aldine.

_____ and Joan W. Scott. 1978. *Women, Work, and Family*. New York: Holt, Rinehart & Winston.

Treiman, Donald J. and Heidi Hartmann, eds. 1981. *Women, Work, and Wages: Equal Pay for Jobs of Equal Value*. Washington, DC: National Academy Press.

Treiman, Donald J. and Patricia A. Roos. 1983. "Sex and Earnings in Industrial Society: A Nine-Nation Comparison." *American Journal of Sociology* 89:612-650.

Turner, Jonathan H. 1986. "Toward a Unified Theory of Ethnic Antagonism: A Preliminary Synthesis of Three Macro Models." *Sociological Forum* 1:403-427.

U.S. Commission on Civil Rights. 1978. *Social Indicators of Equality for Minorities and Women*. Washington, DC: Author.

Vanek, Joann. 1973. "Keeping Busy: Time Spent in Housework, United States, 1920-1970." Ph.D. dissertation, University of Michigan.

Walder, Andrew G. 1986. *Communist Neo-Traditionalism. Work and Authority in Chinese Industry*. Berkeley: University of California Press.

Waldinger, Roger D. 1986a. *Through the Eye of the Needle: Immigrants and Enterprise in New York's Garment Trades*. New York: New York University Press.

_____ 1986b. "Immigrant Enterprise: A Critique and Reformulation." *Theory and Society* 15: 249-285.

_____, Robin Ward, and Howard Aldrich. 1985. "Ethnic Business and Occupational Mobility in Advanced Societies." *Sociology* 19:586-597.

Wallace, Anthony F.C. 1978. *Rockdale. The Growth*

of an American Village in the Early Industrial Revolution. New York: Knopf.

Weber, Max. 1968. "The Economic Relationships of Organized Groups." Pp 339-355 in *Economy and Society*, edited by Guenther Roth and Claus Wittich. New York: Bedminster Press. (original work published 1921)

Weitzman, Martin. 1984. *The Share Economy: Conquering Stagflation*. Cambridge, MA: Harvard University Press.

White, Harrison C. 1970. *Chains of Opportunity: System Models of Mobility in Organizations*. Cambridge, MA: Harvard University Press.

Whyte, William Foote. 1955. *Money and Motivation: An Analysis of Incentives in Industry*. New York: Harper and Brothers.

Williamson, Jeffrey. 1985. *Did British Capitalism Breed Inequality?* Boston: Allen & Unwin.

Williamson, Jeffrey G. and Peter H. Lindert. 1980. *American Inequality. A Macroeconomic History*. New York: Academic Press.

Williamson, Oliver. 1975. *Markets and Hierarchies*. New York: Free Press.

———. 1985. *The Economic Institutions of Capitalism*. New York: Free Press.

———, M. Wachter, and J. Harris. 1975. "Understanding the Employment Relation: The Analysis of Idiosyncratic Exchange." *Bell Journal of Economics* 6:250-278.

Willms, Angelika. 1983. *Auf dem Weg zur beruflichen Gleichstellung von Männern und Frauen? Entwicklungstendenzen der geschlechtsspezifischen Segregation des Arbeitsmarkts und ihre Determinanten, 1925-1980*. Arbeitspapier 35, VASMA-Projekt, University of Mannheim.

Wilson, William Julius. 1980. *The Declining Significance of Race. Blacks and Changing American Institutions*. Chicago: University of Chicago Press.

Wood, Stephen, ed. 1982. *The Degradation of Work?: Skill, Deskilling and the Labour Process*. London: Hutchinson.

Woodward, Joan. 1970. *Industrial Organization: Behavior and Control*. London: Oxford University Press.

———. 1980. *Industrial Organization: Theory and Practice*. London: Oxford University Press.

Wright, Erik Olin. 1978. *Class, Crisis and the State*. London: NLB.

———. 1985. *Classes*. London: Verso.

———, Cynthia Costello, David Hachen, and Joey Sprague. 1982. "The American Class Structure." *American Sociological Review* 47:709-726.

Zunz, Olivier. 1982. *The Changing Face of Inequality. Urbanization, Industrial Development, and Immigrants in Detroit, 1880-1920*. Chicago: University of Chicago Press.

7

Race and Ethnicity

KATHERINE O'SULLIVAN SEE
WILLIAM J. WILSON

The field of race and ethnic relations is periodically confronted with challenges that do not present themselves in other areas of study. Racial and ethnic flare-ups around the world tend to be highly visible (e.g., South Africa with its ethnic and tribal rivalries, Southeast Asia with the conflicts among the Chinese, Indians, and other native people; Western Europe with the antagonisms directed against immigrants from Eastern Europe and Northern Africa, and the United States with its ethnic rivalries, racial tensions, and manifestations of ethnic pluralism) and often generate heated discussions in the public forum and policy arena. Because patterns of race and ethnic relations represent a good deal of the inequality and injustice in complex societies, much of the literature that is referred to or said to represent sociological analysis is normative in character. In the United States this was particularly true of many of the studies that accompanied or immediately followed the racial protest movements of the 1960s. The heightened awareness of racial inequality during this period resulted in a proliferation of studies that forcefully presented arguments about the evils of racism and discrimination but that lacked analysis of fundamental sociological problems and were seldom based on empirical research.

In addition to the normative character of much of the literature in the field of race and ethnic relations, the problems investigated or selected for research are often based on the public's (or public official's) perception of the issues that ought to be addressed at a given point in time. In some cases the objectives of the research are designed either to be consistent with a public policy agenda or to resolve a controversial public issue. This, along with the normative literature, has contributed to the disproportionate number of studies that have little or no theoretical grounding, studies that are largely descriptive. The field of race relations, in comparison with other fields in sociology, has one of the severest imbalances between descriptive studies and studies grounded in theoretical principles.

The significantly higher proportion of descriptive studies in the field of race and ethnic relations is also a function of the focus and scope of the empirical research. Scholars of the sociology of the family, or the sociology of education, or complex organizations are not likely to consider it crucial to monitor developments in their respective fields in Western Europe, Southern Africa, or Latin America. On the other hand, studies that now represent the core of knowledge in the field of race and ethnic relations are increasingly those based on macro-comparative research, studies that often contrast race or ethnic relations in one society with those in other societies. Although these comparisons often involve the use of theoretical arguments to gauge the influence of different political, economic, and cultural systems, the broad units of investigation result in studies that tend to be *largely descriptive and that lead to the formulation of typologies as opposed to the testing or development of explicit theoretical propositions.*

To the extent that the focus of research in the field of race and ethnic relations tends to be broad, often of whole societies, it also becomes less quantitative. It is interesting to note, therefore, that unlike many other fields in sociology, important factors in the accumulation of knowledge in race and ethnic relations have not been associated with the development and use of quantitative techniques. As R. A. Schermerhorn has appropriately pointed out, the most effective tools of research in sociology are "the very ones fitted for minuscule units of single societies" (1978, p. 252). Although the field of race and ethnic relations is represented by some fine studies based on the sophisticated application of survey methods (Campbell and Schuman, 1968; Greeley and Sheatsley, 1971; Marx, 1970; Schuman, Steele, and Bobo, 1985; Taylor, Sheatsley, and Greeley, 1978) and although some important methodological advances are associated with the development of different indices of dissimilarity in the measure of segregation (Duncan and Duncan, 1955; Lieberson, 1963, 1980; Taeuber and Taeuber, 1965), such studies, as we shall see, are hardly representative of the significant work in the field.

Nonetheless, despite the disproportionate number of descriptive studies, and despite the relative absence of sophisticated quantitative studies, the field of race and ethnic relations has accumulated an impressive array of substantive findings and theoretical arguments that have enhanced our understanding of patterns of intergroup interaction in societies around the world. In the following sections we have organized the studies that represent the basic substantive and theoretical knowledge in the field around two major topics: (1) processes of ethnic group formation and boundary maintenance, and (2) social structure, societal processes, and ethnic boundaries. Our purpose is not to summarize the findings and arguments of the individual studies but to integrate them in terms of these two topics in order to provide a comprehensive overview of what we have learned about race and ethnicity in complex societies. Although most of the following discussion will focus on developments in the sociology of race and ethnic relations, many of the works considered represent important contributions of nonsociologists. However, before turning to this discussion, we should explain our use of the concept "ethnicity."

In an important study of ethnic relations, R. A. Schermerhorn defines an ethnic group "as a collectivity within a larger society having real or common ancestry, memories of a shared historical past, and a cultural focus on one or more symbolic elements defined as the epitome of their peoplehood" (1978, p. 12). Schermerhorn uses the term *ethnicity* to refer "to the fusion of many traits or components that belong to the nature of any ethnic group" (1978, p. 12). Ethnicity, therefore, is embodied in shared beliefs, norms, values, preferences, in-group memories, loyalties, and consciousness of kind. Depending on the ethnic group or situation, such traits vary in terms of their salience, importance, or strength. Although such traits can be altered independently, they tend to vary together, especially when there is a real or perceived threat to the unity or survival of the ethnic group, or when the need for in-group solidarity or collective security diminishes "under conditions of assured safety and/or acceptance" (1978, p. xv). Accordingly, ethnicity and its various components are "relative to time and place" (1978, p. xv).

In this chapter *ethnic group* and *ethnicity* are used as generic terms that incorporate the terms *racial group* and *race*. What distinguishes a racial ethnic group (or a racially defined ethnic group) from a nonracial ethnic group, then, is the inclusion of race as a part of common ancestry. Nonetheless, the definition of "ethnicity" is equally applicable to both groups.

Processes of Ethnic Group Formation and Boundary Maintenance

Group Formation and Ethnic Identity

A fundamental question in the study of intergroup relations is how ethnic identity arises, persists, and is altered. Recent research has documented a psychological proclivity for deep group attachments, a tendency for individuals to value members of their own group over others, regardless of interest. In a series of experiments on individuals' valuation of their group affiliations, for example, Henri Tajfel (1981) has demonstrated that even when assigned to groups with whom they have no face-to-face interaction, individuals will nonetheless demonstrate favoritism toward their assigned group. Regardless of purpose, shared interest with, knowledge of, or contact with the out-group members, individuals will consistently seek to increase the differences in rewards given to members of their own group and those given to others. They do this even when an increase in reward differences may produce a lower reward for their group. In short, this research suggests that the proclivity for invidious intergroup comparison and competition cannot be reduced to materialist factors (Billig, 1976, pp. 343-352; Tajfel, 1981).

In recent years some sociologists, attempting to explain the proclivity for invidious intergroup distinctions and competition, have begun to reassess the importance of human nature in understanding ethnicity (see, e.g., Gordon, 1978; van den Berghe, 1981). As one of the major contributors to this reassessment, Milton Gordon has advanced "a theory of human nature" that distinguishes hereditary factors from social influences, while simultaneously emphasizing "their mutual and constant interaction" (1978, p. 48). Gordon introduces concepts such as "overarching drive motivations," "cognitive capacities," and "emotional capacities" to emphasize the importance of the biological equipment of human needs; and concepts such as "aggression" and "motivation," subdivided into multiple types (e.g., instrumental cooperation, dependency-induced cooperation, authority-induced cooperation, forced-induced cooperation, and normative-induced cooperation) to clarify the patterns of behavior that are derived from the interaction of some elements of the biological equipment of needs with the social and cultural environment.

Gordon argues that because ethnicity, unlike economic class background, cannot "be shed by mobility," it "becomes incorporated into the self" (1978, p. 73). Accordingly, when a person defends the honor or welfare of his ethnic group, he is, in effect, defending himself. Thus the potential for ethnic conflict is always present because the human being is essentially a narcissistic, often aggressive, defender of self. However, it is important to emphasize that this basic biosocial predisposition is mediated both by interaction process variables and by societal variables (Gordon, 1978). Indeed, social, societal, and cultural variables, not biosocial predispositions, determine *variations* in ethnic conflict. Thus if human nature analysis has any real value in the field of race and ethnic relations it is not in enhancing explanations of the persistence, increase, or reduction of ethnic antagonisms and conflicts in particular situations, but in reminding scholars that because ethnic attachment are deeply rooted in biosocial predispositions, there

is an ever-present potential for ethnic or racial conflict in any multiethnic or multiracial society. Accordingly, the burden of *explaining variations* in ethnic intragroup and intergroup behavior will fall on theories that emphasize interaction-process variables, cultural variables, and societal variables.

Even if the question of variations in ethnic behavior is not raised, there is a question of whether the salience of ethnicity has to be explained in terms of human nature, especially if one considers a more sociological explanation of the strength of ethnic identity recently advanced by Stephen Cornell (1985). Cornell has explicated four potential bases of group affiliation: affinity, interest, institutions, and culture. Groups bound by affinity or sentiment are among the most permeable and transient since feelings may be quickly satisfied or diffused. Groups that develop out of a shared interest may last longer, but focus only on partial aspects of members' lives (and hence constitute communities of "limited liability"). Institutional groups are more durable because they are based on regular member contact and because they meet basic daily needs. They too, however, may be isolated in particular spheres of or moments in one's life (e.g., professions, schooling, churches). In contrast to each of these, groups that represent a community of culture "are most closely linked by their participation . . . in systems of meaning and attendant patterns of interaction and behavior which reflect distinctive paradigms of groupness, world views, or ways of being" (1985, p. 5). They therefore have far greater longevity than other groups. "Movement in and out of a community of culture is difficult because it involves putting on and taking off a system of meaning, patterns of customary behavior, a view of the world," states Cornell. "The act is a more vital and comprehensive one, often involving a profound redefinition of the self and its relations with the social environment. Such movement occurs regularly enough, but in general the membership of a community of culture is less volatile than that of other types of groups" (1985, p. 8).

The power of the ethnic community is perhaps evident from these analytic distinctions. The ethnic community evokes both affinal and cultural attachments. Because it is rooted in kinship ties (real or purported), ethnic identity appeals to the bonds of family, blood origin, descent; it promises membership in a community that transcends the particulars of time and space. The ethnic group constitutes a community of culture, but its resilience and power are variable, subject to the vicissitudes of social change (Banton, 1983, pp. 140-169; Isaacs, 1976; Mazuri, 1975). As in the family, so in ethnicity, the boundaries are not permanent. Without patterns of endogamy and some institutional base, ethnic attachments are likely to attenuate and ethnic groups are likely to assimilate. For individuals, the allegiance to ethnic identity, and for groups, the permeability of boundaries, depend in part on the extent to which interests are satisfied by group membership (Alba, 1985; Patterson, 1977). But they also depend on the extent to which cultural identity is encapsulated within the institutions that protect and reward group membership. Ethnic groups then persist to the extent they become composite communities, combining culture, affinity, institutional protection, and a shared interest (Cornell, 1985). But the cultural, institutional, and/or interest bases of ethnic boundaries may erode as dramatic social changes (migration, urbanization, industrialization, technological growth) alter the bases for shared values. We will turn to those processes, but must first seek to identify the underlying psychological, ideological, and behavioral bases that shape ethnic responses to processes of social change.

Psychological Aspects of Intergroup Boundaries

In its earliest incarnation as a field of specialization, scholars in the area of race and ethnic relations devoted a good deal of attention to the psychological and ideological aspects of intergroup relations, especially the development and decline of prejudice and racism. Our understanding of ethnic and racial boundary formation is rooted in this early work, so it deserves careful consideration.

Persistent ethnic stereotypes and prejudicial attitudes are one of the major factors in limiting intergroup contact and preserving ethnic boundaries. Seeking to interpret the virulence of anti-Semitism and racism in the 1940s and 1950s, which persisted despite patterns of group acculturation, social psychologists sought to apply psychoanalytic theories of individual-level behavior to groups, to locate prejudice and discrimination in subconscious processes, and to delineate the conditions under which these processes might be social as well as individual (Adorno et al., 1950; Allport, 1954; Allport and Kramer, 1946; Dollard, 1937; Dollard et al., 1939; Williams, 1944).

Psychoanalytic theory emphasizes the effects of early socialization on character formation; it posits that when the individual is frustrated in

efforts to secure a valued object or form a symbolic attachment, he or she will repress the inevitable resentment against those powerful individuals who block satisfaction. Repression of individual longing generates a generalized state of anxiety that can be alleviated only if the individual releases the mounting frustration. However, given the initial experience of denial and rejection by the powerful, the release becomes an act of aggression directed onto a vulnerable target. The prejudiced personality is more likely to be someone whose character development was distorted by rejecting parents, who experienced chronic anxiety as a result of these rejections, and who is therefore predisposed to see others as menacing. At its most extreme, individuals may develop an authoritarian personality, a complex of characteristics that predisposes them to reject out-groups and to display deep prejudice. The authoritarian personality is rigid in outlook, intolerant of ambiguity, superstitious, chronically anxious, defensive, and outwardly submissive but inwardly resentful (Adorno et al., 1950).

At the societal level, these theorists have argued that a similar situation occurs when a group experiences a significant period of frustration (due, for instance, to unemployment, status insecurity, or political powerlessness) followed by a sense of chronic anxiety. The diffused feeling of hostility is then displaced onto culturally sanctioned victims. At the macro level, when a society proscribes certain forms of behavior and members of that society fail to meet the stringent standards, they may project their failure onto other groups (e.g., the development of the stereotypes of the licentious slave may have been rooted in the masters' violation of the Protestant ethic of sexual self-restraint).

In the past several decades, psychodynamic theories have been subjected to a series of methodological and theoretical critiques that have emphasized that these theories are plagued by the difficulty of measuring early childhood experiences, fail to explain functional alternatives to ethnic and racial prejudice and hence to predict the likely targets of aggressive action, and are unable to explain social situations in which prejudice is "normal" and it is the psychologically "maladjusted" who are not prejudiced. Given the difficulties in relating micro-level psychodynamic processes to group attitudes, behaviors, and beliefs, contemporary social psychologists have tended to focus on cognitive and social learning approaches and to study prejudice as a defense of group position.

Social learning theories emphasize the importance of social norms and socialization in generating positive or negative affective responses to particular groups. Early socialization generates a set of psychological predispositions, a cognitive readiness to attach affect to symbols of group identity. The self develops in a societal context and each individual must constantly synthesize and resynthesize a coherent identity in changing social circumstances. Ethnic identity can facilitate this by providing a continuity, a link to early childhood as well as to one's future. Because part of early individuation is the process of identification and differentiation, ethnic boundaries can provide the basis for both a sense of commonality and of counteridentification (Harre, 1979; Weinrich, 1983, 1985).

Ethnic boundaries provide a standard for viewing the self as a member of a moral community; they partly create and reinforce psychological boundaries that connect one sense of a continuous self with ethnic identity (Myerhoff, 1978). A child from a dominant group who is reared in an ethnically conscious environment will tend to attach positive affect to the set of traits that are associated with his or her "own kind." A child from a dominant group who is reared in a prejudicial setting will tend to attach a negative affect to minority groups and will be open to believing social stereotypes about those groups. In a prejudiced society, the dominant group's evaluation of the minority group creates different perceptions or forms of identification among individual minority members. Psychologists regularly document a process of "part identification" by members of pariah or socially despised group with members of the socially respected groups. This process of ambivalent identification generates more complex ethnic boundaries: Sometimes it produces a drive to abandon one's origins and seek to assimilate; at other times it may fuel a complete rejection of the "respected" dominant group culture (Horowitz, 1985, pp. 166-184; Weinrich, 1983).

Psychological studies of prejudice do not provide clues as to which of these two responses is likely to occur under certain situations. However, sociological studies of race and ethnic relations have advanced hypotheses stating that the attempt among certain members of a minority group to abandon their racial origin and seek to assimilate in the dominant culture is more likely to occur when a society is undergoing a process of deracialization—that is, when steps are being taken to eliminate artificial racial barriers to social mobility—whereas the move to reject the dominant culture and trumpet the culture of the minority or pariah group is far more likely to occur in a rigid racially stratified society that is experiencing increasing racial intolerance (van den Berghe, 1967; Wilson, 1976, 1987). If empirical research is to shed some light on this issue, attention will have to be directed to the different conditions that are likely to influence individual decisions, attitudes, and perceptions of opportunity—conditions that not only include individual and group variables but cultural and structural variables as well. It would be especially important to distinguish between the concepts of "prejudice" and "racism" when these conditions are identified and specified.

Prejudice refers to the attitudinal dimension of intergroup relations, to the process of stereotyping and aversion that may persist even in the face of countervailing evidence. Racism is a more complex belief system that prescribes and legitimates a minority group's or an out-group's subordination by claiming that the group is either biogenetically or culturally inferior. From our perspective, there are two components to racism that are not present in prejudice: an ideology that justifies social avoidance and domination by reference to the "unalterable" characteristics of particular groups and a set of norms that prescribes differential treatment for these groups. Whereas prejudice is an attitude held by an individual, racism is an ideology of exploitation and is therefore equated with a society's culture. Even if prejudice is an attribute characteristic of most members of a society, "its focus, nonetheless, remains the individual and it is not analyzed in terms of institutional processes but in terms of the psychological processes of categorization, displacement, and rationalization" (Noel, 1972, p. 159). Accordingly, although prejudice is likely to flourish in a racist culture, a racist culture is not a prerequisite or necessary condition for the development, growth, spread, or enhancement of prejudice. Regardless of the existence of racism, a sufficient basis for the existence of prejudice may exist if the competition for scarce resources in a society takes place along racial group lines. As Noel has so vividly put it:

An individual can be described as prejudiced or racist—or both; but a culture can only be described as racist. However, acceptance of a belief in inherent racial superiority—inferiority by some or even a majority of the members of the society is not sufficient to demonstrate the existence of an ideology of racism. Conversely, a society can be racist even if only a minority of its members are racist. Racism is not an aggregation of individual ideas; it is rather a distinct cultural orientation sustained and expressed by the society's basic institutions. A society is racist

—or more accurately, its structure is supported by a racist ideology—only if the idea of group superiority-inferiority is incorporated into the institutional structure. To the extent that the institutions of society convey the idea and function in accord with the assumption that ability is dependent upon race, the society is racist [1972, p. 159].

Because it is likely to be embodied in the norms of social institutions, racism is much more difficult to eradicate than prejudice (Frederickson, 1971; Rex, 1970; Wilson, 1976, pp. 32-34). Theorists posit that normal individuals will gradually relinquish prejudicial attitudes in situations where the dominant norms are egalitarian and where intergroup contact is cooperative and noncompetitive (Allport, 1954; Smith, 1981). However, even among groups that had been cooperative or on friendly terms, sustained competition can foster antagonistic feelings (Sherif and Sherif, 1953). Does this mean that ethnic and racial boundaries will dissipate only under conditions of cooperation? Do changes in institutional support for racial bias help erode prejudice? These questions have been a major focus of social psychological work in the last several decades.

Most of what we know is based on studies of the impact of racial desegregation on prejudicial attitudes. Although hundreds of papers have been published on the thesis that equal-status contact reduces prejudices, until recently, few studies have been rigorous enough to yield major conclusions (for a review, see McConahy, 1976). However, recent work does seem to provide qualified support for the view that equal-status contact reduces prejudices. Some studies indicate that the disconfirmation of prejudicial beliefs following equal-status contact between ethnic groups will occur only where explicit efforts are made to challenge those beliefs (Cohen, 1984). Others indicate that interracial work groups—even without direct challenge to prior prejudices—will increase tolerance. Experimental studies document a reduction of prejudice in situations where students work together on class projects, are involved in peer tutoring, or play sports together (Cohen, 1984; DeVries, Edwards, and Slavin, 1978; Patchen et al., 1977; Rogers et al., 1984; Slavin and Madden, 1979). However, research by Cook (1984) suggests that although cooperative and equal-status contacts will reduce prejudice and hostility in a particular setting, individuals do not necessarily alter their attitudes outside that setting.

Some analysts have argued that even in situations of declining intergroup competition for valued resources, traditional negative views of the out-group may persist but may be expressed in a language that does not clash with new or contemporary social norms. For example, descriptions of the out-group may no longer include categorical statements about biogenetic or cultural inferiority but rather may focus on the "illegitimate" demands for changes in the racial status quo or on the group's violation of widely shared social values.

The research in this area is sparse and does not definitively establish the extent to which shifts in the verbally and publicly expressed views of in-group members toward the out-group are influenced by more liberal social norms. However, there is some research that could be interpreted as suggesting a connection between individual beliefs and the expression of negative views toward the out-group in a socially acceptable language. For example, Kluegel and Smith (1984) and Sears and Allen (1984) have found a high correlation between expressions of opposition to public policies that are perceived to favor blacks (views that are no longer socially acceptable) and explanations of social inequality that emphasize individual deficiencies (views that are socially acceptable). However, much more research is needed to establish clearly the relationship between social norms, expressions of ethnic/racial feelings, and actual beliefs.

Any theory of ethnic and race relations must recognize that ethnically related preferences and prejudices are never wholly rational. They are inextricably connected to the formation and development of identity and to conceptions and meanings given to one's existence. As such, they are loaded with moral power. It is clear that the cognitive element plays a complex role in the dynamics of individual and group attitudes, one that is not yet well comprehended.

Instrumental Explanations of Ethnic Boundaries

In the last several decades, some sociologists have sought to refine our understanding of ethnic and racial boundaries by introducing rational choice or instrumentalist assumptions into models of intergroup behavior. Building on the work of Mancur Olsen in economics (1965) and exchange theorists in sociology (Homans, 1961, 1962; Blau, 1964), this approach assumes that members of ethnic groups behave like all rational individuals and seek to maximize their social advantages in particular situations (Banton, 1983; Barth, 1969; Blalock, 1967; Blalock and Wilken, 1979; Hechter, 1982; Wilson, 1976). If individuals follow a logic of rationality, calculating the costs and benefits of efforts to realize their preferences, then we can predict patterns of ethnic group formation and dissolution. Assimilation is the result of accumulated individual choices based on the perceived benefits of abandoning group identities and cultural attributes. One type of assimilation, based on the individual choice to alter ethnic attachment (e.g., intermarriage, conversion), is a form of population exchange that does not necessarily threaten ethnic or racial categories. The attenuation of group boundaries—a weakening in the distinction between groups—is more important to intergroup relations. This form of assimilation will occur when members of several groups perceive greater advantages in individual, not group, competition. Similarly, ethnic boundaries will be preserved when it appears that greater advantage can be attained through group identification.

Although members of one group may seek to assimilate and abandon their group identities and cultural attributes, ethnic boundaries will persist if a more powerful group attaches importance to categorical ethnic distinctions. We do not fully understand the conditions that give rise to different individual and group assessments of the importance of ethnic boundaries, but these conditions are sufficiently complex to cast doubt on purely rational choice or instrumentalist explanation of the development, persistence, or attenuation of such boundaries. We make this argument for three specific reasons. There is, first, a problem with the very concept of "rational behavior" when applied to ethnic groups. Action to preserve a cultural attribute may be rational from one stance (institutional protection) but irrational from another (market competition). Because they assume a preeminent rationality in a social system, instrumentalists have not yet refined a model that can interpret contexts of competing "rationalities." In order to address the problem of competing rationalities, we need a substantive model of the relations among spheres of intergroup relations within a society, since some arenas may be characterized by segregated ethnic collectivities and others by intergroup competition (Smith, 1985, pp. 490-492). We also need to appreciate the power of ideologies in *defining* perceived interests that are not necessarily rational. The extensive research on racism indicates the determinative impact of ideology in fostering group preferences in situations where greater benefits would be secured from intergroup alliances (Rex, 1970; See, 1986a, 1986c; Wilson, 1980).

A second problem with the instrumental approach is the tendency to reduce group interests to the aggregate interests of individual members. As many have recognized, the interests of *some* members of the group or a minority of the group members are often defined as those of the group as a whole. In some situations this is mainly the result of the nonparticipating "free rider" who receives the benefits of any collective action without necessarily risking potential costs. In other situations it underscores the superior ability of class elites to define group interests in terms of their own concerns.

A third problem with the instrumentalist approach is that it inadequately considers racial and ethnic boundaries that are ascribed or denied, not asserted. Although some instrumentalists are sensitive to this problem by, for example, associating ethnic identification with the notion of inclusion (assertion of identity) and racial identification with that of exclusion (ascription of identity), they fail to spell out the different processes by which assertion or ascription of group identity takes place (Banton, 1983), including the process that creates a "double identification" whereby groups may assert a particular identity because they have been denied another (e.g., in the late 1960s many Afro-Americans trumpeted an ethnicity based on their African heritage because of their limited inclusion in Anglo-American culture).

Although some commentators present the analytic distinction between subjective and objective processes in group formation as an unbreachable chasm, most recognize that ethnic boundaries are psychological, ideological, and instrumental. As Pierre van den Berghe has so succinctly put it, "There can be no ethnicity (or race) without some conception and consciousness of a distinction between 'them' and 'us.' But these subjective perceptions do not develop at random; they crystallize around clusters of objective characteristics that become badges of inclusion or exclusion" (1978, p. xvii). In the following section we present a discussion of the social structures and developmental processes that shape these clusters or ethnic boundaries.

Social Structure, Societal Processes, and Ethnic Boundaries

Conditions of intergroup contact and structures of intergroup inequality that emerge from this contact are crucial to the development and persistence of ethnic and racial boundaries. Together, conditions of intergroup contact and structures of intergroup inequality determine group resources, differential interests, cultural and institutional infrastructure, and hence the likelihood of particular patterns of accommodation or assertion. Rational choice is easy to calculate in a symmetrical situation in which individuals can achieve a maximal advantage. But because such situations are rare, and even symmetrical exchanges will generate inequalities, the limits on free and equal bargaining are substantial. Indeed, in the field of race and ethnic relations, choices are almost invariably made in situations of inequality. Hence, the analytic task is to identify the structural conditions under which collective actions will be perceived as beneficial. The range of such situations can be organized into two model forms of ethnic stratification: (a) hierarchical or vertical systems in which resources are unequally distributed among ethnically identified groups or regions, for instance, the coercive slave system of plantations; ethnoregional colonial and internal colonial regimes; indentured and contract labor systems; sojourner and migrant labor; segregated dual labor markets; and (b) segmentary systems in which ethnic groups occupy specialized economic niches, for example, middlemen minorities and complementary ethnic group pluralism (Hechter, 1975). Although both forms of ethnic stratification have elements of differential power, the hierarchical division is more likely to be the product of force or coercion. In such situations there is a greater propensity among subordinate ethnic group members to challenge ethnic boundaries in order to redistribute social benefits and powers. In the case of segmentary systems, congregation in a certain occupational niche provides more of an incentive among subordinate group ethnics to preserve ethnic categories (Hechter, 1975, p. 131). In either case, there is a basis for subordinate ethnic group mobilization—but the calculation of costs and the kinds of resources available to generate such action will differ dramatically, depending on the conditions of intergroup contact, the economic class structure, and the nature of the state system.

Patterns of Intergroup Contact

The sequences of intergroup contact that are significant for race and ethnic relations are those that are likely to generate competition beyond individual market situations, to sharpen group boundaries, and to enhance cultural differences. The major patterns of contact are: annexation and conquest; colonization and frontier expan-

sion; involuntary and forced migration; and voluntary migration (Rex 1982; Schermerhorn, 1978; See, 1986c).

Annexation and conquest refer to the efforts to incorporate contiguous territories either by force or by purchase. Invasions of territory by any "foreign" group is likely to reinforce boundary consciousness. The group that is invaded may seek to protect its territory by developing a military and political infrastructure, adopting myths of origin and symbols and rituals of solidarity to mobilize the population. Similarly, invaders or frontier migrants will seek to consolidate their access to and control over the territory through developing structures of group protection. They will legitimate their invasions with ideological claims about prior rights. The early invasion of North America exemplifies this process as dispossession of the land of indigenes was rationalized both by claims about their savagery and by the doctrine of vacuum docilium, which asserted that land that had not been cultivated was open to settlement. Annexation and conquest need not entail settlement; the dominant group may maintain merely a military presence or it may seek indigenes to administer a region on behalf of the conquerors (as in the Soviet invasion and conquest of Afghanistan). In any case, the very process of annexation is likely to generate or underscore ethnic boundaries.

Colonization and frontier expansion is the control of a specific territory by a nonindigenous group through the process of settlement. Colonies of limited settlement may result from early warfare, conquest, and annexation as the metropole seeks to sustain its administrative control over a particular region. Typical of such colonization was the settlement of Ireland in the thirteenth century, of the Cape of South Africa by the Dutch East Indies Company in the mid-seventeenth century, and of French Canada in the sixteenth and seventeenth centuries. The primary interest in such limited colonies tends to be control of territory and resources—not labor. In such circumstances there may be severe conflicts with the indigenes leading to displacement or decimation of the native population. But settlers may also develop amicable relations of trade with the natives, intermarry, and adopt their language and customs. Or they may tolerate very separate spheres, encouraging complementary trade relations but also encouraging social segregation. All three patterns (severe conflicts, amicable relations, toleration of separate spheres) occurred in the relation between Irish and English outside the Pale in early colonial Ireland, between the Khoikhoi and the Boers in South Africa, and between French fur trappers and Indians in early Canada.

More extensive settlement colonies aim to control territory for extraction of resources, exploitation of labor, market of surplus, and development of metropolitan markets. Such colonies will seek to draw the indigenous population into the economy as indentured servants, tenants or workers on commercial farms, and wage labor in mining or other extractive and industrial concerns. Such colonies not only compete for land usage; they disrupt traditional divisions of labor and political structures. The political infrastructure develops to protect the interests of the colonial regime. Indigenes are hired as low-level functionaries or as collaborators in governance, but clear status lines are drawn restricting their mobility. There is, most evident here, a strong material base for a hierarchical division of labor to preserve and promote the process of colonization. Pockets of the economy are preserved as "native rights," thus generating more segmentary ethnic labor. India and South Africa in the eighteenth century constitute classic cases of limited colonial settlement.

As the number of colonists increase and access to resources constricts, colonies begin a process of frontier expansion into the interior that may produce greater competition with the indigenous population. In such a situation, there is increased independence from the metropole. Settlers seek to develop the economy and polity of the colony and begin to see themselves as having distinctive interests and identities. A "national identity" develops among the colonialists, legitimating their articulation of independence from the metropole and their right to control expanding territory. More comprehensive racial and national ideologies develop, such as claims about "the white man's burden," the differential capacities of the "races," and the legitimacy of cultural and social pluralism. This was evident in the settlement and expansion of North America in the eighteenth century, in the Afrikaaner ethnic mobilization in the Boer Republics of the nineteenth century, and in the European colonies of Asia and Africa in the nineteenth and twentieth centuries.

Forced migration (e.g., slave transfers, indentured and contract labor), a third type of intergroup sequence, frequently results from colonial situations where the native population is small or cannot be subdued to labor on behalf of the settlers. Colonists import labor from other colonies or from the metropole; such migrants have limited rights and are subordinated through coercive control, political exclusion, and economic dependence. The importation of slaves to the antebellum American South and to the Caribbean are classic examples; so too was the importation of Irish slave labor to the Americas, of indentured Indians to the South African Natal, and of Chinese to Malaysia. But forced migration can also be a product of expulsion movements in which indigenes are forced to new territories. Stripped of their resources, such refugees must preserve their ethnic identities in situations of powerlessness. Jacksonian America's "Indian Removal" and forced westward movement is a classic example.

Finally, *voluntary migration* refers to the movement of numerically smaller groups to a larger society. Generally labor transfers generated by changing economic needs and opportunities, voluntary migration situations can range from the admission of sojourners or temporary workers to receipts of permanent immigrants. Of the four types of ethnic contact, voluntary migration represents a situation of greatest freedom of choice and movement of minority ethnic groups. Hence the degree of domination is not as great as in situations involving forced migration, colonization and frontier expansion, and annexation—situations that are more closely associated with hierarchial systems of ethnic stratification. Although voluntary migration can also lead to hierarchical systems of ethnic stratification, "especially in racially ordered societies where the immigrant group finds itself in direct competition with certain segments of the dominant group for scarce goods and positions" (Wilson, 1976, p. 21), insofar as there is an element of voluntarism, migrants are likely to be receptive to host cultures or to find an occupational niche that does not compete with host labor (Lieberson, 1980). In other words, voluntary migration is more closely associated with segmentary systems of ethnic stratification. However, the range of voluntary migration is vast and, to the extent there is resource competition (for land, jobs, schooling, housing), the potential for ethnic conflict increases.

These sequences of intergroup contact can overlap and a particular sequence does not necessarily *fix* ethnic boundaries. Rather, even when a vertical or segmentary system of stratification is established, it is likely to be altered under conditions of social change. We turn now to the effects of economic and state structures on these patterns; we will then examine the impact of modernization processes.

Economic Organization, Class Process, and the Cultural Division of Labor

Perhaps no issue is more central to the field of intergroup relations than the relationship between economic organization and the cultural division of labor (i.e., the stratification of groups into occupations according to race or ethnicity). This complex relationship has been the focus of a good deal of theoretical attention, especially among those writers who have attempted to explain the important interplay between economic class stratification and the cultural division of labor. The most influential economic-based models represent different levels of explanation and include world-systems theory, internal-colonial theory, split labor-market theory, and middlemen-minority theory. Let us briefly discuss how these theoretical models have been applied to the relationship between class and ethnic stratification.

World-systems theory posits that cultural divisions of labor are inextricably connected to the historic growth and concentration of capitalism in the European core states and their expansion through the exploitation of labor and extraction of resources from colonized areas. Competition between core states and the trade barriers that ensued helped congeal national boundaries and obscured the shared class situations of workers and peasants. Colonization of peripheral areas facilitated a process of uneven global development in which the superexploitation of colonial regions and labor provided core states with the resources to solve internal problems of labor control and capital growth. Higher wages and higher-status jobs were preserved for members of the metropolitan labor force, who constituted an international labor aristocracy. Judicial and political structures (e.g., citizenship rights) reinforced these privileges. Since these divisions also reflected racial or ethnic differences, an ideology of racism developed to rationalize and promote this international system of stratification, legitimating the exploitation of natural resources in the peripheral regions and thereby providing a continuous supply of cheap labor to the regions of the core.

Industrial policies that resulted in the heavy extraction of natural resources from the periphery, land-use policies that limited the indigeneous population's access to land in the periphery, and labor-market policies that promoted either the use of workers from the periphery as contract laborers or the use of slave transfer from the periphery to the core regions as coerced labor all resulted in a steady stream of cheap labor migrants to the regions of the core, creating cultural divisions of labor that resembled those in the periphery.

Internal-colonial theory also focuses on the exploitation of economically dependent regions with ethnically distinct populations. However, it argues that this process can take place within core states as a result of state policies. Particular regions within the core may be explicitly underdeveloped (e.g., Ireland within Great Britain, Quebec within Canada; native American reservations in the United States). The division of labor that grows out of this process is both regional and ethnic, giving a political salience to ethnic markers and providing a basis for of ethnoregional politics (Hechter, 1975). Variations of this model have been applied to the development of inner-city ghetto areas where a racially identified surplus labor force is prevented from accumulating competitive resources through such mechanisms as exclusionary zoning, differential taxation, and residential discrimination (Blauner, 1972).

World-systems theory and internal-colonial theory rightly point to the significance of Western imperialism and capitalist development in shaping an international racial division of labor. However, neither can make adequate distinctions among peripheral regions to explain differential patterns of development. For example, some ethnoregions that fit the definition of "internal colonies" have become well developed economically (e.g., Scotland, Catalonia, Brittany). Furthermore, these models cannot explain ethnic and racial divisions that were drawn within particular states as a result of intergroup competition in noneconomic sectors (e.g., schooling, residental turf). Finally, these models completely ignore the ethnic division of labor in societies outside the orbit of Western expansion. One-third of the world's population lives in ethnically plural Communist states without a substantial Western colonial legacy. Accordingly, the failure of these models to address the social experiences of this segment of the world raises questions about the relative importance of different economic systems in determining patterns of intergroup interaction.

Split labor-market theory, in contradistinction to world-systems theory and internal-colonial theory, disputes the central proposition that ethnic and racial antagonisms are the product of capitalist or elite efforts to deflect class struggle. Edna Bonacich, the architect of the split labor-market model, argues that the processes of uneven development do create ethnically and racially distinguishable labor forces and that employers have the incentive to undermine the power of an indigenous proletariat by replacing higher priced with cheaper labor. But the split labor-market theory envisions ethnic boundaries to be the result of a three-way struggle between capital, indigenous high-priced labor, and an ethnically distinct low-wage labor force. If unconstrained, employers would ignore ethnic differences and hire the cheapest labor available. However, given the processes of uneven capitalist development, high-wage laborers tend to possess political resources (citizenship, solidarity, unions) that allow them to protect successfully their market position against the encroachment of low-wage labor through exclusionary movements, job segregation, and job protectionist policies (Bonacich, 1972). This model has been expanded to explain the reactive ethnicity of an indigenous petit bourgeoisie when it is displaced by larger corporate firms willing to employ ethnic labor (e.g., Protestants in postwar Ulster). It has also been applied to the protectionist response of American workers to the relocation of multinationals in areas of cheap labor overseas (Bonacich, 1972).

Critics note a number of limitations in the explanatory import of the split labor-market theory. It rests entirely on an argument about the price of labor and the ways in which employers seek to maximize profits. This simple cause-and-effect theory obscures the complex relationship among capital growth, the rationalization of labor, and the rate of profit. The model may only apply in situations where cheap labor is needed precisely because the rate of profit is low; hence it may not successfully explain situations of monopoly in which ethnic stratification persists (Wilson, 1980). Moreover, it applies *only* to labor-market situations, whereas much ethnic antagonism originates in rivalries over residential space, political turf, and symbols of group prestige (Budge and O'Leary, 1970; Katznelson, 1981). The real problem is that the conditions that are necessary for a split labor market to exist occur with less frequency in the late twentieth century. Certainly, we still find the use of migrant labor and ethnic occupational segregation; but with the growth of trade unions and expansion of monopoly capitalism, direct intergroup competition and displacement is infrequent (Wilson, 1980). Finally, it should also be pointed out that in a survey of postcolonial Asian and African ethnic conflicts, Donald Horowitz was able to locate only a single case that resulted from a split labor market (1985, p. 126).

Middleman-minority theory examines the role of those minorities that may foster both vertical and segmentary divisions of labor. Such minorities often serve as procurers of cheap ethnic labor (e.g., the use of immigrant labor or extended family labor in homogeneous ethnic shops), thereby fostering a split labor market by undercutting the indigenous work force. Or middlemen may occupy certain economic niches between consumers and producers as traders, retailers, and small shopkeepers. In either case, they are successful because they use ethnic institutions and networks (rotating credit associations, family labor) to lower business costs and to monopolize an economic niche. Since such practices invariably undercut business rivals or displace other workers, ethnic antagonisms ensue. Because the success of middlemen minorities is based on ethnic institutions, normal business and labor rivalries are articulated in racist/ethnocentric language. Middleman-minority theory has been used to explain the anti-Asian expulsion movement in California, the antagonisms directed against Korean small businesses in California, anti-Semitism in post-Weimar Germany, and the ethnic hostilities encountered by the Chinese in Mississippi (Bonacich, 1973, 1975; Bonacich and Modell, 1980; Light, 1972; Loewen, 1971). Unlike the other models, the middleman theory recognizes the important intervening role of cultural institutions in shaping ethnic divisions of labor. But this model does not deal with the extent to which middlemen may *restrict* intergroup antagonisms by limiting the number of ethnic differences in an occupation, thereby undercutting competition and ensuring a kind of complementary pluralism (e.g., the situation of Lebanese in West Africa and the Chaldeans in Detroit). Nor does it consider the extent to which such middlemen have consumer support because they can provide goods at cheaper costs (Horowitz, 1985). This model applies only in situations where there is direct economic competition—that is, in the early stages of ethnic segmentation. The ethnic antagonisms expressed at other stages may be more the result of a process of frustration/displacement, of competition over symbols of prestige, or of political clout.

It is important to stress that none of the four economic class-based models addresses the fact that associations between ethnicity and types of occupations can congeal and persist beyond their economic motivations. Ethnic boundaries may be generated by the use of ethnic institutions: schooling, religious training, rotating credit associations that provide members with both the resources and the inclination to adopt certain trades. Ascriptive group ties facilitate the use of kin networks to locate opportunities, to support (or suppress) occupational aspirations, and to develop and sustain businesses. Ethnically based craft associations and neighborhood networks help in preserving such monopolies, socializing a set of work expectations, and informing members about opportunities. Although exclusionary in some sense, these processes of segmented ethnic labor also reflect the voluntaristic components of ethnic associations—a fact that economic-class theories neglect. The social factors that support working with one's "own kind" can reinforce stereotypes about special group aptitudes and appropriate work for certain types of groups (Horowitz, 1985, pp. 108-111). The persistence of such ethnic occupational niches depends, in part, on the structure of the state and on the impact of processes of development on intergroup contact and economic opportunity.

State Structures and Group Interests

Because of its explicit concern with social cohesion, the state is a crucial determinant of ethnic boundaries and rivalries, and of resources and interests. As Daniel Bell argues, ethnicity is a significant factor in political allegiance precisely because it combines objective bases for cohesion (interest, culture, institutions) with a common symbolism and shared consciousness (1975, p. 165). But individuals do not automatically make political claims in terms of ethnic identity. Whether and how ethnic claims are made depends to a significant degree on the policy toward and methods of ethnic incorporation into the state. There are four political systems that either facilitate or limit ethnic/racial stratification and minority mobilization (Gordon, 1975).

(1) *Racist systems that deny political equality and civil rights to particular groups.* Racist systems are likely to define interests in primarily racial and ethnic terms and to limit ethnic mobilization to the dominant group that controls the coercive apparatus of the state.

(2) *Assimilationist systems that seek to dissolve all ethnic identities.* Assimilation systems prohibit ethnically based parties and policies and insist on common languages and institutions. Nonetheless, occupational segmentation can persist in such systems to the extent that there is freedom of association.

(3) *Liberal pluralist regimes that prohibit official recognition of or favoritism toward ethnic or racial groups.* Such systems will tolerate a cultural division of labor, voluntary ethnic associations and institutions, and ethnic politics as long as particular group interests are not incorporated into public policies and practices. These states will neither encourage nor foster ethnicity by supporting such institutions.

(4) *Corporate pluralist systems in which ethnic/racial groups retain a separate but equivalent legal status and in which political rewards are distributed on the basis of ethnic quotas or ethnoregional rights.* Such systems may have federal schemes to ensure equal outcomes along ethnic lines, will tolerate and support segregated institutions, and will adopt policies that seek to preserve ethnicity. A segmented division of labor is likely in such regimes, but cultural hierarchies will be resisted by state policies.

It is obvious that the first (racist system) and last (corporate pluralist systems) offer the greatest potential for political cleavage along ethnic lines. But any regime type may encourage ethnic politics. For example, the substantive policy of an assimilationist regime may encourage absorption into the culture of a dominant group, and what appears to be a nonethnic policy may actually be a policy geared toward the destruction of all cultures except that of the most dominant. Hence, assimilation itself may generate ethnic politics, particularly where such policies would undermine ethnic resources, interests, or culture (e.g., American policies toward Native Americans in the early twentieth century). A particular state may combine several of these policies over time. Nonetheless, the analytic distinction allows us to measure the *propensity* toward group politics and the likely form that intergroup competition may take. Moreover, the analytic distinction draws our attention to the way the political system may shape the impact of development processes on the state, fashion bureaucratic growth, expand welfare functions, and promote educational development. Nowhere is this more evident than in South Africa, whose state bureaucratic structures were developed to encapsulate and promote the ethnic hegemony of Afrikaanerdom. Any challenge to the racial order requires dismantling an extensive bureaucratic structure that has created a large number of jobs dependent on the administration of apartheid (Adam and Giliomee, 1979). In contrast, American bureaucratic expansion has occurred simultaneously with the development of corporate pluralist policies that seek to equalize opportunities for racial minorities. As a result, attacks on the bureaucracy that administers such policies *threaten* the interests of Afro-Americans whose economic status depends on public sector jobs and state-supported firms (Collins, 1983; Wilson, 1980). In short, state policy toward ethnicity and the structure of state institutions play a significant role in determining group interests, attitudes toward ethnic identity, and resources for ethnic mobilization.

Few states fit neatly into any of these four analytic categories. Over time, a regime may change from one predominant tendency to another. However, the ethnic division of labor and cultural hegemony generated in one era will shape the political salience of ethnicity even with regime change. Nowhere is this more evident than in the postcolonial world. To illustrate this and to indicate the crucial role of the state in preserving all of the dimensions of ethnicity we have examined, we will briefly consider the impact of colonial state forms on ethnic group relations and the difficulties such forms have generated for the development of modern pluralist states.

Colonial regimes represent a paradigm of plural societies in which ethnic and racial differences were preserved in segregated social institutions and the subject people were differentially incorporated into the economy and polity. The state constituted the primary means of controlling the indigenous populace, frequently through an indigenous elite that provided military and administrative support on behalf of metropolitan interests. Colonial policies created and reinforced ethnic boundaries in a number of ways: missionary education often focused on particular groups, thereby promoting different patterns of acculturation; politics of development often "protected" certain regions and groups from modernization, thereby encouraging uneven economic growth; immigration policies brought cheaper labor and middlemen into the colonial economies; states designated particular groups as agents of governance or military rule, sometimes reinforcing traditional ethnic hierarchies, sometimes creating new ones and displacing local elites (Fallers, 1973; Horowitz, 1985; Young, 1976). Racist ideologies and ethnic stereotypes shaped and buttressed colonial policies, reinforcing the ethnic differences in the colonial opportunity structure. Recruitment of particular tribes to colonial offices or migration of selected groups for wage labor, for example, would be justified by claims that the selected groups possessed certain ethnic skills. This congealed ethnic and occupational categories and stereotypes.

The anticolonial nationalist movements deliberately eschewed ethnic differences in their mobilization for independence. They embraced a rhetoric of universality and assimilation. But, if colonialism built on or distorted ethnocultural distinctions, the postcolonial regimes retain a legacy of this history. Descendants of colonial agents and immigrants favored by the administration had particular skills and resources at the time of independence and have been able, frequently, to monopolize positions in the independent state bureaucracy. In such cases, policies of assimilation are indeed evidence of an effort to continue an ethnic hegemony. Policies of schooling, bureaucratic recruitment, and state credit often reflect dominant group interests. Family and kin groups and ethnic associations have been able to elaborate an ethnic division of labor so specialized that government offices are frequently the monopoly of a particular group (Brass, 1985; Horowitz, 1985; Keyes, 1981; Nagata, 1975; Rothschild, 1981). All of this has intensified an ethnic, rather than an individual, basis for competition for state advantages.

A second legacy of colonialism is ideological. In nearly every colonial state, metropolitan dominance was legitimated by racist ideologies —claims about the capability of indigenes or of particular groups for self-governance. Policies of acculturation often encouraged selected colonial subjects to absorb metropolitan culture, language, and values and hence to absorb the invidious distinctions and dichotomous thinking that characterized imperial rule. Those subjects who sought to acculturate were both praised as "more civilized" and mocked as "imitators." The denigration of indigenous culture and mode of invidious evaluation that resulted has had complex effects. National movements frequently absorbed such comparative thinking, asserting the special mission of the "sons of the soil" and excluding those "recent" migrants who came during the colonial period. This is evident in the historical debates about the appropriate inclusion of Indians in antiapartheid movements in South Africa; and in past colonial expulsion movements against Asians in East Africa.

Postcolonial societies are not alone in such processes. Similar patterns are evident in the old metropoles (Rex, 1973). However much more comparative analysis is necessary, especially in noncapitalist states, if we are to cull out the basic structures and processes of the state in relation to ethnicity (Connor, 1984). Historic inclusion of groups in the polity, combined with the official policies, will determine the salience of ethnicity as a basis of mobilization. State structures both facilitate ethnic group boundaries and direct or constrain group politics. They may provide groups with the resources (e.g., bureaucratic access, communication networks, rights of assembly, legislative allies) to challenge and mobilize against particular policies. As Wilson has stated, the direction and form of ethnic politics is constrained by "a group's belief regarding its ability or inability to produce change . . . based on perceptions of both its own relative power resources and the magnitude of the problem to be solved" (1976, p. 49). But neither these beliefs nor the power resources are fixed. We now turn to the development processes that can alter group interests, resources, and competition.

Developmental Processes and Ethnic Mobilization

Classical social theorists assumed that modernization processes (industrialization, more complex forms of social organization, urbanization, bureaucratic rationalization, secularization) would erode traditional communities and bases of ethnic group affiliation (Alford, 1963; Lipset and Rokkan, 1967; Nairn, 1977). Continued ethnic attachment constitutes the atavistic responses to the temporary alienation that results from the dislocating effects of modernization on one's identity. Ethnic activism, from this perspective, occurs when the forces of assimilation (common schooling, language, familiarity with modern values) do not proceed as quickly as the processes of social change (Apter, 1963; Deutsch, 1969; Eisenstadt, 1966; Smelser, 1968). This theory of development as a trajectory simplifies the myriad ways in which modernization processes foster ethnic allegiance, competition for resources, and political activism. Drawing from studies of development and race, we have identified six interlocking developmental processes that encourage ethnic boundaries and politics: industrialization, urbanization, multinational organization, technological growth, state expansion, and dissemination of principles of self-determination (Nagel and Olzak, 1982; See, 1986a, 1986c; Wilson, 1973).

On the face of it, industrialization, with its ethos of rationality, contractually based relations, impersonal market rules, and need for free labor mobility, should facilitate individualistic relations of production and exchange and undermine traditional racial orders. Extensive research, however, indicates that there is no such inevitable effect. In the early stages of indus-

trialization, firms frequently adhere to traditional racial norms—sometimes because of a split labor market, sometimes because of consumer demands. As industrialization expands, groups organize in ethnically exclusive associations to monopolize new occupational sectors, or employers may seek to break up former monopolies in order to decrease production costs. Both patterns increase the level of direct competition between groups and foster ethnopolitical antagonisms and efforts to develop or reconstitute a racial division of labor (Blumer, 1965; Wilson, 1976, pp. 60-64). Moreover, once established, racial stratification may persist without deliberate intent if industrial firms are located in areas that happen to be populated by a particular racial/ethnic group.

Urbanization has an even more substantial effect on ethnic conflict. Migrants from rural areas may cluster in particular neighborhoods where traditional networks and ethnic associations persist. Or residential competition may lead to efforts at segregation and ghettoization. Urbanization also shifts the resources available; neighborhood concentrations provide the numbers and physical proximity needed to develop viable minority institutions and organizations. They constitute potential voting blocs and a terrain on which a sense of solidarity, strength, and invulnerability can grow. Metropolitan growth facilitates this process even more, generating an ethnic or racial mosaic in which particular groups occupy distinct jurisdictions and erect boundaries to preserve their "own" turf (zoning regulations, housing covenants, discrimination in financing). Such patterns of segregation can replicate forms of vertical stratification over a spatial area, especially if—as in the United States—there is a correlation between residential and industrial decentralization (Wilson, 1980).

When industrialization and urbanization combine with modern mass communication, there is a multiplier effect. Some means of communication is essential to the development of ethnic identities and ideologies. Previously isolated groups may come into contact with each other through communication systems. Radio and television, especially with satellite communication, provide a potent media of mobilization: an arena for documenting group grievances, undermining isolation, providing an audience for persuasion and support. Ethnic leaders can propagandize, appealing within and across group boundaries. Evidence of parallel success can be illustrated, demonstrating the benefits of ethnic activism. Although technology does encourage a standardization of culture, it can also provide information about relative group position, disseminate ideologies of group rights, and spread information about successful mobilization elsewhere. The potency of the television camera as a resource was evident in the United States' Civil Rights movement and was even more apparent in South Africa's state control over mass communication, especially during recent periods of political insurgency.

Expansion of the state sector introduces new arenas for intergroup competition and new resources for mobilization. State builders may encourage the integration of ethnically distinct groups in order to consolidate territorial interests. A growing administrative bureaucracy, access to the benefits of public employment and social services, state involvement in fiscal and industrial growth, financial and labor regulations, and welfare make group access to political power crucial. All require some distributive policy and a basis for making group claims. Redistributive policies, state guarantees of ethnoregional claims, and affirmative-action regulations emphasize ascriptive boundaries over other potential bases of identification and encourage group mobilization. Hence, they constitute both resources and arenas for conflict. State development can also underscore the connection between cultural identity and individual interest. Certainly where language and religious differences exist, the potential arenas of conflict and competition (schools, courts, legislature, bureaucracies) escalate (Nagel and Olzak, 1982; See, 1986c).

Multinational corporations and supranational organizations can alter a cultural division of labor and resources for group competition. Multinational corporations, for example, may undermine local capital by bringing in their "own" nationals, displacing local firms, and generating economic antagonisms. Alternatively, they may provide occupational niches by hiring particular ethnic members for middlemen positions as local management for advertising and public relations. Supranational organizations can provide allies and publicity for previously isolated groups with grievances or disrupt ethnically based patronage systems through international aid requirements. In short, the processes of modernization can have precisely the opposite effect to that hypothesized by class theory—they can foster ethnic boundaries, disrupt traditional power relations, and provide new resources that facilitate intergroup competition.

Not all processes of change are material. The dissemination of principles of self-determination, of the right of peoples to self-governance have been broadly disseminated by supranational organizations. When states acknowledge such principles, they may activate and legitimate ethnic group demands. More specifically, such principles not only undermine deterministic racial ideologies, they also facilitate group-based claims by defining ethnonations as a legitimate people. Appeals can be made linking individual grievances to these values and to traditional ethnic norms thereby providing an integrative ideology in which numerous grievances and varying interests can be subsumed under the mantle of the nation (Connor, 1972; See, 1986c).

If all of these processes facilitate ethnic claims, however, they do not explain the patterns of ethnic politics. Studies of ethnic movements indicate that patterns of mobilization can be predicted only through an analysis of the sociohistorical context under conditions of social change. However, there are important intermediate variables that contribute to the direction of group action. Specifically, tactics, strategies, and demands will be shaped by the restrictiveness of the political regime, the number of potential allies, the institutional infrastructure of the minority community, and the influence of minority leaders. In a racially restrictive environment (high vertical stratification, a racist regime, few allies, few viable organizations), a subordinate racial group is likely to avoid those direct confrontations likely to invite coercive responses. In such a case, apparent accommodation, appeals to external audiences, use of the "rules of the system," and documentation of injustices are more likely patterns. However, as new resources become available, minority political entrepreneurs will undertake more direct and focused challenges.

Without extensive institutional networks, individuals are likely to interpret their situations in highly localized ways. Ethnic institutions and kinship networks provide a base for organizing and a structure of incentives for participating in group action. Regular interaction takes place within such associations and makes them an essential base for recruiting support, directing group action, and overcoming the "free rider" problem (Gamson, 1975, pp. 66-71; McAdam, 1982, pp. 44-47; Levi and Hechter, 1985; Wilson, 1976, pp. 63-64). A crucial role in channeling political action in an ethnic direction is played by "cultural entrepreneurs" who seek to interpret grievances in group terms. These leaders seek to forge a change in consciousness by emphasizing the low benefits of individual action and the advantage of group solidarity. Ideologies emphasizing a unique group history and culture, group responsibilities and rights, and the injustice of present arrangements evoke ethnic solidarity and outgroup hostility. Once again, we should stress the potency of ethnicity as a basis for such networking: Rooted in family and kinship, there is a "natural" incentive for participation in the ethnic polity.

To summarize, ethnic politics are most likely to congeal in the context of socioeconomic changes that weaken a traditional cultural division of labor, expand group political opportunity, and foster a climate for the growth of ethnic institutions and organizations. Leaders will draw on the myths of group history and ideologies of self-determination to define the situation as unjust and as requiring group-based action. The particular direction of the challenge will depend upon the relative group resources, areas of intergroup competition, and dominant ideologies of group rights.

Conclusion: Race and Ethnic Relations and Societal Organization

The preceding discussion of the diverse theories of and approaches to the study of ethnic boundaries reflects one of the major problems in the field of race and ethnic relations—the lack of a single comprehensive framework to integrate these disparate theories and approaches. It would be ideal if a general theory of ethnic relations were available not only to explain the emergence of ethnic stratification in general but also to account for both the development of different forms of ethnic stratification, in either the same society on in different societies, and the persistence of or changes in these forms over time. For example, ethnic stratification represented by employment segregation, supported by dominant group workers to control or eliminate economic competition from minority group workers, is substantially different from ethnic stratification embodied in the exploitation of the labor of minority group workers by the business and management class of the dominant group. This fact is often obscured in theoretical discussions of race and ethnic relations because of a tendency to discuss issues in terms of "dominant group" versus "subordinate group" or "majority" versus "minority."

It is important to underline that different types of ethnic stratification are not only structured by different arrangements of the economy and the polity, they are also shaped by the participants within the intergroup arena. In order to explain fully the ultimate form of ethnic stratification in a given society, it is necessary to consider the ways in which different segments of the dominant group interact with different segments of the subordinate group, especially in more industrialized societies with their elaborate class structures and complex divisions of labor.

It is true, as our previous discussion reveals, that economic-class theories of ethnic stratification do discuss variations in intraethnic group behavior. However, they tend to focus solely on the ethnic antagonisms that are tied to basic economic arrangements and therefore fail to address either the politically based aspects of ethnic conflicts (emphasized in the writings of plural society analysts) or the strength of ethnic differentiation, which may have been grounded in economic matters but which have become firmly institutionalized and persist in educational institutions, residential areas, or other parts of the social system. Indeed, factors that contribute to the persistence of ethnic stratification in different societies are less understood than factors that contribute to the emergence of and changes in ethnic stratification.

There has been some work on the role of value consensus in maintaining ethnic boundaries (Shibutani and Kwan, 1965; Schermerhorn, 1978). However, as Barth and Noel have pointed out, complex multiracial or multiethnic societies groups are so heavily interdependent that they develop mutual commitments to the maintenance of order, commitments that discourage radical or disruptive social change and encourage social systems to "be receptive to modifications to assure that they will not be destroyed by their own rigidity in the face of internal contradictions and environmental changes" (1972, pp. 340-341). In other words, the existence of interdependent racial and ethnic groups tends to give rise to either social stability or an ordered process of change that does not disrupt the social system. Increased role differentiation and specialization have forced disparate ethnic groups to cooperate "to achieve a variety of goals which they cannot achieve alone" (1972, p. 340).

However, as Morris Janowitz has argued, despite these interdependent groups, the capacity of a social system to achieve self-regulation is decreasing in modern industrial society because political institutions are finding it increasingly difficult to mediate conflicting group interests and resolve economic and social conflict. He states:

The focal point of disarticulation are two-fold. One set rests within and between the bureaucratic hierarchies—industrial and service—in which labor violence has been replaced to a large extent by the adversary model. The other nexus of disarticulation results from increased separation of place of work and community of residence; this serves to fragment social and political relations. The result is hardly the emergence of a population of "isolated" persons and households but, rather, a complex of ordered social groups with striking primary group similarities [1978, p. 548].

If this analysis is applicable to the problems of race and ethnicity, particularly in recent periods with the sharp increase in ethnic antagonisms around the world (Patterson, 1977), it suggests that a study of the persistence of or changes in racial or ethnic stratification would of necessity be part of a larger investigation of the social system. It may be, as one author has already argued, that the field of race and ethnic relations has "little claim for autonomous theoretical status" (van den Berghe, 1978, p. 6); and that a comprehensive framework needed to integrate the disparate approaches and theories discussed in the previous sections would, in the final analysis, be a theory of societal organization that could explain different patterns of race and ethnic relations.

In other words, problems associated with race or ethnicity would be related to the broader issues of societal organization—"the working arrangements of society, including those that have emanated from previous arrangements, that specifically involve processes of ordering relations and action with respect to given social ends, and that represent the material outcome of those processes" (Wilson, 1987, p. 133). For example, an analysis of changes in the pattern of race and ethnic relations would have to consider the effects of the increased separation of place of work and place of residence. And, as suggested by the economic-based theories of ethnic boundaries, an analysis of changes in economic organization, including shifts in labor-management relations, may be necessary before we can fully grasp changes in the intergroup arena.

Moreover, it is important to recognize that significant changes in *intragroup* behavior and experience may accompany changes in the larger society. A consideration of intragroup behavior is important because in modern industrial society the economic class position of subordinate ethnic group members determines in large measure their perception and definition of the problems of racial or ethnic inequality, the solutions they propose and support to eliminate the problems, and their selection and mobilization of resources to address the problems. Moreover, the benefits that individual subordinate ethnic group members receive from changes in a society's ethnic or racial policies also tend to be related to their economic class position (Wilson, 1980, 1987).

In summary, to study the problems of race and ethnicity in terms of societal organization is to recognize that the institutional processes of ordering actions and relations in terms of given social ends impose constraints on racial and ethnic group interaction whereby intergroup relations are structured, antagonisms are channeled, and group access to rewards and privileges is differentiated. As these processes undergo change, they bring about changes not only in patterns of intergroup interaction but in the differences in intragroup experiences as well.

REFERENCES

Alford, Robert. 1963. *Party and Society: The Anglo-American Democracies*. Chicago: Rand McNally.

Adam, Heribert and Hermann Giliomee. 1979. *Ethnic Power Mobilized: Can South Africa Change?*. New Haven, CT: Yale University Press.

Adorno, Theodore W., Else Frenckel-Brenswick, D. J. Levinson, and R. N. Sanford. 1950. *The Authoritarian Personality*. New York: Harper.

Alba, Richard D. 1985. "The Twilight of Ethnicity among Americans of European Ancestry: The Case of Italians." *Ethnic and Racial Studies* 8:134-157.

Allport, Gordon. 1954. *The Nature of Prejudice*. Reading, MA: Addison-Wesley.

———— and B. M. Kramer. 1946. "Some Roots of Prejudice." *Journal of Psychology* 22:9-39.

Apter, David. 1963. "Political Religion in the New Nations." Pp. 15-46 in *Old Societies and New States*, edited by Clifford Geertz. New York: Free Press.

Banton, Michael. 1983. *Racial and Ethnic Competition*. Cambridge, England: Cambridge University Press.

Barth, Ernest A.T. and Donald L. Noel. 1972. "Conceptual Frameworks for the Analysis of Race Relations: An Evaluation." *Social Forces* 50: 333-348.

Barth, Frederick, ed. 1969. *Ethnic Groups and Boundaries*. Boston: Little, Brown.

Bell, Daniel. 1975. "Ethnicity and Social Change." Pp. 141-176 in *Ethnicity: Theory and Experience*, edited by Nathan Glazer and Daniel

Patrick Moynihan. Cambridge, MA: Harvard University Press.

Beer, William R. 1980. *The Unexpected Rebellion: Ethnic Activism in Contemporary France*. New York: Columbia University Press.

Billig, Michael. 1976. *Social Psychology and Intergroup Relations*. New York: Academic Press.

Blalock, Hubert M. 1967. *Toward a Theory of Minority Group Relations*. New York: John Wiley.

———— and Paul I. Wilken. 1979. *Intergroup Processes: A Micro-Macro Approach*. New York: Free Press.

Blau, Peter M. 1964. *Exchange and Power in Social Life*. New York: John Wiley.

Blauner, Robert. 1972. *Racial Oppression in America*. New York: Harper & Row.

Blumer, Herbert. 1965. "Industrialization and Race Relations." Pp. 200-253 in *Industrialization and Race Relations*, edited by Guy Hunter. London: Oxford University Press.

Bonacich, Edna. 1972. "A Theory of Ethnic Antagonism: The Split Labor Market." *American Sociological Review* 37:547-559.

———— 1973. "A Theory of Middlemen Minorities." *American Sociological Review* 38:583-594.

———— 1975. "Small Business and Japanese American Ethnic Solidarity." *Amerasian Journal* 3: 96-112.

———— 1979. "The Past, Present and Future of Split Labor Market Theory." Pp. 17-54 in *Research in Race and Ethnic Relations*, edited by Cora Marrett and Cheryl Leggon. Greenwich, CT: JAI.

———— and John Modell. 1980. *The Economic Basis of Ethnic Solidarity: Small Business in the Japanese American Community*. Berkeley: University of California Press.

Brass, Paul, ed. 1985. *Ethnic Groups and the State*. Totowa, NJ: Barnes & Noble.

Budge, Ian and Cornelius O'Leary. 1970. *Belfast: Approach to Crisis. A Study of Belfast Politics, 1630-1970*. New York: Macmillan.

Campbell, Angus and Howard Schuman. 1968. *Racial Attitudes in Fifteen American Cities*. National Advisory Commission on Civil Disorders, Supplemental Studies. Washington, DC: Government Printing Office.

Cohen, Elizabeth G. 1984. "The Desegregated School: Problems in Status and Interethnic Climate." Pp. 77-96 in *Groups in Contact: The Psychology of School Desegregation*, edited by Norman Miller and Marilyn Brewer. New York: Academic Press.

Coleman, James S. 1969. *Nigeria: Background to Nationalism*. Berkeley: University of California Press.

Collins, Sharon. 1983. "The Making of the Black Middle Class." *Social Problems* 30:369-382.

Connor, Walker. 1972. "Nation Building or Nation-Destroying?" *World Politics* 24:319-355.

———— 1984. *The National Question in Marxist and Leninist Theory and Strategy*. Princeton, NJ: Princeton University Press.

Cook, Stuart W. 1984. "Cooperative Interaction in Multiethnic Contexts." Pp. 156-186 in *Groups in Contact: The Psychology of School Desegregation*, edited by Norman Miller and Marilyn Brewer. New York: Academic Press.

Cornell, Steven. 1985. "Communities of Culture, Communities of Interest: On the Variable Nature of Ethnic Groups." Paper presented at the Conference on Ethnic Labels/Signs of Class, Center for Study of Industrial Societies, University of Chicago, October.

Deutsch, Karl. 1969. *Nationalism and Its Alternatives*. New York: Knopf.

DeVries, D. L., K. J. Edwards, and R. E. Slavin. 1978 "Biracial Learning Teams and Race Relations in the Classroom." *Journal of Educational Psychology* 70:356-372.

Dollard, John. 1937. *Caste and Class in a Southern Town*. New York: Social Science Research Council.

————, Leonard Doob, N. E. Miller, O. H. Mowrer, and R. R. Sears. 1939. *Frustration and Aggression*. New Haven, CT: Yale University Press.

Duncan, Otis Dudley and Beverly Duncan. 1955. "A Methodological Analysis of Segregation Indexes." *American Sociological Review* 20:210-217.

Eisenstadt, S. N. 1966. *Modernization: Protest and Change*. Englewood Cliffs, NJ: Prentice-Hall.

Fallers, Lloyd. 1973. *Inequality: Social Stratification Revisited*. Chicago: University of Chicago Press.

Frederickson, George M. 1971. "Toward a Social Interpretation of the Development of American Racism." In *Key Issues in the Afro-American Experience*, edited by Nathan Huggins et al. New York: Harcourt, Brace, Jovanovich.

———— 1981. *White Supremacy: A Comparative Study in American and South African History*. New York: Oxford University Press.

Gamson, Ted. 1975. *The Strategy of Social Protest*. Homewood, IL: Dorsey Press.

Gordon, Milton. 1975. "Toward a General Theory of Racial and Ethnic Group Relations." In *Ethnicity: Theory and Experience*, edited by Nathan Glazer and Daniel Patrick Moynihan. Cambridge, MA: Harvard University Press.

———— 1978. *Human Nature, Class, and Ethnicity*. New York: Oxford University Press.

Gourevitch, Peter Alexis. 1979. "The Reemergence of 'Peripheral Nationalism.'" *Comparative Studies in Social History* 21:303-327.

Greeley, Andrew and Paul S. Sheatsley. 1971. "Attitudes toward Racial Integration." *Scientific American* 225:13-19.

Harre, R. 1979. *Social Being*. Oxford: Basil Blackwell.

Hechter, Michael. 1975. *Internal Colonialism: The Celtic Fringe in British National Development, 1536-1966*. Berkeley: University of California Press.

———— 1982. "A Theory of Group Solidarity." Pp. 16-57 in *The Microfoundations of Macrosociology*, edited by Michael Hechter. Philadelphia: Temple University Press.

Hechter, Michael and Margaret Levi. 1979. "The Comparative Analysis of Ethnoregional Movements." *Ethnic and Racial Studies* 2:260-274.

Homans, George C. 1961. *Social Behavior: Its Elementary Forms*. London: Routledge & Kegan Paul.

———. 1962. *Sentiments and Activity*. New York: Free Press.

Horowitz, Donald. 1985. *Ethnic Groups in Conflict*. Berkeley: University of California Press.

Isaacs, Harold. 1976. *Idols of the Tribe: Group Identity and Political Change*. New York: Harper & Row.

Janowitz, Morris. 1978. *The Last Half Century*. Chicago: University of Chicago Press.

Katznelson, Ira. 1981. *City Trenches: Urban Politics and the Patterning of Class in the United States*. New York: Pantheon.

Keyes, Charles, ed. 1981. *Ethnic Change*. Seattle: University of Washington Press.

Kluegel, Charles and Eliot R. Smith. 1984. "Beliefs and Attitudes about Women's Opportunity: A Comparison with Beliefs about Blacks." *Social Psychology Quarterly* 1:81-95.

Levi, Margaret and Michael Hechter. 1985. "A Rational Choice Approach to the Rise and Decline of Ethnoregional Political Parties." Pp. 128-146 in *New Nationalisms of the Developed West*, edited by Edward Tiryakian and Ronald Rogowski. London: George Allen & Unwin.

Light, Ivan. 1972. *Ethnic Enterprise in America*. Berkeley: University of California Press.

Lieberson, Stanley. 1963. *Ethnic Patterns in American Cities*. New York: Free Press.

———. 1980. *A Piece of the Pie: Blacks and White Immigrants since 1890*. Berkeley: University of California Press.

Loewen, James W. 1971. *The Mississippi Chinese: Between Black and White*. Cambridge, MA: Harvard University Press.

Lipset, Seymour and Stein Rokkan. 1967. *Party Systems and Voter Alignments*. New York: Free Press.

Marx, Gary T. 1970. *Protest and Prejudice: A Study of Belief in the Black Community*. New York: Harper & Row.

Mazuri, Ali A. 1975. *Soldiers and Kinsmen in Uganda: The Making of a Military Ethnocracy*. Beverly Hills, CA: Sage.

McAdam, Doug. 1982. *Political Process and the Development of Black Insurgency, 1930-1970*. Chicago: University of Chicago Press.

McConahy, J. B. and J. C. Hough. 1976. "Symbolic Racism." *Journal of Social Issues* 32:23-45.

Myerhoff, Barbara. 1978. *Number Our Days: Old Age in an Urban Jewish Ghetto*. New York: Simon & Schuster.

Nagata, Judith, ed. 1975. *Pluralism in Malaysia: Myth and Reality*. Leider: Brill.

Nagel, Joane and Susan Olzak. 1982. "Ethnic Mobilization in New and Old States: An Extension of the Competition Model." *Social Problems* 30:127-143.

Nairn, Tom. 1977. *The Break-Up of Britain*. London: New Left Books.

Noel, Donald. 1972. *The Origins of American Slavery and Racism*. Columbus, OH: Merrill.

Olsen, Mancur. 1965. *The Logic of Collective Action: Public Goods and the Theory of Groups*. Cambridge, MA: Harvard University Press.

Olzak, Susan. 1983. "Contemporary Ethnic Mobilization." *American Sociological Review* 9:355-374.

Patchen, M., J. D. Davidson, G. Hofman, and W. R. Brown. 1977. "Student Interracial Behavior and Opinon Change." *Sociology of Education* 50:55-75.

Patterson, Orlando. 1977. *Ethnic Chauvinism: The Reactionary Impulse*. Cambridge, MA: Harvard University Press.

Rex, John. 1970. "The Concept of Race in Sociological Theory," in *Race and Racialism*, edited by Sami Zubaide. London: Tavistock.

———. 1973. *Race, Colonialism and the City*. London: Routledge & Kegan Paul.

———. 1982. "Convergence in the Sociology of Race Relations and Minority Groups." Pp. 173-200 in *Sociology: The State of the Art*, edited by Tom Bottomore, Stefan Nowak, and Magdalena Sokolowska. London: Sage.

Rogers, Marian, Karen Hemingway, Craig Bowman, and Norman Miller. 1984. "Intergroup Acceptance in Classroom and Playground Settings." Pp. 214-228 in *Groups in Contact: The Psychology of Desegregation*, edited by Norman Miller and Marily Brewer. New York: Academic Press.

Ronen, Dov. 1980. *The Quest for Self-Determination*. New Haven, CT: Yale University Press.

Rothschild, Joseph. 1981. *Ethnopolitics: A Conceptual Framework*. New York: Columbia University Press.

Schermerhorn, R. A. 1978. *Comparative Ethnic Relations: A Framework for Theory and Research*. Chicago: University of Chicago Press.

Schuman, Howard, Charlotte Steele, and Lawrence Bobo. 1985. *Racial Attitudes in America: Trends and Interpretations*. Cambridge, MA: Harvard University Press.

Sears, David O. and Harris M. Allen. 1984. "The Trajectory of Local Desegregation Controversies and Whites' Opposition to Busing." Pp. 123-151 in *Groups in Contact: The Psychology of Desegregation*, edited by Norman Miller and Marilyn B. Brewer. New York: Academic Press.

Sears, David O. and David R. Kinder. 1981. "Prejudice and Politics: Symbolic Racism versus Racial Threats to the Good Life." *Journal of Personality and Symbolic Psychology* 40:414-431.

See, Katherine O'Sullivan. 1986a. "Ideology and Racial Inequality: A Theoretical Juxtaposition." *International Journal of Sociology and Social Policy* 6:75-89.

———. 1986b. "For God and Crown: Protestant Politics and Class Relations in Northern Ireland." In *Ethnic Competition*, edited by Susan Olzak and Joanne Nagel. New York: Academic Press.

_____ 1986c. *First World Nationalisms: Ethnic and Class Politics in Northern Ireland and Quebec.* Chicago: University of Chicago Press.

Sherif, Muzafer and Carolyn W. Sherif. 1953. *Groups in Harmony and Tension.* New York: Harper & Row.

Shibutani, Tamotso and Kian M. Kwan. 1965. *Ethnic Stratification: A Comparative Approach.* New York: Macmillan.

Slavin R. E. and N. A. Madden. 1979. "School Practices That Improve Race Relations." *American Educational Research Journal* 16:169-180.

Smelser, Neil J. 1968. *Essays in Sociological Explanation.* Englewood Cliffs, NJ: Prentice-Hall.

Smith, A. Wade. 1981. "Racial Tolerance as a Function of Group Position." *American Sociological Review* 46:558-573.

Smith, M. G. 1985. "Race and Ethnic Relations as Matters of Rational Choice." *Ethnic and Racial Studies* 8:484-499.

Taeuber, Karl and Alma Taeuber. 1965. *Negroes in Cities.* Chicago: Aldine.

Tajfel, Henri. 1981. *Human Groups and Social Categories.* Cambridge, England: Cambridge University Press.

Taylor, David Garth, Paul B. Sheatsley, and Andrew M. Greeley. 1978. "Attitudes toward Racial Integration." *Scientific American* 238:39-42.

van den Berghe, Pierre. 1978. *Race and Racism: A Comparative Perspective.* New York: John Wiley.

_____ 1981. *The Ethnic Phenomenon.* New York: Elsevier.

Wallerstein, Immanuel. 1985. "Racism, Nationalism, Ethnicity: The Construction of Peoplehood." Paper presented at the Conference on Ethnic Labels/Signs of Class, Center for the Study of Industrial Societies, University of Chicago, October.

Weinrich, Peter. 1983. "Psychodynamics of Personal and Social Identity." In *Identity: Personal and Sociocultural*, edited by A. Jocobson Widding. New York: Humanities Press.

_____ 1985. "Rationality and Irrationality in Racial and Ethnic Relations: A Metatheoretical Framework." *Ethnic and Racial Studies* 8:500-515.

Williams, Robin M. 1944. *The Reduction of Intergroup Tensions.* New York: Social Science Research Council.

Wilson, William J. 1973. *Power, Racism and Privilege: Race Relations in Theoretical and Sociohistorical Perspective.* New York: Macmillan.

_____ 1976. *Power, Racism and Privilege: Race Relations in Theoretical and Sociohistorical Perspective.* New York: Free Press.

_____ 1980. *The Declining Significance of Race: Blacks and Changing American Institutions.* Chicago: University of Chicago Press.

_____ 1987. *The Truly Disadvantaged: The Inner City, The Underclass and Public Policy.* Chicago: University of Chicago Press.

Young, Crawford. 1976. *The Politics of Cultural Pluralism.* Madison: University of Wisconsin Press.

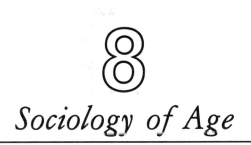

Sociology of Age

MATILDA WHITE RILEY
ANNE FONER
JOAN WARING

A sociology of age is concerned with two major topics: (1) aging over the life course as a social process and (2) age as a structural feature of changing societies and groups, as both people and roles are differentiated by age. In this chapter we describe this emerging special field of sociological work that crosscuts other sociological fields and also makes a unique contribution in showing how these two topics, each clearly distinct and significant in its own right, are interdependent. Neither can be understood without the other. Aging processes and age structures form a *system* of interdependent parts that we refer to as an "age stratification system."

Sociological Background. Age, though only in recent decades accorded specific sociological attention, has always permeated the sociological enterprise. Pitirim Sorokin (1947, 1969) spoke of age as one of the major bases of social organization, shaping the structure of groups and social systems, molding the characteristics and behaviors of individuals, channeling funda-

mental social processes and even the course of history. Mannheim (1928/1952) pointed to the power of age in social arrangements by proposing the provocative thought experiment: What if nobody in society died? What if individuals did not grow older but forever remained children, middle-aged adults, or the oldest old? What if social institutions were never again challenged to make way for new cohorts of people or to extrude old ones? Other sociologists (including Cottrell, 1942; Eisenstadt, 1956; Lenski, 1966; Parsons, 1942) have pointed to age as a focal point for group formation and intergroup relations, as a basis of social inequality, and as an intrinsic source of social change as new cohorts because of their particular historical experiences make unique contributions to social structures (e.g., Cain, 1964; Ryder, 1965).

Aging as a process has also been a continuing focus of sociological work. Using diaries and letters (Thomas and Znaniecki, 1918), panel studies (Lazarsfeld, Berelson, and Gaudet, 1944/1960), or longitudinal analyses (Elder, 1974), sociologists have shown how people change, as they age, in their family involvements, work behaviors, political beliefs, and subjective orientations—and how these changes have been affected by prevailing social conditions (see the models of human development in Clausen, 1972, 1986a; Neugarten, 1968; Strauss, 1959).

In empirical research, age has long been

This chapter was written in association with John W. Riley, Jr. We are deeply appreciative of editorial help on earlier versions of this chapter from Dale Dannefer, Beth B. Hess, David Kertzer, John Meyer, Bernice Neugarten, and Harris Schrank; of special suggestions from Kathleen Bond, Dennis Hogan, and Norman Ryder; and of invaluable assistance in manuscript preparation from Diane Zablotsky.

among the standard variables that inform (and sometimes misinform) sociological analysis. In fact, it was our review (Riley and Foner, 1968) of a wide range of empirical studies using age as an explanatory factor that gave impetus and direction to defining age as a sociological specialty. In sorting out which studies made authentic contributions to knowledge of age and aging and which were flawed by improper methodologies or fallacious interpretations, the need for a conceptual framework became apparent. Sociologists were prompted to take serious account of two interdependent dynamisms: the aging of people in successive cohorts who grow old, die, and are replaced by other people; and the changes in social structure as people of different ages pass through the social institutions that are organized by age to accommodate them.

Synopsis of the Chapter. The emerging understandings of aging processes, changing age structures, and the complex interplay between them are illustrated in this chapter by a few sociological studies, old and new. The studies selected are described only as they abstract those aspects relating to age. There are many necessary exclusions of work on other countries, on policy implications, or on statistical procedures (though the extensive bibliography points to excluded aspects of the diverse and scattered literature). Following the introduction of a conceptual framework (Section I) for use in locating the works under review, the chapter arbitrarily arranges the discussion of age stratification systems in three sections. Studies on *aging* or the "life course" (Section II) focus on individuals whose lives are shaped through interactions with the social structure. Studies on *age structure* (Section IV) focus on an age structure of roles—changing as society changes—in which age defines the social locations of people alive at any given time. Linking these two sets of studies, and described in Section III, are studies of *cohort flow*, as cohorts of people born at approximately the same time not only express changing patterns in the aging process but also form the structures of people who occupy the various roles in the age strata. Since these chapter divisions describe three interdependent parts of age stratification as a system, there can be no logical beginning and no logical end.

I. An Age Stratification System

A set of broad concepts and postulated relationships among the age-related aspects of social

systems is defined in the heuristic model of an age stratification system (Riley, Johnson, and Foner, 1972). This model, designed as an aid for interpreting data on age and integrating them into a larger conceptual framework, focuses on the central topics of the chapter: individual aging, changing age structures, and the interdependence of these two as they are linked through the succession of cohorts.

Process and Structures

Figure 8.1 depicts schematically these elements of an age stratification system. The diagram is a social space with two time-related boundaries. The vertical axis is marked off by years of age, calling attention both to the ongoing changes that occur in people's lives as they grow older and to age criteria for entering and leaving roles. The horizontal axis is marked off by dates, calling attention to the changes—economic, political, cultural, and so on—that occur in societies with the passage of time. The diagonal bars represent cohorts of people born in the same time period who are aging—that is, moving across time and upward with age. The perpendicular lines at particular dates identify the people, and associated roles, comprising the age structure of the society. These cross-sectional slices indicate how people from many cohorts, who are at different stages of their lives and are involved in different social roles and institutions, are organized roughly in socially recognized age divisions or strata, from the youngest to the oldest.

This schematization is, of course, highly oversimplified. The figure cannot show how the strata are crosscut by other major divisions based on class, gender, race, and so on. The diagonal lines give no hint of the varied paths by which individuals grow older, the extent of differentiation within cohorts, or the differences in cohort size and changes in size as people move away or die. The vertical lines do not show the roles available in the several strata, but the complex organization of age roles within the many social groups and institutions is suggested in Figure 8.2. Figures 8.1 and 8.2, like the conceptual framework they illustrate, merely provide a lens for locating within the full complexity of the social system those aspects that refer to age.

Two Dynamisms: Aging and the Changing Social Structure

Peculiarly sociological in this conceptual framework is the interplay between the two dynamisms: aging of individuals in successive cohorts and changing age structures of society, as each can transform the other (Riley, 1982). Each dynamism is distinct; neither is reducible to the other. Each has its own tempo. People, as they age, move along the axis of the life course (the diagonals in Figure 8.1), are born and die according to a rhythm that is set by the approximate length of the human lifetime. In contrast, the full set of age strata, with their age roles and the age distribution of people within them, coexist, influence each other, and change together as society changes (as in the vertical cross-sectional slices in Figure 8.1). And social change moves along its own axis of historical time, as imbalances, strains, and conflicts within the age stratification system are influenced by factors extrinsic to it (such as social and environmental events or evolutionary changes in the organism). Because the two dynamisms of individual aging and structural change, though interdependent, can never be perfectly synchronized with one another, the asynchrony between them often imposes strains and pressures for further change upon both individual and society (see also Strauss, 1959).

This asynchrony can be apprehended by tracing one diagonal in Figure 8.1: While individuals within a particular cohort are aging, the society is changing. People start their lives in one historical period, when all the age strata and people's definitions and evaluations of these strata and their feelings about them are organized in one particular way; but as these people age, the full set of age strata is continually being reorganized from one period to the next. For example, people who were young earlier in this century learned appropriate age patterns of behavior and internalized norms of that period; most went to school for no more than six or seven years—adequate education for the jobs then held by the boys' fathers or older siblings, more than adequate for the girls whose mothers, if they worked outside the home at all, tended to have menial jobs. That cohort of young people developed images of old age from the characteristics of their few surviving grandparents. But now that these people have themselves grown old, the society is very different from that of their grandparents. They have outdistanced the world for which they were initially prepared. Similarly, cohorts of people who are young today see the entire occupational ladder before it will be transformed by fast-breaking technological innovations and accompanying changes in the age structure. For them, promotion and retirement as currently institutionalized are viewed as entitlements. But these young people will not be old in the same society in which they began. They too must move through a society that is changing.

Note on Use of the Framework

As a heuristic device, this conceptual framework sets criteria for sociological studies of age

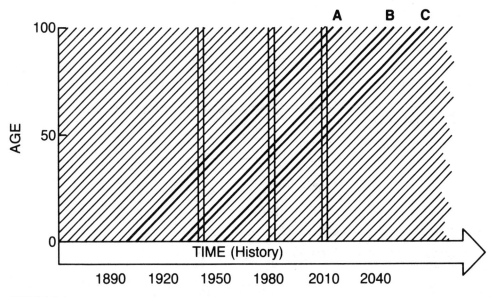

FIGURE 8.1
The Age Stratification System: A Schematic View

as requiring both dynamic and cross-sectional views (see Featherman and Lerner, 1985), both objective and subjective understandings, and analyses of both the age-stratified society and the micro-level processes of growing older in age-related social roles. Moreover, the framework draws attention to age as representing a special perspective on a great many phenomena of sociological as well as interdisciplinary concern. On the one hand, the developing sociology of age draws on sociology, benefiting from reexamination of established sociological fields (e.g., social psychology, social stratification) and from reinterpretation of familiar sociological concepts (e.g., socialization, social control, the "family cycle," social change). On the other hand, research on age is raising fresh questions about established sociological fields and giving emphasis to connections with related disciplines like biology and psychology.

With continuing use of such an age stratification model for locating, interpreting, and integrating research findings, and for formulating testable hypotheses and appropriate research designs, a set of working principles (referred to throughout the chapter as WP) has been predicated, and several persistent fallacies have been identified (Featherman, 1981; Riley, 1973, 1979, 1985).[1] These are listed in Tables 8.1 and

8.2 and will be discussed at appropriate points in this chapter.

For parsimony, the framework abstracts only the most general concepts, selecting terms from the varied empirical literature and the diverse "schools" of sociological thought, and defining these terms—sometimes arbitrarily—so as to transcend parochial usages. Briefly, these are as follows:

• "aging"—a life-course process of growing up and growing *older* from birth to death, not simply growing *old* beyond some arbitrary point in the life course (see adoption of this usage as by Featherman and Lerner, 1985).

• "cohort"—a set of people born (or entering a particular system such as a hospital, school, or a community of scientists) at approximately the same period. (The word "generation" is reserved for the kinship context—see Kertzer, 1983; Ryder, 1968.) Each cohort has distinctive properties (e.g., initial size and composition, age-specific mortality rates), and the life-course experiences of its members reflect a particular period of history. The term "birth cohort" is preferred to "age cohort."

• "age strata" (in preference to "age categories" or "age groups")—as the rough divi-

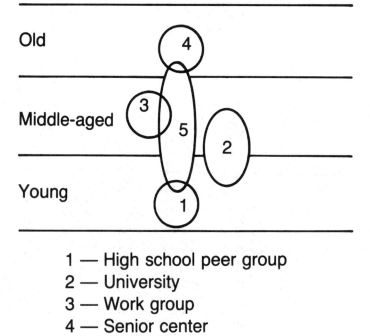

1 — High school peer group
2 — University
3 — Work group
4 — Senior center
5 — Family

FIGURE 8.2
Relation of Groups to Age Strata (A Schematic View)

sions by age of people and roles within a society or group. The strata form a series from younger to older, often resulting in inequalities. These partitions of the society (or group) have meaning as age strata only as they reflect socially significant aspects of people or of the roles they perform.

- "people"—as members of society or "actors," not mere demographic aggregates or "populations."

- "age roles" (used for parsimony to include both "role" and "status")—as positions in societies or groups where age criteria govern en-

TABLE 8.1
Selected Working Principles

Referring to the Age Strata

WP-1: Every society is stratified by age, just as it is stratified by class and gender (and in some societies by ethnicity); and the character of age stratification varies across societies and over historical time.

WP-2: Age strata are produced by the ongoing interplay between (a) changes in society involving wide variations in age-related roles and (b) the processes of aging and cohort flow, which are universal as long as the society endures.

WP-3: Age strata are interdependent, so that changes in one stratum can have repercussions on other strata.

WP-4: *Within* a stratum, people's similarity in age and cohort membership contributes to mutuality of experiences, perceptions, and interests that may lead to integration or even to age-based groups and collective movements.

WP-5: Integration within an age stratum contains potentials for cleavage *between* age strata. Moreover, the differences among strata in age and cohort membership imply differences in experiences, perceptions, and interests that could lead to indifference or divisiveness and pressures toward social change.

WP-6: Within each age stratum, individuals actively engage in a complex of roles (e.g., at work, in the family) that can influence the way they grow older, their capacities and attitudes, and the other people with whom they interact; these roles set limits on, but also provide opportunity for, individual initiative and enterprise.

WP-7: Individuals who are growing older in any one age stratum interact with members of other strata, allowing either for affiliation and reciprocal socialization or for age-based tension and conflict.

Referring to Aging

WP-8: Aging is a life-long process of growing *older* from birth to death, moving through all the strata in society.

WP-9: Aging is multifaceted, composed of interrelated biological, psychological, and social processes.

WP-10: The ways people age are affected by the social locations through which they move, by the social and cultural conditions to which they are exposed at particular ages, and by the life-course experiences of others with whom they interact as they grow older.

Referring to Aging and Social Change

WP-11: The ways people age are affected by the character of the cohort to which they belong and by those social, cultural, and environmental changes to which their cohort is exposed in moving through each of the successive age strata. Because society changes, members of successive cohorts age in different ways.

WP-12: When many individuals in the same cohort are affected by social change in similar ways, the change in their collective lives can produce changes in social structure that in turn further influence the process of aging. That is, new patterns of aging are not only caused by social change; they also contribute to it.

WP-13: Individual aging and social change involve separate dynamisms, and their intrinsic lack of synchronization with one another produces strains for both individual and society.

NOTE: See Riley (1973, 1979); Foner (1974); Featherman (1981a).

try or exit, or define expectations, facilities, and sanctions for performance. Age criteria can be either formal or informal, and can consist either of factual age regularities or of normative age prescriptions.

The word "age" itself takes on varied meanings depending on the context. With reference to people, chronological age is usually a mere index reflecting past experiences undergone or future experiences anticipated, and carrying with it widely varying probabilities of attitudes, behaviors, and characteristics. In role structures, however, chronological age criteria are often built explicitly into laws or customs, as entering school or drawing a pension or punishment for a crime can depend on years of age. There are numerous surrogates for chronological age, such as attaining puberty or completing school; and in some less complex societies age is not calculated by birthdate but by generation in a family, the appearance of a physical sign, the accomplishment of some feat, or the assumption of certain social roles (e.g., Foner and Kertzer, 1978).

II. Aging

Understanding aging processes is in large part a sociological matter. Because of their broad concern with both social structures and the lives of individuals in society, sociologists have taken the lead in integrating the divergent and often confusing biological, psychological, and sociological

TABLE 8.2
Common Misinterpretations and Fallacies

• The *life-course fallacy*—erroneously assuming that cross-sectional age differences, essential for examining age structures at particular periods, refer instead to the process of aging.

• The fallacy of *cohortcentrism*—erroneously assuming that members of all cohorts will age in exactly the same fashion as members of our own cohort.

• The fallacy of age *reification*—treating chronological age in itself as a causal life-course variable without specifying what factors may be influencing the aging process (e.g., because he is 40, someone "becomes his own man").

• The fallacy of *reifying historical time*—treating historical change as a causal variable without specifying what aspects of historical change may be pertinent to understanding particular shifts in the aging process or in age structures.

perspectives on the ways individuals grow older. Despite the ineluctable facts of birth and death, and the persistent beliefs that aging is biologically determined and psychologically constrained by early childhood experience, research makes clear that the aging process varies with social structures and social change.

A central theme of sociological work on aging relates to the social character of this variability. This theme takes two main forms. On the one hand, there is *plasticity* in the aging process *within* each individual life, as social processes interact with biological and psychological processes to influence the ways in which people change from childhood through adulthood to old age. On the other hand, there is *diversity among* individuals in the ways they grow older, depending on their locations in a society, their relationships with other people, and their development of a social self. This theme of socially structured variability, both individual plasticity and collective diversity, is illustrated by selected studies that focus on several topics: how people as they grow older move through the changing society, how sequences of age roles and role transitions are experienced over the life course, and how aging people are articulated with the role structures in society through lifelong processes of socialization and allocation.

Growing Older

The accumulating information about how people grow older points to the plasticity of the individual life course. Aging is a multifaceted process (see WP 6 in Table 8.1) in which alterations in the brain, in mental and physiological processes, and in social processes are all intertwined. The changes that accompany the move from infancy to childhood, adolescence, and young and mature adulthood are multidetermined and multidimensional. There are patterns, to be sure, but also much diversity. And there is no single source of either the patterning or the wide diversity in the ways people grow older; biological and psychological, as well as social, factors are involved.

INDIVIDUAL PLASTICITY

The aging process is far more malleable and far less programmed than once thought. Not long ago numerous putatively scientific studies reported (often erroneously) inevitable declines from young adulthood to old age in such physiological functions as nerve conduction velocity, heart output, and maximum breathing capacity;

and in such behavioral functions as sensation and perception, complex sensorimotor responses, and the ability to learn, remember, and think intelligently. These reports were based largely on cross-sectional data, despite the fact that findings of cross-section differences among age strata are often traceable, not to the aging process, but to the differing experiences of cohort members (see life-course fallacy, Table 8.2; also Section III). With the growing sophistication of research on aging, and the mounting evidence that social interventions can reverse age-related declines (Riley and Bond, 1983), the erroneous belief in immutability of the life course is gradually being clarified and corrected.

Like the inaccurate assumption of inevitable biological decline in later life, the assumption that early-life experiences inevitably constrain the characteristics of adolescence and adulthood is under challenge. Findings from numerous empirical studies examining the degree to which individuals change over the life course are summarized in *Constancy and Change in Human Development*, edited by Brim and Kagan (1980). In their review of several chapters on physical growth, health, cognitive development, personality, social attitudes and beliefs, occupational careers, psychoses, and criminal behavior, Brim and Kagan conclude that "there are important growth changes across the life span from birth to death, many individuals retain a great capacity for change, and the consequences of the events of early childhood are continually transformed by later experiences, making the course of human development more open than many have believed" (p. 1). For example, longitudinal studies show that children who have illness early in life are only a little more likely than other children to have illness later. Attitudes, including those that reflect "basic values," change even among older adults (Glenn, 1980; see also Foner, 1972). All such characteristics show considerable plasticity in the aging process.

Such findings, of course, do not mean that early life experiences have no enduring effects. There is much evidence of the interconnectedness of early life with late life as, for example, hardships in childhood or disadvantaged career beginnings influence what happens in middle and later life (e.g., Elder and Liker, 1982; O'Rand and Henretta, 1982). What the findings on constancy and change do mean is that the belief in an immutable process of aging is no longer tenable.

Increasingly, sociologists are focusing attention on the plasticity of specific aspects of the aging process. Mental and physical health,

though the primary province of other disciplines, are dimensions of aging that affect the contributions individuals make as members of social systems. Studies of intellectual functioning (see Baltes and Willis, 1982; Schale, 1983) demonstrate, contrary to conventional wisdom, that healthy individuals up to age 60, and most of those up to age 80, do now show declines with aging; and that those who do show declines can be greatly improved through interventions in the social environment. Thus the social situation plays an important part in the maintenance of functioning in old age. Collaborative work between sociologists and psychologists is investigating unrecognized components of intelligence that may develop in later life; for example, the accumulation of experience may enhance decision-making ability, interpersonal competence, or "wisdom" (Dittman-Kohli and Baltes, in press; Riley and Riley, 1986; Schooler and Schaie, 1986).

Of interest to sociologists in regard to health is the still puzzling question of whether marked increases in longevity mean greater or less morbidity at the older ages (Manton, 1982; Shanas and Maddox, 1985). In particular, why is it that women, though they live longer than men, report more illnesses (see Mechanic, 1983)? Lois Verbrugge's (1985) review of age-related gender differences shows how reproductive conditions (at ages 17 to 55) account for little of the excess morbidity of women over men, and that women at every age are less likely than men to suffer from life-threatening and disabling diseases. Because women pay greater attention to symptoms and the emotional content of disease, they receive better health care than men in earlier life, which may diminish the severity of disease in later life and help to extend their lives.

Sociologists are also paying attention to sources of variability in the interplay among social, biological, and psychological processes.[2] There are studies of secular changes, including genetic changes, in the potential for "human development" (Featherman and Lerner, 1985); of the interaction of biological and social factors in the sexual behavior of adolescents (Smith, Udry, and Morris, 1985); of the lifelong physical and mental sequelae, as well as the social and economic consequences, for school-age mothers and their babies (Furstenberg, 1976; Presser, 1974); of the neurobiological changes implicated in the maturing mother's relation to her offspring (Rossi, 1977, 1984); and of older people's increased susceptibility to physical and psychological deterioration when age segregation undermines the social stimulation and support provided in work roles or kinship roles (House, Robbins, and Metzner, 1982).

COLLECTIVE DIVERSITY

While interdisciplinary approaches enhance understanding of plasticity of individual aging, the diversity among individual aging patterns is ignored by many theorists from other disciplines who argue that development and aging go through fixed "stages" (e.g., Levinson, 1978; Vaillant, 1974) and by life span psychologists who aggregate individual data into statistical averages treated as maturational or "normative" models of ontogenetic development (see the review by Baltes, Reese, and Lipsitt, 1980). Dannefer (1984), calling this practice "ontogenetic reductionism," points to the weakness of many widely accepted findings that, through aggregation and the use of averages, obscure significant clues to differences, not only in genetic makeup, but also in socioculturally patterned variations in the ways people grow older.

Of course, sociologists take for granted that individuals are influenced by their locations in society. Yet much sociological work similarly fails to identify the wide diversity of age-linked patterns that are hidden in the averages. Fortunately, there are exceptions. For example, Spanier and Glick (1980) examine the relationship of demographic variables to the timing of events in the family lives of American women, reporting such findings as these: the lower the level of educational attainment, the earlier a woman begins her family life trajectory; long-standing differences between blacks and whites with regard to life-course events tend to be minimized when educational level is controlled; the younger a woman is at termination of her first marriage, the more likely she is to marry again (see also Hagestad and Neugarten, 1985; Winsborough, 1979).

STATUS ATTAINMENT AND AGING

Very different from mental or physical functioning over the life course is "status attainment," the socioeconomic dimension of the aging process (Blau and Duncan, 1967; Sewell and Hauser, 1975). Studies focusing on social mobility investigate life-long trajectories of achievement behaviors, using longitudinal and causal modeling to examine the interconnections among such variables as family background, scholastic achievement, succession of jobs, and employment and unemployment (summarized by Featherman, 1981).

The findings demonstrate both the plasticity within individual lives and the diversity among life-course patterns that result in inequalities of income and prestige. For example, a person's educational experience is influenced by such family characteristics as occupation and education of the family head, number of siblings, family stability, or race. In turn, a person's education has considerable effect on occupational achievement. Of course, subpopulations differ: for example, there is greater continuity between achievement in school and in work for men than there is for women, whose work lives are more often interrupted by their family lives. Extension of this status attainment model into old age (e.g., Henretta and Campbell, 1978) suggests how education and occupation in early life can influence health and labor force participation in later life, and how these in turn contribute to income and assets in old age. This body of work provides considerable understanding of how certain background characteristics and early events can affect later events and role changes in a person's life.

Aging and Role Sequences

Complementary to the work on how people grow older are studies of the role sequences associated with aging. Since much of the variability in life-course patterns is socially structured, sociologists are examining how people's lives depend on the particular roles they play, the situations they encounter, the others who become significant to them, and how these others in turn act, think, and feel. Over the life course, each person interacts in many roles and complexes of roles and the accumulated experience has consequences for acquisition of styles of thinking, coping, and relating to others; personal approaches to discontinuities and problems of identity; and development of active, innovative, creative attacks on living (see Riley, 1984).

AGE ROLES

The roles open to people of a particular age are parts of the larger social structure. Yet for people viewing their individual lives, the sequential roles they perform (e.g., school child, wife, mother, grandmother) appear as if torn from the societal framework, and strung along the person's own life course. In research, roles are often treated as if they were merely contextual characteristics of individuals, and indeed, at any given point in a single life course, the individual is located in a particular age stratum and subject to the influences of the particular age complexes in that stratum (see WP 6 in Table 8.1).

The centrality of age roles to people's lives has been documented in numerous life-course studies of the economy, the educational system, and the polity. For example, a study of ex-nuns (San Giovanni, 1978), who as teenagers had withdrawn from lay society to enter a convent, found that away from the conventional social environment they aged differently from their secular peers. When they left the convent to return to the lay world, these adult women had to resume life where they left off—at age 17. They had to learn such conventional adult roles as consumer, worker, friend, or lover. Without having an adolescence, they had to create their own avenues to the modal roles for mature women in the society. In a different example involving types of work role structures, Sorensen (1986) shows that the life course may be primarily shaped in a "closed" position system by the opportunities and constraints of the social structure, but in an "open" position by changes in the individual's own capacities and efforts.

INTERACTION BETWEEN PERSON AND AGE ROLE

Aging in any role does not imply, of course, passive compliance with expectations about age-appropriate behavior. The person being influenced by the role is also an active participant. Within each role, the *person* who is aging contributes the motivations and capacities to perform, as well as actual performances; and in turn *others* contribute age-related expectations, facilities and supports, rewards and punishments. In this interplay, both aging people and age-related roles change. The person's active participation mediates the impact of the role on the aging process. For example, nursing home residents often resist succumbing to the expected dependency, and by being independent may reshape the role itself by altering the expectations and responses of their caretakers (see Gubrium, 1975; Litwak and Spilerman, 1978). Other research (Kohn and Schooler, 1978, 1983; Miller, Slomczynski, and Kohn, 1985) shows that people as they grow older do not simply fit into and mold their jobs, but that their intellectual functioning is also affected by the jobs they have. Thus individuals who are intellectually flexible come to have jobs characterized by substantive complexity, and in turn substantively complex jobs enhance intellectual flexibility.

AGE CRITERIA

The age criteria governing role occupancy and role performance may be factual as well as normative (see Marini, 1984). Factual age criteria (such as average ages of entering or leaving roles, or modal age patterns of role performance) operate subtly and indirectly as expectations and sanctions, whether or not they become translated into overt age norms. Such factual criteria are often a response to prevailing opportunity structures as, for example, when elderly widows are enabled to maintain separate households because incomes become adequate or housing becomes available; or when high school graduates are unemployed because there are not enough suitable jobs (see Section III on cohort experience and age-related performance).

ROLE SEQUENCES

Sociologists have also described the sequencing of roles over the life course. In an early synthesis focusing on roles, Cain (1964) showed that aging processes involve "successive statuses" in family, religious, political, economic, legal, educational, welfare, and other institutional spheres. His formulation, a landmark development in the sociology of age, has been followed by others who pay special attention to the micro-level interaction between person and role in analyzing the life course (see Clausen, 1972).

More recently, Rosow (1985) postulates different patterns of life-course change. For example, "institutional roles," which relate to work both outside and inside the home, follow an inverted U-curve over the life course, peaking in mid-adulthood. "Tenuous roles," which involve the major mid-life statuses but with reduced activities and responsibilities, follow a U-curve that peaks in early and again in late life. Since tenuous roles are likely to be "emptied of functions," individuals in both childhood and old age are more likely to be evaluated on the basis of age than of performance criteria.

John Meyer's (1986) essay, "The Institutionalization of the Life Course and its Effects on the Self" argues that such "institutional" properties of the individual as education, occupational status, or pensions—individual properties that are socially valued, and into which modern social systems pour their resources—serve to integrate the life course with the social structure. With age criteria central to the social system, the formal distinctions among individuals are based more on age than on capacity or performance. One objective consequence, according to Meyer, involves invidious distinctions based on age that, in view of modern commitment to equalitarianism, would be unacceptable, even unconstitutional, based on criteria of race, sex, or religion. (See also Section IV.)

SUBJECTIVE CONTINUITIES

Only recently has systematic sociological attention been paid to the lifelong interplay between subjective experience and social relationships. Clausen (1972, 1986a) has analyzed the developing sense of the "self" of individuals striving to integrate the past into the present as they age through the sequence of roles, as personality becomes anchored in the network of personal relationships, and as the other people in these groups continually reinforce one's sense of "being" the same person.[3]

In Meyer's (1986) view, the total society as organized around the individual life course affects subjective as well as objective aspects of aging. Meyer speculates about the lack of private continuity in the self, as each transition requires a change in identity, in contrast to the predictability of the sequence of roles in the public identity of the "institutionalized" life course. By substituting age criteria for performance criteria, he notes, such a system helps to protect the self. One consequence is to equalize selves, as self-esteem can be derived from minor situational variations, rather than major differences in power or wealth. The big gainers in self-conception are persons with the greatest status disadvantages: the young and old, and those middle aged who are in inferior occupations.

A study by Lorence and Mortimer (1985) probes into the life-long plasticity of the self-conception in respect to the meaning and importance of work. Using panel data from three different age strata, these researchers find that job involvement is volatile among those in early stages of their careers, but more stable among the older workers at life stages when work environment is also more stable. Their findings support the hypothesis of a point in life at which individuals, without necessarily becoming rigid, consolidate their own identity, which then becomes a basis for further evaluations and selections. Variability in orientations over 50 years of people's lives is further specified in Clausen's (1986b) continuing analyses of the Berkeley longitudinal data, which show that stability over the entire life course of commitments to marriage for both men and women, and to careers for men are strongly related to "planfulness" and competence as assessed in adolescence. Despite great changes in many aspects of personality and heterogeneity in the styles of adaptation and decision making in old age, realistic choices made by these individuals early in their adult years are reflected in high attainment and satisfaction in later years.

Subjective experience with aging depends in part on choice of reference group. Comparisons of the self with others of one's own age can produce quite different evaluations from comparisons with members of other age strata or with one's self at earlier ages. For example, Rosow (1967) argues that older people's self-image is enhanced by housing arrangements that bring together those of like age; older workers' satisfaction with income in late middle age is higher when compared with own earlier income than when compared with the income of younger adults who began their careers with higher entry-level earnings.

The subjective meanings attached to the life course have objective consequences both for individual lives and for societal norms and institutions (Riley, 1978; see Section III).[4] For example, because the ills of old age were long regarded as inevitable, older people often received inadequate medical treatment: They took their aches and pains for granted, and doctors spent less time with older than with younger patients (Kane et al., 1980). Estes, Swan, and Gerard (1982) argue that public stereotypes of "ageism" both reflect and reinforce the invidious status of older people in a class-based society.

AGING AND SOCIAL STRUCTURE

Life-course research on the structural determinants of work-related inequalities (for a summary, see Kalleberg, 1983) illustrate a multilevel approach that focuses on social structure as well as on aging individuals. Termed the *new structuralism* (Baron and Bielby, 1980), this perspective on the work trajectories of individuals examines how work roles are arranged and rewarded in different industries, occupations, social classes, or organizations (e.g., Sorenson, 1986; Wright et al., 1982). As one example, Baron and Bielby (1985), investigating several hundred California work organizations between 1959 and 1979, found that sex segregation is pervasive and is sustained by diverse organizational structures and processes such as division of labor, promotion ladders, and supervisory hierarchies. Organizational constraints block career paths more for women than for men.

Such linking of individual life-course experience with social structure avoids "life span reductionism," in which the structure is reduced to contextual characteristics of individuals (see Dannefer, 1984; Riley, 1985). This widespread form of reductionism neglects the complexity of social institutions and the systematic ways in which schools, families, and work organizations sort individuals and differentiate their lives. Baron and Bielby (1985) and Kalleberg (1983) point out that it is particularly misleading to infer organizational arrangements from observed career paths of individuals, as many studies of status attainment have done, or to infer societal stratification systems of either age or class from aggregated information about individual lives.

Role Transitions

Hagestad and Neugarten (1985) define role transitions, or the many role entrances and exits each person makes over the life course, as the central concern of the life course approach, as distinct from the concern with growing older *within* roles. Sociological studies of role transitions (see Glaser and Strauss, 1971; Hogan and Astone, 1987; Riley and Waring, 1976) help to explain variability in the aging process, as individuals find ways to reshape old roles or adapt to new ones during turning points in their lives. Most sociological studies analyze particular transitions (avoiding the aggregation of diverse "stressful life events" criticized by Brim and Ryff, 1980), with many studies illustrating the linkages between individual transitions and age structures.

ORDERING, TIMING, AND DURATION

The circumstances of life-course transitions, often affected by location in the social structure, influence people's subsequent lives (see Hogan, 1978; Marini, 1985; Winsborough, 1979). For example, persons of lower socioeconomic status are more likely to be married earlier, have children earlier, start and leave work earlier, and die earlier than persons at higher socioeconomic levels (Abeles, Steele, and Wise, 1980). Postponing a role change, or inverting the customary order, may have lingering effects. Glen Elder (1986) shows how wartime military service interrupts schooling and occupational careers and delays marriage and parenthood, but can sometimes provide escape from an early life of disadvantage into a more promising future. In another example (Udry and Cliquet, 1982), women with early menarche tend to marry earlier and to have earlier first births than do women with later onset of puberty—a life-course pattern observed consistently across a range of cultures and subpopulations within cultures. Here the timing of a biological event, itself associated with social factors, triggers social and cultural interpretations of readiness for the subsequent transitions of marriage and reproduction.

COUNTERPART TRANSITIONS

As individuals move because of aging from one role to another, their significant others undergo counterpart transitions (WP 10). A few studies have begun to trace the consequences of such interdependent life-course events. For example, when many fathers lost their jobs during the Great Depression, there were often lifelong repercussions throughout the family system (Elder, 1974). One person's marriage changes the lives of the spouse and relatives on both sides. A family crisis, such as divorce, requires simultaneous role transitions by all family members, with complex economic as well as social consequences for the lives of the children, and also for the grandparents (Cherlin and Furstenberg, 1986; Duncan and Morgan, 1985). Historical accounts of western Europe show how the timing of the death or retirement of the older farmer affected the timing of marriage and independence of the sons and their families (Gaunt, 1983); and in the contemporary United States, the husband's retirement can influence the timing of his wife's retirement (O'Rand and Henretta, 1982), potentially creating a future family stage in which, as increasing numbers of women workers reach old age, the husband, but not the wife, is retired. Becoming a mother has consequences, including socially significant biological consequences, for the infant as well as for the mother (Rossi, 1977). Dying, the last transition, though reported in national surveys to be more painful for the survivor than for the person dying, appears to be less grievous in its long-term consequences than is generally believed (Hyman, 1983; J. Riley, 1983). Despite the reportedly high rates of mortality following death of a spouse, one controlled study (Helsing et al., 1981) finds that widowed males, but not widowed females, experience excess mortality during the years following bereavement—unless they remarry, as most do.

LIFE-COURSE OUTCOMES

A good deal of current research documents people's resilience in the face of life-course discontinuities. For example, the transition to retirement shows few adverse consequences when only the "average" impact is considered (Ekerdt and Bosse, 1982; see also early studies by Streib and others reported in Riley et al., 1968). However, reports of "average" impact, without regard to the social context of the meanings for the individuals involved, may obscure essential features of the transition. For example, there may be more stress in enduring a hated role than in making the transition to a new one.

In a study that does probe into differences in the context and implications of life-course changes, McLanahan and Sorensen (1985) examined changes in employment, residence, or household composition occurring within a single year in a national sample of heads of households. After establishing that nearly all of these life changes are age related (i.e., occur more frequently in certain age strata than in others), they find that most of the self-reported life changes have a negative effect on satisfaction with self. This effect is heightened when the change occurs at the "wrong" age (is "off time"), when it is involuntary rather than voluntary, and when children are present.

Other studies investigate conditions influencing the ease or difficulty of the transition experience. Transitions are more problematic when individuals are ahead of (or behind) the schedule that is customary or socially acceptable under prevailing conditions (Neugarten, Moore, and Lowe, 1965). For example, Glick and Norton reported in 1977 that marriages occurring earlier or later than the modal age were especially likely to end in divorce. Blau found in 1961 that young widows had more difficulty finding friends than did older widows who were surrounded by large numbers of women who themselves were widows. Special difficulties may be posed by "emergent passages," defined by Glaser and Strauss (1971) as situations in a changing environment where persons either create new roles or modify the institutionalized pathways of existing ones (see San Giovanni's 1978 study of ex-nuns). However, transitions may be eased by age criteria that are flexible and within an individual's control. Foner and Kertzer (1978) show how in African age-set societies some freedom of choice in entering or leaving an age set helps to minimize discrepancies between individual inclinations and the formal rules of societal age-grade systems.

GENERAL NATURE OF TRANSITIONS

Research is gradually clarifying and specifying earlier attempts to theorize about transitions (see Van Gennep, 1908/1960) and their life-course implications. Regarding transitions to the

roles of later life, two earlier formulations attracted considerable attention: "disengagement theory" (Cummings and Henry, 1961), which postulated a mutual and satisfactory process of withdrawal from social roles and social relationships on the part of both the individual and the society, in anticipation of the older person's approaching death; and the opposing "activity theory" (Havighurst and Albrecht, 1953; Burgess, 1960), which held that "successful" aging is achieved by the older person's continuation of social interaction and the substitution of new roles for those taken away (Hochschild, 1975). Continuing research shows that, depending on the social and cultural conditions, individuals differ markedly in their pathways through particular transitions to particular life-course outcomes (see Maddox and Campbell, 1985).

Lifelong Socialization and Allocation

Successive life-course transitions, as well as the ongoing experiences of growing older, are facilitated by socialization and allocation—familiar sociological processes that are redefined within the age stratification system as continually operating to articulate people who are aging with the age-appropriate roles. Responsive to social structures but impinging directly on individuals, these processes are understood in a sociology of age as shaping differentiated patterns of behaviors and orientations throughout life, helping to explain both the diversities and the commonalities in life-course patterns.

LIFELONG SOCIALIZATIONS

Traditionally defined as the problem of how to rear the young to become adequate adult members of society, socialization is now recognized as continuing throughout life (Brim, 1966; Clausen, 1968; Mortimer and Simmons, 1978; Strauss, 1959). A person's beliefs, values, and competencies are not indelibly imprinted in childhood but can change at every age (Glenn, 1980); and most roles provide opportunity for maintaining or altering current performances and for learning new ones (see Wheeler, 1966).

This recognition of socialization as an ongoing process of aligning capacities and performances with age-related role expectations brings to attention its special features. First, socialization is not a one-way but a *reciprocal* process, in which both the socializer and the person being socialized learn from each other (as noted early by Goslin, 1969; Mannheim, 1928/1952). Not only are parents themselves socialized by the demands of their children, but also adolescent peer group relationships (see Eisenstadt, 1956) and most adult relationships between socializer and the person being socialized (including those between parent and offspring) involve mutual influence. Second, the driving force in life-long socialization may be *expectations*, rather than simply imitation as students of childhood socialization often claim. Studies of adolescent socialization have shown how parents, by teaching normative expectations as standards for the future, encourage their offspring to transcend the limits of the parents' own experience (Johnson, 1976); and Rosow (1967) notes the continuing importance of expectations in socialization even among very old people.

LIFELONG ALLOCATION

Parallel to socialization, but less widely studied, allocation operates to guide people to the age-appropriate roles over their life course (see Eisenstadt, 1956; Riley, Johnson, and Foner, 1972). The processes of role assignment are often obscure. Even when they seem clear (as in being hired or fired from a job at a particular age), the visible aspects may constitute only a small part of much broader social, economic, or political forces of which people are largely unaware. Studies of allocation deal with such topics as how support from older and more experienced colleagues as allocators can encourage young workers to remain in a job (Schrank and Riley, 1976); or how lack of suitable rewards can discourage junior scientists from continuing as researchers instead of becoming teachers or administrators (Cole, 1979; Zuckerman and Merton, 1972).

While allocation, like socialization, is a reciprocal process, age relationships between allocators and candidates are likely to be asymmetrical. To be sure, candidates can decide whether to apply for a job, to enter college, or to retire early, and they can act as their own allocators to such roles as friend or marital partner. Yet candidates have little or no control over many decisions—being born, entering the first grade, being chosen from among competitors for scarce jobs or scarce training opportunities, or being mandated to retire.

A Note on Methods and Data

Before turning to Section III on the successive cohorts of individuals who are aging, we note the substantial methodological development that has stimulated (and been stimulated by) sociological research on aging. Because of its dynamic emphasis, research on aging often requires methods for tracing individuals over extended time intervals; because of its multifaceted emphasis, it often requires methods for interrelating many complex variables. From the baseline work of Paul Lazarsfeld (with Berelson and Gaudet, 1944), who elucidated the necessity for focusing directly on individual change rather than "net change" for a sample of individuals, and who also set out stochastic models for transition processes, sociologists have gone far to adapt methods used in other disciplines and to develop new methods for the purposes at hand. Otis Dudley Duncan (1966) introduced path analysis and structural equation models as a tool for postulating time order and causal connections of variables, and for partitioning statistical correlations into paths of direct and indirect influence among them. This tool and other developing methods of longitudinal analysis continue to make noteworthy sociological contributions both to substantive research on aging and to methodology generally.[5] Correlative to such methodological advances has been the development of computerized data banks for longitudinal and cohort analysis, as well as computer programs for analyzing such data (e.g., Karweit and Kertzer, 1986). These accumulating techniques and data have both actual and potential utility, though untutored applications sometimes threaten to outstrip the use of relevant theory or appropriate interpretation. An important challenge for future research on aging is the development of new methods that can translate into operations both the postulated multilevel relations between aging and social structure, and between aging and historical change (see Riley and Nelson, 1971).

III. Cohort Flow

Studies of cohort flow—as new members are born into a social system, move through the age strata as they grow older, and eventually die—have been the source of some of the most crucial contributions to sociological understanding of age. They have been instrumental in undermining the biological and psychological determinism that characterized so much of the early opinion on aging. They have challenged efforts at stereotyping age-related behaviors. They have shown how age-graded institutions operate in the society, and have illuminated the processes of social change.

When viewed within the larger framework of the age stratification system, cohort flow can be seen as the link between the aging of individuals and the changing societal age structures—the two dynamisms outlined in Section I. Because society changes, members of successive cohorts age in different ways; when many individuals in the same cohort are affected by social change in similar ways, the change in their collective lives can produce changes in social structure, which in turn affect the aging process (WP 11 and 12). As research probes further into the mechanisms linking cohort differences in individual aging to social structure and social change, the feedback loops within the age stratification system are gradually becoming clearer.

The Cohort Approach: Conceptual and Procedural Aspects

In this Section, we give examples of sociological work on cohort flow as it helps to explain (1) the aging process and (2) the formation of age structures, as well as the complex interplay between the two. Longitudinal studies (which trace a single diagonal, Figure 8.1) are used for understanding aging; but cohort comparisons (longitudinal studies along several diagonals) are needed to show how aging varies with historical conditions. Cross-sectional studies (the vertical slices through all the cohorts in Figure 8.1) are essential for describing age structures and their changes; but the cohort approach is needed for investigating *how* age structures arise and change. The set of cohorts that coexist at a given time, and confront the age-related roles, *are* the components of the age structure of people.

THEORETICAL BACKGROUND

The seminal sociological work on cohort flow is by Norman Ryder (1964, 1965). Ryder observes that because those whose ages differ at any given time are members of different cohorts, age has a double meaning: as temporal location in terms *both* of personal career and of history (Ryder, 1968, vol. 5). In respect to age structure, his notion of "social metabolism"—that is, the continual replacement of former cohorts by new ones—is central to the study of social change. Cohorts are differentiated from one another by the process of change, and they operate to bring about change.

Ryder's work also draws on that of earlier sociologists, notably Mannheim (1928/1952), who alerted sociologists to the importance of studying "generations"—using this term for the concept of "cohort" as used in this chapter. Like social class, Mannheim's generation provides a "location" in society, from which the person derives a unique configuration of predispositions to thought and action. These predispositions, as embodied in and objectified by successive generations of actors, then become the "stuff" of social change.

NATURE OF THE APPROACH

When such complex conceptualizations are translated into empirical studies, complementary research methods are required, from historical analyses to mathematical modeling and rigorous tests of specific hypotheses. One widely used tool in large-scale studies is "cohort analysis" in the form of direct comparison of particular characteristics or life-course experiences of members of successive cohorts, with the potentially explanatory variables not specifically defined but indexed only by age and date. Early cohort analyses involved topics on which age-specific data were available over long periods of time, such as fertility (see Ryder, 1968, vol. 5; Whelpton, 1954) and political attitudes (see Evan, 1965; Foner, 1972). Epidemiologists helped to develop and promote the approach. Susser (1969), a sociologically oriented epidemiologist, demonstrated in detail how cohort analysis could tease out the aging pattern of an early-life peak in death from tuberculosis—a pattern obscured in the cross-sectional data that (because of historical reductions in prevalence of the disease) erroneously suggested a secondary peak in old age. Susser also demonstrated how periods of economic prosperity or depression affected suicide rates in all the different cohorts, not just those at the most vulnerable ages.

The two illustrations of cohort analyses that follow help to clarify the dual relationship of cohort flow to individual aging and to the formation of societal age structures (and also illustrate the confusions deriving from the misinterpretation of the intrinsically atheoretical variables of age and date). In each example the exploratory analysis starts with inspection of the cross-sectional data for any empirical regularities in the structure, and is followed by the cohort approach with its search for interpretative clues. The first step focuses on *aging*. The data are examined longitudinally to ask not only how individuals are aging *within* each single cohort, but also how aging patterns differ *across* successive cohorts. The second step focuses on the *formation of structure.* Here the data are reexamined to see how aging patterns of the successive cohorts influence the shape, and changes in the shape, of the age structure. At each of these steps, the purpose is exploratory: to scrutinize the empirical regularities for possible clues to the processes affecting individual aging or social change and to the implications for future aging and future change.

EXAMPLE OF CONTRACEPTIVE USE

One illustration is provided by Westoff and Bumpass (1973) on the use of contraceptives by Catholic women. The data for this study are shown in Figure 8.3. In the conventional analysis (reading down the columns) there are few consistent age differences in the first three time periods. This finding suggests that, at least until 1970, there was no clear "generation gap" in attitudes on this issue between mature Catholic women and those young enough to be their daughters.

However, to infer from this that contraceptive practice does not change with aging would constitute a cross-sectional fallacy (Table 8.2). In the *cohort analysis* of the same data (reading up the diagonals), the relevance of age becomes clear. First, in respect to *aging*, in each of the cohorts contraceptive use tends to rise with in-

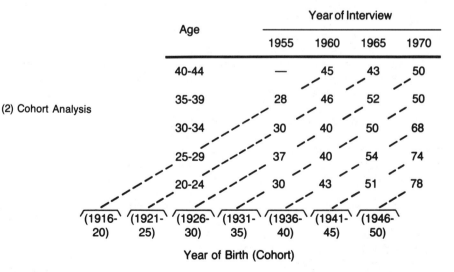

FIGURE 8.3
Percentage of White, Married Catholic Women Using Birth Control Not Conforming to Church Teaching

SOURCE: Westoff and Bumpass, 1973 (adapted)

creasing age up to the late thirties. In possible explanation, this aging pattern points to the influence of completed family size and perhaps to changed sexual activity after age 40. When cohorts in the several diagonals are compared, further insights appear: The *shape* of the aging pattern is fairly stable, but there is a marked change in the *level* of contraceptive use. Reading across the bottom row, thereby comparing successive cohorts at the age of entry to adulthood, the percentage of users rises steadily and dramatically from 30 in the earliest-born cohort to 78 in the most recent. How can this change be interpreted? Perhaps as reflecting social changes in availability of new contraceptive techniques, in norms of acceptance, or in regard for the legitimacy of teachings of the Church. For research focused on the aging process, then, looking at cohorts can uncover unsuspected patterns of age-related behavior, and attention can then be directed to possible explanations not immediately apparent from cross-sectional data.

Turning as the second step to the focus on *formation of the structure*, cohort analysis also investigates how the successive cohorts fit together at times to create the age strata of people. Here the analysis shows that the particular pattern of aging, and the cohort changes in this pattern, account for the age structure in ways that could not have been discerned in a cross-sectional sample for one time period. In this instance, aging and cohort flow empirically counteract each other, leading to the absence of clear age differentiation in the first three time periods. On the one hand, the tendency for contraceptive use to rise with aging obviously means that use will tend to be higher in the *older* as compared with the younger strata at a particular period. On the other hand, whenever successive cohorts (compared age for age) increase their use, this heightening of use will be observed in the *younger* as compared with the older strata (the more recent cohorts constitute the younger, rather than the older). Because of these counteracting tendencies, few differences appeared among the age strata until 1970. Then the pronounced increase in contraceptive use by the youngest members (i.e., the most recent cohort) "washed out" the effect of aging, and thus changed the earlier pattern in the age structure. (For general rules for such derivation of cross-sectional structural configurations from processual information about the aging patterns of successive cohorts, see Ryder, 1963; Susser, 1969; Riley, 1973, 1976).

Incidentally, this finding of increased differentiation in the age strata in 1970 is important because it demonstrates how cohort flow,

not the aging process, accounts for the societal change among women in their twenties. General rules (for details see Riley 1973, 1976) are useful for understanding the relationship of these processes of aging and cohort flow to change in the cross-sectional age strata. A pertinent rule here is: When two or more time periods are compared, observed shifts in the behavior or attitudes of particular age strata are the consequence not of aging per se, but of differences (in level, slope, or shape) of aging patterns across cohorts. This rule is a formal statement of Ryder's (1964, p. 461) pronouncement: that social change occurs only to the extent that "successive cohorts do something other than merely repeat the patterns of behavior of their predecessors." Social change and cohort differences are interdependent. It is this principle that brings cohorts to center stage in understanding how human lives are implicated in social change.

EXAMPLE OF WOMEN'S LABOR FORCE PARTICIPATION

A second example of cohort analysis (as examined by Riley, Johnson, and Foner, 1972) refers to the well-known twentieth-century rise in American women's participation in the labor force. Historical data are displayed in Figure 8.4 as graphs of age-specific participation rates, arranged first in cross section, and then as age curves for successive cohorts (Kreps and Leaper, 1976; Taeuber and Sweet, 1976). In cross Section, the graph for 1940 shows a single peak at age 20 in the proportion of women in the labor force, followed by marked drops at all the subsequent ages. By 1960, however, a revolutionary change had occurred; the cross-sectional pattern still shows a peak at age 20, then a dip, but then a new and pronounced secondary peak at about age 50—a near doubling in the participation rates of women in the middle years. These cross-sectional age changes not only describe the proportions of women in the labor force at various ages, but also raise such structural issues (section IV) as the age-related match or mismatch between work roles available and women seeking work; the age inequalities of rewards, relations between middle-aged women who are working, their spouses, their elderly parents, and their daughters who are also likely to be in the labor force.

However, the cross-sectional data are not directly useful for understanding how individual women in different cohorts pattern labor force participation over their lives, or how these cohort differences in life-course patterns underlie the age stratification of work. For this purpose, the data are rearranged by cohorts in Figure 8.4 (2), from those born about 1890 to those born about 1970. In respect to *aging*, this refocusing of the analysis discloses striking cohort differences both in level and in shape of the life-course curves of labor force participation (because of these differences, reasoning from a single curve would produce a fallacy of cohort-centrism, Table 8.2). Most obvious is the long-term rise in labor force participation (the entire curve for each more recent cohort is higher than its predecessor), but note also the complete reversal in women's participation as they grow older: While members of the earliest cohort did *not* increase their participation after age 20, those in the most recent cohort enter the labor force in *increasing* numbers as they age. There has been a veritable transformation over the century in the work life of women. The striking cohort differences in aging patterns raises macro-level questions: e.g., as to how women in one cohort came to behave differently from women in another cohort, how rising educational levels have altered expectations, what rearrangements of work and family are involved, or what values have changed.

Turning to the focus on *formation of structure*, the differing cohorts fit together to form the set of age strata at given time periods. For example, the two peaks in the cross-sectional configuration are the outcome of differences between the aging patterns of earlier and more recent cohorts. Moreover, the changing cross-sectional picture reflects the interplay among the many varied cohorts of women passing through the strata and the changing age criteria governing women's work roles. For example, comparing cohorts of women reaching age 50 early in the century with those reaching 50 by mid-century suggests possible change in structural relationships between employers and older women workers. In the historical study of women at work, then, the cohort approach calls attention to empirical regularities that might otherwise be undiscovered, and rephrases interpretations in terms of cohort flow in relation both to the work lives of women and to the age structure of the work force.

POTENTIALS AND PROBLEMS OF THE APPROACH

Many similar analyses have been used to tease out the implications, both for aging and structural formation and change, of the flow of cohorts through political, economic, familial, and religious institutions, and through smaller social systems (work organizations, hospitals, the

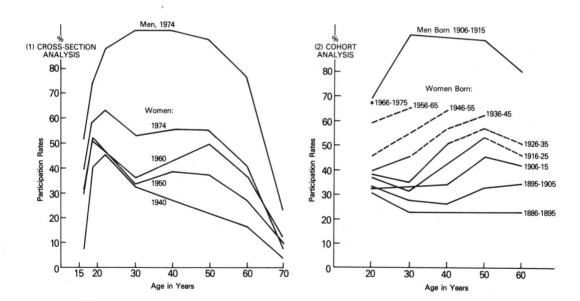

FIGURE 8.4
Labor Force Participation Rates by Age for Women

SOURCE: Kreps and Leaper, 1976 (adapted)

scientific community) where cohorts are often identified by date of entry rather than by birth (e.g., Liu and Manton, 1984; Schrank and Waring, 1983; Zuckerman and Merton, 1972). Information from cohort studies about the formation of age strata distinguishes them from cross-cultural studies. Though both are laboratories for examining life-course patterns under varied sociocultural conditions, what cross-cultural studies of aging cannot do (without cohort comparisons in the same societies) is to show how the varied life-course patterns fit together at given times to influence, and be influenced by, social structures and social change.

Useful as cohort analysis can be, there are many stubborn problems for which diverse solutions are being attempted. The data are complex, and oversimplified conceptualizations or facile statistical manipulations are often misleading.[6] When the research focus of the cohort approach is on individual aging, the identity of the individuals can be lost. For example, life-course changes that counteract each other will be obscured in "net shifts" in the aggregated cohort data. Individual shifts may be undetected if the measures are not continuous over time; or compositions shifts within a cohort (because of migration or mortality) may be erroneously interpreted as aging changes in individuals. Such obstacles are somewhat reduced when the research focus is on cohort contributions to age structures; here, too, however, special effort is needed to avoid submerging individual lives in the cohort aggregates (see Dannefer, 1987; Hagestad and Neugarten, 1985), or to avoid generalizing from the selectively biased survivors of earlier cohorts.

Uhlenberg (1969) illustrates an approach to cohort studies of aging that attacks the problems of obscuring within-cohort differences in life-course patterns by aggregation, and of compositional changes in the cohort through mortality. For cohorts of women born between 1830 and 1920, Uhlenberg uses census data on ages of marriage, having children, widowhood, and death in order to classify individual life-course patterns into several types. The genius of the approach is in taking mortality into account by tracing the lives of *all* women initially born into each cohort; this contrasts with the usual procedure of basing the average age of marriage or other events on only those selected women who survive. The analysis shows that the most frequent pattern for those born in 1830 was woman dying before age 20; whereas in the "typical" pattern for those born in 1890 or later, the woman survives to age 20, marries, has children,

and survives with her husband alive to at least age 55.

Other studies find various ways of handling difficulties of the cohort approach through modeling of continuous time measures (Liu and Manton, 1984); through compositional analysis, which holds constant across cohorts those factors known to operate selectively on mortality or migration (see Maddox, 1963); or through longitudinal studies of successive cohorts (see Schaie, 1983)—though these entail their own problems of sample mortality and representativeness (see Streib, 1966). Where statistical data are unavailable or limited in sociotemporal scope, or fail to provide needed detail on subjective orientations, other studies rely on documents, diaries, letters, or historical accounts (see Hareven, 1982; Kohli, 1985; Smelser, 1968; Vinovskis, 1982). As Ryder puts it (1965), considerable research investment is necessary "to study a long-lived species experiencing structural transformations."

Among the most widely discussed of the difficulties of research on cohorts is the "age-period-cohort problem," which is not intrinsic to cohort analysis but only to the particular form in which the data often appear: namely, where the variables are indexed by only two measures, date and age (as in Figures 8.3 and 8.4). In this form, the analysis encounters the "identification problem" (Blalock, 1967), familiar in sociological studies of social mobility or marital duration, where just two measures are used for determining the separate effects of three different concepts. While various procedures (see Fienberg and Mason, 1979; Mason and Fienberg, 1985) have been devised for interpreting such data, these procedures essentially require either knowledge or assumptions "that certain of the parameters are zero (or some other known value)," as Blalock put it (1967, p. 799; see also Cohn, 1972).

The most appropriate solution is to specify and measure directly the theoretical variables for which age, period, and cohort are used as indirect indicators in the particular analysis (Rodgers, 1982). For example, as early as 1955, Samuel Stouffer, finding that older people were less tolerant of nonconformity than were younger people, used educational level as an index of cohort membership in order to separate the influence of growing old from that of cohort differences in early socialization experience (for a similar example, see Dowd, 1980). More recently, Hoge and Hoge (1984) take care to specify the particular "age effects" on values of college alumni as "occupation-related influences" or "family-related influences." Gay and Campbell (1985), searching for the sources of personal well-being in either the cohort-size factors postulated by Easterlin (1980) or the aging theories of Levinson (1978), choose dates that reflect the "boom or bust" periods in Easterlin's work and ages that reflect Levinson's scheme. Ryder argues (1979) that, whatever the behavior under scrutiny in such studies, the collective members of the "cohort" constitute the behaving entity, the "period" is a surrogate for information about the social context at the time of observation, and "age" indexes information about the cohort.

Cohort Flow and Aging

Much of the work on cohort flow examines the relationship between social change and cohort differences in patterns of individual *aging*. The objective here is to probe into how and when particular social and cultural conditions and changes in these conditions influence the aging process. By comparing the aging experiences of members of successive cohorts, the life-course approach (Section II) is extended. In effect, cohort membership is treated as a contextual characteristic of the individuals who are aging.

The search for cohort differences can also lead to discovery of cohort *likenesses*, uncovering patterns of behavioral as well as biological aging that persist relatively intact. Such persistence could, of course, be ontogenic, but may also be shaped by enduring features of social organization. For example, over the last half-century in the United States there has been considerable stability in ages of labor market entry or retirement, reflecting an historically stable age-graded environment (Dannefer, 1984; Kalleberg and Loscocco, 1983). When similarities in life-course patterns are observed, despite variations in the conditions under which people live—as in the long-term evidence that crime rates peak between adolescence and adulthood (Hirschi and Gottfredson, 1983; Greenberg, 1985)—they may point to the relative importance of biological or psychological explanations (e.g., maturation) over social ones (e.g., the adolescent gap between needs and resources). While there is no "pure" process of aging (human beings do not grow up in laboratories but in complex and shifting social environments), the similarities across many cultures suggest those features of aging that most nearly approximate universals.

However, most cohort analyses emphasize *differences* among cohorts, and may be interpreted as modal changes in the aging process that are mediated by prevailing social conditions: for example, the timing of menarche seems related to the adequacy of nutrition available to successive cohorts; perceptions of "reading readiness" are affected by the pedagogical ideologies to which different cohorts of children are exposed; or the role of retiree may disappear for cohorts under the demands of war mobilization, or arrive in life's prime for members of cohorts experiencing economic retrenchments.

Other studies of cohort differences reinforce and begin to specify the general principle (WP 11) that aging is not immutable or entirely fixed by biology, but varies with social and cultural change (see Section II). For example, members of cohorts now in childhood differ from those who were children in the past in respect to number of parents surviving or living together, number of siblings, experience with day care, exposure to chronic diseases, and so on. Members of cohorts now old differ from those who were old in the past in respect to educational level, family history, work history, diet and exercise, standard of living, number of years in retirement, and—perhaps most significant of all—the number of years they can expect to survive. Cohort membership is a characteristic that not only marks a person at birth, but also has consequences at every age. The varied directions of cohort studies focused on the aging process can be illustrated by work on the impact of historical events, the timing of transitions, and the consequences of the lengthening life course.

IMPACT OF HISTORICAL CHANGES

Some studies examine specific aspects of historical change that cut across the coexisting cohorts at given periods to produce changes in the way aging occurs. For example, Vinovskis (1982) examines the lives of three cohorts of ministers in seventeenth- and eighteenth-century America, illustrating how the status and care of the elderly deteriorated, not because of age as such, but because of the effects of long-term declines in economic prosperity and spiritual ardor. Simkus (1982), focusing on the relationship between individuals' socioeconomic careers and radical changes in socioeconomic structures in Hungary during the previous 50 years, demonstrates how a rapid transition from agriculture to industry and intensive state intervention can bring substantial alterations in the aging process both through within-career shifts and through cross-cohort differences (see Featherman and Sorensen, 1982). Hofferth (1985), using the Panel Study of Income Dynamics (1960-1980), does not find cohort differences when she traces the modal life-course patterns up to age 17 of six cohorts of black and white children in "traditional" two-parent families. She shows how the break-up of families, though consistently higher for blacks than whites, comes at similar ages for all cohorts.

Other studies examine how short-term "period events" affect the aging process differentially as they impinge on coexisting cohorts. Elder (Elder and Rockwell, 1979), looking at consequences of the Great Depression for the future lives of members of different cohorts, finds that boys who were younger at the time of the event were more susceptible than older boys to the effects of the traumatic social change on family patterns and resources. Handl et al. (1979) show how the acceptance of women working during World War II in Germany, combined with the tendency to recruit only the youngest women to the newly developing industries, meant that women, unlike men, were increasingly likely to spend their entire work lives in these industries.

TIMING OF TRANSITIONS

Several sociologists have been concerned with cohort differences in the timing or ordering of life-course transitions (Hogan and Astone, 1987). Winsborough (1979) found that among cohorts of men born between 1911 and 1941, men in the more recent cohort moved more rapidly than their predecessors through role transitions associated with becoming an adult. This pace increased for many years (see Hareven, 1982; Modell, Furstenberg, and Hershberg, 1976) due to secular declines in the age of leaving the parental home. There is speculation about the implications of such piling up of role changes, as men in those more recent cohorts experienced a near simultaneity of entry or exit from their several overlapping roles in education, work, the military, their parental family, and their own new family. Whatever the consequences for the aging process, for the age structure the boundary to the age stratum of adulthood became more clearly defined during that period (see Kohli, 1985).

THE LENGTHENING LIFE COURSE

Among the major cohort differences in the aging process that have emerged in this century (see Riley and Riley, 1986) is the remarkable ex-

tension of longevity—in developed countries like the United States from an average life expectancy at birth of less than 50 years in 1900 to 70 for males and nearly 80 for females by the 1980s. The fact that in recent cohorts most people live to be old has sociological significance for the shape of the life course and the way it is subjectively experienced (Parsons, 1963; Preston, 1976). Many roles have been prolonged. Prolonged roles mean the accumulation of varied experiences (Riley, 1984), a "socially expected duration" (Merton, 1984) that allows ordering life in new ways; and they mean extended opportunities either to build or to dissolve commitments and solidary relationships (Turner, 1970; Hagestad, 1981). The extended life course has allowed education to be prolonged (see Parsons and Platt, 1972): Colonial children rarely went beyond grammar school, but the percentage graduating from high school rose to 38 in cohorts entering adulthood early in the century and to over 70 in the 1970s and 1980s. Retirement, which scarcely existed early in the century, now typically occupies over one-fourth of the adult life course. Role relationships are protracted: In couples marrying a century ago, one or both partners were likely to have died before the children were reared; today they can anticipate surviving together (apart from divorce) for 40 or 50 years on the average (Uhlenberg, 1969, 1980). Today, parents and children live a larger share of their lives as age-status equals than in the adult-dependent child relationship (Hess and Waring, 1978; Menken, 1985).

RELATION TO HEALTH

One critical, but still unanswered question about the postponement of mortality is whether the age-specific health status of the population has been improving from one cohort to another, or deteriorating because many disabled or ill people are now being kept alive (see Feldman, 1983; Manton, 1982). Verbrugge's (1985) review of the literature, while acknowledging indications of deteriorating health in recent decades in the United States, also points to practices that encourage increasing manifestation of ill health: the continuing emphasis by the medical profession on treatment rather than prevention, the trend toward screening and earlier detection of cancer and other diseases, and the willingness of old people to use poor health as the grounds for suspended work activities.

The confused relationship between health and the extended life course applies to the younger as well as the older ages. Modern medicine preserves the lives of infants with incurable congenital impairments and of youthful accident victims who would have died under earlier conditions. Among women at the reproductive ages, infertility (the reduced ability to conceive and bear a live child) became an "issue" with the cohort increases in childlessness during the 1960s and 1970s. Menken (1985) notes that biological infertility is thought to rise only moderately with aging up to the late thirties or early forties, so that the question is whether cohort comparisons are showing actual age-specific infertility increases over time, or whether the increases are associated with surgical sterilization or other contraceptive practices. A more important factor behind the concern may be the high level of interest in infertility currently shown by physicians and childless couples.

Cohort Flow and the Age Structure

Complementing the work on cohort differences in the aging process are studies of how cohort flow contributes to the formation of the age strata (see Section IV). Cohort flow affects *the age structure of people* in two ways. First, cohort flow affects the *numbers* and *kinds* of people in particular strata, as each cohort starts the life course with a characteristic size and composition (genetic makeup, sex ratio, proportions of different races, and so on), properties that are subsequently modified through migration and through the mortality of cohort members (as men tend to die earlier than women, or blacks earlier than whites). Second, cohort flow affects the *capacities, attitudes, and actions* of people in particular strata as the members of each cohort bring to the social structure their experiences with the social and environmental events spanned by their previous lifetime. As the different cohorts of people enter concurrently into the strata, they encounter the exigencies of the *age-related roles*, and they interact with people in other strata who differ from them in age and cohort experience.

Only a few strands of sociological work break into this intricate age system to describe the real-world meanings of the interdependent relationships between cohort flow and the age structure. A few examples, though not cognate with each other, begin to specify how cohort flow, through differences in size, composition, and life-course experiences, affect particular cross-sectional age configurations. Although for parsimony, we shall ordinarily speak of averages for each cohort, it is understood that *within* each cohort different kinds of people, contending with different kinds of social situations, act and think in very different ways.

COHORT SIZE AND THE AGE STRUCTURE OF PEOPLE

That differences in cohort size affect the age strata is evident to all who have observed the baby boom cohort of the 1950s. This cohort is creating role strain followed by role slack as it progresses through the strata, requiring expansion followed by contraction of the educational system, confusing the age-related operations of the work force in the late twentieth century, presaging an unprecedented "aging" of the population early in the twenty-first century (see Espenshade and Braun, 1983), not to mention creating an echo baby "boomlet" in the 1970s and 1980s. Yet, these baby booms appear as temporary interruptions when compared with the long-term downward trends in both fertility and mortality. The structure of society as we know it today reflects at least a century of past cohort experience, and portends at least another century of future cohort experience. People in the oldest stratum today were born under fertility conditions affecting the cohort of their mothers a century ago; and the survival of those in the youngest stratum today will depend on mortality conditions affecting their cohort over the next century.

The cohorts born during the past hundred years have been marked by a world decline in *mortality* equalling the entire decline in all previous human history (Preston, 1976). In the United States, declines in mortality in earlier cohorts, when most deaths occurred in infancy, added to the size of the younger age strata. More recently, however, as members of successive cohorts have increasingly withstood the ills of childhood and middle age until the great majority now survive to at least age 65, mortality declines are contributing to the growing numbers of people in the middle strata and currently to the stratum of the "oldest old," age 85 and over (Suzman and Riley, 1985). Because longevity has increased faster for women than for men, women now predominate in the older strata—by the year 2000 the ratio of women to men is estimated at 150 to 100 at age 65 and over, and at 350 to 100 at age 85 and over.

As cohort differences in longevity result in increasing numbers of people in the middle-aged and older strata, all social institutions are affected. The age structure of the kin network has become more complex (Section IV), as four generations of many families now survive: For example, in 1900 fewer than half of middle-aged couples had surviving elderly parents, whereas today half have two or more parents still alive (Uhlenberg, 1980). Menken (1985), using simulations of age-specific cohort differences in survival and family status, estimates a dramatic change in the proportions of 50-year-old women in the middle-aged strata who have a surviving mother: an increase from 37% to 65% between 1940 and 1980, which is even greater when 1980 is compared with 1900 or 1800. (Note the effects of cohort increases in longevity in prolonging role relationships between mothers and daughters, described above.) Menken also uses simulations to estimate the combined effects of cohort changes in mortality and fertility on the coexistence in a single family of all three generations of women. The expected number of years that a woman will have simultaneously *both* a child under 18 and a parent over 65 peaks at about eight years in 1960 and then decreases again (reflecting both the long-term cohort increases in the ages to which parents survive, and the cohort declines in fertility).

As cohort differences in mortality and fertility affect the sizes of the particular age strata, other changes ensue. Changes in family structure interact with changes produced by related cohort differences in other institutions (Section IV): For example, the same middle-strata women who, as the primary caretakers in the family, are sandwiched between their parents and their children are also increasingly active in the labor force (see Taeuber and Sweet, 1976), and encounter the economic "squeeze" between age-related family income and needs described by Valerie Oppenheimer (1981).

Long-term declines in mortality have undoubtedly contributed to the long-term declines in *fertility*: from 8 to 10 children born to each woman in eighteenth-century cohorts, to about 5 for mid-nineteenth-century cohorts, and down to approximately 2 today (Taeuber and Sweet, 1976, p. 48). The processes linking fertility declines to declines in mortality are age related (Davis, 1963). Instead of bearing enough children so that at least a few would survive, successive cohorts of young people earlier in the century were increasingly motivated to use whatever means of fertility control they knew in order to reduce the number of children they bore. Menken (1985), looking at the recent cohorts of young women who now become mothers later, if at all, and have fewer children, suggests that, because of longevity, fertility changes may also reflect concern about incurring lasting obligations.

Of course, such studies of the effects of cohort size on age strata size also point to related changes in age patterns of marrying or having children, as well as to shifts in the roles occupied by young parents or elderly daughters. As Mannheim put it originally (also Ryder, 1968), the demographic facts of size and composition provide opportunities for social process and social change, but cannot account for particular features of any given modification. Like all social processes, cohort flow is embedded in and realized through structured social relationships, reflecting ties to the social locations and the basic values and personal interests of the participants, and reflecting the interplay with the age structure of roles. Moreover, these processes operate not only in society as a whole but also in smaller systems, where entrance and exit of successive cohorts form the age structure. For example, Zuckerman and Merton (1972) show how, with the rapid growth of science, the rising numbers of newly trained scientists had a "juvenescent effect" on the age structure of scientists; or the small numbers of new cohorts of academicians is leading to an "aging" of the professoriate.

COHORT SIZE AND THE AGE STRUCTURE OF ROLES

Another strand of sociological work addresses the linkages through which differences in cohort size and composition affect the age structure of roles and the criteria for role assignment and role performance. Waring (1975) coined the term *disordered cohort flow* for situations in which incoming cohorts that are too large or too small for the roles available in the age strata evoke societal alterations in the age-related roles themselves. By formulating the issues, Waring set forth an agenda still demanding further research.

The effect of cohort size on role structures is the theme of Easterlin's (1980) book, *Birth and Fortune: The Impact of Numbers on Personal Welfare*. He shows how the relative size of cohorts since World War II seem to have "determined" the economic fortunes of cohort members. In small cohorts, job opportunities were comparatively plentiful, and families could be started easily, while in large cohorts jobs and advancement were harder to obtain; couples postponed marriages, and children and family life were subject to greater economic pressure.

Waring's analysis identifies processes that, by operating to redress the balance between people and roles, can either modify existing roles or change what roles are allocated and how they are allocated. For the most part, Waring argues (see also Ryder, 1965), new cohorts are ushered into and earlier cohorts eased out of successive role complexes without disturbing usual social arrangements. First graders become second graders and are replaced by a new cohort of first graders without upsetting the school operations. However, when the fit between the cohort and the role system is poor, the customary orderly flow of cohorts becomes so disordered as to undermine the established age grading arrangements, and to elicit alterations in age criteria and in age role structures. These alterations are sometimes made deliberately; more often they occur through ad hoc responses of diverse agencies to situational changes. Moreover, these alterations in turn can disrupt the life course of the people involved, and cause further changes in the affected stratum and other strata.

In instances where no radical institutional changes are necessary, the balance is redressed simply by changing the numbers of roles: for instance, building new schools or nursing homes for excessive numbers of pupils or elderly patients, or making room at the top in firms pressed by a large cohort of middle-aged executives (Easterlin, 1980, p. 152). When cohorts are relatively small, vacancies can sometimes be filled by retraining retirees, or by teaching new skills to displaced younger workers. Some imbalances are handled through migration. In the late nineteenth century, countries undergoing economic expansion welcomed young immigrants to work in agriculture or industry (see Thomas and Znaniecki, 1918). Though long-term declines in migration of unskilled young people to the United States have markedly reduced the proportion of foreign-born in cohorts recently entering old age strata, international labor migrations, both legal and illegal, are now furnishing workers at various ages for underdemanded occupations.

In other instances, in line with Waring's formulation, major role changes occur that tend to redress imbalances between people and roles. Such changes include modifications in age criteria for role entry or role exit, or in age-related role expectations, facilities, and sanctions. Familiar examples of *changing age criteria* for role occupancy show how, as a consequence, the rate of flow from one role to another is altered. In the wake of the baby boom, the age of entry to educational institutions was first raised; subsequently, with the dwindling of applications for college, age restrictions on entry of older adults were often removed. The supply of older workers has also been increased or decreased by changes in age of eligibility for retirement benefits. Such changes in age criteria

are made *directly* (as through legislation) or *indirectly* (as budgetary cutbacks can postpone the age at which many frail old people enter nursing homes; or as improved screening can lower the age at which people are diagnosed as having cancer).

Less explicit than such age regulations are changes in age-related expectations, facilities, or sanctions that have the effect of controlling the *rate of cohort flow*. The flow through schools of an oversupply of children is accelerated if summer sessions are added. Raising or lowering standards for admission to colleges will decelerate or accelerate the flow of entrants. The flow of young people into the work force is decelerated if job requirements protract the period of education. The movement of adult workers into the higher echelons slowed through "down grading," which Easterlin (1980, p. 151) describes as analogous to being "left back" in school, and which limits mobility opportunities for the newer cohort further down the line. Early retirement of older workers in the United States, stimulated following World War II by the Social Security Act, is further encouraged through pension plans, special incentives, or failure to promote or rehire after a period of unemployment (e.g., Pampel and Park, 1986). Manipulation of reimbursement plans accelerates or decelerates the flow of frail old people into nursing homes.

Still other age-related processes influence people's *level of performance* when, in response to people-role imbalances, age-related expectations, facilities, or rewards change. Studies show how, when role opportunities exceed the numbers of people, household management is rearranged to increase the usefulness of children in the family; special lighting, equipment, and work conditions are adjusted to increase the productivity of older workers; or self-help devices are introduced to improve the functioning of elderly residents in nursing homes. If elderly patients are rewarded for being independent and caring for themselves, they are likely to show improvements in health; whereas the underdemanded who are "warehoused" in situations of dependence tend to deteriorate. Where older workers or new military recruits are comparatively scarce, challenge and the promise of rewards encourage them to try harder, whereas lack of stimulation and incentives discourages effort, often producing its own form of deviance.

Just as diverse changes in age roles may be evoked by disordered cohort flow, changes in any one stratum will affect other strata as well, often with unintended consequences (see

Winsborough, 1979). For example, China's one-child policy will have consequences for the kinship structure, virtually eliminating the role of sibling, reducing the scope of aunt, uncle, or cousin, and creating new problems of old age support (Kertzer, personal communication). Or in the example of college faculties in the 1980s, with the population bulge at the older ages and little room for young recruits, efforts were made to encourage early retirements. Having intentionally accelerated the flow out of faculty roles, college administrators must then make renewed efforts to accelerate the flow back into these roles.

COHORT EXPERIENCE AND
AGE-RELATED PERFORMANCE

Cohort differences in life-course experience can also affect both people and roles in the age strata, in turn contributing to further cohort differences and to the continuing dialectic between aging and social change. Here a related process is at work, *cohort norm formation* (Mannheim, 1928/1952; Riley, 1978), when behaviors and attitudes that develop within a cohort in response to social change become institutionalized as norms that then pervade all the age strata. Several studies illustrate this process, as members of the same cohort, responding to shared experiences, develop common patterns of response, common definitions, and common norms.

Age criteria, though operating as social controls, arise in many complex ways (see Section II), sometimes as normatively prescribed, sometimes as factual age regularities (Hagestad and Neugarten, 1985; Riley, Johnson, and Foner, 1972; Rosow, 1985). Factual age criteria (e.g., average or modal ages of entering or leaving roles, age patterns of role performance) are formed when societywide conditions and changes converge upon particular age categories in the population, as the recent emergence of nursery schools for 3- to 5-year olds followed changes in women's labor force participation. Often, age regularities in cohort behavior translate indirectly into *age norms*, and may then become institutionalized in the role structure through shared expectations, formal regulations, contracts, or laws (Cain, 1964). In other instances, normative age criteria derive from widespread beliefs about the capacities and reactions of people at particular ages, beliefs that are frequently unfounded and subject to change. Beliefs as to what children or old people can do then shade into ideological notions about what they *ought* to do. For example,

historians describe long periods in Western history when age norms for children differed little from those for adults because no distinctive value was placed on the needs of children.

The evolution of age criteria, first factual and then becoming normative, can be seen in historical accounts of how changes wrought by the Industrial Revolution affected successive cohorts entering the age stratum called childhood. In contrast with the preindustrial era in England (Smelser, 1968), when a father typically apprenticed his older sons to his trade, the introduction of a new technology that routinized tasks meant that the entire family could work together as a unit either in the factory or in the home. Thus parents attempted to counter economic change through new behavior patterns in which, even though the children's work lasted from sunup to sundown, parents could nevertheless provide discipline and even some recreation.

With further technological developments, these family patterns broke down (spinners were required to hire more assistants than they had children, and home weavers were forced to send their children into the factories) and, as fathers lost direct control and protection of their offspring, the state interceded with legislation limiting children's working hours to 8 (while parents worked for 12), and providing schools for children during several hours of the parent's working day. This splitting apart of parents and children paved the way for entirely new stages such as childhood and adolescence, which were publicly defined as real and objective by "experts" in childhood.

Some general understanding of the process of cohort norm formation can be gleaned from this and similar detailed studies (see Schrank and Waring, 1983). The process (Riley, 1978) can be described as follows: (a) in response to social change, people in a cohort begin to develop new age-typical patterns and regularities of behavior (changes in aging); (b) these behavior patterns then become defined as age-appropriate norms and rules, are reinforced by "authorities," affect other strata, and thereby become institutionalized in the role structure of society (social change); (c) in turn these changes in age norms and social structures redirect age-related behaviors (further changes in aging). In such ways, each cohort exerts a collective force as it moves through the age-stratified society, pressing for adjustments in social roles and social values.

Varied studies shed further light on the nature of this process (see Hagestad and Neugarten, 1985, for a summary). Analyzing marked cohort differences in the age of marriage during the Great Depression and World War II, Modell (1980) concludes that economic changes evoked the alterations in behavior, which were only then reflected in norms about the appropriate timing of marriage. Another study (McGee and Wells, 1982) suggests how, in response to increases in paid employment for women in successive cohorts, tendencies toward androgyny and decreased gender typing might characterize members of these cohorts as they reach the older age strata. Sutton (1983), reporting on shifts in the legal status of children in the United States, shows how variations in formal age criteria occur as successive cohorts of reformers move through society to influence such changes. Refuges and reform schools, set up early in the nineteenth century, gradually took over all the functions of parents, not only assuming complete control over the children, but also attempting to reform the entire society through its children. Rossi (1982), in a study of women in politics, details how a succession of several cohorts is required for structural change to be effected. The first cohort, angered by the limits imposed on them as women, struggles to achieve certain structural changes. The second cohort lives in the new set of social relationships, experiencing both the freedom and the limits of the restructured world. The third cohort takes the freedom for granted but experiences the limits acutely, thus reverting to the struggles of the first cohort to remove these restraints (see Ferree and Hess, 1985).

Such analyses suggest how age norms may be formed when values and attitudes that developed within a cohort in response to social change become institutionalized and pervade all the age strata. Cohort flow is seen as an independent source of social change, as people and roles modify each other.

FUTURE DIRECTIONS

Apart from the theoretical importance of cohort flow as a major vehicle for social change, it is clear that the cohort approach also has practical utility in improving future forecasts of the age structure of society. Members of every cohort currently alive already have a past history, about which much is known or can be learned, and this history can be used to anticipate the future lives of these cohort members and their contributions to the future state of society. As one illustration, Uhlenberg (1979), projecting the characteristics of old people in the year 2000, reconstructs the life-course patterns of cohorts born in 1890, 1900, and 1930. By tracing the

cumulative impact on these lives of major demographic variables (mortality, fertility, marital formation and dissolution, immigration, and urbanization), he is able to describe declines in poverty and inadequate health care in the changing old age strata, and also to warn of the widening gap between the generally improving abilities of older people and their decreasing opportunities to participate in the future labor force or the family. Along similar lines, Glick (1979) summarizes some of the estimates: The percentage of elderly women (65 and over) living alone will rise from 38% in 1976 to over 50% by 2000; and among women 65 to 79, the proportion ever divorced will nearly double (from 12% to 22%).

Cohort approaches to forecasting are increasingly common in both popular speculation and sophisticated mathematical modeling (see Singer, Manton, and Suzman, in press); some are reaching the popular media and informing public policy. Several of the predicted tendencies (reminiscent of earlier warnings by Sorokin, 1941, or Spengler, 1926-28) against assuming continuing unilinear "progress'" point to possible reversals in some long-standing cross-sectional advantages of younger over older strata. Although in the past the more recent cohorts started their life course at *higher* levels of advantage than their predecessors, in certain respects current cohorts in the United States are starting at *lower* levels. Reports from the United States Bureau of the Census and other sources show that for the decades between the 1950s and the 1980s, for example the median inflation-adjusted wage for a 30-year-old male head of household has dropped; the percentage of wages needed by a 30-year-old head of household for mortgage payments on a median-priced house has risen sharply; the percentages of infants born out of wedlock and of children living in female-headed households has risen—changes that are even more drastic for blacks than whites; cohorts reaching old age by the turn of the century will no longer be significantly inferior to younger people in educational attainment; and in performance on achievement tests, cohorts of high school students in the United States have shown declines. Such cohort differences, to the extent that they persist through the years remaining in the lives of these cohort members, could erode the superiority of the younger over the older strata in economic level, family stability, or educational accreditation and recency (for similar possibilities of reversal of past tendencies, see Kohli, 1985).

However, all estimates of the future rest on assumptions (see, for example, the caveats in Liu and Manton, 1984). These assumptions are precarious under current conditions of rapid social and ideological change and little-understood increases in longevity; and they require far more specification of *how* cohort flow affects particular structural configurations. Yet the recognition of cohort differences, past and future, with their implications for individual aging over the life course and their repercussions throughout the age strata, lay the groundwork for examining the nature of the age strata and their distributive and evaluative characteristics.

IV. Age Structure

Studies of age structure focus on the social divisions based on age (age strata) that cut across the society and its institutions at given points in time. Age strata in society are like the grades in a modern school: Both consist of people of similar age, similarly guided by age criteria defining their expected behaviors and goals. Unlike the school grade, which involves a single age-related role, however, each stratum in the society embraces a complex of age-related roles.

Section III has shown how age strata form and change through the continuing interplay between changes in society with its age-related roles and the aging of successive cohorts of people. Section IV reviews studies of the age structure itself: its configurations, operations, intrinsic dynamics; its place within social systems and institutional spheres; and the location of individuals within it. Studies range from those showing how age defines criteria for social positions that influence people's performances and attitudes, to those exploring age as a basis of inequality and conflict, following the Marxian tradition, or as a basis of integration and solidarity, following Durkheim. They illustrate several working principles (WP; Table 8.1): age-based relationships of cohesion or conflict (WP 4 and 5); the interdependence of the several age strata (WP 3); pressures toward change inherent in age stratification systems (WP 13); and intersections of age systems with other stratification systems.

The Nature of Age Structures

In every society both people and roles are stratified by age. There are broad social divisions, for example, among children, youths, adults, and old people, and age criteria for roles that are often reinforced by laws or bureaucratic rules. The age structure of social roles and institutions tends to persist beyond the lifetime of particular individuals. Many studies have noted how these age structures vary across societies and change over historical time.

AGE STRUCTURES OF ROLES

The pervasiveness of age structures has prompted investigations of how age is built into social institutions and into the criteria for role incumbency and role performance. Some explanations emphasize cohort flow and the articulating processes of socialization and allocation. Thus Cain (1964) sees the formation of age systems as a solution to problems of succession: As cohorts of individuals age, they must be prepared for successive statuses (roles in our terminology), absorbed into these roles, and removed from roles formerly occupied. In a similar vein, Eisenstadt (1956) sees youth groups forming to ease the transition to adulthood in those societies where, because attainment of full adult status requires meeting standards of achievement and universalism, kinship groups are unsuited to the socialization task.

Other studies of age role structures emphasize the aging process. Meyer (1986), in proposing the "institutionalization of the life course" (Section II, Role Sequences), traces a broad social and cultural shift from traditional views of individuals and their actions as derivative of family, tribal, communal, ethnic, or status groups to a Western view of society as a product of individual choice (see Fortes, 1984). Gradually, these Western individualistic views have lost their earlier utilitarian, romanticist, or Calvinist forms and have become bureaucratized, so that the "central social categories of modern society are those socially defining the actor's place in the life cycle and linking steps in this cycle." In accounting for such institutionalization of the life course, Mayer and Mueller (1982) emphasize the role of the state in defining "ports of entry and exit" that turn life-course transitions into public events. Kohli (1986) argues rather for the primacy of the modern system of labor, as institutionalization of the life course serves to meet such problems in the social organization of work as pressures for rationalization, social control, and orderly succession. In effect, the age strata as they currently exist have been socially constructed to fit the life-course patterns of individuals, with transition points constituting the structural boundaries between age strata in the society at given periods. This view of age in the life course of individuals as central to the structure of modern Western societies contrasts with the contention of other scholars that age is a more powerful base of social organization in many less complex societies (as in age-set societies; Foner and Kertzer, 1978; Bernardi, 1985).

One aspect of age structure, the status of old people, has been attributed to features of modernization. Cowgill (1974), for example, accounts for the declining status of older people in terms of such modernization processes as technological advances, industrialization, and educational upgrading. This "modernization theory" has been challenged for being too global, and inapplicable either to preindustrial or postindustrial eras (Foner, 1986; Pampel, 1981; Quadagno, 1982). Calling for qualifications, Quadagno cites the nineteenth-century English example of elderly seamstresses whose status actually improved with industrialization, because the newly invented sewing machine increased the value of the piecework produced at home.

AGE STRUCTURE OF PEOPLE

Studies of people who perform the roles in these age structures focus not only on people's capacities and motivations but also on their distributions across the strata (see Figure 8.5). Special attention has been paid to the widespread twentieth-century phenomenon of "population aging": Unlike individuals, populations can grow not only older but also younger, as, for example, the baby boom at its inception disproportionately enlarged the younger strata. In "The Sociology of Population Aging," Davis and Combs (1950) lay the groundwork for many subsequent treatments. They emphasize that the growing numbers of older people in American society are inseparable from the increasing complexity of the society and its institutions, for "it is only in a changing, mobile, industrial, and urban society that birth and death rates fall so rapidly and so low that a heavy proportion of aged people is produced" (p. 151; see Cowgill, 1974). In such a society, even apart from their numerical proportions, the status of the aged is altered. The isolation of the modern family, the competitiveness of economic organization, geographical and social mobility, and the rapid pace of social change all would make older people more useless and insecure and hence turn them into a social problem even if their proportion in the population were small. The chang-

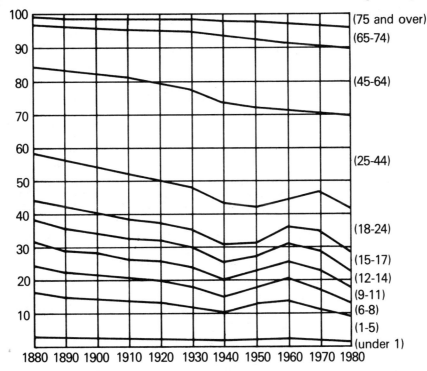

FIGURE 8.5
Distribution of United States Population by Age Strata, 1880-1980

ing age distribution simply adds to the magnitude of the problem.

Other implications of the aging of society's population have also been explored (Pifer and Bronte, 1986). For example, will high proportions of old people necessarily produce a conservative society? Davis and Combs's answer is negative: Whether or not individuals become more conservative with aging, the kind of society that can reduce its mortality and fertility is also likely to be more innovative—as characterized by education, cities, industrial technology—than other societies that are demographically more youthful. Or what are the consequences of a top-heavy population for public expenditures? Pampel and Williamson (1986) find in advanced industrial democracies that per capita expenditures for public pensions are associated with the size of the aged population. However, the particular mechanisms by which such policies are implemented are subject to debate (e.g., DeViney, 1984; Myles, 1984; Shalev, 1983; see also Section 4, Age and the Structure of Politics).

In sum, the status of people in any age stratum depends on both their numbers and personal characteristics, and on the age-related rights and duties prescribed in the particular society. Studies in three selected institutional spheres—the economy, the polity, and the family—will describe these age structures of people and roles, their relationships to aging and cohort flow, and their implications for age stratification systems as a whole.

Age and the Structure of Work

In modern societies, where work is a major activity in the adult strata, the age stratification of work roles provides a key illustration. Education prepares young people for work, and retirement from work contributes to the definition of old age (see Foner and Schwab, 1981). The changing age distribution of work, education, and retirement in the United States since 1900 is shown in Figure 8.6. In all societies (Cowgill, 1986) age has played a part in assigning productive roles in the economy, largely because of perceived age-related abilities and performances. With the institutionalization of retirement as the typical pattern for older workers, however, chronological age itself has become the basis for leaving the work force. Entry into the labor force is also age graded, indirectly through establishment of educational criteria for many jobs, but also directly as in chronological ages prescribed in child labor laws.

THE AGE PATTERN OF WORK

In advanced societies, the cross-sectional age pattern of labor force participation is curvilinear: high rates of participation among people age 25 to 54 and lower rates among those 16 to 24 and over 55, with those 65 and over having by far the lowest rates. While women's participation currently tends to follow this same broad pattern, their rates are generally lower than men's.

There are also age differences in the kinds of jobs people hold. Kaufman and Spilerman (1982) report that occupations with relatively high proportions of self-employed (e.g., the independent professions, tailor, barber, or taxi driver) have a relatively high concentration of older workers, as self-employment provides some flexibility in the scheduling of work. In contrast, physically demanding jobs, many entry-level positions, and openings in new fields such as computer industries tend to be "young-age" occupations. Jobs filled by the middle aged, though more varied, involve many supervisory and middle-level tasks such as school administrators or sales manager.

Not only the kinds of jobs people hold, but also the overall age distribution of the work force itself, change drastically with industrialization. In colonial America, children—sometimes as young as six or seven—were often sent out to work as servants or apprentices (Demos, 1970). Preindustrial societies, from hunting and gathering or horticultural groups to large-scale agricultural societies, typically utilize the productive capacity of children as well as of older people, who continue to work as long as they are able, switching to easier tasks or tapering off gradually as necessary. Even in early factory production, young children were part of the work force, often under the supervision of their parents (Marx, 1906; Smelser, 1968); and there was no set age among older workers for withdrawal from their jobs. Child labor and labor force participation by older men are still common in many developing societies today.

THE CHANGING AGE
STRUCTURE OF WORK

The voluminous multidisciplinary literature on the institutionalization of retirement in the modern era (e.g., Foner, 1986; Foner and Schwab, 1981; Graebner, 1980; Pampel and Weiss, 1983; Riley and Foner, 1968) points to many common factors in the nonemployment of children, teenagers, and older people. One factor is the form of productive activity. Where securing and growing food are predominant, work is organized to accommodate the labor of young and old. By contrast, in more advanced societies, with a wide variety of jobs—some of which require special training—educational credentials are used to screen job seekers and thus to delay entry into the work force (see Coleman, 1974).

Problems of succession, which require no special measures in nonindustrial societies where high mortality rates ensure spaces for younger workers, are handled in more developed societies by formal and informal rules of employee replacement (Foner and Schwab, 1981). Modern work organizations characteristically operate according to bureaucratic rules that apply to all workers. At younger ages, rules are typically reinforced by state regulations barring child labor. At older ages, bureaucratic rules often

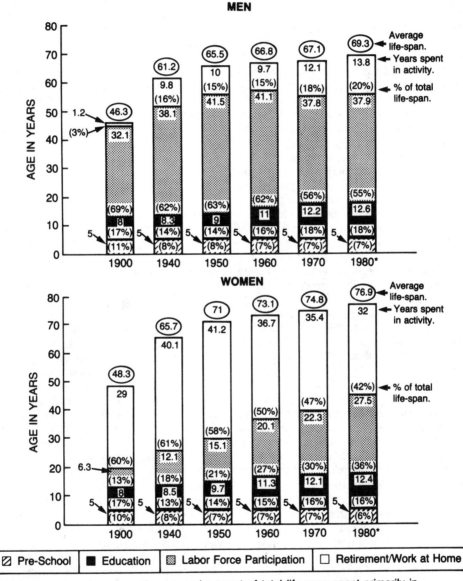

Divisions represent number of years and percent of total life-span spent primarily in these activities.

FIGURE 8.6
Distribution of the United States Population by Years of Education, Labor Force Participation, Work in the Home, and Retirement, 1900-1980

SOURCE: United States Senate and the American Association of Retired Persons, 1985, *Aging America*, p. 45

prevent workers from tapering off gradually or mandate retirement at given ages. Retirement-related rules deal with problems of succession by relieving the pressure by middle-aged workers for promotion and facilitating the employment of younger workers. They also forestall time consuming and potentially painful decisions based on individual cases.

Another factor that affects older workers in particular is the perception—often inaccurate—of their qualifications to do the work. In all societies, the aging process takes a toll of many of the oldest workers in diminished strength, sensory impairment, or activity limitations due to chronic disease. Yet in preindustrial societies the experience and accumulated knowledge of older people was often an economic asset that compensated for many physical decrements. In today's more advanced societies, despite widespread chronic ailments and impairments, the great majority of older people report that they can carry on normal activities. Among those who remain in the work force there is great variation in productivity, perhaps more than among younger workers; yet, on average, the performance of older workers is not significantly inferior to that of younger workers (Foner and Schwab, 1981; Riley and Bond, 1983; Robinson, Coberly, and Paul, 1985). Further, many jobs in the modern era are not physically taxing, and there is much evidence that older workers are able to learn new methods if given the opportunity. Facts about older workers' abilities notwithstanding, however, it is employers' beliefs that are critical, and there are still widespread negative stereotypes about the ability of older workers.

On one important qualification for work, many older people are disadvantaged in the modern era: They are less likely than younger applicants to have the educational credentials required by employers, although the age gap in educational attainment is speedily narrowing and expected to be nearly closed by the 1990s (Taeuber, 1983). Further, the training of older workers who do have such credentials is typically outdated, although adult education and retraining is increasingly frequent.

The estimated costs of retraining or hiring an older worker also influence employers' decisions, as older employees enjoy relatively high wages or salaries and fringe benefits as a result of long tenure on the job. Younger workers, in contrast, have typically low entry-level salaries, their basic training has been financed privately or with state subsidies, and the indirect costs of their on-the-job training can be spread over many decades (Foner, 1986).

Labor market conditions also affect the participation of both younger and older workers. Where youth unemployment is particularly high, as in several countries in the 1980s, many young people cannot get a toehold in the work force, have little hope of securing regular employment in the future, and often remove themselves from the labor force entirely. Older workers who lose jobs when plants close or who move away face longer periods of unemployment than do younger workers, and many then decide to retire from the work force (Robinson, Coberly, and Paul, 1985).

Another key factor is the development of alternative sources of income. The establishment of Social Security insurance and other public programs for the old, combined with the spread of private pensions, has helped to pull older workers out of the work force by providing a foundation of support for those who cannot or do not wish to work or for whom there are no jobs.

CONSEQUENCES

Nonparticipation in the work force provides the young with a period in which to prepare for work and the old with leisure after a lifetime of work. Insofar as money is centrally valued in a society, however, nonparticipation means that on average both young and old tend to be relatively deprived. In the United States in the mid-1980s the youngest and especially the oldest adults reported median incomes far below those of people aged 35 to 64. In the mid-1980s, poverty rates were highest for young people. The percentage of elderly below the poverty level has been lowered due to extensions of Social Security benefits, but remains higher than among adults 25 to 64 and is especially severe among the very old, widows, and nonwhites. However, there are wide differences among individuals, and income levels are especially diverse among older people, a few of whom have large accumulated assets that are income producing.

Insofar as positions of economic power provide access to other forms of power, the overall status of both young and old is affected. The age patterns of inequality differ from those found in nonindustrial societies, where the old are often the most advantaged, at least until advanced old age or when disabilities set in (N. Foner, 1984). The advantages of the old (particularly older men) in these societies often rests on ownership or control of land or livestock, on knowledge and experience as economic assets, and on such noneconomic factors as ritual knowledge or closeness to ancestors. Younger people, who have not had time to accumulate or inherit these resources and are dependent on older kin, generally have low status.

The age status of individuals in economic life has consequences for the family and other social institutions. In preindustrial societies, there can be intergenerational conflicts, as young men challenge their fathers to cede economic assets to them (N. Foner, 1984). Among the old in advanced societies, although most express high levels of satisfaction with retirement (see Foner and Schwab, 1981), some husbands and wives realign roles, and some retired men feel uncomfortable in intergenerational contacts that remind them of their loss of power (Dowd, 1980). The exclusion of certain age strata from the labor force also has a societal impact; for example, provision of work for young and old, or the extent of societal responsibility for those out of the work force, can become political issues (see Section IV). Moreover, unemployment among the young may be associated with deviant behaviors (Horwitz, 1984).

THE AGE STRATIFICATION
OF WORK ORGANIZATIONS

Of special sociological interest is age stratification within employing organizations. Studies have traced the relationship or organizational exigencies and age-graded policies to the experiences of individuals who confront the age structures of these organizations. In one analysis, Schrank and Waring (1983) show how the age stratification of work emerges and plays itself out within the modern firm (see also Pfeffer, 1981), where both people and roles are stratified by age. Employees are ordered by organizational age (time with the firm), job age (tenure on a particular job), as well as chronological age. Age, however indexed, tends to qualify individuals for particular jobs, and to set norms defining the kinds of jobs appropriate for them.

To be sure, not all organizational roles are governed by age criteria (e.g., elevator operator or cafeteria worker), which suggests that there may be multiple age structures within firms. If labor markets are segmented (see, for example, Kalleberg and Sorensen, 1979), then Schrank and Waring's analysis should be most applicable to occupations in the core or primary sectors of the labor market. Age norms governing many blue-collar and lower-level white-collar jobs in the periphery or secondary sectors appear applicable to only certain aspects of their jobs (degree of job protection or eligibility for fringe benefits, for example) and to be less clearly defined.

Schrank and Waring also use the example of the firm to illustrate the dynamic character of an age stratification system. The age structure of people is replenished as new cohorts of employees are hired, while others leave, become disabled, or are terminated. External events such as a military draft or changing college enrollments influence the age structure of people in the firm, which is also subject to internal changes as job descriptions are revised, or particular jobs are created or eliminated.

Despite tendencies toward change, a fairly stable age structure is generally discernible in a firm. A familiar categorization is that of newcomer, veteran, and senior, with each stratum having more or less understood age boundaries. Lawrence (1984) found that employees used age as a criterion for defining career levels, basing their rough judgments on the age distribution of the career level of the coworkers around them. In fact, the perceived age ranges were narrower than the actual age ranges of workers at each level, suggesting that workers engage in a kind of reification of age.

A concomitant of the age structure in firms is that higher ranks, with their higher rewards, are deemed appropriate for the most senior members. Schrank and Waring suggest that such a reward structure has considerable legitimacy, with age a surrogate for valued characteristics such as insider know-how and experience. Further, by allocating highest rewards to the oldest members, the firm prevents the premature closure of leadership roles and ensures turnover at the top ranks. This pattern also motivates younger employees and serves as an inducement for them to stay with the company.

Although Schrank and Waring do not address the question of job satisfaction directly, their analysis points to one factor behind the consistent finding of relatively low levels of satisfaction among younger, as compared to middle-aged and older, employees (Quinn, Staines, & McCullough, 1974): the mismatch of the rank and compensation of young employees with their perception of their own abilities. Given the pyramidal structure of many firms, young employees may see a long wait ahead to achieve the rewards they believe commensurate with their current contributions.

In short, in patterns somewhat parallel to those found at the societal level, the age structure of firms is an organizational "solution" to problems associated with aging and cohort flow: the continual shifting of firm membership as cohorts of individuals enter, gain seniority, and then leave. Age structure as a solution has costs as well as benefits: for the firm, a loss or underutilization of talent; for the individual, concomitant dislocations and dissatisfactions (see Dannefer, 1983).

To be sure, the model age structure Schrank and Waring describe is best adapted to the salaried and managerial components of large, well-established firms, and many jobs are not built around an age-related hierarchy. For example, firms in new industries may try to avoid clear age norms through participatory decision making, job rotation, and so on, and may never develop age structures like those found in older firms.

Age and the Structure of Politics

Research on political life affords further insights into age stratification systems. Age affects organized as well as unorganized political activity (e.g., voting, following public affairs in the media, participation in age-based interest groups), and particular age strata are involved in such political issues as old age pensions, student loans, the military draft, or aid to public education. Increasingly, as age-related issues have come to the fore and as age-based political movements and conflicts have erupted, sociological attention has turned to age—along with the earlier attention to class and ethnicity—as a key social identity affecting the individual's political stance and as a focal point for political divisions or coalitions in the society.

AGE AND THE INDIVIDUAL POLITICAL ACTOR

Studies of political attitudes and behaviors generally present an apparent paradox: People in the lower socioeconomic strata, though presumably having much to gain from political activity in a democracy, are the least likely to express interest or take part in it; yet older people, although relatively disadvantaged, show relatively high levels of both political interest and voting from the 1940s to the 1980s (Berelson, Lazarsfeld, and McPhee, 1954; Glenn and Grimes, 1968; Lazarsfeld, Berelson, and Gaudet, 1944; Lipset, 1960; Miller, Miller, and Schneider, 1980).

In political attitudes, older people are generally more conservative than younger ones on such issues as civil liberties, law and order, life style, racial or sexual equality, and self-labeling. On issues where their self-interest is involved, however—such as government support of pensions or health care—older people are often more liberal than middle-aged (on some issues

it is the youngest who are the most conservative). The cross-sectional age differences, which are generally small, do not mean that people adhere rigidly to ideas they adopted in their youth, or that when they do change they necessarily become more conservative. Various longitudinal analyses show that on many issues people change their political attitudes as they grow older, even up to their sixties or seventies, with the changes sometimes in the more liberal direction, sometimes in the more conservative—depending on trends in the society as a whole (Foner, 1974; Glenn, 1980).

AGE AND COLLECTIVE POLITICAL ACTION

Voting and party politics are only one form of political activity: The organized activities of age groups constitute another mode of political influence. Such activities attempt to unify voters of a given age around particular candidates or issues or more militant forms of political expression. Given the long history of youth movements (Braungart, 1984) and the public attention to the student rebellions of the 1960s and 1970s, it is not surprising that sociological analyses of age-based movements have focused on the younger strata. Yet there have been political movements of the old in the past and new old-age movements are likely to emerge in the future. Because of their increasing numbers, coupled with their high interest in politics and their citizenship participation, older people in the last few decades constitute a potentially powerful political force. What, then, are the general conditions under which societal-wide age-based solidarity (or age-based conflict) is likely to arise and which age groups are most likely to be involved?

Foner (1974), drawing on sociological analyses of class solidarity and conflict (e.g., Giddens, 1973; Morris and Murphy, 1966), explores conditions fostering common attitudes and interests, and coalescence into age-based groups. People of similar age have similar roles and confront similar life-stage problems. In the younger and older strata, age peers face common difficulties associated with their relative powerlessness and deprivation of material and social rewards. As members of the same cohort, age peers' exposure to social, cultural, or political events at similar junctures in their lives can forge similar approaches to public issues and similar views about desirable goals. Age segregation in social life, by providing opportunities for people of like age to communicate with each other and helping to insulate them from contrary views of other age strata, reinforces common attitudes and a sense of community among age peers. Once people of like age feel impelled to organize to achieve their goals, age segregation in colleges, schools, and communities provides a ready base for new recruits to organizations already formed (Foner, 1972, 1975; Lipset, 1976).

While there have been societal-wide age-based movements among both old and young, the youth movements have been most likely to erupt into conflicts. But such conflicts have been sporadic, inhibited by several factors. Young people are generally willing to bear with deprivations that they feel are only temporary. Their relatively low incomes and limited power are legitimated by relative inexperience and the likelihood that their turn will come. Moreover, as the young look forward to their adult roles, there is considerable anticipatory socialization to the views of people who are older than they, and frequent unwillingness to undertake militant actions that might jeopardize their future.

Additionally, motivation to engage in conflict and the capacity of age-based groups to mobilize (see Coser, 1956) are reduced by the crosscutting of age strata by class, ethnic, or gender groups. These other groupings often have greater salience than age. Further, mutual socialization and commitments in the family or at work can bind together people of different ages. Disputes that do arise in these settings are submerged when broad political issues affecting the welfare of the whole group are involved.

Foner distinguishes between two types of political issues, and proposes that mechanisms reducing age conflict are most likely to be effective when "material issues"—those involving the distribution of economic rewards—dominate political discourse, in contrast to "ideal issues"—those involving questions of right and wrong, war and peace, the rights of all people (see Berelson, Lazarsfeld, and McPhee, 1954; Gusfield, 1966; Weber, cited in Gerth and Mills, 1958). Many material issues divide the public along lines of class rather than age. Even when certain material issues—like taxation policies burdening certain age groups—do divide the public along age lines, class interests are generally still involved and often override the age divisions (see Foner, 1984). Many ideal issues dividing age strata are not seen as involving particular class interests and are thus less likely to bring into play crosscutting lines of cleavage. The expectation of future improvement is unlikely to influence the young if the issues involve everyone's rights, not just their own, or if the issues concern war and peace, raising doubts about whether they will have a future at all.

Consistent with this formulation, experience shows that age conflicts, typically initiated by the young, tend to occur where ideal issues are involved. The young, regarded by Mannheim (1928/1952) as especially receptive to new worldviews when they first come of political age, often present challenges on precisely those ideal issues that threaten the way of life to which the mature strata have become accustomed. Faced with resistance from older people on such issues, the young, with little access to positions of power or political resources, often resort to demonstrations and other noninstitutionalized political actions. In particular, student youth not yet connected to adult roles feel they have little to lose by participating in such activity. In contrast, the old have rarely spearheaded societal-wide age conflict, in part because the issues that typically arouse them are material issues subject to conflict-reducing mechanisms; indeed, organized political action among the old has frequently been takenin coalition with other age groups. Further, because older people have access to institutionalized power through voting and established organizations, they have little motivation to engage in confrontational politics.

Both types of age movements—younger people's movements in conflict with their elders and older people's movements that have cooperated with other age groups—have had a modicum of success. The student movement of the 1960s and 1970s changed power relationships in the university and contributed to anti-Vietnam war sentiment in the society (Foner, 1979; Lipset, 1976); and the 1930s Townsend Movement helped set the stage for Social Security legislation in the United States (Quadagno, 1984).

Important insights into social movements have been provided recently by resource mobilization theorists, who explain several movements more in terms of group resources, organization, and opportunities for collective action than of increasing grievances (Jenkins, 1983). In regard to age-based movements, however, it seems to be the ebb and flow of issues before the polity that are crucial for understanding the birth and death of movements. Resource mobilization theorists stress that while grievances are ever present, it is the ability to mobilize resources that is key; but in the case of age movements it can be argued that although mobilization opportunities have been fairly stable, it is the emergence of issues that triggers the conflict.

Age and the Family

Few social institutions are as clearly age graded as the family, for age and sex are its major bases of differentiation. The anthropological, historical, and sociological record is clear. Societies have implicit and often explicit criteria for appropriate ages to marry and bear children, there are norms affecting the relationships among family members of different ages and generations, and the processes of aging and cohort flow continually shape and reshape the structure of particular families. Moreover, unlike work organizations or political life, the age structure of the family includes both the very young and the very old.

Since most family units consist of at least two generations, an overriding interest has been the nature of intergenerational relationships, as affected by two contradictory forces: bonds of affection born of close and regular contacts, and inequalities of power and other social benefits that constitute a latent source of conflict. The potential for intergenerational conflict is heightened because the generations in the family differ in age and belong to different cohorts that have experienced widely different social circumstances. Just how these forces operate depends on the stage of the "family cycle" at which the structure of intergenerational relationships is observed, since the structure of a family changes as its members age.

Most studies of intergenerational relationships focus on one stage of the family and one set of relationships, either parent/teenager or elderly/adult offspring (but see Bengtson, 1975; Hill et al., 1970). In the 1950s there was considerable emphasis on child socialization (e.g., Parsons and Bales, 1955). In the 1960s—a period when many young people were rejecting established ways—there was special interest in relationships between adolescents and their parents (e.g., Bengtson, 1970; Coleman, 1961; Feuer, 1969; Riley, Riley, and Moore, 1961). In the 1970s and 1980s, with more older people surviving to advanced ages, attention turned to relationships between elderly and their adult children and between grandparents and grandchildren. The nature of such relationships varies with ethnicity, gender, education, and residence in addition to ages of grandchild and grandparent (Bengtson and Robertson, 1985).

One familiar theme has been the impact of modernization and industrialization on kinship structures: on the family roles of young and old, age-related residential patterns, age at marriage, relative ages of marital partners, in addition to intergenerational relationships. Recent studies have considered the implications for family age patterns of the changing roles of women, high divorce rates, social welfare policies, and increasing longevity (e.g., Hagestad, 1986; Riley, 1983; Rossi, 1986; Sussman, 1985). It is the increase in longevity that makes the four-generation family a common reality—indeed, more of a reality than in preindustrial societies where such a family might have been an ideal, but where high mortality rates made it a rarity; and there is current interest in the complexities of relationships in four- and, in the rare case, five-generation families, where the middle-generation grandchild is herself a grandmother (Kruse, 1984; Shanas et al., 1968).

AGE RELATIONSHIPS IN THE FAMILY

Relationships between *adolescents and their parents* in the modern era are commonly thought to be sensitive and tense, as adolescents try to assert their independence and parents to maintain their authority; and as young people adopt new attitudes in line with changing societal conditions. Adolescent rebellion, though not found in many tribal groups, was thought to be a "normal" maturational process in modern societies; yet much evidence of adolescent/parent solidarity was found in the United States from the 1950s to the late 1970s (Bengtson, 1975; Caplow et al., 1983; Johnson, 1976).

In attempting to understand this apparent anomaly, Foner (1978) explores the structural bases of both solidarity and conflict between generations, comparing conditions in the nineteenth and twentieth centuries. Despite the inequalities and differential experiences that can spark conflicts, several other conditions encourage closeness between parents and children. The small size of the modern family, which permits frequent and intense interaction between parents and children, can support the growth of emotional bonds. Few adolescents today are required to face long delays in the transition to adulthood because they must contribute to the family's economic welfare. Moreover, the value agreement observed between parents and children benefits from reciprocal socialization: While parents influence the views of their children, the offspring also socialize and resocialize their parents who, guided by modern values, pay attention to their children.

To be sure, there are many disagreements between adolescents and their parents, and various studies indicate that disputes arise particularly over the exercise of parental power. More serious are the widespread reports of parental abuse of children and less frequent instances of adolescent assaults on parents (Gelles and Cornell, 1985; Strauss, 1980). Such tensions are not unique to modern societies. Analysis of ethnographic reports of 60 nonindustrial societies (N. Foner, 1984) also shows power differentials and economic inequalities as important sources of intergenerational conflict. Young adult sons waiting for the wherewithal to marry and to gain control over economic assets have been known to attack their fathers, and even to commit patricide.

The forces affecting the younger age strata also influence the relationships of *elderly parents and their adult offspring*. The pronounced stereotype that, in modern societies, elderly parents are neglected by their children derives from an idealized image of intergenerational solidarity in earlier times, coupled with the fact that currently most older people (including the widowed) live by themselves. As with other stereotypes, research demonstrates that the supposed complete isolation of the elderly from their adult children is fallacious. The major cross-national studies by Shanas and her collaborators (1968) show that living apart from children does not necessarily mean abandonment. The great majority of the old live near at least one of their children, there is frequent contact between most elderly and their offspring, and children provide the great bulk of the care when other family members are disabled. To be sure, emotional compensations to parents for care of young children may exceed those to adults for care of their elderly parents, buttressing the desire for independence among the old (Davis and Combs, 1950).

Hess and Waring (1978) throw light on several conditions influencing the relationships between older people and their children. There are forces in modern societies operating to loosen ties between the generations: social welfare measures that permit the elderly to live independently; laws freeing offspring of legal responsibility for their aged parents; proliferation of agencies to provide services to older people; the multiple demands placed on middle-aged parents by their own children, jobs, and community responsibilities; and attitudinal differences deriving from the varying experiences of the generations. Yet, as Hess and Waring point out, the nature of the family itself serves to strengthen intergenerational ties. Ties built and reinforced over many years are not easily repudiated, and they are buttressed by current exchanges of gifts and services, and long-term exchanges as children compensate parents for the care received in their childhood and youth

(Mutran and Reitzes, 1984). Furthermore, adult children, anticipating their own old age, often want to provide examples to their children of the proper treatment of the elderly.

Although most studies have focused on family relationships among people of different ages, the modern similarity in age of marital partners and of siblings has produced a considerable literature on *age peers* in the family. Even in the United States, where power differentials are relatively narrow, husbands still typically hold the balance of power. The older the husband relative to his wife, the greater his opportunity to have accumulated such power resources as money and education. While the long-term decline in age differences of spouses at first marriage reinforces the trend toward marital equalitarianism, the norm remains for the husband to be at least a few years older than the wife. Moreover, age differences at remarriage tend to be greater than at first marriage and, given high rates of divorce and remarriage, a growing proportion of marriages will display a considerable age gap between partners. Presser (1974) notes that age differences between spouses can have different implications at different family stages. Though a 10-year difference may have few consequences in the early years of marriage, in later life, wives much younger than their husbands often face retiring after their husbands, having to care for an ill spouse, and having to spend years in widowhood.

In regard to siblings, the decline in family size has brought them closer in age than in the nineteenth and early twentieth centuries. In a family with five or six children, there is considerable age difference between the youngest and oldest. Smaller families, combined with close spacing of children, result in siblings nearer in age. Hagestad (1986) reports from Norwegian census material that among children born during the 1920s, close to one-third were age 16 or older when their youngest sibling was born; whereas among firstborns from the 1950s, less than one-tenth have such an age gap between them and their youngest sibling. Whether these newer patterns foster sibling solidarity or competition is not clear. Nor can we predict the impact of the introduction of stepbrothers and stepsisters of varying ages into families reconstituted after divorce, in contrast with the widespread earlier remarriage after the spouse's death (Cherlin and Furstenberg, 1986; Furstenberg et al., 1983; Furstenberg, Spanier, and Rothschild, 1982).

CHANGING FAMILY STRUCTURES

Broad social trends, including age-related

demographic shifts, have implications for family life: for instance, not only the dramatic changes in age at marriage and in the stages of family life (to be discussed here), but also the increase of single-person households among both young and old, the rise in the numbers of women in their thirties bearing their first child, the widening age range of divorce and remarriage, and the postponement of widowhood to the later years (e.g., Glick, 1977; Glick and Park, 1965; Meyers, 1985; Siegel and Taeuber, 1986; Spanier and Glick, 1980).

Norms about the appropriate *age for marrying* vary across societies and over time. In some African societies, males must delay marriage until they accumulate an adequate bride price. In some agricultural societies, poor families who cannot afford dowries may marry off daughters when they are children, their labor compensating for lack of a dowry. Among the European aristocracy, child marriages were contracted to solidify economic and political alliances. In the United States, from the end of the nineteenth century until the 1970s there was a downward trend in age at marriage, as families could manage without economic contributions from their young adult offspring. After 1970 this trend was reversed (Masnick and Bane, 1980), as young people delayed marriage to finish their education, as cohabitation became more widespread, or as increases in women's labor force participation reduced the pressure to secure economic support through early marriage (Cherlin, 1980).

These shifts in age of marriage affect other family patterns. If a woman delays marriage, she is likely to delay childbearing, and in turn to have fewer children. If marriage and childbearing are delayed, so that parents are considerably older than their offspring, the nature of parenting is likely to be altered. Age at marriage also appears to influence marital relations, as people who marry at young ages (under age 20) have higher rates of divorce than people marrying at the customary ages (Leslie and Korman, 1985). Another consequence of increasing numbers of women waiting until their thirties to bear their first child is to counterbalance the effect of increased longevity in producing multigeneration families.

The nature of the "family cycle," as children grow up and leave home, has also varied historically and cross-culturally. It is now known that in many agricultural societies at any given time, few families consisted of the proverbial three or more generations residing together continuously—with exceptional brief periods before newly married couples could establish their own households, or when widowed parents lived with their children (Berkner, 1972; Laslett, 1985). In the nineteenth-century United States, another pattern—taking in boarders—occurred in working-class families (Modell and Hareven, 1973), with children of these families often living as boarders elsewhere where they could find jobs. The discontinuities in membership of family/household units, as people moved in and out, were strongly related to the economic needs of the family unit and of individual family members.

In the contemporary United States the structure of the family varies by stages. At least until recently, there was typically a sustained period when parents and growing children lived together, followed by a substantial one-generational postparental stage after children left to establish their own households (Glick and Parke, 1965; Glick, 1977). The existence of this postparental stage was brought about by several trends: lower mortality rates, resulting in joint survival of spouses; lower fertility rates and closer spacing of children, shortening the period before the last child left home; and the tendency of elderly parents to live independently, thanks to pensions, savings, and social welfare.

This pattern of two relatively stable periods of family life is giving way to more complex arrangements. Some families exhibit the discontinuities of earlier times, but for different reasons: The disruption of marriages is now caused more frequently by divorce than by death of one spouse (Cherlin, 1980). After balancing the trends in divorce with the trends in widowhood, Griffith and associates (1985) have shown that the probability of disruption of first marriage by age 70 has increased for women from 56% for the 1906-1910 birth cohort to 71% for the 1946-1950 cohort. As such disruption brings in its wake single parenthood, remarriages, and reconstituted families, the structure of family units changes, requiring family members to face continual relational adjustments within the residential unit and with former and newly acquired kin outside the household (Riley, 1983). One other alteration in the "family cycle" is increasingly predictable: Because of greater longevity and retrenchment of social welfare programs, more families will confront the need—widespread in less developed societies—to provide care for their frail elderly parents or to take them into their homes. The major burden will fall on the middle-aged and young-old, especially women (Hagestad, 1986; Shanas, 1968).

As such changes—precipitated by social, economic, political, and demographic factors in the society—are felt in the family, family problems and responses generate pressures on other social institutions. For example, courts have been involved, sometimes acting to protect grandparents' relationships with grandchildren when threatened by divorce (Kornhaber, 1985). More broadly, declining fertility rates, in part the result of changing age of marriage and childbearing, contribute to lowering the ratio of working-age adults to dependent older persons, a ratio that affects the soundness of Social Security funds (Siegel and Taeuber, 1986), thus becoming a political issue. Such social and demographic currents may have certain positive implications, as they convert the kinship structure into a larger and more complex "matrix of latent relationships," within which individuals have increased opportunity to select and intensify particular relationships—whether grandparent with grandchild, or adult son with stepfather—that are earned rather than ascribed (Riley, 1983).

Structural Sources of Change

These accounts of age structures in society and its institutions emphasize the intersections between age stratification and other systems of stratification based on class, gender, or ethnicity (Foner, 1975, 1984; Lenski, 1966; Sorokin, 1947). Within each age stratum, individuals who are similar in age are subject to widely divergent influences from their locations in these other systems. The crosscutting lines of stratification affect age-based social relationships, tending to reduce within-stratum solidarity and to mute interstrata conflict (Coser, 1964). At the societal level, age stratification systems and other stratification systems are parts of the same social environment, with each system influencing all the others. For example, age inequalities within class strata or within racial divisions (Hess, 1985; Jackson, 1985; Markides, 1983; Streib, 1985) all contribute to the overall pattern of inequality that determines the consequences for societal conflict and change.

Within the age stratification system, the variabilities and changes described in this Section bring to attention a central feature of social dynamics: the age structure itself as one unique source of social change. Noted elsewhere in this chapter are several other sets of pressures toward change in age stratification systems and related changes in the environing society: (1) from sources outside the age system (e.g., conquest, economic growth or decline, developments in technology or in mass culture); (2) from processes of aging and cohort flow; and (3) from the

basic lack of synchronization between individual aging and social change (WP 13). Noted here is a fourth set of pressures for change that arises from the operation of age structures themselves: value conflicts between young and old, faulty operation of allocation and socialization, inequalities among age strata, and imbalances within particular strata between available roles and numbers of people able and motivated to perform these roles. We focus on these last two—age inequality and age imbalances, both at the center of policy debates in the United States in the 1980s—as they illustrate the structural dynamics under consideration.

AGE INEQUALITY

Inequalities are endemic in all age systems and, depending on the values of the society or the preferences of members of the age strata, they are often regarded as inequities. (Some have contended that, though both young and old in the United States are comparatively deprived of the rewards of economic activity, both may value the rewards of freedom in preference to the constraints of work—e.g., Linton, 1942).

One political issue concerns "intergenerational equity," or more precisely the inequitable allocation of resources between age strata.[7] Preston (1984) spurred the debate by presenting evidence of improvement since 1960 in income and public support for the well-being of older people, concomitant with the deterioration of such support for the well-being of children. Several factors contribute to the worsening relative position of children, including the apparent decline in the quality of schools in the United States, the instability of the nuclear family, the political weakness of children to effect changes in their own behalf, and the political inactivity of parents of young children.

Several policy issues are involved in the debate: whether age differences are outweighed by the "common stake" of all strata in the good of each one (Kingson, Hirshorn, and Corman, 1986); whether crosscutting divisions by income or by health require pluralistic policies for the entire society without reference to age (see Crystal, 1982; Neugarten and Neugarten, 1986); whether age inequalities are ultimately reducible to inequalities based entirely on class, race, or gender (Foner, 1986); or whether, indeed, the age inequalities are regarded as inequities. According to Preston, the fundamental issue is whether to return further responsibility for children to the family—weak vessel that it appears to be—or to recognize public expenditures on children as an investment in the future as well as in current consumption.

While debate on such issues can influence public policy, the terms of debate, the guiding ideologies, and the sides taken by particular age strata change over time. As recently as the mid-twentieth century, American society was viewed as "child-centered," and neglect of the problems of old people was decried (e.g., Davis and Combs, 1985). For the future, though the baby boom cohorts may advocate support for the young while they are young themselves, as they grow older they are likely to opt for stronger backing of older people's interests. As such issues are played out in public life, age structures change.

AGE IMBALANCE

Another structural source of change is the mismatch between age structures of people and of roles—not merely the short-term failure of institutions to adapt to disordered cohort flow (as with the baby boom), but more especially the long-term failure of institutions to accommodate the steady rise in the proportion of people who are old. Because of the aging of society, large strata of older people have been added at the top of the traditional age pyramid, but no comparable activities have been prescribed for them either in the work force or the family, and no adjustments made for the repercussions in the other strata. The age structure of roles has lagged behind the unprecedented changes in the age structure of people.

Proposed alternative solutions to this problem of lag in the role structure include either accepting the situation or working to change it. For example, Rosow (1967, 1985), accepting the assumption that older people have little chance of remaining in the roles of prime life, proposes that they should be resocialized for informal roles in voluntary associations or social networks. Documenting his recommendations from his studies of older people's friendships, Rosow advocates age-segregated housing, because it can stimulate spontaneous social ties and protect against invidious comparisons with younger people as reference groups.

Others, (e.g., Burgess, 1960; Estes, 1979; Foner and Schwab, 1983), emphasizing the problems for society and older people themselves of the "roleless role," propose various interventions to modify the role structure rather than accepting it: for example, retraining older adults or preparing them for new careers; providing opportunities for constructive use of free time; or encouraging educational leaves, part-time work, job sharing, or extended vacations that would spread education, work, and leisure more evenly over the life course (Riley and Riley, 1986). It has been suggested that the oldest age stratum can afford entirely new models for a "good society," where individuals at every age have opportunity to exercise their capacities through new uses of leisure (White, 1961); or that roles should be redefined for older people so as to build on their competence as "stabilizers of desirable change" (Parsons, 1962); or that older people, because they have already achieved and have little to risk, can spark significant innovations (Schrank and Waring, 1983). Social reorganization to integrate the old with activities viewed as essential could result in shorter working hours and paid vacations in all age strata, higher education for all youths, or nonemployment of mothers of young children (Davis and Combs, 1950). As Hauser (1953) put it over 30 years ago, "We have . . . succeeded in adding years to life; we are only beginning to turn to the task of adding life to years."

****

With every indication that, barring major disasters, the populations of all societies will continue to age, the strains engendered by such age-related imbalances between people and roles will predictably result in further accretions of change in the social structure. Not predictable are the future responses to the varied pressures to adapt to the strains or to redress the imbalances. Also unpredictable are the outcomes for the shape and significance of the age strata or for the nature of individual lives. Much of the change will depend not only on the concrete operations of age stratification systems, but also on future directions in the ideologies defining rights and powers of children or old people, in cultural stereotypes of people's capacities at differing ages, and in the basic values by which rewards are assessed. Sociologists have been working in an era when wealth and power are highly regarded, with social class as one of the deepest lines of intergroup differentiation, solidarity, and conflict. Yet, as Sorokin emphasized (1968, p. 408), social class (in its modern form as "multibonded" through occupational, economic, and sociopolitical similarities of its members, and as "legally open but actually semi-closed") has held sway in the Western world only since the eighteenth century. If, as Sorokin suggests, other combinations of groups and interests come to dominate the future course of human history, the place of age in society will change. Such basic issues cannot be overlooked in the continuing agenda for work in the sociology of age.

NOTES

1. The conceptual framework is continually being amplified, amended, and specified through the range of studies illustrated here, and through several reviews (e.g., Elder, 1985; Foner, 1980; Maddox, 1979) and textbooks (e.g., Hess and Markson, 1980; Foner, 1986; Ward, 1979).

2. Moreover, sociologists participate widely in multidisciplinary symposia on aging and the life course (see Elder, 1985; Kertzer and Keith, 1984; Kiesler, Morgan, and Oppenheimer, 1981; Riley, 1979; Riley, Abeles, and Teitelbaum, 1981; Riley, Matarozzo, and Baum, 1987; Sorenson, Weinert, and Sherrod, 1986).

3. For other aspects of the linkages between aging processes and subjective development, see, for example, the discussion by Parsons and Bales (1955) of the developing orientations of the child who relates sequentially to mother and to father; or Giele's (1980) suggestion that currently eroding age- and sex-role constraints can enlarge individual opportunities for growth and unification of the self.

4. Merton's self-fulfilling prophesy or the dictum of W. I. Thomas, if situations are defined as real, they are real in their consequences. Berger and Berger (1972) use a life-course framework to explain the social construction of society and institutions.

5. For details, see Coleman (1981); Featherman (1981); Featherman and Lerner, (1985); Goodman (1962); Tuma and Hannan (1984).

6. Details of the procedural problems of sampling, data gathering, analysis, and interpretation of sociological data on age cannot be presented here; but see, for example, Riley, Johnson, and Foner (1972: appendix), Duncan and Morgan, 1985.

7. In the population as a whole, where parents and children of all ages are intermingled, the age gap in resources between generations of particular families tends to disappear.

REFERENCES

Abeles, Ronald P., L. Steel, and L. L. Wise. 1980. "Patterns and Implications of Life-Course Organization." Pp. 307-337 in *Life-Span Development and Behavior*, vol. 3, edited by Paul Baltes and O. G. Brim. New York: Academic Press.

Alford, Robert R. and Roger Friedland. 1975. "Political Participation and Public Policy." *Annual Review of Sociology* 1:429-79.

Baker, Kendal L., Russell J. Dalton, and Kai Hildebrandt. 1981. *Germany Transformed: Political Culture and the New Politics*. Cambridge, MA: Harvard University Press.

Baltes, Paul B. and Sherry L. Willis. 1982. "Enhancement (plasticity) of Intellectual Functioning in Old Age: Penn State's Adult Development and Enrichment Project (ADEPT)." In *Aging and Cognitive Processes*, edited by F.I.M. Craik and S. E. Trehub. New York: Plenum.

———, H. Reese, and L. Lipsitt. 1980. "Lifespan Developmental Psychology." *Annual Review of Psychology*. 31:65-110.

Baron, James N. and William T. Bielby. 1980. "Bringing the Firms Back in: Stratification Segmentation, and the Organization of Work." *American Sociological Review* 45:737-765.

——— 1985. "Organizational Barriers to Gender Equality: Sex Segregation of Job Opportunities." Pp. 233-251 in *Gender and the Life Course*, edited by A. S. Rossi. New York: Aldine.

Benedict, Ruth. 1938. "Continuities and Discontinuities in Cultural Conditioning." *Psychiatry* 1:161-167.

Bengtson, Vern L. 1970. "The Generation Gap: A Review and Typology of Social-psychological Perspectives." *Youth and Society* 2:7-32.

——— 1975. "Generation and Family Effects in Value Socialization." *American Sociological Review* 40:358-371.

——— and Joan F. Robertson, eds. 1985. *Grandparenthood*. Beverly Hills, CA: Sage.

Berelson, Bernard, R., Paul F. Lazarsfeld, and William N. McPhee. 1954. *Voting*. Chicago: University of Chicago Press.

Berger, Peter L. and Brigitte Berger. 1972. *Sociology: A Biographical Approach*. New York: Basic Books.

Berkner, Lutz I. 1972. "The Stem Family and the Developmental Cycle of the Peasant Household: An Eighteenth-century Austrian Example." *American Historical Review* 77:398-418.

Bernardi, Bernardo. 1985. *Age Class Systems: Social Institutions and Polities Based on Age*, translated by David Kertzer. Cambridge, England: Cambridge University Press.

Blalock, Hubert M. Jr. 1967. "Status Inconsistency, Social Mobility, Status Integration, and Structural Effects." *American Sociological Review* 32:790-801.

Blau, Peter and Otis D. Duncan. 1967. *The American Occupational Structure*. New York: John Wiley.

Blau, Zena Smith. 1961. "Structural Constraints on Friendship and Old Age." *American Sociological Review* 26:429-439.

Braungart, Richard G. 1984. "Historical and Generational Patterns of Youth Movements: A Global Perspective." *Comparative Social Research* 7:3-62.

Brim, Orville G. Jr. 1966. "Socialization through the life cycle." Pp. 368-388 in *Socialization after Childhood: Two Essays*, edited by Orville G. Brim, Jr., and Stanton Wheeler. New York: John Wiley.

——— and Jerome Kagan, eds. 1980. *Constancy and*

Change in Human Development. Cambridge, MA: Harvard University Press.

Brim, Orville G. Jr. and Carol D. Ryff. 1980. "On the Properties of Life Events." Pp. 368-388 in *Life-Span Development and Behavior*, vol. 3, edited by Paul B. Baltes and Orville G. Brim, Jr. New York: Academic Press.

Burgess, Ernest W., ed. 1960. *Aging in Western Societies*. Chicago: University of Chicago Press.

Cain, Leonard D. 1964. "Life Course and Social Structure." Pp. 272-309 in *Handbook of Modern Sociology*, edited by Robert E.L. Faris. Chicago: Rand McNally.

Caplow, Theodore, Howard M. Bahr, Bruce A. Chadwick, Reuben Hill, and Margaret Holmes Williamson. 1983. *Middletown Families: Fifty Years of Change and Continuities*. New York: Bantam Books.

Cherlin, Andrew. 1980. *Marriage, Divorce, Remarriage*. Cambridge, MA: Harvard University Press.

_____ and Frank F. Furstenberg, Jr. 1986. *The New Grandparent*. New York: Basic Books.

Clausen, John A. 1968. *Socialization and Society*. Boston: Little, Brown.

_____ 1972. "The life course of individuals." Pp. 457-514 in *Aging and Society: A Sociology of Age Stratification*, vol. III, edited by Matilda White Riley, Marilyn Johnson, and Anne Foner. New York: Russell Sage Foundation.

_____ 1986a. *The Life Course: A Sociological Perspective*. Englewood Cliffs, NJ: Prentice-Hall.

_____ 1986b. "Early Adult Choices and the Life Course." Paper presented at the 1986 annual meeting of the American Sociological Association.

Cohn, Richard. 1972. "On Interpretation of Cohort and Period Analyses: A Mathematical Note." Pp. 85-88 in *Aging and Society: A Sociology of Age Stratification*, vol. III, edited by Matilda White Riley, Marilyn Johnson, and Anne Foner. New York: Russell Sage Foundation.

Cole, Stephen. 1979. "Age and Scientific Performance." *American Journal of Sociology* 84:958-977.

Coleman, James S. 1961. *The Adolescent Society*. Glencoe, IL: Free Press.

_____ 1981. *Longitudinal Data Analysis*. New York: Basic Books.

_____ et al. 1974. *Youth:Transition to Adulthood*. Chicago: University of Chicago Press.

Coser, Lewis A. 1956. *The Functions of Social Conflict*. New York: Free Press.

Cottrell, Leonard, S. Jr. 1942. "The Adjustment of the Individual to His Age and Sex Roles." *American Sociological Review* 7:617-620.

Cowgill, Donald O. 1974. "The Aging of Populations and Societies." *The Annals of the American Academy of Political and Social Science* 415:1-18.

_____ 1986. *Aging Around the World*. Belmont, CA: Wadsworth.

Crystal, Stephen. 1982. *America's Old Age Crisis*. New York: Basic Books.

Cummings, Elane and William F. Henry. 1961. *Growing Old: The Process of Disengagement*. New York: Basic Books.

Dannefer, Dale. 1983. "Age Structure, Values, and the Organization of Work: Some Implications for Research and Policy." *Futurics* 7:8-13.

_____ 1984. "Adult Development and Social Theory: A Paradigmatic Reappraisal." *American Sociological Review* 49:100-116.

_____ 1987. "Aging as Intracohort Differentiation: Accentuation, the Matthew Effect, and the Life Course." *Sociological Forum* 2 (spring): 211-236.

Davis, Kingsley. 1940. "The Sociology of Parent-Youth Conflict." *American Sociological Review* 5:523-535.

_____ 1963. "The Theory of Change and Response in Modern Demographic History." *Population Index*. Pp. 345-365.

_____ and J. W. Combs Jr. 1950. "The Sociology of an Aging Population." Pp. 146-170 in *The Social and Biological Challenge of our Aging Population*, edited by D. B. Armstrong. New York: Columbia University Press.

Demos, John. 1970. *A Little Commonwealth: Family Life in Plymouth Colony*. New York: Oxford University Press.

DeViney, Stanley. 1984. "The Political Economy of Public Pensions: A Cross-national Analysis." *Journal of Political and Military Sociology*. 12:295-310.

Dittman-Kohli, Freya N. and Paul B. Baltes. In press. "Toward a Neofunctionalist Conception of Adult Intellectual Growth." In *Beyond Formal Operations: Alternative Endpoints to Human Development*, edited by C. Alexander and E. Langer.

Dowd, James. 1980. *Stratification Among the Aged*. Monterey, CA: Brooks/Cole.

_____ 1980. "Prejudice and Proximity." *Research on Aging*. 2:23-48.

Duncan, Greg J. and James N. Morgan. 1985. "The Panel Study of Income Dynamics." Pp. 50-73 in *Life Course Dynamics*, edited by G. H. Elder. Ithaca, NY: Cornell University Press.

Duncan, Otis Dudley. 1966. "Path Analysis: Sociological Examples." *American Journal of Sociology*. 72:1-16.

Easterlin, Richard A. 1978. "What Will 1984 Be Like? Socioeconomic Implications of Recent Twist in Age Structure." *Demography* 15:397-432.

_____ 1980. *Birth and Fortune: The Impact of Numbers on Personal Welfare*. New York: Basic Books.

Eisenstadt, S. N. 1956. *From Generation to Generation: Age Groups and Social Structure*. Glencoe, IL: Free Press.

Ekerdt, D. J. and R. Bosse. 1982. "Change in Self Reported Health with Retirement." *International Journal of Aging and Human Development*. 15:213-223.

Elder, Glenn H. Jr. 1974. *Children of the Great*

Depression. Chicago: University of Chicago Press.

——— 1985. *Life Course Dynamics*. Ithaca, NY: Cornell University Press.

——— 1986. "Military Times and Turning Points in Men's Lives." *Developmental Psychology* 22:233-245.

——— and Jeffrey K. Liker. 1982. "Hard Times in Women's Lives: Historical Influences Across 40 Years." *American Journal of Sociology* 88:241-269.

Elder, Glenn H. Jr. and R. C. Rockwell. 1979. "Economic Depression and Postwar Opportunity in Men's Lives: A Study of Life Patterns and Mental Health." In *Research in Community and Mental Health*, vol. 1, edited by R. G. Simmons. Greenwich, CT: JAI Press.

Erikson, Erik H. 1968. "Life Cycle." Pp. 286-292 in *International Encyclopedia of the Social Sciences*, vol. 9. New York: Macmillan.

Espenshade, Thomas J. and Rachel Eisenberg Braun. 1983. "Economic Aspects of an Aging Population and the Material Well-being of Older Persons." Pp. 25-51 in *Aging in Society: Selected Reviews of Recent Research*, edited by Matilda White Riley, Beth B. Hess, and Kathleen Bond. Hillsdale, NJ: Lawrence Erlbaum.

Estes, Carroll. 1979. *The Aging Enterprise*. San Francisco: Jossey-Bass.

———, James H. Swan, and Leonore E. Gerard. 1982. *Ageing and Society*. 2:151-164.

Evan, William M. 1965. "Cohort Analysis of Attitude Data." Pp. 117-142 in *Computer Methods in the Analysis of Large-Scale Social Systems*, edited by J. M. Beshers. Cambridge, MA: Harvard University Press.

Featherman, David L. 1981. "The Life-span Perspective." Pp. 621-648 in *The National Science Foundation's 5-Year Outlook on Science and Technology*, vol. 2. Washington, DC: Government Printing Office.

——— and Richard M. Lerner. 1985. "Ontogenesis and Sociogenesis: Problematics for Theory and Research About Development and Socialization Across the Lifespan." *American Sociological Review* 50:659-676.

Featherman, David L. and Annemette Sorensen. 1982. "Societal Transformation in Norway and Change in the Life Course Transition into Adulthood." Paper presented at the Population Association of America, San Diego.

Feldman, Jacob J. 1983. "Work Ability of the Aged under Conditions of Improving Mortality." in *Milbank Memorial Fund Quarterly/Health and Society* 61:430-444. (Statement before the National Commission on Social Security Reform, June 21, 1982.)

Ferree, Myra Marx and Beth B. Hess. 1985. *Controversy and Coalition: The New Feminist Movement*. Boston: Twayne.

Feuer, Lewis. 1969. *The Conflict of Generations*. New York: Basic Books.

Fienberg, Stephen E. and Mason, William M. 1979.

"Identification and Estimation of Age-cohort Models in the Analysis of Discrete Archival Data." *Sociological Methodology* Pp. 1-67.

Foner, Anne, 1972. "The Polity." Pp. 115-159 in *Aging and Society: A Sociology of Age Stratification*, vol. III, edited by Matilda White Riley, Marilyn Johnson, and Anne Foner. New York: Russell Sage Foundation.

——— 1974. "Age Stratification and Age Conflict in Political Life." *American Sociological Review* 39:187-196.

——— 1975. "Age in Society: Structure and Change." *American Behavioral Scientist* 19:144-168.

——— 1978. "Age Stratification and the Changing Family." Pp. 340-365 in *Turning Points: Historical and Sociological Essays on the Family*, edited by John Demos and Sarane Spence Boocock. Chicago: University of Chicago Press.

——— 1980. "The Sociology of Age Stratification: A Review of Some Recent Publications." *Contemporary Sociology* (November):771-779.

——— 1982. "Perspectives on Changing Age Systems." In *Aging from Birth to Death, vol. II. Sociotemporal Perspectives*, edited by Matilda White Riley, Ronald P. Abeles, and Michael S. Teitelbaum. Boulder, CO: Westview.

——— 1984. "The Issues of Age Conflict in Political Life." Pp. 170-175 in *Intergenerational Relationships*, edited by Vjenka Garms-Homolova, Erika M. Hoerning, and Doris Schaeffer. Lewiston, NY: C. J. Hogrefe.

——— 1986. *Aging and Old Age: New Perspectives*. Englewood Cliffs, NJ: Prentice-Hall.

——— and David I. Kertzer. 1978. "Transitions Over the Life Course: Lessons from Age-Set Societies." *Americal Journal of Sociology* 83:1081-1104.

Foner, Anne and Karen Schwab. 1981. *Aging and Retirement*. Monterey, CA: Brooks/Cole.

——— 1983. "Work and Retirement in a Changing Society." Pp. 71-93 in *Aging in Society: Selected Reviews of Recent Research*, edited by Matilda White Riley, Beth B. Hess, and Kathleen Bond. Hillsdale, NJ: Lawrence Erlbaum.

Foner, Nancy. 1984. *Ages in Conflict: A Cross-Cultural Perspective on Inequality Between Old and Young*. New York: Columbia University Press.

Fortes, Meyer. 1984. "Age, Generation, and Social Structure." Pp. 99-122 in *Age and Anthropological Theory*, edited by David I. Kertzer and Jennie Keith. Ithaca: Cornell University Press.

Furstenberg, Frank F. Jr. 1976. *Unplanned Parenthood: The Social Consequences of Teenage Child Bearing*. New York: Free Press.

———, Christine Winquist Nord, James L. Peterson, and Nicholas Zill. 1983. "The Life Course of Children of Divorce." *American Sociological Review* 48:656-668.

Furstenburg, Frank F. Jr., Graham Spanier, and Nancy Rothschild. 1982. "Patterns of Parenting in the Transition From Divorce to Remarriage.'' Pp. 325-343 in *Women: A Developmental Perspective*, edited by Phyllis W. Berman and Estelle R. Ramey. NIH Publication 82-2298, Department of Health and Human Services, National Institutes of Health, Washington, DC.

Freeman, Jo. 1975. *The Politics of Women's Liberation*. New York: David McKay.

Gaunt, David. 1983. ''The Property and Kin Relationships of Retired Farmers in Northern and Central Europe.'' Pp. 249-279 in *Family Firms in Historical Europe* edited by Richard Wall, Jean Robin, and Peter Laslett. New York: Cambridge University Press.

Gay, David A. and Richard T. Campbell. 1985. ''The Role of Age and Cohort in Well-Being Over the Life Course: Comparing the Levinson and Easterlin Hypotheses.'' Paper presented at the annual meeting of the Southern Sociological Society.

Gelles, Richard J. and Clair Pedrick Cornell. 1985. *Intimate Violence in Families*. Beverly Hills, CA: Sage.

Gerth, Hans H. and C. Wright Mills, eds. 1958. *From Max Weber*. New York: Oxford University Press.

Giddens, Anthony. 1973. *The Class Structure of the Advanced Societies*. New York: Harper & Row.

Giele, Janet Zollinger. 1980. ''Adulthood as Transcendence of Age and Sex.'' Pp. 151-73 in *Themes of Work and Love in Adulthood*, edited by Neil J. Smelser and Erik H. Erikson. Cambridge, MA: Harvard University Press.

Glaser, Barney G. and Anselm L. Strauss. 1971. *Theory of Status Passage*. Chicago: Aldine.

Glenn, Norval D. 1980. ''Values, Attitudes, and Beliefs.'' Pp. 596-640 in *Constancy and Change in Human Development*, edited by Orville G. Brim, Jr. and J. Kagan. Cambridge, MA: Harvard University Press.

———— and Michael Grimes. 1968. ''Aging, Voting, and Political Interest.'' *American Sociological Review* 33:563-575.

Glick, Paul C. 1977. ''Updating the Life Cycle of the Family.'' *Journal of Marriage and the Family* 39:5-13.

———— 1979. ''The Future Marital Status and Living Arrangements of the Elderly.'' *The Gerontologist* 19:301-309.

———— and Arthur J. Norton. 1977. ''Marrying, Divorcing, and Living Together in the U.S. Today.'' *Population Bulletin* 32:15.

Glick, Paul C. and Robert Parke Jr. 1965. ''New Approaches in Studying the Life Cycle of the Family.'' *Demography* 2:187-202.

Goodman, Leo A. 1962. ''Statistical Methods for Analyzing Processes of Change.'' *American Journal of Sociology* 68:57-78.

Goslin, David A. 1969. *Handbook of Socialization Theory and Research*. Chicago: Rand McNally.

Graebner, William. 1980. *A History of Retirement*. New Haven, CT: Yale University Press.

Greenberg, David F. 1985. ''Age, Crime, and Social Explanation.'' *American Journal of Sociology* 91:1-21.

Griffith, Janet D., C. M. Suchindran, and Helen P. Koo. ''Cohort Change in the Marital Life Course.'' Paper presented at the 1985 annual meeting of the Population Association of America.

Gubrium, Jaber F. 1975. *Living and Dying at Murrey Manor*. New York: St. Martin's.

Gusfield, Joseph R. 1966. *Symbolic Crusade*. Urbana. University of Illinois Press.

Hagestad, Gunhild O. 1981. ''Problems and Promises in the Social Psychology of Intergenerational Relations.'' Pp. 11-46 in *Aging: Stability and Change in the Family*, edited by Robert W. Fogel et al. New York: Academic Press.

———— 1986. ''The Aging Society as a Context for Family Life.'' *Daedalus* 115:119-139.

Hagestad, Gunnhild O. and Bernice L. Neugarten. 1985. ''Age and the Life Course.'' Pp. 35-61 in *Handbook of Aging and the Social Sciences*, edited by R. H. Binstock and E. Shanas. New York: Von Nostrand Reinhold.

Handl, Johann, Karl Ulrich Mayer, Walter Mueller, and Angelika Williams. 1979. ''Prozesse Sozialstrukturellen Wandels am Beispiel der Entwicklung von Qualifikations und Erwerbsstruktur der Frauen. Im Deutschen Reich und der Bundersrepublik Deutschland.'' Paper presented at the 19th Deutschen Soziologentag, Berlin.

Hareven, Tamara. 1982. *Industrial Time and Family Time*. Cambridge, England: Cambridge University Press.

Hauser, Philip M. 1953. ''Facing the Implications of an Aging Population.'' *Social Review* 26:162-176.

Havighurst, Robert and R. Albrecht. 1953. *Older People*. New York: Longmans Green.

Henretta, John C. and Richart T. Campbell. 1978. ''Net Worth as an Aspect of Status.'' *American Journal of Sociology* 83:204-223.

Hess, Beth. 1972. ''Friendship.'' Pp. 357-393 in *Aging and Society: A Sociology of Age Stratification*, vol. III, edited by Matilda White Riley, Marilyn Johnson, and Anne Foner. New York: Russell Sage Foundation.

———— 1985. ''Aging Policies and Old Women: The Hidden Agenda.'' Pp. 319-331 in *Gender and the Life Course*, edited by Alice S. Rossi. Chicago: Aldine.

———— and Elizabeth W. Markson. 1980. *Aging and Old Age: An Introduction to Social Gerontology*. New York: Macmillan.

Hess, Beth B. and Joan M. Waring. 1978. ''Parent and Child in Later Life: Rethinking the Relationship.'' Pp. 241-273 in *Child Influences in Marital Interaction*, edited by R. M. Lerner and G. B. Spanier. New York: Academic Press.

Hill, Reuben and associates. 1970. *Family Development in Three Generations*. Cambridge, MA:

Shenkman.

Hirschi, Travis and Michael Gottfredson. 1983. "Age and the Explanation of Crime." *American Journal of Sociology* 89:552-584.

Hochschild, Arlie. 1975. "Disengagement Theory: A Critique and a Proposal." *American Sociological Review* 40:553-569.

Hofferth, Sandra L. 1985. "Children's Life Course: Family Structure and Living Arrangements in Cohort Perspective." Pp. 75-112 in *Life Course Dynamics*, edited by G. E. Elder. Ithaca, NY: Cornell University Press.

Hogan, Dennis P. 1978. "The Variable Order of Events in the Life Course." *American Sociological Review* 43:537-586.

_____ and Nan Marie Astone. 1987. "The Transition to Adulthood." *Annual Review of Sociology* 13:109-130.

Hoge, Dean R. and Jann L. Hoge. 1984. "Period Effects and Specific Age Effects Influencing Values of Alumni in the Decade after College." *Social Forces* 62:941-962.

Horwitz, Allan V. 1984. "The Economy and Social Pathology." *Annual Review of Sociology* 10:95-116.

House, James S., Cynthia Robbins, and Helen L. Metzner. 1982. "The Association of Social Relationships and Activities with Mortality: Prospective Evidence from the Tecumseh Community Health Study." *American Journal of Epidemiology* 116:123-140.

Hyman, H. H. 1983. *Of Time and Widowhood: Nationwide Studies of Enduring Effects*. Durham, NC: Duke University Press.

Jackson, Jacquelyne Johnson. 1985. "Race, National Origin, Ethnicity and Aging." Pp. 264-303 in *Handbook of Aging and the Social Sciences*, edited by Robert H. Binstock and Ethel Shanas. New York: Van Nostrand Reinhold.

Jenkins, J. Craig. 1983. "Resource Mobilization Theory and the Study of Social Movements." *Annual Review of Sociology* 9:527-553.

Johnson, Marilyn. 1976. "The Role of Perceived Parental Models, Expectations and Socializing Behaviors in the Self-expectations of Adolescents, from the U.S. and West Germany." Ph.D. dissertation, Rutgers University.

Kalleberg, Arne L. 1983. "Work and Stratification." *Work and Occupations* 10:251-259.

_____ and Karyn Loscocco. 1983. "Aging, Values, and Rewards: Explaining Age Differences in Job Stratification." *American Sociological Review* 48:78-90.

Kalleberg, Arne L. and Aage B. Sorensen. 1979. "The Sociology of Labor Markets." *Annual Review of Sociology* 5:351-379.

Kane, Robert, D. Solomon, J. Beck, E. Keeler, and R. Kane. 1980. "The Future Need for Geriatric Manpower in the United States." *New England Journal of Medicine* 302: 1327-1332.

Karweit, Nancy and David I. Kertzer. 1986. "Data Base Management for Life Course Family Data."

In *Family Relations in Life Course Perspective*, edited by David I. Kertzer. Greenwich, CT: JAI.

Kaufman, Robert L. and Seymour Spilerman. 1982. "The Age Structure of Occupations and Jobs." *American Journal of Sociology* 87:827-851.

Kertzer, David I. 1983. "Generation as a Sociological Problem." *Annual Review of Sociology* 9:125-149.

Kertzer, David I. and Jennie Keith, eds. 1984. *Age and Anthropological Theory*. Ithaca, NY: Cornell University Press.

Kiesler, Sara B., James N. Morgan, and Valerie Kincaid Oppenheimer, eds. 1981. *Aging: Social Change*. New York: Academic Press.

Kingson, Eric R., Barbara Hirshorn, and John M. Cornman. 1986. *Ties That Bind: The Interdependence of Generations*. Washington, DC: Seven Locks Press.

Kohli, Martin, 1985. "The World We Forgot: An Historical Review of the Life Course." In *Later Life: The Social Psychology of Aging*, edited by Victor W. Marshall. Beverly Hills, CA: Sage.

Kohn, Melvin and Carmi Schooler. 1978. "The Reciprocal Effects of the Substantive Complexity of Work and Intellectual Flexibility." *American Journal of Sociology* 84:24-52.

Kohn, Melvin and Carmi Schooler. 1983. *Work and Personality: An Inquiry Into the Impact of Social Stratification*. Norwood, NJ: Ablex Press.

Kornhaber, Arthur. 1985. "Grandparenthood and the 'New Social Contract.' " Pp. 159-171 in *Grandparenthood*, edited by Vern L. Bengtson and Joan F. Robertson. Beverly Hills, CA: Sage.

Kreps, Juanita M. and R. John Leaper. 1976. "Home Work, Market Work, and the Allocation of Time." Pp. 61-81 in *Women and the American Economy* edited by Juanita M. Kreps. Englewood Cliffs, NJ: Prentice-Hall.

Kruse, Andrea, 1984. "The Five-Generation Family—a Pilot Study." Pp. 115-124 in *International Relationships*, edited by Vjenka Garms-Homolova, Erika M. Hoerning, and Doris Schaeffer. Lewiston, NY: Hogrefe.

Laslett, Peter. 1985. "Societal Development and Aging." Pp. 173-198 *Handbook of Aging and Social Sciences*, edited by Robert H. Binstock and Ethel Shanas. New York: Van Nostrand Reinhold.

Lawrence, Barbara S. 1984. "Age Grading: The Implicit Organizational Timetable." *Journal of Occupational Behaviour* 5:23-35.

Lazarsfeld, Paul F., Bernard Berelson, and Hazel Gaudet. 1960. *The People's Choice*. New York: Columbia University Press. (Original work published 1944)

Lenski, Gerhard E. 1966. *Power and Privilege*. New York: McGraw-Hill.

Leslie, Gerald R. and Sheila K. Korman. 1985. *The Family in Social Context*. New York: Oxford University Press.

Levinson, Daniel J. 1978. *The Seasons of a Man's Life*. New York: Knopf.

Linton, Ralph. 1942. "Age and Sex Categories." *American Sociological Review* 7:589-603.

Lipset, Seymour Martin. 1960. *Political Man: The Social Bases of Politics*. Garden City, NY: Doubleday & Co.

Litwak, Eugene and Seymour Spilerman. 1978. "Organizational Structure and Nursing Home Policy for Health Care Problems." Paper delivered at the World Congress of Sociology, Uppsala, Sweden.

Liu, Korbin and Kenneth Manton. 1984. "The Characteristics and Utilization Pattern of an Admission Cohort of Nursing Home Patients." *The Gerontologist* 24:70-76.

Lorence, Jon and Jeylan T. Mortimer. 1985. "Job Involvement." *American Sociological Review*. 50:618-638.

Maddox, George L. 1963. "Activity and Morale: A Longitudinal Study of Selected Elderly Subjects." *Social Forces*. 42:195-204.

――――― 1979. "Sociology of later life." *Annual Review of Sociology* 5:113-135.

Maddox, George L. and Richard T. Campbell. 1985. "Scope, Concepts, and Methods of Study of Aging." Pp. 3-33 in *Handbook of Aging and the Social Sciences*, edited by Robert Binstock and Ethel Shanas. New York: Van Nostrand Reinhold.

Manton, Kenneth G. 1982. "Changing Concepts of Morbidity and Mortality in the Elderly Population." *Milbank Memorial Fund Quarterly/ Health and Society* 60:183-244.

Mannheim, Karl. 1952. "The Problem of Generations." Pp. 276-322 in *Essays on the Sociology of Knowledge*, edited and translated by Paul Kecskemeti. London: Routledge & Kegan Paul. (Original work published 1928)

Marini, Margaret Mooney. 1984. "Age and Sequencing Norms in the Transition to Adulthood." *Social Forces* 63:229-244.

――――― 1985. "Determinants of the Timing of Adult Role Entry." *Social Science Research*. 14:309-350.

Markides, Kyriados S. 1983. "Minority aging." Pp. 115-37 in *Aging in Society: Selected Reviews of Recent Research*, edited by Matilda White Riley, Beth B. Hess, and Kathleen Bond. Hillsdale, NJ: Lawrence Erlbaum.

Marx, Karl. 1906. *Capital*, vol. 1. Chicago: Charles H. Kerr. (Original work published 1867)

Masnick, George and Mary Jo Bane. 1980. *The Nation's Families: 1960-1990*. Cambridge, MA: Joint Center for Urban Studies of MIT and Harvard University.

Mason, William M. and Stephen E. Fienberg. 1985. *Cohort Analysis in Social Research*. New York: Springer-Verlag.

Mayer, Karl Ulrich and Walter Muller. 1982. "The State and the Structure of the Life Course." Presented at the Intergenerational Conference of Life-Course Research on Human Development, Berlin.

McGee, Jeanne and Kathleen Wells. 1982. "Gender Typing and Androgyny in Later Life." *Human Development* 25:116-139.

McLanahan, Sara S. and Aage B. Sorensen. 1985. "Life Events and Psychological Well-Being over the Life Course." Pp. 217-38 in *Life Course Dynamics*, edited by Glenn H. Elder. Ithaca, NY: Cornell University Press.

McPherson, Barry D. 1983. *Aging as a Social Process*. Toronto: Butterworth.

Mechanic, David. 1983. "The Experience and Expression of Distress: The Study of Illness Behavior and Medical Utilization" Pp. 591-607 in *Handbook of Health, Health Care, and the Health Profession*, edited by David Mechanic. New York: Free Press.

Menken, Jane L. 1985. "Age and Fertility: How Late Can You Wait?" *Demography* 22:469-484.

Merton, Robert K. 1968. "The Matthew Effect in Science: The Reward and Communications Systems of Science." *Science* 199:55-63.

――――― 1984. "Socially Expected Durations: I. A Case Study of Concept Formation in Sociology." Pp. 262-86 in *Conflict and Consensus: A Festschrift for Lewis A. Coser*, edited by W. W. Powell and Richard Robbins. New York: Free Press.

Meyer, John. 1986. "The Institutionalization of the Life Course and its Effect on the Self." Pp. 199-216 in *Human Development: Interdisciplinary Perspectives*, edited by A. B. Sorenson, F. E. Weinert, and L. R. Sherrod. Hillsdale, NJ: Lawrence Erlbaum.

Miller, Joanne, Kazimierz M. Slomczynski, and Melvin L. Kohn. 1985. "Continuity of Learning-Generalization: The Effect of Job on Men's Intellective Process in the United States and Poland." *American Journal of Sociology*. 91: 593-615.

Miller, Warren E., Arthur H. Miller, and Edward J. Schneider. 1980. *American National Election Studies: Data Sourcebook 1952-1978*. Cambridge, MA: Harvard University Press.

Modell, John. 1980. "Normative Aspects of American Marriage Timing Since World War II." *Journal of Family History*. 5:210-234.

――――― and Tamara K. Hareven. 1973. "Urbanization and the Malleable Household: An Examination of Boarding and Lodging in American Families." *Journal of Marriage and the Family* 35:467-479.

Modell, John, Frank Furstenberg, and Theodore Hershberg. 1976. "Social Change and Transitions to Adulthood in Historical Perspective." *Journal of Family History* 1:7-31.

Morris, Richard and Raymond J. Murphy. 1966. "A Paradigm for the Study of Class Consciousness." *Sociology and Social Research*, 50:297-313.

Mortimer, Jeylan T. and Roberta G. Simmons. 1978. "Adult Socialization." *Annual Review of Sociology* 4:421-454.

Mutran, Elizabeth and Donald C. Reitzes. 1984. "Intergenerational Support Activities and Well-being.'' *American Sociological Review* 49:117-130.

Myers, George C. 1985. ''Aging and Worldwide Population Change.'' Pp. 173-198 in *Handbook of Aging and the Social Sciences*, edited by Richard H. Binstock and Ethel Shanas. New York: Van Nostrand Reinhold.

Myles, John. 1984. *Old Age in the Welfare State: The Political Economy of Public Pensions*. Boston: Little, Brown.

Nathanson, Constance A. 1984. ''Sex Differences in Mortality.'' Pp. 191-213 in *Annual Review of Sociology* vol. 10, edited by Ralph H. Turner and James F. Short. Palo Alto, CA: Annual Reviews.

Neugarten, Bernice L., ed. 1968. *Middle Age and Aging*. Chicago: University of Chicago Press.

Neugarten, Bernice L. and Dail A. Neugarten. 1986. ''Age in the Aging Society.'' *Daedalus* 115:31-49.

Neugarten, Bernice L., Joan W. Moore, and John C. Lowe. 1965. ''Age Norms, Age Constraints, and Adult Socialization.'' *American Journal of Sociology* 70:710-717.

Oppenheimer, Valerie Kincade. 1981. ''The Changing Nature of Life-Cycle Squeezes: Implications for the Socioeconomic Position of the Elderly.'' Pp. 47-82 in *Aging: Stability and Change in the Family*, edited by Robert W. Fogel et al. New York: Academic Press.

O'Rand, Angela M. and John C. Henretta. 1982. ''Delayed Career Entry, Industrial Pension Structure and Early Retirement in a Cohort of Unmarried Women.'' *American Sociological Review* 47:365-474.

Pampel, Fred C. 1981. *Social Change and the Aged*. Lexington, MA: D.C. Heath.

_____ and Sookja Park. 1986. ''Cross-national Patterns and Determinants of Female Retirement.'' *American Journal of Sociology* 91:932-955.

Pampel, Fred C. and Jane A. Weiss. 1983. ''Economic Development, Pension Policies, and the Labor Force Participation of Aged Males: A Cross-National, Longitudinal Approach.'' *American Journal of Sociology* 89:350-372.

Pampel, Fred C. and John B. Williamson. 1985. ''Age Structure, Politics, and Cross-National Patterns of Public Pension Expenditures.'' *American Sociological Review* 50:782-799.

Parsons, Talcott. 1942. ''Age and Sex in the Social Structure of the United States.'' *American Sociological Review* 7:604-616.

_____ 1962. ''The Cultural Background of Today's Aged.'' Pp. 3-15 in *Politics of Aging*, edited by Wilma Donahue and Clark Tibbitts. Ann Arbor: University of Michigan.

_____ 1963. ''Death in American Society: A Brief Working Paper.'' *American Behavioral Scientist* 6:61-65.

Parsons, Talcott and Gerald M. Platt. 1972. ''Higher Education and Changing Socialization.'' Pp.

236-93 in *Aging and Society: A Sociology of Age Stratification*, vol. III, edited by Matilda White Riley, Marilyn Johnson, and Anne Foner. New York: Russell Sage Foundation.

Pfeffer, Jeffrey. 1981. ''Some Consequences of Organizational Demography: Potential Impacts of an Aging Work Force on Formal Organizations.'' Pp. 291-345 in *Aging: Social Change* edited by Sara B. Kiesler, James N. Morgan, and Valerie K. Oppenheimer. New York: Academic Press.

Pifer, Alan and D. Lydia Bronte. 1986. *Our Aging Society*. New York: Norton.

Presser, Harriet. 1974. ''Early motherhood: Ignorance or bliss?'' *Family Planning Perspective* 6:8-14.

Preston, Samuel H. 1976. *Mortality Patterns in National Populations: With Special Reference to Recorded Causes of Death*. New York: Academic Press.

_____ 1984. ''Children and the Elderly: Divergent Paths for America's Dependents.'' *Demography* 21:435-457.

Quadagno, Jill. 1982. *Aging in Early Industrial Society: Work, Family, and Social Policy in Nineteenth-Century England*. New York: Academic Press.

_____ 1984. ''Welfare Capitalism and the Social Security Act of 1935.'' *American Sociological Review* 49:623-647.

Quinn, Robert A., Graham L. Staines, and M. R. McCullough. 1974. ''Job Satisfaction: Is There a Trend?'' Manpower Research Monograph No. 30. U.S. Department of Labor. Washington, D.C.: Governing Printing Office.

Riley, John W., Jr. 1983. ''Dying and the Meanings of Death: Sociological Inquiries.'' *Annual Review of Sociology* 9:191-216.

Riley, Matilda White. 1973. ''Aging and Cohort Succession: Interpretations and Misinterpretation.'' *Public Opinion Quarterly* 37:35-49.

_____ 1976. ''Age Strata in Social Systems.'' Pp. 189-217 in *Handbook of Aging and the Social Sciences*, edited by Robert H. Binstock and Ethel Shanas. New York: Van Nostrand Reinhold.

_____ 1978. ''Aging, Social Change, and the Power of Ideas.'' *Daedalus* 107:39-52.

_____ 1979. ''Introduction: Life-Course Perspectives.'' Pp. 3-13 in AAAS Selected Symposium 30, *Aging from Birth to Death: Interdisciplinary Perspectives*, vol. 1, edited by Matilda White Riley. Boulder, CO: Westview Press.

_____ 1980. ''Age and Aging:From Theory Generation To Theory Testing.'' Pp. 339-348 in *Sociological Theory and Research: A Critical Appraisal*, edited by Hubert Blalock, Jr. New York: Free Press.

_____ 1982. ''Aging and Social Change.'' Pp. 11-26 in AAAS Selected Symposium 79. *Aging from Birth to Death: Sociotemporal Perspectives*, vol. II, edited by Matilda White Riley, Ronald P. Abeles, and Michael S. Teitelbaum. Boulder, CO: Westview Press.

———— 1983. "The Family in an Aging Society: A Matrix of Latent Relationships." *Journal of Family Issues* 4:439-454.

———— 1984. "Women, Men, and the Lengthening Life Course." Pp. 333-347 in *Gender and the Life Course*, edited by A. Rossi. New York: Aldine.

———— 1985. "Age Strata in Social Systems." In *Handbook on Aging and the Social Sciences*, edited by Robert H. Binstock and Ethel Shanas. New York: Van Nostrand Reinhold.

———— 1986. "Overview and Highlights of a Sociological Perspective." In *Human Development: Interdisciplinary Perspectives*, edited by Aage B. Sorenson, Franz E. Weinert, and Lonnie R. Sherrod. Hillsdale, NJ: Lawrence Erlbaum.

———— and Kathleen Bond. 1983. "Beyond Ageism: Postponing the Onset of Disability." Pp. 243-52 in *Aging in Society: Selected Reviews of Recent Research*, edited by Matilda White Riley, Beth B. Hess, and Kathleen Bond. Hillsdale, NJ: Lawrence Erlbaum.

Riley, Matilda White, and Anne Foner, in association with Mary E. Moore, Beth Hess, and Barbara K. Roth. 1968. *Aging and Society: An Inventory of Research Findings*, vol. 1. New York: Russell Sage.

Riley, Matilda White and Edward E. Nelson. 1971. "Research on Stability and Change in Social Systems." Pp. 407-449 in *Stability and Social Change: A Volume in Honor of Talcott Parsons*, edited by Bernard Barber and Alex Inkeles. Boston: Little, Brown.

Riley, Matilda White and John W. Riley, Jr. 1986. "Longevity and Social Structure: The Added Years." *Daedalus* 115:51-75.

Riley, Matilda White and Joan Waring. 1976. "Age and aging." Pp. 357-410 in *Contemporary Social Problems*, edited by Robert K. Merton and Robert Nisbet. New York: Harcourt Brace Jovanovich.

Riley, Matilda White, Ronald P. Abeles, and Michael S. Teitelbaum, eds. 1981. AAAS Selected Symposium 79, *Aging from Birth to Death, Vol. II: Sociotemporal Perspectives*. Boulder, CO: Westview Press.

Riley, Matilda White, Andrew S. Baum, and Joseph Matarazzo. 1986. *Perspectives on Behavioral Medicine: Biomedical and Psychological Dimensions*, vol. IV. New York: Academic Press.

Riley, Matilda White, Marilyn Johnson, and Anne Foner. 1972. *Aging and Society, Vol. III: A Sociology of Age Stratification*. New York: Russell Sage Foundation.

Riley, Matilda White, John W. Riley, Jr., and Mary E. Moore. 1961. "Adolescent Values and the Riesman Typology." Pp. 370-386 in *Culture and Social Character*, edited by S. M. Lipset and L. Lowenthal. Glencoe, IL:Free Press.

Robinson, Pauline K., Sally Coberly, Carolyn S. Paul. 1985. "Work and retirement." Pp. 503-527 in *Handbook of Aging and the Social Sciences*, edited by Robert H. Binstock and Ethel Shanas. New York: Van Nostrand Reinhold.

Rodgers, Willard L. 1982. "Estimable Functions of Age, Period, and Cohort Effects." *American Sociological Review* 47:774-787.

Rosow, Irving. 1967. *Social Integration of the Aged*. New York: Free Press.

———— 1985. "Status and Role Change Through the Life Cycle." Pp. 62-93 in *Handbook of Aging and the Social Sciences*, edited by R. H. Binstock and E. Shanas. New York: Van Nostrand Reinhold.

Rossi, Alice S. 1977. "A Biosocial Perspective on Parenting." *Daedalus* 106:1-31.

———— 1982. *Feminists in Politics: A Panel Analysis of the First National Women's Conference*. New York: Academic Press.

———— 1984. "Gender and Parenthood." *American Sociological Review* 49:1-19.

————, ed. 1984. *Gender and the Life Course*. New York: Aldine.

———— 1986. "Sex and Gender in an Aging Society." *Daedalus* 115:141-169.

Ryder, Norman B. 1963. "The Translation Model of Demographic Change." *Milbank Memorial Fund* Pp. 65-81.

———— 1964. "Notes on the Concept of a Population." *American Journal of Sociology* 69:447-463.

———— 1965. "The Cohort as a Concept in the Study of Social Change." *American Sociological Review* 30:843-861.

———— 1968. "Cohort Analysis." *International Encyclopedia of the Social Sciences* 5:546-550.

———— 1979. "Commentary on Cohorts, Periods, and Ages." Paper prepared for conference sponsored by the Social Science Research Council.

San Giovanni, Lucinda. 1978. *Ex-nuns: A Study of Emergent Role Passages*. Norwood, NJ: Ablex.

Schaie, K. Warner, ed. 1983. *Longitudinal Studies of Adult Psychological Development*. New York: Guilford Press.

Schooler, Carmi and K. Warner Schaie, eds. 1986. *Cognitive Functioning and Social Structure Over the Life Course*. Norwood, NJ: Ablex.

Schrank, Harris T. and John W. Riley, Jr. 1976. "Women in Work Organizations." In *Women in the American Economy: A Look to the 1980s*, edited by Juanita M. Kreps. Englewood Cliffs, NJ: Prentice-Hall.

Schrank, Harris T. and Joan M. Waring. 1983. "Aging and Work Organizations." Pp. 53-70 in *Aging in Society: Selected Reviews of Recent Research*, edited by Matilda W. Riley, Beth B. Hess, and Kathleen Bond. Hillsdale, NJ: Lawrence Erlbaum.

Sewell, W. H. and Hauser, R. M. 1975. *Education, Occupation, and Earnings*. New York: Academic Press.

Shalev, Michael. 1983. "The Social Democratic Model and Beyond: Two 'Generations' of Comparative Research on the Welfare State." Pp. 315-51 in *Comparative Social Research, Volume 6: The Welfare State, 1883-1983*, edited by Richard F. Tomasson.

Shanas, Ethel. 1979. "Social Myths as Hypothesis: the Case of the Family Relations of Old People." *Gerontologist* 19:2-9.

————— and George L. Maddox. 1985. "Health, Health Resources, and the Utilization of Care." Pp. 697-726 in *Handbook of Aging and the Social Sciences*, edited by R. H. Binstock and E. Shanas. New York: Van Nostrand Reinhold.

Shanas, Ethel, Peter Townsend, Dorothy Wedderburn, Hennig Friis, P. Milhj, and Jan Stehouwer. 1968. *Old People in Three Industrial Societies*. New York: Atherton Press.

Siegel, Jacob S. and Cynthia M. Taeuber. 1986. "Demographic Perspectives on the Long-Lived Society." *Daedalus* 115:77-117.

Simkus, Albert. 1982. "Socioeconomic Careers in the Context of Radical Social Change: Evidence from Hungary." Pp. 163-180 in *Aging from Birth to Death: Sociotemporal Perspectives*, edited by Matilda White Riley, Ronald P. Abeles, and Michael S. Teitelbaum. Boulder, CO: Westview Press.

Singer, Burton, Kenneth G. Manton, and Richard Suzman. In press. *Forecasting Life Expectancy*.

Smelser, Neil J. 1968. "Sociological History: The Industrial Revolution and the British Working Class Family." Pp. 76-91 in *Essays in Sociological Explanation*, edited by Neil J. Smelser. Englewood Cliffs, NJ: Prentice-Hall.

Smith, Edward J., J. Richard Udry, and Naomi M. Morris. 1985. "Pubertal Development and Friends: A Biosocial Explanation of Adolescent Sexual Behavior." *Journal of Health and Social Behavior* 26:183-192.

Sorenson, Aage B. 1986. Pp. 177-197 in *Human Development: Interdisciplinary Perspectives*, edited by A. B. Sorenson, F. E. Weinert, and L. R. Sherrod. Hillsdate, NJ: Lawrence Erlbaum.

Sorenson, Aage B., F. E. Weinert, and L. R. Sherrod, eds. 1986. *Human Development: Interdisciplinary Perspectives*. Hillsdale, NJ: Lawrence Erlbaum.

Sorokin, Pitirim A. 1959. *Social and Cultural Mobility*. New York: Free Press. (Original work published 1927)

————— 1941. *Social and Cultural Dynamics: Basic Problems, Principles, and Methods*, vol. 4. New York: American Book Company.

————— 1947. *Society, Culture and Personality*. New York: Harper and Brothers.

————— 1969. "Social differentiation." Pp. 406-409 in *International Encyclopedia of the Social Sciences*, edited by David L. Sills. New York: Macmillan.

Spanier, Graham B. and Paul C. Glick. 1980. "The life cycle of American families: An expanded analysis." *Journal of Family History* 5:97-111.

Spengler, Oswald. 1926-1928. *The Decline of the West* (vols. 1 and 2) (1918-1922), translated by C. F. Atkinson. New York: Knopf.

Stouffer, Samuel A. 1955. *Communism, Conformity, and Civil Liberties*. New York: Doubleday.

Strauss, Anselm. 1959. *Mirrors and Masks*. Glencoe, IL: Free Press.

Strauss, Murray. 1980. *Behind Closed Doors: Violence in the American Family*. Garden City, NY: Anchor.

Streib, Gordon F. 1966. "Participants and Dropouts in a Longitudinal Study." *Journal of Gerontology*. 2:200-209.

————— 1985. "Social stratification and aging." Pp. 339-368 in *Handbook of Aging and the Social Sciences*, edited by Herbert H. Binstock and Ethel Shanas. New York: Van Nostrand Reinhold.

Susser, Mervyn. 1969. "Aging and the Field of Public Health." Pp. 114-160 in *Aging and Society, Volume II: Aging and Professionals*, edited by Matilda White Riley, John W. Riley, Jr., and Marilyn E. Johnson. New York: Russell Sage Foundation.

Sussman, Marvin B. 1985. "The Family Life of Old People." Pp. 415-449 in *Handbook of Aging and the Social Sciences*, edited by Robert H. Binstock and Ethel Shanas. New York: Van Nostrand Reinhold.

Sutton, John R. 1983. "Social Structure, Institutions, and the Legal Status of Children in the United States." *American Journal of Sociology* 88: 915-947.

Suzman, Richard and Matilda White Riley, eds. 1985. "The Oldest Old." *Milbank Memorial Fund Quarterly*. (Entire issue)

Taeuber, Cynthia M. 1983. *America in Transition: An Aging Society*. Series P-23, no. 128, U.S. Bureau of the Census. Washington, DC: Government Printing Office.

Taeuber, Karl E. and James A. Sweet. 1976. Pp. 31-60 in *Women and the American Economy*, edited by Juanita M. Kreps. New York: Columbia University Press.

Thomas, William I. and Florian Znaniecki. 1918. *The Polish Peasant in Europe and America*. Chicago: University of Chicago Press.

Torrey, Barbara B. 1982. "The Lengthening of Retirement." Pp. 181-196 in *Aging from Birth to Death: Sociotemporal Perspectives*, edited by Matilda White Riley, Ronald P. Abeles, and Michael S. Teitelbaum. Boulder, CO: Westview Press.

Tuma, Nancy B. and Michael T. Hannan. 1984. *Social Dynamics: Models and Methods*. Orlando, FL: Academic Press.

Turner, Ralph H. 1970. *Family Interaction*. New York: John Wiley.

————— 1978. "The Role and the Person." *American Journal of Sociology* 84:1-23.

Udry, J. Richard and R. L. Cliquet. 1982. "A Cross-cultural Examination of the Relationship between Ages at Menarche, Marriage, and First

Birth.'' *Demography* 19:53-63.

Uhlenberg, Peter. 1969. ''A Study of Cohort Life Cycles: Cohorts of Native Born Massachusetts Women, 1830-1920.'' *Population Studies* 23: 407-420.

———— 1979. ''Demographic Change and Problems of the Aged.'' Pp. 153-166 in *Aging from Birth to Death: Interdisciplinary Perspectives*, edited by Matilda White Riley. Boulder, CO: Westview Press.

———— 1980. ''Death and the Family.'' *Journal of Family History* 5:313-320.

Vaillant, George E. 1974. *Adaptation to Life*. Boston: Little, Brown.

Van Gennep, Arnold. 1960. *The Rites of Passage*, translated by Monike B. Visedom and Gabrielle L. Caffee. Chicago: University of Chicago Press. (Original work published 1908)

Verbrugge, Lois M. 1985. ''Gender and Health: An Update on Hypotheses and Evidence.'' *Journal of Health and Social Behavior* 26:156-182.

Vinovskis, Maris A. 1982. ''Aged Servants of the Lord: Changes in the Status and Treatment of Elderly Ministers in Colonial America.'' Pp. 105-137 in AAAS Selected Symposium 79, *Aging from Birth to Death: Sociotemporal Perspectives*, vol. II, edited by Matilda White Riley, Ronald P. Abeles, and Michael S. Teitelbaum. Boulder, CO: Westview Press.

Ward, Russell A. 1984. *The Aging Experience: An Introduction to Social Gerontology*. New York: Harper & Row.

Waring, Joan M. 1975. ''Social Replenishment and Social Change.'' *American Behavioral Scientist* 19:237-256.

Westoff, C. F. and L. Bumpass. 1973. ''The Revolution in Birth Control Practices of U.S. Roman Catholics.'' *Science* 19:237-265.

Wheeler, Stanton. 1966. ''The Structure of Formally Organized Socialization Settings.'' Pp. 51-116 in *Socialization After Childhood*, edited by Orville G. Brim and S. Wheeler. New York: John Wiley.

Whelpton, Pascal K. 1954. *Cohort Fertility: Native White Women in the United States*. Princeton, NJ: Princeton University Press.

White, Winston. 1961. *Beyond Conformity*. New York: Free Press.

Winsborough, Halliman H. 1979. ''Changes in the Transition to Adulthood.'' Pp. 137-152 in AAAS Selected Symposium 30, *Aging from Birth to Death: Interdisciplinary Perspectives*, vol. 1, edited by Matilda White Riley. Boulder, CO: Westview Press.

Wright, Eric O., C. Costello, D. Hachen, and J. Sprague. 1982. ''The American Class Structure.'' *American Sociological Review* 47:709-726.

Zuckerman, Harriet and Robert K. Merton. 1972. ''Age, Aging and Age Structure in Science.'' Pp. 292-356 in *Aging and Society: Volume II, A Sociology of Age Stratification*, edited by Matilda White Riley, Marilyn Johnson, and Anne Foner. New York: Russell Sage Foundation.

9

Gender and Sex Roles

JANET Z. GIELE

Several dramatic social changes since World War II have affected not only the relative status of women and men but also the sociology of gender. Women's labor force participation in the United States rose dramatically from 30% in 1940 to 64% of women under 65 in 1986 (Bergmann, 1986, p. 21). A surprising number of legal and economic disabilities were uncovered by the Commission on the Status of Women appointed by President Kennedy in 1961 (Mead and Kaplan, 1965). These and other developments helped to fuel a new woman's movement during the sixties that sought equal pay, educational and employment opportunities, reproductive rights, and greater public support for traditional women's activities such as child care.

Changes in women's status inevitably affected the intellectual frameworks with which scholars and the general public interpreted the events of everyday life. The functionalist sociology of Parsons (1942; Parsons and Bales, 1955) had seemed adequate to explain the sexual division of labor based on male (instrumental) breadwinner roles and female (expressive) homemaker

roles, which had characterized middle-class nuclear families of the late nineteenth and early twentieth centuries. But a new generation of sociologists sharply criticized this framework because it no longer conformed to the reality of their experience. Alice S. Rossi (1964) in her now-classic article, "Equality between the Sexes," called for a critical evaluation of the existing gender system. Her essay was a radical departure from the prevailing sociology of the period in that she unabashedly examined social relations from the standpoint of women and envisioned both sexes as subjects with the power to change the family and workplace rather than as objects who were totally constrained by existing social relations. In the ensuing decade a number of other sociologists noted that in much sociological research (1) women were frequently omitted or underrepresented as subjects, (2) the topics studied were often more central to men's than women's lives, (3) women's experiences were sometimes distorted by the models or methods used, and (4) men's experience was usually taken as the norm (Bernard, 1973; Lipman-Blumen and Tickamyer, 1975; R. E. Smith, 1979; Ward and Grant, 1985).

As changes in social relations between the sexes become more visible, not only the popular ideology of gender relations began to change but also the nature of sociological discourse. The amount of scholarly work on the status of

I wish especially to thank Barrie Thorne and Francesca Cancian, who each gave a very thorough reading to an earlier draft and provided many helpful comments and references. In addition I benefited from conversations about the chapter with Lise Vogel, Joan Huber, Mirra Komarovsky, Beatrice Whiting, and Natalie Sokoloff.

291

women, sexuality, and male and female differences and men's roles rose dramatically. The proportion of articles devoted to sex roles and sexuality in 10 major sociological journals grew from 14% in 1974 to 21% in 1983 (Ward and Grant, 1985).[1] Where once the major reviews of sociology—*Sociology Today* (Merton, Broom, and Cottrell, 1959) and the *Handbook of Modern Sociology* (Faris, 1964)—contained no chapters on sex roles or gender, every major sociological textbook in the 1980s contained a gender chapter.

Growing popular interest and the new women's movement partly explained the changing character of sociological research on sex and gender. But a major impetus also came from increasing numbers of women sociologists. Sociologists for Women in Society was founded in 1969; the Sex Roles section of the American Sociological Association was organized at the same time. Other disciplines also fostered an energetic outpouring of research on women: section W of the American Association of University Professors; the women's caucus of the American Economic Association; and similar groups in psychology, history, and literature. New journals sprang up: *Feminist Studies* (1972), *Women's Studies* (1972), *Signs* (1974), *Sex Roles* (1975), *Psychology of Women Quarterly* (1976), *Women's Law Reporter* (1976), and most recently, *Gender and Society* (1987).

Several features distinguish the growing sociological literature on gender and sex roles from other types of sociological inquiry. A large proportion of the researchers are women, and their perspective tends to be critical of mainstream sociology (Bernard, 1973). Methods are often "feminist" in the sense that they use participant observation or fieldwork and treat the persons observed as subjects not objects (D. E. Smith, 1979). Partly because scholars in the new gender field frequently take the standpoint of women, much of the new gender research treats commonplace subjects of everyday life: emotions, sexuality, housework, and the informal and private contexts in which people live their daily lives. Finally, research on gender is often accompanied by implicit or explicit arguments for social justice and social change.

This review attempts to organize the vast sociological literature on sex and gender first by placing it in a context of changing ideologies and alternative epistemologies and then by grouping the principal studies according to their relevance for macro or micro levels of social organization. It focuses primarily on sociological research since 1970. However, since the study

of sex and gender is not confined to works by sociologists it also refers to a few key sources in neighboring fields.

Alternative Perspectives on Gender Organization

An important aspect of any inquiry is the conceptual framework that organizes the questions and findings. Pioneers in the gender field found no ready paradigms that made sense out of women's experience as they knew it. Sociologist Dorothy E. Smith (1979) wrote: "Inquiry does not begin within the conceptual organization or relevances of the sociological discourse but in actual experience . . ." Philosophers Harding and Hintikka (1983, p. x) went even further to claim that "women's experience systematically differs from the male experience upon which knowledge claims have been grounded." Therefore the feminist "deconstructive" project is to show the incompleteness of current established masculine properties in each field, and the "reconstructive" project is to show what is required in scientific inquiry to make women's experience into a foundation for a more adequate and truly human epistemology.

The Problem of Knowing

Scientist and mathematician Evelyn Fox Keller (1985) suggests that women are quite capable of scientific thought, but of a different kind that sees the inquirer as related to the subject of inquiry, not separate and emotionally uninvolved. Reinharz (1979) in a more general fashion holds that the social scientist is most insightful when beginning from observations based on her own subjective experience.

Students of gender thus emphasize that the gender of the knower will affect the scientific enterprise. Their insights recall the reasoning of Marx and Engels (1846) and Mannheim (1936) concerning the sociology of knowledge. Because knowledge and beliefs vary according to the social location of the knower, males, who are generally in a socially dominant position, will have a different view of the social order than women, who are normally in subordinate roles.

But are males always dominant? Several theoretical perspectives are available that characterize the gender and sex role system differently and result in somewhat different projections about the outlook for sex equality.

Liberal, Marxist, Radical, and Socialist Perspectives

As scholars sought conceptual frameworks to map the emerging gender field, they found in liberal and socialist theories of class stratification a natural starting point for analogs in gender theory (Andersen, 1983; H. Eisenstein, 1983; Jaggar, 1983).

Liberal feminist theory drew on the Enlightenment ideas of individual rights, justice, and freedom. It envisioned a time when women could enjoy equality with men if they were given equal opportunity for civil rights, education, and employment. The founders of the National Organization for Women and feminists like Betty Friedan (1963) were among the leaders who articulated this view (Carden, 1974). A great deal of the sociology of gender falls within the liberal tradition because it emphasizes the structural bases for sex inequality and implies such remedies as affirmative action that are possible within the limits of the existing democratic and economic order. Thus, for example, Kanter (1977c) hypothesizes that either a very high or very low proportion of women in a job will lead to patterns of discrimination that can be remedied by a hiring policy that avoids such imbalances.

Traditional Marxist feminist theory traced oppression of women to relations in production and advocated the abolition of private property as the principal vehicle for the liberation of women (Andersen, 1983, pp. 267-275). However, Marxist theory had a flaw in that it largely overlooked relations in the household, which were more relevant to gender than to analysis of class inequality. Recent theorists have invested considerable effort in elaborating the implications of household labor and reproductive work for gender relations (Vogel, 1983). Sociological work that examines the relation between means of subsistence, political economy, and gender relations draws a number of insights from this tradition (Blumberg, 1976b, 1984).

Radical feminist theory focused on the immutable physical differences between the sexes as the principal source of women's oppression. Women by the fact of being the childbearers and nurturers of the young are vulnerable to dependency and limitations on activity. Radical lesbians suggest that communities of women are one means to circumvent oppression of women (G. Rubin, 1975). Sociological work in this tradition tends to be pessimistic about the possibilities for sex equality through a restructuring of the social order and shows instead the extent to which females are disproportionately the victims of battering, rape, and sexual abuse (Barry, 1979).

Socialist feminist theory, according to Jaggar (1983), combines the insights of both traditional Marxist and radical theories. Along with restructuring relations in production, socialist feminists would restructure reproductive relations by socializing (getting state or community support for) such private family functions as housework and child care. Sociological work relevant to this tradition examines the kibbutz and modern socialist states in their successes and failures at equalizing the status of the sexes (Blumberg, 1976b; Scott, 1974; Stacey, 1983).

Sociology of Gender

How do these alternative feminist theories relate to the sociology of sex and gender? First, they contain the main elements of a more comprehensive sociological theory of gender stratification. Second, their focus on the hierarchical aspect of gender implicitly raises questions about possible sex and gender differences that are not inherently hierarchical.

Theory of gender stratification. Taken together, these feminist theories begin to articulate a conceptual framework that links the structure of gender relations to degree of equality between the sexes. Three factors not emphasized by established status attainment theories are given particular attention: (1) the relevance of the *structure of the larger society* (democratic, capitalist, socialist, etc.); (2) the nature of *gender relations in production* (the workplace); and (3) the nature of *gender relations in reproductive activities* (the household).

Most American sociologists have used a status-attainment model based on individual background and performance to explain social class differences. Since this model takes for granted the larger societal context and ignores such structural barriers to gender equality as the unequal division of labor between the sexes in the household, it does not explain very well the differences in educational and occupational attainment that persist among men and women even when they come from the same social background (Acker, 1973; Sokoloff, 1980).

The important contribution of the feminist theories and the sociological theories that have followed in their wake is to highlight the institutional structures that help to explain inequality between the sexes, particularly the political economy that gives women and men different roles in production and reproduction (Benston, 1969). Harriet Holter (1970) was among the first sociologists to attempt a general theory of sex stratification by describing conditions in a single country, Norway. She pointed to values, beliefs about inborn traits, economic roles, and other perceptions as determinants of degree of gender differentiation. In a capitalist society such as the United States, Stockard and Johnson (1980) attribute special importance to the traditional belief that woman's place is in the home. Women's reproductive activities are expected to take precedence over their paid work; they are vulnerable to work interruption and are expected to invest human capital in their children, not themselves. Gender stratification is reflected in pay inequity and flatter career paths for women than men because men are expected to achieve through their work, and women through their families. Sociological theories now recognize that the nature of the societal economy as well as its work and family structures bear on the pattern of gender stratification (Huber, 1986).

Horizontal differentiation by sex. Theories of gender stratification by their silence on non-hierarchical aspects of gender differentiation make one wonder whether there are other frameworks for interpreting sex role systems that do not use equality as the principal dependent variable. For example, are there qualitative differences in the experience of males and females that are not reducible to questions of dominance or subordination? Judith Brown (1981, p. 603) suggests that anthropological studies of gender difference have concentrated all too much on status differences between the sexes to the exclusion of other important questions. The present review recognizes that along with an examination of the nature and bases of gender stratification, which have been central to the sociology of gender, there are other valid frameworks for organizing the field. Recent studies have dealt with gender differences in role performance, interaction in informal groups, methods of play, cognitive style, moral reasoning, and various physiological responses. Explanations range from historical period and cultural milieu to possible psychological and biological bases for sex differentiation.

Gender and Social Organization

Gender enters into social reality at many different levels of social organization and experience; societies, institutions, small groups, and the individual. The effects of gender vary according to the specific context but are fre-quently lumped together and referred to as gender or sex roles.

Definition of Gender and Sex Role

The terms *gender* and *sex role* are used almost interchangeably. But since 1970 there has been a growing consensus on the distinction between sex and gender. Sex more often refers to the biologically determined sex characteristics of male and female; gender, to the culturally and socially defined elements of male and female role expectations.

The terms sex or gender *roles* present a more difficult problem. Lopata and Thorne (1978) argue that "sex role" makes no more sense than "class role" or "race role"; that role terminology masks power differences while alluding to presumed gender differences in roles that result from stratification, not sex. Instead Thorne proposes specific terms for different dimensions of gender differentiation such as "male and female symbolic associations" (culture), "division of labor by sex" (roles), or "gender identification" (individual differences).

Although the use of sex role terminology is often loose and undiscriminating, the concept of sex role is nevertheless an efficient way of referring to the sum total of sex-differentiated expectations in a particular setting. Sociological use of the term *role* has traditionally included all the internalized cultural and normative expectations that an individual brings to a particular social location (Merton, 1957; Komarovsky, 1973; Parsons, 1951). Cultural, normative, and psychological dimensions, while analytically separable, are closely intertwined in their influence on the actions of the individual. Sex role or gender roles thus refer "to normative expectations about the division of labor between the sexes and to gender-related rules about social interactions that exist within a particular cultural and historical context" (Spence, Deaux, Helmreich, 1985, p. 150).

Gender in Society, Institutions, Groups, Individuals

The relevant dimensions of gender and sex role vary depending on the level of social organization that is being observed. In this essay I distinguish four principal levels. At the macro level, gender organization differs across *societies* according to national culture and the economic system. Also at the macro level, the major *in-*

stitutions of society—government, family, the economy, education, and organized religion—develop implicit or explicit norms out of a multitude of micro situations that divide the labor between men and women and differentially allocate responsibilities and rewards. The result is a system of rules that operate more or less consistently across institutional boundaries.

At the micro level, concrete interaction between the sexes is observable in small groups and individual behavior. In *face-to-face groups*, activities and social interaction of males and females are the basis for inferences about social roles of each sex (Giddens, 1984). Roles may be differentiated vertically (by status and rank) and horizontally (by function in the division of labor). Another important variable is the sex ratio of the membership. Within *the individual*, various modes of cognitive, emotional, or instrumental behavior are the basis for inferences about sex differences based on some combination of innate disposition, socialization, or current social expectations.

All these levels of social organization are dynamically linked in such fashion that changes in one will usually have repercussions for the others. Changes generally begin either in altered material conditions that affect population size and the division of labor (Boserup, 1970; Easterlin, 1980) or in changing values, norms, and beliefs (Norton, 1980; Parsons, 1966; Slater, 1968; Smelser, 1963). Material conditions as well as changing cultural expectations are thus potential sources of change or stability in the existing sex/gender system as shown in Figure 9.1.

Societal Variation

In a cross-national study for UNESCO Duverger (1955) demonstrated a nearly invariable rule in women's occupational stratification: the higher, the fewer. Feminist theorists like De Beauvoir (1952), Millett (1970) and Rowbotham (1972) also pointed to an almost universal pattern of patriarchy or male dominance throughout human societies. Even the anthropologists Rosaldo and Lamphere (1974, p. 3) after extensive comparative work had to conclude,

Everywhere we find that women are excluded from certain crucial economic or political activities, that their roles as wives and mothers are associated with fewer powers and prerogatives than are the roles of men. It seems fair to say then, that all

contemporary societies are to some extent male-dominated, and although the degree and expression of female subordination vary greatly, sexual asymmetry is presently a universal fact of human social life.

Structural and cultural variations among societies, however, challenge the proposition that patriarchy is universal. Prior to the feminist revolution sociologists and anthropologists collected considerable evidence of both structural and cultural bases for variation in gender roles. Modern studies have elaborated these themes while introducing further precision and qualification.

Variation in Societal Complexity

Early sociologists such as Spencer (1883), Toennies (1887), and Durkheim (1893) implied that status based on any ascribed characteristics such as gender would eventually decline. Urbanization and modernization would diminish the importance of unchangeable biological or familial attributes and increase the importance of self-controlled performance and effort (Freedman, 1952; Linton, 1936). Later evidence that women in modern society continued to suffer from limitations on their opportunities and achievement represented a challenge to this meritocratic theory.

Now contemporary social scientists have reformulated the structural hypothesis by linking societal complexity to gender inequality in a more complicated way. There appears to be no simple linear relation between societal development and female status. Instead the relationship is curvilinear with higher relative status of women at each end of the development continuum. Lowest status of women appears in peasant societies that are found at an intermediate level of structural complexity.

The new theoretical framework was based on Lenski's comparative work on social stratification. Lenski (1966) discovered a curvilinear relationship between societal complexity and social inequality. More egalitarian class structures were found in both simple (hunter-gatherer and horticultural) societies and in complex modern economies. Class inequality was at its peak in peasant agricultures, empires, and contemporary preindustrial societies where any surplus was concentrated in the hands of a few.

Blumberg (1974, 1984), Giele (1977), and Chafetz (1984) built on Lenski's model to elaborate its implications for gender stratification. They delineated a curvilinear relationship similar to Lenski's where gender *in*equality was highest in societies at intermediate levels of complexity and lower at the two extremes. However, instead of political structure and class differentiation as the primary mechanism for unequal distribution of resources, they focused on the sexual division of labor in the family and community. Like Sacks (1974) and Sanday (1974) their findings suggest that where women have a greater role in production *and* participated in decision making, their status is higher.

The curvilinear model of sex equality appears to be supported by a number of cross-cultural studies (Goode, 1963; Martin and Voorhies, 1975; Friedl, 1975; Whyte, 1978). Ester Boserup (1970), the Danish economist, associated egalitarian relations between the sexes with low population pressure and female farming systems where men cleared land and women cultivated with hoes. With the introduction of the plow,

women became less valuable as producers, and their status declined relative to men. Even in patriarchal peasant societies, however, women were acknowledged as having considerable informal power within the family; they managed property and mediated between kin groups (Lamphere, 1974; Stamm, 1984). However, their contribution to production, while considerable, was often undervalued and unacknowledged, probably because men held ultimate control.

This structural explanation of gender equality now provides an interpretation for what have seemed contradictory findings on the effects of modernization and development on the status of women. On the one hand, modernization and development seemed to emancipate women as it brought them higher education, birth control, and suffrage. On the other hand, development often seemed to have an adverse impact

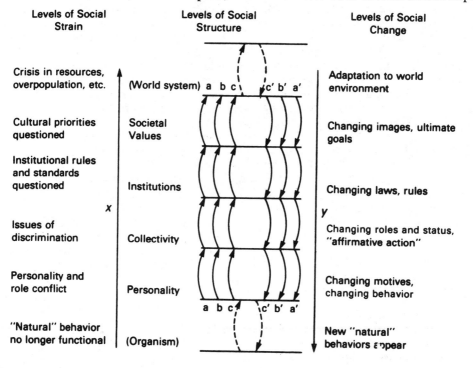

a, a′   elements of reform ideology, and institutionalization of that ideology
b, b′   research and scientific study, and application of that research
c, c′   political interests, and new political consensus

X   The reform process moves up the hierarchy of control
Y   The institutionalization of change moves down the hierarchy of control

Strain may be contained at any one level or it may pass further up the hierarchy before causing change at a higher level which in turn trickles down to lower ones.

FIGURE 9.1
A Model of Change in Sex Roles

by removing women from productive labor, placing them on a pedestal, or oppressing them as low-paid workers in a growing urban proletariat. The curvilinear hypothesis gives a context for interpreting both positive effects that come from the gains associated with emphasis on merit and performance and negative effects stemming from loss of women's roles in production.

Positive and Negative Effects of Development

From the mid-nineteenth century until the mid-twentieth century most people believed that modernization was a boon to women. Democracy and a rising standard of living seemed to bring emancipation. Not just in the United States and western Europe, but throughout the world, women gained the vote, found access to higher education, and increasingly served in public office, the professions, and the nonagricultural labor force (Haavio-Mannila, 1971; Giele and Smock, 1977). Sex-role egali-

tarianism grew in cultures as diverse as Arabic Islam, India, China, the United States, and Japan (Goode, 1963).

These positive changes appeared in part because of the increased importance of the conjugal family and a decline in patriarchal extended families (Goode, 1963). Revolutionary ideas of the Enlightenment helped to legitimate women's rights to citizenship (Banks, 1981; Norton, 1900). The industrial revolution by splitting work from family life and freeing adults as well as children from complete family control probably also contributed to women's new sense of individuality (Smelser, 1959). The Puritan tradition and its religious individualism embodied in the nineteenth-century revivals provided an additional basis for women's sense of moral autonomy (Ryan, 1981). Colleges and universities began to open their doors to women (Solomon, 1985). The women's suffrage movement launched at Seneca Falls in 1848 spread across America and Europe in the early 1900s and by 1975 all of the developed countries of the world had granted women the vote as shown in Table 9.1 (Pharr, 1981, p. 174).

TABLE 9.1
Granting of Suffrage to Women in Selected Countries, by Year

FOURTH WAVE* (1972—)	THIRD WAVE (1950-1971)	SECOND WAVE (1923-1949)	FIRST WAVE (1893-1922)
Islamic Third World Countries	Newly-Independent Third World Countries	Late Developing Societies (Catholic Europe, Eastern Europe, "most developed" countries of the Third World)	Advanced Western Societies (non-Catholic Europe, U.S., USSR, "Europeanized" British colonies)
Saudi Arabia	Pakistan (1950)	Turkey (1934)	New Zealand (1893)
Nigeria	Indonesia (1950)	India (1935)	Australia (1902)
(Northern States)	Nicaragua (1955)	Philippines (1937)	Denmark (1915)
Jordon	Upper Volta (1960)	Cuba (1940)	Soviet Union (1917)
Yemen	Malta (1964)	Quebec (1940)	England (1918)
Kuwait	Tunisia (1969)	France (1944)	Luxembourg (1919)
Liechtenstein	Kenya (1969)	Japan (1945)	Netherlands (1919)
	Syria (1969)	Hungary (1945)	Austria (1919)
	Somalia (1970)	Yugoslavia (1946)	United States (1920)
	Switzerland (1971)	Italy (1947)	Sweden (1921)
		Argentina (1947)	Thailand (1921)
		Belgium (1948)	Canada (except Quebec)
		Chile (1949)	(1922)

SOURCE: For states that granted suffrage prior to 1950, dates are those that appear in U.S. Department of Labor, Women's Bureau, "Women's Suffrage among the Nations," September 1950, or in Josephine F. Milburn, *Women as Citizens: A Comparative Review* (Sage, 1976). Where the dates given in the two sources conflict, the earlier date is given. For third and fourth waves, data are as reported by the states to the United Nations as of 1970-1971. United Nations General Assembly Report No. 8132, *Derechos Politicos de la Mujer* (New York, December 15, 1970), and Report No. 8481, *Droits Politiques de la Femme* (New York, November 30, 1971).

*Countries where women were not eligible to vote as of 1971.

From *Political Women in Japan: The Search for a Place in Political Life* by Susan J. Pharr. Copyright © 1981 The Regents of the University of California.

Contrasting with the benign impact of modernization on women were both historical and contemporary cases that illustrated negative effects. Cott (1977) and Douglas (1977) noted that American women in the 1830s lost a sense of useful involvement in productive work and sought meaningful activity in a narrower feminized sphere of family and cultural life that was represented by "the cult of true womanhood" (Welter, 1976). Restraints on physical activity, the ideology that middle-class homemakers should not work, the association of women with love and men with work, and the "feminine mystique" of the 1950s were all outgrowths of an industrial economy that removed production from the home and narrowed women's domain to the sphere of emotional work and social reproduction (Cancian, 1987).

Contemporary accounts continue to feed skepticism about the positive impact of economic development on women. By 1975 numerous reports documented the displacement of women from agricultural production and the possible worsening of women's status relative to men. The population of dependent female-headed families living in the poor sections of urban centers like Mexico City or Jakarta was growing rapidly. Offshore factories located in the Third World were employing women at low pay. Development schemes often omitted women, reinforced stereotypic inequalities, or added new ones based on Western notions of the proper relations of men and women (Nash and Fernandez-Kelly, 1983; Papanek, 1977; Tinker, 1976). Resources went to expensive sprayers and trucks for production and transport of cash crops (Fortmann, 1981). Women directed their efforts away from food production and their families grew hungry (Boulding, 1977).

Women displaced from the rural economy entered marginal urban occupations as domestic servants, street vendors, or prostitutes. Unable to eke out sufficient living by themselves, they often sought a male partner and had another child in an effort to cement a relationship (Blumberg, 1976a; Youssef, 1976). Although in the short run, urban women's high fertility was rational because their older children could help as vendors or baby-sitters, their extra children in the long run only pushed them further into the urban underclass.

Even in the industrial sector in such industries as food processing, textiles, and electronics where thousands of women worked in "offshore" factories, the working conditions were poor, pay and job security low, and demands for performance and obedience very high (Lim, 1981; Srinivasan, 1981).

This dual assessment of the impact of modernization on gender roles continues in projections for the future. An optimistic outlook comes from those social scientists who see a continuing trend toward crossover between what were traditional sex roles. As more women participate in the workplace as well as the home, and more men take responsibility in household work and child care, the status gap seems likely to narrow (Huber, 1986). Studies of dual-career households provide some evidence of such a trend (Rapoport and Rapoport, 1976; Hertz, 1986). In addition, the ideology and life structure of males appears to be headed toward greater recognition of men's responsibilities to intimate relationships as well as to work (Pleck, 1975, 1976, 1979, 1981; Cancian, 1987). Ideology and life structure of females also gives greater emphasis to competence and productivity as well as to nurturance and caring (Baruch and Barnett, 1983; Giele, 1982).

However, a more pessimistic view is found among scholars who emphasize the continued and almost universal economic dependency of women. The overall wage gap between the sexes in the United States has changed very little despite women's improved education, their more continuous work histories, and legislation barring sex discrimination in employment; moreover, a similar wage gap exists in other countries because of the differences in occupations held by women and men (Roos, 1985). An increasing proportion of the poor are women and children because fewer of them live in traditional two-parent nuclear families (Gerson, 1985). Moreover, those women who do work for pay continue to bear a "double burden" of household responsibility as well as employment. Men's contributions to the family and social programs for child care are still far from reducing women's burden to the extent that would equalize the relative status of the sexes (Hewlett, 1986).

Historical and Cultural Variation

Cultural as well as structural explanations have been put forward by historians, anthropologists, and others to account for differences in gender relations. These cultural factors vary both among and within societies.

CULTURE, RELIGION, POLITICAL VALUES

Even among societies at roughly similar stages of technological and economic development, quite different attributes and values may be associated with each sex. Ruth Benedict (1934) found that both sexes among the Pueblos participated in the Apollonian values of moderation. Margaret Mead (1935) likewise saw little difference between male and female attitudes in two societies—the cooperative culture of the Arapesh and the ruthless aggressive Mundugumor. In a third, the Tchambuli, male and female attitudes were differentiated but in ways opposite to the West: the women were dominant, impersonal, and managerial while the men were less responsible and more emotionally dependent. Youssef (1974) has shown in contemporary developing societies that Latin American cultures are much more encouraging to the emancipation of women than Islamic traditions, where strict separation of the sexes militates against female participation in public life. Among economically advanced societies, it appears that political traditions are especially critical. Socialism seems to be more conducive to women's public participation than the capitalist legacy, which for many decades supported a female ideal of domesticity and voluntary participation in cultural affairs rather than paid employment and public office holding (Haavio-Mannila, 1971; Salaff and Merkle, 1973; Giele and Smock, 1977, p. 17).

RACE, ETHNICITY, AND CLASS

Just as gender roles and inequality vary across societies, they also vary within societies. Women's liberation is differently understood according to race, class, and ethnic location. For black women domestics who up to World War II constituted 60% of all household workers, the opportunity *not* to work outside their own home was usually considered a luxury. But the black middle class during the 1950s, unlike the whites who were caught in the "feminine mystique," valued the economically successful woman who managed to combine career with family (Jones, 1985). Asian immigrant women had yet a different experience; they worked as domestics to gain autonomy from their families as well as to contribute to family income (Glenn, 1980). The perspective of white working-class women is not altogether clear. Many young working-class women value education and employment and are more likely to desire a future with marriage and career than as full-time homemakers (Seifer, 1973). But others sound as though they would rather be full-time homemakers than many middle-class women (Komarovsky, 1964; L. Rubin, 1976). Catholics and other religious groups who believe in a high degree of gender differentiation are more likely to accept men's

dominance over women, encourage high fertility, and keep women closely tied to the family (Scanzoni, 1975). Clearly, gender roles and the values associated with them are quite different according to race, class, and ethnicity and must be taken into account if false universal statements are to be avoided.

MALE AND FEMALE QUALITIES AND VALUES

Race and class variation in what is considered the female ideal points up a larger question: Are there any universal dimensions by which males and females can be described? Whereas in early work Margaret Mead developed a relativistic scheme to characterize male and female personality in similar terms (Bateson, 1984), she had by the time of *Male and Female* (1949) begun to search for such basic regularities in human sex development as male concern with potency and female concern with receptivity (although her central message continued to be the arbitrary nature of sex distinctions and the desirability of developing the full range of human potential in each sex). Parsons and Bales (1955) associated the female more often with expressive functions and an orientation to the internal workings of a group whereas men were associated with instrumental functions and an external orientation. Such analytic efforts to distinguish sex characteristics were sharply criticized by feminists and social scientists alike (Friedan, 1963; Rossi, 1964). For a time, particularly in the 1970s, social scientists were influenced by what Lorber (1981) has called a "minimalist" feminist ideology—a belief that differences between the sexes were minimal and mostly due to socialization and situational influence.

Yet contemporary feminists as well as social scientists have continued the effort to characterize male and female traits in order to highlight women's contributions and to ask how they might be more justly rewarded. Radical feminists call for a woman-centered value system based on nurturance and caring that will drastically reorient priorities and give women their due (H. Eisenstein, 1983). Sociologist Jessie Bernard (1981) describes the female world of love and support and suggests that it be given a place of equal honor with the male world of rational exchange. Such a perspective is akin to what Lorber (1981) has called a "maximalist" feminist ideology, one that emphasizes male and female difference and particularly calls for the rediscovery of valuable female qualities that need to be encouraged for the benefit of the whole society. Similar analyses abound in the fields of political science and philosophy (Bologh, 1984).

In her review of women's place in Western political thought Okin (1979) discovers an androcentric bias in all the classic political theories that separate public and private worlds and mete out different kinds of justice to each gender (Elshtain, 1981). Women because of maternity disproportionately bear the responsibilities and costs for social reproduction in the private world of child care and human care. Their consequent disadvantage in the public world of production and paid employment does not so much result from their personal characteristics as from the priorities of society.

Institutional Structure and Gender Relations

As women's labor force participation, even among mothers of preschool children, continued to rise dramatically, scholars probed the nature and degree of sex differentiation in the workplace. The market did not simply reward individuals for their education and continuous attachment but produced a persistent overall earnings gap of 40% between the sexes and 20% between women and men with comparable training and qualifications (Barrett, 1979, p. 38; Bianchi and Spain, 1986, p. 175).

Efforts to explain the earnings gap led in three major directions: (1) examination of the *workplace*, particularly hiring and promotion practices; (2) description of time spent in the *family*, in household work and child care; and (3) analysis of *social policies* related to education,

employment, and family life that could alleviate the inequality between traditional homemaker and breadwinner roles. While early sociological works treated initial policy efforts for sex equity in a wide variety of fields (Bernard, 1971; Giele, 1978; Lipman-Blumen and Bernard, 1979; Safilios-Rothschild, 1974), this review focuses primarily on gender as it relates to three institutions cconomy, family, and polity.

Gender in the Workplace

The most dramatic postwar change in women's lives was the rise in *labor force participation*. Between 1947 and 1978, married women's rate increased from 20% to 48% (Smith, 1979, p. 4) as shown in Table 9.2. After 1940 older married women were drawn into the labor market; old rules against employment of married women in such professions as schoolteaching were gradually dropped (Oppenheimer, 1970); by 1977, 42% of married women with children under six years old were employed, compared with 26% in 1967 (Smith, 1979, pp. 14, 83).

Oppenheimer (1970) attributed the remarkable postwar rise in married women's employment to a short supply of young unmarried women and a growing demand in such female-labeled occupations as teaching, nursing, and clerical work. Economists explained the rising employment of married women by the rising opportunity cost of wives' and mothers' "leisure," which outstripped the cost of replacing their services in the home. Models developed by Mincer (1962), Cain (1966), Bowen and Finegan (1969), and Polachek (1979) suggested

TABLE 9.2
Sex Differentials in Labor Force Participation Rates Since 1940 (Percentage)

Year	Men[a] 25-54	Women[a] 25-54	Married Women[b]	Mothers of children[c] Under 6 yrs	6-18 yrs	Women with 4 yrs[d] High School	College
1947/1948	96.6	35.0	21.0	10.8	26.0		
1950	96.5	36.8	23.8	11.9	28.0		
1955	97.4	39.8	27.7	16.2	34.7		
1960	97.0	42.9	30.5	18.6	39.0	34.3	41.6
1965	96.7	45.2	34.7	23.3	42.7		
1970	95.8	50.1	40.8	30.3	49.2	44.4	53.4
1975	94.4	55.1	44.4	36.7	52.2		
1980	94.2	64.0	50.1	45.1	61.7	61.7	74.8
1983	93.8	67.1	51.8	49.9	63.8		

SOURCES: a. Bianchi and Spain (1968, p. 143); U.S. Department of Labor (1983), Tables 2 and 3; U.S. Department of Labor (1984), Table 3. b. Bianchi and Spain (1986, p. 201); U.S. Department of Labor (1982), Tables C-3 and C-6; U.S. Bureau of the Census (1987, p. 383), Table 654. c. Bianchi and Spain (1986, p. 226); Waldman (1983), Table 2, p. 18; Hayghe (1984), Table 1, p. 32; U.S. Bureau of the Census (1975, p. 134), series D 63-74. d. Bianchi and Spain (1986, p. 131); 1960, 1970, and 1980 Census 1/1,000 Public Use Microdata Sample. Figures here are for women 25-34 years of age who completed four years of high school and four years of college.

that women with more education (human capital), lower husband's income, and older children were more likely to be employed.

Studies by Corcoran, Duncan, and Ponza (1983), however, failed to uphold the related human capital hypothesis that differences in labor force attachment would account for sex differences in earnings. Women who had not worked continuously had incomes very similar to those who had worked. Moreover, Easterlin (1980) located some of the push for women's employment in the worsening economic situation of younger men. Husband's incomes, unlike those of their fathers, were less capable of supporting a family and required supplementation by wives. Oppenheimer (1982) saw little prospect that this pattern would cease with an economic upturn and smaller cohorts entering the labor force. She proposed instead that two foreseeable types of "life cycle squeeze" would keep women in the labor force: first, the initial start-up phase of family life when husband's income was low and purchase of household durables put particular pressure on working white-collar couples; and second, when costs of older children again created a particular need for wife's supplemental income.

The second principal focus of scholarly research on sex roles in the workplace has been explanation of *labor market segmentation*. Men predominate in management, high-prestige professions, sales and production jobs; women are the vast majority in the lower-prestige professions, high-prestige clerical work, and low-status sales and production jobs. These patterns are strikingly similar across the industrialized nations, and although women's and men's occupations are similar in *status and prestige*, they differ in *earnings and promotion opportunities* (Roos, 1985). Some of the earliest descriptive studies of sex segregation were done by sociologists regarding the academic world and other professions (Bernard, 1964; Epstein, 1970; Rossi and Calderwood, 1973).

Major explanations for gender inequalities at work first came from economists (Blau and Jusenius, 1976). The more individually oriented *human capital theory* explained sex differences in occupational attainments by sex differences in skills, experience, and motivation. Men supposedly reached different jobs and were better paid because they had more human capital. The more structurally oriented *dual labor market theory* explained job differences and the earnings gap by employers' hiring and promotion practices. More fortunate workers (native born, whites, males) were hired into primary-sector jobs with better benefits and pay and better op-portunities for training and advancement. Less fortunate workers (immigrants, blacks, females) were steered into less well paid and more expendable secondary jobs (Thurow, 1969).

Sociologists tested these alternative perspectives both cross-nationally and at home. After extensive comparison of data from 12 industrialized nations, Roos (1985) found more support for the dual market model than the human capital model as explanation for the widespread and persistent differences in male and female occupations and earnings. Women had lower returns to education than men; single and married women had very similar earnings. In their extensive study of 290 diverse California firms, Bielby and Baron (1986) found not only the familiar distribution of twice as many men in managerial occupations and three times as many women in clerical work but *sex labeling in job assignment even within the same detailed (nine-digit) occupational classification categories*! Such complete job-level segregation by sex indeed suggests that there is a structural or systemic basis for sex differences in promotion opportunities, occupational status, and earnings trajectories.

Employers appear to be counting *gender* over and above actual education, work attachment, or family responsibilities as a proxy for the likely return on future investments in the worker. The case brought by the Equal Employment Opportunities Commission (EEOC) against American Telephone and Telegraph in 1972 prohibited such discriminatory hiring practices. Men *with no prior training* were steered to jobs as linemen and repairmen that offered higher pay and greater opportunity for advancement. Women, however (also *with no prior training*) were directed to dead-end and low-paid jobs as operators (Equal Employment Opportunities Commission, 1972, pp. E1244-E1245; Hacker, 1979).

Gender in the Household

During the same period that the sex composition of the labor force changed, *family behavior* was also changing, as shown in Table 9.3. Young and Willmott (1973) described the "symmetrical family" as a product of the modern era that brought greater equality to women and men in the home as well as at work. Dual-career families were becoming more common (Holmstrom, 1972; Rapoport and Rapoport, 1976). But so also were single-parent families and female-headed households. The proportion of family and nonfamily residences maintained by a woman increased from 15% to 26% between 1940 and 1980 (Bianchi and Spain, 1986, p. 90). Fertility fell from 3.8 births per women in 1957 to only 1.8 in 1980. Over 50% of ever-married adults born during the 1950s would experience a divorce (Bianchi and Spain, 1986; Norton and Moorman, 1987).

Possibly the dual responsibilities of carrying both work and family roles became so heavy that fewer people in the 1980s were willing to undertake both commitments. In addition, the traditional male breadwinner ethic may have been weakened in part by the counterdependent ideology of the women's liberation movement (Ehrenreich, 1983). Since men were no longer supposed to tie their self-esteem and masculinity to the size of their paychecks, they could justify their abdication of family responsibilities with claims to individual freedom and choice. Of children under 21 who in 1981 were entitled to child support, only 72% received it, and the average amount received was $2,106. Yet the income of divorced and separated women (with whom the children usually reside) was only $6,386 in 1980 compared with $11,440 of divorced and separated men (Bianchi and Spain, 1986, pp. 213, 217).

Changes in *family forms* also expressed the new gender ideologies, especially the tie between gender and the household division of labor. In a survey of 300 gay, lesbian, married, and cohabiting couples, Blumstein and Schwarz (1983) depicted cohabiting heterosexual couples as avoiding marriage in part because of its traditional association of the male with the breadwinner and of the female with the housekeeper. Similarly, gay and lesbian couples, apart from their distinctive sexual orientation, also resisted

unequal responsibility for earning a living or doing household chores; one of the principal reasons for breakup was loss of this equality when one member of the pair became more dominant and the other more dependent.

With the gender revolution came new interest and scholarship about *housework* (Glazer-Malbin, 1976). Numerous accounts describe the unequal burden that falls on women for child care and housework, even if they are employed. Husbands are likely to have many more working hours and take second jobs, but wives (even those employed part- or full-time) spend about twice as much time with children and two-and-a-half times as much time on housework (Staines and Pleck, 1983). Researchers have been puzzled as to why husbands' time in the household is not more responsive to wife's employment. Pleck (1982) described the work-family role system as comprising "buffers" with asymmetrically permeable boundaries between work and family roles. The wife's work role is more permeable to family demands; the husband's family role, to work demands. Berk (1985, pp. 201-204), noting the consistent apportionment of household work (70% to wives and 10%-15% to husbands) and the legitimacy accorded to these arrangements by the majority of the 335 couples whom she interviewed, concludes that the household is producing not only goods and services but gender identity. The grossly imbalanced division of labor allows male and female to demonstrate behaviorally their sexual categorization, an important part of which is "doing" dominance and submission.

Berk's one-dimensional picture of marital interaction is now called into question by new research on the responsiveness of husband's

TABLE 9.3
Changing Family Behavior of Women and Men, 1940-1985 (Percentage)

Year	Families with Female Heads[a]	Single-Person Households[b]	Divorce Rate[c]	Birth Rate[d]	Adolescent Birth Rate[e]
1940	15.3	7.1	8.8	131.4	7.1
1950	9.4	10.9	10.3	190.4	14.1
1960	9.3	13.1	9.2	252.8	21.6
1970	10.8	17.0	14.9	163.4	26.4
1980	14.6	18.3	22.6	115.1	29.4
1984	15.9	20.0	52.2	107.3	30.0*

SOURCES: a. National Center for Health Statistics (1985) Table 67; U.S. Bureau of the Census (1948, p. 47), Table 48; (1960, p. 41), Table 41. b. U.S. Bureau of the Census (1975, p. 42), series A 335-349; U.S. Bureau of the Census (1985, p. 40), Table 40. c. Divorces per 1000 married women aged 15 and over. U.S. Bureau of the Census (1987, p. 41), Table 51; National Center for Health Statistics (1968, p. 102), Table 2; Bianchi and Spain (1986, p. 36). d. Live births per 1000 women ages 20-24. See Bianchi and Spain (1986, p. 49). U.S. Bureau of the Census (1975, pp. 50-51), series B 11-19; (1987, p. 59), Table 82; (1985, p. 57), Table 83. e. Number of births per 1000 unmarried women ages 15-19. Bianchi and Spain (1986, p. 75).
*[1982].

household work to wife's employment. Pleck (1985), drawing on time use studies, finds that men's share of family work rose from 20% in 1965 to 30% in 1981. In the 1975-1976 Study of Time Use, the role overload of employed wives relative to husbands had all but disappeared to a difference of only 12 minutes a day. Barnett and Baruch (1987) gathered similar findings using detailed measures of wife's sex-role attitudes, hours of employment, husband's attitudes toward fathering, and sex and age of child. With interviews from both mothers and fathers of 160 kindergarten and fourth grade children of both sexes, Barnett and Baruch are able to analyze the factors that affect father's time spent in child care and feminine household tasks. There is still marked disparity in total interaction time (fathers, 29.48 hours per week; mothers, 44.45 hours) and solo time with child (fathers, 4.48 hours per week; mothers, 19.56 hours). In *absolute* time husbands of employed and nonemployed wives were not significantly different. But in *proportional* time (i.e., *relative* to the mothers), husbands whose wives were employed and had nontraditional sex-role attitudes spent significantly more time with their children (30% compared to 20%).

Couples with sufficient income can, of course, hire live-in baby-sitters or part-time domestic help. The result is greater capacity to maintain equality between spouses (Hertz, 1986), but at the cost of pushing the domestic chores outside the family to another class and often another race who may be dehumanized in the relationship (Rollins, 1985). Despite rapid change in women's labor force participation, 8% of all black women workers in 1979 were employed in private household service, compared with only 2% of whites (Fox and Hesse-Biber, 1984, p. 161).

Social Policies to Promote Gender Equality

Much of the analysis of sex inequality in the workplace can ultimately be reduced to issues of female labor supply and demand (Reskin, 1984, pp. 310-313). Similarly, social policies to promote equality generally fall into three categories: (1) *educational* policies that will stimulate or redirect women's labor supply; (2) *employment* policies that will affect the demand side by changing employers' hiring and promotion practices; and (3) *family* policies that will affect both worker supply and employer demand and address women's overburdening in the home.

EDUCATIONAL POLICIES

Education is critically important both to level of labor force participation and to type of occupation a woman enters. Of women with four years of college, half are in the labor force, compared with only a third of those who are not high school graduates. Half of college educated women are in managerial or professional jobs, compared with only 14% of high school graduates. During the 1960s and 1970s women's college enrollment and educational attainments improved dramatically, as shown in Table 9.4. From 12% of all 18- to 24-year-old women enrolled in college in 1960, the figure rose to 25% in 1980, the same proportion as for men. Between 1965 and 1980 the percentage of women receiving doctorates had roughly doubled in the humanities and social sciences, and almost doubled in biological sciences and mathematics. The proportion of medical degrees granted to women rose from 6% in 1960 to 23% in 1980, and law degrees from 2% in 1960 to 30% in 1980 (Bianchi and Spain, 1986, pp. 120, 123).

Yet improved education did not overcome occupational segregation or sex differences in pay. Equal rights legislation such as Title IX of the Educational Amendments Act of 1972 (Sandler, 1973) helped to assure more resources for girls' and women's athletics. Home economics classes were opened to boys and shop classes to girls. But policy proposals continue to address the issue of sex-imbalanced classrooms (Dalton, 1986), to subsidize employers to train men and women for jobs mainly held by the opposite sex (Roos, 1985, p. 160), and to train girls for engineering and the high-paying blue-collar jobs in construction and mechanical repair (Bergmann, 1986, p. 305). Educators themselves call for a critical review of their own classroom and administrative practices. A number of corrective strategies are needed to revise curriculum and teaching materials, monitor classroom behavior of teachers and students, and increase the number of women administrators (Klein, 1985, pp. 501-518). Currently there is great concern to institute better sex education in the schools and stem the tide of adolescent pregnancy, which seriously impairs young women's chances of finishing their education and finding a good job (Furstenberg, 1976).

EQUAL EMPLOYMENT POLICY

The Equal Pay Act of 1963 and Title VII of the 1964 Civil Rights Act prohibit discriminatory hiring and pay practices. Often, however, occupational segregation and pay differences result even when there is no conscious discrimination. Advocates of sex equality have therefore proposed deliberate constructive policies such as affirmative action and comparable worth.

Affirmative action developed as a way to comply with federal guidelines under Executive Order 11246, which bars sex discrimination in institutions receiving over $10,000 of federal contracts (Sandler, 1973). Affirmative action requires the employer to make additional efforts to recruit, employ, and promote qualified members of groups formerly excluded. Although the Reagan administration has opposed such a strategy as a form of reverse discrimination, the Supreme Court in 1987 upheld the practice in *Johnson v. Transit Agency*, where Santa Clara County, California, had promoted a woman rather than an equally qualified man to the position of road dispatcher (*National NOW Times*, 1987). Whether affirmative action will now be used more widely is not yet clear. Bielby and Baron (1986), after discovering virtually complete sex segregation in job assignments, would focus scientific effort on discovering the underlying behavioral principles that account for initial sex stereotypes, the process by which they are enshrined in bureaucratic rules, and might be dismantled. Bergmann (1986, p. 302) focuses on the lax enforcement of antidiscrimination laws and advocates EEOC enforcement that would be as strict as that by the IRS: annual reports, strict audits, and monitoring of employment practices of large employers, especially governmental agencies. Roos (1985, pp. 160-163) and Reskin and Hartmann (1986, p. 121) suggest affirmative action as the main strategy by which to increase men's and women's representation in sex-atypical employment and thereby to raise women's pay. As in Sweden, this could be done by subsidizing

employers who hire men and women in sex-atypical jobs or by imposing sex quotas on firms that receive government aid.

Comparable worth is also an affirmative strategy but one that would change primarily the compensation associated with sex-labeled jobs rather than the sex ratio of the workers who fill those jobs. Studies have documented ironic discrepancies and similarities between tree trimmers and nurses in Denver, female and male prison guards in Washington state, and school teachers and liquor store clerks in Maryland (Whicker and Kronenfeld, 1986). Sociologists and others have described extensively how comparable worth might be instituted by evaluation of job components (training, content, responsibility) and equalization of salaries for jobs with comparable demands (Cain, 1985; Hartmann, Roos, and Treiman, 1985; Ratner, 1980; Treiman and Hartmann, 1981). Although there are a few well-known examples such as the city of San Jose where comparable worth has been instituted among city employees, the policy is still controversial because its critics claim that changes in salary would be negligible. Elaine Sorensen (1986), however, argues on the basis of four state-level comparable worth studies (in Iowa, Michigan, Minnesota, and Washington) that the earnings ratio between women and men could be raised from an average of 76% to an average of 87% if earnings in female-dominated occupations were based on the estimated earnings equation of male-dominated occupations.

FAMILY POLICIES

Increasingly the advocates of equal employment opportunity are pointing to family-related policies as one of the most promising strategies for encouraging nontraditional employment both among workers and employers. Of particular interest are flexible working schedules for parents, corporate or community-based child care, and income supports (Bergmann, 1986; Giele, 1978; Hewlett, 1986; Kanter, 1977b; Roos, 1985).

TABLE 9.4
Sex Differentials in Education and Professional Degrees: 1960, 1970, 1980 (Percentage)

Year	Completed College[a]		Degrees Granted to Women			Doctor in
	Men, 25-34	Women, 25-34	Dentistry	Law	Medicine[b]	Education[c]
1960	14.4	17.4	0.8	2.5	5.5	73.5
1970	19.2	12.3	0.9	5.4	8.4	74.4
1980	26.1	20.7	13.3	30.2	23.4	73.9

SOURCES: a. Bianchi and Spain (1986, p. 131). b. Bianchi and Spain (1986, p. 123). c. Blau and Ferber (1985, p. 35). National Center for Education Statistics (1970-1971; 1979-1980). U.S. Bureau of the Census (1962, p. 137).

Comparative research by Kamerman and Kahn (1978) in 14 countries of western Europe and North America made clear the glaring absence of state support in the United States for child care, parental leaves, and family allowances (see also Lipman-Blumen and Bernard, 1979). The Family and Medical Leave Act introduced in Congress in 1987 would meet some of these needs by provision for up to 26 weeks of unpaid *parental leave* and protection against job loss as a result of childbirth or serious illness of child or parent.

Advocates for a broad spectrum of *child care* have never yet reversed the defeat inflicted by President Nixon's veto of the enabling legislation in 1971. As more married women are employed outside the home, it becomes more difficult for families to provide care for children, the sick and handicapped, and the elderly (Brody, 1981; Horowitz, 1985; Moroney, 1976). Conservatives have fought state-supported child care and oppose the new Medical Leave Act, as they have fought the Equal Rights Amendment (Berry, 1986; Conover and Gray, 1983; Mansbridge, 1986), to resist erosion of women's and men's traditional caretaking and breadwinning roles (Ehrenreich, 1983).

Policy analysts repeatedly call for adequate *income supports* for families with children—especially those in female-headed families, who make up over a third of the population in poverty (Bianchi and Spain, 1986, p. 210). Moynihan (1986) decries the erosion of tax deductions and other important government subsidies for parenting and advocates a family policy not just directed to the poor but to all families with children. While benefit payments to poor families may stimulate higher rates of marital dissolution as suggested by the Seattle-Denver Negative Income Tax experiments (Groeneveld, Tuma, and Hannan, 1980), divorce in many cases is economically disastrous for women. Weitzman (1985) documents the sharp decline in women's economic status after divorce that accompanied the no-fault divorce law in California. Alimony awards dropped almost by half; more awards were transitional than permanent; and divorced men experienced an average 42% rise in their standard of living in the first year after divorce, while divorced women and their children experienced a 73% decline.

Although such policy reforms as child care and income supports are slow to be adopted, there is at least now a public debate about gender justice both in the workplace and in the home. A key question on the future policy agenda is whether social programs can compensate for men's and women's asymmetrical roles in production and reproduction (Gould, 1980).

Group Dynamics and Sex Composition

Small groups and collectivities spell out the rules of gender stratification as they are to be followed in everyday life. In the words of Nancy Henley (1977, p. 178), "Nonverbal power gestures provide the micro-political structure, the thousands of daily acts through which nonverbal influence takes place, which underlies and supports the macropolitical structure." Sociologists have observed the character and composition of informal groups: first, how they differ depending on whether male, female, or mixed; second, how group structure affects male and female participation; and finally, whether male and female interaction are of a distinctly different character.

Gender and Group Membership

The first general descriptive task is to link gender with group dynamics. What is the gender of the membership of volunteer groups, classrooms, families, work groups, play groups? And how do the groups differ depending on whether men or women, boys or girls are in the majority?

Surveys of *volunteer groups* show that instrumental job-related groups tend to have more heterogeneous memberships, whereas expressive groups are more likely to be either male or female. Male memberships also lead to a wider network of contacts, 37 as compared with 29 for female memberships (McPherson and Smith-Lovin, 1986). Arlene Kaplan Daniels (1975, 1985) has long insisted, however, that the expressive activities of women's volunteer organizations—although often devoted to giving parties for the symphony or other worthy causes—are not merely expressive but instrumental in the sense that they require effort and promote the goals of the organization.

Classrooms are another object of sociological interest because women are so often the teachers. Lightfoot (1975) in her intensive studies of teacher-student interaction notes the significant gender component in the classroom relationship. While teachers make more negatively evaluative statements about boys, their statements indicate more overall personal involvement with them. Society recognizes that many of the qualities of a good teacher—nurturance and sensitivity—are stereotypically feminine, and that good male teachers are often more like women in having these characteristics; yet these qualities are devalued and receive little reward. In the continuing effort to attain sex equity in the classroom teachers are now being advised to encourage cooperative cross-sex learning, to monitor their own (teacher) behavior to be sure that they reward male and female students equally, and actively familiarize students with gender-atypical roles by assigning them specific duties as leaders, recording secretary, and so on (Lockheed, 1985). There is also growing recognition that same-sex interaction in the early grades is more common than cross-sex interaction, and may be used to positive effect in the educational process (Klein, 1985).

Families are other collectivities to scrutinize for patterns of gendered behavior. Blumberg's (1984) macro model of gender stratification implies that power between husbands and wives, like women's general status in society, is a reflection of women's economic stake. The more contribution a wife's income makes to the family economy, the greater say she will have in family decision making and the more egalitarian her own and her husband's sex-role attitudes (Hertz, 1986; Huber and Spitze, 1983). In a nationally representative sample of employed persons examining how much domestic labor husbands perform, Coverman (1985) finds that husband's participation is greater among younger men who have children, employed wives, and jobs that do not require long hours. The demands on the husband's capacity to respond explains husband's domestic labor better than wife's socioeconomic power or husband's egalitarian sex-role ideology. Fishman (1983) has conducted detailed content analysis of tape recorded conversations between couples and finds that men are less expressive but more in control of topics of conversation. Wives do more of the ''work'' of bringing out information and asking questions, but more topics introduced by the husband are explored while those introduced by the wife are more often not pursued.

Gendered interaction in the *workplace* very often takes place in a context of sex segregation. A number of historians examining the women's colleges have argued that within the all-female institution, women were promoted and paid on a level that was rare to achieve within a mixed faculty (Schwager, 1987; Solomon, 1985). Within both the mixed and sex-segregated workplace there appears to be an expressive dimension that has only recently been noticed.

Kanter (1977a), observing the secretaries in a large corporation, and Feldberg and Glenn (1979), describing the routine jobs of data entry clerks, all note the personal rewards that women workers find in the sociability of the job. It may be that male work groups offer similar expressive rewards to men. Sociologists have been so fixed on separation of the workplace from intimate relationships that they may have failed to note the importance to work of men's sociability and emotional ties except where it is negative, as in the case of illicit affairs or sexual harassment (Schneider, 1985).

Children's *play groups* are another source of insight about the daily worlds of male and female. Lever's (1976, 1978) classic studies showed that girls were more likely to play in dyads or very small groups and to play at imitative and turn-taking games, while boys played in larger groups and at games governed by complex rules. Thorne (1985), however, argues that treating boys' and girls' play groups as separate worlds has hindered contextual understanding of gender and social relations among children. She calls for more complex conceptualization. Segregation between boys and girls provides gender differentiated contexts for learning as do cross-gender groups that teach strategies for intimacy and accomplishment in adult life.

Dynamics of Gender Discrimination

Sociologists have tried to discover the particular circumstances of interaction in which gender discrimination is likely to occur. Three major factors have received attention: (1) sex imbalance in numbers; (2) devaluation of women and higher valuation of males; and (3) social control and boundary maintenance that reinforces structural and symbolic inequality.

Regarding sex imbalance in *numbers*, Kanter (1977c) hypothesized that greatly skewed sex ratios themselves lead to prejudicial behavior on the part of the majority. The token minority members have heightened visibility; their differences are exaggerated; and the tokens' attributes are distorted to fit preexisting generalizations about their nature. Ferber (1986) illustrates another consequence of skewed proportions of each gender in the field of economics. She casts doubt on the validity of Cole's (1979) citation analysis to judge relative scholarly achievements of men and women. Her empirical analysis of citations in 608 articles that appeared in four issues of the *Journal of Economic Literature* showed that men and women authors were each significantly more likely to cite authors of their own sex. Noting that fewer than 9.7% of the articles were written by women, 82.6% by men, and 7.7% by both males and females, she demonstrates by a series of mathematical calculations that strongly skewed gender proportions will work to the marked advantage of the majority sex and marked disadvantage of the minority, regardless of merit.

Devaluation of females and *higher valuation* of males is another powerful force that perpetuates inequality. Wagner, Ford, and Ford (1986) in a small group experiment manipulated feedback that they gave to female and male subjects regarding their performance on an assigned task. Males were less sensitive to negative information about their own performance than females; apparently more general processes of status organization outside the group influenced each gender's evaluation of their own worth. At the same time the group experiment also showed that communication about performance was to some degree situation specific; gender inequality was reduced on well-defined tasks with clear performance standards and unambiguous demonstration of ability.

Boundary maintaining processes within a group further reinforce the negative effects of skewed sex ratios and unequal validation. Hall and Sandler (1982) describe how social control and labeling work to create a ''chilly'' classroom climate for many women. Nonverbal behavior of professors who ignore, talk down to, or ridicule female students subtly devalues them and in some instances unconsciously rewards and encourages the males. The concept of the chilly classroom was recently central to a self-study of the first decade of coeducation at Phillips Academy in Andover, Massachusetts. By examination of the historical record, classroom size and sex ratios, course enrollments, dormitory life, participation in athletics, and student and faculty surveys, the school was able to identify aspects of school life that put students at a disadvantage who did not fit the image of a ''good Andover boy.'' Many girls and some of the boys, rather than being independent achievers, derived much satisfaction from giving friendly support to others, yet only a few school structures rewarded this valuable alternative type of person, a condition that the school has since submitted to critical review (Dalton, 1986).

The Character of Male and Female Interaction

The modern gender revolution, in addition to stimulating much work on the group dy-namics of sex discrimination, has also prompted an exciting array of investigations into the distinctive character of male and female interaction. These studies examine subtle features of language and gesture such as smiling, accepting interruptions, and allowing others to talk that are more often found in female behavior and that are also routinely associated with lower power and greater vulnerability (Goffman, 1979; Thorne, Kramarae, and Henley, 1983). Henley (1977) applies Roger Brown's ''universal norm'' of language usage to gender relations. She suggests that just as the form used between intimates is more likely to be used to inferiors, it is also more likely to be used to women and the form used between strangers and toward superiors is more likely to be used to men.

Particularly noteworthy are the new investigations of love, emotion, and management of feeling that until a decade ago were unknown in the sociological literature. The theme of this literature is the mixture of emotion with control and rationality rather than the distillation of a pure expressive or instrumental behavior. These new investigations take place against the backdrop of Parsons and Bales's (1955) typology of instrumental and expressive functions that have been the predominant concepts for characterizing male and female roles (Spence, Deaux, Helmreich, 1985). Bezdek and Strodtbeck's (1970) empirical investigations showed male contributions to group interaction to be more means oriented and female contributions more goal oriented. Even though some readers concluded that male or father-son-brother roles were *always* instrumental and female or mother-daughter-sister roles were *always* expressive, Parsons's scheme was more complicated and relative. The mother was instrumentally oriented in dyadic relationship to the child. Parsons (1942) had also noted a number of domains where sex differentiation was on the decline, as in dressing little girls in overalls or imposing similar requirements on males and females in public school and liberal arts colleges. The type of sex role change that particularly interested Parsons (1966) was the elimination of gender differentiation by adaptive upgrading and inclusion of women in rational and instrumental activities.

What is characteristic of the modern feminist interactionists is their examination of rationality and control in relation to the expressive domain. Hochschild (1979) delves into the ways of controlling emotions and doing expressive ''work'' that are particularly characteristic of female occupational and family roles. She calls this field of inquiry the sociology of feeling and emotion and shows that it has been neglected because of a too rational emphasis on individuals as either calculating or unconsciously emotional. She calls for recognition of the sentient actor as one who uses feeling rules to express anger downward and channel awe and liking upward. Expression of feelings is especially relevant to the world of women and men, for women inhabit a more *hostile* emotional world as the result of accepting the anger of higher-ups, men a more *benign* environment as the recipients of positive feelings from persons of lower status.

Hochschild (1983) applies these insights to airline flight attendants and emerges with an analysis of why women in our society are expected to do more emotional work than men. Lacking other resources, women learn to make a resource out of feelings that they offer to men as a gift in return for material support. In childhood females receive a different training of the heart and therefore specialize in the "flight attendant" side of emotion and men in the "bill collection" side. Women also have a weaker "status shield" against negative displaced feelings of others. Power differences between the sexes result in women's being expected to turn their beauty, charm, and relational skills to instrumental use, while men are expected to use anger and threats for the benefit of their jobs.

Swidler (1980) explores the emotional side of adulthood by probing the meaning of love. Love in modern society has been transformed from being a one-time commitment to being a vehicle for continuing growth and adult development. This transformation makes even more problematic women's traditional commitment to the family as the avenue for self-sacrifice and emotional investment in the lives of others. Love as a continuing process of self-discovery is part of a new concept of adult development that is now life-long, not just settled once and for all by finding one "true" love. At times the new love seems itself endangered by the rationality that pervades it. Yet this new ideology is consistent with age and gender roles that are more fluid. The developmental tasks of adulthood in both love and work do not simply end at one stage of life but recur throughout the life course. Cancian (1985) carries the theme of fluid instrumental and expressive worlds even further. She shows that a man may show his love by an instrumental act such as washing his wife's car. Women, however, tend not to recognize these instrumental forms of expressing love. They instead are likely to turn their performance of work into expressive activity. The result is that each sex is likely to talk past the other: men showing love through "work"; women doing work through expressions of "love."

Gender and the Individual

Thirty years of change in sex roles have reoriented the study of individual sex-typing. Sociologists and psychologists used to ask how the child acquired gender identity as part of self-concept. Today there is a more critical view of traditional gender expectations and with it more ambivalence about the nature of the gender identity that is acquired (Spence, Deaux, and Helmreich, 1985). Social scientists now recognize that masculinity and femininity are not mutually exclusive polarities. Males and females share certain characteristics with the opposite sex, and distinctive male and female behavior varies according to activity and situational context (Huston, 1983).

Theorists differ in their explanations of sex differences. Among psychologists, for example, social learning theorists emphasize the role of culture and socialization, whereas cognitive developmentalists see the child developing a concept of gender from within (Huston, 1983). More sociologists incline toward structural than dispositional explanations of sex differences in individual behavior. Yet Alice S. Rossi (1985, 1977) is a notable exception for her repeated emphasis on the sociological ramifications of biologically based sex differences. Most social scientists take the view that the study of individual sex differences, to be adequate, must consider both culture and innate disposition. This review organizes the principal sociological studies of individual behavior in descending order by degree to which gendered behaviors (attitudes, life course patterns, psychological traits, and sexuality) are likely to be influenced by social and cultural definitions of gender as compared with innate disposition.

Attitudes

Sex-role attitudes refer to individuals' *beliefs*, *values*, and *preferences* concerning sex roles. Since attitudes are particularly influenced by social experience, the remarkable changes in women's roles over the last three decades have eventually been reflected in more favorable opinion toward women's employment, child care for working mothers, husband's participation in household work, and the suitability of women for public office. Summaries of these attitude changes appear in historical accounts (Chafe, 1972; Kessler-Harris, 1982; Pleck and Pleck, 1980, pp. 1-49) as well as in the social science literature (Oppenheimer, 1970, chap. 2; 1982, pp. 28-31; Spence, Deaux, and Helmreich, 1985; Bianchi and Spain, 1986, pp. 237-239).

Sociologists have been particularly interested in the ways that historical and social location are related to sex-role ideology. Although Oppenheimer (1970; 1982, p. 30) concluded that sex-role attitudes changed *after* and not *before* women's massive entry into the labor force, the shift was nonetheless dramatic: A 1937 poll showed 82% of the population *against* the employment of a married woman if her husband was capable of supporting her, while a 1972 poll found 68% *in favor of* married women working (Cherlin and Walters, 1981). From 1964 to 1974 there was a marked drop in proportion of women who believed maternal employment harmful to a child (Mason, Czajka and Arber, 1976). As more women enter the work force, receive more education, and delay marriage and childbearing, it seems likely that previous trends toward liberalization of sex role attitudes will continue. By 1980 only 19% of respondents to a Harris poll believed that "raising children should be the responsibility of the mother, not the father, whether or not she works" (Bianchi and Spain, 1986, p. 239). Within families, daughters in 1980 expressed more egalitarian sex-role attitudes in 1980 than their mothers in 1962 (Thornton, Alwin, Camburn, 1983).

Sex-role attitudes not only became more liberal in the aggregate as women's employment increased, but individual attitudes were correlated with individual experience. More positive opinions about wife's employment were expressed in those couples where the wife was employed (Huber and Spitze, 1983). A mother's own employment was positively correlated with her daughter's work orientation (Bianchi and Spain, 1986). Even on such a controversial topic as abortion, women's attitudes varied in relation to their own role pattern. Kristin Luker (1984) found that women who opposed abortion deferred to their husbands, were less well educated, and were less likely to be employed than pro-choice advocates; they considered motherhood to be their most important social role. Political scientists found that women's voting patterns were also affected by women's changing roles. Those with more education and work experience were more likely to vote and to hold egalitarian sex-role attitudes (Baxter and Lansing, 1983).

Yet a new term, the "gender gap," describes more general differences in men's and women's voting patterns that have emerged in the 1980s—a tendency for women to vote for more liberal candidates, to favor domestic social programs, oppose defense spending, and support active peace initiatives. This phenomenon raises a more fundamental question about possibly universal differences in attitudinal orientation of males and females. Parsons and Bales's (1955) association of males with instrumental roles and females with expressive roles is one of the most famous bipolar conceptualizations and has been used by many psychologists to assess masculine and feminine orientation (Spence, Deaux, and Helmreich, 1985, p. 152). Similar distinctions appear in Bakan's (1966) contrast of male *agentic* orientation with female *communal* orientation, Erikson's (1964) contrast of male preoccupation with *external* space and females with *inner space*, and McClelland's (1975) description of male power based on assertiveness and control compared with female power based on a sense of interdependence and cooperation.

Ortner and Whitehead (1981) argue that such consistent description of each sex's attributes, which are reflected in the social sciences as well as in popular thought, are the result of systematic cultural and sociological processes rather than of innate differences between males and females. Males are almost universally associated with public roles beyond the kinship group that *encompass* the particularistic and domestic roles held by females. Levi-Strauss (1969) and Rubin (1975) note that in preliterate societies it is *males* who exchange women, expand political loyalties beyond narrow kinship groups, and thereby attain greater power than women, who cannot initiate such exchange on their own behalf because their activities are confined to a particular domestic circle.

Such dichotomies as instrumental and expressive have gained a powerful grip on the conceptualization of gender differences in attributes, attitudes, and behaviors. But Spence, Deaux, and Helmreich (1985, p. 159) warn that all such polarizations are highly suspect unless they recognize that masculinity and femininity are *multidimensional* rather than unidimensional. The two do not necessarily covary; behavior and attitudes do not appear correlated with self-rating; each dimension has a different history within the individual. Moreover, as public and private life become more closely interwoven and more women are active outside the home, such clear contrasts are likely to erode.

*Life Course Patterns
and Adult Development*

The most familiar sociological explanation of individual sex typing is the socialization process that continues throughout the life span. Detailed studies of early socialization tend to be the work of psychologists and anthropologists. Sociologists have given relatively more attention to adulthood—historical change in the life patterns of both sexes, early experience that shapes adult roles, and the quality of life (health, illness, satisfaction) associated with major alternative patterns.

HISTORICAL CHANGE IN LIFE PATTERNS

By using panel studies and cohort analysis, it is now possible to compare changes in the life course of women and men over the past half-century. Hogan (1981) used census data to chart changes in life patterns of men born between 1907 and 1952. The most noteworthy long-term historical trend was a decrease in the amount of time that younger cohorts required to complete passage from adolescence to adulthood, primarily because of longer school attendance and general increase in modernity of the social structure. At the same time that school leaving was delayed, marriage was occurring earlier, thereby intermixing the transitional events rather than neatly ordering them in serial array. Featherman and Sorensen (1983) have studied Norwegian cohorts of males born in the late 1920s and early 1930s and found a quickening of life events, greater overlap in simultaneous roles, and higher educational and occupational attainment. Similar changes appear in the lives of women who graduated from college since the 1930s—more events, rising educational and occupational attainments, multiple roles, and nontraditional role patterns by women of modest social origins (Giele, 1987). These trends in the lives of both sexes appear to be correlated with the modernization process.

IMPACT OF EARLY EXPERIENCE

Elder (1974) in *Children of the Great Depression* examined a cohort of children born in the 1920s who were affected by the Great Depression. He showed that a number of males of middle-class deprived families attained higher occupational status than the nondeprived. Girls of deprived families were less likely to have careers and more likely to marry early and be full-time homemakers than nondeprived girls

who completed their education, married later, and combined employment with family life.

ADULT ROLES AND QUALITY OF LIFE

A number of studies have noted that mental distress, especially depression, is higher in women than men (Belle, 1982; Weissman and Klerman, 1977). Married people report higher life satisfaction. Satisfaction is notably lower among women with young children (Campbell, Converse, and Rodgers, 1976; Veroff, Kulka, and Douvan, 1981).

Cancian (1987) links the different sources of health and illness in men and women to split gender roles. Men are much more likely to suffer illness or to die from loss of an intimate emotional relationship, while women may become depressed from too little opportunity for independence. Baruch and Barnett's (1983) findings on Boston-area women support this thesis; they discovered that women who combine both work and family roles have higher sense of life satisfaction than those who have one role without the other. The two-role combination appears to meet needs for competence and intimacy better than either family or employment alone.

Implicit in the ideal adult role for either sex is often an idea of androgyny in which the best of male and female qualities are combined in the individual. The popularity of the androgynous ideal waxed with research by Bem (1974, 1976) suggesting healthier and more adaptive behavior by persons who combined masculine and feminine properties; but psychologists gradually grew skeptical about androgyny as they discovered that it was not a unitary concept (Spence, Deaux, and Helmreich, 1985). Nevertheless, the concept of the whole person (with masculine and feminine qualities) reappears in a number of theories about adult development. David Gutmann (1977) sees women becoming more executive and men more nurturant as they complete the process of parenting. Erikson (1950), Levinson (1978), and Gould (1978) find in mid-life a search to complete the self—men for ways to be more expressive; women, for independence and achievement.

*Psychological Functioning
and Early Socialization*

Most sociologists turn to psychologists for a precise description and interpretation of sex differences as they relate to individual cognition, moral development, and personality traits. But the expert testimony of psychologists is contradictory. On the one hand, we learn from Maccoby and Jacklin (1974) that there are very few stable sex differences, that one of the few is that boys are more aggressive than girls, and that almost any difference that appears initially can be attenuated by a different pattern of socialization. But Jeanne Block's (1976) meticulous critique of Maccoby and Jacklin's summary reintroduces a list of sex differences based on several key studies: *girls' higher scores*, on average, on "verbal ability, school grades, suggestibility, anxiety level, fears, social and affiliative interests, and fear of failure"; and *boys' higher scores*, on average, on "quantitative ability, spatial ability, restructuring or breaking set, adult achievements, aggressivity, field independence, realistic assessment of own performance, and difficulty in controlling impulse" (p. 285).

What sociologists have contributed to this discussion is close analysis of the socialization process to identify what elements may be contributing to same or different outcomes for each sex. Nancy Chodorow in *The Reproduction of Mothering* (1978) has made a leading contribution by explicating the different object relations between mother and son and mother and daughter. Since a boy ultimately has to give up identification with his mother in order to become a man, he learns to separate himself from her by repressing his feelings of separation and loss and focusing instead on objective goals by thinking unemotionally and analytically. Females, who never have to disassociate self from the mother in order to become a woman, develop a different emotional and cognitive style. They see issues in terms of context and relationship and find it more difficult to think analytically; but emotionally they are more sensitive and empathetic. Chodorow's theory makes understandable McClelland's observations that men see power as a test of control, while women see it in terms of interdependence. Her theory is also consistent with Gilligan's (1982) observations that moral decisions for women revolve around questions of relationship and care but for men are tied to issues of individual rights and justice.

Rose Coser (1986) uses the logic of socialization and internalization of objects to demonstrate that there will likely be greater convergence in girls' and boys' intellectual performance and emotional style as schools and families subject children of each sex to increasingly comparable experience. Drawing on a wide variety of studies of the use of social space, Coser shows that intelligent organisms, female or male, are much more capable of analytic and abstract thought when they have opportunity to move freely about their environment and to extend their visual horizons. Females, if exposed to the same size play groups, allowed the same range of physical movement, and permitted the same latitude in social contacts as boys, will according to Coser show greater ability in mathematics and abstract thought. In the last decade differences in the quantitative test scores of male and female high schools students have narrowed. Coser suggests that this trend will continue because of changing role expectations for women that both encourage achievement in careers and bind them less closely to the home.

If caring behavior is as valuable to social systems as Bologh (1984) contends, and if such behaviors are in fact not innate but the result of the socialization process, it should be possible to foster them in males as well as in females. So far sociological studies of child rearing have found few significant differences in the way that parents reported treating the two sexes (Duncan and Duncan, 1978). Chodorow's work, however, implies that sons could become more nurturant through fathers' greater involvement in the child-rearing process. Then the symmetrical identification of sons with fathers would be parallel with daughters and mothers and would lead to greater capacity for sympathy and caregiving behavior. The best evidence that boys can learn caretaking responsibility is from the work of Carol Ember (1981) on the Luo of Kenya. She found that the boys who did inside "feminine" work such as housework and babysitting had lower levels of egoistic aggression and increased prosocial behavior (behavior that satisfies the needs of others).

Sexuality, Aggression, and Reproduction

Even if most sex-typing were culturally determined, it is still the case that only females can bear children and nurse them. Sociologists therefore ask to what degree this basic biological difference affects other types of social functioning. Relevant evidence comes from human evolution, adolescent development, and adult reproductive behavior.

SEX-ROLE DIFFERENTIATION AND HUMAN EVOLUTION

Alice S. Rossi (1977, 1985) contends that sociologists have given too little attention to the biological basis for sex-differentiated behavior. She hypothesizes that

> all sexually dimorphic characteristics contribute to the species function of reproduction and, hence, have persisted as biological predispositions across cultures and through historical time [Rossi, 1985, p. 182].

An apparent predisposition in the female to be responsive to people and sounds gives her an edge in communication, whereas males appear to have the advantage in spatial perception, gross motor control, visual acuity, and capacity to separate emotional from cognitive responses. A number of scholars have been alarmed by Rossi's emphasis on biological underpinnings of gendered behavior, fearing that such assertions will reinforce stereotypes and undermine alternative explanations based on environmental or cultural conditions (Lowe, 1983; Gould, 1980). Rossi, however, argues that facing the biological components of gender is necessary if society is to promote true gender equality.

Konner (1981) and Ember (1981) both caution against common fallacies in the study of physical sex differences: (1) *developmental fallacies* that extrapolate from differences at birth to the nature of the adult organism; (2) *cross-cultural fallacies*, which infer innate or genetic origins from widespread incidence; (3) *cross-species fallacies* that derive biological determination from similar sex differences found in non-human primates; and (4) *evolutionary fallacies*, which assume that behaviors advantageous for survival are of necessity innate rather than learned.

Until recently the predominant theory of sex differences among the higher primates and early hominids was that males evolved as hunters and women as nonmobile nurturers of the young. Now challenging the male hunter model of society is a theory that early human societies first become possible when females developed the digging tools, gathering containers, and infant carriers that permitted them to care for the young over a long period of gestation and infancy (Fedigan, 1986; Tanner and Zihlman, 1976). Women possibly selected those males who would be stable members of the small food-gathering group. Male hunting and female gathering were thus interrelated (Zihlman, 1978).

EFFECTS OF PUBERTY ON SELF CONCEPT

Rossi (1985) notes that hormonal sex differences are pronounced in fetal development,

puberty, and pregnancy. Ember (1981) in cross-cultural studies finds only negligible developmental differences between the sexes before puberty. Bardwick (1970) provides striking evidence that psychological functioning in women after puberty is directly influenced by hormonal fluctuation. At time of ovulation young women told stories that were very positive and self-confident. Prior to menstruation the very same women conversed on topics or remembered events that were pervaded by images of death and mutilation.

Puberty appears to be relevant to social role and self-concept, especially among girls in sixth grade and junior high school. Simmons et al. (1979) found that the transition to junior high school was harder for the girls with early menarche. Adaptation to a new social role was apparently more difficult for girls who menstruated early because the onset of puberty challenged body image and sense of self.

Boys' social functioning is affected in a quite different way during puberty and adolescence by greater probability of involvement with deviant behavior. Throughout the world and across time, crime and delinquency are primarily male phenomena (Gove, 1985). The rates are sufficiently stable that Gove contends they cannot be explained solely by structure of society or by sex-role socialization. Gove suggests that biological factors may be contributing to such underlying traits as physical aggressiveness that are associated with male deviance.

SEX DIFFERENCES IN PARENTING

The impact of sex differences on parenthood is probably more visible than in any other social role. Since pregnancy and lactation occur only in females, it is difficult not to ascribe all sorts of sex differences in parenting to biological causes. Rossi (1977) has argued that 40,000 years of human development selected for a special capacity in the female to bond to the infant over the long period of its socialization and dependency. Anthropologist Lila Leibowitz (1978), however, argues that there is great flexibility in parenting capacity and only limited genetic programming of nurturing behavior. In place of either sexual dimorphism or distinct male and female roles, Leibowitz emphasizes the importance of environmental conditions and adaptive learning. Using examples from pre-hominid family units Leibowitz (1978) describes sex roles of Japanese monkeys in two very different ecological settings. One group that was moved to a beach from its traditional environment in the trees was plentifully supplied with food and developed whole new patterns in its sexual division of labor and care of the young.

The wide variation in mothers' roles has been more widely studied by social scientists than the universals of sex differences in parenting roles. Judith K. Brown (1970) demonstrated that women's involvement in food production depended on the compatibility of the technology with carrying infants and watching toddlers. Deep sea fishing, ploughing, and hunting were relatively incompatible, whereas gathering, hoe culture, and shallow water fishing encouraged women's involvement in production.

A number of other studies have examined reasons for variations in parenting roles at time of birth. Paige and Paige (1973) find mother's activity limitations and patriarchal control of birth practices in those societies where fraternal kin groups are in control of property. Brown (1981) shows that presence or absence of ceremonies marking the female life cycle is explained by a number of variables ranging from infant socialization to kinship structure. The elegant work of Monroe, Monroe, and Whiting (1981) explains the couvade in terms of ambivalent male sex-role identification found most often in those cultures where absence of patrilineages and close mother-infant contact have encouraged male identification with the female role. In sum, it appears that the *social* roles of parents, like attitudes, life patterns, and psychological functioning, are surprisingly susceptible to variation in culture and social structure.

Dynamics of Change

Gender roles result from the complex interplay of many levels of the social system—cultural, institutional, interactional, and individual. Gender roles change as a result of two vertical dynamics that connect these systems—one "top-down" process linking ideas, values, and *consciousness* of the human condition to the social structure and individual psyche; the other "bottom-up" process linking *material conditions* such as technology, individual health, and population to social structure and culture. These two dynamics and their links to each system level are pictured in Figure 9.1, shown earlier.

Changing Consciousness

The new women's movement of the 1960s prompted an outpouring of historical research on both the nineteenth-century suffrage movement and the new women's liberation movement. Sociologists have particularly examined the social origins and actions of these collective efforts to change the social rules governing women's roles. Gusfield (1963) understood the Women's Christian Temperance Movement to be concerned with status protection and documented its gradual decline in power and prestige as prohibition receded. Buechler (1986) attributed success of the nineteenth-century women's movement to a coalition between suffrage and party interests and effective resource mobilization by the National American Women's Suffrage Organization. Others, however, link the growth of historic feminism to more fundamental changes in women's roles. Temperance and missionary women expanded women's domestic role into the community, and the suffrage movement eventually legitimated the professional and political activities of women in the public sphere (Giele, 1961; in press).

The modern women's movement encompassed both structureless consciousness-raising groups and more bureaucratic women's organizations such as NOW (Freeman, 1975). Carden (1974) was among the first sociologists to interview active feminists and discern why they joined modern women's liberation groups. Ferree and Hess (1985) have since interpreted modern feminism as a social movement with the same issues of recruitment, organization, and growth that face other movements. By analyzing the sources of pro-choice and right-to-life groups, Luker (1984) demonstrates the close connections between women's own roles and their sex-role ideology: The homemaker women are more likely to oppose abortion, whereas the professional and more highly educated women are likely to support it.

Corresponding with investigations of the women's movement are a few studies of the modern men's movement. Pleck (1981) traces strains in the masculine role to insecurity about being sufficiently independent, potent, and aggressive. American males are now recognizing that there is strain and inconsistency in sex-role definitions. Rather than try to overcompensate by supermasculinity, writers on male liberation say it is necessary to confront stereotyped demands and adopt more realistic goals that permit emotional expression and interdependence (Franklin, 1984).

Rotondo (1982, 1983) outlines the historical construction of American "manhood." As mothers become the more dominant parent during the nineteenth century, father's roles became less clear and the masculine ideal was exaggerated. Yet men also learned to venerate the female world with its links to affectionate nurture and restraint of impulse, enjoyment of rest, and cultivation of leisured pleasures. Rotondo interprets current trends in middle-class manhood as being in part a reaction to women's pressure to change traditional male domains— the workplace, the polling booth, and the saloon. The defensive solution is to recover an exaggerated masculine ideal by emphasis on the male animal. Another solution is to adopt a new success ethic of team play that replaces the model of self-made success.

Changes in traditional gender roles appear to be closely associated with increased awareness and study of homosexual alternatives. D'Emilio (1983) and Humphries and Miller (1980) have recently detailed the evolution of the homosexual identity in the gay rights movement. *Signs* (1984), the leading women's studies journal, has also published a special issue on lesbianism. In general, however, sociologists have not yet explained why acceptance of gay alternatives and gay rights has occurred at the same time as changing sex-role definitions for heterosexuals.

Social movements ultimately strive for changes in social norms, social policy, and everyday behavior. Effects of the new women's movement are evident in rules and policies supporting affirmative action and sex equity in education. Sex-role attitudes about child care, women's employment, and fathers' roles have also changed in recent decades. Changing consciousness, social movements, and advocacy for policy and behavior change are thus the key *ideological* feedback mechanisms that affect future sex-role structures. The other key feedback mechanisms stem from changing *material* conditions.

Changing Material Conditions

Changes in the physical environment, especially technology, health, and reproduction, affect the magnitude and importance of physical differences between the sexes. Changing *technology* can diminish the importance of physical differences between the sexes. Bielby and Baron (1986) have already noted that sex segregation is most extreme in mining and construction, where men predominate, and in occupations requiring dexterity, where women predominate. The introduction of automatic weapons and communication devices to police work, of power machinery to various crafts, or of the computer to a variety of other fields lessens the importance of sex differences in strength and physical capacity, even though gender styles vary in *use*

of the computer (Turkle, 1984). As Dauber and Cain (1981) show, however, technological changes may also remove women from the labor force in underdeveloped countries as technology is directed to sectors of the economy where men have predominated.

Changes in *health and reproductive behavior* affect gender roles through changing the relative importance of child bearing and mothering. As the life span lengthens, the period of women's lives devoted to child bearing is drastically reduced, allowing 30 to 40 years of productive activity after the last child goes to school (Glick, 1977; Van Dusen and Sheldon, 1976; Uhlenberg 1969). Control over conception also allows women to limit their child bearing and more closely approximate the work roles of men. (As Linda Gordon [1976] notes, however, the use of birth control was as much a product as a cause of women's new independence.)

Ultimately, improved technology and health affect the *cohort size of specific age-sex groups*. Opportunity is considerably increased for persons in smaller cohorts. Women born in the late 1920s and early 1930s were pulled into the labor force during the 1950s because they were from a relatively small birth cohort and were needed in the burgeoning service economy (Oppenheimer, 1970). On the other hand, a large baby boom cohort clogs the labor market and decreases the salaries of sons relative to their fathers, thereby encouraging wives to round out family income (Easterlin, 1980).

Conclusion

The sociology of gender and sex roles has been constructed at the intersection of two perennial debates, the terms of which are shared by many other disciplines. The first debate concerns *sex differences*. Do such differences actually exist, and if so, what are they? Some works focus on the similar capacities of the sexes (Coser, 1986; Maccoby and Jacklin, 1974; Pleck, 1981; Rossi, 1964). Others emphasize the deep and continuing differences in power, activities, and thought of women and men (Bernard, 1981; Bielby and Baron, 1986; Block, 1976; Chodorow, 1978; Gilligan, 1982; Henley, 1977; Ortner, 1974; Rossi, 1985). Just as a recent Equal Employment Opportunities Commission case against Sears Roebuck for sex discrimination was decided in favor of the company, in part because of greater weight given to historian Rosalind Rosenberg's testimony about women's traditional work and family choices than to historian Alice Kessler-Harris's testimony on historical sex discrimination in the retail trades (*Signs*, 1986), sociologists are particularly concerned that emphasis on sex differences may be used in a conservative way to preserve existing gender inequity rather than to accomplish change (Lorber, 1981).

A second debate revolves around *nature vs. nurture* as an explanation of sex differences. Are gender contrasts primarily due to cultural and social influence or to innate psychological or physical disposition? Some works emphasize the cultural and sociological construction of sex difference and the immense variation in sex roles according to situational context (Blumberg, 1984; Chafetz, 1984; Kanter, 1977c; Ortner and Whitehead, 1981; Spence, Deaux, and Helmreich, 1985). Others focus on nearly universal sex differences that point to psychological processes or physical differences as at least part of the explanation (Block, 1976; Chodorow, 1978; Rossi, 1977, 1985).

It is natural enough to look for a clear resolution to both of these debates. But the truth is that there are no simple answers to either the sex difference or nature-nurture question. Sociology makes its distinctive contribution by spelling out the issues and developing an appropriate research methodology.

To *measure* sex differences, sociologists have made a major conceptual contribution by specifying the significant dimensions to be compared. They share an interest with psychologists in sex-typing of beliefs, cognitions, and preferences. Like anthropologists, they are interested in cultural variation. Sociologists' distinctive focus, however, is on *gender stratification*—the conditions that promote social equality or inequality between the sexes. Using degree of inequality as a dependent variable they are able to make comparisons across different societies, groups, and individuals by controlling on some factors, while examining the effects of others.

To *explain* sex inequality, sociologists turn to the surrounding and interacting systems that affect all human behavior—culture, macro- and microsocial structure, individual psychology, and the human organism. Individual sex differences and gender differences at the microsociological level cannot be fully understood without reference to institutions and culture. Nor can the gendered nature of culture and social structure be fully understood without some reference to organic and developmental constraints.

At every system level, sociological studies have formulated explanations of gender difference by examining the effects of variation in adjacent systems. Thus, for example, it is possible to explain societal differences in gender inequality by reference both to differences in overarching cultural tradition (Ortner and Whitehead, 1981; Youssef, 1974) and to institutional variation in economic and political structure (Blumberg, 1974; Chafetz, 1984). Similarly, power differences within a work group can be understood as resulting in part from larger institutional forces such as sex typing among occupations (Bielby and Baron, 1986) or from the internal sex ratio in a particular department or firm (Kanter, 1977a, 1977c).

The feminist revolution may not have brought to sociology the dramatic reorientation of its central paradigms that occurred in history and anthropology (Stacey and Thorne, 1985). But sociology has accurately reflected the complexities and ambiguities that are inherent in the study of gender difference. Any sociologist who argues that it is only a matter of time until men's and women's roles are truly equal will be reminded that job segregation is still a powerful reality. Those who hold that males and females differ right down to their hormones will be shown converging test scores and changing attitudes. These debates make for a vital and growing field and deserve celebration as well as continued endeavor.

NOTE

1. Ward and Grant (1985) reviewed all issues of ten major sociology journals published between 1974 and 1983. Included were the *American Journal of Sociology*, the *American Sociological Review*, the *Journal of Health and Social Behavior*, the *Pacific Sociological Review* (later retitled *Sociological Perspectives*), *Social Forces*, *Social Problems*, *Social Psychology Quarterly* (formerly *Sociometry*), *Sociological Quarterly*, *Sociology of Education*, and *Work and Occupations* (formerly *Sociology of Work and Occupations*. Those designated as gender articles had titles and/or abstracts which mentioned such terms as *women, men's roles, sex, gender, male, female, or sexuality*. The review covered 3,674 articles of which 705 were gender articles.

REFERENCES

Acker, Joan. 1973. "Women and Social Stratification: A Case of Intellectual Sexism." Pp. 174-183 in *Changing Women in a Changing Society*, edited by Joan Huber. Chicago: University of Chicago Press.

Andersen, Margaret L. 1983. *Thinking about Women*. New York: Macmillan.

Bakan, David. 1966. *The Duality of Human Existence*. Chicago: Rand McNally.

Banks, Olive. 1981. *Faces of Feminism: A Study of Feminism as a Social Movement*. New York: St. Martin's.

Bardwick, Judith M. 1970. "Psychological Conflict and the Reproductive System." Pp. 3-28 in *Feminine Personality and Conflict*, edited by J. M. Bardwick et al. Belmont, CA: Brooks/Cole.

Barnett, Rosalind C. and Grace K. Baruch. 1987. "Determinants of Fathers' Participation in Family Work." *Journal of Marriage and the Family* 49:29-40.

Barrett, Nancy S. 1979. "Women in the Job Market: Occupations, Earnings, and Career Opportunities." Pp. 31-61 in *The Subtle Revolution: Women at Work*, edited by R. E. Smith. Washington, DC: Urban Institute.

Barry, Kathleen. 1979. *Female Sexual Slavery*. Englewood Cliffs, NJ: Prentice-Hall.

Baruch, Grace K. and Rosalind Barnett. 1983. *Lifeprints: New Patterns of Love and Work for Today's Women*. New York: McGraw-Hill.

Bateson, Mary Catherine. 1984. *With a Daughter's Eye: A Memoir of Margaret Mead and Gregory Bateson*. New York: William Morrow.

Baxter, Sandra and Marjorie Lansing. 1983. *Women in Politics*. Ann Arbor: University of Michigan Press.

Belle, Deborah, ed. 1982. *Lives in Stress: Women and Depression*. Beverly Hills, CA: Sage.

Bem, Sandra Lipsitz. 1974. "The Measurement of Psychological Androgyny." *Journal of Consulting and Clinical Psychology* 42:155-162.

———— 1976. "Probing the Promise of Androgyny." Pp. 48-62 in *Beyond Sex-Role Stereotypes: Readings Toward a Psychology of Androgyny*, edited by A. G. Kaplan and J. P. Bean. Boston: Little, Brown.

Benedict, Ruth. 1934. *Patterns of Culture*. Boston: Houghton Mifflin.

Benston, Margaret. 1969. "The Political Economy of Women's Liberation." *Monthly Review* 21:13-27.

Bergmann, Barbara R. 1986. *The Economic Emergence of Women*. New York: Basic Books.

Berk, Sarah Fenstermaker. 1985. *The Gender Factory*. New York: Plenum.

Bernard, Jessie. 1964. *Academic Women*. University Park: Pennsylvania State University Press.

———— 1971. *Women and the Public Interest*. Chicago: Aldine.

———— 1973. "My Four Revolutions: An Autobiographical History of the ASA." Pp. 11-29 in *Changing Women in a Changing Society*, edited by J. Huber. Chicago: University of Chicago Press.

———— 1981. *The Female World*. New York: Free Press.

Berry, Mary Frances. 1986. *Why ERA Failed: Politics, Women's Rights, and the Amending Process of the Constitution*. Bloomington: Indiana University Press.

Bezdek, William and Fred L. Strodtbeck. 1970. "Sex-role Identity and Pragmatic Action." *American Sociological Review* 35:491-502.

Bianchi, Suzanne M. and Daphne Spain. 1986. *American Women in Transition*. Report for the National Committee for Research on the 1980 Census. New York: Russell Sage Foundation.

Bielby, William T. and James N. Baron. 1986. "Men and Women at Work: Sex Segregation and Statistical Discrimination." *American Journal of Sociology* 91:759-799.

Blau, Francine D. and Marianne Ferber. 1985. "Women in the Labor Market: The Last Twenty Years." Pp. 19-49 in *Women and Work: An Annual Review*, edited by Laurie Larwood. Beverly Hills, CA: Sage.

Blau, Francine D. and Carol L. Jusenius. 1976. "Economists' Approaches to Sex Segregation in the Labor Market: An Appraisal." *Signs* 1:181-199.

Block, Jeanne H. 1976. "Issues, Problems, and Pitfalls in Assessing Sex Differences: A Critical Review of *The Psychology of Sex Differences*." *Merrill-Palmer Quarterly* 22:283-308.

Blumberg, Rae Lesser. 1974. "A Paradigm for Predicting the Position of Women: Policy Implications and Problems." Pp. 113-142 in *Sex Roles and Social Policy*, edited by J. Lipman-Blumen and J. Bernard. Beverly Hills, CA: Sage.

———— 1976a. "Fairy Tales and Facts: Economy, Family, Fertility, and the Female." Pp. 12-21 in *Women and World Development*, edited by I. Tinker and M. B. Bramsen. Washington, DC: Overseas Development Council.

———— 1976b. "Kibbutz Women: From the Fields of Revolution to the Laundries of Discontent." Pp. 319-44 in *Women in the World: A Comparative Study*, edited by L. Iglitzin and R. Ross. Santa Barbara, CA: ABC Clio.

———— 1984. "A General Theory of Gender Stratification." Pp. 23-101 in *Sociological Theory 1984*, edited by R. Collins. San Francisco: Jossey-Bass.

Blumstein, Phillip and Pepper Schwarz. 1983. *American Couples: Money, Work, Sex*. New York: William Morrow.

Bologh, Roslyn Wallach. 1984. "Feminist Social Theorizing and Moral Reasoning: On Difference and Dialectic." Pp. 373-393 in *Sociological Theory 1984*, edited by R. Collins. San Francisco: Jossey-Bass.

Boserup, Ester. 1970. *Women's Role in Economic Development*. London: Allen & Unwin.

Boulding, Elise. 1977. *Women in the Twentieth Century World*. New York: Halsted Press.

Bowen, William G. and T. Aldrich Finegan. 1969. *The Economics of Labor Force Participation*. Princeton, NJ: Princeton University Press.

Brody, Elaine M. 1981. "Women in the Middle and Family Help to Older People." *The Geron-*

tologist 21:471-480.

Brown, Judith K. 1970. "A Note on the Division of Labor by Sex." *American Anthropologist* 72: 1073-1078.

_____ 1981. "Cross-cultural Perspectives on the Female Life Cycle." Pp. 581-610 in *Handbook of Cross-Cultural Human Development*, edited by R. H. Munroe, R. L. Munroe, and B. B. Whiting. New York: Garland STPM Press.

Buechler, Steven M. 1986. *The Transformation of the Woman Suffrage Movement: The Case of Illinois, 1850-1920*. Princeton, NJ: Princeton University Press.

Cain, Glen G. 1966. *Married Women in the Labor Force: An Economic Analysis*. Chicago: University of Chicago Press.

Cain, Pamela Stone. 1985. "Prospects for Pay Equity in a Changing Economy." Pp. 137-165 in *Comparable Worth: New Directions for Research*, edited by H. I. Hartmann. Washington, DC: National Academy Press.

Campbell, Angus, Philip E. Converse, and Willard L. Rodgers. 1976. *The Quality of American Life: Perceptions, Evaluations, and Satisfactions*. New York: Russell Sage Foundation.

Cancian, Francesca M. 1985. "Gender Politics: Love and Power in the Private and Public Spheres." Pp. 253-264 in *Gender and the Life Course*, edited by A. S. Rossi. New York: Aldine.

_____ 1986. "The Feminization of Love." *Signs* 11:692-709.

_____ 1987. *Love in America: Gender and Self-Development*. New York: Cambridge University Press.

Carden, Maren Lockwood. 1974. *The New Feminist Movement*. New York: Russell Sage Foundation.

Chafe, William H. 1972. *The American Woman: Her Changing Social, Economic, and Political Roles, 1920-1970*. New York: Oxford University Press.

Chafetz, Janet Saltzman. 1984. *Sex and Advantage: A Comparative, Macro-Structural Theory of Sex Stratification*. Totowa, NJ: Rowman & Allanheld.

Cherlin, Andrew J. and Pamela B. Walters. 1981. "Trends in United States Men's and Women's Sex-Role Attitudes: 1972 to 1978." *American Sociological Review* 46:453-460.

Chodorow, Nancy. 1978. *The Reproduction of Mothering*. Berkeley: University of California Press.

Cole, Jonathan R. 1979. *Fair Science: Women in the Scientific Community*. New York: Free Press.

Conover, Pamela Johnston and Virginia Gray. 1983. *Feminism and the New Right: Conflict over the American Family*. New York: Praeger.

Corcoran, Mary, Greg J. Duncan, and Michael Ponza. 1983. "Work Experience and Wage Growth of Women Workers." Pp. 249-323 in *Five Thousand American Families—Patterns of Economic Progress*, vol. X., edited by G. J. Duncan and J. N. Morgan. Ann Arbor: Institute for Social Research, University of Michigan.

Coser, Rose Laub. 1986. "Cognitive Structure and the Use of Social Space." *Sociological Forum* 1:1-26.

Cott, Nancy F. 1977. *The Bonds of Womanhood: "Woman's Sphere" in New England, 1780-1835*. New Haven, CT: Yale University Press.

Coverman, Shelley. 1985. "Explaining Husbands' Participation in Domestic Labor." *Sociological Quarterly* 26:81-97.

Dalton, Kathleen M. 1986. *A Portrait of a School: Coeducation at Andover*. Report on research of the Committee on Coeducation. Andover, MA: Phillips Academy.

Daniels, Arlene Kaplan. 1975. "Feminist Perspectives in Sociological Research." Pp. 340-380 in *Another Voice: Feminist Perspectives on Social Life and Social Science*, edited by M. Millman and R. M. Kanter. New York: Anchor.

_____ 1985. "Good Times and Good Works: The Place of Sociability in the Work of Women Volunteers." *Social Problems* 32:363-374.

Dauber, Roslyn and Melinda L. Cain, eds. 1981. *AAAS Selected Symposium 53: Women and Technological Change in Developing Countries*. Boulder, CO: Westview Press.

De Beauvoir, Simone. 1952. *The Second Sex*. New York: Knopf.

D'Emilio, John. 1983. *Sexual Politics, Sexual Communities: The Making of a Homosexual Minority in the U.S.* Chicago: University of Chicago Press.

Douglas, Ann. 1977. *The Feminization of American Culture*. New York: Knopf.

Duncan, Beverly and Otis Dudley Duncan. 1978. *Sex Typing and Social Roles: A Research Report*. New York: Academic Press.

Durkheim, Emile. 1960. *The Division of Labor in Society*, translated by George Simpson. New York: Free Press. (Original work published 1893)

Duverger, Maurice. 1955. *The Political Role of Women*. Paris: Unesco.

Easterlin, Richard A. 1980. *Birth and Fortune: The Impact of Numbers on Personal Welfare*. New York: Basic Books.

Ehrenreich, Barbara. 1983. *The Hearts of Men: American Dreams and the Flight from Commitment*. Garden City, NY: Anchor/Doubleday.

Eisenstein, Hester. 1983. *Contemporary Feminist Thought*. Boston: G. K. Hall.

Elder, Glen H., Jr. 1974. *Children of the Great Depression: Social Change in Life Experience*. Chicago: University of Chicago Press.

Ember, Carol R. 1981. "A Cross-cultural Perspective on Sex Differences." Pp. 531-580 in *Handbook of Cross-Cultural Human Development*, edited by R. H. Monroe, R. L. Monroe, and B. B. Whiting. New York: Garland STPM Press.

Elshtain, Jean Bethke. 1981. *Public Man, Private Woman: Women in Social and Political Thought*. Princeton, NJ: Princeton University Press.

Epstein, Cynthia Fuchs. 1970. *Women's Place: Options and Limits in Professional Careers*.

Berkeley, CA: University of California Press.

Equal Employment Opportunity Commission. 1972. "A Unique Competence: A Study of Equal Employment Opportunity in the Bell System." *Congressional Record* 17: E1243-E1268.

Erikson, Erik H. 1950. *Childhood and Society*. New York: W. W. Norton.

———— 1964. "Inner and Outer Space: Reflections on Womanhood." *Daedalus* 93:1-25.

Faris, Robert E. L., ed. 1964. *Handbook of Modern Sociology*. Chicago: Rand McNally.

Featherman, David L. and Annemette Sorenson. 1983. "Societal Transformation in Norway and Change in the Life Course Transition into Adulthood." *Acta Sociologica* 26:105-126.

Fedigan, Linda Marie. 1986. "The Changing Role of Women in Models of Human Evolution." *Annual Review of Anthropology* 15:25-66.

Feldberg, Roslyn L. and Evelyn Nakano Glenn. 1979. "Male and Female: Job versus Gender Models in the Sociology of Work." *Social Problems* 26:524-538.

Ferber, Marianne A. 1986. "Citations: Are They an Objective Measure of Scholarly Merit?" *Signs* 11:381-389.

Ferree, Myra Marx and Beth B. Hess. 1985. *Controversy and Coalition: The New Feminist Movement*. Boston: Twayne.

Fishman, Pamela M. 1983. "Interaction: The Work Women Do." Pp. 89-101 in *Language, Gender and Society*, edited by B. Thorne, C. Kramarae, and N. Henley. Rowley, MA: Newbury House.

Fortmann, Louise. 1981. "The Plight of the Invisible Farmer: The Effect of National Agricultural Policy on Women in Africa." Pp. 205-214 in *AAAS Selected Symposium 53: Women and Technological Change in Developing Countries*, edited by R. Dauber and M. L. Cain. Boulder, CO: Westview Press.

Fox, Mary Frank and Sharlene Hesse-Biber. 1984. *Women at Work*. Palo Alto, CA: Mayfield.

Franklin, Clyde. 1984. *The Changing Definition of Masculinity*. New York: Plenum.

Freedman, Ronald, Amos H. Hawley, Werner S. Landecker, Gerhard Lenski, and Horace M. Miner. 1952. *Principles of Sociology: A Text with Readings*. New York: Holt.

Freeman, Jo. 1975. *The Politics of Women's Liberation*. New York: David McKay.

Friedan, Betty. 1963. *The Feminine Mystique*. New York: W. W. Norton.

Friedl, Ernestine. 1975. *Women and Men: An Anthropologist's View*. New York: Holt, Rinehart and Winston.

Furstenberg, Frank. 1976. *Unplanned Parenthood: The Social Consequences of Teenage Childbearing*. New York: Free Press.

Gerson, Kathleen. 1985. *Hard Choices: How Women Decide about Work, Career, and Motherhood*. Berkeley: University of California Press.

Giddens, Anthony. 1984. *The Constitution of Society: Outline of the Theory of Structuration*. Berkeley: University of California Press.

Giele, Janet Zollinger. 1961. *Social Change in the Feminine Role: A Comparison of the Woman's Suffrage and Woman's Temperance Movements, 1870-1920*. Ph.D. dissertation, Harvard University.

———— 1977. "Introduction: The Status of Women in Comparative Perspective." Pp. 3-31 in *Women: Roles and Status in Eight Countries*, edited by J. Z. Giele and A. C. Smock. New York: Wiley-Interscience.

———— 1978. *Women and the Future: Changing Sex Roles in Modern America*. New York: Free Press.

———— 1982. *Women in the Middle Years: Current Knowledge and Directions for Research and Policy*, edited by J. Z. Giele. New York: Wiley-Interscience.

———— 1987. "Modernity and the Changing Structure of the Life Course." Paper presented at the annual meeting of the American Sociological Association, Chicago.

———— In press. *Two Paths to Equality: Woman's Suffrage and Woman's Temperance, 1830-1920*. Boston: Twayne Press.

Gilligan, Carol. 1982. *In A Different Voice*. Cambridge, MA: Harvard University Press.

Glazer-Malbin, Nona. 1976. "Housework." *Signs* 1:905-922.

Glenn, Evelyn Nakano. 1980. "Dialectics of Wage Work: Japanese-American Women and Domestic Service, 1905-1940." *Feminist Studies* 6:432-471.

Glick, Paul C. 1977. "Updating the Life Cycle of the Family." *Journal of Marriage and Family* 39: 5-13.

Goffman, Erving. 1979. *Gender Advertisements*. Cambridge, MA: Harvard University Press.

Goode, William J. 1963. *World Revolution and Family Patterns*. New York: Free Press.

Gordon, Linda. 1976. *Woman's Body, Woman's Right*. New York: Penguin.

Gould, Meredith. 1980. "The New Sociology." *Signs* 5:459-467.

Gould, Roger L. 1978. *Transformations: Growth and Change in Adult Life*. New York: Simon & Schuster.

Gove, Walter R. 1985. "The Effect of Age and Gender on Deviant Behavior: A Biopsychological Perspective." Pp. 115-144 in *Gender and the Life Course*, edited by A. S. Rossi. Hawthorne, NY: Aldine.

Groeneveld, Lyle P., Nancy Brandon Tuma, and Michael T. Hannan. 1980. "The Effects of Negative Income Tax Programs on Marital Dissolution." *Journal of Human Resources* 15:654-674.

Gusfield, Joseph R. 1963. *Symbolic Crusade: Status Politics and the American Temperance Movement*. Urbana: University of Illinois Press.

Gutmann, David. 1977. "The Cross-cultural Perspective: Notes Toward a Comparative Psychology of Aging." Pp. 302-326 in *Handbook of the Psychology of Aging*, edited by J. E. Birren and K. W. Schaie. New York: Van Nostrand

Rheinhold.

Haavio-Mannila, Elina. 1971. "Convergences Between East and West: Tradition and Modernity in Sex Roles in Sweden, Finland and the Soviet Union." *Acta Sociologica* 14:114-125.

Hacker, Sally L. 1979. "Sex Stratification, Technology, and Organizational Change: A Longitudinal Case Study of AT&T." *Social Problems* 26:539-557.

Hall, Roberta M. and Bernice R. Sandler. 1982. *The Classroom Climate: A Chilly One for Women?"* Report of the Project on Status and Education of Women. Washington, DC: Association of American Colleges.

Harding, Sandra and Merrill B. Hintikka, eds. 1983. *Discovering Reality: Feminist Perspectives on Epistemology, Metaphysics, Methodology, and Philosophy of Science*. Dordrecht, Holland: D. Reidel.

Hartmann, Heidi I., Patricia A. Roos, and Donald J. Treiman. 1985. "An Agenda for Basic Research on Comparable Worth." Pp. 3-33 in *Comparable Worth: New Directions for Research*, edited by H. I. Hartmann. Washington, DC: National Academy Press.

Hayghe, Howard. 1984. "Working Mothers Reach Record Number in 1984." *Monthly Labor Review* 107:31-39.

Henley, Nancy. 1977. *Body Politics: Power, Sex, and Nonverbal Communication*. Englewood Cliffs, NJ: Prentice-Hall.

Hertz, Rosanna. 1986. *More Equal than Others: Women and Men in Dual Career Marriages*. Berkeley: University of California Press.

Hewlett, Sylvia. 1986. *A Lesser Life: The Myth of Women's Liberation in America*. New York: William Morrow.

Hochschild, Arlie Russell. 1979. "Emotion Work, Feeling Rules, and Social Structure." *American Journal of Sociology* 85:551-575.

————. 1983. *The Managed Heart: Commercialization of Human Feeling*. Berkeley: University of California Press.

Hogan, Dennis P. 1981. *Transitions and Social Change: The Early Lives of American Men*. New York: Academic Press.

Holmstrom, Lynda Lytle. 1972. *The Two-Career Family*. Cambridge, MA: Schenkman.

Holter, Harriet. 1970. *Sex Roles and Social Structure*. Oslo, Norway: Universitetsforlaget.

Horowitz, Amy. 1985. "Sons and Daughters as Caregivers to Older Parents: Differences in Role Performance and Consequences." *The Gerontologist* 25:612-617.

Huber, Joan. 1986. "Trends in Gender Stratification, 1970-1985." *Sociological Forum* 1:476-495.

————— and Glenna Spitze. 1983. *Sex Stratification: Children, Housework, and Jobs*. New York: Academic Press.

Humphries, Laud and Brian Miller. 1980. "Identities in the Emerging Gay Culture." Pp. 142-156 in *Homosexual Behavior: A Modern Reappraisal*, edited by Judd Marmor. New York: Basic Books.

Huston, Aletha C. 1983. "Sex-typing." Pp. 387-468 in *Handbook of Child Psychology*, vol. 4, edited by Paul H. Mussen. New York: John Wiley.

Jaggar, Alison M. 1983. *Feminist Politics and Human Nature*. Totowa, NJ: Rowman & Allanheld.

Jones, Jacqueline. 1985. *Labor of Love, Labor of Sorrow: Black Women, Work, and the Family from Slavery to the Present*. New York: Basic Books.

Kamerman, Sheila B. and Alfred J. Kahn, eds. 1978. *Family Policy: Government and Families in Fourteen Countries*. New York: Columbia University Press.

Kanter, Rosabeth Moss. 1977a. *Men and Women of the Corporation*. New York: Basic Books.

————— 1977b. *Work and Family in the United States: A Critical Review and Agenda for Research and Policy*. New York: Russell Sage Foundation.

————— 1977c. "Some Effects of Proportions on Group Life: Skewed Sex Ratios and Responses to Token Women." *American Journal of Sociology* 82:965-990.

Keller, Evelyn Fox. 1985. *Reflections on Gender and Science*. New Haven, CT: Yale University Press.

Kessler-Harris, Alice. 1982. *Out to Work: A History of Wage-Earning Women in the United States*. New York: Oxford University Press.

Klein, Susan S., ed. 1985. *Handbook for Achieving Sex Equity through Education*. Baltimore, MD: Johns Hopkins University Press.

Komarovsky, Mirra. 1964. *Blue-collar Marriage*. New York: Random House.

————— 1973. "Some Problems in Role Analysis." *American Sociological Review* 38:649-662.

Konner, Melvin J. 1981. "Evolution of Human Behavior Development." Pp. 3-51 in *Handbook of Cross-Cultural Human Development*, edited by R. H. Monroe, R. L. Monroe, and B. B. Whiting. New York: Garland STPM Press.

Lamphere, Louise. 1974. "Strategies, Cooperation, and Conflict Among Women in Domestic Groups." Pp. 97-112 in *Woman, Culture, and Society*, edited by M. Z. Rosaldo and L. Lamphere. Stanford, CA: Stanford University Press.

Lenski, Gerhard. 1966. *Power and Privilege: A Theory of Social Stratification*. New York: McGraw-Hill.

Leibowitz, Lila. 1978. *Females, Males, Families: A Biosocial Approach*. North Scituate, MA: Duxbury Press.

Lever, Janet. 1976. "Sex Differences in the Games Children Play." *Social Problems* 23:478-487.

————— 1978. "Sex Differences in the Complexity of Children's Play and Games." *American Sociological Review* 43:471-483.

Levinson, Daniel J. 1978. *The Seasons of a Man's Life*. New York: Knopf.

Levi-Strauss, Claude. 1969. *The Elementary Structures of Kinship*, translated by J. H. Bell, J. R. von Sturmer, and R. Needham. Boston: Beacon.

Lightfoot, Sarah Lawrence. 1975. "Sociology of Education: Perspectives on Women." Pp. 106-143 in *Another Voice: Feminist Perspectives on Social Life and Social Science*, edited by M.

Millman and R. M. Kanter. New York: Anchor.

Lim, Linda Y.C. 1981. "Women's Work in Multinational Electronics Factories." Pp. 181-190 in *AAAS Selected Symposium 53: Women and Technological Change in Developing Countries*, edited by R. Dauber and M. L. Cain. Boulder, CO: Westview Press.

Linton, Ralph. 1936. *The Study of Man: An Introduction*. New York: Appleton-Century.

Lipman-Blumen, Jean and Jessie Bernard, eds. 1979. *Sex Roles and Social Policy: A Complex Social Science Equation*. Beverly Hills, CA: Sage.

Lipman-Blumen, Jean and Ann R. Tickamyer. 1975. "Sex Roles in Transition: A Ten-year Perspective." *Annual Review of Sociology* 1:297-337.

Lockheed, Marlaine. 1985. "Sex Equity in Classroom Organization and Climate." Pp. 189-217 in *Handbook for Achieving Sex Equity through Education*, edited by Susan S. Klein. Baltimore, MD: Johns Hopkins University Press.

Lopata, Helena Z. and Barrie Thorne. 1978. "On the Term 'Sex Roles.' " *Signs* 3:718-772.

Lorber, Judith. 1981. "Minimalist and Maximalist Feminist Ideologies and Strategies for Change." *Quarterly Journal of Ideology* 5:61-66.

Lowe, Marian. 1983. "The Dialectic of Biology and Culture." Pp. 39-62 in *Woman's Nature: Rationalizations of Inequality*, edited by M. Lowe and R. Hubbard. New York: Pergamon Press.

Luker, Kristin. 1984. *Abortion and the Politics of Motherhood*. Berkeley: University of California Press.

Maccoby, Eleanor Emmons and Carol Nagy Jacklin. 1974. *The Psychology of Sex Differences*. Stanford, CA: Stanford University Press.

Mannheim, Karl. 1936. *Ideology and Utopia*. New York: Harcourt, Brace and World.

Mansbridge, Jane J. 1986. *Why We Lost the ERA*. Chicago: University of Chicago Press.

McClelland, David C. 1975. *Power: The Inner Experience*. New York: Irvington.

McPherson, J. Miller and Lynn Smith-Lovin. 1986. "Sex Segregation in Voluntary Associations." *American Sociological Review* 51:61-79.

Martin, M. Kay and Barbara Voorhies. 1975. *Female of the Species*. New York: Columbia University Press.

Marx, Karl and Friedrich Engels. 1959. *The German Ideology*. Excerpts on pp. 246-260 in *Marx and Engels: Basic Writings on Politics and Philosophy*, edited by L. S. Feuer. Garden City, NY: Doubleday/Anchor. (Original work published 1846)

Mason, Karen Oppenheim, John L. Czajka, and Sara Arber. 1976. "Change in U. S. Women's Sex-Role Attitudes, 1964-1974." *American Sociological Review* 41:573-596.

Mead, Margaret. 1935. *Sex and Temperament in Three Primitive Societies*. New York: William Morrow.

———— 1949. *Male and Female: A Study of the Sexes in a Changing World*. New York: Dell.

———— and Frances Balgley Kaplan, eds. 1965. *American Women: The Report of the President's Commission on the Status of Women and Other Publications of the Commission, 1963*. New York: Scribner's.

Merton, Robert K. 1957. *Social Theory and Social Structure*. New York: Free Press.

————, Leonard Broom, and Leonard S. Cottrell. 1959. *Sociology Today: Problems and Prospects*. New York: Basic Books.

Millett, Kate. 1970. *Sexual Politics*. Garden City, NY: Doubleday.

Mincer, Jacob. 1962. "Labor-force Participation of Married Women: A Study of Labor Supply." Pp. 63-105 in *Aspects of Labor Economics*. Report of the National Bureau of Economic Research. Princeton, NJ: Universities-National Bureau Committee of Economic Research.

Monroe, Robert L., Ruth H. Munroe, and John W.M. Whiting. 1981. "Male Sex-role Resolutions." Pp. 611-632 in *Handbook of Cross-Cultural Human Development*, edited by R. H. Monroe, R. L. Monroe, and B. B. Whiting. New York: Garland STPM Press.

Moroney, Robert. 1976. *The Family and the State*. London: Longmans.

Moynihan, Daniel Patrick. 1986. *Family and Nation*. San Diego: Harcourt, Brace Jovanovich.

Nash, June and Maria Patricia Fernandez-Kelly, eds. 1983. *Women, Men and the International Division of Labor*. Albany: State University of New York Press.

National Center for Education Statistics. 1970-1971. *Earned Degrees Conferred*. Washington, DC: Government Printing Office.

————. 1979-1980. *Earned Degrees Conferred*. Washington, DC: Government Printing Office.

National Center for Health Statistics. 1968. *Vital Statistics Rates in the United States 1940-1960*, vol. 83. Washington, DC: Government Printing Office.

———— 1985. *Vital Statistics of the United States*. Washington, DC: Government Printing Office.

National NOW Times. 1987. "Court Rejects Reagan; Upholds Affirmative Action for Women." *National NOW Times* (April):1.

Norton, Mary Beth. 1980. *Liberty's Daughters: The Revolutionary Experience of American Women, 1750-1800*. Boston: Little, Brown.

Norton, Arthur J. and Jeanne E. Moorman. 1987. "Current Trends in Marriage and Divorce among American Women." *Journal of Marriage and the Family* 49:3-14.

Okin, Susan Moller. 1979. *Women in Western Political Thought*. Princeton, NJ: Princeton University Press.

Oppenheimer, Valerie Kincaide. 1970. *The Female Labor Force in the United States*. Population Monograph Series no. 5. Berkeley: University of California.

———— 1982. *Work and the Family: A Study in Social Demography*. New York: Academic.

Ortner, Sherry B. 1974. "Is Female to Male as Nature is to Culture?" Pp. 67-87 in *Woman, Culture, and Society*, edited by M. Z. Rosaldo and L. Lamphere. Stanford, CA: Stanford University Press.

———— and Harriet Whitehead. 1981. *Sexual Meanings: The Cultural Construction of Gender and Sexuality*. New York: Cambridge University Press.

Paige, Karen and Jeffrey Paige. 1973. "The Politics of Birth Practices: A Strategic Analysis." *American Sociological Review* 38:663-676.

Papanek, Hanna. 1977. "Development Planning for Women." *Signs* 3:14-21.

Parsons, Talcott. 1942. "Age and Sex in the Social Structure of the United States." *American Sociological Review* 7:604-616.

———— 1951. *The Social System*. New York: Free Press.

———— 1966. *Societies: Evolutionary and Comparative Perspectives*. Englewood Cliffs, NJ: Prentice-Hall.

———— and Robert F. Bales. 1955. *Family, Socialization, and Interaction Process*. New York: Free Press.

Pharr, Susan J. 1981. *Political Women in Japan: The Search for a Place in Political Life*. Berkeley: University of California Press.

Pleck, Joseph H. 1975. "Masculinity-femininity: Current and Alternative Paradigms." *Sex Roles* 1:161-178.

———— 1976. "The Male Sex Role: Definitions, Problems, and Sources of Change." *Journal of Social Issues* 32:144-164.

———— 1979. "Married men: Work and Family." Pp. 387-411 in *Families Today: A Research Sampler on Families and Children*, vol. 1, edited by E. Corfman. Washington, DC: Government Printing Office.

———— 1981. *The Myth of Masculinity*. Cambridge: MIT Press.

———— 1982. "The Work-Family Role System." Pp. 101-10 in *Women and Work: Problems and Perspectives*, edited by Rachel Kahn-Hut, Arlene Kaplan-Daniels, and Richard Colvard. New York: Oxford University Press.

———— 1985. *Working Wives/Working Husbands*. Beverly Hills, CA: Sage.

Pleck, Elizabeth H. and Joseph H. Pleck, eds. 1980. *The American Man*. Englewood Cliffs, NJ: Prentice-Hall.

Polachek, Solomon W. 1979. "Occupational Segregation Among Women: Theory, Evidence, and a Prognosis." Pp. 137-57 in *Sex, Discrimination, and the Division of Labor*, edited by Cynthia B. Lloyd. New York: Columbia University Press.

Rapoport, Rhona and Robert Rapoport. 1976. *Dual-Career Families Reexamined*. New York: Harper & Row.

Ratner, Ronnie Steinberg, eds. 1980. *Equal Employment Policy for Women: Strategies for Implementation in the United States, Canada, and Western Europe*. Philadelphia: Temple University Press.

Reinharz, Shulamit. 1979. *On Becoming a Social Scientist*. San Francisco: Jossey-Bass.

Reskin, Barbara F., ed. 1984. *Sex Segregation in the Workplace: Trends, Explanations, Remedies*. Washington, DC: National Academy Press.

———— and Heidi I. Hartmann, eds. 1986. *Women's Work, Men's Work: Sex Segregation on the Job*. Washington, DC: National Academy Press.

Riley, Matilda W., Anne Foner, and Joan Waring. 1988. "Sociology of Age." Pp. 243-291 in *Handbook of Sociology*, edited by N. J. Smelser. Newbury Park, CA: Sage.

Rollins, Judith. 1985. *Between Women: Domestics and Their Employers*. Philadelphia: Temple University Press.

Roos, Patricia A. 1985. *Gender and Work: A Comparative Analysis of Industrial Societies*. Albany: State University of New York Press.

Rosaldo, M. Z. and L. Lamphere., eds. 1974. *Woman, Culture, and Society*. Stanford, CA: Stanford University Press.

Rossi, Alice S. 1964. "Equality Between the Sexes: An Immodest Proposal." Pp. 98-143 in *The Woman in America*, edited by R. J. Lifton. Boston: Beacon.

———— 1977. "A Biosocial Perspective on Parenting." *Daedalus* 106:1-31.

————, ed. 1985. "Gender and Parenthood." Pp. 161-191 in *Gender and the Life Course*. Hawthorne, NY: Aldine.

———— and Ann Calderwood, eds. 1973. *Academic Women on the Move*. New York: Russell Sage Foundation.

Rotondo, E. Anthony. 1982. "Manhood in America: The Northern Middle Class, 1770-1920." Ph.D. dissertation, Brandeis University.

———— 1983. "Body and Soul: Changing Ideals of American Middle-Class Manhood, 1770-1920." *Journal of Social History* 16:23-38.

Rowbotham, Sheila. 1972. *Women, Resistance, and Revolution*. New York: Pantheon.

Rubin, Gayle. 1975. "The Traffic in Women: Notes on the 'Political Economy' of Sex." Pp. 157-210 in *Toward an Anthropology of Women*, edited by R. R. Reiter. New York: Monthly Review Press.

Rubin, Lillian B. 1976. *Worlds of Pain: Life in the Working-Class Family*. New York: Basic Books.

Ryan, Mary P. 1981. *Cradle of the Middle Class: The Family in Oneida County, New York, 1790-1865*. New York: Cambridge University Press.

Sacks, Karen. 1974. "Engels Revisited: Women, the Organization of Production, and Private Property." Pp. 207-222 in *Woman, Culture, and Society*, edited by M. Z. Rosaldo and L. Lamphere. Stanford, CA: Stanford University Press.

Safilios-Rothschild, Constantina. 1974. *Women and Social Policy*. Englewood Cliffs, NJ: Prentice-Hall.

Salaff, Janet and Judith Merkle. 1973. "Women and

Revolution: The Lessons of the Soviet Union and China.'' Pp. 145-177 in *Women in China: Studies in Social Change and Feminism*, edited by M. B. Young. Ann Arbor, MI: Center for Chinese Studies, University of Michigan.

Sanday, Peggy R. 1974. "Female Status in the Public Domain." Pp. 189-206 in *Woman, Culture, and Society*, edited by M. Z. Rosaldo and L. Lamphere. Stanford, CA: Stanford University Press.

Sandler, Bernice. 1973. "A Little Help from our Government: WEAL and Contract Compliance." Pp. 439-462 in *Academic Women on the Move*, edited by A. S. Rossi and A. Calderwood. New York: Russell Sage Foundation.

Scanzoni, John H. 1975. *Sex Roles, Life Styles, and Childbearing*. New York: Free Press.

Schneider, Beth E. 1985. "The Sexualization of the Workplace: A Challenge to Sociological Theory." Presented at the annual meetings of the American Sociological Association, Washington, DC.

Schwager, Sally. 1987. "Educating Women in America." *Signs* 12:333-372.

Scott, Hilda. 1974. *Does Socialism Liberate Women? Experiences from Eastern Europe*. Boston: Beacon.

Seifer, Nancy. 1973. *Absent from the Majority: Working Class Women in America*. New York: American Jewish Committee.

Signs: Journal of Women in Culture and Society. 1984. "The Lesbian Issue." *Signs* 9:553-791.

_____ 1986. "Women's History Goes to Trial." *Signs* 11:751-779.

Simmons, R. G., D. A. Blyth, F. Van Cleave, and D. M. Bush. 1979. "Entry Into Early Adolescence: The Impact of School Structure, Puberty, and Early Dating on Self-Esteem." *American Sociological Review* 44:948-967.

Slater, Philip E. 1968. *The Glory of Hera: Greek Mythology and the Greek Family*. Boston: Beacon.

Smelser, Neil J. 1959. *Social Change in the Industrial Revolution*. Chicago: University of Chicago Press.

_____ 1963. *Theory of Collective Behavior*. New York: Free Press.

Smith, Dorothy E. 1979. "A Sociology for Women." Pp. 135-187 in *The Prism of Sex: Essays in the Sociology of Knowledge*, edited by J. A. Sherman and E. T. Beck. Madison: University of Wisconsin Press.

Smith, Ralph E., ed. 1979. *The Subtle Revolution: Women at Work*. Washington, DC: The Urban Institute.

Sokoloff, Natalie J. 1980. *Between Money and Love: The Dialectics of Women's Home and Market Work*. New York: Praeger.

Solomon, Barbara Miller. 1985. *In the Company of Educated Women: A History of Women and Higher Education in America*. New Haven, CT: Yale University Press.

Sorensen, Elaine. 1986. "Implementing Comparable Worth: A Survey of Recent Job Evaluation Studies." *AEA Papers and Proceedings* 76:364-367.

Spence, Janet T., Kay Deaux, and Robert L. Helmreich. 1985. "Sex Roles in Contemporary American Society." Pp. 149-178 in *Handbook of Social Psychology*, vol. 1, edited by Gardner Lindzey and Elliot Aronson. New York: Random House.

Spencer, Herbert. 1883. *Ceremonial Institutions*. Part IV of *Principles of Sociology*. New York: Appleton.

Srinivasan, Mangalam. 1981. "Impact of Selected Industrial Technologies on Women in Mexico." Pp. 89-108 in *AAAS Selected Symposium 53: Women and Technological Change in Developing Countries*, edited by R. Dauber and M. L. Cain. Boulder, CO: Westview Press.

Stacey, Judith. 1983. *Patriarchy and the Socialist Revolution in China*. Berkeley: University of California Press.

_____ and Barrie Thorne. 1985. "The Missing Feminist Revolution in Sociology." *Social Problems* 32:301-316.

Staines, Graham L. and Joseph H. Pleck. 1983. *The Impact of Work Schedules on the Family*. Ann Arbor: Institute for Social Research, University of Michigan.

Stamm, Liesa. 1984. "Differential Power of Women Over the Life Course: A Case Study of Age-roles as an Indicator of Power." Pp. 15-35 in *AAAS Selected Symposium 96: Social Power and Influence of Women*, edited by L. Stamm and C. D. Ryff. Boulder, CO: Westview Press.

Stockard, Jean and Miriam M. Johnson. 1980. *Sex Roles: Sex Inequality and Sex Role Development*. Englewood Cliffs, NJ: Prentice-Hall.

Swidler, Ann. 1980. "Love and Adulthood in American Culture." Pp. 120-147 in *Themes of Work and Love in Adulthood*, edited by N. J. Smelser and E. H. Erikson. Cambridge, MA: Harvard University Press.

Tanner, Nancy and Adrienne Zihlman. 1976. "Women in Evolution. Part I: Innovation and Selection in Human Origins." *Signs* 1:585-608.

Thorne, Barrie. 1985. "Girls and Boys Together . . . But Mostly Apart: Gender Arrangements in Elementary Schools." Pp. 167-184 in *Relationships and Development*, edited by W. W. Hartup and Z. Rubin. Hillsdale, NJ: Lawrence Erlbaum.

_____ 1986. Personal communication (August).

Thorne, Barrie, Cheris Kramarae, and Nancy Henley, eds. 1983. *Language, Gender and Society*. Rowley, MA: Newbury House.

Thornton, Arland, Duane F. Alwin, and Donald Camburn. 1983. "Causes and Consequences of Sex-Role Attitudes and Attitude Change." *American Sociological Review* 48:211-227.

Thurow, Lester C. 1969. *Poverty and Discrimination*. Washington, DC: Brookings Institution.

Tinker, Irene. 1976. "The Adverse Impact of Development on Women." Pp. 22-34 in *Women and World Development*, edited by I. Tinker and M. B. Bramsen. Washington, DC: Overseas Development Council.

Toennies, Ferdinand. 1940. *Fundamental Concepts of Sociology (Gemeinschaft und Gesellschaft)*, translated and supplemented by Charles P. Loomis. New York: American Book Company. (Original work published 1887)

Treiman, Donald J. and Heidi I. Hartmann, eds. 1981. *Women, Work, and Wages: Equal Pay for Jobs of Equal Value*. Washington, DC: National Academy Press.

Turkle, Sherry. 1984. *The Second Self: Computers and the Human Spirit*. New York: Simon & Schuster.

Uhlenberg, Peter. 1969. "A Study of Cohort Life Cycles: Cohorts of Native-born Massachusetts Women, 1830-1920." *Population Studies* 23:407-420.

U.S. Bureau of the Census. 1948. *Statistical Abstract of the United States*. Washington, DC: Government Printing Office.

———— 1960. *Statistical Abstract of the United States*. Washington, DC: Government Printing Office.

———— 1962. *Statistical Abstract of the United States*. Washington, DC: Government Printing Office.

———— 1975. *Historical Statistics of the United States: Colonial Times to 1970*. Washington, DC: Government Printing Office.

———— 1985. *Statistical Abstract of the United States*. Washington, DC: Government Printing Office.

———— 1987. *Statistical Abstract of the United States*. Washington, DC: Government Printing Office.

U.S. Department of Labor, Bureau of Labor Statistics. 1982. *Labor Force Statistics Derived from the Current Population Survey: A Databook*, vol. I, bulletin 2096. Washington, DC: Government Printing Office.

———— 1983. *Handbook of Labor Statistics*. Washington, DC: Government Printing Office.

———— 1984. *Employment and Earnings*, vol. 31. Washington, DC: Government Printing Office.

Van Dusen, Roxann and Eleanor Bernert Sheldon. 1976. "The Changing Status of American Women: A Life Cycle Perspective." *American Psychologist* (February):106-116.

Veroff, Joseph, Richard A. Kulka, and Elizabeth Douvan. 1981. *Mental Health in America: Patterns of Help-Seeking from 1957 to 1976*. New York: Basic Books.

Vogel, Lise. 1983. *Marxism and the Oppression of Women: Toward a Unitary Theory*. New Brunswick, NJ: Rutgers University Press.

Wagner, David G., Rebecca S. Ford, and Thomas W. Ford. 1986. "Can Gender Inequalities Be Reduced?" *American Sociological Review* 51:47-61.

Waldman, Elizabeth. 1983. "Labor Force Statistics from a Family Perspective." *Monthly Labor Review* 106:16-20.

Ward, Kathryn B. and Linda Grant. 1985. "The Feminist Critique and a Decade of Published Research in Sociology Journals." *Sociological Quarterly* 26:139-157.

Weissman, Myrna M. and Gerald L. Klerman. 1977. "Sex Differences and the Epidemiology of Depression." *Archives of General Psychiatry* 34:98-111.

Weitzman, Lenore. 1985. *The Divorce Revolution: The Unexpected Social and Economic Consequences for Women and Children in America*. New York: Free Press.

Welter, Barbara. 1976. *Dimity Convictions: The American Woman in the Nineteenth Century*. Athens, OH: Ohio University Press.

Whicker, Marcia Lynn and Jennie Jacobs Kronenfeld. 1986. *Sex Role Changes: Technology, Politics, and Policy*. New York: Praeger.

Whyte, Martin King. 1978. *The Status of Women in Pre-Industrial Societies*. Princeton, NJ: Princeton University Press.

Young, Michael and Peter Willmott. 1973. *The Symmetrical Family*. New York: Pantheon.

Youssef, Nadia Haggag. 1974. *Women and Work in Developing Societies*. Berkeley: Institute of International Studies, University of California.

———— 1976. "Women in Development: Urban Life and Labor." Pp. 70-77 in *Women and World Development*, edited by I. Tinker and M. B. Bramsen. Washington, DC: Overseas Development Council.

Zihlman, Adrienne L. 1978. "Women and Evolution, Part II: Subsistence and Social Organization among Early Hominids." *Signs* 4:4-20.

Part III

MAJOR INSTITUTIONAL AND ORGANIZATIONAL SETTINGS

10
Jobs and Work

JOANNE MILLER

If one aspect of social life can be said to dominate views of society, it is the organization of production. Work relations enter virtually all models of social organization and associated images of man or woman as an actor in and product of structured relationships. Moreover, the workplace per se, as a strategic location in which work arrangements are staged, has been a central laboratory for investigating social order and the dynamics of change. In the wake of the industrial revolution, the organization of production inevitably focused attention on the physical setting of the workplace—the factory. The physical plant and social organization for manufacturing technology became the symbol—indeed, part of the definition—of industrial society. Further, individual conduct and mental life were intimately tied to the secular, money economy built around the institutions of work. For social philosophers of the nineteenth century, industrialization and urbanization had transformed the relationship of person to society and thus the individual. Alienation in industrial life was a pervasive theme (Nisbet, 1966). Subjugation to economic institutions separating workers from the management of their labor (Marx), trivialization of the individual stemming from economic specialization,

leveling forces of democracy, and secular reasoning (Tocqueville, Weber), isolation in the division of labor separated from community (Durkheim), and estrangement from the intense and impersonal stimuli of the metropolis (Simmel) were a fate projected for the industrial worker.

Preoccupation with the enterprise of work and its staging heightened further as industrial society evolved and postindustrial forms were foreshadowed. With increasing complexity in operations and diversification, industrial society became organizational society. Manufacturing technology no longer served as the prototype for work relations or task structuring. Rather, bureaucracy was recognized as the generic structure organizing jobs and workers. Industrial experiments in managing increasing scale and productivity attested to the efficiency of the form. As Weber (1958, p. 229) had foreseen, "The objective indispensability of the once-existing apparatus, with its peculiar 'impersonal' character, means that the mechanism . . . is easily made to work for anybody who knows how to gain control over it." Taylor's applied methods of scientific management focused on hierarchical planning and direction, the disaggregation and coordination of task activity, personnel requirements, and formal incentive systems. Their success contributed to increasing specialization and formalization of production activity and the growth of management and personnel administration.

This work was supported, in part, by a fellowship from the Russell Sage Foundation.

Responses to work experiences also entered applied research in studies of recruitment and adjustment, human factors underlying motivation and productivity, and conflict resolution. In analyzing "labor problems," workers could no longer be treated as identical elements in machine processing. Recognition of individual differences was required before they could be managed. More important, workers could not be conceptualized as unconnected actors in the workplace. Rather, behavior had to be placed in the context of membership and affiliation. Socialization and group dynamics became central in analyses of labor behavior. The workplace took on new significance as a social system of formal and informal relationships in which work was enacted.

Through these transitions, the workplace—whether as the site of production, organizational structure, or arena of social interaction and exchange—remained core to the study of social organization. The combination of theoretical ideas and applied issues of management coalescing in the workplace spawned a subfield of study focusing on jobs and work behavior in society. The terms *industrial relations*, *industrial sociology*, and *the sociology of work* express expanding conceptions of the field that progressively broadened from a focus on the terms and management of production and the conditions of work to systems of social stratification, social interaction, and organizational functioning. Studies of the professions, occupations, organizations, and community combined with the study of industry as forerunners to this broader approach to work behavior (see overview by Miller and Form, 1980, pp. 6-14).

The sociology of work developed in tandem with the sociological study of the economy. During the 1950s theorists returned to the classical issues of economy and society. Parsons and Smelser were leaders in forging integration of economic and sociological theory (see Swedberg, Himmelstrand, and Brulin, 1987, on the paradigm of economic sociology). They challenged neoclassical economics to move beyond the market and to study economic activity in terms of intersecting social systems. Concrete elaboration of behavior in firms became the central domain incorporating research on the sociology of work and, in turn, influencing its development. Classical concern with the organization of production activity and its psychological consequences was reformulated in terms of organizational functioning in the larger economy.

This contemporary stance on jobs and work emphasizes the micro-level processes and institutional factors operating within firms to organize work and determining its outcomes. Work and workers' behavior are treated as socially constructed phenomena embedded in the structured relationships of organizational life and the larger society. The model is social-psychological in its dual emphasis on the *structure* of role relationships in work and their *construction*. Following cognitive theories of organizational behavior, action is not assumed to be situationally predetermined or purposively rational. Rather, it is viewed as part of an emergent and unfolding process of enactment and the reciprocal product of job and worker. Social patterning evolves through the institutionalization of practice, meaning, and roles.[1] As Zucker points out (1977, p. 726), "Social knowledge once institutionalized exists as a fact, as part of objective reality, and can be transmitted directly on that basis." Definitions and social understandings of the workplace, while cognitively constructed and in this sense intrasubjective to individual actors, come to be objectified and no longer properties of actors' independent resolution. They are simply ways of life accepted by the participants and enacted through routine. The negotiated realities of the workplace thus come to have a persistent structure and bounded pattern of social relationships.

In emphasizing both the cognitive construction and social structuring of the workplace, I describe social behavior in which meaning both *derives from* the structure of social relationships and *produces* structured relations. This is a familiar stance. For example, Giddens (1984) depicts the structural properties of social systems as both the medium and outcome of the practices they recursively organize. They do not exist outside of action but are chronically implicated in its production and reproduction. Actors are assumed to monitor reflexively the context in which they operate and to gain a "knowledgeability" about the situated character of their circumstances. Normative patterning emerges from the constraints of a position within a social system that both *limits the options* of actors and *creates opportunity* for purposive action. Strategic conduct within the system of social relationships is thus defined and reproduced.

In this chapter, I review contemporary research to show how social knowledge of structured relationships is implemented in the workplace: what factors predominate conceptual maps of work and how these templates are reflexively interpreted and operationalized. After addressing the social construction of jobs, I move to the process through which workers derive meaning from work and the psychological outcomes of job experience.

The Social Construction of a Job

Work conducted in places of formal employment ordinarily consists of aggregated activities sufficiently cohesive to be categorized under an administrative job title. However, the similarity of work performed under one job title compared to others is difficult to judge. The terms in which activities are described and conceptually aggregated are highly diverse in content and nomenclature. In practice, definitions and standards can appear more arbitrary than systematic.[2] Most firms in the private sector are probably not using any formal method of job classification (U.S. Commission on Civil Rights, 1985; also see historical growth of job analysis empirically documented in Baron, Dobbin, and Jennings, 1986, p. 354). Shared understandings of meaningful task units, their place in the production process, and what constitutes a job must be deciphered. These operational definitions of work are important for what they reveal about underlying perceptions of labor, cognitive maps of work, and the structure of role relationships. Moreover, the reflection of these orientations in organizational structures are part of the concrete realities that embody and shape labor markets.

Although the study of shared meanings, normative expectations, and cognitive systems of information processing are ripe for analysis, jobs per se are a strangely neglected topic of research—especially in contrast to the attention focused on occupations. Perhaps the common occupational labels applied to jobs are deceiving in the familiarity they evoke about work, masking the complexities that underlie their origin and maintenance. Sociological knowledge of how jobs come to be defined and work arrangements organized is disparate and incomplete. Yet, parts of the process can be pieced together by examining (1) how organizations interpret external frames of reference and (2) individual negotiation of work roles. I begin by focusing on four factors that have dominated contemporary research on work: gender, education, occupations, and technology. Then individual negotiation of work roles is discussed.

Organizational Interpretations of External Frames of Reference

GENDER AND THE PERCEPTION OF WORK

Current interest in perceptions of work and job definitions has been stimulated by debates surrounding the comparable worth of jobs. Subjectivity in evaluation criteria is poignantly illustrated in case examples and aggregate statistics showing systematic downrating of women's occupational characteristics and monetary value (see review by Treiman and Hartmann, 1981). However, there is relatively little research addressing the processes that contribute to selective perceptions of work behavior.

Most of the existing work focuses on the liability of female status for individual outcomes. There is accumulating evidence that female workers are underrated in their abilities, performance, and work commitment in a manner that parallels other social judgments about women in society (see review by Shepela and Viviano, 1984). Gender appears to operate as a highly diffuse status cue, broadly affecting expectations held about participants that ultimately structure task-oriented behavior (see reviews by Berger, Rosenholtz, and Zelditch, 1980; Meeker and Weitzel-O'Neill, 1977; Walker and Fennell, 1986). Experimental studies, case studies, and survey research all point to processes of attribution that result in the devaluation of female labor.

However, these lines of research are limited by an exclusive focus on perceptions of the individual. Treiman (1979, p. 45) notes that most studies of gender and work focus on the evaluation of people *not jobs*. Yet, the mechanisms through which sex stereotyping is activated appears closely connected with the treatment of job content in organizations. Analysis of U.S. Employment Service data shows that a proliferation of job titles for similar job tasks (beyond what would be expected based on occupational functions) is an important mechanism through which men and women are segregated in firms (Baron and Bielby, 1985). In addition, jobs are sex segregated in terms of sex-exclusive and sex-discriminating promotion ladders. Baron, Davis-Blake, and Bielby (1986) report nearly 80% of promotions ladders to be completely segregated by sex and 73% of integrated ladders to exclusively select men into superordinate positions.

Case studies show selective perception of job content to be a significant source of variation in the value attached to (and treatment of) occupations dominated by women. A classic example of selective perceptions of job content affecting ratings of work is AT&T's crediting of managerial jobs for work involving customer contact but allowing almost no recognition of contact in the wage determination of nonmanagerial telephone operators (a practice later revised; Steinberg, 1985, p. 47). Further illustrations abound (see for example, Acker, 1987; Baron and Bielby, 1985; Treiman, 1979, pp. 45-46). A review of the procedures used in 16 systems of job evaluation revealed that operationalizations of job content repeatedly ignored dimensions of job stress, disagreeable working conditions, responsibility, and skill in jobs dominated by women (Steinberg and Haignere, 1987).

The importance of job content in the valuation of work is also shown in experimental studies. Schwab and Grams's (1985) manipulation of the reported pay and sex composition of jobs showed raters to be sensitive to pay levels but the sex ratio to have no independent effect on the evaluation of job content. These findings suggest that *occupational* sex stereotyping is largely activated through the selective perception of job content and status rather than as direct attributions based on the gender composition of occupations. This is not to say, however, that gender is not an independent factor influencing *job* evaluation.

It is important to distinguish between the sex composition of job holders as a group and gender as an individual attribute of workers. McArthur and Obrant (1986) found that a job's reported salary, desirability, and the *sex of the incumbent* operated as independent predictors of raters' perceptions of job content. Jobs enacted by men were rated as requiring more decision making, as being more critical to the company's assets and operations, as being less structured, as involving more responsibility, and as having greater monetary worth than the same jobs enacted by women. But the *sex composition of the occupation* had no impact on job evaluation—a finding consistent with Schwab and Grams's study results.[3] In other words, the effect of a worker's gender on raters' perceptions of job content can be interpreted as the valuation of a personal attribute carried by the worker regardless of the sex composition of jobholders overall—a finding that parallels the impact of gender on the evaluation of individual performance. As a result, the significance of gender is likely to be more pervasive than if it operated solely in terms of the sex composition of abstract occupational categories. The work of women in nontraditional and sex-neutral occupations would be selectively evaluated as would those in female-dominated occupations.

It is interesting that the gender of evaluators appears irrelevant to perceptions of job content. The studies of job evaluation by McArthur and Obrant (1986), Schwab and Grams (1985), and Doverspike et al. (1983) show no systematic effects of the sex of the evaluator on ratings.

Similarly, sex-linked attributions about individual performance appear to be maintained by both male and female respondents (see conclusions of Landy and Farr, 1983: 123; Ross and Fletcher, 1985, p. 91). Although Arvey, Pasino, and Lounsburg (1977) find women's ratings of job content to differ from men's, the effect operates irrespective of the sex of the incumbent. The values and practices exhibited in gender biases appear highly institutionalized—reliably reproduced even across sex of evaluator.

The evaluation of women's abilities and performance in the workplace appears to mirror the beliefs and expectations held about females more generally in society. At the same time, employers interpret job content in relationship to gender, which results in selective recognition of task components, required skills, and job conditions. This extension not only reflects existing beliefs about women, it generates new dimensions of gender stratification. It places women in lower hierarchical ranks, laterally segregated units or job titles, and bounded promotion tracks. The selective treatment of job content in the workplace thus transforms sex-biased expectations into a self-fulfilling prophecy through the structural circumstances it creates (Kanter, 1977, 1982). Women have fewer opportunities to demonstrate (and be recognized for) their competencies. They have fewer resources to draw upon to be successful in demonstrations that are open to them. And, irrespective of demonstrated value, the structural position of women's jobs itself lowers the worth attached to the work and ultimately the incumbent. From the treatment of job content, values are both sustained and derived. Studies of comparable worth not only draw attention to the social criteria used in judging work but highlight the significance of organizational interpretations in a system of values (Roos and Reskin, 1984).

INTERPRETATION OF EDUCATIONAL QUALIFICATIONS

Perceptions of work and the labor force are also revealed in patterns of recruitment and selection. Organizations differ in their selection criteria and in their methods of screening applicants. For example, employers may establish crude eligibility requirements that eliminate gross classes of workers from consideration, accept all applications for review and apply detailed screening procedures; or mix crude and detailed assessments in their procedures. In addition, particular qualifications may be assessed in only one or multiple points in the process of recruiting and selecting candidates. Both the criteria and methods used in hiring decisions reflect how the organization conceptualizes the job and the worker. Although the structure of hiring decisions undoubtedly depends upon the resources of the organization and the size of the labor pool to be processed under different eligibility requirements, it also embodies conceptual distinctions.

Employers' treatment of educational qualifications has received the most concentrated research attention (see review by Bills 1986a, 1986b). Economic models of human capital traditionally interpreted schooling as training that developed requisite skills for job performance (Becker, 1964; Mincer, 1958). The employer screening on education would be seen as projecting a direct link between education and labor productivity. Subsequent refinement of this model, however, qualified this relationship by interpreting educational criteria as a filter separating out those of lesser general ability and leaving those capable of performing a job, if not specifically prepared for it (Albrecht, 1981; Arrow, 1973; Riley, 1976; Spence 1973; Stiglitz, 1975; Wolpin, 1977). Here the implication is that capacity to perform may or may not have been transformed into productive skill, necessitating a more complex or multistaged hiring decision.

Alternatively, education can be viewed as a credential providing rights of passage that are unrelated to either the capacity or likely productivity of the worker (Berg, 1971; Collins, 1979; Dore, 1976). From this perspective, screening on education would be viewed as either counterproductive or irrelevant to job performance. Employers using educational criteria would be selecting for factors extrinsic to job performance —for instance, social status and cultural values. If recognized as a credential and not an indicator of ability, the specific skills and potential of job candidates would have to be individually assessed, not assumed. If erroneously interpreted as an indicator of ability, the likelihood of mismatching person to job increases in hiring decisions.

The degree to which reliance on education criteria has resulted in the inefficient employment of labor is debated. Demographic analysis documents rapid educational upgrading of work over the past decade (especially in occupations not previously held by college graduates), raising the issue of occupational mismatches (Clogg and Shockey, 1984). However, there is very little research that examines the actual structure of hiring decisions. Even in applied contexts, it is the measurement of job elements and individual capacities that are studied, not the decision-making process and its organizational frame of reference. We know little about what information is actually exchanged, how it is sequenced and evaluated by employers, and what type and level of information successfully predict job performance.

A comparison of the educational requirements rated in the *Dictionary of Occupational Titles* (DOT) and employers' requirements for those jobs suggests that educational requirements are interpreted within a particular organizational context. Ruchlin (1971) finds that employers report higher requirements for sales, clerical, and service jobs and lower requirements for skilled and semiskilled occupations than apparently required by task characteristics. Although the discrepancies were not specifically analyzed, employers' educational requirements are sensitive to organizational characteristics (size) that have no significant effect on the DOT's rating. The organizational context of educational requirements is also evidenced in Cohen and Pfeffer's (1986) analysis of hiring standards showing interorganizational variation in relationship to promotion and training practices, unionization, and the presence of a personnel department. Diamond and Bedrosian (U.S. Department of Labor, 1970, p. 4) suggest that between-firm variation in schooling requirements for the same occupations is related to whether the employer equates education with the ability to communicate and comprehend instructions. Not only are the presence and level of schooling requirements at issue, but also their prominence in the decision-making process. In case studies of hiring decisions in several organizations in Chicago, Bills (1986a) found that rigid educational criteria were mainly instituted through gross eligibility markers prescreening pools of candidates. Education generally failed to reenter as a primary or exclusive criterion in later stages of hiring decisions. Although particular organizations did exhibit predilections for educational credentials as indicators of "image" and "fit" to the organization, most firms believed that their educational requirements selected for specific, job-related skills—though not an exclusive source of those skills.

These findings suggest that the educational requirements of work are made prominent by their temporal position in the structure of organizational decision making and their rigidity. The "educationally unqualified" are typically never seen or not further evaluated. Sometimes this is legitimized by professional certification. In other instances, it is produced through systems of recruitment organized through (or by) educational institutions that have taken a role in placing graduates. This eligibility screen, however, remains coarse. Once in a proximate position to the individual, the meaning of educational credentials blurs and the candidate's performance capacity must be evidenced by experience, job history, and the candidate's personal presentation of abilities and potential— *rather than more detailed (individual) assessment of education for the job*. Despite employers' assertions to the contrary, the temporal position and crude form of the information used in the decision-making process suggest that, in practice, educational criteria are used as a filtering mechanism and not an indicator of specific skills predicting job performance.

The failure of educational information to reenter in later stages of the decision-making process or to become more refined does not, however, resolve the question of whether the filter operates to select on general capacity to do the work or on social characteristics. It is instructive to note that every age cohort has experienced educational upgrading in its work— not just young, entry-level workers (Clogg and Shockey, 1984). Job experience does not appear to protect workers from changing educational criteria for employment. The case-study findings suggest that prescreening on education contributes to the disadvantage of cohorts with less education in their occupational labor markets. The apparent failure of job experience to substitute as information about capacity to do the job *at the prescreening phase of decision making* suggests that educational criteria are employed less as indicators of capacity than as credentials providing rights of passage. Employers' sense to the contrary probably results from the use of job experience criteria in later stages of decision making (after prescreening).

The sequencing of information in decision making is central in making educational criteria prominent in the evaluation of jobs and workers. Yet the origins of these practices and variation in different labor markets receive little attention. The meaning attached to education remains ambiguous. The organizational treatment of educational requirements suggests that they are not specifically equated with job performance. The general capacities and social position associated with education are more difficult to disentangle, especially in particular kinds of work. For example, Cain and Green (1983) report that the DOT's ratings of educational requirements (particularly in math) for clerical, service, and sales occupations have lower reliability that is mainly due to "rater" as opposed to "description" sources of error. Perhaps there

is general ambivalence about the significance of education for these occupations. The rationales underlying educational screens are critical for establishing what elements of social stratification are most prominent in structuring work relationships.

OCCUPATIONAL STRUCTURING OF WORK

Sociological understandings of work have developed predominantly in terms of named occupations. Lines of research vary in whether they treat occupations as discrete entities, aggregated categories, or hierarchical continuum. The emphasis attests not so much to the intellectual inventiveness of the discipline but to the meaningfulness of these labels in society. In the prototypic exchange, "What do you do? I am a sales clerk," the questioner infers considerable information about the respondent's particular work activities, supervisory relations, salary, and so on. However, more important than the information conveyed in common usage is the significance of the occupational label in the workplace. In the example above, if the respondent had replied that he or she was a sales "person" rather than a "clerk," the general questioner may not have made any different inferences about the work performed. In contrast, the job analyst using the *Dictionary of Occupational Titles* (U.S. Department of Labor, 1977) would have inferred that a "clerk" was selling a wide variety of merchandise and had little knowledge of the products beyond price, while a sales "person" was doing work that was more complex by virtue of requiring specialized knowledge about products and advising buyers about purchases.

It is important to remember that an occupational profile is a conceptual composite of numerous jobs—itself derived from a particular social context (Garnsey, 1981). The U.S. Department of Labor defines over 12,000 occupational titles by which to classify the millions of jobs in the American economy and identifies over 8,500 alternate labels for these titles (Miller et al., 1980). The compilation is itself the result of a particular procedural history. The distribution of titles is not representative of the labor force. Its areas of greater and lesser differentiation are known only in the crudest respects. Examples of disparities in coverage [recognition of 70 kinds of "sewing machine operators, garment" but only 6 kinds of "secretary" (Cain and Treiman, 1981, p. 260) show its selective view of occupations—a view of unknown consequence in the world of employment in which it is applied.[4]

Case examination of occupational nomenclature and systems of classification suggest a rich political and social history underlying the terms in which occupations are classified. Margo Conk's (1980) history of U.S. occupational statistics documents the embodiment of conceptions of social mobility, urbanization, and industrialization in the Census Bureau's systems of classification between 1870 and 1940. Take, for example, the treatment of manufacturing occupations. Conk notes of the classification system used between 1870 and 1910 that "laborers" were not included in manufacturing occupations:

> Until 1910, 91 percent of 100 percent of the nonagricultural laborers were listed under the "service" occupations—along with doctors, lawyers, servants and barbers, for example. The critical relationship defined by such a classification was not the skill level—but rather the relationship of the person to the "person" or "group" served. A laborer in the 1870 Census classification was assumed to be in a personal, almost feudal relationship either to an artisan . . . or to the society as a whole. . . . There was no place in the classification scheme for a "laborer" to serve a corporation; to do so he had to become an "employee" and stand in a different social position [1980, p. 30].

Later, the skill and ability of the worker became the critical criteria for classification. In 1910 laborers moved into the ranks of the manufacturing occupations differentiated by industry and from the semiskilled operatives and skilled or managerial occupations that retained individually listed names. In practice, however, categorization by skill continued to reflect aspects of social position. Alba Edwards writes of the classification scheme that

> certain specific occupations which technically, are skilled occupations were classified as semi-skilled because the enumerators returned so many children, young persons, and women as pursuing these occupations as to render the occupations semiskilled, even though each of them did contain some skilled workers [Conk, 1980, p. 43].

A specific example of such downgrading is the occupation of dressmaker, considered in 1910 to be a skilled trade. A total of 99% of workers in this occupation were female. In 1940 the occupation was rated as semiskilled, although tailoring—an occupation dominated by men—retained its classification as skilled work (Conk, 1980, p. 146).

While there is little disagreement that occupational structures are historically dynamic and transforming (Davies, 1980; Hauser and Featherman, 1977; Katz, 1972; Sharlin, 1979), there is debate over the factors underlying social change in the position of occupations and the nature of the work they embody. These include the size and composition of the labor force, the skill and expertise required in the work, the relative level of professionalization, career trajectories, the bureaucratic treatment of the occupation, and its market position. Case studies and aggregate statistics document the changing character of the occupational structure in each respect but there are no simple generalizations to be made about the interrelationships of these factors, global trends across occupations, or historical periods. Even conclusions about specific occupations remain tentative, generally reflecting singular interpretations. There is no comprehensive theory of occupations by which to characterize the process of transformation. Nonetheless, there is ample face evidence that conceptions of occupations are socially derived.

Current literature is dominated by the theme of social control (see reviews by Rothman, 1979; Simpson, 1985), whether from the perspective of labor attempting to expand its autonomy over work and labor markets (see, for example, Etzioni, 1969; Freidson, 1970; Larson, 1977; Montgomery, 1979) or owners attempting to exercise increased control over production through the division of labor (for example, see Braverman, 1974; Kraft, 1977; Stone, 1974). As Rothman notes:

> Occupations are the point of convergence of the activities and competing demands of a number of groups controlling resources. Groups with resources may be in a position to define tasks, areas of expertise, enforce deference and subordination, control access and socialization, and in many other ways control the evolution of specific roles [1979, p. 496].

The occupational treatment of administrative and clerical work serves as a useful illustration of the multiplicity of factors to be disentangled.

Historical accounts of office work (Anderson, 1976; Braverman, 1974; Davies, 1982; DiPrete, 1985b; Lockwood, 1958) indicate that up to the early twentieth century, administrative work was treated as an aggregate function. While status hierarchies existed within clerical service, the transcription, accounting, and management of records were tasks requiring literacy and falling under the aegis of workers classified as clerks. Without romanticizing the circumstances of black-coated workers in Victorian times (note cautions by Attewell, 1987; Cohn, 1985; and Form, 1980), the breadth of the occupational category contrasts with its contemporary usage denoting a subordinate position entailing only routine office functions and conceptually distinct from professional and managerial work.

There is no question that the expanding administrative component of production across industries and the growth of the service sector increased demand for clerical workers. At initial stages, the importance of administrative functions and literacy requirements restricting supply appear to have collectively maintained the position of clerks and minimized grade and pay differentials. But greater differentiation of administrative activities was soon to follow with recognition of managerial responsibilities and specialized (higher) knowledge. Ultimately, clerical work was occupationally separated and hierarchically differentiated from professional and executive functions.

While the outlines of the story are generally agreed upon, its dynamics are widely discussed. The account portrays an implicit link between organization growth and task differentiation stemming from the increasing size and cost of the nonmanual-labor component of production (Edwards, 1979; Mills, 1951). However, there is debate over the preconditions that made such differentiation initially profitable and maintained its profitability. Braverman (1974) and others (Davies, 1982; Rotella, 1981) focus on the technical deskilling of clerical work as a critical mechanism of control over labor costs, allowing the substitution of less expensive workers (presumably less skilled or using fewer of their skills) in the bulk of administrative-support positions. Although Braverman emphasizes the technical fragmentation and time/motion efficiencies of ''deskilling'' as the origin of increased profit, the fragmentation of clerical work need not have actually lowered the skill level of the clerical job to have been profitable. Indeed, the contention that clerical occupations have, on balance, decreased in skill has been challenged in both historical (Cohn, 1985) and contemporary contexts (see reviews by Kraft, 1985, and Attewell, 1987). As Edwards (1979) points out, the social control achieved through technological restructuring can be the more important origin of profit. Although clerical workers were not paid less in absolute terms as a result of occupational differentiation (Cohn, 1985, pp. 69-77), there is evidence that the separation of professional and managerial positions placed a relative cap on the salary range and altered the distribution of salaries (DiPrete, 1988). This rescaling dramatically altered the relative advantage of white-

collar over blue-collar labor, making their salary distributions far more overlapping (Crozier, 1971; Lockwood, 1958).

In this context, the transformation of clerical occupations, although apparently rationalized on the basis of reduced skill requirements, hinged on (1) a supply of labor accepting of the new occupational definition, its career ladder, and pay scales and (2) the orderly separation of higher-level clerical workers needed in professional and managerial functions. Research on the feminization of clerical work and the professionalization of management is central in these regards.

The reconceptualization of clerical work was accompanied by a dramatic change in the composition of its work force from male to female labor. While in part a function of their increasing entry into the labor force, the recruitment of women does not explain their disproportionate employment in clerical occupations (Rotella, 1981). White-collar work was an attractive option compared to manual labor, especially for literate women of middle-class social origin (Davies, 1982). But the supply of female labor —while a necessary condition—would not alone maintain the concentration of women in lower-level clerical positions over time. As new employees, women were largely entry level, less experienced workers for whom immediate eligibility for promotion into newly created managerial and professional positions would not be at issue. Exiting from the labor force and part-time patterns of work during family formation truncated careers; turnover could be synthetically enforced by explicit bars to employment after marriage (Cohn, 1985, pp. 97-109). Unlike alternative sources of cheap labor (juveniles and minority and least qualified men), the employment of women minimized later problems of absorption into higher-paid positions and increased pay based on tenure (Cohn, 1985, pp. 198-217).

The mobility of men out of clerical ranks further transformed the status of the occupation into a subordinate position (Crompton and Jones, 1984). Executive and professional positions, initially filled by high-level clerks, came to form a separate labor market for management and specialized professions (Carey, 1969; DiPrete, 1988; Kocka, 1980; Previts and Merino, 1979; Strom, 1985). The exclusion of women from these markets further concentrated women in clerical work, irrespective of turnover. Moreover, the development of professional and managerial staff reinforced the division between supervisory and nonsupervisory lines that formalized bureaucratic rationales for occupational distinctions. As Edwards (1979) points out, bureaucratic control first emerged in white-collar industry and extended the basis for differentiating labor:

Stratification is no longer limited by the firm's ability either to divide delegated power or to find technologically rooted differences. Now social or organizational distinctions (always supplemented, of course, by differences both in power and in technical function) become the basis for ranking and advancement [1979, p. 135].

The interrelationships of the factors converging in the social transformation of office work cannot be definitively stated. Their joint impact on clerical occupations proved dramatic in creating and sustaining subordinate positions with restricted functions, substitutable personnel, and controlled salary ranges. Whatever its origins, conceptions of clerical work became rationalized through the bureaucratic treatment of occupational distinctions. Most striking in the account is how reliably organizations reproduced these distinctions, even in circumstances where the economic conditions and organizational growth initially producing the division of labor did not apply. The transformation of clerical work evidences the importance of occupational distinctions in the division of labor and its powerful impact on work arrangements.

Although one would reasonably infer that conceptions of occupations are imported into organizations through the external labor market's pricing and treatment, firm behavior is not a simple translation of these definitions and standards. Exclusive preoccupation with global economic divisions of labor markets (sectors, industries, or occupations) has proved an inadequate depiction of the dynamics organizing jobs and workers (Althauser and Kalleberg, 1981; Baron and Bielby, 1980, 1984; Granovetter, 1981; Hodson, 1984; Lorence, 1987). There is substantial variation within occupational divisions of the labor market: Finlay's (1983) case study of longshore crane operators illustrates a single occupation in which two labor markets operate; Baron and Bielby's (1986; Bielby and Baron, 1986) statistical analysis of job titles shows that organizations having the same mix of occupations and skills can differ significantly in how they structure and label work roles; Smith's (1983) study of coaches illustrates the operation of submarkets within an occupation stratified by prestige. Occupations appear to serve as a critical template for the organization of work; it is a framework, however, that is

molded to fit particular organizational structures and interorganizational relationships.

Organizational explanations of job structures place occupational distinctions in the context of two general imperatives: organizational scale and personnel management. Both can alter or extend occupational frames of reference. With increasing size, firms are structurally managed through the differentiation and specialization of functions (Blau and Schoenherr, 1971; Child, 1973). Not only do multiple hierarchical levels emerge but lateral distinctions according to location, products, and markets may appear depending on the complexity of the external environment. Occupational distinctions are refined and customized in this context and come to produce job configurations that are particular to operations of a certain scale and increasingly firm specific. Similarly, problems of personnel management can produce job configurations that embody pay and status differences that extend beyond occupational distinctions. Job structures influence, for example, the need to create incentives for increased proficiency encourage longer attachment to the firm, promote apprenticeship relationships, and attract and retain specific types of workers. Baron and Bielby's (1986) analysis of the proliferation of job titles beyond that associated with conventional occupational distinctions shows the importance of these factors. They find that firms tend to proliferate job titles when they are large, employ personnel specialists, operate in complex environments, and have high proportions of nonentry employees in addition to high proportions of professional, technical, and managerial workers.

Research on job ladders and career lines within organizations shows that job sequences are constrained by the organizational demography of job vacancies (see review by Baron, 1984) and again reflect distinctions that extend beyond occupational or skill groupings. Analysis of job transitions reported in the 1970 census (Spenner, Otto, and Call, 1982, chap. 5) shows skill level to be only weakly related to differentiation in the number of job avenues open from the job held in 1965 or to the skill distance of the job transition. Although the number of ports of entry and exit and the percentage entering from outside the labor force are more strongly related to skill level, order in job chains is more consistently related to sector location. DiPrete's (1987) preliminary analyses of the Washington office of four bureaus of the federal government between 1975 and 1978 show the permeability of occupationally based job series. Particularly striking is the crossing of occupational boundaries in filling professional vacancies (presumably requiring task-specific expertise) and the importance of positional location within a division for job sequencing.

TECHNOLOGICAL DETERMINISM OF WORK

A technological basis for work structures and control was a pervasive theme of organizational research during the 1960s (Blauner, 1964; Harvey, 1968; Perrow, 1967; Stinchcombe, 1965; Woodward, 1965). While unidimensional treatments of technology proved oversimplified (Burns and Stalker, 1961; Hickson, Pugh, and Pheysey, 1969; Lawrence and Lorsch, 1969), technology remained a critical feature defining organizational environments and requisite modes of organizing work and labor. Alternate technologies varying in their mix of labor and capital expenditures might exist; once selected, the formal design of the technology became a given. Technological changes in modes of production were assumed to follow a specific organizing logic affecting the social organization of production.

The imperatives of technology have, however, been questioned in both "sociotechnical" (Cooper and Foster, 1971; Trist, 1981) and "conflict" (Zimbalist, 1979, pp. xii-xvii) models of innovation. While it is assumed that technological change affects the organization of work, a range of possible modes of implementation are also assumed. The effects of technology on jobs and the work force are no longer viewed as inevitable outcomes but the product of multiple and reciprocal constraints of a technical and nontechnical nature. In this context, attempts to make economywide or even industrialwide generalizations about new technologies (let alone forecasts—see critique by Hunt and Hunt, 1985) are seldom received without controversy. In particular, two related issues have received considerable attention: the technological displacement of workers and the impact of technology on the content of work.

There is general agreement that technological innovation has the capacity to create new jobs and eliminate others. However, the location of these shifts and their net impact on employment can vary dramatically across technologies, industries, commodities, and combinations thereof. Two independent reviews of studies examining employment patterns associated with the implementation of technology fail to identify consistent outcomes (Attewell and Rule, 1984; Kraft, 1985). Moreover, each assessment notes alternative interpretations of changes in occupational distributions, including the supply

of labor and economic expansion. Similarly, the impact of technology on the content of work is found to be quite variable, reducing requisite skills in some respects but increasing others (see reviews by Attewell, 1987; Attewell and Rule, 1984; Kraft, 1985; Spenner, 1983, 1985). And, again, changes in job content can be linked to variables other than any inherent technological imperative.

Recognition of the contingencies surrounding the implementation of technology has developed largely with increasing knowledge of the diffusion of innovations—a social process in which subjectively perceived information is communicated, evaluated, and adapted (Rogers, 1983). While the vast body of diffusion research examines *individual* recognition and adoption of technology, recent attempts to develop organizational models of innovation are informed by this research and have been modified to fit an organizational context. Rogers outlines the following stages in the innovation process in organizations (1983, p. 363):

I. Initiation
1. *Agenda-setting*. General organizational problems, which may create a perceived need for an innovation, are defined; the environment is searched for innovations of potential value to the organization.
2. *Matching*. A problem from the organization's agenda is considered together with an innovation, and the fit between them is planned and designed.

II. Implementation
3. *Redefining/Restructuring*
   (a) The innovation is modified and re-invented to fit the situation of the particular organization and its perceived problem.
   (b) Organizational structures are altered to accommodate the innovation.
4. *Clarifying*. The relationship between the innovation and the organization is defined more clearly as the innovation is put into full and regular use.
5. *Routinizing*. The innovation eventually loses its separate identity and becomes an element in the organization's ongoing activities.

The model emphasizes the negotiated character of innovation and uncertainty of outcomes. Information about technology is itself structured by communication channels, interpreted in the context of existing social arrangements, conceptually fitted to the particular organizational framework, and accordingly acted upon itself—

furthering emergent understandings of the technology. Organizations are not merely receptive or unreceptive to technological change but themselves defining of its forms of implementation. They are the creators of the structural and administrative imperatives with which the technology comes to be associated. However, in contrast to the substantial literature on the diffusion of technology, the managerial practices associated with technology have received little attention. Kimberly (1981, p. 87) hypothesizes that organizations may be especially sensitive to the status of organizations previously adopting the innovation and establish managerial practices by imitation. The widespread sense of technologies as having inherent administrative imperatives may stem from an automatic, prepackaged acceptance of the managerial forms accompanying technological innovations.

The mechanisms producing such a rapid diffusion and consistency of practice to be characterized as imitation are, however, in question. It is generally agreed that uncertainties about the costs and benefits of innovation are seldom individually resolved (Rogers, 1983, chap. 8). The greater the ambiguity about the innovation, the more likely that network ties will be a significant basis for defining acceptable practice and risk. Kimberly (1981, p. 87) argues that an important feature of managerial innovation is its less tangible basis of evaluation, making it especially subject to network influence. Moreover, the status of having adopted a new technology may strengthen ties such that consensus about the appropriate organization of jobs and labor in relation to the technology is quickly achieved.

While not imperative, the managerial practices associated with new technology can take on a standardized form seemingly unquestioned by adopters. Ironically, the organization need not have identified internal problems that the managerial innovation addresses. Rather, the mere knowledge of an innovative form can spur organizational review (March, 1981). Indeed, Rogers (1983, p. 363) depicts organizations as continuously scanning for innovations in general and matching any promising innovation found with some relevant problem.

Although such boundary scanning could operate through interpersonal communication networks in which the cohesive forces of frequent and empathic communication lead to a mutually derived consensus about the costs and benefits of innovation (Coleman, Katz, and Menzel, 1966), the pace and consistency of diffusion characterized as "imitation" suggests a network model based on structural equivalence (Burt, 1982). In this model, innovation is evaluated in the context of competitive relationships.

> [T]he trigger to ego's adoption is adoption by the people with whom he jointly occupies a position in the social structure, the people who could replace him in his role relations if he were removed from the social structure. . . . Once the occupants of his status begin adopting, ego is expected to follow suit rapidly in order to avoid the embarrassment of being the last to espouse a belief or practice that has become a recognized feature of occupying his status [Burt, 1987, p. 1294].

In the structural equivalence model, personal contact and exchange are not essential for behavioral consensus. As DiMaggio and Powell note of mimetic processes (1983, p. 151), "The modeled organization may be unaware of the modeling or may have no desire to be copied; it merely serves as a convenient source of practices that the borrowing organization may use." In the absence of interpersonal exchange, diffusion can be rapid and practices are unlikely to be modified.

The impression of technology as creating administrative imperatives appears to stem more from the social structure of competitive relationships in the market rather than interpersonal patterns of influence. For example, David Noble's (1979) account of automated, machine-tracing technology points to competition for U.S. Air Force contracts as a principal force underpinning the diffusion of hi-tech numerical control technology over more cost-effective methods of machine tracing among military contractors. He finds that alternate methods fell into the status of quaint, simplistic options unattractive to the producers of automation. Hi-tech solutions were required for competitive status. Commercial users, not operating on a "cost-plus" basis and producing smaller lots, though aware of alternative modes of tracing technology, failed to pursue their implementation, following instead the lead of the large military contractors. Noble attributes the decision to emulate the military contractors to common management ideologies about profitability. For example, the separation of programming and cutting operations was viewed as eliminating the human error of machinists on the shop floor and enforcing pacing specifications. Technology was copied as part of a constellation of management practices associated with the most profitable applications of machine-tracing, the military contract. Although seemingly natural to follow from the technology, neither management objective was achieved. The close attention and intervention of machinists on the shop floor were still required and pacing specifications were routinely overridden. In practice, alternate modes of implementing the technology evolved, modifying a system that was initially copied as a management imperative for the technology.

External frames of reference decidedly affect organizational conceptions of labor and task activity. Yet, in reviewing the treatment of gender, education, occupation, and technology, in no instance are organizational interpretations a simple translation of these macro-templates. Jobs are defined and structured within an organizational milieu capable of refining and transforming these broad conceptual maps. It is instructive to note the general fluidity of job sets within organizations. Rosenbaum (1984) reports that over a three-year period in the large corporation studied, only 76% of nonmanagement jobs, 73% of foreman-level jobs, and 56% of lower management jobs were in existence at the beginning and end of the period. Over a 13-year period the stabilities dropped to 53%, 46%, and 22%, respectively. Such dramatic change in the set of jobs composing task structures suggests that job configurations do not solely reflect the attributes of the labor force, occupational distinctions, or technology. Rather, the treatment of jobs must be organizationally based. Such fluidity also directs attention to individual control over work arrangements.

Individual Negotiation of the Work Role: Job Molding

The preceding sections treat the workplace as a preestablished environment in which workers hold jobs. The job exists independent of and prior to the person, and the named job is assumed to be clearly defined and precisely placed. Although the separation of person from office and formalization are fundamental to the prototype of bureaucratic organization, in practice jobs are seldom as concretely defined as the model implies. Recognition of the ambiguities surrounding job content developed mainly from studies of organizational socialization investigating the level of correspondence between workers' and employers' beliefs and expectations about the work process (see overviews by Graen, 1983; Katz, 1980, pp. 92-102; Roos and Starke, 1981, pp. 296-297; Sproull, 1981, pp. 212-214; Wanous, 1980). These studies evidence the uncertainties facing entering employees and processes of resolution in which work roles are

enacted. Under extreme ambiguity, jobs are better described as negotiated than learned. Strauss et al.'s (1963) study of experimental psychiatric wards is a poignant example of staff negotiation of work roles and coins the term "negotiated order." Similarly, evolved work roles have been reported by Blau and Alba (1982) in a psychiatric facility for severely disturbed and handicapped children. Their quantitative analysis of network relationships showed the influence derived from bureaucratic bases of power to be mitigated by strategic responsibility (the degree of unit involvement with children on a daily basis) and system integration (the level of exchange with other units).

Underlying developmental models of job enactment is the assumption that individuals actively pursue order and meaning in their experiences and that they will strive to achieve strategic influence over their activities (Dachler and Wilpert, 1978; Katz, 1980; Weick, 1969). Even in circumstances of limited manipulation, the inventiveness and imagination of workers to construct strategic games has been repeatedly observed (Burawoy, 1979; Crozier, 1964; Garson, 1975; Roethlisberger and Dickson, 1939; Roy, 1958; Terkel, 1974). However, despite recognition that jobs evolve in the context of interpersonal interaction, job molding as a general phenomenon and its organizational significance has not received concentrated attention. Rather, a more delimited context has been emphasized —workers' attempts to influence or circumvent a preexisting production process. Thus, for example, employees' pacing of work has been largely addressed as a control or resistance strategy (Roy, 1952; Shapiro-Perl, 1984) rather than as job defining. Yet, there is evidence that employees' patterns of pacing become incorporated into the local management of the production process and fundamental to making the job work out for the employee and the company. For example, Burawoy's (1979) telling account points to the cooperation and participation of foremen and scheduling men in output restriction, which establishes a continuity in the production process that is relied upon by management.

More systematic knowledge of the degree of latitude open to workers in how they carry out their jobs, the relative time frame for achieving such adjustments, and the scope of change possible remains fragmentary. Over half (54%) of the workers surveyed in the 1977 Quality of Employment Survey (Quinn and Staines, 1979, p. 193) estimate that they would have at least some difficulty getting particular duties of their jobs changed. Studies of employees' participation in management show workers' perceived control to seldom reach desired influence or to be equal with that of management (Bartolke et al., 1982; Kavcic and Tannenbaum, 1981; Long, 1981; Tannenbaum et al., 1974). Moreover, even in systems conceptually designed to promote workers' participation, workers' control appears to erode over time (Derber and Schwartz, 1983; Kavcic and Tannenbaum, 1981; Long, 1981; Russell, 1985). Specific control over shop floor activities, skill utilization, and job design remains minimal (Koopman et al., 1981; Strauss, 1982, pp. 248-249).

Although workers develop specialized knowledge about task idiosyncrasies (Williamson, 1975), workers' control over task activity appears limited and only gradually implemented. Incompatibilities with formal hierarchical structures, the division of labor, contract provisions, and individual expertise and motivation, have all been cited as constraints (Dachler and Wilpert, 1978; Russell, 1985, pp. 53-64; Serrin, 1986; Whyte et al., 1983). Kohn and Schooler's (1983) national longitudinal study of the reciprocal effects of work and personality flags the strong impact of men's intellectual flexibility on job conditions, but their analysis suggests that men's control over job conditions is primarily achieved through job changes. To the extent that job molding occurs, it is primarily a gradual (longitudinal) process, not contemporaneous. This interpretation is consistent with developmental theories of organizational socialization that view worker-initiated innovation as possible only after the employee has established a role identity and situational definitions (Feldman, 1976; Katz, 1980). Moreover, jobs vary in malleability and the initiative they inspire. Nicholson's (1984) model of work role transitions highlights the interplay of job and person and the bounded character of job molding. He posits that individual initiative in role innovation is determined by the level of discretion open to the worker, novelty of job demands, and prior job socialization.

Current research on job molding provides only a general outline of the scope of workers' influence over job redesign and has not addressed the reciprocal relationship between job and worker.[5] Limited manipulation of tasks and procedures appears commonplace and fundamental to the enactment of work roles. However, the conditions under which job characteristics are dramatically transformed and organizationally redefined as a result of individual initiative are certainly more rare. Even work programs promoting cooperative participation in decision making appear to reach bounds that,

in practice, grant workers input but not authority. This is not to say, however, that job molding of limited scope is inconsequential.

The concept of evolved jobs and their enduring significance for job structures is pursued in the work of Miner and Estler (Miner, 1985; Miner and Estler, 1985). Evolved jobs are identified as task configurations that transcend expected patterns of job growth and transition and develop around the activities and abilities of the incumbent. They hypothesize that evolved jobs may be a significant vehicle by which organizations can experiment and possibly "discover" new organizing logics for particular work. In Miner's study of nonfaculty university personnel (1985), between 1% and 2% of jobs per year were officially reclassified as new positions created around the evolved duties of the incumbent. Moreover, evolved jobs were more likely to appear in departments with greater resource uncertainty and mission ambiguity—exactly the circumstances in which individual motivation for role management and the organization's need to be adaptive should be greatest. If retained beyond the initiator's incumbency, such positions could, over time, dramatically alter job structures and be an important component of organizational change.

There is some evidence that evolved jobs can, over time, have substantial impact on organizational functioning. Stewman (1986) identifies job evolution and relocation in an organizational structure as an important source of job vacancies. In his study of state police, he found that 22%-27% of the vacancies in top management positions between 1949 and 1969 could be attributed to jobs that had been redefined and relocated in the organization. Although forces external to the organization may stimulate such redefinition, Stewman focuses attention on internal processes involved in job evolution. In particular, he points to the role of job incumbents in such change.

Perhaps even more fundamental for work organizations than the evolution of new positions are the integrative functions of job molding. Even the limited accommodation of job to person is increasingly viewed as a critical mechanism maintaining social cohesion within the workplace (Burawoy, 1979; Crozier and Friedberg, 1980, pp. 45-63; Derber and Schwartz, 1983). Workers' manipulation of the people, machines, and procedures regulating the conditions of work creates the individual challenge and felt autonomy essential for job involvement and required for strategic functioning on the job. Workers thus engaged become part of the cooperative fabric of the production process that sustains the organizational system. As long as the worker can achieve some mastery over his or her work role, the playing of the game itself legitimizes its rules and contributes to its continued viability. The individual achieves a sense of competence and control from these job experiences—and probably financial reward for optimum performance. The company benefits from the enhanced functioning and stability of the production structure it created.

The significance of job molding in working life is also suggested by the importance workers attach to the intrinsic attributes of their jobs. Autonomy, self-direction, and the psychological engagement of challenging and interesting tasks are repeatedly cited as critical features of work. Studies of the relative emphasis and concern placed on specific job characteristics (Agassi, 1982; Quinn and Shepard, 1974; Sheppard and Herrick, 1972), the job conditions defining a "good" job (Jencks, Perman, and Rainwater, 1988); and the psychological consequences of job conditions (discussed below) support the contention that meaning in work is derived from its content and that workers recognize and pursue such engagement. Although job molding may, in practice, be highly delimited in its scope, it appears to be a significant process through which work roles are negotiated, involvement is elicited, and the social cohesion necessary for production is maintained. Further, it focuses attention on the process through which meaning is derived from work and its individual consequences.

The Psychological Outcomes of Work Experience

Vocational guidance and personnel management have been dominated by theories of career development that stress proper selection into jobs as the critical determinant of personal adjustment and good job performance (Holland, 1973; Lofquist and Dawis, 1969). This view of employment outcomes deemphasizes adult socialization to work roles after organizational entry, the social context that shapes perceptions of task activities, and the impact of job conditions on the individual. The perspective reflects its origins. The approach is rooted in educational research addressing career preparation, occupational knowledge, and vocational interests— aspects of development directly influenced by schooling and embodied in its product. In this context, specific conditions of employment represent a separate domain in the sense that they are established after schooling and are not directly influenced by the educational institution. The application of "selection" models in personnel management may reflect its historical connections to education professions. It is also instructive to note the physical separation of personnel departments from production units where the consequences of work conditions would be more directly viewed (Jacoby, 1985). More important, however, was the advent of scientific management, which stressed the matching of the employee to the demands of task activity. Attention was thus focused on the fit of the person to the job (getting the right person for the job) and away from job conditions and their effects on workers.

This perspective complemented a neoclassical economic view of human capital. As Spenner (1985, p. 199) summarizes, "In neoclassical economics, workers' tastes and preferences are features of labor supply and, therefore, are exogenous to the job structure. Tastes and preferences are: (a) more or less fixed upon entry into the labor force; (b) causes of occupational selection and productivity in jobs; and (c) are largely impervious to occupational experiences (Cain, 1976; Darity, 1982)." In addition, psychology's concentration on child and adolescent development implicitly left adult functioning to be treated as given until the point of biological deterioration.

The impetus for detailed investigation of the effects of work experience on the individual stemmed from: (1) behavioral research on productivity within industry (Roethlisberger and Dickson, 1939; Trist and Bamforth, 1951), (2) social critiques of technological change and the dysfunctions of bureaucracy (Bell, 1956; Merton, 1968, pp. 249-260, 616-627), and (3) research on professional socialization (see review by Mortimer and Simmons, 1978, pp. 434-440). Though later research following these traditions retained distinctive features, each evolved to focus on the structural differentiation of work environments and workers' reactions to job conditions. Building on behavioral approaches, Turner and Lawrence (1965) conceived of "requisite task attributes" as the objective dimensions of work that define its fundamental nature, allow the conditions of work in different occupations and industries to be compared, and directly affect work attitudes, behavior, and health—a path also pursued by Kornhauser (1965). Blauner (1964) investigated the diversity of industrial contexts in terms of varying technologies, the conditions of work they create, and the resulting psychological alienation of the worker (also see Seeman, 1967). Similarly, research on increasingly occupational socialization elaborated the organizational context of work roles and individual functioning. For example, Kahn et al. (1964) investigated the organizational antecedents of role relationships, sources of stress in these role relationships, and the physical and mental health outcomes of these experiences.

In focusing on the structural differentiation of job conditions, a fundamental question was posed by each of these lines of inquiry: From what underlying factors do task activities derive their significance for the individual? The depiction of motion, cognition, and communication in work had to be formed into a conceptual model that described its nature.

The Conceptualization of Task Activity and its Effects

Conceptual schemes for analyzing task characteristics abound.[6] Each attempts to profile critical dimensions of work conditions, work behaviors, and/or work demands. In some schemes, job information is organized in relationship to a behavioral model of work. For example, McCormick, Jeanneret, and Mecham (1972) emphasize a job's information input, mediation processes, work output, and relationships to others. While such an approach describes what the worker is doing and its context, it does not draw out the cognitive significance of the task activity. In contrast, social-psychological models of task activities emphasize sources of gratification/deprivation in work that give it meaning. For example, the performance of skilled activities would not be coded in terms of their frequency or importance in the job but in terms of their level of complexity, autonomy, responsibility, interest, or challenge. A distinction between job conditions emanating from the intrinsic features of task activity (what Herzberg, 1976, called "motivators") and the extrinsic circumstances of the job (so-called hygiene factors) is common in this research. Though it is sometimes difficult to decide what is inherent to the doing of tasks and what is a peripheral circumstance or condition, it is believed that the psychological gratification/deprivation derived from these realms are different. For example, Herzberg (1976) contended that the pay and benefits of a job might create dissatisfactions, but did not in themselves make work enriching and thus would not be expected to be primary determinants of job involvement. While the dichotomy is certainly too simplistic a model of work's psychological ramifications, it has been useful in drawing attention to the inherent qualities of task activity from which meaning is derived.

Though social-psychological approaches to job analysis share a concern with the significance of task activity for the individual, there is by no means agreement on what are the most critical dimensions of work or the processes through which they have impact. Most perspectives view the worker as a purposive organism and a reflexive monitor of the environment. Employment is treated as task experience that differentially activates (engages) the organism depending on its conditions. From here, however, approaches diverge. A need for self-actualization is ordinarily incorporated (or not inconsistent) as motivating attention to work stimuli and defining classes of stimuli as positive (rewarding) or negative. However, needs for self-actualization can be treated as universal (Herzberg, 1976), hierarchically activated (Maslow, 1943; and Alderfer's revision, 1972), or conditional on personality (Hackman and Lawler, 1971; Kahn et al., 1964) and background (Hulin and Blood, 1968; Turner and Lawrence, 1965). Further, need for self-actualization in work is alternatively viewed as innate to the organism or itself the product of social experience and/or cognition (see Gurin and Brim's discussion of psychological needs and their implications for adult change in self, 1984, pp. 298-309).

At the root of these variations are important differences in the depiction of the dynamics through which job conditions affect behavior and orientations. In sociology, three perspectives have been especially prominent: (1) learning theory, (2) expectations theory, and (3) theories of stress and coping processes. While each perspective has developed to incorporate aspects of the others, distinctions remain and represent different research foci.

LEARNING THEORY

Classical and social learning theory has been drawn upon in depictions of work as a stimulus-complex to which the organism responds. As such, task activity and the work environment is a source of experiential feedback providing reinforcement (Skinner, 1953), social comparison (Festinger, 1954), and models of response that are imitated (Miller and Dollard, 1941). Behavior is conceptualized as a response to its consequences—its instrumental rewards and deprivations. Moreover, there is an implicit psychological response in which the organism seeks outcomes that are satisfying and learns to avoid behavior that is expected to evoke negative feedback. Not only is behavior affected by experience but so are abstract orientations toward objects and processes. Drawing on Parsons's theory of action (Parsons et al., 1951), Breer and Locke (1965) identify cognitive knowledge of instrumentality, cathectic attachment toward rewarded behavior, and evaluation of legitimacy as learned in task experience as well. These "lessons" of experience provide for the transfer of learning. In abstracting from the specific circumstances of stimuli-response-feedback, behavior and orientations are generalized to other domains. Despite concern with the mental processing of experience implicit in "generalized response" to reinforcement (Skinner, 1953), "generalized psychological pattern" (Festinger, 1957), and "generalized imitation" (Gewirtz and Stingle, 1968), learning theory retains its emphasis on the nature of stimuli and the consequences of behavior. It remains a model of "observables" (Lott and Lott, 1985).

Not surprisingly, research on responses to task experience that apply this perspective emphasizes the objective conditions of task activity. Kohn and Schooler's (1983) study of the effects of job conditions illustrates the approach. They use detailed descriptions of task activity involving data, people, and things; reported repetitiveness and variety of tasks; and reports about how much latitude is allowed and how supervisory control is exercised to measure self-directed work experience. Note that it is the intention of this approach (within the constraints of a survey interview framework) to measure what a worker does, who determines how it is done, and its social circumstances rather than the worker's appraisal of whether he or she is doing complex work, whether it is boring or interesting, and the worker's felt sense of freedom. Yet, the model is far from behavioral; for it is the social-psychological experience of self-direction that is hypothesized to underlie the impact of these job conditions on the worker. Kohn and Schooler are silent on whether self-direction gratifies a need for self-actualization in the organism; however, self-direction in work is always characterized as a positive, enhancing experience and of importance for diverse aspects of psychological functioning. It appears, then, to be a fundamental reward of work and a stimulus to which the organism is attentive. If self-direction is central because of needs for self-actualization, the need is treated as universal. Kohn and Schooler's basic model examines the effects of job conditions as general determinants of psychological functioning—not conditional on growth needs, background, or other internal motivations. Also in keeping with the learning-generalization model is Kohn and

Schooler's depiction of the process as a direct transfer of learning, without attention to how job experience is cognitively or emotionally interpreted. Psychological reactions to job conditions (for example, felt satisfaction or stress) would themselves be viewed as learned responses, the product of objective job conditions. There is no assumption that the nature of job experience need be consciously realized for it to affect the worker.

EXPECTANCY THEORY

Expectancy theory is not so much an alternative to learning theory's stimulus-response model of behavior as a particular line of elaboration in which the cognitive interpretation of stimuli and feedback are emphasized (Lawler, 1973; Vroom, 1964). As in learning theory, attention to stimuli is related to the needs and purposeful orientation of the organism (Vroom, 1964, p. 13). However, as developed by Lawler (1973, pp. 11-40), needs and need strength are viewed as differentiating perceptions of stimuli and the importance (valence) that will be attached to particular stimulus. Lawler draws upon Maslow's (1943) and Alderfer's (1972) need classifications to specify what will be valued and thus the more critical source of reward/deprivation for an individual at any given time. In Lawler's elaboration there is an important distinction been learning theory and expectancy theory in that the "value" placed on a particular experience is not learned in responding to stimuli. Rather, the valence of stimuli is linked to needs that are viewed as the product of heredity and childhood experience (Lawler, 1973, p. 38). This contrast is less clear in Vroom's writings. Vroom (1964, p. 15) treats the perceived valence of stimuli as a function of anticipated satisfaction—a property learned, in part, in response to stimuli. However, individuals are presumed to differ in the satisfaction derived from response to the same stimuli depending on value. Vroom does not pursue the origins of differential gratification. In any case, in both treatments response to a particular stimulus is conditional on the perception of its valence.

The mechanisms producing a connection between stimuli and response (what is learned from the consequences of behavior) also differ in expectancy and learning theory. Social learning theory focuses on abstract orientations toward emitted behavior—cathectic attachment toward rewarded behavior, cognitive knowledge of instrumentality, and evaluation of legitimacy. Expectancy theory focuses on the interpreted efficiency of behavior—the subjective probability that an act will be followed by an outcome. Though overlapping with cognitive knowledge of instrumentality and perhaps evaluation of legitimacy (a normative judgment), it is a narrower and more particular definition of what is learned from the consequences of behavior. It is explicitly a model of *subjective beliefs* motivating response to stimuli.

Kalleberg's (1977) research on work values and job rewards incorporates central elements of expectancy theory and illustrates its applied ramifications. Using the 1972-1973 Quality of Employment Survey, the study delineates job "rewards" that consist of the worker's reports of the *perceived* level of particular job characteristics in their work. In many instances, it is the worker's assessment of the quality of the task experience (e.g., the work is interesting; the pay is good), not its objective character that is reported. The measures are defended as capturing the critical nature of task activity as the worker experiences it. This operationalization of job conditions is, of course, also the product of the survey instrument. But in this case, the limitations of the data are themselves revealing, for the design of the questionnaire was itself influenced by expectancy theory (Cammann et al., 1983). Kalleberg's model also incorporates the value (importance) the worker places on particular job conditions in an effort to capture the conscious meaning that the worker attaches to the work role. Together, work values and work rewards are used to measure workers' subjective assessments of the jobs they perform—perceptions that are hypothesized to determine their job satisfaction.

STRESS AND COPING THEORIES

Stress and coping theories of job outcomes also focus on the subjective experience of job conditions but more precisely develop the nature of the relationship between objective and perceived conditions of work and the conditions under which this relationship results in positive or negative outcomes. In contrast to learning and expectancy theories, this approach gives less attention to what activates attention to job stimuli or what lessons are learned through task activity. In this sense, it is not a stimulus-response model of behavior. Rather, it is better described as a model of fit in which the capacities and resources of the organism and demands of the job interact. Stress and coping research can also be understood in terms of its association with studies of medical pathology—a model that emphasizes trauma, vulnerability,

and dysfunction (see review by Kessler, Price, and Wortman, 1985). The approach has ramifications for (1) what dimensions of work are viewed as significant experience, (2) the psychological mechanisms depicted as underlying reactions to work, and (3) the specific outcomes addressed.

Stress models of job conditions have ordinarily focused on sources of adversity in job experience: disruptive events and chronic pressures (Pearlin et al., 1981), role conflict and ambiguity (Kahn et al., 1964), and relative deprivations and pressures resulting from mismatching of the preferences/abilities of the worker to the demands/rewards of the job (Caplan et al., 1980; French, Caplan, and Van Harrison, 1982; Pearlin and Schooler, 1978). The description of task activity is not addressed from the neutral stance of "stimuli" activating the organism. Rather, the job is assessed in terms of "stressors," that is, agitation of the organism. Note that the activation of the organism is not the result of excitation but trauma—an abnormal state, the disruption of homeostasis. In this context, unexpected events or changing conditions, disequilibrium in role expectations, and misfit between job and worker are the natural places to look for the wounds of work.

The adequacy of this view of task activity as a description of job experience depends upon the meaning of the poles of the scales used to reflect stressors and the range of circumstances examined. For example, the absence of "negative" work events or situations need not be equivalent to the absence of "positive" work circumstances. Exclusive preoccupation with the adverse pole may distort the conditions experienced by the worker. Also, the significance of opposite poles (and what should be interpreted as an agitator) will vary by what is being predicted. For example, French et al. (1982, appendix C) show that demands/rewards of work in *relative excess* of abilities/preferences versus *relative deficiency* versus *poor fit in either direction* vary widely in their correlations with psychological outcomes. Defining agitators in the objective work environment (independent of its outcomes) is itself a difficult theoretical question still unresolved.

Although stress models recognize disequilibrium to exist in objective circumstances, the subjective assessment of component conditions and their relative balance is considered the critical definition of stressors. As in expectancy theory, subjective perception is the dynamic motivating the organism. Response to stressors is thus treated as inherently conditional on organism interpretation. In stress theory, however, there is the biomedical assumption that equilibrium is the normal state for the organism and that there will be efforts to adapt in order to maintain balance—just as bodily processes in normal functioning promote healing. Stress models explicitly posit both subjective perceptions and reactions to job conditions to be conditional on the individual's ability to adapt through coping resources, which include both personal attributes and situational factors. In other words, vulnerabilities are taken into account in the prognosis of outcomes.[7]

Finally, the clinical orientation of stress research is seen in the outcomes investigated. Mental health (depression, anxiety, dissatisfaction, self-concept) and physical health have been the central focus of stress research (see review by Kessler et al., 1985). In contrast, research following learning theory perspectives has generally addressed a broader spectrum of personality outcomes, including intellective processes and social orientations, but few physical outcomes. In not applying biomedical assumptions, expectancy theory has closely focused on the work orientations resulting from the subjective assessment of task activities.

Some variants of the stress and coping model described above are noteworthy because they draw upon elements more characteristic of learning theory and expectancy theory approaches. These include: (1) the elaboration of coping techniques and the integration of more general psychological states as outcomes of experience and (2) the inclusion of objective job conditions.

Most studies of coping resources have focused on external sources of support. There have, however, been efforts to investigate the internal resources through which people cope (Lazarus, 1966; Pearlin et al., 1981). These psychological and action strategies are not treated as personality traits but strategies learned and applied in the context of specific problems (Pearlin and Schooler, 1978, and Folkman and Lazarus, 1980). Menaghan and Merves (1984) explicitly present coping efforts as responses to current occupational problems that are selectively employed, in part, on the basis of past experience with earlier problems and the effectiveness of coping strategies. Similarly, general cognitive orientations, such as mastery and self-esteem (Pearlin et al., 1981) and fatalism and inflexibility (Wheaton, 1980, 1983) have been investigated as consequences of stressors and not solely as conditioning variables.

There have also been efforts to measure and assess the direct effects of objective job conditions on the perceived stress and psychological outcomes of work. House (1980) uses company

and expert judges' rating of job demands for 21 *occupational* groupings to predict factory workers' perceptions of stress and health outcomes in over 200 different jobs. While he finds objective ratings of occupational conditions to be related to the perceived stress of particular jobs, the correlations are weak.[8] James and Jones (1980) show a stronger relationship using the objective ratings of *job* characteristics but again show discrepancy between objective and perceived conditions.

These findings underscore the subjective nature of *perceived* stress. For example, House (1980) finds *objective* job rewards to be positively correlated with the *objective* demands of the job. But workers *perceive* job rewards as incommensurate with *perceived* demands (they are negatively correlated). The lack of correspondence between objective and subjective measures of job stressors points to the need to elaborate the process of cognitive appraisal that operates. If perceived stressors exist apart from objective task dimensions, the question arises whether perceived stress can be conceptually and causally differentiated from the psychological outcomes they predict.[9] James and Jones (1980) show that the perception of job conditions to be reciprocally related to job satisfaction, with job satisfaction having a far greater impact on perceptions than the reverse (beta = .60 versus .24). Similar conclusions are reached by O'Reilly, Parlette, and Bloom (1980) and Caldwell and O'Reilly (1982) in studies designed to hold job conditions constant.

One perspective addressing the lack of correspondence between objective and perceived job conditions is the information-processing model proposed by Salancik and Pfeffer (1978). This perspective suggests that the meaning of task activity will be interpreted in the context of information in the social environment and the individual's past attitudes and behaviors. There is some experimental evidence that subjects' perceptions of task characteristics will be influenced by the social information they are given about task content. O'Reilly and Caldwell (1979), Weiss and Shaw (1979), and White and Mitchell (1979) manipulated external information about tasks as being enriching or depriving work experiences. These studies found that external ratings independently influenced subjects' evaluation of task content. Salancik and Pfeffer (1978) also point to instances of cognitive dissonance (e.g., hard work with insufficient justification) resulting in positive responses to task circumstances as evidence of behavior-influencing interpretation of task activity.

The inclusion of objective job conditions in

stress and coping research also opens the question of whether vulnerabilities are themselves the product of objective job circumstances. Take, for instance, the place of work in social support. Social support is clearly contingent on access to people and resources. Employment per se greatly expands one's social capital. Moreover, access varies by the circumstances of employment. Fischer (1982, pp. 103-105) finds in his study of northern Californian communities that involvement with coworkers is affected by number of hours worked, shift, self-employed/employee status, and years at present job. Lincoln and Miller (1979) find in a study of organizations employing professionals that both instrumental and friendship ties are structured by positional authority. Similarly, Olson and Miller's (1983) study of a white-collar firm shows that positional rank has a strong effect on the level of contact, support, and influence derived from social networks in the workplace because of centrality in patterns of interaction. Pugliesi (1986) suggests that the complexity and autonomy/control of task activity can affect the social support derived from work relationships by constraining the level and type of personal interactions in which the worker is involved. Her study of employed women suggests that job characteristics influence the availability and use of intimate contacts. Although House (1980, p. 148) fails to find a relationship between *occupational* conditions and perceived social support (but see note 8), the findings discussed above call for further investigation of the issue.

The Effects of Job on Person

As noted at the beginning of this section, the effects of job conditions on the individual stand in contrast to an interpretation that views the outcomes of work as a matter of selection, properly or improperly implemented. In the extreme, "selection" models imply that there is a correspondence between job conditions and workers' orientations only because of self-selection and recruitment, which deliberately or inadvertently select for individual predispositions or personality types. This unidirectional view (person determines job outcome) is not supported by longitudinal research able to control for earlier functioning and disaggregate the reciprocal relationship between job conditions and psychological functioning. Kohn and Schooler's (1983) national study of men in the civilian labor force shows selection to operate but demonstrates that workers are also responsive to numerous conditions of their employment—

especially the substantive complexity of the work.[10] Similarly, Mortimer, Lorence, and Kumka's (1986) analysis of a follow-up of the Michigan Student Study shows work autonomy to affect self-concept, work involvement, and occupational values. The Quality of Employment Surveys panel data document the effects of work autonomy on work involvement (Lorence and Mortimer, 1985). Spenner and Otto (1985) find work history to affect self-concept in the Washington State Career Development Sample. Using the National Longitudinal Study of the High School Class of 1972, Lindsay and Knox (1984) show that job characteristics independently affect work values. However, these findings do not dispel more sophisticated versions of the selection hypothesis. Particularly prominent are models positing "buffering" and "mediation" of the effects of job on the worker.

THE BUFFERING HYPOTHESIS

Both expectancy theory and stress and coping research view workers reactions to job conditions as *conditional* on the "fit" of the worker to the job. Outcomes are not the direct consequences of job conditions but contingent on the personality, expectations, and resources of the worker. The contrast between learning theory and "fit" hypotheses is clearest in their prototypic answers to the question, "Why do two people doing the same type of work respond differently?" "Fit" models contend that individual differences in how conditions are perceived and reacted to are the obvious explanation. Learning theory directs attention to differences in the particular conditions of each's job and conditions outside of the job to which the worker also is responding.

Social support has probably received the greatest attention as a factor conditioning reactions to stress. There is substantial evidence that social support is itself psychologically beneficial; whether such support serves as a buffer against the deleterious effects of stressful life circumstances is debated (see, for example, the exchange between LaRocco, 1983, and Thoits, 1983). Studies investigating vulnerability to stressful life events with large samples and general population data are mixed in their findings. In their review of such community studies, Kessler and McLeod (1985) make a convincing case that extensiveness of network affiliations and frequency of contact do not have buffering effects. As Pearlin et al. (1981, p. 340) emphasize, there is an important distinction between potential resources from a social network and the support actually derived in times of trouble.[11]

While the empirical evidence marshalled by Kessler and McLeod points to emotional support as the more critical factor for buffering, the findings are again mixed—especially among longitudinal studies. Even those studies evidencing this conditional outcome must be closely examined. For example, Pearlin et al.'s (1981) Chicago panel study of stress and coping shows emotional intimacy to buffer against adverse effects of job disruption on self-esteem and mastery but not depression. Although emotional support may condition the deleterious outcomes of stressful circumstances, it appears to operate selectively.

The Chicago data also indicate that even if the impact of acute events (such as the loss of a job or demotion) may be partially ameliorated by effective coping mechanisms, the individual is not necessary protected from persistent job pressures. Menaghan and Merves's (1984) detailed analysis of chronic job stressors (work overload, depersonalization, inadequate extrinsic rewards, and noxious work environment) and individual coping efforts (direct action, relative comparisons, selective attention, and restricted expectations) shows no buffering of chronic work stressors on distress.

Reactions to job conditions have also been hypothesized to be conditional on the importance the worker places on particular job rewards. As discussed earlier, expectancy theory emphasizes selective sensitivities to perceived job experiences depending on the worker's values. Typically, however, the conditional impact of job conditions is not systematically tested against alternative specifications. Kalleberg (1977) shows that while job values and job rewards additively affect workers, an interaction model fails to increase the total variance explained. He also finds that highly valued rewards do not necessarily have greater impact on the worker than rewards that are unimportant to the worker.

More general personality factors have also been examined as conditioning reactions to stressors, including locus of control (Johnson and Sarason, 1978; Lefcourt, 1980), fatalism and inflexibility (Husaini et al., 1982; Wheaton, 1983), composite "hardiness" (Kobasa, Maddi, and Courington, 1981; Kobasa, Maddi, and Kahn, 1982), and Type A personality (French, Caplan, and van Harrison, 1982; House, 1980). Findings are again mixed, with stressful life events *in the aggregate* sometimes showing conditional effects depending on personality. However, studies specifically focusing on the effects of chronic job experiences do not find

systematic differences in the effects of job on person depending on personality (French, Caplan, and van Harrison, 1982; House, 1980).

It would be unfair to conclude at present that the effects of chronic job stressors are unconditional irrespective of social support, coping strategies, values, or personality. But even those studies commonly cited as evidencing buffering effects for job outcomes, in fact, report a mixed set of results. For example, LaRocco, House, and French (1980, p. 211) conclude from their cross-sectional analysis of the effects of role conflict, ambiguity, underutilization, participation, and workload, "there is no evidence that support buffers the relationship of perceived job stressors to job strains, such as job dissatisfaction and boredom with work." Further, buffering effects on mental health (depression, irritation, anxiety, somatic complaints) are selective and sometimes marginal ($p < .10$; see LaRocco, House, and French, 1980, Table 3, p. 210). House (1980) also notes interactions involving perceived social support in his cross-sectional study of factory workers. However, the directions of these effects are not only to buffer against deleterious outcomes. House's findings suggest that social support is as likely to dampen the benefits of positive job experiences. Such a pattern of results suggests detachment, not buffering. In some instances social support is found to amplify the stress-inducing effects of job characteristics. Only in the case of rather severe manifest symptoms (neurotic behavior, ulcers, and cough and phlegm) does social support buffer workers against the deleterious consequences of perceived job stressors and felt occupational distress. In sum, the buffering effects of social support again appear selective.

The Michigan study of Job Demands and Worker Health (Caplan et al., 1980; French, Caplan, and Van Harrison, 1982) also reports evidence of conditional job outcomes depending on the fit of a job relative to the preferences and abilities of the worker. In this work, the interaction between characteristics of the job and the person is measured as either a difference score or as a perceived-fit indicator such as the perceived underutilization of skills. The ability to differentiate "fit" from the additive components of these scores is critical. Unfortunately, the causal analyses employ a strategy that sidesteps a direct test of the additive versus fit model by using the single form of the variable that is the best predictor of a particular job outcome (Caplan et al., 1980, p. 63; French, Caplan, and Van Harrison, 1982, p. 62). While there is evidence that the fit of the person to a job has selective effects, it is never clear how much these effects would be attenuated if the effects of the additive components of the fit measures were included. Burris (1983) shows, for example, that the impact on job satisfaction of being over-educated for one's job is quite small when the additive effects of one's education and the educational requirements for the job are controlled. Only workers grossly overeducated for their positions appear to be somewhat more dissatisfied than one would predict. While fit is probably of some consequence for workers, the strength of its effect must be questioned.

In toto, the evidence of buffering against job stressors remains sketchy and ill-specified. Differential vulnerability to stressors may well operate but its role in determining the consequences of job experiences appears selective. It is difficult to draw general conclusions about what forms of vulnerabilities condition reactions to particular job experiences and the outcomes to which they are related. Very few studies focus on *chronic* conditions and none explicitly contrast different forms of vulnerability in this realm. The lack of systematic evidence documenting buffers against job stressors, focuses attention on the general psychological model of *additive* sources of experience that explain psychological functioning.

THE MEDIATION OF JOB EFFECTS

Buffering effects aside, stress and coping theories also posit *intervening* psychological states and resources that indirectly modify the effects of job conditions. Such explanations of how job conditions come to affect psychological functioning and illness are important because they imply that the deleterious consequences of job experiences can be counterbalanced by improving workers' coping resources and decreasing felt strain, which have positive benefits. In contrast, a learning-generalization model views the effects of job experiences as direct, not operating through felt strain, other aspects of personality, or social support. Regardless of whether a worker feels distressed by job circumstances or has resources to deal with problems, job experiences are posited to affect the worker. These contrasting perspectives raise two important questions: (1) Do job conditions (objective or perceived) have independent effects on functioning, irrespective of resources or the felt strains experienced by the worker? (2) If so, what is the relative importance of job conditions compared to these factors in determining the outcomes of work?

Although these questions are straightforward, they are difficult to answer because few studies have assessed both the direct and indirect effects of the relevant variables. Virtually all studies of stress/coping show social support, coping strategies, and felt strain to affect individual functioning; virtually all studies of work conditions show job characteristics (objective or perceived) to affect individual functioning. Very few studies have assessed both as competing explanations in an additive model that allows main effects to be statistically disaggregated in a fully controlled model. Pointing to the need for replication, the following analyses inform the issue.

Menaghan and Merves (1984) analyze the relative impact of chronic job stressors (work overload, depersonalization, inadequate extrinsic rewards, and noxious work environment) and coping efforts on occupational distress, controlling for background and social circumstances. While effective coping strategies (avoiding restricted expectations and optimistic comparisons) directly affect felt occupational distress, job stressors are by far the strongest direct determinants of occupational distress. Pearlin et al. (1981) focus on job disruption and income adequacy. The chronic pressure of income adequacy is found to be the major determinant of changes in self-esteem and mastery; job disruption, though less important, also exceeded the relative impact of coping and social support on self-concept. House (1980, p. 185) reports that in an additive model of the effects of social support and job conditions (perceived and objective) on job satisfaction and self-esteem, job conditions are the more important determinants. Social support has but a small effect on job satisfaction and no independent effect on self-esteem. Though the evidence is limited, all these analyses show job conditions to have independent direct effects on workers' self-concept and job satisfaction that are more important than the direct effects of social support or coping strategies.

As noted earlier, stress and coping models also posit that felt job distress (such as job satisfaction and self-concept) mediates the effects of objective or perceived job conditions on mental and physical health. This hypothesis is more difficult to evaluate because it makes the assumption that job distress is conceptually distinct from other psychological and physical states it is used to predict, and not itself a reflection or product of these states. However, even accepting this causal assumption, job conditions have been shown to have direct effects on mental and physical health. Pearlin et al. (1981) show that the direct effects of both job disruption and income adequacy on depression are as strong as the direct effects of self-esteem and mastery on depression. Only the effect of income adequacy is attenuated when self-esteem and mastery are controlled. In contrast, the effects of social support and coping techniques are totally mediated by these psychological states and they are shown to have no direct effects on depression. Similarly, House (1980) shows the effects of objective and perceived job conditions to be, in most cases, only slightly attenuated by the inclusion of job satisfaction and occupational self-esteem in models predicting life satisfaction and neurotic symptoms and these effects are significant. For physical health, the attenuation is trivial if it exists at all. Again, the direct effects of job experiences on functioning are underscored.

Available evidence indicates that job conditions directly affect both job distress and more general dimensions of functioning. The findings are consistent with a learning-generalization model—a process in which learning from the job is generalized to other realms of life, independently of social support, coping resources and self-concept, or felt strain. However, this evidence of learning-generalization is but a flag. It has not specified what is being learned or how. As noted earlier, social learning theory focuses on the abstract mental processing of experience—cathectic attachment toward rewarded behavior, cognitive knowledge of instrumentality, and evaluation of legitimacy (normative evaluation). However, we know little about how such reactions to job stimuli are derived and organized.

Cognitive interpretations of learned behavior (the view dominating psychology) link perceptions of activity and their outcomes to systems of representational encoding that exist apart from immediate experience. Selective perception and response are depicted as bias in cognitive schema (see review by Markus and Zajonc, 1985). In essence, the separation of mind from the environment (stimulus-complex) to which the actor responds extracts the worker from the workplace for further examination of his or her head. Although the failure of psychology to elaborate the interactive connection between cognitive structures and the environment receives increasing attention (Bandura, 1986), few psychologists are radical in their reinterpretation of *social* perception and learning.

An important and instructive exception is an approach termed an ecological perspective (see the collected papers of James Gibson edited by Reed and Jones, 1982: particularly chapter 4; Bickhard and Richie, 1983; and McArthur and Baron, 1983; Shaw, Turvey, and Mace, 1982).

It challenges cognitive models of perception to reincorporate dimensions of learning theory— the world of observables and the information they carry. Cognitive structures are not reified as independent, higher-order, representational entities existing in the head. Rather, ecological approaches stress the knowledge acquired through interaction with the environment. The perspective elaborates upon stimulus-response models in the emphasis placed on (1) the nature of stimulus-complexes, (2) the relationship between the perceiver and the perceived, and (3) the active involvement of the perceiver in extracting information from stimuli.

The mental processing involved is one of direct knowledge acquisition (learning) in which information is extracted from the detection of patterning. Awareness of structure is itself learned in interacting with stimuli. Thus it contrasts with a cognitive perspective in which patterning is indirectly inferred from the representational encoding of stimuli. What is learned may be selective, but its origin is in the structure of the patterning detected and not "bias" in cognitive representations. In a very real sense, from an ecological perspective, "perception is guided by opportunities for action in the environment" (Showers and Cantor, 1985, p. 280).

The model emphasizes that individual functioning must be analyzed in the context of structured relationships governing: (1) opportunities for interaction with stimuli, (2) the form, constancy, and consistency of patterning experienced, and (3) content. For, in this structuring, the observer/actor not only learns about the multifaceted properties of stimuli but their "affordances," *opportunities for acting or being acted upon, with reference to the observer.* These inform the observer about particular constraints and utilities that create sensitivities to particular stimulus information and guide adaptation. Two observers may well differ in their perceptions of stimuli but neither need be in "error." Rather, the differences may be explained by differences in affordances inherent in the structural position of each vis-a-vis the stimulus-complex. In other words, attention to stimuli and properties detected are interactively educated in the context of structure.

In work experiences, a social basis for structuring is readily seen in task differentiation and hierarchical groupings. In essence, the ecological perspective leads to a theory of job outcomes that intimately links perception to social structure. In exploratory work, Schwalbe (1985) investigates the kinds of information that workers draw out of job conditions that is relevant to self-esteem. He finds that information about the self is derived from diverse facets of job stimuli. Not only does the worker gain self-knowledge of actualization in doing autonomous work, but finds meaning in reflected appraisals and social comparisons. For example, the worker is able to detect supervisory evaluation of competence as well as relative social status in having autonomous work. Schwalbe's findings suggest that a coherent perception of one's self in the workplace stems in part from structured consistency in the information being detected. Not only has the content of "knowledge structures" been linked to the social structuring of stimuli but fundamental organizing logics also appear to be learned as a consequence of job experience (Kohn and Schooler, 1983). There is emerging agreement that intellectual flexibility may be one of the critical mechanisms governing the dynamics of information-processing (Kohn, 1980; Showers and Cantor, 1985; Wheaton, 1983).

If perception is a product of experiencing such structured patterning in stimuli and their learned affordances, then similar "realities" should be detected by persons similarly positioned in the social world. However, the significance of position must be thoroughly examined. Traditionally, sociology has emphasized socialization processes as mechanisms that imbue individuals with social knowledge of their roles and normative behavior. One's position in a social structure determines socialization experiences, and *when internalized*, these experiences influence orientations and behavior in circumstances where the role is salient. But, in the absence of a structural context specifying the *affordances* learned in interaction with stimuli, socialization (though a product of social structure) inevitably leads back to a view of perception that rests on mental encoding of stimuli as appropriate or inappropriate for one's role set. In contrast, ecological models go on to introduce the structural context of interaction with stimuli, by specifying the constraints and opportunities of action. Perception is grounded in the social context of stimulation, not the higher-order, mental representation of that knowledge.

The affordances of job stimuli and their importance in deriving meaning from work experiences can be illustrated by considering the structural context of supervision. It is common for workers doing very simple and routine tasks to have little direct supervision in their task activities. It is also common for workers doing very complex and variable tasks to have little supervision. Yet, the absence of supervision is likely to have entirely different "meanings" in these

two circumstances. In the latter case, the absence of supervision is likely to denote opportunity for self-direction, but in simple work, the absence of supervision may signify no autonomy by virtue of tasks being entirely prescribed. While one might hypothesize that differential socialization has lead these workers to behave differently in their respective jobs and thus initiate and sense different levels of self-direction in the absence of supervision, their structural circumstances cannot be ignored. Absence of supervision is experienced in the context of the structural autonomy of the actor: his or her centrality in a set of relationships and substitutability. Note that this information would be interactively derived in the course of doing one's job and thus has its origin in the stimulus-complex and not necessarily in socialization for role performance.

To my knowledge, the distinction between socialization and structural autonomy in work experience has not been empirically investigated. Typically, the effects of job on worker are described as evidencing socialization processes (in contrast to selection processes) without attending to the structural context underlying meanings of work. Yet virtually every study examining the consequences of job conditions has found some dimension of self-directedness (whether labeled as autonomy, independence, challenge, complexity, interest, participation, control, or power) to affect the worker. To interpret self-direction as an internal construction of the worker based on socialization and current task experience (narrowly defined), is to ignore important avenues through which social structure impinges on individual functioning. These findings not only evidence the psychological significance of self-directed task experience but flag the structural conditions from which self-direction is derived. This paper argues that it is the affordances of job experience—the opportunities for acting or being acted upon—that are critical in determining the outcomes of job experience.

Research on the Social Construction of Jobs and the Psychological Outcomes of Work Experience: Overview

In this paper, I have reviewed contemporary literature on jobs and work to show how jobs are defined and organized within the workplace. Particular emphasis was placed on social knowledge of gender, education, occupations, and technology and their interpretation in the workplace. While each of these frames of reference strongly affect work arrangements, none operates outside of an organizational context. In each instance, the global frame of reference is interpreted and customized to fit particular organizational structures and interorganizational relationships. Research investigating the elaboration of macro-templates in firm behavior is essential for understanding the process of institutionalization and how systems of values are maintained and change.

Socialization within a dominant system of values is insufficient to explain the particular *form* in which values are expressed. Swidler (1986) points out that varying "strategies of action" can be constructed from the amorphous body of a cultural repertoire. For example, Milkman (1987) shows conflicting idioms for occupational segregation across industries in World War II that nonetheless acted in concert to consistently maintain gender stratification in work arrangements. Structural theories of action are compelling models by which to understand such organizational isomorphism and variations on theme (Burt, 1982; DiMaggio and Powell, 1983; and the distinct but related views of Giddens, 1984).

Structural models place action in the context of the structured role relationships of markets and institutional environments. Behavior is reproduced through the role relationships defining statuses in a network and the interdependency of interests among actors jointly occupying a status/role set. From this perspective, understanding the social construction of jobs requires knowledge of the productive and institutional environment that structures: (1) autonomy, (2) the perception of utility, and (3) the pursuit of advantage in interrelationships. Two dynamics can operate to determine organizational interpretations: (1) forces of cohesion and (2) structural equivalence. Cohesion is based on communication and interpersonal influence—a process implying direct exchange between actors in which normative consensus is jointly derived. Structural equivalence is based on role-playing. Actors need not jointly devise strategies for action but emulate forms that are behaviorally normative in their role position. Both processes can operate, but one or the other may dominate particular classes of behavior or particular types of networks. Behavior reproduced as a result of operating under similar positional constraints or copied as part of a constellation of behavior indicates processes of structural equivalence. The social construction of jobs in firms appears to be dominated by structural equivalence in organizational relationships.

Structural theories of action can also be applied to individual role relationships. Accounts of job molding in the workplace evidence the pursuit of autonomy, the advantage perceived in even limited opportunities for self-direction, and structural relationships that constrain or facilitate opportunities for action in role negotiation. Participatory ideology appears to be inconsequential apart from workers' structural autonomy to control their task activities in a competitive system of relationships structured in terms of role sets. Further, meanings of work for the individual appear intimately linked to the structured relationships experienced in opportunities for acting or being acted upon.

There is accumulating evidence that work experience has diverse psychological consequences, including effects on intellectual flexibility, self-concept, worldview, and affective states. A process of learning-generalization is hypothesized to operate. However, the knowledge acquired in work experience and its origin remain ill-specified. At the heart of the issue are the dynamics of *social* perception. Theories of socialization emphasize the structure of role relationships. However, it is the values and expectations learned in role performance that are traditionally stressed as affecting perception. Conformity is linked to the internalization of values apart from the forces of coercion, self-interest, and selective enactment of prescribed behaviors (see Wrong's classic critique, 1961). This cultural view of role behavior contrasts with ecological views of perception that place role socialization in the context of specific constraints and opportunities for action in an environment. Attention is focused on the competitive exchange relationships learned in the course of interaction with stimuli and agency in role performance.

NOTES

1. For more complete citations to this literature see Pfeffer's (1985) review of organizational literature, Hedberg's (1981) overview of psychological models applied to organizational learning, and Fine's (1984) integration of sociological views of negotiated order in organizations. Also see Stryker and Statham (1985) for an excellent discussion of symbolic interactionist and role theory views of structure in social interaction.

2. Treiman (1979) notes in his review of job evaluation systems that the first step in analyzing job content typically involves a job description upon which all subsequent evaluation is based. Yet, there have

been no systematic studies assessing the validity of their content (Treiman, 1979, p. 40; McCormick, 1979, pp. 133-134), despite recognition among job analysts of their subjective nature (McCormick, 1979, pp. 33-34). There is also evidence that assessed job content varies depending upon the method of data collection (Jenkins et al., 1975) and that there is variable interrater reliability across job characteristics (Hackman and Oldham, 1975). These technical problems not only point to the difficultly of measuring job content; they suggest a complex process of information processing from which the meaning of work is derived.

3. Although Arvey, Passino, and Lounsburg (1977) fail to find an effect of incumbent's sex on rated job descriptions, this may be due to methodological factors (see McArthur and Obrant, 1986, for details). Also note that the simulated job description included the writing of affirmative action reports, a strong cue on sex bias.

4. Miller et al. (1980) report distribution of the *Dictionary of Occupational Titles* to government agencies, educational institutions, private for-profit companies, and nonprofit agencies for uses including career and vocational counselling, personnel management, employment placement, and statistical reporting.

5. There is growing consensus that more detailed knowledge of the constraints and opportunities governing job restructuring will require systematic measurement and assessment of what aspects of job characteristics change over time and the interrelationships of task components (Hackman and Oldham, 1975; Roberts and Glick, 1981). As Dachler and Wilpert note (1978, p. 8), "It has never been clear what characteristics participatory social arrangements have (or should have) [to make them self-actualizing] according to theories of human growth and development."

6. Methods frequently applied in psychological and sociological research include the dimensional schemes associated with the Job Diagnostic Survey (Hackman and Oldham, 1980), Position Analysis Questionnaire (McCormick, Jeanneret, and Mecham, 1972), *Dictionary of Occupational Titles* (Miller et al., 1980), Michigan Organizational Assessment Questionnaire (Cammann et al., 1983), and indices of occupational self-direction and other facets of job conditions developed by Kohn and Schooler (1983). Also see Fleishman and Quaintance (1984) for an overview of current methods of job analysis.

7. It is customary for stress and coping models to investigate the main effects of coping resources on psychological functioning in addition to their buffering capacity. This discussion does not focus on the possible benefits of these resources irrespective of exposure to job stressors (see Wheaton, 1985, for an instructive summary of model specifications in stress research).

8. Note that House aggregated data on jobs into occupational groupings because of the lack of variance

in company reports of objective job rewards within these groupings. Also, expert raters were instructed to evaluate job stressors for occupational groupings as a whole, although they were given the list of jobs comprising the occupational categories. Oddly, most of the variation in *perceived* stress occurs *within* occupational groupings, in these data.

9. Although House (1980, p. 188) acknowledges reciprocal causation, his interpretation and handling of the data assumes that perceived stress determines job satisfaction and self-esteem. If perceived stress is redundant information—that is, the product of distress or an additional measure of distress—it is not properly interpreted as a competing explanation of the personal reality that affects distress. House finds the objective stressors and deprivations included in his study to have no effects on distress when perceived stressors are controlled. Because the findings challenge models based on the assumption of direct learning generalization, they warrant careful consideration (but see note 8).

10. Educationally heterogeneous samples (Kohn and Schooler, 1983; Lindsay and Knox, 1984; Lorence and Mortimer, 1985) show selection into jobs based on educational attainment. Selection on psychological functioning appears to mainly involve cognitive abilities. There is strong selection on intellectual flexibility (Kohn and Schooler, 1983) but much weaker selection by self-concept (Kohn and Schooler, 1983; Mortimer et al., 1986; Spenner and Otto, 1985) or work values and involvement (Miller, 1980, Lindsay and Knox, 1984; Lorence and Mortimer, 1985; Spenner and Otto, 1985; and Mortimer, Lorence, and Kumka, 1986).

11. Analysis of data from Rand's Health Insurance Experiment (4603 respondents sampled from low- and middle-income populations) shows felt emotional ties to have low correlations with the extensiveness and frequency of social contact ranging between .08 and .22 (Donald and Ware, 1982, p. 89).

REFERENCES

Acker, Joan. 1987. "Sex Bias in Job Evaluation: A Comparable Worth Issue." Pp. 183-196 in *Ingredients for Women's Employment Policy*, edited by Christine Bose and Glenna Spitze. Albany: State University of New York Press.

Alderfer, Clayton P. 1972. *Existence, Relatedness, and Growth: Human Needs in Organizational Settings*. New York: Free Press.

Agassi, Judith Buber. 1982. *Comparing the Work Attitudes of Women and Men*. Lexington, MA: D. C. Heath.

Albrecht, James W. 1981. "A Procedure for Testing the Signalling Hypothesis." *Journal of Public Economics* 15:123-132.

Althauser, Robert P. and Arne L. Kalleberg. 1981. "Firms, Occupations, and the Structure of Labor

Markets: A Conceptual Analysis." Pp. 119-149 in *Sociological Perspectives on Labor Markets*, edited by Ivar Berg. New York: Academic Press.

Anderson, Gregory. 1976. *Victorian Clerks*. New York: Kelley.

Arrow, Kenneth J. 1973. "Higher Education as a Filter." *Journal of Public Economics* 2:193-216.

Arvey, Richard D., Emily M. Passino, and John W. Lounsbury. 1977. "Job Analysis Results as Influenced by Sex of Incumbent and Sex of Analyst." *Journal of Applied Psychology* 62:411-416.

Attewell, Paul. 1987. "The De-Skilling Controversy." *Work and Occupations* 14:323-346.

—— and James Rule. 1984. "Computing and Organizations: What We Know And What We Don't Know." *Communications of the ACM* 27:1184-1192.

Bandura, Albert. 1986. *Social Foundations of Thought and Action: A Social Cognitive Theory*. Englewood Cliffs, NJ: Prentice-Hall.

Baron, James N. 1984. "Organizational Perspectives on Stratification." Pp. 37-69 in *Annual Review of Sociology*, vol. 10, edited by Ralph H. Turner and James F. Short, Jr. Palo Alto, CA: Annual Reviews Inc.

—— and William T. Bielby. 1980. "Bringing the Firms Back In: Stratification, Segmentation, and the Organization of Work." *American Sociological Review* 45:737-765.

—— 1984. "The Organization of Work in a Segmented Economy." *American Sociological Review* 49:454-473.

—— 1985. "Organizational Barriers to Gender Equality: Sex Segregation of Jobs and Opportunities." Pp. 233-251 in *Gender and the Life Course*, edited by Alice S. Rossi. New York: Aldine.

—— 1986. "The Proliferation of Job Titles in Organizations." *Administrative Science Quarterly* 31:561-586.

Baron, James N., Alison Davis-Blake, and William T. Bielby. 1986. "The Structure of Opportunity: How Promotion Ladders Vary within and among Organizations." *Administrative Science Quarterly* 31:248-273.

Baron, James N., Frank R. Dobbin, and P. Devereaux Jennings. 1986. "War and Peace: The Evolution of Modern Personnel Administration in U.S. Industry." *American Journal of Sociology* 92:350-383.

Bartolke, Klaus, Walter Eschweiler, Dieter Flechsenberger, and Arnold S. Tannenbaum. 1982. "Workers' Participation and the Distribution of Control as Perceived by Members of Ten German Companies." *Administrative Science Quarterly* 27:380-397.

Becker, Gary S. 1964. *Human Capital*. New York: National Bureau of Economic Research.

Bell, Daniel. 1956. *Work and Its Discontents*. Boston: Beacon Press.

Berg, Ivar. 1971. *Education and Jobs: The Great Training Robbery*. Boston: Beacon.

Berger, Joseph, Susan J. Rosenholtz, and Morris Zelditch. 1980. "Status Organizing Process." Pp. 479-508 in *Annual Review of Sociology*, vol. 6, edited by Alex Inkeles, Neil J. Smelser, and Ralph H. Turner. Palo Alto, CA: Annual Reviews Inc.

Bickhard, Mark H., and D. Michael Richie. 1983. *On the Nature of Representation: A Case Study of James Gibson's Theory of Perception*. New York: Praeger.

Bielby, William T. and James N. Baron. 1986. "Men and Women at Work: Sex Segregation and Statistical Discrimination." *American Journal of Sociology* 91:759-799.

Bills, David B. 1986a. "Educational Credentials and Hiring Decisions: What Employers Look for in Entry Level Employees." Unpublished manuscript, University of Iowa.

—— 1986b. "Employer Entrance Requirements and Qualifications of Entry Level Workers: A Survey of Employer Surveys." Unpublished paper, College of Education, University of Iowa.

Blau, Judith R. and Richard D. Alba. 1982. "Empowering Nets of Participation." *Administrative Science Quarterly* 27:363-379.

Blau, Peter M. and Richard A. Schoenherr. 1971. *The Structure of Organizations*. New York: Basic Books.

Blauner, Robert. 1964. *Alienation and Freedom: The Factory Worker and His Industry*. Chicago: University of Chicago Press.

Braverman, Harry. 1974. *Labor and Monopoly Capital: The Degradation of Work in the Twentieth Century*. New York: Monthly Review Press.

Breer, Paul E. and Edwin A. Locke. 1965. *Task Experience as a Source of Attitudes*. Homewood, IL: Dorsey.

Burawoy, Michael. 1979. *Manufacturing Consent: Changes in the Labor Process Under Monopoly Capitalism*. Chicago: University of Chicago Press.

Burns, Tom and G. M. Stalker. 1961. *The Management of Innovation*. London: Tavistock.

Burris, Val. 1983. "The Social and Political Consequences of Overeducation." *American Sociological Review* 48:454-467.

Burt, Ronald S. 1982. *Toward A Structural Theory of Action: Network Models of Social Structure, Perception, and Action*. New York: Academic Press.

—— 1987. "Social Contagion and Innovation: Cohesion versus Structural Equivalence." *American Journal of Sociology* 92:1287-1335.

Cain, Glen G. 1976. "The Challenge of Segmented Labor Market Theories to Orthodox Theory: A Survey." *Journal of Economic Literature* 14:1215-1257.

Cain, Pamela S. and Bert F. Green. 1983. "Reliabilities of Selected Ratings Available From the

Dictionary of Occupational Titles." *Journal of Applied Psychology* 68:155-165.

Cain, Pamela S. and Donald J. Treiman. 1981. "The Dictionary of Occupational Titles as a Source of Occupational Data." *American Sociological Review* 46:253-278.

Caldwell, David F. and Charles A. O'Reilly III. 1982. "Task Perceptions and Job Satisfaction: A Question of Causality." *Journal of Applied Psychology* 67:361-369.

Cammann, Cortlandt, Mark Fichman, G. Douglas Jenkins, Jr., and John R. Klesh. 1983. "Assessing the Attitudes and Perceptions of Organizational Members." Pp. 71-138 in *Assessing Organizational Change: A Guide to Methods, Measures, and Practices*, edited by Stanley E. Seashore, Edward E. Lawler, III, Philip H. Mirvis, and Cortlandt Cammann. New York: John Wiley.

Caplan, Robert D., Sidney Cobb, John R.P. French, Jr., R. Van Harrison, and S. R. Pinneau, Jr. 1980. *Job Demands and Worker Health: Main Effects and Occupational Differences*. Ann Arbor: Survey Research Center, Institute for Social Research, University of Michigan.

Carey, John L. 1969. *The Rise of the Accounting Profession: From Technician to Professional 1896-1936*. New York: American Institute of Certified Public Accountants.

Child, John. 1973. "Predicting and Understanding Organization Structure." *Administrative Science Quarterly* 8:168-185.

Clogg, Clifford C. and James W. Shockey. 1984. "Mismatch Between Occupation and Schooling: A Prevalence Measure, Recent Trends and Demographic Analysis." *Demography* 21:235-257.

Cohen, Yinon and Jeffrey Pfeffer. 1986. "Organizational Hiring Standards." *Administrative Science Quarterly* 31:1-24.

Cohn, Samuel. 1985. *The Process of Occupational Sex-Typing: The Feminization of Clerical Labor in Great Britain*. Philadelphia: Temple University Press.

Coleman, James S., Elihu Katz, and Herbert Menzel. 1966. *Medical Innovation*. Indianapolis: Bobbs-Merrill.

Collins, Randall. 1979. *The Credential Society: An Historical Sociology of Education and Stratification*. New York: Academic Press.

Conk, Margo Anderson. 1980. *The United States Census and Labor Force Change: A History of Occupational Statistics, 1870-1940*. Ann Arbor: UMI Research Press.

Cooper, Robert and Michael Foster. 1971. "Sociotechnical Systems." *American Psychologist* 26:467-474.

Crompton, Rosemary and Gareth Jones. 1984. *White Collar Proletariat: Deskilling and Gender in Clerical Work*. Philadelphia: Temple University Press.

Crozier, Michel. 1964. *The Bureaucratic Phenomenon*. Chicago: University of Chicago Press.

_____. 1971. *The World of the Office Worker*. Chicago: University of Chicago Press.

_____ and Erhard Friedberg. 1980. *Actors and Systems: The Politics of Collective Action*. Chicago: University of Chicago Press.

Dachler, H. Peter and Bernhard Wilpert. 1978. "Conceptual Dimensions and Boundaries of Participation in Organizations: A Critical Evaluation." *Administrative Science Quarterly* 23:1-39.

Darity, William A. Jr. 1982. "The Human Capital Approach to Black-White Earnings Inequality: Some Unsettled Questions." *Journal of Human Resources* 17:73-93.

Davies, Celia. 1980. "Making Sense of the Census in Britain and the U.S.A.: The Changing Occupational Classification and the Position of Nurses." *Sociological Review* 28:581-609.

Davies, Margery W. 1982. *Woman's Place Is at the Typewriter: Office Work and Office Workers, 1870-1930*. Philadelphia: Temple University Press.

Derber, Charles and William Schwartz. 1983. "Toward a Theory of Worker Participation." *Sociological Inquiry* 53:61-78.

DiMaggio, Paul J. and Walter W. Powell. 1983. "The Iron Cage Revisited: Institutional Isomorphism and Collective Rationality in Organizational Fields." *American Sociological Review* 48:147-160.

DiPrete, Thomas A. 1987. "Horizontal and Vertical Mobility in Organizations." *Administrative Science Quarterly* 32:422-444.

_____. 1985b. "The Upgrading and Downgrading of Occupations: The Case of Government Clerks." *Social Forces* 66:725-746.

Donald, Cathy A. and John E. Ware, Jr. 1982. *The Quantification of Social Contacts and Resources*. Report R-2937. Santa Monica, CA: Rand Corp.

Dore, Ronald P. 1976. *The Diploma Disease: Education, Qualification and Development*. London: Allen & Unwin.

Doverspike, Dennis, Anne Marie Carlisi, Gerald V. Barrett, and Ralph A. Alexander. 1983. "Generalizability Analysis of a Point-Method Job Evaluation Instrument." *Journal of Applied Psychology* 68:476-483.

Edwards, Richard. 1979. *Contested Terrain: The Transformation of the Workplace in the Twentieth Century*. New York: Basic Books.

Etzioni, Amitai, ed. 1969. *The Semi-Professions and Their Organization: Teachers, Nurses, Social Workers*. New York: Free Press.

Festinger, Leon. 1954. "A Theory of Social Comparison Processes." *Human Relations* 7:117-140.

_____. 1957. *A Theory of Cognitive Dissonance*. Evanston: Row, Peterson.

Feldman, Daniel C. 1976. "A Contingency Theory of Socialization." *Administrative Science Quarterly* 21:433-452.

Fine, Gary Alan. 1984. "Negotiated Orders and Organizational Cultures." Pp. 239-262 in *Annual Review of Sociology*, vol. 10, edited by Ralph H. Turner and James F. Short, Jr. Palo Alto, CA: Annual Reviews Inc.

Finlay, William. 1983. "One Occupation, Two Labor Markets: The Case of Longshore Crane Operators." *American Sociological Review* 48: 306-315.

Fischer, Claude S. 1982. *To Dwell Among Friends: Personal Networks in Town and City*. Chicago: University of Chicago Press.

Fleishman, Edwin A. and Marilyn K. Quaintance. 1984. *Taxonomies of Human Performance: The Description of Human Tasks*. Orlando, FL: Academic Press.

Folkman, Susan and Richard S. Lazarus. 1980. "An Analysis of Coping in a Middle-Aged Community Sample." *Journal of Health and Social Behavior* 21:219-239.

Form, William. 1980. "Resolving Ideological Issues on the Division of Labor." Pp. 110-155 in *Sociological Theory and Research: A Critical Appraisal*, edited by Hubert M. Blalock, Jr. New York: Free Press.

Freidson, Eliot. 1970. *Professional Dominance: The Social Structure of Medical Care*. New York: Atherton Press.

French, John R. P., Jr., Robert D. Caplan, and R. Van Harrison. 1982. *The Mechanisms of Job Stress and Strain*. New York: John Wiley.

Garnsey, Elizabeth. 1981. "The Rediscovery of the Division of Labor." *Theory and Society* 10: 337-358.

Garson, Barbara. 1975. *All the Livelong Day: The Meaning and Demeaning of Routine Work*. New York: Penguin.

Gewirtz, Jacob L. and Karen G. Stingle. 1968. "Learning of Generalized Imitation as the Basis for Identification." *Psychological Review* 75: 374-397.

Giddens, Anthony. 1984. *The Constitution of Society: Outline of the Theory of Structuration*. Berkeley: University of California Press.

Graen, George. 1983. "Role-Making Processes within Complex Organizations." Pp. 1201-1245 in *Handbook of Industrial and Organizational Psychology*, edited by Marvin D. Dunnette. New York: John Wiley.

Granovetter, Mark. 1981. "Toward a Sociological Theory of Income Differences." Pp. 11-47 in *Sociological Perspectives on Labor Markets*, edited by Ivar Berg. New York: Academic Press.

Gurin, Patricia and Orville G. Brim, Jr. 1984. "Change in Self in Adulthood: The Example of Sense of Control." Pp. 281-334 in *Life-Span Development and Behavior*, vol. 6, edited by Paul B. Baltes and Orville G. Brim, Jr. New York: Academic Press.

Hackman, J. Richard and Edward E. Lawler III. 1971. "Employee Reactions to Job Characteristics." *Journal of Applied Psychology* 55:259-286.

Hackman, J. Richard and Greg R. Oldham. 1975. "Development of the Job Diagnostic Survey." *Journal of Applied Psychology* 60:159-170.
———. 1980. *Work Redesign*. Reading, MA: Addison-Wesley.

Harvey, Edward. 1968. "Technology and the Structure of Organizations." *American Sociological Review* 33:247-259.

Hauser, Robert M. and David L. Featherman. 1977. *The Process of Stratification: Trends and Analyses*. New York: Academic Press.

Hedberg, Bo. 1981. "How Organizations Learn and Unlearn." Pp. 3-27 in *Handbook of Organizational Design: vol. 1: Adapting Organizations to Their Environments*, edited by Paul C. Nystrom and William H. Starbuck. New York: Oxford University Press.

Herzberg, Frederick. 1976. *The Managerial Choice: To Be Efficient and to Be Human*. Homewood, IL: Dow Jones-Irwin.

Hickson, David J., Derek S. Pugh, and Diana C. Pheysey. 1969. "Operational Technology and Organization Structure: An Empirical Reappraisal." *Administrative Science Quarterly* 14:378-397.

Hodson, Randy. 1984. "Companies, Industries and the Measurement of Economic Segmentation." *American Sociological Review* 49:335-348.

Holland, John L. 1973. *Making Vocational Choices: A Theory of Careers*. Englewood Cliffs, NJ: Prentice-Hall.

House, James S. 1980. *Occupational Stress and the Mental and Physical Health of Factory Workers*. Ann Arbor: Survey Research Center, Institute for Social Research, University of Michigan.

Hulin, Charles L. and Milton R. Blood. 1968. "Job Enlargement, Individual Differences, and Worker Responses." *Psychological Bulletin* 69: 41-55.

Hunt, Timothy L. and H. Allan Hunt. 1985. "An Assessment of Data Sources to Study the Employment Effects of Technological Change." Pp. 1-116 in *Technology and Employment Effects: Interim Report*, Panel on Technology and Women's Employment. Washington, DC: National Academy Press.

Husaini, Baqar A., James Alan Neff, J. R. Newbrough, and Michael C. Moore. 1982. "The Stress-Buffering Role of Social Support and Personal Competence among the Rural Married." *Journal of Community Psychology* 10:409-426.

Jacoby, Sanford M. 1985. *Employing Bureaucracy: Managers, Unions, and the Transformation of Work in American Industry, 1900-1945*. New York: Columbia University Press.

James, Lawrence R. and Allan P. Jones. 1980. "Perceived Job Characteristics and Job Satisfaction: An Examination of Reciprocal Causation." *Personnel Psychology* 33:97-135.

Jencks, Christopher, Lauri Perman, and Lee Rainwater. 1988. "What is a Good Job? A New Measure of Labor Market Success." *American*

Journal of Sociology 93:1322-1357.

Jenkins, G. Douglas, Jr., David A. Nadler, Edward E. Lawler III, and Cortland Cammann. 1975. "Standardized Observations: An Approach to Measuring the Nature of Jobs." *Journal of Applied Psychology* 60:171-181.

Johnson, James H. and Irwin G. Sarason. 1978. "Life Stress, Depression and Anxiety: Internal-External Control as a Moderator Variable." *Journal of Psychosomatic Research* 22:205-208.

Jones, Allen P. and Lawrence R. James. 1979. "Psychological Climate: Dimensions and Relationships of Individual and Aggregated Work Environment Perceptions." *Organizational Behavior and Work Performance* 23:201-250.

Kahn, Robert L., Donald M. Wolfe, Robert P. Quinn, and J. Diedrick Snoek. 1964. *Organizational Stress: Studies in Role Conflict and Ambiguity*. New York: John Wiley.

Kalleberg, Arne L. 1977. "Work Values and Job Rewards: A Theory of Job Satisfaction." *American Sociological Review* 42:124-143.

Kanter, Rosabeth Moss. 1977. *Men and Women of the Corporation*. New York: Basic Books.

———. 1982. "The Impact of Hierarchical Structures on the Work Behavior of Women and Men." Pp. 234-247 in *Women and Work: Problems and Perspectives*, edited by Rachel Kahn-Hut, Arlene Kaplan Daniels, and Richard Colvard. New York: Oxford University Press.

Katz, Michael B. 1972. "Occupational Classification in History." *Journal of Interdisciplinary History* 3:63-88.

Katz, Ralph. 1980. "Time and Work: Toward an Integrative Perspective." Pp. 81-127 in *Research in Organizational Behavior: An Annual Series of Analytical Essays and Critical Reviews*, vol. 2, edited by Barry M. Staw and L. L. Cummings. Greenwich, CT: JAI Press.

Kavcic, Bogdan and Arnold S. Tannenbaum. 1981. "A Longitudinal Study of the Distribution of Control in Yugoslav Organizations." *Human Relations* 34:397-417.

Kessler, Ronald C. and Jane D. McLeod. 1985. "Social Support and Mental Health in Community Samples." Pp. 219-240 in *Social Support and Health*, edited by Sheldon Cohen and S. Leonard Syme. Orland, FL: Academic Press.

Kessler, Ronald C., Richard H. Price, and Camille B. Wortman. 1985. "Social Factors in Psychopathology: Stress, Social Support, and Coping Processes." Pp. 531-572 in *Annual Review of Psychology*, vol. 36, edited by Mark R. Rosenzweig and Lyman W. Porter. Palo Alto, CA: Annual Reviews.

Kimberly, John M. 1981. "Managerial Innovation." Pp. 84-104 in *Handbook of Organizational Design: vol. 1, Adapting Organizations to Their Environments*, edited by Paul C. Nystrom and William H. Starbuck. New York: Oxford University Press.

Kobasa, Suzanne C., Salvatore R. Maddi, and Sheila

Courington. 1981. "Personality and Constitution as Mediators in the Stress-Illness Relationship." *Journal of Health and Social Behavior* 22:368-378.

Kobasa, Suzanne C., Salvatore R. Maddi, and Stephen Kahn. 1982. "Hardiness and Health: A Prospective Study." *Journal of Personality and Social Psychology* 42:168-177.

Kocka, Jurgen. 1980. *White Collar Workers in America 1890-1940: A Social-Political History in International Perspective*. Beverly Hills, CA: Sage.

Kohn, Melvin L. 1980. "Job Complexity and Adult Personality." Pp. 193-210 in *Themes of Work and Love in Adulthood*, edited by Neil J. Smelser and Erik H. Erikson. Cambridge, MA: Harvard University Press.

——— and Carmi Schooler. 1983. *Work and Personality: An Inquiry into the Impact of Social Stratification*. Norwood, NJ: Ablex.

Koopman, Paul L., Pieter J.D. Drenth, Frans B.M. Bus, Agaath J. Kruyswijk, and Andre F.M. Wierdsma. 1981. "Content, Process, and Effects of Participative Decision Making on the Shop Floor: Three Cases in the Netherlands." *Human Relations* 34:657-676.

Kornhauser, Arthur. 1965. *Mental Health of the Industrial Worker: A Detroit Study*. New York: John Wiley.

Kraft, Philip. 1977. *Programmers and Managers. The Routinization of Computer Programming in the United States.* New York: Springer-Verlag.

——— 1985. "A Review of Empirical Studies of the Consequences of Technological Change on Work and Workers in the United States." Pp. 117-150 in *Technology and Employment Effects: Interim Report*, Panel on Technology and Women's Employment. Washington, DC: National Academy Press.

Landy, Frank J. and James L. Farr. 1983. *The Measurement of Work Performance: Methods, Theory, and Applications*. New York: Academy Press.

LaRocco, James M. 1983. "Theoretical Distinctions Between Causal and Interaction Effects of Social Support." *Journal of Health and Social Behavior* 24:91-92.

———, James S. House, and John R.P. French, Jr. 1980. "Social Support, Occupational Stress, and Health." *Journal of Health and Social Behavior* 21:202-218.

Larson, Magali Sarfatti. 1977. *The Rise of Professionalism: A Sociological Analysis*. Berkeley: University of California Press.

Lawler, Edward E. III. 1973. *Motivation in Work Organizations*. Monterey, CA: Brooks/Cole.

Lawrence, Paul R. and Jay W. Lorsch. 1969. *Organization and Environment: Managing Differentiation and Integration*. Homewood, IL: Richard D. Irwin.

Lazarus, Richard S. 1966. *Psychological Stress and the Coping Process*. New York: McGraw-Hill.

Lefcourt, Herbert M. 1980. "Locus of Control and

Coping with Life's Events." Pp. 201-235 in *Personality: Basic Aspects and Current Research*, edited by Ervin Staub. Englewood Cliffs, NJ: Prentice-Hill.

Lindsay, Paul and William E. Knox. 1984. "Continuity and Change in Work Values among Young Adults: A Longitudinal Study." *American Journal of Sociology* 89:918-931.

Lincoln, James R. and Jon Miller. 1979. "Work and Friendship Ties in Organizations: A Comparative Analysis of Relational Networks." *Administrative Science Quarterly* 24:181-199.

Lockwood, David. 1958. *The Blackcoated Worker: A Study in Class Consciousness*. London: Allen & Unwin.

Lofquist, Lloyd H. and Dawis, Rene V. 1969. *Adjustment to Work*. New York: Meredith.

Long, Richard J. 1981. "The Effects of Formal Employee Participation in Ownership and Decision Making on Perceived and Desired Patterns of Organizational Influence: A Longitudinal Study." *Human Relations* 34:847-876.

Lorence, Jon. 1987. "Intraoccupational Earnings Inequality: Human Capital and Institutional Determinants." *Work and Occupations* 14:236-260.

———— and Jeylan T. Mortimer. 1985. "Job Involvement Through the Life Course: A Panel Study of Three Age Groups." *American Sociological Review* 50:618-638.

Lott, Bernice and Albert J. Lott. 1985. "Learning Theory in Contemporary Social Psychology." Pp. 109-135 in *Handbook of Social Psychology, vol. 1: Theory and Method*, edited by Gardner Lindzey and Elliot Aronson. New York: Random House.

March, James G. 1981. "Footnotes to Organizational Change." *Administrative Science Quarterly* 26:563-577.

Markus, Hazel and R.B. Zajonc. 1985. "The Cognitive Perspective in Social Psychology." Pp. 137-230 in *Handbook of Social Psychology, vol. I: Theory and Method*, edited by Gardner Lindzey and Elliot Aronson. New York: Random House.

Maslow, A. H. 1943. "A Theory of Human Motivation." *Psychological Review* 50:370-396.

McArthur, Leslie Zebrowitz and Reuben M. Baron. 1983. "Toward and Ecological Theory of Social Perception." *Psychological Review* 90:215-238.

McArthur, Leslie Zebrowitz and Sarah W. Obrant. 1986. "Sex Biases in Comparable Worth Analyses." *Journal of Applied Social Psychology* 16:757-770.

McCormick, Ernest J. 1979. *Job Analysis: Methods and Applications*. New York: AMACOM, A Division of American Management Associations.

————, Paul R. Jeanneret, and Robert C. Mecham. 1972. "A Study of Job Characteristics and Job Dimensions as Based on the Position Analysis Questionnaire (PAQ)." *Journal of Applied Psychology Monograph* 56:347-368.

Meeker, B. F. and P. A. Weitzel-O'Neill. 1977. "Sex Roles and Interpersonal Behavior in Task-Oriented Groups." *American Sociological Review* 42:91-105.

Menaghan, Elizabeth G. and Esther S. Merves. 1984. "Coping with Occupational Problems: The Limits of Individual Efforts." *Journal of Health and Social Behavior* 25:406-423.

Merton, Robert K. 1968. *Social Theory and Social Structure*. New York: Free Press.

Milkman, Ruth. 1987. *Gender at Work: The Dynamics of Job Segregation by Sex during World War II*. Urbana: University of Illinois Press.

Miller, Ann R., Donald J. Treiman, Pamela S. Cain, and Patricia A. Roos, eds. 1980. *Work, Jobs, and Occupations: A Critical Review of the Dictionary of Occupational Titles*. Washington, DC: National Academy Press.

Miller, Delbert C. and William H. Form. 1980. *Industrial Sociology: Work in Organizational Life*. New York: Harper & Row.

Miller, Joanne. 1980. "Individual and Occupational Determinants of Job Satisfaction: A Focus on Gender Differences." *Sociology of Work and Occupations* 7:337-366.

Miller, Neal E. and John Dollard. 1941. *Social Learning and Immitation*. New Haven, CT: Yale University Press.

Mills, C. Wright. 1951. *White Collar*. New York: Oxford University Press.

Mincer, Jacob. 1958. "Investment in Human Capital and Personal Income Distribution." *Journal of Political Economy* 66:281-302.

Miner, Anne S. 1985. "The Strategy of Serendipity: Ambiguity, Uncertainty and Idiosyncratic Jobs." Ph.D. dissertation, Graduate School of Business, Stanford University.

———— and Suzanne E. Estler. 1985. "Accrual Mobility: Job Mobility in Higher Education through Responsibility Accrual." *Journal of Higher Education* 56:122-143.

Montgomery, David. 1979. *Workers Control in America: Studies in the History of Work, Technology, and Labor Struggles*. Cambridge, England: Cambridge University Press.

Mortimer, Jeylan T., Jon Lorence, and Donald S. Kumka. 1986. *Work, Family, and Personality: Transition to Adulthood*. Norwood, NJ: Ablex.

Mortimer, Jeylan T. and Roberta G. Simmons. 1978. "Adult Socialization." Pp. 421-454 in *Annual Review of Sociology*, vol. 4, edited by Ralph H. Turner, James Coleman, and Renee C. Fox. Palo Alto, CA: Annual Reviews.

Nicholson, Nigel. 1984 "A Theory of Work Role Transitions." *Administrative Science Quarterly* 29:172-191.

Nisbet, Robert A. 1966. *The Sociological Tradition*. New York: Basic Books.

Noble, David F. 1979. "Social Choice in Machine Design: The Case of Automatically Controlled Machine Tools." Pp. 18-50. in *Case Studies on the Labor Process*, edited by Andrew Zimbalist.

New York: Monthly Review Press.

Olson, Jon and Jon Miller. 1983. "Gender and Interaction in the Workplace." Pp. 35-58 in *Research in the Interweave of Social Roles: Jobs and Families*, vol. 3, edited by Helena Z. Lopata and Joseph H. Pleck. Greenwich, CT: JAI Press.

O'Reilly, Charles A. III and David F. Caldwell. 1979. "Informational Influence as a Determinant of Perceived Task Characteristics and Job Satisfaction." *Journal of Applied Psychology* 64:157-165.

O'Reilly, Charles A. III, G. Nicholas Parlette, and Joan R. Bloom. 1980. "Perceptual Measures of Task Characteristics: The Biasing Affects of Different Frames of Reference and Job Attitudes." *Academy of Management Journal* 23:118-131.

Parsons, Talcott, Edward A. Shils, Gordon W. Allport, Clyde Kluckhohn, Henry A. Murray, Robert R. Sears, Richard C. Sheldon, Samuel A. Stouffer, Edward C. Tolman. 1951. "Some Fundamental Categories of the Theory of Action: A General Statement." Pp. 3-29 in *Toward a General Theory of Action*, edited by Talcott Parsons and Edward A. Shils. Cambridge, MA: Harvard Univesity Press.

Pearlin, Leonard I. and Carmi Schooler. 1978. "The Structure of Coping." *Journal of Health and Social Behavior* 19:2-21.

Pearlin, Leonard I., Morton A. Lieberman, Elizabeth G. Menaghan, and Joseph T. Mullan. 1981. "The Stress Process." *Journal of Health and Social Behavior* 22:337-356.

Perrow, Charles. 1967. "A Framework for the Comparative Analysis of Organizations." *American Sociology Review* 32:194-208.

Pfeffer, Jeffrey. 1985. "Organizations and Organization Theory." Pp. 379-440 in *Handbook of Social Psychology: vol. I, Theory and Method*, edited by Gardner Lindzey and Elliot Aronson. New York: Random House.

Previts, Gary John and Barbara Dubis Merino. 1979. *A History of Accounting* in America: An Historical Interpretation of the Cultural Significance of Accounting. New York: John Wiley.

Pugliesi, Karen. 1986. "Work, Social Support and the Well-Being of Women." Unpublished paper, Department of Sociology, State University of New York, Plattsburgh.

Quinn, Robert P. and Linda J. Shepard. 1974. *The 1972-73 Quality of Employment Survey: Descriptive Statistics with Comparison Data from the 1969-70 Survery of Working Conditions*. Ann Arbor: Survey Research Center, Institute for Social Research, University of Michigan.

Quinn, Robert P. and Graham L. Staines. 1979. *The 1977 Quality of Employment Survey: Descriptive Statistics with Comparison Data from the 1969-70 and the 1972-73 Surveys*. Ann Arbor: Survey Research Center, Institute for Social Research, University of Michigan.

Reed, Edward and Rebecca Jones. 1982. *Reasons for Realism: Selected Essays of James J. Gibson*.

Hillsdale, NJ: Lawrence Erlbaum.

Riley, John G. 1976. "Information, Screening and Human Capital." *American Economic Review* 66:254-260.

Roberts, Karlene H. and William Glick. 1981. "The Job Characteristics Approach to Task Design: A Critical Review." *Journal of Applied Psychology* 66:193-217.

Roethlisberger, F. J. and William J. Dickson. 1939. *Management and the Worker*. Cambridge, MA: Harvard University Press.

Rogers, Everett M. 1983. *Diffusion of Innovations*. New York: Free Press.

Roos, Leslie L., Jr. and Frederick A. Starke. 1981. "Organizational Roles." Pp. 290-308 in *Handbook of Organizational Design, vol. 1: Adapting Organizations to Their Environments*, edited by Paul C. Nystrom and William H. Starbuck. New York: Oxford University Press.

Roos, Patricia A. and Barbara F. Reskin. 1984. "Institutional Factors Contributing to Sex Segregation in the Workplace." Pp. 235-260 in *Sex Segregation in the Workplace*, edited by Barbara F. Reskin. Washington, DC: National Academy Press.

Rosenbaum, James E. 1984. *Career Mobility in a Corporate Hierarchy*. Orlando, FL: Academic Press.

Ross, Michael and Garth J. O. Fletcher. 1985. "Attribution and Social Perception." Pp. 73-122 in *Handbook of Social Psychology, vol. II, Special Fields and Applications*, edited by Gardner Lindzey and Elliot Aronson. New York: Random House.

Rotella, Elyce J. 1981. *From Home to Office: U.S. Women at Work, 1870-1930*. Ann Arbor: UMI Research Press.

Rothman, Robert A. 1979. "Occupational Roles: Power and Negotiation in the Division of Labor." *Sociological Quarterly* 20:495-515.

Roy, Donald. 1952. "Quota Restriction and Goldbricking in a Machine Shop." *American Journal of Sociology* 57:427-442.

_____ 1958. " 'Banana Time': Job Satisfaction and Informal Interaction." *Human Organization* 18:158-168.

Ruchlin, Hirsch S. 1971. "Education as a Labor Market Variable." *Industrial Relations* 10:287-303.

Russell, Raymond. 1985. *Sharing Ownership in the Workplace*. Albany: State University of New York Press.

Salancik, Gerald R. and Jeffrey Pfeffer. 1978. "A Social Information Processing Approach to Job Attitudes and Task Design." *Administrative Science Quarterly* 23:224-251.

Schwab, Donald P. and Robert Grams. 1985. "Sex-Related Errors in Job Evaluation: A 'Real-World' Test." *Journal of Applied Psychology* 70:533-539.

Schwalbe, Michael L. 1985. "Autonomy in Work and Self-Esteem." *The Sociological Quarterly* 26:519-535.

Seeman, Melvin. 1967. "On the Personal Consequences of Alienation in Work." *American Sociological Review* 32:273-285.

Serrin, William. 1986. "Wariness Seen on Sharing Workplace Power." *New York Times* (March 9): sec. L, p. 26.

Shapiro-Perl, Nina. 1984. "Resistance Strategies: The Routine Struggle for Bread and Roses." Pp. 193-208 in *My Troubles Are Going to Have Trouble With Me*, edited by Karen Brodkin Sacks and Dorothy Remy. New Brunswick, NJ: Rutgers University Press.

Sharlin, Allan. 1979. "From the Study of Social Mobility to the Study of Society." *American Journal of Sociology* 85:338-360.

Shaw, Robert, M. T. Turvey, and William Mace. 1982. "Ecological Psychology: The Consequence of a Commitment to Realism." Pp. 159-226 in *Cognition and the Symbolic Processes*, vol. 2, edited by Walter B. Weimer and David S. Palermo. Hillsdale, NJ: Lawrence Erlbaum.

Shepela, Sharon Toffey and Ann T. Viviano. 1984. "Some Psychological Factors Affecting Job Segregation and Wages." Pp. 47-58 in *Comparable Worth and Wage Discrimination: Technical Possibilities and Political Realities*, edited by Helen Remick. Philadelphia: Temple University Press.

Sheppard, Harold L. and Neal Q. Herrick. 1972. *Where Have All the Robots Gone? Workers Dissatisfaction in the '70s*. New York: Free Press.

Showers, Caroline and Nancy Cantor. 1985. "Social Cognition: A Look at Motivated Strategies." Pp. 275-305 in *Annual Review of Psychology*, vol. 36, edited by Mark R. Rosenzweig and Lyman W. Porter. Palo Alto, CA: Annual Reviews.

Simpson, Richard L. 1985. "Social Control of Occupations and Work." Pp. 415-436 in *Annual Review of Sociology*, vol. 11, edited by Ralph H. Turner and James F. Short, Jr. Palo Alto, CA: Annual Reviews.

Skinner, Burrhus F. 1953. *Science and Human Behavior*. New York: Macmillan.

Smith, D. Randall. 1983. "Mobility in Professional Occupational-Internal Labor Markets: Stratification, Segmentation and Vacancy Chains." *American Sociological Review* 48:289-305.

Spence, Michael. 1973. "Job Market Signaling." *Quarterly Journal of Economics* 87:355-374.

Spenner, Kenneth I. 1983. "Deciphering Prometheus: Temporal Change in the Skill Level of Work." *American Sociological Review* 48:824-837.

_____ 1985. "The Upgrading and Downgrading of Occupations: Issues, Evidence, and Implications for Education." *Review of Educational Research* 55:125-154.

_____ and Luther B. Otto. 1985. "Work and Self-Concept: Selection and Socialization in the Early Career." Pp. 197-235 in *Research in Sociology of Education and Socialization*, vol. 5, edited

by Alan C. Kerckhoff. Greenwich, CT: JAI Press.

_____ and Vaughn R.A. Call. 1982. *Career Lines and Careers*. Lexington, MA: D. C. Heath.

Sproull, Lee S. 1981. "Beliefs in Organizations." Pp. 203-224 in *Handbook of Organizational Design, vol. 2: Remodeling Organizations and Their Environments*, edited by Paul C. Nystrom and William H. Starbuck. New York: Oxford University Press.

Steinberg. Ronnie J. 1985. "Evaluating Jobs." *Society* 22:44-54.

_____ and Lois Haignere. 1987. "Equitable Compensation: Methodological Criteria for Comparable Worth." Pp. 157-182 in *Ingredients for Women's Employment Policy*, edited by Christine Bose and Glenna Spitze. Albany: State University of New York Press.

Stewman, Shelby. 1986. "Demographic Models of Internal Labor Markets." *Administrative Science Quarterly* 31:212-247.

Stiglitz, Joseph E. 1975. "The Theory of 'Screening,' Education, and the Distribution of Income." *American Economic Review* 65:238-300.

Stinchcombe, Arthur L. 1965. "Social Structure and Organizations." Pp. 142- 193 in *Handbook of Organizations*, edited by James G. March. Chicago: Rand McNally.

Stone, Katherine. 1974. "The Origins of Job Structures in the Steel Industry." *Review of Radical Political Economics* 6:61-97.

Strauss, Anselm, Leonard Schatzman, Danuta Ehrlich, Rue Bucher, and Melvin Sabshin. 1963. "The Hospital and its Negotiated Order." Pp. 147-169 in *The Hospital in Modern Society*, edited by Eliot Freidson. New York: Free Press.

Strauss, George. 1982. "Workers Participation in Management: An International Perspective." Pp. 173-265 in *Research in Organizational Behavior: An Annual Series of Analytical Essays and Critical Reviews*, vol. 4, edited by Barry M. Staw and L. L. Cummings. Greenwich, CT: JAI Press.

Strom, Sharon Hartman. 1985. *Technology, the Office, and the Changing Sexual Division of Labor, 1910-1940*. Commissioned by the Panel on Technology and Women's Employment, National Academy of Sciences, Washington, DC.

Stryker, Sheldon and Anne Statham. 1985. "Symbolic Interaction and Role Theory." Pp. 311-378 in *Handbook of Social Psychology, vol. I: Theory and Method*, edited by Gardner Lindzey and Elliot Aronson. New York: Random House.

Swedberg, Richard, Ulf Himmelstrand, and Goran Brulin. 1987. "The Paradigm of Economic Sociology: Premises and Promises." *Theory and Society* 16:169-213.

Swidler, Ann. 1986. "Culture in Action: Symbols and Strategies." *American Sociological Review* 51:273-286.

Tannenbaum, Arnold S., Bogdan Kavcic, Menachem

Rosner, Mino Vianello, and Georg Wieser. 1974. *Hierarchy in Organizations*. San Francisco: Jossey-Bass.

Thoits, Peggy A. 1983. "Reply to LaRocco." *Journal of Health and Social Behavior* 24:92-95.

Treiman, Donald J. 1979. *Job Evaluation: An Analytic Review: Interim Report to the Equal Employment Opportunity Commission*. Washington, DC: National Academy of Sciences.

—— and Heidi I. Hartmann. 1981. *Women, Work and Wages: Equal Pay for Jobs of Equal Value*. Washington, DC: National Academy Press.

Trist, Eric L. 1981. "The Sociotechnical Perspective: The Evolution of Sociotechnical Systems as a Conceptual Framework and as an Action Research Program." Pp. 19-75 in *Perspectives on Organization Design and Behavior*, edited by Andrew H. Van de Ven and William F. Joyce. New York: John Wiley.

—— and K. W. Bamforth. 1951. "Some Social and Psychological Consequences of the Longwall Method of Goal Getting." *Human Relations* 4:3-38.

Terkel, Studs. 1974. *Working: People Talk About What They Do All Day and How They Feel About What They Do*. New York: Pantheon.

Turner, Arthur N. and Paul R. Lawrence. 1965. *Industrial Jobs and the Worker: An Investigation of Response to Task Attributes*. Cambridge, MA: Harvard University, Division of Research, Graduate School of Business Administration.

U.S. Commission on Civil Rights. 1985. *Comparable Worth: An Analysis and Recommendations*. Washington, DC: Government Printing Office.

U.S. Department of Labor, Manpower Administration. 1970. *Hiring Standards and Job Performance*. Manpower Research Monograph No. 18. Washington, DC: Government Printing Office.

——. Employment and Training Administration. 1977. *Dictionary of Occupational Titles*. Washington, DC: Government Printing Office.

Vroom, Victor H. 1964. *Work and Motivation*. New York: John Wiley.

Walker, Henry A. and Mary L. Fennell. 1986. "Gender Differences in Role Differentiation and Organizational Task Performance." Pp. 255-275 in *Annual Review of Sociology*, vol. 12, edited by Ralph H. Turner and James R. Short, Jr. Palo Alto, CA: Annual Reviews.

Wanous, John P. 1980. *Organizational Entry: Recruitment, Selection, and Socialization of Newcomers*. Reading, MA: Addison-Wesley.

Weber, Max. 1958. *From Max Weber: Essays in Sociology*, translated and edited by H. H. Gerth and C. Wright Mills. New York: Oxford University Press.

Weick, Karl E. 1969. *The Social Psychology of Organizing*. Reading, MA: Addison-Wesley.

Weiss, Howard M. and James B. Shaw. 1979. "Social Influences on Judgment about Tasks." *Organizational Behavior and Human Performance* 24:126-140.

Wheaton, Blair. 1980. "The Sociogenesis of Psychological Disorder: An Attributional Theory" *Journal of Health and Social Behavior* 21:100-124.

—— 1983. "Stress, Personal Coping Resources, and Psychiatric Symptoms: An Investigation of Interactive Models." *Journal of Health and Social Behavior* 24:208-229.

—— 1985. "Models for the Stress-Buffering Functions of Coping Resources." *Journal and Health and Social Behavior* 26:352-364.

White, Sam E. and Terrence R. Mitchell. 1979. "Job Enrichment Versus Social Cues: A Comparison and Competitive Test." *Journal of Applied Psychology* 64:1-9.

Whyte, William Foote, Tove Helland Hammer, Christopher B. Meet, Reed Nelson, and Robert N. Stern. 1983. *Worker Participation and Ownership: Cooperative Strategies for Strengthening Local Economies*. Ithaca, NY: ILR Press.

Williamson, Oliver E. 1975. *Markets and Hierarchies, Analysis and Anti-Trust Implications: A Study in the Economics of Internal Organization*. New York: Free Press.

Wolpin, Kenneth I. 1977. "Education and Screening." *American Economic Review* 67:949-958.

Woodward, Joan. 1965. *Industrial Organization: Theory and Practice*. London: Oxford University Press.

Wrong, Dennis H. 1961. "The Oversocialized Conception of Man in Modern Society." *American Sociological Review* 26:183-193.

Zimbalist, Andrew. 1979. *Case Studies on the Labor Process*. New York: Monthly Review Press.

Zucker, Lynne G. 1977. "The Role of Institutionalization in Cultural Persistence." *American Sociological Review* 42:726-743.

11

Environments and Organizations

HOWARD E. ALDRICH
PETER V. MARSDEN

Organizations—producing goods, delivering services, maintaining order, challenging the established order—are the fundamental building blocks of modern societies, the basic vehicles through which collective action is undertaken. The prominence of organizations in contemporary society is apparent when we consider some consequences of their actions.

Above all, organizations coordinate the actions of people in pursuit of activities too broad in scope to be accomplished by individuals alone. For example, in ancient and medieval Chinese civilization, the bureaucracy of the scholar-official class coordinated large-scale activities essential to the society, including the maintenance of a calendar, a system of weights and measures, water works to guard against both floods and droughts, and a system of currency (Balazs, 1964). In the United States, railroads were the first large corporations, and they struggled to find methods of overcoming the problem of coordinating the passage of shipments across then-vast distances (Chandler, 1977).

More recently, the production of mass-market consumption goods, such as automobiles and televisions, has entailed the rise of large, vertically integrated manufacturing firms. Similarly, in the public sector, the development of welfare-state social policies necessitated the development of large government agencies (Orloff and Skocpol, 1984). When the United States found itself behind in the "race into space" in the early 1960s, President Kennedy committed the nation to putting a man on the moon within the decade, and he created an enormous organization—the National Aeronautics and Space Administration—to accomplish the task.

The concentration of power in organizations contributes not only to the attainment of large-scale goals in complex societies, but also to some of the most troublesome actions affecting us. When the American auto industry experienced a slump in 1980, firms laid off one-fourth of their employees, putting over 200,000 people out of work. Hazardous waste contamination, as in the "Love Canal" episode in Buffalo, New York, is a result of the careless disposal of unwanted hazardous materials by chemical manufacturers. In the Love Canal case, New York State and the U.S. government spent millions of dollars in dealing with the problem (Brown, 1979; Levine, 1982). Perrow (1984) discussed the "normal accidents" to be expected in complex technical systems managed by organizations, such as airline transportation or nuclear

This has been a fully collaborative effort, and the order of authorship is alphabetical. Thanks to Priscilla Preston for help in preparing the manuscript. We wish to thank the following persons for their helpful comments on previous drafts: Steven Andrews, Nicole W. Biggart, Glenn Carroll, Lee Clarke, Karen E. Campbell, Joseph Galaskiewicz, Arne Kalleberg, W. Richard Scott, Jitendra Singh, and Neil Smelser.

power plants. Less dramatic, but still illustrative of the capacity of organizations to do harm as well as good, are accounts of price-fixing scandals (Geis, 1967) and insurance fraud (Vaughan, 1983).

Organizations pervade our lives, and we tend to take their existence for granted. Consider, however, that much of an individual's biography could be written in terms of encounters with organizations: born in a hospital, educated in a school system, licensed to drive by a state agency, loaned money by a financial institution, employed by a corporation, cared for by a hospital and/or a nursing home, and at death served by as many as five organizations—a law firm, a probate court, a religious organization, a mortician, and a florist. Even one's use of leisure time is constrained by the options offered by certain organizations (Hirsch, 1972).

Increasingly, major tasks in society are addressed not by single organizations, but by sets of interdependent organizations. Shrum, Wuthnow, and Beniger (1985) described "technical systems" for the production of research, including government agencies, laboratories, private firms, and universities. Laumann, Knoke, and Kim (1985) studied "policy domains" consisting of government bodies, corporations, political groups, and nonprofit associations that collectively influence governmental policy formation and agenda-setting. Scott and Black (1986) reviewed interorganizational arrangements that have replaced the asylum for the delivery of mental health services at the community and societal levels. McCarthy and Zald (1977) discussed social movement "industries" and "sectors" that mobilize collective protest and articulate demands for social change.

Our plan for this chapter is as follows. We first consider the question of what constitutes an organization. Next, we present an overview of the field of organizational studies, focusing on the growth of several new theoretical orientations in the past decade. We then review some major research issues that are common themes in much of the recent research on organizations, and turn to some aspects of environments that complicate organizational research. Having presented the background to and central issues facing modern organizational analysis, in the second half of the chapter we review and evaluate research findings in three areas: the structural diversity of organizations, organizational change processes, and the nature of organizational fields. We conclude with some speculations about promising trends in organizational studies.

What Is an Organization?

Definitions of organizations abound. Typically included are such characteristics as goal orientation, deliberateness of design, and the existence of boundaries. Sociologists often add other criteria, such as the existence of a status structure, patterned understandings between participants, orientation to an environment, possession of a technical system for accomplishing tasks, and interchangeability of personnel.

We will not add to debates over which characteristics must be part of the definition of an "organization." Goal orientation and deliberate design of activity systems are, however, often cited as distinctive features discriminating between organizations and other collectivities. Organizations are purposive systems, and to an observer, members of organizations behave as if their organizations have goals. Concerted collective action toward an apparent common purpose distinguishes organizations from social units such as informal groups, friendship circles, and audiences or mass publics.

Organizations have activity systems—or technologies—for accomplishing work, that is, for processing raw materials, information, or people. Activity systems consist of bounded sets of interdependent role behaviors; the nature of the interdependencies is often contingent upon the techniques used. Organizations differ from other social units in the extent to which their activity systems are deliberately designed toward the accomplishment of specific goals. The formal structure of an organization, including a division of labor, authority relationships, prescribed communication channels, and so forth, reflects this purposeful design.

Other key elements of organizations are shared with other types of collectivities, but are no less essential to an understanding of organizations. The establishment of an "organization" implies a distinction between members and nonmembers (Weber, 1947). Maintaining the distinction requires boundary-maintenance activity, because boundaries may be permeable. This often involves the establishment of an authoritative process to enforce membership distinctions.

Organizations, with few exceptions, are typically incomplete social systems dependent on interchanges with their environments. Goal setting must take into account the sometimes contrary preferences of other organizations, as activity systems are fueled by resources obtained from outside a given organization's boundaries.

For example, participants must be enticed or coerced into contributing to the organization's activities. Because organizations are not self-sufficient, they are subject to uncertainties, and may be vulnerable to exploitation or external control by the outsiders on whom they depend. Much recent organizational theory and research is concerned with how these external dependencies are managed by organizations.

Within an organization, goal attainment and boundary maintenance manifest themselves as issues of coordination and control. Organizational authorities construct arrangements for allocating resources or integrating work flows. These internal structures affect the perceived meaning and satisfaction of individual participants by, for example, differentially allocating power and affecting the characteristics of jobs. Control structures—shaping the way participants are directed, evaluated, and rewarded—are constrained by participants' multiple external social roles, some complementing, but others conflicting with, organizational roles. Over the past few decades, organizational sociology has gradually expanded its scope to include more of the external uncertainties associated with organizational life, as we discuss below.

Overview of the Field of Organizational Studies

Historical Antecedents

Organizational sociology, as a field of specialization, has emerged rather recently. In 1947 the index of the *American Journal of Sociology* for the previous 52 years contained no subject references to "organization," "formal organization," or "complex organization" (Freeman, 1982). There were no entries under "bureaucracy," and readers were referred to "government" or "institutions." Six years later, the index to the *American Sociological Review* had no category for "organization" and only six entries under "bureaucracy." In the period since 1960, however, growth has been substantial.

Our overview of the field is indebted to Scott's (1987) comprehensive review. He described theoretical trends involving a shift from *closed-system rational* views, which treat organizations as tools and focus on internal management problems, toward *open-system*

natural views that see goal-setting as problematic and emphasize organization-environment relations.

Some pre-1960 political sociologists were concerned with the external environment of organizations, but most of the early work on organizations was guided by more practical considerations: investigators focused on management problems from the perspective of those interested in improving the efficiency and effectiveness of profit-oriented organizations.

With their normative commitment to improving the performance of organizations, closed-system rationalists emphasized the formal, manipulable features of organizations. Their social psychology was rather elementary, stressing pecuniary incentives for inducing participants to play their proper roles and fulfill their obligations to the putative higher rationality represented by managers or leaders. For example, Frederick W. Taylor (1947) argued that through scientific investigation, work processes and remuneration could be structured to encourage workers to obey management. As a result of this, both employees and organizations would achieve their maximum potential as well as serve their own economic interests, and there would be no basis for intraorganizational conflict.

A second set of theorists, whom Scott (1987) labeled *natural system* theorists, treated organizations as evolving social communities that had to meet certain needs if they were to persist. Natural system theorists emphasized the informal structure of organizations and the local adaptations participants made to the situations they experienced. For investigators trained in industrial psychology or related fields—such as the "human relations" tradition—a concern for effectiveness was translated into a search for organizational designs and leadership styles that would increase levels of participant satisfaction and commitment. The human relations school drew on a more elaborate theory of motivation than did the closed-system rationalists, emphasizing the morale of participants as a means to enhanced effectiveness. Barnard (1938) and Selznick (1948), in developing an institutional theory of leadership, highlighted the nonrational aspects of organizations that must be shaped into a unique organizational competence by leaders.

As Scott (1987, pp. 72-75) noted, closed-system rational and natural theorists took some account of environments, but neither had an explicit conceptualization of them. Beginning in the 1950s, the closed-system view was gradually challenged by open-system models giving increased weight to organization-environment interchanges. At first the new perspective worked within the boundaries of rational models, highlighting the organizational design issues posed by systems thinking and emphasized effectiveness and efficiency. Eventually, as the natural systems perspective gained a foothold in sociological studies of organizations, open-system natural models gained prominence.

Sociological studies, as opposed to industrial- or social-psychological studies, began addressing different problems from those of their predecessors, based on observations of the natural history of organizations. In the 1950s an "expose" tradition relying on case studies asked why organizations sometimes stray from pursuing their stated goals (Perrow, 1979). By the 1960s, sociologists taking a less normative approach began studying large (by comparative standards of the day) samples of organizations. They were interested in documenting, dimensionalizing, and explaining the diversity of organizations found in complex industrial societies. Initially, these efforts were directed toward achieving a unified general theory of organizations, as in the work of the Aston Group (Pugh et al., 1969a, 1969b) or Blau (1970), but eventually competing theories emerged (e.g. Hannan and Freeman, 1977; March and Olson, 1976; Meyer and Scott, 1983; Williamson, 1975). Aspects of the environment were central to most of the theories set forth after 1970.

Growth of the New Orientation

Several forces stand out as responsible for increasing the concern for "environments" in organizational studies: problems changed, political sociology began to contribute insights, new sources of funds arose, and interorganizational studies became popular in certain subfields.

A growing awareness of the anomalies and imperfections of closed-system views was partially responsible for development of new theories. There were no "critical experiments" or crucial tests that the traditional models failed, however. Indeed, many organizational psychologists and management theorists today are still pursuing research agendas laid down by founders of the human relations and cooperative management schools (Tosi, Rizzo, and Carroll, 1986). Rather, the incompleteness of closed-system views became apparent when research outside the confines of American business schools introduced new, more sociological issues into organizational analysis.

Early sociological attention to organizations was shaped by investigators with strong roots in political sociology. Selznick's (1949) study of the Tennessee Valley Authority, Dalton's (1959) study of relations between staff and line managers, Gouldner's (1954) analysis of a gypsum mine, Blau's (1955) analysis of two public agencies, and Lipset, Trow, and Coleman's (1956) investigation of the social structural roots of democracy within the International Typographical Union treated organizational activities as highly politicized, and "placed heavy emphasis on conflict as an endemic feature of organizational life" (Freeman, 1982, p. 25). "Power" was featured as an important force within organizations and in relations between them and their environments.

In the mid-1950s and early 1960s, a natural system perspective on organizational analysis became influential, as students of Robert Merton—Selznick, Blau, and Gouldner, among others—conducted historically informed case studies of organizations (see Merton, Gray, Hockey, and Selvin, 1952, for an early glimpse of the subsequent changes). Several sociologists —many of them students of Selznick—conducted research projects showing the powerful effects of environments as sources of goal displacement. One of the best known was Clark's (1956) study of adult education, showing that the pressures of an "enrollment economy" undermined the academic integrity of the program. In another, Zald and Denton (1963) documented the transformation of the YMCA from a highly specialized evangelical organization to an all-purpose service organization as its environment became increasingly secularized and economic prosperity permitted increased leisure time for people of all ages.

New sources of funds for organizational research facilitated research using an open-natural systems approach. The Ford Foundation and other nonprofit philanthropic agencies sponsored research on urban community organization (Moynihan, 1970). During the 1960s, the federal government funded hundreds of studies of social services sector organizations, focusing on ways of facilitating service coordination and avoiding duplication of effort. These studies of what Warren (1967) called "interorganizational fields" emphasized the external context of social services organizations and their power-dependence relations with local governmental units.

Perhaps no article did more toward demonstrating the potential of explicitly introducing the "environment" into organizational analysis than Stinchcombe's essay on "Social Structure and Organizations" (1965). Using a variety of case examples and secondary data, Stinchcombe showed that structural analysis at the organization level could illuminate the study of revolutions, social inequality and mobility, and other social phenomena.

Several other theoretical streams of work came together in the 1960s and early 1970s to shape an understanding of "environments." From human ecology, Hawley's (1950) writings spawned an interest in the ecological analysis of organizations. Katz and Kahn's (1966) melding of open systems and social-psychological analysis attracted the interest of business school departments of organization and management, and Buckley's (1967) review of open-systems thinking performed the same function in sociology departments. Contingency theory, asserting that effective organizational design required a matching of structure to environment, was advanced through the writings of Woodward (1965) and especially Lawrence and Lorsch (1967).

The remainder of this chapter will discuss the work conducted within this developing orientation. The bodies of research giving rise to an environmental perspective on organizations have been only partially integrated at best, and disputes begun in the early literature continue to the present. Our review concentrates on research and theorizing that takes organizations as units of analysis: how changes in organizational forms are affected by environments, how organizations may in turn influence or structure their environments, and how they are tied together into organizational fields. Research in related subfields draws on organizational theory to help explain phenomena such as inequality or individual responses to work settings; for coverage of these subjects, however, the reader is referred to other chapters in this book, such as those by Granovetter and Tilly and by Miller.

Major Research Issues on Environments and Organizations

Sociologists interested in organization studies have been concerned, on the one hand, with basic problems of social organization, and, on the other, with issues of efficiency and effectiveness. On the basic research front, two fundamental, related social science problems are central: organizational diversity and change processes. Most applied concern is focused on the issue of organizational effectiveness. The differences between these kinds of work should not be overemphasized, because they inform one another, but the distinction does point to important differences in emphasis between investigators.

Varieties of Organizations

The term *organization*, however defined, covers a very diverse set of social units. In this section we review conceptual schemes that have been proposed to apprehend this diversity. (For a more comprehensive review, see Scott, 1981, chapter 2.)

The number of organizations in industrial societies is very large. A conservative estimate of the number of businesses in the United States during 1982, for example, is 4.6 million.[1] To these must be added numerous governmental, nonprofit, membership and voluntary associations (e.g., Smith and Freedman, 1972; Knoke, 1986).

Business organizations are highly stratified by size, and large firms have more resources with which to resist and counter environmental pressures. The vast majority of organizations are small, however. Most business establishments employ fewer than 100 workers (Granovetter, 1984), while typical voluntary associations have fewer than 50 members (McPherson and Smith-Lovin, 1986). Most organizations are more vulnerable to environmental forces than literature focusing on cases such as General Motors, IBM, or Exxon might suggest. A representative sample of organizations would thus yield predominantly small ones.

If, however, interest lies in the impact of organizations on society, then we must recognize the substantial social power that is concentrated in a very small number of large organizations (Coleman, 1974). In the United States, more than 50% of the civilian labor force is employed by only 2% of employing units (Faber, 1973). In manufacturing, the top 200 firms control about 60% of all assets (Useem, 1984, p. 35). Kerbo (1983) reported that 50% of all banking assets are controlled by 30 out of 14,000 banks, and that eight out of approximately 1,800 insurance companies hold half of the assets in that industry. Some sociologists argue that this concentration points to a fundamental aspect of the environments of large organizations: Competitive forces are muted so effectively that survival is not nearly the issue it is for small ones (e.g., Perrow, 1986).

Organizations vary in many ways besides size, of course, and analysts have suggested dozens of concepts for capturing such variation. These have given rise to classifications and dimensionalizations based on inputs or raw materials, throughputs or organizational structures, and outputs or products.

INPUTS

Classifications based on inputs often overlap substantially with concepts used to describe environmental diversity, which we consider below. One that does not, however, emphasizes raw materials (Perrow, 1970): Are they homogeneous, or are many exceptional cases encountered? Are they human (and therefore reactive) or not? Differences such as these affect the level of uncertainty faced by an organization, and arguably its form as well.

STRUCTURES OR THROUGHPUTS

Structural diversity among organizations reflects differing responses to two fundamental problems of social organization—those of differentiation and integration. Differentiation refers to the division of labor among different roles and subunits; for example, employees may be divided into departments such as sales, finance, and manufacturing. As such, it is a centrifugal force that can threaten the coherence of social units. Integration, by contrast, refers to procedures through which coherence is maintained, as diverse roles are linked and activities coordinated. Examples of integrative processes include the holding of weekly departmental meetings or the circulation of interoffice memos.

Structural dimensions emphasizing differentiation concentrate on *complexity*—the extent and nature of specialization (e.g., Hall, 1987: pp. 58-65). Complexity increases with the number of different subparts, and may be horizontal (tasks spread over many roles or units), vertical (many levels in a hierarchy of authority), or spatial (many operating sites). Beyond the form of differentiation, some analysts (Mintzberg, 1979, chapter 7) concentrate on its content, asking whether tasks are grouped by products/market (soap, paper products, foods, and so on) or by function (finance, production, marketing, and so forth).

Problems of coordination are present for any activity system, but especially for a complex one. Many concepts used to describe organization structure involve alternative processes used in attempts to achieve integration. Mintzberg (1979, 1983), for example, conceptualized organizational design in terms of five coordinating mechanisms, which some analysts interpret as control mechanisms (Salaman, 1980): direct supervision, formalization, and three forms of standardization.

With *direct supervision*, or "simple control" in Edwards's (1979) view, persons at the top of a hierarchy make decisions that lower-level personnel simply carry out. This means that decision making is highly centralized. This coordination pattern was prevalent in preindustrial organizations, and today is especially likely within small organizations.

Formalization, termed "bureaucratic control" by Edwards (1979), seeks to achieve coordination through rules and procedures. Rules for arriving at work on time, for processing orders, for assembling and packaging products, or for conducting screening interviews for clients are examples. A formalized organization may appear decentralized, since few explicit commands are given and lower-level participants have freedom in making decisions within the rules. The rules may, however, be so restrictive as to leave little room for discretion, thus yielding little more than an illusion of decentralization.

Coordination also can be attained through standardizing work processes, skills, or outputs. With *standardized work processes*, coordination is built into machinery, as in an assembly line. This is Edwards's (1979) technical control." Most discretion is eliminated by the design of the technical system, and what remains is centralized in the upper echelons.

Standardization of skills involves considerable training and indoctrination of personnel, so that participants will carry out organizational policies with minimal oversight. Organizations employing large numbers of professionals are likely to rely on this coordination strategy. Professionalized participants enjoy considerable autonomy in making decisions, but their prior socialization sets most decision premises for them.

By producing products with *standard properties*, subunits of an organization are able to work independently of one another; if they use each other's outputs, the standards tell them what to anticipate. For example, large clothing firms produce massive runs of identical garments, and thus the various departments within firms know precisely what to expect from one another as they follow daily routines.

OUTPUTS

A final way to conceptualize the diversity among organizations involves their products or outputs. Again, many classifications are available. For example, establishments can be classified using the Standard Industrial Classification (SIC; Office of Management and the Budget,

1972). Parsons (1960) proposed that organizations should be classified according to their goals, or the social functions they serve. Thus he distinguished among organizations that help acquire resources, attain goals, maintain coordination, or create and transmit cultural patterns.

An oft-cited typology based on outputs is Blau and Scott's (1962) classification on the basis of the prime beneficiaries of organizational action: owners, members, clients, or the general public. Another output-based classification contrasts generalist and specialist organizations and hypothesizes that each type thrives in different kinds of environments (Hannan and Freeman, 1977).[2]

The conceptual schemes we have reviewed convey a sense of the great variety among organizations. Many typological efforts have not, however, been extensively used in empirical research, and none is consensually accepted by organizational analysts.

Understanding Diversity in Structural Form

The large number and variety of organizations makes organizational sociology a fertile research site for studies of how and why social structures differ. Diversity was not, however, a central issue in the early studies of intraorganizational phenomena; most theorists were working under the assumption that "all organizations are pretty much alike" (McKelvey and Aldrich, 1983) and that there was "one best way to organize." At the opposite end of the spectrum, rich case-study descriptions of single organizations often pointed to so many unique features as to make cross-organization generalizations inherently suspect. Neither approach was a fruitful point of departure for understanding organizational heterogeneity.

Early efforts at bringing diversity into organizational theory were largely descriptive, leading to some of the typologies discussed previously; examples are those based on routineness of technology (Perrow, 1967), compliance structure (Etzioni, 1964), or beneficiary (Blau and Scott, 1962). Some took an empirical approach to classification, attempting to build typologies by analyzing the cooccurrence of properties in samples of organizations (Hall, Haas, and Johnson, 1967; Pugh, Hickson, and Hinings, 1969a). Calls for the development of taxonomies of organizations continue, from population ecologists (Hannan and Freeman, 1977; McKelvey,

1982) and business strategy theorists (Porter, 1980).

Approaches to understanding differences in structural form span the entire scope of organizational theory. In the 1960s and 1970s, comparative studies of organizations (e.g. Blau and Schoenherr, 1971) emphasized structural forces, especially size, as correlates of differences in levels of differentiation, administrative intensity, formalization, and so forth. Scott (1987) referred to such theorists as open-system rationalists, because their explanations were framed in terms of administrative concerns for efficiency, and assumed that the relationships identified were more or less the same for all kinds of organizations.

Open-systems thinking sparked interest in explaining organizational diversity. Both empirical studies (Burns and Stalker, 1961; Lawrence and Lorsch, 1967; Woodward, 1965) and theoretical treatises (Thompson, 1967) suggested that organizations differ in form because they are situated within different social environments. These scholars often assumed "norms of rationality," but their explanations of diversity were much more sensitive than those of closed-system rationalists to the social contexts of organizations. This body of work came to be known as *contingency theory*, and its insights have been developed in several directions by contemporary schools of thought on sources of organizational diversity, notably population ecology and institutional theory.

Environments and Organizational Change

Parsons (1961) argued that the study of structure is logically prior to understanding structural change, but knowledge of change processes can also inform explanations of diversity in structure at a given time. During the 1970s there was great controversy in the area of organization studies concerning the mechanisms through which organization-environment relationships affect change within particular organizations. Child (1972) helped to structure the terms of the debate by contrasting what he perceived as technological and environmental determinist models of the 1960s with a more political model of "strategic choice." Although the distinction between the models that Child discussed can be framed as one of determinism versus voluntarism (Astley and Van de Ven, 1983), both kinds of models suggest that organizations adapt to their environments by changing their structures.

A radically different view of change processes is presented by the population ecology approach advocated by Hannan and Freeman (1977). They posited that there are strong inertial forces at work in organizations, and that individual organizations rarely change form. Most changes in diversity at the aggregate or population level come about not through transformation of existing organizations, but instead through turnover in units: the creation of new organizations and the dissolution of old ones. The fundamental process generating organizational diversity is thus one of environmental *selection*, driven by competition for resources and other environmental constraints.

Corning (1983) classified change theories by their supposed precipitating causes: purpose, necessity, or chance. Theorists attributing organizational change to *purposeful* action operate within Scott's (1987) rational system perspective. They assume that people make decisions on the basis of a consistent set of preferences, and that choices are directed toward a specific goal (Pfeffer, 1982, p. 6). Purpose may come from within, as in the case of goal-setting inspired by a charismatic leader, or be imposed from without, as in government agencies or corporate subsidiaries. Perspectives placing an emphasis on purpose include contingency theory, transaction cost economizing (Williamson, 1981), and any approach stressing "leadership" as an essential component of change.

Theories stressing *necessity* as an explanation for change tend to focus on unanticipated consequences of internal requisites for maintaining an organization (e.g., "technological imperatives"), or on external constraints that limit prospects for autonomous action (Pfeffer and Salancik, 1978). Such theories fall within what Scott (1987) called the natural and open-systems perspectives, and their explanations tend to avoid variables that describe an organization in favor of those focusing on its environment. Population ecology, institutional theory, resource dependency theory, and other approaches emphasizing situational constraints fall within this domain.

Theories attributing change to *chance* are neither especially prominent nor popular within the social sciences. Some models used in research on work and occupations and in the study of organizational cultures are sympathetic to chance explanations, as they emphasize emergent outcomes growing out of negotiated orders and situational ambiguity (Benson, 1977; Fine, 1984). Ecological models presume a large random component to change, particularly in the generation of variations from which organiza-

tional forms are selected. Such models differ from early deterministic "evolutionary" models because they make no predictions about the future course of change (Aldrich, 1979, pp. 52-54). Accidental combinations of resources and constraints are doubtless common in the creation of organizations. The "garbage can" model of change in "organized anarchies" (Cohen, March, and Olson, 1972) attracted attention and critical praise (Perrow, 1979) when first proposed, but it has not generated a great deal of research (March and Olsen, 1976; Padgett, 1980).

Purpose, necessity, and chance are not mutually exclusive in their application, and theories are distinguished primarily by the extent to which they emphasize one set of forces over another. For example, ecological models may posit that the behaviors of individual actors are best modeled by a random walk process, but explain changes in organizational forms primarily through external constraints. Astley and Van de Ven (1983) argued that many apparent conflicts between perspectives actually reflect differences in their levels of analysis, with many purposive models focusing on individual behaviors and necessity models focusing on organizational or population levels. Following this reasoning, the path to integrative, comprehensive applied research remains open.

Organizational Effectiveness

Practitioners and citizens look to organizational theory for guidance on how organizational performance might be improved, or at least for explanations of differences in performance. Assessing effectiveness has proved to be a less straightforward enterprise than it might seem at first blush, however. For some organizations, especially businesses, there are clear performance standards based on financial indicators and clear market tests of whether they are effective. Nevertheless, assessments might differ depending on whether, for example, one adopts a long- or short-run perspective.

Determining effectiveness grows even more difficult when clear or measurable performance standards are lacking. For example, is the effective police department one that makes a large number of arrests, or one that forestalls criminal activity with surveillance and handles domestic disputes with conflict resolution work—and therefore makes few arrests? How are we to know how well an educational institution achieves vague goals such as inculcating a love of learning or the capacity to be a responsible citizen?

Ambiguity in the assessment of organizational outputs has led to different concepts of effectiveness. The "system resource" approach of Yuchtman and Seashore (1967) transformed the issue into one of survival: The effective organization was one that succeeded in acquiring from its environment the resources it required to persist. A related notion of effectiveness is put forth by institutional theories (e.g. Meyer and Scott, 1983), which suggest that in the absence of clear output tests, organizations will be evaluated on the basis of the appropriateness of their structures and processes, as judged by relevant environmental actors. Effectiveness is thus defined in terms of conformity to norms of the wider society about proper ways to organize, regardless of whether these have demonstrable links to the production of output. By conforming to "rationalized myths" about effective structure and processes, organizations maintain their legitimacy and retain access to needed resources from the environment (Meyer and Rowan, 1977).

Both system resource and institutional conceptions of effectiveness are based on factors external to an organization. Attainment of effectiveness thus defined may depend more on adept political work outside of the organization than on instrumental work within it.

Aspects of Environments

The "environment" figures prominently in almost all contemporary organization theory but is rarely defined in other than a residual way, as everything outside the boundaries of an "organization." Theorists and researchers have attempted more precise specification by pointing to several distinct elements of environments, including informational, resource, cultural, and temporal aspects. In this section we review these efforts at dimensionalizing environments, after a discussion of differing levels of analysis for organization/environment studies.

Levels of Analysis

The appropriate conception of "environment" depends in part on the analytic focus of a study. Researchers must decide whether all organizations in a given area or sector face the same environment, or whether environments must be defined uniquely for each organization. Carroll (1984a) distinguished organizational, population, and community levels. One of the classic organization-environment studies (Lawrence and Lorsch, 1967) drew even finer distinctions, noting that different subunits of a single firm may face quite dissimilar environments.

Early writing, and most subsequent research, focused on individual organizations and regarded "the environment" as everything external to a focal unit that was relevant to the unit's goal setting or attainment. Dill (1958) coined the term *task environment* as a label for what lay beyond organizational boundaries, and Evan (1972) called for attention to the "organization set," consisting of the other organizations with which a focal organization interacted when procuring inputs or disposing of outputs. These concepts encouraged a view that environments were composed of other organizations, and stressed instrumental transactions between them and focal organizations. They were not developed into systematic statements of how environments of different organizations vary, however.

Lawrence and Lorsch (1967, pp. 19-20) used a focal organization approach, but also assumed that industrial context was an important feature of the environment. Because they were concerned with the management of uncertainty, they studied firms in three industries having different rates of technological innovation. Their characterization of the three industry contexts pointed the way toward later efforts at developing summary indicators of the state of an organization's environment, by making use of "contextual" measures.

Some more recent studies have treated collections of organizations as objects of analysis, and required correspondingly different conceptions of environments. Population analysis, stimulated by Hannan and Freeman's (1977) programmatic statement, is concerned with aggregates of similar organizations competing for the same resources. Resource combinations that are sufficient to support organizational forms are termed niches. Organizations in a population may have either symbiotic or competitive relations with one another.[3]

The community level of analysis is concerned with sets of interacting organizations, or with interdependent populations of organizations. Inclusion of an organization in a community may be based on either functional interdependence or geographic location (Laumann, Galaskiewicz, and Marsden, 1978). Functional criteria restrict the set of organizations to those sharing a common or collective goal; social service delivery systems are a commonly studied example. Scott (1987) used the term *field* in place of "community" to avoid geographic connotations, as functional and geographic definitions of organizational communities need not coincide.

When populations or communities/fields are studied, researchers typically use contextual measures for the relevant area as indicators of environmental states. Among the explanatory variables used in over-time studies of organizational founding rates, for example, are human population size and immigration rates (Hannan and Freeman, 1987) and the occurrence of events such as political turbulence, economic prosperity, or depression (Delacroix and Carroll, 1983). Few comparative studies of organizational fields have been conducted, but these undoubtably require similar kinds of environmental measures.

Environments as Stocks of Information and Resources

The need for measures of environments that could be compared across organizations grew with the introduction of open-system approaches. In keeping with purposive assumptions, many theorists emphasized technical aspects of environments—that is, features that facilitated or impeded the efforts of organizations to accomplish their principal tasks. One view saw environments as sources of information that could present problems of uncertainty. Another, complementary, view treated environments as pools of resources for which organizations compete, stressing the dependence of the organization on environmental actors (Aldrich and Mindlin, 1978). These dimensions were used jointly by Lawrence and Dyer (1983) in their study of the competitiveness and potential for innovation and renewal of American industry.

Investigators studying organizational uses of information are concerned with decision processes inside organizations and with the conditions under which information is received and processed by participants. The effect of uncertainty on people's decision-making capacity is highlighted, and emphasis is placed on transformations of organizational structures to cope with uncertainty. Thus organizations are hypothesized to "buffer" their core activity subunits by creating boundary subunits charged with uncertainty absorption (Thompson, 1967) and to institute uncertainty reduction processes including forecasting, stockpiling, and the like.

A resource view of environments points to the incompleteness of organizations as social systems, and asks about their bargaining power vis-à-vis the environment, insofar as obtaining necessary inputs is concerned. The autonomy of a focal organization relative to its environment depends on access to resources and competition for them (Burt, 1980a). Analyses examine bridging efforts to limit competition or mitigate dependency through creating interorganizational relations like contracts, consortia, joint ventures, or, in the extreme case, mergers.

Aldrich (1979, pp. 63-74) surveyed the literature and identified six abstract dimensions that were relevant to informational and resource views of environments. Scott (1987, p. 128), in a similar listing, specified seven. Among those identified were the following:

(1) Environmental capacity or munificence: the supply of resources in the environment. In general, organizations are more dependent on lean environments than on rich ones;

(2) Environmental heterogeneity: the diversity of elements in an organization set. More heterogeneous environments tend to create more uncertainty;

(3) Environmental instability: the rate of turnover in elements of an organization set. Higher levels of instability increase uncertainty;

(4) Environmental concentration: the extent to which necessary resources are controlled by a small number of environmental actors. High concentration entails dependence because a focal organization is less able to place environmental elements in competition with each other;

(5) Environmental coordination: the density of relationships between relevant environmental actors, indicative of their capacity to act collectively. High coordination increases dependence for the same reason that concentration does, but reduces uncertainty; and

(6) Environmental hostility or threat: the disposition of environmental actors toward a focal organization. This reflects the organization's legitimacy and indicates its vulnerability. Uncertainty is increased in threatening environments.

Dess and Beard (1984) and Burt (1983) conducted research directed toward obtaining operational measures of environmental dimensions. Dess and Beard (1984) studied 52 four-digit SIC manufacturing industries in an attempt to validate five of Aldrich's (1979) environmental dimensions. They constructed four or five scales for each, measuring characteristics of inputs, outputs, and member firms within industries. Factor analysis of the scales produced three factors with acceptable reliability: munificence, heterogeneity, and instability. Dess and Beard suggested that their results could be used to generate measures for any SIC industry, but to date no investigators have done this.

Burt (1983) adopted a structural approach to describing environments, using data on two-and four-digit SIC manufacturing industries, which he regarded as market contexts within which individual firms operate. His work focused on a network of sales and purchase transactions, as given by input-output tables assembled by the U.S. Department of Commerce, and on industry concentration (oligopoly) levels. His measure of "constraint" combined elements of heterogeneity, concentration, and coordination as discussed above. Firms operating within a market are highly constrained to the extent that they purchase outputs from, and sell inputs to, only one other industrial sector, and this constraint increases to the degree that the sectors with which they must deal are noncompetitive, that is, oligopolistic or concentrated. In addition, firms are constrained to the extent that they have many competitors, i.e., when concentration in their own market is low.

Cultural Conceptions of Environments

One of the first explicit statements on organizational environments as institutional or cultural phenomena appeared in Parsons's (1956a, 1956b) essays in the inaugural volume of the *Administrative Science Quarterly*. In Parsons's model, organizations survive only insofar as they achieve legitimacy through their contributions to the wider society. Thus organizations are never truly independent: They must adapt to the institutional structure and agencies of superordinate social systems.

Parsons sustained the Weberian perspective on organizations that Selznick (1948, 1949) and his students advocated in the 1940s and 1950s. They argued that societal institutions give rise to organizations in their own images, reflecting a conception of environments as supraorganizational meaning systems defining appropriate patterns of organizational activity.

Some studies of functional organizational fields—social service delivery systems—pointed to "institutionalized thought structures" (Warren, Rose, and Bergunder, 1974) as bases for organizational survival. Interorganizational conflict is minimized to the extent that units within a field achieve "domain consensus" (Litwak and Hylton, 1962); that is, agree on a common set of rules governing their activities. A "group ethic" of corespective behavior (Baran and Sweezy, 1966) serves a similar purpose among business firms. Culture is thus viewed as a set of norms and values shared by interacting organizations or business elites and governmental officials (e.g., Galaskiewicz, 1985a).

The most influential recent statement on a cultural conception of environments is by Meyer and Rowan (1977). They adopted a much more inclusive view of the culture affecting organizational activities, pointing to the rules, understandings, and meanings attached to institutionalized social structures. Meyer and Rowan (1977, p. 343) argued that

> [m]any of the positions, policies, programs and procedures of modern organizations are enforced by public opinion, by the views of important constituents, by knowledge legitimated through the educational system, by social prestige, and by the definitions of negligence and prudence used by the courts.

They referred to the normatively approved structures and activities as rationalized myths, since the institutional environment exerts pressure to adopt them irrespective of the extent to which they are "efficient" within some means-ends calculus. These myths about appropriate organizational forms are taken-for-granted and nearly invisible to most participants, making them highly resistant to change.

Norms, values, and like concepts are defined at a high level of abstraction, and are not amenable to precise measurement. Most work on institutional environments thus relies on indirect indicators that differentiate between settings thought to place greater or lesser institutional pressure on the organizations within them. Some investigators infer the importance of culture when a techno-rational model does not work out as expected. Some "culture" studies have contrasted organizations operating in different countries (Lammers and Hickson, 1979) or at different times (Tolbert and Zucker, 1983). Others analyze particular fields or sectors, such as education or medical care, where effects of specific laws or rules can be examined (Meyer and Scott, 1983).

Temporal Elements

One of the influential early discussions of environments (Emery and Trist, 1965) revolved around environmental "turbulence." Emery and Trist argued that developments in advanced industrial societies had produced environments that were changing in poorly understood ways, and that individual organizations were seeking collective solutions in managing problems produced by the changes. Since that classic article, organizational sociologists have become more conscious of the need for explicitly including time in models of environments.

Hannan and Freeman (1977), in introducing population ecology models, specified three environmental concepts—uncertainty, variability, and grain—the last two of which refer to environmental change. Variability indexes the typical span separating states between which the environment varies (e.g., the amplitude of a business cycle), while grain refers to the typical length of time (relative to an average organization's life span) that the environment is in any given state. These concepts represent a specification and expansion of the concept of stability proposed by earlier investigators.

Taking a long-term view of the temporal aspects, Scott (1983) focused on the historical dimension. The history of an organization's environment encompasses relevant past conditions including the time at which an organization was created (Stinchcombe, 1965), the number and rate of change in competitor organizations (Hannan and Freeman, 1987), and differences across historical eras—including levels of political unrest or changes in legal institutions. For example, the sociopolitical environment for the health care system in the United States changed dramatically after World War II with the passage of the Hill-Burton Act, which subsidized the construction of hospitals in many communities that previously could not afford them. Hospital founding rates increased substantially, as did founding rates of new organizational forms symbiotically linked to hospitals (Alexander and Amburgery, 1987).

Problems in the Conceptualization of Environments

Analysts have come a long way from residual, "everything else" definitions of an organizational environment, but many problems remain. Although useful for pedagogic purposes, typologies obtained by cross-classifying sets of environmental dimensions have not notably informed empirical research (McKelvey, 1982). Typological dead ends might reflect a failure to resolve the level of analysis issue: The environmental attributes most relevant to explaining organizational form and change differ by kind of organization, by industry, and over time (Carroll, 1984a). In addition, highly abstracted typologies can miss important attributes at the local level. Still, if the area of organization studies is to move toward empirically verified generalizations about the effects of environments on the form and change of organizations, populations, and organizational fields, developments toward generalized conceptions and measures of environments must continue.

Another persistent issue concerns whether environments affect organizations chiefly through the way in which they are perceived by participants, or whether they have an objective presence independent of perceptions. Dill (1962) first suggested the perceptual emphasis, while some later theorists (e.g., Weick, 1979) expressed interest only in participants' cognitions. Others have been concerned both with events and their perception (Bacharach and Lawler, 1976). Several investigators have studied the disjuncture between perceptual measures and objective indicators of environmental states, particularly for the measurement of environmental uncertainty (Downey, Hellriegel, and Slocum, 1975; Tosi, Aldag, and Storey, 1973).

A late 1970s survey of past issues of the *Administrative Science Quarterly* (Downey and Ireland, 1979) found 27 articles that dealt directly with how organizational environments were conceptualized. Most investigators had presumed a dichotomy between "objective" and "subjective" measures, depending on whether they were gathered from archival sources or participants. Downey and Ireland noted that such a dichotomy was unfortunate, and suggested differentiating between what is being measured and how measurement is conducted. Environments can be conceptualized in terms of either the perceptions of participants or attributes that exist independent of individual actors; and one can measure each via both quantitative (surveys, archival sources) or qualitative (in-depth observation) techniques.

Research on Structural Diversity

When researchers became sensitive to diversity among organizations during the 1950s and 1960s, they began devoting attention to explaining differences in structure. The theoretical framework used in these efforts was one of contingency theory, broadly conceived. Contingency theory specified that particular structures were appropriate adjustments to certain situations, and that organizational effectiveness depended on an appropriate matching of design to circumstance. Most research has examined the structural hypothesis; less attention has been devoted to effectiveness.

Contingency theory departed from the "one best way to organize" prescriptions of early organization theory. In common with those approaches, however, it tended to treat organizational structures as the result of rational decisions by managers seeking to administer organizations efficiently. Thus it implied that organizational diversity was the result of adaptations of structures to varying situations. Later waves of research, which we review below, treated diversity as the outcome of processes of organizational change driven by environmental selection.

Research designs for early studies on diversity were typically cross-sectional, comparing numerous organizations in different situations and drawing inferences about how a given organization would change as it moved from one situation to another. These designs differed from the case study designs of prior studies, and increased confidence in the representativeness of results. At the same time, because organizations were not followed over time, this design left basic questions unanswered. In particular, adaptation of structure to circumstance had to be inferred from cross-sectional correlations, under the implicit assumption that an equilibrium state had been reached.

We briefly review research on three major situational factors that have captured the attention of researchers: size, technology, and environment. Though some of the size and technology research does not specifically deal with environmental issues, we review it because it formed the context within which later research was conducted. Our review is necessarily selective, as far more research was conducted on each factor than we have space to review here. We have attempted to highlight major themes and research projects that provide empirical support for generalizations about diversity.

Size

Few propositions in the organizational literature are better documented than those involving the covariation of size and organizational structure. Size, usually measured as the number of employees, permits increased specialization and division of labor, and thereby results in greater structural complexity. This proposition was set forth by Blau (1970), who provided support for it from a sample of U.S. public employment agencies. Blau argued that due to diminishing economies of scale, differentiation should

increase with size at a decreasing rate. This finding has been replicated for several other kinds of organizations in the United States (Blau, 1972; Miller and Conaty, 1980), for British business organizations (Child, 1973), and for Japanese factories (Marsh and Mannari, 1981).

Substantial research attention has been given to the relationship between size and coordination mechanisms, especially regarding the amount of resources devoted to administration, usually measured as the "administrative ratio" —the number of administrators per production worker. Initial disagreements arose over how the proportionate size of the administrative component varies with organization size (Scott, 1987, p. 242), but the bulk of the available results, for several kinds of organizations, indicate that administrative ratios decline with size (Blau, 1972; Blau and Meyer, 1987, p. 95).

Administrative economies are thus available in larger organizations; these come, however, at a decreasing rate with size. Decreasing returns to size occur because reduced costs of supervising the larger and more homogeneous subunits of larger organizations are balanced by increasing costs of coordinating their more numerous subunits (Blau, 1970). Size and the administrative ratio are more strongly related for growing than for declining organizations (Freeman and Hannan, 1975; McKinley, 1987), suggesting that political, in addition to rational, elements play a part in organizational design. Administrators are apparently reluctant to eliminate their own positions in the course of work force reductions.

The size of an organization also covaries with measures of formalization and standardization of procedures. Blau and Schoenherr (1971) indicated that personnel regulations increase with size; Van de Ven, Delbecq, and Koenig (1976) showed that the use of plans and rules rises with subunit size; Pugh, Hickson, and Hinings (1969a) found a strong relationship between size and "structuring of activities"; and Marsh and Mannari (1981) found a more modest association between size and their formalization scale. Contrary to stereotype, however, the level of centralization of decision making appears to be lower in larger organizations, according to the results of Blau and Schoenherr (1971), Child (1972), and Mansfield (1973). Delegation of discretion is more extensive in larger organizations having more levels of authority.

Empirically, size is the most important correlate of diversity in organization structure, but the theoretical status of "size" as an explanatory variable is unclear. Kimberly (1976) pointed to alternative conceptual meanings of size and noted that different measures of size usually, but not always, covary strongly. An organization's size is usually viewed as an indicator of environmental demand for its product (Blau and Meyer, 1987); it also reflects technological economies of scale (Chandler, 1977). Size is thus seen as a factor intervening between environmental conditions and organizational form (Aldrich, 1972).

Technology

Woodward (1965), who was one of the first researchers to systematically document structural diversity among organizations, stressed their activity systems as the factor behind differences in structure. She classified her sample of English manufacturing firms by the complexity of their technical processes: small batch or custom producers; large batch or mass producers; and continuous process or bulk producers. She found that this classification was associated with numerous differences in organizational structure. Some structural features were related directly to technical complexity: vertical differentiation, capital intensity, and the administrative ratio are examples. In other respects, the small batch and process firms were similar. In particular, they tended to have smaller first-line work units and more "organic" (as distinct from "mechanistic") management systems than the large batch firms. Woodward's research thus supported the proposition that the character of technical systems had strong implications for the administrative structures of organizations.

Subsequent theoretical work stressed the complexity, uncertainty, and interdependence of technical processes guiding the structuring of organizations. Scott (1987, p. 214) summarized the relevant hypotheses: that technical complexity will be mirrored by structural complexity; that technical uncertainty will lead to decentralization and a deemphasis on formalization; and that highly interdependent work flows will tend to require more resources for coordination.

These hypotheses have received mixed support in empirical studies conducted since Woodward's. Hickson, Pugh, and Pheysey (1969) studied 46 "diverse" organizations, and found that a measure of work flow integration was correlated with formalization, specialization, and decentralization. These correlations were weaker, however, for a subsample of 31 manufacturing organizations; size was, in general, more strongly associated with structural form than was work flow integration. Blau et al. (1976) obtained similar results in their study of

large (200 or more employees) manufacturing establishments. Marsh and Mannari's (1981) findings for Japanese factories showed that size is a better predictor of differentiation than "automaticity"—a measure of the degree of automation in the production process—but automaticity is a stronger correlate than size of three other variables: the mix of direct and indirect workers, the typical education of employees, and labor intensity. Both size and automaticity were associated with increased formalization in the Marsh-Mannari study. Singh's (1986) reanalysis of Marsh and Mannari's data suggests that these issues remain open.

The research results for technology hardly justify the notion of a technological "imperative," but neither do they show technological factors to be irrelevant. Some of the inconsistent findings are surely attributable to difficulties in conceptualizing and measuring an organization's technology. Listing 23 different indicators of technology, Scott (1975) noted that the concept of "technology" can refer to the materials, operations, or knowledge involved in an organization's activity system. Each of these facets may be applied to different stages of processing (inputs, throughputs, and outputs), so many concepts and measures of technology are possible.

Research on structural effects of technology is also complicated by the problem of choosing an appropriate level of analysis. Work processes are quite heterogeneous within organizations; consider, for example, the manufacturing and marketing units of a corporation, or the emergency, nursing, and accounting departments of a hospital. Obtaining a single summary measure of technology for an entire organization under such conditions is a demanding task, and there are further differences in work processes for individual employees within subunits. We are thus not surprised that some of the more convincing studies of technology and organizational form were conducted at the subunit level (Comstock and Scott, 1977; Van de Ven, Delbecq, and Koenig, 1976). Indeed, many analysts conclude that technology as a situational factor is most relevant to the structuring of the core subunits comprising an activity system, especially small work groups (Hickson, Pugh, and Pheysey, 1969; Mintzberg, 1979; Scott, 1987).

Environment

Emphasis on the environment as a contingency factor was stimulated by field studies conducted during the 1950s and 1960s comparing relatively small numbers of organizations. Burns and Stalker (1961) undertook a retrospective study of firms in Scotland and England, focusing on how organizations dealt with change in their market situations and technical systems. "Mechanistically" structured organizations responded to change by elaborating on already established bureaucratic procedures, whereas "organically" structured ones increased lateral communications, created more flexible job definitions, and so forth. The organic form seemed more suited to rapidly changing circumstances, while the mechanistic one did best in stable conditions. This was not, however, a study of organizational adaptation, for no matter how poorly they "fit" their environmental conditions, few organizations changed form (Burns and Stalker, 1961, p. xi).

In the United States, Lawrence and Lorsch (1967) studied a high- and a low-performing firm in each of three industries—plastics, food processing, and standardized containers. They concluded that the appropriate level of internal differentiation and the requisite mechanisms for coordination and dispute resolution were contingent on the nature of the environmental demands faced by subunits. They found that differentiation and integration were better matched to the state of the environment in the high-performing firms.

These exemplars led to studies that examined the association between measures of environmental properties and diverse aspects of organizational structure or functioning. Environmental uncertainty received the most attention; the guiding hypothesis was that under conditions of uncertainty, structures would tend to be more organic (less formalized, less centralized). Considerable attention was devoted to accounting for differences in organizational effectiveness.

The orienting ideas of environmental contingency theory remain provocative. Research on environments, structure, and effectiveness has been conducted, however, at several levels of analysis, from the individual employee to the cluster of organizations. It has also measured environmental properties in numerous ways, almost none of which have been used by more than one investigator. For these reasons, findings have been inconsistent, and it is difficult to reach firm empirical generalizations as to environmental correlates of organizational diversity. We review selected studies covering major themes.

HETEROGENEITY

Comparative studies of organizations conducted in the 1960s were designed to study variations in structure by size and technology, and contained limited information about environmental properties.[4] Blau and Schoenherr (1971, chapter 8) did find, however, that the specialization of local employment agencies was related to the heterogeneity of local populations. DuBick's (1978) findings on the structure of major metropolitan newspaper organizations revealed a similar association between diversity and structure. Daily newspapers with more diverse local populations tended to have more departments and a more heterogeneous staff distribution. Of particular note to the contingency perspective is the result that newspapers in competitive situations were more responsive to their environments than those in monopoly positions.

MUNIFICENCE

On the dimension of environmental munificence, Bidwell and Kasarda (1975) found, for school districts, that per capita revenue lowered pupil-teacher ratios while raising numbers of professional support staff and staff qualifications. Staw and Szwajkowski (1975) reported that businesses operating in profitable industries were less likely to be cited for unfair market practices or restraints of trade.

Fennell (1980) conducted a panel study of small localized populations, or "clusters," of hospitals within SMSAs. She found that the range of services within a cluster was more responsive to the supply of medical service providers than to the nature of the local population, casting doubt on the idea that structure is strictly a reflection of patient demand. Fennell inferred that institutional elements of the environment were more important than characteristics of the patient base. Perhaps most interesting, she found that hospital clusters grew more differentiated as they became larger. This was contrary to her expectation that duplication of services would increase as hospitals competed for patients, but it is consistent with Carroll's (1985) resource-partitioning model positing that organizations specialize within niches of a resource space, thereby avoiding competitive pressures.

UNCERTAINTY

At the subunit level, Argote (1982) obtained findings consistent with the effectiveness proposition of contingency theory. She found, for hospital emergency units, that programmed means of coordination were effective in providing efficient patient care when units dealt with few patient conditions, but that nonprogrammed means were advantageous when a greater variety of conditions was handled. She did not, however, isolate any general tendency for high-uncertainty units to use nonprogrammed means. Schoonhoven (1981) also obtained results supportive of contingency propositions in a study of operating room suites in hospitals. Leblebici and Salancik (1981) studied the decision-making processes of loan officers in Illinois banks. They found that environmental diversity was associated with permanent organizational routines for loan processing, while volatility was handled on a case-by-case basis. Hirsch's (1972) work on industries engaged in the production and mass distribution of cultural products—books, music recordings, and motion pictures—described structural devices used to cope with input and market uncertainty, including considerable numbers of boundary-spanning personnel charged with locating talent and seeking publicity for products.

The contingency perspective has thus proved informative in some studies, but it is by no means an unqualified success. Arguments that uncertainty influences structure and effectiveness have been called into serious question by other studies. Pennings (1975) studied 40 branch brokerage offices, finding that "none of the environmental variables seemed to be relevant for understanding why organizations differed structurally" (p. 403) and that "[t]he goodness of fit between environmental and structural variables has little bearing on the effectiveness of the organization" (p. 405). Osborn and Hunt (1974) found no association between environmental complexity and the perceived effectiveness of 26 social service agencies. These results, among others, have forced analysts to reconsider the propositions of contingency theory, and have stimulated calls for more precise specification of how structure and effectiveness are to be "fit" to environmental conditions (Schoonhoven, 1981; Drazin and Van de Ven, 1985).

DEPENDENCE

Mintzberg (1979) and Scott (1987) argued that environmental effects should be sharpest in the "peripheral" sectors of organizations, those at or near their boundaries. Indeed, research results focusing on structures buffering and bridging organizational boundaries have been more consistent than other findings. Recent research has highlighted the dependence of organizations on their environments, and has

argued that interorganizational relations are constructed as a consequence of resource dependencies. Managers are said to construct bridging ties with cooptive intent; that is, with the objective of stabilizing relationships with critical external elements.

Pfeffer (1987) reviewed research on intercorporate relations, most of which is consistent with a resource-dependency perspective. Data on interlocking corporate directorates are publicly available, so they have been the object of much analysis. Pfeffer (1972a) found that the size and composition of boards of directors could be understood in relation to environmental features; for example, companies with higher debt/equity ratios tended to have more bankers on their boards, while regulated corporations tended to have more outside directors. Using his measure of the extent of market constraint between industries, Burt (1983) reported that outside directors tend to come from those industries on which a firm is most dependent.[5]

The same resource-dependence logic has been used in the study of other kinds of more tangible interorganizational ties. Pfeffer and Nowak (1976) found that joint ventures are more likely between corporations in interdependent industries tan in industries having little to do with each other. Pfeffer (1972b) obtained a similar finding in his study of mergers. Likewise, Burt (1983) reported that cross-industry ownership ties tend to follow patterns of interindustry dependence.

An organization's dependence on its environment is also correlated with the distribution of power and influence within it. The Aston group (Pugh et al., 1969b) reported a correlation between dependence on the environment and the concentration of authority. Studies of budget decision making within universities (Pfeffer and Salancik, 1974) show that subunits tend to be regarded as powerful when they are sources of external funds from grants or contracts, and that powerful departments receive larger budget allocations, net of their size and other bureaucratic bases of resource distribution.

Research on Organizational Change Processes

As the above survey indicates, contingency perspectives generated a great deal of research on the fit between organizations and their environments, but often failed to address the question of how a fit was achieved. The presumption was that fitness resulted from the transformation of structures toward consistency with environmental constraints and opportunities. The prevailing cross-sectional research designs could not, however, either verify or contradict the assumption of organizational adaptation.

Organizational theory has brought dynamic issues to the forefront in the past decade; several theories have been advanced to account for empirical generalizations on environments and structural form established by contingency-oriented research. Managerially based theories continue in the tradition of open-system, rational-purposive perspectives. Prominent among these is transaction-cost economizing (Williamson, 1975, 1981), contending that organizational boundaries will be set, and "governance" structures established, to minimize the costs of coordinating work in an activity system. Transactions can become costly when they are conducted under conditions of uncertainty and imperfectly distributed information, and when small numbers of opportunistically inclined buyers and sellers are potential parties to them. Under these circumstances, this perspective claims, the administrative overhead of an organization will provide more efficient coordination than market transactions between independent producers. Thus if changes in technological conditions or market structures alter the environments for transactions, efficiency considerations would lead to creations or structural transformations of organizations. Vertical integration and movement from unitary to multidivisional structures are examples (Chandler, 1977).

Institutional theories (Meyer and Scott, 1983) focus instead on external conditions for persistence or transformation, highlighting industrywide or societal values and norms to which organizations must conform. When cause-effect relations between organizational structures and outcomes are poorly understood, maintaining a secure flow of resources requires that organizations adopt externally legitimated practices. Change is thus thought to follow from altered definitions of appropriate structure and process promulgated by external bodies such as professional associations or state agencies.

An interesting implication of this line of reasoning is that it forecasts increasing homogeneity of organizations within fields (DiMaggio and Powell, 1983), as they are typically subject to the same external pressures. Structural similarity should rise as organizations in a field adopt practices prescribed by law or by normative pressure from professional associations. Similarity should also increase as new organizations entering a field copy the structures of already existing units, or as existing units mimic forms and procedures of one another. Ouchi (1981) gave one example of the latter process: Large American corporations, in their attempts to be internationally competitive, are turning to Japan for models of workplace organization. To the extent that managers consciously adopt other organizations' practices in pursuit of effectiveness, such models mix purpose and necessity in their explanations for organizational change.

By contrast, population ecology (Hannan and Freeman, 1977) gives little attention to transformation. Instead, ecologists maintain that structural and societal pressures toward structural inertia place severe limits on organizational adaptive capacity. Organization-environment fit is, therefore, achieved through demographic processes—more fit forms are created more rapidly than they are dissolved. This perspective thus focuses on competition, selection, and differences in net mortality among organizational forms, with fitness judged by the extent to which births exceed deaths.

Research conducted in conjunction with current perspectives has sought study designs that are faithful to theoretical concerns with processes of organizational change. Over-time studies have become much more common, and knowledge about correlates of birth and death rates is beginning to accumulate. Key issues remain, however, especially regarding the pivotal question of organizational adaptive capacity. Our review of research on change follows the organizational life course: We first cover foundings, or the creation of new organizations; we then turn to transformations, the modification of existing ones; and finally to dissolutions, the death or absorption of existing organizations.

Foundings

It is commonplace to observe, as we have, that contemporary society is organizationally based (e.g., Presthus, 1978), but there have been relatively few studies that permit us to say just what conditions have facilitated or required the creation of organizations. Theoretical ideas advanced by Stinchcombe (1965) have greatly influenced work in this area. He argued that societal demands for special-purpose organizations increased with urbanization and differentiation in society, while the supply of factors needed to construct them grew with the development of a money economy and the spread of literacy. The emphasis of institutional theory on the facilitative part played by changes in legal institutions is also pertinent. Coleman (1974) reviewed changes in the law that first gave recognized social standing to impersonal corporate actors, and institutionalists contend that the initial organizations developed within these laws served as cultural models for the creation of others.

An emphasis on the broad societal conditions generating or facilitating the formation of organizations is very different from typical accounts drawn from research on entrepreneurship (see Aldrich and Zimmer, 1986). Many of these are personality-based theories stressing traits such as internal control, ambition, tolerance for risk, and the like. Such psychological constructs might help to explain which individuals in a society perceive and act on available opportunities, though the evidence is by no means clear on this point. Sociological approaches to the issue of who becomes an entrepreneur ask instead about how individuals are tied to information and other resources necessary to building an organization. Personality-based approaches are of little assistance in understanding why there are niches to be entered, or opportunities to be seized.

CREATION RATES

Data on founding rates are not especially abundant, but available information shows that new organizations are established fairly frequently. Birch (1979) estimated birth rates for business establishments in the United States as the percentage of new units added relative to the number existing at the beginning of a period, giving a rate of 14.7% for 1972-1974 and 13.4% for 1974-1976. The Small Business Administration (1986) estimated the annual birth rate during 1980-1982 at 10.4%, with that for 1982-1984 at 12.5%. Similar results are emerging for other Western nations: Research conducted for the Department of Trade and Industry of the British government found that the business birth rate there in 1981 was 9.6% (Ganguly, 1982). For New Zealand in 1981, the rate was 8.3% (Bollard and Harper, 1986).

ENVIRONMENTAL CONDITIONS
FOR FOUNDINGS

Explanations for variation in rates of creation have stressed opportunities for or stimuli toward foundings, the existence of technological and social infrastructures, and population processes. Brittain and Freeman (1980) traced the development of the semiconductor industry, noting that

innovations in both products and production processes for transistors, integrated circuits, and microprocessors opened niches for new firms to enter. Delacroix and Solt (1988) reported that increasing imports of foreign wine actually increased the founding of new American wineries, as increasing consumption was a sign to potential entrepreneurs that a niche was opening.

Pennings (1982) examined interurban variation in birth frequencies for three industries in which creation rates are relatively high: plastics, telecommunications, and electronic components. He found that city size had a positive zero-order correlation with birth frequencies, though this disappeared when other factors were controlled. Occupational and industrial differentiation had a curvilinear relationship to creations; Pennings argued that moderate differentiation would create specialized or "adjacent" niches (Aldrich and Pfeffer, 1976), but that extreme differentiation would involve fragmentation and hence depress creations. Munificence, too, seemed important: Creation frequencies rose with a measure of capital availability, but fell with bank concentration, which Pennings treated as an inverse indicator of the availability of venture capital.

Other studies present additional data on population size and creations. Carroll and Huo (1986) reported a negative relationship between size and creation rates for newspapers in the San Francisco-Oakland-San Jose region, but this became positive when certain other environmental variables were controlled. Aldrich, Anderson, and Grams (1976) found that Councils of Governments (COGs) tended to be established earlier and more frequently in large SMSAs. They also showed that COGs were established in places with higher per-capita revenues and with more local governmental units; these results suggest effects of munificence and demands for coordination, but Aldrich et al. do not present results of multivariate analysis.

Stinchcombe's (1965) essay suggested that periods of political upheaval or revolution could stimulate new organizational structures by freeing resources from previous uses. Historical research on newspaper creation rates is consistent with this reasoning. Political turbulence was the best predictor of creation rates in Delacroix and Carroll's (1983) study of Irish and Argentine newspapers, and Carroll and Huo (1986) replicated this result. During turbulent periods, rival factions created newspapers to publicize and promote their causes. In the California study, turmoil increased the founding rate for all newspapers, not just explicitly political ones.

INFRASTRUCTURE

Chandler (1977) repeatedly noted that the emergence of modern industrial corporations became possible only with the development of fast, efficient means of transportation and communication. Much recent work has examined the social, rather than technological, infrastructure within which new organizations are created. Marrett (1980) studied the establishment of women's medical societies in seven cities during the late nineteenth century, comparing them to seven matched cities lacking women's societies. She found that in the cities with women's societies, women physicians were more active in the primary local medical society and were more likely to be linked via partnerships or institutions. She concluded that these conditions allowed women to acquire organizational skills and build networks, which in turn facilitated establishment of a women's society. Sabel (1982) used a similar argument in explaining the high rate of founding of small metalworking shops and artisanal businesses in small towns near Bologna, Italy, pointing to the dense network of ties between craft workers there.

Research findings on ethnic business support the proposition that social density encourages creations. Light (1972) and Bonacich (1973) argued that the internal organizing capacity of an ethnic community is a condition for business efforts, and that this helps to explain the differing business fortunes of, for example, Chinese and blacks. The most salient feature of early business ventures by ethnic groups is their dependence on an infrastructure built by fellow immigrants (Aldrich et al., 1985). Mutual benefit associations, cooperative housing and buying arrangements, joint capital-raising activities, and other collective actions provide support for potential entrepreneurs.

Voluntary associations, trade associations, public agencies, and other sorts of "broker" social units can increase opportunities for people to contact one another, and thereby facilitate creations. The pattern of social organization in the Silicon Valley region of California illustrates this: Well-known "watering holes" and restaurants, together with family and friendship networks, supported a high start-up rate (Rogers and Larson, 1984). However, as McPherson and Smith-Lovin (1988) showed, the presence of other organizations competing for the same kinds of members inhibits the growth chances of voluntary associations.

Creations may also be encouraged through spinoffs from loosely coupled organizations operating in high-innovation environments. Under such conditions, engineers may see the potential of a new technique that superiors fail to grasp, or sales and marketing staff may learn about unfilled market needs, as illustrated in Brittain and Freeman's (1980) study of the semiconductor industry.

POPULATION PROCESSES

Population ecologists study demographic conditions and events relevant to the creation of new organizations, including population size, recent births, recent deaths, competition among forms, and capacity constraints. A principal concern has been with *density dependence*. In the initial stages of the growth of a form, birth rates tend to rise with the number of similar organizations, as they begin to exploit resource opportunities. As the number of organizations nears the carrying capacity of the environment, however, birth rates tend to fall as a consequence of intrapopulation competitive processes.

These predictions of ecological theory were confirmed in Hannan and Freeman's (1987) study of founding rates for national labor unions. The rate of founding was curvilinearly related to the prior number of unions. Moreover, interform competition was evident: Increases in the number of industrial unions inhibited the creation rate for craft unions, though no reverse competitive effect was apparent. The competition model yields similar findings for semiconductor firms and newspapers (Hannan and Freeman, 1988). Pennings's (1982) findings also support the notion of density dependence, in that birth frequencies for manufacturing concerns rose with the number of preexisting firms, but fell as the environment grew less munificent.

Creations are influenced not only by prior population size, but also by recent demographic events. Delacroix and Carroll (1983) estimated a "population dynamics" model of newspaper foundings. They hypothesized that recent births would increase creation rates by providing successful models to emulate. Modest recent death rates were likewise thought to permit new formations by freeing resources, but high death rates would be a signal that a form was no longer viable. The Delacroix and Carroll results supported these propositions. Carroll and Huo (1986) replicated the findings for recent birth rates, but not those for recent deaths. A positive dependence of creation rates on recent birth rates was also found for national labor unions in Hannan and Freeman's (1987) study. Delacroix and Solt (1988) obtained similar results for the American wine industry, finding that the number of wineries founded increased foundings in subsequent years.

Transformations

The issues of how frequently and under what conditions organizations change has provoked some of the most spirited debates in contemporary organization studies (Astley and Van de Ven, 1983). The polar positions of the controversies are taken up by strategic choice theorists arguing for managerial autonomy and adaptability, and population ecologists stressing organizational inertia. The enthusiasm of theoretical dispute in this area has not been matched by a corresponding volume of research results, so some of the most attractive opportunities for new work lie here.

INERTIA

The argument for managerial choice and adaptation has been reviewed above, so we discuss the case against it here. Hannan and Freeman (1984), drawing on Stinchcombe (1965), argued that the early period of an organization's existence is a crucial and fragile one, during which operating routines are worked out and external legitimacy established. Organizations in their early years are subject to a liability of newness, or high ''infant mortality'' rate (see below). Hannan and Freeman concluded that organizations surviving past infancy will be reluctant to alter structures and processes, anticipating what might be termed a ''liability of reorganization.''

A case for organizational inertia can be built on the basis of environmental factors as well. Hannan and Freeman asserted that the institutional environment of contemporary society rewards organizations for reliability and accountability. The structures and processes that produce these, in turn, discourage innovation.

Moreover, many of the mechanisms used to coordinate work in organizations will permit change to occur slowly, if at all. Organizational routines built around elaborate structures of formalized rules or automated technology cannot be changed overnight; decentralization of authority and loose coupling may permit autonomous work and responsiveness, but they can also lead to the creation of numerous ''veto groups,'' any of which has the potential to block proposals for change.

These considerations have interesting implications for the relative strength of inertial forces in large and small organizations. On the one hand, the superior resources of large organizations give them more wherewithal for adapting to external conditions. On the other hand, the simple structures of small organizations can be changed more readily (Mintzberg, 1979). Accordingly, small organizations may attempt reorganization more often, but also fail more often in the effort, as Hannan and Freeman (1984) suggested. Large ones may appear more adaptive, not because they are more innovative but because they are better equipped to ride out disruptive effects of reorganization. We are aware of little systematic data bearing on this issue, but a few interesting studies exist.

Two articles based on longitudinal studies have some bearing on the contention that there is a liability of reorganization; they yield contradictory results, however. Carroll's (1984b) study of publisher succession in the newspaper industry was an indirect test; he found that death rates of newspaper organizations increased in the wake of succession, presumably due to concomitant attempts at reorganization. Singh, Tucker, and House (1986) studied the impact of various organizational changes, including major structural change, on the death rates of voluntary social service organizations in metropolitan Toronto. They found that most changes had little effect on the death rate, and changing the chief executive actually lowered the death rate. Singh et al. speculated that their results might reflect the fact that the organizations they studied are highly institutionalized ones, dependent more on legitimizing themselves with the environment than on the outcome of competitive struggles with one another.

Advocates of the inertia position can point to Romanelli's (1986) historical study of the American minicomputer industry, which found that two-thirds of all firms used the same basic marketing strategy over the course of their lives. The firms that did change during the formative years of the industry tended to stick with their new strategy rather than adjusting further as the industry matured. Boeker's (1988) study of semiconductor firms in Silicon Valley also found that organizations were set on a path at their founding from which change was difficult.

One implication of the structural inertia argument is that, on occasion, ''creative destruction'' may be the only way in which to engineer transformation. Biggart's (1977) study of reorganization at the United States Postal Service showed that radical changes in leadership and personnel were required to inculcate a marketing orientation. Starbuck (1983) described the near-fatal inertia of the Facit Office Machine Company, which continued to produce electromechanical calculators when the market was moving toward electronic office machines and computers. Disaster was averted only when the entire top management was replaced.

Institutionalists can point to studies showing that prevailing definitions of appropriate organizational forms engender transformations. For example, Rothschild-Whitt (1979) studied a collectivist school in Santa Barbara that tried to maintain an antibureaucratic, no-written-records policy. It was forced by other local educational organizations to keep records so that its students would be able to transfer into the larger organizational field if they chose. Tolbert and Zucker (1983) showed that local governments adopted civil service reform fastest when this was prescribed by state law, while others adopted as reform gradually became legitimated. Jacoby (1984) attributed the development of internal labor markets in manufacturing firms to "new social norms of employment" rather than to organizational complexity. In discussing the same innovation, Kochan, Katz, and McKersie (1986) focused on the power of industrial relations specialists who drew on externally defined professional standards to develop personnel practices.

STRATEGY AND ADAPTATION

Studies that bolster the adaptationist view that organizations change in response to their environments can also be found. Miles and Cameron (1982) studied the response of large firms in the tobacco industry to the smoking and health controversy that began in the 1960s. Their work described strategic responses, at both the organizational and communal levels, including domain defense through the creation of political joint ventures and diversification into other industries. They contended that the situation left considerable latitude for strategic action, finding that some firms successfully diversified whereas others failed. Miles and Cameron asserted that appropriate diversification required allegiance to an underlying "corporate character."

Some results of Fligstein's (1985) study of the adoption of the multidivisional form (MDF) by American corporations also yield support for a strategic management perspective. Fligstein found that firms pursuing product-related or product-unrelated strategies were more likely to adopt the MDF than those concentrated in a single line of business. Mimetic effects were evident as well, as adoption rose with the number of prior adoptions in a corporation's industry. Fligstein noted that his study design did not permit a strong test of the ecological argument for structural inertia.

Our brief review makes it obvious that issues of transformation are by no means closed. Certainly some instances of successful transformation have been documented, but many occurred only in the face of imminent hostile action by environmental elements. Hrebiniak and Joyce (1985) suggested that both environmental determinism and strategic choice may be important in a given situation, and that it is not fruitful to pose the central issue as a question of whether one or the other is valid. Instead, researchers should study the extent to which environmental conditions allow flexibility in responses and the capacity of a given organization to formulate and implement a strategy.

Dissolutions: Organizational Mortality

If all newly founded organizations lived forever, the study of organizational change would be limited to the issues of creation, adaptation, and inertia. Organizational existence is much more precarious than this, however. Organizations dissolve at a reasonably high rate, and advocates of environmental perspectives on organizations have sought to isolate properties that influence death rates. In keeping with the emphasis of ecology on population dynamics, almost all research on dissolutions has been conducted within an ecological frame of reference.

DISSOLUTION RATES

Organizations can cease to exist as separate entities in two ways: by completely dissolving, with their resources freed for other uses, or by becoming part of a different entity through merger or acquisition. Freeman, Carroll, and Hannan (1983) have pointed out that the causes of mergers and failures might differ substantially, and that the two should be separated in analyses of dissolutions. For example, economically successful firms are among the most attractive targets for acquisitions, while economically marginal ones are most at risk of failure.

The more dramatic event, merger, has attracted more publicity in recent years, but the actual frequency of mergers is comparatively low. The number of "economically significant" mergers has averaged fewer than 2500 per year. By contrast, there were 70,644 business bankruptcies in 1985, and almost 400,000 business "deaths." Between 1976 and 1984, the annual rate of dissolution in the business population ran at about 10% (Small Business Administration, 1986). Of course, the volume of resources involved in most dissolutions is far lower than in the typical economically significant merger.

LIABILITIES OF NEWNESS AND SMALLNESS

Two internal characteristics—age and size—appear to affect mortality rates regardless of environmental conditions. Carroll (1983, p. 304), reviewing findings from 52 data sets on organizational mortality, stated that "the most common finding is that organizational death rates decrease with age." This holds under controls for size, historical period, and other factors, and confirms Stinchcombe's (1965) thesis of a liability of newness. In addition to internal liabilities revolving around attracting qualified employees and creating and clarifying roles and structures, new organizations are subject to external liabilities stemming from barriers to entry that make acquisition and mobilization of resources difficult. Singh, Tucker, and House's (1986) research on social services organizations attributed a modest liability of newness in that population to differential success in establishing external legitimacy.

Dissolution rates are also consistently higher, irrespective of age, for small organizations than for large ones. Birch (1979), for example, found that death rates were highest for establishments having fewer than 21 employees. Liabilities of smallness include problems in raising capital, meeting governmental rules and regulations, and competing for labor with larger organizations that pay higher wages and offer more benefits (Aldrich and Auster, 1986).

Institutional legitimacy is clearly a factor in organizational mortality. Carroll and Delacroix (1982) showed that an increase in the political and economic legitimacy of the Argentine press reduced death rates over time. Halliday, Powell, and Granfors (1987) found that as the novel form of "state bar association" became legitimated, death rates for bar associations declined to zero.

POPULATION PROCESSES

Organizations of the same form occupying the same niche compete for resources, and the more densely packed the niche, the tighter the competition. The expected population growth curve is S-shaped, with a rapid initial increase while the ratio of competitors to resources is low, and a gradual leveling off as carrying capacity is reached. Death rates, like creations, are thought to be curvilinearly related to population size, falling as a form gains a foothold and then rising as competitive pressures increase. Few studies give data on density-dependence of death rates, however.

Carroll and Huo (1986) studied the population dynamics of death rates, examining the implications of recent birth and death rates for current death rates. They found that rates of death for newspapers rose with the number of foundings in the previous year, but that the death rate was insensitive to recent disappearances. They concluded that high birth rates heighten competition, but that high death rates do not necessarily reduce it.

Another effect of competition, as Hawley (1950) pointed out, is to increase population differentiation. This could occur through adaptive processes, as less fit competitors enter adjacent, noncompeting niches. Carroll's (1985) resource-partitioning model suggests instead that increased differentiation results from the dissolution of unsuccessful competitors and concomitant foundings in adjacent niches. In either case, we observe symbiotic as well as competitive relations between population elements.

Carroll (1985) tested the resource-partitioning model in a study of all newspapers founded in seven American cities between 1800 and 1975. He distinguished between generalist newspapers that attempt to cover the mass urban market, and specialists that serve a specific subpopulation (e.g., an ethnic neighborhood). As the concentration of the mass market for which generalists compete grew, death rates of generalists rose as they spread themselves thin in attempts to cover all of it. The death rates of specialists decreased at the same time, however; Carroll reasoned that they benefited by focusing on newly formed narrow niches that generalists could not cover adequately. Several other industries, including music recording, book publishing, and brewing, show a mix of organizational forms that may well be produced by similar dynamics.

NICHE WIDTH AND MORTALITY

When environments are certain, or changing in predictable ways, specialism is always an optimal strategy, as specialist forms can concentrate on that portion of the environment in which they do best. Under uncertainty, the situation is more complex. In their discussion of niche width, Freeman and Hannan (1983) argued that the implications of uncertainty for the differential survival of forms are contingent on the extent to which organizations can tolerate extreme environmental conditions. If many organizations can survive at the extremes ("convex" fitness sets), generalists would be favored in all uncertain environments. If, however, most organizations cannot survive at any extreme ("concave" fitness sets), specialists would be favored when change is rapid ("fine-grained"), because they will encounter favorable conditions often enough to ride out difficult environmental states. No form would do very well when change is slow and unpredictable, though Freeman and Hannan hypothesized that generalists would outperform specialists.

Freeman and Hannan (1983) tested part of this model in a three-year study of restaurants in 18 California cities. They assumed a concave fitness set, so their study applied to only part of the model, but they found relatively strong support for their predictions. "Full-menu" restaurants (which they classified as generalists) were much more likely to persist in seasonal, high-variability environments, but under other conditions more specialized restaurants had better survival chances. Carroll and Huo (1988) found that a specialist strategy had opposing effects at different stages in the life course of local assemblies of the Knights of Labor. Specialist assemblies (organized around a single trade) had higher initial death rates, lower rates in the next two years, and thereafter were indistinguishable from generalists (organized around multiple trades). Their findings imply not only that different strategies are appropriate for different environments, but also that the effectiveness of strategies may vary over organizational life-course stages.

Discussion

Significant progress has been made toward dynamic models of how environments affect organizational change. Appreciable developments in both study designs and analytic methods (e.g., Tuma and Hannan, 1984) have occurred. Almost all generalizations about change processes are based on research conducted during the past decade. Without minimizing the achievements of these studies, we note that there are a number of reasons for caution in interpreting their results.

We have mentioned the relative inattention given to issues of transformation in empirical studies. Ecological work has been reluctant to examine differences in organizational form other than specialism-generalism, and its ability to inform the study of other aspects of structural diversity—such as differentiation, formalization, and the like—has been correspondingly limited.

Many methodological issues are open as well. Much of the research conducted on change relies heavily on archival and historical data having limited epistemic correlations with environmental conditions. Indicators of institutionalization tend to be especially indirect. Moreover, controls for competing explanations have been less than fully adequate. Enthusiasm for environmental perspectives should not deter investigators from gathering detailed information on administrative and strategic differences between organizations within a population. Competition and environmental pressure may place an upper limit on the number of organizations that can survive in a niche, but those organizations that do survive are not necessarily randomly drawn.

Organizational Fields

The study of organizational fields marks an important shift in the level of analysis and the kind of interorganizational interdependence examined. The object of study is not an individual organization or a set of potential competitors, but a set of organizations oriented toward some collective end. This could be, for example, the determination of public policy, either national (Knoke and Laumann, 1982) or local (Galaskiewicz, 1979); the representation of industry interests (Miles and Cameron, 1982; Staber, 1985); or the delivery of social services (Rogers and Whetten, 1982; Morrissey, Tausig, and Lindsey, 1986). Tension often exists between the objectives of the individual organizations composing a field and its collective purpose, and thus much attention has been directed toward the question of how cooperation at the field level can be attained without sacrificing the autonomy of individual units. In studies on the social services sector, investigators have emphasized the conditions leading to the establishment of domain consensus, thus avoiding interagency competition and the charge of duplication of effort, and guaranteeing each component unit a secure niche (Levine and White, 1961).

Types of Fields

Several typologies of organizational fields have been offered. These are generally based on the extent and legitimacy of coordination within a field. Warren (1967) distinguished between social choice, coalitional, federative, and unitary contexts. In the social-choice setting, cooperation among organizations is based on individually defined interests, and participation in collective action is voluntary; as one moves toward the unitary context, hierarchy develops with the establishment of central coordinating authorities, and the participation of individual organizations tends to become mandatory.

Laumann, Galaskiewicz, and Marsden (1978) referred to competitive, contingent, and mandated contexts for network formation. These categories contrast fields in terms of the discretion of component units, as well as in terms of the legitimacy of joint action. Cooperation is encouraged in contingent and mandated fields, but is viewed with suspicion in the competitive setting. Whetten (1982) observed that interorganizational research in the public sector has had the objective of promoting agency coordination, but studies of private-sector fields are concerned with preventing it. Downs (1967) described the competition for policy domains by public agencies, which fight to control "their" territory.

Themes in Theory and Research

A great deal of interorganizational research has been devoted to the question of how organizations can enter relationships with one another while maintaining their independence, drawing on exchange theory (Cook, 1977; Levine and White, 1961) for theoretical motivation. Research conducted in this area overlaps substantially with that on the resource-dependence models used in the study of bridging structures, which were reviewed above (see also Galaskiewicz, 1985b).

In addition to studies of the structure and behavior of individual organizations embedded within fields, there has been some work on the form of fields themselves. One line of theorizing is reminiscent of structuralist work on organizational diversity, as it relates different features of field structure to one another. Phillips (1960) offered generalizations about the formalization of "interfirm organizations" in oligopolistic markets. Formalization would become more crucial as the number of firms grew and as power was dispersed among them. Formalization would also grow more necessary as the firms in the environment became better organized and more efficient, if the oligopoly was to maintain a given level of efficiency.

Turk (1977) stressed the importance of pre-existing linkages among field organizations for resource mobilization and coalition formation, and provided supporting data from interurban comparisons. Knoke and Laumann (1982) offered a set of hypotheses relating aspects of field structure, including centralization and polarization, to the outcomes of agenda-setting processes within policy domains.

Institutional theorists have related the structuring of fields to properties of their environments. Scott and Meyer (1983) proposed hypotheses linking the centralization of decision making within societal sectors to conditions in their environments, such as professionalization, and to outcomes including the development of interlevel control among organizations in the sector. DiMaggio and Powell (1983) focused on sources of homogeneity or "institutional isomorphism" among field organizations. They pointed to external conditions including power-dependence relations, state pressure, and the visibility of alternative organizational models as predictors of the extent of and rate of change in isomorphism.

Much research at the field level deals with interorganizational relationships; emphasis on collective action within organizational fields has predisposed investigators toward the study of coordinating ties, or of conditions that hinder coordination. From the standpoint of individual organizations within a field, interorganizational ties are seen as devices through which uncertainty is reduced or dependence mitigated. We have studies of information linkages (Galaskiewicz, 1979; Laumann, Knoke, Kim, 1985), personnel flows (Baty, Evan, and Rothermel, 1971), influence and assistance ties (Lincoln and McBride, 1985), and joint programs and written agreements (Knoke and Rogers, 1979).

As noted above, interlocking directorates have been studied as cooptive devices from the standpoint of individual corporations, but other analysts adopt a systemic or field perspective on them. Directorate ties are treated as devices through which the unity of the business community (Mintz and Schwartz, 1985) or the capitalist class (Useem, 1984) is maintained. A consistent finding in such research is that banks and other financial institutions tend to be central in an interlock network. This has been taken as supportive of a thesis of bank hegemony over the community (Mintz and Schwartz, 1985), but the finding of bank centrality is also consistent with what resource dependency theory would predict from the perspective of an individual organization. Because fluid capital is an important resource for many corporations, one would expect cooptive efforts to place bankers on a board, which in turn would would yield central positions for banks when a set of overlapping boards is analyzed.

Discussion

The study of organizational fields is both more recent and less developed than that of diversity or change in individual organizations. Some practical obstacles to research in the area were overcome with the development of network models and methods (e.g., Burt, 1980b; Marsden and Laumann, 1984). The data requirements of such methods are rather extensive, however, because information on many organizations and their ties to one another must be assembled for each organizational field. For this reason, studies comparing fields to one another are comparatively rare, and many hypotheses concerning fields virtually untested. Most studies have been cross-sectional (two exceptions are Galaskiewicz and Wasserman, 1981, and Mizruchi, 1982), and many have had a descriptive flavor.

Interest in organizational fields or "communities" (Carroll, 1984a) is likely to increase with the rise in the organizational density of society. There is substantial room for theoretical and empirical work here, both on the structure and functioning of fields and on their origin, development, and failure. Interest in the new internationally competitive business environment and industrial policies to meet changing competitive conditions should spark more interest in the generation of new organizational forms, and rekindle interest in field-level interaction between organizations. New forms of organization (as opposed to new organizations with traditional forms) may be facilitated by infrastructural developments at the field level, such as new financial arrangements between capital sources, consortia among technically innovative organizations, or export support from public agencies. Although the debate over industrial policy ignited by the 1984 U.S. presidential campaign has died down, controversy over the best way to meet the Japanese challenge clearly involves possible restructuring of competitive and symbiotic interorganizational relations at the field level. This could involve new sorts of ties between business, government, and organized labor (see Ouchi, 1984), and research interest in collaborative organizational arrangements—joint ventures, licensing, and so forth—seems to be increasing.

Conclusion

Organization studies have displayed a good deal of intellectual vitality during the past decade. A series of provocative developments in theory during the late 1970s has been followed by a period of consolidation in which the beginnings of a solid empirical foundation have been laid. In closing this review, we comment briefly on some trends in the field, and some important open issues.

We observe an increase in theoretical crossfertilization. Advocates of competing perspectives have grown more willing to take one another seriously, and points of complementarity as well as conflict have been found. A prominent example lies in the exchange between population ecology and institutional theory: Differentials in establishing legitimacy have come to be regarded as important elements of competitive processes in analyses of creations and dissolutions. Researchers could profitably study the processes by which ideas about the legitimacy of new organizational forms are established (e.g., Biggart, in press).

Organizational perspectives have achieved notable penetration into related areas of sociology. This is clearest in the area of work and stratification (see Baron, 1984), where analysts commonly treat organizations as arenas for such processes as career mobility and income attainment. Elite studies in political sociology now routinely take organizations as key units of analysis, or at least regard organizational affiliations as key resource bases for elite individuals.

The increase in dynamic and cross-national organizational studies has encouraged other connections between organization studies and general sociology. Many studies of organizational change have covered reasonably long time frames, during which large-scale social changes altered environments. More sensitivity to the "long-term" opens up the possibility of dialogues with historical approaches to the study of social change. Comparative studies of organizations in different institutional and cultural settings (e.g., Lincoln, Hanada, and McBride, 1986) present other opportunities to link the study of organizations to macrosociological concerns.

We applaud these trends. The potential they represent will be realized, however, only as the study of environments and organizations continues to build on its theoretical and empirical basis. We have entered various remarks throughout this essay on topics that present clear opportunities for new research. We see a need for attention to clarification of key concepts; for example, a clear delineation of organizational forms, even on a within-population basis, would advance the study of transformations. There is also reason for caution in the uncritical adoption of theoretical frameworks from other disciplines. We have learned a great deal from theories that draw on foundations in biology and economics, for example, but there are important differences between organizations and organisms, and the social structure in which organizations develop differs in appreciable ways from what some economic approaches assume (Granovetter, 1985). Sociologists using such models might profitably reexamine the work of economic historians (Robins, 1987).

Some methodological issues also require attention. We have noted the lack of consensus on measures of both organizational and environmental properties. Another barrier to codification has been the relative inattention to sampling issues in organizational research. Clear sampling frames for organizational studies are yet to be developed. According to a comprehensive study conducted by Drabek et al. (1982), only 13% of articles on organizations published between 1965 and 1979 used simple or stratified random sampling; the rest used saturation, purposive, or convenience samples. Few samples contain more than 100 cases. Thus knowledge about organizations has only a weak claim to representativeness.

A related issue is that of replication. With some exceptions that we have noted, few hypotheses have been examined repeatedly. While replication is not the most glamorous of scientific activities, it is essential to the building of an empirically verified body of theory. We would hope to see it become more common in the 1990s, as research on organizations pursues and develops the leads we have reviewed here.

NOTES

1. *County Business Patterns* (U.S. Bureau of the Census, 1982). This source reports only nonfarm business establishments with one or more employees. Internal Revenue Service (Small Business Administration, 1986) figures on business income tax returns filed use a less restrictive definition of business, including even single part-time persons with no employees. In 1983, 15.2 million business income tax returns were filed.

2. Note, though, that this classification could equally well be termed an input or environmental one, since generalists by definition draw on many environmental resources in wide "niches," while specialists are found in comparatively narrow niches.

3. McPherson (1983) modeled competition among voluntary associations for members. He measured niche overlap as the extent to which types of associations recruit persons of similar age, occupation, sex, and education.

4. Udy (1962) is an exception.

5. Most research on interlocking directorates has been cross-sectional. Palmer, Freidland, and Singh (1986) conducted a longitudinal study of accidentally disrupted directorate ties, and found that directed ones—in which an officer of one corporation sits on the board of another, with no reciprocal relationship—tend to get reestablished. They argued that interlocking is associated with formal coordination and may be required for its persistence. Stearns and Mizruchi (1986) studied "functional" reconstitution of broken ties, which occurs when a new tie is established to a corporation in the same industry as the one involved in the previous link. They found that quite different factors are associated with direct and functional reconstitution.

REFERENCES

Aldrich, Brian C., Theodore R. Anderson, and Robert W. Grams. 1976. "Predicting New Urban Social Organization: Councils of Governments." *Sociological Focus* 9:73-87.

Aldrich, Howard E. 1972. "Technology and Organization Structure: A Reexamination of the Findings of the Aston Group." *Administrative Science Quarterly* 17:26-43.

Aldrich, Howard E. 1979. *Organizations and Environments*. Englewood Cliffs, NJ: Prentice-Hall.

———— and Ellen Auster. 1986. "Even Dwarfs Started Small: Liabilities of Age and Size and Their Strategic Implications." Pp. 165-198 in *Research in Organizational Behavior*, vol. 8, edited by Barry Staw and L. L. Cummings. Greenwich, CT: JAI Press.

Aldrich, Howard E., John Cater, Trevor Jones, David McEvoy, and Paul Velleman. 1985. "Ethnic Residential Concentration and the Protected Market Hypothesis." *Social Forces* 63:996-1009.

Aldrich, Howard E. and Sergio Mindlin. 1978. "Uncertainty and Dependence: Two Perspectives on Environment." Pp. 149-170 in *Organization and Environment*, edited by Lucien Karpik. Beverly Hills, CA: Sage.

Aldrich, Howard E. and Jeffrey Pfeffer. 1976. "Environments of Organizations." *Annual Review of Sociology* 2:79-105.

Aldrich, Howard E. and Catherine Zimmer 1986. "Entrepreneurship Through Social Networks." Pp. 3-23 in *The Art and Science of Entrepreneurship*, edited by Donald Sexton and Raymond Smilor. New York: Ballinger.

Alexander, Jeffrey and Terry Amburgey. 1987. "The Dynamics of Change in the American Hospital

Industry: Transformation or Selection?" *Medical Care Review* 44:279-321.

Argote, Linda. 1982. "Input Uncertainty and Organizational Coordination in Hospital Emergency Units." *Administrative Science Quarterly* 27:420-434.

Astley, W. Graham and Andrew H. Van de Ven. 1983. "Central Perspectives and Debates in Organization Theory." *Administrative Science Quarterly* 28:245-273.

Bacharach, Samuel and Edward J. Lawler. 1976. "The Perception of Power." *Social Forces* 55:123-134.

Balazs, Etienne. 1964. *Chinese Civilization and Bureaucracy: Variations on a Theme.* New Haven, CT: Yale University Press.

Baran, Paul and Paul Sweezy. 1966. *Monopoly Capital.* New York: Monthly Review Press.

Barnard, Chester I. 1938. *The Functions of the Executive.* Cambridge, MA: Harvard University Press.

Baron, James N. 1984. "Organizational Perspectives on Stratification." *Annual Review of Sociology* 10:37-69.

Baty, Gordon B., William M. Evan, and Terry W. Rothermel. 1971. "Personnel Flows as Interorganizational Relations." *Administrative Science Quarterly* 16:430-443.

Benson, J. Kenneth. 1977. "Organizations: A Dialectical View." *Administrative Science Quarterly* 22:1-21.

Bidwell, Charles E. and John D. Kasarda. 1975. "School District Organization and Student Achievement." *American Sociological Review* 40:55-70.

Biggart, Nicole W. 1977. "The Creative-Destructive Process of Organizational Change: The Case of the Post Office." *Administrative Science Quarterly* 22:410-426.

_____ In press. *Charismatic Capitalism.* Chicago: University of Chicago Press.

Birch, D. 1979. *The Job Generation Process.* Cambridge: MIT Program on Neighborhood and Regional Change.

Blau, Peter M. 1955. *The Dynamics of Bureaucracy.* Chicago: University of Chicago Press.

_____ 1970. "A Formal Theory of Differentiation in Organizations." *American Sociological Review* 35:201-218.

_____ 1972. "Interdependence and Hierarchy in Organizations." *Social Science Research* 1:1-24.

_____, Cecilia McHugh Falbe, William McKinley, and Phelps K. Tracy. 1976. "Technology and Organization in Manufacturing." *Administrative Science Quarterly* 21:20-40.

Blau, Peter M. and Marshall W. Meyer. 1987. *Bureaucracy in Modern Society.* New York: Random House.

Blau, Peter M. and Richard A. Schoenherr. 1971. *The Structure of Organizations.* New York: Basic Books.

Blau, Peter M. and W. Richard Scott. 1962. *Formal Organizations.* San Francisco: Chandler.

Boeker, Warren. 1988. "Organizational Origins: Entrepreneurial and Environmental Imprinting at the Time of Founding." Pp. 33-52 in *Ecological Models of Organization*, edited by Glenn Carroll. Cambridge, MA: Ballinger.

Bollard, Alan and David Harper. 1986. "Employment Generation and Establishment Size in New Zealand Manufacturing." *International Small Business Review* 4:10-28.

Bonacich, Edna. 1973. "A Theory of Middleman Minorities." *American Sociological Review* 38:583-594.

Brittain, Jack and John Freeman. 1980. "Organizational Proliferation and Density-Dependent Selection." Pp. 291-338 in *The Organizational Life Cycle*, edited by John Kimberly and Robert Miles. San Francisco: Jossey-Bass.

Brown, Michael. 1979. *Laying Waste.* New York: Pantheon.

Buckley, Walter. 1967. *Sociology and Modern Systems Theory.* Englewood Cliffs, NJ: Prentice-Hall.

Burns, Tom and George M. Stalker. 1961. *The Management of Innovation.* London: Tavistock.

Burt, Ronald S. 1980a. "Autonomy in a Social Topology." *American Journal of Sociology* 85:892-925.

_____ 1980b. "Models of Network Structure." *Annual Review of Sociology* 6:79-141.

_____ 1983. *Corporate Profits and Cooptation.* New York: Academic Press.

Carroll, Glenn R. 1983. "A Stochastic Model of Organizational Mortality: Review and Reanalysis." *Social Science Research* 12:303-329.

_____ 1984a. "Organizational Ecology." *Annual Review of Sociology* 10:71-93.

_____ 1984b. "Dynamics of Publisher Control in Newspaper Organizations: A Test of the Succession-Crisis Hypothesis." *Administrative Science Quarterly* 29:93-113.

_____ 1985. "Concentration and Specialization: Dynamics of Niche Width in Populations of Organizations." *American Journal of Sociology* 90:1262-1283.

_____ and Jacques Delacroix. 1982. "Organizational Mortality in the Newspaper Industries of Argentina and Ireland." *Administrative Science Quarterly* 27:169-198.

Carroll, Glenn R. and Yangchung Paul Huo. 1986. "Organizational Task and Institutional Environments in Evolutionary Perspective: Findings from the Local Newspaper Industry." *American Journal of Sociology* 91:838-873.

_____ 1988. "Organizational and Electoral Paradoxes of the Knights of Labor." Pp. 175-194 in *Ecological Models of Organization*, edited by Glenn R. Carroll. Cambridge, MA: Ballinger.

Chandler, Alfred D. 1977. *The Visible Hand: The Managerial Revolution in American Business.* Cambridge, MA: Harvard University Press.

Child, John. 1972. "Organizational Structure, Environment, and Performance: The Role of Stra-

tegic Choice." *Sociology* 6:1-22.
————. 1973. "Predicting and Understanding Organization Structure." *Administrative Science Quarterly* 18:168-185.

Clark, Burton R. 1956. *Adult Education in Transition.* Berkeley: University of California Press.

Cohen, Michael D., James G. March, and Johan P. Olsen. 1972. "A Garbage Can Model of Organizational Choice." *Administrative Science Quarterly* 17:1-25.

Coleman, James S. 1974. *Power and the Structure of Society.* New York: W.W. Norton.

Comstock, Donald E. and W. Richard Scott. 1977. "Technology and the Structure of Subunits: Distinguishing Individual and Workgroup Effects." *Administrative Science Quarterly* 22: 177-202.

Cook, Karen S. 1977. "Exchange and Power in Networks of Interorganizational Relations." *The Sociological Quarterly* 18:62-82.

Corning, P. A. 1983. *The Synergism Hypothesis.* New York: McGraw-Hill.

Dalton, Melville. 1959. *Men Who Manage.* New York: John Wiley.

Delacroix, Jacques and Glenn R. Carroll. 1983. "Organizational Founding: An Ecological Study of the Newspaper Industries of Argentina and Ireland." *Administrative Science Quarterly* 28: 274-291.

Delacroix, Jacques and Micheal E. Solt. 1988. "Niche Formation and Foundings in the California Wine Industry, 1941-84." Pp. 53-70 in *Ecological Models of Organization,* edited by Glenn Carroll. Cambridge, MA: Ballinger.

Dess, Gregory G. and Donald W. Beard 1984. "Dimensions of Organizational Task Environments." *Administrative Science Quarterly* 29: 52-73.

Dill, William R. 1958. "Environment as an Influence on Managerial Autonomy." *Administrative Science Quarterly* 2:409-425.

————. 1962. "The Impact of Environment on Organizational Development." Pp. 29-48 in *Concepts and Issues in Administrative Behavior,* edited by S. Mailick and E. H. VanNess. Englewood Cliffs, NJ: Prentice-Hall.

DiMaggio, Paul J. and Walter W. Powell. 1983. "The Iron Cage Revisited: Institutional Isomorphism and Collective Rationality in Organizational Fields." *American Sociological Review* 48:147-160.

Downey, H. Kirk, Don Hellriegel, and John W. Slocum, Jr. 1975. "Environmental Uncertainty: The Construct and Its Application." *Administrative Science Quarterly* 20:613-629.

Downey, H. Kirk and R. Duane Ireland. 1979. "Quantitative versus Qualitative: Environmental Assessment in Organizational Studies." *Administrative Science Quarterly* 24:630-637.

Downs, Anthony. 1967. *Inside Bureaucracy.* Boston: Little, Brown.

Drabek, Thomas E., Rita Braito, Cynthia C. Cook, James R. Powell, and David Rogers. 1982. "Selecting Samples of Organizations: Central Issues and Emergent Trends." *Pacific Sociological Review* 25:377-400.

Drazin, Robert and Andrew H. Van de Ven. 1985. "Alternative Forms of Fit in Contingency Theory." *Administrative Science Quarterly* 30: 514-539.

DuBick, Michael A. 1978. "The Organizational Structure of Newspapers in Relation to Their Metropolitan Environments." *Administrative Science Quarterly* 23:418-433.

Edwards, Richard C. 1979. *Contested Terrain: The Transformation of the Workplace in the Twentieth Century.* New York: Basic Books.

Emery, F. E. and E. L. Trist 1965. "The Causal Texture of Organizational Environments." *Human Relations* 18:21-32.

Etzioni, Amitai. 1964. *Modern Organizations.* Englewood Cliffs, NJ: Prentice-Hall.

Evan, William. 1972. "An Organization-Set Model of Interorganizational Relations." Pp. 181-200 in *Interorganizational Decision-Making,* edited by M. Tuite, M. Radnor, and R. Chisholm. Chicago: Aldine.

Faber, Homo. 1973. "Introduction." Pp. 1-28 in *Special Task Force to the Secretary of Health, Education, and Welfare: Work in America.* Cambridge, MA: MIT Press.

Fennell, Mary L. 1980. "The Effects of Environmental Characteristics on the Structure of Hospital Clusters." *Administrative Science Quarterly* 25:485-510.

Fine, Gary A. 1984. "Negotiated Orders and Organizational Cultures." *Annual Review of Sociology* 11:281-304.

Fligstein, Neil 1985. "The Spread of the Multidivisional Form among Large Firms, 1919-1979." *American Sociological Review* 50:377-391.

Freeman, John H. 1982. "Organizational Life Cycles and Natural Selection Processes." Pp. 1-32 in *Research in Organizational Behavior,* vol. 4, edited by Barry Staw and L. L. Cummings. Greenwich, CT: JAI Press.

————, Glenn R. Carroll, and Michael T. Hannan. 1983. "The Liability of Newness: Age Dependence in Organizational Death Rates." *American Sociological Review* 48:692-710.

Freeman, John H. and Michael T. Hannan. 1975. "Growth and Decline Processes in Organizations." *American Sociological Review* 40:215-228.

————. 1983. "Niche Wideth and the Dynamics of Organizational Populations." *American Journal of Sociology* 88:1116-1145.

Galaskiewicz, Joseph. 1979. *Exchange Networks and Community Politics.* Beverly Hills, CA: Sage.

————. 1985a. *Social Organization of an Urban Grants Economy.* New York: Academic Press.

————. 1985b. "Interorganizational Relations." *Annual Review of Sociology* 11:281-304.

————. and Stanley Wasserman. 1981. "A Dynamic

Study of Change in a Regional Corporate Network.'' *American Sociological Review* 46:475-484.

Ganguly, Pom. 1982. ''Births and Deaths of Firms in the UK in 1980.'' *British Business* 29:1-2.

Geis, Gilbert. 1967. ''White Collar Crime: The Heavy Electrical Equipment Antitrust Cases of 1961.'' Pp. 140-151 in *Criminal Behavior Systems: A Typology*, edited by Marshall B. Clinard and Richard Quinney. New York: Holt, Rinehard and Winston.

Gouldner, Alvin W. 1954. *Patterns of Industrial Bureaucracy*. Glencoe, IL: Free Press.

Granovetter, Mark S. 1984. ''Small is Bountiful: Labor Markets and Establishment Size.'' *American Sociological Review* 49: 323-334.

Granovetter, Mark S. 1985. ''Economic Action and Social Structure: The Problem of Embeddedness.'' *American Journal of Sociology* 91:481-510.

Hall, Richard H. 1987. *Organizations: Structures, Processes and Outcomes*. Englewood Cliffs, NJ: Prentice-Hall.

_____, J. Eugene Haas, and Norman J. Johnson. 1967. ''Organizational Size, Complexity, and Formalization.'' *American Sociological Review* 32:903-912.

Halliday, Terrence, Michael Powell, and Mark Granfors. 1987. ''Minimalist Organizations: Vital Events in State Bar Associations, 1870-1930.'' *American Sociological Review* 52:456-471.

Hannan, Michael T. and John Freeman. 1977. ''The Population Ecology of Organizations.'' *American Journal of Sociology* 82:929-964.

_____ 1984. ''Structural Inertia and Organizational Change.'' *American Sociological Review* 49: 149-164.

_____ 1987. ''The Ecology of Organizational Founding: American Labor Unions, 1836-1985.'' *American Journal of Sociology* 92:910-943.

_____ 1988. ''Density Dependence in the Growth of Organizational Populations.'' Pp. 7-32 in *Ecological Models of Organization*, edited by Glenn Carroll. Cambridge, MA: Ballinger.

Hawley, Amos H. 1950. *Human Ecology*. New York: Ronald Press.

Hickson, David J., D. S. Pugh, and Diana C. Pheysey. 1969. ''Operations Technology and Organization Structure: An Empirical Reappraisal.'' *Administrative Science Quarterly* 14: 378-397.

Hirsch, Paul M. 1972. ''Processing Fads and Fashions: An Organization-Set Analysis of Cultural Industry Systems.'' *American Journal of Sociology* 77:639-659.

Hrebiniak, Lawrence G. and William F. Joyce. 1985. ''Organizational Adaptation: Strategic Choice and Environmental Determinism.'' *Administrative Science Quarterly* 30:336-349.

Jacoby, Sanford M. 1984. ''The Development of Internal Labor Markets in American Manufacturing Firms.'' Pp. 23-69 in *Internal Labor Markets*, edited by Paul Osterman. Cambridge, MA: MIT Press.

Katz, Daniel and Robert L. Kahn. 1966. *The Social Psychology of Organizations*. New York: John Wiley.

Kerbo, Harold. 1983. *Social Stratification and Inequality*. New York: McGraw-Hill.

Kimberly, John. 1976. ''Organizational Size and the Structuralist Perspective: A Review, Critique, and Proposal.'' *Administrative Science Quarterly* 21:571-597.

Knoke, David. 1986. ''Associations and Interest Groups.'' *Annual Review of Sociology* 12:1-21.

_____ and Edward O. Laumann. 1982. ''The Social Organization of National Policy Domains.'' Pp. 255-270 in *Social Structure and Network Analysis*, edited by Peter V. Marsden and Nan Lin. Beverly Hills, CA: Sage.

Knoke, David and David L. Rogers. 1979. ''A Blockmodel Analysis of Interorganizational Networks.'' *Sociology and Social Research* 64:28-52.

Kochan, Thomas, Harry Katz, and Robert McKersie. 1986. *The Transformation of American Industrial Relations*. New York: Basic Books.

Lammers, Cornelius J. and David J. Hickson 1979. ''A Cross-National and Cross-Institutional Typology of Organizations.'' Pp. 420-434 in *Organizations Alike and Unlike*, edited by C. J. Lammers and D. J. Hickson. London: Routledge & Kegan Paul.

Laumann, Edward O., Joseph Galaskiewicz, and Peter V. Marsden. 1978. ''Community Structure as Interorganizational Linkages.'' *Annual Review of Sociology* 4:455-484.

Laumann, Edward O., David Knoke, and Yong-Hak Kim. 1985. ''An Organizational Approach to State Policy Formation: A Comparative Study of Energy and Health Domains.'' *American Sociological Review* 50:1-19.

Lawrence, Paul R. and Davis Dyer. 1983. *Renewing American Industry*. New York: Free Press.

Lawrence, Paul R. and Jay W. Lorsch. 1967. *Organization and Environment: Managing Differentiation and Integration*. Boston: Graduate School of Business Administration, Harvard University.

Leblebici, Huseyin and Gerald R. Salancik. 1981. ''Effects of Environmental Uncertainty on Information and Decision Processes in Banks.'' *Administrative Science Quarterly* 26:578-596.

Levine, Adeline 1982. *Love Canal: Science, Politics, and People*. Lexington, MA: D. C. Heath.

Levine, Sol and Paul E. White. 1961. ''Exchange as a Conceptual Framework for the Study of Interorganizational Relationships.'' *Administrative Science Quarterly* 5:583-601.

Light, Ivan H. 1972. *Ethnic Enterprise in America*. Berkeley: University of California Press.

Lincoln, James R. and Kerry McBride. 1985. ''Resources, Homophily, and Dependence: Organizational Attributes and Asymmetric Ties in Human Service Networks.'' *Social Science Re-*

search 14:1-30.

Lincoln, James R., Mitsuyo Hanada and Kerry McBride. 1986. "Organizational Structures in Japanese and U.S. Manufacturing." *Administrative Science Quarterly* 31:338-364.

Lipset, Seymour Martin, Martin A. Trow, and James S. Coleman. 1956. *Union Democracy*. Glencoe, IL: Free Press.

Litwak, Eugene and Lydia Hylton. 1962. "Interorganizational Analysis: A Hypothesis on Coordination." *Administrative Science Quarterly* 6:395-420.

Mansfield, Roger. 1973. "Bureaucracy and Centralization: An Examination of Organizational Structure." *Administrative Science Quarterly* 18:77-88.

March, James G. and Johan P. Olsen. 1976. *Ambiguity and Choice in Organizations*. Bergen, Norway: Universitetsforlaget.

Marrett, Cora Bagley. 1980. "Influences on the Rise of New Organizations: The Formation of Women's Medical Societies." *Administrative Science Quarterly* 25:185-199.

Marsden, Peter V. and Edward O. Laumann. 1984. "Mathematical Ideas in Social Structural Analysis." *Journal of Mathematical Sociology* 10:271-294.

Marsh, Robert M. and Hiroshi Mannari. 1981. "Technology and Size as Determinants of the Organizational Structure of Japanese Factories." *Administrative Science Quarterly* 26:33-57.

McCarthy, John D. and Mayer N. Zald. 1977. "Resource Mobilization and Social Movements: A Partial Theory." *American Journal of Sociology* 82:1212-1241.

McKelvey, Bill. 1982. *Organizational Systematics*. Berkeley: University of California Press.

———— and Howard Aldrich. 1983. "Populations, Natural Selection, and Applied Organizational Science." *Administrative Science Quarterly* 28:101-128.

McKinley, William. 1987. "Complexity and Administrative Intensity: The Case of Declining Organizations." *Administrative Science Quarterly* 32:87-105.

McPherson, J. Miller. 1983. "An Ecology of Affiliation." *American Sociological Review* 48:519-532.

———— and Lynn Smith-Lovin. 1986. "Sex Segregation in Voluntary Associations." *American Sociological Review* 51:61-79.

———— 1988. "A Comparative Ecology of Five Nations: Testing a Model of Competition Among Voluntary Organizations." Pp. 85-110 in *Ecological Models of Organization*, edited by Glenn Carroll. Cambridge, MA: Ballinger.

Merton, Robert K., Ailsa Gray, Barbara Hockey, and Hanan C. Selvin. 1952. *Reader in Bureaucracy*. Glencoe, IL: Free Press.

Meyer, John W. and Brian Rowan. 1977. "Institutionalized Organizations: Formal Structure as Myth and Ceremony." *American Journal of Sociology* 83:340-363.

Meyer, John W. and W. Richard Scott. 1983. *Organizational Environments: Ritual and Rationality*. Beverly Hills, CA: Sage.

Miles, Robert H. with Kim S. Cameron. 1982. *Coffin Nails and Corporate Strategies*. Englewood Cliffs, NJ: Prentice-Hall.

Miller, George A. and Joseph Conaty. 1980. "Differentiation in Organizations: Replication and Cumulation." *Social Forces* 59:265-274.

Mintz, Beth and Michael Schwartz. 1985. *The Power Structure of American Business*. Chicago: University of Chicago Press.

Mintzberg, Henry. 1979. *The Structuring of Organizations*. Englewood Cliffs, NJ: Prentice-Hall.

———— 1983. *Structure in Fives: Designing Effective Organizations*. Englewood Cliffs, NJ: Prentice-Hall.

Mizruchi, Mark. 1982. *The American Corporate Network, 1904-1974*. Beverly Hills, CA: Sage.

Morrissey, Joseph P., Mark Tausig, and Michael L. Lindsey. 1986. "Interorganizational Networks in Mental Health Systems: Assessing Community Support Programs for the Chronically Mentally Ill." Pp. 197-230 in *The Organization of Mental Health Services: Societal and Community Systems*, edited by W. Richard Scott and Bruce L. Black. Beverly Hills, CA: Sage.

Moynihan, Daniel P. 1970. *Maximum Feasible Misunderstanding*. New York: Free Press.

Office of Management and the Budget, Statistical Policy Division. 1972. *Standard Industrial Classification Manual*. Washington, DC: Government Printing Office.

Orloff, Ann Shola and Theda Skocpol. 1984. "Why Not Equal Protection? Explaining the Politics of Public Social Spending in Britain, 1900-1911, and the United States, 1880s-1920." *American Sociological Review* 49:726-750.

Osborn, Richard N. and James G. Hunt. 1974. "Environment and Organizational Effectiveness." *Administrative Science Quarterly* 19:231-246.

Ouchi, William G. 1981. *Theory Z*. Reading, MA: Addison-Wesley.

———— 1984. *The M-Form Society*. Reading, MA: Addison-Wesley.

Padgett, John. 1980. "Managing Garbage Can Hierarchies." *Administrative Science Quarterly* 25:563-604.

Palmer, Donald, Roger Friedland, and Jitendra Singh. 1986. "The Ties that Bind: Organizational and Class Bases of Stability in A Corporate Interlock Network." *American Sociological Review* 51:781-796.

Parsons, Talcott. 1956a. "Suggestions for a Sociological Approach to the Theory of Organizations-I." *Administrative Science Quarterly* 1:63-85.

———— 1956b. "Suggestions for a Sociological Approach to the Theory of Organizations-II." *Administrative Science Quarterly* 1:225-239.

———— 1960. *Structure and Process in Modern Societies*. New York: Free Press.

_____ 1961. "Some Considerations on the Theory of Social Change." *Rural Sociology* 26:219-239.

Pennings, Johannes. 1975. "The Relevance of the Structural-Contingency Model for Organizational Effectiveness." *Administrative Science Quarterly* 20:393-410.

_____ 1982. "Organizational Birth Frequencies: An Empirical Investigation." *Administrative Science Quarterly* 27:120-144.

Perrow, Charles. 1967. "A Framework for the Comparative Analysis of Organizations." *American Sociological Review* 32:194-208.

_____ 1970. *Organizational Analysis: A Sociological View.* Belmont, CA: Wadsworth.

_____ 1979. *Complex Organizations: A Critical Essay.* Glenview, IL: Scott, Foresman.

_____ 1984. *Normal Accidents: Living With High-Risk Technologies.* New York: Basic Books.

_____ 1986. *Complex Organizations: A Critical Essay.* New York: Random House.

Pfeffer, Jeffrey. 1972a. "Size and Composition of Corporate Boards of Directors: The Organization and Its Environment." *Administrative Science Quarterly* 17:218-228.

_____ 1972b. "Merger as a Response to Organizational Interdependence." *Administrative Science Quarterly* 17:382-392.

_____ 1982. *Organizations and Organization Theory.* Marshfield, MA: Pitman Press.

_____ 1987. "A Resource Dependence Perspective on Intercorporate Relations." In *Structural Analysis of Business,* edited by Mark Mizruchi and Michael Schwartz. New York: Cambridge University Press.

_____ and Philip Nowak. 1976. "Joint Ventures and Interorganizational Dependence." *Administrative Science Quarterly* 21:398-418.

Pfeffer, Jeffrey and Gerald R. Salancik. 1974. "Organizational Decision-Making as a Political Process: The Case of a University." *Administrative Science Quarterly* 19:135-151.

_____ 1978. *The External Control of Organizations.* New York: Harper & Row.

Phillips, Almarin. 1960. "A Theory of Interfirm Organization." *Quarterly Journal of Economics* 74:602-613.

Porter, Michael E. 1980. *Competitive Strategy.* New York: Free Press.

Presthus, Robert. 1978. *The Organizational Society.* New York: St. Martin's.

Pugh, D. S., D. J. Hickson, and C. R. Hinings. 1969a. "An Empirical Taxonomy of Structures of Work Organizations." *Administrative Science Quarterly* 14:115-126.

_____ and C. Turner. 1969b. "The Context of Organization Structures." *Administrative Science Quarterly* 14:91-114.

Robins, James A. 1987. "Organizational Economics: Notes on the Use of Transaction-Cost Theory in the Study of Organizations." *Administrative Science Quarterly* 32:68-86.

Rogers, David L. and David A. Whetten. 1982. *Inter-organizational Coordination: Theory, Research, and Implementation.* Ames: Iowa State University Press.

Rogers, Everett M. and Judith K. Larson. 1984. *Silicon Valley Fever: Growth of High Technology Culture.* New York: Basic Books.

Romanelli, Elaine. 1986. "Organizational Persistence and Adaptation: A Comparison of Alternative Theoretical Models." Paper presented at the Academy of Management meetings, Chicago.

Rothschild-Whitt, Joyce. 1979. "The Collectivist Organization: An Alternative to Rational Bureaucracy." *American Sociological Review* 44:509-527.

Sabel, Charles. 1982. *Work and Politics: The Division of Labor in Industry.* Cambridge, England: Cambridge University Press.

Salaman, Graeme. 1980. "Classification of Organizations and Organization Structure: The Main Elements and Interrelationships." Pp. 56-84 in *Control and Ideology in Organizations,* edited by Graeme Salaman and Kenneth Thompson. Cambridge: MIT Press.

Schoonhoven, Claudia Bird. 1981. "Problems with Contingency Theory: Testing Assumptions Hidden within the Language of Contingency Theory." *Administrative Science Quarterly* 26:349-377.

Scott, W. Richard. 1975. "Organizational Structure." *Annual Review of Sociology* 1:1-20.

_____ 1981. *Organizations: Rational, Natural, and Open Systems.* Englewood Cliffs, NJ: Prentice-Hall.

_____ 1983. "The Organization of Environments: Network, Cultural, and Historical Elements." Pp. 155-175 in *Organizational Environments: Ritual and Rationality,* edited by John W. Meyer and W. Richard Scott. Beverly Hills, CA: Sage.

_____ 1987. *Organizations: Rational, Natural, and Open Systems.* Englewood Cliffs, NJ: Prentice-Hall.

_____ and Bruce L. Black. 1986. *The Organization of Mental Health Services: Societal and Community Systems.* Beverly Hills, CA: Sage.

Scott, W. Richard and John W. Meyer. 1983. "The Organization of Societal Sectors." Pp. 129-154 in *Organizational Environments: Ritual and Rationality,* edited by John W. Meyer and W. Richard Scott. Beverly Hills: Sage.

Selznick, Philip. 1948. "Foundations of the Theory of Organization." *American Sociological Review* 13:25-35.

_____ 1949. *TVA and the Grass Roots.* Berkeley: University of California Press.

Shrum, Wesley, Robert Wuthnow, and James Beniger. 1985. "The Organization of Technology in Advanced Industrial Society: A Hypothesis on Technical Systems." *Social Forces* 64:46-63.

Singh, Jitendra V. 1986. "Technology, Size, and Organizational Structure: A Reexamination of the Okayama Study Data." *Academy of Man-*

agement Journal 29:800-812.

———, David J. Tucker, and Robert J. House. 1986. "Organizational Legitimacy and the Liability of Newness." *Administrative Science Quarterly* 31:171-193.

Small Business Administration. 1986. *The State of Small Business*. Washington, DC: Government Printing Office.

Smith, Constance and Anne Freedman. 1972. *Voluntary Associations: Perspective on the Literature*. Cambridge, MA: Harvard.

Staber, Udo. 1985. "A Population Perspective on Collective Action as an Organizational Form: The Case of Trade Associations." Pp. 181-220 in *Research in the Sociology of Organizations*, vol. 4, edited by Samuel B. Bacharach and Stephen M. Mitchell. Greenwich, CT: JAI Press.

Starbuck, William. 1983. "Organizations as Action Generators." *American Sociological Review* 48:91-102.

Staw, Barry M. and Eugene Szwajkowski. 1975. "The Scarcity-Munificence Components of Organizational Environments and the Commission of Illegal Acts." *Administrative Science Quarterly* 20:345-354.

Stearns, Linda Brewster and Mark S. Mizruchi. 1986. "Broken-Tie Reconstitution and the Functions of Interorganizational Interlocks: A Reexamination." *Administrative Science Quarterly* 31: 522-538.

Stinchcombe, Arthur L. 1965. "Social Structure and Organizations." Pp. 142-193 in *Handbook of Organizations*, edited by James G. March. Chicago: Rand-McNally.

Taylor, Frederick W. 1947. *Scientific Management*. New York: Harper and Brothers.

Thompson, James D. 1967. *Organizations in Action*. New York: McGraw-Hill.

Tolbert, Pamela S. and Lynne G. Zucker. 1983. "Institutional Sources of Change in the Formal Structure of Organizations: The Diffusion of Civil Service Reform, 1880-1935." *Administrative Science Quarterly* 28:22-39.

Tosi, Henry, Ramon Aldag, and Ronald Storey. 1973. "On the Measurement of the Environment: An Assessment of the Lawrence and Lorsch Environmental Uncertainty Subscale." *Administrative Science Quarterly* 18:27-36.

———, John R. Rizzo, and Stephen J. Carroll. 1986. *Managing Organizational Behavior*. Marshfield, MA: Pitman.

Tuma, Nancy Brandon and Michael T. Hannan. 1984. *Social Dynamics: Models and Methods*. New York: Academic Press.

Turk, Herman. 1977. *Organizations in Modern Life*. San Francisco: Jossey-Bass.

Udy, Stanley. 1962. "Administrative Rationality, Social Setting, and Organizational Development." *American Journal of Sociology* 68:299-308.

U.S. Bureau of the Census. 1982. *County Business Patterns*. Washington, DC: Government Printing Office.

Useem, Michael. 1984. *The Inner Circle*. New York: Oxford University Press.

Van de Ven, Andrew H., Andre L. Delbecq, and Richard Koenig, Jr. 1976. "Determinants of Coordination Modes within Organizations." *American Sociological Review* 41:322-338.

Vaughan, Diane. 1983. *Controlling Unlawful Organizational Behavior: Social Structure and Corporate Misconduct*. Chicago: University of Chicago Press.

Warren, Roland L. 1967. "The Interorganizational Field as a Focus for Investigation." *Administrative Science Quarterly* 12:396-419.

———, Stephen Rose, and Ann Bergunder 1974. *The Structure of Urban Reform*. Lexington, MA: D.C. Heath.

Weber, Max. 1947. *The Theory of Social and Economic Organization*, edited by A. H. Henderson and Talcott Parsons. Glencoe, IL: Free Press.

Weick, Karl. 1979. *The Social Psychology of Organizing*. Reading, MA: Addison-Wesley.

Whetten, David A. 1982. "Objectives and Issues: Setting the Stage." Pp. 3-8 in *Interorganizational Coordination*, edited by David L. Rogers and David A. Whetten. Ames: Iowa State University Press.

Williamson, Oliver E. 1975. *Markets and Hierarchies: Analysis and Antitrust Implications*. New York: Free Press.

——— 1981. "The Economics of Organization: The Transaction Cost Approach." *American Journal of Sociology* 87:548-577.

Woodward, Joan. 1965. *Industrial Organization: Theory and Practice*. New York: Oxford University Press.

Yuchtman, Ephraim and Stanley E. Seashore. 1967. "A System Resource Approach to Organizational Effectiveness." *American Sociological Review* 32:891-903.

Zald, Mayer N. and Patricia Denton. 1963. "From Evangelism to General Service: The Transformation of the YMCA." *Administrative Science Quarterly* 8:214-234.

12
Political Sociology

ANTHONY M. ORUM

Political sociology is a field that bridges some of the concerns of political science with those of sociology. It had its modern beginnings sometime after World War II, although its theoretical roots go back in history far longer. A number of scholars have substantially helped to contribute to the growth and development of the field, including Reinhard Bendix and Seymour Martin Lipset, among sociologists, and Robert Dahl, among political scientists. The field has become notable, much like other of the social sciences, for the rise and fall of different intellectual perspectives and different theoretical problems. Thirty years ago, scholarly attention was centered almost exclusively on the nature of democracy—on what it was and how it was produced. In retrospect, it now is clear that this focus resulted from issues raised during the course of World War II, and further highlighted in the Cold War era. Today, however, there are new questions that dominate the research done in political sociology, questions such as the "relative autonomy of the state," many of which spring from the outpouring of scholars who consider themselves neo-Marxists. Consequently, anyone who is interested in taking up this branch of work as a full-time scholar and professional must be prepared to appreciate and to tolerate the variety of work done by those who call themselves political sociologists. It is a field that is broad and wide-ranging and, because of this, a field that demands considerable knowledge as well as the cognitive capacity to tolerate and to explore problematic differences among competing ideas and intellectual perspectives.

In light of the considerable breadth and diversity of the field, this chapter will highlight some of the significant viewpoints that ground the research and thought of political sociologists, old and new, alike. The chapter also will seek to identify some of the important empirical conclusions that have emerged from the last 40 years of research, particularly on American society, by political scientists, sociologists, and political sociologists. Where there are important differences of opinion and interpretation, they, too, will be noted. So far as novelty or important breakthroughs are concerned, I have deliberately refrained from pushing any single point of view in the body of the chapter. Rather, my intention is to provide the reader with a catholic introduction to the main ideas and issues for the political sociologist. Nevertheless, at the conclusion of the chapter I shall engage in a far more speculative and normative line of thought, and will push very strongly for the general directions in which I believe political sociology *ought* to move. Finally, let me add that this chapter will not engage in any extended discussion either of nation-states or of collective behavior/social movements. While I believe that both topics are an integral part of the work of political sociology, and have dealt with them as such in other writings (see, for example, Orum, 1988), in this book they are treated separately in different chapters, including the one by Doug McAdam, John McCarthy, and Mayer Zald.

Competing Imageries of States and Societies

There are several key imageries that guide and shape the work of contemporary political sociology. By imagery here I mean certain conceptual maps and claims about the nature and structure of the world, including claims about the logic of relations that exist in the world as well as the logic of scientific inference that is to be employed to obtain knowledge. The imageries are such that they represent self-contained wholes of the elements purported to constitute the world. Moreover, they themselves are not subject to empirical proof or disproof, although the lower-level claims they make about the world may, in fact, be so (Stinchcombe, 1968). There are four such imageries that are crucial to the work of contemporary political sociology—those of Karl Marx, Max Weber, Talcott Parsons, and, those several theorists who collectively have inspired modern elite theory, namely, Robert Michels, Gaetano Mosca, and Vilfredo Pareto.

The Imagery of Karl Marx

Everyone has his or her own Karl Marx. I will provide a brief capsule version of my reading of the imagery of Marx, which draws on a host of his writings, and then single out the neo-Marxist writings that have had the most influence over modern political sociology. The central feature of life, according to Marx, is production (1932/1978b). The act of production furnishes the seeds of the human being's alienation, or divorce from his or her own *species-being*, as from one's fellow human beings. As the mode of production changes, so too does the nature of social relations, and the general character of the superstructural, or nonproduction elements (1848/1978d). With alienation as with production, the world becomes divided into struggling social classes. Class struggle is the constant fact of history, although the form of the struggle, like the mode of production, will vary from one major historical epoch to another, and the outward signs of the struggle will vary as well (1848/1978d). History—or more precisely, prehistory—to Marx will terminate with the overcoming of the class struggle (Avineri, 1968); with its conclusion there will be a gradual disappearance of inequality as well as alienation and exploitation (1848/1978b).

Alienation, production, and class struggle each represent prominent themes in the writings of Marx, from the earliest works to the later ones; each element, moreover, furnishes a key part of his imagery of the world. Marx's earliest work is concerned with a substantial critique of the thought of the great German philosopher G.W.F. Hegel (1843/1978a) and, in particular, of Hegel's claim that the world represents the evolution of *der Geist* (Hegel, 1807/1967). Marx argued that Hegel was fundamentally mistaken about the nature of reality, and that Hegel's emphasis on the spiritual foundations of the world must instead be replaced by an assumption of material reality (1932/1978b). Thus, quite apart from any intuitive truth to his argument about the importance of production to life, Marx's claims about the significance of production derive from his dialogue, critique, and transcendence (*Aufhebung*) of Hegel's worldview. But Marx was quite unclear about the nature and limits of such materialism, thereby leaving his life-long colleague, Friedrich Engels, to give a rather broad range to the applicability of the doctrines of *historical materialism* and *dialectical materialism* (Engels, 1892/1940; 1892/1950b).

In his more mature writings, Marx (1887/1961) shifted from a very abstract, virtually Hegelian analysis of alienation and production to a far more systematic and scientific treatment of the nature of labor in society, of social class, of class struggles, and of the underlying laws of modern capitalism. In his writings on the historical circumstances of the French Third Republic, for instance, Marx (1852/1972) characterizes in very concrete terms the political struggles among the French, and he clearly suggests that such struggles emanate from differences in the class basis of various groups. In his great works on the nature of modern capitalism, furthermore, Marx (1887/1961) delves deeply into the heart of the economic system, and reveals the principles, such as the theory of surplus value, that he believes ultimately will undermine capitalist civilization, and with it the dominance of the capitalist class.

Politics and, in general, the institutions of the state, play a secondary role in the worldview of Marx. Again, Marx's view of the state machinery, and of struggles among elements located or represented within the state, seems clearly fashioned in an effort to transcend disagreements he had with Hegel. His effort to articulate the nature and the role of the state, however, is never very detailed or clear, thus leading to numerous controversies among his dedicated followers as well as his interpreters. At the most basic, or abstract, level of analysis, the state, or politics, represents a reflection of and functions to sustain the dominance of the reigning social class. Thus in his early writings Marx (1843/1978a) inverts Hegel's imagery of the subordination of civil society to the state. In a somewhat later argument he maintains that "(t)he Executive of the Modern State is but a committee for managing the common affairs of the whole bourgeoisie" (1848/1978d, p. 475). Engels himself adds immeasurably to one's understanding of the general Marxian imagery of the state by claiming that the state arises to mediate the contradictions of society, and to moderate between conflicting social classes (1884/1950a, pp. 288ff). In light of the fact that class struggle and fundamental contradictions lie at the heart of Marx's imagery of the world, this particular claim about the functions of the state is of singular consequence.

At more concrete levels of analysis, Marx makes a host of other claims, noting, for example, in the instance of France in the nineteenth century that political differences among contending groups somehow coincide with differences in the nature of their position in the labor process (Marx, 1852/1972). The most difficult historical event for Marx to grasp within the framework of his view of dominance of the production system, or civil society, over the political system, or the state, was the reign of Louis Bonaparte in France. Did the reign of Bonaparte represent an exception to the laws of the development of modern capitalism, or could it be incorporated into Marx's general framework? Marx himself seems to suggest that the Bonapartist state was able to free itself from its class basis, hence to achieve, on the one hand, some autonomy from the class system, yet on the other, he insisted that the Bonapartist state aided the actual development and progress of capitalism, itself (Marx, 1852/1972). Marx's claims about Bonaparte, and the fact of the Bonapartist state itself, have provoked considerable contemporary speculation and debate about these issues (see, for example, McLellan, 1978).

There are other elements that figure into this Marxian picture of the world. Ideas and their production through the institutions of society play a crucial role in the Marxian imagery, but principally as illusions that help to maintain the dominance of the ruling class. "The ideas of the ruling class are in every epoch the ruling ideas," Marx once wrote (1932/1978b, p. 172). These ideas, or ideologies as Marx came to call them, must not be underestimated in the Marxian worldview, despite his critique of Hegel. They work to sustain the hegemony of the dominant class, or classes, by disguising the true nature of exploitation, particularly under capitalism. Furthermore, they must be penetrated even by Marxian scientific endeavors in order to arrive at the truth of the world (Althusser, 1977, chap. 6; Lefebvre, 1969, pp. 59-88). Likewise, the logic of change and development, according to Marx, is built on principles of self-contradiction of the laws of development of each historical epoch—modern capitalism, in particular. Marx devotes considerable attention in the first volume of *Capital* (1887/1961) to outlining the fundamental principles of modern capitalism, as well as to demonstrating how such principles as the law of surplus value, or the organic composition of capital, work in the long run to undermine the very system they have built. Marx's conception of self-contradiction in the laws of society was a profound element of his theoretical view of the world, one that informs, among other things, his very claims about the historical omnipresence of the class struggle.

Like writings by Marx, criticisms of him abound. There are philosophers such as Karl Popper (1957) who entirely reject Marx's imagery on grounds of its historicism. Recently, G. A. Cohen (1978), however, has come forward in very rigorous and compelling terms to defend Marx's historical logic, seeking thereby to overcome the Popperian critique. Questions also have been raised about the historical foundations that Marx purports for the rise of modern capitalism, including the critique of Joseph Schumpeter (1947/1962, p. 17) that Marx had failed effectively to ground his claims about the nature of primitive accumulation. There are also equally sound criticisms of Marx's general imagery, including questions about the soundness of dialectics as a logic of change, and about the details of the theoretical imagery that he uses to posit his distinctive view of the relative weight of production and other institutions and processes in the world. Why, many analysts have asked, should production and labor necessarily take precedence over power and politics, even in the long-run character and shape of any historical society? In what sense, they ask, are production and labor necessarily determinative of the other elements of society, even of a system of nation-states?

But, today at least, the aficionados and devotees far outweigh the basic critics of Marx.

In the course of the twentieth century, many embellishments and modifications have been made in the basic Marxian imagery (Anderson, 1979; McLellan, 1978). V. I. Lenin helped to make the basic framework accommodate more of the political and historical realities of the twentieth century, for example. He (1917/ 1975b) devoted far more attention to the nature of the state, and to state power and its machinery than Marx, and he also traced out the international development of capitalism in the course of this century in his profoundly influential work *Imperialism* (1917/1975a). Likewise, Antonio Gramsci (1948-1951/1971a, 1971b) has had a very influential role in the current understanding of the Marxian imagery, pointing, among other things, to the various political, economic, and ideological forces of the state that serve to sustain the dominance, or as he termed it, the hegemony, of the leading social classes.

In the 1960s and 1970s, with the decline of Soviet domination over other Communist nations and parties in Europe, there was almost a parallel rise in revision and reinterpretation of the writings of Marx. Among the most influential were the French structuralists, led by Louis Althusser (1977; Althusser and Balibar, 1970), who furnished very novel reassessments of the Marxian imagery. Althusser argued that the mature Marx had decisively broken from his Hegelian concerns and in the process had invented a thoroughly novel form of philosophy and science. Althusser's most striking contribution, and also his most controversial, was his suggestion that the complex totality of ideological, political, and economic relations shaped the visible practices and institutions of modern capitalism; in other words, the economic sphere did not always dominate the Marxian landscape (1977). This claim, building to some extent on the insights of Lenin and Gramsci, modified the basic Marxian imagery considerably, and at the same time provided a platform on which Althusser's student, Nicos Poulantzas, could provide new speculations on the nature of the state. Poulantzas himself argued that the complex interconnection of the ideological, political, and economic structures of modern capitalism sustained its hegemony. Furthermore, he insisted, the institutions of the state, in particular, could only be understood in the context of these structures, and as elements designed to cope with the internal contradictions of modern capitalism. Poulantzas also maintained that the state, under the leadership of different fractions of capitalism, could achieve a "relative degree of autonomy" from the class foundations of capitalism. Nevertheless, he argued, state power

always is grounded in the class struggle and capitalist exploitation, and therefore even if certain fractions of classes capture the state apparatus, they could never exercise state power independently of its class base (see, for example, Poulantzas, 1978).

Poulantzas's worldview, which differs considerably from that of orthodox Marxism, has become very popular in recent years. Moreover, in a very widely cited article, David Gold, Clarence Lo, and Erik Olin Wright (1975a, 1975b; but also see Mollenkopf, 1975) have claimed an important distinction between the so-called structuralist view of the state, associated with the position of Poulantzas, and the so-called instrumentalist view of the state, which they identify with the work of Ralph Miliband (1969), among others. The one position, they maintain, claims that the state operates on the basis of objective structures in society, and that it sustains class rule independently of the conscious and willing exercise of state power by class members. As Poulantzas himself has framed it:

> The *direct* participation of members of the capitalist class in the state apparatus and in the government, even where it exists, is not the important side of the matter. The relation between the bourgeois class and the state is an *objective relation*. This means that if the *function* of the state in a determinate social formation and the *interests* of the dominant class in this formation coincide, it is by reason of the system itself: the direct participation of members of the ruling class in the state apparatus is not the *cause* but the effect, and moreover a chance and contingent one, of this objective coincidence [Poulantzas, 1969, pp. 73-74; italics in the original].

By contrast, the instrumentalist view, they argue, insists rather simplistically that the machinery of the state is controlled by members of the ruling class. The problem with this latter view, they further suggest, is that it portrays the state merely as a tool in the hands of the ruling class, when, as history shows, the relationship between class domination and the operations of the state, itself, is considerably more complex. *The theoretical trouble here is not due to any misreadings of Marx either by Miliband or by Poulantzas: It is due exclusively to the ambiguities evident in the writings of Marx himself*. Not the least of the ambiguities is that Marx was a self-proclaimed humanist in his early works, emphasizing "man" and "man's development" over and above the spiritualism of Hegel, but in his later works he seems to have subdued his humanism for economic science (but see Ollman, 1976, for a different view). His followers thus are left to squabble over such issues as the degree to which any human agents, acting individually or collectively, may exercise their will within the realm of state power, or whether, instead, they are somehow mere "vessels" for the operations of "objective" forces. This issue is one to which we shall return at the conclusion of this review, but in a different manner.

The Imagery of Max Weber

Karl Marx was essentially a philosopher and a theorist, whereas Max Weber essentially was a historian. The difference is important, and it helps to explain the two scholars' very different orientations to the world. While Marx clearly and consciously seemed to develop a worldview at different levels of abstraction, involving among other things assumptions about the lawlike nature of society, Weber equally as consciously sought instead to draw careful inferences about historical events and institutions, and was particularly intent on drawing systematic comparisons between Western and Eastern societies. Weber's broadest task was to account for the rationalization of Western societies, not to account for the development and maintenance of capitalism. Moreover, Weber sought to explain history through the mechanisms of the real interests of human beings, both material and ideal ones, and thus in strong contrast to Marx, turned ultimately to the intentions of the historical actors and subjects to assess the viability of his arguments rather than to so-called objective conditions. His worldview invoked the purposes of the actor to explain the character of social action rather than the purposes of classes and systems (for an excellent discussion of these matters, see the introduction to Weber, 1975). Nevertheless, his extraordinary outpouring of written work offered important insights and springboards for further analysis of classes, and of the important role of state institutions in the makings of history.

The study and exploration of societies, Weber insisted, must involve a broad historical compass. Human beings are not only producers, as Marx would argue, but they also are driven by a host of different material and ideal interests in the course of their action (Bendix, 1962; Collins, 1968). Weber argued that the view that classes are the leading agents of history underemphasizes the role of ideas and of power. Thus,

in one of his more widely known writings (see discussion in Weber, 1968, pp. 284-306), he claimed that at different times and in different places in history, status groups and political parties also have a prominent role in the making of important historical events and in the construction of social institutions. In the case of the modern West, for example, he insisted that certain professional groups, such as lawyers, could become prominent agents, in part because they were the masters of legal expertise, and law represented the basic foundations of authority in the West (1919/1958). Yet, while Weber's worldview clearly admitted a greater variety of motives and agents to play a leading part than that of Marx, at the same time Weber concurred with Marx that struggle and conflict lay at the heart of history, and that domination and insubordination were continuous facts of life (Collins, 1968).

The theme that dominated much of Weber's attention in his historical work, and which has inspired much contemporary reflection as well, is that of rationality. Weber saw elements and traces of rationality in many institutional spheres of modern Western institutions. He saw it in the philosophical contemplations of the Enlightenment philosophers, particularly in those of his fellow German, Immanuel Kant. He found it too in the practices and in the spirit of modern science, which sought through such processes as the scientific method to arrive at the grounded truths of the world. And he found it ultimately creeping into the very foundations of organizational life throughout modern societies, ranging from the organization of the military to the organization of business practices (Weber, 1904-1905/1958; 1919/1958). But what he further perceived was that rationality in the modern world was one of only two prominent forms that had existed historically. Modern rationality—that which occupied contemporary science—for example, emphasized the adjustment of means to ends, and stressed that the means used to attain given ends should be clear, precise, specific, efficient, and, if possible, permit formal and technical representation. Such rationality, however, he believed, represented a very different form from that which was concerned mainly with the ends of social life, and inquired into matters such as the fundamental nature of truth, beauty, justice, and the good life (Weber, 1947, pp. 35ff). If one could impute the view to Weber that human beings in modern times indeed suffered, it would be because contemporary societies had created institutions that replaced a fundamental concern for the ends of life with a concern for the technically most efficient means (Weber, 1919/ 1958, pp. 155-156).

Far more than Marx, Weber truly appreciated the nature of power in history, and the complex issues of domination and the state. No group, not even social classes, ruled automatically. The rule of every group had to be grounded in some form of authority, whether conveyed through tradition and custom, or through law, as in the modern West (Weber, 1968, pp. 212-269). Moreover, Weber seemed to believe that the rulers of the modern state could exercise a decisive role over the course of history, in part because the state itself held a monopoly over the legitimate use of force in the modern world (Weber, 1919/1958, p. 78). Weber's appreciation of the independent and determinative role of the state could best be seen in his analysis of nineteenth-century Germany, and particularly the role of Bismarck (Weber, 1917/1968, pp. 1381-1428). Bismarck, in Weber's eyes, played a leading role in shaping the construction of modern Germany, and he did so in ways that ran contrary to the interests of the landed nobility that he represented. But at the same time it would be too simple-minded, in Weber's view, to see the state and its rulers simply as automatic agents able to acquire and direct power. The state, to a degree, like society at large, represented an arena of autonomous conflict, a conflict that could involve, as in the German case, battles between parliamentary representative and the large body of civil servants. Furthermore, if there were a single body that could be claimed by Weber to hold the key to the future directions of the modern state, it would be the vast corps of civil servants and the bureaucratic machinery they had erected. This machinery, far more than any previous form of state administration, thrived on technically rational standards, and through its collective hegemony could ultimately dominate other sectors of society (Weber, 1917/1968, p. 1393-1401 ff).

Like the writings of Marx, the works of Weber and his general worldview have been subject to considerable reassessment and reinterpretation in the twentieth century. He has inspired considerable work in the research and theory about the role and nature of organizations in modern life (Blau and Meyer, 1971). Moreover, critical social theorists such as Herbert Marcuse (1968) and Jürgen Habermas (1975) have built upon as well as criticized Weber's insights into the character of rationality in the modern West. Weber's work on the nature of authority and of power has had broad impact, leading to many standard insights and claims about the nature of power, but until recently no scholar has developed Weber's understandings about the nature of the modern state. It is only with the very recent works of Theda Skocpol (1979, 1981) that any political sociologist has sought to take Weber's claims about the constitution and immanent significance of the state very seriously. The one other theme of Weber's that has captured some recent attention is that of the grounding of rulership in the world in conditions that purport to make its exercise legitimate. Seymour Martin Lipset (1963; Lipset and Schneider, 1983), and, more recently, Habermas have attended to this feature of society systematically; the latter has even employed the conception, in a very broad sense, to provide his own interpretation of the present crisis of modern capitalism.

The Imagery of Talcott Parsons

Talcott Parsons's construction of the nature of the world offers yet a very different but equally important approach to the study of states and societies. Of the several views discussed here, Parsons's view is clearly the most theoretically developed and sophisticated. Unlike Weber, he was fully committed to elaborating a comprehensive theoretical scheme to depict the nature of reality, and unlike Marx he was more appreciative of the role that many institutions could play in history.

Parsons was committed to a highly complex and analytically differentiated view of the world. He sought systematically to distinguish the nature of analytical constructs from the concrete, empirical objects and processes to which they were intended to correspond. In his early, pathbreaking work, *The Structure of Social Action*, Parsons reminded the reader not to confuse analytical constructs and claims with the concrete empirical objects of the world-about-us (1937/1968, I, p. 29). In taking this step, Parsons in a fashion prepared the reader, and later scholars, for his life works. What he succeeded in producing during a lifetime of extraordinary productivity was a set of schemes that were designed to aid and to direct the attention of the scientific student of society. The theoretical apparatus provided a blueprint to study a reality that, in fact, was not there. Like any good neo-Kantian, Parsons firmly believed that reality did not present itself to our senses in an orderly fashion, but rather had to be consciously ordered and classified for us to apprehend it. This belief thus accounts for the many layers of conceptual schemes that Parsons created; in effect, since he believed there were no actual laws operating in the social world, he was compelled to provide the mental machinery to direct our attention to the world. Such mental machinery would help us to make sense of the chaos that existed. This task, of course, stood worlds apart from that approach of Marx, who sought to emancipate human beings through urging a constant interplay between theory and practice, as from Weber who was firmly committed to an historicist approach to the nature of reality.

Parsons took the view that society could be seen as analogous to a system. To him this meant that society was a self-contained entity, that it possessed a broader environment to which it had to adapt, and that it entailed a variety of structures and processes that would sustain it (Parsons, 1966, 1971). In particular, society could be thought to consist of several different institutional spheres or subsystems, each of which performed a function crucial to its survival. There were four such spheres in all. An economic subsystem accounted for the adaption of society to its environment; a political subsystem provided the overall directions and goals for the society; a societal subsystem furnished the institutional means for the integration of diverse rules and institutions of society; and a latency subsystem furnished the means whereby the basic institutions and patterns of society could be reproduced over time. Furthermore, one could conceptualize not only different processes, or functions, but also different levels of social structure. Structure meant a means whereby regular patterns of interaction would be created. Again, there were four key components, ranging from roles at the most concrete level of reality to values that stood at the most abstract. Parsons maintained throughout his life that social structural elements helped to sustain social order in fact as well as in theory, and that norms and values, in particular, were crucial to the survival of any society—indeed, civilization (see, for example, Parsons, 1966, pp. 18-19). In this regard, of course, he helped to carry on the tradition in sociology begun with the works of Emile Durkheim (Parsons, 1937/1968, I).

This general imagery of the world, once supplemented with additional claims, then permits some application to the study of power, politics, and their connections to the other institutions of society. In a rather stunning, and very controversial, claim, Parsons insisted that power should be conceived as a medium that, like money, circulated through its corresponding subsystem, namely, the polity. Power, moreover, was available to the holders of official political positions for the attainment of the collective goals of the policy, as to the overall society, itself. He argued (Parsons, 1957), in a famous review of C. Wright Mills's *The Power Elite*, that Mills had mistakenly believed in a zero-sum conception of power. Contrary to this view, which purports that there is only so much power available in a society, and that what one group possesses is thus unavailable to another group, Parsons asserted that power is a property of the system that could be expanded. It was not a matter of elites versus masses in the struggles for power, but rather the effective use of power by officials on behalf of the entire society (Parsons, 1969, chap. 14). Parsons's imagery also held suggestive implications for broad relations and interactions among the institutions of society. Unlike Marx, who took the view that material conditions in the abstract, and productive ones in the concrete, exercised a long-range effect over the shape of a society, Parsons believed that each of the subsystems was crucial for maintaining the society, and that the economic possessed no more weight, in the long run, than any other. In his later writings, Parsons (1966) insisted that the long-run realities of societies and history in general were to be determined more by cultural innovations than by the dominance of one class over another. Indeed, at one point, Parsons (1937/1968, I, p. xiv) dismisses Marx as a thinker whose writings about the nature of the social world and its underpinnings have been superseded.

Further, Parsons possessed a very rigorous and powerful comprehension of the nature of social change. He distinguished between processes that sustain a society on a regular basis, such as the circulation of goods, from systemic and structural transformations, which produce widespread changes. Such transformations, Parsons maintained, could be identified analytically as originating in the strains experienced by individuals, and ultimately would produce changes in the structures of society itself (Parsons, 1961, pp. 70 ff). Moreover, owing to the very explicit way in which he had construed the social world, Parsons was able to demonstrate that transformations in one institutional sphere of society— let us say, the religious one—would necessarily have impact on the other institutional spheres as well (Parsons, 1961, 1966, 1971).

Parsons's themes and imagery have not had nearly the influence for the study of societies and states as those of Marx and Weber. In large part, this is the overall result of his schema, which is so abstract and complex that many scholars find it too unwieldy to mine for insights. Nevertheless, there are some recent scholars who have used parallel notions in the study of the political system, such as David Easton (1953), and used them to great profit. Others, such as Lipset and Rokkan (1967), even have used Parsons's notions of pattern variables to suggest new angles for undertaking comparative analyses of political systems worldwide. Lipset (1963) has also relied heavily on Parsons for his analysis of the founding and development of American society, an analysis that emphasizes the role of values in creating societies. And, more recently, Habermas (1975) has assimilated Parsons's system concepts into his own scheme, and used them to spell out more clearly how modern capitalism has failed in certain functional respects.

The Imagery of Robert Michels, Gaetano Mosca and Vilfredo Pareto

There is one last comprehensive set of images about states and societies that hold reign among a segment of political sociologists. This imagery is based upon the collective writings of three figures whose work on politics was inspired in large part by a reaction to the influence and popularity of socialist doctrines in Europe, particularly the works of Marx (Field and Higley, 1984). Although the claims of each of these scholars are quite different from one another, what they share is a similar dislike and distrust of the Marxian argument that hope lies in the future of the rule of the organized majority of people. All three figures vigorously disagree with this claim, and all three assert, in effect, that the history of rulership in society is but the history of endless succession of different minority groups, or, as Pareto put it in a famous phrase, history is "the graveyard of aristocracies" (Bottomore, 1964, p. 42).

Gaetano Mosca and Vilfredo Pareto each wrote in response to the ascendance of radical left-wing groups in Italy. Each scholar claimed that there is an inevitable split between the large, unorganized masses of people in a society, and the small, organized groups that possess the reigns of power. For Pareto, in particular, there existed two segments of society: the elites and the nonelites. Furthermore, there was an additional separation between the governing elites and that element of the elite class that did not rule (Bottomore, 1964; Pareto, 1915-1919/ 1935). Mosca was unequivocal in his claims about the rule of the minority:

> Among the constant facts and tendencies that are to be found in all political organisms, one is so obvious that it is apparent to the most casual eye. In all societies—from

societies that are very meagerly developed and have barely attained the dawnings of civilization, down to the most advanced and powerful societies—two classes of people appear—a class that rules and a class that is ruled. The first class, always the less numerous, performs all political functions, monopolizes power and enjoys the advantages that power brings, whereas the second, the more numerous class, is directed and controlled by the first [1939, p. 50].

To Pareto the split was due to the uneven distribution of talents among human beings. Some people stood in the possession of greater strength or gifts of rhetoric, and thus were able to attain a position in society of dominance over others (Bottomore, 1964). Mosca gave evidence of a similar assumption, although his view took into account the privilege of talent along with the privilege of social inheritance (1939, p. 61).

Robert Michels, Max Weber's contemporary and friend, took the issue of political rule very seriously, and sought in a famous work, *Political Parties* (1915/1962), to provide the empirical detail necessary to uphold the thesis of elite domination. Michels insisted that even where democratic ideologies were proposed for organizations, in particular, in the case of the German Social Democratic party, such organizations necessarily produced rule of the organized minority, or oligarchy. This constant and ever-present tendency for organizations to create the domination of the minority came about for many reasons. Some were psychological, according to Michels, such as the inevitable "veneration for leaders" by the masses, and their equally strong predisposition to be indifferent or apathetic to the interests of the group. But some were clearly tied to the very features of organizational and modern life. Michels, for instance, clearly echoed a theme of Weber's when he insisted that even in the case of the Socialist party, the "professional . . . give(s) place to the permanent and dilettantism . . . yield(s) to professionalism" (1915/1962, p. 107). But there were a host of other reasons that accompanied the development of organization life, including the automatic monopoly over the instruments of leadership by the officials, and their natural inclination to reproduce their leadership through such practices as cooptation: "(T)here arises in the leaders a tendency to isolate themselves, as it were, with a wall, within which they will admit those only who are of their own way of thinking" (1915/1962, p. 126). It is of interest to note that Michels perceived no difference whatsoever between his claims about the inevitable emergence of an oligarchy to continuously dominate groups, and Marx's insistence of the ultimate disappearance of classes and class struggle. "The existence of a political class does not conflict with the essential content of marxism," he wrote, ". . . for in each particular instance the dominance of a political class arises as the resultant of the relationships between different social forces competing for supremacy" (1915/1962, pp. 354).

All three figures, furthermore, more or less agreed that history does not represent the progressive and ultimate emancipation of human beings, as Marx was led to believe, but that the domination of the minority leaders was sustained continuously through a variety of forces. Pareto, for one, spoke of the *circulation des elites*, by which he meant that rulership would always continue to lie in the hands of the minority, but that the composition of the minority would change from time to time based upon the qualities of the leaders themselves. Michels, in contrast, claimed that the small minority always sought to replace itself through active recruitment into its ranks. Where its replacement efforts failed, then the organization, or society at large, would be due for a change; but the change only meant a replacement by another elite force. Michels also agreed with Marx that history was replete with struggles, but such struggles occurred among contending factions, never between the leaders and their followers.

It is self-evident that this imagery of societies, and of political rule, is in fact very different from that of Marx, not to say a theorist like Parsons. Unlike Marx, the three scholars—Michels, Mosca and Pareto—are unconcerned with developing a strong intellectual argument about the general nature of society that will produce a division between the leaders and the led. They are further unconcerned with the sorts of philosophical issues that preoccupied Marx, such as the fundamental difference between an idealist account of history and a materialist one. For Marx, materialism ran throughout his theoretical imagery, as did such notions as alienation and exploitation. His was a view that saw theory as an active force in the making of the world (Marx, 1845/1978c), whereas Michels, Mosca, and Pareto each believed in a theory that sought to capture the hard-surface verities of politics and social life. In the final analysis, hope sprang eternal to Marx; to Michels, Mosca, and Pareto, hope represented an intellectual sham perpetrated by power-hungry oligarchs.

Marxists, of course, criticize this sort of imagery for, among other things, the same sorts of claims they level at themselves: namely, that it focuses too much on individual persons, and too little on the broad historical and structural context in which struggles are fought. They also disapprove of the elite imagery for its failure to take a strong critical stance toward the nature of modern capitalism—in this instance, a sort of parallel criticism to that leveled at Weber by Herbert Marcuse (1968) and Habermas among others. Nonetheless, this package of images is widely popular among students of politics. A recent textbook in political sociology by Martin Marger (1981) in fact organizes its analysis along the lines of the elite-mass division. Among political scientists, there are a number of important books that treat modern society essentially in terms of the division between the leaders and the led, including works by Michael Parenti (1980), Robert Putnam (1976), and the very popular works of Thomas Dye and Harmon Ziegler (1981). Most of these works, of course, were inspired by the classical analysis of American society in terms of elite rule, that of Mills (1959), to which we shall turn in detail shortly. Among modern scholars, no one has taken this imagery more seriously than two political scientists/sociologists, G. Lowell Field and John Higley (1980). Field and Higley insist that "elitism" occupies a place in the intellectual firmament as grand as that of Marxism (Field and Higley, 1984). They have proceeded in their various works to demonstrate how elite rule varies, from forms of consensual elites to disunified elites, but also how elites have maintained rule in all historically known societies from the past to the present. The essential problem that scholars like Field and Higley face, apart from the inclination common to many sociologists and political scientists not to believe in rule by elites, is that their claims almost seem to be truisms. Regardless, there is every reason to suspect that the elite-mass imagery will continue to hold great appeal for many students of politics.

The Nature of Power and Authority

If it may be said that some fundamental concepts underlie the thought and research of political sociologists, those concepts would have to be the notions of power and authority. At least since the profound insights of Niccolo Machiavelli (1532/1947) and Thomas Hobbes (1651/1968), students of the political arena have been fascinated with assessing the character of power, and either how it is sustained or overturned. Machiavelli, of course, was the grand master for modern political theory, inspiring even the writings of neo-Marxists such as Gramsci (1948-1951/1971a, 1971b). His were the insights of the political strategist who believed that the key to the effective use and display of power lay in shifting with the winds. Hobbes, in contrast, claimed by Hannah Arendt (1958) to be the main philosophical servant of modern capitalism, insisted that at base human beings were evil, and that the machinery of the state was crucial to the establishment of order in society. As is well known, Hobbes inspired not only grand work on the nature of power among students of politics, but propelled Parsons (1937/1968) to create his vision of a world controlled not by force, but by social norms.

So far as the principal images behind political sociology go today, there are notable differences about the exact character of power and authority. Most neo-Marxists would agree with Gramsci that the domination of capitalism, and of the capitalistic class, occurs through a variety of different mechanisms, all of which constitute the virtual invincibility of modern society to any assault by proletarian, or other forces. But some will emphasize the economic and political mechanisms that sustain power (for example, Paul Baran and Paul Sweezy, 1968; or James F. O'Connor, 1973; or even a complementary analysis such as that of Frances Fox Piven and Richard Cloward, 1971), whereas others, particularly those of the Frankfurt school, will emphasize the symbolic and ideological elements (for example, Habermas, 1975, or, much earlier, Lukacs (1918-1930/1971). Parsons offered a stimulating view of power (1969, chap. 14) as a collective entity, but grounded his deeper view of authority on common values and sanctions (see Orum, 1988, chap. 4), thus leading to the attribution of him as a so-called consensual theorist (Dahrendorf, 1958). The band of three scholars who support one variant or another of elite rule clearly believe that power springs from political position and its use of the instruments of force and coercion, as well as those of persuasion. Indeed, to Michels, Mosca and Pareto, the occupancy of the offices of the state, or of organization, provided the occupants with the clear edge in rulership over society. Of all the principal images conveyed to us by the main theorists, however, it is Weber's analysis of power and authority that has generated the most influence and provided the most enduring insights.

Weber (1947, pp. 152) insisted that the power of one party, A, over another party, B, lay in the ability of the former to exercise his will over the latter despite the latter's resistance. All contemporary students of power tend to agree with this claim. They would differ with Weber only on the matter of will; most, I believe, would insist today that the power of A over B lies in the capacity of the former to get the latter to act contrary to his or her own interests (see, for example, Lukes, 1974). Further, as Weber also pointed out, no society or group can continue to operate over the long haul based simply upon the power exercised by one party, A, over the other party, B. Thus something else must be added to the concept of power to make it work continuously; that something else is values that make power legitimate. In traditional settings, such values are essentially those of veneration or custom, whereas in modern, capitalist societies such values are those of rational legality, or law (Weber, 1968, pp. 217 ff). Weber, and later Parsons who adopted his view, believed then that the matter of power became transformed into the matter of authority. B thus acts contrary to her own interest, and obeys A because she grants to A the right to govern her. Now, note, in this formulation there will persist an underlying tension inasmuch as Weber would grant to party, B, interests other than those of party A. It is perhaps precisely for that reason that Bendix (1962, p. 292) has insisted that authority or, *Herrschaft*, would better be identified as *domination*, for the latter includes a sense of resistance, coercion, and force (see, also, Dahrendorf, 1959). At the same time, this essentially Weberian treatment of power and authority entails some important ramifications. Not the least of them is that this notion of power represents the very obverse of autonomy. Those who possess power can, by virtue of their exercise of it, limit the choices of those who are subject to it, and at the same time free themselves to engage in a wide range of actions. Power, in brief, guarantees freedom to one party but denies it to the other. These and other features of power have been nicely incorporated into the work of Michel Crozier and Erhard Friedberg (1980, pp. 32-37).

In the next couple of sections of this review, we shall turn to discuss in detail empirical research and generalizations about power and authority in modern society and in urban areas, in particular. For these purposes, we shall rely upon a rather straightforward conception of power. We shall adopt the formulation that *power represents the social capacity to make binding decisions that have major consequences over the directions in which a society moves.* This formulation holds implicit some of the Weberian concerns above. It also recognizes that power is a social capacity, and, further, it collapses the distinction between power and authority by referring to the "binding decisions." Finally, it speaks to the outcome of power by referring to the "major consequences" for the direction of society. Such consequences are part and parcel of any definition, and in the above treatment are contained in the outcome of B's actions for the fulfillment of A's interests. This definition, furthermore, will permit us to get into empirical matters. It should be added, however, that there are many other facets of power; for example, the resources that underlie it are worthy of further study and reflection (see, for example, Lukes, 1974, Olsen, 1970a, as well as Wrong, 1979).[1]

Power in Modern Society

The landmark research that has influenced the study of politics in modern societies over the last three decades, particularly research in the United States, is that of Mills in his classic study, *The Power Elite* (1959). Mills effectively put his finger on a number of themes that then and now continue to be evident in American politics. First, he insisted that historical trends in American society were such that corporations had replaced small private firms as the seat of power. This meant, in effect, that corporate leadership positions had become more crucial to the exercise of great decisions than either those of personal or family backgrounds, or those of small private firms. Here Mills took up an insight previously acknowledged by Adolph Berle and Gardner Means (1932/1968). Second, Mills argued that the federal government—in particular, the executive branch as well as certain key posts in legislative and judicial branches—had come to play an increasingly prominent role in the making of political decisions. This meant, among other things, that the role of state and local governments had considerably diminished over time, leaving officials of such institutions virtually without power. Third, Mills argued that the military also had come to play an increasingly pivotal role in American decision making, particularly after World War II. As a result of all three basic historical trends, Mills insisted, American society in the Cold War era had become dominated by a few individuals exercising their power and influence from a small handful of institutional positions.

To say that the claims of Mills have had an important impact on research into the character of power and authority in modern society is grossly to understate the case. Mills's work, even though three decades old, continues to shape the discussion of many issues of power and even to exercise an influence over the writings of a number of Marxists and non-Marxists alike, including Miliband (1969), Poulantzas (1978), Dye (1976), Domhoff (1967, 1983), and Parenti (1980), and among many, many writers. Mills's view, however, is not without its critics. At roughly the same time, another view was put forward, by Robert Dahl (1961), which claimed that power in American society was rather evenly dispersed among a number of contending groups, and that there were multiple interests represented in the American polity. A somewhat parallel view was also put forward by David Riesman (1954/1961), who in effect argued that power and authority had become virtually neutralized in America, replaced instead by a congeries of contending "veto groups." Other views, which also endorsed the dispersal rather than concentration of power, such as that of Truman (1953), also held sway over scholarly opinion at the time. But Mills's work still represents the touchstone of scholarly writing on power in America, and we shall use it to organize our discussion of certain empirical highlights on the nature of power in America today. (For a fascinating review by an orthodox Marxist contemporary of Mills, see Sweezy, 1956).

POWER AS COMMON SOCIAL POSITION/STRUCTURE

There is one line of research that owes itself to the work of Mills, that of students of social position—or what is sometimes known as power structure research (Domhoff, 1975). Mills argued that the triumvirate of elite groups,—in brief, the power elite—came to share a similar worldview, and hence they acted, to some degree, in concert with one another. Subsequent scholarship has followed up on this line of reasoning, and has sought, in a host of ways, to identify how elite figures act in concert, and how their common worldview may have been shaped. One large body of research has shown, for example, that a number of the figures who occupy the prominent positions in the government also are men and women who come from backgrounds of wealth and privilege. Students such as G. William Domhoff (1971, 1983) and Miliband (1969) represent the key figures in this line of research, each having argued that there exists not merely a power elite in modern society, but a ruling class as well—a ruling class that dominates the direction of society through its control of key positions in the government, or state (see also Allen, 1974; Burch, 1980; and Zeitlin, 1974, among many others). Others have attacked the problem in a somewhat different manner. Dye and his colleagues (1976), for example, demonstrate that there is a corporate interlock among a host of different firms and institutions in the governmental and business worlds. They argue, then, that key positions are in fact concentrated among a relative handful of citizens. A somewhat similar line of reasoning, and set of findings also emerge from the research of Gwen Moore (1979). Michael Useem (1979) also has found that in the United States there seems to exist a small circle within the capitalist class, a group commonly linked to one another. And, in a recent work, Useem (1984) has further refined his claims that there is an "inner circle" of the capitalist class by showing its existence in the United States as well as in Great Britain. Moreover, it seems to run much as Mills had envisioned the operations of the power elite.

There are many critics of this line of research and of the specific findings. As I have noted above, some neo-Marxists criticize the work of Miliband and Domhoff, as well as Mills, for its assumption that the state operates merely as an automatic reflex of the wishes of its occupants. Poulantzas charged, for example, that the emphasis on the backgrounds and interconnections among individual leaders ignored the far more profound structural mechanisms and contradictions evident in modern capitalism (1969). Other opponents, including Berle and Means (1932/1968), emphasize that managers have taken over the direction of corporations, or that such corporations operate to serve their broad stock-holding public, so that it cannot be said that a small group of individuals, whether called an elite or a ruling class, dominates the corporate world.

POWER AS POLITICAL PROCESS

When the democratic theorists, such as Dahl, criticized Mills's vision of the world, or similar ones, they often charged, as Polsby (1963) noted, a bias toward the assumption that if a capitalist class exists, it automatically rules. They then turned their attention strictly away from a concern with the structural background and/or position of individuals to examine in detail the nature of the political process. Dahl and his colleagues (1961), for instance, found that many different players seemed to be involved in the emergence and resolution of policy questions, thereby leading to the support for their argument on the dispersal of power. There were

other students of politics who found somewhat complementary patterns. John Kenneth Galbraith (1971), for example, insisted that in the modern government it was not the officials who ran the operations, but rather the large body of technical experts. Among the most interesting works in this vein are those that seek to get behind the power associated with the position, particularly in the high offices of the federal government, to see how power is managed. Richard Neustadt's work (1980) on these matters is among the most interesting, as he shows in detail what distinguishes between the effective and ineffective use of a position of power. There are a host of other informative works that provide great insight on these internal workings of governmental institutions (see, for example, Burns, 1978; Halberstam, 1973).

POWER AS THE REPRODUCTION OF INEQUALITY

Neo-Marxists criticize the followers both of Mills and of Dahl for adopting a view that focuses far too heavily on the role of human agents in the exercise of power. They claim, in effect, that power is far more in evidence in certain structural processes under modern capitalism, processes that permit the exploitation of one class by another. Moreover, such critics argue, the research into social positions or political process fails to take note of the basic contradictions and class struggles under modern capitalism. Such tensions, it is argued, prompt actions of the state, as an institution, in the effort to sustain the inequalities and exploitation under capitalism (Offe, 1972). Various scholars have used this framework recently to explain certain empirical phenomena. In a widely known work, Piven and Cloward (1971) argue, among other things, that under the presidential administration of Lyndon Johnson, welfare expenditures for the poor were increased precisely to defuse discontent. O'Connor (1973), in an equally influential work, insists that under late capitalism the state intervenes closely in order to offset the flaws of the capitalist order, in particular, the tendencies toward disaccumulation rather than accumulation of surplus value. A number of other recent works also take this general point of view, and seek to show ways in which the institutions of the state and of the capitalist economy are intertwined (see the excellent discussion in Carnoy, 1984; chaps. 7-9).

THE CONTEMPORARY CRISIS OF POWER

In the late 1960s, it became evident in the United States as well as in other Western nations that large segments of citizens had grown disenchanted with the institutions of government. Protest took place on a scale unprecedented in the history of many nations. A number of studies at the time and subsequently have revealed a continuing decline in the trust people place in such institutions as the presidency or the government as a whole (Ladd, 1976-1977; Miller, 1974). The issue soon moved beyond a mere secular blip to invoke explanations at different levels of abstraction. An observer like Walter Dean Burnham (1971), for example, suggested that the growing disaffection may have resulted from major changes taking place in the party system, whereas others, such as Arthur Miller (1974) claimed that the growing public disenchantment resulted from the absence of effective policymaking by government officials (see also remarks by Citrin, 1974). But far deeper explanations were produced as well, the most penetrating and influential being that of Habermas (1975). Habermas argues that the late capitalist societies are in the throes of major upheavals, and that the present decline of trust and loss of faith in public institutions is the result of a decline in the very foundations of legitimacy of Western institutions. Critical political sociologists continue to pursue this line of thought (Offe, 1972; and Wolfe, 1977), and maintain that today there remains a profound crisis of authority in modern capitalism. However, on the matter of public confidence in American institutions, recent research by Seymour Martin Lipset and William Schneider (1983) challenges this argument.

SYNOPSIS

Many different interpretations can be supported by the empirical materials uncovered on the workings of power in modern societies. In the case of the United States, in particular, studies showing the presence of interlocking corporate directorates, wealthy individuals who serve on the boards of agencies of major policy influence such as the Council on Foreign Relations, signs of growing distrust among citizens, and the vast power of the federal government to shape the direction of society all can be taken to provide support for a neo-Marxist, a neo-Weberian, or even an elitist interpretation of the world. The vision of someone like Mills still remains influential today because it incorporates so much of what we know about the empirical world into a theoretical framework composed eclectically from the insights of Marx, Weber, and Pareto.

Power in Urban Settings

Urban settings have furnished students of politics with a unique opportunity to examine some of their perspectives on power and authority more closely. The very first research on urban, or community, politics suggested that power was vested in the hands of very small groups of individuals, virtually ruling cliques or oligarchy. But as research on the nature of power in urban settings proceeded, two very different pictures of power emerged.

ELITIST

The first portrait grew easily out of the early research on urban areas and seemed clearly to support the view that power in such places was highly concentrated. Floyd Hunter (1954), in a work that stood to the study of urban power as that of Mills had to the study of national power, argued that a relatively small number of people wielded power in the community he studied in the early 1950s—Atlanta, Georgia. Those who stood at the pinnacle of power were, in Hunter's terms, the policymakers, and their policies were implemented through the work of a second tier of figures, the policy implementers. The policymakers mainly included prominent businessmen from Atlanta, whereas the policy implementers consisted of figures such as the editor of the newspaper. Hunter further maintained that the individuals who sat at the pinnacle of power shared common viewpoints on many key matters, the product mainly of their common friendships and activities with one another. Hunter's work pioneered not only a point of view about power, which clearly echoes the imagery of theorists like Pareto and Michels, but it brought to the forefront of modern research the study of social networks and the determination of who holds power by an assessment of the reputation of individuals. Many similar pieces of work were spawned by the research of Hunter, including that of Sayre and Kaufman (1960). The most recent work along these lines is that of Domhoff (1978), who undertook a rich and penetrating study of the wielders of power in New Haven.

PLURALIST

A very different portrait of power emerged from the minds of a number of political scientists in the 1950s and 1960s. It was claimed, principally through the masterful work of Robert Dahl and his associates (Dahl, 1961; Polsby, 1963), that the social world ought to be construed in a more open-minded fashion than that of Hunter. Dahl charged that Hunter had adopted a common view that the ruling class, or wealthy economic figures, naturally will dominate the workings of an urban place, whereas, in fact, the real issue is whether anyone governs at all. Dahl proceeded to develop a very comprehensive and theoretically rich and diverse portrait of the world. He insisted, something like Parsons had, that there were different spheres of society. There was, for example, an economic sphere, a social sphere, and a political sphere, and such spheres did not necessarily overlap with one another. Thus one could not automatically assume that those who were dominant in the economic sphere necessarily were dominant in the political one as well. Through a close study of New Haven, Dahl then proceeded to demonstrate that, in fact, many individuals and groups were involved in political decision making, and that the actual participants varied according to the particular issue in question. In effect, there appeared to be multiple centers of power in New Haven. If any participant were prominent in the overall process, it was the Mayor, Richard Lee. But no business figures were very influential within the confines of the political arena. Dahl's portrait, moreover, did not go so far as to suggest that democracy reigned in fact as well as in theory in New Haven, for he further demonstrated that only a small number of individuals actually took part in the political process. As between his claims and those of Hunter, it was really a difference in the number and type of leading figures rather than a matter of emphasizing heavy citizen involvement over the involvement of just a handful of people. Dahl's picture of New Haven became transformed into a portrait of America, and his view soon became one of the most influential among students of American politics. Naturally, his research also was confirmed by a number of other studies of urban settings (see, for example, Banfield, 1961, and Presthus, 1964).

CRITIQUES

The work of Hunter, Dahl, and of their respective followers came open to criticism as well as admiration. Hunter was criticized by Dahl, among others, for the manner in which he studied power. It was claimed that reputation for power is not the same as its exercise, and therefore Hunter's results probably were faulty. Dahl in turn was criticized for the manner in which he studied power. Some (Domhoff, 1978) charged him with a failure to systematically trace

out the ways in which business figures in New Haven influenced the outcome of policy debates. Bachrach and Baratz (1962) leveled the most serious charges at Dahl, claiming that because he and his colleagues only examined how issues were decided in public, they had missed the ways in which power can operate even to prevent certain crucial questions from ever reaching the public venue (see also Crenson, 1971; Lukes, 1974).[2]

POWER, AND THE CONSTRUCTION OF THE CITY

The late 1960s and the 1970s saw a whole new set of questions arise about the nature of politics and power in urban areas. These studies developed not so much in response to the debates between the elitists and the pluralists, but in reaction to the perceived deficiencies in the reigning paradigm of urban land use among sociologists (Castells, 1977). The basic paradigm, which was the product of the Chicago school of sociology (Park, 1952), suggested that broad ecological processes took place in urban areas with regard to the use of land, and that such processes involved aggregates of people in competition with one another for such land. Conflict, displacement, and other disruptions occurred in the urban centers. Moreover, it was claimed, the competition for land ultimately determined its value as well. This neo-Darwinian model of urban land use (Park, 1952) was challenged in the 1970s by a whole host of other urban students, many of whom were neo-Marxists and had fashioned entirely novel perspectives on the urban setting (Castells, 1983; Harvey, 1978; Pahl, 1977). Manuel Castells, perhaps the leading figure in the assault, had in fact developed his views as a result of study with Althusser and, like Althusser, offered an argument premised on the operations of fundamental structures in the world.

What these new ideas and debates did for the study of urban politics was significant and refreshing. First of all, they forced the study of urban areas to confront directly questions of the overall character of the city, particularly issues such as its growth and decline. Harvey Molotch (1976), in a seminal argument, proposed that urban areas are something like "growth machines," and he asserted that actors within them engage in political struggle in order to promote the city's growth. He further argued that the *rentier* class holds an especially important role, since it seeks to gain the most profit from land sales, but that other urban actors, such as political officials, also come to play a prominent part in providing direction over the shape of city policy. This work thus suggested that politics in cities must be seen in a broader context, and only within that context did political questions come to matter. Other work along somewhat similar lines also arose about this time, suggesting that the battles within urban settings were shaped by fundamental differences between consumption units, rather than as part of a neo-Darwinian struggle over land and space (Castells, 1977; see also Harvey, 1978).

This new line of questioning also opened up important new questions about power and politics for debate and analysis. John Mollenkopf (1983), in an important work, has argued that the state, or federal government, played a very key role in the construction of urban areas in America, particularly during the New Deal. He insists that political entrepreneurs within the state actively promoted policies for the growth of such areas, in large part as a device to secure electoral support. Joe Feagin (1984, 1985) has undertaken a detailed analysis of the development of Houston, and he suggests that the growth of this city can only be understood in terms of the development of certain basic resources, and how individual actors have sought to manipulate those resources. Feagin further believes that the growth of Houston must be seen within the broader contexts of the capitalist world economy and the operations of the local and federal branches of the state. Work by Anthony Orum (1987a, 1987b) on the history of development in central Texas and Austin, in particular, reveals that various coalitions emerged, linking the federal to the local levels of government—coalitions without which key decisions on the very survival of certain urban places could never have been made. Orum also suggests that urban policymaking must be seen in broad ideological context, one that promotes the value of growth and helps to shape the cultural agenda for urban decisions. The bulk of this work further suggests that the research of the elitists and pluralists alike was far too limited and circumscribed, ignoring, among other things, the place of the city in the broader national and/or environmental context, as well as the long history of decisions (Domhoff, 1978). Work in other countries as well, including that of Raymond Pahl (1977) in England, underscores the key role that state managers play in the development of urban areas.

ANTECEDENTS AND CONSEQUENCES OF URBAN POWER

The circumscribed character of urban places has permitted analysts to study power and

authority within them in different ways. One of the more interesting angles has to do with the potential antecedents and consequences of the concentration of urban power. Several studies have pointed to the interesting ways in which the concentration of urban power could be determined by various external influences. Terry Clark (1971) asked whether an expansion in the industrial base of the community might affect the nature of power within it. He reasoned that as the community became more diverse, there would be a fragmentation of power among competing elites. His study of 51 different American cities revealed that as the industrial base of a community became diversified, so too its process of decision making became more decentralized. Likewise, John Walton (1967) also believed that as outside interests came to bear upon a city, there would result more conflict and competition among the various centers of power. His data confirmed this hypothesis.

Amos Hawley (1963) was interested in the consequences of the concentration of urban power rather than in the antecedents, and produced one of the more intriguing and provocative analyses ever done of urban politics. He argued that as the power in a city became more concentrated, then the city as a whole would be better able to develop policies to sustain itself. He developed novel measures of each dimension: The relative proportion of managers, officials, and proprietors in a city became his measure of the concentration of power, while the city's level of implementation of urban renewal plans became his measure of the implementation of policies. As he expected, the higher the concentration of power, the more likely an urban center embarked on, and fully implemented, urban renewal. Hawley's work spawned some other research as well (Straits, 1965) but it did not entirely support Hawley's own thesis.

MOBILIZING THE URBAN MASSES

How active are the masses of residents in urban areas? Are they generally satisfied with the exercise of power on their behalf, or are their interests ignored? These are the sorts of questions that have intrigued modern students of politics, and those of urban politics, in particular. The answers, moreover, are by no means clear.

Robert Dahl has argued that the mass of citizens in American cities tend to be indifferent and inactive in urban politics, primarily because they are satisfied with the exercise of power by officials. At least in one sense, Dahl would seem right. Few Americans seem to take an active part in local affairs. Usually only 40% of Americans participate in local elections; even fewer, 20%, actively pursue issues and problems at the local level (Alford and Lee, 1968; Milbrath and Goel, 1977; Verba and Nie, 1972). But do officials truly exercise power on behalf of their local constituents? Studies of some of the *major domos* in recent American urban history clearly suggest that power is often exercised to benefit an official's party, or the official himself, and not so much the public. A whole line of research on urban bosses and their machines dating from the great work of M. Ostrogorski (1902), and most recently evident in the works of Mike Royko (1971) and Robert Caro (1974), strongly argues that positions of power frequently are abused by their occupants.

By the same token, urban residents do not take abuse and corruption of power lightly. The widespread riots of the 1960s, for example, revealed that many residents clearly were disenchanted with workings of their urban governments. (Feagin and Hahn, 1973). In a few notable instances, moreover, the urban poor and underclasses were able to bring pressure to bear against insensitive urban landlords in order to effect important changes (Lipsky, 1968, 1970). Moreover, in cities like Chicago or Buffalo, where there had been widespread dissatisfaction, political strategists were able to come in and effectively mobilize residents to protest against perceived injustices (Alinsky, 1971). In the mid-1970s, moreover, the character of protest shifted, from racial uprisings to very widespread activities among urban neighborhoods. The neighborhood movement, as it has come to be called, has fostered a good deal of interest by urban experts (Crenson, 1983). As cities continue to grow or to decline, we expect the neighborhood will more and more come to be the source of intense political activity on the part of urban dwellers (see especially Castells, 1983).

Parties, Interest Groups And Participation

While one entire stream of theory and empirical research on the nature of politics has been devoted to macrosociological and macropolitical issues, another stream has been concerned with the internal character of politics of nations and, in particular, with the nature of involvement among the large body of citizens. Much of this line of work has been conducted by political scientists, but sociologists have engaged in this work as well. Indeed, some (Hyman, 1959) have helped to inspire an important intellectual development, the study of political socialization.

Political Parties

Political parties essentially are a product of the twentieth century. Although notable forerunners exist, in political clubs in England, for example, it has not been until the twentieth century that mass politics demanded anything like a modern political party, with vigorous campaigns, highly developed political platforms, and intense competition among candidates competing for party nomination (Chambers, 1963). There are two enduring questions in the study of political parties for contemporary political sociologists. First, what is the structure of parties, and what influences their structures? And, second, how deeply does partisanship penetrate into the consciousness of members of the mass public?[3]

STRUCTURE

Some of the most interesting work done by students of politics early in this century dealt with the nature of party structure, and how it had developed. M. Ostrogorski (1902) broke important new ground in his pioneering work on the emergence of political parties in Great Britain and in the United States. Ostrogorski examined the emergence of the Liberal Party in Great Britain, and the Democratic Party in America. He discovered that such parties grew rapidly in the course of the nineteenth century, through the development of a host of campaign techniques required by the challenges of the widening political arena as well as group discontent, and through ingenious organizational devices created by party stalwarts such as Joseph Gladstone in Great Britain. He also observed important differences between the party structures in Great Britain and the United States, finding in the latter case a looser organization to the party as well as more intricate and, in his eyes, nefarious ties with wealthy individuals and business firms. In the United States, moreover, Ostrogorski noted that in many states and localities party officials had abused their offices, using patronage as a means of securing special favors in the business community as well as with the larger public. Ostrogorski's critical voice came to be heard the same time as others were, especially those of the muckrakers like Lincoln Steffens.

Another landmark study on the nature of political parties was performed by the French political sociologist, Maurice Duverger (1959/ 1972). Duverger introduced certain concepts to aid the comparative analysis of party structures. For example, he suggested that in terms of membership recruitment an important difference lay between the *cadre* and *mass* party structures. The former, which tended to be characteristic of American parties, relied on the continuous activity of small numbers of people who directed the operations of the party, whereas the latter, which were found mainly in European countries, sought vigorously to engage the energies of the mass public. The cadre party, moreover, was a loosely run organization that prepared itself mainly for electoral contests, whereas the mass party attempted to create a more permanent and active organization among citizens, seeking to shape their view on many issues. The difference, Duverger believed, meant much for the nature of politics in the societies where one or the other form prevailed, in the one case limiting the degree to which parties could operate in society, in the other providing them with a basis for reshaping the nature of government itself. Duverger went on to depict additional differences in party structures, noting, for example, that some organizations were based on the principle of the *caucus*, a temporary form of organization designed mainly to gather for the nomination of candidates, whereas others, the *cell* and the *branch*, were created to fashion a more intense public involvement devoted, among other things, to teaching an ideology. Duverger's novel concepts were very illuminating, and were particularly helpful in demonstrating the very different role that parties play in America as compared to that in countries such as France.

One of the most intriguing questions pursued by students of the structure of modern political parties emanates from the work of Robert Michels, whose ideas we discussed earlier. Michels insisted that under virtually all conditions, regardless even of the ideological stripe of a party, party organization entailed the dominance of an elite, or oligarchy. Michels's own empirical conclusion became known as the "iron law of oligarchy." Among students of politics, it has spawned some very interesting research. Samuel Eldersveld (1964), for example, made a systematic study of local party organizations in Michigan. He found that instead of a single elite at the top, there were several different elites that were only loosely aligned with one another. He also maintained that the local party organizations, rather than consisting of a single hierarchy of control, could better be identified as constituted of layers of organization, each only loosely coordinated with the others. The most novel study of this question came from an intense examination of the internal operations of the International Typographers Union (ITU) in New York. Seymour Martin Lipset, Martin Trow, and James Coleman (1956) found that the I.T.U. possessed a competitive political system rather than an oligarchic one. Why, they wondered, did no socalled iron law of oligarchy operate? Their analysis suggested, among other things, that the level of education of the typographers, coupled with the typographers' generally deep commitment to the union's political activities, fostered regular competition for office rather than dominance of a single group. The issue of the internal oligarchic rule of parties, or even of other political organizations, remains a very important one, and has even figured into the study of political movements (Gamson, 1975).

PARTISANSHIP

Most of the empirical research on political parties over the last three decades has been devoted to examining the partisanship of the mass public. Two central issues animate this research: First, how deeply does partisanship penetrate into the consciousness of citizens? And second, on what basis do citizens actually decide to vote?

The landmark study of partisanship in the mass public was conducted by Angus Campbell (1960) and his colleagues at Michigan, although earlier, significant work had been done by survey researchers at Columbia (see, for example, Berelson, 1954). The Campbell study found that almost three-quarters of the American electorate identified with either of the two major political parties. Of this figure, about 45% identified with the Democrats, and another roughly 28% identified with the Republicans. Over the period of several presidential elections, these percentages seemed to be more or less stable (1960, p. 124). But partisanship did not penetrate very deeply into the consciousness of citizens. Campbell and his colleagues found that they could only classify 10% of the American public as truly "ideologues," that is, as people who thought about the political world in terms of clear political issues and principles. Most citizens, about 65% seemed to think of party identification as merely a label to be used every now and then in the voter's booth. A later piece of research, by Phillip Converse (1964), a longtime associate of the Campbell team, proved to be even more provocative and famous. Converse assessed the degree of issue-oriented thinking in a sample of the American public. He found little evidence that Americans thought conceptually about politics. He went on to insist that the vast majority of citizens do not think of politics in terms of basic ideological principles. Later, he and Georges Dupeux (Converse and Depeux, 1966) reaffirmed conclusions about the low level of political awareness in the American public by showing that party identification, and socialization to politics, was far more pronounced in France than in America. Their observations in this regard underscored Duverger's structural analysis of the role of party organizations in the two countries.

In the last 20 years or so, however, there have been some very important changes in the whole character of partisanship among American citizens. For one thing, there is clear evidence that more and more people now disclaim any identification with a political party, preferring instead to call themselves independents (Glenn, 1972; Ladd and Hadley, 1978). At the same time, fewer people now identify themselves as Democrats, whereas more identify themselves as Republicans. According to a famous theory, first put forward by the prominent political scientist V. O. Key (1955), what could explain these sorts of changes is that the United States party system has undergone a period of "critical realignment." Large segments of the citizens, so the theory goes, will align themselves for a long period of time behind a dominant party, just as many voters had done under the banner of the Democrats beginning in the 1930s. But after a while, owing to a host of external circumstances such as profound crises in the economy and the failure of party policies to deal effectively with world events, voters will begin to shift their loyalties to the other of the two main parties. This argument was revived by Walter Dean Burnham in the early 1970s to suggest that the American party system may have been in the midst of a period of realignment, and that such a realignment was the product in part of the changing nature of the American social and economic topography. Yet since Burnham's pronouncement, there are no clear signs that the majority of American voters have sided with the Republicans, despite the Republican presidential victories that have taken place.

Still a second major finding also has emerged from voting research in recent years. An increasingly large number of citizens now show some signs of conceptual thinking, or, in empirically defined terms, attitude consistency, in their perception of the political world. Norman Nie

and Kristi Andersen (1974) undertook a replication of the analysis of Converse, and found much greater consistency in the recent samples of the electorate as compared to earlier ones (See also Nie, Verba, and Petrocik, 1979). This result, coupled with the other patterns about declining partisanship, suggest to some observers that the United States is in the midst not of party realignment, but of party *dealignment* (Ladd, 1982, p. 77; Ladd and Hadley, 1978; and also Burnham, 1971, chap. 6), a period in which people are becoming increasingly sophisticated about politics, and concurrently are relying less and less automatically on the dictates of a single party. In brief, the American public, according to this view, is becoming more deliberative and thoughtful about their choices at election time, a pattern that is in keeping with certain theories about the ideal working of citizens in a democratic system (see, for example, Thompson, 1970).

The next question then becomes, Why are these changes taking place? For some researchers, the changes are happening simply because of a changing composition in the electorate. Abramson (1976) and Glenn (1972) both have shown that the new independents in the American public are the younger generations of voters. They are better educated than earlier cohorts of the voting public, a fact that may help to account both for their detachment from parties and for their higher levels of conceptual thinking. But a much stronger argument has been that the political party system in America itself is in a period of sharp decline. The political parties themselves, it is maintained, are to be held responsible for the diminishing partisanship in the electorate: Weakening parties make for weakening attachments. This argument has often been made about the American parties, even prompting committees of the American Political Science Association to engage in extended discussion about how to remedy the matter.

Not all students of parties, however, buy this line. In a series of very illuminating studies of local and state party organizations, the team of James L. Gibson, Cornelius Cotter, John F. Bibby, and Robert J. Huckshorn (Cotter, Gibson, Bibby, and Huckshorn, 1984; Cotter and Bibby, 1980; Gibson, Cotter, and Bibby, 1983; and Gibson, Cotter, Bibby, and Huckshorn, 1985) recently have argued and effectively demonstrated that the strength of organizations of the Republicans and Democrats at the local and state party levels have not declined or diminished in recent years. If anything, the party organizations have increased in strength, particularly those of the Republicans. The research of these scholars thus commends serious reconsideration of the exact factors that have brought about the current changes in partisanship in the American electorate (see also Craig, 1985).

THE SOCIAL BASES OF PARTISANSHIP

The imageries of states and societies of different social theorists, but especially Marx and Weber, have made their way into the study of mass politics through research on the social foundations of partisanship. A number of students of parties have sought to identify the ways in which parties intersect with the interests of social classes, among other major groups. Do people from different social classes, they ask, identify with the political party that appears to express and defend their own class interests? The answers are by no means unambiguous. In the United States, the long-standing modern links between the electorate and the political parties were fashioned under the regime of the New Deal and Franklin Roosevelt. Roosevelt and his allies actively sought to represent themselves as the party of the poor and the downtrodden, but they ultimately secured the affiliation of the majority of Americans, including many middle-class citizens. Close analytical examinations of the statistical correlation between social class, as measured in terms of socioeconomic status—a Weberian concept rather than Marxian concept —reveals, however, that in the United States there is only a weak correspondence between class and party affiliation (Knoke, 1972). The American case may be somewhat exceptional. A broad study undertaken by Robert Alford (1963) revealed that the correspondence between social class and party was far stronger in Great Britain and Australia than in the United States. Even in Europe, however, there is no perfect correspondence. In Great Britain, for example, there are countless instances in which workers will vote for the Tory Party, and in which middle-class people will vote for the more radical Labour or socialist parties (Nordlinger, 1967). Furthermore, since the 1960s it has been found (Ladd, 1982; Kelley, McAllister, and Mugham, 1985) that as a result of economic growth and other changes, the alignment of specific social classes behind particular political parties has diminished almost everywhere, including the United States; in other words, there is a progressively diminishing correspondence between social class interests and political party choices. A large part of the problem in assessing the social bases of partisanship here arises from a very powerful and often unrecognized

insight—namely that political parties do not merely reflect the interests of social classes, as Marxian imagery suggests, but are themselves autonomous agents capable of molding the ideas of social classes, a notion far more compatible with the Weberian imagery (see, for example, Sartori, 1968).

THE SOCIAL AND PSYCHOLOGICAL ROOTS OF PARTISANSHIP

Owing to the seminal work of Herbert Hyman (1959), a considerable amount of writing and thinking took place in the 1950s through the 1970s on what came to be called the study of political socialization. The study of political socialization represented the effort to learn how people think about the political world, and to learn further how they develop an attachment to political organizations. Sometimes observers took the view that such inquiries were important as a way of determining how individuals internalized or developed a political worldview (Greenstein, 1965; Hess and Tornery, 1967), whereas at other times investigators were far more curious about the vital signs of the political system itself (Easton and Dennis, 1967). Whether the one or the other point of view was assumed, some very revealing insights emerged from this research. It was discovered, for example, that the party identification of children tends to be learned very early in life. Other features of the child's political worldview, such as knowledge, or the power to conceptualize different aspects of politics, develop far later, and also seem to be far more likely to change (Greenstein, 1965; Jennings and Niemi, 1974). Second, students of political socialization also found that parents and schools play very little role in influencing the worldview of the child, except insofar as attachment to a party is concerned (Jennings and Niemi, 1974). Further, it was learned that there are important differences in the political worldviews of children from different social classes and ethnic backgrounds. Children from the working class, for example, seem to possess a far more idealized picture of the political world, whereas those from the middle and upper classes are far more apt to demonstrate a realism, if not cynicism, about politics (Greenstein, 1965). Ethnic groups also make a difference in the child's worldview. Children from Appalachia, for example, tend to view political figures and institutions in a far more cynical light than urban, middle-class youngsters (Jaros, Hirsch, and Fleron, 1968). Likewise, there are notable differences between black and white youngsters, with the former demonstrating considerably lower affection for offices such as that of the president (Orum and Cohen, 1973). There even is evidence of important sex differences in the political worldviews of children. Young boys, for example, tend to demonstrate more informed views of the world of politics (Hess and Tornery, 1967). Yet in the early 1970s, at least, there were signs that these differences are diminishing, and that young girls are developing more realistic and informed conceptions (Orum, Cohen, Grasmuck, and Orum, 1974). Recent years have seen a dramatic fall-off in the attention devoted to the issues of political socialization; an article by Cook (1985) critically assesses this pattern, and also offers a provocative new way to conceive how children learn to think about politics.

Interest Groups

Political parties are only one of the organizational means through which the interests of the public are channeled and/or molded. The other principal means in modern society are interest groups. According to contemporary theories of democracy, such groups are claimed to play a very vital role. In the eyes of Gabriel Almond and G. Bingham Powell (1966, chap. 5), for instance, these groups, like parties, serve as a device for organizing the diverse interests of the public, and then for communicating them effectively to the institutions and leaders of the government. Likewise, for theorists of pluralist democracy, such as Dahl (1971), and Truman (1953), interest groups are major vehicles for the expression of public concerns to those who make public policies. Indeed, to such scholars, it would seem, the political arena is largely setting in which different interests compete for the attention of policymakers, almost an exact model of Joseph Schumpeter's (1947/1962) famous conception of democratic politics, and later for Anthony Downs's (1957) pioneering work on the economic interpretation of democratic political contests. Moreover, in the eyes of figures like Dahl, no interest is dominant in the political arena, testimony therefore to the open and competitive character of democratic politics. This image is not totally unrelated to the concerns of sociological theorists. In the late nineteenth century, Emile Durkheim (1897) formulated a somewhat similar conception of the ideal state, a conception in which the occupational interests of the laboring classes would be voiced and received treatment from the leaders of the state. In turn, Durkheim's work would show up at mid-

twentieth century in the once very influential model of pluralist democracy proposed by William Kornhauser (1959), under the title of *The Politics of Mass Society*.

The theory of interest groups is far more robust and intriguing than the empirical work on such groups (for an excellent recent overview, see Wilson, 1981). There are standard excursions into the role of trade unions and agencies like the American Medical Association, as lobbying organizations, in the political process (see, for example, Hall, 1969), but very few systematic social scientific treatises. This is especially surprising in light of events over the course of the last few years. There are some very vigorous interest group activities evident in the efforts of organizations like Ralph Nader's Consumer Advocates. Even more to the point in the United States, there has been a revival and reshaping of interest groups in the electoral process through the emergence of political action committees (PACs). To the news media, if not to social scientists, the political action committees clearly have come to play a formidable role in the electoral process, channeling many millions of dollars into the hands not only of presidential candidates, but state and local ones as well.

Interest groups do not work the same way everywhere, and that argument lies at the heart of some recent theory and empirical work on what has come to be called "neo-corporatism." According to proponents of this view (see especially Schmitter and Lehmbruch, 1979), the modern state is not entirely as the proponents of pluralism depict. Whereas it is true that in American society interest groups act to mediate between the efforts of government and the interests of the public (see especially Wilson, 1982), that is not true in many European countries. Philippe Schmitter and Gerhard Lehmbruch, in fact, argue that in certain countries, such as Austria, corporatism is a far better picture of the nature of politics than pluralism. What distinguishes the corporatist version of political reality from the pluralist version is that in the case of the former, interest groups are formally recognized by the state, are interdependent with one another, and may be organized in terms of a vertical hierarchy, linking themselves from the state to the mass public (Schmitter, 1979). The proponents of this view further propose to distinguish between a kind of loose societal corporatism, in which societal interests easily are expressed, from a tight political corporatism, as evident, they say, in cases like Nazi Germany, in which the state exercises great restraint over the interest groups.

This line of work has proved stimulating in recent years to students of interest groups, and is apt to provide whole new sets of empirical information and analytical principles with regard to the nature of interest groups.

Participation

The views of many theorists of democratic politics, including the pluralists to whom we refer above, suggest that the participation of citizen is absolutely vital to the well-being of the polity. One very clear voice along these lines was that of Alexis de Tocqueville (1862/1945), who insisted that voluntary associations and organizations constituted the very fabric of American society, and helped to sustain its principles of equality. Others, like Dennis Thompson (1970) and Carole Pateman (1970), have made similar assessments on the importance of political participation. A great deal of empirical research has been done on the nature of political participation, particularly since the advent of widespread survey research, and the results have helped us better to comprehend the character of such activity.

DIMENSIONS OF PARTICIPATION

There are different ways to carve up the meaning of political participation. Lester Milbrath and M. W. Goel (1977), for example, suggest that participation be divided into several levels, ranging from the least active, or spectator, to the most active, or gladiator. By far the best conceptual and empirical work on the notion has been done by Sidney Verba and Norman Nie (1972). Using a set of survey materials from 1967, the authors demonstrate that there are six major types of political participation. At the least active level, there are the *inactives*, who account for 22% of the public. The other segments, ranging from least to most active, are *voting specialists*, 21%; *parochial participants*, who contact state or local officials on personal matters, 4%; *communalists*, who engage in action only on local issues, 20%; *campaigners*, who engage in campaign activities, 15%; and, finally, *complete activists*, who do everything, 11%.

THE SOCIAL BASES OF PARTICIPATION

There are some very different views of how social and economic interests might be linked to participation in various political activities. Some radical observers, such as Robert Alford and Roger Friedland (1975), argue that participation in politics serves no purpose whatsoever. The poor and the underclasses, they claim, gain no benefits from their participation in political activities; regardless of how much they become involved in politics, the upper classes still get the greatest benefits. Others, however, argue that participation may work to the definite advantage of groups and that therefore one should expect to discover noticeable differences in the rates of participation as between, let us say, working-class people and middle-class citizens. One point of view has it that the working and the middle classes can effectively use their participation to gain definite advantages for themselves (Cloward and Piven, 1977). And yet another argument is that the more privileged groups will use their involvement in organizations to maintain their edge in society. Obviously, this argument is a clear echo of the kind of view espoused by the elite theorists such as Michels (1915/1962). Once we examine the actual empirical materials on participation between different social groups, some of these arguments fall to the side. Virtually every study ever done of the correspondence between social class, in the Weberian sense of socioeconomic status, and participation finds that the more privileged segments of the population participate far more heavily (Lane, 1959). The most exacting research on this matter, by Verba and Nie (1972) finds, moreover, a very marked difference in the rates of participation of people from less privileged and those from more privileged backgrounds. Socioeconomic status, as it turns out, explains fully 25% of the variation among individuals in their rates of participation. There are also noticeable differences in the rates of participation of people from different ethnic groups. One of the recurrent results of research over the past couple of decades is that blacks generally participate less than whites in political activities, but that once comparisons are made between blacks and whites in comparable socioeconomic groupings the picture changes. In particular, blacks in the middle and upper ranks of privilege and education are no less apt to participate than their white counterparts; in fact, those of highest privilege and education belong in heavier proportions than whites. Blacks, generally, also are more active in organizations than whites. Among the explanations for this phenomenon is that blacks may use organizational involvement as a means of attaining specific ends, not the least of which is to secure their collective sense of ethnic identity (Olsen, 1970b; Orum, 1966, Verba and Nie, 1972).

PSYCHOLOGICAL ROOTS AND RAMIFICATIONS OF PARTICIPATION

Apart from social class and other group affiliations that can promote, or dampen, tendencies to participate in organizations, what are the psychological implications of political participation? Does it spring from a sense of confidence, or does it spring from a sense of hopelessness? A good deal of the empirical research on participation focused precisely on such matters in the 1960s and 1970s. For example, it was found that participation in social and political activities is clearly linked to the degree to which people feel competent about themselves, and about their capacity to influence government. Generally speaking, those people who feel competent are more likely to participate in a whole variety of social and political activities than those who feel incompetent (Aberbach, 1969). And the direction of the relationship between competence and participation is not a simple one. A recent study demonstrates that participation in electoral and campaign activities may enhance the sense of competence of people over a period of time (Finkel, 1985), thereby underscoring the claims of various political strategists (Alinsky, 1971). There are other psychological and quasi-psychological correlates of participation as well. A number of studies demonstrate that the more attentive and knowledgeable people are about politics, the more likely they will participate in political activities, generally (for a review, see Orum, 1988, chap. 10). Finally, it must be noted that the political efforts to intervene and to promote participation among people, particularly among the very poor, with an eye to attaining psychological benefits for them seem only partly successful. Saul Alinsky's famous experiments with neighborhood groups worked to stir up people for special events and periods of crisis, but they did not work to promote people's activity over a long period of time. As a number of recent observers of broad organizational activity in society have noted, the issue of participation may be less one of the psychological benefits it might entail, and more one of the effectiveness of organizations in mobilizing people as well as in attaining substantial benefits through their actions (Castells, 1983; Cloward and Piven, 1977; Gamson, 1968, 1975).[4]

Conclusion: Forward into the Past

> Men make their own history, but they do not make it just as they please; they do not make it under circumstances chosen by themselves, but under circumstances directly found, given and transmitted from the past [Karl Marx, 1852/1972].

In the concluding section of this review, I shall take the liberty to engage in some speculative and normative discussion of the directions for the field of political sociology. I shall assert my own preferences here, but do so in the course of drawing a rough distinction among the types of approaches that are employed under the rubric of political sociology.

As we have discovered in the process of reviewing a number of different theoretical and empirical works, there are a host of ways in which the political world can be construed, and a wide assortment of empirical claims that can be advanced. Political sociology is a field virtually replete with differences of interpretation as well as arguments among competing points of view. Inasmuch as it is unlikely that such conflicts ever will be settled once and for all the reader might ask: Well, okay, so you have different points of view? But which one is *really* the *best* one, and *why?* Here I wish to state a strong case on behalf of a single point of view. To do so, I must draw attention to certain features of different theoretical imageries that have only been tangentially noted in my earlier discussion.

Let us consider that there are two major criteria whereby social scientific theories may be classified. The first criterion deals with the form of causal imagery employed by the theory.[5] Two imageries dominate in the social scientific approaches we have discussed here. One speaks of broad systems, such as social systems, or capitalist civilizations, or societies that consist of certain contending social groups. This imagery claims that some sort of basic mechanisms operate in the system (or civilization or whatever) to sustain it as well as to account for its changes over the course of time. The approach may draw upon a classical functionalist imagery, such as that of Durkheim (1985/1950b), or it may draw upon a kind of dialectical imagery. The other main imagery speaks of historical actors, including, perhaps, even individuals. It typically is couched in terms of concrete societies. Its claims about causality, furthermore, are made in terms of the actions of human beings seen as at work within a broader spectrum of events and contexts. There are no fundamental or deep laws in history, according to this view. Indeed, history in this imagery is recognized as a highly diverse and variable set of happenings, but happenings that may reveal patterns and repetitions.

The second criterion deals with the purposes to which theory is, or can be, turned. Here I shall speak only to the conscious intentions of the theorist, and draw upon a distinction made evident in the writings of Habermas. We may think of two primary purposes to theory in the social sciences. One is to employ theory as a means of critically assessing the world, and with an eye to transforming it. Karl Marx put this element of theory as well as anyone ever has: "The philosophers have only *interpreted* the world, in various ways; the point, however, is to *change* it" (Marx, 1845/1978c, p. 145). Theory, in this sense, is seen as one side of a dialogue that is actively carried on with the world; the other side of the dialogue is the actual practices in the world, however they may be construed. The theorist, moreover, is not considered as apart from the world itself but rather plays an active and integral role in shaping the world. The other purpose of theory is to use it simply to inform the theorist, and his or her audience, about the world. Theory, even though analytical, is intended to depict a world out there. There is the further assumption that the theorist is effectively not even a member of the world. The hope is to understand and to comprehend the operations of the world, but to disavow any active intention to intervene in the processes of the world, itself.

Now let us use the two separate criteria to create a fourfold scheme, always the pride and joy of social theorists. We discover in Figure 12.1 that there are four resulting cells, and types of theory. Down the side are the two types of causal imageries, systemic and historicist. Across the top are the two types of purposes, emancipatory and interpretive. The four types of theory then are systemic-emancipatory, systemic-interpretive, historicist-interpretive, and historicist-emancipatory. Figure 12.1 further reveals there

are clear individual representatives of each type of theory, most of whom have figured into our earlier discussions. Much of the early writing of Marx, I would argue, qualifies as systemic-emancipatory; so, too, does the great work, *Capital* (1887/1961). The reasons are self-evident. Marx's vision was couched in terms of a system, that of capitalism; spoke further about the basic mechanisms of the system, those of self-contradictions; and possessed a clear view of change. The theoretical imagery, of course, also was designed to be emancipatory. Jürgen Habermas, among contemporary thinkers, also stands out as an example of this sort of theorist. Others who come to mind are writers such as Louis Althusser and Georg Lukacs. Talcott Parsons, in contrast, qualifies as the preeminent representative of a theorist who possesses all the systemic imagery, but whose intent plainly is to provide the conceptual apparatus to acquire knowledge about the world. Again, it is helpful, especially to those familiar with some philosophy, to think of Parsons as a true neo-Kantian rather than, as Marx, a true neo-Hegelian. Parsons seemed to believe, with Kant, that the intentions of a theorist were to create the cognitive bases for grasping reality, and, in particular, for uncovering the grounds of social order. Theory to him was regarded as something apart, perhaps even above, the world rather than an integral part of it.

So far as the remaining examples of theorists are concerned, we find that Weber stands as the representative of the historicist-interpretive mode. Weber quite clearly was an historian above all else, and almost self-consciously disavowed any effort to create a grand system within which all reality could be depicted. There is that famous set of lines at the conclusion of *The Protestant Ethic and the Spirit of Capitalism* where Weber expresses this sentiment directly:

It is, of course, not my aim to substitute for a one-sided materialistic an equally one-sided spiritualistic causal interpretation of culture and of history. Each is equally possible, but each, if it does not serve as the

PURPOSES

		Emancipatory	Interpretive
CAUSAL IMAGERY	Systemic	Marx Habermas	Parsons
	Historicist	E.P. Thompson	Weber

FIGURE 12.1
Types of Theories and Representative Theorists

preparation, but as the conclusion of an investigation, accomplishes equally little in the interest of *historical* truth [Weber, 1904-1905/1958, p. 183; italics mine].

Weber was especially sensitive to the vagaries and varieties of history, to how the changes in time and in place corresponded to differences in the nature of human beings and of social institutions. Moreover, like Parsons, Weber was something of a neo-Kantian. He believed that society could not be understood without understanding how human beings themselves grasped the world through the framing devices of ideas and ideals. People's ideals, in Weber's eyes, assumed considerable importance in the shaping of the world, in the battles between them for dominance over one another. Yet, possibly because of his deep pessimism about the "iron cage" of contemporary life, Weber did not firmly believe human beings—much less he himself, as a theorist—could hope to free the world from the course on which it had been set.

And now to my favored type of theory, that for which a figure such as E. P. Thompson stands as a representative. Thompson, as the reader may know, wrote a classic book on the creation of the English working class over the course of the late eighteenth and early nineteenth centuries. It is a landmark piece of scholarship in many ways. Perhaps most significantly, it addressed the lives of everyday citizens, and sought to dignify them through its intense examination of how they had developed a consciousness of being members of the working class. It considered lives of a host of different occupational groups, including artisans and weavers, as well as how the common people came to engage in political rebellions, such as the Chartist Movement of the 1830s and 1840s. What makes this work so compelling is that it concerns itself with the histories of classes of individual human beings and it seeks to do so in part in order to furnish insights useful for present-day workers. As Thompson so aptly puts it, "the greater part of the world today is still undergoing problems of industrialization, analogous in many ways to our own experience during the Industrial Revolution. Causes which were lost in England might, in Asia or Africa, yet be won" (1953, p. 13). Although this work does not possess a deep emancipatory design—perhaps no historical work ever could—it still is propelled, both in terms of its subject matter and in terms of its general intentions, to provide some kind of intellectual leverage for those who wish to free themselves and/or others from the traps of modern life.

Judging from the reception given to current works by social historians, the historicist mode of theorizing clearly is very popular today. But more than that, I would argue, this sort of work is *far preferable* to the kind created by the other three sorts of theoretical modes. Why? For one thing, we have learned that the transhistorical, or systemic imageries, are so broad and abstract as to defy any easy and precise application to the world we inhabit, that of human beings. The sort of understanding permitted by this kind of writing is invariably useless. Much, although not all—for example, the *Eighteenth Brumaire*—of Marx's own scholarship has this character. His imagery of the connections between production and the other sectors of society is so very broad that it leaves not only non-Marxists cold, but it also proves problematic even for neo-Marxists. Nowhere is this fact more evident than in the attempt by countless Marxists, including Marx himself, to explain the rise and success of Louis Bonaparte. Bonaparte wielded power in nineteenth-century France on behalf of peasants, and seemed notably indifferent to the claims of various sectors of the bourgeoisie. Marx had great trouble making sense of Bonaparte within his frame of reference. Contemporary scholars such as Poulantzas (1978) seem to have pushed Marx to the limits in order to achieve apparently satisfactory explanations. In light of Poulantzas's problems, there is an obvious choice: Abandon the broad systemic imagery, or just consider Bonaparte an anomaly. But many Marxists do not want to abandon the imagery. Thus they must necessarily consider Bonaparte a theoretical misfit. But if they do so, it seems to me, they also must consider equally anomalous a number of so-called totalitarian and authoritarian regimes of the twentieth century, such as those under Nazi Germany, the Soviet Union, or the volatile Muammar Quaddafi. If so many exceptions exist, it is self-evident that there are some deep problems with the claims put forward on behalf of this transhistorical set of arguments.

We are thus brought naturally, I believe, to assume the historicist imagery, and to seek to account for more of the world at lower levels of abstraction. Not any historicist position will do, however. Weber, and many others, believed that historical scholarship could be divorced from its normative foundations and ramifications. Today that position is absolutely untenable. All work is informed by some sort of value. The argument that scientific work in the social sciences is objective and nonnormative is itself a position of value, for at a very minimum such a position entails the claim that some other position is both wrong and bad. To impute value to a theoretical stance is by definition to place it in the the context of normative evaluation. In other words, science cannot provide its own justification, but must itself rest on nonscientific standards and judgments. (In twentieth-century philosophy, this has involved the need for a meta-language of theory.) Such standards, moreover, are themselves fashioned in the course of historical and social development, as the important but often unrecognized research of Robert Merton (1970) on the origins of science in seventeenth-century England attests, and as much subsequent work in the sociology of science further underscores. To understand the justification, then, of science is to understand its own place in time, and to grasp how practicing scientists attempt to justify themselves in the broader real of right and wrong, good and bad in the world. This position, moreover, is advocated no longer simply by radical left-wingers, like Marxists, but has come even to be avowed in a very strong and sophisticated fashion by other social scientists such as Robert Bellah and his colleagues (1985, also note other references therein).

What this position on history further entails is a strong concern with the enduring issues of humanist scholarship. At root, humanist concerns invoke a sense of the dignity of human life, as Margaret Mead once put it, a sense that scholarship about the social world must concern human beings as the object of its attention (Orum, 1985). Even more than that, I would maintain, such work must envision its audience as human beings in the broader society—as you and me—rather than as a small, self-contained group of academics, trapped by the insidious intricacies of their limited hold on the world. On this matter, many neo-Marxists find themselves in difficulty too, for their own work is directed largely at one another, and is so technical—if not obscure—that it cannot possibly inform, or direct, everyday discussion and life. Mainly descriptive studies by the critical muckraking journalists, such as Robert Caro (1974), offer far more usefulness in the way of emancipatory-historical work on the nature of political life than the writings of figures such as Althusser. Many people today claim that modern sociology is not particularly relevant to the world of everyday life. That belief, with which I concur entirely, is true because many sociologists no longer work in the realm of human life. Instead, they are mired in the realm of technical processes and conceptions that, to all appearances, have nothing to do with life whatsoever.

In sum, then, I would argue on behalf of a vision of the political world that seeks to follow the historicist-emancipatory mode of social theory. Such work, by inviting critical inquiries into the past of human life, can help us all to achieve the promise of a brighter and thus better practical future.

NOTES

1. The French structuralists Althusser, (Althusser and Balibar, 1970); Foucault (1980); and Poulantzas (1969, 1978), among others, possess a radically different notion of power. It assumes the exercise of power lies beyond the willing and conscious control of human agents, and is instead animated by diverse structural forces, including language. Readers interested in these matters should consult these works.

2. For other excellent work on these matters, see, for example, Presthus (1964) and for a recent way in which these issues have been reconceptualized and overcome, to a degree, see Stone (1980).

3. For a superb analysis of parties, see Epstein (1967).

4. For a very different view of this matter, see Olson (1971).

5. The distinction here was suggested by my reading of Stinchcombe (1968), but I have turned his distinction to my own purposes. For an entirely different treatment of historicism, see the eminently lucid *Poverty of Historicism* by Popper (1957).

REFERENCES

Aberbach, Joel D. 1969. "Alienation and Political Behavior." *American Political Science Review* 63:86-99.

Abramson, Paul R. 1976. "Generational Change and the Decline of Party Identification in America." *American Political Science Review* 70:469-478.

_____ 1978. "Class Voting in the 1976 Presidential Election." *The Journal of Politics* 40:1066-1072.

Alford, Robert. 1963. *Party and Society: The Anglo-American Democracies*. Chicago: Rand McNally.

_____ and Eugene C. Lee. 1968. "Voting Turnout in American Cities." *American Political Science Review* 62:796-813.

Alford, Robert and Roger Friedland. 1975. "Political Participation." Pp. 429-479 in *Annual Review of Sociology*, vol. I, edited by Alex Inkeles, James Coleman, and Neil Smelser. Palo Alto, CA: Annual Reviews.

Alinsky, Saul. 1971. *Rules for Radicals*. New York: Random House.

Allen, Michael Patrick. 1974. "The Structure of Interorganizational Elite Cooperation: Interlocking Corporate Directorates." *American Sociological Review* 39:393-406.

Althusser, Louis. 1977. *For Marx*, translated by Ben Brewster. London: NLB.

_____ and Etienne Balibar. 1970. *Reading Capital*, translated by Ben Brewster. London: NLB.

Almond, Gabriel and G. Bingham Powell, Jr. 1966. *Comparative Politics: A Developmental Approach*. Boston: Little, Brown.

Anderson, Perry. 1979. *Considerations on Western Marxism*. London: Verso.

Arendt, Hannah. 1958. *The Origins of Totalitarianism*. Cleveland: World Publishing.

Avineri, Schlomo. 1968. *The Social and Political Thought of Karl Marx*. Cambridge, England: Cambridge University Press.

Bachrach, Peter and Morton S. Baratz. 1962. "Two Faces of Power." *American Political Science Review* 51:947-952.

Banfield, Edward. 1961. *Political Influence*. New York: Free Press.

Baran, Paul A. and Paul M. Sweezy. 1968. *Monopoly Capital: An Essay on the American Economic and Social Order*. New York: Monthly Review Press.

Bellah, Robert N. et al. 1985. "Social Science as Public Philosophy." Pp. 297-307 in *Habits of the Heart: Individualism and Commitment in American Life*, edited by Bellah et al. Berkeley: University of California Press.

Bendix, Reinhard. 1962. *Max Weber: An Intellectual Portrait*. Garden City, NY: Doubleday.

Berelson, Bernard, Paul F. Lazarsfeld, and William N. McPhee. 1954. *Voting*. Chicago: University of Chicago Press.

Berle, Adolphe A., Jr. and Gardiner C. Means. 1968. *The Modern Corporation and Private Property*. New York: Harcourt, Brace and World. (Original work published 1932)

Blau, Peter M. and Marshall W. Meyer. 1971. *Bureaucracy in Modern Society*. New York: Random House.

Bottomore, T. B. 1964. *Elites and Society*. London: C. A. Watts.

Burch, Philip H., Jr. 1980. *Elites in American History: The New Deal to the Carter Administration*. New York: Holmes & Meier.

Burnham, Walter Dean. 1970. *Critical Elections in the Main Springs of American Politics*. New York: W. W. Norton.

Burns, James MacGregor. 1978. *Leadership*. New York: Harper & Row.

Campbell, Angus et al. 1960. *The American Voter*. New York: John Wiley.

Carnoy, Martin. 1984. *The State and Political Theory*. Princeton, NJ: Princeton University Press.

Caro, Robert. 1974. *The Power Broker: Robert Moses and the Fall of New York*. New York: Knopf.

Castells, Manuel. 1977. *The Urban Question*. London: Edward Arnold.

_____ 1983. *The City and The Grassroots*. Berkeley: University of California Press.

Chambers, William Nisbet. 1963. *Political Parties in A New Nation: The American Experience, 1776-1809*. New York: Oxford University Press.

Citrin, Jack. 1974. "Comment: The Political Relevance of Trust in Government." *American Political Science Review* 68:973-988.

Clark, Gordon C. and Michael Dear. 1984. *State Apparatus: Structures and Language of Legitimacy*. Boston: Allen & Unwin.

Clark, Terry N. 1971. "Community Structure, Decision Making, Budget Expenditures, and Urban Renewal in 51 American Communities." Pp. 293-313 in *Community Politics: A Behavioral Approach*, edited by Charles M. Bonjean, Terry N. Clark, and Robert L. Lineberry. New York: Free Press.

Cloward, Richard and Frances Fox Piven. 1977. *Poor Peoples Movements*. New York: Pantheon.

Cohen, G. A. 1978. *Karl Marx's Theory of History: A Defence*. Princeton, NJ: Princeton University Press.

Collins, Randall. 1968. "A Comparative Approach to Political Sociology." Pp. 42-67 in *State and Society: A Reader in Comparative Political Sociology*, edited by Reinhard Bendix. Boston: Little, Brown.

Converse, Philip E. 1964. "The Nature of Belief Systems in the Mass Public." Chapter 6 in *Ideology and Discontent*, edited by David Apter. New York: Free Press.

_____ and Georges Dupeux. 1966. "Politicization of the Electorate in France and the United States." Pp. 269-291 in *Elections and the Political Order* by Angus Campbell et al. New York: John Wiley.

Cook, Timothy E. 1985. "The Bear Market in Political Socialization and the Costs of Misunderstood Psychological Theories." *American Political Science Review* 79:1079-1093.

Cotter, Cornelius P. and John F. Bibby. 1980. "Institutional Development of Parties and the Thesis of Party Decline." *Political Science Quarterly* 95:1-27.

Cotter, Cornelius P., James L. Gibson, John F. Bibby, and Robert J. Huckshorn. 1984. *Party Organizations in American Politics*. New York: Praeger.

Craig, Stephen C. 1985. "Partisanship, Independence, and No Preference: Another Look at the Measurement of Party Identification." *American Journal of Political Science* 29:274-290.

Crenson, Matthew. 1971. *The Un-Politics of Air Pollution: A Study of Non-Decision Making in the Cities*. Baltimore: Johns Hopkins University Press.

_____ 1983. *Neighborhood Politics*. Cambridge, MA: Harvard University Press.

Crozier, Michel and Erhard Friedberg. 1980. *Actors & Systems: The Politics of Collective Action*, translated by Arthur Goldhammer. Chicago: University of Chicago Press.

Dahl, Robert A. 1971. *Polyarchy: Participation and Oppositiion*. New Haven, CT: Yale University Press.

_____ 1961. *Who Governs: Democracy and Power in An American City*. New Haven, CT: Yale University Press.

Dahrendorf, Ralf. 1958. "Out of Utopia: Toward a Reorientation of Sociological Analysis." *American Journal of Sociology* 64:115-127.

_____ 1959. *Class and Class Conflict in Industrial Society*. Stanford, CA: Stanford University Press.

de Tocqueville, Alexis. 1945. *Democracy in America*, vols. I and II, translated by Henry Reeve. New York. Random House. (Original work published 1862)

Domhoff, G. William. 1967. *Who Rules America?* Englewood Cliffs, NJ: Prentice-Hall.

_____ 1971. *The Higher Circles: Governing Class in America*. New York: Vintage.

_____ 1975, ed. *The Insurgent Sociologist*. Eugene: University of Oregon.

_____ 1978. *Who Really Rules: New Haven and Community Power Re-examined*. Pacific Palisades, CA: Goodyear.

_____ 1983. *Who Rules America Now?* Englewood Cliffs, NJ: Prentice-Hall.

Downs, Anthony. 1957. *An Economic Theory of Democracy*. New York: Harper & Row.

Durkheim, Emile. 1950a. *The Rules of the Sociological Method*, translated by Sarah A. Solvay and John H. Mueller, edited by George E.G. Catlin. New York: Free Press. (Original work published 1895)

_____ 1950b. *Suicide*. New York: Free Press. (Original work published 1897)

Duverger, Maurice. 1959. *Political Parties: Their Organization and Activity in the Modern State*, translated by Barbara North and Robert North. New York: John Wiley.

_____ 1972. *Party Politics and Pressure Groups: A Comparative Introduction*, translated by Robert Wagoner. London: Nelson.

Dye, Thomas L. 1976. *Who's Running America? Institutional Leadership in the United States*. Englewood Cliffs, NJ: Prentice-Hall.

Dye, Thomas R. and L. Harmon Ziegler. 1981. *The Irony of Democracy*. Monterey, CA: Duxbury Press.

Easton, David. 1953. *The Political System*. New York: Knopf.

_____ and Jack Dennis. 1967. "The Child's Acquisition of Regime Norms." *American Political Science Review* 61:25-38.

Eldersveld, Samuel. 1964. *Political Parties: A Behavioral Analysis*. Chicago: Rand McNally.

Engels, Frederick. 1940. *On Historical Materialism*. New York: International Publishers. (Original work published 1892)

_____ 1950. "The Origin of the Family, Private Property and the State." Pp. 155-296 in *Karl Marx and Frederick Engels: Selected Works in Two Volumes*, vol. II. London: Lawrence and Wishart. (Original work published 1884)

_____ 1950. "Socialism: Utopian and Scientific." Pp. 86-142 in *Karl Marx and Frederick Engels:*

Selected Works in Two Volumes, vol. II. London: Lawrence and Wishat. (1892)

Epstein, Leon. 1967. *Political Parties in Western Democracies*. New York: Praeger.

Feagin, Joe R. 1984. "The Role of the State in the Urban Development: The Case of Houston Texas." *Environment and Planning D: Society and Space* 2:447-460.

_____ 1985. "The Global Context of Metropolitan Growth: Houston and the Oil Industry." *American Journal of Sociology* 90:1204-1230.

_____ and Harlan Hahn. 1973. *Ghetto Revolts*. New York: Macmillan.

Field, G. Lowell and John Higley. 1980. *Elitism*. London: Routledge & Kegan Paul.

_____ 1984. "Marxism and Elite Theory." Paper presented at the annual meetings of the American Sociological Association, San Antonio, Texas.

Finkel, Steven E. 1985. "Reciprocal Effects of Participation and Political Efficacy: A Panel Analysis. *American Journal of Political Science* 29(4):891-913.

Foucault, Michel. 1980. *Power/Knowledge: Selected Interviews and Other Writings*, translated by Colin Gordon, Leo Marshall, John Mepham, and Kate Soper. New York: Pentagon.

Galbraith, John Kenneth. 1971. *The New Industrial State*. Boston: Houghton Mifflin.

Gamson, William A. 1968. *Power and Discontent*. Homewood, IL: Dorsey.

_____ 1975. *The Strategy of Social Protest*. Homewood, IL: Dorsey Press.

Gibson, James L., Cornelius P. Cotter, and John F. Bibby. 1983. "Assessing Party Organizational Strength." *American Journal of Political Science* 27:193-222.

_____ and Robert J. Huckshorn. 1985. "Whither Local Parties? A Cross-Sectional Analysis of the Strength of Party Organizations." *American Journal of Political Science* 29:139-160.

Glenn, Norval D. 1972. "Sources of the Shift to Political Independence: Some Evidence from a Cohort Analysis." *Social Science Quarterly* 53: 494-519.

Gold, David Clarence, Y. H. Lo, and Eric Olin Wright. 1975a. "Recent Developments in Marxist Theories of the State." *Monthly Review Press* 27:29-43.

_____ 1975b. "Recent Developments in Marxist Theories of the State, part 2. *Monthly Review Press* 27:36-51.

Gramsci, Antonio. 1971a. "The Modern Prince." Pp. 123-205 in *Selections from the Prison Notebooks of Antonio Gramsci*, translated and edited by Quintin Hoare and Geoffrey Nowell Smith. New York: International Publishers. (Original work written 1948-1951)

_____ 1971b. "State and Civil Society." Pp. 206-276 in *Selections from the Prison Notebooks of Antonio Gramsci*, translated and edited by Quintin Hoare and Geoffrey Nowell Smith. New

York: International Publishers. (Original work written 1948-1951)

Greenstein, Fred. 1965. *Children and Politics*. New Haven, CT: Yale University Press.

Habermas, Jurgen. 1975. *Legitimation Crisis*, translated by Thomas McCarthy. Boston: Beacon.

Halberstam, David. 1973. *The Best and the Brightest*. Greenwich, CT: Fawcett.

Hall, Donald R. 1969. *Cooperative Lobbying: The Power of Pressure*. Tucson: University of Arizona Press.

Harvey, David. 1978. "The Urban Process Under Capitalism: A Framework for Analysis." *International Journal of Urban and Regional Research* 2:101-31.

Hawley, Amos H. 1963. "Community Power and Urban Renewal Success." *American Journal of Sociology* 68:422-431.

Hegel, G.W.F. 1967. *The Phenomenology of Mind*, translated with notes by J. B. Baillie. New York: Harper & Row. (Original work published 1807)

Hess, Robert and Judith Torney. 1967. *The Development of Political Attitudes in Children*. Chicago: Aldin.

Hobbes, Thomas. 1968. *Leviathan*. Middlesex, England: Penguin. (Original work published 1651)

Hunter, Floyd. 1963. *Community Power Structure: A Study of Decision Makers*. New York: Doubleday. (Original work published 1954)

Hyman, Herbert H. 1959. *Political Socialization*. New York: Free Press.

Jaros, Dean, Herbert Hirsch, and Frederic Fleron, Jr. 1968. "The Malevolent Leader: Political Socialization in An American Sub-Culture." *American Political Science Review* 62:564-575.

Jennings, M. Kent and Richard G. Niemi. 1974. *The Political Character of Adolescence*. Princeton, NJ: Princeton University Press.

Kelley, Jonathan, Ian McAllister, and Anthony Mugham. 1985. "The Decline of Class Revisited: Class and Party in England, 1964-1979." *American Political Science Review* 79:719-737.

Key, V.O., Jr. 1955. "A Theory of Critical Elections." *Journal of Politics* 17:3-18.

Knoke, David. 1972. "A Causal Model for Political Party Preference." *American Sociological Review* 37:679-689.

Kornhauser, William. 1959. *The Politics of Mass Society*. Glencoe, IL: Free Press.

Ladd, Everett Carl. 1976-1977. "The Polls: The Question of Confidence." *Public Opinion Quarterly* 40:544-552.

_____. 1982. *Where Have All The Voters Gone?*. New York: W. W. Norton.

Ladd, Everett Carl and Charles D. Hadley. 1978. *Transformation of the American Party System*. New York: W. W. Norton.

Lane, Robert E. 1959. *Political Life: Why People Get Involved in Politics*. Glencoe, IL: Free Press.

Lefebrve, Henri. 1969. *The Sociology of Marx*. New York: Random House.

Lehmbruch, Gerhard and Philippe C. Schmitter, eds. 1982. *Patterns of Corporatist Policy-making*. Beverly Hills, CA: Sage.

Lenin, V. I. 1975a. "Imperialism: The Highest Stage of Capitalism." Pp. 204-274 in *The Lenin Anthology*, edited by Robert C. Tucker. New York: W. W. Norton. (Original work published 1917)

_____. 1975b. "The State and Revolution." Pp. 311-398 in *The Lenin Anthology* edited by Robert C. Tucker. New York: W. W. Norton. (Original work published 1917)

Lipset, Seymour Martin. 1963. *The First New Nation*. New York: Doubleday.

_____. 1982. *Political Man: The Social Basis of Politics*. Baltimore: Johns Hopkins Press.

_____ and Stein Rokkan, eds. 1967. *Party Systems and Voter Alignments*. New York: Free Press.

Lipset, Seymour Martin and William Schneider. 1983. *The Confidence Gap: Business, Labor, and Government in Public Mind*. New York: Free Press.

Lipset, Seymour Martin, Martin Trow, and James S. Coleman. 1956. *Union Democracy: The Internal Politics of the International Typographers Union*. Garden City, NY: Anchor.

Lipsky, Michael. 1968. "Protest As A Political Resource." *American Political Science Review* 62:1144-1158.

_____. 1970. *Protest in City Politics*. Chicago: Rand McNally.

Lukacs, Georg. 1971. *History and Class Consciousness: Studies in Marxist Dialectics*. Cambridge: MIT Press. (Original works published 1918-1930)

Lukes, Steven. 1974. *Power: A Radical View*. London: Macmillan.

Machiavelli, Niccolo. 1947. *The Prince*, translated and edited by Thomas G. Bergin. New York: Appleton-Century-Crofts. (Original work published 1532)

Marcuse, Herbert. 1963. *One Dimensional Man*. Boston: Beacon.

_____. 1968. "Industrialization and Capitalism in the Work of Max Weber." Pp. 201-226 in *Negotiations: Essays in Critical Theory*. Boston: Beacon Press.

Marger, Martin N. 1981. *Elites and Masses: An Introduction to Political Sociology*. New York: D. Van Nostrand.

Marx, Karl. 1961. *Capital*, vol. I. Moscow: Foreign Languages Publishing House. (Original work published 1887)

_____. 1972. "The Eighteenth Brumaire of Louis Bonaparte." Pp. 436-525 in *The Marx-Engels Reader*, edited by Robert C. Tucker. New York: W. W. Norton. (Original work published 1852)

_____. 1978a. "Contribution to the Critique of Hegel's *Philosophy of Right*." Pp. 16-25 in *The Marx-Engels Reader*, edited by Robert C. Tucker. New York: W. W. Norton. (Original work published 1843)

_____. 1978b. "The German Ideology: Part I." Pp. 146-200 in *The Marx-Engels Reader*, edited by

Robert C. Tucker. New York: W. W. Norton & Company. (Original work published 1932)

―――― 1978c. "Theses on Feuerbach." Pp. 143-145 in *The Marx-Engels Reader*, edited by Robert C. Tucker. New York: W. W. Norton. (Original work published 1845)

―――― 1978d. "Manifesto of the Communist Party." Pp. 469-500 in *The Marx-Engels Reader*, edited by Robert C. Tucker. New York: W. W. Norton. (Original work published 1848)

McClellan, David. 1978. *Karl Marx*. New York: Penguin.

Merton, Robert K. 1970. *Science, Technology and Society in Seventeenth-Century England*. New York: Harper & Row.

Michels, Robert 1962. *Political Parties: A Sociological Study of The Oligarchical Tendencies of Modern Democracy*. New York: Collier-Macmillan. (Original work published 1915)

Milbrath, Lester W. and M. L. Goel. 1977. *Political Participation: How and Why Do People Get Involved in Politics?*. Chicago: Rand McNally.

Miliband, Ralph. 1969. *The State in Capitalist Society*. London: Weidenfeld & Nicolson.

Miller, Arthur H. 1974. "Political Issues and Trust in Government: 1964-1970." *American Political Science Review* 68:951-972.

Mills, C. Wright. 1959. *The Power Elite*. New York: Oxford University Press.

Mollenkopf, John. 1975. "Theories of the State and Power Structure Research." *The Insurgent Sociologist* 5:245-264.

―――― 1983. *The Contested City*. Princeton, NJ: Princeton University Press.

Molotch, Harvey. 1976. "The City As A Growth Machine: Toward A Political Economy of Place." *American Journal of Sociology* 82:309-333.

Moore, Gwen. 1979. "The Structure of a National Elite Network." *American Sociological Review* 44:673-692.

Morris, Milton D. 1975. *The Politics of Black America*. New York: Harper & Row.

Mosca, Gaetano. 1939. *The Ruling Class*, translated by Hannah D. Kahn. New York: McGraw-Hill. (Original work published 1896)

Neustadt, Richard E. 1980. *Presidential Power*. New York: John Wiley.

Nie, Norman H. with Kristi Andersen. 1974. "Mass Belief Systems Revisited: Political Change and Attitude Structure." *Journal of Politics* 36: 540-591.

Nie, Norman H., Sidney Verba, and John Petrocik. 1979. *The Changing American Voter*. Cambridge, MA: Harvard University Press.

Nordlinger, Eric A. 1967. *The Working-Class Tories: Authority, Deference, and Stable Democracy*. Berkeley: University of California Press.

O'Connor, James F. 1973. *The Fiscal Crisis of the State*. New York: St. Martin's Press.

Offe, Claus. 1972. "Advanced Capitalism and the Welfare State." *Politics and Society* 1:479-488.

Ollman, Bertel. 1976. *Alienation: Marx's Conception of Man in Capitalist Society*. Cambridge, England: Cambridge University Press.

Olsen, Marvin E, ed. 1970a. *Power in Societies*. New York: Macmillan.

―――― 1970b. "The Social and Political Participation of Blacks." *American Sociological Review* 35:682-697.

Olson, Mancur. 1971. *The Logic of Collective Action: Public Goods and the Theory of Groups*. Cambridge, MA: Harvard University Press.

Orum, Anthony M. 1966. "A Re-appraisal of the Social and Political Participation of Negroes." *American Journal of Sociology* 72:32-46.

―――― 1988. *Introduction to Political Sociology*. Englewood Cliffs, NJ: Prentice-Hall.

―――― 1985. "Why Places Grow: An Argument on Behalf of Human Dreams, Human Decisions and Human Dignity." Presented at the annual meetings of the American Sociological Association, Washington, DC.

―――― 1987a. "City Politics and City Growth." In *Research in Political Sociology*, vol. III, edited by Richard G. Braungart. Greenwich, CT: JAI Press.

―――― 1987b. *Power, Money & the People: The Making of Modern Austin*. Austin: Texas Monthly Press.

―――― and Roberta S. Cohen. 1973. "The Development of Political Orientations Among Black and White Children." *American Sociological Review* 38:62-74.

―――― , Sherri Grasmuck, and Amy W. Orum. 1974. "Sex, Socialization and Politics." *American Sociological Review* 39: 197-209.

Ostrogorski, M. 1902. *Democracy and the Organization of Political Parties*, vols. I and II, translated by Frederick Clarke. New York: Macmillan.

Pahl, Raymond. 1977. "Managers, Technical Experts, and the State." Pp. 49-60 in *Captive Cities* edited by Michael Harloe. London: John Wiley.

Parenti, Michael. 1980. *Democracy for the Few*. New York: St. Martin's.

Pareto, Vilfredo. 1935. *The Mind and Society*, vols. I-IV. London: Jonathan Cape. (Original works published 1915-1919)

Park, Robert E. 1952. *Human Communities*. New York: Free Press.

Parsons, Talcott. 1957. "The Distribution of Power in American Society." *World Politics* 10:123-143.

―――― 1961. "An Outline of the Social System." Pp. 30-79 in *Theories of Society*, vol. I, edited by Talcott Parsons et al. New York: Free Press.

―――― 1966. *Societies: Evolutionary and Comparative Perspectives*. Englewood Cliffs, NJ: Prentice-Hall.

―――― 1968. *The Structure of Social Action*, vols. I and II. New York: Free Press. (Original work published 1937)

―――― 1969. *Politics and Social Structure*. New York: Free Press.

———— 1971. *The System of Modern Societies*. Englewood Cliffs, NJ: Prentice-Hall.

Pateman, Carole. 1970. *Participation and Democratic Theory*. Cambridge, England: Cambridge University Press.

Piven, Frances Fox and Richard A. Cloward. 1971. *Regulating the Poor*. New York: Pantheon.

Polsby, Nelson W. 1963. *Community Power and Political Theory*. New Haven, CT: Yale University Press.

Popper, Karl. 1957. *The Poverty of Historicism*. Boston: Beacon Press.

Poulantzas, Nicos. 1969. "The Problem of the Capitalist State." *New Left Review* 58:67-78.

———— 1978. *Political Power and Social Classes*. London: Verso.

Presthus, Robert. 1964. *Men at the Top: A Study in Community Power*. New York: Oxford University Press.

Putnam, Robert D. 1976. *The Comparative Study of Political Elites*. Englewood Cliffs, NJ: Prentice-Hall.

Riesman, David. 1961. *The Lonely Crowd*. New Haven, CT: Yale University Press. (Original work published 1954)

Royko, Mike. 1971. *Boss: Richard J. Daley of Chicago*. New York: NAL.

Sartori, Giovanni. 1968. "The Sociology of Parties: A Critical Review." Pp. 1-25 in *Party Systems, Party Organizations and the Politics of New Masses*, edited by Seymour Martin Lipset and Stein Rokkan. Berlin: Institut für politische Wissenscheft an der Freien Universität Berlin Institut.

Sayre, Wallace S. and Herbert Kaufman. 1960. *Governing New York City*. New York: Russell Sage Foundation.

Schmitter, Philippe. 1979. "Still the Century of Corporatism?" Pp. 7-52 in *Trends Toward Corporatist Intermediation*, edited by Philippe C. Schmitter and Gerhard Lehmbruch. Beverly Hills, CA: Sage.

———— and Gerhard Lehmbruch, eds. 1979. *Trends Toward Corporatist Intermediation*. Beverly Hills, CA: Sage.

Schumpeter, Joseph. 1962. *Capitalism, Socialism and Democracy*. New York: Harper & Row. (Original work published 1947)

Seeman, Melvin. 1975. "Alienation Studies." Pp. 91-123 in *Annual Review of Sociology*, edited by Alex Inkeles, James Coleman, and Neil J. Smelser. Palo Alto, CA: Annual Reviews.

Skocpol, Theda. 1979. *States and Social Revolutions: A Comparative Analysis of France, Russia and China*. New York: Cambridge University Press.

———— 1981. "Political Response to the Capitalist Crisis: Neo-Marxist Theories of the State and the New Deal." *Politics and Society* 10:155-201.

Stinchcombe, Arthur L. 1968. *Constructing Social Theories*. New York: Harcourt, Brace & World.

Stone, Clarence. 1980. "Systemic Power in Community Decision-Making: A Restatement of

Stratification Theory." *American Political Science Review* 74:978-90.

Straits, Bruce C. 1965. "Community Adoption and Implementation of Urban Renewal." *American Journal of Sociology* 71:77-82.

Sweezy, Paul M. 1956. *Power Elite or Ruling Class?* New York: Monthly Review Press.

Therborn, Goran. 1978. *What Does the Ruling Class Do When It Rules?* London: NLB.

Thompson, Dennis F. 1970. *The Democratic Citizen*. Cambridge, England: Cambridge University Press.

Thompson, E. P. 1963. *The Making of the English Working Class*. London: Victor Gollancz.

Truman, David. 1953. *The Governmental Process*. New York: Knopf.

Useem, Michael. 1979. "The Social Organization of the American Business Elite." *American Sociological Review* 44:553-572.

———— 1984. *The Inner Circle: Large Corporations and the Rise of Political Activity in the U.S. and U.K.* New York: Oxford University Press.

Verba, Sidney and Norman Nie. 1972. *Participation in America: Political Democracy and Social Equality*. New York: Harper & Row.

Walton, John. 1967. "The Vertical Axis of Community Organization and the Structure of Power." *Social Science Quarterly* 48:353-368.

Wattenberg, Martin P. and Arthur H. Miller. 1981. "Decay in Regional Party Coalitions: 1952-1980." Pp. 341-367 in *Party Coalitions in the 1980s*, edited by Seymour Martin Lipset. San Francisco: Institute for Contemporary Studies.

Weber, Max. 1947. *The Theory of Social and Economic Organization*, translated by A. M. Henderson and Talcott Parsons. New York: Oxford University Press.

———— 1958a. *The Protestant Ethic and the Spirit of Capitalism*, translated by Talcott Parsons. New York: Scribner's.

———— 1958b. "Politics as a Vocation." Pp. 77-128 in *From Max Weber: Essays in Sociology*, translated, edited, and with an introduction by H. H. Gerth and C. Wright Mills. New York: Oxford University Press. (Original work published 1919)

———— 1958c. "Science As A Vocation." Pp. 129-56 in *From Max Weber: Essays in Sociology*, translated, edited and with an introduction by Hans Gerth and C. Wright Mills. New York: Oxford University Press. (Original work published 1919)

———— 1968. *Economy and Society*, vol. I-III. New York: Bedminster Press.

———— 1975. *Roscher and Knies: The Logical Problems of Historical Economics*, translated and with an introduction by Guy Oakes. New York: Free Press.

Wilson, Graham K. 1981. *Interest Groups in the United States*. Oxford, England: Clarendon Press.

———— 1982. "Why Is There No Corporatism in the United States?" Pp. 219-236 in *Patterns of Cor-*

poratist Policy-Making, edited by Gerhard Lehmbruch and Philippe C. Schmitter. Beverly Hills, CA: Sage.

Wolfe, Alan. 1977. *The Limits of Legitimacy: Political Contradictions of Contemporary Capitalism*. New York: Free Press.

Wrong, Dennis. 1979. *Power: Its Form, Bases and Uses*. New York: Harper & Row.

Zeitlin, Maurice. 1974. "Corporate Ownership and Control: The Large Corporation and the Capitalist Class." *American Journal of Sociology* 79:1073-1119.

13

Trends in Family Sociology

JOAN HUBER
GLENNA SPITZE

Reviews of research on the family typically define it by relating its functions to the environment. The definitions represent a search for theory; the field rests on a weak base. Macro theory has been slighted. Micro theory, having neglected comparative and historical data, remains mute on the topic of change. We discuss past research to explain how this came about. Then, to suggest principles for a macro-level theory, we show how various subsistence technologies permitted or encouraged certain patterns. We use these principles to explain trends in family formation and dissolution, change in motivation to divorce and remarry, untraditional dyadic relations, and parent-child relations.

A theory of moral progress dominated nineteenth-century Western thought about the family: from sexual promiscuity, group marriage, matriarchy, and polygyny to, finally, monogamy. It was replaced by new data and perspectives from several fields. Anthropology had benefited from improvements in field methods early in the century. By 1937 Murdock had assembled the Human Relations Area Files.

Family sociology began with Burgess and Ogburn's insight that industrialization had reduced family functions and isolated the nuclear family. The scholars who fully developed these themes were few but they included Parsons, 1943; Levy, 1945; Smelser, 1959; Goode, 1959; Zelditch, 1964; and Farber, 1968. By the mid-1950s a large literature questioned the extent of kin isolation (Sussman, 1965) but it was agreed that economic ties had decreased. Then P. Laslett (1965) demonstrated that the nuclear family also dominated preindustrial Europe. His (1977, 1983) work in historical demography links midcentury macrosociology with later work in social history and historical sociology, for example, B. Laslett's (1975) evidence that the nuclear family was dominant in preindustrial Los Angeles.

Social psychology was also indebted to Burgess: Having lost functions, the family was primarily a unity of interacting personalities. Research should show how they could interact in harmony. However, efforts to predict marital "disorganization" produced contradictory findings and, as research became more applied, theory tended to disappear. But this perspective prevailed.

Criticism has persistently dogged the field: It was shackled by superstition (Komarovsky and Waller, 1945). Much of it failed to address important problems or yield significant knowledge (Cottrell, 1948). In a benchmark volume spon-

For support of part of this research, we are grateful to the National Science Foundation for grant SES 831 9139 to Glenna Spitze. We are grateful to William Form for critical comment, to Lisa Ransdell for unflagging research assistance, and to Judith Essig for help in preparing the manuscript. The order of our names is an accident of the alphabet. We are coauthors.

425

sored by the American Sociological Association, Goode (1959) blasted the neglect of theory. In a major encyclopedia Smith (1969) concluded that knowledge about the family remained rudimentary. These criticisms were not isolated. In the 1950s and 1960s many scholars noted problems and suggested ways to improve the field. The prescriptions were of two kinds.

First, identify major frameworks. In 1957 Hill named seven: institutional, interactional, situational, structural functional, developmental, learning theory, and home management. Broderick's (1970) review reported only three in use: symbolic interactional, structural functional, and developmental. Several minor ones (game, balance, exchange) and a major one (systems) were new. Holman and Burr (1980) regrouped them: major (symbolic interaction, systems and exchange theory), minor (conflict, developmental, and ecosystems theory, phenomenology and behaviorism), or peripheral (psychoanalysis and learning theory). Structural functionalism, game theory, and the institutional and situational frameworks were dropped. Exchange theory predominated; no feasible alternatives could provide testable hypotheses (Aldous, 1977).

Another way to improve the field was to construct middle-range axiomatic theories, exemplified in Burr et al. (1979, vols. 1, 2). Volume 1 covered inductive theory building; volume 2, the application of general theory. However, integrating phenomenology, symbolic interaction, systems, exchange, and conflict theories with lesser ones proved difficult. The methodology provided neither adequate terms nor guidelines. Burr et al. (1979, vol. 2, p. xi) concluded that the field was still in early stages of theory construction.

Other authors in Burr et al. (1979, vol. 1) and Berardo (1980) agreed. Research quality was too low for causal assertions (Lee, 1980), it was descriptive, based on inadequate methods (Clayton and Bokemeier, 1980; Otto, 1979), it consisted of ad hoc generalizations (Gelles, 1980; Scanzoni and Fox, 1980; Steinmetz, 1979)—and the field had moved no closer to a general theory (Holman and Burr, 1980).

What had gone wrong? After so much hard work, why did the problems so stubbornly persist? There are several answers.

First, adequate data for general theory were not available from relevant disciplines until recently. The Human Relations Area Files posed severe measurement problems. Demography's contribution was limited by neglect of history and underdeveloped theory. History had long focused on great men and great events, neglecting social data.

The use of social psychological frameworks that slighted comparative and historical data also created problems. Some frameworks were hard to test. Many failed to yield findings that went beyond common sense. All findings were bound by time and place.

In the 1970s two events moved family study closer to general theory. First, a new wave of the women's movement made women's status a variable to be explained thus marking the conceptual birth of gender stratification. If the societal division of labor spawns strata of varying power and prestige, does the domestic division of labor similarly affect the family? How do forms of marriage and family relate to sex stratification? New questions thrown to the fore could be addressed only with comparative and historical data.

Second, new data and methods appeared. Historical demography, historical sociology, and social history expanded the midcentury macroanalyses of industrialization's effect on families. One stream culminated in the life-course perspective, a mix of history, social psychology, and demography with formidable quantitative techniques. Previously unanswerable questions can be addressed with panel and longitudinal data (Elder, 1985; Hareven, 1978).

Another stream depended more on anthropology. Focusing on ecology, technology, and stratification, Lenski (1970) showed how subsistence technology affects social organization worldwide and over time. Comparisons of work, stratification, and inheritance in foraging, hoe, and plow societies suggested causal explanations of marriage and family types (Friedl, 1975; Goody, 1976). Since their work is not well known in sociology, we show how it helps to explain family patterns in four preindustrial societies, thereby deriving principles that can apply to Western marriage and family types.

We begin with Friedl's basic questions: Why do men and women in foraging and hoe cultures perform certain tasks, and which ones give the most prestige and power? The answers suggest three principles of sex stratification that help to relate production, reproduction, and stratification to forms of marriage and family in foraging, hoe, herding, and plow societies.

The first principle applies at family level. Those who produce have more power and prestige than those who consume. But which spouse performs the most productive tasks? Who produces the most food—and why? The second principle provides answers. The work women do results from the way it meshes with the functional requirements of pregnancy and lactation. The third principle applies at societal level. The most power and prestige accrue to those who control the distribution of valued goods beyond the family. The following account shows how these principles apply in four societal types.

Subsistence Technology and Family Patterns

Foragers hunted large animals and gathered berries, nuts, and insects. Food was scarce. Groups averaged 50 persons. They moved when food in an area was used up. Polygyny was rare; food was too scarce to supply more than one set of affinal relatives. Divorce was common because it little affected the subsistence of either spouse or the children. Premarital sex relations were usually permitted.

Labor was divided by age and sex. Men hunted large animals. They could therefore distribute food beyond the family. Women never hunted. It required an uncertain time away from camp, which made nursing impossible. During their most vigorous years women were constantly pregnant or nursing children (up to age four) to offset high death rates. The need for population replacement thus excluded women from the work that yielded the most power.

In simple hoe cultures the main tool, a wooden digging stick, produces more food than foraging, but the group—200 persons on average—moved every few years to seek fertile soil. In advanced hoe cultures (pre-Columbian Mexico and sub-Saharan Africa) the tip of the hoe is metal. A larger surplus permits a 60-fold population increase, a greater division of labor, much greater inequality, and the use of war to increase the surplus.

The sexual division of labor varied but men monopolized land clearing and, after the invention of metallurgy, warfare. Clearing land gives less chance to allot food beyond the family than does warfare. Men therefore outrank women more in advanced than simple hoe cultures. In both types of cultures women's food production equals men's on average. Since divorce little affects the subsistence of mother and children, divorce rates were high (Friedl, 1975). Matrilocality and matrilineality, which improve women's status, occur most often in hoe cultures. Complex kinship systems organize individuals against risk. Women's ability to provide for children permits what we call populist polygyny: Although women marry young and

men marry old (as in sub-Saharan Africa), most persons marry.

Herding societies occur where low rainfall, a short season, or mountains preclude growing crops. The need for water and grazing rights makes war important and enables elites to control economy and polity. Since warfare and herding (tending animals far from home over long periods) mesh badly with nursing, women lack access to the major tools of food production. What we call elite polygyny—only rich men have plural wives—can occur in these circumstances.

The use of the plow in Eurasia vastly increased the food supply but it depressed the status of commonfolk. A food surplus in the countryside coupled with the availability of iron weapons tempts elites to extract as much as possible from impoverished peasants, probably worse off than their foraging ancestors (Lenski, 1970). Men monopolized the plow. Larger fields further from home made it hard to arrange work to suit a nursling (Blumberg, 1978). Women's share of food production fell relative to that in hoe societies.

The plow lowered women's status in other ways (Goody, 1976). Hoe peoples moved when the soil was exhausted. The plow permits land to be used indefinitely. It therefore becomes the chief form of wealth. Since it tends to be an impartible inheritance—with a given technology, it supports only a given number—the production of legal heirs must be controlled. Monogamy therefore predominates. Divorce is nearly impossible. Women's sexual behavior is constrained by law and custom lest a man's property go to another man's child. The wealthier her family, the greater the constraints.

Did constraints such as suttee and footbinding occur in Europe? Were European women less constrained than Asian women in the plow era? If so, why? Goody's (1983) work suggests less constraint, an unplanned outcome of Church efforts to increase its wealth. Such research might also explain why the age of marriage was higher west than east of a line from Leningrad to Trieste (Hajnal, 1965).

Since the Church needed property to grow, it had to control marriage and the legitimation of children in order to influence inheritance patterns. After 325 A.D., various measures decreased the supply of close relatives to induce testators to leave property to the Church. Encouraging celibacy, forbidding close cousin marriage and adoption (widespread in biblical and Roman times), condemning polygyny and divorce, and discouraging remarriage greatly reduced the number of male heirs. Church emphasis on mutual consent as a requirement decreased child marriage and also the chance that a marriage would serve family interests. Women could avoid marriage by entering the cloister, which increased their control over property and chance that the Church would acquire it (Goody, 1983).

Church strategy worked. By the eighth century, for instance, it owned a third of productive French land. These measures permitted women more independence in Europe than in Asia for a millennium before the Industrial Revolution, conceivably helping them to adapt to change.

The preceding discussion of foraging, hoe, herding, and plow societies suggests how ecology and technology affected preindustrial types of family and marriage. The extended family type cannot become dominant unless the elderly control major resources, as in plow cultures. The conjugal type occurs when the elderly cannot control resources, as in foraging societies, or when family resources go from parents to children, as in industrial societies.

Polygyny takes two forms. Populist polygyny occurs only if a woman can support herself and her children. Nearly everyone marries, but women marry young and men marry old, as in many hoe cultures. Elite polygyny occurs only if the food supply permits a man to support more than one family and when women lack access to major subsistence tools. A few rich men have plural wives, as in many herding societies. Polygyny rarely occurs in foraging societies because of the poor food supply. Plow cultures typically ban both types because monogamy more efficiently limits the number of legal heirs. Postindustrial societies inherited lifetime monogamy, but its major prop, the impartibility of land, now counts for much less. Lifetime monogamy has also been buffeted by the following four trends that occurred during industrialization in the West.

A *decline in infant mortality* reduced the number of pregnancies needed for population replacement. Ariès's (1962) often-cited claim that it also increased parents' attachment to children has been rejected by a number of scholars on empirical grounds. Le Roy Ladurie (1975, p. 307) states that the documentation is entirely based on ad hoc citations and on the magnificent collection of pictures that Ariès's had assembled in his imaginery museum of childhood.

Industrialization sometimes increased infant deaths. French data support Friedl's (1975) view that women's work shapes child-rearing practices rather than vice versa. High rents and low wages made household production necessary for survival. Heavy workloads induced wives to send babies out to nurse despite the increased death rates for such babies (Garden, 1975). In Paris only 1 baby in 30 was nursed by its mother around 1800 (Sussman, 1982).

Today the decline affects adults more than children. Despite a rise in divorce, the mean duration of marriages has risen and an increasing number of middle-aged couples have living parents. An unknown number are involved in parent care (Brody, 1985).

Education was compulsory in most of the West by 1880. Recent research stresses its effects on parents' ability to control their children's labor (Lesthaeghe, 1980). Education restructures the family economy by redirecting family wealth flows (Caldwell, 1976). Mass education destroys patterns that made children responsible for current family survival and instead encourages wealth flows from parents to children. A generation of mass schooling suffices to begin a fertility decline (Caldwell, 1980).

A *fertility decline* was spurred by the mortality decline, mass education, and rapid economic growth. Between 1860 and 1910 real income doubled. Economic growth triggers demographic change because a rise in real income fuels ambition, opens opportunities, and makes people feel more independent. In turn, the economic calculus of later generations responds to new preferences (Lesthaeghe, 1983). In 1946 the Baby Boom became an upward blip in a long fertility decline but the decline soon began again. Total fertility halved from 1960 to 1977. It has been below replacement since the early 1970s. Recent birth increases reflect the larger number of women aged 15 to 45.

In the West an increase in current fertility levels seems unlikely. Disincentives are formidable. Direct costs of rearing a child continue to rise. The high opportunity cost of the mother's time adds a heavy deterrent. The prospect and experience of divorce highlight child costs and result in lower fertility (Becker, 1981). Pension plans provide retirement security. Grown children may live far away. The emotional benefits of parenting seem low to offset such powerful disincentives. Research on parent-child relations, presented later, illuminates these issues.

Married women's entry into market work increased primarily in this century, following the transitions in mortality, education, and fertility. Since 1700 European women's productivity has tended to follow a U-curve: high in the preindustrial household economy, lower in industrial economies, and higher again with the development of the tertiary sector (Tilly and Scott, 1978). Men's earlier entry to market work spawned a men's movement comprised of socialist and labor groups that excluded women from high-wage work—and most women still work in feminized occupations, those whose wages are too low to attract men qualified to du the jub. The sex-wage issue is often thought to stem from the shift of work site from home to a place away from home but the real issue centers on the use of the most productive tools, not the work site. Preindustrial women did more labor-intensive work than men even away from home (Rosenfeld, 1985). Industrialization enabled men to continue to use the most productive tools, ensuring that their wages would be higher than women's.

In sum, at the outset of industrialization husbands supplied a large share of family subsistence needs, which decreased as wives entered the work force. The fertility decline and the development of safe methods of bottle feeding after 1910 made market work easier for wives. However, the division of household labor is little changed (Miller and Garrison, 1982), few women hold elite positions, and male prerogatives in task bargains remain strong (Hiller and Philliber, 1986). We discuss prospects for change in the conclusion.

We now turn to the literature on divorce and remarriage, nontraditional dyads, and parent-child relations, three areas that have been much affected by the decline in the complementary-role type of marriage. Some topics overlap, for example, the effect of the one-parent household on children. We discuss its economic effects in the section on divorce, since they fall on ex-wives, too. We discuss other effects in the parent-child section.

Divorce and Remarriage

The sparse research on divorce before 1960 rose in the 1960s and mushroomed in the 1970s. The *Journal of Marriage and the Family*'s decade review for the 1960s subsumed divorce under marital quality—a decade later it merited a separate chapter. We review the literature on marital dissolution through divorce or separation, on the divorce process, and on remarriage. We cover aggregate- and individual-level trends, explanations, theories, and methodological issues. We emphasize demographic and quantitative studies.

Macrolevel Trends

Recent high divorce levels in the West are part of a long-term trend—in the United States, back to the mid-1800s—that can be viewed from a period or cohort perspective. Period divorce rates (relative to the married population) increased slowly in the late 1800s, leveled off in the early 1900s, increased dramatically during both world wars, and were low between the wars, particularly in the Great Depression (Cherlin, 1981; Furstenberg and Spanier, 1984; South, 1985). They were increasing but below the trend in the 1950s and have increased sharply since the 1960s.

Cohort rates (the proportion of marriages contracted in a given year that ended or are projected to end in divorce) have increased more steadily over that period, with a recent accelerated rate. From about 5% for the 1867 cohort (Preston and McDonald, 1979), most recent estimates expect 46% for the 1948-1950 cohort (Schoen et al., 1985) and close to 50% for recent marriages (Glick, 1984). Divorce timing has changed. The average age at divorce has declined for both sexes (Schoen et al., 1985). Dissolution rates due to divorce *or* death have varied less: about 33 per 1000 marriages from 1860 to 1970, increasing to around 40 only since 1970 (Cherlin, 1981).

Female employment rates affect recent United States and Swedish divorce trends (Schoen and Urton, 1979). However, Davis (1984) thinks that after rising divorce rates reach a threshhold, married women enter the labor force as insurance. Other factors may include changes in contraceptive technology and trends in postponed fertility (Cherlin, 1981). Both trend and longitudinal data show that attitude changes result from rather than cause increased divorce rates (Thornton, 1985). Nor do legal changes (e.g., the switch to no-fault divorce) raise divorce rates (Wright and Stetson, 1978).

Micro level theories from sociology and economics dominate the study of marital dissolution. Levinger's (1979) theory posits that marital dissolution is affected by attractions to the marriage, alternatives to it, and barriers to dissolution. Based on exchange theory, it sees marital cohesion as a special case of group cohesion. Attractions to a marriage relate to perceived rewards and costs, weighted by subjective probability. Barriers hold a marriage together, sometimes as an empty shell. Alternative attractions include other partners or types of fulfillment. A wider field of alternatives yields greater marital power, more often for husbands than wives. The model does not specify how these factors interact.

From Becker's theory of marriage, Becker, Landes, and Michael (1977) derive a theory of dissolution that shares much with Levinger's but uses different terms. It assumes that individual marital strategies maximize the value of the lifetime stream of commodities consumed, including monetary and nonmonetary "income." A dissolution decision may occur because full information was lacking at marriage or because changed circumstances (e.g., children grew up) altered its utility. They suggest that most divorces stem from unexpected outcomes due to uncertainty since they most often occur early in marriage. Probability of divorce decreases with accumulation of marital-specific capital such as children or property, whose value decreases if the marriage dissolves.

Both theories' basic elements include weighing attractions in and out of marriage and barriers that hold a marriage together. Two major differences are, first, that Levinger gives more latitude to social forces (e.g., religious constraints or kin pressures) and symbolic or attitudinal rewards. Economic theory is not limited to monetary rewards but it tends to focus on individual rational decision processes. Second, economic theory is more aware of the dynamic process, including changes in information over time. Both theories have been tested with moderate success.

Data Problems

Analyses of individual-level causes of divorce use a variety of methods and data. Each has problems. Such analyses should be based on longitudinal data because many variables that contribute to divorce also change in consequence. For example, a wife's employment increases the probability of divorce but women's employment responds to experience of divorce. Studies that use cross-sectional data with ever-divorced status as dependent variable risk confusing cause and effect. A compromise is to match data on marital histories with change data on other independent variables (e.g., Morgan and Rindfuss, 1985). Longitudinal data do not quite eradicate risk of confusing cause and effect since some variables change before divorce in response to its increased likelihood—for example, women at higher risk of divorce have higher employment levels (Greene and Quester, 1982; Johnson and Skinner, 1986).

A major problem in using longitudinal data to predict divorce probabilities is the dependent variable's skewness. Since few marriages dissolve in the short run—4% in four years (Cherlin, 1979)—even large surveys like the National Longitudinal Survey (NLS) or the Panel Study of Income Dynamics (PSID) note few divorces. Using such surveys in secondary analysis also limits availability of needed variables. We discuss alternatives below.

Quantitative Evidence on Individual Determinants

Variables that affect divorce probabilities fall under three rubrics: preparation for marriage, investment in it, and outside market forces. They relate only in part to the theoretical factors noted earlier but they more readily permit filing the research variables actually used into mutually exclusive bins.

Under "preparation," either spouse's education decreases dissolution (Bahr and Galligan, 1984; Moore and Waite, 1981). Some nonlinearity occurs: Women with graduate education are more likely to disrupt, especially if it was acquired after marriage (Houseknecht and Spanier, 1980). Also, women who fail to complete a given level of schooling disrupt more often, the "Glick effect" (Thornton, 1978).

Age at marriage is a strong and widely documented determinant of divorce, perhaps due to maturity (Thornton, 1978) or factors related to underpreparation (disinterest in school, desire to leave home) that lead to poor marital role performance (Bahr and Galligan, 1984). It may also be due to the normal changes of early adulthood that then occur in the period of early marriage, causing marital strains (Morgan and Rindfuss, 1985). Alternatively, age at marriage can indicate search time; those who marry early are more apt to find more desirable partners after the marriage (Becker, Landes, Michael, 1977).

Under "investment" (economists' marital-specific capital), children have long been thought to deter dissolution—although Monahan (1955) argued that the relation was spurious; younger couples were most likely to divorce and have few children. Waite, Haggstrom, and Kanuse (1985a) argue that children could affect marital stability either way since they increase dissolution costs but decrease marital quality. Their results are somewhat inconsistent, like those of Cherlin (1977) and Morgan and Rindfuss (1985), although preschoolers, especially, had some deterrent effect. A premarital birth increases risk of divorce, especially for whites who married young, but a premarital pregnancy has no effect (Teachman, 1983).

Home ownership, another investment, decreases dissolution (Becker, Landes, Michael, 1977; Moore and Waite, 1981). However, couples at greater risk may be less likely to invest.

Many studies have linked marital duration to dissolution probabilities. At least two processes are involved. Marriages that have lasted build up more marital capital and, due to selection, they last for reasons not easy to measure. Recent analyses have separated effects of time-related variables and found age at marriage and age to be more salient than marital duration (Thornton and Rodgers, 1984; Morgan and Rindfuss, 1985). Sorting out how determinants vary across marital durations may be more fruitful (e.g., Morgan and Rindfuss, 1985; South and Spitze, 1986).

Another factor that relates to investment is marriage order. Becker pointed out that higher-order marriages tend to have less marital-specific capital (children and property) and, in fact, such marriages dissolve at higher rates and sooner than first marriages. The presence of children from earlier marriages also relates to divorce (Aguirre and Parr, 1982).

In explaining the lower stability of higher-order marriages, Cherlin (1978) denies that divorced persons have personality disorders or that divorced men are poor providers. Instead, the normlessness of remarriage creates strains that reduce stability, especially if stepchildren are present (White and Booth, 1985).

Furstenberg and Spanier (1984) challenge Cherlin. They agree that normlessness creates strains. They question that the strains increase divorce. Instead, they distinguish movers and stayers. Stayers, who oppose divorce more (perhaps for religious reasons), are less likely to divorce. They found no support for Cherlin's contention that remarriages involving stepchildren are less happy. The argument hinges on whether remarriages are less happy than first ones or simply less stable at a given happiness level.

An economic explanation stresses search time. Due to economic need or loneliness, remarriages may occur without due thought (Becker, Landes, Michael, 1977; see also Fergusson, Horwood, and Dimond, 1985). Also, less marital-specific capital is gained in remarriage than first marriage.

Psychological investment in marriage may vary with attitudes to divorce, in turn related to religion or early experience. Such attitudes have been linked to religious group membership and religiosity with mixed results. Thornton (1978) reported that Baptists and Fundamentalists had higher dissolution rates than Catholics or the residual category. Catholics had the lowest rates

(Teachman, 1983). Parental divorce also increases positive attitudes to divorce among college students (Greenberg and Nay, 1982).

Under "market forces" we include employment and economic factors and subgroup or areal differences that reflect economic and marriage markets. A number of studies have found divorce more likely when wives work for pay (Mott and Moore, 1979), due to the independence effect of her earnings (Ross and Sawhill, 1975) or to the disruptive effect of change in traditional roles (Cherlin, 1979). No definitive study sorts these explanations out. Wives' work hours may affect spousal levels of disagreement or interaction time (Booth, Johnson, and White, 1984; Hill, 1984; Spitze and South, 1985).

Indicators of husband's socioeconomic level inversely affect dissolution probabilities (Cherlin, 1979; Hampton, 1979; Mott and Moore, 1979), not the absolute level so much as unexpected change in them. Couples experiencing lower income than usual for the year, those in which the husband experienced serious unemployment, and those in which the husband, given his attributes, earned more or less than expected are more likely to dissolve (Ross and Sawhill, 1975). Variables representing the husband's socioeconomic position likely have countervailing effects, since husbands who do well may feel more competitive in the marriage market while they will also be more attractive to the current spouse.

Government payments provide an alternative income source. The impact of their availability on marital dissolution has generated much ideological controversy. Experimental evidence on income maintenance suggests that the relative impact of income versus independence effects depends on the level of income during and before the experiment (Hannan, Tuma, Groenveld, 1977). Longitudinal survey data reveal no effect of welfare payments on marital dissolution (Draper, 1981; Kitson et al., 1985; Ross and Sawhill, 1975).

People in large metropolitan areas probably feel more pressure to dissolve marriages, since both economic and marriage alternatives diverge more (Preston, 1984). Attitudes in such areas are also less conducive to stability (Elder, 1978). However, empirical results have been mixed (Moore and Waite, 1981; Mott and Moore, 1979).

Racial and Ethnic Differences

Although many studies include race as a variable, most of the marital dissolution literature ignores race and ethnic differences in prevalence and experience, partly due to lack of data. A national sample includes few subgroup divorces. Yet some things are known about subgroup breakups.

Blacks experience dissolution more often than whites, even with controls for key variables (Espenshade, 1983; Moore and Waite, 1981; Thornton, 1978), over the entire life span (Thornton, 1978) but black women's remarriages (unlike whites') are less likely to disrupt than first ones; black women tend to be separated longer than whites (Espenshade, 1983). Since black women are more likely to separate permanently and less likely to remarry, racial differences are fewer in divorce than in dissolution (McCarthy, 1979).

Many correlates of disruption are akin for blacks and whites: education (McCarthy, 1979), religiosity (Hampton, 1979), husband's earnings, marital duration and age (Mott and Moore, 1979). Some variables may not signify for blacks owing to small sample sizes. For example, black marriages are not affected by respondent's living in an SMSA, by wife's having lived with both parents at age 14, or wife's employment, suggesting that different community norms may interact with these variables. Separating effects of early first births for blacks and whites, Moore and Waite (1981) report that for whites, early marriage is the key factor increasing dissolution. Premaritally pregnant whites tend more than blacks to marry. For blacks, an early first birth increases dissolution.

As part of social scientists' negative view of black families (Mathis, 1978; Staples, 1985), blacks' higher dissolution rates were once attributed to subcultural differences arising from historical experience, but past history cannot explain a legacy that accelerated in the 1950s (Engerman, 1977). Recent explanations note lack of good jobs (Kitson et al., 1985; Patterson, 1982).

Compared to blacks, Puerto Ricans, and non-Hispanic whites, Mexican-Americans and Cubans have lower dissolution rates, with controls for education and age at first marriage. Education and age effects resemble those for other groups except that not completing a given level has no effect (Frisbie, 1986; Frisbie, Opitz, Kelly, 1985). Divorce rates for Hispanic groups have risen in recent years along with those of the rest of the population (Mirand, 1985).

To our knowledge no divorce research focuses on other ethnic or racial groups. Family research on such groups as Asian Americans or Native Americans has been neglected (Staples and Mirande, 1980).

Age Patterns in Divorce

Much divorce literature is biased toward young adults. They divorce oftener. Older divorcing persons have fewer peers sharing the experience (Hagestad and Smyer, 1982). In the future the experience of divorce will be more common among the elderly (Uhlenberg and Myers, 1981).

Several studies have tested whether divorce determinants vary by age or marital duration (Becker, Landes, Michael, 1977; Morgan and Rindfuss, 1985; South and Spitze, 1986). Most variable effects remain although age-of-marriage effects taper off (Morgan and Rindfuss, 1985) and education's negative impact becomes positive (South and Spitze, 1986).

Marital Dissolution as Process

Everyone knows that marriages dissolve gradually but most research treats dissolution as a discrete event. Separation and divorce even become a single variable. There are good reasons for these practices. Government statistics are available for divorce but not separation. Most cross-sectional surveys report marital status and sometimes ever-divorced status. Longitudinal surveys report marital status changes. Unfortunately, processual data in depth must be gathered by the researcher, who can ask a representative sample of married persons about a possible divorce or else ask a sample (convenience or based on court records) of separated or divorced persons retrospectively about the process.

Using representative samples, Booth and White (1980) and Huber and Spitze (1980) asked respondents if they had ever thought about divorce. Wives said yes more often. Many divorce predictors signified in one or both studies. Using thought of divorce instead of divorce as dependent variable allows separating motivation by gender. Given marital work role differences, even with both spouses employed, a wife's sense of inequity may affect some dissolutions. Retrospective complaints may increase after a bitter divorce. In surveying currently married spouses, one can relate thought of divorce to marital characteristics queried elsewhere in the interview. Huber and Spitze (1980) found that wives' but not husbands' thoughts were affected by the division of household labor and their own attitudes to housework. Booth et al. (1984a, 1985) furthered this work by creating a marital instability index to measure the incidence of behaviors and thoughts that sometimes lead to divorce.

Both Udry (1981) and Booth, Johnson and White (1984a) tested Levinger's (1979) three-factor theory of marital cohesion. Udry measured respondent perceptions of marital alternatives. They correlate as expected with own and spouse's objective resources, they are independent of marital satisfaction, and they predict marital disruption over a two year period. Booth et al. (1985) measure all three factors, using a combination of objective and subjective indicators. All factors help to predict which couples with high instability will divorce during a three-year period and which ones with low instability will move toward divorce or higher instability.

A number of studies, often based on court records, examined separation and divorce processes from retrospective accounts. One of the most comprehensive, Spanier and Thompson (1984), interviewed 210 persons who had separated within two years. They obtained accounts of the pre- and postseparation period and the role of kin and friends to isolate factors that facilitate marital adjustment.

Qualitative studies on causes of divorce that use retrospective data tend to focus on marital complaints. A review of this research reveals a shift over time from instrumental toward interpersonal, intrapsychic issues (Kitson et al., 1985). The typical complaints (personality problems, communication difficulties, extramarital sex) are hard to relate to the demographic correlates in quantitative studies. Few attempts have been made to do so. Nor are many data available on similarities of partners' complaints. The key issue, how inputs from two partners with different interests form a single final outcome, has yet to be fully modeled or explained.

Consequences

Recent research on divorce consequences for parents and children has turned from earlier emphasis on emotional ones, using small qualitative studies, to large demographic studies. Although some earlier work examined differences in socioeconomic attainment between those who had experienced parental divorce as a child (Hernandez, 1986), recent work relies more on longitudinal data that examine actual status changes over time.

The most serious consequence of divorce for women and children may be the low income of the female-headed household. Almost all states now base custody awards on the child's best interest (Freed and Walker, 1985), but mothers receive custody in 90% of cases (Weitzman, 1985). Several recent studies using Panel Survey of Income Dynamics or National Longitudinal Survey data examined changes in both spouses' economic situation after separation or divorce. Hoffman (1977) found decreases in income relative to family needs for women and children and increases for men. Similarly, women are more likely to become poor and less likely to move out of poverty than men or continuously married women (Espenshade, 1979). Women's economic losses result from loss of economies of scale, decreased access to husband's income, low female earnings, and low rates of award and payment of child support and alimony (Espenshade, 1979). Decreases in the economic status of women who do not remarry continue for at least five years after the divorce (Weiss, 1984).

Women often respond to divorce by entering or staying in the labor force. Divorced women who were nonemployed before divorce were 10 times more likely to take jobs than go on welfare (Hoffman, 1977). Receiving child support does not affect employment incentives (Beller and Graham, 1985). Divorce increases women's employment rates both before and after remarriage (Johnson and Skinner, 1986).

Although the average number of children per divorce has fallen (Waite, Haggstrom, and Kanuse, 1985a), parental divorce has become a more common experience for children. Recent demographic analyses (Bumpass, 1984a; Bumpass and Rindfuss, 1979; Furstenberg et al., 1983) estimate that a child's cumulative probability of experiencing parental marital dissolution at some time is about 40%; black children's rates are substantially higher than white children's. The chance of living in a single-parent family, including those that result from premarital births, is closer to 50%. A majority of children have little or no contact with the noncustodial parent.

Remarriage

Until recently, the slim literature that addressed remarriage saw it as an attempt to rebuild the ideal nuclear family (Furstenberg and Spanier, 1984). A few recent works discuss remarriage and new family patterns (blended or reconstituted) sociologically (Cherlin, 1978; Furstenberg and Spanier, 1984). Recent demographic work reports that women's marriage or remarriage prospects diminish rapidly after age 25. At ages 40-49, for example, for every 10 college-educated single women, fewer than 3 college-educated single men are available, owing partly to social disapproval of women's marrying younger men (Goldman, Westoff, Hammerslough, 1984).

Remarriage rates and the percentage of marriages involving a divorced person recently rose due to a larger pool of divorced persons. Their probability of remarriage is projected to continue a slight downward trend (Glick, 1984; Schoen et al., 1985).

Until recently data on the composition of United States families of remarriage were poor or nonexistent. Including detailed marital and fertility histories in the June 1980 Current Population Survey has generated better estimates. In 1980 a fifth of all married households included a previously divorced spouse. Of these, 35% included a previously divorced husband; 30% a wife; and 35% both (Cherlin and McCarthy, 1985).

In 1980, 96% of children lived with their mothers; of these, 72% lived with both natural parents, 19% with the mother alone, and 9% with a mother and a stepfather. Focusing only on children whose mothers remarried since 1965 and when they were under age 18, Bumpass (1984b) estimated that half of the children under age five and a sixth of those aged 10 to 13 at the time of remarriage acquire a half-sib. Since two-thirds of the remarriages involve a previously married man, many children acquire step-sibs. Two-thirds will have a half-sib or step-sib and a sixth will have both. However, only a tiny fraction of families will include children from both previous marriages and the remarriage, the most complex family type. Higher fertility in the wife's first marriage decreases the probability of another birth in the remarriage.

Since a majority of divorced persons remarry —1980 period rates were 83% for men and 78% for women (Schoen et al., 1985)—analyses of remarriage determinants tend to focus on timing rather than on who will remarry, and to use longitudinal or marital history data. As in analyses of first marriage and divorce, congruence between theory and variables tested is problematic. Using NLS Young Women data, Mott and Moore (1983) found that the probability of remarriage within five years of divorce is related to lower educational levels, non-SMSA residence, lack of health problems, and nonemployment. Consistent with past research, the presence of children from the previous marriage had no effect on remarriage.

Postdivorce childbearing affects remarriage, especially for whites (Suchindran, Koo, Griffith, 1985). Those more likely to remarry are whites, less educated women, those younger at divorce,

and white non-Catholics. For blacks the time between separation and divorce increases remarriage; blacks apparently divorce when they want to remarry (Beller and Graham, 1985). Nor does divorced status harm women in the marriage market. If remarriage would make women downwardly mobile, they remain divorced (Mueller and Pope, 1980).

Although remarriage may solve financial problems for divorced women and their custodial children, it can make other problems. Cherlin (1978) notes the lack of legal and normative guidelines for a remarriage's complex relations—and no names for them. What does a child call a stepmother? Children in stepfamilies have more problems than those in one-parent families (Cherlin, 1981).

In contrast, Furstenberg and Spanier (1984) emphasize positive aspects of reconstituted families, such as adaptation and the benefits for children of acquiring many weak ties through remarriage chains. This concept extends Bohannon's (1970) "divorce chains," the chain of relationships formed among spouses and their ex-spouses.

In sum, new family types make work for everybody. Children and their divorced parents may hold different conceptions of family rights and duties. Legislators can find no political solutions to value questions raised by family troubles. Society does not know how to ensure marital stability and cannot know when it is worth preserving or when dissolution is better for everyone, including children (Steiner, 1981). Sociologists need to rethink concepts such as "family of orientation" that now lack precise meaning (Bumpass, 1984b). What is the family size or birth order of an only child whose mother remarries a man with custody of four children, older and younger? What is the child's father's occupation?

New family types also arouse anxiety. Having choices makes people nervous. Peasants, serfs, and slaves rarely faced the disruption of social mobility. Our Victorian ancestors rarely faced the disruption of marital mobility. A stable marriage may not be happy but if law and custom forbid divorce, then miserable couples can blame the system, not themselves, if they fail to attain it.

Untraditional Dyadic Relations

The factors that have increased divorce and decreased fertility have also encouraged the emergence of untraditional dyads, household partnerships that provide some of the benefits of marriage. During the 1970s and 1980s two forms of nonlegal dyadic relations increased in number and acceptability: cross-sex nonmarital cohabitation and same-sex (gay or lesbian) relationships. Recent demographic accounts (Spanier, 1983) report that cross-sex nonmarital cohabitation rates doubled between 1975 and 1980. Such couples represented 4% of U.S. male-female couples living together in 1981; 28% of their households include children. The majority of cohabiting men and women are under age 35, with a decreasing proportion (but a steady number) of such couples over 65 who tend to be disproportionately black and urban. The convergence of married and unmarried couples' socioeconomic characteristics suggests that cohabitation should be viewed as normative rather than as an alternative lifestyle (Spanier, 1983).

Other research on nonmarital cohabitation (see Macklin, 1978, 1980) is sparse and tends to be found in family journals. Apart from demographic accounts based on Current Population Survey data, cited above, this research often uses small nonprobability samples of college students. Findings cannot apply to less-studied cohabitants who were previously married or are elderly (Newcomb, 1979). This research focuses on such issues as whether cohabitants break up or marry (e.g., Risman et al., 1981) and compares their behavior to that of married couples. Cohabitants' division of household labor resembles that of married couples (Stafford et al., 1977). Cohabitants who marry are just as likely to divorce as those who did not cohabit (Newcomb, 1979). Marital quality equals or is less than that of couples who did not cohabit (DeMaris and Leslie, 1984).

Several recent articles have reviewed the even sparser literature on lesbian and gay male relationships (Macklin, 1980; Peplau, 1982; Tuller, 1978). This literature is mainly in books and in the *Journal of Homosexuality*—seldom in family journals (but see Harry, 1979; Jensen, 1974; Voeller and Walters, 1978). Research is currently moving toward use of community (rather than clinical) samples and a focus on lesbians as well as gay males. It still tends to rely on small samples (e.g., Tanner, 1978) of middle-class respondents and on unstructured interviews. Research on gay/lesbian couples tends to be psychological. It often counters stereotypes by showing that such couples have lasting relationships that are less often based on stereotyped gender roles than are heterosexual relationships (Marecek, Finn, and Cardell, 1982). Other topics include values about and quality of rela-

tionships (e.g., Peplau, Padeski, and Hamilton, 1982), the role of sexuality and exclusivity (e.g., Harry, 1979) and differences of lesbians and gay men.

The tiny literature on gay and lesbian parenting focuses more on mothering than fathering. Miller, Jacobsen, Bigger (1981) found no important differences between children's home environments provided by lesbian and heterosexual mothers, except that lesbian mothers have less money—presumably in comparison to married heterosexual women. Miller (1979) tries to dispel myths about homosexual fathers by showing that they do not molest their children, do not rear children as a cover, and their children do not tend to become homosexual. Hitchens (1979-1980) discusses legal issues in custody cases for lesbian and gay parents.

A unique study compares cohabiting cross-sex, gay, lesbian, and married couples on handling money, market and house work, and sexual relations using a nonprobability sample because three of the four types are uncommon and stigmatized (Blumstein and Schwartz, 1983). However, the study has a larger N and more issues than previous ones. By comparing four groups it avoids viewing gay males and lesbians as special breeds with special problems. The sample yielded 12,000 questionnaires; 300 couples were interviewed intensively and a larger group received follow-up questionnaires 18 months later.

In that period about 5% of the married couples and from 12% to 22% of the other couples broke up. Breakups related to topics the couples argued about and thus do not parallel demographic divorce studies. Married couples and cross-sex cohabitants are more likely to disrupt if she has money to leave and if he is *not* ambitious or she *is*. Conflict over housework leads to divorce only when he thinks she does too little. Interaction time decreases breakups for all groups. Factors associated with stability of gay male and lesbian couples were also akin to those of cross-sex couples. Those who broke up tended to have argued about money, income level, work, or to include a person more dependent or more ambitious than the other. Gay relationships apparently need to be symmetrical to last.

Parents' and Children's Effects on Each Other

Sociological research typically sees children as passive objects of parental behavior. Only recently has research taken the child's viewpoint or seen it as affecting parents. This section reviews literature on children's impact on parents' marital and work behavior and mental well-being; parents' influence on children's lives; and grown children's lives; and grown children's relations with elderly parents.

Children's Effects on Parents' Marriages

Long ago Monahan (1955) noted the widespread belief that children increase marital happiness despite research that showed otherwise. Reviews of 1960s research noted the same finding, which was was elaborated in the 1970s and early 1980s with small samples, national samples, and longitudinally. The negative relation holds for almost all subgroups defined by sex, race, religion, and employment although the impact was near-zero for whites with four or more children (Glenn and McLanahan, 1982). Effects appear greater for women, blacks (especially men), and parents of younger children (Glenn and McLanahan, 1982; Glenn and Weaver, 1978; Spanier and Lewis, 1980).

Children's negative impact is explained by their strain on time, energy, and resources (Ross and Huber, 1985; Spanier and Lewis, 1980). They may interfere with parental interaction; a larger number creates a system with more problem potential (Glenn and Weaver, 1978). Children may also cement unhappy marriages, creating a biased sample over time as unhappy childless couples divorce.

Stepchildren make problems for families of remarriage (Ambert, 1984). Using national sample data for a three-year period, White and Booth (1985) found no evidence that remarriages have lower quality than first ones, but a double remarriage and presence of stepchildren additively affect divorce. Parents in families with stepchildren report more problems getting along with children. Stepchildren are more likely to move (or be moved) from home at earlier ages.

Research on own children's effects on parental divorce is less consistent than on marital satisfaction, probably because children stabilize marriage by increasing monetary and emotional costs of dissolution while decreasing marital quality. Early reports that children deterred dissolution had failed to control for marital duration. Even so, recent conclusions remain inconsistent (Cherlin, 1977; Koo and Janowitz, 1983; Thornton, 1977; Waite, Haggstrom, and Kanouse, 1985—see also Haggstrom et al., 1984).

Conclusions about these relations are premature. Children probably do not increase marital dissolution despite their impact on satisfaction. The decrease in marital satisfaction seems well offset by higher dissolution costs. (Relations between other factors that affect dissolution and fertility may also be spurious.) None of the research above has data on the process by which children affect marital quality or divorce, although Hill (1984) reports differences in marital interaction time by parental status. This is a fruitful area for research, especially for longitudinal studies that follow changes in marital quality along with demographic factors.

Children's Effects on Parental Well-Being

Children could conceivably provide gratification to offset the decline in marital satisfaction but Glenn and Weaver (1979) show that children also decrease global life satisfaction. However, they conclude that overall parents are not less satisfied with their lives than are nonparents due to offsetting effects of higher income and marriage.

Popular opinion holds that children reduce old age loneliness. Might this offset the negative effects of young children? Two studies say no. Glenn and McLanahan (1981) find few significant differences in psychological well-being between the elderly with or without children and these few are both positive and negative. Having offspring affects black men and highly educated white men negatively. Rempel's (1985) Canadian data are similar. Parents have more friends and slightly higher life satisfaction; the childless have better health. However, Mutran and Reitzes (1984) report that the presence of adult children improves well-being of the elderly.

A large literature addresses parents' psychological effects on children; the other direction is neglected. The impact of a first birth on parents' self-esteem and locus of control over the first two years are slight (Haggstrom et al., 1984). Psychological effects on mothers of first children depend on prior work roles and attitudes (Pistrang, 1984). Voluntary organization membership and political activities decline during children's preschool years but parents of school-age children participate more in organizations than nonparents (Haggstrom et al., 1984).

*Children's Effect on
Parental Economic Status*

might cost $184,000 through age 17. College attendance would raise costs.

Children's strongest economic impact is on the mother's employment (Hofferth, 1983). Much research documents effects across subgroups and with attention to causal ordering. Child care, the salient link between employment and fertility, constrains employment. Presser and Baldwin (1980) report that 18% of the nonemployed, 24% of part-time employed, and 12% of full-time workers would work more hours if affordable child care were available. Constraints are greater on young, black single women with low levels of education and income. Child-care arrangements are often changed (Floge, 1985), reflecting changing preferences as children age but also lack of satisfactory arrangements. Stolzenberg and Waite (1984) creatively demonstrate child-care constraints. After separate analyses of 409 SMSAs, the coefficients relating children's ages to mother's employment are regressed on characteristics of those SMSAs. Number of child-care workers, rather than their earnings, relates most consistently to the extent to which children constrain maternal employment.

Timing of childbearing has short- and long-term effects on maternal economic status. Women who bear children later are more highly educated, have fewer children, and higher family incomes per capita. They work fewer hours at age 27, but this probably reflects timing differences that reverse later (Hofferth and Moore, 1979). After age 60, women who bore a first child after age 30 were better off financially, especially if they had only one or two, than those who remained childless or had an early birth (Hofferth, 1984).

In the short term, children reduce young families' savings (mainly due to decreased maternal employment) but increase savings at marital durations above five years. Births early in marriage induce a switch from financial to durable goods assets. Contrary to popular belief, young parents with young children actually decrease family consumption levels (Smith and Ward, 1980).

An alternative to assessing children's financial impact is to measure parental expenditures on them. Using survey data on consumer expenditures Espenshade (1984) derives estimates that vary by SES, mother's employment status, family size, region, and inflation level. Assuming a full-time employed mother, medium SES and medium inflation, a first child born in 1981

*Parent's Marital Status
Effects on Children*

Parents' entries and exits from marital and parental statuses affect children's lives in many ways. The greatest public concern has been for the consequences of teenage births. In 1977 Planned Parenthood's brochure on an epidemic of 11 million teenage pregnancies directed public attention to their rising proportion of total fertility. This statement was true but misleading. Teenage fertility had declined from 1957 to 1977 but not as fast as total fertility. Also, the proportion of nonmarital teenage births increased substantially because of the sharp decline in marital fertility (Chilman, 1980).

Yet concern is still appropriate. Children of teenage parents tend to suffer medically and cognitively, to spend more time in a one-parent household, to attain less education, and to marry earlier and oftener than children of older parents (Baldwin and Cain, 1980). Most effects disappear with SES controls except those leading to lower education level and earlier marriage (Card, 1981).

Much recent research examines how parental divorce and single parenthood affect children psychologically. Longfellow (1979) and Bleckman (1982) reviewed research on psychological impacts to counter the deficit model (Walters and Walters, 1980) that looks only for negative effects. Many one-parent studies fail to control for covariates, thus missing possible positive effects in a zealous search for negative ones. Despite use of identical objective measures, teachers rate one-parent children as being less adjusted. Yet the causal order may go the other way: Problem children can create enough stress to contribute to divorce.

Father absence is not the major psychological problem. In reconstituted families children have more problems than in one-parent families. Fox and Inazu (1982) found no evidence that black or white teenage daughters in maritally nonintact homes had to take on quasi-adult companionate roles or chores. Divorce's negative impact on children depends on the level of family conflict, parental mental health, the social network of families after divorce and on children's age (Longfellow, 1979; Wallerstein and Kelly, 1980). In fact, children's self-esteem is hurt more by conflict-ridden two-parent homes than by single-parent homes (Cooper, Holman, and Braithwaite, 1983). But children's stress can interact with other factors like low income or parental stress (Hodges, Tierney, and Buchsbaum, 1984)—recently divorced women tend to experience other stressful events (McLanahan, 1983).

Children of divorce, especially black men and white women, tend less to marry at given ages (Kobrin and Waite, 1984). Mueller and Pope (1977) found them more likely to divorce (but see Hanson and Tuch, 1984). Parental divorce reduces psychological well-being among adults, especially women, through increased probability of divorce (Glenn and Kramer, 1985). Women reared in one-parent families tend to marry and bear children early, to experience premarital births and marital dissolution (McLanahan and Bumpass, 1986).

Several studies surveyed college students to identify behavior and attitudes resulting from parental divorce that might decrease future marital success. Greenberg and Nay (1982) report only one difference: attitudes about divorce. Booth, Brinkerhoff, and White (1984) found another: children exposed to more post-divorce parental conflict were less satisfied with their own courtship behavior.

Parents' marital status may most affect children's household situation. Hofferth (1985), projecting children's life course, compares likely patterns for those born in 1980 to those of earlier cohorts. Of children born in 1980, 70% of the white and 94% of the black will spend time in a one-parent family by age 17. As noted in the divorce section, period rates in the 1970s imply that about half of all children will live in a one-parent household at some time. After 5 years over half (Bumpass, 1984a) and after 10 years, 38% of whites and 73% of black children will still be there (Bumpass, 1984b). Only 17% see the noncustodial father weekly (Furstenberg et al., 1983). Most children never sleep at the noncustodial parent's home (Furstenberg and Nord, 1985). Children who live apart from biological parents reduce ties if a functional equivalent is present (Bianchi and Seltzer, 1986). Children living with a biological parent and a stepparent resemble those living with both biological ones; adopted children were better off than both (Bachrach, 1985).

Out-of-wedlock children's relations with their fathers have received little attention. Furstenberg and Talvitie (1980) report a five-year follow-up of a convenience sample of black children and parents. About half of the parents married during the five-year period but half of them later divorced, leaving one child in five

with a father present after five years. Parents who never married provided substantial contact and financial support, akin to that of divorced fathers. About a quarter of the children saw their never-married fathers at least once a week.

Frequent status changes and the complexity of reconstituted families makes the concept of family problematic. In 1980 about a sixth of children under 18 lived in remarried-couple households (Cherlin and McCarthy, 1985). Furstenberg and Nord (1985) asked children of divorce whom they include in their family. The majority who had stepparents include them; only half include noncustodial biological parents, which is substantial given the low level of contact with them. The degree to which stepfathers assume paternal duties evidences the increasing salience of sociological (rather than biological) parenthood, especially for fathers.

Effects of Parents' Economic Status on Children

The one-parent family's low income seriously affects children. Since it also affects ex-wives, we discussed it in the section on divorce.

Parental SES effects on children's status attainment has been a major research tradition since the 1960s. Early on most studies focused on paternal effects. In the 1950s interest in mothers had focused on alleged harmful effects of her employment but this topic has not concerned sociologists recently (Etaugh, 1980). Instead, the attainment model has been used to study maternal employment effects on children's work and sex-role attitudes.

Both mother's employment and occupational status affect daughter's employment status (Stevens and Boyd, 1980). The impact of maternal employment on children's attitudes is complex, depending on her status and attitude to her job. Macke and Morgan (1978) report both positive and negative modeling among black and white high school seniors. For adult respondents, the mother's employment affects sons' but not daughters' sex-role attitudes (Powell and Steelman, 1982). Maternal employment in low-status jobs decreases maternal influence on children; children of mothers in higher-status jobs had less traditional attitudes—but the relation may be spurious (Acock, Barker, and Bengtson, 1982).

Several studies report parents' influence on children. Parents have more influence than peers for both sexes (Davies and Kandel, 1981; Elder, 1984). Early influence of parental SES and family size outrank later ones in determining school achievement (Alwin and Thornton, 1984). Sons whose fathers behaved explosively tended later to exhibit low levels of impulse control (Elder, Caspi, and Downey, 1985).

Family Size Effects on Children

Until recently, attainment research tended to neglect family size. It was used most often in psychological research on intelligence and personality, for example, Clausen and Clausen's (1973) excellent review and Heer's (1985) more recent one. Much recent research tests the "dilution of resources" model (Blake, 1981) or Zajonc's (1976) confluence model, which explains both family size and birth order effects in relation to family members' average mental age. This theory predicts lower IQ outcomes for children of larger families and later-born children. A teaching effect explains discontinuities for only and last-born children—children benefit from teaching younger sibs.

Recent research shows that family size matters (Heer, 1985). Birth order (research on it has been revived) does not (Hauser and Sewell, 1985). Blake (1981, 1985), tested family size effects with national survey data. Her findings are consistent with a dilution model: Sibs must share family resources such as parental attention. Using college plans, education, and IQ as outcomes, parental encouragement, which cannot be bought and becomes most diluted with family size, has greatest impact. There is no evidence of birth order effects or of detriments for only children. Using data on grade schoolers, Steelman and Mercy (1980) support Blake's findings on family size and report no birth-order effects. Nor did birth order affect the attainment of Wisconsin high school graduates in 1957 (Hauser and Sewell, 1985).

Parents can little change their own SES characteristics but they can control the number of their children. Hence family size is salient to the study of transmitted inequality. Heer (1985) argues that choosing the number and spacing of children is one of the most important ways married couples can affect child outcomes; funds to gather better data to study these issues would be well spent.

The foregoing review shows that, first, research about children's effects on parents still sees children as passive. Parents affect children by their behavior, status, and specific attitudes. Children affect parents simply by their presence. At most, their impact varies with age and gender. For example, we know of no research on the effect of teenagers' attitudes or behaviors

on parents. Second, to the extent that children measurably affect parents, the effects seem rather negative.

A slim literature indicates that actual and expected costs and benefits of childbearing differ. The actual costs have been reported above. A number of recent studies have queried beliefs about the benefits of children to test their effects on fertility plans. Fried, Hofferth, and Udry (1980) and Thomson (1983) stress the greater impact of emotional than economic factors.

Adult Children and Elderly Parents

Recent fertility and mortality trends have changed the ratio of aging parents to grown children and the composition of the parent group (Brody, 1985; Streib and Beck, 1980; Treas, 1977). Increased life expectancy has increased the probability that a middle-aged adult will have surviving parents. A 40-year-old couple in 1980 had nearly identical numbers of living parents and children (2.6 and 2.7). At current rates these figures will stabilize at 2.9 and 1.8 (Preston, 1984). Increased life expectancy and a larger sex gap in mortality has also increased the proportion of the total population over age 65 and changed the sex/age composition of the over-65 population (Treas, 1977). This group increasingly includes persons over 75, who have more health impairments (Smyer and Hofland, 1982), and women. In turn, their adult children will be older and, born in the 1930s, have fewer sibs to share duties.

Such trends further strain generational contact patterns related to shared or independent households or geographic proximity (Hess and Waring, 1978; Streib and Beck, 1980). Shared households, viewed as a last resort, increase in number with the parent's age (Troll, Miller, and Atchley, 1979). During transitions either generation may use the shared household strategy. Its incidence is higher in longitudinal than cross-sectional studies (Beck and Beck, 1984).

Sex, marital status, age, and class differences mark contact patterns, which tend to be maintained by women. Unmarried daughters are more likely than sons to share a residence with parents (Hess and Waring, 1978; Troll, Miller, and Atchley, 1979). The recent rise in older women's independent living may stem partly from the decreasing supply of unmarried adult daughters (Thomas and Wister, 1984). While widowers are less likely than widows to live with children, they are also likely to be younger and better off financially.

In the exchange of gifts and services that often occurs between adult generations, more help flows upward as parents age and are widowed (Streib and Beck, 1980) but financial assistance beyond token gifts is rare (Hess and Waring, 1978). Services tend to be provided more by women (Lopata, 1973; Treas, 1977). Brody (1985) calls "family care" a euphemism for daughters-in-law and adult daughters; except for her work, this issue has been given no attention in the context of the division of household labor.

Class and ethnic effects on contact patterns include middle-class parents' helping their adult children more, especially with money (Troll, Miller, and Atchley, 1979). Working-class parents tend to give services and receive financial aid (Hess and Waring, 1978). Among the urban poor, generational expectations may conflict (Seelbach, 1977). Puerto Rican families in New York City exhibit higher levels of intergenerational contact and exchange than a comparable Anglo sample from the Midwest (Rogler and Cooney, 1984).

Several weaknesses mar most work on contact patterns. It is mostly descriptive. Even when it is quantitative rather than anecdotal, it is theoretically weak. Most of it focuses on aid givers or receivers; the same study rarely includes both types, hence little is known about how flows of help relate to each other. Few studies use probability samples. None has used a longitudinal design. These flaws in 1960s research continued in the 1970s (Streib and Beck, 1980). Finally, little of it includes two major factors in intergenerational exchange: women's employment patterns and divorce.

Since grown daughters provide most services for elderly parents, women's changing work patterns affect intergenerational relations. Middle-aged women are caught between needs of parents who live longer and children who remain dependent longer or become so during marital disruptions (Hagestad, Smyer, Stierman, 1984). The empty nest may refill with aging parents or adult children.

Few empirical studies have compared parental service patterns of employed and nonemployed daughters. More weekly aid was given by women who were not employed, unmarried, or living with the parent (Lang and Brody, 1983) but Cicirelli (1981, p. 144) reported no impact of women's employment on helping behavior. Both studies, based on small nonprobability samples, fail to control for relevant variables. Stoller (1983) study, based on a large probability sample, concluded that employment status limits sons' but not daughters' helping be-

havior; but since she dichotomizes employment status, it is not clear whether women's hours of work might affect or be affected by parents' demands.

Implications of grown children's divorce for generational relations has also been studied (Treas, 1977; Troll, Miller, and Atchley, 1979; Smyer and Hofland, 1982; Hagestad, Smyer, Stierman, 1984), partly due to concern about disruption of grandparent-grandchild contacts. With few exceptions these studies tend to use the divorcing adult(s) as respondents. Samples are often small and nonprobability. Using the divorcing adult's perspective may affect whether consequences are seen as positive or negative. For example, Furstenberg and Spanier (1984) suggest that divorce and remarriage of a child's parents may beneficially increase the child's network of relatives. From the grandparents' viewpoint, divorce and remarriage imply that they must share a grandchild just when low fertility is decreasing the supply (Matthews and Sprey, 1984). A child's divorce, especially a son's, affects an older mother negatively (Johnson, 1981).

Family ties with aging parents are mediated through the person whose kin they are (Anspach, 1976). Thus divorce may disrupt ties with former in-laws (Matthews and Sprey, 1984). Such contacts decrease for both spouses. They may be maintained by a custodial mother for her children's sake (Anspach, 1976; Spicer and Hampe, 1975). Contacts may decrease even further upon remarriage. Contact with own parents often increases (Anspach, 1976; Spicer and Hampe, 1975) sometimes to the point of coresidence for a period.

Since divorce decreases wives' and children's income and increases husbands', it may modify prior assistance patterns. Divorced wives need more help—money and child care (Furstenberg and Spanier, 1984)—and have less time or money to give (Cherlin, 1983). Evidence, often anecdotal, suggests that divorced wives (especially if they have custody and have not remarried) will receive help from own kin and sometimes from former in-laws (Johnson, 1981; Matthews and Sprey, 1984). Custodial fathers tend to have older children (Matthews and Sprey, 1984) and need fewer child-care services but they have more time and money to help aging parents, at least until remarriage. Spicer and Hampe (1975) suggest that divorced fathers without child custody see their parents more than do fathers with custody. The only study that examined patterns of aid by marital history compared convenience samples of persons with disrupted and intact marriages. Remarrieds helped parents less than first marrieds but the effect of disruption had to be inferred since the data were cross-sectional (Cicirelli, 1981).

Half of recent marriages are expected to end in divorce. This implies that generational relations merit far more attention than they have received, including the use of appropriate data.

Conclusions

Except for the industrial era, family sociology has lacked theories that explain world patterns over time. A generation ago a handful of scholars analyzed industrial effects on families but lacked data to go beyond that period. Recent work in historical demography, social history, comparative sociology, and anthropology now suggest how the variables involving food production permit or encourage monogamy, polygyny, and the conjugal or extended family.

Industrial technology altered costs and benefits of marriage and child rearing in plow cultures. Family wealth flows reversed direction. Economic ties dwindled among kin. Family functions shifted. Retirement plans now cover individual risk. Improved contraceptives reduce costs of avoiding pregnancy. Wives' employment still grows. By 2000 AD young women's earnings will approach young men's (Smith and Ward, 1984). Incentives to marry for life and rear children are thus eroded. Current research confirms response to these stimuli. Since 1960 age at first marriage, divorce, and untraditional household formation are up. Remarriage and fertility are down. The economic cement that once bound spouses for life has been replaced by love, a thin glue for a 50-year contract.

These changes pose new questions. Theory suggests answers to some. Will the division of household labor shift? Probably. As women's rates of labor force attachment and wages approach men's, it will become harder for him to go fishing while she cleans house.

For other questions even speculation is difficult, owing to offsetting variables. Will the divorce rate fall, level off, or rise? How high is "too high"? Is there a "too low"? Why or why not? Much work remains to be done (see also Zelditch, 1964).

However, one question may swamp all others because it directly affects so many people. Can Western countries maintain fertility at levels adequate to support their retirement systems? The direct economic benefits of child rearing currently go to the elderly according to their wage-related contributions. The persons who rear the child receive no direct economic benefits. Is child rearing rewarding enough to offset such costs? Does an innate factor drive humans to reproduce regardless of disincentives? It is plausible (but not proven) that such a factor could exist. If so, it will need to be strong.

REFERENCES

Acock, Alan and Vern Bengtson. 1980. "Actual Versus Perceived Similarity Among Parents and Youth." *Journal of Marriage and the Family* 42:501-516.

Acock, Alan, Deborah Barker, and Vern Bengtson. 1982. "Mothers' Employment and Parent-youth Similarity." *Journal of Marriage and the Family* 44:441-458.

Aguirre, B. E. and W. C. Parr. 1982. "Husbands' Marriage Order and the Stability of First and Second Marriages of White and Black Women." *Journal of Marriage and the Family* 44:605-620.

Aldous, Joan. 1977. "Family Interaction Patterns." *Annual Review of Sociology* 3:105-135.

Alwin, Duane. 1984. "Trends in Parental Socialization Values: Detroit. 1958-83." *American Journal of Sociology* 90:359-382.

_____ and Arland Thornton. 1984. "Family Origins and Schooling." *American Sociological Review* 49:784-802.

Ambert, Anne-Marie. 1984. "Longitudinal Changes in Children's Behavior Toward Custodial Parents." *Journal of Marriage and the Family* 46:463-467.

Anspach, Donald. 1976. "Kinship and Divorce." *Journal of Marriage and the Family* 38:323-330.

Ariès, Philippe. 1962. *Centuries of Childhood*, translated by Robert Baldick. New York: Random.

Bachrach, Christine. 1985. "Children in Families: Characteristics of Biological, Step- and Adopted Children." *Journal of Marriage and the Family* 45:171-180.

Bahr, Stephen and Richard Galligan. 1984. "Teenage Marriage and Marital Stability." *Youth and Society* 15:387-400.

Baldwin, Wendy and Virginia Cain. 1980. "Children of Teenage Parents." *Family Planning Perspectives* 12:34-43.

Beck, Scott and Rubye Beck. 1984. "The Formation of Extended Households During Middle Age." *Journal of Marriage and the Family* 46:277-288.

Becker, Gary. 1981. *A Treatise on the Family*. Cambridge, MA: Harvard University Press.

_____, Elisabeth Landes, and Robert Michael. 1977. "An Economic Analysis of Marital Instability." *Journal of Political Economy* 85:1141-1187.

Beller, Andrea and John Graham. 1985. "Variations in Child Support Income." Pp. 471-509 in *Horizontal Equity, Uncertainty, and Economic Wellbeing. Studies in Income and Wealth 49*, edited by M. David and T. Smeeding. Cambridge, MA: NBER.

Berardo, Felix, ed. 1980. *Decade Review: Family Research. 1970-1979. Journal of Marriage and the Family* 42. (Entire issue)

Bianchi, Suzanne and Judith Seltzer. 1986. "Children's Contact with Absent Parents." Paper presented at the annual meeting of the Population Association of America.

Biddle, Bruce, Barbara Bank, and Marjorie Marlin. 1980. "Parent and Peer Influence on Adolescents." *Social Forces* 58:1057-1079.

Bielby, William and James Baron. In press. "Undoing Discrimination." In *Ingredients for Women's Employment Policy*, edited by C. Bose and G. Spitze. Albany: SUNY Press.

Blake, Judith. 1981. "Family Size and the Quality of Children." *Demography* 18:421-422.

_____ 1985. "Number of Siblings and Educational Mobility." *American Sociological Review* 50: 84-93.

Bleckman, Elaine. 1982. "Are Children with One Parent at Psychological Risk? A Methodological Review." *Journal of Marriage and the Family* 44:179-198.

Bloom, David. 1982. "What's Happening to Age at First Birth in the United States? A Study of Recent Cohorts." *Demography* 19:351-370.

Blumberg, Rae Lesser. 1978. *Stratification: Socioeconomic and Sexual Inequality*. Dubuque, IA: Brown.

Blumstein, Philip and Pepper Schwartz. 1983. *American Couples: Money, Work, Sex*. New York: Pocket Books.

Bohannan, Paul. 1970. "Divorce Chains, Households of Remarriage, Multiple Divorcers." Pp. 137-139 in *Divorce and After*, edited by P. Bohannon. New York: Doubleday.

Booth, Alan and Lynn White. 1980. "Thinking about Divorce." *Journal of Marriage and Family* 42:605-616.

Booth, Alan, David Johnson, and Lynn White. 1984. "Women, Outside Employment, and Marital Instability." *American Journal of Sociology* 90: 567-583.

Booth, Alan, David Brinkerhoff, and Lynn White. 1984. "The Impact of Parental Divorce on Courtship." *Journal of Marriage and the Family* 46:85-94.

Booth, Alan, David Johnson, Lynn White, John Edwards. 1985. "Predicting Divorce and Permanent Separation." *Journal of Family Issues* 6: 337-346.

Broderick, Carlford. 1970. "Behind the Five Conceptual Frameworks: A Decade of Development in Family Theory." Pp. 3-23 in *A Decade of Family Research and Action*, edited by Carlford Broderick. Minneapolis: Council on Family Relations.

Brody, Charles and Lala Carr Steelman. 1985. "Sibling Structure and Parental Sex Typing of Children's Household Tasks." *Journal of Marriage and the Family* 47:265-274.

Brody, Elaine. 1985. "Parent Care as a Normative Family Stress." *The Gerontologist* 35:19-29.

_____, Pauline Johnson, and Mark Fulcomer. 1984. "What Should Adult Children Do for Elderly Parents?" *Journal of Gerontology* 39:736-746.

Bumpass, Larry. 1984a. "Children and Marital Dissolution." *Demography* 21:71-82.

_____ 1984b. "Some Characteristics of Children's Second Families." *American Journal of Sociology* 90:608-623.

_____ and Ronald Rindfuss. 1979. "Children's Experience of Marital Disruption." *American Journal of Sociology* 85:49-65.

Burr, Wesley, Reuben Hill, Ivan Nye, and Ira Reiss, eds. 1979. *Contemporary Theories about the Family*. New York: Free Press.

Caldwell, John. 1976. "Toward a Restatement of Demographic Transition Theory." *Population and Development Review* 2:321-366.

_____ 1980. "Mass Education as a Determinant of the Timing of the Fertility Decline." *Population and Development Review* 6:225-256.

Card, Josefina. 1981. "Longterm Consequences for Children of Teenage Parents." *Demography* 18: 137-156.

Cherlin, Andrew. 1977. "The Effect of Children on Marital Dissolution." *Demography* 14:265-272.

_____ 1978. "Remarriage as an Incomplete Institution." *American Journal of Sociology* 84:634-650.

_____ 1979. "Work Life and Marital Dissolution." Pp. 151-66 in *Divorce and Separation*, edited by G. Levinger and O. Moles. New York: Basic Books.

_____ 1981. *Marriage, Divorce, Remarriage*. Cambridge, MA: Harvard University Press.

_____ 1983. "Recent Research on Aging and the Family." Pp. 5-23 in *Aging in Society*, edited by M. W. Riley, B. Hess, and K. Bond. Hillsdale, NJ: Lawrence Erlbaum.

_____ and James McCarthy. 1985. "Remarried Couple Households: Data from the June 1980 Current Population Survey." *Journal of Marriage and the Family* 47:23-30.

Chilman, Catherine. 1980. "Social and Psychological Research Concerning Adolescent Childbearing: 1970-1980." *Journal of Marriage and the Family* 42:793-805.

Cicirelli, Victor. 1981. *Helping Elderly Parents*. Boston: Auburn House.

_____ 1983. "Adult Children and Their Elderly Parents." Pp. 31-46 in *Family Relationships in Later Life*, edited by T. Brubaker. Beverly Hills, CA: Sage.

Clausen, John and Suzanne R. Clausen. 1973. "Effects of Family Size on Parents and Children." Pp. 185-208 in *Psychological Perspectives on Population*, edited by J. Fawcett. New York: Basic Books.

Clayton, Richard and Janet Bokemeier. 1980. "Premarital Sex in the Seventies." *Journal of Marriage and the Family* 40:759-776.

Cooper, Judith, Jacqueline Holman, and Valerie

Braithwaite. 1983. "Self Esteem and Family Cohesion: The Child's Perspective and Adjustment." *Journal of Marriage and the Family* 45: 153-158.

Cottrell, Leonard. 1948. "The Present Status and Future Orientation of Research on the Family." *American Sociological Review* 13:123-129.

Crimmins, Eileen, Richard Easterlin, and Lee Ohanian. 1984. "Changes in Labor Force Participation of Older Men and Women since 1940: A Time Series Analysis." Manuscript.

Davies, Mark and Denise Kandel. 1981. "Parental and Peer Influences on Adolescents' Educational Plans." *American Journal of Sociology* 87:363-387.

Davis, Kingsley. 1984. "Wives and Work: The Sex Role Revolution and Its Consequences." *Population and Development Review* 10:397-417.

DeMaris, Alfred and Gerald Leslie. 1984. "Cohabitation with Future Spouse: Its Influence on Marital Satisfaction and Communication." *Journal of Marriage and Family* 46:77-84.

Draper, Thomas. 1981. "On the Relationships between Welfare and Marital Stability: A Research Note." *Journal of Marriage and the Family* 43:293-299.

Dyson, Tim and Mike Murphy. 1985. "The Onset of Fertility Transition." *Population and Development Review* 11:399-440.

Easterlin, Richard. 1980. *Birth and Fortune*. New York: Basic Books.

Elder, Glen. 1978. "Family History and the Life Course." Pp. 17-64 in *Transitions: The Life Course in Historical Perspective*, edited by T. Hareven. New York: Academic Press.

———— 1984. "Families, Kin, and the Life Course: A Sociological Perspective." Pp. 80-137 in *Review of Child Development Research 7: The Family*, edited by R. Parke. Chicago: University of Chicago Press.

————, ed. 1985. *Life Course Dynamics*. Ithaca, NY: Cornell University Press.

————, Avshalom Caspi, and Geraldine Downey. 1985. "Problem Behavior and Family Relations." Pp. 293-340 in *Human Development*, edited by A. Sorensen, F. Weinert, and L. Sherrod. Hillsdale NJ: Lawrence Erlbaum.

Engerman, Stanley. 1977. "Black Fertility and Family Structure in the U.S., 1880-1940." *Journal of Family History* 2:117-138.

Espenshade, Thomas J. 1979. "The Economic Consequences of Divorce." *Journal of Marriage and the Family* 41:615-625.

———— 1983. "Black-White Differences in Marriage, Separation, Divorce and Remarriage." Paper presented at the annual meeting of the Population Association of America.

———— 1984. *Investing in Children*. Washington, DC: Urban Institute.

———— 1985. "Marriage Trends in America: Estimates, Implications, and Underlying Causes." *Population and Development Review* 11:193-245.

Etaugh, Claire. 1980. "Effects of nonmaternal childcare." *American Psychologist* 35:309-319.

Farber, Bernard. 1968. *Comparative Kinship Systems*. New York: John Wiley.

Fergusson, D. M., L. J. Horwood, and M. E. Dimond. 1985. "A Survival Analysis of Childhood Family History." *Journal of Marriage and the Family* 47:287-295.

Floge, Liliane. 1985. "The Dynamics of Child Care Use and Some Implications for Women's Employment." *Journal of Marriage and the Family* 47:143-154.

Fox, Greer Litton and Judith Inazu. 1982. "Influence of Mother's Marital History on Mother-Daughter Relationship in Black and White Households." *Journal of Marriage and the Family* 44:143-144.

Freed, Doris Jonas and Timothy Walker. 1985. "Family Law in the Fifty States." *Family Law Quarterly* 18:369-471.

Fried, Ellen Shapiro, Sandra Lynn Hofferth, Richard Udry. 1980. "Parity-Specific and Two-Sex Utility Models of Reproductive Intentions." *Demography* 17:1-12.

Friedl, Ernestine. 1975. *Women and Men: An Anthropologist's View*. New York: Holt, Rinehart and Winston.

Frisbie, Parker. 1986. "Variation in Pattern of Marital Instability among Hispanics." *Journal of Marriage and the Family* 48:99-106.

————, Wolfgang Opitz, William R. Kelly. 1985. "Marital Instability Trends among Mexican Americans as Compared to Blacks and Anglos." *Social Science Quarterly* 66:587-601.

Furstenberg, Frank and Kathy Gordon Talvitie. 1980. "Children's Names and Paternal Claims: Bonds between Unmarried Fathers and Their Children." *Journal of Family Issues* 1:31-57.

Furstenberg, Frank, Christine Nord, James Peterson, and Nicholas Zill. 1983. "The Life Course of Children of Divorce." *American Sociological Review* 48:656-667.

Furstenberg, Frank and Graham Spanier. 1984. *Recycling the Family*. Beverly Hills, CA: Sage.

Furstenberg, Frank and Christine Winquist Nord. 1985. "Parenting Apart." *Journal of Marriage and the Family* 47:893-904.

Garden, Maurice. 1975. *Lyon et les Lyonnais au XVIIIe Siècle*. Paris: Flammarion.

Gelles, Richard. 1980. "Violence in the Family." *Journal of Marriage and the Family* 42:873-886.

Glenn, Norval and Charles Weaver. 1978. "A Multivariate, Multisurvey Study of Marital Happiness." *Journal of Marriage and the Family* 40:269-282.

———— 1979. "Family Situation and Global Happiness." *Social Forces* 57:960-967.

Glenn, Norval and Sara McLanahan. 1981. "The Effects of Offspring on the Psychological Wellbeing of Older Adults." *Journal of Marriage and the Family* 43:409-421.

———— 1982. "Children and Marital Happiness." *Journal of Marriage and the Family* 44:63-72.

Glenn, Norval and Kathryn Kramer. 1985. "The

Psychological Wellbeing of Adult Children of Divorce." *Journal of Marriage and the Family* 47:905-912.

Glick, Paul. 1984. "Marriage, Divorce, and Living Arrangements: Prospective Changes." *Journal of Family Issues* 5:7-26.

Goldman, Noreen, Charles Westoff, and Charles Hammerslough. 1984. "Demography of the US Marriage Market." *Population Index* 50:5-25.

Goode, William J. 1959. "The Sociology of the Family." Pp. 178-196 in *Sociology Today*, edited by R. Merton, L. Broome, and L. Cottrell. New York: Free Press.

Goody, Jack. 1976. *Production and Reproduction*. Cambridge, England: Cambridge University Press.

———— 1983. *The Development of Family and Marriage in Europe*. Cambridge: Cambridge University Press.

Greenberg, Ellen and Robert Nay. 1982. "The Intergenerational Transmission of Marital Instability Reconsidered." *Journal of Marriage and the Family* 44:335-348.

Greene, William and Aline Quester. 1982. "Divorce Risk and Wives' Labor Supply Behavior." *Social Science Quarterly* 63:16-27.

Hagestad, Gunhild and Michael Smyer. 1982. "Dissolving Long Term Relationships: Patterns of Divorcing in Middle Age." Pp. 155-88 in *Personal Relationships 4: Dissolving Personal Relationships*, edited by S. Duck. New York: Academic Press.

———— and Karen Stierman. 1984. "The Impact of Divorce in Middle Age." Pp. 247-262 in *Parenthood*, edited by R. Cohen, B. Cohler, and S. Weissman. New York: Guilford.

Haggstrom, Gus, Linda Waite, David Kanouse, and Thomas Blaschke. 1984. *Changes in the Lifestyles of New Parents*. Santa Monica, CA: Rand.

Hajnal, John. 1965. "European Marriage Patterns in Perspective." Pp. 101-143 in *Population in History*, edited by D. Glass and E. Eversley. London: Edward Arnold.

Hampton, Robert. 1979. "Husband's Characteristics and Marital Disruption in Black Families." *Sociological Quarterly* 20:255-266.

Hannan, Michael, Nancy Brandon Tuma, and Lyle Groenveld. 1977. "Income and Marital Events." *American Journal of Sociology* 82:1186-1211.

Hanson, Sandra and Steven Tuch. 1984. "Some Methodological Issues in the Determinants of Marital Stability." *Journal of Marriage and the Family* 46:631-642.

Hareven, Tamara, ed. 1978. *Transitions: The Family and the Life Course in Historical Perspective*. New York: Academic.

Harry, Joseph. 1979. "The 'Marital' Liaisons of Gay Men." *Family Coordinator* 28:622-629.

Hauser, Robert and William Sewell. 1985. "Birth Order and Educational Attainment in Full Sibships." *American Educational Research Journal* 22:1-23.

———— 1985. "Effects of Sibling Number on Child Outcomes." *Annual Review of Sociology* 11:27-47.

Heer, David. 1985. "Effect of Sibling Number on Child Outcomes." *Annual Review of Sociology* 11:27-47.

Hernandez, Donald. 1986. "The Sociology of Childhood." *Annual Review of Sociology* 12:159-180.

———— and David Myers. In Press. *America's Children since the Great Depression*. New York: Basic Books.

Hess, Beth and Joan Waring. 1978. "Parent and Child in Later Life." Chapter 9 in *Child Influences on Marital and Family Interaction: A Life-Span Perspective*, edited by R. Lerner and G. Spanier. New York: Academic Press.

Hill, Martha. 1984. "Marital Instability: Effects of Spouses' Time Together." Presented at the PAA meeting, Minneapolis.

Hiller, Dana and William Philliber. 1986. "Role Expectations and Perceptions of Partner's Role Expectations in Contemporary Marriage." *Social Problems* 33:191-201.

Hitchens, Donna. 1979-1980. "Social Attitudes, Legal Standards, and Personal Trauma in Child Custody Cases." *Journal of Homosexuality* 5:85-95.

Hofferth, Sandra. 1983. "Childbearing Decisionmaking and Family Wellbeing." *American Sociological Review* 48:533-545.

———— 1984. "Longterm Economic Consequences for Women of Delayed Childbearing and Reduced Family Size." *Demography* 21:141-55.

———— 1985. "Updating Children's Life Course." *Journal of Marriage and the Family* 47:93-115.

———— and Kristin Moore. 1979. "Early Childbearing and Later Economic Wellbeing." *American Sociological Review* 44:784-815.

Hoffman, Saul. 1977. "Marital Instability and Women's Economic Status." *Demography* 14:67-76.

Hodges, William, Carol Tierney, and Helen Buchsbaum. 1984. "The Cumulative Effect of Stress on Preschool Children of Divorced and Intact Families." *Journal of Marriage and the Family* 46:611-618.

Hoge, Dean, Gregory Petrillo, and Ella Smith. 1982. "Transmission of Religious and Social Values from Parents to Teenage Children." *Journal of Marriage and the Family* 44:469-580.

Holman, Thomas and Wesley Burr. 1980. "Beyond the Beyond: The Growth of Family Theories in the 1970s." *Journal of Marriage and the Family* 42:729-741.

Houseknecht, Sharon. 1982. "Voluntary Childlessness." *Journal of Family Issues* 3:459-471.

Houseknecht, Sharon and Graham Spanier. 1980. "Marital Disruption and Higher Education among Women in the United States." *Sociological Quarterly* 21:375-389.

Huber, Joan and Glenna Spitze. 1980. "Considering Divorce." *American Journal of Sociology* 86:75-89.

———. 1983. *Sex Stratification: Children, House-work, and Jobs.* New York: Academic Press.

Jensen, M. S. 1974. "Role Differentiation in Female Homosexual and Quasi-Marital Unions." *Journal of Marriage and the Family* 36:360-367.

Johnson, Elizabeth. 1981. "Older Mother's Percep-tions of their Child's Divorce." *The Geron-tologist* 21:395-401.

Johnson, William and Jonathan Skinner. 1986. "Labor Supply and Marital Separation." *American Economic Review* 76:455-469.

Kitson, Gaye, Karen Benson-Babri, and Mary Joan Roach. "Who Divorces and Why: A Review." *Journal of Family Issues* 6:255-294.

Komarofsky, Mirra and Willard Waller. 1945. "Studies of the Family." *American Journal of Sociology* 50:443-451.

Koo, Helen and Barbara Janowitz. 1983. "Interrela-tionships between Fertility and Marital Dissolu-tion: Results of a Simultaneous Logit Model." *Demography* 20:129-146.

Lang, Abigail and Elaine Brody. 1983. "Character-istics of Middle-aged Daughters and Help to Their Elderly Mothers." *Journal of Marriage and the Family* 45:193-202.

Laslett, Barbara. 1975. "Household Structure on an American Frontier." *American Journal of Soci-ology* 81:109-128.

Laslett, Peter. 1965. *The World We Have Lost.* Lon-don: Methuen.

———. 1977. "Characteristics of the Western Fam-ily Considered over Time." *Journal of Family History* 2:89-116.

———. 1983. "Family and Household as Work and Kin Group." Pp. 513-563 in *Family Forms in Historic Europe*, edited by R. Wall. Cambridge, England: Cambridge University Press.

Lee, Gary. 1980. "Effects of Social Networks on the Family." Pp. 27-56 in *Contemporary Theories about the Family*, edited by W. Burr et al. New York: Free Press.

Lenski, Gerhard. 1970. *Human Societies.* New York: McGraw-Hill.

Le Roy Ladurie, Emmanuel. 1975. *Montaillou, Vil-lage Occitan de 1994 a 1324.* Paris: Gallimard.

Lesthaeghe, Ron. 1980. "On the Social Control of Reproduction." *Population and Development Review* 6:527-548.

———. 1983. "A Century of Demographic and Cultural Change in Western Europe." *Popula-tion and Development Review* 9:411-435.

Levinger, George. 1979. "A Social Psychological Perspective on Marital Dissolution." Pp. 37-60 in *Divorce and Separation*, edited by G. Levinger and O. Moles. New York: Basic Books.

Levy, Marion. 1949. *The Family in China.* Cam-bridge, MA: Harvard University Press.

Lewis, Robert and Graham Spanier. 1979. "Theoriz-ing about the Quality and Stability of Mar-riage." Pp. 268-294 in *Contemporary Theories about the Family*, edited by W. Burr et al. New York: Free Press.

Longfellow, Cynthia. 1979. "Divorce Impact on Children." Pp. 287-306 in *Divorce and Separa-tion*, edited by G. Levinger and O. Moles. New York: Basic Books.

Lopata, Helena. 1973. *Widowhood in an American City.* Cambridge, MA: Schenkman.

Macke, Anne Statham and William Morgan. 1978. "Maternal Employment, Race, and Work Orien-tation of High School Girls." *Social Forces* 57:187-204.

Macklin, E. D.. 1978. "Nontraditional Heterosex-ual Cohabitation: A Research Review." *Marriage & Family Review* 1:1-12.

———. 1980. "Nontraditional Family Forms: A Decade of Research." *Journal of Marriage and the Family* 42:905-922.

Maracek, Jeanne, Stephen Finn, and Mona Cardell. 1982. "Gender Roles in the Relationships of Les-bians and Gay Men." *Journal of Homosexual-ity* 7:49-58.

Mathis, Arthur. 1978. "Contrasting Approaches to the Study of Black Families." *Journal of Mar-riage and the Family* 40:667-676.

Matthews, Sarah and Jetse Sprey. 1984. "Divorce Im-pact on Grandparenthood." *The Gerontologist* 24:41-47.

McCarthy, James. 1979. "Racial Differences in U.S. Marriage Dissolution." Paper presented at the annual meeting of the Population Association of America.

McLanahan, Sara. 1983. "Family Structure and Stress: Longitudinal Comparison of Two-parent and Female-headed Families." *Journal of Marriage and the Family* 45:347-358.

———. 1985. "Family Structure and the Reproduc-tion of Poverty." *American Journal of Sociology* 90:873-901.

——— and Larry Bumpass. 1986. "Intergenerational Consequences of Marital Disruption." Mimeo-graphed. Department of Sociology, University of Wisconsin.

Miller, Joanne and Howard Garrison. 1982. "Sex Roles: The Division of Labor at Home and in the Work Place." *Annual Review of Sociology* 9:237-262.

Miller, Brian. 1979. "Gay Fathers and their Chil-dren." *The Family Coordinator* 28:544-552.

Miller, Judith, Brooke Jacobsen, and Jerry Bigner. 1981. "The Child's Home Environment for Les-bian vs. Heterosexual Mothers: A Neglected Area of Research." *Journal of Homosexuality* 7:49-58.

Mirande, Alfredo. 1985. *The Chicano Experience.* Notre Dame: University of Notre Dame Press.

Monahan, Thomas. 1955. "Is Childlessness Related to Family Stability?" *American Sociological Review* 20:446-456.

Moore, Kristin and Linda Waite. 1981. "Marital Dissolution, Early Motherhood and Early Mar-riage." *Social Forces* 60:20-40.

Morgan, Philip and Ronald Rindfuss. 1985. "Marital Disruption." *American Journal of Sociology* 90:1055-1077.

Mott, Frank and Sylvia Moore. 1979. "The Causes of Marital Disruption among Young American Women." *Journal of Marriage and the Family* 41:355-365.

———. 1983. "The Tempo of Remarriage among Young American Women." *Journal of Marriage and the Family* 45:427-435.

Mueller, Charles and Hallowell Pope. 1977. "Marital Instability: A Study of Its Transmission between Generations." *Journal of Marriage and the Family* 39:83-93.

——— 1980. "Divorce and Female Remarriage Mobility." *Social Forces* 58:726-738.

Mutran, Elizabeth and Donald Reitzes. 1984. "Intergenerational Support Activities and Well-being among the Elderly." *American Sociological Review* 49:117-130.

Newcomb, Paul. 1979. "Cohabitation in America: An Assessment of its Consequences." *Journal of Marriage and the Family* 41:597-603.

Otto, Luther. 1979. "Antecedents and Consequents of Marital Timing." Pp. 101-126 in *Contemporary Theories of the Family*, edited by W. Burr et al. New York: Free Press.

Parsons, Talcott. 1943. "The Kinship System of the Contemporary United States." *American Anthropologist* 45:22-38.

Patterson, Orlando. 1982. "Persistence, Continuity, and Change in the Jamaican Working Class Family." *Journal of Family History* 7:135-161.

Peplau, Letitia Anne. 1982. "Research on Homosexual Couples." *Journal of Homosexuality* 8:3-8.

———, Christine Padesky, and Mykol Hamilton. 1982. "Satisfaction in Lesbian Relationships." *Journal of Homosexuality* 8:23-36.

Pistrang, Nancy. 1984. "Women's Work Involvement and Experience of New Motherhood." *Journal of Marriage and the Family* 46:433-448.

Powell, Brian and Lala Carr Steelman. 1982. "Maternal Effects on Sons' and Daughters' Attitudes toward Women in the Labor Force." *Journal of Marriage and the Family* 44:349-358.

Presser, Harriet and Wendy Baldwin. 1980. "Child Care as a Constraint on Employment." *American Journal of Sociology* 85:1202-1213.

Preston, Samuel. 1984. "Children and the Elderly." *Demography* 21:435-457.

——— and John McDonald. 1979. "The Incidence of Divorce within Cohorts of American Marriages Contracted since the Civil War." *Demography* 16:1-25.

Rempel, Judith. 1985. "Childless Elderly." *Journal of Marriage and the Family* 47:343-348.

Risman, Barbara, Charles Hill, Zick Rubin, and Letitia Anne Peplau. 1981. "Living Together in College: Implications for Courtship." *Journal of Marriage and the Family* 43:77-84.

Rogler, Lloyd and Rosemary Sontana Cooney. 1984. *Puerto Rican Families in New York City: Inter-generational Processes*. Maplewood, NJ: Waterfront Press.

Rosenfeld, Rachel. 1985. *Farm Women*. Chapel Hill: University of North Carolina Press.

Ross, Catherine and Joan Huber. 1985. "Hardship and Depression." *Health and Social Behavior* 26:312-327.

Ross, Heather and Isabel Sawhill. 1975. *Time of Transition: The Growth of Families Headed by Women*. Washington DC: The Urban Institute.

Rossi, Alice, ed. 1985. *Gender and the Life Course*. New York: Aldine.

Ryder, Norman. 1975. "The Future of American Fertility." *Social Problems* 26:359-370.

Sanders, Ruth. 1985. *Child Support and Alimony: 1983*. Bureau of the Census, Current Population Reports. Special Studies Series P-23, No. 141. Washington, DC: Government Printing Office.

Scanzoni, John and Greer Litton Fox. 1980. "Sex Roles, the Family, and Society: The Seventies and Beyond." *Journal of Marriage and the Family* 42:2-33.

Schoen, Robert and William Urton. 1979. "A Theoretical Perspective on Cohort Marriage and Divorce in Twentieth Century Sweden." *Journal of Marriage and the Family* 41:4090-4416.

———, Karen Woodrow and John Baj. 1985. "Marriage and Divorce in Twentieth Century American Cohorts." *Demography* 22:101-114.

Seelbach, Wayne. 1977. "Gender Differences in Expectations for Filial Responsibility." *The Gerontologist* 17:421-425.

Smelser, Neil. 1959. *Social Change in the Industrial Revolution: An Application of Theory to the British Cotton Industry*. Chicago: University of Chicago Press.

Smith, James P. and Michael Ward. 1980. "Asset Accumulation and Family Size." *Demography* 17:243-260.

——— 1984. "Women's Wages and Work in the Twentieth Century." Santa Monica, CA: Rand.

Smith, Raymond. 1968. "Family." Pp. 301-312 in *International Encyclopedia of Social Science 5*, edited by D. Sills. New York: Macmillan.

Smyer, Michael and Brian Hofland. 1982. "Divorce and Support in Later Life." *Journal of Family Issues* 3:61-77.

South, Scott. 1985. "Economic Conditions and the Divorce Rate: A Time-series Analysis of the Postwar U.S." *Journal of Marriage and the Family* 47:31-41.

——— and Glenna Spitze. 1986. "Determinants of Divorce Over the Marital Life Course." *American Sociological Review* 51:583-590.

Spanier, Graham. 1983. "Married and Unmarried Cohabitation in the United States: 1980." *Journal of Marriage and the Family* 45:277-278.

——— and Robert Lewis. 1980. "Marital Quality: A Review of the Seventies." *Journal of Marriage and the Family* 42:825-840.

Spanier, Graham and Linda Thompson. 1984. *Part-*

ing: *The Aftermath of Separation and Divorce*. Beverly Hills, CA: Sage.

Spicer, Jerry and Gary Hampe. 1975. "Kin Interaction after Divorce." *Journal of Marriage and the Family* 37:11-19.

Spitze, Glenna and Joan Huber. 1980. "Changing Attitudes Toward Women's Nonfamily Roles, 1939-1978." *Work and Occupations* 7:317-335.

Spitze, Glenna and Scott South. 1985. "Women's Employment, Time Expenditure, and Divorce." *Journal of Family Issues* 6.307-330.

Stafford, Rebecca, Elaine Backman, and Pamela Dibona. 1977. "The Division of Labor among Cohabiting and Married Couples." *Journal of Marriage and the Family* 39:43-47.

Staples, Robert. 1985. "Changes in Black Family Structure." *Journal of Marriage and the Family* 47:1005-1013.

_____ and Alfredo Mirande. 1980. "Racial and Cultural Variations among American Families: A Decennial Review." *Journal of Marriage and the Family* 42:887-904.

Steelman, Lala Carr and James Mercy. 1980. "Unfounding the Confluence Model: Sibship Size and Birth Order Effects on Intelligence." *American Sociological Review* 45:571-582.

Steiner, Gilbert. 1981. *The Futility of Family Policy*. Washington, DC: Brookings Institution.

Steinmetz, Suzanne. 1979. "Disciplinary Techniques, Aggressiveness, Dependency, and Conscience." Pp. 405-438 in *Contemporary Theories about the Family*, edited by W. Burr et al. New York: Free Press.

Stevens, Gillian and Monica Boyd. 1980. "The Importance of Mother: Labor Force Participation and Intergenerational Mobility of Women." *Social Forces* 59:186-199.

Stoller, Eleanor Palo. 1983. "Parental Caregiving by Adult Children." *Journal of Marriage and the Family* 45:851-858.

Stolzenberg, Ross and Linda Waite. 1984. "Local Labor Markets, Children and Labor Force Participation of Wives." *Demography* 21:157-170.

Streib, Gordon and Rubye Wilkerson Beck. 1980. "Older Families." *Journal of Marriage and the Family* 42:937-958.

Suchindran, Chirayath, Helen Koo, and Janet Griffith. 1985. "The Effects of Postmarital Childbearing on Divorce and Remarriage." *Population Studies* 39:471-86.

Sussman, George. 1982. *Selling Mothers' Milk*. Urbana: University of Illinois Press.

Sussman, Marvin. 1965. "Relations of Adult Children with their Parents." Pp. 62-92 in *Social Structure and the Family: Generational Relations*, edited by E. Shanas and G. Streib. Englewood Cliffs, NJ: Prentice-Hall.

Szalai, Alexander. 1973. *The Use of Time in Twelve Countries*. The Hague: Mouton.

Tanner, Donna. 1978. *The Lesbian Couple*. Lexington, MA: D. C. Heath.

Teachman, Jay. 1983. "Early Marriage, Premarital

Fertility, and Marital Dissolution." *Journal of Family Issues* 4:105-126.

Thomas, Kausar and Andrew Wister. 1984. "Living Arrangements of Older Women: The Ethnic Dimension." *Journal of Marriage and the Family* 47:301-312.

Thompson, Linda and Alexis Walker. 1984. "Mothers and Daughters: Aid Patterns and Attachment." *Journal of Marriage and the Family* 46:313-322.

Thomson, Elizabeth. 1983. "Individual and Couple Utility of Children." *Demography* 20:507-518.

Thornton, Arland. 1977. "Children and Marital Stability." *Journal of Marriage and the Family* 39:531-540.

_____ 1978. "Marital Instability Differentials and Interactions: Multivariate Contingency Table Analysis." *Sociology and Social Research* 62: 570-595.

_____ 1985. "Changing Attitudes toward Separation and Divorce: Causes and Consequences." *American Journal of Sociology* 90:856-872.

Tilly, Louise and Joan Scott. 1978. *Women, Work and Family*. New York: Holt, Rinehart and Winston.

Treas, Judith. 1977. "Family Support Systems for the Aged." *The Gerontologist* 17:486-491.

Trimberger, Rosemary and Michael MacLean. 1982. "Maternal Employment: The Child's Perspective." *Journal of Marriage and the Family* 44: 469-476.

Troll, Lillian, Sheila Miller, and Robert Atchley. 1979. *Families in Later Life*. Belmont, CA: Wadsworth.

Tuller, N. R. 1978. Couples: "The Hidden Segment of the Gay World." *Journal of Homosexuality* 3:331-343.

Udry, Richard. 1981. "Marital Alternatives and Marital Disruption." *Journal of Marriage and the Family* 43:889-897.

Uhlenberg, Peter and Mary Anne Myers. 1981. "Divorce and the Elderly." *The Gerontologist* 21:276-282.

Veevers, J. E. 1979. "Voluntary Childlessness." *Marriage & Family Review* 2:1-26.

Veroff, Joseph, Elizabeth Douvan, and Richard Kulka. 1981. *The Inner American*. New York: Basic Books.

Voeller, B. and J. Walters. 1978. "Gay Fathers." *The Family Coordinator* 27:149-157.

Waite, Linda. 1981. "U.S. Women at Work." *Population Bulletin* 36:1-43.

_____, Gus Haggstrom, and David Kanouse. 1985a. "The Consequences of Parenthood for the Marital Stability of Young Adults." *American Sociological Review* 50:850-857.

_____ 1985b. "Changes in the Employment Activities of New Parents." *American Sociological Review* 50:263-282.

Wallerstein, J. and J. Kelly. 1980. *Surviving the Breakup: How Children and Parents Cope with Divorce*. New York: Basic Books.

Walters, James and Lynda Henly Walters. 1980. "Parent-Child Relationships: A Review, 1970-79." *Journal of Marriage and the Family* 42: 807-824.

Watson, J. and R. Kivett. 1976. "Influences on the Life Satisfaction of Older Fathers." *Family Coordinator* 25:482-488.

Weiss, Robert. 1984. "The Impact of Marital Dissolution on Income and Consumption in Single Parent Households." *Journal of Marriage and the Family* 46:115-128.

Weitzman, Lenore. 1985. *The Divorce Revolution.* New York: Free Press.

White, Lynn and Alan Booth. 1985. "The Quality and Stability of Remarriages: The Role of Stepchildren." *American Sociological Review* 50:689-698.

Wright, Gerald, and Dorothy Stetson. 1978. "The Impact of No-Fault Divorce Law Reform on Divorce in the American States." *Journal of Marriage and the Family* 40:575-584.

Zajonc, R. B. 1976. "Family Configuration and Intelligence." *Science* 192:227-235.

Zelditch, Morris. 1964. "Family, Marriage, and Kinship." Pp. 680-733 in *Handbook of Modern Sociology*, edited by Robert Faris. Chicago: Rand McNally.

14

The Sociology of Education

CHARLES E. BIDWELL
NOAH E. FRIEDKIN

Commentary on education can be found in the writings of the first generation of American sociologists, including Ellsworth Faris (1928), Albion Small (1897), and Lester Ward (1883). During the early years of European sociology, Emile Durkheim (1961/ 1925; 1956/1903, 1906, 1911; 1977/1938) and Max Weber (1946/1906, 1922) gave substantial attention to educational matters. From these beginnings, an intimate relationship between sociological theory and social practice has produced a highly variegated research literature.

Various lines of work have yielded important findings about educational structures and processes. For example, certain sociologists of education have applied theories of formal organization to schools and colleges (e.g., Bidwell, 1965; Meyer, 1970). Others have applied ideas about work and occupations to school teaching and administration and have analyzed the roles of teacher and administrator (e.g., Gordon, 1957; Gross, Mason, and McEachern, 1958; Lortie, 1975). Still others have probed the subcultures of schools and colleges (e.g., Coleman, 1961; Trow, 1962; Wallace, 1966), and there is a large comparative literature on the development and

structure of national systems of education (e.g., Clark, 1983; Meyer et al., 1977; Organisation for Economic Co-operation and Development, 1971; Teichler and Sanyal, 1982; Trow, 1984).

However, most central to the sociological study of education is the analysis of educational activities—their form and content, their embeddedness in broader social structures, and their outcomes for individuals and collectivities. We shall focus on these topics. Reflecting the principal achievements in the field, we shall give special attention to relationships between education and social stratification and mobility and to issues of justice that are raised by the hierarchical distribution of education in modern societies.

This chapter is divided into two main parts. The first part is a chronological review. It traces the intellectual origins of the sociology of education in the writings of the first generation of American and European sociologists. We shall see that what they had to say about education defines a scholarly agenda in which institutional analysis is central. The aim of this agenda is to discover how educational mechanisms that affect life chances are embedded in the institutional fabric of society. How these mechanisms act is affected by public policy, so that work on education and social stratification is complemented by studies of the political processes through which educational polices are formed.

The authors are grateful to William T. Bielby and Mary C. Brinton, who read and commented on an earlier draft. A portion of this chapter is drawn from Charles Bidwell's Hawley Lecture, "Schools, Learning, and Status," delivered at the University of North Carolina, Chapel Hill on April 24, 1987.

449

We shall see that subsequent sociological studies of education have departed substantially from this agenda. Although the concern for relationships between education and social stratification persists, attention has shifted from institutional topics to an individual-centered analysis of the sources of educational attainments and of the contribution of these attainments to status inheritance and social mobility. Established early among American sociologists, this line of work on individual attainments and concern for the welfare of individuals were reinforced by post-World War II liberal political programs in Great Britain, Europe, and the United States (Wexler, 1976).

In the second part of the chapter, we shall turn to a theoretical statement. Our review will have shown that despite sustained research on relationships between educational attainment and social mobility, the constituent processes have not been analyzed in sufficient detail. We shall present an elaborated theoretical approach to certain of these processes. This approach leads into classroom-level studies of the social organization of education and into society-level sociopolitical analyses of institutional change in education.

A Review of the Field

From about 1880 until World War II, the question of social control dominated sociology and sociological studies of education. The Americans and Europeans approached the issue from different starting points and therefore presented different analyses.

Education and Social Control: The Americans

For the Americans, exemplified by Lester Ward's *Dynamic Sociology* (1883), social control was primarily a matter of social betterment. Its principal goal was to increase individual liberties in a context of general prosperity, enlightenment, and civility. The principal mechanisms of social betterment envisioned by these sociologists were mechanisms of individual improvement. They assumed that changes in people would sum to changes in society, so that education, by virtue of its beneficial effects on a person's values and knowledge, was among the chief instruments of social progress.

When the social organization of education—its institutional structures, organizational forms, and instructional processes—was examined, the aim was to discover how schools could be made more effective means of individual improvement. These writers assumed that an understanding of social life and the skills of social participation were learned mainly through the experience of social relationships themselves. Moreover, they knew that school was at the center of the student's everyday world. Therefore, because school pervaded students' lives, the social organization of the school could be a powerful tool to prepare young people to understand the nature of society and to be productive members of it. According to this argument, a key task of educators was to order the small society of the school to present students with opportunities to become effective members of adult society. The objective was to form students' capacity for independent, critical social practice.

The social philosopher, John Dewey (1900), was the most articulate proponent of this view, but sociologists also promoted it. Albion Small (1897), who was Dewey's colleague at the University of Chicago, attacked the then-accepted idea that the school curriculum should be based upon faculty psychology, which asserted a radical separation of mental capacities. Small contended that this curriculum had become compartmentalized to the point that students could neither learn about social life as a whole nor develop the practical skills required to live effectively in it.

Education and Social Control: The Europeans

Emile Durkheim and Max Weber proceeded from the assumption that in the West traditional values had given way under the onslaught of industrialization, rational science, and an expansive state. In contrast to the American sociologists, they thought that the rise of national societies was fast eroding the moral base of human conduct and attenuating human community.

DURKHEIM

Durkheim, who lectured on pedagogy throughout his career, proceeded from an instrumentalist starting point toward the same idea that informed the American writings—that everyday participation in the social life of the school forms students' habits, values, and skills. The question for Durkheim, as for Dewey and Small, was how to order the classroom so that what students learned would fit them for productive lives in the larger society. However, when he specified the nature of the classroom society and the content of classroom activities, Durkheim differed sharply from the Americans.

In France common education had come under state control despite the strong opposition of the Catholic church. Durkheim (1961), supporting this move, argued that only the state, in contrast to the family, religious orders, or other parochial groups, could educate with sufficient disinterest to serve a whole nation. He gave special emphasis to elementary education. The elementary school was to form a common national identity and inculcate habits of conduct that would secure social integration in a secular age.

Durkheim thought that these common values and habits would be hard to develop (given the decline of traditional community), and he wanted teachers to attend to this task before they turned to the development of students' individual capabilities. The Americans, who were less worried about the question of national loyalty and identity, believed that the schools' chief task was to educate for critical thought and practical action.

In Durkheim's analysis, the elementary school classroom had three fundamental social organizational properties that made it a natural instrument for socializing pupils in secular morality. First, the regular tasks of the student mirrored the requirements for regularity in the workplace and other of the more formal settings of the adult world. Second, the teacher's authority (as an adult and as a civil servant) reproduced the authority of the state in relation to the citizen. Third, the pupil group itself represented the first experience of a society of equals. From participation in this small social order, Durkheim argued, children would acquire social habits that could evolve into identification with the nation, capacity for commitment to collective enterprise, and the orderly conduct required of effective citizens, workers, and group members.

Durkheim did not ignore what he called "autonomy" or "self-direction," with a denotation that was close to the Americans' notion of capacity for individually governed action. As Durkheim saw it, studying such subjects as science in later school grades would make students skillful rational analysts. They could then solve problems of everyday life with an independence and initiative that were secured within the frame of discipline and duty.

In the Third Republic, where schooling was becoming a state function, education was drawn inexorably into partisan politics, and Durkheim was an active reformist participant. Moreover, in lectures at the Sorbonne, he (Durkheim, 1977) had treated the development of French education from the Middle Ages through the first three-quarters of the nineteenth century as an outcome of interest group action. Nevertheless, he glossed over contemporary educational politics, preferring to think of modern educational policy as a product of scientific analysis by professional ministry officials and school inspectors. He seemed to think that these bureaucrat-professionals, prepared by university study for sound, scientific judgment, would be insulated by office and the surrounding governmental apparatus from partisan considerations.

WEBER

Weber was not much interested in the common school. He did not attend to educational professions or bureaucracy, despite his thesis that bureaucratization is a master social trend. He was drawn to educational topics by his analysis of social stratification. He noted that as the nineteenth century progressed, university education had become an increasingly useful means to legitimate traditional status honor. It provided this legitimation by virtue of study in a liberal curriculum that prepared students not for work but for "the conduct of a life" (Weber, 1946, pp. 242-243, 426).

Proceeding apace, however, was the rise of rationalized, specialized occupations. University training for occupations like engineering and law brought heightened status advantage to graduates, fostering the rise of new, bourgeois status groups. These groups, defined by the distinctive occupations of their members and the economic nature of their life chances, were challenging traditional status groups for honor and power. Hence, university education was evolving into an arena of intense status group competition.

Weber thought that this competition would be conducted through parents' efforts to realize their conceptions of the kinds and amounts of university training that their sons should receive. For a status group to influence university curricula or access would give its members an edge in their struggle for life chances. The state, through its policymaking and administrative organs, would provide major tools for such action, especially for status-seeking groups without other channels through which to influence events in the universities. Matters of university curriculum and finance (and, by implication, questions of access to the secondary education that opened university doors) would necessarily become issues of partisan contention, having become matters of state policy and governmental action.

Education and Social Stratification

By 1930 in the United States, as the discipline of sociology developed, it turned from its earlier instrumentalism toward a more generalized, analytic interest in social organization and process. The Great Depression had eroded the optimism of the earlier American sociological generation, and interest in social practice intersected with more general analytical concerns. The forms and mechanisms of social stratification were among the prime topics.

The stage was set to incorporate educational topics into the emerging analytical agenda. Willard Waller (1932) accomplished a trenchant analysis of the school as in itself a system of power, but the Russian emigre sociologist Pitirim Sorokin, by linking education to broader systems of social stratification, took an especially interesting step. Like Weber, he stressed institutional relationships between the distribution of amounts and kinds of schooling, the rise and fall of status groups, and the movement of individuals and families through a competitive stratification order.

In *Social and Cultural Mobility*, Sorokin (1927, part 2) gave extensive attention to the way in which the institutional structure of societies provides channels for vertical social mobility, especially for elite formation. These channeling institutions, he argued, provide mechanisms through which individuals are selected into positions of greater or lesser economic or political power. Schools, he said, are among these mobility channels, along with the church, the military, the government and polity, and the organized occupations.

Sorokin argued that when families command the economic and cultural resources required for social participation, the aggregate result is a very high level of status inheritance from one generation to the next and strong ascriptive biases in the distribution of life chances and social standing. Only when the hold of the family on status resources weakens (e.g., with the rise of formally free labor) does status inheritance decline, and then only if relatively autonomous mobility channels are available to sort and allocate persons to status positions according to nonascriptive criteria.

Sorokin thought that education had become an important, autonomous mobility channel in contemporary society. He saw a relatively low level of "preselection" (selection according to family origins) in the recruitment of students to schools. He argued that a decline of direct family control over the life chances of offspring and the fungibility of school attainment in labor markets (the latter in contrast to the narrower, institution-specific opportunities created by such institutions as the military or the church) had produced this result.

In the presence of strong preselection, Sorokin continued, schooling—both the substance of what children learn and the certificates they receive—reinforces family effects on status allocation. The school extends the family's status-allocating influence. As preselection weakens, how students are judged and rewarded and what they learn occur in increasing independence of their family origins. The correlation of school attainment with family status declines, and students' educational and later life chances become more dependent on academic ability, curriculum content, and teachers' standards than on social ascription. The school has gained institutional autonomy.

Sorokin brought education squarely into the institutional analysis of societies. He presented the form and content of education as functions of broader institutional provisions for the accumulation, maintenance, and transmission of wealth, power, and honor. He argued, further, that the relative autonomy of the schools (e.g., to fix curricula and to test and select students) is itself historically determined by the scope and security of family control of status resources.

In Sorokin's view, such educational activities as training, testing, and sorting could not be analyzed fruitfully apart from their institutional context. At the points of entry to school, one would show how these activities were related to external criteria of recruitment to kinds and levels of schooling (e.g., family-linked criteria). At the points of departure from school, one would show how these activities were related to students' entry into the labor force and other major sectors of social participation. Thus the principal reason for studying education was not its intrinsic significance, but rather its significance for structures of wealth, power, and prestige.

Sorokin dismissed the view of his sociological predecessors in the United States, that education is a great democratizer. In Sorokin's view, schooling is no "leveler" of populations. When schools gain institutional autonomy in the allocation of social status, this allocation occurs on the basis of the schools' own tests and standards of judgment. Individual ability, character, and academic attainment then replace family origins as the principal criteria of social mobility. He wrote (1927, pp. 189-190):

> Contrary to the common opinion, universal education . . . leads not so much to an obliteration of mental and social differences as to their increase. The school, even the most democratic school, open to everybody, if it performs its task properly, is a machinery of the "aristocratization" and stratification of society, not of "leveling" and "democratization."

Sorokin's analysis is consistent with Weber's assertion that occupational specialization requires families to secure their children's favorable educational placement if they are to secure their favorable occupational placement. Moreover, they must do so in a regime of educational allocation that relies more on capability and attainment than on the rights or perquisites of social standing.

Sorokin was not clear about whether the autonomous action of schools in social allocation necessarily weakens status inheritance. Even though family origins per se may then be less significant among the criteria of status allocation, individual capability or character may still be strongly related to status origins.

Education and Status Attainment

After World War II, liberal-democratic efforts to open an era of social equity led political and governmental leaders to echo a sociological theme—that in a world dominated by work and the specialized occupations, removing ascriptive obstacles to school and university attendance would result in a more equitable distribution of life chances. Opportunities for income, power, and honor would be less dependent on accidents of birth and more dependent on individuals' performance and conduct.

Sociologists translated this policy objective into research questions. Although they might have been posed at the levels of both institutional process and individual mobility, the individualistic orientation of the policymakers was echoed by the sociologists' preoccupation with the relationship between individuals' schooling and life chances. In this way, Sorokin's idea of the institutional autonomy of the schools was constrained to the individual level of analysis. Sorokin had presented two indicators that would let one infer the amount of institutional autonomy of education from data about individuals' social mobility:

(1) the degree to which individuals' educational attainment is independent of ascriptive characteristics; and

(2) the degree to which individuals' occupational attainment depends upon the kinds and amounts of schooling attained.

The postwar studies of educational and occupational status attainment gave prime attention to these indicators. However, they did not press on to consider the mechanisms by which the organization of schooling affects status attainment or the importance of the institutional context in which these mechanisms act.

There have been certain exceptions, most notably Turner's (1960) speculative comparison of British "sponsored" and American "contest" mobility and Kerckhoff's (1974) empirical test of Turner's ideas. However, although this work has been well received and has stimulated sociological interest, it has not led to a substantial body of institutionally oriented research. Ironically, this neglect of the institutional context of status attainment has occurred in societies marked by the very institutional developments foreseen by Weber and central to Sorokin's depiction of the modern West.

Sociological studies of education turned not only from the institutional aspects of educational status allocation, but also from Durkheim's interest in the internal organization and processes of schools. Instead, the investigators assumed an essential substitutability of educational content with respect to postschool social destinations. Given this assumption, educational attainment could be conveniently indexed for everyone by the number of school years completed or by scores on nationally normed tests of verbal or quantitative achievement.

As the substance of education disappeared from analytical view, this research centered increasingly on family and other social environments outside the school that might influence students' work in school. The school or university as a social-organizational entity or as a cluster of social processes (Durkheim, Waller), along with the content of what was taught or learned (Dewey, Small, Ward, Durkheim, Weber) left the research field. Thus, in Great Britain and Europe, work on education and status attainment has been concerned primarily with imparities attributable to economic circumstances and class placement (e.g., Boudon, 1974; Bourdieu and Passeron, 1979; Fagerlind, 1975; Floud, Halsey, and Martin, 1957). In the United States this research has extended as well to imparities that are associated with race, ethnicity, and gender.

American research on education and occupational mobility was prefigured by the ethnographic community studies of W. L. Warner and his collaborators (e.g., Hollingshead, 1949; Warner, Havighurst, and Loeb, 1944; Warner, Meeker, and Eells, 1949). They had found that community status orders afforded limited opportunities for occupational mobility and that the schools were less avenues of mobility than agents of status maintenance. Then came the seminal studies of Duncan and Hodge (1963) and Blau and Duncan (1967) that documented the importance of educational attainment for occupational attainment by white males in the United States. Their work located the sources of occupational status inheritance primarily in a strong correlation between father's occupational standing and son's years of completed schooling. This work was soon followed by an expanding literature that provided further evidence of these relationships, including the incorporation of black males into the dominant, education-based attainment process (e.g., Featherman and Hauser, 1978; Sewell, Hauser, and Featherman, 1976).

With respect to educational attainment itself, the pathbreaking survey of the distribution of educational opportunity in this country by Coleman and his associates (1966) set the substantive and methodological frame for virtually all subsequent investigations. This research has focused on the capacity of schooling to overcome the ascriptively-based disadvantge in educational attainment (e.g., Alexander, Cook, and McDill, 1978; Alexander, Eckland, and Griffin, 1975; Jencks, Crouse, and Mueser, 1983; Jencks et al., 1972, 1979; Sewell and Hauser, 1975; Sewell, Hauser, and Featherman, 1976).

EDUCATION AND OCCUPATIONAL ATTAINMENT

We shall open our discussion of the attainment research with findings that pertain to the second of Sorokin's indicators—the relationship between educational attainment and occupational mobility. There is a voluminous literature on this relationship, but few of these studies speak directly to our understanding of the institution, organization, or processes of education. We shall limit ourselves to the most pertinent works.

Studies of educational and occupational attainment in economically developed societies consistently document a very strong relationship for males between the years of schooling that an individual completes and his later attainment of occupational prestige and income. These relationships have received two contrasting interpretations, as indicating either "credentialism" or "human capital" formation. On the credentialist side, Collins (1979) has argued that the relationships arise primarily because schools award certificates that employers are willing to accept, however close or distant the connection between award of the certificate and what the student has learned. Indeed, Meyer (1977) would place school instruction on the periphery of the schools' core social functions—namely, classifying and certifying students as more or less fitted for varieties of employment and for other aspects of social participation. On the human capital side, the sociologists Rosenbaum (1976) and Hope (1984) and such economists as Schultz (1963), Bowman (1969), Becker (1964), Mincer (1974), and Fagerlind (1975) have argued that schooling endows individuals with cognitive and motivational resources that are not otherwise available and that are essential for productive life on the job and elsewhere.

It is not clear that these interpretations can be distinguished empirically. What is learned and what is certified as having been learned on average are strongly related, making it very difficult to determine the degree to which labor markets are responsive to workers' capabilities or credentials. It may be more judicious to regard learning and gaining credentials as tightly linked mechanisms through which schooling affects employability.

A major exception to the tendency of attainment researchers to index education solely as completed schooling or test performance is a study by Miller, Kohn, and Schooler (1986). They reopened the Durkheimian question of schooling and habituation. Using longitudinal data about a large sample of American males, they found that students gain capacity for self-direction in proportion to their opportunities in school for self-directed activities. They have also shown that schooling affects occupational attainment by virtue of this relationship. These in-school opportunities are probably greater in academic than nonacademic high school tracks by virtue of differences in the substantive complexity of schoolwork and in the degree to which this work is performed without close teacher supervision (the two elements of the Miller et al. measurement of educational self-direction). Perhaps they also are greater for students who are active than for those who are inactive in the extra-curriculum and greater for students in some extra-curricular activities than others (e.g., debate versus team sports).

In the light of the human capital approach, the Miller-Kohn-Schooler findings suggest the presence of reinforcing effects of cognitive learning, habituation, and motivation that could easily have substantial influence on many kinds of adult social participation. In fact, earlier research on samples of the American adult population has shown that years of schooling correlates with such beliefs or predispositions as civil libertarianism and tolerance of heterodoxy (Hyman, Wright, and Reed, 1975; Stember, 1961; Stouffer, 1955), while Jennings (1981) has reported a relationship between educational level and rates of political participation.

SCHOOLING AND EDUCATIONAL ATTAINMENT

Strong effects of schooling on occupational attainment can occur whatever the degree of institutional autonomy that schools enjoy. Indeed, when the school-to-work link is strong, those parents in the best position to do so are likely to press for educational allocation that reflects and reinforces status origins. Thus we must turn to the other of Sorokin's prime questions—the mechanisms that affect the allocation of educational opportunities and the distribution of educational attainment.

Advocates of the view that schools have gained an institutionally autonomous role (e.g., Jencks et al., 1972) have emphasized the modest proportion of variance in completed years of school that is attributable to status origins. Proponents of the view that educational attainment is ascriptively biased (e.g., Bowles and Gintis, 1976) have emphasized the substantial coefficients obtained in regressions of years of education on students' status origins.

Although these contrasting interpretations are based on different estimates of the relationship between status origins and attainment, they use the same body of evidence about educational achievement in the United States (Alexander, Cook, and McDill, 1978; Alexander, Eckland, and Griffin, 1975; Blau and Duncan, 1967; Duncan and Hodge, 1963; Featherman and Hauser, 1978; Jencks et al., 1972, 1979; Jencks, Crouse, and Mueser, 1983; Sewell and Hauser, 1975; Sewell, Hauser, and Featherman, 1976). Even the most technically sound of these studies attribute from less than one-fifth to over one-half of the variance in completed years of schooling to individuals' status origins (Bielby, 1981). The larger estimates have come from sibling studies in which the covariance of sibs' educational attainment is attributed to their similar family origins (Hauser and Mossel, 1985; Jencks et al., 1972, 1979; Olneck, 1977).

However, regardless of the proportion of variance that is explained by status origins, these studies have obtained statistically significant coefficients from regressions of attainment on origins. These coefficients show that social strata differ with respect to the probability of attainment. For certain pairs of social strata, these differences are substantial.

Sewell and Hauser (1976), for example, studied the educational attainment of a large sample of young Wisconsin men. Although more than four-fifths of the variance in their subjects' educational attainment was independent of status origins, the effects of origins on attainment were large. They (Sewell and Hauser, 1976, p. 13) summed up by saying:

> Whatever measure of socioeconomic status we use—parental income, father's or mother's education, father's occupation, or any combination of them—we find enormous differences in the educational attainments of the socioeconomic groups. These differences are large regardless of how broadly or restrictively educational attainment is defined—whether it is defined as merely continuation in some kind of education beyond high school, college entry, college graduation, or professional and graduate study.

Dividing their index of socioeconomic status into quartiles, they found that the highest quartile had a 4-to-1 advantage over the lowest in entering college, a 6-to-1 advantage in college graduation, and a 9-to-1 advantage in graduate or professional education.

In short, studies like Sewell and Hauser's have shown over and over that in the contemporary United States status origins have a powerful influence on the odds of attaining a given level of schooling. Even though the spread of the distribution of educational attainment within a social stratum is substantial, so that stratum membership is an imprecise predictor of an individual's attainment, the central tendencies of these distributions are likely to be lower among lower strata and higher among higher strata. These differences often entail substantial discrepancies in the odds of attaining given levels of education, which suggests systematic biasing effects of status origins on individuals' educational life chances.

There are three possible explanations for this difference of odds. First, personal traits that affect students' academic attainment may be related to their status origins. For example, if students of higher status origins have higher academic aspirations than others, they probably will work harder in school.

Second, students' access to educational resources may be biased according to status origins. To use Sorokin's term, this bias would result from preselection into schools or instructional programs within schools. For example, high schools in affluent suburbs may offer more subjects, more advanced courses, and a richer extracurriculum than high schools in central cities. Similar resource differences may distinguish college preparatory tracks from other tracks in comprehensive high schools.

Third, school social organization—both the formal organization of instruction and informal social relationships—may be related to students' status origins in a way that produces ascriptively biased attainment. For example, lower-status high school students may find that course prerequisites or grade requirements bar the way from a vocational or general to a college preparatory track. High school teachers may spend more time with students of higher than of lower social standing and give them greater encouragement to take college preparatory courses. High-status students may be more likely than others to have school friends who aspire to college.

These three sets of mechanisms may affect academic attainment independently, but they may also interact. For example, students who are more highly motivated may take greater advantage of educational resources and be more responsive to teachers' encouragement than students with weaker academic aspirations. In addition, the mechanisms may be causally related. For example, resource-rich schools, more often than less well-endowed schools, may teach in ways that encourage students to do well.

The findings of the academic attainment literature are quite consistent. They suggest that the primary sources of individual differences in educational life chances arise more from the traits of students than from differences of access to school resources or exposure to school social organization. This literature consists primarily of studies that use data about American high school students to estimate predictive models. In these models, the criterion variables include intended or completed years of schooling, achievement test scores, or such measures of educational aspirations as plans for college attendance. Measures of status origins are exogenous and variously include parental occupational prestige, education, and income; material and cultural aspects of the home; race and ethnicity; and gender. The intervening variables variously include academic ability and performance, the student's academic and occupational goals, sources of interpersonal support and influence, and school organizational variables.

Whatever the criterion variable, the effects of status origins on academic performance and college-attendance plans and activities are substantially mediated by the intervening variables that the model contains. In the dominant pattern, the largest of these indirect effects are transmitted by academic ability and prior academic performance (see Alexander, Eckland, and Griffin, 1975; Hauser and Featherman, 1976; Jencks, Crouse, and Mueser, 1983; Sewell and Hauser, 1976). Somewhat smaller effects are mediated by prior educational goals and parental and peer social support (see Alexander, Eckland, and Griffin, 1975; Alwin, 1976; Hauser and Featherman, 1976; Jencks, Crouse, and Mueser, 1983; Sewell and Hauser, 1976; Spenner and Featherman, 1978). The indirect effects of track placement, the school variable most often considered, are still smaller (see Alexander and Cook, 1982; Alexander and Eckland, 1975; Alexander, Cook, and McDill, 1978; Alexander and McDill, 1976; Alwin, 1976; Bain and Anderson, 1974; Hauser, 1971; Hauser, Sewell, and Alwin, 1976; Rehberg and Rosenthal, 1978).

Despite the trend in these findings, it is hard to accept the conclusion that school resources or social organization have only minor effects on academic attainment unless we assume that cognitive ability is a strong function of status origins. Although Eckland (1967) has argued for the existence of genetically determined cognitive differences between socioeconomic strata, there is no convincing evidence for strong differences of this kind. In their absence, any relationship of status origins with academic ability, performance, persistence, or aspirations must be mediated by, and therefore the cumulative result of, education and socialization in other settings, primarily the family.

The evidence does not let us disentangle the mediating action of education from that of other forms of socialization. However, a considerable part of the origins-attainment relationship is undoubtedly a function of schooling, as a consequence (independent or joint) of the distribution of educational resources and school social organization. Indeed, if the social organization of the school represents a basic allocation of the energies and activities of teachers and students, then opportunities for and constraints on academic attainment, including those that mediate status inheritance, must be distributed within the school's organization. In other words, status inheritance through education should be a strong function of status biases in the way schools distribute academic opportunities and constraints. Recent studies support these state-

THE SOCIOLOGY OF EDUCATION

ments, although they have not successfully described the mechanisms by which school resources or social organization have their effects.

Coleman et al. (1966) discovered that students' race had only weak biasing effects on access to well or poorly endowed public high schools. However, more recent work has documented sharper differences of resource access between curricular tracks within comprehensive high schools. These studies report a strong tendency for students of lower socioeconomic origins and of minority status to enroll in the less-advantaged tracks (Heyns, 1974; Rosenbaum, 1976; Vanfossen, Jones, and Spade, 1987).

Orfield and Paul (1987), studying the educational trajectories of young people in five U.S. cities, found that because of differences in access to resources, teachers, and counselors, black and Hispanic youth, by comparison with whites, encountered cumulative deficits of academic preparation. These deficits effectively blocked their enrollment in four-year colleges and universities. We can reasonably conclude that a portion of the origins-attainment relationship arises from imparities in the distribution of educational resources and, hence, from status-based preselection of students into schools and tracks.

That school social organization may have its own status-biasing effects on students' attainment is suggested by the mediating effects of peer ties, as well as those of track placement, in the educational attainment models. In view of the strong tendency among youth to form socially homophilic friendships (Cohen, 1983; Kandel, 1978), it is likely that school friendships channel interpersonal influence and social support in ways that encourage attainment among students of higher-status origins and discourage it among students of lower standing. Preselection of students into schools or tracks may reinforce this effect of peer homophily. Alexander and Campbell (1965) observed an effect on students' educational aspirations seemingly produced by the socioeconomic composition of high school student bodies. However, they discovered that this effect could be traced to constraints of student body composition on the probability of having school friends with high or low aspirations.

As for track placement itself, a tracked high school undoubtedly distributes resources, interpersonal ties (with teachers as well as peers), and instructional and related experiences in ways that translate differences of status origins into differences of attainment. Some years ago, Talcott Parsons (1959) argued that the differential distribution of educational experiences across high school tracks would yield a corresponding distribution of chances to learn subject matter, values, and motives (e.g., differences in the independence and initiative required by school work and consequent differences in students' capacities for independence and initiative). Subsequent studies have tended to support Parsons.

We have already reviewed the evidence of disproportionate resource allocation among tracks (Heyns, 1974; Rosenbaum, 1976), and intertrack differences evidently extend to the availability of academically informative and supportive counseling (Cicourel and Kitsuse, 1963; Rosenbaum, 1976). They also extend to matters more specifically instructional. Vanfossen, Jones, and Spade (1987) have documented between-track differences in the number of courses that students take and in students' reports of their schools' disciplinary climate and of teachers' morale, fairness, and supportiveness. Each of these differences is in a direction that should favor attainment by students in the college preparatory track.

There is growing evidence that such differences affect attainment outcomes. We have noted that Miller, Kohn, and Schooler's (1986) findings imply that tracks differ in opportunities for the self-directed school work that affects occupational attainment. Enrollment in the college preparatory track, in contrast to either the general or vocational track, may yield more rapid and more complex cognitive development and subject-matter learning (Alexander and Pallas, 1984; Rosenbaum, 1976). Gamoran (1987), using a sample of the American high school student population, has demonstrated larger differences in cognitive development between tracks than between students and dropouts, implying a greater effect of being in one or another track than of remaining in high school past the school-leaving age. He could attribute a substantial part of this effect to between-track differences of course offerings. Lee and Bryk (1987) found that public high school track has significant effects on the probability of enrolling in courses that demand academic effort. They demonstrated that this relationship in part mediates the association between parental social standing and students' academic accomplishment.

Vanfossen, Jones, and Spade (1987) found that between the sophomore and senior years of high school, study in a college preparatory track has positive effects on changes in students' educational aspirations, school performance, occupational aspirations, and post-high school enrollment. These effects occurred after controls for status origins and prior school performance and experience. Coupled with their finding of similar effects on course taking, liking for school, self-esteem, and friends' educational and occupational aspirations, these findings strongly suggest that tracks constitute distinctive environments for learning. This study is among those that document ascriptive preselection of students into tracks, so that there appears to be a systematic tendency for students of higher-status origins to enjoy the more favorable learning environments.

Curricular differentiation need not occur through formal means (as in a tracked high school) to have such effects. Lee and Eckstrom (1987) reported that in untracked high schools where students choose their own programs from an array of electives, preference for academically demanding courses is a function of status origins, irrespective of ability, in part as a result of differences in the provision of information about educational life chances by parents and counselors.

In sum, there are good reasons to pursue the proposition that ascriptive biases in educational attainment follow from ascriptive biases in the ways schools distribute educational resources and organize teaching and student life. A theory that accounts satisfactorily for the educational mediation of status inheritance must consider how access to educational resources, informal social relationships in school, and the social organization of instruction intervene between status origins and educational attainment.

In the next section, we shall present such a theory. To do so, we shall look beyond the walls of the U.S. high school. There are two reasons to do so. First, ascriptive bias in educational attainment is not peculiar to the United States (Bourdieu, 1977; Bourdieu and Passeron, 1977; Matras, 1980; Robinson and Garnier, 1985), yet differences in the organization of national systems of education imply important cross-national differences in the mechanisms that generate the relationship (Kerckhoff, 1974).

Second, academic attainment is cumulative, so that what students accomplish in high school or later may have significant roots in the educational resources and school social organization that they encountered in earlier grades. There is some evidence that students are admitted to high school tracks primarily on the basis of test scores and grades, with little overt attention to class, race, ethnicity, or gender (Rehberg and Rosenthal, 1978). These schools appear to be operating with the autonomy that Sorokin envisioned, yet their students are ascriptively

preselected into tracks. If so, the educational sources of status biases in the allocation of students to tracks must be traced to events earlier in school.

A Theory of Educational Status Allocation

Our theoretical discussion has three parts. We shall consider first how differences between national systems may effect differences in the mechanisms of educational attainment. Then, for the illustrative case of the United States, we shall discuss what these mechanisms may be. Finally, continuing with the United States, we shall examine how socially ordered events in the earlier years of school may affect the operation of these mechanisms.

Comparative Structures of Educational Allocation

We begin with the premise that students' educational achievements (how far they go in school, what grades and diplomas they earn, and what and how much they learn) are a function of decisions about what schools to attend, what programs and courses to take, and how much effort to spend toward what ends. The question is, Who makes these decisions and how tightly do they bind students' actions?.

Some of these decisions necessarily are made by the students themselves. These are everyday decisions about time, effort, and the most proximate ends of school work. However, other sorts of decisions may be made by other persons— parents, teachers, principals, or admissions officers, for example. The most central of these decisions are, first, where a student will be located in the educational system (if anywhere) and, second, how far to continue once placed in the system. These decisions have strong consequences for educational attainment because they frame the educational opportunities that it is possible for a student to realize through capacity and effort.

Who makes these framing decisions should be a strong function of curricular differentiation in national educational systems (e.g., the "streams" of European secondary education or the tracks of American high schools). As a national curriculum becomes more intensively differentiated and the boundaries between its various streams or tracks become less permeable, framing decisions become more consequential for occupational and other significant social destinations. Less permeable boundaries mean fewer points at which framing decisions can be made. As the number of these points decreases, their significance to the involved actors should increase, if only because it becomes harder to recoup from a "bad" decision.

Therefore, as curricula become more differentiated and as stream or track boundaries harden, framing decisions should be made increasingly by parents and educators rather than students, because each decision has become more consequential for everyone who has an interest in a student's educational trajectory. Decision making itself should become more subject to formal rules and definitions of decision-making rights as a result of efforts, especially by educators, to secure decision-making claims. Finally, even students' own everyday decisions about academic effort should come more and more under parental and teacher influence (at least in the upper reaches of the differentiated system), as these actors put pressure on students to follow through once the consequential framing decisions have been made.

The educational systems of Great Britain, Europe, and Japan provide good examples of relatively intensive curricular differentiation (Altbach, Arnove, and Kelly, 1982). In these streamed systems, some secondary schools lead to university, others to various technical occupations that do not require university training, and still others to less exalted forms of work. Access to secondary education, especially the grammar school, lyce, or gymnasium and various technical high schools, has been comparatively limited.

In Japan (Rohlen, 1983), the high schools offer either academic or vocational curricula. Each school sets its own entrance examination, and within cities and prefectures the high schools are ranked by their reported effects on students' chances of admission to the "top" universities. In these universities, student places are severely limited, and the universities differ in the access that they are thought to give to desirable jobs.

In each of these educational systems, the number of points at which choices about educational destinations can be made is relatively restricted. Once made, such decisions tend to be irrevocable, although there may be some provision for students placed in "too high" a stream to move down. The framing decisions are quite formalized, with substantial reliance on examinations, interviews, and other such paraphernalia. As a result of these structural-temporal properties of educational allocation, parents and school officials are dominant actors in decisions about where and for how long a young person will continue schooling and, at least in Japan, about how hard to work. Students have a relatively subordinate place as educational decision makers (Brinton, 1987; Clark, 1985; Dore, 1976).

In the United States, the balance of decision-making power is more favorable to the students. The educational system, with its array of comprehensive high schools and its multitude of competing community and liberal arts colleges and universities, is less intensively differentiated than the streamed systems, and its internal boundaries are more permeable. It is true that the greater number of American high schools are tracked. However, at least in principle, it has often been possible for students to change tracks. Moreover, the American high school curriculum has been expanding steadily into a growing array of subject matters and courses at varying levels of difficulty. In this diversified curriculum, the student plans his or her own program of study, often with minimal counseling (Cusick, 1983; Powell, Farrar, and Cohen, 1985).

In the United States, high school graduates who seek postsecondary education usually find an institution that will accept them. It has been estimated, for example, that 90% of the class of 1972 who applied to college had been accepted by the end of the senior year (Hilton and Rhett, 1973). The situation probably is not much different for the graduates of four-year colleges who seek advanced degrees. This aspect of the U.S. educational system is reinforced by the market-driven nature of its postsecondary component. One can find some set of colleges that compete for students of virtually any level of capacity and motivation or virtually any ascriptive social stripe (Ben-David, 1972).

Of course, certain American high schools and universities are highly selective on such criteria as ability, achievement, religion, and gender. More generally, there is a substantial amount of formal allocation of students, especially at the time of high school graduation and during subsequent transitions within higher education. Nevertheless, the effect of this allocation is to set a series of thresholds below which the range of self-selection (into a college or into the labor force) is relatively restricted. Above these thresholds (especially at higher levels, such as those that mark relatively high probabilities of admission to prestigious colleges), the range of opportunity for self-selection is quite wide.

In sum, the number of transitions and thus the number of choice points in the American student career are comparatively large. Many of these transitions are marked by much less formal evaluation than is college or university entrance (e.g., the decision to drop out of high school upon reaching the school-leaving age).

Consequently, by comparison with Britain, Europe, or Japan, in the United States students are more likely themselves to make the decisions that frame their educational trajectories, and they are probably subject to relatively weak influence by parents and teachers when they make the more immediate decisions about academic effort. Parent and teacher influence is more likely to be indirect, via persuasion or the limiting or channeling of opportunities—for example, parents deciding where to live (and therefore which public schools will be available to their children) or whether to underwrite college expenses.

Students' Decisions and Educational Attainment

If these contrasts are valid, then a theory that accounts for relationships between status origins and educational attainment must be specific to the institutional conditions under which schooling and academic attainment occur. We turn now to a theory applicable to the United States. It treats institutional and social-psychological variables that channel or constrain students' framing decisions.

Ascriptive biases in these decisions and their consequences for educational attainment surely arise in part from status-linked differences in students' decision criteria and in willingness to follow through on decisions once made. Such differences must be attributed largely to differences in the status-related subcultures in which students are reared.

To some further extent, these biases probably arise from social structural correlates of students' status origins. Some of these correlates may be exogenous to schooling itself—for example, information about educational opportunities or the quality of schooling available where students live. Others may be endogenous to schooling— for example, high school track assignment. We shall focus on these endogenous variables.

The decision-making processes that we shall discuss should become more pervasive and consequential as students move through the school and age grades. As American students get older, the decision-making power of their parents and teachers should decline. The results of framing decisions come nearer, and the decision tree itself narrows, while an increasingly diverse curriculum and school social structure provide more

numerous and complex occasions for these decisions. However, because schooling is cumulative, we shall see later that roots of the decision-making process reach back into the early school years.

We proceed from the classic social-psychological axiom that social participation leads to a definition of the situation in which the participation occurs (Thomas, 1923). This definition embraces understandings about collective aims, opportunities and requirements for action, and appropriate modes of conduct. It allows one to assess the fit between collective and personal aims and between socially structured opportunities and requirements and personal capabilities. In this way, the desirability of further participation can be judged.

We shall argue that school social structure makes schooling psychologically punishing for all students and more punishing than rewarding psychologically for most. It follows that going to school imposes psychological costs on every student and substantial costs on all but a few. However, we shall also argue that students to varying degrees can tolerate the punishing aspects of education and thus discount these costs.

We assume that students are rational actors, so that they tend to define the educational situation by assessing the costs and benefits of schooling, on the one hand, and personal capacity to gain benefits and reduce costs, on the other. Students' framing decisions in large part are about exposure to relative amounts of academic demand, such as subject matter difficulty or the rigor of instructional standards—how much demand and for how long.

The extent to which students' framing decisions point toward educational attainment— toward demanding programs or further enrollment—should be influenced by their definitions of the educational situation and therefore by their expectations about the punishing and rewarding aspects of further education and their capacity to tolerate the punishment. Consequently, educational attainment should be a function of whatever affects students' experiences of academic punishment and reward and their capacity to tolerate education. We shall argue that these influences, which are grounded in school social structure, create a strong tendency toward status inheritance through education.

THE PUNISHMENT-REWARD RATIO

The psychologically punishing nature of schooling and the psychological rewards that schooling entails derive from the evaluative character of school work. School work involves performance to a standard, sometimes embodied in formal statements of academic requirements, but more often in teachers' discretionary demands and judgments and, to a degree, in students' own collective understandings about the quality of academic work.

There may be substantial differences between teachers' and students' standards, and teachers and students each may differ in the criteria that they use to evaluate academic performance. Our theory is concerned with the punishing or rewarding character of working to a standard, so that these disagreements are of limited pertinence. Note, though, that agreement may increase the rigor and consistency with which performance standards are enforced, while disagreement may increase the likelihood of variation in students' experience of punishment and reward. In any event, failure to meet a performance standard is punishing; meeting it is rewarding; and exceeding it is more rewarding still.

The nature of academic evaluation makes it unlikely that any student will escape the punishing aspect of schooling. Because they are judged, and tend to judge themselves, according to degrees of excellence, few students find themselves consistently at or above standard. All fall short on occasion, and most students fall short often. It follows that all students are subject to some degree of punishing academic stress and that most experience such punishment most of the time.

Academic reward and punishment may be mediated interpersonally or impersonally, but the dominant medium is interpersonal. In either case, the experience is socially ordered. With respect to interpersonal mediation, the teacher is the central punishing and rewarding agent. The central mediating act is the teacher's formal evaluation of recitation, tests, exercises, or papers, although such subtle media as the gesture, facial expression, or tone of voice also tell students what teachers think of them. Fellow students, too, are important punishing and rewarding agents, by virtue of their individual and collective judgments about the quality of peers' work and the accuracy and fairness of teachers' evaluations (again expressed in both explicit and implicit ways).

Two aspects of school social structure make school work a potent interpersonal source of punishment and reward—the authoritative relationship between teacher and student and the public nature of academic work. First, the student is a novice and as such is subordinated to the expert teacher. In this relationship, the teacher's subject matter-based authority is reinforced by an authority that inheres in age and office (Bidwell, 1970; Durkheim, 1961; Waller, 1932).

Second, students are taught in groups, which means that their academic work and teachers' and fellow students' responses to it are public and that the audience is an audience of similarly situated peers (Dreeben, 1968). This public situation constrains the teacher toward a common standard for all students, especially in the upper grades, where specialized classes lose much of the communal character of the "self-contained" primary school classroom. The public nature of instruction also invites competition among classmates that, because it is focused on striving for the scarce good of satisfactory performance, intensifies the punishing aspect of academic work (Bossert, 1979).

As for the impersonal mediation of academic reward and punishment, the social organization of instruction creates academically ranked instructional categories, such as high school tracks, advanced placement versus less elevated high school courses, and elementary school ability groups. These categories classify students according to levels of academic performance. Belonging to one or another group may, through social labeling, undergird a portion of the interpersonal mediation of academic reward and punishment (e.g., Rosenbaum, 1976), but when students know the category ranks, the sheer fact of being in one or another track, class, or ability group is likely to be rewarding or punishing.

Instruction has a temporal as well as a social structure. It is temporally organized as a set of successive, delimited tasks. This temporal structure subjects students' academic work to fairly constant monitoring by school staff and fellow students. Therefore, students are likely to be anxious most of the time about meeting academic standards, the more so the greater the substantive rigor of the standards and the severity of enforcement. Rewards, by contrast, are likely to be intermittent, a nonroutine response to exceptional academic work.

As a result of the nature of academic evaluation, the social organization of instruction, and the differing schedules of punishment and reward, schools should be more punishing than rewarding, up to some threshold at which accomplishment is sufficiently outstanding to result in very frequent and intense rewards. Hence, for all students, schooling to a degree should be punishing. For students below the performance threshold, the ratio of punishments to rewards should be unfavorable, the more so the more demanding the educational situation (i.e., the higher the performance standards and the tougher their enforcement) and the lower the students' academic performance.

The degree to which a student's definition of the educational situation envisions punishment as the probable net outcome of academic work should be a function of a summary punishment-reward ratio that averages this aspect of the student's experience of schooling. Other things being equal (including tolerance for education, to which we shall turn in a moment), the larger this ratio, the lower the odds of a framing decision that leads to academic attainment—to enrollment in a demanding school or program or to long-term enrollment. Thus we expect (ceteris paribus) that at any average level of performance, the greater the academic demand that the student has experienced, the lower the odds of further academic attainment. We also expect (ceteris paribus) that at any average level of academic demand, the poorer the student's overall performance, the lower these odds.

In addition, as the distribution of punishment-reward values narrows over the span of a student's schooling, the less ambiguous the definition of the educational situation should become. The student then has fewer opportunities for experiences that are inconsistent with the average. Therefore, as this distribution becomes less dispersed, the effect of the average punishment-reward ratio on framing decisions should become stronger.

Our argument about the punishment-reward ratio is supported by reported associations between school achievement and students' conduct, self-esteem, and attitudes about schooling (Demo and Savin-Williams, 1983; Rosenberg and Simmons, 1972; Stinchcombe, 1964). Evidently, high rates of punishing experiences are likely to leave a youth either humbled and subdued or resentful and rebellious; high rates of rewarding experiences tend to result in self-confidence and engagement with schooling. Note also the findings of a "frog pond" effect in schools (Alwin and Otto, 1977; Davis, 1966). That is, surrounding a student with pupils of substantially higher performance than his or her own tends to depress the student's academic aspirations, presumably by subjecting this student to consistently punishing comparisons with peers. This relationship seems to hold for students at all achievement levels.

Our theory specifies a three-step mechanism that makes schooling status-maintaining. This mechanism involves the successive action of family socialization, via students' cognitive and motivational traits, and school social organization. First, there is considerable evidence of

social class differences in child rearing that give the middle-class child a significant cognitive and motivational advantage by the time schooling begins (e.g., Bloom, 1976; DiMaggio, 1982; Douglas, 1964). Second, these initial differences are introduced into a social organization of schooling that channels punishments toward lower-performing students. Third, this channeling should result in an ascriptively biased distribution of educational attainment. Indeed, recent findings suggest that the decision to drop out of high school can be predicted accurately by students' elementary school reading performance (Hess and Greer, 1987).

TOLERANCE FOR EDUCATION

Students' status origins should affect educational attainment not only by virtue of academic punishments and rewards, but also as a result of tolerance for education. Tolerance for education denotes a student's capacity to adapt to the psychological stresses induced by schoolwork (Bielby, 1981, p. 11).

Just as the definition of the educational situation presumably includes a summary of experiences of academic punishment and reward, so it also presumably includes a summary assessment of capacity to adapt to academic stress. We assume that a student's relative degree of past adaptation (e.g., more or less successful completion of a demanding course or program) induces the expectation of a similar degree of adaptation in the future. This expectation should take into account both the past level of academic demand and self-assessed capacity to cope with this demand, so that the expectation would be adjusted up or down according to the anticipated difficulty of further studies.

Students should discount the value of the punishment-reward ratio according to their anticipated adaptive capacity. Thus we predict that the higher a student's tolerance for education, the weaker the negative effects of expected academic punishment on students' framing decisions and the stronger the positive effects of expected academic rewards.

The likely sources of tolerance for education are socially ordered in ways that should produce higher tolerance the higher a student's status origins are. These sources are to be found in group and interpersonal affiliations and in instrumental calculations about the future. We shall turn now to three significant examples.

First, as students progress through the school grades, they make increasingly frequent, realistic calculations about the relationship between schooling and adult social destinations (primarily occupational and marital). Given our rational actor assumption, we expect that the higher the value of the material or social goods to which a student aspires and the stronger the perceived effect of education on their realization, the higher the student's tolerance for education. In other words, we are proposing a reciprocal relationship between academic performance and educational and postschool aspirations, in which these aspirations reinforce performance, just as they are reinforced by performance via the definition of the educational situation.

Second, students may acquire extracurricular memberships and interpersonal ties with fellow students or teachers that provide opportunities for collective and interpersonal identifications and consequent commitments that reinforce the propensity to continue in school or to undertake demanding studies. These commitments, in turn, should increase students' capacities to adapt to the punishing aspects of academic work.

The relationship between affiliations and tolerance for education should be more problematic in the upper than in the lower school grades. From Durkheim's (1961) analysis of the primary school classroom, it follows that this class itself has binding, affirmative effects on students, fostering an identification with the class that tends to generalize to academic tasks and performance. As the social structure of higher school grades differentiates, separating the academic from the nonacademic and the more academically advanced and demanding from the less, this generalization effect should become less secure. Students then can find avenues of collective and interpersonal identification in school that have very little to do with course work and study (compare Coleman, 1961).

Whatever the normative content of a student's affiliations, we expect that the more numerous these affiliations and the stronger the student's commitment to them, the greater the student's tolerance for education. However, unless the affiliation is either coercively or voluntaristically linked to substantive school achievement (e.g., grade point minima for participation in varsity athletics or the self-selection of abler students to staff school publications), students are not likely to discount the punishment-reward ratio very heavily. Then, the affiliation effect should be short term, probably restricted to the timing of dropping out.

When the linkage of affiliation and achievement has been effected, the discounting should be heavier because the reward value of academic work has moved toward the center of the student's social world in school. This phenomenon may account for the "common school effect" described by Coleman, Hoffer, and Kilgore (1982) and for the relative uniformity of academic outcomes documented by Bryk et al. (1984), in each case for Roman Catholic high schools.

Interpersonal networks and extracurricular groups are arenas not only for the formation of commitments, but also for gaining and losing reputations. Reputations in prospect are likely to have substantial motivating effects on what students do, while reputations gained are likely to affect students' behavior by virtue of self-evaluation and others' expectations. When a student's in-school affiliations provide opportunities for reputational gains or losses that are based proportionally on academic achievment, they should increase the student's willingness to endure the punishing aspects of school work.

Finally, interpersonal ties are sources of affective support and channels of interpersonal influence. Because of their potential significance as sources of affective support, interpersonal ties probably have stronger effects than group affiliations per se on tolerance for education. Ties to teachers and achievement-oriented peers integrate affectivity and performance and thereby should provide social support that reinforces a student's predilection toward hard work and further schooling (Blau and Duncan, 1967, pp. 296). They also are channels for interpersonal influence that encourages the student to do well academically.

Thus we would expect that the more extensive, cohesive, and normatively consistent a student's network of peer and teacher ties, the greater the positive effect on a student's tolerance for education. By contrast, if a student has strong ties to school friends who themselves do not value educational attainment, the student may stay in school for a time to enjoy the friendship, but student and friends alike will probably leave school as soon as it is practicable to do so.

Third, some schools are characterized by an ethos or tradition that is more than ordinarily focused on educational attainment and by such collective representations as prize days and academic assemblies that reinforce the tradition and bind students to it. Schools with distinctive missions or with access to a distinctive occupational field or clientele often have this character—for example, select private schools (Cookson and Persell, 1985; Weinberg, 1967; Wilkinson, 1964) parochial schools (Bryk et al., 1984), and professional schools and programs (Meyer, 1970). Identification with such a school tends to heighten tolerance for education for both consummatory and instrumental reasons—for example, high stress, which serves as a badge of elite student status, or academic rigor, which provides a prelude to elite adult standing. Note that this same argument can be made about the identification of students with tracks or other distinctive programs within schools.

In each of these examples, the tolerance-influencing factor should be correlated with students' status origins. Hence, the higher a student's status origins, the heavier the probable discounting of the punishment-reward ratio. Certain of these correlations should arise from the differing life circumstances of the social strata (sources exogenous to school). Thus there is substantial evidence that students' assessments of their occupational prospects are powerful covariates of family social class (Kerckhoff, 1974; Sewell and Hauser, 1975, 1980). Other correlations with status origins may arise from ascriptive preselection to schools or curricula. The odds of encountering academically supportive school affiliations and social ties are a function of such preselection (Alexander and Campbell, 1964; Cohen, 1983; Hallinan and Sorensen, 1985; Rosenbaum, 1976). We lack evidence concerning such effects on the chances of encountering a strong academic school tradition, but a similar selection bias probably obtains.

To sum up our argument so far, our theory elaborates a significant relationship between students' cumulative academic performance and their eventual educational attainments. For the United States, we have postulated the duration and academic demand level of students' enrollment as a strong function of student choice. Accordingly, a student's educational attainment trajectory must be understood as an outcome of how the student defines the educational situation when he or she makes framing decisions. We have identified two key components of the definition of the educational situation: (1) the ratio of punishments and rewards averaged over a student's cumulative experience of schooling and (2) tolerance for education (the capacity to adapt to the stresses of academic work). We expect the probability of students' prolonging their education or enrolling in demanding schools or curricula to fall as the average punishment-reward ratio rises or as tolerance for education declines.

This analysis of the social psychology of students' framing decisions explains how initial individual differences of cognitive capacity and motivation are translated into later differences of educational attainment. This explanation is predicated on two social organizational condi-

tions in schools. The first condition is a social organization of academic punishment and reward that directs more punishments and fewer rewards to those students whose academic performance is low relative to that of fellow students. As a result, status-linked performance differences lead to ascriptive biases in later distributions of educational attainment. We have discussed this condition, noting how a positive relationship between status origins and tolerance for education and a negative relationship between status origins and school performance foster the educational mediation of status inheritance.

The second condition, to which we shall turn next, is the social organization of opportunities to learn. These opportunities are structured as a sequentially contingent chain that allocates opportunities to students in accordance with prior academic performance. As a result, early associations between children's social origins and their academic capabilities and motivation have cumulative effects on their academic performance and attendant punishments and rewards. The existence of this opportunity chain makes it hard to modify students' relative academic standing and, in turn, alter the relative amounts of academic punishments and rewards that they receive. Hence, it has strong implications for the origins-performance relationship.

OPPORTUNITIES TO LEARN

A few sociologists of education, reviving the Durkheimian tradition, have begun studies of the social organization of instruction in relation to the provision of learning opportunities. (See, especially, Barr and Dreeben, 1983, and Hallinan and Sorensen, 1983, 1985. A microeconomic analysis of the instructional process in classrooms by Thomas, 1977, also is of interest.) Hallinan and Sorensen (1985) reminded us that schools cannot teach and students cannot learn in school what they have not encountered in class or in their texts and other instructional materials. From the premise that exposure varies among schools, teachers, and classrooms, they inferred that the amount of exposure, calculated subject by subject, is a measure of what students might learn in school. Hallinan and Sorensen called this quantity "opportunities for learning."

Because earlier learning sets a foundation for later learning, Hallinan and Sorensen reasoned that capacity to exploit present learning opportunities depends on earlier opportunities and what was done with them (compare Thomas, 1977). These cumulative learning effects initially may be quite generalized, as in the early acquisition of language and number skills. Later, they may be more confined to sequentially ordered subject matters like mathematics or physics.

In virtually all American elementary and high schools, instructional resources (e.g., teachers' skills, materials, and curriculum content) are distributed across ability groups and tracks so that learning opportunities are a positive function of the ability level of the students in the group or track (Heyns, 1974; Rosenbaum, 1976). Consequently, by virtue of the postulated cumulative effect of academic performance on further exploitation of learning opportunities, grouping and tracking are prime sources of ascriptive biases in learning. Note that this effect would occur even if, in the later grades, school resources, social relations, and instruction were distributed in a status-neutral way.

Sorensen and Hallinan (1986) have documented that in elementary school classrooms, high-ability groups not only afford more opportunities to learn than low-ability groups, but also are characterized by greater use of these opportunities. As they argue, this difference may arise from differences in pupils' average prior learning, their average academic effort, or the effectiveness with which they are taught. Gamoran (1986) has shown that differences of instructional effectiveness help explain why ability groups differ in the rate at which pupils learn what they are taught. Moreover, Dreeben and Gamoran (1986) have reported a substantial correlation of race and socioeconomic status with the reading achievement of a sample of first graders. They have shown that with academic aptitude controlled, these relationships are substantially accounted for by variation in reading instruction in ability groups of differing level.

Ability groups and tracks are structured in a way that reduces the likelihood that students, once assigned to one or another of these pathways, will be reassigned, even if official school policy allows such movement. A portion of this immobility can be attributed to curricular content, especially in the high school, where subject matter sequences are likely to make it hard to move from less to more advanced tracks. To make such a move would require the student to backtrack too far into subject matter if, as almost everyone prefers, the student is to graduate "on time."

Downward mobility also is difficult because of constraints produced by organizational practice. Once resources are distributed among groups or tracks, there is an inertial presumption against their redistribution. This redistribu-

tion is a cost to the elementary school teacher and to the staff of the tracked high school. In addition, because students compete with one another for the limited places in a group or a track, in order to a student to move down, another student usually must move up. However, unless the performance criteria that admit students to groups or tracks are made strictly relative, such neatly balanced movement between groups or tracks may not be possible. Indeed, in an ethnographic study of elementary school classrooms, Eder (1981) found that teachers are more likely to adjust their judgments of students' performance than they are to move them from one ability group to another.

As a result, Sorensen (1987) argued that instructional grouping and tracking create a system of contingent vacancies in which early assignments become crucial for students' educational careers. Despite the egalitarian policies of American schools, elementary school teachers tend to group students at the year's start on the basis of information supplied by the previous teacher (Eder, 1981), and in high schools (Cicourel and Kitsuse, 1963) teachers' and counselors' advice to students more often than not works to stabilize track placements, even when official policy allows students to elect their own tracks. Thus Sorensen (1987, p. 13) describes an educational system as

> a promotion system where more and more students are left without promotion chances as they progress . . . in a manner similar to how internal labor market systems leave more and more employees without further promotion chances as they age.

Under these circumstances, we would expect early associations between status origins and capacity for school work to have cumulative, strengthening consequences for learning and academic performance. Orfield (1984) and Paul (1987) documented such cumulative biases in the educational histories of urban Black and Hispanic youth. The primary school classroom is undoubtedly the seedbed for such patterns of ascriptively biased educational attainment.

To sum up our theory of educational status allocation, we have proposed that as national school curricula become less intensively differentiated, students become more active in determining and making the decisions that frame their educational trajectories. Hence, a theory that explains variation in distributions of educational achievement must be specific to the institutional (i.e., curricular) conditions of national educational systems.

Turning to the comparatively undifferentiated case of the United States, we have proposed mechanisms embedded in the social organization of the school that should make students' decisions about academic effort and persistence a strong function of their status origins, as a consequence of family socialization and the cumulative effects of opportunities to learn in school, and another tendency for tolerance for education to vary directly with status origins.

Cross-National Evidence on Educational Attainment

Although research outside the United States does not allow us to press very far into the comparative, cross-national analysis of educational attainment, it provides a useful perspective on the U.S. findings. The bulk of this work has been conducted in Great Britain and on the Continent, with respect especially to effects of streaming on learning rates and labor force entry.

In two important aspects, the findings are similar to those obtained for educational attainment in the United States. First, both subject-matter learning and more general cognitive development evidently occur more rapidly and lead to more complex outcomes, the more academically oriented the stream in which a student is located (Fagerlind, 1975; Rutter et al., 1979). Second, schooling apparently mediates status inheritance, by virtue of cumulative ascriptive biases in the distribution of opportunities to learn (Boudon, 1974; Hope, 1984; Rutter et al., 1979). If these findings give an accurate picture of educational attainment in developed societies, then we must conclude that in none have the schools approached the institutional autonomy that Sorokin envisioned for them.

However, writing some twenty years ago, Duncan (1968) examined the United States and concluded that the schools were serving as both mediators of status inheritence and springboards of occupational mobility. Research by Hope (1984) offers similar evidence for Scotland. In a longitudinal study, he traced the school histories, cognitive achievement, and occupational destinations of a large sample of adults drawn from a Scottish birth cohort. Although the findings document substantial status inheritance via schooling, they also show that the schools produced substantial learning and mobility effects that were independent of students' status origins. The Scottish schools do

appear to have gained a measure of the autonomy that Sorokin envisioned. This autonomy evidently resulted from a state policy that was designed explicitly to remove socioeconomic barriers to secondary school and university attendance, within an allocative system that maintained strong stress on the recognition of academic merit.

Duncan's and Hope's findings tell us that any social mobility regime will contain elements of both status inheritance and institutionally autonomous selection and allocation. Evidence of status inheritance through education need not preclude autonomous selection and allocation by schools. Hope makes the cogent point that teachers' professional standards and judgments may dominate the allocation and evaluation of students, even when there is a strong ascriptive bias in educational attainment. Our earlier theoretical argument led to this same conclusion.

This point amplifies Sorokin's treatment of the institutional autonomy of the schools. For Sorokin, schools gain autonomy to the degree that family influence on the allocation of educational opportunities weakens, and teachers' own standards come to the fore in testing and screening pupils. He left unclear the degree to which the basis of autonomy is structural or normative. It follows from Hope's argument that the institutional autonomy of the schools is strengthened normatively to the degree that the standards used to evaluate students are universalistic, even when the allocation of students to schools or curricula is ascriptively neutral.

Perhaps these standards are more often universalistic, the more structurally autonomous the schools' evaluative and allocative procedures (e.g., control of these procedures by a national ministry rather than a local school board). Nevertheless, whatever the structure of control, it is easy to imagine schools in which teachers encourage not only the ablest of their students, but also those whose bearing and breeding seem to fit them for adult success, while at the same time vigorously defending the sanctity of their professional, decision-making domain. Here, we would find a close fit between students' status origins and teachers' allocation of learning opportunities.

Comparative Educational Politics

Effective policymaking and implementation require one to understand not only the issues but also the policy processes. In the educational realm, the principal statements on these political processes remain those of Weber and Durkheim. Both gave a central place to interest group action in the emerging national state. However, while Weber pointed to interest group competition as the principal contemporary determinant of policy outcomes, Durkheim rested his hopes for modern educational reform on disinterested decisions by the professionals in a powerful state educational bureaucracy.

To address topics of this kind, we need comparative studies of educational policymaking, focused on relations between educational organizations, interest groups, political parties, and governments. Only recently have such questions appeared on the agenda of the sociology of education. This work suggests that national systems of education in the West have indeed been objects of fairly intense interest group competition. Elites for the most part have pressed for system structures that would enhance the educational life chances of their own offspring and reduce the educational life chances of the offspring of others. They have resisted the expansion of common education and have sought highly stratified (e.g., intensively streamed) arrangements for secondary and higher education. Workers' organizations and professional educators have been especially active opponents of these policies, seeking to expand common school enrollments and opportunities for more advanced education.

However, the policies that have shaped national educational systems have by no means been a simple expression of dominant interests. Interest group action has been channeled and expressed in different ways in differently structured polities. Evidently, national systems of education tend to acquire a more differentiated form, the more varied and similar in power the interest groups involved in educational politics. Decentralized polities may be more accessible to less powerful interest groups than those political systems that are more markedly hierarchical. When parties cross class lines (e.g., parties based on ethnic or religious divisions), class action to affect system structure tends to be muted, fostering mass enrollment. (See Archer, 1984, on systems of common education and Clark, 1983, on university systems. Rubinson, 1986, gives particular attention to the role of political structure in forming national educational systems.)

This work, much of it based on careful historical scholarship, has revived study of the formation, persistence, and change of national systems of education. This work gains added point if, as we have suggested, such formal properties of national systems as their curricular differentiation affect the distribution of opportunities to learn, the way framing decisions are made, and, consequently, the ways in which education affects status inheritance and mobility.

Conclusion

We can expect further sociological studies of education to develop in close connection with the movement of social policy. Indeed, a key to good sociology is not to sunder this connection but to bring sociological imagination to work on central problems of social practice. The evident tendency for ascriptively based intracohort differences of academic competence, performance, and plans to be maintained and even to grow during the course of schooling raises a vexing policy issue for a liberal society. In any population, the distribution of cognitive endowment probably is substantially independent of status origins. A large portion of the biasing effects of status origins appears to be transmitted by mechanisms that in principle are susceptible to control by educators—for example, the balance of rewards and punishments in classroom life.

To take the United States as a case in point, one would expect that after so many years of public and professional debate about equality of educational opportunity, American elementary and high schools would have taken effective steps against ascriptive biases in educational opportunities and achievement. Instead, American common schools seemingly transmit these biases, strengthening them in the process. The reasons for this failure are many, but in part they reside in the failure of social scientists to respond to this policy issue with sustained theoretical imagination.

The literature has moved some distance toward specifying mechanisms of educational attainment and educationally mediated status inheritance, but much remains to be done. We require more elaborated models, informed by a social theory of school learning, that show what happens in school to create and maintain status-linked patterns of punishment and reward, learning, motivation, and movement through student careers. Sorensen and Hallinan (1986) and Sorensen (1987) have pointed us in an interesting theoretical direction toward work that will further specify these mechanisms and trace their precise effects on academic attainment.

Such studies of school learning and educational attainment should be complemented by historical and contemporary comparative work on the rise and change of national educational systems. These comparative studies would lay the groundwork for society-specific theories of educational status attainment. Then it would be possible to trace consequences of variation or change of system form for the rise or decline of educationally mediated status inheritance. By broadening and deepening our understanding of the nature and action of the institution of education, this research program would increase our capacity to make wise, effective policy in pursuit of an equitable distribution of educational life chances.

REFERENCES

Alexander, C. N. and E. Q. Campbell. 1964. "Peer Influence on Adolescent Educational Aspirations and Attainments." *American Sociological Review* 29:568-575.

Alexander, K. L. and M. Cook. 1982. "Curricula and Coursework." *American Sociological Review* 47:626-640.

———— and E. L. McDill. 1978. "Curriculum Tracking and Educational Stratification: Some Further Evidence." *American Sociological Review* 43:47-66.

Alexander, K. L. and B. K. Eckland. 1974. "Sex Differences in the Educational Attainment Process." *American Sociological Review* 39:668-682.

———— 1975. "Contextual Effects in the High School Attainment Process." *American Sociological Review* 40:402-416.

———— 1975. "The Wisconsin Model of Socioeconomic Achievement: A Replication." *American Journal of Sociology* 41:324-363.

Alexander, K. L., S. Holupka, and A. M. Pallas. 1987. "Social Background and Academic Determinants of Two-year vs. Four-year College Attendance: Evidence from Two Cohorts a Decade Apart." *American Journal of Education* 96:56-80.

Alexander, K. L. and E. L. McDill. 1976. "Selection and Allocation within Schools." *American Sociological Review* 41:963-980.

Alexander, K. L. and A. M. Pallas. 1984. "Curricular Reform and School Performance." *American Journal of Education* 92:391-420.

Altbach, P. G., R. F. Arnove, and G. P. Kelly, eds. 1982. *Comparative Education*. New York: Macmillan.

Alwin, D. F. 1976. "Socioeconomic Background, Colleges, and Postsecondary Achievement." Pp. 343-372 in *Schooling and Achievement in American Society*, edited by W. H. Sewell, R. M. Hauser, and D. L. Featherman. New York: Academic Press.

———— 1984. "Trends in Parental Socialization Values: Detroit, 1958-1963." *American Journal of Sociology* 90:359-382.

———— and L. B. Otto. 1977. "High School Context Effects on Aspirations." *American Sociological Review* 50:259-273.

Alwin, D. F. and A. Thornton. 1984. "Family Origins and the Schooling Process: Early Versus Late Influence of Parental Characteristics." *American Sociological Review* 49:784-802.

Archer, M. S. 1984. *Social Origins of Educational Systems*. Beverly Hills, CA: Sage.

Bain, R. K. and J. G. Anderson. 1974. "School Context and Peer Influences on Educational Plans of Adolescents." *Review of Educational Research* 44:429-445.

Barker Lunn, J. C. 1970. *Streaming in the Primary School*. London: National Foundation for Educational Research in England and Wales.

Barr, R. and R. Dreeben. 1983. *How Schools Work*. Chicago: University of Chicago Press.

Becker, G. S. 1964. *Human Capital*. New York: Columbia.

Ben-David, J. 1972. *American Higher Education*. New York: McGraw-Hill.

Bidwell, C. E. 1965. "The School as a Formal Organization" Pp. 972-1022 in *Handbook of Organizations*. J. G. March, ed. Chicago: Rand McNally.

———— 1970. "Students and Schools: Observations on Trust in Client-serving Organizations." Pp. 37-70 in *Organizations and Clients*, edited by W. R. Rosengren and M. Lefton. Columbus, OH: Merrill.

Bielby, W. T. 1981. "Models of Status Attainment." *Research in Social Stratification and Mobility* 1:3-26.

Blau, P. M. and O. D. Duncan. 1967. *The American Occupational Structure*. New York: John Wiley.

Bloom, B. S. 1976. *Human Characteristics and School Learning*. New York: McGraw-Hill.

Borg, W. 1965. "Ability Grouping in the Public Schools." *Journal of Experimental Education* 34:1-31.

Bossert, S. T. 1979. *Tasks and Social Relationships in Classrooms*. New York: Cambridge University Press.

Boudon, R. 1974. *Education, Opportunity, and Social Inequality*. New York: John Wiley.

Bourdieu, P. 1977. "Cultural Reproduction and Social Reproduction." Pp. 487-511 in *Power and Ideology in Education*, edited by J. Karabel and A. H. Halsey. New York; Oxford University Press.

———— and J.-C. Passeron. 1979. *The Inheritors*. Chicago: University of Chicago Press.

Bowles, S. and H. Gintis. 1976. *Schooling in Capitalist America*. New York: Basic Books.

Bowman, M. J. 1969. "Economics of Education." *Review of Educational Research* 39:641-670.

Brinton, M. C. 1987. "Gender Stratification and Human Capital Development Systems." Department of Sociology, University of Chicago.

Bryk, A. S., P. B. Holland, V. E. Lee, and R. A. Carriedo. 1984. *Effective Catholic Schools: An Exploration*. Washington, DC: National Catholic Education Association.

Cicourel, A. V. and J. I. Kitsuse. 1963. *The Educational Decision-Makers*. Indianapolis: Bobbs-Merrill.

Clark, B. R. 1983. *The Higher Education System*. Berkeley: University of California Press.

_____ , ed. 1985. *The School and the University*. Berkeley: University of California Press.

Cohen, J. 1983. "Peer Influence on College Aspirations with Initial Aspirations Controlled." *American Sociological Review* 48:728-734.

Coleman, J. S. 1961. *The Adolescent Society*. Glencoe, IL: Free Press.

_____ , E. Q. Campbell C. J. Hobson, J. McPartland, A. J. Mood, F. D. Weinfeld, and R. L. York. 1966. *Equality of Educational Opportunity*. Washington, DC: Government Printing Office.

Coleman, J. S., T. Hoffer, and S. Kilgore. 1982. *High School Achievement: Public, Catholic, and Other Private Schools Compared*. New York: Basic Books.

Collins, R. 1979. *The Credential Society*. New York: Academic.

Cookson, P. W. and C. H. Persell. 1985. *Preparing for Power: America's Elite Boarding Schools*. New York: Basic Books.

Cusick, P. A. 1983. *The Egalitarian Ideal and the American Public School*. New York: Longman.

Dahloff, U. 1971. *Ability Grouping, Content Validity, and Curriculum Process Analysis*. New York: Teachers College Press.

Davis, J. S. 1966. "The Campus as a Frog Pond: An Application of the Theory of Relative Deprivation to Career Decisions of College Men." *American Journal of Sociology* 72:17-31.

Demo, D. H. and R. C. Savin-Williams. 1983. "Early Adolescent Self-esteem as a Function of Social Class: Rosenberg and Pearlin Revisited." *American Journal of Sociology* 88:763-774.

Dewey, J. 1900. *The School and Society*. Chicago: University of Chicago Press.

DiMaggio, P. 1982. "Cultural Capital and School Success: The Impact of Status Culture Participation on the Grades of U.S. High School Students." *American Sociological Review* 47: 189-201.

Dore, R. P. 1976. *The Diploma Disease*. Berkeley: University of California Press.

Douglas, J.W.B. 1964. *The Home and the School*. London: Macgibbon and Kee.

Dreeben, R. 1968. *On What Is Learned in School*. Reading, MA: Addison-Wesley.

_____ and A. Gamoran. 1986. "Race, Instruction, and Learning." *American Sociological Review* 51:660-669.

Duncan, O. D. 1968. "Ability and Achievement." *Eugenics Quarterly* 15:1-11.

Duncan, O. D. and R. W. Hodge. 1963. "Education and Occupational Mobility: A Regression Analysis." *American Journal of Sociology* 68: 629-644.

Durkheim, E. 1956. *Education and Sociology*. Glencoe, IL: Free Press. (Original works written 1903, 1906, 1911)

_____ 1961. *Moral Education*. Glencoe, IL: Free Press. (Original work published 1925)

_____ 1977. *The Evolution of Educational Thought*. London: Routledge & Kegan Paul. (Original work published 1938)

Eckland, B. 1967. "Genetics and Sociology: A Reconsideration." *American Sociological Review* 32: 173-194.

Eder, D. 1981. "Ability Grouping as a Self-fulfilling Prophecy." *Sociology of Education* 54:151-161.

Fagerlind, I. 1975. *Formal Education and Adult Earnings*. Stockholm: Almqvist and Wiksell.

Faris, E. 1928. "The Sociologist and the Educator." *American Journal of Sociology* 33:796-801.

Featherman, D. L. and R. M. Hauser. 1978. *Opportunity and Change*. New York: Academic.

Floud, J. E., A. H. Halsey, and F. M. Martin. 1957. *Social Class and Educational Opportunity*. London: Heinemann.

Gamoran, A. 1986. "Instructional and Institutional Effects of Ability Grouping." *Sociology of Education* 59:185-198.

_____ 1987. "The Stratification of High School Learning Opportunities." *Sociology of Education* 60:135-155.

Gordon, C. W. 1957. *The Social System of the High School*. Glencoe, IL: Free Press.

Gross, N., W. S. Mason, and A. W. McEachern. 1958. *Explorations in Role Analysis*. New York: John Wiley.

Hallinan, M. and A. B. Sorensen. 1983. "The Formation and Stability of Instructional Groups." *American Sociological Review* 48:838-851.

_____ 1985. "Ability Grouping and Student Friendships." *American Educational Research Journal* 22:485-499.

Hauser, R. B. 1971. *Socioeconomic Background and Educational Performance*. Washington, DC: Rose Monograph Series, American Sociological Association.

Hauser, R. M. and D. L. Featherman. 1976. "Equality of Schooling." *Sociology of Education* 49: 99-120.

Hauser, R. M. and P. A. Mossel. 1985. "Fraternal Resemblance in Educational Attainment and Occupational Status." *American Journal of Sociology* 91:650-673.

Hauser, R. M., W. H. Sewell, and D. F. Alwin. 1976. "High School Effects on Achievement." Pp. 309-341 in *Schooling and Achievement in American Society*, edited by W. H. Sewell, R. M. Hauser, and D. L. Featherman. New York: Academic.

Hess, G. A., Jr. and J. L. Greer. 1987. *Bending the Twig: The Elementary Years and Dropout Rates in the Chicago Public Schools*. Chicago: Chicago Panel on Public School Policy and Finance.

Heyns, B. 1974. "Selection and Stratification in Schools." *American Journal of Sociology* 79: 1434-1451.

Hilton, T. L. and H. Rhett. 1973. *Final Report: The Base-Year Study of the Longitudinal Study of the High School Class of 1972*. Princeton, NJ: Educational Testing Service.

Hollingshead, A. B. 1949. *Elmtown's Youth*. New York: John Wiley.

Hope, K. 1984. *As Others See Us: Schooling and Social Mobility in Scotland and the United States*. Cambridge, England: Cambridge University Press.

Hout, M. and W. R. Morgan. 1975. "Race and Sex Variations in the Causes of the Expected Attainments of High School Seniors." *American Journal of Sociology* 81:342-364.

Hyman, H. H., C. R. Wright, and J. S. Reed. 1975. *The Enduring Effects of Education*. Chicago: University of Chicago Press.

Jencks, C., J. Crouse, and P. Mueser. 1983. "The Wisconsin Model of Status Attainment: A National Replication with Improved Measures of Ability and Aspiration." *Sociology of Education* 56:3-19.

Jencks, C., M. Smith, H. Acland, M. J. Bane, D. Cohen, H. Gintis, B. Heyns, and S. Michelson. 1972. *Inequality*. New York: Basic Books.

Jencks, C., S. Bartlett, M. Corcoran, J. Crouse, D. Eaglesfield, G. Jackson, K. McClelland, P. Mueser, M. Olneck, J. Schwartz, S. Ward, and J. Williams. 1979. *Who Gets Ahead?* New York: Basic Books.

Jennings, M. K. 1981. *Generations and Politics: A Panel Study of Young Adults and Their Parents*. Princeton, NJ: Princeton University Press.

Kandel, D. B. 1978. "Homophily, Selection, and Socialization in Adolescent Friendship." *American Journal of Sociology* 84:427-436.

Kerckhoff, A. C. 1974. "Stratification Processes and Outcomes in England and the U.S." *American Sociological Review* 39:789-801.

Lee, V. E. and A. S. Bryk. 1987. "Curriculum Tracking as Mediating the Social Distribution of Achievement in Catholic and Public Secondary Schools." Working paper 87-01-02, Benton Center for Curriculum and Instruction, University of Chicago.

Lee, V. E. and R. B. Eckstrom. 1987. "Student Access to Guidance Counseling in High School." *American Educational Research Journal* 24:287-310.

Looker, E. D. and P. C. Pineo. 1983. "Social Psychological Variables and Their Relevance to the Status Attainment of Teenagers." *American Journal of Sociology* 88:1195-1219.

Lortie, D. C. 1975. *Schoolteacher*. Chicago: University of Chicago Press.

Marini, M. M. 1984. "Women's Educational Attainment and the Timing of Entry into Parenthood." *American Sociological Review* 49:491-511.

Matras, J. 1980. "Comparative Social Mobility." *Annual Review of Sociology* 6:401-431.

Meyer, J. W. 1970. "The Charter: Conditions of Diffuse Socialization in Schools." Pp. 564-578 in *Social Processes and Social Structures*, edited by W. R. Scott. New York: Holt, Rinehart, and Winston.

———— 1977. "The Effects of Education as an Institution." *American Journal of Sociology* 83:55-77.

Meyer, J. W., F. O. Ramirez, R. Rubinson, and J. Boli-Bennett. 1977. "The World Educational Revolution, 1950-1970." *Sociology of Education* 50:242-258.

Miller, K. A., M. L. Kohn, and C. Schooler. 1986. "Educational Self-direction and Personality." *American Sociological Review* 51:372-390.

Mincer, J. 1974. *Schooling, Experience, and Earnings*. New York: National Bureau of Economic Research.

Morgan, W. R., D. F. Alwin, and L. J. Griffin. 1979. "Social Origins, Parental Values, and the Transmission of Inequality." *American Journal of Sociology* 85:156-166.

Olneck, M. R. 1977. "On the Use of Sibling Data to Estimate Effects of Family Background, Cognitive Skills, and Schooling: Results from the Kalamazoo Brothers Study." Pp. 125-162 in *Kinometrics: Determinants of Socioeconomic Success Within and Between Families*, edited by P. Taubman. Amsterdam: North-Holland.

Orfield, G. 1984. *The Chicago Study of Access and Choice in Higher Education*. Chicago: Committee on Public Policy Studies, University of Chicago.

———— and F. Paul. 1988. "Patterns of Decline in Minority Access to Higher Education in Five Metropolitan Areas." *Educational Record* 69: 52-56.

Organisation for Economic Co-operation and Development. 1971. *Development of Higher Education, 1950-1967: Analytical Report*. Paris: OECD.

Parsons, T. 1959. "The School Class as a Social System." *Harvard Educational Review* 29:297-318.

Paul, F. 1987. *Declining Access to Educational Opportunities in Metropolitan Chicago, 1980-1985*. Chicago: Metropolitan Opportunity Project, University of Chicago.

Powell, A. G., E. Farrar, and D. K. Cohen. 1985. *The Shopping Mall High School: Winners and Losers in the Educational Marketplace*. Boston: Houghton Mifflin.

Rehberg, R. A. and E. R. Rosenthal. 1978. *Class and Merit in the American High School*. New York: Longman.

Robinson, R. V. and M. A. Garnier. 1985. "Class Reproduction among Men and Women in

France: Reproduction Theory on its Home Ground." *American Journal of Sociology* 91: 250-280.

Rohlen, T. P. 1983. *Japan's High Schools*. Berkeley: University of California Press.

Rosenbaum, J. E. 1976. *Making Inequality*. New York: John Wiley.

Rosenberg, M. I. and R. Simmons. 1972. *Black and White Self-Esteem: The Urban School Child*. Washington, DC: Rose Monograph Series, American Sociological Association.

Rubinson, R. 1986. "Class Formation, Politics, and Institutions: Schooling in the United States." *American Journal of Sociology* 92:519-548.

Rutter, M., B. Maughan, P. Mortimore, J. Ouston, and A. Smith. 1979. *Fifteen Thousand Hours: Secondary Schools and Their Effects on Children*. Cambridge: Harvard University Press.

Schultz, T. W. 1963. *The Economic Value of Education*. New York: Columbia University Press.

Sewell, W. H., R. M. Hauser, and W. C. Wolf. 1980. "Sex, Schooling, and Occupational Status." demic.

—————— 1976. "Causes and Consequences of Higher Education: Models of the Status Attainment Process." Pp. 9-27 in *Schooling and Achievement in American Society*, edited by W. H. Sewell, R. M. Hauser, and D. L. Featherman. New York: Academic Press.

—————— 1980. "The Wisconsin Longitudinal Study of Social and Psychological Factors in Aspirations and Achievements." Pp. 59-99 in *Longitudinal Perspectives on Educational Attainment*, edited by A. C. Kerckhoff. Greenwich, CT: JAI Press.

—————— and D. L. Featherman, eds. 1976. *Schooling and Achievement in American Society*. New York: Academic Press.

Sewell, W. H., R. M. Hauser, and W. C. Wolf. 1980. "Sex, schooling, and occupational status." *American Journal of Sociology* 86:551-583.

Small A. W. 1897. "Some Demands of Sociology upon Pedagogy." *American Journal of Sociology* 2:839-851.

Sorensen, A. B. 1987. "The Organizational Differentiation of Students in Schools as an Opportunity Structure." Pp. 103-129 in *Conceptualizations of School Organization and Schooling Processes*, edited by M. T. Hallinan. New York: Plenum.

—————— and M. T. Hallinan. 1986. "Effects of Ability Grouping on Growth in Academic Achievement." *American Educational Research Journal* 23:519-542.

Sorokin, P. A. 1927. *Social and Cultural Mobility*. New York: Harper.

Spenner, K. I. and D. L. Featherman. 1978. "Achievement Ambitions." *Annual Review of Sociology* 4:373-420.

Stember, C. H. 1961. *Education and Attitude Change*. New York: Institute of Human Relations Press.

Stinchcombe, A. L. 1964. *Rebellion in a High School*. Chicago: Quadrangle.

Stouffer, S. A. 1955. *Communism, Conformity, and Civil Liberties*. Garden City, NY: Doubleday.

Teichler, U. and B. C. Sanyal. 1982. *Higher Education and the Labor Market in the Federal Republic of Germany*. Paris: International Institute for Educational Planning, UNESCO.

Thomas, J. A. 1977. *Resource Allocation in Classrooms*. Final Report, Project No. 4-0794, National Institute of Education. Chicago: Department of Education, University of Chicago.

Thomas, W. I. 1923. *The Unadjusted Girl*. Boston: Little, Brown.

Trow, M. A. 1962. "The Democratization of Higher Education in America." *European Journal of Sociology* 3:231-262.

Trow, M. A. 1984. "The Analysis of Status." Pp. 132-164 in *Perspectives on Higher Education: Eight Disciplinary and Comparative Views*, edited by B. R. Clark. Berkeley, CA: University of California Press.

Trow, M. A. 1961. "The Second Transformation of American Secondary Education." *International Journal of Comparative Sociology* 2:144-166.

Turner, R. H. 1960. "Sponsored and Contest Mobility and the School System." *American Sociological Review* 25:855-867.

Vanfossen, B. E., J. D. Jones, and J. Z. Spade. 1987. "Curriculum Tracking and Status Maintenance." *Sociology of Education* 6104-6122.

Wallace, W. L. 1966. *Student Culture: Social Structure and Continuity in a Liberal Arts College*. Chicago: Aldine.

Waller, W. W. 1932. *The Sociology of Teaching*. New York: John Wiley.

Ward, L. F. 1883. *Dynamic Sociology*, vol. 2. New York: Appleton.

Warner, W. L., R. J. Havighurst, and M. B. Loeb. 1944. *Who Shall Be Educated?* New York: Harper.

Warner, W. L., M. Meeker, and K. Eells. 1949. *Social Class in America*. Chicago: Science Research Associates.

Weber, M. 1946. *The Theory of Social and Economic Organization*. Glencoe, IL: Free Press. (Original works published 1906, 1922)

Wexler, P. 1976. *The Sociology of Education: Beyond Equality*. Indianapolis: Bobbs-Merrill.

Weinberg, I. 1967. *The English Public Schools*. New York: Atherton.

Wilkinson, R. 1964. *Gentlemanly Power*. Oxford, England: Oxford University Press.

15
Sociology of Religion

ROBERT J. WUTHNOW

The fact that religion is one of the oldest, and yet one of the most dynamic, social institutions has made it a subject of enduring interest to sociologists. Virtually all of the discipline's founding fathers—Marx, Weber, Comte, Durkheim, Spencer, Simmel—devoted special attention to the changing role of religion in modern society. From their work have come many of the concepts and theoretical perspectives that continue to guide sociological investigations of religion. In addition, many contributions have been made by more recent scholars, including Talcott Parsons, Peter Berger, Clifford Geertz, Robert N. Bellah, Mary Douglas, Niklas Luhmann, Thomas Luckmann, Bryan Wilson, and others. Currently, the field displays much vitality, both in research projects and in theoretical ferment. Approximately 500 sociologists in the United States alone claim professional interest in it, with important work being done in a number of other countries as well; more than a hundred graduate departments offer training in the subject; three professional organizations are concerned with it (Society for the Scientific Study of Religion, Association for the Sociology of Religion, and Religious Research Association); and each year between two and three hundred articles on the topic are published in major sociology journals and in specialty journals, of which there are three in the United States and an equal number in Europe.[1] As the discipline has expanded, soci-

ology of religion has become more clearly differentiated as a separate subdiscipline; yet it continues to overlap intellectually with a number of other subdisciplines, including sociological theory, social psychology, collective behavior, formal organizations, and cultural change.

An extremely wide variety of problems presently occupies the interest of researchers trained in sociology of religion. Much research is currently devoted to practical problems facing religious organizations (e.g., membership, attendance, contributions, staffing, etc.). This research typically utilizes sociological methods of data collection and analysis, but its primary concern is generally not with the theoretical development of the discipline. Another research focus concerns the social history of contemporary religion. Often prompted by the emergence of religious movements and religious conflicts, it seeks to describe religious developments and interpret their potential significance for public affairs. Still another body of literature has been concerned with the development of theories relating religious systems to their social environments. It is this last body of literature with which the present survey is concerned.

Definitional Issues

Sociological definitions of religion seek to identify the religious phenomenon in the most general terms. Implicit in these definitions are assumptions about the relevance of social conditions to the understanding of religion. In addition, many point implicitly to the importance of religion as a universal, or nearly universal, feature of human societies. Since religions vary widely in substantive teachings and practices, most sociological definitions attempt to identify religion in terms of *functions* rather than substance. Specifying the functions of religion necessarily requires some assumptions to be made about the character of society and, indeed, about human nature. For this reason, any definition of religion implies a certain theoretical perspective as well as a purely formal statement about religion itself.

One of the more systematic definitional treatments of religion defines it as "a system of symbols which acts to establish powerful, pervasive, and long-lasting moods and motivations in men by formulating conceptions of a general order of existence and clothing these conceptions with such an aura of factuality that the moods and motivations seem uniquely realistic" (Geertz, 1973, pp. 87). Other popular definitions focus on similar characteristics (see Bellah, 1970; Berger, 1969). In each case religion is conceptualized as a cultural system that provides meaning and purpose in some ultimate sense by creating a conception of reality that can be regarded as sacred, holistic, or transcendent. The operative feature of religion consists less of the moods generated, as Geertz's definition suggests, than of its all-encompassing vision of reality.

The theoretical framework underlying these conceptions includes an assumption that humans construct the realities in which they live through the use of symbols (see Berger and Luckmann, 1966). Symbols consist of objects, acts, utterances, and events that convey meaning; they are created, objectified, and internalized through social interaction. As a symbol system, therefore, religion is inevitably rooted in social processes. A further assumption on which this view of religion rests is that humans require a *meaningful* (i.e., orderly, comprehensible) reality, both in order to orient themselves psychologically to the world and in order to sustain social relationships. Meaning is understood to depend on the context in which a symbol occurs (just as the meaning of a word is given by the sentence in which it appears). Many of the meanings required in everyday life occur within relatively circumscribed spheres of relevance (e.g. cooking, commuting, lovemaking, etc.). However, these discrete spheres of relevance also require broader conceptualizations that integrate

them and provide them with meaning. Symbols are needed to integrate a person's biography, to provide answers to questions about meaning and purpose in life, and to interpret experiences of great anguish or great ecstasy that fall at the margins of everyday life. Thus it becomes possible to posit a level of symbolism dealing with reality at the most general (inclusive, holistic, transcendent) level. Symbols providing meaning at this level are identified as religion. These symbols may be organized into highly elaborate systems, such as Christianity and Judaism, or consist of relatively simple statements (e.g., about "luck"), rituals, and objects (e.g., a mandala, cross, or gesture of obeisance).

Research tends to support the assumptions on which functional definitions of religion are based. Questions about meaning and purpose in life appear to occupy virtually everyone's attention at one time or another. Meaning and purpose is derived from everyday life, especially work and family, but also depends on more encompassing symbol systems. The desire for coherence among different spheres of personal life is widespread and, for many, religion provides such a sense of coherence. Experiences falling outside the realm of everyday reality—suffering, grief, ecstasy—are particularly productive of questions about meaning and purpose and of religious interpretations. Research also indicates that the images evoked by such experiences include not only formal religious symbols but also an eclectic synthesis of symbols from nature, culture, and personal background that perform similar functions (reviewed in Wuthnow, 1986a).

Functional definitions of religion are sufficiently broad to encompass self-proclaimed religions (such as Christianity) and other symbol systems (such as Marxism or Freudianism) that may perform comparable functions. Objections to functional definitions indicate that they may be too broad and suggest defining religion more narrowly in terms of belief in the supernatural (e.g., Glock and Stark, 1965; Spiro, 1966). Substantive definitions, however, run into difficulty because many non-Western religions do not include conceptions of the supernatural; and even in the Western tradition, certain definitions of God have become difficult to associate with simple distinctions between the natural and supernatural (e.g., Tillich, 1963; Pannenberg, 1983; Peukert, 1984). The solution is to employ functional definitions that err on the side of being overly inclusive, but to specify additional parameters that permit one kind of religion to be distinguished from others (e.g., supernaturalistic/humanistic, dualistic/monistic, etc.).[2]

Inclusive definitions of religion obviously enlarge the scope of the sociology of religion. Until a few decades ago most work in this field dealt with organized religion; since then, much work continues to focus on organized religion, but increasing interest is evident in other topics as well, such as secular belief systems that provide transcendent frameworks of meaning, social movements that combine religious and political aims, moral codes, rituals of all kinds, and similarities between religious and nonreligious ideologies. As a result, much of the current work is of broader relevance than to those interested only in religion.

A wholesale reexamination of the idea of *secularization*, as advanced in the classical literature, has also been one of the significant consequences of conceptualizing religion in inclusive, functional terms. The assumption that religion in modern societies would gradually diminish in importance or else become less capable of influencing public life was once widely accepted; indeed, much of the research on religion was informed by the assumption that secularization was an inevitable trend. That assumption has now become a matter of dispute. Many continue to stress conflict between religion and modernization; others argue that the entire secularization thesis should be abandoned; still others suggest modifications that leave open the direction of religious change in specific historical periods.[3] Most evident is the need to rethink the relations between religion and the social environment. Modern religion is resilient and yet subject to cultural influences; it does not merely survive or decline, but adapts to its environment in complex ways.

The Social Environment

Some general points must first be made before turning to more substantive topics. In particular, the reasons for examining religion in relation to the social environment need to be understood. A convenient starting place is the observation that a great many varieties of religious expression have existed. This diversity makes comparisons possible that allow variations in religious expression to be related to variations in social environments. Further, it does not seem likely (intuitively or logically) that variations in religious patterns have been strictly random with respect to social environments. In other words, some correlations probably exist between kinds of religious patterns and different types of environments. Moreover, variations in religious patterns, while quite numerous, are still fewer than the number of variations conceivable (any number of new "religions" might be generated, for example, simply by developing a list of the major tenets of the world's religions and having a computer create random combinations of these tenets). Since only some variations among all conceivable variations have actually come into being, we can say that a process of "selection" has been at work.

Focusing on the correlations between religious patterns and social environments can be contrasted with an alternative approach to the sociology of religion. That approach emphasizes the meaning of religious symbols (e.g., Bellah, 1970, pp. 237-259). Instead of relating religious symbols to the social environment, it stresses the richness of religion itself. This approach is appealing since many of the classical approaches tried to "explain away" religion. Moreover, an adequate job of relating religious symbols to the social environment cannot begin until some understanding of the symbols themselves has been gained. Yet the quest to understand the meaning of religious symbols has proven difficult for several reasons (see Wuthnow, 1981a; Wuthnow et al., 1984). One is that the meaning of any religious symbol, located as it is in the subjective consciousness of the individual, is extremely difficult to elicit, sometimes even for the person holding it (e.g., what does "God" mean to you?). In short, subjective meanings are unobservables as far as sociology is concerned. Another problem is that these meanings are inevitably contingent on the situation in which they occur. Some progress may be made toward explicating the meanings present in one situation, but these meanings will be different in the next situation; indeed, the same person is likely to attribute slightly different meanings to a symbol in another context or at a different time. This is not an insuperable problem. It does imply, however, that a degree of generalization and simplification is always going to be present, despite the ideal of probing fully into the richness of symbolic meanings. And third, the meaning of religious symbols most obviously depends on the religious texts in which these symbols are embedded (or in comparable documents and folk traditions). Examining the relations among symbols in such texts is, of course, what theologians, ethnologists, and students of comparative religion have done for many years with great skill. Clearly sociologists can learn from these studies, but it may not be expedient for sociologists to attempt to duplicate what others with more specialized skills have already been doing. The special contribution that sociologists can make remains that of examining how social conditions affect religious patterns.

But this task is not one of explicating the meaning of religious symbols. It focuses instead on identifying conditions that contribute to the *meaningfulness* of symbols. In other words, the central question shifts from "what is the meaning of a symbol" to "what makes a symbol meaningful"? For instance, rather than pretending to know what the Virgin Mary means to everyone we study, we examine the social conditions under which people consider the Virgin Mary a meaningful symbol. Focusing on the meaning of a symbol forces the observer to pay primary attention to the subjective consciousness of individuals, whereas an emphasis on the conditions that make a symbol meaningful puts the symbol itself back in the spotlight. Research ceases to be a variant of social psychology and makes religious symbolism itself an object of investigation. In societies where religious conviction has become a deeply personal matter, the relation between religion and the individual can still be examined within this framework. But the relation is examined as an objective feature of symbolism—observable in utterances, texts, and rituals—rather than making claims about the hidden functioning of hearts and minds. This problem shift makes the sociology of religion both more promising and less pretentious. It becomes more promising because it seeks only conditions that make some observable symbol meaningful, where the evidence of something being meaningful is that it is used. That is, an assumption is made that symbols that are meaningful are more likely to be in use than are symbols that are not meaningful.[4] And research becomes less pretentious because it claims only to have specified some of these conditions, not to have discovered what the meaning of a religious symbol "really" is.

A number of factors can be identified that contribute to the meaningfulness of any religious symbol. For example, an utterance about religious beliefs is probably more likely to be meaningful if the speaker is assumed to be speaking sincerely or truthfully. Similarly, the meaningfulness of a religious utterance is likely to depend on what is actually true, and to an important extent on the language with which it is conveyed. Specifying social conditions that also make a contribution, therefore, does not "explain away" the power or truth of a religious symbol. The norms and values, patterns of interaction, institutions, distributions of power, and other social conditions that make a religious utterance seem more or less meaningful in a

given situation can obviously be investigated without engaging in any kind of sociological reductionism.

To focus on social conditions at all requires some a priori reason for expecting these conditions to bear on the presence, absence, or use of different religious symbols. That reason, most simply, has to do with the dependence of religious symbols on social resources. The development and perpetuation of any religious system requires social resources. These may range from self-evident resources such as the financial means necessary to support a professional clergy to less obvious resources such as the sacrifice of options entailed in the moral behavior of any individual who is committed to a religious creed (e.g., deciding not to have an abortion). In this sense, religious symbols are inevitably products of their social environments. They vary according to the amount and kinds of social, material, political, and cultural resources available. Religions have, in fact, often been conceived of as social systems that extract resources from their environments and that process these resources for their own maintenance and diffusion (for a recent example, see Luhmann, 1984, 1985). Religions define a "moral community" or set of moral obligations that reveal how persons should behave toward one another. Moral obligations are necessary components of social relations, especially where these relations cannot be controlled merely by force or fiduciary calculations. Religious symbolism assists in communicating what the nature of these obligations is (e.g., "love your neighbor as yourself"), thereby reducing some of the uncertainty that complicates social relations. It also provides legitimation that enhances the obligatory nature of moral commitments by making them seem inevitable, by attaching them to sacred values, and by articulating reasons commitment is desirable ("love others because God has loved you"). The nature of these obligations will depend to some extent on the distribution of social resources, will in turn affect this distribution, and will involve an expenditure of resources in the maintenance of symbolic communication.

The relation between a religious system and its environment is a dynamic relation. In extracting resources a religious system necessarily manifests dependence on its environment; yet in turning these resources to its own use, it may significantly modify the environment. The religious peace movement, for example, extracts resources from its environment, but also affects the environment by challenging prevailing views on nuclear weapons. What constitutes the religious system at issue and what constitutes its environment depends, of course, on the problem under consideration. For purposes of examining a specific religious symbol or ritual, the environment may include much of the religious community in which that symbol or ritual occurs. For the purpose of comparing religious organizations, part of the relevant environment is likely to consist of the resources already captured by these organizations at a previous time as well as the resources external to the organization. For determining the correlations between religious systems in a general sense and the societies in which they occur, it may be sufficient to focus mainly on broad patterns of resources in the larger societal milieu.

The importance of social resources becomes more readily apparent when it is seen that religious systems often engage in *competition* with one another for scarce resources. One of the reasons competition so frequently exists is that multiple religious movements often arise in response to a particular social stimulus and then compete with one another to develop a stable niche in the social environment. Other reasons include migration, cultural contact, and pluralistic religious traditions. In competing with one another, religious systems come face to face with the effects of the social environment. Specific environments, it appears, "select for" certain religious patterns and "select against" others.

Implicit in these considerations, therefore, is a dialectic framework that may be useful for discussing the relations between religious systems and the social environment. It consists of a "phase" or "moment" of *production* in which variations in religious systems are initiated, often by the emergence of religious movements; a competitive phase in which a process of *selection* reinforces the success of certain religious patterns and the failure of others; and a phase of *institutionalization* in which successful religious patterns develop features that make them less vulnerable to changes in their environments (see Wuthnow, 1981b). The three moments of this dialectic may occur in a temporal sequence or may be distinguishable only as analytic considerations. The following discussion deals first with the topic of religious movements, then with the selective relationships evident between several types of religious systems and the social environment, and finally with several aspects of religious institutionalization. In considering these topics, it will be possible not only to mention a number of the research interests that have been evident in the field in recent years but also to demonstrate some theoretical relationships among these interests that might otherwise be missed.

Religious Movements

If sociology has retreated from its more ambitious goal, evident in classical theory, of accounting for the initial appearance or "elementary forms" of religion, the discipline nevertheless manifests a continuing interest in the question of why, and under what circumstances, *variations* in religious forms are produced. In general, reasons for this interest can be traced to questions about the nature of social order and social change. The production of religious innovations represents an instance of cultural adaptation that may have important ramifications for societal values. More concretely, the production of variations in religious forms serves as a starting point for examining the interconnections between specific types of religious symbolism and characteristics of the social environment.

The question of how variations in religious forms are produced has been addressed most explicitly in the literature on religious movements. Surveys of this literature generally *follow* the discussion of more institutionalized types of religion, especially in presentations treating religious movements as examples of deviance from accepted religious patterns. For a dialectic treatment of the relations between religion and the social environment, however, the topic of religious production obviously precedes that of religious institutionalization. This topic has been the subject of much discussion, partly because of the large number of religious movements that have appeared in recent decades.[5] It is also a topic that sheds special light on the relations between religion and the social environment, since the environments in which religious movements are generated can be compared with others less productive of movement activity.

One of the more familiar approaches to religious movements focuses on relative deprivation (Glock, 1973; Schwartz, 1970; Stark and Bainbridge, 1980). Economic distress, downward social mobility, loneliness, anomie, and problems with physical health have all been identified as potential sources of religious movements. Religion allegedly appeals to the deprived by offering other-worldly substitutes for the ordinary gratifications they desire. Relative deprivation, and related approaches, such as those emphasizing social dislocation, have been criticized for casting religion in a purely negative light, portraying it as a coping device used by those who cannot get along in some more effective way (e.g., Bruce, 1983). Criticisms have also focused on the fact that relative deprivation elicits other responses than religious movements (alcoholism, deviance, passive withdrawal), and that the relation between relative deprivation and religious movements seems to be largely indeterminate in empirical cases (Hine, 1974; Wilson, 1982, pp. 115-118). A number of studies, consequently, have emphasized the importance of additional social conditions: the presence of a religious worldview predisposing the deprived to seek religious solutions, social networks and other means of recruitment or assembling, charismatic leadership, and broader resources such as organizational expertise, financial means, and access to communication channels (e.g., Beckford, 1975; Gerlach and Hine, 1970; Richardson, 1982; Zald, 1982). While most of these studies take issue with the relative deprivation approach, many can be interpreted as attempts to add specification to this approach by identifying factors likely to be important in translating the perception of deprivation into an organized religious movement. The thrust of this work has been less concerned with the relations between religious movements and the broader social environment than with the strategies used by religious movements themselves to mobilize resources. An appealing feature of this approach, of course, is that it highlights the importance of social movement activity itself in shaping beliefs and attitudes.

Another criticism of the relative deprivation approach, challenging it at a more fundamental level, is that it inherently emphasizes internal psychological states such as anxiety and other felt needs, and thus fails to provide a conception of the relation between religion and the social environment that is sufficiently *sociological*. As an alternative, it might be suggested that some insights from relative deprivation theory be retained, but that they be reconceptualized as part of the social order itself, rather than being treated simply as motivational factors. That is, religion might be understood as an ideological system with a distinctly social character, as opposed to whatever psychological functions it may perform for the individual. The basis for adopting this perspective is that religion, among other things, always contains propositions about moral obligations (see Bellah, 1973; Durkheim, 1915/1965). The character of these obligations is evident in the fact that religious propositions, depending on the

setting, are closely associated with patron-client relations, with loyalties to local communities, with groups' conceptions of themselves as a people or nation, with standards of interpersonal morality, and with conceptions of equity and justice (e.g., Eisenstadt and Roniger, 1980; Scott, 1977; Tipton, 1982). These propositions, clothed in conceptions of the sacred or divine, specify how social relations should be conducted, and therefore affect the nature of social exchange as well as the distribution of social resources. Conversely, insofar as ideological systems require social resources in order to be maintained, any disturbance of social resources that results in uncertainties about the nature of moral obligations is likely to result in some modification at the level of ideology.[6] As such, this perspective is concerned primarily with explaining the emergence of new variations in religious ideology, rather than the emergence of religious movements as social organizations, but it implicitly includes religious movements as the agents responsible for producing ideological variations. Several important observations follow from this line of analysis.

One is that disturbances in social resources need not lead directly to the production of alterations in religious ideology, nor are the disturbances that do necessarily the kind that result in feelings of deprivation on the part of the individual. Rather, disturbances in moral obligations—uncertainties in cultural definitions of the manner in which individuals and groups should relate to one another—appear to be the most likely sources of alterations in religious ideology. Moral obligations themselves bear some relation to the nature of social resources, but this relation is not strictly determined by those resources. Indeed, the role of moral obligations in many cases is to anticipate disturbances in social resources and to provide for the maintenance of social order in the presence of such disturbances. Research on peasant societies, for example, indicates that a "moral economy" is often present—a set of expectations about peasants' obligations to one another and about the reciprocal obligations between peasants and landlords (often dramatized ritually)—which buffers the community against recurrent subsistence crises (Scott, 1976). In these settings, the occurrence of a subsistence crisis would not necessarily be expected to result in new or unusual religious patterns. If, however, conditions were to change in such a way as to render inoperable or uncertain the system of moral obligations, then some degree of ideological effort would undoubtedly be expended to reconstruct, as it were, the nature of those obligations.

The intrusion of foreign powers into peasant economies, for example, has often been accompanied by an upsurge of novel religious activity because, from this perspective, local elites are drawn into external alliances that permanently alter their relations to the existing moral economy of peasant life (for examples, see Scott, 1977; Wuthnow, 1980).

In this example, some degree of subjective deprivation may well be experienced on the part of peasant clients who suffer a loss of patronage from local elites. Still, clients and patrons alike may experience the new conditions as a kind of liberation, or as a situation that poses new potential. Whether this is the case or not, the change of moral order effected at the local level may in fact present an opportunity in terms of its potential for ideological innovation. The disruption of established moral expectations creates a situation in which new symbols can be advanced as interpretations of what the moral order should include. The capacity to exploit these moments of opportunity will depend, of course, on the availability of symbolic leaders, their capacity to generate recruits, and the kind of cultural materials present from which to construct new interpretations. Disruptions of the moral economy in peasant societies, for example, have seemingly been more productive of millenarian religious movements than have disruptions of moral order among the urban proletariat—one reason being that folk beliefs, community rituals, and potential leaders remain more readily available in the peasant than in the proletarian setting. Other things being equal, religious movements are also more likely to emerge when whole collectivities are affected by changes in moral obligations than when individuals are subjected to uncertainties and risks solely as individuals or as family units.

An emphasis on moments of opportunity provided by uncertainties at the level of moral obligations requires no assumptions about individual anxieties or individual needs as the inspiration for religious innovation. Rather, it posits a requirement strictly at the social level for communication about the nature of moral expectations. It also posits that religious codes provide a means of dramatizing and clarifying such expectations. Religion creates, as it were, models of moral order that can be visualized and experimented with symbolically, enacted in ritual or in idealized religious communities, and implemented as a way of reconstructing social relations (see Comaroff, 1985). Accordingly, any ambiguity in moral obligations creates possibilities for innovative religious interpretations to be presented.

A second observation is that disruptions of the moral order generally elicit not one, but multiple ideological responses. The religious responses to changes in economic and political circumstances in the sixteenth century, for example, included not only Lutheranism and Calvinism but also myriad Erasmian, Arminian, and Anabaptist formulations, as well as counter-formulations within Roman Catholicism, and scattered episodes of mysticism and witchcraft. Similarly, the social disruption of the late 1960s in the United States was accompanied by "new religions" as varied as Zen and Synanon and by various syntheses and modifications in Christianity, Judaism, and quasi-religious disciplines such as Scientology. Multiple ideological responses occur partly because a disruption of the moral order, by definition, involves ambiguity—which evokes uncertainty as to which response may be most compelling. The presence of this uncertainty is especially likely to evoke multiple responses in situations characterized by a high degree of cultural, political, or economic diversity (e.g., Central Europe in the sixteenth century and the United States in the 1960s). In addition, multiple responses often result from the fact that the various entities that have been tied together by moral obligations may now find themselves separated and having to respond to different circumstances. Part of the diversity of responses in the sixteenth century, for example, can be attributed to the fact that the rising commercialization of Central Europe opened different types of opportunities for urban merchants, artisans, landlords, and peasants. Studies of other periods of religious innovation, such as the early nineteenth century in the United States, also point to the importance of rising differentiation among various economic and occupational strata (e.g., Johnson, 1978). Multiple responses are also generated by the fact that movements' initiatives often invite counter-initiatives. The moral order conceived by one set of actors is likely to structure resources in a way that other actors perceive as inequitable or threatening. The sheer opportunities provided by uncertainty in the moral order may lead individuals to consolidate forces in hopes of protecting these opportunities once an alternative vision begins to predominate. As a result, religious movements and countermovements frequently emerge in roughly the same contexts.

Another observation that follows from the foregoing is that the emergence of multiple ideological responses invites competition among the various movements associated with these responses. This means that religious movements, often from the beginning, are compelled to compete with one another for scarce resources (e.g., members, leaders, finances), and that some effort must be made to carve out a suitable niche that ensures access to resources and perpetuates the movement's ideology. It is often this competition that transforms previously diffuse religious sentiments into an articulated religious ideology. Tai's (1983) study of Vietnam, for example, demonstrates that Maitreyan millenarianism and communism emerged at about the same time, both responding to the opportunities provided by France's declining position as a colonial power in the years immediately prior to World War II, and each attempting to define a vision of the future in competition with the other. This example also illustrates another reason episodes of *multiple* ideologies are likely to emerge—namely, that competing movements themselves add to the environmental uncertainty that ideologies attempt to restructure.

The presence of multiple, competing religious movements means that efforts to typologize or categorize kinds of movements may have practical, as well as theoretical, implications. Such efforts have in fact resulted in a proliferation of typological schemes, differentiated partly by differing conceptual and theoretical purposes, but also differentiated by the fact of focusing on different periods of religious unrest or sets of religious responses, each of which is of course historically unique (e.g., Beckford, 1986; Robbins and Anthony, 1981; Wallis, 1984). But the fact that religious movements are related to one another not only in observers' typologies but also in the competitive reality of the social world means that modes of differentiation must be a part of the strategic ideology of any religious movement. Symbolic markers must be adopted that set each movement off from its competitors and that cause it to be identified with certain classes of religions rather than others. These are the materials that observers have sometimes made use of in constructing their own typologies. But the markers and classification schemes evident in religious movements' ideologies themselves remain a subject that has been little investigated. What appears probable is that these markers do not emerge simply as orientations toward the world in general, as some religious typologies imply, but as orientations aimed specifically at setting one movement off from its competitors. Gager (1983), for example, suggests that anti-Semitism emerged in early Christianity at least partly because Judaism posed a strong competitor to Christianity. In other settings, Anabaptists have taken their very name from opposing confessional

Protestants, as have Protestants from opposing conciliar theological settlements; Marxists set themselves apart from Blanquists; black Muslims define themselves against black Christian churches; pro-life against pro-choice; populists against statists; ultrafundamentalists against moderate evangelicals; and so on (e.g., Heinz, 1983; Luker, 1984).

A further observation is that the role of disturbances in moral obligations need not be limited to the emergence of religious movements as such. The same logic applies to minor variations in the content of religious teachings or to the development of beliefs that modify rather than change fundamentally the nature of existing religious codes. For example, Carroll's (1983, 1986) detailed investigation of the elevation of the Virgin Mary to the status of a near-deity in the fourth-century Roman Empire demonstrates its relation to the political changes that took place under the rule of Constantine. The effect of Constantine's rule was to alter radically the existing moral order by giving Christianity official recognition. Including such tangible resources as government funding for the erection of churches, this recognition permitted Christianity to expand beyond the relatively narrow niche it had previously occupied among the urban merchant class. As Christianity diffused among the population at large, which consisted mainly of the rural poor, it encountered a different type of family structure—a structure that had supported local goddess cults for several centuries. This environment also provided a niche conducive to the development of a goddess cult around the Virgin Mary.[7]

Once generated, religious movements then become engaged in a struggle, as it were, to develop a suitable mode of adaptation to their environment. Decisions may be made according to rational calculations about maximizing potential adherents, securing favorable access to the media, instilling recruits with zeal for the movement's ideology, and cultivating respect for movement leaders. The ways in which movements adapt are often not this rational, however. Immediate crises call for short-term solutions, which are decided upon within the context of various opportunities and constraints presented by the movement's environment. What may be "selected for" or "selected against" are not always entire movements in all their complexity, but particular ideological styles or themes that become characteristic of a wide variety of movements or become diffused far beyond specific movements. Any number of such themes might be identified: utopianism, millenarianism, mysticism, nostalgia, collectivism, thaumaturgic motifs, and so on. In the following sections three religious patterns having quite far-reaching applications—popular religion (and fundamentalism), individualism, and rationality —are considered in order to illustrate the selective relationships between religious patterns and social environments.

Popular Religion and Fundamentalism

The role of social environments in selecting from among the various strands of competing religious ideology that are produced in any historical period is a problem that has received little attention of an explicit sort. Usually religious movements are examined in isolation from one another and their success or failure is attributed largely to internal factors such as leadership styles or modes of organization. Even if greater attention were devoted to comparisons, it remains unclear whether or not the selective effect of environmental characteristics would be evident in such limited contexts. On the other hand, a number of efforts have been made to identify general themes or patterns among religious manifestations, some of which appear more common in certain circumstances than in others.

Research has come increasingly to recognize the importance of what has been termed "popular religion." Whereas formal religion is characterized by codified doctrines, ecclesiastical organizations, and a professional clergy, popular religion consists of relatively amorphous beliefs, is extra-ecclesiastical, and is located among the common people (Vrijhof and Waardenburg, 1979). Popular religion tends to be syncretistic, drawing simultaneously from indigenous folklore [the "little tradition," in Redfield's (1956) terms] and the more formalized symbols ("great tradition") associated with historic or world religions (see Scott, 1977). Symbols are drawn from a wide variety of common sources —nature, work, food, music—rather than systematic theology, and yet these symbols are distinguished from ordinary folklore in that beliefs are incorporated about divine or supernatural intervention in the realm of everyday experience. Examples include beliefs about demons and witchcraft, spiritualism, astrology, magic, miracles, and superstitions.

In a valuable introduction to the study of popular religion, Williams (1980, p. 65) identifies six subject headings under which the beliefs and practices of popular religion can be classified: food, health and sickness, major transitions in the life cycle, death and the dead, predictions of the future, and problems of evil and misfortune. These kinds of beliefs and practices also suggest some clues about the relations between popular religion and the social environment. Popular religion has been most evident in relatively nonmodern societies. Studies of medieval and early modern Europe, of Third World countries, and of traditional settlements in North America, such as Amish and Hutterite communities, give ample testimony to the importance of popular superstitions, charms and amulets, stories of miraculous happenings, and so on.[8] From these studies, it might seem that popular religion does not do well in modern contexts. Yet recent research has begun to challenge this notion. Studies now suggest that popular religion may be remarkably robust even in the most modernized settings. Beliefs in astrology and extrasensory communication, contact with the dead and out-of-body experiences, superstitions about lucky numbers, mystical experiences, and trances, not to mention the quasi-sacred character of many holidays, sports events, and emblems of nature, all seem to be relatively common in settings such as the United States and Western Europe.[9] The question has arisen, therefore, of how beliefs and practices that on the surface seem incompatible with the secular, scientific norms of modern culture could have proven so adaptable. Scattered research suggests at least a partial answer.

First, popular religion usually lacks much formal structure. It appears to consist of sayings, dictums, and aphorisms ("the luck of the draw"), even though systematic treatments of its tenets sometimes appear, for example, in the form of theological treatises on spiritualism. The moral maxims of popular religion, moreover, are illustrated and substantiated by anecdotes or narratives rather than by formal argument. This looseness of symbolic structure probably also permits if not encourages another feature of popular religion: its syncretism, whereby discrete elements that might in principle be contradictory in a tighter logical system are in fact loosely linked without apparent feelings of inconsistency or discomfort on the part of believers (see Firth, 1984; Van Baaren, 1984).

More formally, popular religion can be described as a symbol system comprising a relatively large number of elements, but with a low number of definite relations among pairs of elements. Other things being equal, a disconnected system of this kind tends to withstand external shocks relatively well, since an alteration in any specific element or subsystem of elements need not affect the entire system.[10] Belief in demon possession, for example, might decline; yet if this belief is not logically related to other elements of popular religion, this decline could occur without affecting, say, the tendency to believe in life after death or the credibility of astrology.

A second point is that popular religion tends to gravitate toward the interstices of modern society. Most of the beliefs and practices in Williams's sixfold typology deal with the marginal or unanticipated—illness, death, misfortune—or with those transitional states that Turner (1977) and others have associated with "liminality"; that is, a feeling of being "betwixt and between." Even seemingly ordinary beliefs and practices in this schema, such as those dealing with food preparation, turn out to be most concerned with high feast days and festivals and, as Mary Douglas (1966, 1984) has shown, symbolize deeper boundaries in social relations and understandings. Much of the impetus for popular religion, it appears, comes from what Berger (1969) has identified as experiences of "marginality," which fall at the edges of ordinarily constructed realities.

The fact that popular religion falls within the interstices of ordinary reality means that it is concerned with experiences that happen to nearly everyone at some time or another (e.g., illness, bereavement, tragedy), even in modern societies, but that are generally not dealt with adequately by the dominant institutions in these societies. Death and bereavement notoriously fail to be handled satisfactorily except to be insulated from the rest of society.[11] Illness and tragedy, while subject to risk reduction and insurance schemes, continue to raise problems of personal adjustment because of their unpredictability and undesirability. And life passages often fail to be adequately handled because they occur precisely at those points of exit and entry between major institutions (e.g., school and work). The result is that popular religion is able to occupy a relatively enduring and important niche in modern society, just as it does in traditional society. Less obviously, the nature of this niche also reinforces the disconnectedness evident among tenets of popular religion. The events to which it relates are themselves disconnected, separated in time from one another in the typical individual's biography, largely unanticipated, and in most cases relatively limited in frequency and duration.

A third feature of popular religion, stemming from its association with crisis events, is that it often occurs in informal gatherings of close relatives and friends. Whether at birthdays or

weddings, hospital visits, wakes, or other times of crisis, a small community of intimates is likely to be present. Even when it occurs in modern societies, therefore, popular religion is likely to take place amidst small, solidarist communities, just as it does in traditional societies.

Its association with small, solidarist groups also affords a further insight into the character and persistence of popular religion. From Bernstein's (1975) research on linguistic codes, it can be said that solidarist groups are more likely to generate "restricted" codes rather than "elaborated" codes. That is, the high degree of shared understandings in solidarist groups means that fewer words actually have to be spoken for communication to take place.[12] Because it is evoked in the presence of solidarist groups, popular religion is likely to share the characteristics of restricted codes: much is left unspoken, few of the relations among its various tenets are spelled out, and what is spoken tends to be intertwined with the anecdotes and experiences—the folklore—of a particular group. In addition, the relative isolation of these experiences and gatherings from institutional life increases the likelihood that the material used to construct popular religious discourse will be the events of one's childhood, ancestors, or immediate acquaintances. As a result, "discourse" is indeed likely to consist of *discourse*—an oral tradition—rather than becoming subject to greater systematization through written formalization. Rumors of miracles, strange happenings, confirmations of superstitious beliefs thrive on verbal retelling in intimate settings. In these situations, many of the more penetrating questions that might be asked remain unspoken because of common experiences and bonds of trust.

Finally, another body of research permits an interpretation to be given for the frequency with which popular religion seems to manifest a belief in, or experience of, divine intervention. A substantial body of empirical literature contains the idea, on the one hand, that major "life events" tend to evince stress, including emotional and physical symptoms, and that these events, on the other hand, evoke a wide variety of religious responses, ranging from mere questioning of the purpose of life to experiences of divine contact or revelation (see Dohrenwend and Dohrenwend, 1974; Stokes, 1982; Thoits, 1981). The connection between stressful events and religious experiences is in some ways obvious, since the questions elicited by these events may have culturally specified answers that fall into the domain of religious interpretations ("it was God's will," "the devil made him do it").

This line of reasoning, of course, leads directly to the observation that *formalized* religious beliefs frequently play a role during crisis events, and less directly to the observation that popular religion may also be elicited (since it too is culturally available). But a cultural interpretation of this kind does less well at accounting for events in which an extraordinary intervention of the supernatural is actually *experienced*.

Here, a combination of psychological, sociological, and cultural explanations seems necessary. At the psychological level, a well-established body of research indicates a connection between crisis-induced stress and propensities to hallucinate, including visual and auditory components (e.g., Bender, 1970; Jaffe, 1966). At the sociological level, research suggests that patterns of family socialization may affect the propensity to have experiences of the supernatural. Specifically, families that require children to act on behalf of the family itself (as opposed to expressing purely individual interests) encourage a tendency for the child to feel constrained by purposes other than his or her own; as a result, such individuals are more susceptible to having hallucinatory experiences in which they feel possessed by some external power (Swanson, 1978a, 1978b). And at the cultural level, evidence from studies of religious experiences points to the importance of either preconceived frameworks with which to interpret one's experience, or else of associates who suggest an interpretation for what is at first a seemingly ordinary or ambiguous event (Carroll, 1986; Laski, 1961). One person's "terror in the night" can clearly be another person's "visitation of the Lord."

Placing these arguments beside one another therefore suggests that the persistence of popular religion in modern societies can be understood in terms of a distinct relation between its ideological structure and the social environment. The niches in modern society to which popular religion adapts are relatively common (as common as illness and death). Yet in actuality, from the standpoint of the specific person or group most immediately involved, these niches are relatively narrow, unstable, and discrete: narrow in the sense of happening to only a few people at a time who have contact with one another, unstable in terms of unpredictability of occurrence and duration, and discrete as far as any particular individual's biography is concerned as well as falling into the interstices between social institutions. The tenets of popular religion that are preferentially selected by this kind of environment also tend to be relatively discrete elements with few systematic relations with one another, thus permitting them to adapt with relative flexibility to diverse and changing circumstances.

In some respects, *fundamentalism* may appear to be the polar opposite of popular religion; indeed, fundamentalists have generally been harsh opponents of astrology, magic, and popular superstitions. Strict adherence to doctrinal orthodoxy, a rigid conception of faith, and a lack of tolerance for superstition and the occult all seem to set fundamentalism apart from popular religion. Yet the two bear certain similarities to one another. Like popular religion, fundamentalism has been studied mainly as an anomaly of modern culture that is presumably better suited to more traditional settings. Its origins have been sought in social crises that breed hostile reactions to the modernization process. Its content is described as a totalistic worldview, organized around absolute values, and representing a countertrend to the process of cultural differentiation (see Lechner, 1983). Implicitly, fundamentalism is generally assumed to be a short-term phenomenon unlikely to survive in the modern milieu. But (again like popular religion) fundamentalism has surprised many observers by its persistence and, in some cases, growth.

Kelly's (1972) research on the growth of fundamentalist churches in the United States initiated a wave of renewed interest in the study of fundamentalism (see Hunter, 1985). This interest was further stimulated by American fundamentalists' move toward political activism and by an apparent resurgence of fundamentalism in the Islamic world and in Judaism (Antoun and Hegland, 1986). While most of this research has been limited to the American case, some general lines of interpretation have emerged. One is the view (just mentioned) that fundamentalism is a reaction against certain modernizing tendencies, such as greater emphasis on higher education and the penetration of local communities by the national state. Another is that fundamentalism, while rooted in traditional communities, is rapidly accommodating to modernity itself, gaining resources in the process, but losing many of its distinctive qualities (Hunter, 1983, 1986). Both of these interpretations predict a relatively limited future for fundamentalism. A third view is that fundamentalism has grown mainly by default as liberal denominations have abandoned ultimate concerns to engage in social activism (Kelly, 1972). Finally, it has been suggested that fundamentalism's growth reflects little more than high fertility rates among its members (Bibby and Brinkerhoff, 1983). All of these interpretations have some empirical support, but each is somewhat limited in its conceptualization of fundamentalism.

Participant-observer studies of fundamentalist groups have begun to fault the idea that fundamentalism is a totalistic worldview, tightly integrating behavioral norms with central values, and lacking in usual kinds of cognitive differentiation. What these studies suggest is that fundamentalist beliefs focus on several highly salient aspects of behavior (family, for example) but leave most others up to the individual's discretion (Ammerman, 1983; Ault, 1983). In addition, the relation between central values and prescribed norms often appears to rest more on custom than on clearly articulated arguments. Survey studies of fundamentalists support these conclusions, revealing relatively low correlations between fundamentalist beliefs and many other attitudes, and demonstrating that identification with local custom is the principal link binding attitudes with beliefs (e.g., Roof, 1978; Rothenberg and Newport, 1984).

In formal terms, fundamentalism appears to be an example of an ideological system comprising relatively few elements that are strongly related to one another. The elements generally considered essential in Christian fundamentalism in the United States—the so-called fundamentals—are limited to no more than five or six beliefs (concerning biblical inerrancy, the divinity of Jesus, his resurrection, the individual's need for salvation, and so on). These, and the relations among them, were codified in great detail in a series of volumes published between 1910 and 1915 (Marsden, 1980). Empirical studies generally reveal a high degree of consistency in believers' answers to these questions (e.g., Glock and Stark, 1965). Other attitudes popularly associated with fundamentalism (e.g., premillennialist views, attitudes toward tobacco and alcohol, political conservatism), however, tend to vary widely among different fundamentalist groups. Indeed, the division of fundamentalists into numerous small denominations means that, from the standpoint of formal ideology, the core tenets of fundamentalism are connected in widely diverse ways with other beliefs and attitudes.

In comparison with popular religion, therefore, fundamentalism consists of fewer elements with stronger relations. As an ideological system it is somewhat less stable than popular religion, since the strong relations among its elements mean that a change in any one is likely to affect all the others. But fundamentalism is more stable than a comparable ideological system having large numbers of elements. It is, on the

whole, a conceivable candidate on formal grounds to persist in an otherwise changing environment. Fundamentalism has in fact demonstrated remarkable resilience in relation to processes such as urbanization and industrialization and shifts in political and economic patterns. Its weakness has been mainly in relation to cultural processes of rationalization that add to the number of elements that are interrelated and thus increase the likelihood of change occurring in the system. Increased levels of education, imposing a greater consistency on diverse ideological elements, has been one such process (for an interesting empirical study, see Hammond and Hunter, 1984). Political movements and moral crusades, welding tighter relations between religious beliefs and social attitudes, have been another. Of the two, education appears to have the most serious consequences. The reason may not be, as often assumed, that education provides alternative values that make more sense. Rather, the effect of education may be to encourage a more rational systematization among fundamental beliefs, transforming them from the "more fragmented and less internally consistent" beliefs characteristic of the less educated (Scott, 1977, p. 6), but at the same time making them more vulnerable to environmental disturbances.

For these reasons, fundamentalism appears to function best in relatively homogeneous niches within the larger environment in which the connections between core tenets and lifestyle issues can remain implicit. The introduction of heterogeneity into such settings frequently proves disruptive to the ideology, causing either a sectarian schism to occur, which recreates homogeneity within each splinter group, or an attempt at rationalization, which may produce further strain among the ideological elements. Under these circumstances, it is not uncommon to find ideological flexibility being increased by a shift toward greater emphasis on the individual.

Religious Individualism

The importance of individualism in religion was identified by nearly all the classical theorists, thereby rendering it an issue bearing on a broad range of theoretical questions as well as substantive questions pertaining uniquely to the study of religion. Certain developments in contemporary religion have also opened new lines of inquiry into its nature. Like popular religion and fundamentalism, it can be examined beneficially in relation to the kinds of social environments in which it tends to be selected.

In the classical tradition, religious individualism gained prominence in the work of Marx and Weber, and to a lesser extent in the work of Durkheim. For Marx and Weber, it was regarded as an ideology uniquely compatible with capitalism. According to Marx, the emergence of capitalism, particularly in seventeenth-century England, necessitated an ideology that had a corrosive effect on traditional solidarist groups standing in the way of market relations and that legitimated individual property rights. While in some ways present in all of the Reformation doctrines, this ideology became prominent in an especially powerful form in English Puritanism. Weber's interpretation differed from Marx's in terms of the priority accorded to religious ideology as an independent contributor to economic change, but it also emphasized the unique compatibility between capitalism and Puritanism (Seaver, 1985; Zaret, 1985). Durkheim, finally, differed from Weber and Marx in giving causal priority to different factors, but he also envisaged a general increase in "the cult of the individual," as he described it, during the course of modernization.

The characteristics of Puritanism that, to the classical theorists, qualified it as religious individualism include the high priority it attached to personal salvation and direct accountability to God, its delegitimation of sacraments and offices associated with the ecclesiastical hierarchy, and the considerable degree of ethical responsibility it assigned to individual behavior. In Puritanism the individual stood alone before God, faced with ultimate uncertainty about personal salvation, and yet was free to make ethical decisions from which evidence of his or her moral worth could be discerned. Such accountability obviously bore a strong resemblance to the conditions under which entrepreneurs functioned in the capitalist marketplace.

The more recent sociological literature has provided theoretical and empirical evidence bearing on these initial formulations and has extended the idea of religious individualism into other areas. Much of this work has consisted of relatively technical reconsiderations of the classical materials themselves, constituting a body of literature falling largely outside of the purview of the present discussion. There have been, however, a number of important contributions that focus directly on the conceptualization of religious individualism and its relation to features of the social environment. Rather than viewing individualism as a coherent philosophical system in its own right, it may be more pro-

ductive to treat it as a formal characteristic that can infuse many types of ideology. That is, individualism, in the same sense as popular religion and fundamentalism, can encompass a relatively wide variety of substantive tenets, but common to all of these variants are certain formal properties that distinguish the structure of the ideology itself. In the case of religious individualism, the most general effect of a strong emphasis on the individual appears to be a tendency to "decouple" the substantive tenets of any formalized set of doctrines or creeds. If religious belief is defined as a matter of individual interpretation, for example, then it becomes possible for particular ideas to be put together in any number of ways. The effect of this decoupling is somewhat similar to that accomplished in popular religion but at a different level of ideological organization. Whereas popular religious tenets tend to be disaggregated by virtue of their intrinsic aphoristic quality and lack of formal codification, individualistic religious orientations are disaggregated at the level of the individual believer. Accordingly, for any particular individual, a highly integrated worldview may exist, but the components of that worldview may be quite dissimilar from those of any other person's worldview. The extreme manifestation of religious individualism, therefore, lies in the dual formulation "do your own thing" and "anything goes."

Fortunately, perhaps, religious individualism seldom takes this extreme form. Rather, a total disaggregation of religious elements is usually prevented by specifying some relations among individuals; that is, moral obligations. The individual may be emphasized as decision maker, but is nevertheless bound to other individuals by notions of ethical responsibility, community, and so on. Several implications follow from this observation.

Above all, any religious ideology that can be characterized as individualistic requires a number of markers or cues in the religious discourse itself that *individuate* its structure. Phrases like "in my view" or "I tend to think" dramatize the connection between beliefs and individual believers. These cues may be "given" explicitly as part of the propositional content of religious discourse, or "given off" implicitly as part of the illocutionary force of that discourse (Brummer, 1982; Searle, 1969; Taylor, 1984). In either case, they must heighten the importance of an utterance's connection with its speaker as an individual (or in some cases, with the hearer as an individual).

Foucault's (1965, 1970, 1972, 1975, 1979) work on cultural developments in eighteenth-

and nineteenth-century Europe, while not concerned explicitly with religion, provide examples of the ways in which discourse became individuated. In the realm of criminality individuation developed in conjunction with theories and sentences that emphasized the individual's *body* as a relevant object of discipline and punishment. Notions of insanity, Foucault suggests, developed in tandem with heightened conceptions of the mind and with medical concepts that dramatized disturbances of the mind. Even the development of modern social sciences, he argues, required the individual to be invented before it could be studied. More generally, Foucault's framework for the analysis of knowledge emphasizes the importance of "formations" that make it appropriate for the individual to speak, for individuals to be objects of speech, and for them to be related to other objects of speech. Prominent examples of such individuating formations in modern societies include institutionalized norms of child rearing, standardized educational systems, occupational credentials, citizenship rights, and conceptions of the life course, all of which define the individual in public or cultural terms, rather than leaving such matters strictly up to the subjective processes of the individual (Boli-Bennett and Meyer, 1978; Meyer, 1984).

In the case of religious discourse, examples are readily available that evidence the high degree to which individuation is generally present. The fact that religious beliefs are usually referred to as beliefs, rather than as teachings or symbols, implies that they are to be associated chiefly with individuals rather than larger institutions or uniform cultural systems. The Protestant reformers' emphasis on the "priesthood of the believer" clearly sought to reassociate what had been an institutional role with the common person. Believer's baptism further emphasized the choice-making capacity of the individual, as have more recent pastoral emphases on conversion, being "born again," personal "faith development," and so on.

Several empirical studies have examined the nature of individuation in religious discourse. McGuire (1982), in a study of Catholic Pentecostalism, has demonstrated the importance of conversion testimonials for associating religious teachings with individual biographies. Hunter (1983), in a systematic content analysis of evangelical literature, has found evidence of a strong tendency to associate subjective concerns, such as emotional problems, guilt, worry, and personal adjustment, with religious assertions. Cuddihy (1978) observes that religious discourse now frequently is prefaced with such personalizing phrases as "in my experience" or "my own view of it is," which, he suggests, make religion increasingly a matter of individual preference and serves to introduce an element of civility into pluralistic religious gatherings. Bellah and his associates (1985) present evidence of a fairly radical individuation of religious commitments in America in both liberal and conservative churches. One of the people they interviewed even had a unique religion entirely of her own making—"Sheilaism." Other research shows statistically significant tendencies among respondents in survey studies for beliefs about the importance of the individual to be associated with beliefs about the importance of religion (e.g., Apostle et al., 1983; Wuthnow, 1976). In all of these cases, the evidence suggests a relatively prevalent tendency toward individuation in modern religion, raising the question, therefore, about the ways in which this tendency may be preferentially selected in modern social environments.

Marx's interpretation was that the market system, especially under capitalism, reinforced individuation by forcing buyers and sellers to compete with one another as individuals whose relations were defined strictly by the supply-demand-price mechanism. Along similar lines, Durkheim argued that market exchange led to greater and greater specialization, thereby breaking down homogeneous groups and causing individuals to be more differentiated from one another. Foucault's work has added flesh to these assertions, demonstrating that individuation was reinforced through the very physical manipulation of persons. Holding pens gave way to individual cells in prisons, narrenschiffe were replaced by the psychoanalyst's couch, military regiments placed soldiers into distinct positions and gave them clearly defined duties to fulfill, and assembly lines eventually broke down the group character of work itself.

What has often seemed anomalous is how individuation could advance at the same time that bureaucracies became bigger and social institutions in general became more complex. Foucault's examples illustrate that individuation may go hand in hand with the means by which effort in these large-scale entities is coordinated. Studies of the state point in the same direction. As Bendix (1977) has suggested, individuation on a societal scale may serve usefully in the state-building process. Autonomous individuals, he suggests, are easier to control than are tribes, ethnic groups, collectives, unions, or other solidaristic entities. Thus modern bureaucratic states have generally advanced individuation through, on the one hand, standardization—

especially through schooling and language uniformities—which makes persons relatively interchangeable with one another, and, on the other hand, through personalization, which attaches rights and responsibilities—such as voting and paying taxes—to the individual. In short, individuation in ideology and individuation in social structure seem to be prominent features of modern society.

But individuation and individualism are not exactly the same. Following Turner's (1983, pp. 160-161) valuable discussion, individualism may be defined as "a doctrine of individual rights, which may be expressed in a variety of religious, political, economic or legal forms," as contrasted with individuation, which consists only of "marks, numbers, signs and codes" which identify and separate "persons as differentiated bodies." The key to distinguishing individualism from individuation, therefore, lies in the idea of rights, and these always connote *responsibilities* as well.

The idea of rights and responsibilities helps to explain why Puritanism qualifies as an example of religious individualism. Puritanism not only contributed to the individuation of religious persons (as did religious doctrines as different as Anabaptism and mystical contemplation); it also specified definite rights and responsibilities among religious persons. Puritans stood alone before God, and yet they also felt a duty, as Weber recognized, to work for the improvement of humanity and to abide by the discipline and norms of the religious community. It was out of this conception of responsibility that the Lockean theory of property rights was formed. It was this sense of a moral relationship that also permitted the American Puritans to mold strong communities—moral communities that defined that distinctive brand of American individualism that Tocqueville was to describe in the phrase "self-interest rightly understood."

Individualism, then, is an ideological form, based on a sharply individuated sense of the person, which defines certain rights and responsibilities among individuals. Several features of this ideological form are crucial to its coherence and also constitute the components to which religious imagery is usually related. First, the individual must be conceived of as possessing rights; second, the individual must be free to choose; and finally, the individual must be conceptualized as having moral obligations.

With respect to the idea of rights, the individual cannot be regarded simply as a self or as a conjuncture of interests and instincts. Instead, the individual must possess something that defines him or her as a member of some larger

system (e.g., property or citizenship). In religious conceptions, salvation, sanctification, or election have served to define individuals as members in good standing with rights to certain privileges. Not surprisingly, "religious tests" have often been associated with the right to enjoy other privileges, such as holding office, voting, owning property, and so on.

Freedom to act as a locus of choice is a considerably more complicated issue. As an ideological tenet, it performs a dual function. It adds ideological flexibility by crediting the individual with the capacity to make decisions. This is particularly important in religion, since individual freedom connotes the ability to render doctrinal interpretations and thus to adapt universalistic ideas to particular situations. In addition, the concept of individual freedom seems to provide the essential link between individual rights and individual responsibilities in that freedom is necessary for the individual to be held morally accountable. That is, any sense of moral obligation requires that the individual be free to do otherwise; if not, no sense of having fulfilled these moral obligations is possible (one can scarcely take moral credit for doing something that could not have been avoided). Consequently, it is not surprising to find religious individualism strongly associated in many instances with notions of personal morality. Indeed, modern religions that strongly emphasize freedom of belief are often the most "moralistic" in defining standards of personal conduct.

The sense of moral obligation, finally, is primarily an "other-directed" concept, defining normative relations between the individual and others. The individual is not simply free, but is free to exercise certain responsibilities. This concept, of course, necessarily implies some notion of a community or social system with which one shares contractual obligations. Mary Douglas's (1973) idea of "grid" and "group" captures this notion: As a cell in a grid, an individual is individuated but also knows clearly his or her place in relation to other cells in the system; in contrast, an individual who is simply an unspecified member of a group does not know what his or her obligations are, and a person who has neither group nor grid is in the worst situation of all with respect to having clearly defined roles.

Returning then to the question of how the social environment selects for religious individualism, it can be seen that individualism is unlikely to flourish in a situation of strictly autonomous monads (desert hermits, for example). It is more likely to flourish where the environment demands some degree of coordinated but flexible relationships. Such conditions are likely to be present in an environment with heterogeneous resources (e.g., a diversity of natural resources or a high degree of occupational specialization) and where the environment is organized across these various heterogeneous resources; that is, requiring coordination rather than the mere coexistence of largely separate, internally homogeneous entities. *Heterogeneity* in this context can be defined formally as the probability that any two randomly selected subunits of the environment will be different (e.g., raw materials, occupations, ethnic-identities, forms of industrial organizations, etc.). Obviously this is the kind of environment that becomes relevant whenever a market system spans a relatively large area and when it leads to a kind of internal division of labor such that interdependence (organic solidarity, in Durkheim's terms) is present.

Historical studies generally support the idea that religious individualism became more prominent in areas characterized by market conditions. Indeed, it is the appearance of market conditions, rather than capitalism as such, that appears to be most closely associated with the rise of individualism. As trade expanded in the thirteenth century, for example, a heightened sense of individualism appears to have developed in various areas of Europe, particularly in the trading areas of Italy and England. In the sixteenth century, towns that were engaged in commerce over long distances, rather than local trade, seem to have been especially prominent in adopting the new ideas of the Reformation (Wuthnow, 1986b). Davis (1981) suggests that part of the appeal was the fact that Protestantism conceived of social relations more as a network of responsibilities among individuals rather than as membership in predefined local collectivities. Later still, the globalization of markets during the nineteenth century seems to have been accompanied by another wave of individualism. Thomas (1979), for example, has provided statistical evidence for the United States between 1870 and 1890 that indicates a close relation between the spread of capitalist agriculture and the diffusion of individualistic religious beliefs—especially Methodism (for an earlier period, see Pritchard, 1984).

The topic of religious individualism has not only been studied historically. Other studies have been prompted by recent discussions of narcissism and privatism in religion. Writers have identified a type of individualism—identified variously as narcissism, civil privatism, and expressive individualism—that seems to be a prominent feature of contemporary culture (Bellah et al., 1985; Habermas, 1975, pp. 75-92; Lasch, 1978; Sennett, 1978). Since this kind of individualism appears different from its historical counterpart, it has been useful to give it a different name. Turner (1983, p. 162), for example, suggests the term *individuality*, instead of individualism, by which he means "a romantic theory of the subjective interior of persons, which is concerned with the growth of sensibility, taste, consciousness and will." The contrast is perhaps best drawn by saying that individualism emphasizes a concern for the moral responsibility of individuals toward other individuals, whereas individuality focuses on the moral responsibility of the individual toward his or her own self. In the one, relationships are specified among individuals; in the other, relationships are specified among the internal components of the self. Individuation is an important precondition of both, but the two differ sharply in the kinds of relationships emphasized.

Discussions of narcissism and civil privatism correspond well with this definition of individuality. According to Sennett, the main feature of narcissism is its inability to distinguish among parts of the self—as in the case of Narcissus, who confuses his image reflected in the spring with himself and thus eventually falls in and drowns. The result, Sennett suggests, is a tendency to become preoccupied with relations purely within the self and, therefore, to become withdrawn from public roles; that is, from moral relationships with other individuals. Habermas's discussion of civil privatism flows along similar lines, suggesting that withdrawal from public roles is accompanied by an inner search for meaning and purpose.

Examples of individuality in religion are not hard to find. Troeltsch's (1960/1911, pp. 691-806) contrast between mysticism and sectarianism in some ways parallels the distinction between individuality and individualism. Whereas the sectarian may emphasize individualism (in the form of religious rights and duties) as a protest against more organized churchlike religions, the mystic is more likely to withdraw from public roles and engage in a life of contemplative introspection. Public roles, such as political and economic participation, are thought to require too many compromises of one's ideas; consequently the mystic carves out an inner realm over which greater control can be exercised. It has also been suggested that many of the "new age" spiritual disciplines that have become attractive in the West may represent this kind of individuality. Certainly those who are attracted to mystical religious movements and the various human potential movements are more likely to focus on fantasy, new insights about themselves, and symbolism (Wuthnow, 1976). What these movements appear to accomplish in many cases is a clarification of the various components of the self. Specifically, an inner self is often identified as a kind of command center that then becomes capable of defining the relations among other component selves (Fingarette, 1963; Tipton, 1982; Westley, 1983).

The social conditions promoting these orientations remain inadequately examined, but several plausible hypotheses have been put forth. One is that life in modern bureaucratic institutions becomes so well organized—so regimented—that any sense of free choice, and thus of moral responsibility, becomes incomprehensible; consequently, persons who have been socialized to value freedom and moral responsibility shift increasingly to private or inner pursuits over which they have greater discretion (see Wilensky, 1964). An alternative hypothesis is that individuality stems not so much from overorganization, but from the greater degree of flexibility required in role performances in the professions or, indeed, in any complex situation where the different components of the self may need to become operative at different times (see Bell, 1977; Swanson, 1980; Yankelovich, 1982). According to this hypothesis, multiple role requirements lead to multiple selves, which in the extreme can lead to problems in forming a stable self-identity, and therefore, to a preoccupation with self-exploration.

Where there is greater agreement is that individuality, whatever the source, poses relatively serious implications for religion. Rather than an ethical religion, which attaches importance to strict moral obligations, individuality seems likely to be associated with a highly relativistic religion that focuses on inward pursuits and leaves public or collective values to be informed primarily by secular considerations (Luckmann, 1967). At this writing, much debate has in fact begun to appear over the ramifications of such an orientation for the stability of modern societies (e.g., Bellah, 1982; Bellah et al., 1985; Neuhaus, 1984).

Religion and Rationality

Another theme of importance, particularly in light of Weber's (1922/1963) work on rationalization, has been the role of rationality in religion. Discussions of this topic have some-

times been cast simply in terms of an apparent conflict between religion (presumably nonrational) and rationality. Weber's principal contribution, however, was to identify rationality as a characteristic of modern religion itself. In his treatment of the Protestant ethic, for example, he envisioned a relatively high degree of rationality in the teachings of the Protestant reformers and suggested that the resultant ethical system would erode the mysteriousness of religion itself.

Rationality, unfortunately, has several different technical meanings and some vague popular connotations (see Habermas, 1984). To Weber, it meant a systematization of means or norms in relation to an end or goal, or else a systematization among goals themselves. Behavior could be considered rational insofar as it conformed to the norms that were accepted as efficient and effective means of attaining one's designated goal. In purely formal terms, rational belief systems are thus ones in which the various elements (i.e., designations of means and ends) bear relatively strong relationships to one another. In addition, these relationships are subjected to a kind of performance calculation such that failure to attain specified ends casts into question the nature of the elements that are identified as means. All of this obviously suggests a relatively high degree of reflection or self-consciousness about the relationships among the elements of a rational belief system: an application of "reason" or argumentation. Rational belief systems are also likely to be characterized by a high degree of universalism; that is, a conviction that the underlying procedures used to arrive at specified relationships between means and ends can be generalized to a wide variety of situations.

In seeking relations between rationality and social environments, anthropologists have pointed out that rationality is not limited to modern societies; it also exists in primitive settings once thought to be governed only by magic and superstition (see Wilson, 1970; Geraets, 1979). Nevertheless, the anthropological literature seems to be oriented more toward recognizing that a certain logic exists within nonmodern belief systems, rather than saying that the specific kind of rationality identified in Weber's work is present.[13] If the application of reason to practical tasks seems to be evident in virtually all societies, the development of a systematized, means-ends calculus oriented toward performance and conforming to universalistic norms appears to be limited to a much smaller set of social environments.

Other things being equal, rationality (so

defined) seems to have an elective affinity with heterogeneous environments. The reason can be specified along several different lines. One is that a heterogeneous environment presents a sphere in which learning can take place. In contrast with an entirely homogeneous environment, the presence of diverse stimuli means that comparisons can be made, and as a result, learning can be acquired about the means that produce different consequences. Only if heterogeneous resources are distributed completely at random (e.g., an island fishing economy in which schools of fish swim around the island in entirely random patterns) is learning sufficiently unlikely that the most efficient means of maximizing results may be one that also randomizes behavior (e.g., certain types of magic). In short, the attempt to make achievement predictable through a rational systematization of means and ends appears likely to prove most successful in an environment with heterogeneous but nonrandomly distributed resources. A differentiated market economy—some laborers having skills at bookkeeping, others at mining, and so on—is, of course, such an environment. Capitalists quickly learn how to combine rationally the right resources to achieve their ends.

Another line of reasoning points to the need for greater coordination in heterogeneous environments. If the niche occupied by a population is sufficiently broad that diverse resources have to be utilized, a complex system of social exchange will have to be developed. However, the greater the degree of complexity in an exchange system—that is, the larger the number of actors and the more diverse the tasks involved—the greater will be the potential for uncertainty (in the entire system) and unpredictability (for any specific outcome). For interaction to be effectively orchestrated under such conditions, therefore, a high degree of communication must take place (see Beniger, 1986). Any belief system that imposes predictability on actors or facilitates communication is likely to be favorably selected in this kind of environment. For example, rational law and rational educational philosophies impose predictability on individuals in complex modern societies; expectations about systematizing theological beliefs and publicizing them in sermons and written treatises encourage communication.

Yet another line of reasoning is suggested by this last observation concerning the need for communication. As mentioned earlier, Bernstein's (1975) work on language codes suggests that "elaborated" codes are likely to be more effective than "restricted" codes in highly diverse settings where communication is needed

among actors with few shared understandings. Rational belief systems represent a type of elaborated code in that they have explicitly articulated relationships among their various elements and are framed in such a way as to be presumably applicable to a wide variety of settings. It would again, therefore, be expected that rational belief systems should be preferentially selected in heterogeneous environments.

Many of the more familiar examples dealing with the development of rational belief systems in the West give prima facie support to arguments about the importance of heterogeneous social environments. Weber's own treatment of inner-worldly asceticism, epitomized in Puritan Calvinism, stressed the high degree of systematization that this orientation imposed on ideas about ethical behavior as well as the predictability that accompanied this systematization as far as the individual's behavior was concerned (see Schluchter, 1981). Both of these characteristics were, in his view, deeply compatible with the kinds of complex calculations required by the expansion of capitalism in the seventeenth century. During the same period, as Merton's (1938/1970) application of Weber has suggested, Puritanism and capitalism appear to have provided conducive environments for the growth of rational experimental procedures in the natural sciences. In the following century, the extension of rational procedures to moral and political philosophy—indeed, the triumph of these procedures in the Enlightenment—appears to have been reinforced not only by a further expansion of the mercantile economy but also by a tremendous expansion of the bureaucratic state, which added greatly to the complexities and uncertainties involved in formulating public policies.

Research dealing with less obvious examples has also pointed strongly to the role of environmental heterogeneity in the development of rational belief systems. LeGoff's (1984) magisterial history of the idea of purgatory, particularly of its development in the twelfth century, argues that the acceptance of teachings about purgatory need to be understood in the context of changes taking place in the Medieval social system. Among these was the rapid spread of a particular type of feudalism marked by a dual hierarchy of lords versus peasants and high nobility versus chevaliers. In addition, a tripartite system of estates came into being distinguishing the ecclesiastical, military, and laboring orders (respectively, *oratores, bellatores,* and *laboratores*). Other changes included geographic expansion, both in trade and in military conquests, monastic reforms, and a more detailed system of contract law, penal codes, and bookkeeping procedures. The idea of purgatory, LeGoff argues, was both an adaptation to and an extension of this increasingly complex social and cultural milieu. It added an important intermediate category between heaven and hell, just at the time that intermediate categories were being recognized in the social structure; it corresponded with a whole set of ternary logical models evident in social, legal, and philosophical classifications; and above all it introduced into eschatological visions a new kind of calculation, similar to that being introduced in the courts, in which fixed terms or "sentences" served as a more realistic mode of reckoning between behavior, rewards, and punishments.

In a quite different setting, Geertz (1968) has provided an insightful illustration of the shift toward religious rationalization that frequently appears to accompany the integration of localized social systems into the broader context of world markets and export trade. Both in Morocco and in Indonesia Geertz observes a period in which Islam placed increasing emphasis on "scripturalism," including greater demands for strict adherence to Islamic doctrine and greater interest in religious schools. In both cases these tendencies toward rationalization accompanied waves of commercial expansion that eroded the personalized moral bonds between cultivators and rural landlords and gave merchants a stronger hand in establishing economic links with the outside world. Much the same phenomenon, it appears, took place in Brazil at a time when merchant classes were concerned with restricting spirit worship and other local folk beliefs and were seeking greater legitimacy with the church outside of Brazil (Ribeiro de Oliveira, 1979).

In a number of cases, the process of religious rationalization appears to be mediated by the state, rather than simply being a diffuse, undirected instance of cultural adaptation. In the Reformation, for example, the relatively high degree of rationality evident in both Lutheranism and Calvinism (especially in matters of church government and in procedures for settling theological disputes) appears to have emerged as a direct result of church leaders seeking the involvement of secular princes, courts, and parliamentary assemblies in ecclesiastical controversies. One result of this involvement was the development of standardized procedures that permitted these faiths to operate in relatively broad, heterogeneous environments. Similarly, in the case of early scientific development, the scientific academies not only received direct patronage from the state but also consciously borrowed parliamentary procedures from the state for the conduct of their meetings. In other cases, the vehicle of rationalization was not the state but direct borrowing from other highly rationalized bureaucracies (e.g., the adoption of corporate methods of organization by many denominations in the United States during the last quarter of the nineteenth century).

An aspect of the issue of religious rationality that has apparently remained relatively overlooked is that, notwithstanding its seeming adaptability to heterogeneous environments, it is highly vulnerable to instabilities in its environment. This is because its structure, in formal terms, consists of large numbers of elements that are systematically related to one another. Unlike folk religions or fundamentalism, therefore, rational belief systems can be easily subjected to internal strain by a significant change in any subset of their many elements. On the surface, this feature may appear counterintuitive; yet the relative frequency and suddenness with which highly rationalized systems such as scientific theories or theological perspectives change suggests that there may be some truth to the matter. It is perhaps because of this susceptibility to instability that rationalized belief systems appear frequently to incorporate one or both of two other formal properties.

One of these is individualism, which, as already seen, serves as a decoupling mechanism in religious systems, heightening their flexibility by giving individuals the right to combine ideological elements largely as they choose. A further advantage of combining individualism with rational belief systems is that assertions about the responsibility of the individual may be sufficient to lend the kind of predictability that is required in complex social environments. It needs to be added, however, that the radical relativism that comes with certain types of individualism is in some ways incompatible with a rationalistic orientation in a strict sense (see Jarvie, 1983). The other property is a kind of formal "blocking" of rational belief systems into discrete subsystems. The division of knowledge into specified disciplines, specialties, and theoretical perspectives accomplishes this task in science. As a result of this division, alterations in one subsystem become less likely to have ramifications for the entire system. In religion, a similar function is fulfilled by formal divisions along denominational lines. These divisions, occurring in the context of certain shared beliefs that are common to all denominations, create what is sometimes called a "federated" structure that is usually highly adaptable to complex and changing circumstances (see Hannan and Freeman, 1977). Both of these properties—individualism and denominational blocking—help, incidentally, to explain why religious commitment has remained at remarkably high levels in the otherwise deeply rationalized context of American culture.

Blocking of a distinct kind often takes the form of distinguishing core tenets of the faith, which presumably need to remain constant, from their ethical applications, which may be regarded as situationally variable. This distinction gives added flexibility to rationalized belief systems by allowing them to be adapted in diverse ways in different environments. Communist ideology in China, for example, formally incorporated a distinction between "theory" (Marxist-Leninist doctrine) and "thought" (Mao Zedong's more practical interpretations), making it possible for the Chinese to develop their own programs even to the extent of critically distancing themselves from the Soviet Union (Schurmann, 1968). In the United States leaders of the "new religious right" have found it expedient to separate "morality," which they claim is agreed on by a large majority of the public, from "religion," which they acknowledge is divided according to sectarian preferences (Wuthnow, 1983). If other conditions are constant, extreme fluctuations in the official reception given a belief system appear to promote this kind of blocking. Gager's (1975) study of early Christianity, for example, suggests a close relation between the variable reception given it by different governorships and the emergence of a sharp distinction between universal millenarian doctrines and the more temporal apostolic teachings concerned with establishing Christian communities.

At another level, rational belief systems appear to be particularly susceptible to processes of internal differentiation in response to changes in their environment. Internal differentiation represents a method of reintegrating elements that have become seemingly incompatible by identifying a higher order of generalization to which these elements can be related. Modern religious systems are often characterized, as Weber recognized, by a type of rational integration that differs from that evident in more traditional religions. Specifically, purely substantive modes of integration that relate religious elements in terms of logical content (e.g., scholasticism) tend to be replaced by types of integration emphasizing underlying procedures or techniques. Emphasis on conscience, methods of biblical criticism, rules of textual hermeneutics, and norms of tolerance, therefore, may provide the level at which otherwise conflicting religious beliefs become integrated.

The manner in which religious systems become internally differentiated has in fact been the subject of much exploration. Several comprehensive schemes have been put forth summarizing a complex evolutionary process marked by increasing differentiation. These schemes need to be understood, first, as having particular, if not unique, relevance to rational belief systems, as opposed to other varieties such as folk religions that may be less vulnerable to environmental shocks; and second, the process of internal differentiation needs to be clearly recognized as a mode of adaptation to fundamental changes in the social and cultural environment.

One of the most systematic treatments of the process of religious differentiation within a broad evolutionary framework remains that of Bellah (1970, pp. 20-50). Five stages of religious evolution are distinguished, ranging from the relatively undifferentiated to the most highly differentiated: primitive, archaic, historic, early modern, and modern. In the primitive stage mythical realities and the actual world remain undifferentiated, whereas in the archaic stage mythical beings begin to be objectified as distinct gods. This process continues in the historic stage, which begins to distinguish clearly between the present world and a supernatural or transcendent reality. The early modern stage (notably Protestantism) breaks out the individual from other realities, making salvation more contingent on personal choice. Finally, the modern stage generates a more "multiplex" version of reality in which multiple realities replace the dualistic worldview of previous stages. Other aspects of religion, such as religious action, religious organization, and ethical systems, show corresponding increases in differentiation. With each successive increase in differentiation, religious systems presumably gain greater capacities to adapt to complex environments.

Habermas (1979a, 1979b) has taken Bellah's scheme, modified it by collapsing the early modern into the modern stage, and attempted to specify some further theoretical distinctions. In Habermas's version, religious evolution is even more clearly specified in terms of increasing differentiation. At the initial (neolithic) stage, motives and behavioral consequences remain undifferentiated, as do actions and worldviews, human and divine events, natural and social phenomena, and tradition and myth. In the next (archaic) stage, greater degrees of differentiation occur between all these categories, producing a clearer sense of the linearity of history, providing for calculated action oriented toward the control of nature, and giving rise to rational law and the state. The third (developed) stage replaces myth and tradition with unified cosmologies and religions oriented toward high (monotheistic) gods, includes better defined moral precepts, and posits universalistic norms and values. The final (modern) stage is typified by an erosion of confidence in the validity of these higher-order principles, replaces absolute laws with reflective applications of reason to collective problems, and invokes a greater degree of self-consciousness about the procedures used to test the validity of statements about religion and morality. In Habermas's scheme, therefore, it becomes clear that the process of internal differentiation is closely linked with the rationalization of religion. Each successive stage introduces a higher order of abstraction, usually focusing increasingly on procedural modes of integration, which resolve problems at the previous stage. These problems occur principally as economic and political systems develop to the point of having to coordinate activities over larger and more diverse environments.

Bellah's and Habermas's schemes are presented at a sufficiently high level of generality that their connection with concrete historical events is not always evident. What they suggest, however, is that the process of religious rationalization represents a response to the inherent instabilities of rational belief systems against changes in the social environment. Evolutionary differentiation appears to be the basic method of gaining greater stability in more complex environments. But this process is clearly more applicable to religious systems characterized by a high degree of rationality than it is to other kinds of religious systems.

The obverse of the relationship between religious rationality and heterogeneous social environments is, of course, that nonrational religious systems are more likely to be evident in relatively narrow social niches in which resources are homogeneous rather than heterogeneous. What nonrationality does is to inhibit communication with other environments, thus in a way protecting local resources from becoming subject to exploitation in broader environments. It is not uncommon in such niches, therefore, to find religious expressions such as trance states, emotionalism, glossalalia, snake handling, and so on, which seem unintelligible to the outsider (see Scott, 1977, for examples). These religious expressions serve as dramatizations of a particular religious style, just as other religious expressions, such as theological discourse, bureau-

cratic structures, and formalized creeds, provide public dramatization of a "rational" style (see Meyer and Rowan, 1977).

Rituals and Organizations

In stressing the environment's selective influence over religious systems, objections can be raised that religion is accorded too passive a role. These objections can be overcome, however, by reintroducing the third element—institutionalization—of the dialectic framework set forth at the outset. The process of becoming an institution involves developing a relatively stable means of securing resources, an internal structure for processing these resources, some degree of legitimacy with respect to societal values and procedural norms, and sufficient autonomy from other institutions to be able to establish and pursue independent goals. A religious system that has become fully institutionalized, therefore, is capable of not only withstanding considerable alterations in its environment but also producing some of these alterations itself. The dynamics of institutionalization can be illustrated with respect to rituals, organizations, and the relations between religion and the state.

Much of the ambiguity surrounding the study of religious rituals can be avoided if it is recognized that their chief function is communication. Like verbal utterances, rituals are behavioral acts that explicitly or implicitly express something about actors' relations to one another. Rituals may be consciously orchestrated according to preestablished norms to commemorate or initiate some important event in the life of a community (weddings, holidays, etc.) —in which case the term *ceremony* may be more appropriate. Other rituals consist of relatively simple acts that nevertheless convey meaning (e.g., a soldier's salute or an automobile driver's signal to turn). Even acts that are primarily conducted for purely instrumental purposes (e.g., digging a ditch) may have expressive roles, depending on how they are performed. Thus it appears that ritual may be more appropriately described as an analytic dimension of behavior than as a totally discrete type of behavior. Ritual is symbolic-expressive and, in order to accomplish this communicative task, it often conforms to formalized norms and has built-in redundancy, which gives it an elaborated or ceremonialized character.[14]

Rituals are generated in much the same manner as other ideological systems, such as religious movements. They appear in situations of uncertainty in the moral order and assist in clarifying the moral obligations constituting that order. Erikson's (1966) study of witch hunting in colonial Massachusetts remains the classic example. On three occasions the colony's moral order became tenuous, either from outside threats or from conflicts within the community. On each of these occasions an episode of witch hunting broke out; each time the ensuing trial became instrumental in reaffirming the community's basic values and in clarifying its moral boundaries in relation to other values. Erikson's study has served as inspiration for a number of more recent studies applying the same logic to other kinds of rituals, such as political show trials, lynchings, and religious heresy hunts (e.g., Inverarity, 1976; Ben-Yehuda, 1980; Bergesen, 1977, 1978, 1980, 1984; Bergesen and Warr, 1979; Kurtz, 1983, 1986; Lauderdale, 1976).

In the case of religion, rituals not only serve as a response to broader ambiguities but are part of the function of the institution itself. That is, religious organizations produce rituals as a kind of service to their members, in return for which resources are contributed. Worship services, funerals, weddings, and christenings are all examples. A religious organization's effectiveness in conducting rituals is likely to be one of the ways in which its beliefs are perpetuated. Its rituals are also likely to be one of the means by which it shields itself from its environment. Where this becomes most evident is in rituals that not only utilize resources but also manufacture them.

One of the obvious ways in which rituals manufacture resources is by generating enthusiasm (what Durkheim called "collective effervescence"). Research on religious rituals emphasizes the role of charismatic leaders in evoking such enthusiasm. Studies have also come to greater recognition that enthusiasm, once generated, has to be carefully controlled in order to channel it toward realization of the organization's goals (see especially McGuire, 1982). For this reason, a strong charismatic leader may again be necessary. Or in other settings, carefully prescribed rules appear to operate to set limits on what may otherwise seem to be purely spontaneous behavior (Bainbridge, 1978; Zablocki, 1980).

Religious rituals also manufacture resources by providing collective confirmation of promised rewards. Testimonials play a special function in this regard since they not only confirm to the believer a particular alteration of self-identity but provide the collectivity with evidence that its beliefs are efficacious. Seemingly supernatural claims acquire pragmatic justification as members point to the fact that "lives are changed" (Ault, 1983). Testimonials also dramatize the collectivity's legitimacy by demonstrating the "acts of grace" that have befallen its members (e.g., anything from good fortune in locating parking places to miraculous healings). The ritual publicizes these happenings: Believers are thus encouraged to selectively perceive such acts of grace in order to have something to "share"; and otherwise infrequent or random occurrences seem to become more common by virtue of being communicated to the entire collectivity (Downton, 1979; Kroll-Smith, 1980).

Rituals also help stabilize religious systems by solving the so-called "free rider" problem; that is, the tendency for members of organizations to reap collective rewards without contributing resources (Hilke, 1980; Olson, 1971). This is a particular problem for religions that attach a high degree of importance to individual conscience, thus bestowing on the individual the capacity to communicate directly with God and the expectation of receiving supernatural rewards directly. In part, the tendency for such beliefs to reduce involvement in religious organizations is mitigated, as Weber recognized, by the radical uncertainty that besets the individual with regard to salvation and thus the need for confirmation through legitimate membership in a religious collectivity. In addition, most religious organizations orchestrate rituals in such a way as to prevent the full benefits of the organization from being distributed to persons who are not actively contributing members. Persons having contributed at specially high levels may be accorded recognition in leadership roles as part of the organization's rituals, access to privileged information may require participating in rituals, having individual needs met may require making these needs known in ritual settings, and the belief system may simply define as high rewards such benefits as "fellowship" or "the worship experience," which can only be attained through ritual participation. Most established religions in the West continue to rely mainly on these kinds of collective processes to ensure that sufficient contributions of time and energy are received to maintain their organizations. However, the professionalization of many of the welfare and charity services that religious organizations have traditionally provided their members may have eroded some of this capacity. In response, a tendency has become evident in some religious organizations to offer programs on a fee-for-service basis (e.g., educational programs, youth activities, and counseling) or to simply establish membership dues. Another potential problem for religious organizations, also deriving from believers' tendency to get religious gratifications without participating in religious rituals, is the impact of religious television programming (Hadden and Swan, 1981; Horsfield, 1984). The question raised by the rapid rise of such programming is whether its convenience and availability to "free riders" may detract from personal involvement in religious rituals and organizations. Preliminary results from the United States suggest that this has *not* been the case in the short run but leave open the question of longer-term effects (Gallup Organization, 1984).

Religious *organizations*, in addition to serving as a focus for religious rituals, represent a higher level of institutionalization than rituals alone in that they constitute an ongoing application of resources to the advancement of specific religious beliefs. Organizations serve as mechanisms not only for the extraction of resources from the environment but also for the coordination of these resources around the accomplishment of specific objectives, some of which may effect transformations in the environment itself. Thus the essential components of a religious organization include a system of drawing in resources, a relatively stable system of processing these resources, and a set of goals or tasks to which processed resources are committed. These components obviously do not apply only to religious organizations, but the nature of religious systems often causes them to differ from their counterparts in other types of organizations.[15]

Beginning with Troeltsch, a basic distinction has been drawn between two types of religious organizations: *churches* and *sects*. The meaning of these terms has often been ambiguous because inductive evidence was cited rather than developing more formal conceptions. In keeping with an emphasis on the extractive relations between religious organizations and their environments, churches may be defined as religious organizations that extract resources in a relatively nonintensive way from a large segment of the environment, while sects may be defined as religious organizations that extract resources intensively from a smaller segment of the environment.[16]

This way of distinguishing churches and sects clearly rests on not one but two distinctions: the *size* of the environmental segment from which resources are drawn (large/small), and the *intensity* with which these resources are drawn (low/high). Other things being equal, churches are more likely to be relatively large but make shallow demands; sects are more likely to be smaller but make deeper demands. Another way of making the same point is to say that churches attempt to regulate or fulfill a few of the activities or needs of large numbers of people; sects attempt to regulate or fill many of the activities or needs of small numbers of people. An attractive feature of this distinction is that it corresponds well with common usage of the two terms. The term *church* is typified by various national churches that encompass an entire society but elicit minimal levels of commitment by fulfilling such limited functions as administration of sacraments; sects are typified by denominations that (though sometimes quite large) are small in comparison with national churches but provide an all-encompassing set of activities for their members and obtain high levels of commitment in time and money in return. Also typical of many contemporary churches are organizations that supply a wide variety of services but that involve any given member in relatively few of these activities (e.g., choir for one, youth activities for another).

An important implication of this way of defining churches and sects is that *both* can be viable means of adapting to the modern social environment. Contrary to an assumption prevalent in the literature, sects need not follow some inevitable path toward becoming churches. Indeed, the persistence of sects should itself be sufficient to cast doubt on this notion. Sects can maintain themselves by adapting to relatively discrete niches in the environment and by giving much but also demanding much. Churches can adapt by demanding little but specializing in services that at least secure a little commitment from large numbers of people. Increasingly, too, religious organizations have adapted by combining elements of both styles, resulting in what sometimes looks like an inverted pyramid, with many members having few commitments and a few members having many commitments. Established religious organizations and new religious movements have incorporated this strategy, providing low-commitment services such as public meetings and open classes, but also providing more intensive training for the few willing to make a commitment (for some examples, see Popenoe and Popenoe, 1984). Some of the problems characteristic of sects and churches also seem to be closely linked with their particular modes of competing for resources. Sects, for example, turn their "consumers" into "employees" by relying on intensive commitment from small numbers of people; but this strategy increases the likelihood of having "labor" problems; hence, one of the traits typical of sectarianism is a tendency toward internal disputes, often resulting in relatively high rates of schismatic factionalism. Churches, in contrast, tend to follow mass market strategies oriented toward the casual consumer with relatively low levels of product awareness; as a result, educational programs are often underemphasized, audience-like behavior is cultivated, high levels of organizational switching (low product loyalty) are evident, withdrawal becomes more common than efforts at reform, and organizational initiatives tend to come less from lay members than from the more heavily involved bureaucratic staff.

Churches and sects, however, represent only two of the four types of organizations that can be identified by cross-classifying size and intensity. Also conceivable are large-intensive organizations and small-nonintensive organizations. The former appears to indeed represent a nearly ''empty cell'' as far as modern societies are concerned. Institutional differentiation, resulting in many functions and resources being dissipated among other organizations, appears to preclude large numbers of people giving total commitment to religious organizations. The other option (small nonintensive), however, appears to be a nonempty but neglected category of religious organization. This category is represented by relatively small religious organizations that make specialized demands on their members and fulfill specialized functions. The most appropriate term to describe these organizations is perhaps *special purpose groups.*

Special purpose religious groups are exemplified by religious movements oriented toward the reform of some larger religious body or the larger society, by interest groups and professional organizations among laity or among religious specialists, and by coalitions that integrate or bridge interest groups across the boundaries of established religious organizations. Rather than dealing inclusively with core religious concerns such as worship and instruction, they tend to be oriented toward more specialized aims (e.g., music, evangelism, or church policies on race). For this reason, many are characterized by fleeting existence or fleeting memberships. The intensity of commitment required may be quite high (as in other social movements), but in formal terms tends to be routinized either as a professional interest or as a focused commitment, in contrast with the model of religious communities, which purports to encompass all of an individual's interests and activities. Special purpose groups have a long history alongside churches and sects, but their numbers and memberships have apparently risen dramatically over the past half century or so (Wuthnow, 1985a).

The rising importance of special purpose religious groups appears in part to represent an isomorphism between religious organizations and secular organizations; for example, feminist movements in churches, black caucuses in churches, and so on. In addition, it appears that special purpose groups may be especially adaptable to the modern environment. In more narrowly focusing the goals of an organization greater adaptability may be gained in relation to an environment that is heterogeneous and rapidly changing. Special purpose groups may arise in relation to a specific social or political concern, but then disband once this concern has passed. By differentiating the special purpose group clearly from established churches and sects, resources can be channeled in more specific directions.

Research on religious organizations has also concentrated heavily on the internal structure of religious organizations and on leadership patterns, especially clergy roles. The most apparent tendency in this research has been a shift away from purely normative models that focused on formal conceptions and internalized roles toward more dynamic models emphasizing bargaining among constituencies within the organization and in the external environment. Churches' capacity to pursue transcendent ideals, such as civil rights activism, for example, may be largely determined by structural conditions such as denominational control over local churches, ministerial networks in the community, methods of local dispute settlement, and the degree of organization among lay members (e.g., Wood, 1981). Similarly, the capacity to mount large religio-moral movements, such as the Moral Majority, has been shown to depend on factors such as clergy autonomy, clergy networks, and prior experience in creating and managing large ecclesiastical organizations (Liebman, 1983). One highly beneficial result of this reorientation has been greater sensitivity to the ''supply'' side of religious commitment. Whereas it was once common for religious commitment to be examined entirely with reference to the social psychological needs that created a demand for religion on the part of the individual, explanations now give greater weight to the resources commanded by religious organizations and the ways in which these resources are mobilized to provide attractive services for the religious market.

Religion and the State

A final aspect of religious institutionalization that merits attention is the relation between religion and the state. This relation was ignored for a considerable time because of theoretical perspectives that concentrated on the growth of institutional differentiation between religion and the state.[17] Insofar as any continuing interaction was seen, it tended to be portrayed in terms of religious organizations fighting a rear guard action against the intrusion of the state into areas formerly under ecclesiastical jurisdiction. From this perspective it seemed evident that even by the end of the nineteenth century the church had withdrawn into comfortable isolation from the public affairs now supervised by the state. Yet recent developments in a number of societies, particularly in Latin America and the Middle East, have heightened awareness of the complexities of the relations between religion and the state. In the last few years a number of solid empirical studies have been produced.[18] Many have of necessity been preoccupied with the task of developing a descriptive empirical base; others have been devoted to questions of practical, legal, and ecclesiastical concern. Consequently, the literature in this area continues to lack rigorous theoretical systematization. For this reason, little more can be attempted here than a broad outline of the theoretical questions needing to be addressed.

The topic of *civil religion* is one area in which new thinking has been generated about the relations between religion and the state. Civil religion has been defined as "that religious dimension, found . . . in the life of every people, through which it interprets its historical experience in the light of transcendent reality" (Bellah, 1975, p. 3). In practice, civil religion generally consists of god-language used in reference to the nation; e.g., biblical quotations in presidential addresses, religious jeremiads directed at government policies, and so on. A society's civil religion includes a "myth of origin" that relates (and often reconstructs) the nation's history, a conception of the nation's purpose or destiny in history and in the world, definitions of what constitutes legitimate membership in the nation, and various taboos that define the society's external boundaries and differentiate it from other societies. Like religion generally, civil religion performs a dual function for the society: it legitimates the social order, evoking commitment and consensus; and it permits specific social policies to be criticized in light of transcendent ideals.[19]

Civil religion can be thought of as an instance of incomplete differentiation between religion and the state. It represents an intermingling of religious and political symbolism at the cultural level. Despite formal separation of church and state, the presence of a civil religion allows religious values to influence the state, on the one hand, and gives the state a means of influencing religion, on the other. The fact that these influences remain possible in highly industrialized societies suggests that the relations between religion and the state may be more complex than a strict conception of institutional differentiation would imply. Two empirical questions follow: One is whether religious organizations tend to benefit by having this form of access to the state or whether civil religion generally forces them to compromise; the other is whether the state benefits from having access to religious arguments or whether it functions more effectively in terms of purely secular norms. Both of these questions remain open, but available evidence indicates that answers are likely to vary from society to society depending on the nature of the state and the strength of different religious traditions.

The key limitation of studies concerned with civil religion to date is that they have concentrated almost entirely on matters of symbolism rather than including considerations of the institutional structure of the state and of religion. Greater attention needs to be given to the ways in which organizational constraints, resources, interest groups, and social cleavages affect the relations between religion and the state. For analytic purposes, these factors can be investigated at one or both of two distinct levels. At the societal level, the state becomes a relevant consideration chiefly as an element of the resource environment. At the institutional level, specific alliances and other forms of interaction between religious organizations and political organizations can be examined.

As a feature of the resource environment, the state influences religion in a number of indirect ways. Other things being equal, the presence of a centralized state with legitimate rule over a sizable territory defines an environment that encompasses local and regional niches of considerable heterogeneity. Indeed, the expansion of the nation-state typically takes place at the expense of local and regional autonomy. In this manner, state expansion is likely to create an environment that selects for the kinds of religious systems that adapt most easily to broad heterogeneous niches. As the defender of uniform laws and regulations, the state also in a sense establishes "rules of the game" to which religious institutions must conform. The state not only defines the environment but also monopolizes many of the resources in the environment. To the extent that its monopoly over resources needed by religious systems—charters, educational facilities, public buildings, communications media—is complete, religious competition may be reduced to an inconsequential minimum (as in the case of theocratic states or states banning all forms of religious practice). On the other hand, states whose own legitimacy is in doubt or whose capacity to elicit consensus is weak are likely by default to create niches in which religious opposition is able to flourish. That is, pockets of opposition to the state become recognizable social niches in which alternative religions can develop. In these niches, more established religions may be unable to succeed because of their identification with the norms and values of the state. A strong sense of internal solidarity may also give rise to collective symbolism and rituals which take on religious connotations. Examples include such diverse movements as Shi'ism among the technical intelligentsia in Iran, Protestant Pentecostalism among ethnic minorities in Latin America, and Eastern-mystical religions among American youth during the Vietnam War.

In its capacity to manipulate resources, the state also produces alterations in the social environment that affect the capacity of established religious communities to maintain themselves. Matters as seemingly remote as government expenditures on space exploration and military installations can have significant ramifications for religious communities. In a society characterized by a high degree of religious involvement, such as the United States, commitments to the educational upgrading involved in space exploration and other highly technological programs lead indirectly to serious cleavages within religious bodies by altering the educational and occupational statuses of the members of these bodies; similarly, decisions to locate military installations in previously localized cultures give the religions of these areas greater interest in and access to national agendas (Hunter, 1980; Sweet, 1984; Wacker, 1984). These effects, it should be noted, cannot be summarized simply in terms of a decline in religious influence but rather have to be examined in terms of the restructuring of religious resources, organizations, and commitments. If religious systems constitute moral communities with patterned relations to their environments, then cleavages and other changes in the social environment are likely to produce a significant restructuring of religious organizations, commitments, and ideologies.

The other—institutional—level of investigation focuses on formal and informal interactions between religious organizations and agencies of the state. These interactions take place within the context of considerable complexity on the sides of both the state and religion. For its part, the state cannot be viewed as a static or mono-lithic entity, but must be conceived of as a set of interdependent organizations, with both representative and intrinsic interests, having to secure resources from a changing environment, and subject to internal cleavages as a result of differential relations to the environment.[20] On the religious side, different religious organizations are likely to be in competition with one another (and with secular organizations), will be characterized by different levels of resources, and will adopt strategies aimed at protecting or enlarging their niche in the environment.

During much of the period extending from the beginning of the sixteenth century to the middle of the nineteenth century the relations between states and religious organizations in the West were deeply influenced by the break-up of ecclesiastical universalism and by the internal conflict between representative Estates and central administrative agencies that accompanied the transition from medieval *standestadten* to the modern bureaucratic state. Competition among religious organizations was typically resolved by different organizations forming alliances with Estates or central administrative agencies, the outcome of which was greatly affected by changes in the broader economic base and by the various groups' access to these resources (see Wuthnow, 1985b). Fulbrook's (1983) comparative study of Puritanism in seventeenth-century England and Pietism in eighteenth-century Prussia and Württemberg illustrates the dynamics of this process. In Württemberg, Pietism was absorbed relatively easily into the state church and, for this reason, did not engage in direct political agitation as a means of enlarging its resources. In Prussia the economic and military expansion of the eighteenth century led to an enlarged cleavage between the landed aristoccracy and the central bureaucracy, with Lutheranism maintaining its traditional alliance with the landed elite. As a result, the central bureaucracy threw its support behind the Pietist opposition, in return for which Prussian Pietism came to associate fairly closely with proabsolutist sentiments. In contrast, English Puritanism developed strong anti-absolutist sentiments despite a close resemblance between its purely religious style and that of Prussian Pietism. The difference, Fulbrook argues, was the fact that Anglicanism had been closely allied with the central bureaucracy, thus heightening the chances of an alliance between the Puritan religious opposition and the parliamentary political opposition. At an earlier stage of political development some of these processes are also evident in the religious conflicts surrounding the Reformation in the sixteenth century. Parts of Central Europe, Scandinavia, and England underwent rapid commercial expansion, providing central administrators and urban magistrates with resources no longer associated with the rural aristocracy. In these areas Protestant reformers were able to gain strong support from central administrators despite resistance from the land-owning classes. Other areas such as Poland, France, and Spain benefited less significantly from commercial expansion or acquired military obligations that retained the state's fiscal and administrative dependence on the landed elites. These areas experienced Protestant agitation in many urban areas but ultimately remained Catholic in the face of strong pressures from the land-owning sector on the central bureaucracies (Wuthnow, 1986b).

In the twentieth century interactions between religious organizations and states in industrialized societies have been marked chiefly by the ambivalent character of the modern welfare state. On the one hand, the modern welfare state continues to function in accordance with classical laissez faire conceptions that define its role as a guarantor of open market competition. On the other hand, it has taken an increasingly active role in providing for public welfare, making available public services, regulating and promoting economic growth, and supervising a greatly enlarged set of civil rights. Many observers have commented on the tendency of welfare functions and civil rights regulations to interfere with the traditional activities of religious groups, thereby producing a seemingly endless series of litigations (e.g., Robbins, 1985). These conflicts have been taken as ready evidence of the further erosion of religious institutions in modern societies. Yet, closer examination indicates that the state's own ambivalence has played a role in these relations with religion and that religious organizations have adopted a wide variety of strategies in dealing with the state.

As a rule, religious organizations have supported the laissez faire conception of the state, at least in matters where religion is concerned, perhaps largely because the long history of religio-political conflicts has generated norms favoring religious tolerance and some degree of separation between church and state. Most religions, it appears, have adapted to the modern situation by developing quasi-commercial strategies that allow them to compete in the marketplace rather than relying heavily on the state for resources (e.g., see White, 1972). This, of course, has been more the case in religiously diverse societies than in societies where a single religion can overpower all the others. In return, religious organizations' support of free market conditions in religion has often provided proponents of minimalist state intervention in economic affairs with ideological ammunition, if not supportive constituencies (e.g., Novak, 1982, 1984).

Where the strategies of religious organizations have been more varied is with respect to the welfare, service, and regulatory functions of the state. In part, these strategies can be analyzed in relatively straightforward terms based on the kinds of interests involved. For example, religious organizations with large investments in private schools are more likely to support tax vouchers than organizations without such investments. Not all of the relations can be analyzed this simply, however. Both the issue under consideration and the broader social position of the religious organizations involved are likely to influence the nature of the interaction.

Animating many of the relations between religious organizations and the state is the fact that religion tends to be concerned not only with human-divine relations but with moral or ethical questions. The expansion of the welfare state into a broader range of regulatory and service functions has made it a relevant resource for religious organizations to attempt to exploit in implementing their moral and ethical programs. Religious organizations of all theological orientations have attempted to forge coalitions with state agencies and have greatly expanded their use of the courts in order to promote particular moral crusades, whether these crusades consist of drives against racial segregation, lobbying for gender equality, antipornography campaigns, efforts to promote prayer in schools, or movements in favor of or against abortion. The difference in religious organizations' attitude toward government involvement has typically depended more on the issue concerned than on general orientations toward church and state.

At the same time, religious organizations' relations to the state are also affected by their position in the larger society. Again, access to resources appears to be a decisive consideration. Minority religions with limited resources are likely to favor relatively strict separation between church and state, since religious freedom allows them to retain control over the limited resources they have acquired. Claims to religious freedom by Amish groups and Jehovah's Witnesses provide cases in point. At the other extreme, religious organizations with such an ample supply of resources as to be able to dominate the religious market also tend to support policies of government noninterference (except of course in the extreme case of theocracies). These establishments have sufficient resources to achieve many of their own programs without government assistance; in arguing for strict noninterference they in effect pit their substantial resources against other religious organizations with fewer resources (see Lindblom, 1977, for a related economic argument). From this perspective, it is not surprising that large organizations such as the National Council of Churches or the Southern Baptist Convention have generally been strong advocates of strict separation between church and state. The groups most likely to support government intervention, other things being equal, therefore, are those in the middle—groups having enough resources to entertain hopes of being successful in relations with the state, yet lacking the resources needed to win over their competitors in strictly open religious competition. The recent political activism of fundamentalist and evangelical clergy, coming in the wake of an increase in their own organizational resources, seems to fit this pattern. Such groups are particularly likely to become involved in the political process when actions of the state or changes in political climate give them a sense of political *entitlement* (e.g., Wuthnow, 1983).

None of this implies that religious organizations act according to strictly rational resource maximization strategies or that these organizations are, after all, more concerned with pragmatic matters than with articulating worshipful responses to the sacred. But social environments characterized by rational, pragmatic, technical procedures necessarily impose certain constraints on the manner in which religious organizations can function. How religion adapts—whether it maintains a critical role in relation to its environment or whether it compromises in serious ways—bears importantly on the direction of culture itself.

Conclusion

In viewing the sociology of religion as a whole, many significant developments have obviously taken place over the past several decades; yet, it appears regrettable that the field has grown more rapidly in inductive empirical research and in subspecializations than it has in attempts to identify theoretically integrative concepts and to develop formulations that would permit the field to interact more beneficially with the rest of the discipline. Fragmentation in terms of social psychological versus organizational approaches, micro versus macro levels of analysis, studies of institutional religion versus studies of new religious movements, and cultural perspectives versus social structural perspectives remains altogether too common. Even to attempt a survey of the field, giving it some semblance of conceptual coherence, necessitates imposing greater unity on the field than actually exists. The problem is not one of lively disagreement over serious intellectual disputes but an absence of unifying constructs with which such communication might be advanced.

Cues from the discipline at large are of questionable value since, with the exception of purely technical advances in statistical methods, little evidence of theoretical convergence can be found there either. Yet possibilities may exist for the study of religion to benefit from conceptual modifications that encourage greater interaction with developments in other areas. Certainly it is arguable that many of the classical writers were good sociologists of religion because they were good sociologists.

Emphasis on the relations between social systems and their environments has been increasingly evident in the discipline more generally, as have related perspectives such as those dealing with the network structure of social systems and the structural arrangement of social resources. While there may well be characteristics of religious systems that make them different from other social entities, it seems clear that many of the distinctive concepts of the field can either be abandoned or translated in ways that make them more compatible with formulations having wider use in the discipline. Thus to speak of various processes of social production, selection, and institutionalization in religion is to speak in words that have become relevant in other parts of the discipline as well.

What is perhaps of equal value to the study of religion is the possibility of developing concepts capable of bridging its various subspecializations. Until recently, languages of quite different vintage had to be employed in order to discuss the social psychology of religious belief, the organizational properties of religious institutions, and the dynamics of religious culture. Yet, as the foregoing has sought to illustrate, it is often possible to conceptualize the characteristics of religious movements, religious beliefs, and religious organizations in more compatible terms. A rigorous orthodoxy of deductive generalizations is neither the likely nor the desirable outcome of such conceptual integration. But conceptual integration is essential for greater communication in the future about the significance of empirical work.

NOTES

1. These are: *Journal for the Scientific Study of Religion, Sociological Analysis, Review of Religious Research, Social Compass, Archives de Sociologie des Religions*, and *Internationales Jahrbuch für Religionssoziologie*. Also of relevance is the annual volume of proceedings, *Actes de la Conference Internationale du Sociologie Religieux*. Useful overviews of the field are available in several recent introductory texts; see especially McGuire (1981), Chalfant, Beckley, and Palmer (1981), Roberts (1984), and Moberg (1984). Edited volumes that provide useful overviews of the field include Hammond (1985), McNamara (1984), and O'Dea and O'Dea (1973). The literature on social psychology of religion is surveyed in Batson and Ventis (1982), Paloutzian (1983), Byrnes (1984), Spilka, Gorsuch, and Hood (1984), and Meadow and Kahoe (1984). Secondary discussions of the classical literature on religion are numerous; see especially Budd (1973), Glock and Hammond (1973), Turner (1983), and O'Toole (1984).

2. The literature on empirical measures of specific types of religious beliefs and practices is quite extensive; for a useful overview, see Roof (1979).

3. For a comprehensive bibliographic review of the literature on secularization, see Dobbelaere (1981). Among the studies challenging the secularization thesis are Caplow, Bahr, and Chadwick (1983), Douglas (1983), Neuhaus (1984), Stark and Bainbridge (1985), and Greeley (1982).

4. The conditions under which this assumption is more or less likely to hold true are also subject to empirical investigation, of course.

5. Several useful anthologies and bibliographic guides to this literature are available: Glock and Bellah (1976), Robbins, Anthony, and Richardson (1978), Robbins and Anthony (1981), Barker (1982), Wallis (1984), Choquette (1985), Kilbourne (1985), and Beckford (1986).

6. "Disturbance" is used here as an umbrella concept to indicate relatively abrupt or dramatic changes in the amount or distribution of social resources (e.g., an increase in trade flows, an invention of new means of disseminating literature, a redistribution of welfare benefits through legislative actions). Specific examples are given in the following sections. "Uncertainty" in moral obligations can be of several varieties (see Wuthnow, 1981b).

7. In addition to research on the origin of religious movements as collectivities, much sociological work has also focused on the nature of religious conversion at the individual level; see Rambo (1982) for an extensive interdisciplinary review of the literature. Also see Long and Hadden (1983) for a critical discussion of sociological theories of conversion. Another useful overview of the literature is found in Snow and Machalek (1983).

8. Some of the more interesting of these studies, by subject matter, are as follows: Middle Ages— Lerner (1972), Moore (1975); Early Modern Europe—

Bruckner (1968), Thomas (1971), LeRoy Ladurie (1979); Third World—Wilson (1973); American rural south—Browne (1958), Rickles (1965), Genovese (1974); Amish—Hostetler (1968); Hutterites—Peters (1965), Hostetler and Huntington (1967); Judaism— Trachtenberg (1970), Poll (1969), Friedman (1975).

9. For some statistical studies, see Greeley (1975), Gallup (1982), Wuthnow (1978), Krarup (1983), and Towler (1983). For the survival of the occult, see also Kerr and Crow (1983); and on folklore, see Brunvand (1981, 1984). On holidays, see Caplow and Williamson (1980), Caplow (1982), and Caplow, Bahr, and Chadwick (1983); and on sports and other media events, see Owens (1980) and Goethels (1981).

10. For a mathematical proof of this assertion, see May (1973). I am indebted to James R. Beniger for this insight; see Beniger (1981).

11. Among the relatively large number of discussions of this topic, several of which bear on the subject of religion include: Parsons (1951, pp. 297-321; 1978, pp. 264-299, 331-351), Cook and Wimberley (1983), Aris (1981), and Hochschild (1978).

12. This relationship appears to have gained empirical confirmation in a wide variety of settings; see, for example, Bergesen (1979) and Cerulo (1985).

13. Recent contributions to the debate on rationality and cultural relativism include Geertz (1984) and the essays in Hollis and Lukes (1982).

14. Studies of ritual remain more the domain of anthropologists than of sociologists, but several useful overviews of the literature are available that raise issues of relevance to sociology. Grimes (1982) surveys a number of major theoretical approaches in addition to providing some empirical cases; Skorupski (1976) is one of the most valuable discussions because it sets ritual in the context of broader considerations on the nature and functions of symbolism; a number of shorter essays on ritual are available in Shaughnessy (1973) and d'Aguili, Laughlin, and McManus (1979); several notable empirical studies are those of Lane (1981), Paige and Paige (1981), and Westley (1983, pp. 115ff). Douglas (1973, pp. 19-39) continues to be a useful discussion of misconceptions concerning ritual, while the nature of ritual as communication is effectively illustrated by Leach (1964), Barthes (1972), Bossy (1981), Burguiere (1978), Davis (1975), McCarl (1979), and Darnton (1984).

15. For reviews of the literature on religious organizations, including an annotated bibliography, see Beckford (1973, 1984). Beckford conceives of religious organizations as "open systems" that interact with their environments and with one another in competition for resources. More recently, valuable evidence on religious organizations can be found in Scherer (1980), Wood (1981), and Moberg (1984).

16. A third concept—cult—is often introduced as well. By one set of criteria, a cult differs from a sect chiefly by virtue of originating as an independent organization rather than as a splinter group from an established organization; in other treatments, cults are simply less stable or more dependent on a charismatic leader than are sects. It would appear

preferable to retain these questions about the origins and evolutions of religious movements as empirical matters rather than prejudge them by the definitional process. On the debate over terminology, see especially Stark and Bainbridge (1979) and Bainbridge and Stark (1980).

17. Representatives of this perspective include Vallier (1970) and Smith (1970); for a critique, see Levine (1979; 1981, pp. 24-25).

18. On Latin America, see especially Levine (1980, 1981), Smith (1982), Dussel (1981), Bruneau (1982); also see Levine (1985) for a wide-ranging review of the literature; studies of religion and politics in the Middle East include Esposito (1983), Arjomand (1984a, 1984b), Piscatori (1982), Voll (1982), Haddad (1982), Fischer (1980), Keddie (1983), and Pipes (1983). Recent work has also focused on Poland (Pomian-Srzednicki, 1982), Italy (Kertzer, 1980), Ireland (Bowen, 1983; Gallagher and Worrall, 1982), and Israel (Elazar, 1983; Liebman and Don-Yehiya, 1983, 1984). Work on the United States has been somewhat more scattered, often dealing with specific religio-political movements or with the relations between religion and voting; several studies of more general use include Kelly (1983), Benson and Williams (1982), Mechling (1978), Sorauf (1976), Bourg (1980), and Robertson (1981). Earlier works that are still valuable include Stokes and Pfeffer (1964), Pfeffer (1967), and Stroup (1967). An excellent source for more specific studies is the *Journal of Church and State*.

19. For an extensive review of the literature on civil religion, see Gehrig (1979); also see Hammond (1976) and Wilson (1979). Most of the work on civil religion has been limited to the American case, but several valuable studies that provide comparisons are also available; see especially Moodie (1975), Liebman and Don-Yehiya (1983), and the essays in Bellah and Hammond (1980).

20. Increasingly, the larger environment in which both states and religious organizations function has been analyzed as a ''world-system''; essays applying this approach specifically to religion include Robertson (1985a, 1985b), Wuthnow (1978, 1980, 1983), Hunter (1986), and Thomas (1986).

REFERENCES

Ammerman, Nancy Taton. 1983. ''The Fundamentalist Worldview: Ideology and Social Structure in an Independent Fundamental Church.'' Ph.D. dissertation, Yale University.

Antoun, Richard and Mary Hegland, eds. 1986. *Religious Resurgence in Comparative Perspective*. Syracuse: Syracuse University Press.

Apostle, Richard A., Charles Y. Glock, Thomas Piazza, and Marijean Suelzle. 1983. *The Anatomy of Racial Attitudes*. Berkeley: University of California Press.

Aris, Philippe. 1981. *The Hour of Our Death*. New York: Knopf.

Arjomand, Said Amir. 1984a. *The Shadow of God and the Hidden Imam: Religion, Political Order, and Societal Change in Shi'ite Iran from the Beginning to 1890*. Chicago: University of Chicago Press.

_____, ed. 1984b. *From Nationalism to Revolutionary Islam*. Albany: State University of New York Press.

Ault, James M., Jr. 1983. ''The Shawmut Valley Baptist Church: Reconstructing a Traditional Order of Family Life in a Fundamentalist Community.'' Unpublished Paper, Pembroke Center, Brown University.

Bainbridge, William Sims. 1978. *Satan's Power: A Deviant Psychotherapy Cult*. Berkeley: University of California Press.

_____ and Rodney Stark. 1980. ''Sectarian Tension.'' *Review of Religious Research* 22:105-124.

Barker, Eileen, ed. 1982. *New Religious Movements.: A Perspective for Understanding Society*. New York: Edwin Mellen.

Barthes, Roland. 1972. *Mythologies*. New York: Hill and Wang.

Batson, C. Daniel and W. Larry Ventis. 1982. *The Religious Experience*. New York: Oxford University Press.

Beckford, James A. 1973. ''Religious Organization: A Trend Report and Bibliography.'' *Current Sociology* 21:1-170.

_____ 1975. *The Trumpet of Prophecy: A Sociological Study of the Jehovah's Witnesses*. New York: John Wiley.

_____ 1984. ''Religious Organization: A Survey of Some Recent Publications.'' *Archives de Sciences Sociales des Religions* 57:83-102.

_____ 1986. *Cult Controversies*. London: Tavistock.

Bell, Daniel. 1977. ''Beyond Modernism, Beyond Self.'' Pp. 213-253 in *Art, Politics, and Will: Essays in Honor of Lionel Trilling*, edited by Quentin Anderson, Stephen Donadio, and Steven Marcus. New York: Basic Books.

Bellah, Robert N. 1970. *Beyond Belief: Essays on Religion in a Post-Traditional World*. New York: Harper & Row.

_____, ed. 1973. ''Introduction.'' Pp. ix-lv in *Emile Durkheim on Morality and Society*. Chicago: University of Chicago Press.

_____ 1975. *The Broken Covenant*. New York: Seabury.

_____ 1982. ''Cultural Pluralism and Religious Particularism.'' Pp. 33-52 in *Freedom of Religion in America: Historical Roots, Philosophical Concepts, and Contemporary Problems*, edited by Henry B. Clark II. New Brunswick, NJ: Transaction Books.

_____ and Phillip E. Hammond. 1980. *Varieties of Civil Religion*. New York: Harper & Row.

Bellah, Robert N., Richard Madsen, William M. Sullivan, Ann Swidler, and Steven M. Tipton. 1985. *Habits of the Heart: Individualism and Com-*

mitment in American Life. Berkeley: University of California Press.

Ben-Yehuda, Nachman. 1980. "The European Witch Craze of the 14th to 17th Centuries: A Sociologist's Perspective." *American Journal of Sociology* 86:1-31.

Bender, Lauretta. 1970. "The Maturation Process and Hallucinations in Children." Pp. 95-101 in *Origins and Mechanisms of Hallucinations*, edited by Wolfram Keup. New York: Plenum.

Bendix, Reinhard. 1977. *Nation-Building and Citizenship*. Berkeley: University of California Press.

Beniger, James R. 1981. "Ideology as a Dynamic System: Complexity vs. Stability." Unpublished paper, Department of Sociology, Princeton University.

———. 1986. *The Control Revolution: Technological and Economic Origins of the Information Society*. Cambridge, MA: Harvard University Press.

Benson, Peter L. and Dorothy L. Williams. 1982. *Religion on Capital Hill: Myths and Realities*. New York: Harper & Row.

Berger, Peter L. 1969. *The Sacred Canopy: Elements of a Sociological Theory of Religion*. Garden City, NY: Doubleday.

——— and Thomas Luckmann. 1966. *The Social Construction of Reality*. Garden City, NY: Doubleday.

Bergesen, Albert. 1977. "Political Witch-Hunts: The Sacred and the Subversive in Cross-National Perspective." *American Sociological Review* 42:220-233.

———. 1978. "A Durkheimian Theory of Political Witch-Hunts with the Chinese Cultural Revolution of 1966-1969 as an Example." *Journal for the Scientific Study of Religion* 17:19-29.

———. 1979. "Spirituals, Jazz, Blues, and Soul Music: The Role of Elaborated and Restricted Codes in the Maintenance of Social Solidarity." Pp. 333-350 in *The Religious Dimension*, edited by Robert Wuthnow. New York: Academic.

———. 1980. "Official Violence During the Watts, Newark, and Detroit Race Riots of the 1960s." Pp. 138-174 in *A Political Analysis of Deviance*, edited by Pat Lauderdale. Minneapolis: University of Minnesota Press.

———. 1984. *The Sacred and the Subversive: Political Witch-Hunts as National Rituals*. Storrs, CT: Society for the Scientific Study of Religion Monograph Series.

——— and Mark Warr. 1979. "A Crisis in the Moral Order: The Effects of Watergate upon Confidence in Social Institutions" Pp. 227-298 in *The Religious Dimension*, edited by Robert Wuthnow, New York: Academic Press.

Bernstein, Basil. 1975. *Class, Codes and Control*. New York: Schocken.

Bibby, R. and M. Brinkerhoff. 1973. "The Circulation of the Saints." *Journal for the Scientific Study of Religion* 12:273-285.

———. 1983. "Circulation of the Saints Revisited: A Longitudinal Look at Conservative Church Growth." *Journal for the Scientific Study of Religion* 22:253-262.

Boli-Bennett, John and John W. Meyer. 1978. "The Ideology of Childhood and the State: Rules Distinguishing Children in National Constitutions, 1870-1970." *American Sociological Review* 43:797-812.

Bossy, John. 1981. "Essai de sociographie de la masse, 1200-1700." *Annales E.S.C.* 36:44-70.

Bourg, Carroll J. 1980. "Politics and Religion." *Sociological Analysis* 41:297-315.

Bowen, Kurt. 1983. *Protestants in a Catholic State: Ireland's Privileged Minority*. Montreal: McGill-Queens University Press.

Browne, Ray B. 1958. *Popular Beliefs and Practices from Alabama*. Berkeley: University of California Press.

Bruce, Steve. 1983. "Social Change and Collective Behaviour: The Revival in Eighteenth-Century Rossshire. " *British Journal of Sociology* 34: 554-572.

Bruckner, Wolfgang. 1968. "Popular Piety in Central Europe." *Journal of the Folklore Institute* 5:158-174.

Brummer, Vincent. 1982. *Theology and Philosophical Inquiry*. Philadelphia: Westminster.

Bruneau, Thomas C. 1982. *The Church in Brazil: The Politics of Religion*. Austin, TX: University of Texas Press.

Brunvand, Jan. 1981. *The Vanishing Hitchhiker*. New York: W.W. Norton.

———. 1984. *The Choking Doberman*. New York: W.W. Norton.

Budd, Susan. 1973. *Sociologists and Religion*. London: Collier-Macmillan.

Burguiere, A. 1978. "Le rituel du mariage en France: Pratiques ecclesiastiques et pratiques populaires (XVIe - XVIIIe siecle)." *Annales E.S.C.* 33: 637-649.

Byrnes, Joseph F. 1984. *The Psychology of Religion*. New York: Free Press.

Caplow, Theodore. 1982. "Christmas Gifts and Kin Networks." *American Sociological Review* 47: 383-392.

———, Howard M. Bahr, and Bruce A. Chadwick. 1983. *All Faithful People: Change and Continuity in Middletown's Religion*. Minneapolis: University of Minnesota Press.

Caplow, Theodore and Margaret Holmes Williamson. 1980. "Decoding Middletown's Easter Bunny: A Study in American Iconography." *Semiotica* 32:221-232.

Carroll, Michael P. 1983. "Visions of the Virgin Mary: The Effect of Family Structures on Marian Apparitions." *Journal for the Scientific Study of Religion* 22:205-221.

Carroll, Michael P. 1986. *Ave Maria, Gratia Plena: The Social Origins of the Mary Cult*. Princeton, NJ: Princeton University Press.

Cerulo, Karen A. 1985. *Music as Symbolic Communication: The Case of the National Anthem*. Ph.D. dissertation, Princeton University.

Chalfant, H. Paul, Robert E. Beckley, and C. Eddie Palmer. 1981. *Religion in Contemporary Society*. Sherman Oaks, CA: Alfred.

Choquette, Diane. 1985. *New Religious Movements in the United States and Canada: A Critical Assessment and Annotated Bibliography*. Westport, CT: Greenwood Press.

Comaroff, Jean. 1985. *Body of Power, Spirit of Resistance: The Culture and History of a South African People*. Chicago: University of Chicago Press.

Cook, Judith A. and Dale W. Wimberley. 1983. "If I Should Die Before I Wake: Religious Commitment and Adjustment to the Death of a Child." *Journal for the Scientific Study of Religion* 22: 222-239.

Cuddihy, John. 1978. *No Offense: Civil Religion and Protestant Taste*. New York: Seabury.

d'Aguili, Eugene G., Charles D. Laughlin, Jr., and John McManus, eds. 1979. *The Spectrum of Ritual: A Biogenetic Structural Analysis*. New York: Columbia University Press.

Darnton, Robert. 1984. *The Great Cat Massacre*. New York: Basic Books.

Davis, Natalie Zemon. 1975. *Society and Culture in Early Modern France*. Stanford, CA: Stanford University Press.

Dobbelaere, Karel. 1981. "Secularization: A Multi-Dimensional Concept." *Current Sociology* 29: 1-216.

Dohrenwend, Bruce P. and Barbara S. Dohrenwend, eds. 1974. *Stressful Life Events: Their Nature and Effects*. New York: John Wiley.

Douglas, Mary. 1966. *Purity and Danger: An Analysis of Concepts of Pollution and Taboo*. London: Penguin.

———— 1973. *Natural Symbols*. New York: Vintage.

———— 1983. "The Effects of Modernization on Religious Change." Pp. 25-43 in *Religion and America: Spirituality in a Secular Age*, edited by Mary Douglas and Steven M. Tipton. Boston: Beacon.

————, ed. 1984. *Food in the Social Order: Studies of Food and Festivities in Three American Communities*. New York: Russell Sage.

Downton, James V., Jr. 1979. *Sacred Journeys: The Conversion of Young Americans to Divine Light Mission*. New York: Columbia University Press.

Durkheim, Emile. 1965. *The Elementary Forms of the Religious Life*. New York: Free Press. (Original work published 1915)

Dussel, Enrique. 1981. *A History of the Church in Latin America: Colonialism to Liberation*. Grand Rapids, Mich.: Eerdmans.

Eisenstadt, S. N. and Louis Roniger. 1980. "Patron-Client Relations as a Model of Structuring Social Exchange." *Comparative Studies in Society and History* 22:42-77.

Elazar, Daniel J., ed. 1983. *Kinship and Consent: The Jewish Political Tradition and Its Contemporary Uses*. Washington, DC: University Press of America.

Erikson, Kai T. 1966. *Wayward Puritans: A Study in the Sociology of Deviance*. New York: John Wiley.

Esposito, John L., ed. 1983. *Voices of Resurgent Islam*. Oxford: Oxford University Press.

Fingarette, Herbert. 1963. *The Self in Transformation: Psychoanalysis, Philosophy and the Life of the Spirit*. New York: Harper & Row.

Firth, Raymond. 1984. "The Plasticity of Myth: Cases from Tikopia." Pp. 207-216 in *Sacred Narrative: Readings in the Theory of Myth*, edited by Alan Dundes. Berkeley: University of California Press.

Fischer, Michael M.J. 1980. *Iran: From Religious Dispute to Revolution*. Cambridge, MA: Harvard University Press.

Foucault, Michel. 1965. *Madness and Civilization: A History of Insanity in the Age of Reason*. New York: Random House.

———— 1970. *The Order of Things: An Archeology of the Human Sciences*. New York: Random House.

———— 1972. *The Archeology of Knowledge*. New York: Random House.

———— 1975. *The Birth of the Clinic: An Archeology of Medical Perception*. New York: Random House.

———— 1979. *Discipline and Punish: The Birth of the Prison*. New York: Vintage.

Friedman, Norman L. 1975. "Jewish Popular Culture in Contemporary America." *Judaism* 24:263-277.

Fulbrook, Mary. 1983. *Piety and Politics: Religion and the Rise of Absolutism in England, Württemberg, and Prussia*. Cambridge: Cambridge University Press.

Gager, John. 1975. *Kingdom and Community: The Social World of Early Christianity*. Englewood Cliffs, NJ: Prentice-Hall.

———— 1983. *The Origins of Anti-Semitism: Attitudes Toward Judaism in Pagan and Christian Antiquity*. Oxford: Oxford University Press.

Gallagher, Eric and Stanley Worrall. 1982. *Christians in Ulster, 1968-1980*. Oxford: Oxford University Press.

Gallup, George, Jr. 1982. *Adventures in Immortality: A Look Beyond the Threshold of Death*. New York: McGraw-Hill.

Gallup Organization. 1984. *Religious Television in America*. Princeton, NJ: Author.

Geertz, Clifford. 1968. *Islam Observed: Religious Development in Morocco and Indonesia*. Chicago: University of Chicago Press.

———— 1973. *The Interpretation of Cultures*. New York: Basic Books.

———— 1984. "Distinguished Lecture: Anti Anti-Relativism." *American Anthropologist* 86:263-278.

Gehrig, Gail. 1979. *American Civil Religion: An Assessment*. Storrs, CT: Society for the Scientific Study of Religion Monograph Series, No. 3.

Genovese, Eugene D. 1974. *Roll, Jordan, Roll: The World the Slaves Made*. New York: Random

House.

Geraets, Thomas, ed. 1979. *Rationality Today*. Ottowa: University of Ottowa Press.

Gerlach, Luther P. and Virginia Hine. 1970. *People, Power, Change: Movements of Social Transformation*. Indianapolis: Bobbs-Merrill.

Glock, Charles Y. 1973. "On the Origin and Evolution of Religious Groups." Pp. 207-220 in *Religion in Sociological Perspective*, edited by Charles Y. Glock. Belmont, CA: Wadsworth.

———— and Robert N. Bellah, eds. 1976. *The New Religious Consciousness*. Berkeley: University of California Press.

Glock, Charles Y. and Phillip E. Hammond, eds. 1973. *Beyond the Classics? Essays in the Scientific Study of Religion*. New York: Harper & Row.

Glock, Charles Y. and Rodney Stark. 1965. *Religion and Society in Tension*. Chicago: Rand McNally.

Goethels, Gregor T. 1981. *The TV Ritual: Worship at the Video Altar*. Boston: Beacon.

Greeley, Andrew M. 1975. *The Sociology of the Paranormal: A Reconnaissance*. Beverly Hills, CA: Sage.

———— 1982. *Religion: A Secular Theory*. New York: Free Press.

Grimes, Ronald L. 1982. *Beginnings in Ritual Studies*. Washington, DC: University Press of America.

Habermas, Jürgen. 1975. *Legitimation Crisis*. Boston: Beacon.

———— 1979a. *Communication and the Evolution of Society*. Boston: Beacon.

———— 1979b. "History and Evolution." *Telos* 39: 5-44.

———— 1984. *The Theory of Communicative Action, vol. 1: Reason and the Rationalization of Society*. Boston: Beacon.

Haddad, Yvonne Yazbeck. 1982. *Contemporary Islam and the Challenge of History*. Albany: State University of New York Press.

Hadden, Jeffrey and Charles Swan. 1981. *Primetime Preachers: The Rising Power of Televangelism*. Reading, MA: Addison-Wesley.

Hammond, Phillip E. 1976. "The Sociology of American Civil Religion: A Bibliographic Essay." *Sociological Analysis* 37:169-182.

————, ed. 1985. *The Sacred in a Secular Age: Toward Revision in the Scientific Study of Religion*. Berkeley: University of California Press.

———— and James Davison Hunter. 1984. "On Maintaining Plausibility: The Worldview of Evangelical College Students." *Journal for the Scientific Study of Religion* 23:221-239.

Hannan, Michael T. and John Freeman. 1977. "The Population Ecology of Organizations." *American Journal of Sociology* 82:929-964.

Heinz, Donald. 1983. "The Struggle to Define America." Pp. 133-149 in *The New Christian Right*, edited by Robert C. Liebman and Robert Wuthnow. New York: Aldine.

Hilke, John C. 1980. "Voluntary Contributions and Monitoring Efforts: Revealed Preference for the Services of Religious Organizations." *Journal for the Scientific Study of Religion* 19:138-145.

Hine, Virginia H. 1974. "The Deprivation and Disorganization Theories of Social Movements." Pp. 646-664 in *Religious Movements in Contemporary America*, edited by Irving I. Zaretsky and Mark P. Leone. Princeton, NJ: Princeton University Press.

Hochschild, Arlie Russell. 1978. *The Unexpected Community: Portrait of an Old Age Subculture*. Berkeley: University of California Press.

Hollis, M. and S. Lukes, eds. 1982. *Rationality and Relativism*. Cambridge, MA: MIT Press.

Horsfield, Peter G. 1984. *Religious Television: The American Experience*. New York: Longman.

Hostetler, John A. 1968. *Amish Society*. Baltimore, MD: Johns Hopkins Press.

———— and Gertrude Enders Huntington. 1967. *The Hutterites in North America*. New York: Holt, Rinehart and Winston.

Hunter, James Davison. 1980. "The New Class and the Young Evangelicals." *Review of Religious Research* 22:155-169.

———— 1983. *American Evangelicalism: Conservative Religion and the Quandary of Modernity*. New Brunswick, NJ: Rutgers University Press.

———— 1985. "Conservative Protestantism." In *The Sacred in a Secular Age*, edited by Phillip E. Hammond. Berkeley: University of California Press.

———— 1986. *Evangelicalism: The Coming Generation of America*. Chicago: University of Chicago Press.

Inverarity, James M. 1976. "Populism and Lynching in Louisiana, 1889-1896: A Test of Erikson's Theory of the Relationship between Boundary Crises and Repressive Justice." *American Sociological Review* 41:262-280.

Jaffe, Steven. 1966. "Hallucinations in Children at a State Hospital." *Psychiatric Quarterly* 40:88-95.

Jarvie, I. C. 1983. "Rationality and Relativism." *British Journal of Sociology* 34:44-60.

Johnson, Paul E. 1978. *A Shopkeeper's Millennium: Society and Revivals in Rochester, New York, 1815-1837*. New York: Hill and Wang.

Keddie, Nikki R., ed. 1983. *Religion and Politics in Iran: Shi'ism from Quietism to Revolution*. New Haven, CT: Yale University Press.

Kelly, Dean M. 1972. *Why Conservative Churches Are Growing*. New York: Harper & Row.

Kelly, George Armstrong. 1983. *Politics and Religious Consciousness in America*. New Brunswick, NJ: Transaction.

Kerr, Howard and Charles L. Crow, eds. 1983. *The Occult in America: New Historical Perspectives*. Urbana: University of Illinois Press.

Kertzer, David I. 1980. *Comrades and Christians: Religion and Political Struggle in Communist Italy*. New York: Cambridge University Press.

Kilbourne, Brock K., ed. 1985. *Scientific Research*

and New Religions: Divergent Perspectives. San Francisco: American Association for the Advancement of Science.

Krarup, Helen. 1983. "Conventional Religion and Common Religion in Leeds' Interview Schedule: Basic Frequencies by Question." *Religious Research Papers* (University of Leeds, Department of Sociology).

Kroll-Smith, J. Stephen. 1980. "The Testimony as Performance: The Relationship of an Expressive Event to the Belief System of a Holiness Sect." *Journal for the Scientific Study of Religion* 19: 16-25.

Kurtz, Lester R. 1983. "The Politics of Heresy." *American Journal of Sociology* 88:1085-1116.

———. 1986. *The Politics of Heresy: The Modernist Crisis in Roman Catholicism.* Berkeley: University of California Press.

Lane, Christel. 1981. *The Rites of Rulers: Ritual in Industrial Society—the Soviet Case.* Cambridge, England: Cambridge University Press.

Lasch, Christopher. 1978. *The Culture of Narcissism: American Life in an Age of Diminishing Expectations.* New York: W.W. Norton.

Laski, M. 1961. *Ecstasy: A Study of Some Secular and Religious Experiences.* London: Cresset.

Lauderdale, Pat. 1976. "Deviance and Moral Boundaries." *American Sociological Review* 41:660-676.

Leach, E. R. 1964. *Political Systems of Highland Burma.* Boston: Beacon.

Lechner, Frank J. 1983. "Fundamentalism and Sociocultural Revitalization in America: A Sociological Interpretation." Paper presented at the annual meeting of the Association for the Sociology of Religion, Detroit.

LeGoff, Jacques. 1984. *The Birth of Purgatory.* Chicago: University of Chicago Press.

Lerner, Robert E. 1972. *The Heresy of the Free Spirit in the Later Middle Ages.* Berkeley: University of California Press.

LeRoy Ladurie, Emmanuel. 1979. *Montaillou: The Promised Land of Error.* New York: Vintage.

Levine, Daniel H. 1979. "Religion and Politics, Politics and Religion: An Introduction." *Journal of Interamerican Studies and World Affairs* 21:5-29.

———. 1981. *Religion and Politics in Latin America: The Catholic Church in Venezuela and Colombia.* Princeton, NJ: Princeton University Press.

———. 1985. "Religion and Politics: Drawing Lines, Understanding Change." *Latin American Research Review* 20:20-39.

———, ed. 1980. *Churches and Politics in Latin America.* Beverly Hills, CA: Sage.

Liebman, Robert C. 1983. "Mobilizing the Moral Majority." Pp. 50-74 in *The New Christian Right*, edited by Robert C. Liebman and Robert Wuthnow. New York: Aldine.

Liebman, Charles S. and Eliezer Don-Yehiya. 1983. *Civil Religion in Israel: Traditional Judaism and*

Political Culture in the Jewish State. Berkeley: University of California Press.

———. 1984. *Religion and Politics in Israel.* Bloomington: Indiana University Press.

Lindblom, Charles E. 1977. *Politics and Markets.* New York: Basic Books.

Long, Theodore E. and Jeffrey K. Hadden. 1983. "Religious Conversion and the Concept of Socialization: Integrating the Brainwashing and Drift Models." *Journal for the Scientific Study of Religion* 22:1 -14.

Luckmann, Thomas. 1967. *The Invisible Religion: The Transformation of Symbols in Industrial Society.* New York: Macmillan.

Luhmann, Niklas. 1984. *Religious Dogmatics and the Evolution of Societies.* New York: Edwin Mellen.

———. 1985. "Society, Meaning, Religion—Based on Self-Reference." *Sociological Analysis* 46:5-20.

Luker, Kristin. 1984. *Abortion and the Politics of Motherhood.* Berkeley: University of California Press.

Marsden, George M. 1980. *Fundamentalism and American Culture: The Shaping of Twentieth Century Evangelicalism.* Oxford, England: Oxford University Press.

May, Robert M. 1973. *Stability and Complexity in Model Ecosystems.* Princeton, NJ: Princeton University Press.

McCarl, Robert S., Jr. 1979. "Smokejumper Initiation: Ritualized Communication in a Modern Occupation." *Journal of American Folklore* 89: 49-66.

McGuire, Meredith B. 1981. *Religion: Social Context.* Belmont, CA: Wadsworth.

———. 1982. *Pentecostal Catholics: Power, Charisma, and Order in a Religious Movement.* Philadelphia: Temple University Press.

McNamara, Patrick. 1984. *Religion: North American Style.* Belmont, CA: Wadsworth.

Meadow, Mary Jo and Richard D. Kahoe. 1984. *Psychology of Religion: Religion in Individual Lives.* New York: Harper & Row.

Mechling, Jay, ed. 1978. *Church, State, and Public Policy: The New Shape of the Church-State Debate.* Washington, DC: American Enterprise Institute.

Merton, Robert K. 1970. *Science, Technology and Society in Seventeenth-Century England.* New York: Harper & Row. (Original work published 1938)

Meyer, John W. 1984. "The Self and the Institutionalization of the Life Course." Unpublished paper, Stanford University.

——— and Brian Rowan. 1977. "Institutionalized Organizations: Formal Structure as Myth and Ceremony." *American Journal of Sociology* 83:340-363.

Moberg, David D. 1984. *The Church as a Social Institution.* Grand Rapids, MI: Baker Book House.

Moodie, T. Dunbar. 1975. *The Rise of Afrikanerdom:*

Power, Apartheid, and the Afrikaner Civil Religion. Berkeley: University of California Press.

Moore, R. I. 1975. *The Birth of Popular Heresy*. London: Edward Arnold.

Neuhaus, Richard John. 1984. *The Naked Public Square: Religion and Democracy in America*. Grand Rapids, MI: Eerdmans.

Novak, Michael. 1982. *The Spirit of Democratic Capitalism*. New York: Simon & Schuster.

———— 1984. *Freedom with Justice: Catholic Social Thought and Liberal Institutions*. New York: Harper & Row.

O'Dea, Thomas F. and Janet K. O'Dea. 1973. *Readings on the Sociology of Religion*. Englewood Cliffs, NJ: Prentice-Hall.

O'Toole, Roger. 1984. *Religion: Classical Sociological Approaches*. Toronto: McGraw-Hill Ryerson.

Olson, Mancur. 1971. *The Logic of Collective Action: Public Goods and the Theory of Groups*. Cambridge, MA: Harvard University Press.

Owens, Virginia Stem. 1980. *The Total Image: Or Selling Jesus in the Modern Age*. Grand Rapids, MI: Eerdmans.

Paige, Karen Ericksen and Jeffery Paige. 1981. *The Politics of Reproductive Ritual*. Berkeley: University of California Press.

Paloutzian, Raymond F. 1983. *Invitation to the Psychology of Religion*. Glenview, IL: Scott, Foresman.

Pannenberg, Wolfhart. 1983. *Christian Spirituality*. Philadelphia: Westminster.

Parsons, Talcott. 1951. *The Social System*. New York: Free Press.

———— 1978. *Action Theory and the Human Condition*. New York: Free Press.

Peters, Victor. 1965. *All Things Common: The Hutterian Way of Life*. New York: Harper & Row.

Peukert, Helmut. 1984. *Science, Action, and Fundamental Theology*. Cambridge, MA: MIT Press.

Pfeffer, Leo. 1967. *Church, State, and Freedom*. Boston: Beacon.

Pipes, Daniel. 1983. *In the Path of God: Islam and Political Power*. New York: Basic Books.

Piscatori, James P., ed. 1982. *Islam in the Political Process*. New York: Cambridge University Press.

Poll, Solomon. 1969. *The Hasidic Community of Williamsburg: A Study in the Sociology of Religion*. New York: Schocken.

Pomian-Srzednicki, Maciej. 1982. *Religious Change in Contemporary Poland: Secularization and Politics*. London: Routledge & Kegan Paul.

Popenoe, Cris and Oliver Popenoe. 1984. *Seeds of Tomorrow: New Age Communities that Work*. New York: Harper & Row.

Pritchard, Linda. 1984. "The Burned-Over District Reconsidered: A Portent of Evolving Religious Pluralism in the United States." *Social Science History* 8:243-265.

Rambo, Lewis R. 1982. "Current Research on Religious Conversion." *Religious Studies Review* 8:146-159.

Redfield, Robert. 1956. *Peasant Society and Culture*. Chicago: University of Chicago Press.

Ribeiro de Oliveira, Pedro A. 1979. "The 'Romanization' of Catholicism and Agrarian Capitalism in Brazil." *Social Compass* 26:309-329.

Richardson, James T. 1982. "Financing the New Religions: Comparative and Theoretical Considerations." *Journal for the Scientific Study of Religion* 21:255-267.

Rickles, Patricia K. 1965. "The Folklore of Sacraments and Sacramentals in South Louisiana." *Louisiana Folklore Miscellany* 2:27-44.

Robbins, Thomas. 1985. "Government Regulatory Powers and Church Autonomy: Deviant Groups as Test Cases." *Journal for the Scientific Study of Religion* 24:237-252.

———— and Dick Anthony, eds. 1981. *In Gods We Trust: New Patterns of Religious Pluralism in America*. New Brunswick, NJ:Transaction.

———— and James Richardson. 1978. "Theory and Research on Today's New Religions." *Sociological Analysis* 39:95-122.

Roberts, Keith A. 1984. *Religion in Sociological Perspective*. Homewood, IL: Dorsey.

Robertson, Roland. 1981. "Considerations from within the American Context on the Significance of Church-State Tension." *Sociological Analysis* 42:193-208.

———— 1985a. "The Sacred and the World System." Pp. 347-358 in *The Sacred in a Secular Age*, edited by Phillip E. Hammond. Berkeley: University of California Press.

———— 1985b. "Modernization, Globalization and the Problem of Culture in World-System Theory." *Theory, Culture and Society* 4:111-126.

Roof, Wade Clark. 1978. *Community and Commitment: Religious Plausibility in a Liberal Protestant Church*. New York: Elsevier.

———— 1979. "Concepts and Indicators of Religious Commitment: A Critical Review." Pp. 17-46 in *The Religious Dimension*, edited by Robert Wuthnow. New York: Academic Press.

Rothenberg, Stuart and Frank Newport. 1984. *The Evangelical Voter: Religion and Politics in America*. Washington, DC: Institute for Government and Politics.

Scherer, Ross P., ed. 1980. *American Denominational Organization: A Sociological View*. Pasadena, CA: William Carey Library.

Schluchter, Wolfgang. 1981. *The Rise of Western Rationalism: Max Weber's Developmental History*. Berkeley: University of California Press.

Schurmann, Franz. 1968. *Ideology and Organization in Communist China*. Berkeley: University of California Press.

Schwartz, Gary. 1970. *Sect Ideologies and Social Status*. Chicago: University of Chicago Press.

Scott, James C. 1976. *The Moral Economy of the Peasant: Rebellion and Subsistence in Southeast*

Asia. New Haven, CT: Yale University Press.

———. 1977. "Protest and Profanation: Agrarian Revolt and the Little Tradition." *Theory and Society* 4:1-38; 211-246.

Searle, John R. 1969. *Speech Acts: An Essay in the Philosophy of Language.* Cambridge, England: Cambridge University Press.

Seaver, Paul S. 1985. *Wallington's World: A Puritan Artisan in Seventeenth-Century London.* Stanford, CA: Stanford University Press.

Sennett, Richard. 1978. *The Fall of Public Man: On the Social Psychology of Capitalism.* New York: Vintage.

Shaughnessy, James D., ed. 1973. *The Roots of Ritual.* Grand Rapids, MI: Eerdmans.

Skorupski, John. 1976. *Symbol and Theory: A Philosopohical Study of Theories of Religion in Social Anthropology.* Cambridge, England: Cambridge University Press.

Smith, Brian H. 1982. *The Church and Politics in Chile: Challenges to Modern Catholicism.* Princeton, NJ: Princeton University Press.

Smith, Donald Eugene. 1970. *Religion and Political Development.* Boston: Little, Brown.

Snow, David A. and Richard Machalek. 1983. "The Convert as a Social Type." Pp. 259-288 in *Sociological Theory,* edited by Randall Collins. San Francisco: Jossey-Bass.

Sorauf, Frank J. 1976. *The Wall of Separation: The Constitutional Politics of Church and State.* Princeton, NJ: Princeton University Press.

Spilka, Bernard, Richard L. Gorsuch, and Ralph W. Hood, Jr. 1984. *The Psychology of Religion: An Empirical Approach.* Englewood Cliffs, NJ: Prentice-Hall.

Spiro, Melford. 1966. "Religion: Problems of Definition and Explanation." Pp. 85-126 in *Anthropological Approaches to the Study of Religion,* edited by Michael Banton. London: Tavistock.

Stark, Rodney and William Sims Bainbridge. 1979. "Of Churches, Sects, and Cults: Preliminary Concepts for a Theory of Religious Movements." *Journal for the Scientific Study of Religion* 18:117-131.

———. 1980. "Towards a Theory of Religious Commitment." *Journal for the Scientific Study of Religion* 19:114-128.

———. 1985. *The Future of Religion: Secularization, Revival and Cult Formation.* Berkeley: University of California Press.

Stokes, Anson Phelps and Leo Pfeffer. 1964. *Church and State in the United States.* New York: Harper & Row.

Stokes, Kenneth E., ed. 1982. *Faith Development in the Adult Life Cycle.* New York: Sadlier.

Stroup, Herbert. 1967. *Church and State in Confrontation.* New York: Seabury.

Swanson, Guy E. 1978a. "Travels through Inner Space: Family Structure and Openness to Absorbing Experiences." *American Journal of Sociology* 83:890-919.

———. 1978b. "Trance and Possession: Studies of Charismatic Influence." *Review of Religious Research* 19:253-278.

———. 1980. "A Basis of Authority and Identity in Post-Industrial Society." Pp. 190-217 in *Identity and Authority: Explorations in the Theory of Society,* edited by Roland Robertson and Burkart Holzner. New York: St. Martin's.

Sweet, Leonard I. 1984. "The 1960s: The Crises of Liberal Christianity and the Public Emergence of Evangelicalism." Pp. 29-45 in *Evangelicalism and Modern America,* edited by George Marsden. Grand Rapids, MI: Eerdmans.

Tai, Hue-Tam Ho. 1983. *Millenarianism and Peasant Politics in Vietnam.* Cambridge, MA: Harvard University Press.

Taylor, Mark C. 1984. *Erring: A Postmodern A/theology.* Chicago: University of Chicago Press.

Thoits, Peggy A. 1981. "Undesirable Life Events and Psychophysiological Distress: A Problem of Operational Confounding." *American Sociological Review* 46:97-109.

Thomas, George. 1979. "Rational Exchange and Individualism: Revival Religion in the U.S., 1870-1890." Pp. 351-372 in *The Religious Dimension,* edited by Robert Wuthnow. New York: Academic Press.

———. 1986. *Christianity and Culture in the 19th-Century United States: The Dynamics of Evangelical Revivalism, Nationbuilding, and the Market.* Berkeley: University of California Press.

Thomas, Keith. 1971. *Religion and the Decline of Magic.* New York: Scribner's.

Tillich, Paul. 1963. *The Eternal Now.* New York: Scribner's.

Tipton, Steven M. 1982. *Getting Saved from the Sixties: Moral Meaning in Conversion and Cultural Change.* Berkeley: University of California Press.

Towler, Robert. 1983. "Conventional Religion and Common Religion in Great Britain." *Religious Research Papers* (University of Leeds, Department of Sociology).

Trachtenberg, Joshua. 1970. *Jewish Magic and Superstition: A Study in Folk Religion.* New York: Atheneum.

Troeltsch, Ernst. 1960. *The Social Teaching of the Christian Churches.* New York: Harper & Row. (Original work published 1911)

Turner, Bryan S. 1983. *Religion and Social Theory.* London: Heinemann.

Turner, Victor. 1974. *Dramas, Fields, and Metaphors: Symbolic Action in Human Society.* Ithaca, NY: Cornell University Press.

———. 1977. *The Ritual Process: Structure and Anti-Structure.* Ithaca, NY: Cornell University Press.

Vallier, Ivan. 1970. *Catholicism, Social Control, and Modernization in Latin America.* Englewood Cliffs, NJ: Prentice-Hall.

Van Baaren, Th. P. 1984. "The Flexibility of Myth." Pp. 217-224 in *Sacred Narrative: Readings in the Theory of Myth,* edited by Alan Dundes. Berkeley: University of California Press.

Voll, John Obert. 1982. *Islam: Continuity and Change in the Modern World*. Boulder, CO: Westview Press.

Vrijhof, Pieter Hendrik and Jacques Waardenburg, eds. 1979. *Official and Popular Religion: Analysis of a Theme for Religious Studies*. The Hague: Mouton.

Wacker, Grant. 1984. "Uneasy in Zion: Evangelicals in Postmodern Society." Pp. 17-28 in *Evangelicalism and Modern America*, edited by George Marsden. Grand Rapids, MI: Eerdmans.

Wallis, Roy. 1984. *The Elementary Forms of the New Religious Life*. London: Routledge & Kegan Paul.

Weber, Max. 1963. *The Sociology of Religion*. Boston: Beacon. (Original work published 1922)

Westley, Frances. 1983. *The Complex Forms of the Religious Life: A Durkheimian View of New Religious Movements*. Chico, CA: Scholars Press.

White, O. K., Jr. 1972. "Constituting Norms and the Formal Organization of America's Churches." *Sociological Analysis* 33:95-109.

Wilensky, Harold. 1964. "Mass Society and Mass Culture: Interdependence or Independence?" *American Sociological Review* 29:173-197.

Williams, Peter W. 1980. *Popular Religion in America: Symbolic Change and the Modernization Process in Historical Perspective*. Englewood Cliffs, NJ: Prentice-Hall.

Wilson, Bryan R., ed. 1970. *Rationality*. London: Basil Blackwell.

———— 1973. *Magic and the Millennium: A Sociological Study of Religious Movements of Protest among Tribal and Third-World Peoples*. London: Heinemann.

———— 1982. *Religion in Sociological Perspective*. Oxford: Oxford University Press.

Wilson, John F. 1979. *Public Religion in American Culture*. Philadelphia: Temple University Press.

Wood, James R. 1981. *Leadership in Voluntary Organizations: The Controversy over Social Action in Protestant Churches*. New Brunswick, NJ: Rutgers University Press.

Wuthnow, Robert. 1976. *The Consciousness Reformation*. Berkeley: University of California Press.

———— 1978. *Experimentation in American Religion*. Berkeley: University of California Press.

———— 1980. "World Order and Religious Movements." Pp. 57-75 in *Studies of the Modern World-System*, edited by Albert Bergesen. New York: Academic.

———— 1981a. "Two Traditions in the Study of Religion." *Journal for the Scientific Study of Religion* 20:16-32.

———— 1981b. "Comparative Ideology." *International Journal of Comparative Sociology* 22: 121-140.

———— 1983. "The Political Rebirth of American Evangelicals." Pp. 168-185 in *The New Christian Right: Mobilization and Legitimation*, edited by Robert C. Liebman and Robert Wuthnow. New York: Aldine.

———— 1985a. "The Growth of Religious Reform Movements." *Annals of the American Academy of Political and Social Science* 480:106-116.

———— 1985b. "State Structures and Ideological Outcomes." *American Sociological Review* 50(6)799-821.

———— 1986a. "Religion as Sacred Canopy." In *Making Sense of Modern Times: Peter L. Berger and the Vision of Interpretive Sociology*, edited by James Davison Hunter and Stephen C. Ainlay. London: Routledge & Kegan Paul.

———— 1986b. "Towns, Regimes, and Religious Movements in the Reformation." In *Geographic Perspectives in History*, edited by Eugene Genovese and Leonard Hochberg. London: Basil Blackwell.

————, James Davison Hunter, Albert Bergesen, and Edith Kurzweil. 1984. *Cultural Analysis: The Work of Peter L. Berger, Mary Douglas, Michel Foucault, and Jürgen Habermas*. London: Routledge & Kegan Paul.

Yankelovich, Daniel. 1982. *New Rules: Searching for Self-Fulfillment in a World Turned Upside Down*. New York: Bantam.

Zablocki, Benjamin. 1980. *Alienation and Charisma: A Study of Contemporary American Communes*. New York: Free Press.

Zald, Mayer N. 1982. "Theological Crucibles: Social Movements in and of Religion." *Review of Religious Research* 23:317-336.

Zaret, David. 1985. *The Heavenly Contract: Ideology and Organization in Pre-Revolutionary Puritanism*. Chicago: University of Chicago Press.

16

The Sociology of Science

HARRIET ZUCKERMAN

About a decade ago, a distinguished historian of science argued that science may be the most significant social institution in modern society. "It has transformed the lives and destinies of more of the world's peoples than any . . . religious or political event"; it controls the "economic and military" strength of nations and "the quality of life of their populations" (Price 1976, p. 1). This strong statement is, however, moot since there is no metric for comparing the relative impact of social institutions. Still, it is clear that science has significant social consequences and it is also clear that until recently, comparatively few sociologists have paid much attention to it.

The sociology of science examines a variety of connected matters: the effects of science on society; in turn, the ways in which it is conditioned by its social and cultural contexts; its social structure, and the processes involved in the production of scientific knowledge. As a specialty, it resembles the sociologies of art, law, religion, politics, economy, and the family, since each examines institutional organization, structure, processes, contexts, and products.

One way of conveying a sense of what the sociology of science is like is to describe it from the perspective of a sociologist of science; that is, to outline its distinctive social attributes, its research agenda—what sociologists of science study and why—and to indicate how work in the specialty ties in with sociological research more generally. This we shall do and then turn in greater detail to a series of questions that have occupied sociologists of science in the West over the last several decades. (See Milic, 1980, for developments in Eastern Europe).

Some Social Attributes of the Specialty

As sociological specialties go, the sociology of science is comparatively young. (See Cole and Zuckerman, 1975, for an account of its origins and development. Recent reviews include Ben-David and Sullivan, 1975; Mulkay, 1980a; and Collins, 1983. For a personal account, see Merton, 1979.) In the United States, at least, the first doctoral degrees in sociology were given late in the nineteenth century but the earliest degrees in a subject at all resembling what we now call the sociology of science were not conferred until 1936, when S. C. Gilfillan presented his dissertation on the sociology of invention at Columbia. (It was published in 1935.) That same year, Robert Merton received his degree from Harvard; his dissertation analyzed the emergence of modern science in seventeenth-century England and the social, economic, and

Research for this chapter was supported by the National Science Foundation (NSF-SES 84-11152) and the Russell Sage Foundation.

technological contexts shaping the selection of problems for scientific investigation (1938/1970). This is still the focus of much scholarly attention and is one of the longer-lived dissertations in American sociology. These auspicious beginnings were not followed by much active work for some time. The field of inquiry was not widely cultivated in the 1940s and 1950s and few sociologists were attracted to what was emerging as the sociology of science, although there were some exceptions both in the United States and abroad. (See, for example, Barber, 1952; Merton, 1942/1973b, 1949/1973c, 1952/1973d; among others.)

The sociology of science did not begin to coalesce as a specialty until the late 1950s, when it developed a theoretical orientation and a research agenda together with a social infrastructure (arrangements for the support and training of new recruits, for communicating of new research through meetings and journals, providing research funding and linkages to the larger discipline). It was then that a concatenation of circumstances, both outside and inside the specialty, brought it into being. As had been forecast (Merton, 1952/1973d), it was when science and associated technologies had been socially defined as a serious social problem as well as great social asset that appreciable numbers of sociologists would turn their attention to it. And, at that time, the field of sociology was flourishing; research in new areas seemed promising and comparatively easy to support.

Moreover, two theoretical developments in the emerging specialty sharpened its cognitive focus: the publication in 1957 of Merton's "Priorities in Scientific Discovery" and in 1962 of Kuhn's *Structure of Scientific Revolutions*. Each set out new perspectives on the social organization of scientific inquiry and its patterns of growth, and each led to major lines of inquiry. Most of those who began work on the sociology of science at the time were new Ph.D.s, and as is often the case with new specialties, many of the major contributors were quite young.

Now, in the late 1980s, these early contributors, now in their middle years, have been supplemented by a series of new academic generations (which emerge quite rapidly). A cadre of sociologists define themselves and are defined by others as sociologists of science and, since the field is still small, they are apt to know one another, keep track of one another's work, and to engage in considerable informal as well as formal communication. In the interim, a professional association, the Society for Social

Studies of Science (4S) was founded in 1975 and first met in 1976. It serves to advance interdisciplinary research on science. A batch of journals and annuals devoted primarily or entirely to publishing research in science studies have also come into being.[1] Major departments of sociology in the United States include sociologists of science. Federal agencies and private foundations support research in the field, although, of course, specialists find that support far from copious. In short, the specialty is well institutionalized with science considered a legitimate subject of sociological study.

Still, science is decidedly not taken by many sociologists to be a central concern of the discipline. Most college and university departments do not yet consider the sociology of science as central as more traditional specialties such as the family, religion, and crime or juvenile delinquency. This is itself an interesting intellectual and institutional phenomenon. There appears to be a somewhat ambivalent attitude toward the sociology of science; many sociologists profess an interest in the field, especially when the science being studied is sociology itself, but most seem unaware of its potential contributions to the development of the discipline.

The specialty has two other important and rather atypical attributes. What is known as the social studies of science have become distinctly interdisciplinary. The sociology of science has sometimes uneasy connections to the history and philosophy of science, science policy studies, and the still nascent field of the psychology of science. (On linkages between the history and sociology of science, see Beaver, 1978; Shapin, 1982.) Science studies has also attracted the interest of physical and biological scientists, some of them being avid consumers of the research literature. Having one's "subjects" of study be actively interested in ongoing research in the field adds a piquant note to the enterprise and raises intriguing questions about the grounds on which accounts of cognitive and social realities by participants or observers should be taken as valid.

Not unlike other specialties, this one is marked also by warm and lively, if not always cordial, interaction between adherents of different theoretical orientations, no one of which holds sway: constructivism, discourse analysis, relativism, structural analysis, functional analysis, and conflict theory. These diverse perspectives are sometimes linked with differences in foci of attention and nationality, such that cognitive conflict is sometimes transformed into social conflict. Those focusing on the sociology of scientific knowledge—largely, though far from all, being English and European researchers—have often been at odds with those focusing on the social structure of science—largely, though far from all, being American researchers. Distinct and sometimes conflicting views are held within each "theory group," this tending to polarize discussion on complex and subtle problems further. Indeed, as Collins (1983a, p. 265) notes, even though work on the sociology of scientific knowledge "has only begun to fulfill its potential, disagreements are now taking up more space than substantive contributions."

Almost a decade ago, Joseph Ben-David (1978) observed that some of these differences in approach to the sociology of science derive from differences in the education and social location of American and British sociologists of science--the one having typically been educated first as sociologists, largely located in departments of sociology and oriented to graduate training in the discipline; the other, in contrast, have often come to the sociology of science from other fields, often been employed in science studies units outside the traditional disciplinary structures of universities, and often engaging in undergraduate teaching, with its distinctive concerns and rhetoric. Such differences, Ben-David claims, have shaped the intellectual tenor of the specialty; they have perhaps made for sharper controversy than in more socially and cognitively homogeneous specialties, where most have had similar histories and structural positions.

The Research Agenda of the Sociology of Science

Analytically, the current research agenda divides into three parts: first, problems concerning the social and cognitive organization of scientific work; second, problems in the sociology of scientific knowledge; and third, the reciprocal connections between science and its social contexts—the social consequences that flow from science and the influence of other social institutions and culture upon science. This formal classification only hints at the range and diversity of problems sociologists of science actually study. It also can be taken to imply that questions about the development of scientific knowledge can fruitfully be isolated from its social organization, that the cognitive and social domains of science are separable. This is not the case. The two are intricately interconnected, though some current research on the social organization of science tends to underplay the cognitive aspects of science, while some current

research on the sociology of scientific knowledge tends to underplay the social organization of science. This division of labor is understandable. In fact, sociologists of science working in the early period adopted the self-conscious research strategy of addressing problems in the social organization of science before tackling problems of the sociology of scientific knowledge. As we shall see, however, the sharp division that now obtains is neither necessary nor, in the long run, likely to be fruitful. I shall be examining both classes of work but will exclude many contributions since each has a copious literature to draw on.[2]

Theoretical differences in the sociology of science reflect marked differences in conceptions of science, centering on the question of whether it has any special cognitive warrant, more so than other types of knowledge claims. As we shall see in the final section of the chapter, that is a question central to the sociology of scientific knowledge. (See Bloor, 1976, for one view and Ben-David, 1981, for another.) Putting these matters to one side, it is nevertheless useful to identify three ways of thinking about the nature of science: first, of course, it is a body of certified knowledge, comprising theories, observations, and empirical generalizations about the natural and social worlds, provisionally accepted by scientists in the given field at a given time and forming the substance of what has been put the published archive.[3] Science is also a set of procedures for finding things out,[4] which is to say that scientific knowledge develops in accord with a set of rules—some mutable, others fixed; with those that are fixed including the requirement that scientific knowledge be logically consistent and confirmable, or in Popper's terms, falsifiable (see Popper, 1959, for the translation of Popper's *Logic of Scientific Discovery*, published first in 1935). And third, science is a social enterprise, a culture or tradition, and a set of social arrangements for developing, certifying, and communicating knowledge. Sociologists of science are interested in all three accounts as they apply to the physical, biological, behavioral, and social sciences, these all being considered legitimate subjects for sociological analysis.

Finally, the sociology of science has the engaging feature of being self-exemplifying much of the time (Merton, 1963/1973g, pp. 382; 1973a, p. ix). The specialty exhibits the very characteristics that its practitioners study. Thus the study of modes of problem choice in science, why scientists elect to take up certain problems and neglect others, is itself an example of problem choice for the sociologists of science who study this matter. Or, as we shall see in the section on growth and decline of scientific specialties, the development of the sociology of science as a specialty exemplifies features of specialty development generally. And as I have suggested, the analysis of theoretical controversy by sociologists of science has itself not been free of controversy.

The self-exemplifying character of the sociology of science marks it off from other sociological specialties and enables sociologists of science to draw upon their own experience in thinking about the problems they study since they are at once observers of this kind of behavior and participants in it.

Modes of Connection Between the Specialty and the Parent Discipline

Certain theories, concepts, problems and procedures used in the sociology of science are generic, found in sociology generally, while others are subject-specific, limited to the study of science alone. As an example of the first, a considerable body of research has focused on social stratification in science, on its structure, determinants, and consequences for scientists' careers. These studies are pertinent not just to science but also to stratification in the society at large. Similarly, studies of deviant behavior in science—fraud and plagiarism—and modes of their social control draw upon and enlarge sociological knowledge of deviant behavior.

Other problems, concepts, theories, and methods are subject-specific, particular to the sociology of science, and are not readily generalizable beyond its subject matter, broadly conceived.[5] The nature of replication or the filiation of ideas in science and methods for studying them are distinctive of the specialty. In examining the research agenda in the sociology of science, I shall periodically indicate aspects that are generic and spell out how they contribute to the sociological enterprise and also periodically indicate concepts, problems, and procedures that are subject-specific. This will convey some idea of the ties between specialty and discipline and indicate how specialty development proceeds independently while drawing upon and contributing to the discipline.

Problems in the Social Structure and Culture of Science

Most studies in the sociology of science readily divide into three classes: the social structure and culture of science, the sociology of scientific knowledge, and the interaction of science and its sociocultural contexts. As I have noted, however, this division is both descriptive of current research and somewhat misleading insofar as it makes for a separation of the social and cognitive domains, which are in practice interconnected. That caveat reiterated, this part of the chapter treats five questions in the social structure of science that have occupied the research attention of sociologists.

Is There an Ethos of Science? Do Scientists Conform to It? Does It Contribute to the Extension of Scientific Knowledge?

These seemingly innocent questions have been controversial for decades. Centering on a theory of the normative structure of science proposed some 45 years ago (Merton, 1942/1973b), the controversy did not develop immediately. During the 1950s and 1960s, the theory was expanded, reformulated, and subjected to limited empirical tests (Barber, 1952; Hagstrom, 1965; Storer, 1966; West, 1960).[6] When Kuhn's widely read *Structure of Scientific Revolutions* (1962/1970) appeared, some took it as an alternative theoretical orientation (unlike, as we shall see, Kuhn himself). In recent years, criticism has shifted from Kuhnian to phenomenological and "economic" accounts, reflecting increasing interest among sociologists of science in these other perspectives on scientists' behavior.

Merton's initial statement held that "the institutional goal of science is the extension of certified knowledge," knowledge comprising "empirically confirmed and logically consistent statements of regularities (. . . in effect, predictions)" (1942/1973b, p. 270). As a social institution, science is marked by an

ethos . . . [or an] affectively toned complex of values and norms which are held to be binding on scientists. The norms are expressed in the form of prescriptions, proscriptions, preferences, and permissions. They are legitimized in terms of institutional values. These imperatives [or norms], transmitted by precept and example and reinforced by sanctions are in varying degrees internalized by the scientist, thus fashioning his scientific conscience.. . . Although the ethos of science has not been codified, it can be inferred from the moral consensus of scientists as expressed in use and wont, in countless writings on the scientific spirit and in moral indignation directed toward contraventions of the ethos [1942/1973b, pp. 268-269].

This compact paragraph lays out much of the theory: it holds that the institution of science has a distinctive set of norms and values; that these are legitimized by its principal goal, the extension of certified knowledge; that these are transmitted by socialization and reinforced by rewards and punishments; that the ethos or code of science can be inferred from what scientists write about science and from how they behave, particularly from scientists' responses to departures from the posited norms.[7]

Furthermore, "the mores [norms] of science possess a methodologic rationale, but they are binding, not only because they are procedurally efficient but because they are believed right and good" (1942/1973b, p. 270). Here the double claim is made that the ethos of science contributes to the institutional goal of advancing knowledge and also has strong expressive significance.

What then are the norms of science that "are expressed in use and wont and in countless writings"? The ethos is composed of two sorts of norms: "technical" and "moral" or latterly, cognitive and social. "The technical [or cognitive] norm of empirical evidence, adequate and reliable, is a prerequisite for sustained true prediction; the technical norm of logical consistency, a prerequisite for systematic and valid prediction. The entire structure of technical and moral norms implements the final objective" of extending certified knowledge (1942/1973b, p. 270). The moral or social norms were also treated briefly. Just four were proposed in the original statement.

(1) The norm of "*universalism*" refers to the requirement that scientific contributions be judged according to "preestablished impersonal criteria." Social attributes of contributors such as their race, religion, class origins, or gender are deemed "irrelevant" in such judgments (1942/1973b, pp. 270-271). The norm of universalism also requires that scientists be rewarded in accord with the extent of their contributions to science (1957/1973e).

(2) The norm of "*communism*," or as Barber retermed it during the McCarthy era, "communalism" (1952, p. 130), prescribes that knowledge, which is the product of collective effort by the scientific community, must be shared—not kept secret. Indeed, the only way scientists can be sure that they will acquire property rights to their contributions is, paradox-ically, to give them away to their scientific peers—that is, to publish them promptly (1942/1973b, pp. 273-275). As Hull (1985) observes, science is organized so as to make group goals and individual goals coincide; that is, that scientists are "forced" to make their work public or forgo priority and credit for it.

(3) "*Disinterestedness*," or the curbing of personal bias, involves institutional control over the motives for doing science so as to advance scientific knowledge. Put another way, the intrinsic reward of discovering new knowledge and sharing it will elicit other rewards, notably peer recognition. This prescription does not require scientists to feel altruistic—social arrangements depending wholly on altruism are notably unstable—rather, the reward and punishment systems of science generally make it in scientists' own interest to act in such a disinterested manner (1942/1973b, pp. 275-277).

(4) Last, "*organized skepticism*" is "both a methodologic and an institutional mandate" that calls for "the suspension of judgment" until the requisite evidence is there. Once again, in this account of the normative structure of the institution of science, the emphasis is on its institutional arrangements. This calls for "organized" skepticism, for arrangements such as refereeing and other critical appraisals of work by competent peers; not necessarily for each scientist to feel uniformly skeptical.

Fifteen years later, Merton returned to these problems in his analysis of priority disputes in science (1957/1973e)—those frequent arguments scientists have concerning who has been first to make a particular discovery. Here, the analysis examines the twin significance of both "originality" in science and collegial recognition—on being first in contributing new knowledge and in being recognized for it—and often the ironic consequences of this institutionalized pattern. Intense competition and, in certain instances, even fraud and other forms of seriously deviant behavior occur when the desire for recognition outstrips commitment or capacity to extend knowledge (1957/1973e, 1963/1973g, 1968, 1976a).

The ethos of science, as with norms generally, specifies shared expectations or ideals, how scientists should act in their work and vis-a-vis other scientists. No more than in other domains does every scientist uniformly live up to every norm on each and every occasion. In science, as in other institutions, there is often a "painful contrast" between normative expectations and actual behavior (Merton, 1976a, p. 40). This "painful contrast" does not mean that the norms of science do not exercise patterned control over behavior any more than occasional homicides mean that norms prohibiting murder are either absent or inconsequential. Sociologists seldom need to be reminded that norms and behavior are never perfectly correlated.

Why, then, has this proposal of norms in science provoked such prolonged and heated discussion? From the vantage point of the 1980s, it seems to have provided an occasion for sociologists of science adopting a relativist or phenomenological stance to claim shortcomings not just of the normative theory but of the Mertonian research program, in general. It also became an occasion for laying out alternative accounts of scientific practice; what norms are and their role in the production of knowledge; and last, how scientists behave in relation to them. (See Toren, 1983, for a similar view.) Moreover, the controversy has not occurred in a theoretical vacuum. It has also reflected a growing tendency in the discipline at large to question structural and functional perspectives, closely associated with Talcott Parsons and, in a variant, with Merton, as well as a lack of consensus among sociologists on the character of social norms, their influence on behavior, and on modes of studying normative structures.[8] In short, it is a self-exemplifying instance of the norm of organized skepticism in practice.

And, of course, the normative theory as first proposed is exceedingly brief, almost elliptically so. It does not adequately anticipate potential criticisms nor does it place the theory in the framework of social and cognitive (or, in Merton's terms, "moral" and "technical") norms in science, much less in the larger framework of cultural structures generally.[9] This left room for critics and supporters to interpret the theory in ways that were not necessarily consistent with the expressed intentions of the author.

In the wake of controversy, as I noted, sociologists of science have splintered into several contending groups—some of whom think most headway can be made by examining the social structure of science, others who focus on its links to the larger society, and a third and growing group comprising those who take one or another form of the sociology of scientific knowledge to be the most fruitful focus for research. Few sociologists of science do research combining all these differing foci of attention. Divisions of this sort may have developed in any event, but they were surely encouraged by the controversy over the ethos of science. Since its early phase, when a proliferation of programmatic papers appeared calling for interpretative or relativist studies in

the sociology of scientific knowledge, a considerable literature of ethnographic, historical case studies and discourse analyses has come into being. I shall get to these in the last section of the chapter.

THE CHARACTER OF THE NORMS

Most critics of the Mertonian formulation are not normative nihilists. Few think that science has no normative structure at all but rather focus on such questions as the nature of norms that govern scientists' actions; the purposes they serve; the extent to which norms are shared by scientists; the proposal that this configuration of norms is unique to science; and the interpretation that overt conformity to the norms signals commitment to them.

Growing out of the Kuhnian mode of analysis is the claim that only cognitive, not social, norms really count in science. Cognitive norms are said to derive from the paradigm prevailing in a given field or specialty, along lines spelled out by Kuhn (Barnes and Dolby, 1970). Just what sorts of norms are contained in such paradigms has not been explicated in detail but, following Kuhn's (1962/1970, p. 187) amplification of his initial views, it would seem that forms of generally accepted problem solutions provide the main constituents of cognitive norms. Although this position reflects the "immense influence" of Kuhn's writings, as Stehr (1978) has put it, for his part, Kuhn finds the supposed opposition of his views and those of Merton seriously "misdirected" (1978, p. xxi).[10]

The conception that cognitive norms are paramount involves the hypothesis that these alone are binding on scientists and the only ones to which they actually conform (Dolby, 1975; Mulkay, 1980a). Only cognitive norms are said to be institutionalized since scientists are rewarded only for conforming to them (Mulkay, 1976, p. 641) but not so allegedly for social norms. The first assertion is an empirical assertion, of course, on which the data are far from adequate. For one thing, the imperfect evidence in hand mainly concerns commitment and conformity to social not cognitive norms. The evidence on conformity to cognitive norms is limited mainly to case studies and to what scientists put in print.[11] Not surprisingly, the published record of science indicates widespread conformity to cognitive norms, at least among those whose papers are accepted for publication, else the papers would hardly have been found acceptable. The published archive is therefore a biased source of evidence on conformity to these norms. When it comes to conformity to social norms, the evidence, as we shall see, is mixed. Scientists neither invariably act in accord with them nor in opposition to them. As I have noted, however, commitment and conformity to norms are not the same; whether scientists do or do not conform in particular instances is quite distinct from whether they believe the norms are legitimate. Were this not so, phenomena of guilt in violating accepted norms would not be a familiar human experience. Although Mulkay makes the claim that positive rewards are given not for conformity to social but only to cognitive norms, rewards appear to be conferred for conformity to both sets of norms; that is, those whose work accords with prevailing cognitive standards and who contribute to scientific knowledge, according to standards prescribed by the social norms, are by and large more copiously rewarded than those who do not. Moreover, it is not the case that institutionalization requires that acts of conformity be positively rewarded. Conformity to all sorts of thoroughly institutionalized norms —the prohibitions on forgery and theft of data, for example—are not rewarded, but detected violations are of course punished.

This is not all to Mulkay's (1976) views about social and cognitive norms. He goes on to contend that scientists' normative statements do not express their own commitments, but they are simply ideological statements designed to defend the autonomy of science. They are "vocabularies of justification," rationales for noninterference rather than authentic ethical principles. This account of the norms differs from, but is not inconsistent with, the interpretative or phenomenological perspective, which emphasizes that sociological observers must discern not static rules or norms, but the process through which actors negotiate, interpret, and evaluate actions (Cicourel 1973). Drawing on his detailed studies of the behavior of radio astronomers, Mulkay has more recently claimed that the normative statements scientists invoke to explain their acts are highly contingent on the context in which they are embedded. Astronomers call on a complex repertoire of rules that they differentially apply depending on the situation. The connections then between rules and specific acts are said to be "indeterminate." There is then no single coherent code dominant in science (Mulkay, 1980b).

Others (Barnes and Dolby, 1970; Schmaus, 1983) dispute the uniqueness of the scientific ethos. Universalism, organized skepticism, communism, and disinterestedness each turn up in other societal contexts and the norms can therefore provide no solid ground for demarcating science from other activities. Perhaps so. Scientists and philosophers have struggled for some time with the complex issues involved in demarcating science from nonscience and still have not come to a satisfactory conclusion. But, as Gaston (1978) has observed, the main point with respect to the ethos of science is not the uniqueness of this or that norm, but rather of the entire configuration and the interdependence of its parts.

Some 20 years have passed since the controversy over the norms of science began. It now appears that efforts to oppose cognitive and social norms are theoretically unsound and misleading. The institution of science is a complex set of arrangements, cognitive and social, for learning about nature and society with the evidence on hand indicating that scientists are committed to both the cognitive and social norms, although not all invariably act in accord with them.[12] Nonetheless, cognitive and social norms are analytically separable even if they are intertwined in practice. It is useful to think about the cognitive or technical norms as specifying what should be studied and how and the social or moral norms as specifying scientists' attitudes and behavior in relation to one another and their research.[13] Both, it can be argued, implement the goal of scientific activity and both are binding. We recall the Durkheimian rule that expressions of moral indignation upon (posited) social norms testify to their social significance. Applying that rule to science, we note the uniformly intensive and angry responses of scientists to fraud, plagiarism, misallocation of recognition, efforts to impose curbs on free communication and to major errors of procedure, analysis, or interpretation subjected to "organized skepticism." This places these norms at a great distance from merely ideological statements designed to defend the autonomy of science and from mere rationalizations of action offered after the fact.

SCIENTISTS' COMMITMENT AND CONFORMITY TO NORMS

Expressions of moral indignation and contempt for violations provide one sort of indicator of scientists' being committed to social and cognitive norms. Another is provided by systematic empirical studies of scientists' attitudes and behavior. Here the data are, to say the least, sketchy. Two of the three pertinent studies (Mitroff, 1974; West, 1960) draw on very small samples, and the indicators used in the third (Blisset, 1972) often confuse behavior and expectations, making it difficult to draw conclusions about the extent and distribution of scientists' commitments to the norms. This much said by way of caution, West's (1960) study shows that the 57 scientists he studied reported being committed to certain norms but not to others, while Blisset's (1972) findings showed considerable variation in attitudes toward the norms among scientists in different disciplines and types of universities. Mitroff's (1974) qualitative study examines the commitments to the ethos expressed by 42 Apollo moon scientists and finds both the Mertonian norms and counternorms opposing the ethos being invoked, in accord with Merton's (1963/1973g; 1976b) analysis of normative ambivalence in science invoking a set of dominant norms and a subsidiary set of counternorms.[14] For Mitroff, such opposing commitments advance science by enabling scientists to maintain their own unconventional ideas in the face of collegial criticism. Normative systems are never perfectly integrated and often call for conflicting behaviors in differing contexts. Individuals adapt to such conflicting normative expectations by oscillating between normatively legitimated but inconsistent behaviors, and in the process accommodate to the special demands of given situations.[15]

Other empirical studies of the ethos focus specifically on the norm of communism and behavior related to it: that is, on scientists' communicating their work freely to fellow scientists or keeping it secret. Hagstrom (1974, p. 9), Gaston (1971, p. 118), and Sullivan (1975, p. 238) all report a readiness among most scientists to discuss their work even before publication; the small fraction who restrict communication of their ideas do so principally to protect their claims to priority and recognition. Still other studies have focused on the ethos of science to examine the normative commitments of industrial scientists (e.g., Box and Cotgrove, 1970; Krohn, 1972), reporting less marked commitment among such scientists. In light of the growing share of scientists at work in industry rather than the academy, such differences can be consequential. Indeed, Ziman (1985) asserts that the model in which scientists exchange communications for professional recognition "is not yet out of date" but must be radically modified to take account of "collectivized science"—not only in industrial corporations but also in the large-scale academic science that requires considerable management and coordination. Further comparative evidence finds that scientists trained in the U.S.S.R. and the United States share the ethos of science but differ in their views about the proper role of science in society (Toren, 1980).

The evidence on the extent to which scientists, in the aggregate, subscribe to the norms is also incomplete. The available data show variability in the extent and depth of commitment to the norms, but in the absence of good measures and good samples, firm conclusions would be premature. The available evidence on the extent to which scientists actually conform to the norms is somewhat better but also not free of complexity. It might be said, for example, that the superabundant evidence showing that many scientists publish little or not at all implies that they feel no obligation to contribute to the advancement of knowledge. But of course there are many roles besides research roles in the domain of science. Publication of research is not the only way of contributing to knowledge. Teaching and the administering of research are indispensable to the system of science, and in industrial science, proprietary or national constraints on publication are common. Publication as an indicator is not all it is sometimes taken to be.

The large literature on social stratification in science, on inequalities in the distribution of rewards and resources for research, also bears upon the ethos of science, primarily on the norm of universalism. The findings here are more complex than uniformly clear-cut. Many studies examine the extent to which universalism and particularism obtain in allocating rewards to scientists for their work. Universalism dictates that scientific merit and the quality of role performance be the sole basis for decisions on appointments, promotions, fellowships, publication, proposals for research funds, and honors. Particularism, in contrast, takes personal relations, social origins, and social statuses as the basis of such decisions. The studies show that in practice, processes of allocation are neither wholly universalistic nor wholly particularistic (Cole and Cole, 1973; Gaston, 1971, 1978). Cole, Rubin, and Cole (1977), Stewart (1983), and Zuckerman (1977b) all report strong connections between the extent to which scientists have contributed to the advancement of knowledge and the resources and rewards they have received. However, Crane (1965); Reskin (1976, 1977, 1978, 1979); Long (1978); Long, Allison, and McGinnis (1979); Zuckerman (1977b, 1978); Cole (1979); and Chubin, Porter, and Boeckmann (1981) variously find that particularism modifies such decisions and is applied along with quality of role performance. Having a degree from a prestigious university and having powerful sponsors are advantageous for upward mobility, while having been trained in a less than distinguished department and being female are decidedly disadvantageous; the last of these is especially true in gaining appointments to tenured posts in major universities (Cole, 1979; Zuckerman, 1987a). Similarly mixed results appear in research focused on the outcomes of the refereeing of papers submitted for publication.

All these studies of scientists' behavior in the aggregate imply that the ethos is neither consistently honored nor consistently flouted. Rather, studies of the reward system show that particularism is most apt to operate in the absence of convincing evidence on role performance (as, for example, in the allocation of jobs to new Ph.D.s or in the choices between candidates whose role performance is about equal). Next steps in research on this matter require better specification of the conditions under which the norms are binding and those in which they may be abridged or outright violated, as well as those calling counternorms into play. More needs to be learned also about the invoking of norms to account for various kinds of behaviors and about the nature of normative repertoires. The connections between normative commitments and behavior must also be examined to assess the claim that observed conformity to the ethos of science need not indicate commitment to the norms since it might result from self-interest and calculations of how best to survive the competition for resources and rewards (Bourdieu, 1975; Mulkay, 1980b). This last holds special interest as a theme that has appeared in several ethnographic studies of science. Latour and Woolgar (1979, p. 207) draw a sharp distinction between normative constraints and self-interest. Thus they hold that scientists assess the value of colleagues' contributions not because the norms require it, but because they depend on those contributions for their own work. They adopt a utilitarian mode of analysis of exchange in science in which scientists gain "capital" that can be reinvested when others use their work. As they put it, "a successful investment" for a scientist "might mean that people phone him, his abstracts are accepted, others show interest in his work, he is believed more easily and listed to with greater attention, he is offered better positions, . . . [his] data . . . form a more credible picture." Knorr-Cetina (1981) does not subscribe to this account but she too is inclined to think that self-interest and competition for resources account for what appears to be conformity to the norms. An earlier theoretical formulation, however, refers to the simultaneous operation of these analytically separate components as "those happy circumstances in which self-interest and

moral obligation coincide and fuse" (Merton, 1957/1973e, p. 293).

THE ETHOS OF SCIENCE AND THE ADVANCEMENT OF KNOWLEDGE

Does the ethos of science advance scientific knowledge? Two sorts of evidence are germane here: first, comparative data on the development of scientific knowledge in societies that permit conformity to the ethos and in those that do not and, second, data on the connections between individual contributions to science and commitment and conformity to the ethos. Again, the evidence is complex and far from satisfactory on both counts. Studies of science in totalitarian regimes, which limit conformity to the ethos, suggest that science does not suffer uniformly in such regimes; rather, some sciences fare well and others do not. Such regimes foster the development of some sciences while discouraging others. The social sciences are considerably more vulnerable to interference in totalitarian regimes than the biological sciences and both, in turn, fare worse than the physical sciences and mathematics (Graham, 1981; Joravsky, 1986; Mehrtens, 1987; Solomon, 1975). "Although the most diverse social structures have provided some measure of support to science," comparative data are far from simple to interpret since it is not just the survival of the sciences that is in point, but the "ratio of scientific achievement to scientific potentialities." (Merton, 1942/1973b, p. 269). The proper comparative analyses have yet to be done.

The connections between individual commitment to the ethos and role performance are even less clear. For one thing, the normative theory, as it was originally proposed, asserts the ethos is "procedurally efficient" at the institutional level and makes no claim that this should hold for individuals. Thus the assertion (Mitroff, 1974) that compliance with the norms stands in the way of scientists' maintaining unorthodox views and, as a consequence, can undermine their contributing to science may not be theoretically pertinent. [There is always the question of how efficient it is for the development of knowledge for scientists to continue to hold views that remain unacceptable to their peers, as Polanyi (1963) perceptively observed long ago.] Beyond this, there is no evidence, pro or con, to indicate whether major contributors to scientific knowledge are also more committed to the ethos and conform to it more assiduously than others.

Research now in progress on the sociocultural structure of science focuses on the growing involvement of scientists in industry and politics and the growing importance of science in both these domains. Such involvements produce a good deal of strain and conflict for individual scientists who experience incompatible role demands, and this will exert pressure for the emergence of new norms more consonant with the hybrid activities of "entrepreneurial science," as Etzkowitz (1983) has termed it. (On this issue, see also Nelkin 1984). If so, the success of science in generating certified or reliable knowledge may have the ironic consequence of undermining the normative arrangements making for that success.

Deviant Behavior in Science

Sociologists' interest in deviant behavior in science (Merton, 1957/1973e; Mulkay, 1969; Gaston, 1973; Hagstrom, 1974) long predated the recent flurry of attention it has received in the mass media (Broad and Wade, 1983) but has accelerated since then.[16,17] Not only are deviance and social control important generic problems in sociology, but they also provide strategic sites for examining the ethos of science in practice. Indeed, the "great emphasis on original and significant discoveries [in the ethos], may occasionally generate incentives for eclipsing rivals by illicit or dubious means" (Merton, 1957/1973e). Paradoxically, while prescribing the terms of conformity, the normative structure can also generate deviance.

FORMS OF DEVIANT BEHAVIOR IN SCIENCE

Deviant behavior in science, as in other institutional domains, involves departures from institutional norms: here, departures from both social and cognitive norms specifying what individuals should and should not do in their role as scientists.[18] As noted earlier, social and cognitive norms are analytically separable but empirically intertwined in the ethos of science, and this is patently so in the case of deviance. Various forms of deviance involve departures from both classes of norms simultaneously, highlighting their close connections. The social and cognitive aspects are also tightly linked in the modes of social control of deviance. As we shall see, replicability of scientific work, a central feature of cognitive control, is also a prime mechanism for social control. Replication may detect deviance after it has occurred and its possibility may deter it before the fact, thus giving it double relevance in the system of social control.

As we have seen, cognitive norms comprise both generic technical or methodological canons, the requirements of logical consistency and empirical confirmability or falsifiability, and also norms specific to particular disciplines and specialties. Departures from the methodological canons that mark off science from nonscience, include adventures into such exotic areas as the occult, astrology, and parapsychology. These are commonly defined by scientists as deviant because the phenomena they would examine have not been scientifically established, cannot be consistently replicated, and purported results do not generally measure up to scientific criteria.[19]

DEPARTURES FROM COGNITIVE NORMS

Discipline- and specialty-specific cognitive norms designate the theories, problems, procedures, and solutions that are prescribed, proscribed, permitted, and preferred. Scientific innovations involving departures are allowed, but these must be within the framework of methodological canons of the time. Scientists who propose novel ideas or report unusual findings have the burden of persuading peers in their sector of the scientific community that their work can be connected with canonical or accepted knowledge. Some fail to do so altogether. (See Wynne, 1976, for the case of Barkla and the J phenomenon.) Others ultimately succeed only after a long period or rejection or neglect. As a major example, in the early 1950s the biologist Barbara McClintock proposed that genes are mobile rather than fixed on the chromosome, like pearls on a string. In doing so, she challenged widely held views about the nature of genes and gene expression (Keller, 1985). Yet neither she nor anyone else at the time was able to link her ideas to prevailing theories. Although most geneticists did not know how to proceed with McClintock's ideas or indeed understand quite what they meant, they were not defined as deviant. Although departing from prevailing theoretical commitments, they conformed to methodological canons. When the significance of McClintock's work became clear years later, it was quickly incorporated into canonical knowledge and she was rewarded copiously for it.[20] The tension between tradition and change, conservation and innovation (Kuhn, 1978), has been characteristic of science right along. This finds expression in the seemingly incompatible requirements that scientists conform to cognitive norms while simultaneously being called on to innovate. But when the rejection of prevailing theories and findings occurs within the framework of the methodological canons, this is plainly in line with the institutional goal of extending certified knowledge. It constitutes nonconforming but not aberrant behavior—that is, behavior in which nonconformers publicly announce their dissent, challenge the legitimacy of what they reject, and openly aim to change those accepted ideas, their departures are acknowledged to be disinterested and often draw upon ultimate values (here, the extension of certified knowledge) in the process (Merton 1976a, pp. 29-31).

Violations of cognitive norms prescribing proper research procedures are quite another matter. Scientists recognize that occasional error is to be expected; it is a hazard of doing science. Even the most experienced and skilled investigators can and do make mistakes. However, scientists implicitly differentiate between "reputable" and "disreputable" errors (Zuckerman, 1977a, pp. 110-113). Reputable errors occur even when investigators follow appropriate scientific practice--that is, abide by cognitive norms. Disreputable errors are those that occur when cognitive norms are neglected or flouted. Not using proper experimental controls or random assignment of subjects, not protecting samples from contamination, not arranging for double-blind designs, not using replicate observers, or not making repeated measurements are familiar violations of basic procedural norms in certain fields and times.[21] These are counterparts in science of negligence.[22] Since disreputable errors can be avoided and since they encourage others to follow up on erroneous results, they are taken as serious violations by the scientific community when discovered. Such errors greatly compromise the future credibility of scientists responsible for them.

The discovery of "polywater" is one of the better documented examples of disreputable error in science. After 10 years of work, it proved only to be a contaminated sample, not an anomalous new form of water as originally claimed (see Franks, 1980; Kohn, 1986). During those 10 years, theorists attempted to account for its structure and experimenters tried to identify its constituents. Once it became clear that polywater was only an artifact, the credibility of its "discoverer," Boris Deryagin, was seriously damaged. He had broken two unwritten commandments in the domain of science: "Thou shalt not mislead thy colleagues" and "Thou shalt not waste their time."

Disreputable error arises from failure to live up to cognitive norms specifying procedures that build skepticism into the research process. Procedural norms, when followed, reduce the probability that scientists will deceive themselves and their colleagues. These procedural norms are reinforced by the social norm of organized skepticism, which requires investigators to be skeptical about their work and legitimizes the evaluation system that assesses the probable validity and value of new contributions. Disreputable error thus violates both cognitive and social norms.

DEPARTURES FROM SOCIAL NORMS

The two most serious violations of the social norms of science are fraud and plagiarism[23]—making deliberately deceptive truth claims and making deliberately deceptive claims to ownership of intellectual property. Fraud usually involves departures from the social norms of disinterestedness and organized skepticism. It occurs when scientists knowingly engage in deceptive activities in order to receive peer recognition or financial gain. In the case of plagiarism, the norms of communism and universalism are violated because those scientists who are legitimately entitled to credit for work have had it taken from them. Applying the Durkheimian principle, mentioned earlier, that moral indignation signals the violation of an important norm, scientists' responses to fraud and plagiarism make it clear that they take these deviant acts very seriously. The language they use is sociologically significant: according to the immunologist Peter Medawar (1976), fraud is "heinous"; for the molecular biologist Salvadore Luria, it is a "scandal" with a "quality of desecration about it" (1975); it is, for the medical scientist Robert Petersdorf, "shocking" (1986), and for the biochemist and editor of *Science* Daniel Koshland, it is simply "intolerable" (1987). Scientists do not take these episodes casually. Fraud and plagiarism undermine the widely held belief in the scientific community that what other scientists say can be taken as reliable most of the time. That belief makes it possible to avoid the immense—indeed, the impossible—time and effort that would be required to verify what others have reported in each and every case. "The institution of science involves an implicit social contract between scientists so that each can depend on the trustworthiness of the rest . . . the entire cognitive system of science is rooted in the moral integrity of individual scientists" (Zuckerman, 1977a, pp. 113).

Fraud, the generic term for deliberate deception, comes in three forms, as Charles Babbage (1830/1976) put it—"forging," or data fabrication, "trimming," or data manipulation, and "cooking," or data suppression. "Cooking" may seem a less serious threat to the integrity of scientific knowledge than the other two since no untruths are reported. Yet cooking misleads since the whole known and relevant truth is not told. Data suppression is difficult to identify; scientists must make judgments about which data are trustworthy and which are not. Deviance occurs only when unreported data are hidden and reasonable accounts cannot be given for their not having been made public. Yet it is sometimes difficult to distinguish fraud from error. In principle, what separates the two are scientists' intent; whether they deliberately meant to deceive. In practice, this test is not readily applied (see Stewart and Feder, 1987, on the wide array of errors and apparent frauds detected in papers coauthored by John Darsee).

Plagiarism also involves deliberate deception; credit is claimed where credit is not due. The theft of texts is relatively easy to detect but this is not the case when evidence or ideas are appropriated. The phenomenon of multiple simultaneous discovery (discussed later) makes it possible that these ideas or findings were arrived at independently. The normative status of plagiarism is complicated further by the absence of agreement on what constitutes property rights in science and whether rights to ideas are as strictly protected as printed text. This remains an ill-defined normative area. It thus provides the basis for profound disagreements among scientists on rights to credit for contributions. In any event, plagiarism, while a serious departure from social norms in science as elsewhere, is also illegal. However, it does not alter the fabric of scientific knowledge and thus is described by Joravsky (1983, pp. 3-4) as "a pecadillo compared to the mortal sin of fabrication."

Other departures from the social norms of science are variously serious. But none of these are as consequential as the three forms of fraud for the development of knowledge or for the trust that scientists have in one another. Plagiarism is also serious but makes only for inequity rather than undermining the cognitive enterprise. Both, as we shall see, when discovered, call forth severe punishment, often severe enough to wreck the careers of those involved.

SOURCES OF DEVIANT
BEHAVIOR IN SCIENCE

Three kinds of explanations have been proposed to account for deviant behavior in science and a whole host of subsidiary conditions have been identified that may contribute to it. These in turn derive from major types of sociological and psychological theories of deviant behavior: anomie theory, psychopathology, and conflict theory.[24] We have already noted that the great premium science puts on originality and peer recognition, producing intense competition. Among investigators who believe that they cannot achieve these goals legitimately, a few have turned to illicit means, this being an application of anomie theory designed to account for deviant behavior in science (Merton, 1957/ 1973e; 1968; 1984). Thus, on occasion, scientists have falsified evidence, stolen others' work, become secretive, or falsely accused others of plagiarism in order to gain recognition for themselves. It only seems paradoxical that in such instances the source of deviance is an excess, not an insufficiency of commitment to values incorporated in science. These instances are also marked by insufficient commitment to normatively approved means of reaching the goals to which they are so strongly committed.

A second explanation holds that deviance in science typically results from individual psychopathology—a view many scientists share. In testimony before Congress, Phillip Handler, then president of the National Academy of Sciences, asserted that fraud is perpetrated by the "deranged" (testimony, March 31, 1981, hearings before the House of Representatives Subcommittee on Oversight and Investigation of the Science and Technology Committee.) A variant of this explanation holds that fraud results from pathological self-deception. Scientists are said to believe that their ideas are correct and would be supported by the evidence, if only the evidence could be properly marshalled; hence, why not contrive or invent that evidence? The line between such deviant behavior and routine behavior in science is clear. Scientists know that good ideas are often not supported by evidence and that the evidence, not the ideas, may be at fault; even so, they do not proceed to shape evidence fraudulently to be in accord with what they believe must be so.

A third explanation is essentially Marxist and tied to conflict theories of deviance. It holds that deviant behavior results from the industrialization of science in large corporate and academic laboratories and the resulting alienation of scientists from their labor. "Alienation does tend to make it difficult to 'live for' science, to pursue science 'only in the cause of science itself,' to maintain 'disinterestedness.' And fraud is one possible outcome when the 'rigorous policing' becomes loose" (Weinstein 1977, p. 643).

Others seek to account for deviant behavior by specific structural sources. Fraud is said to derive from the pressure to get grants and to publish (Woolf, 1986), from the "hyperkinetic environment of science" and the absence of time to supervise students and assistants and from interdisciplinary research in which co-authors cannot check one anothers' work (Kennedy, 1987; Petersdorf, 1986), and a host of other observations about conditions in science making for fraudulent practices. (See also Koshland, 1987; Meadows and Meadows, 1983).

Theories of deviance in science differ primarily in the sources they identify: anomie theory focuses on the immense value science places on originality and peer recognition and the way these exert pressures for deviance; psychopathological accounts put prime weight on the individual; and variants of Marxist theory point to the industrialization of science, which alienates investigators from their work and leads to the decline of "rigorous policing." Each of these theories implies that deviant behavior should be more frequent in certain groups of scientists than others. Yet there has been no systematic effort to investigate the extent to which the theories square with data on incidence of deviance or to investigate the structural conditions held conducive to deviance. There are good reasons for the absence of such research; the actual frequency and distribution of deviant behavior, in general, imperfectly estimated, is altogether unknown in science.

THE INCIDENCE OF DEVIANT BEHAVIOR

Scientists believe that outright fraud is rare and, indeed, act in accord with that belief.[25] Thus they do not routinely replicate the work of others they use in their own research. When results appear implausible and prove not to be replicable, scientists generally assume that error, not fraud, intervened. Others, however, believe that fraud is comparatively frequent. The science journalists, Broad and Wade (1983), identified a total of 34 cases of "known or suspected" fraud from the second century BC to 1981 in all fields of science, but go on to assert that the actual numbers must be of far greater magnitude: "For every major fraud that comes to light, a hundred or so are undetected. For each major fraud, perhaps a thousand minor fakeries are perpetrated . . . every major case of fraud that becomes public is the representative of some 100,000 others, major and minor combined, that lie in the marshy wastes of the scientific literature" (1983, p. 87). The grounds for these estimates are not made evident.

Claims both of high and low rates must be treated with caution. No one knows the actual frequency or distribution of fraud in science. No method has been developed to gauge the ratio between the small number of cases that have come to public light and those that may lie undetected. There is reason to suppose that reported cases do not tell the full story since we know that cases of error have remained undetected in the literature for some time and it is therefore likely that the same holds for fraud.

The impression that fraud has become more frequent may arise from the increased number of reports of such episodes in the press. This impression may also be reinforced by the journalistic practice of reiterating charges every time developments in the same episode are reported; this of course amplifies the mentions rather than the episodes. This pattern has been identified in other instances of press coverage, such as Joseph McCarthy's accusations against the physicist E. U. Condon, and probably holds here also (Klapper and Glock, 1949).

The absence of data on the incidence of deviance means that there is no social epidemiology of deviance in science—no systematic analysis of its distribution, sources, or control. By way of a poor substitute, one can only piece together scattered quantitative evidence and turn to qualitative case studies. For example, I have already described studies in which scientists were asked anonymously about their inclinations to be secretive. Few reported that they withheld information about their work (Gaston, 1973; Hagstrom, 1974; Sullivan, 1975).[26] This, in turn, implies that few of them believe their work will be plagiarized.

Self-reports are one way of assessing the incidence of deviant behavior; reports of having been victimized, so-called victimization data, are another. The only available data pertain not to fraud in science but to the less serious infraction of improper citation of prior work. Hagstrom (1974) reports that about one-fourth of the scientists he queried said their work had not been properly cited by those who knew it; however, self-serving misperceptions may of course account for some of these instances. The third sort of evidence traditionally used in studies of deviance is official crime statistics; notoriously biased, they are at least available for many forms of deviant behavior. In science, however, official statistics on deviance are not collected. Institutionalized procedures for dealing with misconduct are only now beginning to be put in place and there are still no procedures for assembling data of this kind. Finally, informants' estimates are sometimes used to gauge the incidence of deviant behavior. But here, the few studies available are based on such poor or nonsamples that no sound conclusions on incidence can be drawn from them.

Case studies cannot, of course, provide a basis for judging the incidence of deviant behavior, but they do provide cues to the sorts of scientists who engage in seriously deviant acts and the circumstances that are conducive to them. The small number of current cases in hand imply that junior scientists are more often directly involved than seniors, that these episodes occur more often in biomedical science, and in laboratories with conspicuously high rates of publication (Woolf, 1986). But such materials cannot of course answer such questions as: Do eminent scientists depart from the norms more often or less than others? Does serious misconduct occur more often in settings that put a high premium on publication and grant getting, and more often in interdisciplinary research, where coworkers are not in a position to check on one another?

Understandably, the historical cases of apparent deviant behavior that have come to light disproportionately involve figures of great standing in science, not junior investigators who hold no great interest for posterity. These include Ptolemy, Newton, and Mendel. Close scrutiny of such cases indicates that it is difficult to determine with reasonable assurance whether misconduct did or did not occur, according to standards in force at the time. The verdict is still out on Newton (see Cohen, 1974; Westfall, 1973). But it appears now that neither Ptolemy nor Mendel departed significantly from practices prevailing in their times (Dunn, 1965; Fisher, 1936; Gingerich, 1976; Kohn, 1986; Neugebauer, 1975). Other distinguished if less epoch-making scientists have also been accused of fraud. R. A. Millikan, the great American physicist, may have "cooked" evidence on the oil drop experiment. Experts disagree (Franklin, 1981; Holton, 1978). They also disagree in the case of Cyril Burt, although Burt now has few supporters (Dorfman, 1978; Hearnshaw, 1979; Stigler, 1979; see also Gieryn and Figert, 1986). Yet these highly visible instances are too small in number to shed light on the question of whether famous scientists are more or less apt to deviate than others.

There is no firm basis, then, for assessing rival claims that deviance in science is frequent or rare, that its rate is increasing, stable, or decreasing, or that it is less frequent in science than in other social domains. Such claims are plainly based on impressions of varying degrees of reliability. Indeed, the hard work of identifying the pertinent units of analysis has yet to be done—it is not clear how rates should be estimated—whether they should be figured per capita, per experiment, per paper, or even per finding, however these might be counted. In light of all this, it is tempting to settle for the reasonable but impressionistic conclusion drawn by the geneticist Norton Zinder (private communication) that fraud, at least, can neither have been very frequent in the past nor be very frequent now; else science would scarcely be the successful enterprise it has proved to be. However, this judicious conclusion leaves almost entirely open questions of the incidence of deviance and its epidemiology.

SOCIAL CONTROL OF DEVIANT BEHAVIOR

Standard sociological lore has it that social control of deviance always involves procedures for deterrence, detection, and punishment. The inculcation of norms through socialization is one means of deterrence. But in general, it is a necessary though not wholly effective means of preventing deviance. Thus the fact that scientists learn early in their careers that various acts are proscribed is doubtless not enough to ensure conformity. Probably more effective and certainly more interesting sociologically is the part played in science by the methodological canon of reproducibility and by actual replication; the first serves as a mechanism for deterring fraudulent evidence, and the second as a means of detecting it when it does occur.[27] Knowing that fraud in all its forms may be detected at some time in the future in the process of replication may deter some potential departures from the norms.[28]

The reproducibility of scientific work does not mean, of course, that actual replication is common practice. Indeed, given the emphasis in science on making original contributions and receiving the rewards that go with them, and given the expense and impracticality of replication in various sciences, it is not surprising that deliberate replication does not occur routinely (see Sterling, 1959; Bahr, Caplow, and Chadwick, 1983; Mulkay, 1984). This, however, does not mean that replication is rare in any form. Rather, it appears that as they go about their work in attempting to extend others' contributions, scientists engage in much inadvertent replication. They do not carry out precisely the same experiments or calculations as others before them. Rather, as they work at related research, inconsistent results of prior work can be identified and lead to questions being raised about validity. Moreover, it appears that the more significant earlier work is for the development of scientific knowledge, the more often and the more rapidly will others try to extend it and, the more often it will be subjected to such inadvertent tests of validity. Such inadvertent replication will not distinguish fraud from error; it will call results into question. Scientists are not apt to keep silent about important work they find unreliable.[29] From the standpoint of the development of knowledge, this may be enough.

Not all contributions are equally reproducible. There are great differences, associated with cognitive texture of scientific disciplines, in the extent to which experiments are readily replicated. There are differences in potentials for replication, especially between the observational and experimental sciences; differences also in the nature of phenomena being examined, those subject to maturation effects, testing effects, and social change being less reproducible than those that are not; and, of course, differences in the cost of replication, with expensive large-scale studies less likely to be fully replicated. It follows then that opportunities for engaging in undetected fraud vary in differing fields and sorts of research. Whether such differing potentials are actually exploited, we cannot say.

This line of analysis on the role of replicability and of inadvertent replication in the social control of deviance (and indeed in demarcating science from nonscience) is not shared by all sociologists of science. Those who adopt a radically relativist position hold that exact replication is not possible. Collins (1975, 1982, 1985), an exceedingly articulate exponent of the relativist view, argues that so much tacit knowledge of experiments is required to repeat an experiment that real replication simply cannot occur. Rather, he holds, scientists decide whether competent experiments have been done and negotiate about the extent to which a given set of experiments has or has not replicated earlier work. Replication therefore provides no firm basis for identifying error or fraud and also no firm ground for marking off science from pseudoscience. Knorr-Cetina (1977, 1981), an ethnographer of science and advocate of the constructivist perspective, does not deny the possibility of replication but doubts that the outcomes of research can often be validated. This is so because scientific "facts," which are constructed by scientists, are strongly affected by their local contexts and thus scientists do not

produce a body of "invariant knowledge." Discourse analysts take still a third view of replication (and thus of its possible role in detecting and deterring deviance) that is consistent with their general position—"there is no single coherent story [about] . . . 'replication,' [it] has multiple meanings" (Mulkay, 1984, p. 278). Scientists themselves, Mulkay and Gilbert (1986) say, deny engaging in "mere replication." Rather, Mulkay and Gilbert report that scientists produce a complex combination of "realist" and "constructionist" accounts in describing what they take to be replication. One can however just as easily identify scientists, even sophisticated falsificationists, who reject the constructionist view. These scientists conclude that replication does serve to deter error of all kinds and thus provides adequate safeguards against fraud (Franklin, 1984).

In the continuing absence of systematic analysis of what scientists in various fields actually make of replication, it is premature to decide whether they believe in it in principle. Given the divergent views about the nature of replication, there can be no agreement among sociologists about its effectiveness in detecting error and fraud. This also holds for the effectiveness of peer review of papers submitted for publication. Designed to assess the plausibility of claims and the publishability of papers and not to detect misconduct, this procedure is sometimes rejected as ineffectual (Broad and Wade, 1983; Stewart and Feder, 1987) because error and fraud sometimes appear in the published literature in spite of its having been peer reviewed. That surely does show that peer review is imperfect. However, the published record alone scarcely provides strong evidence regarding the effectiveness of peer review in the absence of systematic evidence on the relative number of papers rejected for publication because referees judged them not to meet acceptable evidentiary standards.

So much for deterrence and detection of deviance in science. How is punishment meted out and how severe is it? Science has been far less organized in dealing with misconduct than other learned professions such as medicine and law. Codes of scientific conduct and procedures for review and punishment been formalized only recently, not just for individuals but also for the institutions with which they are affiliated.[30] This does not mean that scientists judged to be deviant have only recently been subjected to system-exercised punishment. Those who have been judged guilty of fraud or plagiarism have generally been expelled from the scientific community. Their acts are defined as unacceptable assaults on the social integrity of science. In science, it is not common to have the slate wiped clean after penance is done. But the system of imposing punishments is still not formalized. There is ambiguity, not just about the proper match between crime and punishment, but also about how far scientists' responsibilities for misconduct extend. Some would exempt senior scientists whose assistants went astray without their knowledge; others would not. The severe line, taken by Nobel Laureate Rosalyn Yalow, for example, holds that "those who take the fame, have to take the blame" (quoted in *The New York Times*, July 13, 1987, p. 27).

It should be clear that the basic evidence is lacking on the incidence, distribution, and effectiveness of various controls of deviant behavior in science. Yet it provides a particularly interesting and possibly unique domain for the study of deviant behavior. The very pressures that make for deviant behavior, the intense culturally reinforced ambition to receive credit for original contributions, also makes for the greater likelihood of its detection, since the more important the claim and the greater the amount of credit at stake, the greater the chances that follow-up inquiry will occur and deviance will be discovered. The same conditions that provide incentives for deviance in science then also provide for its detection.

Stratification in Science

The scientific community is not a company of equals. It is sharply stratified; a small number of scientists contribute disproportionately to the advancement of science and receive a disproportionately large share of rewards and resources needed for research. Moreover, these inequalities tend to be self-reinforcing over the course of scientists' careers. All this is largely invisible to outsiders, who see science as an occupation of comparatively high prestige and ample rewards.[31]

Stratification in science has been a central focus of research for sociologists of science since the early 1960s, a time when research on stratification was flourishing in the discipline at large. Yet the focus on stratification in science has derived more from the research program laid out in Merton's "Priorities in Scientific Discovery" (1957) than from an interest in the generic problem. The issue posed then has pervaded research on the subject ever since: Do scientists live up in practice to the normative principle of universalism in the allocation of rewards—that is, are they rewarded primarily or solely to the

extent that their contributions advance knowledge? If not, what sorts of particularism obtain, which social attributes of scientists and of their affiliations affect their life chances in science? Some, though decidedly not all, early research found that universalism largely did pertain; that rewards in science by and large went to those who had contributed most (Cole and Cole, 1967). This led to the speculation that science was "special," as social institutions go, not in being wholly meritocratic, but in being more meritocratic than others. In the interim, these early findings and the assertion that science is special have been questioned, though not entirely overturned.

THE STRUCTURE OF STRATIFICATION IN SCIENCE

Stratification is ubiquitous in science. Individuals, groups, laboratories, institutes, universities, journals, fields and specialties, theories, and methods are incessantly ranked and sharply graded in prestige. Even awards for assessed contributions are themselves graded. The topmost layer of each hierarchy is made up of an elite whose composition rests on socially assessed role performance or, in the case of fields, specialties, theories, and findings, on their cognitive standing.[32] While high-quality role performance in science generally brings material rewards, as well as peer recognition in science, the latter is particularly important.

The quest for peer recognition. Why is peer recognition so important? It is simply this: Recognition from those relatively competent to judge is the prime indicator scientists have of their having contributed to the advancement of knowledge. The intrinsic pleasure of discovery is one thing and their belief that what they have done is new and important is another, but recognition of their work by the collectivity of competent peers is the only unambiguous demonstration that what they have done matters to science (Merton, 1957/1973e). Thus it is the ne plus ultra of rewards in science. Scientists are therefore greatly concerned about peer judgments and this concern is institutionally generated. (See Hagstrom, 1965, for a different but congruent account of why scientists are concerned with peer recognition.) One concrete expression of peer recognition of work in science is in its use—that is, by scientists first building on contributions and then referring to them in published work. Collegial recognition is also expressed in a vast array of honorific awards including all manner of prizes, fellowships, named lectureships, and professorships and, in fairly rare instances, by eponymy—the naming of all or part of a discovery after its discoverer, Halley's Comet, Boyle's Law, and Mendelian genetics being familiar examples.[33]

This account of peer recognition and its importance in science is more or less canonical; that is, accepted by most sociologists of science interested in its social organization. Most scientists report that it accords with their own experience. Latour and Woolgar (1979, chap. 5), however, have proposed an alternative "economic" account that emphasizes scientists' concern not with gaining peer recognition, but with accumulating, using, and converting credibility into other resources. They portray science as a market in which scientists "invest" their credibility in problems they believe will yield further credible evidence, which in turn helps them get more support for their work and in the process enhance their career attainments— the objective of the enterprise being to speed up the credibility cycle, just described, as much as possible. They claim that this model allows for all sorts of motivations in science and does not require the analyst to posit scientists' having an interest in recognition. Latour and Woolgar are correct, in the current period at least, that scientists must be dedicated to maintaining their laboratories, research funding, research performance, and careers and that such a cycle cannot be interrupted for long without catastrophic results. Yet they also imply that scientific activity is no more than an accelerated and never-ending cycle of information production. That model does not explain the intense concern of scientists in receiving peer recognition for their contributions. Such concerns are not incompatible with their account even though they play down the intrinsic significance peer recognition holds for scientists and its institutional derivation and maintenance. (Knorr-Cetina, 1981, has other objections to the Latour and Woolgar thesis: They limit their focus to scientific communities rather extend it to "transepistemic arenas." And, as she terms it, the thesis "functionalizes" the relations between the credibility of the objects produced and scientists' positions, power, and dominance.) But if patterned motives for doing science are now at issue, the resulting structure of stratification is not.

Recognition and rewards in science are not just graded but highly stratified. They are greatly concentrated among a relatively small number of recipients—a few scientists and a few laboratories and a few universities get the lion's share. By way of example, a crude but service-able gauge of recognition is the extent of citation to scientists' work in research publications of their peers.[34] Like other indicators of collegial recognition, citation counts are highly skewed. Of scientist-authors whose work was cited at all during the two decades between 1961 and 1980, 62% were cited no more than five times, just 6% were cited as many as 100 times and at the peak, 1% were cited 500 times or more (Institute for Scientific Information, 1981).

When it comes to awards, Cole and Cole (1973) report that about half of a national sample of American academic physicists had received some award, with most of these being postdoctoral fellowships. Only 15% had received an award other than a "post-doc," and 11% of the physicists had received 70% of all the awards. Although there are no sound estimates of the distribution of awards across fields, the Coles's findings hold also for another national sample of American rank-and-file physical and biological scientists (Zuckerman, 1977b). Similar concentrations of recognition and standing appear also among organizations. Just five universities employ half of all American Nobel laureates (Zuckerman, 1977, p. 241). Members of the National Academy of Sciences—the principal honorific scientific academy in the United States—are only slightly more dispersed. Ten universities account for half of all members of the Academy (Kash et al., 1972).[35] It turns out also that promising students, or more precisely, students who later became highly recognized for their scientific accomplishments, cluster at a few universities. Half of all American laureates took their doctoral degrees from five universities (not quite the same ones that later employ them); these same five also graduated 18% of all Ph.D.s in the sciences but as many as 46% of future members of the Academy (Zuckerman, 1977b, p. 90).[36]

Rewards in science are readily transmuted into resources for research.[37] Highly recognized scientists and research institutions are more successful than their less recognized colleagues in getting resources for future research. Thus the same concentrations, noted earlier, also appear in research funding. Ten universities were granted 21% of all the funds available to American colleges and universities in 1979-1980 with the next 20 having an additional 43%; the remaining 3000 or so institutions thus shared the remaining 36% (National Center for Educational Statistics, 1981, p. 1). These highly skewed distributions of resources have been in effect for many years. Thus the same few institutions continue, year after year, to be better supported than all the rest, meanwhile attracting notable scientists and the most promising students. The concentration then of human and financial resources in organizations are plainly interrelated and continually reinforced. Thus scientists, differentially located in the system, encounter vastly different structures of opportunity to do research and to contribute to knowledge. Those who have done well in the past are given a better chance of doing so in the future, and to that extent, meritocracy makes for markedly steep structures of stratification.

SOURCES OF INEQUALITY

Why is the distribution of rewards so sharply graded? How much does it reflect the distribution of role performance in science, as the principle of universalism suggests it should, and how much do other processes contribute to these high concentrations?

No procedure now in hand satisfactorily measures all aspects of scientists' role performance. But not all aspects of role performance are defined as equally important. Given the emphasis in science on advancing knowledge, research contributions are generally given prime weight. The extent of scientists' research publication, the mere number of papers they have published, is often used as one rough measure of contribution. Although it does not hold, of course, in every individual case—many a scientist has published much but contributed little—on the average, the sheer number of publications has been found to correlate with other assessments of quality of contribution. Beyond the number of publications is the frequency of peer citations to them as an indicator of performance. These measures clearly have their limitations. For one thing, as we have noted, scientific role performance is not limited to research and publication. Teaching, administration, and citizenship in the community of science also contribute to the advancement of knowledge in less obvious ways. For another, all published papers are of course not equally important, nor are citations of a piece as indicators of intellectual influence. Still, sociologists of science have found these useful measures of role performance, or more specifically, of research performance, inasmuch as they have been found to be correlated with other more direct gauges of performance such as ongoing assessments by peers. (Again, it should be repeated: Correlation is not identity. This holds in the aggregate but not in every individual case.) This correlation is not surprising. Since scientific knowledge is public knowledge, publication in science is important. New ideas and findings do not qualify as scientific until

they are published, exposed to the scrutiny of competent judges, and provisionally certified as valid contributions to knowledge. As a result, the work that scientists publish and the number of citations to it become a useful if imperfect indicator of their contributions to knowledge. (See Fox, 1983, for a review of studies of scientific productivity.) Together and separately, published productivity and extent of citation are the most common measures of research performance used by sociologists of science.

Judging from these indicators, there is enormous inequality in the scientists' research performance and in the performance of research organizations (Irvine and Martin, 1984). As we have seen, most individuals publish little. Scientists, on average, publish an estimated 3-6 papers over the course of their careers while only about 1% publish more than 10 papers (Price, 1986; Ziman, 1976, p. 105). In strong contrast, the most prolific publish 40 or more papers a year—a paper every two weeks or so. As Lotka (1926) observed a half-century ago, the distribution of scientists' publications is described by the inverse square law; the chances that a scientist will publish as many as n papers is $1/n^2$. Put another way, about 16% of scientists are responsible for about half of all scientific publications (Price, 1986).[38]

Citations are also highly skewed, as we have seen, and strongly correlated with the extent of publication.[39] But as we have also noted, there are important departures from the rule that the more scientists publish, the greater the cognitive impact of their work; in fact, some scientists are "perfectionists" and publish few papers, each of which is highly cited, while others are "mass producers" who publish many papers but receive comparatively few citations (Cole and Cole, 1973; Gaston, 1978).

THE RELATION BETWEEN RESEARCH PERFORMANCE AND REWARDS

This brings us to central questions addressed in studies of stratification in science: How well does research performance correlate with the rewards individuals receive? Is the observed correlation authentic or spurious?

Available evidence suggests an appreciable connection between performance and reward toward the upper reaches of the stratification system. For example, Nobel laureates-to-be were cited 230 times a year before they receive their awards; on average, two-and-a-half times as often as scientists about to be elected to the National Academy of Sciences, who received 90 citations in the same period. Future academicians, in turn, were cited six times as often as the average scientist-author. It is also the case that "perfectionist" authors tend to be more copiously rewarded than "mass producers" who churn out great numbers of less consequential papers. Such evidence suggests that universalism does hold, that the greater the extent of assessed contribution, by these measures, the greater the recognition conferred. But, of course, the most-cited scientists of all do not necessarily become Nobelists and Academicians. In part, this results from patterns of citation; the most cited papers in the literature report methods or procedures, useful but not necessarily challenging or theoretically significant work. But there are basic structural reasons as well. There are far fewer top-level awards available in science than there are qualified candidates for them. Consequently, when recipients are selected from the pools of more or less equally qualified candidates, thus approximating the norm of universalism, it appears that particularistic criteria are often introduced as secondary criteria. Further fine-grained research is needed to discover the extent and distribution of this composite process of cognitive and social selection. What we do know is that the scarcity of awards also contributes to the skewness of the distribution of rewards, as we shall see.

All apart from citation data, there is considerable evidence showing that the more scientists are judged to have contributed, the more they are rewarded. The Coles (1973) found that in a sample of physicists' research performance, measured by published productivity and particularly by the extent of citation, was the strongest determinant of scientists' reputations among their peers and also of gaining a post at a university department of high prestige.[40] Stephen Cole's (1978) later research shows that the findings for physics were much like those for four other sciences. More than any other variable, the "quality" of scientists' contributions as perceived by fellow scientists influences the allocation of rewards. He draws the double conclusion that the assessed significance of scientists' research is the strongest determinant of the honors they receive and that the structures of the reward systems in the fields he studied were remarkably similar. In short, a marked tendency toward universalism does hold not just in this or that science but in the sciences generally.[41] The findings from the Coles's work in mapping out connections between the extent of scientists' contributions and the rewards they receive and Stephen Cole's (1970) analysis of the impact of scientists' standing on the speed of reception of their research are borne out in Gaston's (1978)

work on British physicists, in numerous papers analyzing the connections between productivity and the prestige of departmental affiliation of scientists, the relations between extent of citation and academic salaries (Diamond, 1984) and my own examination of the careers of Nobel laureates compared with those of other scientists (Zuckerman, 1977b).

In the allocation of research funds, universalism in the form of peer judgments of proposals have been found to be the most important determinant of their acceptance or rejection (Cole and Cole, 1977; Cole, Cole and Simon, 1981; Mullins, 1985).[42,43] It also governs decisions on scientific publication—in some measure. "Problematic" papers submitted to the outstanding journal of physics—that is, papers considered questionable by referees—were no more likely to be accepted when submitted by distinguished scientists than by unknown ones (Zuckerman and Merton, 1971, p. 55). We also found that the disproportionately large share of the literature published by well-known scientists resulted from their submitting more papers for publication and not necessarily from their having received favored treatment, as others have supposed.[44] Yet the findings indicating that universalistic standards largely apply in the evaluation of scientists' work and the allocation of certain rewards are not the whole story.

For one thing, not all scholars agree that the correlation between research performance, as measured by citations, and the rewards scientists receive provides valid evidence of universalism. Mulkay (1980, p. 33), for one, holds that it is spurious or at least that universalism has not been demonstrated. The connection between citations and awards *"merely . . . show[s] that both kinds of rewards tend to go to the same people"* (italics his). The fundamental question why these scientists "receive an unusually large share of both these types of rewards . . . remains untouched" (1980, pp. 33-34). Does some particularistic process underlie both citing practices and the allocation of rewards? Possibly. Yet in light of the way in which citations are generated, this seems unlikely. Although a relatively few scientists publish a great deal and therefore account disproportionately for the number of citations conferred in the literature, such vast numbers of citations are conferred in the aggregate of most disciplines within even a short time period that a few authors cannot monopolize the citation process. Citations are not exclusively controlled by an elite (as many other rewards are), nor are they, in the aggregate, the product of deliberate collective decisions by particular groups. Indeed, highly cited authors are referenced as often in papers by comparatively uncited authors as in those by highly cited authors (J. Cole, 1970). Still, not enough is known about scientists' citing practices to estimate the extent to which they might result from particularistic or localistic judgments. Yet, it seems unlikely that the rank-and-file scientists who are responsible for most citations are motivated to reward the elite, beyond what they take to be their due.

However, there is more direct evidence for the operation of some degree of particularism in the allocation of resources and rewards in science—although these data, as do those indicating universalism, also contain their own ambiguities.

For example, the prestige of the departments where scientists get their degrees is related to the prestige of the departments where they find jobs, particularly their first jobs, and this holds regardless of research performance. Early research by Crane (1967) and Hargens and Hagstrom (1967) on the correlations between prestige of degree-granting departments and current affiliations, has been substantiated by careful analysis of longitudinal data by Long (1978); Long, Allison, and McGinnis (1979); Reskin (1976, 1977, 1978, 1979); and Chubin, Porter, and Boeckmann (1981). They find that where scientists start out (whether they studied in a highly reputed department) and who they studied with (whether they were sponsored by a scientist of high repute) strongly affects where they end up, even when the extent of research performance is taken into account. Moreover, Long and McGinnis (1981) show that the scientists' research performance is determined more by the departments with which they come to be affiliated than the reverse, and that scientists' performance comes to resemble the performance of those with whom they become associated. This work is important. But it still leaves open the question of the possible additional effects of self-selection, whether scientists choose employment in departments that demand levels of performance they find congenial.

These data indicating the effects of particularism are consistent with my own studies of Nobel laureates, which show the effects on scientists' careers of having a distinguished sponsor. Half of all American laureates studied with prior Nobel laureates. More in point, those who did received the prize nine years sooner than the rest, whose prize-winning work was not done later and was, on average, apt to be no less distinguished. More pertinent for the scientific community at large, historical and socio-

logical research on the careers of men and women scientists shows marked gender disparities in rank (except at the level of assistant professor), salary, promotion rates, positions of influence, and honorific awards. (See Rossiter, 1982, on the history of women scientists and Zuckerman, 1987a, for a review of current sociological research.) They also show great disparities between men and women in published research performance. On average, women publish about 60% as many papers and are cited at a similarly lower rate than men of the same professional ages, in the same fields, and with the same educational origins (Cole and Zuckerman, 1984). In part, the gender disparities in rewards are attributable to gender disparities in performance. However, such disparities in performance are found not to account for women being promoted more slowly and less often to posts in the most distinguished university departments than men with comparable records of performance (Cole, 1979).[45] Since academic rank is both a reward and a resource for continuing research achievement, such gender differences are consequential for women's research performance later in their careers.

In short, the evidence indicates that the stratification system of science is neither exclusively universalistic nor exclusively particularistic. Particularistic standards are often applied early in scientists' careers before they have had much chance to demonstrate how they will perform. At this stage, informal assessments of promise by sponsors count in the allocation of resources and rewards. Later, the impact of sponsorship and of the prestige of the department granting the Ph.D. is attenuated and research performance, gauged by publication and citation, become more important in shaping the allocation of rewards. However since current research performance is in part the product in part of prior experiences with particularism, evidence of the application of universalism later in the career does not mean that it holds exclusive sway.

In light of this mixed set of findings, is science meritocratic? Not entirely. Is it more meritocratic than other institutions? Possibly, but we cannot say without systematic comparative institutional analysis. At this reading, it appears to exhibit some of the same structures of discrimination as other occupations (Bielby, in press; Fox, 1985), but it also is marked by an intense commitment to achievement over ascription. The compelling evidence is plainly not in.

THE THEORY OF ACCUMULATION
OF ADVANTAGE AND DISADVANTAGE:
CONCENTRATION OF REWARDS
IN SCIENCE

Rewards in science are, as we noted, concentrated among a few scientists, a few laboratories, and a few institutions. This results in some measure, as we have seen, from skewness in performance. It also results from the enormous significance given to priority in science. The recognition that goes to those who first make a scientific discovery is incomparably greater than what also-rans receive. The skewness of rewards is also a product of their scarcity. But most of all, the marked concentration of rewards and resources in science results from processes of accumulation of advantage. These shape the distribution of rewards in science and lead to increasing disparities between the "haves" and "have nots" over the course of scientists' careers.

The theory of the accumulation of advantage provides a dynamic structural account of how role performance and recognition in science, and possibly other domains, come to be as sharply concentrated as they are.[46]

Processes of individual self-selection and institutional social-selection interact to affect successive probabilities of access to the opportunity-structure in a given field. . . . When the role-performance of an individual measures up to demanding . . . standards . . . this initiates a process of cumulative advantage in which the individual acquires successively enlarged opportunities to advance his work (and the rewards that go with it) . . . [those who find their] way into [elite] institutions ha[ve] the heightened potential of acquiring differentially accumulating advantage [Merton, 1977, p. 89].

Processes of accumulation of advantage therefore work in such a way that "certain individuals and groups repeatedly receive resources and rewards that enrich recipients at an accelerating rate and conversely impoverish (relatively) the non-recipients" (Zuckerman, 1977b, pp. 59-60). In principle, it does not matter whether criteria for allocating resources and rewards are achieved or ascribed, "these processes [which affect access to the opportunity structure] contribute to elite formation and ultimately produce sharply graded systems of stratification" (Zuckerman, 1977, pp. 59-60).[47]

The theory holds first that early access to resources is singularly important in benefiting particular individuals. The earlier they gain access to various kinds of resources, the earlier they develop and the earlier they gain a head start over their age peers. Correlatively, the longer they are kept from those resources, the more hampered is their future development. Second, the accumulation of advantage operates in systems in which rewards can be transformed into resources for further achievement. This produces an upward spiraling of achievements and rewards. Third, the opportunity structures that scientists encounter at successive stages of their careers to a degree reflect their past achievement, just as performance in the present shapes opportunities in the future. Fourth, by making past achievements the prime criterion for allocating resources and rewards, the accumulation of advantage is, on the face of it, universalistic at any given time but also inadvertently particularistic over the long run since it greatly enlarges disparities in performance and rewards between recipients and nonrecipients, far beyond the disparities that pertained at the outset. And last, the accumulation of advantage calls attention to the impact of the rewards on performance—not just the reverse—and the continuing interplay between performance, rewards, and access to the means of scientific production. In short, the accumulation of advantage produces a "class structure" in science much as similar processes of stratified access do in the society at large.

By and large, the evidence in hand squares with the theory of accumulation of advantage. As we have seen, there are marked disparities in role performance in science, as well as in access to resources and rewards. The data also show that such disparities increase as scientists move through their careers; that is, the gap in levels of performance among age peers is far greater several decades into the career than it was initially, and the same is true for the rewards conferred on scientists. Other evidence is also consistent with the theory: Disparities in scientists' access to resources for research, including time, research funds, assistance, and the like also grow with time. Moreover "reinforcement effects" seem to be at work such that those scientists whose work is recognized early in their careers subsequently become more productive than others with equivalent records of performance who were not early beneficiaries of rewards (Cole and Cole, 1973; Reskin, 1977; and Cole and Zuckerman, 1984, find this is less true for women scientists than for men).

The Matthew Effect as a special case. Processes of accumulation of advantage are accentuated by the operation of the "Matthew Effect," in which "eminent scientists get disproportionately great credit for their contributions . . . while relatively unknown scientists tend to get disproportionately little credit for comparable contributions. . . .This complex pattern of misallocation of credit for scientific work" is named after the Gospel of St. Matthew: "For unto everyone that hath shall be given and he shall have abundance: but from him that hath not shall be taken away even that which he hath" (Merton, 1968, pp. 443, 445). The Matthew Effect is especially evident in cases that are not just vaguely comparable but much the same: ...i collaborations between scientists of greatly differing standing where credit goes to those who are already eminent and in cases of independent multiple discovery (see later section on theory of discovery), episodes in which the same discovery arrived at independently and more or less simultaneously are credited to the better-known discoverer.

The Matthew Effect is the outcome of evaluation and communication processes in science. Having learned the value of attending to the work of certain investigators in the past, and faced with a literature of unmanageable proportions, scientists tend to notice the work of well-known scientists, take it more seriously, and ultimately use it more intensively. The Matthew Effect therefore enlarges differences in reputation and rewards over and above those attributable to differences in performance and to processes of accumulation of advantage, and thereby introduces its own variety of particularism into the system.

Processes of accumulation of advantage not only shape the distribution of rewards in science, they also provide for its justification. Because those who are most copiously rewarded have by and large performed at the highest levels, the accumulation of advantage fosters an ideology claiming that evaluation processes are effective and that the reward system is meritocratic and fair. However, there is no way of knowing the extent to which this is so, given the self-confirming nature of the processes involved. That is, there is no way of determining after the fact how well those who had limited access to opportunity would have done had they benefited more than they did at the outset. In light of this, the idea of accumulation of advantage casts doubt on the assumption that marked differences in performance in science invariably reflect equally marked differences in capacity to do scientific work.

THE REWARD SYSTEM,
STRATIFICATION AND THE
GROWTH OF KNOWLEDGE

In principle, the evaluation and reward systems and the resulting system of stratification have evolved through processes briefly sketched out in these pages.

As we have seen, resources are allocated largely on the basis of assessed prior achievement, with this being institutionally assumed as the best criterion for doing so. But this has not been decisively demonstrated. The reward system does appear to reinforce scientists' motivations to work on important problems insofar as solutions to such problems bring considerable amounts of recognition. But the same reward system may lead many scientists to focus mainly on problems that can be solved rapidly. On this reading, difficult, intractable but important problems may tend to be bypassed by many scientists as they seek immediate rather than distant rewards. Similarly, the system appears to be arranged to inhibit extremely unconventional views to the extent that recognition is given for doing research that helps as many others as possible get on with their own work. It may also divert scientists from problems in applied science and in comparatively unfashionable fields and specialties. By conferring honors of various sorts, the reward system does call attention to problems assessed as important and to research assessed as excellent by making them visible, both within and outside the community of science. However, the comparative scarcity of the most prestigious honors means, of course, that only some of the highest-quality contributions are recognized and made visible by formal awards. The connections between stratification and mobility, the allocation of resources and rewards, and the extension of knowledge have begun to be studied by sociologists of science. Hargens, Mullins, and Hecht (1980) made a good start in showing the effects of cognitive structure on stratification—on how working in a new research area affects scientists' productivity and standing—while Hargens and Hagstrom (1982) and Hargens and Felmlee (1984) have examined the effects of several aspects of cognitive structure, such as the extent of consensus on research priorities and techniques and growth rates of the sciences, on patterns of status attainment and the speed with which younger people are upwardly mobile. These linkages between cognitive structure and stratification patterns represent an important next step for research. Another requires more intensive study of the organizational bases of stratification in science—the ways in which processes internal to organizations work to rank and reward scientists —a line of analysis now receiving much attention in studies of stratification generally. Conversely, students of social stratification in the discipline at large might take note of processes of accumulation of advantage and disadvantage and their effects, not least the unintended but nonetheless potent contribution of meritocracy to inequality.

Is Science a Young Person's Game?

A widely shared belief holds that scientists do their best work when they are young. Thus the physicist P.A.M. Dirac versified:

Age is, of course, a fever chill
that every physicist must fear.
He's better dead then living still
when once he's past his thirtieth year.[48]

Many scientists also believe that the young are more apt than others to adopt new ideas, particularly new revolutionary ideas. It follows then, as the epochal theoretical physicist Max Planck put it, that:

a new scientific truth does not triumph by convincing its opponents and making them see the light, but rather because its opponents eventually die, and a new generation grows up that is familiar with it [Planck, 1949, pp. 33-34].

This proposes that major changes in scientific ideas come about through the inevitable succession of generations, not because scientists change their minds about the validity of new ideas. An interesting and oft-quoted hypothesis.

In the final section of the chapter, we take up the possible connections between the outcomes of scientists' research and their social statuses and ideologies. Here, we examine the two cognate questions presented to us by Dirac and Planck: Do young scientists contribute more than other age groups and is youth more receptive than age to new ideas? Such age-stratified patterns, if they actually occur, would plainly be consequential not just for the research careers of individual scientists but also, and more important, for the development of the corpus of scientific ideas. (See Zuckerman and Merton, 1973, for an analysis of age and age structure in science.)

The idea that science is a young person's game, that the young are the most "creative" age stratum in science, was greatly reinforced by

the studies of psychologist Harvey Lehman (1953). These seemed to find that major works in science and mathematics were mainly contributions of the young; further, this obtained in music, poetry, and other creative endeavors, as well. He suggested that there was something special about being young that encouraged intellectual daring and creativity.[49]

How well do these beliefs square with the evidence? Not very well, in spite of Lehman's reports, which have since been shown to be flawed. (See Zuckerman and Merton, 1973; and Cole, 1979, for critical analysis.) Later investigations, using more exacting measures of the quality of scientific contributions—published productivity, citations and peer-assigned awards —show little evidence that youth was related to outstanding research performance (for reviews, see Bayer and Dutton, 1977; and Reskin, 1979). Rather, some research finds that the relations between age and various measures of research performance are mildly curvilinear; that is, the extent and impact of scientists' work increases slightly in middle age and then declines slightly as scientists age (Cole, 1979; Zuckerman, 1977b), while other research finds markedly different patterns in different scientific disciplines. In some sciences, individuals' published productivity rises, declines, and then rises again in later years, while in others, an initial spurt is followed by slow decline (Bayer and Dutton, 1977; Blackburn, Beyhmer, and Hall, 1978; Helmreich, Spence, and Thorbecke, 1981; Horner, Rushton, and Vernon, 1986; Over, 1982; Stern, 1978).[50] These various patterns call for further investigation but it is evident that in general not all nor even most of scientists' major work is done when they are young. And, of course, as ample evidence testifies, scientists of the same age vary considerably both in rates of publication and in the significance of their work.[51] Thus systematic inquiry of aggregates of scientists does not find that age in itself either chronological or professional age (that is, the number of years elapsed since the doctorate was conferred) makes for patterned differences in rates and kinds of creative scientific work.

Why, then, do some scientists believe that the best work is done by the young? In part, no doubt, because they know this to be true of particular major discoveries in science. Many of the great heroes of science were quite young when they did their transforming work. Thus Newton was 24 when he largely invented the calculus and took his early steps toward the law of universal gravitation. Just as Einstein was 26 when he published the papers on the special theory of relativity, the photoelectric effect, and Brown-ian motion. Darwin was an advanced 29 when he identified the essentials of the theory of natural selection (which he delayed publishing until he was 50). Moreover, 9 out of the 10 physicists generally credited with bringing about the quantum revolution in physics were in their twenties at the time (Zuckerman and Merton, 1973, p. 513). Monumental cases in point. Yet, what is true for these epoch-making events need not hold for the connections between age and scientific contribution generally. These universally known incomparable instances understandably invite the belief that it is generally the case that scientists do their best work when they are young. That belief may also be reinforced by selective perception. Major discoveries by very young investigators elicit much attention and are then easily recalled and reiterated; the many more discoveries of like kind by middle-aged scientists are not expressly linked to the age of their discoverers. At this time, however, systematic study indicates that science is not a young man's or woman's game but rather a game of the middle aged. Thus, to take a summary example, Nobel laureates in physics were on average 36 years of age when they did the research that brought them the prize; those in chemistry were 39, and those in the biological sciences were 41, far from being precociously young, but not old, either (Zuckerman, 1977, p. 166).

Although the evidence so far makes it unlikely that age in and of itself influences scientific performance, this still leaves open the possibility that age-related social and cognitive variables affect scientific performance over the shorter run among subsets of scientists.[52] Only a few studies report on the social attributes of scientists who exhibit particular patterns of research performance throughout the life course but reasonably good data show that a large fraction of scientists spend a decreasing share of their time at research as they age, and that this apparently accounts in part for variously observed declines in rates of scientific publication with aging (Allison and Stewart, 1974; Zuckerman and Merton, 1973, pp. 519-528). Selective attrition of research scientists may also attenuate possible relationships between age and the ongoing extent of new scientific contributions. It has been noted that when their early work is recognized and rewarded, scientists more often continue to be productive, while those whose earlier efforts were neglected are more likely to stop research and turn to other activities. Thus the reward system of science may help to explain persisting and comparatively high rates of publication throughout the careers of some scientists, along with marked reductions in publication by others over the years (Cole, 1979; Cole and Cole, 1973; Cole and Zuckerman, 1984).

Age-related patterns of research performance may be linked to the cognitive structure of science as well. Youthful contributions may be more likely and more visible in the comparatively well-codified sciences—that is, the disciplines in which empirical knowledge is consolidated into "succinct and interdependent theoretical formulations" and "particulars are knit together by general ideas" (Zuckerman and Merton, 1972, pp. 506-519). There, young people can more readily learn what is needed to make significant contributions than in less theoretically integrated disciplines. Truly innovative work in well-codified fields may be more readily identified, irrespective of source. The bias of the Matthew Effect may be less severe, and youth more often given its due. These conjectures are consistent with data on the ages at which scientists in more and less codified fields are elected to major academies and do research of Nobel Prize caliber, but S. Cole (1979) finds no support for them in his studies of the scientists in six disciplines. The jury is still out on the interconnections between the codification of scientific knowledge and age stratification in research performance.

New work by Levin and Stephen (1986) also links cognitive structure to age and research performance. This suggests that entire age cohorts may benefit from "vintage effects"—that is, being trained at a time when a science or specialty is just opening up and there are unusual opportunities for major contributions to be made. In solid state physics, Levin and Stephen report, beneficiaries of "vintage effects" are apt to be more productive initially and throughout their careers than those who came into the field in less innovative times. This promising line of inquiry awaits more comprehensive data and analysis. Meanwhile, it and earlier work on the codification of scientific knowledge illustrate once again the intricate linkages between the cognitive and social structures of science.

Possible connections between age of scientists and receptivity to new ideas are also complicated and they too are not in line with widespread belief. Thus, Gieryn's (1978) study of problem choice among contemporary astronomers finds no greater inclination for younger ones to move into the newest areas of research. McCann's (1978) historical studies of the chemical revolution in the latter eighteenth century found that younger scientists more readily accepted the oxygen paradigm than their seniors. But on closer inspection, those who accepted it first were middle aged rather than young. Similarly, Hull, Tessner, and Diamond (1978) found that Darwinian theory was accepted slightly more quickly by young scientists than by older ones. Yet these ideas were accepted by most English scientists within the decade after they were published. In the years after 1869, older scientists predominated among the few who continued to resist the theory. Messeri's (1988) analysis of contemporary geologists' responses to the revolutionary ideas associated with plate tectonics is consistent with the main import of these earlier studies. He reports a complex interaction between age, social position, and early adoption of new ideas. Age was indeed related to geologists' responses to ideas associated with plate tectonics. But contrary to widespread belief, it was largely middle-aged and comparatively well-established scientists who adopted these ideas while they were still controversial and speculative; younger scientists followed only after the research potentials of these ideas had become clear. Thus age and social position are linked to the reception of intellectual innovation in ways that would elude those sociologists who focus their research interest exclusively on the cognitive or the social domains of science.

The Growth and Decline of Scientific Specialties

The study of scientific specialties by sociologists of science is particularly self-exemplifying. During the late 1960s and all through the 1970s, much research focused on processes of growth and decline of new specialties, comprising groups of scientists working on similar problems and regularly communicating with one another.[53] (For review of research on specialties and disciplines, see Chubin, 1976; Lemaine et al., 1977.) Indeed, the study of specialties itself became a sort of specialty in the field. In the 1980s, however, with the shift in research attention to the microsociology of scientific knowledge, the study of specialties has declined markedly among sociologists. By then, however, an impressive array of case studies of specialty development had appeared. These include the Ben-David and Collins's analysis of the rise of experimental psychology (1966), Mullins's *Theories and Theory Groups in American Sociology* (1973) and Edge and Mulkay's *Astronomy Transformed* (1976). They were accompanied by a spate of inquiries using co-citation analysis, a procedure based on shared citations, developed by Henry Small (1973), in collaboration with Belver Griffith et al. (1974), for identify-

ing the membership and cognitive foci of specialties. But once these initial studies were done, the next steps were far from clear. The study of specialties evolved no well-defined "research programme" that is, no agreed upon "paths of research to avoid" and "paths of research to pursue" (Lakatos, 1970, p. 132). As this illustrates, without an agenda or program, research tends to falter and researchers tend to turn elsewhere. Some sociological research on specialties continues but not at the earlier pace. In marked contrast, historians of science continue to think of specialties and disciplines as key social formations in the growth of scientific knowledge (Fye, 1987; Kohler 1982; Thackray et al., 1987; see Graham, Lepenies, and Weingart, 1983, on uses of disciplinary histories).

In the sociology of science, however, the study of specialties now shows the symptoms of incipient decay typically found in later stages of specialty development. Experienced researchers have turned to other problems, few young recruits have begun to work in the area, and there is little agreement about problems needing further investigation.

Yet the reasons that led sociologists of science to study the development of specialties in the first place still appear to be valid, in general, if not in all specific detail. Specialties have been identified as the "building blocks of science" (Small and Griffith, 1974, pp. 17-18).[54] Specialty formation is therefore taken as a "strategic research site" (Merton, 1987) for examining the connections between the growth of scientific knowledge and its social organization since new lines of inquiry are developed and elaborated in the social context of specialties. But these were not the only reasons for thinking specialties important. It is clear that the number of invisible colleges, specialties, and disciplines have multiplied greatly as scientific knowledge has expanded and that this growing elaborate division of scientific labor calls for explanation and understanding (Price, 1963/1986, chaps. 1 and 6). Empirical evidence, drawn largely but not entirely from analyses of scientific literatures, also showed that specialties and invisible colleges do not live on indefinitely; they emerge, grow up, mature, and often decline (Crane, 1972; Goffman, 1966). At any given time, the sciences comprise a multiplicity of specialties in various states of development and decay. This fluid structure is made all the more so by scientists not remaining permanently wedded to one specialty but often moving from specialty to specialty (Gieryn, 1978) and occasionally even from discipline to discipline (Harmon, 1965). Thus the population of disciplines and specialties is in flux as is the population of scientists who work in them.⁵⁵ In light of these structural aspects of scientific knowledge and its social organization, systematic attempts to understand the growth of scientific knowledge must take boundaries and interactions of specialties into account.

Research on specialties has focused on four problems: What leads to their emergence? What are their patterns of development? Why do certain specialties decline and die? And what can be learned, if anything, about specialties and the structure of science from the procedure of co-citation analysis? After a brief review research on these questions, we turn to further new directions of inquiry.

THE EMERGENCE OF NEW SPECIALTIES

In one of the earliest and still most penetrating accounts of the emergence of new specialties, Holton notes that specialties arise out of scientists' intense competitiveness and interest in making new discoveries (1962/1972). As he puts it, "the growth of knowledge proceeds by the *escalation* of knowledge—or perhaps rather of new areas of ignorance—instead of by mere accumulation" (1962, p. 394). Or, as it has been formulated in the notion of "*specified* ignorance": "as the history of thought, both great and small, attests, specified ignorance is often a first step toward supplanting that ignorance with knowledge" (Merton, 1957, p. 417; 1987, pp. 6-10). Thus, says Holton, "the most original people will transfer. . . to a new area of ignorance" and produce an air of excitement in it (1962, p. 394). One might say that this is especially so when interesting problems in the areas in which they have been working have begun to be exhausted, much as a lode of ore in a mine will eventually thin out as numbers of active miners (scientists) work in it. Not surprisingly, the speed with which interesting problems are exhausted is a function of the numbers of scientists working in them. New specialties thus branch out from old ones, as scientists migrate from problem area to problem area. In doing so, they engage in "the socially defined role of the scientist which calls for both the augmenting of knowledge and the specifying of ignorance" (Merton, 1987, p. 10).

In accord with Holton's imagery, Mulkay (1975) alone and with Gilbert and Woolgar (1975) proposed a branching model of specialty development in which scientists migrate from old areas to new ones, but they emphasize the special importance of borrowing ideas and techniques that originate outside new specialties.

This model squares well with the evidence, as Edge and Mulkay show in a detailed review of a half dozen studies of specialty development (Ben-David, 1971; Ben-David and Collins, 1966; Dolby, 1975; Edge and Mulkay, 1976; Law, 1973; Mullins, 1972). Taken together, the Holton and the Mulkay-Gilbert-Woolgar models help account for several pathways taken by emerging specialties: those that arise from "new insights" within fields, such as nuclear or particle physics, and those that arise from the transfer of previously unconnected ideas or techniques, such as molecular biology or astrophysics. (See Law, 1973, on types of specialties.)

PATTERNS OF DEVELOPMENT

If new ideas are the foundations of scientific specialties and research agendas are critical to their maintenance, new ideas are not, in and of themselves, enough. New specialties and disciplines also require the presence of a social infrastructure for research to become institutionalized. The pioneering work by Ben-David and Collins (1966) on the emergence of experimental psychology indicated the need, first, of creating a new social role for the practitioners of the new specialty and second, for research in the area to proceed, there must be positions for them in the academy—or in some other historically determined organizational framework. That field of experimental psychology, brought into being in German universities in the nineteenth century, required physiologists wanting to study mental phenomena to invent a hybrid role (joining physiology and philosophy) and to utilize the structure of professorial recruitment so that they could become candidates for vacant posts, not in their own field where there were few openings, but in philosophy, where places were available. This recurrent pattern suggests that both new ideas and new structural arrangements are needed for the founding of new specialties.

Case studies of the development of other specialties (Cole and Zuckerman, 1975; Edge and Mulkay, 1976; Thackray and Merton, 1972; Mullins, 1973) also examine the significance of social arrangements for maintaining both "cognitive and professional identities" and diffusing research in new specialties. They variously make the case for the need to establish institutional structures for training students, seeing to their employment, obtaining support for research, providing for both formal and informal communication among workers in the new field through journals, meetings, and specialized scientific societies. These interlocking institutional arrangements do not evolve automatically. They are created, often at great effort (as in the case of George Sarton and the self-exemplifying emergence of the history of science as a university field of study). In conjunction with the "cognitive leaders"[56]—scientists who set the research agenda and whose ideas stimulate others to work in the new area—organizational innovators are crucial to the emergence of specialties. But there is no question that in the evaluation system of science, ideas are prime. Those credited with being founders of disciplines and specialties are almost exclusively cognitive rather than organizational leaders.

Research on specialties has focused principally on their stages of development.[57] Accounts vary; some have proposed three stages (Mulkay, Gilbert, and Woolgar, 1975), others, four (Crane, 1972; Mullins, 1973) but all agreed that specialties mature in predictable sequence with intellectual and social development tending to go together. Thus Crane (1972) observed rates of communication, interaction, and publication in the specialties she studied to follow a logistic curve, this leading her to Kuhnian (1962/1970) ideas of paradigm development. The early phase of slow rise is taken to correspond with the introduction of a new paradigm;[58] the later rapid upswing in growth, with exploration of the paradigm and the development of anomalies, and the final leveling off of the curve, with paradigm exhaustion. In his analysis of the development of theory groups in sociology, Mullins (1973) also emphasizes the joint evolution of social interaction, communication networks and the elaboration of scientific ideas. Cognitive development is facilitated by the "thickening" of communication networks and leads to their further elaboration.

As Mulkay (1980a, pp. 18-22) observes, middle stages in the development of specialties involve increasing consensus on problems to be investigated and the making of significant contributions that become exemplary for further research. In this stage, work in specialties comes to resemble what Kuhn (1962/1970) describes as "normal science." Later, opportunities for making major contributions decline, recruitment of the young slows down and, barring the infusion of funds on the large scale, as in the "War on Cancer" or new potentials for effective application of knowledge (one need look only at the burst of recent activity in genetic engineering for an example of such growth), specialties tend to decline and ultimately to die out. Should major applications materialize, the research agenda of the specialty becomes increasingly significant for and influenced by larger

societal interests all apart from those internal to the specialty itself. The modes of such development have been explored by the Starnberg Group, initially comprising Bohme, van den Daele, and Krohn, under the title of the "Finalization" perspective (Schafer, 1983). Investigators in the philosophy and sociology of science are coming to assess this line of inquiry as a potentially fruitful direction for research, not alone in the study of specialty development, but in moving toward a general theory of scientific change.

Understandably, accounts of the developmental stages of specialties were at first rather schematic. Little effort was made to examine the various patterns of the actual emergence of new fields of inquiry and their institutionalization, particularly the variability attributable to the relationship between new specialties and their parent disciplines.[59] Hagstrom (1965), Griffith and Mullins (1972), Cole and Zuckerman (1975) and Edge and Mulkay (1976) have severally noted, for example, that new specialties do not uniformly challenge prevailing views in their parent disciplines. Some are cognitively radical or rebellious; others, not, the latter being oriented rather to the study of newly identified phenomena or to the use of new techniques that are quite consistent with prevailing theoretical commitments. Rebellious specialties may succeed with a flourish, as in the case of molecular biology. Or they may split off when the larger discipline is taken to be incorrigibly resistant, as in the case of mathematical statistics breaking away from mathematics. Or, again, the new specialty may become largely isolated from the rest of the discipline, which considers their ideas "dangerous or foolish," as Mullins (1973, p. 24) suggests for the case of ethnomethodology in relation to the parent discipline of sociology. Whatever their fate, the developmental patterns of specialties are much affected by their cognitive relations with the parent discipline. As Cole and Zuckerman (1975) have observed, the speed and success with which specialties are institutionalized is also affected by their compatibility with prevailing university structure. The specialties that fit into established departments are more apt to take hold than those requiring structural innovation if they are to find a home. Structural innovation in universities is notoriously difficult and slow, and this is especially so in times of financial stringency. Edge and Mulkay (1976) also trace out in impressive sociohistorical detail how administrative arrangements at important centers of research foster cognitive developments along certain lines and not along others.

THE DECLINE AND DEMISE
OF SPECIALTIES

Are specialties self-terminating? Apparently so. Early accounts of the development of science generally focus on the steady accumulation of scientific knowledge, while modern treatments stress discontinuities, displacements, and opportunistic adaptation in scientific growth. In the case of specialties, as we have seen, some observers assert that "population density" can simply become too great. "This refers not to the obvious differences in the absolute numbers of scientists at work in this or that . . . specialty [rather it] refers to the numbers at work in relation to the significant problematics of the field, some fields are more 'crowded' than others in the sense that many workers are focusing on the same problems" (Merton and Lewis, 1971, p. 157). After a time, the number of "interesting ideas" in a line of inquiry seems to scientists, at least, to thin out and the "most original" among them seek the easier and more stimulating problems offered by new specialties rather than to keep struggling with the recalcitrant ones left over in older areas (Holton, 1962/1972, pp. 393-394). This account of problem choice, emphasizing the diverse cognitive opportunities offered by various specialties agrees in broad outline with Mullins's (1973) observations about the later stages of the theory groups. Ideas that were for a time exciting and fruitful come to be routinized, the cognitive concerns of members diverge, and gradually the scholars who originally comprised the core of the specialty disperse and cease to interact at the earlier rate.[60]

Both Holton and Mullins assume that scientists adopt an opportunistic stance in problem choice and that old specialties lose out to new ones in the ongoing competition for their time and effort. This assumption is fairly consistent with what scientists say about the criteria they apply in problem choice (Zuckerman, 1977). However, in many documented cases, scientists prefer to avoid head-to-head competition with large numbers of other investigators and choose quieter, if less heady, domains of work to keep older or new but less fashionable specialties alive for some time. Max Planck, for example, found his colleagues' lack of interest in his work an "outright boon," and went on to note that "as the significance of the concept of entropy had not yet come to be fully appreciated, nobody paid any attention to the method adopted by me, and I could work out my calculations completely at leisure, with absolute thoroughness, without fear of interference or competition." Moreover, as Mulkay implies, not all scientists

are equally sensitive or demanding in the business of problem choice since "a major part of the innovative work [to be done] is completed before the field has begun to acquire a significant portion of its eventual membership" (1975, p. 197). Specialties decline and die out then in response to changing cognitive and social opportunity structures. In that process, marked changes occur in foci of attention, both for individual scientists and for collectivities of scientists.

CO-CITATION ANALYSIS AND
THE STUDY OF
SCIENTIFIC SPECIALTIES

Various new research procedures have been developed for comprehensive study of specialties and complement the traditional case study method. The technique of co-citation analysis, developed by Henry Small and Belver Griffith, is designed to identify specialties or "nodes" of scientific work and the scientists at work in them. This and related techniques can provide cognitive maps not just of specialties but also of disciplines and interdisciplinary areas. Co-citation analysis earmarks groups of highly cited papers that are frequently cited together. The underlying assumption of the procedure holds that research reports referring to the same papers to some degree share similar subject matters, conceptual schemes, and intellectual origins. "It is assumed," Small says (1977, p. 141), "that co-citation is a rough measure of association between concepts symbolized by highly cited papers." (For details of the procedure of co-citation analysis, see Small, 1973; Griffith et al., 1974; Small and Crane, 1979; Small and Griffith, 1974.) These assumptions have proved reasonable when clusters of papers generated by the procedure have been examined, for example, on collagen research, colloid chemistry, nuclear reaction theory—and on scientific specialties.

When first introduced, the procedure became the subject of considerable disagreement as critics argued that it did not in fact provide an "objective" technique for identifying specialties. It was said to ignore important sociological aspects of specialties. Co-citation analysis assumed that aggregates of scientists who cite the same published work were isomorphic with groups of scientists who interact with one another as members of the same specialty. This, of course, ignores the informal relations among scientists that enter into the development of scientific ideas (Edge, 1977). Various studies have been designed to check the findings of co-citation analysis, with mixed results. Small's

(1977) studies find that scientists' independent identification of the most important innovations and the leading investigators in their specialties square well with co-citation data. From quite a different perspective, Mullins, Hargens, Hecht, and Kick (1977) report that sociometric data provided by scientists working in two specialties (Australian Antigen and Reverse Transcriptase), correspond reasonably well with co-citation data; that is, co-citation clusters identify meaningful social groups. They also find that the density of social interaction and of mutual awareness among scientists in the specialties increase after major discoveries are made and published. Sullivan, White, and Barboni (1977), however, report that co-citation data did not pick up certain events that participants in the history of Weak Interactions took to be important, indicating noted limits of the procedure for reconstructing detailed historical accounts of particular scientific developments.

Co-citation analysis proves most useful for identifying nascent, growing, and changing clusters of ongoing research on given subjects and the linkages among them (Small, 1986). It serves to sketch out evolving and fairly comprehensive cognitive maps. Obviously, as with maps of all sorts, these need to be supplemented by other detailed evidence to round out the membership of specialties and to reconstruct the extent, character, and content of the interactions critical to the development of knowledge. Small himself has developed fine-grained content analyses of how scientists actually use the works they cite. In a series of important studies, he has shown that highly cited papers become "concept symbols" (1978), shorthand notations for complex ideas and findings with their substance being transmitted in this form rather than in rich detail. The diverse perspectives on co-citation analysis now seem to have led, in self-exemplifying style, to a branching of cognitive interests into bibliometric studies, on one side, and studies in the sociology of scientific knowledge, on another.

SPECIALTIES AND THE STRUCTURE OF SCIENCE

The study of specialties has left many questions unanswered. To begin with, are specialties really a primary unit for analysis of how scientific knowledge develops? If they are, how are they socially as well as cognitively organized? To what extent are they integrated by individual and collective competition for resources and rewards, and to what extent do their members share cognitive norms, agreeing on what needs to be studied and how this is to be done? This leads directly to a third question: If specialties and disciplines are structures fundamental to the formation of scientific knowledge, how do they operate as sources of collegial recognition and control of access to resources? Finally, how are these social and cognitive units linked together to form the larger structures of science?

Specialties have proved to be effective units for the sociological analysis of certain problems and rather less for others. Whitley (1978) reports that many of the scientists he studied were unaware of specialty networks pertinent to their work and not particularly interested in them. This opens up the still largely unexplored variations in scientists' orientations toward specialties in which they work and translations of these into sociocognitive behavior. Much historical and sociological evidence suggests that specialties have been prime audiences for many scientists; they are the explicit and tacit audiences—the reference groups—to which they address their work, just as they are the prime sources of wherewithal and rewards for that work. Such evidence comes from investigators of otherwise differing perspectives on the workings of science (e.g., Bourdieu, 1975; S. Cole, 1983; Edge and Mulkay, 1976; Ziman, 1968), all variously suggesting that specialties are significant social and cognitive formations in science. Knorr-Cetina takes a somewhat different tack. She suggests that specialties may be pertinent communities for understanding communication, career mobility, and antagonistic competition for resources, but they are not the "units within which scientific action as observed in the laboratory is contextually organized" (1981, p. 69). In the laboratory, scientists become involved with a great variety of others in what she calls, "resource-relationships," relationships they need to cultivate in order to get on with their work. These are "transscientific," or as she has also called them "transepistemic arenas" (1982). They are not composed only of those at work on similar problems, though they may be included, but of university administrators, institute personnel in control of resources, officials in government agencies, editors of journals or publishers—in short, all varied occupants of positions scientists need to take into account in the course of constructing or "manufacturing" knowledge (Knorr-Cetina, 1981, chap. 4). These observations ring true from the perspective of those dealing with the day-to-day requirements of getting scientific work done. Scientists (not excluding sociologists) inevitably find themselves embedded in a variety of social networks of which specialties are just one. Moreover, specialties do not loom large in the day-to-day research enterprise. All this directs attention to working relationships beyond specialties and the connections of these with the production of scientific knowledge. None of these need substitute wholly for specialties in the various phases of research. As organized for some time now, prospective scientific work in the form of research proposals is assessed primarily by peers drawn from the same specialty or interspecialty, just as it is subjected to peer evaluation when made public through the operation of socially organized skepticism.

Just as the social division of labor in the society at large has long been a prime focus for sociological investigation, so—and for much the same sorts of theoretical reasons—it will probably be a renewed focus of inquiry in the socio-cognitive domain of science. Prior research and reflection direct us to needed further research and reflection on the structure, operation, and sociocognitive consequences of the scientific specialty and related modes of the organization of scientific knowledge. Attention will, as a consequence, need to be paid to how specialties are actually organized and how correct our assumptions about them are; to what extent members are mutually aware of one another's work, how much they actually agree on what research should be done and how. Indeed, not much has been learned about the social organization of specialties and disciplines since the 1970s. Recent studies by S. Cole (1983), designed to examine a quite different question, provide a case in point. He finds high levels of disagreement at the research frontiers of the sciences about the questions requiring research, disagreement manifested in judgments about which researches merit financial support—in distinct contrast to the agreement found about the value of knowledge of the cores of disciplines. Competition for scarce resources in support of research, in turn, amplifies that disagreement. Studies of this sort are germane to the social organization of specialties and disciplines and the nature of their relationships; they also bear upon the prior question whether specialties are a useful unit of analysis, as well as the question regarding linkages between specialties as loci for the production of knowledge and as crucial units in the evaluation and reward systems of science.

Since specialties and disciplines constitute the prime audiences for scientific contributions and since much weight in science is given to peer review, members of these sociocognitive units confer or withhold recognition for work accomplished and resources for work proposed. Yet the connections between specialties and disciplines as knowledge-generating formations and as formations providing for evaluation and the allocation of rewards have hardly been investigated. Whitley (1984) is almost alone in emphasizing the connections between specialty and disciplinary control over reputations, their role in allocating resources and the ways in which these, in turn, shape the sorts of research that gets done. Plainly, the evaluation and reward systems do much to shape the directions, styles, and pace of the development of knowledge just as in reverse. But little enough is yet known about these matters through exacting research.

Several sorts of preliminary steps have been taken to enlarge our understanding of the linkages between specialties and disciplines. As we have seen, Small and colleagues at the Institute for Scientific Information (ISI) have employed bibliometric techniques to develop both maps and histories of selected cognitive areas in the sciences (1986). For some time, Eugene Garfield, founding president of the ISI, and colleagues have been developing a far more comprehensive and detailed *Atlas of Science*. This undertakes the massive task of harnessing the vast ISI database of publications and citations and interpretations of the generated cognitive maps of "research fronts" with the interpretive skills of scientists expert in these fields. Thus the *Atlas of Science: Biotechnology and Molecular Genetics, 1981/82* alone contains well over a hundred chapters, each dealing with an especially active research front in those fields (where "activity" is initially gauged by the amount of publication in each sector). These consolidated quantitative and qualitative mappings of current cognitive areas in the various sciences begin to provide a hitherto unavailable overview of the enormously complex divisions and subdivisions of research work in the major disciplines of today's science (Garfield, 1985, pp. 313-325). This is one sort of beginning.

Another is represented in Donald Campbell's (1969) now classic paper on the structure of the sciences. Viewed up close, specialties are arranged rather like fish scales with overlapping areas of expertise. No specialty is entirely autonomous, having total control over judgments of worth and validity in its domain. Instead, each can be and, to some unknown extent, is monitored by experts in neighboring areas. This structure and evaluative practice thus provide for the exercise of organized skepticism and serve to knit together provisionally separate domains of science. Efforts have also been made to measure the distance between specialties (Krauze, 1972) and to classify disciplines according to their interdependence and task uncertainty, in the process providing a comparative framework for analysis (Whitley, 1984). These various approaches have not been pulled together, nor have they been linked to processes of joint evaluation, along lines such as those laid out by Campbell.

The systematic study of specialties evidently engages many of the principal sociocognitive themes in the sociology (and the history) of science.

The Sociology of Scientific Knowledge

Since its beginnings, questions regarding the reciprocal relations of scientific knowledge and its sociocultural contexts have been central on the research agenda of the sociology of science. Central in the sense that it was clear that such questions had to be addressed, although there was no well-formulated research program then for the sociology of scientific knowledge. Early studies focused on rates of discovery and invention (Merton, 1935; Sorokin and Merton, 1935) and economic and military influences on the foci of scientific attention; that is, on what scientists actually studied at the time (Merton, 1938/ 1970). Ben-David revived this line of work with his own penetrating studies (1960) and those with Zloczower (Ben-David and Zloczower, 1962) on the connections between university structure and the pace of discovery in the medical sciences in the nineteenth century and of the impact of culture on the emergence of the empiricist scientific tradition and the modern scientific role (Ben-David, 1971).

Studies in the sociology of scientific knowledge now divide into two streams: those emphasizing social influences on the structure and development of scientific knowledge and those focusing on the social construction of knowledge itself. The former can be described as "structural" and the latter as "constructionist" studies, these covering a great variety of inquiries, including analyses employing relativist and constructivist perspectives, those treating the impact of social and professional "interests," and discourse and text analysis. The two streams of work differ, as we shall see, not only in their foci of theoretical and research attention but also in the assumptions practitioners make about the nature of scientific knowledge and the extent of its social determination. Practitioners in both streams, however, agree that scientific knowledge is variously influenced by the sociocultural contexts in which it develops

and that the central issues lie in determining just what those influences are, which aspects of knowledge are affected by them, and the processes through which such influences occur.

STRUCTURAL STUDIES IN THE SOCIOLOGY OF SCIENTIFIC KNOWLEDGE

Recent studies focusing on the structure of scientific knowledge, its growth, directions, and pace of development have examined a variety of problems: processes of theory change in the sciences and the extent to which they accord with models proposed by Kuhn, Lakatos, and Popper (S. Cole, 1975; Crane, 1980; Koester, Sullivan, and White, 1982; Messeri, 1988; Mullins, 1975; Nadel, 1980, 1981), forms of discontinuity in scientific development, including resistance to scientific innovation (Aronson, 1986; Barber, 1961; S. Cole, 1970; Stent, 1972), and the sociocultural and cognitive sources of neglect of certain problems and areas of investigation (Murray, 1986-1987; Zuckerman and Lederberg, 1986); the cognitive structure of the sciences, including efforts to measure the extent of consensus, theoretical codification, and their effects (Cole, Cole, and Dietrich, 1978; Hargens, 1988; Zuckerman and Merton, 1973; see also Piaget's distinctive use of this concept, 1977); the comparative growth rates of knowledge in various sciences and their connection, for example, to research funding (see Cozzens, 1986); and most of all, the complex body of research reviewed earlier on the rise and decline of scientific specialties. As noted previously, the intercorrelations between the social and cognitive aspects of science are particularly evident in the development of these important formations in science, but the exact nature of these correlations have not been worked out.

This swift inventory of the sorts of studies being done in the structuralist mode hints at the underlying assumptions many researchers make about scientific knowledge and the respects in which it may be influenced by social and cultural processes. They accept the view that science's pace, directions, modes of change, and structure are amenable to social influences but "they stop . . . short," as Ben-David puts it, of attributing to social conditions the determination of the conceptual and logical structure of scientific arguments. The possibility of the derivation of scientific ideas from social conditions in individual cases [is] admitted, but these [are] not regarded as sociologically . . . instructive" (1981, p. 43). Put another way, rationality and rules of empirical evidence are regarded as primarily determining scientists' acceptance or rejection of truth claims, although, on occasion, nonrational social influences may reinforce that acceptance.[61] As we shall see, sociologists working on the developing structure of knowledge differ from social constructionists in other respects: assessments of the extent to which external realities constrain scientific observation, whether there are important differences between science, on the one hand, and magic and ideology, on the other; the extent to which truth claims in science are not only local but universal; and on an array of specific matters such as the possibility of replication in science and the significance of the predictive power of scientific theories in the matter of theory choice. These perspectives will be examined in a later part of the chapter. Here, however, we take up the phenomenon of multiple independent discoveries in science and its implications for a theory of discovery, as a case in point of structural studies in the sociology of scientific knowledge.

Theories of Discovery: Multiple Independent Discoveries as a Strategic Research Site

The history of science is crowded with episodes of much the same discoveries being made independently and often at the same time by two or more scientists. For just one conspicuous example, the foundations for the calculus were laid in the years 1665-1666 by the epoch-making man of science, Isaac Newton, and simultaneously and independently by the epoch-making mathematician, G. W. Leibniz. Multiple discoveries (or "multiples" as they are called)[62] are not confined to great discoveries, nor to any particular science, nor to any particular period.[63] Scientists see them not as rare curiosities but as predictable facts of the scientific life. Multiple discoveries also provide "strategic research sites" for important problems in the sociology of science (Merton, 1963/1973, pp. 371-382; 1987):

— Are scientific discoveries products of individual talent and genius or are they culturally determined, bound to be made, if not by one scientist then by another because the "time is ripe"?

— Why are multiple discoveries a focus of anxiety for scientists and also often the focus of fierce rivalry and competition? And,

— What light do they shed on the view that scientific discoveries are socially constructed, not depictions of an external reality, but contextually determined and the outcomes of negotiation between investigators in the laboratory?[64]

Such questions tie in, as we have seen with both diverse and shared perspectives among sociologists of science about the nature of scientific knowledge, scientific discovery, and the patterned motives of research scientists.

THE CONCEPT OF MULTIPLES

Whether two or more discoveries are multiples depends, of course, on the criteria taken to qualify them as such. The most extreme set of criteria would require total identity: that their content be precisely the same, that they should have been achieved in precisely the same way and at the very same time, that their consequences for subsequent scientific development be the same, that their discoverers not have had the least inkling of one another's work and that the discoveries convey the identical "central message."[65] To adopt such an extreme concept means, of course, that few if any discoveries can qualify as multiples.

A less demanding but still quite astringent set of criteria was instructively employed by Thomas Kuhn, in his subtle analysis of the discovery of the conservation of energy.[66] Between 1842 and 1847 this fundamental principle was independently hypothesized by a dozen scientists who worked on one or another aspect of the problem. Kuhn indicates that no two of these contributions were precisely the same—nor were they arrived at in the same way, nor did they say the same things at the dates conventionally assigned, nor were the scientists totally ignorant of the other's work. Yet, even in this severely exacting case study, Kuhn finds that, despite the distinct routes taken by this array of scientists, there were significant overlaps of background knowledge, available "conversion processes," deep dispositions "to see a single indestructible force at the root of all natural phenomena," and possibly a variously shared *Naturphilosophie* (1959 in 1977). By his reckoning, then, even though the dozen contributions were not identical, their occurrence was related to cognitive and sociocultural contexts. He concludes the case study with an implicitly general question that directs us to the puzzle and theoretical significance of multiples: "Why, in the years 1830-50, did so many of the experiments and concepts required for a full statement of energy lie so close to the surface of scientific consciousness?'' (1977, p. 104). In short, why the convergence of intellectual interest and the drawing upon a common cognitive base?

Scientists themselves do not adopt the extreme criteria of total identity in defining and experiencing discoveries as multiples. Over the centuries, many scientists have readily acknowledged that their own discoveries were multiples, often doing so against their own interests. This they have done in the most emphatic possible manner by entering into strenuous disputes to establish that their discovery was temporally prior to the same discovery by another scientist. (Recent cases abound, though possibly the best known of such disputes—some would say the most notorious of them—is the one involving the calculus, with the rival advocates of Newton and Leibniz engaging in agitated attacks on one another.) In short, by seeking to establish their priority, scientists define their discoveries as the same, not as different from others. In the actual practice of science, independent multiple discoveries need not be identical in every respect in order to raise the question of how they came to be, as well as the further question of their implications for an understanding of how scientific knowledge develops. It is enough that they be defined as functionally equivalent, by knowledgeable scientists of the time and later, and, not least, by the discoverers themselves. But this still leaves open the question of the frequency of multiples.

HOW OFTEN DO MULTIPLES OCCUR?

Often, many think.[67] Indeed, Merton claims that they are not only frequent but ubiquitous. ''All scientific discoveries are *in principle* multiples'' (italics mine) he writes, ''including those that on the surface appear to be singletons'' (1961/1973, pp. 356ff). This ''extravagant'' and apparently ''incorrigible'' hypothesis, as Merton characterizes it, is actually held much of the time by scientists as they work to achieve priority before others get to the same discovery. There is varied evidence for this principled hypothesis. First, once the historical record is known, discoveries that for a time were taken to be singletons turn out to be rediscoveries of previous work that was unpublished or not widely known.[68] Second, scientists often discontinue a line of research once they learn that others have already published the same work or are about to do so. Third, though forestalled, some scientists nevertheless publish their original work, acknowledging that others have got into print just before them. Fourth, potential

multiples have been transformed into singletons, as scientists join forces to work on the same or converging problems. And most indicative, as we have noted, scientists engaged in research are evidently convinced that multiples are likely since they act in accord with that belief. The ''race for priority'' is a familiar phenomenon in science, as dramatically described by the biologist James D. Watson, in his widely read account of the discovery of the structure of DNA, *The Double Helix* (1968).

Behavior designed to ensure recognition for priority is also far from new. In the seventeenth century, for example, newly institutionalized arrangements emerged for British scientists not yet ready to announce their work publicly to deposit sealed and dated discovery accounts with the Royal Society of London for later use should their priority be contested. A most modern version of the same pattern involves use of a procedure, based on graph theory, by which mathematicians can demonstrate having achieved a full proof of a mathematical theorem without actually providing that proof at the time (Robinson, 1986). Such arrangements designed to provide evidence of priority signal that scientists have been and continue to be concerned about matters of ensuring proper credit in light of possible multiple discoveries.

Empirical studies of American and British scientists indicate that such concerns are not groundless. Hagstrom (1965) found that 63% of a large sample of U.S. academic scientists report having had others anticipate their work at least once in their careers. Gaston's (1978) research on British high-energy physicists found much the same, with 64% of these scientists saying they have been anticipated. This suggests that actual and potential multiple discoveries are commonplace, enough so to be a predictable pattern in scientific discovery. But there are no bases for estimating the proportions of discoveries that are multiples in various fields, times, and places.

WHAT KINDS OF DISCOVERIES ARE APT TO BE MULTIPLES?

The Hagstrom (1965) and Gaston (1978) studies suggest that scientists of every kind, not just eminent ones, find themselves involved in multiple or near-multiples. Practically all contributions to science are, of course, fairly routine—what Kuhn called ''normal science''— with revolutionary or path-breaking discoveries being exceedingly rare. We should therefore expect far larger numbers, if not higher rates, of multiples in the usual run of scientific work. Yet the historical evidence may seem to suggest otherwise, giving the impression that the fundamental discoveries are especially apt to be multiples. That impression is, of course, an illusion. Historical research tends to focus on important discoveries and incidentally take note of multiples among them. There are reasons to suppose that multiples may actually occur less often among truly path-breaking contributions than among routine ones. Presumably, the most radical innovations more often involve a focus on problems not widely identified by the pertinent community as soluble and significant and therefore are not at the focus of work of comparatively large numbers of investigators. The more radical an idea or the more remote a line of scientific investigation is from the consensus in the field, the fewer are likely to work on it and to draw upon a shared knowledge base. In contrast, new but not path-breaking contributions arise directly from the consensus, from the paradigm, exemplars, or research program, as Kuhn (1962/1970) and Lakatos (1970) would put it. This should therefore give rise to a higher rate, not alone a larger number of multiples among this class of contributions.

A collective focus on the same scientific problems—whatever the source of that focus—presumably increases the probability of independent solutions to them. Given scientists' institutionally reinforced concern with gaining recognition for their work, it is not surprising that savage fights about priority have erupted over multiple discoveries, both great and small (Merton 1957/1973e). All the claimants "know" that they have made the discovery on their own. Yet they must share the recognition they feel they alone deserve (see Cohen, 1974, for an account of Newton's priority fights, and Cozzens, 1985, for a contemporary case). Even mild and generous scientists have become fiercely competitive in such circumstances. The renewed cognitive point of such conflicts is that working research scientists do repeatedly identify discoveries as multiples.

WHY DO MULTIPLE DISCOVERIES OCCUR?: THEORIES OF SCIENTIFIC DISCOVERY

At the outset I noted that multiples have been taken as prime evidence for the cultural determination of discovery. Once the main elements of a discovery are available in the body of knowledge and there is a collective focus of research attention, discoveries become are said to become "inevitable," if not by one scientist than by another (Kroeber, 1917; Merton,

1961/1973f; Ogburn and Thomas, 1922). This notion has long been assumed to oppose the one that discoveries are the product of individual genius. A quite different theory holds that the phenomenon of multiple discoveries tells nothing about the sources of discovery. Derek Price (1963/1986) and Dean Keith Simonton (1978, 1979, 1987) argue that multiple discoveries are chance events. According to probabilities, they say, most discoveries should be the work of a single scientist, with successively larger sets of multiples declining in frequency, this in accord with a Poisson or chance distribution. Using vivid imagery, Price (1963/1986, pp. 60-61) asks us to imagine that discoveries are like apples on a tree. If a certain number of blind men (that is, scientists) reached up at random for those apples, the largest number would not be picked at all, the next largest would be picked by one, fewer by two, fewer still by three, and so on. Indeed, Price (1963/1986) found that the Merton-Barber sample of multiples approximates a Poisson distribution as did Simonton (1978) for his large array of multiples over four centuries. Simon concludes that multiples need not mean that discoveries are largely culturally determined.

These theories have been subjected to critical examination and empirical research. To begin with, the evidence for the cultural theory seems is based mainly on the existence of multiple discoveries and their comparative frequency. The very existence of multiples suggests that discovery is not determined only by individual genius. Evidence for the chance theory is more shaky than for the other two. Apart from the questionable imagery that discoveries exist in nature ready to be plucked like apples from a tree, the fact that multiples follow a Poisson distribution need not imply that they are chance events, as Brannigan and Wanner (1983, p. 137) have noted. They also suggest that if the cultural theory is correct, the size of multiple sets (i.e., the number of scientists who have been responsible for given multiples) should be larger in the modern period with its exponentially increased number of scientists than earlier. Moreover, the rate of multiples ought to fluctuate and differ among disciplines and specialties. By contrast, if chance brought them about, they should be approximately constant. Drawing on Simonton's list of multiples, Brannigan and Wanner examine these two hypotheses derived from the cultural theory, and find support for the cultural theory. They also propose a third hypothesis: that the frequency of multiples and their timing are affected by the efficiency of the communication system of science. The more efficient the communication of scientific knowledge, the shorter the interval between the announcements of the first and the "last" discoveries in sets of multiples and the smaller the number of independent codiscoverers involved because other potential discoverers will have heard about the discovery and stopped work on it, just as the original cultural theory assumed in its concept of "forestalled" multiples. The data also support this hypothesis. In response, Simonton (1987) has argued that the same data and independent analyses of the Merton and the Ogburn-Thomas data show no evidence for a negative "contagion" effect that would be required if the communication hypothesis were correct. The lively controversy about the validity of the three theories and their implications continues. Although the weight of evidence supports the theory of sociocultural influences on scientific discovery, there is no agreement yet on what multiples tell us about how scientific knowledge develops.[69]

THE ROLE OF GENIUS IN SCIENTIFIC DISCOVERY

The various theories all seem to minimize the role of individual talent or genius in scientific discovery. At the extreme, the cultural hypothesis suggests that discoveries are inevitable and that particular discoverers are expendable. Indeed, as I have indicated, the explanations of genius and of culture have long been opposed to one another. But Robert Merton argues that this is a false opposition. The two can be consolidated into a single "sociological theory of genius in science." "In this enlarged conception, scientists of genius are precisely those whose work in the end would be eventually rediscovered" (1961/1973f, pp. 366ff). The idea of redundancy of discovery is turned on its head here and made a confirmation rather than refutation of the importance of scientific genius. This hypothesis holds that the greater the scientists, the more discoveries they have made altogether, and the more often they are also involved in multiple discoveries. They have themselves contributed as much to knowledge as the numbers of scientists with whom they have shared multiples. Rather than debasing the role of talent or genius in science, this composite theory gives it great weight. It also suggests that genius or talent may involve greater perceptiveness of the cultural components of discovery. It is not only that genius often sees things that others do not but that it sees more of them and more quickly. Merton goes on to note that near-

ly every important scientist has been involved in many multiple discoveries—Newton, as we have seen, Hooke, Lavoisier, Darwin, Faraday, Kelvin, and Freud are some among the many. With Elinor Barber, Merton studied 400 of Kelvin's 661 scientific communications, finding him to be involved in 32 multiple discoveries with an aggregate of 30 different scientists, many of them also scientists of stature (Merton, 1961/1973f, p. 367). Much the same pattern holds among the talented scientists designated as Nobel prizewinners. At least 11 Nobel prizes have been awarded for multiple discoveries. Moreover, 70 of 264 laureates whose work was studied intensively were found to have been involved in multiple discoveries with other Nobelists, besides those with whom they shared prizes, for the most part before any of them had won the award (Zuckerman, 1977). The laureates, in short, are outstanding men and women scientists of many multiples, typically shared in turn with other outstanding scientists.

What then do multiple discoveries say about the nature of scientific discovery? First, that the imagery of discovery and of discoverers might well be recast. Although each discoverer has the psychological experience of having a creative insight, this does not discount the significance of the "culture base" in focusing attention on certain problems and providing the necessary concepts and tools needed for solution. Second, that major scientists not only make unique contributions but are often engaged in making the same discoveries as others. Third, that it is not yet clear whether the cultural, chance, or communication theory of multiples is preferable or, indeed, that they are in thoroughgoing opposition. However, the nonuniform distribution of multiples across disciplines, types of discoveries, and across time makes an exclusive chance theory less persuasive than the others. Fourth, if we shift our attention from the sources of multiples to their consequences, we note that repeated or multiple discoveries are apt to elicit repeated or enlarged attention. As a result, the history of science would not have been the same if a given discovery was a multiple or a "singleton." The focusing of scientific attention on the subject and findings of a multiple discovery may reinforce its cognitive effects in ways not yet determined. And, of course, the occurrence of multiples provides occasions for periodic and sometimes intense disputes over priority. In such cases, social conflict derives from cognitive developments and the institutional value placed on originality—still another demonstration of the interconnections between the cognitive and social domains of science.

IMPLICATIONS FOR THE SOCIAL CONSTRUCTION OF SCIENTIFIC KNOWLEDGE

Do multiple discoveries have any implications for the conception that scientific knowledge is socially constructed? As I have noted, they do, but not for each and every one of the wide range of views usually given the collective label of constructionism. The occurrence of multiple independent discoveries would seem to create analytical and theoretical problems mainly for those who hold that scientific knowledge is shaped by the specific local context in which it is created. If scientific inquiry is "locally situated [and] occasioned," that is, "situationally contingent" as Knorr-Cetina (1983b, pp. 124ff) has put it, it seems unlikely that scientists working in quite different locations would arrive at the same discovery if this were little more than the result of local events peculiar to this or that laboratory. Evidently, conceptual schemes and the phenomena under theoretically selective examination transcend these idiosyncratic contexts.

There are, of course, ancillary hypotheses designed to counter the import of this observation. It might be argued, for example, that scientists involved in multiples have "simply" shaped their independent discovery accounts in the same or similar culturally prescribed molds. Or, as Brannigan (1981) suggests, two or more independent discoveries are not actually multiples but a simply defined as such.[70] Plainly, such hypotheses that may "save" the theory require their own share of systematic investigation. All this raises the question of how it is that certain discoveries come to be defined as substantially or functionally the same even though their discoverers have worked in quite different local contexts and at times with variant theoretical commitments? Do the phenomena being studied exercise no significant constraint toward convergent observations? And how does it happen that scientists will themselves declare that some of their own culturally prized contributions have also been made independently by others while identifying other contributions as unique rather than duplicated? The phenomena of multiple discoveries raise consequential questions and opportunities for investigation that bears on current sociological theories of scientific knowledge.

The conception that multiples arise from shared ideas of what the scientific community takes to be credible is not far removed from the notion that discoveries are in significant degree culturally determined. But this still does not explain cases of long delayed rediscoveries or anticipations by scientists working in vastly different historical and social contexts. Close analysis of instances claimed to be multiple discoveries will be needed to lay out the respects in which they are authentic multiples, or actually unique and only defined after the fact as similar in terms of a shared cognitive structure, or unique but made to look similar in response to a common cognitive structure. Anticipations and rediscoveries by scientists widely separated in time, place, and community take on a special significance for this theoretical purpose.

Thus it is that multiple discoveries turn out to be far more than esoteric or exotic episodes in the history of science; they are full of implications for an evolving sociology of scientific knowledge.

Constructionist Studies in the Sociology of Scientific Knowledge

Constructionist studies are not all of a conceptual piece;[71] the problems they address differ, as do their methods and their theoretical and epistemological orientations. Yet most exemplify the view that "the project of the sociology of scientific knowledge [is] to work out *in what sense and to what degree* we can speak coherently of knowledge as being rooted in social life" (Knorr-Cetina and Mulkay, 1983, p. 6). Put another way, the sociology of scientific knowledge "is concerned . . . with what comes to count as scientific knowledge and how it comes to count" (Collins, 1983b, p. 267).[72] Social constructionism calls into question the rationalist and objectivist accounts of science, which hold that logic and evidence are prime determinants of scientific validity and of scientists' theory choice.

On the face of it, constructionism, with its focus on the social construction of the content of scientific knowledge, appears quite different from the program examining the structure and development of knowledge. Yet there are affinities between the two. Affinities, particularly, between constructionism and structural studies of discontinuities in the development of scientific knowledge, of the sociocultural sources of resistance to scientific innovation and the neglect of certain problems and areas of investigation. The two streams of work in the sociology of scientific knowledge also share a common interest in how the evaluation system in science, variously construed, affects what comes to count as knowledge and how it does so. As we shall see, such affinities may provide a bridge between the two sorts of research that are often viewed as proceeding on not only different but wholly unrelated tracks (Collins, 1982, p. 300; Knorr-Cetina, 1982a, p. 321).

Four variants of constructionist studies of scientific knowledge have evolved since the papers introducing this perspective were published in the late 1960s and early 1970s (See Collins's 1983 review). These are best characterized by the terms used by the analysts themselves: "relativism," "the interests model," "constructivism," and "discourse analysis."

Relativist studies are so named because they adopt the philosophical position that "assumes neither fixed points in the physical world nor a fixed realm of logic that would compel agreements between unbiased observers or thinkers from radically different cultures. Neither Nature nor Rationality is taken to be a self-evident universal of human culture" (Collins, 1981, p. 267). They begin with the assumption that logic and evidence play little or no part in the construction, transmission, and assessment of knowledge and that these processes are entirely social, or almost so. As a consequence of that assumption, two principal problems are taken as central: how debates in science are closed and how scientists decide on validity even though "formal algorithms" (methods of control and performance of experiments and their replication) fail to explain the outcomes (or "passages") of research (Collins, 1983, p. 273).

The philosophical and conceptual underpinnings of inquiries using *the interests model* are closely allied to those of relativist studies. However, the former emphasize the effects of scientists' social, political, religious, and professional interests, that is, the scientists' concerns about maintaining their standing among their colleagues, on the content of knowledge—observations, interpretations, and theoretical preferences and the ways that these in turn affect the outcomes of controversy. Research on interests continues the long tradition in the sociology of knowledge of focusing on the social determination of knowledge, while rejecting the Mannheimian view that scientific knowledge is exempt from social determination. Some, like Restivo, call for a "critical" sociology of scientific knowledge that would evaluate its social role (Restivo and Laughlin 1987, p. 488), while others, like Barnes and Shapin (1979, p. 10), do not adopt a normative stance on the social roots of scientific knowledge or its social consequences. Much, though not all, research in this genre has been historical and, indeed, it is now often labeled the historical sociology of scientific knowledge.[74]

Constructivist studies focus on contemporary scientific practice, the "production" of knowledge in the laboratory. Laboratory studies, which draw mainly on ethnographic procedures, emphasize the "indexical and contextually contingent properties" of scientific research. Indeed, constructivism "maintains that scientific inquiry may be better understood as a process in which the world is constructed [in the laboratory] rather than depicted." Findings from these studies also challenge the distinction between the social and technical aspects of science (Knorr-Cetina, 1983a, p. 155). And last,

Discourse and Text Analysis are two separate but related kinds of inquiries. The former begins with the observation that different scientists' accounts of the same event are highly variable and context dependent. "The central feature distinguishing discourse analysis from previous approaches to the sociology of science is that . . . it treats participants' discourse as a topic instead of a resource." Thus sociologists cannot use what scientists say, at least for the time being, as evidence for what science is "really like"; rather, attention must shift to "the methodologically prior question, 'How are scientists' accounts of action and belief socially generated?'" (Gilbert and Mulkay, 1984, pp. 13-14). Discourse analysis is related to studies of scientists' writing and the texts they produce—these including Latour and Woolgar's portrayal of "laboratory activity as the organization of persuasion through literary inscription" (1979, p. 88), Knorr-Cetina's (1981) close analysis of the writing of scientific papers as a process of "conversion" from the situationally contingent to the nonlocal and universal; and Bazerman's wide-ranging studies of the emergence and evolution of literary forms in science, and how these, like discourse, are context dependent (1984, 1985).

These four types of work, now defined as constructionist, draw on diverse intellectual antecedents: relativist perspectives in anthropology, Thomas Kuhn's enormously influential ideas (1962/1970),[75] and the continuing, if not always respectable, interest in "externalist" explanations in the history of science. They also draw on antirationalist accounts in philosophy, generally, and in the philosophy of science, particularly.

Indeed, social constructionists take two important philosophical precepts as warrant for their approach to the sociology of scientific knowledge. First is the idea that facts are theory laden, that what we take to be evidence is shaped by our theories and their constituent concepts, other related conceptual schemes, and by our ideas about observation and measurement--a view often attributed to Kuhn and Feyerabend but of course older and not necessarily associated with a strictly relativist perspective. The second is that scientific theories are underdetermined by evidence (generally called the Duhem-Quine thesis, but sometimes the Duhem-Quine-Hesse thesis).[76] Many theories, it is said, can fit the same facts or, put another way, empirical evidence does not provide firm grounds for accepting or rejecting theories. If theories cannot be rejected or accepted on the grounds of the evidence brought to bear on them, then scientists have a good deal of leeway in theory choice. For social constructionists, this means that a variety of nonlogical and possibly social influences, including the process of social negotiation, affect the choices scientists make.

The constructionists' views are not, as noted, universally shared by sociologists of scientific knowledge now,[77] nor were they when constructionists began work in the early 1970s. Social constructionism developed in a intellectual context in which social influences were thought not to affect the content of scientific knowledge, but instead were confined to scientists' choice of problems, ideas they had about how problems might be solved, and their commitment to ideas that already had evidentiary support. Joseph Ben-David has been a vigorous supporter of the limits on the social conditioning of scientific knowledge.

It can be concluded, . . . that although ideological bias (socially determined or not) might have played some role in the blind alleys entered by science, the philosophical assumptions that had become part of the living tradition of science were selected by scientists from the array of competing philosophies for their usefulness in the solution of specific scientific problems and not for any socially determined perspective or motive. . . . Certainly political and economic pressures have directed the attention of scientists to certain important practical problems, but the effect has been much more limited than is usually believed. . . . [Indeed] the possibilities for either an interactional or institutional sociology of the conceptual and theoretical contents of science are extremely limited [1971, pp. 11-12, 13-14].

Nonetheless, by the early 1970s, a number of programmatic papers advocating the constructionist and relativist perspectives had appeared (See Collins's 1983 review). One of the most forceful was David Bloor's "Strong Pro-

gramme in the Sociology of Science" (1976). Bloor, an Englishman trained in philosophy and mathematics, proposed that "all knowledge, whether it be in the empirical sciences or even in mathematics, should be treated through and through, as material for [sociological] investigation" (Bloor, 1976, p. 1). Such investigations should adhere to four tenets: they should be "*causal*" (they should be concerned with conditions that bring about knowledge); they should be "*impartial* with respect to truth and falsity, rationality or irrationality . . . Both sides of these will require explanation;" they should be "*symmetrical*," the same sorts of causes would "explain true and false beliefs" and "[they] would be *reflexive*. In principle, patterns of explanation would have to be applicable to sociology itself" (1976, pp. 4-5; italics mine). [See the philosopher Mary Hesse's acute analysis of the strong program (1984).]

These tenets of "the strong programme" express, in a general way, the views of many who work in the constructivist tradition. They also share three other commitments: the need, first, to treat the technical content of science and research practices of scientists; second, to do detailed empirical investigations, almost always on the microscopic rather than macroscopic level, and, third, to examine *how* scientists do what they do rather than *why*, as Knorr-Cetina and Mulkay (1983, pp. 7-9) put it. This concern with description rather than explanation, they note, means that some investigators, particularly ethnomethodologists (for example, Lynch, Livingston, and Garfinkel, 1983) have self-consciously refrained from theorizing about scientists' purposes and motives although others, such as Knorr-Cetina, have not. Beyond these general commitments, the problems constructionists study, their methods of research, and their conclusions differ and merit separate consideration.

RELATIVIST STUDIES

Had history been otherwise, Ludwik Fleck might well have been a leading pioneer of relativist studies in the sociology of scientific knowledge. But history was otherwise. Comparatively unknown during his lifetime, Fleck, a Polish physician and microbiologist, was a highly original and perceptive observer of science. His *Genesis and Development of a Scientific Fact*, published first in 1935, was practically unobtainable until it was translated and republished in 1979; thus it did not contribute to the emergence of constructionist studies in the early seventies. Fleck's detailed case study of changes in ideas about syphilis and its causes, both within the scientific community and the wider culture, traces how the disease came to be successively defined by the increasingly reliable outcomes of tests for the Wassermann reaction. He proposes that scientists' observations and their definitions of "facts" are shaped by the "thought collectives," or cognitive communities, of which they are members, and by the "thought styles" or assumptions shared in these thought collectives. These ideas presage, of course, Kuhn's analysis of scientific communities and the paradigms to which they subscribe.[78]

Fleck's insistence on scientific knowledge as socially and culturally conditioned is congenial to relativist thinkers. Yet his notion of "passive" connections in knowledge prevent him from being a thoroughgoing relativist who sees scientific findings exclusively as social constructions. Passive connections in knowledge, as opposed to active connections, which are socially constructed, reflect objective constraints in nature; once certain assumptions are accepted by a thought collective,[79] reality will be observed in a particular fashion. Fleck's work is still new and so rich and varied, so allusive and imaginative, that his influence cannot yet be assessed. While he appears to be a precursor of relativism, his ideas about the role of error in science, scientists' efforts to make observations increasingly reproducible, and thought-styles and thought-collectives have relevance also for students of the structure and development of knowledge (see Cohen and Schnelle, 1985).

Although many social constructionists adopt some variant of the relativist perspective, we focus here on those who emphasize processes of social construction of scientific knowledge within the community of science, on "how pieces of knowledge gain acceptance *within science*" (Collins, 1982, p. 300, italics mine), and deal mainly, though not exclusively, with contemporary cases. Harry Collins, the principal exponent of the empirical relativist program, advocates a thoroughgoing relativist position. For Collins, the relativist program must put social explanations of scientific knowledge prior to logic and evidence and must "seek to explain the content of scientific knowledge as far as possible in social terms. *Rationality* (whatever that means) must play little part in explaining how the world comes to appear as it does" (1983, p. 272). Relativism assumes then that an external reality has little effect on what comes to be considered scientific knowledge; "the natural world has a small or non-existent role in the construction of scientific knowledge"

(Collins, 1981, p. 3). And last, the relativist program tries to show that the same scientific methods when applied in different circumstances will produce different outcomes.

> In one set of social circumstances "correct scientific method" applied to a problem would precipitate result p whereas in another set of social circumstances "correct scientific method" applied to the same problem would precipitate result q, where perhaps, q implies not-p [Collins, 1982, p. 302, originally in 1981].

Empirical studies in the relativist tradition have examined the production, transmission, and assessment of knowledge claims in physics, mathematics, and biology, emphasizing the controversial but also treating the uncontroversial: TEA lasers, gravity waves (Collins, 1974, 1975); solar neutrinos (Pinch, 1977, 1981); the J phenomenon (Wynne, 1976); magnetic monopoles (Pickering, 1981); experimental tests of quantum mechanics (Harvey, 1981); number theory in mathematics (Bloor, 1976); and learning in planaria (Travis, 1981). Although studies of marginal science have also been undertaken, the primary strategy has been to select cases in the "hard sciences" in order provide an *a fortiori* demonstration of the social construction of knowledge. This strategy makes sense in terms of the interest relativists have in persuading others that knowledge is socially constructed even in the sciences where that seems least likely, but, given relativists' stated views about knowledge as simply being socially constructed, it seems odd to have them pay such careful attention to the selection of cases for research and to the marshalling of evidence.

As noted, these empirical studies have examined two sets of issues: how formal algorithms (including rules of evidence and logic) fail to explain "passages" of research or what came to be accepted or rejected as scientific knowledge and how scientific consensus is established and maintained—more precisely, how debates are closed in science. It is no easy task to summarize the findings of these studies, much less to assess them. Relativist researchers are persuaded that their studies demonstrate that: "local interpretative flexibility" prevents experiments from being decisive in determining what is taken as scientific knowledge (Collins, 1981, p. 4). Moreover, since there is much "craft" and tacit knowledge in experimental science, scientists are highly skeptical about others' results even if they are confident about their own (Pinch, 1981). Replication is also said to be impossible because so much tacit knowledge is required to do experiments. Thus what is defined as replication amounts to no more than what scientists can persuade one another to accept as such (Collins, 1974, 1975). Such findings are, as noted earlier, important because they suggest that replication, a central cognitive procedure in science, is socially negotiated and thus cannot differentiate reliable knowledge from fraud and error. We shall return to this matter shortly.

Relativist studies also find that controversies are not settled by recourse to unambiguous criteria for assessing knowledge claims. Rather, scientific evidence is ambiguous and so are the criteria. Instead, controversies such as the one over the existence of the magnetic monopole are closed by scientists who are committed to preserving the scientific culture; they decide on that position which undermines as few preexisting agreements on interpretation as possible (Pickering, 1981). They also maintain the consensus by "concealing" results that might prove embarrassing and by using all sorts of rhetorical devices to persuade their fellow scientists of the credibility of particular claims (Wynne, 1976). As we shall see in studies using the "interests model," the conclusion that knowledge is socially negotiated and that debates are closed on social rather than cognitive criteria is not universally shared. When other investigators examine the same or similar evidence, they can come to quite different conclusions (Frankel, 1979; Roll-Hansen, 1979, 1980, 1983; Rudwick, 1985). Thus the question is still open whether the findings of these studies will hold up with further analysis and inquiry.

Putting aside the matter of self-refutation and its potential for undermining all relativist sociological inquiries, three other aspects of these studies merit further comment. First is the claim that the same scientific methods when applied in different social circumstances will yield different outcomes. Plainly, this is for many an empirical question, if relativists will supply evidence for their conclusions. (Rationalists would counter, of course, that ample evidence is already available demonstrating that the same methods yield the same results). Indeed, there are natural experiments in science that provide pertinent evidence in this regard, namely that subset of multiple independent discoveries arising from research using the same procedures. As noted earlier, the phenomenon of multiples is problematic for social constructionists, who contend that scientific inquiry is determined by local social contexts. The point here is that certain multiple discoveries seem to show that the same procedures do yield the same results in different social contexts.

Second, on the matter of replication: As Mary Hesse observes:

> The most noteworthy thing about Collins' accounts is the immense trouble people [scientists] went to *wrestle with material objects* in order to satisfy conditions of replicability, and also the fact that some attempts *fail*, whatever the antecedent social expectations were. Is it conceivable that such problems should arise with sheer manipulation if all questions of replicability could be settled by social fiat without reference to the world? [1986, p. 721].

Hesse's observations are well taken and can be extended to other cases in which evidence and expectation do not accord. If such cases are resolved merely by social fiat, why do members of the community of scientists periodically conclude that their own as well as others' expectations proved to be incorrect because they do not square with the evidence even though they would prefer things to be otherwise?

Moreover, with regard to replication and the social control of deviance noted earlier, the issue is not whether experiments can be precisely copied but rather whether evidence from inadvertent replications, related but not duplicate experiments, is consistent with earlier reported findings.

Third, the assumption that sociological observers must seek social explanations of scientific knowledge and that "*rationality*" must play "little part in explaining how the world comes to appear as it does" (Collins, 1983, p. 272) seems only to prejudge the question of when rationality plays a determining role and how strong its influence is in given cases.

A final observation on relativist studies of the formation and maintenance of consensus in science. They have focused on what Collins calls the "core set," not just on scientists in one laboratory who do a particular experiment, but on the social group who "actively experiment upon and theorize over the controversial topic, and who eventually play a role in the emergent consensus" (Pinch, 1986). Even if one accepts the idea that the content of knowledge has been socially negotiated by the core set, it has not been demonstrated that such groups determine the larger consensus in science. Studies of the formation of consensus have to be extended beyond such groups, especially when the knowledge claim is of major significance to large numbers of scientists. It is here that macrosociological studies are needed of how the evaluation system operates.

STUDIES USING THE INTERESTS MODEL

As noted, studies in this perspective have focused on the role of scientists' social class, religious persuasion, political preferences, and professional concerns in shaping their scientific contributions, assessment of others' research and the conduct and resolution of scientific controversies. Historical research along these lines has been ably reviewed by Shapin (1982), who includes various investigations that examine the "contingency" of experimentation, the effects of vested interests, professional and social, on scientific knowledge, the uses of cultural resources by scientists, and the uses of scientific ideas by the larger society. As he puts it, "In a sociological approach to knowledge-making, people produce knowledge against the background of their culture's inherited knowledge, their collectively situated purposes, and the information they receive from natural reality" (1982, p. 196).[80]

What problems are addressed by newer studies in the "interests" mode, what are their results, and how well do research findings hold up when subjected to critical scrutiny? Recent inquiries have focused on the social conditioning of knowledge by ideology, on social processes involved in the closure of debate, and on the role of professional interests in theory choice, all questions quite compatible with those studied by relativists. As it happens, recent studies have also drawn on quantitative data, largely absent from relativist and interests studies, in order to examine the distribution of intellectual positions in relevant scientific communities; thus extending the more detailed but necessarily more limited perspectives provided by microsociological case studies. Four examples should give a sense of recent work examining scientists' interests and scientific knowledge.

MacKenzie's (1981) historical study of the development of statistics in Britain, 1865-1930, argues first that the ideas of eugenics, the social control of hereditary qualities, was particularly attractive to the rising professional middle class, not just because it emphasized the need for professional expertise in political decision making but also because it proclaimed the biological superiority of that segment of society. Second, it traces the connections between the problems taken up by Galton, Pearson, and Fisher, the three great figures of British statistics in the period, and their interest in the eugenics movement and its ideology. Last, it treats in detail the effects, as the author sees them, of eugenics on Galton's ideas of correlation, how the conflict between the biometricians (represented by

Pearson) and the Mendelians (represented by Bateson) was influenced by Pearson's involvement with eugenics, and how eugenics ideas affected Pearson's proposals for measuring noncontinuous variables. (Fisher, having come on the scene later, when the field was more mature, was far less influenced by eugenics than the other two.) MacKenzie's historical analysis provides strong support for eugenics having played a role in the development of statistics in Britain, particularly in shaping Galton's and Pearson's foci of attention and sustaining their interest eugenically related problems. However, as Stephen Stigler (1986, p. 267), author of what is generally viewed as the definitive history of statistics in this period, quietly reminds us, it is impossible to say just what shaped Galton's ideas: his close family ties to the Darwins, the fact that Darwinian theory captured his imagination, or the social concerns that MacKenzie identifies. If a commitment to eugenics helped shape the problems addressed by statisticians, it seems less clear that it shaped what they found. Indeed, even a sympathetic reviewer, T. M. Porter (1981)—also a historian of statistics—observes that MacKenzie's illustrations of the effects of ideology on the content of statisticians' work are "less impressive" than other instances such as Forman's (1971) analysis of the effects of philosophical views of causality on the Weimar physicists.

Turning from statistics to high-energy physics and from social to professional interests, the "charm-color" debate on the interpretation of the J-psi particle is the focus of Pickering's analysis (1981). He suggests that that debate was settled mainly by the proponents of charm finding a way to tie their ideas successfully to many other lines of inquiry in high-energy physics. Pickering makes the point with admirable clarity:

> The triumphing of charm, then and the eclipse of its rivals, should not be seen in terms of static comparisons between predictions and data. At no point . . . was charm proved to be right or its rivals wrong. The key to charm's success lay in the social and conceptual unification of HEP [high energy physics] practice which was achieved during the November Revolution. . . . [P]rogresive social unification in the common context of gauge theory was intrinsic to the establishment of the new physics in its entirety [1984, pp. 272-273].

Pickering tells us then that the debate was not settled by recourse to evidence but rather because the proponents of one of the theories were more successful in generating "a context in which other traditions could flourish" (Pickering and Nadel, 1987, p. 89). In the process, this made their work part of the interconnected cognitive network of high-energy physics, led to its being identified with the natural world rather than being only a conjecture of its creators, and helped physicists in different traditions get on with their work (1981, p. 130). Pickering's account is appealing; theories that are attractive to large segments of a scientific community, that serve many "professional" interests, are more apt to succeed than those that, other things being equal, have limited significance of that sort. Yet one wonders whether this demonstrates that social rather than cognitive factors accounted for its success. And, of course, experts disagree on whether the color theory was proved wrong. Gingras and Schweber (1986, p. 378) write that "the claim that the 'facts' (however constructed and theory laden) did enter the scene and played a final role in the testing of the theory is indeed tenable, despite Pickering's assertion to the contrary." The question would appear to be open still on whether this debate was or was not closed without recourse to evidence. This is of course central to the thesis, though it does not undermine Pickering's historical inquiry. Recent research by Pickering and Nadel (1987) examines the establishment of the charm theory using co-citation analysis and finds support for Pickering's qualitative account of the principal contributions, the speed with which they came to dominate, and their growth "in symbiosis with a constellation of pre-existing streams of HEP practice" and this, they say, reinforces the earlier interpretation that "the new data constitute an additional constraint upon interpretative flexibility" (1987, pp. 105, 106). Yet this does not address the question of the role experiments played in rejecting the color interpretation.

Quantitative techniques are also used to good effect in Stewart's (1986) analysis of geologists' responses between 1907 and 1950 to the idea of continental drift. Using content analysis of papers and data on geologists' published productivity and fields of specialization, Stewart finds that "productive" geologists were more apt than others to be hostile to the idea of continental drift. This, he observes, might have resulted from their having known more and thus having had grounds to be skeptical, but, given what is known now about the validity of data then available, their stance seems not to have derived from knowledge of "the facts" but from their having a professional stake in other theories. In response, R. Laudan (1987, p. 320) observes that this need not be so since other theories had "greater evidential support than drift" at the time and "hence attracted the support of most earth scientists." Stewart has since countered that geologists should at least have considered drift as a plausible hypothesis. (See Frankel, 1979, for an alternate account.) As the MacKenzie, Pickering, and Stewart cases indicate, the implications of scientific contributions are not immediately spelled out in the scientific publications that report them, but are recast in continuing exchange, thus exemplifying the importance of socially organized skepticism in the evolving content of scientific knowledge and the need for sociological investigation to look beyond the original contributions themselves.

The fourth and last example of recent research does not adopt the interests model of analysis, but it is closely related to it. It considers the validity of ideas associated with the model, examines an instructive historical case, and addresses a major question in this line of work—namely, how scientific controversy proceeds and how closure is reached. This is found in Martin Rudwick's (1985) impressive study of the Devonian Controversy, the dispute that lasted from 1835 to 1850 and focused on "the identification and the correct sequence of strata in the county of Devon . . .[whose implications] from the start . . . were seen to be international, and indeed global" (1985, p. 5). In this superbly delineated case study in the history of science and exemplar of sophisticated sociological analysis of scientific knowledge, Rudwick ultimately comes down on the side of nature and geological evidence in settling the controversy. However his analysis and conclusions tell much about the inadequacy of either an exclusively objectivist position or an exclusively constructionist position. As he puts it,

neither "discovery" nor "construction" is by *itself* an adequate metaphor for the production of scientific knowledge. The outcome of research is neither the unproblematic disclosure of the natural world nor a mere artifact of social negotiation. . . . the Devonian controversy shows how new knowledge is shaped from the materials of the natural world, malleable yet often refractory; but it becomes knowledge only as those materials are forged into new shapes with new meanings, on the anvil of heated argumentative debate. [T]he cumulative empirical evidence . . . can be seen . . . as having had a *differentiating* effect on the course and outcome of the debate, *constraining* the social construction into being a limited, but reliable and indefinitely improvable, representation of a natural reality. . . . What had been *shaped* by the social processes of argument and debate among . . . specialists . . . had been a new piece of reliable scientific *knowledge*. (1985, pp. 454-456)[81]

So much for the claim that empirical evidence cannot be prime when social influences are also at work, even when empirical evidence is prime. Several questions remain about the interests perspective in general and the assertion that scientific knowledge reflects the interests of the groups that produce it. Knorr-Cetina (1982, p. 322) is not alone in arguing that analyses attributing the content of scientific knowledge to social interests fail to "demonstrate exactly *how* and in virtue of which *mechanisms* social factors have indeed entered (and are hence reflected in) particular knowledge claims." The need to identify mechanisms relating interests and ideology on the one hand and knowledge on the other is, of course, a longstanding requirement in the sociology of knowledge. Moreover, scientists, like other members of society, have a great many interests since they all have multiple statuses and roles. Interests studies in the sociology of science have yet to address the basic questions of which interests will be activated in identified types of situations and how it is that scientists of evidently different social "interests" often maintain the same theoretical position. Nor has enough attention been given to those instances in which scientists adopt scientific positions opposed to their apparent "interests," as for example, when they reject theoretical positions they would seem to have a stake in maintaining. (Is this a counterpart in science to false consciousness in the larger class structure?) As we have noted, the general perspective requires further work on the conditions in which social influences may be more likely or less to enter into the production of knowledge and about the strength of such influences relative to logic and empirical evidence.

Domains of scientific knowledge that have immediate social implications—for example, knowledge about race, ethnicity, sex, and gender—may be more subject to social construction than more remote domains.[82] At least this is the strong implication of recent claims by women primatologists and physical anthropologists, which suggests the presence of unexamined male bias in research findings on the behavior of male and female animals in various species, often in the form of neglecting certain aspects of female behavior altogether (see for example, Bleier, 1978; Tiefer, 1978; for the radical view that science, as a whole, is imbued with masculine modes of thought, see Keller, 1985). The evidence for such conclusions plainly requires further analysis to determine whether such interests involve bias in problem choice, observation, interpretation, theory choice, or some combination of these. In any event, research on sex behavior and other matters having direct social implications may serve as strategic research sites for the social construction of knowledge even if they are not the less probable *a fortiori* cases that have often been selected by extreme or strong relativists. Finally, examples of this kind indicate once again that the final shape of knowledge claims is not set when they are first announced but that the sociocognitive process of organized skepticism comes into play to limit or revise the original claims.

CONSTRUCTIVIST STUDIES

Studies in the constructivist mode[83] focus on scientific practice within the laboratory on the premise that the social construction of knowledge begins there, and that is where the constituent processes are most readily observed. The constructivist perspective on science, however, involves more than the claim that the content of scientific knowledge is influenced by social processes. Latour and Woolgar, on the one hand, and Knorr-Cetina, on the other, seek a reflexive understanding of science. As Knorr-Cetina puts it, "scientists not only accomplish (construe) their 'findings,' they also accomplish the meaning of this accomplishment" (1983a, p. 160).

Latour and Woolgar's *Laboratory Life* (1979) and Knorr-Cetina's *The Manufacture of Knowledge* (1981) exemplify the genre. Each has had considerable influence on subsequent research. In these detailed ethnographic field studies of biological laboratories, scientists and the world of the laboratory are viewed much as anthropologists view an exotic culture. Largely consistent in claiming that scientific "evidence" and its meaning are socially constructed, the two studies nonetheless emphasize somewhat different aspects of laboratory practice, draw somewhat different conclusions about how scientific knowledge comes to be constructed, and also about scientists' motives for getting on with their work.

In both investigations, nature or reality is accorded a decidedly second-order role in the process of constructing knowledge. As Latour and Woolgar put it: "reality is the consequence rather than the cause of this construction, this means that a scientist's activity is directed, not toward 'reality,' but toward . . . operations on statements'' (1979, p. 237) that is, toward making them seem more and more ''out there.'' And for Knorr-Cetina, ''nature is not to be found in the laboratory, unless it is defined from the beginning as being the product of scientific work'' (1981, p. 4).[84] Indeed, she vividly demonstrates that, in important respects, scientists' research materials are not ''natural'' but ''constructed.''

> All of the source-materials have been specially grown and selectively bred. Most of the substances and chemicals are purified and have been obtained from the industry which serves science or from other laboratories. But whether bought or prepared by the scientists themselves, these substances are no less the product of human effort than the measurement devices or the papers on their desks [1981, p. 4]

Both investigations also emphasize that scientific knowledge is the outcome of ''locally situated, occasioned . . . selections'' (Knorr-Cetina, 1983a, p. 161) or of ''circumstance'' (Latour and Woolgar, 1979, p. 240), although Knorr-Cetina goes on to make the point that this means that science does not operate according to ''universal standards and criteria'' (1983a, p. 163), while Latour and Woolgar emphasize the processes by which ''circumstance'' disappears from accounts of knowledge. As with most other theoretical perspectives in the sociology of science, scientific knowledge is considered not as an individual achievement but as ''interactively achieved''; however, Latour and Woolgar and Knorr-Cetina go on to describe this as the negotiated outcome of discussion between co-workers of what has been observed. Scientists discuss, argue about, and ultimately decide what they have perceived in the welter of information that is provided by complex instrumentation. Knowledge is not the straightforward outcome of experiment (Knorr-Cetina, 1983, p. 162). Moreover, both studies make much of the ways in which laboratory equipment processes and constructs information rather than reflecting or depicting nature, and is itself the outcome of earlier investigations and social constructions.

Calling on evidence from their fieldwork in a neuroendocrinology laboratory at the Salk Institute as well as from citation and publication data, Latour and Woolgar draw special attention to what they take to be the essentially chaotic character both of scientific practice and also of the evidence scientists try to understand:

> a body of [scientific] practices widely regarded by outsiders as well organized, logical, and coherent, in fact consists of a disordered array of observations with which scientists struggle to produce order . . . we argue that scientists . . . are routinely confronted by a seething mass of alternative interpretations. Despite participants' well-ordered reconstructions, . . . actual scientific practice entails the confrontation and negotiation of utter confusion. The solution adopted by scientists is the imposition of various frameworks by which the extent of background noise can be reduced and against which an apparently coherent signal can be presented [1979, p. 36-37].

Reconstructing the history of one significant discovery in great detail (the structure of TRF or TRH, thyrotropin releasing factor or hormone, a substance released by the brain), Latour and Woolgar report how, for a long time, the evidence was complex, confused, and ambiguous. They suggest that the directions researchers took were far from dictated by the evidence; investigators could have taken routes other than the ones they did on equally logical grounds. They go on to take the much stronger position that ''the list of possible alternatives by which we can evaluate the logic of a deduction is sociologically (rather than logically) determined'' (1979, p. 136).[85]

They also make much of the movement of truth claims from a stage in which the originating scientists describe them only as conjectures to a stage in which their status as ''facts'' is taken for granted (1979, pp. 75ff). As claims move through this process, the language used to make them changes; qualifications about their factual status are removed and their association with particular investigators is erased, making them seem objective and external. This has the consequence, Latour and Woolgar observe, of obliterating traces of the socially constructed nature of scientific knowledge and of making it difficult to detect (1979, p. 175). Finally, Latour and Woolgar make the case that the principal activity of laboratory scientists is writing and their principal objective, publication. Scientists are described as ''compulsive and almost manic writers'' (1979, p. 48). The process of research involves a ''chain of writing operations'' as well as the use of ''inscription devices,'' which ''transform matter into written documents'' (1979, pp. 51, 71). All this serves to produce publications designed to persuade others that what they are saying is true, important, worthy of support, and dictated by an external reality.

Drawing on her study of a plant protein research center located in Berkeley, California, Knorr-Cetina also concludes that the transformation of private laboratory constructions into public products or papers is central to scientific inquiry. That transformation begins with the "conversion" of locally contingent observations into "social objects," that is, into argumentation, and from argumentation into finished papers. One outcome then of the process of "conversion" is the marked disparity between what actually goes on in the laboratory and formal accounts of research that appear in print, an outcome noted not just by sociologists but by scientists themselves, as Latour and Woolgar (1979, p. 28) and Knorr-Cetina recognize (1981, p. 95). Peter Medawar (1963), the immunologist and deeply perceptive observer, calls attention to the gap between science in print and science in the laboratory in his paper, "Is the Scientific Paper a Fraud?" while Robert Merton comments:

> the rock-bound difference between the finished versions of scientific work as they appear in print and the actual course of inquiry followed by the inquirer. The difference is a little like that between textbooks of "scientific method" and the ways in which scientists actually think, feel and go about their work. The books on method . . . do not reproduce the typically untidy, opportunistic adaptations that scientists make in the course of their inquiries. Typically, the scientific paper or monograph presents an immaculate appearance which reproduces little or nothing of the intuitive leaps, false starts, mistakes, loose ends, and happy accidents that actually cluttered up the inquiry. The public record of science therefore fails to provide many of the source materials needed to reconstruct the actual course of scientific developments [1967, p. 4].

Knorr-Cetina goes on to characterize the "conversion" process as also involving "perversion"; a rejection of the original "faith, the original language or the preceding level of organization" (1981, pp. 130-132) of actual laboratory practice. That original practice, she repeatedly emphasizes, is contextually contingent and haphazard (1981, p. 152). Scientists' decisions are opportunistic and draw heavily on tacit knowledge; they are not rational, well planned, or rule governed. She makes the important observation that "scientists do not 'ask questions to nature.' " They

try to make something work in terms of instruments, materials, and interpretations that result from the constructions of other scientists, and they try to make it work in discursive interaction with others within and outside the laboratory. This is . . . [just one] sense in which the "cognitive" core of scientific work appears to be thoroughly social [1983a, p. 169].

The emphasis on research practice as a process of making things work suggests that theories of innovation in science may need to be recast such that innovation is seen as the "transient and temporary end-product of the process," not its beginning (1981, p. 66). Knorr-Cetina's provocative analysis calls for reconsideration of important widely held conceptions of scientific work; as noted, of the universality of rules and decision criteria, the disjunction between the cognitive and social and, indeed, the differences between the natural and social sciences. She suggests that since the natural sciences are the outcomes of practices that are "reflexive and constructive, . . . socially occasioned, subject to an indexical logic, and embodied in discourse which includes its own reference, then a large portion of the presumed distinction between the two sciences disappears" (1983a, p. 171).

These significant proposals, consistent with findings by Latour and Woolgar and other constructivists, merit serious consideration, most particularly in the form of additional field studies of cases chosen with an eye to unanswered questions—for example, about the latitude with which the meaning of experimental evidence can be constructed. Knorr-Cetina and Latour and Woolgar observe that scientists are always alert to possible responses that others will have to their work, suggesting that truth claims are socially constrained before publication, an observation in line with earlier inquiry.[86] But this still leaves open the question of what happens to claims once they are published. The question of why it is that experimental work is so often "frustrating and disappointing" is also left open. As Donald Campbell notes, "The laboratory facts may not be speaking for themselves, but they certainly are not speaking for [the investigator's] hopes and wishes" (1979, p. 198). And as we have noted earlier, the phenomenon of multiple independent discoveries is troublesome for those who claim that the production of scientific knowledge is largely or entirely contingent and local.[87] Indeed, Knorr-Cetina observes that the "complexity of scientific constructions . . . does seem to suggest that scientific products are unlikely to be reproduced in the same way under different circumstances . . . it seems highly improbable that the [research] process could be repeated, unless most of the selections are either fixed or made in a similar fashion." Yet she goes on to say, "Given that scientists working on a problem are related through communication, competition and cooperation, and often share similar educations, instruments and interest structures, the latter situation is not really unusual" (1981, p. 6). This statement suggesting that perhaps repetition is not "really unusual" is amplified by a footnote in which Knorr-Cetina remarks

> This explains the occurrence of simultaneous "discoveries" by scientists who in fact did not steal from one another. Note that scientific institutions and the familiar forms of social control in science can be seen as a comprehensive structure to assure that selections remain to a large degree fixed, and that the remainder are made in a similar, compatible and repeatable way [1981, p. 28, note 25].

Knorr-Cetina then would attribute multiple discoveries in science to constraints imposed not by nature but by socially patterned understandings, processes of communication, competition, and shared scientific culture. This, after all, is not very different from the explanation, examined in an earlier section, which attributes multiple discoveries to a shared knowledge base and a shared research agenda within the acutely competitive social framework of science. That this is so does, however, raise questions about the extent to which scientific practice is simply local and not significantly shaped by the larger social institution of science.

DISCOURSE AND TEXT ANALYSIS

Discourse and text analysis focuses on what scientists say about scientific knowledge, scientific practice, and custom, and how they say it, on what scientists write, and the forms in which they write it. As we have already noted, social constructivists take the production of scientific papers as a central activity of scientists. This line forms one strand of work in text analysis. Latour and Woolgar pay sustained attention to the scientific paper as an effort to persuade the reading audience that a given piece of research is credible, useful, and a reflection of nature. They also attend to the language scientists use in describing the status of truth claims and the progression of claims through stages from possible artifact to provisional truth to taken-for-granted fact. We have also noted that Knorr-

Cetina sees the writing of papers as a process of decontextualization of scientific practice. In a detailed chapter on the evolution of scientific papers from preliminary drafts to final form, she focuses on the marshalling of arguments, on the artful differentiation of scientists' own research from prior work, and on their setting out claims to originality in the body of papers (1981, chap. 5). As we have noted elsewhere (Zuckerman, 1987a), there is good reason both for scientists and sociologists of science alike to pay attention to publication. Scientific knowledge is public, not private knowledge; contributions are not scientific until they are made public and subjected to evaluation by qualified experts.

A second related strand of investigation of scientific texts is historical, often taking as problematic the development of the scientific paper itself (including the form of graphic material). Indeed, such research is not remote from structural and historical analyses of the emergence and evolution of the scientific journal and the scientific paper, although their theoretical justifications are distinctly different. Structural analyses have focused on the rise of the scientific journal in seventeenth-century England as a device that would allow scientists to claim and safeguard intellectual property rights, to induce them "to accept the new norm of free communication through a motivating exchange: open disclosure in exchange for institutionally guaranteed honorific property rights to the new knowledge given to others" (Zuckerman and Merton, 1971, p. 70). Drawing on the writings of the seventeenth-century natural philosopher Robert Boyle, who did much to establish the character of scientific writing in that period, Shapin (1984) examines Boyle's distinctively rich accounts of experiments as "virtual witnessing" as a way of "objectifying" truth claims and of helping readers to envision experiments. By doing so, an audience was created for his own writings and those of other scientists.

Bazerman (1984) adopts a wider focus on scientists as writers and as readers. In one study, he examines the evolution from 1893 to 1980 of the experimental report in physics (with the specialty of spectroscopy taken as a case in point). In this century-long period when physics was, of course, entirely transformed both intellectually and socially, Bazerman finds that physicists' arguments have become increasingly "theory based and knowledge embedded" and that the arguments have become increasingly couched in theoretical terms. This, he suggests, contributed powerfully to the formation of the discipline and indeed the institutionalization of publication is seen as an achievement of scientific disciplines. Correlatively, in another study drawing on interviews with physicists about the ways they read scientific texts, Bazerman finds that reading is "permeated with individual purposes and schema." They read with "maps" of the field in mind and actively assess promising lines of research and potentially effective methods. Such purposes and schema evolve dialectically in response to texts; texts are not static but are perceived in light of evolving research activity (1985).

Discourse analysis, pioneered by Michael Mulkay and Nigel Gilbert (Gilbert and Mulkay, 1984; Mulkay, 1985; Mulkay and Gilbert, 1982), focuses on informal speech but has also treated published text. It begins with the observation that the scientists they interviewed about one development in biochemistry produced disconcertingly variable accounts of the same events, accounts that appeared to be context dependent. Furthermore, what scientists said in informal conversation not surprisingly differed greatly from what they wrote. Mulkay and Gilbert therefore conclude that sociologists cannot use what scientists say as evidence until there is a better understanding of what produces variability (a conclusion that others who bring together data from observation, interviews, and biographical and bibliographic sources do not share). The sociologist's problem, they say, is pushed one step back to what can be learned about the patterned character of scientists' portrayals of science (Mulkay and Gilbert, 1982, p. 315).

In their own inquiry, they have mainly emphasized two kinds of discourse or "interpretative repertoires," empiricist and contingent. The empiricist repertoire is the impersonal mode of expression, long recognized in the institutionalized published text but also, they observe, used in informal conversation as well, in which "the physical world often seems literally to speak and act for itself." The contingent repertoire, used exclusively or nearly so, in informal speech, "emphasizes the part played by social and personal contingencies in scientific action and belief" (Mulkay, Potter, and Yearley, 1983, p. 197). Gilbert and Mulkay (1984) observe that scientists use the empiricist repertoire, for example, in accounting for their own correct beliefs, and the contingent repertoire in accounting for others' errors. This has the consequence of making it difficult—at times, impossible—for scientists to come to agreement on what is valid and what is erroneous. Discourse analysis has been used, at times with perceptive wit, to describe such orthodox subjects as scientists' theories of discovery, replication, and the

development of specialties, and such less orthodox subjects as ceremonial discourse and scientific humor. One conclusion to be drawn from the Gilbert and Mulkay work is that scientists provide multiple and often conflicting accounts of scientific inquiry and that there are no firm grounds for choosing among them. Another is that sociological investigators will have to pay more attention to using multiple indicators of scientists' behavior and not rely exclusively on data from discourse or texts. It is still too soon to generalize about the extent of variability in scientists' accounts of the same research and the conditions and processes bringing about differing degrees of variability. It is also too soon to say what brings about the observed patterning of empiricist and contingent discourse; this is plainly an important item on the research agenda of discourse analysis.

Reprise

The sociology of scientific knowledge, with its focus on the reciprocal connections between cognitive development, on the one hand, and social structure and culture, on the other, has been central in the field since its beginnings. Recent research has focused on selected aspects of the structure and growth of knowledge and on the social construction of knowledge, these separate lines of work mirroring the division in the sociology of science between those adopting the position that the content of scientific knowledge is mainly determined by logic and evidence and those adopting the position that it is socially constructed. The first set of studies finds that the growth of knowledge is often discontinuous and need not have taken the directions it did. Scientific attention gets preempted, scientists' focus on certain aspects of phenomena and neglect others, and resistance to innovation is not unknown. The second set of studies finds that decisions made in the course of research in the laboratory are "locally situated" (Knorr-Cetina, 1983b, p. 123); that "science does not have a set of methodological techniques that can quickly or decisively prove or disprove the existence of natural phenomena . . . [and] that replicability of results does not establish a firm link between theory and observation" (Collins, 1983, p. 280); that decisions scientists make on scientific questions are, in important respects, "sustained by social and political interests" (MacKenzie and Barnes, 1979, pp. 204-205) and that scientist-participants provide multiple accounts of the same events, employ two distinct repertoires in different contexts, and use one to account for correct belief and the other to account for error (Gilbert and Mulkay, 1984).

There are marked differences of opinion on the validity of these findings and on the epistemological assumptions that underlie them, among those working in the constructionist mode as well as between them and others. There are also areas of overlap in foci of research attention, if not in theoretical interpretation, between those adopting the structural and constructionist perspectives: for example, on the significance of the competitive quest for recognition, credit and standing in science,[88] also called "professional interests"; on the importance of scientists' prestige and authority in the reception of truth claims and the settling of disputes; on the central role of publication in scientists' activity and the disjunction between actual scientific practice and published scientific papers. These areas of common concern provide possibilities for convergent development often not recognized.

The findings of constructionist inquiries have also set intriguing directions for further investigation. Specific next steps might include inquiry into the processes by which new knowledge claims are subjected to socially organized skepticism and negotiation once they are published. Scientists do, of course, anticipate others' responses to their work before making it public and such anticipated responses affect the shape and content of their claims. Yet scientific knowledge does not enter the "consensus" precisely in the form that it first emerged from the laboratory, as Collins (1983) and Zuckerman and Lederberg (1986) have variously observed. A related line of inquiry would involve more detailed study of how scientists assess the relative efficacy of opposing knowledge claims in different types of research, for example, whether "interests" have particular influence on the acceptance of claims with significant social implications. Another productive line of investigation would focus on the role of power and authority in the settling of disputes, as Collins has noted (1983, p. 275), recognizing, of course, the difficulty of separating the effects of power and authority from those of logic and evidence where the two overlap, as they often do. Finally, more attention needs to be paid to finding ways of demonstrating to the satisfaction of the unconverted that social structure and process affect the content of scientific knowledge, and if so, how. Short of persuading scientists who work in different contexts to address the same problems, closer study of multiple independent discoveries would seem to be in order.

Evidently, the social and cognitive domains of science are intricately interconnected in studies that focus on the sociology of scientific knowledge just as they are in studies of the social organization of science. Yet recent research in the sociology of science has seen a sharp division of labor between studies of the social structure of science and the sociology of scientific knowledge. As we have learned, while the division of scientific labor often advances knowledge, periodic consolidation can have the same effect. So it would seem in the self-exemplifing specialty of the sociology of science.

APPENDIX A
Lines of Research in the Sociology of Science Not Examined in This Review

(1) The emergence of modern science
(2) The professionalization of science
(3) Patterns of growth of the population of science and its demography
(4) Informal communication in science
(5) Comparative analysis of science in different societies
(6) Science policy
(7) Public attitudes toward science
(8) The reciprocal relations of science and politics
(9) The reciprocal relations of science and the economy
(10) The reciprocal relations of science and the academy
(11) The connections between science and technology
(12) The uses of science in the law

NOTE: Each of these areas of research has its own literature. For pertinent bibliography, see Spiegel-Rosing and Price (1977).

NOTES

1. These include *Social Studies of Science; Scientometrics; Science, Technology and Human Values;, Science and Technology Studies* (the official publication of the professional society); *Sociology of the Sciences Yearbook,* and several more in various stages of planning.

2. See Appendix 1 for a brief listing of areas of work in the sociology of science not treated here.

3. Sociologists of science also examine knowledge claims that have been widely rejected as pseudo-science, including parapsychology and creation "science."

4. The existence of such rules does not imply that scientists follow what has been called "the scientific method." See the later discussion of cognitive norms.

5. This includes the sociology of knowledge since the sociology of science overlaps in large part with it. On links between the sociology of knowledge and the sociology of science, see Milic (1984).

6. Both Hagstrom (1965) and Storer (1966) pose the important question of how social control in science operates: why scientists conform to the norms, do research and publish their work. Both proposed exchange models to deal with that question. For Hagstrom, scientists make gifts of new knowledge to the scientific community in the hope of receiving recognition in return, while for Storer, scientists seek "competent response" to their work, which they can receive only if they make contributions public.

7. This Durkheimian indicator of the significance of norms is often overlooked in writings about the ethos of science. This is particularly so for those claiming that since scientists often violate the norms, there can be no normative code to which they subscribe. Since social relations always involve interaction, social responses to violations are as pertinent as the violations themselves (see Zuckerman, 1984).

8. Rossi's (1979) imaginative development of "vignette analysis" is a new departure in the empirical study of norms and may help make for a consensus on these complex matters.

9. Although this brief paper suggests that the social and cognitive domains of science are interconnected, this line of analysis is not well developed, leading to the claim that Merton neglects the cognitive aspects of science. However, it is odd that the critics make so much of this in light of his early systematic examination of the social, economic, and technological influences on foci of research attention in seventeenth-century English science (1938/1970).

10. Kuhn emphasizes that the social aspects of scientific communities "must be discovered by examining patterns of education and communication before asking which particular research problems engage each group" (1978, p. xxi). To this, Mulkay has responded that Kuhn's views are of "no particular significance . . . Kuhn has supplied no more than . . . a flexible interpretative resource which sociologists have used and revised in a great variety of (and not always compatible ways" (1980b, p. 12).

11. The published archive of science is a highly ritualized and, some contend, partly fictitious, account of how scientists actually do their work (Knorr-Cetina, 1981; Medawar, 1963; Merton, 1968, chap. 1). Case studies of scientific practice provide further evidence on the extent to which scientists are committed to cognitive norms and behave in accord with them in the privacy of their laboratories. These could be fruitfully combined with analysis of the same scientists' expressed attitudes and behaviors in public—in meetings and in print—to get a more complete view of the connections between the norms and public and private acts.

12. This statement would, of course, be rejected by those who see norms only as interpretative accounts and that sociologists can study only what scientists say about what they do.

13. The methodological canons are generic in the sense that at any given time they are much alike in the actual research practices of scientists in all fields.

14. The tensions inherent in science between skepticism and authority and tradition and innovation are enduring themes. Polanyi (1963) eloquently defends the procedural effectiveness of relying on authority (even when theories it rejects ultimately turn out to be accepted), while Kuhn (1978, chap. 9) calls the tension between tradition and innovation "essential" to the enterprise.

15. Ben-David's (1977) observations on the special applicability of the dominant norms once contributions are made public has clarified the norm and counternorm discussion considerably. Mitroff's analysis focuses on scientists' normative commitments in the private phase of their work, not the public one. The developing ideas on normative ambivalence overlap in part with Mulkay's analysis of the contextual contingency of norms.

16. These reports have given some the impression that corruption in science is frequent, that its rate is increasing, and that procedures for curbing it are working poorly (Broad and Wade, 1983). Conversely, these same reports can also be taken to mean that fraud is so rare that when it occurs it merits disproportionate attention of the media.

17. See Bechtel and Pearson (1983); Chubin (1987); Gaston (1983); Kilbourne and Kilbourne (1983); Merton (1984); Mulkay (1980); Mulkay and Gilbert (1986); Schmaus (1983); Suttmeier (1985); Weinstein (1977); Woolf (1981, 1986); among others. The analysis here follows and updates my 1977 treatment of the subject.

18. Other forms of deviance sometimes found in science include the abuse of human and animal subjects, the theft of research funds, and departures from official government regulations of research. These are large and complex subjects deserving separate treatment. On social control of experimentation on human subjects, see Barber et al. (1972).

19. Some who argue that there is no reasonable way of demarcating science from nonscience also take the position that there can be no deviant science; that is, that astrology, for example, does not differ from astronomy and magic from modern science (Bloor, 1976; Collins and Pinch, 1979; Dolby, 1979; Pinch, 1979; see the collection on deviant science edited by Wallis, 1979). See Westrum (1978) for analysis of how deviant ideas are transformed into respectable science as new knowledge becomes available. Schmaus (1983) makes the cognate point that deviant behavior in science differs in no important respects from departures from any occupational norms and thus has no features that mark it off from other violations of occupational integrity (see Zuckerman, 1984, for comment).

20. McClintock received the Nobel Prize in 1983. Accounts in the popular press have claimed that her proposals were dismissed at the time as wrong-headed or false because she was a woman. Careful analysis of references to her and her ideas in writings in that

period indicate otherwise. McClintock was highly respected, if not well understood. As one geneticist put it, "It seemed pretty obscure but if Barbara said it, it was probably right." (See also Caspari, 1951.)

21. Cognitive norms of this sort evolve; many research procedures now considered necessary are comparatively new. As a consequence, accusations of neglect of such procedures in the past are merely anachronistic.

22. The law differentiates between simple and willful negligence, between cases of inadvertent negligence and those involving "reckless disregard" of duty (Black, 1933, p. 1229). Science does not make this distinction.

23. Other less serious departures from social norms include depriving contributors of authorship and gratuitous coauthorship; particularism in judging the significance of contributions, not giving scientists credit that is due because they come from the "wrong" religious group, race, gender, or political party; secrecy in order to enhance financial gain, and making unjustified claims to priority. This list can easily be extended.

24. A fourth major theory of deviance, labeling theory, is not germane here since it accounts mainly for the persistence of deviance. In science, once an individual is labeled as seriously deviant, his or her research career is usually ended. For further discussion of the relevance of anomie theory to deviance in science, see Bechtel and Pearson (1983).

25. Scientists express surprise when misconduct occurs. Moreover, the number of reported episodes of misconduct is exceedingly small. The National Institutes of Health, which has about 20,000 grants in operation each year (and thus supports a much larger number of investigators), reports it received an average of two reports a month between 1982 and 1987 of possible misconduct of all kinds and about "half of these have proven to be factual" (Meiers, 1985).

26. As we have noted, the norm of communism does not apply equally at all stages of research. Scientists are not obliged to make their results public before they are judged ready. Nor are scientists obliged to be skeptical or disinterested in the private phases of their researches (Ben-David, 1977, p. 265).

27. Deviance may also be detected by planned and unplanned scrutiny and then made public by "whistle blowing." The difficulties encountered by Stewart and Feder (1987; see Chubin, 1987) in getting their review of Darsee's publications into print suggest that very great persistence is needed for whistle-blowers to make their case public. A thankless and costly act, whistle-blowing is scarcely a reliable means of social control.

28. There is no statute of limitations in science. It can take a long time for fraud or hoax to be discovered, as in the case of the Piltdown man. In this instance, modern methods were needed to demonstrate that the remains had been doctored.

29. Efforts to replicate are far more common when the scientific or social stakes of research are high. Re-

search on AIDS therapies, for example, has been the subject of multiple efforts to replicate (Barnes, 1987).

30. Agencies providing funds for research have played an important role in encouraging their establishment (Greene et al., 1985).

31. Various studies show that scientists rank near the top of the prestige hierarchy and that rankings of occupational prestige have remained quite stable over many decades in the United States (Hodge, Siegel, and Rossi, 1964).

32. In general, the more "fundamental" the subject matter of a science, the closer it is to the nature of matter, and the more its work is mathematized, the higher its standing.

33. Only seemingly in jest, Stigler (1980, p. 147) asserts that "no scientific discovery is named after its original discoverer," calling attention to the distance in time between the discovery and the eponymous attribution by the scientific community.

34. The Science Citation Index and its younger correlative, the Social Science Citation Index, were established to improve the retrieval of scientific information. Sociologists of science have used these indexes with their millions of entries of scientific reference for the quite different purpose of gauging the cognitive impact of particular contributors and their work. That use as an indicator of impact, let alone of "quality" or significance of scientists' contributions, is being continuously investigated through new analytical procedures. Mere counts are flawed in several respects, as Eugene Garfield, the founder of the Science Citation Index has emphatically observed (1979, chap. 10) and as others such as Edge (1979) have vigorously noted. However, carefully developed citation analyses remains the best available procedure for assessing the intellectual influence of comparatively large numbers of scientists (Zuckerman, 1987b).

35. The concentration of eminent scientists in a few universities is even more marked in England. Cambridge, Oxford, and London dominate the membership of the Royal Society of London, one of the oldest and most distinguished of honorific academies. In 1960, 65% of the Fellows were affiliated with Oxford or London alone, a proportion that has remained stable for half a century, the same period in which a declining proportion of scientists were employed by these institutions (Mulkay, 1976, p. 450).

36. J. Cole (1979, p. 62) reports that, on average, ability scores of scientists are correlated with the prestige of the departments from which they received degrees but the differences are not large.

37. It will be noted that the Latour and Woolgar (1979) model does not depart very much from the longstanding concept of the mutability of resources, rewards, and standing in science. Note too that in certain instances—research fellowships and professorships, for example—resources and rewards are not just mutable but one and the same (Zuckerman, 1970).

38. Lotka's Law holds for for the aggregate of scientists but not for particular subsets (Potter, 1981).

39. Citations are so skewed, in fact, that the Coles (1972) once held that science could manage just as

well with smaller numbers than it then had. Recently, citation counts have been challenged as biased against less well-known scientists (MacRoberts and MacRoberts, 1987), a challenge yet to be demonstrated (Zuckerman, 1987b).

40. The great bulk of research on role performance and rewards in science is limited to academic scientists in the United States and Great Britain. Comparatively little work has been done on the majority of scientists who work in industry or for the government. Not only is the academic career comparatively uniform across institutions, it is also well understood. Moreover, since academic scientists contribute disproportionately to the advancement of fundamental knowledge about science, this focus is scarcely frivolous.

41. S. Cole (1978) also concludes that the cognitive structures of the sciences apparently have little influence on the distribution of rewards, an important finding in light of our poor understanding of differences and similarities among the sciences.

42. The patterns of concentration of funds among scientists of varying levels of prestige are reversed when it comes to the distribution of funds among types of research. Much larger amounts of money are spent on applied science and development than on the more esteemed fundamental research. Of the $106.6 billion spent on research and development in 1985, 66% went to development, 21% to applied research, and a mere 13% to basic research.

43. Cole, Cole, and Simon (1981) also report considerable randomness in referees' decisions on proposals submitted for funding. Since referees disagree on funding decisions and since "luck" governs the assignment of referees to particular proposals, many decisions on funding depend on the chance selection of referees. Given the high degree of self-selection among those applying for research funds (many are highly qualified), this is less surprising than it may seem at first.

44. These data on access to publication must be seen in light of high rates of acceptance of papers submitted for publication in many of the sciences (see Hargens, in press, for recent data) and the multitude of journals that are published. Should a paper be rejected by one, scientists may submit them to another. In conjunction, the moderate degree of universalism and high acceptance rates in the sciences make for an open—perhaps too open—publication system, with its flood of publications.

45. Comparable data on the careers of women scientists in industry also suggest that women are less apt than men to hold managerial posts, that they receive lower salaries and are promoted less rapidly. However, data on role performance are not available and therefore do not permit fine-grained analysis.

46. First stated in a truncated fashion by Merton (1942/1973b) and developed more fully in his later work (1968, 1977), the theory has been elaborated and subject to considerable empirical investigation by Allison, Long, and Krauze (1982); Allison and Stewart (1974); Gaston (1978); Cole and Cole (1973);

Mittermeir and Knorr-Cetina (1979); and Zuckerman (1977b, in press a, in press, b), among others.

47. In practice, it matters a great deal whether processes of accumulation of advantage rest on particularistic or universalistic processes of allocation. If resources go to those who are no more able to use them than the rest, advantage accumulates but not nearly as rapidly as it does when universalistic criteria apply; that is when those who receive resources are not just more qualified by past achievement but can use resources more effectively. In the first instance, advantage accumulates additively, and in the second, multiplicatively (Zuckerman 1977b, pp. 60-61).

48. Quoted in Zuckerman (1977b, p. 164). As noted there, it is fitting that Dirac developed the mathematical theory of the positron at 26 and won his Nobel prize at 31.

49. See Waldman and Avolio (1986) for a critical review of studies of age and job performance in otherwise different spheres. Sociologists of science have practical reasons for being interested in age stratification in the production of new ideas: First, in the correlations between age and job performance, and second in the consequences of declining rates of entry of young people into science in the 1970s and early 1980s. (See S. Cole, 1979, on possible consequences of the "aging" of the scientific population.)

50. Diamond (1984) reports that rates of publication in economics do not vary much over the life course but that rates of citation do, suggesting that the intellectual significance of work by older economists declines even if their output does not. These data are not consistent with those reported by Cole (1979).

51. There is also evidence that disparities in publication within age cohorts increase with age—that is, that the differences between the most and the least productive scientists become ever larger. However, it is less clear that disparities in the impact of scientists' work grow with age (Allison, Long, and Krauze, 1982; Allison and Stewart, 1974).

52. Simonton (1983) departs from others in positing age-related differences in rates of ideation and elaboration. He has proposed that the true relationship between age and creativity is one of constantly decelerating decay.

53. There are no canonical analytical definitions of specialties, sciences, or disciplines. Both are loose groupings of scientists working on similar problems who identify themselves and are identified by others as working in the smaller division, socially and cognitive defined and labeled as a specialty, or in the larger division, similarly defined as a science or discipline. Specialties are comparatively small and fluid, while disciplines are more stable and more often institutionalized in the structure of universities and formal professional societies. The extent to which members of specialties share a "research programme" (Lakatos, 1970) varies, as does their size and the extent of interaction of their members. It is generally agreed that members of specialties are know or know of one another's work, more so than research in their disci-

plines as a whole. They need not interact often but do interact more often than randomly selected members of disciplines. Still smaller groups of scientists who regularly share information with one another are members of "invisible colleges," the evocative term, first used for the "unofficial pioneers" who banded together to found the Royal Society of London in 1660, and adapted by Derek J. de Solla Price to describe these fairly close-knit groups of scientists. Price estimates that an "invisible college" rarely exceeds 100 scientists; after that, communication becomes unwieldy and less effective (1986, pp. 74-76).

54. Two other developments encouraged sociologists' interest in the study of specialties. Empirical studies of communication, published productivity, and stratification in scientific disciplines, to select just a few examples, have produced a set of puzzling findings. So much so, that many have come to believe that specialties might be more promising than disciplines, which appear not to be the proper units for sociological analysis. Some philosophers and historians of science have come to similar conclusions. Lakatos declared that the history of science is not the history of theories but of "research programmes" (1970, p. 132), while Kuhn shifted his attention to "disciplinary matrices," smaller units than the disciplines he originally believed were carriers of paradigms. Toulmin (1972), however, has made a powerful case for disciplines being the socially and intellectually meaningful units of science.

55. In an elegant study of astronomers, Gieryn (1978) found that these scientists continually add new problems to their "problem sets," the array of problems they are studying at a given time, while continuing to work on some old ones. This makes for continuities in the population of specialties and also for a degree of novelty in the work of individual scientists.

56. Cognitive and organizational leaders need not be the same individual. The skills required for the two roles differ significantly. Although, on occasion, they come together in an exceptional individual who sets out the agenda for the field and also does the hard work of setting up arrangements so that others can get on with their work in the field. This familiar division of scientific labor is distantly akin to the empirically based distinction between "instrumental" and "expressive leaders" in small groups (Bales, 1950).

57. As Holton (1972) suggested, an enduring theme in science is the life cycle as an organizing analytic scheme. This is much the case in the study of specialties.

58. Paradigm development was measured here by the number of new variables appearing in the literature of the specialties under examination—a rough but imaginative effort to quantitate a complex set of ideas.

59. For example, certain new perspectives not only challenge prevailing theoretical commitments but also the authority structure and goals of the parent discipline. These may lead to "schools" of thought rather than simply to the successive specification of ignorance. See Amsterdamska (1985) on schools of thought and their dependence on larger institutional structures.

60. Fisher (1967), however, notes that in the case of "invariant theory in mathematics," decay and death set in primarily because no new workers were recruited rather than because the array of interesting problems decreased.

61. This position derives both from Mannheimian (1936) and Durkheimian (1912/1934) traditions in the sociology of knowledge, which hold that the emergence of objective" scientific knowledge is made possible by the development of appropriate social structures, but that once established, its concepts and logic develop independently of its social context. This view is also consistent with that of "rationalist" philosophers of science such as Popper.

62. Robert Merton observes that the hypothesis that discoveries and inventions are inevitable with cultural accumulation is itself a multiple (1961/1973f, pp. 352-356). He identifies no fewer than 18 independent instances in the nineteenth and early twentieth centuries in which multiple discoveries and inventions were noted and some of their implications identified. I draw heavily here on his extended work on the sociological analysis of discovery. (See Merton 1957/1973e, 1961/1973f, 1963/1973g, 1973a.)

63. The phenomenon is also found in technology. One of the sociological earliest studies of multiples is entitled, "Are Inventions Inevitable? A Note on Social Evolution" (Ogburn and Thomas, 1922).

64. His language here presages the concerns both of interests analysts and constructivist sociologists of scientific knowledge. Multiples supplement current emphases in research on the behavior of scientists by conceiving that behavior as a resultant not only of the idiosyncratic characteristics and the local ambiance of scientists, but also of their place in the within the wider "social structure and culture" (1963/1973g, p. 376). In addition to these problems, Merton (1961/1973f) also noted the usefulness of multiples for comparing patterns of development in the various branches of science and for formulating science policy. Policymakers, he observes, might consider fostering rather than trying to eliminate redundancy of discovery in an effort to ensure that scientific advancement will occur along certain lines.

65. The economist Don Patinkin argues (1982, 1983) that that new ideas will stimulate further work—a significant matter for science—if they are explicitly set out as the "central message" of the reported work; that is, the central problems being addressed and the solutions proposed for them. Discoveries are thus equivalent only when they have the same central message. His analysis has focused on whether Keynes's general theory was anticipated by the economist Kalecki and the Stockholm School. He concludes it was not, since neither made all the main elements of the theory their "central message."

66. Kuhn is not alone in taking this severe position. The historian of technology, Jacob Schmookler

(1966), and the historian of science, Yehuda Elkana (1970), also adopt these extremely strong criteria for multiples.

67. Students of multiple discoveries have compiled lists of multiples in science and technology of varying length and for various purposes (Kroeber 1917; Ogburn and Thomas, 1922; Merton in collaboration with Elinor Barber, 1961.) More recently, Simonton (1979) has collected a set of 579 episodes of independent simultaneous discovery for the purpose of quantitative analysis.

68. The most famous of these was the rediscovery of Mendel's work in 1900 by three scientists independently. Recent scholarship suggests that one of these may have known about the work of another (Weinstein, 1977, pp. 362-363). Brannigan (1979) argues that the idea of these being three rediscoveries of Mendelian genetics is a later social construction but this is still moot.

69. See Brannigan's (1981) extended discussion of the social determination of discovery.

70. Cozzens's (1985) analysis of the dynamics involved in the the congeries of discoveries of the opiate receptor identifies the social definition of these multiples. This is not taken to mean that the various researches were not related to the same or similar natural phenomena.

71. So much so that finding an appropriate term to cover all variants of constructionism is no easy task. Gieryn uses the label *relativist/constructivist* program (1982, p. 280), one he describes as "clumsy." In response, Mulkay and Gilbert, the principal advocates of discourse analysis, contend that Gieryn has "divided the field in quite the wrong way. The major division is between discourse analysis and everything else. In particular, it was extremely misleading to put our recent work on scientific discourse in the same category as the 'relativists' or 'constructivists' "(1982, p. 309). Such are the difficulties of trying to locate different strands of inquiry and the scholars who pursue them. I trust that Mulkay and Gilbert and the many others whose work is discussed in the "constructionist" rubric will not be permanently offended by the label.

72. Collins (1983a, p. 267) contrasts this to sociological studies of the social organization of science, "Inquiry based on this program concerns how certain views about the physical and mathematical world come to count as correct within society, rather than how a society can be arranged so that truth will emerge".

73. This is the terminology Pickering (1982, p. 125) uses, though his particular concern with professional or cognitive interests is more focused than Barnes and Shapin's (1979, p. 10), both of whom are interested in the social conditioning of knowledge more generally. They have used the term *naturalism* to describe their perspective, in contrast to traditional Marxist, "evaluative" analyses of science. But this term seems too general to convey the particular concerns of this sort of inquiry.

74. Although it had long been evident that much

could be learned about the development of scientific knowledge by bringing together the perspectives of the history and the sociology of science, there were few, if any, explicit efforts to lay out the problematics of such an undertaking. One such effort, involving Yehuda Elkana, Joshua Lederberg, Robert K. Merton, Arnold Thackray, and Harriet Zuckerman got under way in 1973 at the Center for Advanced Study in the Behavioral Sciences under the title, "Historical Sociology of Scientific Knowledge." The group's intent was to examine "the cognitive and social processes in the development of scientific knowledge" and to "work toward the goal of developing an analytical and interpretative framework through the study of cases in point." (POSTS, 1974, pp. 9-10). With the rapid growth of the field, "the historical sociology of scientific knowledge" has become a matter-of-course expression, as one sees in Shapin's (1981, p. 158) exacting and comprehensive paper.

75. As noted earlier, Kuhn is far from comfortable with the notion that his work encouraged those who rejected the significance of norms and values in science and adopted a radically relativist position.

76. Philosophers far from agree that the Duhem-Quine thesis makes it impossible to reject theories on the basis of evidence under all conditions.

77. Nor were many philosophers of science in accord with these ideas. For one example, see Laudan (1977, chap. 7).

78. In his foreword to the English edition of Fleck, Kuhn observes that he had read Fleck and indeed had cited *Genesis and Development* in the *Structure of Scientific Revolutions* but that he is "almost totally uncertain" as to what he took from him . . . for some years . . . I knew of no one else who saw in the history of science what I was myself finding there. Very probably also, acquaintance with [his] text helped me to realize that the problems which concerned me had a fundamentally sociological dimension." Yet as Kuhn also observes, he found Fleck's "sociology of the collective mind . . . vaguely repulsive" (Fleck, 1979, p. viii, ix).

79. One example Fleck gives of a passive connection is that once syphilis is actively defined as a "carnal scourge," the typically unreliable effect of mercury on the carnal scourge is "inevitable" and "seems real" and "objective." Thus the active and passive in knowledge are connected (Fleck, 1935/1979, p. 10).

80. Shapin also observes that there is no reason to equate "the social with the 'irrational' " unless one wishes to adopt a normative attitude toward rationality. "The role of the social . . . is to prestructure choice, not to preclude choice" (1982, p. 198).

81. Pinch (1986), in his review of Rudwick's book, observes that the evidence was not altogether unproblematic since not all geologists found it convincing, albeit it was marginal scientists who rejected the consensus. However, marginality is itself a social definition and Pinch wonders whether the opinions of marginal scientists would have been considered unimportant had they accepted prevailing views.

82. See Gould (1981, p. 66) for a telling example

of how bias affected his own misreading of the evidence on the cranial capacity of various races.

83. For others, see Lynch (1982); Lynch, Garfinkel, and Livingston (1983); Zenzen and Restivo (1982).

84. The authors of both studies also eschew a relativist position. Latour and Woolgar observe: "We do not wish to say that facts do not exist nor that there is no such thing as reality. In this simple sense our position is not relativist. Our point is that 'out-there-ness' is the consequence of scientific work rather than its cause" (1979, pp. 180-182). While Knorr-Cetina observes that the "constructivist interpretation . . . [is] non-subjectivist exactly in the sense that it considers the self-referential reflexivity of knowledge not in itself as a matter of detached reflection, but as a matter of 'fact,' that is, as a meta-philosophical problem of research" (1983, p. 160).

85. Even so, it is not self-evident that the research decisions they describe, such as Guillemin's announced strategy to go for the structure of TRF, were principally determined by social and not by logical or evidentiary considerations.

86. "Social interaction is related to the development of science in several other ways . . . although the idea of 'other persons' is not employed explicitly in science, it is always tacitly involved. In order to prove a generalization, which for the individual scientists, on the basis of his own private experience, may have attained the status of a valid law, . . . the investigator is compelled to set up critical experiments which will satisfy the other scientists engaged in the same cooperative activity" (Merton, 1938/1970, p. 219).

87. Latour and Woolgar apparently do not think that scientific practice is so local as to preclude multiple discovery since the very case they examine in detail, the discovery of the structure of TRF (TRH), was in important respects a multiple discovery by Roger Guillemin and his colleagues and Andrew Schally and his colleagues. They say that "we ourselves have used the two terms interchangeably. . . . In fact, these alternative formulations corresponded directly to those used in each of the groups led by Guillemin and Schally. It became apparent to us that these terms were different names for the same thing" (1979, p. 111).

88. Paradoxically, Latour and Woolgar report that "our scientists only rarely assessed the success of their operations in terms of formal credit . . . they were only marginally interested in questions of credit and priority" (1979, p. 207). At the same time, they describe in detail their scientists' arguments with the Schally group about alleged misappropriations of credit and issues of priority. Indeed they report that "some bitterness [about the allocation of credit] was apparent as much as seven years later. In response to our sociological enquiries (which undoubtedly had the effect of rekindling the dormant conflict) members of each group carefully set out to compare publication and submission dates so as to establish the 'correct' and 'definitive' allocation of priority" (1979, p. 112).

REFERENCES

Allison, Paul D., J. Scott Long and Tad Krauze. 1982. "Cumulative Advantage and Inequality in Science." *American Sociological Review* 47:615-625.

Allison, Paul D. and John A. Stewart. 1974. "Productivity Differences among Scientists: Evidence for Accumulative Advantage." *American Sociological Review* 39:596-606.

Amsterdamska, Olga. 1985. "Institutions and Schools of Thought: The Neogrammarians." *American Journal of Sociology* 91:332-358.

Aronson, Naomi. 1986. "The Discovery of Resistance." *ISIS* 77:630-646.

Astin, Helen S. 1978. "Factors Affecting Women's Scholarly Productivity." In *The Higher Education of Women: Essays in Honor of Rosemary Park*, edited by H. S. Astin and W. Z. Hirsch. New York: Praeger.

Babbage, Charles. 1976. *Reflections on the Decline of Science in England and Some of Its Causes.* New York: Scholarly. (Original work published 1830)

Bahr, Howard M., Theodore Caplow and B. A. Chadwick. 1983. "Middletown III: Problems of Replication, Longitudinal Measurement, and Triangulation," *Annual Review of Sociology* 9:243-264.

Bales, Robert F. 1950. *Interaction Process Analysis.* Reading, MA: Addison-Wesley.

Barber, Bernard. 1952. *Science and the Social Order.* Glencoe, IL: Free Press.

_____ 1961. "Resistance by Scientists to Scientific Discovery." *Science* 134:596-602.

_____, John Lally, Julia Makarushka, and Daniel Sullivan. 1972. *Research on Human Subjects: Problems of Social Control of Medical Experimentation.* New York: Russell Sage.

Barnes, Deborah, H. 1987. "Debate over Potential AIDs Drug." *Science* 237:128-130.

Barnes, S. B. 1974. *Scientific Knowledge and Sociological Theory.* London: Routledge & Kegan Paul.

_____ and R.G.A. Dolby. 1970. "The Scientific Ethos: A Deviant Viewpoint." *European Journal of Sociology* 11:3-25.

Barnes, Barry and Steven Shapin, eds. 1979. "Introduction." Pp. 9-17 in *Natural Order: Historical Studies of Scientific Culture.* London: Sage.

Bayer, Alan E. and Helen S. Astin. 1975. "Sex Differentials in the Academic Reward System." *Science* 188:796-802.

Bayer, Alan E. and Jeffrey E. Dutton. 1977. "Career Age and Research-Professional Activities of Academic Scientists." *Journal of Higher Education* 48:259-282.

Bazerman, Charles. 1984. "Modern Evolution of the Experimental Report in Physics: Spectroscopic Articles in the Physical Review, 1893-1980." *Social Studies of Science* 14:163-196.

_____ 1985. "Physicists Reading Physics: Schema-Laden Purposes and Purpose-Laden Schema." *Written Communication* 2:3-23.

Beaver, Donald deB. 1978. "Possible Relationships Between the History and Sociology of Science." Pp. 140-161 in Jerry Gaston, ed., *The Sociology of Science: Problems, Approaches and Research*. San Francisco: Jossey-Bass.

Bechtel, Kenneth H., Jr. and Willie Pearson, Jr. 1983. "Deviant Scientists and Scientific Deviance." *Deviant Behavior* 6:237-252.

Ben-David, Joseph. 1960. "Scientific Productivity and Academic Organization in Nineteenth Century Medicine." *American Sociological Review* 23:282-343.

_____ 1971. *The Scientist's Role in Society: A Comparative Study*. Englewood Cliffs, NJ: Prentice-Hall.

_____ 1977. "Organization, Social Control, and Cognitive Change in Science." Pp. 244-265 in *Culture and Its Creators: Essays in Honor of Edward Shils*, edited by J. Ben-David and T. Clark. Chicago: University of Chicago Press.

_____ 1978. "The Emergence of National Traditions in the Sociology of Science: The United States and Great Britain. Pp. 197-218 in *The Sociology of Science: Problems, Approaches and Research*, edited by J. Gaston. San Francisco: Jossey-Bass.

_____ 1980. "The Ethos of Science: The Last Half Century." Pp. 13-27 in *Science and the Polity: Ideals, Illusions and Realities. Silver Jubilee Symposium*, vol. 1, edited by J. R. Philip and T. J. Conlon. Canberra: Australian Academy of Science.

_____ 1981. "Sociology of Scientific Knowledge." Pp. 40-59 in *The State of Sociology: Problems and Prospects*, edited by J. F. Short. Beverly Hills, CA: Sage.

_____ and Randall Collins. 1966. "Social Factors in the Origins of a New Science: The Case of Psychology." *American Sociological Review* 31:451-465.

Ben-David, Joseph and Teresa Sullivan. 1975. "The Sociology of Science." *Annual Review of Sociology* 1:203-222.

Ben-David, Joseph and Awraham Zloczower. 1962. "Universities and Academic Systems in Modern Societies." *European Journal of Sociology* 3:45-84.

Bielby, William T. In press. "Sex Differences in Careers: Is Science a Special Case?" In *Women in Science*, edited by J. R. Cole, H. Zuckerman, and J. Bruer. New York: W. W. Norton.

Black, H. C. 1933. *Black's Law Dictionary*. St. Paul, MN: West.

Blackburn, Richard T., Charles E. Beyhmer and David E. Hall. 1978. "Correlates of Faculty Publications." *Sociology of Education* 51:132-141.

Bleier, Ruth. 1978. "Bias in Biological and Human Sciences: Some Comments." *Signs* 4:159-162.

Blisset, Marlan. 1972. *Politics in Science*. Boston: Little, Brown.

Bourdieu, Pierre. 1975. "The Specificity of the Scientific Field and the Social Conditions of the Progress of Reason." *Social Science Information* 14:19-47.

Box, Steven and Stephen Cotgrove. 1970. *Science, Industry and Society: Studies in the Sociology of Science*. London: Allen & Unwin.

Bloor, David. 1976. *Knowledge and Social Imagery*. London: Routledge & Kegan Paul.

Brannigan, Augustin. 1979. "The Reification of Mendel." *Social Studies of Science* 9:423-454.

_____ 1981. *The Social Basis of Scientific Discovery*. Cambridge, England: Cambridge University Press.

_____ and Richard A. Wanner. 1983. "Multiple Discoveries in Science: A Test of the Communication Theory." *Canadian Journal of Sociology* 8:135-151.

Broad, William and Nicholas Wade. 1983. *Betrayers of the Truth*. New York: Simon & Shuster.

Campbell, Donald T. 1969. "Ethnocentrism of Disciplines and the Fish-Scale Model of Omniscience." Pp. 327-348 in *Interdisciplinary Relationships in the Social Sciences* edited by M. Sherif and C. Sherif. Chicago: Aldine.

_____ 1979. "A Tribal Model of the Social System Vehicle Carrying Scientific Knowledge." *Knowledge* 1:181-201.

Caspari, E. 1951. "Quantitative Biology." *Science* 114:3.

Chubin, Daryl E. 1976. "The Conceptualization of Scientific Specialties." *Sociological Quarterly* 17:448-476.

_____ 1987. "A Soap Opera for Science." *BioScience* 37:259-261.

_____, Alan L. Porter, and Margaret E. Boeckmann. 1981. "Career Patterns of Scientists: A Case for Complementary Data." *American Sociological Review* 46:488-496.

Cicourel, A. V. 1973. *Cognitive Sociology: Language and Meaning in Social Interaction*. London: Penguin.

Cohen, I. Bernard. 1974. "Isaac Newton." Pp. 42-101 in *Dictionary of Scientific Biography*, vol. X, edited by C. C. Gillispie. New York: Scribner's.

Cohen, Robert S. and Thomas Schnelle, eds. 1985. *Cognition and Fact: Materials on Ludwik Fleck*. Boston Studies in the Philosophy of Science, vol. 87. Dordrecht: Reidel.

Cole, Jonathan R. 1970. "Patterns of Intellectual Influence in Scientific Research." *Sociology of Education* 43:377-403.

_____ 1979. *Fair Science: Women in the Scientific Community*. New York: Free Press.

_____ and Stephen Cole. 1972. "The Ortega Hypothesis." *Science* 178:368-374.

_____ 1973. *Social Stratification in Science*. Chicago: University of Chicago Press, 1973.

Cole, Jonathan R. and Harriet Zuckerman. 1975.

"The Emergence of a Scientific Specialty: The Self-Exemplifying Case of the Sociology of Science." Pp. 139-174 in *The Idea of Social Structure: Papers in Honor of Robert K. Merton*, edited by L. A.Coser. New York: Harcourt Brace Jovanovich.

———— 1984. "The Productivity Puzzle: Persistence and Change in Patterns of Publication of Men and Women scientists. Pp. 217-258 in *Advances in Motivation and Achievement*, edited by P. Maehr and M. W. Steinkamp. Greenwich, CT: JAI Press.

———— 1987. "Marriage, Motherhood and Women's Research Performance in Science." *Scientific American* 256:119-125.

Cole, Stephen. 1970. "Professional Standing and the Reception of Scientific Discoveries." *American Journal of Sociology* 76:286-306.

———— 1975. "The Growth of Scientific Knowledge: Theories of Deviance as a Case Study." Pp. 175-220 in *The Idea of Social Structure: Papers in Honor of Robert K. Merton*, edited by L. A. Coser. New York: Harcourt Brace Jovanovich.

———— 1978. "Scientific Reward Systems: A Comparative Analysis." Pp. 167-190 in *Research in Sociology of Knowledge, Sciences and Art*, edited by R. A. Jones.

———— 1979. "Age and Scientific Performance." *American Journal of Sociology* 84:958-977.

———— 1983. "The Hierarchy of the Sciences?" *American Journal of Sociology* 89:111-139.

———— and Jonathan R. Cole. 1967. "Scientific Output and Recognition. *American Sociological Review* 32:377-390.

————, Jonathan R. Cole, and Lorraine Dietrich. 1978. "Measuring the Cognitive State of Scientific Disciplines." Pp. 209-251 in *Toward a Metric of Science: The Advent of Science Indicators*, edited by Y. Elkana et al. New York: John Wiley.

Cole, Stephen, Jonathan R. Cole, and Gary A. Simon. 1981. "Chance and Consensus in Peer Review." *Science* 214:881-886.

Cole, Stephen, Leonard Rubin, and Jonathan R. Cole. 1977. "Peer Review and the Support of Science." *Scientific American* 237:34-41.

Collins, Harry M. 1974. "The TEA-set: Tacit Knowledge and Scientific Networks." *Science Studies* 4:165-186.

———— 1975. "The Seven Sexes: A Study in the Sociology of a Phenomenon, or the Replication of Experiments in Physics." *Sociology* 9:205-224.

———— 1981. "Stages in the Empirical Programme of Relativism." *Social Studies of Science* 11:3-10.

———— 1982. "Knowledge, Norms and Rules in the Sociology of Science." *Social Studies of Science* 12:299-309.

———— 1983a. "The Sociology of Scientific Knowledge: Sudies of Contemporary Science." *Annual Review of Sociology* 9:265-285.

———— 1983b. "An Empirical Relativist Programme

in the Sociology of Scientific Knowledge." Pp. 85-113 in *Science Observed*, edited by K. Knorr-Cetina and M. Mulkay. Beverly Hills, CA: Sage.

———— 1985. *Changing Order: Replication and Induction in Scientific Practice*. London: Sage.

———— and Trevor Pinch. 1979. "The Construction of the Paranormal: Nothing Unscientific is Happening." Pp. 237-270 in R. Wallis, ed., *On the Margins of Science: The Social Construction of Rejected Knowledge*. Sociological Review Monograph #27: Keele.

Cournand, Andre F. and Harriet Zuckerman. 1970. "The Code of Science: Analysis and Some Reflections on Its Future." *Studium Generale* 23:941-962.

Cozzens, Susan. 1985. *The Assignment of Priority in Multiple Discoveries in Science: The Case of the Opiate Receptor Discovery. 1971-1978.* Doctoral dissertation, Department of Sociology, Columbia University.

————, ed. 1986. "Funding and Knowledge Growth: Theme Section." *Social Studies of Science* 16:3-151.

Crane, Diana. 1965. "Scientists at Major and Minor Universities: A Study of Productivity and Recognition." *American Sociological Review* 30:699-713.

———— 1972. *Invisible Colleges: Diffusion of Knowledge in Scientific Comunities*. Chicago: University of Chicago Press.

———— 1980. "An Exploratory Study of Kuhnian Paradigms in Theoretical High Energy Physics." *Social Studies of Science* 10:23-54.

Diamond, A. M. 1984. "An economic model of the life-cycle research productivity of scientists." *Scientometrics* 6:189-196.

Dolby, R.P.A. 1975. "What Can We Usefully Learn from the Velikovsky Affair?" *Social Studies of Science* 5:165-175.

———— 1977. "The Transmission of Two New Scientific Disciplines from Europe to North American in the Late Nineteenth Century." *Annals of Science* 34:287-310.

———— 1979. "Reflections on Deviant Science." Pp. 9-48 in *On the Margins of Science: The Social Construction of Rejected Knowledge*, edited by R. Wallis. Keele Sociological Review Monograph 27.

Dorfman, D. D. 1978. "The Cyril Burt Question: New Findings." *Science* 201:1177-1186.

Dunn, Leslie. 1965. "Mendel, His Work and His Place in History." *Proceedings of the American Philosophical Society*. 109:189-198.

Durkheim, Emile. 1934. *The Elementary Forms of Religious Life*. London: Allen & Unwin. (Original work published 1912)

Edge, David. 1977. "Why I am Not a Co-Citationist." *4S NewsLetter* 2:13-19.

———— 1979. "Quantitative Measures of Communication in Science: A Critical Review." *History of Science* 17:102-134.

———— and Michael J. Mulkay. 1976. *Astronomy

Transformed. New York: Wiley-Interscience.

Elkana, Yehuda. 1970. "The Conservation of Energy: A Case of Simultaneous Discovery? *Archives Internationales D'Histoire Des Sciences* 23:31-60.

———— 1978. "Two-Tier Thiking: Philosohical Realism and Historical Relativism." *Social Studies of Science* 8:309-326.

Etzkowitz, Henry. 1983. "Entrepreneurial Scientists and Entrepreneurial Universities in American Academic Science." *Minerva* 21:198-233.

Fisher, R. A. 1936. "Has Mendel's Work Been Rediscovered?" *Annals of Science* 1:116-137.

Fisher, Charles. 1967. "The Last Invariant Theorists." *European Journal of Sociology* 8:216-244.

Forman, Paul. 1971. "Weimar Culture, Causality and Quantum Theory, 1918-1927." *Historical Studies in the Physical Sciences* 3:1-116.

Fox, Mary Frank. 1983. "Publication Productivity Among Scientists: A Critical Review." *Social Studies of Science* 13:283-305.

———— 1985. "Publication, Performance, and Reward in Science and Scholarship." Pp. 255-277 in *Higher Education: Handbook of Theory and Research*, edited by J. Smart. New York: Agathon.

Fleck, Ludwik. 1979. *Genesis and Development of a Scientific Fact*, edited by T. J. Trenn and R. K. Merton, translated by F. Bradley and T. J. Trenn. Chicago: University of Chicago Press. (Original work published 1935)

Frankel, Henry. 1979. "The Reception and Acceptance of Continental Drift as a Rational Episode in the History of Science." Pp. 51-89 in *The Reception of Unconventional Science*, edited by S. H. Mauskopf. Boulder: Westview.

Franklin Allan. 1981. "Millkan's Published and Unpublished Data on Oil Drops." *Historical Studies in the Physical Sciences* 11:185-201.

———— 1984. "Forging, Cooking, Trimming and Riding on the Bandwagon." *American Journal of Physics* 52:786-793.

Franks, Felix. 1981. *Polywater*. Cambridge: MIT Press.

Fye, W. Bruce. 1987. *The Development of American Physiology: Scientific Medicine in the Nineteenth Century*. Baltimore, MD: Johns Hopkins University Press.

Garfield, Eugene. 1979. *Citation Indexing: Its Theory and Application in Science, Technology and Humanities*. New York: Wiley-Interscience.

———— 1985. "Introducing the ISI Atlas of Science." Pp. 313-325 in *The Awards of Science and Other Essays*, edited by E. Garfield. Philadelphia: ISI Press.

Gaston, Jerry. 1971. "Secretiveness and Competition for Priority of Discovery in Physics." *Minerva* 9:472-492.

———— 1973. *Originality and Competition in Science: A Study of the British High Energy Physics Community*. Chicago: University of Chicago Press.

———— 1978. *The Reward System in British and American Science*. New York: Wiley-Interscience.

———— 1983. "Another Sociological Perspective on Deviance in Science." Pp. 55-65 in *The Dark Side of Science*, edited by B. K. Kilbourne and M. T. Kilbourne. Proceedings of the 63rd Meeting of the American Association for the Advancement of Science, Pacific Division, San Francisco.

Gieryn, Thomas F. 1978. "Problem Retention and Problem Change in Science." *Sociological Inquiry* 48:96-115.

———— 1982. "Relativist/Constructivist Programmes in the Sociology of Science: Redundance and Retreat." *Social Studies of Science* 12:279-297.

———— and Anne E. Figert. 1986. "Scientists Protect Their Cognitive Authority: The Status Degradation Ceremony of Sir Cyril Burt." Pp. 67-86 in *The Knowledge Society*, edited by G. Bohme and N. Stehr. Dordrecht: Reidel.

Gilbert, G. Nigel. 1977. "Competition, Differentiation and Careers in Science." *Social Science Information* 16:103-123.

———— and Michael Mulkay. 1984. *Opening Pandora's Box: A Sociological Analysis of Scientists' Discourse*. Cambridge, England: Cambridge Univerity Press.

Gilfillan, S. C. 1935. *Inventing the Ship*. Chicago: Follett.

Gingerich, Owen. 1976. "On Ptolemy as the Greatest Astronomer of Antiquity: A Review of A History Ancient Mathematical Astronomy." *Science* 193:476-477.

Gingras, Yves and Silvan S. Schweber. 1986. "Constraints on Construction." *Social Studies of Science* 16:372-383.

Goffman, William. 1966. "Mathematical Approach to the Spread of Scientific Ideas: The History of Mast Cell Research." *Nature* 212:449-452.

Gould, Stephen Jay. 1981. *The Mismeasure of Man*. New York: W.W. Norton.

Graham, Loren. 1978. "Concerns About Science and Attempts to Regulate Inquiry," *Daedalus* 107:1-21.

———— 1981. *Between Science and Values*. New York: Columbia University Press.

————, Wolf Lepenies, and Peter Weingart, eds. 1983. *Functions and Uses of Disciplinary Histories*. Dordrecht: Reidel.

Greene, Penelope J., Jane S. Durch, Wendy Horwitz, and Valwyn S. Hopper. 1985. "Policies for Responding to Allegations of Fraud in Research." *Minerva* 23:203-215.

Griffith, Belver C. and Nicholas C. Mullins. 1972. "Coherent Social Groups in Scientific Change." *Science* 177:959-964.

Griffith, Belver C., Henry G. Small, J. A. Stonehill, and S. Dey. 1974. "The Structure of Scientific Literatures II: Toward a Macro-structure and Micro-structure for Science." *Science Studies* 4:339-365.

Hagstrom, Warren. 1965. *The Scientific Commun-*

ity. New York: Basic Books.

———. 1974. "Competition in Science." *American Sociological Review* 39:1-18.

Hargens, Lowell. In press. "A Comparative Analysis of Rejection Rates in Scientific Journals." *American Sociological Review* 53.

——— and Diane Felmlee. 1984. "Structural Determinants of Stratification in Science." *American Sociological Review* 49:685-697.

Hargens, Lowell and Warren Hagstrom. 1967. "Sponsored and Contest Mobility of American Academic Scientists." *Sociology of Education* 40:24-38.

———. 1982. "Scientific Consensus and Academic Status Attainment Patterns." *Sociology of Education* 55:183-196.

Hargens, Lowell. 1988. "Scholarly Concensus and Journal Rejection Rates. *American Sociological Review* 53:139-151.

Harmon, L. R. 1965. *Profiles of Ph.D.s in the Sciences*. National Academy of Sciences-National Research Council Publication 1293, Washington, DC.

Harvey, Bill. 1981. "Plausibility and the Evaluation of Knowledge: A Case-Study of Experimental Quantum Mechanics." *Social Studies of Science* 11:95-130.

Hearnshaw, L. S. 1979. *Cyril Burt: Psychologist*. Ithaca, NY: Cornell University Press.

Helmreich, Robert L., Janet Spence, and William Thorbecke. 1981. "On the Stability of Productivity and Recognition." *Personality and Social Psychology Bulletin*. 7:516-522.

Hesse, Mary. 1984. "The Strong Thesis of Sociology of Science." Pp. 29-60 in *Revolutions and Reconstructions in the Philosophy of Science*. Bloomington: Indiana University Press.

———. 1986. "Changing Concepts and Stable Order Review of H. M. Collins, *Changing Order: Replication and Induction in Scientific Practice*." *Social Studies of Science* 16:714-726.

Hodge, Robert W., Paul Siegel, and Peter Rossi. 1964. "Occupational Prestige in the United States: 1925-1963." *American Journal of Sociology* 70:286-302.

Holton, Gerald. 1972. *Thematic Origins of Scientific Thought: Kepler to Einstein*. Cambridge, MA: Harvard University Press.

———. 1975. "On the Role of Themata in Scientific Thought." *Science* 188:328-334.

———. 1978. "Subelectrons, Presuppositions and the Millikan-Ehrenhaft Dispute." In *The Scientific Imagination*. Cambridge, England: Cambridge University Press.

Horner, Karen L., J. Phillipe Rushton, and Philip A. Vernon. 1986. "Relation between Aging and Research Productivity of Academic Psychologists." *Psychology and Aging* 1:319-324.

Hull, David. 1985. "Openness and Secrecy in Science: Their Origins and Limitations." *Science, Technology and Human Values* 10:4-13.

Hull, David, P. D. Tessner, and A. M. Diamond.

1978. "Planck's Principle." *Science* 202:717-23.

Institute for Scientific Information. 1981. *Science Citation Index: Cumulative Data for 1961-1980*. Philadelphia: ISI.

Jensen, Arthur R. 1976. "On the Trumped-Up Indictment of Sir Cyril Burt." *London Times* (December 9).

Joravsky, David. 1983. "Betrayers of the Truth: Fraud and Deceit in the Halls of Science." *New York Review of Books* 30:3.

———. 1986. *The Lysenko Affair*. Chicago: University of Chicago Press. (Original work published 1970)

Kash, Don E., Irvin L. White, John W. Reuss, and Joseph Leo. 1972. "University Affiliation and Recognition: National Academy of Sciences." *Science* 175:1076-1084.

Keller, Evelyn Fox. 1985. *Reflections on Gender and Science*. New Haven, CT: Yale University Press.

Kennedy, Donald. 1987. "On Fund Raising, Federal Aid and Scientific Fraud: Interview." *The Scientist* 19:14-15.

B. K. Kilbourne and M. T. Kilbourne, eds. 1983. *The Dark Side of Science*. Proceedings of the 63rd meeting of the American Association for the Advancement of Science, Pacific Division, San Francisco.

Klapper, Joseph T. and Charles Y. Glock. 1949. "Trial by Newspaper." *Scientific American* 180: 16-21.

Knorr-Cetina, Karin. 1977. "Producing and Reproducing Knowledge: Descriptive or Constructive." *Social Science Information* 16:669-696.

———. 1981. *The Manufacture of Knowledge: An Essay on the Constructivist and Contextual Nature of Science*. New York: Pergamon Press.

———. 1982a. "Scientific Communities or Transepistemic Arenas of Research? A Critique of Quasi-Economic Models of Science." *Social Studies of Science* 12:101-130.

———. 1982b. "The Constructivist Programme in the Sociology of Science: Retreats or Advances?" *Social Studies of Science* 12:320-324.

———. 1983a. "New Developments in Science Studies: The Ethnographic Challenge." *Canadian Journal of Sociology* 8:153-177.

———. 1983b. "The Ethnographic Study of Scientific Work: Towards a Constructivist Interpretation of Science." Pp. 115-140 in *Science Observed*, edited by K. Knorr-Cetina and M. J. Mulkay. Beverly Hills, CA: Sage.

——— and Michael J. Mulkay. 1983. "Emerging Principles in Social Studies of Science." Pp. 1-17 in *Science Observed*, edited by K. Knorr-Cetina and M. J. Mulkay. London: Sage.

Koester, David, Daniel Sullivan, and D. Hywell White. 1982. "Theory Selection in Particle Physics: A Quantitative Case Study of the Evolution of Weak-Electromagnetic Unification Theory." *Social Studies of Science* 12:73-100.

Kohler, Robert E. 1982. *From Modern Chemistry to Biochemistry: The Making of a Biomedical Dis-*

cipline. Cambridge, England: Cambridge University Press.

Kohn, Alexander. 1986. *False Prophets: Fraud and Error in Science and Medicine*. Oxford: Basil Blackwell.

Koshland, Daniel. 1987. "Fraud in Science." *Science* 235:141.

Krauze, Tadeusz. 1972. "Social and Intellectual Structures of Science: A Mathematical Analysis." *Science Studies* 2:369-378.

Kroeber, Alfred F. 1917. "The Superorganic." *American Anthropologist* 19:163-214.

Krohn, Roger G. 1972. *The Social Shaping of Science*. Westport, CT: Greenwood.

Kuhn, Thomas S., 1970. *The Structure of Scientific Revolutions*. Chicago: University of Chicago Press. (Original work published 1962)

—— 1977. "Energy Conservation as an Example of Simultaneous Discovery." Pp. 66-104 in *The Essential Tension: Selected Studies in Scientific Tradition and Change*. Chicago: University of Chicago Press.

Lakatos, Imre. 1970. "Falsification and the Methodology of Research Programmes." Pp. 91-196 in *Criticism and the Growth of Knowledge*, edited by I. Lakatos and A. Musgrave. Cambridge, England: Cambridge University Press.

Latour, Bruno. 1983. "Give Me a Laboratory and I Will Raise the World." Pp. 141-170 in *Science Observed*, edited by K. Knorr-Cetina and M. J. Mulkay. Beverly Hills, CA: Sage.

—— and Steve Woolgar. 1979. *Laboratory Life: The Social Construction of Scientific Facts*. Beverly Hills, CA: Sage.

Laudan, Larry. 1977. *Progress and Its Problems: Towards A Theory of Scientific Growth*. Berkeley: University of California Press.

Laudan, Rachel. 1987. "Drifting Interests and Colliding Continents: A Response to Stewart." *Social Studies of Science* 17:317-321.

Law, John. 1973. "The Development of Specialties in Science: The Case of X-Ray Protein Crystallography." *Science Studies* 3:275-303.

Lehman, Harvey C. 1953. *Age and Achievement*. Princeton, NJ: Princeton University Press.

Lemaine, Gerard, Roy MacLoed, Michael Mulkay, and Peter Weingart, eds. 1977. *Perspectives on the Emergence of Scientific Disciplines*. Chicago: Aldine.

Levin, Sharon G. and Paula E. Stephen. 1986. "Obsolescence and Scientific Productivity." Presented at the meetings of the Society for Social Studies of Science, September.

Long, J. Scott. 1978. "Productivity and Academic Position in the Scientific Career." *American Sociological Review* 43:889-908.

——, Paul D. Allison, and Robert McGinnis. 1979. "Entrance into the Academic Career." *American Sociological Review* 44:816-830.

Long, J. Scott and Robert McGinnis. 1981. "Organizational Context and Scientific Productivity." *American Sociological Review* 46:422-442.

Lotka, Alfred J. 1926. "The Frequency Distribution of Scientific Productivity." *Journal of the Washington Academy of Sciences* 16:317.

Luria, Salvador. 1975. "What Makes a Scientist Cheat?" *Prism* (May):15-18, 44.

Lynch, Michael. 1982. *Art and Artefact in Laboratory Science: A Study of Shop Work and Shop Talk in a Research Laboratory*. London: Routledge & Kegan Paul.

——, Eric Livingston, and Harold Garfinkel. 1983. "Temporal Order in Laboratory Work." Pp. 205-238 in *Science Observed*, edited by K. Knorr-Cetina and M. J. Mulkay. London: Sage.

McCann, H. Gilman. 1978. *Chemistry Transformed*. Norwood, NJ: Ablex.

MacKenzie, Donald A. 1981. *Statistics in Britain, 1865-1930. The Social Construction of Scientific Knowledge*. Edinburgh: Edinburgh University Press, 1981.

MacRoberts, Michael H. and Barbara R. MacRoberts. 1987. "Testing the Ortega Hypothesis: Facts and Artifacts." *Scientometrics* 12:293-295.

Mannheim, Karl. 1936. *Ideology and Utopia*. London: Routledge & Kegan Paul.

Martin, B. R. and J. Irvine. 1984. "CERN—Past Performance and Future Prospects 1: CERN Position in World High Energy Physics." *Research Policy* 13:183-210.

MacKenzie, Donald and Barry Barnes. 1979. "Scientific Judgment: The Biometrky-Mendelism Controversy." Pp. 191-208 in B. Barnes and S. Shapin, *Natural Order: Historical Studies of Scientific Culture*. Beverly Hills: Sage.

Meadows, Paul and Peter Meadows. 1983. "Anomaly Revisited: Rules and Roles in Research." Pp. 66-89 in *The Dark Side of Science*, edited by B. K. Kilbourne and M. T. Kilbourne. Proceedings of the 63rd meeting of the American Association for the Advancement of Science, Pacific Division, San Francisco.

Medawar, Peter. 1963. "Is the scientific paper a fraud?" *The Listener* (September 12).

—— 1976. "The Strange Case of the Spotted Mice." *New York Review of Books* 23:6-11.

Mehrtens, Herbert. 1987. "The Social System of Mathematics and National Socialism: A Survey." *Sociological Inquiry* 57:59-182.

Meiers, Mary L. 1985. "NIH Perspectives on Misconduct in Science." *American Psychologist* 40:831-835.

Menard, Henry. 1972. *Science, Growth and Change*. Cambridge, MA: Harvard University Press.

Merton, Robert K. 1935. "Fluctuations in the Rate of Industrial Invention." *Quarterly Journal of Economics* 49:454-470.

—— 1967. *On Theoretical Sociology*. New York: Free Press.

—— 1968. *Social Theory and Social Structure*. New York: Free Press. (Original work published 1957)

—— 1970. *Science, Technology and Society in*

Seventeenth Century England. New York: Howard Fertig. (Original work published 1938)

———. 1973a. *The Sociology of Science.* Chicago: University of Chicago Press.

———. 1973b. "The Normative Structure of Science." Chapter 13 in *The Sociology of Science*, by Robert K. Merton. (Original work published 1942)

———. 1973c. "Technical and Moral Dimensions of Policy Research." Chapter 4 in *The Sociology of Science*, by Robert K. Merton. (Original work published 1949)

———. 1973d. "The Neglect of the Sociology of Science." Chapter 10 in *The Sociology of Science*, by Robert K. Merton. (Original work published 1952)

———. 1973e. "Priorities in Scientific Discovery." Chapter 14 in *The Sociology of Science*, by Robert K. Merton. (Original work published 1957)

———. 1973f. "Singletons and Multiples in Science." Chapter 16 in *The Sociology of Science*, by Robert K. Merton. (Original work published 1961)

———. 1973g. "Multiple Discoveries as Strategic Research Site." in *The Sociology of Science*, by Robert K. Merton. (Original work published 1963)

———. 1976a. "The Sociology of Social Problems." Pp. 3-43 in *Contemporary Social Problems*, edited by R. K. Merton and R. Nisbet. New York: Harcourt Brace Jovanovich.

———. 1976b. *Sociological Ambivalence.* New York: Free Press.

———. 1977. *The Sociology of Science: An Episodic Memoir.* Carbondale, IL: Southern Illinois University Press.

———. 1984. "Scientific Fraud and the Fight to be First." *Times Literary Supplement* (November 2):2.

———. 1987. "Three Fragments from a Sociologist's Notebooks: Establishing the Phenomenon, Specified Ignorance, and Strategic Research Materials." *Annual Review of Sociology* 13:1-28.

——— and Richard Lewis. 1971. "The Competitive Pressures: The Race for Priority." *Impact of Science on Society* 21:152-161.

Messeri, Peter. 1988. "Age Differences in the Reception of New Scientific Theories: The Case of Plate Tectonics Theory." *Social Studies of Science* 18:91-112.

Milic, V. 1980. "The Sociology of Science and the Sociology of Science in European Socialist Countries." *Current Sociology* 28:185-342.

———. 1984. "Sociology of Knowledge and Sociology of Science." *Social Science Information* 23:213-273.

Mitroff, Ian. 1974. "Norms and Counternorms in a Select Group of Apollo Moon Scientists: A Case Study in the Ambivalence of Scientists," *American Sociological Review* 39:579-595.

Mittermeir, Roland and Karin D. Knorr-Cetina.

1979. "Scientific Productivity and Accumulative Advantage: A Thesis Reassessed in the Light of International Data." *R&D Management* 9:235-239.

Mulkay, Michael J. 1969. "Some Aspects of Cultural Growth in the Natural Sciences." *Social Research* 36:22-53.

———. 1975. "Three Models of Scientific Development." *Sociological Review* 23:509-526.

———. 1976. "Norms and Ideology in Science." *Social Science Information* 15:627-656.

———. 1979. "Knowledge and Utility: Implications for the Sociology of Knowledge." *Social Studies of Science* 9:63-80.

———. 1980a. "Sociology of Science in the West." *Current Sociology* 28:1-184.

———. 1980b. "Interpretation and the Use of Rules: The Case of the Norms of Science." Pp. 111-125 in *Science and Social Structure: A Festschrift for Robert K. Merton*, edited by T. F. Gieryn. New York: New York Academy of Sciences.

———. 1984. "The Scientist Talks Back: A One-Act Play, with a Moral, about Replication in Science and Reflexivity in Sociology." *Social Studies of Science* 14:265-282.

———. 1985. *The Word and the World: Explorations in the Form of Sociological Analysis.* London: Allen & Unwin.

——— and David Edge. 1973. "Cognitive, Technical and Social Factors in the Growth of Radio Astronomy." *Social Science Information* 12:25-61.

Mulkay, Michael J. and G. Nigel Gilbert. 1982. "What is the Ultimate Question? Some Remarks in Defence of the Analysis of Scientific Discourse." *Social Studies of Science* 12:309-319.

———. 1983. "Scientists' Theory Talk." *Canadian Journal of Sociology* 8:179-197.

———. 1986. "Replication and Mere Replication," *Philosophy of the Social Sciences* 16:21-37.

——— and Steve Woolgar. 1975. "Problem Areas and Research Networks in Science." *Sociology* 9:187-203.

Mulkay, Michael J., Jonathan Potter, and Steven Yearley. 1983. "Why an Analysis of Scientific Discourse is Needed." Pp. 171-203 in *Science Observed*, edited by K. Knorr-Cetina and M. J. Mulkay. London: Sage.

Mullins, Nicholas. 1972. "The Development of a Scientific Specialty: The Phage Group and the Origins of Molecular Biology." *Minerva* 19:52-82

———. 1973. *Theories and Theory Groups in Contemporary American Socology.* New York: Harper & Row.

———. 1975. "A Sociological Study of Scientific Revolution." Pp. 185-204 in *Determinants and Controls of Scientific Development*, edited by K. D. Knorr, H. Strasser, and H. G. Zillian. Dordrecht: Reidel.

———. 1985. "Invisible Colleges as Science Elites." *Scientometrics* 7:357-368.

_____, Lowell L. Hargens, Pamela K. Hecht, and Edward L. Kick. 1977. "The Group Structure of Co-Citation Clusters: A Comparative Study." *American Sociological Review* 42:552-562.

Murray, Stephen O. 1986-1987. "The Postmaturity of Sociolinguistics: Edward Sapir and Personality Studies in the Chicago Department of Sociology." *History of Sociology* (6-7):75-107.

Nadel, Edward. 1980. "Multivariate Citation Analysis and the Changing Cognitive Organization in a Specialty of Physics." *Social Studies of Science* 10:449-473.

_____ 1981. "Citation and Co-citation Indicators of a Phased Impact of the BCS Theory in the Physics of Superconductivity." *Scientometrics* 3:203-221.

National center for Educational Statistics. 1981. "Academic Research Expenditures 1977, 1978, and 1979." *Statistical Highlight*, Report #81-420. Washington, D.C.: Author.

Nelkin, Dorothy. 1976. "Changing Images of Science: New Pressures on Old Stereotypes." *Program on Public Conceptions of Science* Harvard University Newsletter 14.

_____ 1984. *Science as Intellectual Property: Who Controls Scientific Research?* New York: Macmillan.

Neugebauer, Otto. 1975. "Studies in the History of Mathematics and Physical Sciences." Vol. 1 in *A History of Ancient Mathematical Astronomy* (3 vols.) New York: Springer Verlag.

Ogburn, W. F. and Dorothy S. Thomas. 1922. "Are Inventions Inevitable? A Note on Social Evolution." *Political Science Quarterly* 37:83-98.

Over, Ray. 1982. "Is Age a Good Predictor of Research Productivity?" *Australian Psychologist* 17:129-139.

Patinkin, Don. 1983. "Multiple Discoveries and the Central Message." *American Journal of Sociology* 89:306-323.

_____ 1982. *Anticipations of the General Theory? And Other Essays on Keynes*. Chicago: University of Chicago Press.

Petersdorf, Robert G. 1986. "The Pathogenesis of Fraud in Medical Science." *Annals of Internal Medicine* 104:252-254.

Piaget, Jean. 1977. *The Equilibration of Cognitive Structure: The Central Problem of Intellectual Devlopment*, translated by T. Brown and K. S. Thampy. Chicago: University of Chicago Press.

Pickering, Andrew. 1981. "Constraints on Controversy: The Case of the Magnetic Monopole." *Social Studies of Science* 11:63-93.

_____ 1982. "Interests and Analogies." Pp. 125-146 in *Science in Context*, edited by S. B. Barnes and D. Edge. Cambridge: MIT Press.

_____ 1984. *Constructing Quarks: A Sociological History of Particle Physics*. Chicago: University of Chicago Press.

_____ and Edward Nadel. 1987. "Charm Revisited: A Quantitative Analysis of the HEP Literature." *Social Studies of Science* 17:87-113.

Pinch, Trevor. 1977. "What Does a Proof Do If It Does Not Prove? A Study of the Social Conditions and Metaphysical Divisions Leading to David Bohm and John von Neumann Failing to Communicate in Quantum Physics." Pp. 171-215 in *The Social Production of Scientific Kowledge*, edited by E. Mendelsohn, P. Weingartm, and R. Whitley. Dordrecht: Reidel.

_____ 1979. "Normal Explanations of the Paranormal: The Demarcation Problem and Fraud in Parapsychology." *Social Studies of Science* 9:329-348.

_____ 1981. "The Sun-Set: The Presentation of Certainty in Scientific Life." *Social Studies of Science* 11:131-158.

_____ 1986. "Strata Various." *Social Studies of Science* 16:705-713.

Planck, Max. 1949. *Scientific Autobiography and Other Papers*, translated by F. Gaynor. New York: Philosophical Library.

Polanyi, Michael. 1963. "The Potential Theory of Adsorption." *Science* 141:1010-1013.

Popper, Karl. 1959. *The Logic of Scientific Discovery*. New York: Basic Books. (Original work published in 1935)

Porter, Theodore M. 1981. "Social Interests and Statistical Theory." *Science* 214:784.

Potter, William Grey. 1981. "Lotka's Law Revisited." *Library Trends* 30:21-39.

Program on Science, Technology and Society (POSTS). 1974. *Second General Report: September 1, 1973-August 31, 1974*. Stanford, CA: Center for Advanced Study in the Behavioral Sciences.

Price, Derek J. de S. 1965. "Networks of Scientific Papers." *Science* 149:510-515.

_____ 1970. "Citation Measures of Hard Science, Soft Science, Technology and Non-Science." Pp. 3-22 in *Communication Among Scientists and Engineers*, edited by C. Nelson and D. Pollock. Lexington, MA: D. C. Heath.

_____ 1976. "The Nature of Science." Pp. 1-28 in supplement to *Biology*, by R. Goldsby. New York: Harper & Row.

_____ 1986. *Little Science, Big Science . . . and Beyond*. New York: Columbia University Press. (Original work published 1963)

Reskin, Barbara. 1976. "Sex Differences in Status Attainment in Science: The Case of Post-Doctoral Fellowships." *American Sociological Review* 41:597-613.

_____ 1977. "Scientific Productivity and the Reward System of Science." *American Sociological Review* 42:491-504.

_____ 1978. "Academic Sponsorship and Scientists' Careers." *Sociology of Education* 52:129-146.

_____ 1979. "Age and Scientific Productivity: A Critical Review." In *The Demand for New Faculty in Science and Engineering*, edited by Michael S. McPherson for the Commission on Human Resources. Washington, DC: National Academy of Sciences.

Restivo, Sal and Julia Loughlin. 1987. "Critical Sociology of Science and Scientific Validity." *Knowledge* 8:486-508.

Robinson, A. 1986. "How to Keep your Proof a Secret and Yet Convince Your Colleagues that You Have a Proof." *Science* 233:938-939.

Roll-Hansen, Nils. 1979. "Experimental Method and Spontaneous Generation: The Controversy Between Pasteur and Puchet, 1859-1864." *Journal of the History of Medicine* (July):273-292.

——— 1980. "The Controversy Betwen Biometricians and Mendelians: A Test Case for the Sociology of Scientific Knowledge." *Social Science Information* 19:501-517.

——— 1983. "The Death of Spontaneous Generation and the Birth of the Gene: Two Case Studies of Relativism." *Social Studies of Science* 13:481-519.

Rossi, Peter. 1979. "Vignette Analysis: Uncovering the Normative Structure of Complex Judgments." Pp. 176-186 in *Qualitative and Quantitative Social Research: Papers in Honor of Paul F. Lazarsfeld*, edited by R. K. Merton, J. S. Cole, and P. Rossi. New York: Free Press.

Rossiter, Margaret. 1987. "Sexual Segregation in the Sciences: Some Data and a Model." *Signs* 4:146-151.

——— 1982. *Women Scientists in America: Struggles and Strategies to 1940*. Baltimore, MD: Johns Hopkins Press.

Rudwick, Martin. J. S. 1985. *The Great Devonian Controversy: The Social Shaping of Scientific Knowledge Among Gentlemenly Specialists*. Chicago: University of Chicago Press.

Schafer, Wolf, ed. 1983. *Finalization in Science: The Social Orientation of Scientific Progress*, vol. 77, Boston Studies in The Philosophy of Science, edited by R. Cohen and M. Wartofsky, and translated by P. Purgess. Dordrecht: Reidel.

Schmaus, Warren. 1983. "Fraud and the Norms of Science." *Science, Technology and Human Values* 8:12-22.

Schmookler, Jacob. 1966. *Invention and Economic Growth*. Cambridge, MA: Harvard University Press.

Shapin, Steven. 1979. "The Politics of Observation: Cerebral Anatomy and Social Interests in the Edinburgh Phrenology Dispute." Pp. 139-138 in *On the Margins of Science*, edited by R. Wallis. Sociological Review Monograph 27.

——— 1982. "History of Science and Its Sociological Reconstructions." *History of Science* 20:157-211.

——— 1984. "Pump and Circumstance: Robert Boyle's Literary Technology." *Social Studies of Science* 14:481-520.

Simonton, Dean K. 1978. "Independent Discovery in Science and Technology: A Closer Look at the Poisson Distribution." *Social Studies of Science* 8:521-532.

——— 1979. "Multiple Discovery and Invention: Zeitgeist, Genius or Chance?" *Journal of Personality and Social Psychology* 37:1603-1616.

——— 1983. "Creativity, Productivity and Age: A Mathematical Model Based on a Two-Step Cognitive Process." *Developmental Review* 3:97-111.

——— 1985. "Quantity, Quality and Age: The Careers of Ten Distinguished Psychologists." *International Journal of Aging and Human Development* 21:241-254.

——— 1987. "Multiples, Chance, Genius, Creativity and Zeitgeist." Pp. 98-128 in *Scientific Excellence: Origins and Assessment*, edited by D. N. Jackson and J. P. Rushton. Beverly Hills, CA: Sage.

Small, Henry G. 1973. "Co-citation in the Scientific Literature: A New Measure of the Relationship between Two Documents." *Journal of the American Society for Information Science* 24:265-269.

——— 1977. "A Co-Citation Model of a Scientific Specialty: A Longitudinal Study of Collagen Research." *Social Studies of Science* 7:139-166.

——— 1978. "Cited Documents as Concept Symbols." *Social Studies of Science* 8:327-340.

——— 1986. "The Synthesis of Specialty Narratives from Co-Citation Clusters." *Journal of the American Society for Information Science* 37:97-110.

——— and Belver C. Griffith. 1974. "The Structure of Scientific Literatures I: Identifying and Graphing Specialties." *Science Studies* 4:17-40.

Small, Henry G. and Diana Crane. 1979. "Specialties and Disciplines in Science and Social Science: An Examination of Their Structure Using Citation Indexes." *Scientometrics* 1:445-461.

Solomon, Susan. 1975. "Controversy in Social Science: Soviet Rural Studies in the 1920s." *Minerva* 13:554-582.

Sorokin, P. A. and Robert K. Merton. 1935. "The Course of Arabian Intellectual Development, 700-1300 A.D." *ISIS* 22:516-524.

Spiegel-Rosing, Ina and Derek J. de S. Price, eds. 1977. *Science, Technology and Society: A Cross-Disciplinary Perspective*. Beverly Hills, CA: Sage.

Stehr, Nico. 1978. "The Ethos of Science Revisited: Social and Cognitive Norms." *Sociological Inquiry* 48:172-196.

Stent, Gunther. 1972. "Prematurity and Uniqueness in Scientific Discovery." *Scientific American* 227:84-93.

Sterling, Theodore. 1959. "Publication Decisions and their Possible Effects on Inferences Drawn from Texts of Significance or Vice Versa." *Journal of the American Statistical Association* 54:30-34.

Stern, Nancy. 1978. "Age and Achievement in Mathematics: A Case-Study in the Sociology of Science." *Social Studies of Science* 8:127-140.

Storer, Norman. 1966. *The Social System of Science*. New York: Holt, Rhinehart and Winston.

Sullivan, Daniel. 1975. "Competition in Bio-Medical Science: Extent, Structure and Consequences." *Sociology of Education* 48:223-241.

Suttmeier, Richard. 1985. "Corruption in Science:

The Chinese Case." *Science, Technology and Human Values* 10:49-61.

Stewart, John A. 1983. "Achievement and Ascriptive Processes in the Recognition of Scientific Articles." *Social Forces* 62:166-189.

———. 1986. "Drifting Continents and Colliding Interests: A Quantitative Application of the Interests Perspective." *Social Studies of Science* 16:261-279.

Stewart, Walter and Ned Feder. 1987. "The Integrity of the Scientific Literature." *Nature* 325:207-214.

Stigler, George. 1980. "Merton on Multiples, Denied and Affirmed." Pp. 143-146 in *Science and Social Structure: A Festschrift for Robert K. Merton*, edited by T. Gieryn. New York: New York Academy of Sciences.

Stigler, Stephen M. 1979. "Burt's Tables." *Science* 204:242-245.

———. 1980. "Stigler's Law of Eponymy." Pp. 147-157 in *Science and Social Structure: A Festschrift for Robert K. Merton, Transactions of the New York Academy of Sciences*, vol. 39, Series II, edited by T. Gieryn.

———. 1986. *The History of Statistics: The Measurement of Uncertainty Before 1900*. Cambridge, MA: Belknap Press.

Sullivan, Daniel, D. Hywell White, and Edward J. Barboni. 1977. "Co-citation Analyses of Science: An Evaluation." *Social Studies of Science* 7:223-241.

Thackray, Arnold and Robert K. Merton. 1972. "On Discipline Building: The Paradoxes of George Sarton." *ISIS* 63:473-495.

Thackray, Arnold, Jeffrey L. Sturchio, P. Thomas Carroll, and Robert Bud. 1987. *Chemistry in America, 1876-1976*. Dordrecht: Reidel.

Tiefer, Lenore. 1978. "The Context and Consequences of Contemporary Sex Research: A Feminist Perspective." Pp. 363-385 in *Sex and Behavior: Status and Prospectus*, edited by T. E. McGill, D. A. Dewsbury, and B. D. Sachs. New York: Plenum.

Toren, Nina. 1980. "The New Code of Scientists." *IEEE Transactions on Engineering Management* EM-27:79-84.

———. 1983. "The Scientific Ethos Debate: A Meta-Theoretical View." *Social Science and Medicine* 17:1665-1672.

Toulmin, Stephen. 1972. *Human Understanding: The Collective Use and Evolution of Concepts*. Princeton, NJ: Princeton University Press.

Travis, G.D.L. 1981. "Replicating Replicanon: Aspects of the Social Construction Learning in Planarian Worms." *Social Studies of Science* 11:11-32.

Waldman, David A. and Bruce J. Avolio. 1986. "A Meta-Analysis of Age Differences in Job Performance." *Journal of Applied Psychology* 71:33-38.

Wallis, Roy. ed. 1979. *On the Margins of Science: The Social Construction of Rejected Knowledge*.

Sociological Review Monograph #27: Keele.

Weinstein, Alexander. 1977. "How Unknown was Mendel's Paper?" *Journal of the History of Biology* 10:341-364.

West, S. S. 1960. "The Ideology of Academic Scientists." *IRE Transactions of Engineering Management* EM-7:54-62.

Westfall, Richard. 1973. "Newton and the Fudge Factor." *Science* 179:751-758.

Westrum, Ron. 1978. "Science and Social Intelligence about Anomalies: The Case of Meteorites." *Social Studies of Science* 8:461-493.

Whitley, Richard. 1972. "Black Boxism and the Sociology of Science: A Discussion of the Major Developments in the Field." Pp. 61-92 in *The Sociology of Science*, vol. 18, edited by P. Halmis. Sociological Review Monograph.

———. 1978. "Types of Science, Organizational Strategies and Patterns of Work in Research Laboratories in Different Scientific Fields." *Social Science Information* 17:427-447.

———. 1984. *The Intellectual and Social Organization of the Sciences*. Oxford: Clarendon Press.

Woolf, Patricia K. 1981. "Fraud in Science: How Much, How Serious?" *Hastings Center Report* 11:9-14.

———. 1986. "Pressure to Publish and Fraud in Science." *Annals of Internal Medicine* 104:254-256.

Woolgar, Steve. 1981. "Interests and Explanation in the Social Studies of Science." *Social Studies of Science* 11:365-394.

———. 1982. "Laboratory Studies: A Comment on the State of the Art." *Social Studies of Science* 12:481-498.

Wynne, Brian. 1976. "C. G. Barkla and the J Phenomenon." *Social Studies of Science* 6:307-347.

Zenzen, Michael and Sal Restivo. 1982. "The Mysterious Morphology of Immiscible Liquids: A Study of Scientific Practice." *Social Science Information* 21:447-473.

Ziman, John. 1968. *Public Knowledge: An Essay Concerning the Social Dimension of Science*. Cambridge, England: Cambridge University Press.

———. 1976. *The Force of Knowledge*. Cambridge, England: Cambridge University Press.

———. 1985. *An Introduction to Science Studies. The Philosophical and Social Aspects of Science and Technology*. Cambridge: Cambridge University Press.

Zuckerman, Harriet. 1970. "Stratification in American Science." *Sociological Inquiry* 40:235-257.

———. 1977a. "Deviant Behavior and Social Control in Science." Pp. 87-137 in *Deviance and Social Change*, edited by E. A. Sagarin. Beverly Hills, CA: Sage.

———. 1977b. *Scientific Elite: Nobel Laureates in the United States*. New York: Free Press.

———. 1978. "Theory Choice and Problem Choice in Science." *Sociological Inquiry* 48:65-95.

———. 1984. "Norms and Deviant Behavior in

Science." *Science, Technology and Human Values* 9:7-13.

———. 1987a. "Persistence and Change in the Careers of American Men and Women Scientists and Engineers: A Review of Current Research." Pp. 123-156 in *Women: Their Underrepresentation and Career Differentials in Science and Engineering*, edited by Linda S. Dix. Washington, DC: National Academy Press.

———. 1987b. "Citation Analysis and the Complex Problem of Intellectual Influence." *Scientometrics* 12:329-338.

——— and Joshua Lederberg. 1986. "Forty Years of Genetic Recombination in Bacteria: A Postmature Discovery?" *Nature* 324:629-631.

Zuckerman, Harriet and Robert K. Merton. 1971. "Patterns of Evaluation in Science: Institutionalization, Structure and Functions of the Referee System." *Minerva* 9:66-100.

———. 1973. "Age, Aging and Age Structure in Science." Pp. 497-559 in *The Sociology of Science*, by Robert K. Merton. Chicago: University of Chicago Press. (Original work published 1972)

17

Medical Sociology

WILLIAM C. COCKERHAM

How do social factors, such as lifestyle, affect health and illness? What are the social functions of health institutions and organizations? What is the relationship of systems of health care delivery to other social systems? What styles of social behavior characterize health personnel and those people who are the consumers of health care? These are typical questions investigated by medical sociologists. Interest in them and the subject matter of medical sociology generally, as well as extensive funding for sociomedical research, has resulted in medical sociology becoming the largest and one of the most active sociological specialties.

For example, more sociologists work in the area of medical sociology than in any other sociological subdiscipline in the United States and Western Europe. Medical sociologists currently comprise the largest sections of the American, British, and German sociological associations. In the United States, over 10% of the membership of the American Sociological Association belonged to the Medical Sociology Section in 1986, easily making it the largest of ASA's 23 specialty groups. In Europe, over 1500 persons in 27 different countries have been identified as medical sociologists (Claus, 1982) and this population provided the basis for the formation of the European Society for Medical Sociology in 1983. Great Britain has a particularly large number of active medical sociologists whose influence resulted in the 1976 British

Sociological Association meetings being devoted to analysis of health issues. In West Germany, the German Society for Medical Sociology, a separate organization, held its 1985 meeting in Hannover and showed a membership larger than the entire German Sociological Association.

Therefore, when it comes to the things that matter in the development of a sociological specialty; namely, a large proportion of practitioners, funded research, employment opportunities both within and outside of academia, a wide selection of textbooks, and a high volume of publications in specialized and general journals, medical sociology appears to be a success. Since its inception, as Fox (1985, p. 7) points out, the scope of matters pertinent to medical sociology has clearly broadened and grown more inclusive as issues of health, medicine, and illness have become a medium through which fundamental issues and concerns about society have been expressed. From a practical standpoint, medical sociology itself seems to be in a healthy state.

The Direction of the Field

However, as Ruderman (1981) reminds us, medical sociology has an aberrant character when compared to sociology's core fields. Unlike law, religion, politics, modes of economic production, and other basic social processes, medicine was ignored by sociology's early theoreticians because it was not an institution shaping the structure and nature of society. In fact, as reflected in Durkheim's (1961) work, modern sociology evolved in strong opposition to theories advanced in the nineteenth century that explained human social behavior on the basis of innate biological characteristics. Rejection of biologism pushed sociology even further away from a concern with medicine.

Medicine, in a similar fashion, had previously abandoned general interest in the social sciences following the success of Pasteur, Koch, and others in advancing the germ theory of disease in the latter half of the nineteenth century. Medicine's thinking had become dominated by the search for drugs as "magic bullets" that could be shot into the body to kill or control illness (DuBos, 1959). Most members of the medical profession were primarily interested in treating their patients and improving the state of medical technology, rather than developing an interest in the social factors associated with health and disease. What stimulated physicians to consider medical sociology as important for medical practice was the realization that, as medicine moves into the twenty-first century, it is increasingly called upon to deal with problems of the "whole person."

This means that physicians will need to know more about the social behavior of the people they treat if they are to be effective in dealing with contemporary health dysfunctions. The major health disorders in urban-industrial societies are no longer the result of communicable diseases, but instead are chronic problems like heart disease and cancer that require insight into how people at risk and under treatment live their daily lives. Lifestyle, in particular is an important variable in life expectancy, not only in regard to heart disease and cancer, but also for sexually transmitted diseases like Acquired Immune Deficiency Syndrome (AIDS).

Sociologists, on the other hand, eventually organized medical sociology as an area of sociological inquiry because of the realization that medicine represented a distinct segment of society. By virtue of having unique social institutions, social processes, occupations, behavioral settings, and implications for the quality of collective living, medical practice began to attract the attention of increasing numbers of sociologists during the late 1940s. The situation has progressed to the point that there is now greater interest in sociology than ever before by health professionals, and sociologists are in return extensively involved in the study of health and illness.

The notion that medical sociology has an aberrant character stems not only from its neglect by sociology's founders, but, more important, from the fact that it matured in an intellectual climate far different from sociology's traditional specialties with direct roots in nineteenth- and early twentieth-century social thought. Rather, medical sociology faced a set of circumstances in its development unlike that of most other sociological subdisciplines.

Pressure for Applied Research

The circumstance having the greatest impact upon the field has been the pressure to produce work that can be applied to medical practice and the formulation of health policy. This pressure originates from medical and government sources, both of which have considerable influence and power with respect to the conduct and financing of sociomedical research and little or no interest in purely theoretical sociology (Cockerham, 1983, 1986).

Yet the tremendous growth of medical sociology in the United States and Western Europe in recent years would not have been possible without the cooperation of the medical profession and the substantial funding for applied studies by the respective governments. In the United States, where medical sociology has reached its most extensive development, the emergence of the field was greatly stimulated by the expansion of the National Institutes of Health in the late 1940s. Especially significant was the establishment of the National Institute of Mental Health, which was instrumental in encouraging and funding joint social and medical projects. According to Johnson (1975, p. 229), "it was through the impetus provided by this injection of money that sociologists and medical men changed their affiliations and embraced the field of medical sociology."

Thus when Gouldner (1970) described the social sciences as a well-financed government effort to help cope with the problems of industrial society and the welfare state in the West during the post-World War II era, he was certainly describing medical sociology.

For instance, in Europe, Claus (1982) found that government funding of research was *the* initial attraction to the field by the majority of respondents in her survey of medical sociologists. Few were primarily affiliated with university departments or institutes of sociology, and ties to the general discipline of sociology were depicted as weak. Work affiliation rather than professional prerequisites typically determined identification as a medical sociologist, and the dominant employment pattern was in applied research, often in a medical institution. Only one-third had any formal training in medical sociology.

Consequently, there exists the strong possibility of tenuous roots in mainstream sociology for many people working as medical sociologists and a professional perspective oriented toward applied rather than theoretical interests. This situation is reinforced by the tendency of increased levels of funding to correspond with increased demands for applied sociology that can be articulated into public policy by the sponsoring agency. Hence, there is pressure for theory to be "relevant" since the greatest resources are likely to go to those practitioners who can meet the demand for practical application. In this context, as Gouldner (1970) observes, the development of social theory is most vulnerable because "pure" theory is often the least practical component of a social science.

With the funding for teaching positions and research coming almost exclusively from medical schools and government agencies in Western Europe, it is not surprising that European medical sociology developed almost entirely in an applied direction. The heritage of traditional European sociology has been largely neglected. Even in those countries such as Great Britain, where medical sociology best reflects its nation's sociological traditions, medical sociology remains policy oriented (Claus, 1982, 1983; Horobin, 1985). In most countries, it was only after medical sociology was established in medical institutions during the 1960s that links with general sociology were attempted. While medical sociology is, as Claus (1982, p. 85) describes it, "alive and well in Europe," the field has developed with the sponsorship of medicine rather than sociology, and only recently have there been increased efforts to incorporate traditional sociology into medical sociological work.

Medical sociology began somewhat earlier in the United States (the late 1940s as compared to the late 1950s) than in Western Europe, but initially followed the same course. The first use of the term "medical sociology" appeared as early as 1894 in an article by McIntire on the importance of social factors in health, followed by essays on the relationship between medicine and society in 1902 by Blackwell, the first woman medical school graduate in America,

and later by Warbasse in 1909. But these early publications were produced by persons more concerned with medicine than sociology and it was not until 1927 that Stern published the first work from a sociological perspective, which dealt with social factors in medical progress. A few publications followed during the 1930s, but it was not until after World War II that medical sociology began in earnest as significant amounts of federal funding for sociomedical research became available.

Under the auspices of the National Institute of Mental Health, medical sociology's initial alliance with medicine was with psychiatry, a medical specialty that was undergoing a struggle of its own for professional status within its wider discipline. At this time, the discovery and testing of the psychotropic drugs that were to revolutionize psychiatric practice in the mid-1950s had not taken place. A basis for cooperation between sociologists and psychiatrists existed as a result of earlier important epidemiological research such as that conducted in Chicago by Faris and Dunham (1939). A particularly significant result of this postwar cooperation was the publication in 1958 of *Social Class and Mental Illness: A Community Study* by Hollingshead (a sociologist) and Redlich (a psychiatrist). This landmark research produced important evidence that social factors were correlated with different types of mental disorders and the manner in which people received psychiatric care. This study attracted international attention and is probably the best-known single study in the world of the relationship between mental disorder and social class. This book played a key role in the debate during the 1960s leading to the establishment of community mental centers in the United States, as did other significant joint projects involving sociologists and psychiatrists, such as the Midtown Manhattan study of Srole and his colleagues (1962).

Monies from federal and private organizations also helped stimulate cooperation between sociologists and physicians in regard to sociomedical research on problems of physical health. The Russell Sage Foundation funded a program in 1949 to improve the utilization of social science research in medical practice. One result of this program was the publication of *Social Science in Medicine* (Simmons and Wolff, 1954). Other work sponsored by the Sage Foundation came later and included Suchman's *Sociology and the Field of Public Health* (1963). Suchman described how sociology could be applied to the practice of public health. Thus the direction of medical sociology in the United States at the point in the 1940s and 1950s where large-scale funding first became available was principally toward an applied approach.

Parsons

However, a critical event occurred in 1951 that began the reorientation of American medical sociology in a theoretical direction. This was the appearance of Parsons's *The Social System*. This book, written to explain a complex functionalist model of society in which social systems are linked to corresponding systems of personality and culture, contained Parsons's concept of the sick role. Unlike other major social theorists preceding him, Parsons formulated an analysis of the function of medicine in his view of society. In the mid-1930s, Parsons had made the decision to study professional roles in relation to capitalism and socialism (Parsons, 1981). The relationship of the professional to his or her client seemed to fit neither the popular notion of a self-interested, profit-maximizing capitalist nor that of an equalitarian socialist. Among the professions, Parsons choose medicine because it was an area of long-standing interest and one in which he felt he had a relatively good command of empirical material dealing with physician-patient relationships (Parsons, 1951).

In his investigation of the social significance of medical practice, Parsons was led to consider the role of the sick person in relation to the social system within which that person lived. This led him to formulate a concept of the sick role based on four major components: (1) the sick person is exempt from "normal" social roles, (2) the sick person is not responsible for his or her condition, (3) the sick person should try to get well, and (4) the sick person should seek technically competent help. Inherent in this concept is the notion that exemption from normal roles requires legitimation from a physician as the authority on what constitutes sickness, that some curative process apart from personal willpower is needed to recover, and that exemption from usual activities involves an obligation to get well that includes a further obligation to seek help from a technically competent practitioner, typically a physician. The merit of the sick role is that it describes a patterned set of expectations that define the norms and values appropriate to being sick, both for the individual and others who interact with the sick person. This allows us, under certain conditions, both

to understand and to predict the behavior of the ill in Western society.

Yet behind this model, described by some as an ideal representation of acting sick rather than a fixed concept depicting similarities of behavior in all sick people (Cockerham, 1986; Segall, 1976), is a direct link to the classical social theory of Durkheim and Weber and the psychoanalytic theory of Freud. Drawing on Freud's ideas of transference and countertransference, Parsons constructed analogies between the roles of parent-child and physician-patient to demonstrate the dependent status of the sick person. Furthermore, Freud's theories of the structure of the personality and the unconscious assisted Parsons in developing his ideas on the function of individual motivation in social systems. Although Parsons's utilization of psychoanalytic theory in his concept of the sick role is sometimes forgotten (Gerhardt, 1979), Freud's views on motivation are an integral feature of Parsons's perspective. The sick person is presumably motivated to recover (as a result of socialization and the formation of the superego) and yet may perhaps also be motivated, either consciously or unconsciously, to desire the "secondary gain" of privileges and exemptions from normal social roles that accompany sick-role legitimation.

Parsons also uses the work of Durkheim (on moral authority) and Weber (on religious values) to analyze the socialization process inherent in the sick role (Parsons, 1977). Parsons argues that the physician is invested with the function of social control, similar to the role provided historically by priests, to serve as a means to control deviance. In this case, of course, illness and its dysfunctional nature is the deviance. The designation of illness as undesirable is considered by Parsons to have the greatest implications for the healthy in that it reinforces their motivation to stay well. All of this is reflected in the position of health as a positive value in society and the manner in which people are socialized to accept it as such. Therefore, as Muench (1982) notes, Parsons's work allows for a particularly fruitful interpretation of the classics that unites the contributions of Freud, Durkheim, and Weber into a general scheme of social action. By incorporating a consideration of health and illness into this concept, Parsons was the first to demonstrate the controlling function of medicine in macro-level social systems and did so within the parameters of classical theory.

Claims have been advanced that Parsons's concept of the sick role represents the most important single theoretical contribution to medical sociology to date (Fox, 1979; Wolinsky, 1980). The justification for this claim is that Parsons's sick role provides the most consistent and systematic analysis of the behavior of the sick in Western society. Another reason, however, can be offered to support the significance of the concept. That is, just having a theorist of Parsons's stature render the first major theory in medical sociology called needed attention to the young subdiscipline—especially among academic sociologists. Not only was Parsons's concept of the sick role "a penetrating and apt analysis of sickness from a distinctly sociological view" (Freidson, 1970b, p. 62), but it was widely believed in the 1950s that Parsons and his students were charting a future course for all of sociology through the insight to be provided by Parsonian theory generally (Johnson, 1975).

Undoubtedly, Parsons's sick role stimulated a considerable body of research in medical sociology (Arluke, Kennedy, and Kessler, 1979; Berkanovic, 1972; Cockerham, 1986; Gallagher, 1976; Gordon, 1966; Twaddle, 1979; Wolinsky and Wolinsky, 1981). Much of this research was critical of Parsons and focused on how the sick role (1) failed to account for variation in the behavior of different groups, (2) seemed to apply more to acute illness than chronic problems, (3) was a limited version of the physician-patient relationship, and (4) had a middle-class orientation. Although this criticism was to subsequently lessen the acceptance of Parsons's ideas, this does not negate the influence Parsons had on promoting debate and research in medical sociology. Perhaps Gallagher (1976) says it best when he points out that whosoever begins to acquire a sociologically informed understanding of health and illness in contemporary society soon realizes how significantly sociological analysis has benefited from Parsons's formulation of the sick role and how, in comparison, many criticisms of it perhaps seem petty and minor. For example, the finding that some ethnic groups interpret sick role behavior differently (Zborowski, 1952; Zola, 1966) does not erase the fact that Parsons's concept is useful in explaining how members of all socioeconomic strata desire "to get well" (Twaddle, 1979) and how elderly and low-income persons use the sick role to justify a disadvantaged social position (Arluke, Kennedy, and Kessler, 1979; Cole and LeJeune, 1972; Wolinsky and Wolinsky, 1981).

For that matter, it has been argued that in no other area of sociology has Parsons's approach achieved a more influential position than in medical sociology, regardless of the fact that a significant proportion of medical sociologists are not especially sympathetic to the Parsonian view. Others, such as Ruderman (1981), take Parsons to task for removing medical sociology from the purview of medicine. In being a distinctly sociological concept, the sick role had directed the perspective of medical sociologists outside of medicine exclusively toward theoretical sociology. It was Ruderman's position that medical sociology was harmed by the hold of Parsonian theory because it oriented sociological interest in medicine toward the purely social aspects of health situations, thereby leading sociologists to fail to consider the entire experience of being ill and to neglect the actual content of medical knowledge.

To a certain extent Ruderman is correct. Parsons's work did demonstrate that analyses of the medical environment could be conducted within parameters that were strictly sociological and grounded in classical social theory. This stimulated medical sociological research that was more concerned with problems involving sociological rather than medical questions. Yet Parsons's approach provided a theoretical basis for medical sociology that brought the subdiscipline the intellectual recognition that it needed in its early development in the United States. The institutional base for sociology in America was in the universities, where the discipline was established more firmly than anywhere else in the world. Without academic legitimacy and the subsequent participation of such well-known, mainstream academic sociologists as Robert Merton, Everett Hughes, Howard Becker, and Erving Goffman, all of whom published research in the field, medical sociology would lack the theoretical credentials and professional position that it currently has in both academic and applied settings. Functionalism may not be the optimal paradigm for explaining illness, but Parsons formulated a concept of the illness experience in relation to society that had a profound effect on the development of medical sociology: Parsons made medical sociology academically respectable.

Sociology in Medicine and of Medicine

Following Parsons, American medical sociology began showing signs of a division in the 1950s. Although considerable overlap existed, it was nonetheless apparent that two different directions in medical sociology were emerging. As Straus (1957) pointed out, medical sociology had divided itself into a sociology *in* medicine and a sociology *of* medicine. Sociologists in medicine performed applied work in which sociological knowledge and research methods were used to provide information useful to health practitioners in improving health care, health organizations in providing more effective services, and to policymaking bodies for the purpose of developing programs and policies intended to improve health conditions in society. Sociology in medicine was thus characterized as applied research and analysis primarily motivated by a medical problem rather than a sociological problem. Sociologists of medicine, in contrast, use sociological knowledge and research methods to explain, generalize, and predict human social behavior in relation to health situations in order to develop, test, and verify theory and contribute to general knowledge of the subject. Sociologists of medicine share the same goals as other areas of sociology in that they study social phenomenon, in this case the medical environment, from the standpoint of sociological questions rather than medical issues.

This division of labor eventually resulted in a certain amount of tension between sociologists doing medical work in applied situations and those doing largely theoretical work, usually in nonmedical academic settings. The argument that evolved between these two groups was over whether sociologists of medicine had more to contribute to sociology than sociologists in medicine.

While medical sociologists affiliated with departments of sociology in universities were in a stronger position to produce work that satisfied sociologists as good sociology, sociologists in medical institutions had the advantage of participation in medicine and opportunities for research perhaps denied to those outside medical practice. Nevertheless, the requirement for the applied medical sociologist to produce work relevant to patient care, medical education, or health policy was a significant factor constraining efforts to contribute fully to sociological knowledge. This circumstance resulted in lessened professional status for applied medical sociologists, even though their work might be more meaningful for health practitioners, policymakers, and the general public. Furthermore, sociologists in medical institutions had status problems there as well since they were not physicians and did not hold dominant roles. Wolinsky et al. (1980) summarized the situation by saying, "it is generally assumed that to be an applied medical sociologist is somewhat analogous to being a prostitute, while being a pure medical sociologist is clearly synonymous with being a scientist."

It is not accurate to say that Parsons was entirely responsible for this conflict. Instead, the demands of the two work environments, one applied and the other academic, actually produced the dichotomy. Nevertheless, Parsons established the potential of medical sociology for theoretically oriented research and, in doing so, provided sociologists of medicine with the advantage of working within the framework of general sociology. Greater professional status thus accrued to those sociologists who reflected this orientation. Parsons's overall contribution was positive, but contributed significantly to the division between the two groups.

Sociologists in medicine, however, found themselves doubly disadvantaged. Not only were they often outside of academic sociology, but in many cases they were also marginal persons in medicine because they were not medical practitioners and not directly involved in patient care. Moreover, some physicians questioned the relevancy of the social sciences for medical education, although the medical profession generally seemed to acknowledge the need for it. Pflanz (1976), commenting on his experiences in West Germany, which could apply to the United States equally well, noted that some of his physician colleagues thought most medical sociologists were public nuisances. "In the opinion of these doctors," stated Pflanz (1976, p. 12), "not only do sociologists wreak potential damage in the faith of patients in medicine, they also criticize medical institutions and, particularly physicians." Sociologists were also blamed for causing medical students to be dubious of the efficacy of medicine and using an unintelligible jargon to exercise elitist power over physicians and patients (which is an ironic response coming from physicians). In short, Pflanz found that some physicians insisted on controlling the work of sociologists if good cooperation was to be possible.

The issue of subordination to medicine was important for sociologists in the medical field. Medical control could easily result in the sociologist being reduced more or less to the position of providing technical assistance to medical projects without being able to exercise autonomous sociological judgment. In medical settings sociological research can be highly dependent upon medical requirements, sponsorship, approval, and perhaps even definition of the research problem. In addition, such research may be subordinated to medical values that presume medicine is inherently "good" because the objective is to relieve human suffering

(Freidson, 1970a). This so-called halo effect can have the potential of influencing the sociologist to adopt medical views and avoid critical findings since medicine's approaches are supposedly in the best interests of humanity.

This situation, of course, contained serious consequences for all sociologists, not just those working in medicine, because it signifies a loss of professional autonomy and integrity. Pflanz (1975) warned against the field becoming simply a propaganda instrument of medical values, while Gold (1977) found that much of the research concerning patients published in the American Sociological Association's *Journal of Health and Social Behavior* between 1960-1976 did indeed reflect an uncritical view of medicine in the reporting of results.

Yet a state of professional crisis, in the end, did not fully materialize. Much of the credit for this development belongs to the sociologists working in medicine who joined with academic medical sociologists in the 1970s and 1980s to produce studies that were not subordinate to medical views. Some of this work was highly critical and detailed, for example, ineffectual efforts on the part of physicians to regulate medical mistakes by peers (Bosk, 1979; Freidson, 1975; Millman, 1977) and sexist treatment of women patients (Ehrenreich and English, 1979; Fisher, 1984; Howell, 1979; Scully, 1980; Scully and Bart, 1979). Other studies focused on the problems of the poor in obtaining quality medical care and dealing with bureaucratic barriers in welfare medicine (Dutton, 1978; Rundall and Wheeler, 1979). Rather than professional domination by medicine, medical sociology has become a major source of social criticism pertaining to health care providers and the systems they manage.

Besides asserting themselves critically, sociologists in medicine have increased their efforts to incorporate social theory in their research and produce sociological knowledge (Twaddle, 1982). In the meantime, sociologists of medicine began publishing extensively on applied subjects, so that it is increasingly difficult to separate applied from academic medical sociology (Cockerham, 1983). Another important factor bringing about convergence is that the expansion of teaching and research positions in medical sociology has largely occurred in medical institutions, with the result that growing numbers of graduates of medical sociology programs in academic sociology departments are being trained for and employed in medicine. Differences in work orientations have been further reduced as a consequence. Additionally, many medical sociologists hold joint appointments in sociology departments and medical schools, giving them a professional base in sociology and the opportunity to work in medicine.

Current reviews of the state of medical sociology and the research literature comprising the field show that its dominant direction is toward applied sociology in that its research has relevance for health practitioners, organizations, and/or policymaking groups, rather than the development of sociological theory (Cockerham, 1983; Horobin, 1985; Wardwell, 1982). That is, most research in medical sociology today, regardless of whether it is in a sociology department in a university or a medical institution, deals with practical problems. However, the bulk of this literature addresses sociological questions instead of medical definitions of health problems and issues. What is indicated here is that American medical sociology has achieved a state of maturity and professional autonomy that allows it to investigate applied health situations in sociological terms. Contemporary medical sociologists are less concerned with whether or not a piece of work is in the sociology of medicine or sociology in medicine, but rather with how much it increases our understanding of the relationship between social factors and health and the organization and provision of health services. Consequently, the division of the field as outlined by Straus (1957) has lost its distinctiveness in the United States and never really developed abroad.

Classical Studies

Although medical sociology is too new to have produced classical studies that compare directly to those of the great masters of sociological thought, such as Durkheim, Weber, and Simmel around the turn of the century, it has nonetheless compiled a number of studies that are classical in the sense that they are the subdiscipline's seminal works. That is, they are the core studies of the field in their respective areas and qualify as basic works that any serious scholar of medical sociology should be familiar with.

First, of course, is Parsons's (1951) concept of the sick role discussed in the previous section. After Parsons, the attention of many sociologists turned to the study of medical education. Merton and his colleagues in *The Student Physician* (1957) extended the functionalist mode of analysis to the socialization of medical students, with Fox's paper on training for uncertainty ranking as a major contribution.

Shortly thereafter, Becker and his associates published *Boys in White* (1961), a study of medical school socialization conducted from a symbolic interactionist perspective. Taken together, these works explained the medical student experience with reference to loss of idealism, growth of detached concern, and coping with medicine's limitations and uncertainty. *Boys in White* also proved important for both its theoretical and methodological content. The techniques in participant observation employed in this work were the basis for the subsequent innovations in both theory and method developed by Glaser and Strauss in *The Discovery of Grounded Theory* (1967) and *Status Passage* (1971), as well as in *Awareness of Dying* (1965) and *A Time for Dying* (1968). These latter books called attention to the social aspects of dying—particularly the problem of death as a solitary experience in the modern hospital, where the dying patient was often found to be both socially and psychologically isolated. Other research in medical education focused on the training of nurses, and much of it, especially the work of Davis (1972), reflected a symbolic interactionist framework of analysis.

With the introduction of symbolic interactionist research into an area previously dominated by functionalism, medical sociology became an arena of debate between two of sociology's major theoretical schools. During the 1960s, symbolic interactionism emerged as *the* major theoretical perspective in medical sociology. Besides studies of medical and nursing students, symbolic interaction was extensively utilized in sociological research dealing with hospital life, mental patients, and physician-patient interaction. Such research provided rich insight into micro-level processes, but its influence declined in the late 1970s with the increased use in medical sociology of multiple regression techniques and other forms of multivariate analysis and the limitations of symbolic interaction in explaining macro-level processes.

Numerous studies in the interactionist tradition utilized labeling theory. Although labeling theory pertained to deviant behavior generally, the primary center of argument about its merits was focused on the mental patient experience. Scheff, with the publication of his book *Being Mentally Ill* (1966), became the principal proponent of the labeling approach in medical sociology and Gove (1970) his principal critic. Scheff explains how labels are more easily applied to socially marginal persons and how this category of individual is most likely to become an inmate of a mental hospital. Gove notes that the stigma associated with being labeled mentally ill is not necessarily permanent, as Scheff claims. The most important defect in labeling theory, however, is that it does not explain what causes mental disorder other than the reactions of others (the social audience) to it, nor does it explain why certain people become mentally ill and why others in the same social circumstances do not. What seems apparent is that prior to the onset of labeling, there exists a troubled mind independent of the labeling process. Attempts were also made to utilize labeling theory as an explanation of physical illness. For example, Freidson (1970b) used a labeling orientation to propose an alternative concept of the sick role, but this formulation has not been as influential as that of Parsons.

Another major work on mental disorder linked to symbolic interaction was Goffman's *Asylums* (1961), a study of life in a mental hospital, which set forth his concept of "total institutions" that emerged as a significant theoretical statement in the general literature of sociology. All in all, an abundant number of studies were published in the 1960s that resulted in making the sociology of mental disorder a major subfield within medical sociology.

Another prominent category of research at this time was in the area of physician utilization. The process of seeking medical care is and remains an important area of research. The basic study in this regard was Koos's *The Health of Regionville* (1954), which demonstrated a significant relationship between social class and perceived symptoms. Lower-class persons were less likely than members of higher social strata to recognize various symptoms as requiring medical attention, and these beliefs, combined with low income, caused differences in actual use of physician services. As for ethnicity, Suchman (1965a) studied beliefs in and acceptance of modern medicine among several ethnic groups in New York City. Building upon Freidson's (1960) concept of the lay referral system, Suchman found the greatest resistance to using a physician's services was in lower-class neighborhoods characterized by strong ethnic identification and extended family relationships. Freidson had shown that lay avenues of influence existed independently of the physician and served to guide a patient either toward or away from a particular practitioner. Related research by Zborowski (1952) and Zola (1966) also produced important information on ethnic variations in the perception of illness. And Suchman (1965b) made a second major contribution by formulating a model of the illness experience showing the different stages of decision making, behavior, and potential outcomes when dealing with sickness.

Forthcoming in 1970 were two books by Freidson, *Professional Dominance* (1970a) and *Profession of Medicine* (1970b), that became major statements on medical professionalism. The impact of these works on the field is illustrated by Fox's (1985, p. 7) comment that medical sociologists have been practically obsessed with analyzing the professional dominance of physicians, their individual autonomy, their insistence on self-regulation and control, and their paternalism and power over the bodies, minds, and behavior of their patients. All of which was set forth by Freidson in an exceptionally thorough display of scholarship, which established his own reputation as a major figure in medical sociology.

Considerable attention was also paid toward improving research design, instrumentation, and the formulating and testing of quantitative models intended to maximize the amount of variance explained. Much of this work has been atheoretical, such as the model developed by Andersen and his colleagues (Aday and Andersen, 1975; Aday, Andersen, and Fleming, 1980; Andersen, Kravits, and Andersen, 1975) accounting for various predisposing, enabling, and need components in the decision to seek medical care. Yet such models represent advances in methodological techniques and provide useful information by predicting patterns of physician utilization.

Consequently, medical sociology has an impressive foundation of basic literature, showing both theoretical and methodological substance, firmly establishing the subdiscipline as a major area of sociological enterprise. Having discussed the direction of medical sociology and briefly noted its major works, we now turn our focus toward examining areas of research commanding the attention of many contemporary medical sociologists. The topics selected for review here are all areas in medical sociology that are currently experiencing significant change, including: (1) health differences between men and women, (2) social stratification in relation to health and physician utilization, (3) increasing numbers of women physicians, and (4) decline in the status and autonomy of physicians.

Health Differences of Men and Women

As Verbrugge (1985) points out, there is renewed interest in investigating the health differences of men and women because of changes in the way that people now live. The lives of men and women used to be more predictable in that men typically behaved in certain ways and women in others. Thus gender differences in activities, goals, and life expectancy were taken for granted and more or less anticipated. But Verbrugge indicates that important clues are emerging that show the American population may be shifting toward greater equality in mortality between the sexes. This statement is based upon evidence that sex differences for some major causes of death have either become stable, decreased, or only slowly widened. Considerable speculation exists with respect to the possible effects on female longevity posed by their increased participation in the labor force and changes in lifestyle, but it will be several years—until the present cohort dies—before these effects can be fully determined.

Yet we are already seeing such changes as a decline in lung cancer among white males because of reduced smoking, while lung cancer has increased among women as a result of greater numbers of females taking up cigarettes in the 1940s. Figure 17.1 depicts the rapid rise in lung cancer mortality (an average increase of 6.2% annually between 1950 and 1983) among American females. Consequently, as Figure 17.1 shows, lung cancer has moved past stomach and colorectal cancer to nearly overtake breast cancer as the leading cause of cancer deaths among women.

Furthermore, while the proportion of men who smoke declined from 53% in 1964 to 35% in 1983, the proportion of women who smoke has remained at approximately 30% throughout the same period. Among smokers, older men have been quitting smoking at a rate double that of older women. The proportion of adolescent girls who smoke is now about the same as that of boys. Over time these patterns are likely to promote a significant change in differences in life expectancy between men and women.

In the meantime, it is clear that women still have a higher life expectancy than men—showing an average in 1985 of 78.2 years for females and 71.2 years for males. Male death rates generally exceed female deaths at all ages, as well as for the leading causes of death like heart disease, cancer, cerebrovascular diseases, accidents, and pneumonia. Women tend to suffer from more frequent illnesses and disability, but their usual health disorders are often not as serious or as life threatening as those encountered by men. Women, for example, have higher rates of acute illnesses, such as infectious and parasitic diseases and digestive and respiratory conditions. The rates for acute conditions not related to pregnancy is 11 times greater for females than males. Yet women, especially in later life, also die from the same causes as men so what should be kept in mind, as Verbrugge (1985, p. 163) observes, is "that men and women essentially suffer the same *types* of problems; what distinguishes the sexes is the *frequency* of those problems and the *pace* of death." The fact that women are sick more often but live longer and men are sick less often but die sooner contributes to making this situation more complex.

Suggestions have been made that women do not have more illness and disability, but are just more sensitive to their bodily discomforts and more willing to report their symptoms. The best evidence indicates, however, that the differences in morbidity are indeed real (Gove and Hughes, 1979; Nathanson, 1977). When it comes to the risk factors associated with higher mortality, the preponderance of the risks still accrue to males (Waldron, 1983).

Biological and social-psychological differences combine to account for greater male mortality at present. The lessened biological durability of males is evident in mortality rates from the prenatal and neonatal (newborn) stages of life onward. The chances of dying during the prenatal stage are about 12 percent higher for males and 130% greater during the neonatal stages because of a variety of respiratory, circulatory, and other disorders more common to male babies. Males are also subject to more severe bacterial infections as newborns. Females are less

likely to get childhood leukemia and have a better chance of survival when they do, and, as adults, may be protected somewhat from heart disease by sex hormones (estrogen) up to the time of menopause.

The social-psychological aspects of morbidity and mortality attract sociologists to this area and, as Verbrugge (1985) found in her review of relevant studies, these factors appear relatively more important than biological differences in adults. Here the focus of researchers is upon the health risks associated with differential roles, occupational stress, lifestyles, perception of symptoms, and participation in preventive health care. Women consult with physicians more often, assume the sick role more readily, and appear to take better care of themselves in general. Males have more accidents, show greater use of alcohol, illegal drugs, and cigarettes (despite the significant decline in male smokers), and are exposed to greater job-related stress. The lifestyle of the male business executive or professional, with his emphasis upon "career" and "success," as well as a tendency to overwork is believed to contribute strongly to high rates of coronary heart disease. Among lower-class men, higher levels of obesity and smoking, along with less leisure-time exercise and poorer diet, join with the stress that accompanies a life of poverty to produce especially high rates of heart disease for this group, too. The risk of dying from cancer is also higher than average for unemployed or underemployed men who live alone in poor, overcrowded urban neighborhoods because of the lessened chances of early

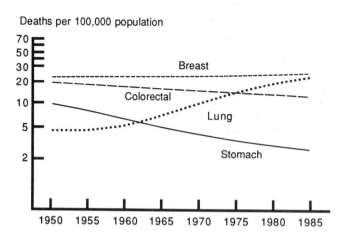

FIGURE 17.1
Age-Adjusted Death Rates for Lung, Breast, Colorectal, and Stomach Cancer Among Females: United States, 1950-83

SOURCE: National Center for Health Statistics, *Health United States, 1985* (Washington, D.C.: U.S. Government Printing Office, 1985)

detection of cancer and exposure to health conditions that make death more likely once cancer occurs (Jenkins, 1983).

When it comes to mental distress, the most disabling disorder, schizophrenia, shows rates about the same for men and women. But certain long-standing differences have remained remarkably persistent over the years, namely the significantly higher rates of depression and anxiety among women and personality disorders among men. While biological factors may be important here, the different social roles and life experiences of men and women appear to also be significant contributing factors. What is needed, as suggested by Dohrenwend and Dohrenwend (1976), is to determine what there is in the endowments and experiences of men and women that push them in these different directions. Relevant research includes analysis of the role of the housewife, the strain of employment outside the home for women concurrent with the raising of children, and the quality of personal relationships between spouses (Cleary and Mechanic, 1983; Gove, Hughes, and Style, 1983: Gove and Tudor, 1973; Mirowsky, 1985). Findings suggest that men and women who are both married and employed are the healthiest, but nonmarried women who are employed and have children have the poorest health. Although research is being done, more work is needed to fully determine the relative contributions of sociological factors relevant to gender in relation to both mental and physical health.

Social Stratification and Health

A particularly active and important area of research in medical sociology involves study of the relationship between social class and health care. Prior to the late 1960s, the socially and economically disadvantaged in American society were significantly less likely to utilize a physician's services than the more affluent (Andersen and Anderson, 1979; Koos, 1954). However, with the advent of Medicare and Medicaid public health insurance programs, persons with the lowest socioeconomic status obtained more equitable access to professional health care. While serious problems remain for the poor with respect to quality of care and the proportion of care they receive relative to their generally poorer levels of health, the literature shows that the financial barrier to health care is no longer so formidable (Dutton, 1978; Rundall and Wheeler, 1979). The result is that the poor are now visiting physicians more often than ever

before. The more affluent, in contrast, have shown a declining rate of physician utilization since the 1970s (Andersen and Anderson, 1979; National Center for Health Statistics, 1983).

The pattern of physician utilization in the United States is clear. The middle and upper socioeconomic groups continue to maintain the highest levels of health and participate more in preventive care. The lower class has more illness and disability and visits physicians more for treatment of symptoms. When overall rates of visits to medical doctors are considered, the lower class visits physicians the most often.

Health Problems of the Poor

Although the poor are showing the highest rates of physician utilization, significant problems remain. Cutbacks in support of welfare programs by the federal government in the 1980s may undermine the ability of the poor to pay for health services and some hospitals have limited the number of Medicare and Medicaid patients they will accept. The poor also have the worst nutrition and housing. They still receive fewer health services in relation to actual need, cope with more bureaucratic agencies, have less quality medical care, and return after treatment to living situations that are less conducive to good health. Nevertheless, the poor are utilizing physicians more frequently than members of higher social strata, and while Medicare and Medicaid may not have met all the needs of the aged and the poor for which they were intended, they have provided health services for these groups where such services were not previously available.

But improved access to medical care by itself cannot reverse the adverse effects of poverty on health. Following World War II, socialized medicine was introduced to Great Britain to provide the lower classes with the same medical care available to the upper classes. Only health care was equalized—poverty and social class differences remained. Results have shown that equalization of health care alone did not reduce the disparity in health between social classes (Susser, Watson, and Hopper, 1985). Even though life expectancy increased for each socioeconomic group, the gap between the rich and poor in mortality remained because living conditions and lifestyle could not be equalized. The physical environment of poverty and poor nutrition continued to adversely affect lower-class health.

Hollingsworth (1981) investigated this situation and suggests that societies wishing to equalize levels of health across social classes should consider equalizing income and educational attainment. Utilizing British data, Hollingsworth hypothesized that as medical technology becomes more effective and the costs increase, there will be a rising public demand for the state to increase its responsibility for providing health services. This will result in greater centralization of decision making. And, as medical care systems come under centralized control, health services should become more accessible to all social classes and regions, thereby producing a convergence in levels of health. In Great Britain, public demand for greater government involvement in providing medical care, influenced by rising costs, did bring about the centralization of care under a National Health Service (NHS). The NHS made those services more accessible to all social classes, but there was not a convergence in levels of health across classes (however, there was some convergence across regions of the country). Mortality rates for all classes declined, but the differences remained. Everyone in Britain tended to live longer than previously, but the upper class continued to live longer than anyone else. This took place even though the lower classes over time began using medical services more often than the middle and upper classes.

In the United States, we find a similar situation in that the middle and upper classes are enjoying the best health and longer lives—despite the availability of public health insurance for the poor. The lower class suffers more from communicable diseases, such as influenza and tuberculosis, that have traditionally made them feel worse and shortened their lives, as well as from accidents, violence, and chronic disorders, including even coronary heart disease, which has traditionally been associated with an affluent way of life. Current research shows that rates of coronary heart disease have declined dramatically in the past 25 years for all Americans, but the decline is significantly greater in the middle and upper classes (Susser, Watson, and Hopper, 1983). The reason for this development is that more obesity and smoking, as well as increased amounts of stressful experiences and weaker coping capabilities occur among people in unskilled and semiskilled occupations, in addition to higher levels of blood pressure, less leisure-time exercise, and poorer diets. Thus heart disease is now concentrated more in the lower socioeconomic brackets, ranging from the working class downward to the lowest echelon of society.

The lower class remains especially disadvantaged in regard to health. This disadvantage extends not only to communicable diseases that are more prevalent in impoverished, overcrowded neighborhoods, but also to chronic disorders like heart disease, arteriosclerosis, and cirrhosis of the liver that are strongly affected by lifestyle. Clearly, there is more to health than the availability of medical care. Several twentieth-century scholars, for example, have found that the decline in deaths from infectious diseases in the second half of the nineteenth century was due more to improvements in diet, housing, public sanitation, and personal hygiene than to medical innovations (Levine, Feldman, and Elinson, 1983; McKeown, 1979; McKinley and McKinley, 1981).

In recent times, lifestyle and social/environmental conditions, along with preventive health measures, primarily determines the level of health maintained by most people. A healthy lifestyle includes the use of good personal habits such as eating properly, getting enough rest, exercising, and avoiding smoking, abusing alcohol, and taking drugs. Yet the type of lifestyle that promotes a healthy existence seems more typical of the upper and middle classes, who have the resources to support it. The most important relationship between social class and health is the manner in which social class affects the opportunities a person has for a generally healthy life. Crowded living conditions, poor diet, inferior housing, low levels of income and education, and enhanced exposure to violence, alcoholism and problem drinking, and drug abuse—all combine to decrease the life chances of the poor.

Attitudes Toward Physicians

Although the health of the lower class remains relatively worse than that of the classes above them, all Americans have seen a general improvement in their health and life expectancy during the twentieth century. Furthermore, increased physician utilization by the poor since the mid-1960s has undoubtedly contributed to a better health situation for this deprived group. Since the utilization rates of the disadvantaged have increased, the question arises over whether their attitudes about going to the doctor have changed as well.

Studies done in the 1950s and 1960s suggested that poverty produced beliefs and values inhibiting the use of physician services (Koos, 1954; Strauss, 1969; Suchman, 1965a; Zola, 1966). This research concluded that the poor generally held beliefs that were not congruent with scientific medical care, were skeptical about the intentions of doctors, and were less sensitive to the meaning of symptoms. The strength of these attitudes and their potential effect upon the manner that lower-class persons managed their health was evident in research reported by Susser and Watson (1971) on physician use in Great Britain during the first 10-15 years after the introduction of socialized medicine. Improved medical care was available at no cost for the poor, yet they continued to use self-treatment if possible and delay in seeking professional care. Susser and Watson suggested that this was a case of cultural lag in which changes in the cultural orientation of the lower class lagged behind the financial and structural changes in the British system of health care delivery. This orientation eventually changed, however, and the poor in Britain now consult with doctors more than members of the other social classes, as is the case in the United States (Reid, 1981).

One would expect that after removing the financial constraints on health care, the attitudes of the disadvantaged toward professional medicine would likewise change. With increasing opportunities for the less privileged to receive health care, such as in Great Britain with socialized medicine and in the United States with Medicare and Medicaid, it seems likely that the attitudes of dependent groups would become more positive. Initially the literature in the United States did not generally support this conclusion. Instead, these studies indicated that the poor continued to hold nonprofessional health orientations and have negative attitudes toward physicians (Dutton, 1978; Rundall and Wheeler, 1979). Perhaps the United States experienced a cultural lag similar to that observed in Great Britain, in which at first, even with financial barriers lessened, the poor persisted in their old attitudes and practices and then gradually adopted new norms about when and from whom to seek health care.

This is what is indicated as more data became available (Stahl and Gardner, 1976; Sharp, Ross, and Cockerham, 1983). Sharp and colleagues (1983), for instance, found that blacks and the less educated had more positive attitudes toward visiting physicians and were more likely than whites and the better educated to think that certain symptoms were serious enough to require the attention of a physician. These findings showed that the attitudes of blacks and less educated persons, coupled with their higher prevalence of reported symptoms, acted to promote physician utilization among these groups. As for persons with higher levels of education, Sharp and colleagues speculated that they may

be taking more responsibility for their health and feeling less inclined to visit a doctor. "More educated persons," state Sharp et al. (1983, p. 261), "may be very (perhaps overly) discriminating in deciding which symptoms warrant a physician's attention because they wish to maintain control over their own health."

Class Differences in Health Self-Management

The literature suggests that the middle and upper classes feel more responsible for maintaining their health. Support for this statement can be found in the tendency of the more affluent to visit doctors for preventive care, while the poor visit physicians primarily for the treatment of overt symptoms of illness (Dutton, 1978). Widespread interest among college-educated persons in health-protective activities like dieting and exercise (i.e., jogging, aerobic dancing) lend credence to such a conclusion (Harris and Guten, 1979; Lueschen, 1983). All of this points toward more of a consumer orientation toward health among the affluent. In a free market situation, health consumers have more power (although they may be subject to more attempts at manipulation by doctors and business enterprises) than they do in a system of socialized or state medicine. The power of the health consumer lies in having the freedom to choose one's source and mode of health care, and laypersons, as Freidson's (1960) discussion of the lay referral system made clear, do judge technical performance regardless of whether they are trained to do so. And they make decisions about doctors based upon these evaluations, usually in consultation with their friends and relatives.

According to Reeder (1972), the concept of a person as a "health consumer" rather than a "patient" became established during the 1960s in the United States. Physicians, in this context, were defined as "health providers." In an age of consumerism, the traditional physician-patient relationship is significantly modified. This modification includes the patient exerting more control and assuming a more equal footing with the doctor in terms of status, decision making, and responsibility for outcomes. The trend toward consumerism in medicine is similar to consumerism in other aspects of American life in which people make informed choices about the services available to them. This activity is thought to be more characteristic of the middle and upper classes than the socially and economically disadvantaged. Consequently, those persons with the lowest socioeconomic status, who are the major participants in welfare medicine, may have a much greater willingness to invest responsibility for their health in the health care delivery system when sick. This suggestion is consistent with Parsons's (1951) concept of the sick role, where it has been found that those persons with low incomes are the most likely to agree that people should not be held responsible for their illnesses (Cole and LeJeune, 1972; Arluke, Kennedy, and Kessler, 1979; Wolinsky and Wolinsky, 1981).

Arluke and colleagues (1979) suggest that acceptance of the notion that illness is not the responsibility of the sick person may be related to broader class differences in imputation of responsibility. That is, lower-class persons may tend to have a more passive orientation toward life in general and less willingness to take responsibility for problems. Certainly this is what is shown by the locus-of-control literature that reports members of the lower class having more fatalistic attitudes and being more accepting of external forces controlling their lives, including situations involving tuberculosis and psychological distress (Ross, Mirowsky, and Cockerham, 1983; Seeman and Evans, 1962; Wheaton, 1980). A weak sense of internal control has been significantly associated with less self-initiated preventive care, less optimism about the effectiveness of early treatment, poorer self-rated health, more illness, more bed confinement, and greater dependence upon physicians (Seeman and Seeman, 1983).

All of this points toward the existence of important perceptual differences between the classes with respect to their health. Studies in the United States (Rosenblatt and Suchman, 1964) and West Germany (Siegrist and Bertram, 1970, 1971) have explained such differences in the utilization of preventive care on the basis of less deferred gratification among the poor. The poor tend to be more present oriented, dealing principally with symptoms as they rise, while the affluent focus more on maintaining their health for the future and thus apply themselves more fully to prevention.

Moreover, d'Houtaud and Field (1984) found in France that upper- and middle- class persons emphasized a personalized view of health as a realization of self. Health was seen as a personal value to be sought and cultivated for one's own personal benefit, such as experiencing increased vitality and enjoyment of life. The lower class, in contrast, expressed a more utilitarian perspective in which health was viewed simply as the ability to work. Health was seen as a means to an end, instead of an end in itself. Results such

as these suggest that the more affluent will engage in a variety of activities to stay fit, while the disadvantaged will use doctors as best they can to keep going.

Since lifestyle appears to be such an important component of this situation, Weber's (1958, 1965) concept of status groups and the lifestyle dimension seems to provide a stronger theoretical explanation than the Marxian model with its emphasis upon material life-chances and social class. It was Weber's position that while class was an objective dimension of social life, signified by amounts of money or property, status was subjective in that it consisted largely of how much esteem a person was accorded by other people. Status was derived particularly from one's lifestyle, but also from education and occupation. As Weber (1958, p. 187) explained it, prestige was "normally expressed by the fact that above all else a specific *style of life* can be expected from all those who wish to belong to the circle." Lifestyle itself was based on what one consumed, rather than what one produced. Thus for Weber the difference between status groups did not lie in their relationship to the means of production, but in their relationship to the means of consumption. Hence, a status group refers to people who share similar material circumstances, prestige, levels of education and occupation, and political influence, as well as displaying the same lifestyle and social perspectives associated with it.

The relevance of this concept for analyzing health is that with increased access to medical care by the poor due to the lowering of the financial barrier, attitudes and personal initiative concerning a person's health may be related more to lifestyle than finances. As previously noted, the type of lifestyle that enhances one's health is thought to be more typical of the middle and upper classes. Yet it was also Weber's contention that lifestyles frequently spread beyond the groups in which they originate. The best example is Weber's analysis of the spread of the *Protestant Ethic* into the general culture of Western society. While lifestyles set people apart, Weber shows us that aspects of a particular group's lifestyle can also gain widespread influence in the larger society.

Cockerham et al. (1986) sought to determine whether lifestyles pertaining to the self-management of one's health had spread throughout society since the poor had gained more equitable access to the health care delivery system. Using data collected from a statewide sample of adults living in Illinois, it was found that considerable similarity existed between status groups in certain lifestyles pertaining to appearance, food habits, exercise, smoking, and alcohol use. Exercise, for example, emerged as a behavioral pattern that people from all social classes accepted as something a person should do and that most people say they attempt in some form, ranging from short walks to participation in sports. When it came to food habits, most people, regardless of socioeconomic position, attempted to obtain the best nutritional value in the food available to them, avoid chemical additives, and the like.

But this study also found important status group differences in respect to symptom perception, physician utilization, and sense of control over one's health situation. Persons with higher socioeconomic status were more consumer-minded and expressed greater personal responsibility for their own health. The poor were less discriminating in deciding which symptoms warranted a doctor's attention. When ill, the poor reported they visited doctors more or less routinely, even for minor ailments, while the more affluent appeared more likely to engage in self-treatment or to recognize minor ailments as self-limiting and likely to disappear in a day or two without a physician's services. The poor also expressed a lessened sense of personal control over their health. Thus the poor seemed to be relatively passive recipients of professional health services with a significantly greater likelihood of investing responsibility for their own health in the health care system than in themselves.

Consequently, when it comes to the self-management of one's health, studies such as the above point to an interesting contrast in the health practices of the poor. Persons in lower socioeconomic groups may be attempting to participate in middle-class health lifestyles in accordance with their level of capability, but adopting a distinctly more dependent posture in interacting with physicians and the health care system. If middle-class values have spread, in a Weberian sense, to the lower class in regard to health advancing behavior, why have they not also spread in relation to coping with medical doctors and institutions?

The answer seems to lie within the cultural context of both poverty and medical practice. The culture of poverty, as summarized by Rundall and Wheeler (1979), is a phenomenon in which poverty, over time, influences the development of certain social and psychological traits among those trapped within it. These traits include dependence, fatalism, inability to delay gratification, and lower valuation of health which, in turn, tends to reinforce the disadvantaged social position of the poor. Research

testing the relative strengths of the financial, cultural, and systems barriers to physician utilization among the lower class found that the culture of poverty barrier still draws some support, although much less so than in the past (Dutton, 1978; Rundall and Wheeler, 1979). The strongest barrier appears to be the systems barrier, which consists largely of adverse psychological reactions to the organization, structure, and bureaucratic administration of welfare medicine. The weakest barrier is financial.

While the culture of poverty may have a lingering significance for explaining physician utilization, initially in delaying use of medical services (Becker, 1974; Berkanovic and Reeder, 1974; Koos, 1954; Langlie, 1977) and more recently in facilitating such use (Sharp, Ross, and Cockerham, 1983; Stahl and Gardner, 1976), another important factor in this situation is the role of medical technology. The development of a complex array of medical equipment and procedures has increasingly taken away the self-management of health from laypersons, but especially from those at the bottom of society with their more limited levels of education and experience with technology. When direct collaboration with medical practitioners is required, the poor become even more dependent.

However, other more able persons have reacted to the professional dominance of physicians with increased skepticism of physicians—service orientation and an emerging belief that physicians should not always be completely in charge of the physician-patient relationship (Haug and Lavin, 1981, 1983). They have assumed more of a consumer position with regard to health care. That is, they are making decisions on their own about which steps are most appropriate for them in dealing with doctors and maintaining their health. In doing so, they are becoming less dependent on physicians and rejecting the traditional physician-patient relationship for one of provider-consumer.

This leads us to consider the influence of the culture of medicine. The culture of medicine neither encourages consumerism among laypersons when direct physician-patient interaction is required, nor provides a context within which such an orientation can grow within the medical environment. Instead, physicians appear as all-powerful individuals with the training and intellect to make life-or-death judgments and patients as completely dependent on those judgments. Consumerism and equality is not promoted because of the physician's requirement to have leverage over the patient. In the medical view, leverage is needed since treatment may be painful and discomforting and the patient typically lacks the expertise to treat the disorder (Parsons, 1951).

Yet physicians have been known to place the technical application of medical procedures ahead of other interests. Van den Berg (1978), for example, notes case histories in which persons suffering terrible physician and mental damage were kept alive by artificial means simply because the doctor was able to do it. The image of the physician that Van den Berg projects is that of a technician who has become so absorbed in the power of medicine that the morality of the situation and the quality of life available to the patient after treatment is neglected. Medicine is depicted as being narrowly oriented toward the preservation of all human life, unconditionally and regardless of the consequences. Such an approach places patients in general, but the poor in particular, in the position of hostages to medical power.

This situation suggests that the culture of medicine is ultimately more important in explaining the health and illness behavior of the poor than that of the culture associated with poverty. One consequence of the increased frequency of contact between the medical profession and the poor appears to be that medical values have spread to the lower class. Accepting responsibility and self-management for diet, exercise, smoking, and other health-advancing behavior is strongly encouraged by the mass media and the medical profession. Physicians actively promote and reinforce the practice of health-advancing behavior. But consumerism and enhanced self-management in dealing with doctors and the health care system is not similarly encouraged or reinforced. Therefore, we have a circumstance in which self-management and responsibility for health among the lower class appears to develop when it is positively sanctioned by social institutions, but fails to flourish where there are negative sanctions.

The trend for the immediate future in the use of physician services seems to be one in which the more affluent and better educated are likely to be more discriminating in their use of doctors. They likely will take a consumer approach, shopping for the appropriate services, making their own decisions about their symptoms and what they mean, and dealing with physicians on a more equal basis than before. The poor, conversely, appear likely to continue seeing doctors more frequently than members of the other social strata, both because they have more illness and disability and because they have more of a tendency to invest responsibility for their problems in the health care delivery system itself. In doing so, they appear less likely to question the authority or judgments of doctors, while assuming doctors will cure them. Whether the lower class evolves toward having more of a consumer orientation in interacting with physicians will have to be determined by future research. The environment to support such a development does not appear to exist at present. Whether it will develop out of participation in lifestyles oriented toward health-advancing behavior remains to be seen, since the poor remain especially dependent upon the medical profession as experts and in this sector increased equality in the nature of a provider-client relationship for doctors and patients is not encouraged.

Women Physicians

In the past the American medical profession has been predominately white and almost exclusively male. In fact, the entire occupational structure of medicine has had decidedly racist and sexist overtones. Most occupations performing patient care can be classified as paramedical because they are organized around the work of the physician and are usually under the physician's direct control. The "doctor's orders" typically provides them with their work requirements. The largest concentration of racial minority persons and women working in medicine is among paramedical workers. Nursing tasks in particular occur in a system of social relationships that are highly stratified by sex. The registered nurse, who has the most advanced training and professional qualifications of any of the workers performing nursing care, is generally a female who is matched occupationally with a physician, whose role is dominant and who is usually a male. The registered nurse, in turn, supervises lesser trained females (practical nurses and nurse's aides) and lesser trained males (orderlies and attendants). Thus emerges the traditional stereotype of the physician as a father figure and the nurse as a mother figure. "This perception," according to Mauksch (1972, p. 217), "creates a woman who serves sacrificially, who supports and protects a dominant male, and who identifies her successes as a nurse with her successes as a woman."

But what is likely to have a far-reaching effect upon this stereotype and perhaps on the medical profession as well is the increasing number of women entering and graduating from medical school. Future studies of medical students, such as that of the Becker et al. book, *Boys in White* (1961), can no longer be titled in a masculine fashion because its contents will no longer reflect an exclusively male experience. Although the majority of medical students in the United States remain white and male, since the 1960s the percentage of racial minorities has risen from 3% to 14%, and women from 9% to 30% of entering medical school classes. While there will be more racial minority doctors in the future, there will be significantly more women doctors, and this development is likely to have especially profound consequences. These consequences include the potential for change in the physician-patient relationship in terms of improved communication and willingness to relate to patients as people and the general image of women held by the medical profession.

Reviews of both past and present medical literature have found images of women patients that depict them as being naturally frail, sickly, incompetent, submissive, and in need of regular consultation with a physician (Ehrenreich and English, 1979; Scully, 1980). Gynecology textbooks attributed inferior sexuality and natural submissiveness to women, as well as relegating them to primary roles in society of reproduction and homemaking (Scully and Bart, 1979). Pediatric textbooks were no better, and portrayed doctors as the champions for children, even over and against their mothers (Howell, 1979). Mothers were sometimes blamed for being unreliable and unable to make accurate judgments about the health of their children. With a relative high percentage of women doctors (nearly one-third) a distinct possibility in the near future, sexist attitudes on the part of male physicians are likely to diminish since these doctors will have had exposure to competent and professional female counterparts in medical school and later in practice.

This is not to claim that sexism in medicine is no longer significant, because several accounts of women medical students and physicians detail the problems women have in being recognized as equal colleagues by male physicians and "real" doctors by patients (Hammond, 1980; Lorber, 1984; West, 1984). But the trend is clear—women physicians will be commonplace in the future and the change should be significant. For example, Lorber (1984) found that when male doctors assessed their accomplishments during their careers, they tended to talk of their skills and choices of appropriate treatment. The personal side of the physician-patient relationship was rarely mentioned. Women doctors, on the other hand, stressed their value to patients and did so using words like "help" and "care." As one woman physician (Lorber, 1984, p. 106) put it: "I think the best thing that I do is simply taking care of patients and being a warm and caring physician."

Outside of patient care, such as in the areas of teaching, research, program development, and other activities, the responses of the male and female physicians in the Lorber study were similar in mentioning their accomplishments. However, women are and continue to be underrepresented in teaching and research. According to Lorber (1984, p. 64), "a career in academic medicine may be attractive to research-oriented women physicians, but appointments at prestigious teaching hospitals are not easy to come by."

The major difference between men and women physicians in the Lorber study was in dealing with patients and it is this difference that medical sociologists will analyze in years to come. The greatest feminist impact in medicine in the immediate future seems most likely in a caring rather than scientific mode, since there appears little difference in the orientation of men and the significantly fewer women who choose research as a career. With women doctors choosing to work in increasing numbers in specialties such as internal medicine, family practice, and even surgery, instead of the usual choices of psychiatry, pediatrics, and pathology, they will be treating a wider range of patients in the future. Thus the potential for change in physician-patient relations is developing.

Decline in Professional Autonomy

Although the health care needs of American society are those of the late twentieth century, organized medicine has continued to pursue a pattern of professional behavior based upon the image of medical practice at the turn of the century when the physician worked as an independent, fee-for-service, private practitioner. This image is that of an entrepreneur who is completely free from lay control and totally in command of providing medical care. Supposedly, medicine's autonomy rests in its orientation toward serving the public, its strong system of ethics and peer regulation, and its professional expertise. Society is therefore justified, the argument goes, in granting the physician professional autonomy since the physician is a member of self-controlled collectivity providing a vital function for society's general good.

In practice this situation has not worked as well as it should. Peer regulation by physicians has generally been weak and ineffectual except in those circumstances where errors and offenses have grossly blatant (Freidson, 1975; Millman, 1977; Bosk, 1979). Confrontation with a colleague was considered distasteful even in private and unthinkable in public. Freidson (1975) observed that rules of etiquette restricted the evaluation of work and discouraged the expression of criticism. Millman (1977) contended that a ''gentleman's agreement'' existed among the physicians in her study to overlook each other's mistakes out of a fear of reprisal and recognition of common interests.

And when it comes to the public interest, the American Medical Association (AMA) has traditionally placed the self-interest of the medical profession over that of public welfare—especially when it comes to protecting the fee-for-service pattern of payment (Stevens, 1971). The medical profession in the United States has a consistent record of resistance to social legislation that in any way reduces the authority, privileges, and income of physicians. The profession, as a group, has opposed worker's compensation social security, voluntary health insurance, and health maintenance organizations (HMOs) in their initial stages. Also opposed were Medicare, Medicaid, Professional Standards Review Organizations (PSROs)—intended to review the quality of medical work in federally funded programs—and national health insurance, as well as Diagnostic Related Groups (DRGs). DRGs establish a schedule of fees placing a ceiling on how much the federal government will pay for services rendered by doctors and hospitals to patients with public health insurance. This situation has reduced societal confidence in medicine more than any other single issue, since physicians in general are often viewed as placing the desire for financial profit ahead of the desire to help people.

There are, of course, other issues of major importance such as the failure to provide quality care to all Americans and the lack of access some people in rural areas and inner-city slums have to health services. But the most important issue in medicine that has attracted public attention in recent years is the high cost of health care. The usual approach to dealing with this problem on the part of the lay public has been to demand increased government involvement in the provision of health services. The response of the federal government has been to support improvements in health care delivery for all segments of the population, but especially for the poor and the elderly. Since the 1960s, legislation pertaining to Medicare, Medicaid, HMOs, PRSOs, DRGs, and the like has passed Congress over the objections of the AMA. Until recently,

as in the case of DRGs, those objections were usually taken into account and incorporated into the legislation.

Nevertheless, these measures signal the increasing involvement of the government in regulating medical practice. As Starr (1982) points out, the sum total of recent regulatory efforts went far beyond what physicians and hospitals wanted; rather, planning was aimed not at expansion but at containment and formally linked with regulation. Government intervention in health care delivery remains limited at present, yet the pattern that is evolving is one of increased government regulation of medical practice.

Thus we are seeing important signs that the professional dominance of the physician may be significantly modified in the future. Three factors appear to be responsible for this development. One is greater government involvement. The second factor is the rise of consumerism in health care in which, as previously discussed, more affluent and better educated people are attempting to take greater control over their health by making their own decisions about what medical services and health practices are best for them and interacting with physicians on more of an equal basis. Health-protective behavior, consisting of various health practices like watching one's weight, exercising, avoiding smoking, and similar measures, and activities like the women's health movement, consisting of largely of well-educated women organized to combat sexism in medicine, are all efforts on the part of individuals to reduce dependence on doctors (Davidson and Gordon, 1979; Harris and Guten, 1979).

Challenge to the dominance of doctors, however, is coming from yet a third and particularly effective direction. This is the takeover of a significant portion of the health market by large business conglomerates. Massive government funding and Medicaid demonstrated that health care could be lucrative, and investors were attracted to put their money in private hospitals and nursing homes. Following this situation closely, corporate chains began purchasing these facilities and shortly thereafter came a wave of mergers, acquisitions, and diversifications, involving not only hospitals and nursing homes but a variety of enterprises such as hospital restaurants and supply companies, medical office buildings, emergency care centers, HMOs, health spas, and hospital management systems. The profit-making corporations expanded into markets that were either underserved or into areas where they could compete successfully with nonprofit institutions. Competition with respect to hospital care would consist of the profit-making hospitals providing more attractive rooms, good food, a friendly staff, and more efficient services than nonprofit hospitals. The higher rates of these hospitals were usually paid by the private health insurance of the patients they attracted. The market for these hospital chains was not in depressed areas where there were large numbers of welfare patients, but in relatively affluent areas where they can serve middle- and upper-class patients whose insurance benefits are likely to exceed those covered exclusively by Medicare or Medicaid. According to Starr (1982, p. 436): "The for-profit chains have an undisguised preference for privately insured patients." They are not interested in patients who cannot pay.

In the context of corporate health care, the physician becomes an employee rather than an independent practitioner. The doctor is bound to the rules, regulations, and procedures for practice established by the corporation, which, in all probability, is managed by people trained in business not medicine. Hence, doctors who do corporate practice are not as likely to play the decisive role in decision making about policy, hospital budgets, capital investments, salaries, promotions, and personnel appointments. There will likely be more regulation of work routine and standards of performance on which the salaries of the doctors will be based. Physicians who do not meet these standards are likely to lose their jobs. It is also certain there will be close scrutiny of mistakes in order to ensure not only quality care but also to avoid corporate liability for malpractice. In sum, the control of corporate medicine tends to be outside the immediate health care facility and in the hands of a management system that is primarily business oriented. Within this system, the doctor's autonomy will be significantly reduced.

To what extent the large health care corporations will be able to extend their control over the medical market is not known. But by the mid-1980s, 20% of all U.S. hospitals were owned by profit-making organizations and the expansion is continuing. It seems apparent, however, that those doctors who practice corporate medicine will constitute a physician group with less control over the conditions of their practice than American physicians in the past. In successfully avoiding government regulation of their work, physicians established the conditions in which corporations could move into and dominate an unregulated area of the economy. This development was materially assisted by increasing numbers of medical school graduates seeking employment and the generous benefits offered to physicians by the corporations wanting their services.

Therefore, indications are that the traditional autonomy and professional dominance of physicians is likely to be diminished in the years ahead. As the twenty-first century approaches, the definition of medicine as a "sovereign profession" shows signs of being increasingly less accurate. This is a situation that will be watched closely by medical sociologists as it represents a dramatic change in the evolution of a profession that has been a model of professional dominance.

With growing corporate control over medical standards and rules, Starr also notes that future studies by sociologists of the socialization of physicians will need to include not just medical school training, but also "corporate socialization" as young doctors learn the ways of the business organization that employs them. Included in the corporate orientation are significant implications for the culture of medicine in which the relationship of profits to services will be closely analyzed. Starr tells us that the marketing of health services will become more commonplace as "health centers" evolve into "profit centers."

What this implies for health care delivery in the United States is not necessarily positive. True, it will mean high-quality care for those who can afford it, but problems of access to such care by the lower class will be further aggravated. Analysis of physician utilization by socioeconomic groups currently shows the pattern of a dual health care system—a "private" system serving a greater proportion of higher income groups and a "public" system with a preponderance of lower-income groups. In the public system, the patient is likely to receive less quality care, spend longer amounts of time in waiting rooms and in obtaining services generally, not have a personal physician, cope with more bureaucratic agencies, and return after treatment to a living situation that is less conducive to good health. With corporate medical facilities catering to the more affluent segments of society, no realistic signs of national health insurance on the horizon, and cutbacks in the public financing of welfare services, health care delivery in the United States may become even more stratified. Access to quality health care thus emerges as an increasingly significant social issue in the years ahead.

Conclusion

The focus of the preceding discussion was upon

four areas of medical sociology—health differences of men and women, physician utilization, health and social stratification, increasing numbers of women physicians, and decline in the autonomy of physicians—all of which are undergoing major changes. But there are numerous areas where important research is being done or needs to be done. There is need for new research pertaining to the socialization of physicians in the corporate environment and the manner in which women medical students are affected by the experience of medical education, as well as the manner in which they in turn affect the institution socializing them. Answers to questions such as those posed by Fox (1985, p. 8) about women doctors need to be answered. Namely, who are these women sociologically speaking, will greater "feminization" of the medical profession take place, and what will be the social and medical consequences of their growing numbers? In addition, more investigation of the role of nursing and various paramedical workers providing technical support to doctors is needed, along with research on those in the health care industry who are involved more in the business and planning side of such services. Much of what we know about social life within medical establishments is based upon studies done in the 1950s and 1960s.

Considerable research is being done in medical sociology on the relationship between stress and physical and mental health. Numerous studies have pointed to the importance of social support in buffering the effects of stress and the types of situations (i.e., unemployment, overcrowding, poverty, various life events) that promote it. Efforts are being spent on refining the methodologies used to measure the psychosocial aspects of stress, while studies dealing with substantative questions clearly point toward rapid change and negative change (as contrasted with change per se) as being exceedingly stressful. It also appears that accumulation of relatively ordinary and frequent stressful incidents in one's life is more pathological than exposure to some extreme but short-lived event such as a natural disaster.

We now see the movement of such research in the direction of determining the manner in which stress is involved in particular health disorders, such as psychological distress (Wheaton, 1980) and chronic diseases (McQueen and Siegrist, 1982). This is an important development because sociologists, especially in the United States, have done little recent work on the experience of being sick. Rather, the focus in this area has been on the health environment itself, the social etiology of disease, the structure of the health care system, and the relationship between health providers and patients, but not so much on what it is actually like to experience illness and the sociological implications of such an experience. Feeling ill and the corresponding effects on one's concept of self, role relationships, and social attributes has not progressed much further beyond the original work of Parsons and Freidson. Fortunately, new sociological works analyzing these dimensions are beginning to appear, such as Fitzpatrick et al.'s *The Experience of Illness* (1984), as well as other studies on coping with physical handicaps (Albrecht and Levy, 1984; Lefton, 1984; Zola, 1982). It is anticipated that such subjects will attract more research in the future.

Yet another area of significant sociological work is the study of the aging population. This population in the future will be healthier, better educated, and more affluent than any groups of elderly persons in U.S. history. There will also be a much greater proportion of them than ever before. In 1980 about 1 in 10 Americans was 65 years of age or older; by the year 2050 this ratio will have increased to 1 in 5. With significantly larger numbers and lifelong exposure to a relatively high standard of living, including experience with the political process, the elderly will have the means to bring about legislation for public services to meet their particular social and health needs. Even though elderly Americans will be healthier than ever before, more pressure is likely to be put on health care delivery systems and public health insurance— that is, Medicare—to keep them fit. The nonphysical aspects of aging will increasingly command the attention of medical sociologists as they study the ways in which the elderly adjust to society and how society adjusts to the elderly.

Also, studies of cross-national comparisons of health policy and health care delivery in different countries are likely to receive greater attention in medical sociology. The experiences of other countries in establishing and maintaining their system of health care delivery is being examined more closely in order to find ways to improve the U.S. system, make American health care more equitable, and reach a deeper understanding of different world societies and their social philosophies. Studies of alternative healers, such as faith healers and folk healers, and the methods and sociological consequences of their practices is another area of research waiting to be fully developed. This is an area that medical sociology shares with medical anthropology.

When it comes to social theory, the outlook for medical sociology is less certain. Medical sociology remains largely an applied field. Yet there appears to be increasing concern with sociological theory in much of the work currently being published. It is almost as if medical sociologists, perhaps especially influenced by those working in applied settings, are searching to establish their roots and professional identity in the foundation common to the wider discipline. In this endeavor, they are demonstrating that they, too, are indeed a core subdiscipline and not a marginal entity whose identification with sociology is spurious at best. The studies reported here show that a substantial literature exists in medical sociology and much of it has direct ties to mainstream sociology.

But there have been few innovations in theory, with the possible exception of attribution theory (Wheaton, 1980) and a growing interest in the potential of conflict and Marxist theory (Krause, 1977; Waitzkin, 1983). Although weak and underdeveloped, Marxist theory currently has the greatest momentum as a newly developing theoretical perspective in medical sociology. Recent Marxist analysis seeks to link physician-patient interaction at the micro level with macro-level structures of professional power and dominance (Waitzkin, 1979). Physicians are seen as cooperating with the capitalist system to maintain worker productivity as a primary goal of health care. Marxist theory also criticizes attempts to reduce responsibility for health to the level of the individual (Waitzkin, 1983). While not denying that individual lifestyle is an important determinant of health, Marxist theorists point out that individuals often lead unhealthy lives because of social structural conditions. An individual's sickness or early death ultimately becomes the individual's own fault. Thus the emphasis on personal lifestyle (a form of reductionism) in capitalist medical sociology does nothing to correct the structural causes of ill health. Other work has examined the role of medical power under capitalism as a general critique of medicine and the state (Navarro, 1976, 1986). New directions as seen in existential sociology, phenomenology, and interpretive sociology have not been reflected in medical sociology to date. Instead, the present appears to be a period when the subdiscipline is generally searching for ways to demonstrate the validity of existing theory within the context of applied research.

Obviously, extensive work in medical sociology remains to be done. But the subdiscipline is firmly established and the potential for further development offers exciting opportunities. Good health is one of the most cherished benefits available to humankind and it is derived from an intricate relationship between mind, body, and the social and physical environment. This is why knowledge of the principles of sociology is essential in the practice of contemporary medicine. Medicine's recognition that sociology can help health practitioners to better understand their patients and provide improved forms of health care and sociology's interest in medicine as a distinct area of social life has combined to bring about a convergence of mutual interest between the two fields. More medical sociologists are being invited to join the staffs of medical institutions and they are participating in more medical research projects, some of which they initiate from a sociological perspective. The tremendous growth of sociological literature on health and illness shows that the subdiscipline is exceptionally active and dynamic—and still evolving.

And it is likely that the subdiscipline will remain a major area of sociological endeavor in terms of both practitioners and resources. For example, the current concern in American society about AIDS and its potential to spread has caused people to adjust their sexual habits and lifestyles, and pay increased attention to the personal side of their social relationships. This disease and its potentially widespread and deadly effects has literally shocked society into being more concerned about the relationship between health and social situations.

REFERENCES

Aday, Lu Ann, and Ronald Andersen. 1975. *Development of Indices of Access to Medical Care.* Ann Arbor, MI: Health Administration Press.
_____ and Gretchen V. Fleming. 1980. *Health Care in the U.S.: Equitable for Whom?* Beverly Hills, CA: Sage.

Albrecht, Gary L. and Judith A. Levy. 1984. "A Sociological Perspective of Physical Disability." Pp. 45-106 in *Advances in Medical Social Science*, vol. 2, edited by J. Ruffini. New York: Gordon and Breach.

Andersen, Ronald and Odin W. Anderson. 1979. "Trends in the Use of Health Services." Pp. 371-391 in *Handbook of Medical Sociology*, edited by H. Freeman, S. Levine, and L. Reeder. Englewood Cliffs, NJ: Prentice-Hall.

Andersen, Ronald, Joanna Kravits, and Odin W. Anderson, eds. 1975. *Equity in Health Services.* Cambridge, MA: Ballinger.

Arluke, Arnold, Louanne Kennedy, and Ronald C. Kessler. 1979. "Reexamining the Sick-Role Concept: An Empirical Assessment." *Journal of Health and Social Behavior* 20:30-36.

Becker, Howard S., Blanche Greer, Everett C.

Hughes, and Anselm Strauss. 1961. *Boys in White: Student Culture in Medical School.* Chicago: University of Chicago Press.

Becker, Marshall H., ed. 1974. *The Health Belief Model and Personal Health Behavior.* San Francisco: Society for Public Health Education.

Berkanovic, Emil 1972. "Lay Conceptions of the Sick Role." *Social Forces* 51:53-63.

———— and Leo G. Reeder 1974. "Can Money Buy the Appropriate Use of Services? Some Notes on the Meaning of Utilization Data." *Journal of Health and Social Behavior* 15:93-99.

Blackwell, Elizabeth. 1902. *Essays in Medical Sociology.* London: Bell.

Bosk, Charles L. 1979. *Forgive and Remember: Managing Medical Failure.* Chicago: University of Chicago Press.

Claus, Lisabeth M. 1982. *The Growth of a Sociological Discipline: On the Development of Medical Sociology in Europe,* vols. I and II. Leuven, Belgium: Katholieke Universitet Leuven.

———— 1983. "The Development of Medical Sociology in Europe." *Social Science and Medicine* 17:1591-1597.

Cleary, Paul D. and David Mechanic. 1983. "Sex Differences in Psychological Distress among Married People." *Journal of Health and Social Behavior* 24:111-121.

Cockerham, William C. 1983. "The State of Medical Sociology in the United States, Great Britain, West Germany, and Austria: Applied vs Pure Theory." *Social Science and Medicine* 17:1513-1527.

———— 1986. *Medical Sociology.* Englewood Cliffs, NJ: Prentice-Hall.

Cockerham, William C., Guenther Lueschen, Gerhard Kunz, and Joe L. Spaeth. 1986. "Social Stratification and Self-Management of Health." *Journal of Health and Social Behavior* 27:1-14.

Cole, Stephen and Robert Lejeune 1972. "Illness and the Legitimation of Failure." *American Sociological Review* 37:347-356.

Davidson, Laurie and Laura Kramer Gordon. 1979. *The Sociology of Gender.* Chicago: Rand McNally.

Davis, Fred. 1972. *Illness, Interaction, and the Self.* Belmont, CA: Wadsworth.

d'Houtaud, A. and Mark G. Field. 1984. "The Image of Health: Variations in Perception by Social Class in a French Population." *Sociology of Health and Illness* 6:30-59.

Dohrenwend, Bruce P. and Barbara Snell Dohrenwend. 1976. "Sex Differences and Psychiatric Disorder." *American Journal of Sociology* 81:1447-1454.

DuBos, Rene. 1959. *Mirage of Health.* New York: Harper and Row.

Durkheim, Emile. 1961. *The Elementary Forms of Religious Life.* New York: Collier.

Dutton, Diana B. 1978. "Explaining the Low Use of Health Services by the Poor: Costs, Attitudes,

or Delivery Systems." *American Sociological Review* 43:348-368.

Ehrenreich, Barbara and Deidre English. 1979. "The 'Sick' Women of the Upper Classes." Pp. 123-143 in *The Cultural Crisis of Modern Medicine,* edited by J. Ehrenreich. New York: Monthly Review Press.

Faris, Robert E. and H. Warren Dunham. 1939. *Mental Disorders in Urban Areas.* Chicago: University of Chicago Press.

Fisher, Sue. 1984. "Doctor-patient Communication: A Social and Micro-Political Performance." *Sociology of Health and Illness* 6:1-27.

Fitzpatrick, Ray, John Hinton, Stanton Newman, Graham Scrambler, and James Thompson. 1984. *The Experience of Illness.* London: Tavistock.

Fox, Renee C. 1979. *Essays in Medical Sociology.* New York: John Wiley.

———— 1985. "Reflections and Opportunities in the Sociology of Medicine." *Journal of Health and Social Behavior* 26:6-15.

Freidson, Eliot. 1960. "Client Control and Medical Practice." *American Journal of Sociology* 65:374-382.

———— 1970a. *Professional Dominance.* Chicago: Aldine.

———— 1970b. *Profession of Medicine.* New York: Dodd and Mead.

———— 1975. *Doctoring Together.* New York: Elsevier.

Gallagher, Eugene B. 1976. "Lines of Reconstruction and Extension in the Parsonian Sociology of Illness." *Social Science and Medicine* 10:207-218.

Gerhardt, Uta. 1979. "The Parsonian Paradigm and the Identity of Medical Sociology." *Sociological Review* 27:229-251.

Glaser, Barney G. and Anselm M. Strauss. 1965. *Awareness of Dying.* Chicago: Aldine.

———— 1967. *The Discovery of Grounded Theory.* Chicago: Aldine.

———— 1968. *A Time for Dying.* Chicago: Aldine.

———— 1971. *Status Passage.* Chicago: Aldine.

Goffman, Erving. 1961. *Asylums.* Garden City, NY: Anchor.

Gold, Margaret. 1977. "A Crisis of Identity: The Case of Medical Sociology." *Journal of Health and Social Behavior* 18:160-168.

Gordon, Gerald. 1966. *Role Theory and Illness.* New Haven, CT: College and University Press.

Gouldner, Alvin W. 1970. *The Coming Crisis of Western Sociology.* New York: Basic Books.

Gove, Walter R. 1970. "Societal Reaction as an Explanation of Mental Illness: An Evaluation." *American Sociological Review* 35:873-884.

———— and Michael Hughes. 1979. "Possible Causes of the Apparent Sex Differences in Physical Health: An Empirical Investigation." *American Sociological Review* 44:126-146.

———— and Carolyn Briggs Style. 1983. "Does Marriage Have Positive Effects on the Psychological Well-being of the Individual?" *Journal of*

Health and Social Behavior 24:122-131.

Gove, Walter R. and Jeanette F. Tudor. 1973. "Adult Sex Roles and Mental Illness." *American Journal of Sociology* 78:812-835.

Hammond, Judith. 1980. "Biography Building to Insure the Future: Women's Negotiation of Gender Relevancy in Medical School." *Symbolic Interaction* 3:35-49.

Harris, Daniel M. and Sharon Guten. 1979. "Health-protective Behavior: An Exploratory Study." *Journal of Health and Social Behavior* 20:17-29.

Haug, Marie and Bebe Lavin. 1981. "Practitioner or Patient--Who's in Charge?" *Journal of Health and Social Behavior* 22:212-229.

———. 1983. *Consumerism in Medicine*. Beverly Hills, CA: Sage.

Hollingshead, August B. and Frederick C. Redlich. 1958. *Social Class and Mental Illness: A Community Study*. New York: John Wiley.

Hollingsworth, J. Rogers. 1981. "Inequality in Levels of Health in England and Wales, 1891-1971." *Journal of Health and Social Behavior* 22:268-283.

Horobin, Gordon. 1985. "Medical Sociology in Britain: True Confessions of an Empiricist." *Sociology of Health and Illness* 7:94-107.

Howell, Mary C. 1979. "Pediatricians and Mothers." Pp. 201-211 in *The Cultural Crisis of Modern Medicine*, edited by J. Ehrenreich. New York: Monthly Review Press.

Jenkins, C. David. 1983. "Social Environment and Cancer Mortality in Men." *New England Journal of Medicine* 308:395-398.

Johnson, Benton. 1975. *Functionalism in Modern Sociology: Understanding Talcott Parsons*. Morristown, NJ: General Learning Press.

Johnson, Malcolm. 1975. "Medical Sociology and Sociological Theory." *Social Science in Medicine* 9:227-232.

Koos, Earl. 1954. *The Health of Regionsville*. New York: Columbia University Press.

Krause, Elliot A. 1977. *Power and Illness*. New York: Elsevier.

Langlie, Jean K. 1977. "Social Networks, Health Beliefs, and Preventive Health Behavior." *Journal of Health and Social Behavior* 18:244-260.

Lefton, Mark. 1984. "Chronic Disease and Applied Sociology: An Essay in Personalized Sociology." *Sociological Inquiry* 54:466-476.

Levine, Sol, Jacob J. Feldman, and Jack Elinson. 1983. "Does Medical Care Do Any Good?" Pp. 394-401 in *Handbook of Health, Health Care, and the Health Professions*, edited by D. Mechanic. New York: Free Press.

Lorber, Judith. 1984. *Women Physicians*. New York: Tavistock.

Lueschen, Guenther. 1983. "The System of Sport: Problems of Methodology, Conflict, and Social Stratification." Pp. 197-203 in *Handbook of Social Science of Sport*, edited by G. Lueschen and G. Sage. Champaign, IL: Stipes.

Mauksch, Hans. 1972. "Nursing: Churning for a

Change?" Pp. 206-300 in *Handbook of Medical Sociology*, edited by H. Freeman, S. Levine, and L. Reeder. Englewood Cliffs, NJ: Prentice-Hall.

McIntire, Charles. 1894. "The Importance of the Study of Medical Sociology." *Bulletin of the American Academy of Medicine* 1:425-434.

McKeown, Thomas. 1979. *The Role of Medicine*. Oxford: Blackwell.

McKinley, John B. and Sonja M. McKinley 1981. "Medical Measures and the Decline of Mortality." Pp. 12-30 in *The Sociology of Health and Illness*, edited by P. Conrad and R. Kern. New York: St. Martin's.

McQueen, David V. and Johannes Siegrist. 1982. "Social Factors in the Etiology of Chronic Disease: An Overview." *Social Science and Medicine* 16:335-367.

Mechanic, David. 1972. *Public Expectations and Health Care*. New York: Wiley-Intersciences.

Merton, Robert K., George G. Reader, and Patricia Kendall. 1957. *The Student-Physician*. Cambridge, MA: Harvard University Press.

Millman, Marcia. 1977. *The Unkindest Cut*. New York: Morrow.

Mirowsky, John. 1985. "Depression and Marital Power: An Equity Model." *American Journal of Sociology* 91:557-592.

Muench, Richard. 1982. "Talcott Parsons and the Theory of Action. II. The Continuity of the Development." *American Journal of Sociology* 87:771-826.

Nathanson, Constance A. 1977. "Sex, Illness, and Medical Care: A Review of Data, Theory, and Method." *Social Science and Medicine* 11:13-25.

National Center for Health Statistics. 1983. *Health, United States 1983*. Washington, DC: Government Printing Office.

———. 1985. *Health, United States 1985*. Washington, DC: Government Printing Office.

Navarro, Vicente. 1976. *Medicine Under Capitalism*. New York: Prodist.

———. 1986. *Crisis, Health, and Medicine: A Social Critique*. New York: Tavistock.

Parsons, Talcott. 1951. *The Social System*. Glencoe, IL: Free Press.

———. 1977. *Social Systems and the Evolution of Action Theory*. New York: Free Press.

———. 1981. "Revisiting the Classics Throughout a Long Career." Pp. 183-194 in *The Future of the Sociological Classics*, edited by B. Rhea. London: Allen & Unwin.

Pflanz, Manfred. 1975. "Relations between Social Scientists, Physicians and Medical Organizations in Health Research." *Social Science and Medicine* 9:7-13.

———. 1976. "Sociology in Community Medicine." Pp. 6-12 in *Seminars in Community Medicine. Vol. 1: Sociology*, edited by R. Acheson and L. Aird. London: Oxford University Press.

Reeder, Leo G. 1972. "The Patient-client as a Consumer: Some Observations on the Changing Professional-client Relationship." *Journal of*

Health and Social Behavior 13:406-412.

Reid, Ivan. 1981. *Social Class Differences in Britain*. London: Grant McIntrye.

Rosenblatt, Daniel and Edward A. Suchman. 1964. "Blue-collar Attitudes and Information toward Health and Illness." Pp. 324-333 in *Studies of the American Worker*, edited by A. Shostak and W. Gomberg. Englewood Cliffs, NJ: Prentice-Hall.

Ross, Catherine, John Mirowsky, and William C. Cockerham. 1983. "Social Class, Mexican Culture, and Fatalism: Their Effects on Psychological Distress." *American Journal of Community Psychology* 11:383-399.

Ruderman, Florence. 1981. "What is Medical Sociology?" *Journal of the American Medical Association* 245:927-929.

Rundall, Thomas G. and John R.C. Wheeler. 1979. "The Effect of Income on Use of Preventive Care: An Evaluation of Alternative Explanations." *Journal of Health and Social Behavior* 20:397-406.

Scheff, Thomas J. 1966. *Being Mentally Ill*. Chicago: Aldine.

Scully, Diane 1980. *Men Who Control Women's Health: The Miseducation of Obstetrician-Gynecologists*. Boston: Houghton Mifflin.

Scully, Diana and Pauline Bart. 1979. "A Funny Thing Happened on the Way to the Orifice: Women in Gynecology Textbooks." Pp. 212-226 in *The Cultural Crisis of Modern Medicine*, edited by J. Ehrenreich. New York: Monthly Review Press.

Seeman, Melvin and J. W. Evans. 1962. "Alienation and Learning in a Hospital Setting." *American Sociological Review* 22:772-783.

Seeman, Melvin and Teresa E. Seeman 1983. "Health Behavior and Personal Autonomy: A Longitudinal Study of the Sense of Control in Illness." *Journal of Health and Social Behavior* 24:144-160.

Segall, Alexander. 1976. "The Sick Role Concept: Understanding Illness Behavior." *Journal of Health and Social Behavior* 17:162-168.

Sharp, Kimberly, Catherine E. Ross, and William C. Cockerham. 1983. "Symptoms, Beliefs, and Use of Physician Services among the Disadvantaged." *Journal of Health and Social Behavior* 24:255-263.

Siegrist, J. and H. Bertram. 1970/1971. "Schichtspezifische Variationen des Krankheitsverhaltens." *Soziale Welt* (20/21):206-218.

Simmons, L. and H. Wolff. 1954. *Science in Medicine*. New York: Russell Sage.

Srole, Leo, T. S. Langner, S. T. Michael, M. K. Opler, and T.A.C. Rennie. 1962. *Mental Health in the Metropolis: The Midtown Manhattan Study*, vol. I and II. New York: McGraw-Hill.

Stahl, Sidney M. and Gilbert Gardner. 1976. "A Contradiction in the Health Care Delivery System: Problems of Access." *Sociological Quarterly* 17:121-129.

Starr, Paul. 1982. *The Social Transformation of American Medicine*. New York: Basic Books.

Stern, Bernard F. 1927. *Social Factors in Medical Progress*. New York: Columbia University Press.

Stevens, Rosemary 1971. *American Medicine and the Public Interest*. New Haven, CT: Yale University Press.

Straus, Robert. 1957. "Nature and Status of Medical Sociology." *American Sociological Review* 22: 200-204.

Strauss, Anselem L. *Mirrors and Masks: The Search for Identity*. San Francisco: Sociological Press.

Suchman, Edward A. 1963. *Sociology and the Field of Public Health*. New York: Russell Sage.

———. 1965a. "Social Patterns of Illness and Medical Care." *Journal of Health and Human Behavior* 6:2-16.

———. 1965b. "Stages of Illness and Medical Care." *Journal of Health and Human Behavior* 6:114-128.

Susser, Mervyn, Kim Hopper, and Judith Richman. 1983. "Society, Culture, and Health." Pp. 23-49 in *Handbook of Health, Health Care, and the Health Professions*, edited by D. Mechanic. New York: Free Press.

Susser, Mervyn W. and William Watson. 1971. *Sociology in Medicine*. London: Oxford University Press.

——— and Kim Hopper. 1985. *Sociology in Medicine*. New York: Oxford University Press.

Twaddle, Andrew C. 1979. *Sickness Behavior and the Sick Role*. Cambridge, MA: Schenkman.

———. 1982. "From Medical Sociology to the Sociology of Health: Some Changing Concerns in the Sociological Study of Sickness and Treatment." Pp. 323-358 in *Sociology: The State of the Art*, edited by T. Bottomote, S. Nowak, and M. Sokolowska. London: Sage.

Van den Berg, Jan Hendrick. 1978. *Medical Power and Medical Ethics*. New York: W. W. Norton.

Verbrugge, Lois M. 1985. "Gender and Health: An Update on Hypotheses and Evidence." *Journal of Health and Social Behavior* 26:156-182.

Waitzkin, Howard. 1979. "Medicine, Superstructure, and Micropolitics." *Social Science and Medicine* 13A:601-609.

———. 1983. *The Second Sickness: Contradictions of Capitalist Health Care*. New York: Free Press.

Waldron, Ingrid. 1983. "Sex Differences in Illness Incidence, Prognosis and Mortality: Issues and Evidence." *Social Science and Medicine* 17: 1107-1123.

Warbasse, James. 1909. *Medical Sociology*. New York: Appleton.

Wardwell, Walter I. 1982. "The State of Medical Sociology—A Review Essay." *Sociological Quarterly* 23:563-571.

Weber, Max. 1958. *From Max Weber: Essays in Sociology*. New York: Oxford University Press.

———. 1965. *The Theory of Social and Economic Organization*, translation and introduction by Talcott Parsons. New York: Free Press.

West, Candace. 1984. "When the Doctor is a 'Lady': Power, Status, and Gender in Physician-Patient Encounters." *Symbolic Interaction* 7:87-106.

Wheaton, Blair. 1980. "The Sociogenesis of Psychological Disorder: An Attributional Theory." *Journal of Health and Social Behavior* 21:100-124.

Wolinsky Frederic D. 1980. *The Sociology of Health.* Boston: Little, Brown.

_____, Gary L. Albrecht, Emil Berkanovic, Una Creditor, and Fred Katz. 1980. "The Medical Sociologist in an Applied Setting: General Observations and Specific Examples." Presented to the Sociology of Health Care Conference, Urbana, IL.

Wolinsky, Frederic D. and Sally R. Wolinsky. 1981. "Expecting Sick-role Legitimation and Getting It." *Journal of Health and Social Behavior* 22:229-242.

Zborowski, Mark. 1952. "Cultural Components in Responses to Pain." *Journal of Social Issues* 8:16-30.

Zola, Irving. 1966. "Culture and Symptoms—An Analysis of Patient's Presenting Complaints." *American Sociology Review* 31:615-630.

_____ 1982. *Missing Pieces: A Chronicle of Living with a Disability*. Philadelphia: Temple University Press.

18

Mass Media Institutions

GAYE TUCHMAN

In recent decades, leading American researchers in mass communications have announced a crisis in their field. In 1959 Bernard Berelson declared that the study of communications was "withering away." He explained, "The innovators have left or are leaving the field, and no ideas of comparable scope and generating power are emerging. The expansion of the field to new centers has certainly slowed down and perhaps even stopped." In 1972 Herbert Gans decried, "Once upon a time, especially in the 1930s and 1940s, mass communications was a vital and productive field in academic sociological research, but ever since it has suffered from a drastic famine that shows no signs of abating."

Berelson's and Gans's statements were probably responses to a shift in paradigms. For even as these respected figures bemoaned the state of the field, in both the United States and Great Britain the past 20 years have seen a general resurgence of sociological studies of the mass media. In both countries, there has been a distinct infusion of new ideas, often antithetical to the notions that dominated the study of media in the 1930s, 1940s, and 1950s. There has also been an increased maturity of what Americans term *mass communications research* and the British refer to as *cultural studies*. (The divergent terms capture divergent histories, theoretical approaches, and research agendas, though there has been cross-fertilization, as well.) Indeed, there is now so much activity in the field of media studies, including the American sociology of media, that in 1983 the *Journal of Communication* (Gerbner and Siefert, 1983) devoted a double issue to a symposium entitled *Ferment in the Field*, containing 35 original essays by 41 authors from 10 countries. Many of these authors were sociologists.

In the face of the awesome diversity represented in the *Journal of Communication*'s symposium and in the many other recently published programmatic essays, this chapter will explore (1) continuities and contrasts between past and present American sociologies of the media; (2) some differences between American and British research; and (3) some directions in which American work seems to be moving. It is particularly important for Americans to be familiar with the British work, because both approaches have vied for influenced in English-speaking universities (see Putnis, 1986) and in other research centers, as well.

My training and perspective are pertinent to this essay. I write as someone trained at Brandeis University by symbolic interactionists, phenomenologists, and Simmelians, in an environment largely sympathetic to German critical theory. I took courses in the sociology of art, but not in the American field of mass communications. I am grateful to a grant from the Markle Foundation, which facilitated this work, to Sooz Walters for research assistance, and to Paul DiMaggio for criticism of an earlier draft. Another excellent review of a complementary literature is Mirkerji and Schudson (1986).

As ever, the discussion of the past presumes specific understandings of the present and prognoses of the future. Consider the essays in the symposium *Ferment in the Field*. Addressing the characteristics of past and present research and suggesting future research programs, these essays sometimes sounded as though they were written about different fields. The divergences are often so extreme that one might speak not simply of "ferment," but rather of "cleavages" in the field. For instance, advocates of a political economy of media (e.g., Garnham, 1983a) posed questions about revolution and ideology, which derive from the development of capitalism. Advocates of a scientific and interactive model of the communications (e.g., Schramm, 1983) also stressed social context, but not its historical derivation. Rather, they wished to delineate a process stressing the active role of both the media and the audience in mass communications.

Furthermore, although some of these cleavages seemed to be responses to the former American dominance in media research, they were not based on author's nationality. Although many of the Europeans contributing to the *Journal of Communication*'s symposium took seemingly ritualistic potshots at past American research, many Americans also did so. Some Europeans and Americans paid equally ritualistic obeisance to the sociologists, political scientists, and psychologists who once dominated the American field, namely Paul Lazarsfeld, Harold Lasswell, Kurt Lewin, and Carl Hovland. Europeans and Americans freely cited and praised the work of members of the Frankfurt School of critical theorists and members of the Birmingham Centre for Contemporary Cultural Studies.[1] Others wrote as though German ideas had never entered American academic discussions and as though many British had never deviated from the American research programs their colleagues and teachers had once embraced.

Understandings of the Past

As Charles Wright (1986) reminded, American sociology has been concerned with the topic of media since its origins at the turn of the century. In 1894 George C. Vincent and Albion Small, then head of the first sociology department in the United States (at the University of Chicago), devoted a chapter of their introductory textbook to the media as "the social nervous system" of the social "organism" (Small and Vincent, 1894).

The sociology of media flourished at Chicago, where Robert Park and his students (see, especially, Hughes, 1940) insistently studied contemporary media in a social context. To learn about the then pressing social issue of assimilating European immigrants and Americans migrants into urban American culture, they analyzed the immigrant press (Park, 1922). Wright (1986) reads Small and Vincent as incorporating social criticism in their functionalist sociology of media, for they included a critique of the shortcoming of newspapers in their chapter on the media as nervous system." I read Park as more critical in today's sense of that term: his *The Immigrant Press and its* **Control** (emphasis added) tackled such issues of political economy as the capital base of the immigrant press, the impact of advertisers on content, and in essence, the instruction of immigrants in American consumerism.

Studies of the media also flourished at other early centers of sociology. Wright (1986) mentions early discussion of the media at Columbia University[2], where Franklin Henry Giddings considered them in an early work on sociological theory (1916) and Robert Lynd and Helen M. Lynd included perceptive and critical discussions of the media in their classic community studies, *Middletown* (1922) and *Middletown in Transition* (1939). Wright catalogues, too, work at the University of Wisconsin undertaken by Edward Alsworth Ross and studies at the University of Washington just after World War II.

The Columbia School of Media Study

By and large, when international scholars discuss traditional "American media sociology," they mean "Columbia sociology" as developed by the Viennese immigrant Paul F. Lazarsfeld, his sometime coauthor Robert K. Merton, and such students as Herbert Hyman and Elihu Katz. Merton (1949) recognized the study of media as part of the sociology of knowledge, but under Lazarsfeld, "Columbia sociology" about "mass communications and public opinion" was generally social psychological research about the impact of the media upon individuals classified by age, race, ethnicity, gender, social class, or religion.

In Austria, Lazarsfeld had published with Marie Jahoda and Hans Zeisel the valuable *Marienthal* (1971/1933), a social-psychological community study of an industrial town where during the Great Depression most of the work force was structurally unemployed. Lazarsfeld's introduction to the American edition emphasized that the researchers were interested in delineating the "sociography" of the community, not the individuals in it. (The English title is *Marienthal: The Sociography of a Community*. The German title, *Die Arbeitlosen von Marienthal*, announces that the book is about the unemployed.) As had Lynd and Lynd in their study of Muncie, Indiana, Lazarsfeld, Jahoda, and Zeisel displayed sophistication about the impact of structural problems on how people experience their lives. As had Lynd and Lynd, they incorporated a concern with the use of diverse media in their study of Marienthal. For instance, focusing on the shame experienced by unemployed men, the research team noted a decrease in the use of newspapers and of the public library. Rather than using their "free time" to read more, the unemployed men lost interest in what had formerly been vital concerns and so men's media use affirmed the authors' thesis that decreased opportunities decreased the aspirations and activities of the structurally unemployed.

Once in the United States, Lazarsfeld's interest in the development of scientific methods of social research led him to turn away from studying the media to focus upon social structure.[3] His work increasingly concentrated upon social psychology. Establishing at the University of Newark a research bureau that was to become Columbia University's Bureau of Applied Social Research, Lazarsfeld put into practice his belief that one could uncover lawlike statements by studying any phenomenon. Like other refugee scientists who established what were first marginal research institutes (Coser, 1984), Lazarsfeld supported himself through his research.

Lazarsfeld quickly forged ties with the communications industry, undertaking studies now characterized as "administrative research." (The term *administrative research* refers to studies that accept industrial and social structures as given and that adopt rather than challenge the presuppositions of industries or state agencies sponsoring the research.) For instance, with Frank Stanton, then a young man with CBS and eventually to become the chief executive officer and chairman of the board of CBS, he designed a method of pretesting the potential popularity of radio programs with audiences. It was intended to help that radio network to maximize its profits by investing in shows that might draw large audiences, whose attention could then be sold to advertisers. Such research was clearly social-psychological analysis in the service of capitalism.

Contemporary scholars have also characterized some of Lazarsfeld's other more academically pertinent studies as administrative research. Gitlin (1978) leveled an influential attack at one of Lazarsfeld's most famous and influential books, *Personal Influence*, whose first author was Elihu Katz, now one of the international deans of communications research (Katz and Lazarsfeld, 1955). An important modification of simple stimulus-response models (sometimes called the "hypodermic-needle theory of media affects"),[4] *Personal Influence* delineates a two-step flow of communication: (1) media make information accessible to opinion leaders (individuals interested in a specific topic who pay particular attention to media information about that topic) and (2) opinion leaders (whose expertise on a topic is socially affirmed) exert personal influence on friends and relatives. Emphasizing the interaction between individuals (those who influenced and those who were influenced), *Personal Influence* was a social-psychological study, whose design would have enabled its financial supporter, Macfadden Publications, to demonstrate to their advertisers that each ad had a potential impact on more individuals than those who had initially attended to it. For the study found that personal influence was more important than media influence in affecting individual decisions about following fashion, buying products for the home, choosing movies to see, and deciding which candidate to vote for.

As Gitlin (1978) points out, Katz and Lazarsfeld's idea of a two-step flow of communications has attained the status of a sociological truism. Even some radicals accept as given their finding that opinion leaders stand between the media and social groups and, by implication, prevent the media from exerting a ideological dominance. All tend to ignore that (1) to qualify for the snowball sample, individuals had to be named as people who had given or received specific sorts of advice, and so the sample was designed to explore and to highlight personal influence, not media influence and (2) the study ignores the power of the media to set the agenda of opinion leaders. For it defines power as the ability to "compel a certain behavior, namely buying; or, in the case of public affairs, it was the power to compel a change in 'attitude' on some current issue" (Gitlin, 1978, p. 215). (3) Opinion leaders had at their disposal information structured by the media (such as the fashionable length of skirts), but not information the media had chosen not to disseminate. In that sense, opinion leaders were passing on information sifted by a vast public relations machine.

Additionally, (4) the 1950 study could not use the then undiscovered concept "parasocial interaction" (Horton and Wohl, 1956/1986). That notion affirms that audience members often react to actors (comedians, musicians, and others featured in the media) as though they had a personal relationship with them. This tendency is most pronounced in the case of television audiences (necessarily excluded from *Personal Influence*) and so may make information on television seem as or more personally compelling than information gleaned from friends or acquaintances.

Finally, (5) in the 1970s and 1980s the media have contained many cross-references to one another.[5] For instance, television carries ads for movies; a variety of media review movies; cable television carries MTV (music television), "videos" designed to promote records; children's television features ads for "action figures" (dolls) who are themselves the characters of children's programs. Hence the media have additional influence as a cross-referenced, self-supporting structure: They presume and create each other's legitimacy within the general context of a much-legitimated consumerism. Indeed, that structured and structural consumerism is so pervasive as often to pass unnoticed as a basis for individual decisions (Why should people wish to dress fashionably? Avoid ring around the collar? Have odor-free feet?) Today, some theorists would claim that Katz and Lazarsfeld's *Personal Influence* was so wrapped up in a series of particular social psychological questions that it could notice neither the assumptions central to the media messages nor the media's power over personal influence.

Similar criticisms have been leveled at an alternative mode of conceiving media effects also developed by Lazarsfeld and his associates. Termed the "uses and gratifications" model, its approach emphasizes that (1) individuals actively use the media in a "goal-directed manner" to gratify certain needs, some of which may have been generated by social factors and (2) the desires that types of individuals bring to the media serve as "intervening variables" in the traditional model of communication effects. More simply, the reasons people use the media help to determine the media's affect on people. To date, most of the implications of this theory remain unexplored. Uses and gratifications researchers have asked people to say what they use different media for and what they claim to get out of their media use. But so far this research has mainly compiled a catalogue of the needs of individuals and the attributes and func-

tions of specific media that might satisfy those needs. It has not yet demonstrated the positive connection between uses and gratifications and media affects.[6]

Uses and gratifications has drawn a variety of criticisms, many prompted by its psychological behaviorism. For researchers in this tradition place great confidence in the ability of people to know what they want and actively to seek and to attain it. The researchers seem to believe that the media do not influence people in undesired ways or in ways of which they are unconscious. For example, uses and gratifications researchers would expect an individual to say that he or she uses advertisements to learn what is available in the marketplace. But they ignore the inability of individuals to report uses or gratifications of which they are or may be unconscious: Typically, survey respondents do not volunteer such statements as, "I believe this to be so, because the media 'manipulated' me" or "Advertisements have taught me that you are what you wear."

Additionally, as is also true of *Personal Influence*, uses and gratifications research implicitly ignores the power of the media to determine the messages available to people. People cannot comment on ideas to which they have not been exposed. Nonetheless, the uses and gratifications approach enables one to learn how individuals of diverse social classes (genders, religions, races, ethnic groups) believe they use the media. It also may enable statements about how cultural contexts influence the meanings people derive from specific content (see Katz and Liebes, 1986).

With Robert K. Merton, Lazarsfeld offered another idea about media effects that remains germane to much contemporary research. They suggested the media may have a "narcotizing dysfunction" (Lazarsfeld and Merton, 1948). That is, news media may lead people who regularly use them to form opinions about topics and then to believe that because they have opinions, they have taken action. Thus modern media may encourage citizens to know more, even to be more opinionated, but to do less about public affairs. Because decreased political participation ultimately debases both the concept and the practice of democracy, Lazarsfeld and Merton term this possibility a "dysfunction." Although few contemporary researchers use such functionalist terms as "narcotizing dysfunction," one major theme in contemporary research is that the media discourage political participation and meaningful social change.

Impact of the Columbia School

I have presented some ways that Lazarsfeld's ideas towered over the sociological study of media. His work was also important in another way. It may have indirectly caused what Gans (1972) identified as the famine in media research.

Reconsider my interpretation of *Personal Influence*.[7] It emphasized that Lazarsfeld and his associates minimized the impact of the media. Some of Lazarsfeld's students made stronger statements about the minimal effects of the media than Lazarsfeld ever did. For instance, the eventual head of the CBS research division, Joseph Klapper (1960), reviewed the accumulated literature to set forth the *Doctrine of Minimal Effects*—an argument that the media mainly reinforce what people already believe.[8] The media's effect on opinions may be significant, only when media offer information about new topics—matters that people do not know about and so about which they have no previous opinions requiring alteration.

Such views about the effect of the media may have prompted three key responses. First, some may have felt the doctrine of minimal effects posed the question, Why bother to study a topic when its importance (its effects) is not demonstrable (Wright, 1986)? Second, any attempt to mount a large-scale survey in order to modify or reject the doctrine of minimal effects would be very costly—although as Gans (1972) pointed out many specialists in such other areas as occupational mobility had solved the problem of funding. Third, as of 1972 no American sociologists had "yet determined effective methods of determining the impact of the mass-media as a whole—either in the short-run or long-run" (Gans, 1972, p. 699).[9] But the supposition seemed to be that if someone discovered an adequate model of the impact of the media as a whole, it would be expensive to test it. That supposition implied that to test a new theory, model, or paradigm, one would need to mount an expensive survey.

However, not all sociologists would agree that the various versions of the doctrine of minimal effects that dominated American media research through the 1960s caused the famine. Other models of effects existed.[10] For instance, Wolfenstein and Leites (1960/1947) used Freudian theory to explore the plots and characters of American movies and so to posit probable effects of cultural themes on individuals. But many sociologists may have felt that like the dominant doctrine, such alternative models posed psychological rather than sociological questions. That feeling might have been exacerbated by the heartiness with which psychologists embraced the topic of effects (Wright, 1986).

Consider Thelma McCormack's and Graham Murdock's separate discussions of media research. Each sociologist assumes that the study of the effects of individual media on individuals is not an appropriate topic for sociological research. Significantly, neither author is American, although McCormack was trained at Columbia University. McCormack (1986) believes that sociologists of mass media have lost their vision by focusing on "the processes of communication—persuasion and influence" and by failing to notice that these processes have been customarily discussed in the context of a conservative social theory. She explains that "the lost vision of communications studies is our failure to concentrate our thinking on social movements and social change, which are the testing grounds, if not the 'killing fields,' of democratic freedoms" (p. 42).

Murdock (1982) shares McCormack's view that American effects models presuppose conservative social theories. He terms it "the individualistic perspective" or "behaviorist project" and even suggests that in studies of the impact of the media on violence, the individualistic perspective is linked to the doctrine of original sin. In traditional American behaviorism, the study of the media concerned "who said what to whom in which channel and with what effect" (Lasswell, 1948) and so presupposed a sequential, linear model. That model failed to embed communications industries in their larger capitalist context and to note how they captured reigning ideologies. Similarly, this model failed to place the media in the context of people's everyday lives, for it failed to see how the media were promulgating doctrines that permeated other major institutions, such as the schools. Rather, the model severed audiences from their social contexts by treating them as individuals —albeit as individuals with (primarily nuclear) families, friends, and acquaintances. Additionally, they ignored how the media as institutions themselves accept presuppositions of Western capitalism and so serve the interests of the capitalist elite. If American sociologists had attended to these issues, they might have asked how, if at all, people resisted the ideas prevailing in the media and how the media contributed to political discourse, including its effects on other institutions, especially those with which it was associated.

This recent British critique of American sociology is now explicit in the writing of some Americans. It is increasingly popular, because it suggests an alternative paradigm to Lasswell's (1948) question of "who says what to whom in which channel with what effect" and to Lazarsfeld's attempt to delineate how the media influence opinion leaders and, through them, other individuals. However, it also demonstrates how the context in which theory develops sets the theoretical and so the research agenda.

An American communications theorist who is not a sociologist has made a similar point. Placing American sociology in a historical perspective, Carey (1983) suggested that paradigms are themselves determined by socioeconomic and sociopolitical conditions. He pointed out that during periods of social ferment or unrest, such as the 1930s and the 1940s, scholars supposed that the media have a powerful impact. During periods of seeming social stability, such as the 1950s and early 1960s, they too celebrated the seeming calm by positing that the media have a minimal impact on society. Carey observed that when social movements again arose in the late 1960s and the 1970s to challenge social inequalities, media scholars challenged the doctrine of minimal effect. Faced with ongoing social change, they insisted the media must matter.

How they matter—or come to matter—is a different issue. Here, especially, one sees the impact of social context and theoretical tradition upon the study of mass-media institutions. The generation of senior media researchers in both Great Britain and the United States owe many a theoretical debt to the Columbia School of Sociology (see, for example, Himmelweit, Oppenheim, and Vince, 1958). However, when in the late 1960s younger media scholars of both countries sought to challenge the reigning model, they did so in very different ways. In the United States, younger researchers developed the "production of culture perspective" (termed "the social production of culture perspective" in Britain).[11] Sometimes, they discussed media institutions in the context of capitalism; sometimes they did not. In Britain, much of the most theoretically interesting work drew upon both British and European Marxist traditions. However, some British researchers still adhered to American empirical traditions.

The Challenge of New Models

Before considering the American production of culture perspective, I will consider the very different context from which British scholars drew intellectual sustenance. Then I will turn to the recent American approach. Finally, I will contrast work in the two countries by juxtaposing two recent books that respectively capture the scholarly transformations of British and American sociology of media.

British Trends

Recent British work differs significantly from most recent American work (that is, American research *not* inspired by European ideas), because younger British scholars are using an approach initially developed in the humanities, not in the social sciences. To oversimplify, much British work asks: "What is the relationship between culture and society, or more generally, between expressive forms, particularly art, and society?" (Carey, 1979, p. 412); while much American work concentrates upon "the conditions under which persuasion occurs" (Carey, 1979, p. 413).[12]

Nicholas Garnham (1983) puts it this way: The failure of British sociologists to secure the large funds necessary to use the "functionalist positivist" American model saved the British from replicating American errors. It also enabled a new generation of British sociologists to return to the source of British media research—literary studies. Citing the work of F. R. Leavis in the 1920s, Garnham explains,

This work focussed upon the corrosive effect upon traditional cultural forms and relations, both elite and popular, of the development of industrial capitalism in general and the industrial forms of mass culture, such as the cinema, in particular. Thus, from the start, British media studies was constructed within a problematic that was critical of capitalism and that saw the mass media as part of a specific and concrete historical development of British social and cultural relations [1983, p. 317].

This problematic need not have produced radical theories. It could have prompted conservative condemnations of contemporary social conditions. However, the British sociologists drew heavily on two leftist interpretations of Leavis's work, each written by a scholar trained in the humanities. These books were Richard Hoggart's *The Uses of Literacy* (1957/1958) and Raymond Williams's *Culture and Society* (1958).[13] Both authors questioned how and why cultural analyses excluded the working class. Both were profoundly concerned with the social impact of contemporary media, but not in the sense that pervaded American sociology. Thus

Hoggart warned, "material improvements can be used so as to incline the body of working people to accept a mean form of materialism as a social philosophy" (1958, p. 323). Williams's study concerns past and contemporary social meanings and social relations among industry, democracy, class, art, and culture—"key words" that permeate his subsequent writings. (See, especially, Williams, 1965/1961, 1975, 1976, 1977.)

Drawing on Hoggart's and Williams's work, as well as E. P. Thompson's *The Making of the English Working-Class* (1963), some British sociologists reformulated the question of effects. Focusing upon resistance, they asked, How did members of recognizable class-based subcultures, such as the Teddy Boys of the 1950s and early 1960s and the punk youth of the 1970s, come to resist dominant middle-class ideologies (see, for example, Hebdige, 1979)? Some of these British studies represent a politically left version of the uses and gratifications perspective developed by Lazarsfeld and his associates. For, to answer their question, researchers gathered ethnographic materials about lower-class youth. These included information about their use of the media and the meaning of the media in their lives. To be sure, researchers found a great deal of dissatisfaction —hostility—toward bourgeois thought and dominance; but researchers could not explain why some groups of working-class youth rebelled culturally, while others did not. Equally important, consideration of these specific "subcultural" groups raised logical contradictions. To explain why these cultural rebellions did not lead to organized political dissent, one must invoke the power of dominant ideology as it exists in the workplace, but also in the media.

This body of work contained another contradiction as well. The researchers came to the question of resistance out of their own political convictions, which would be seen as very liberal to left in the political spectrum of American sociology. Yet the political convictions of the working-class youth whom they studied were conservative. Thus even if the researchers had been able to identify the characteristics of the boys' social situation that led to rejection of the dominant cultural style, they could not have addressed a question implicit in the political thrust of their work: As expressed in the writing of Hans Magnus Enzensberger (1974), that issue is how to resist the ideological dominance of the "consciousness industries" (the media) in order to build socialism.

Finally, research about punks came up against an important characteristic of modern media:

its ability to co-opt dissent. By that I mean rock music may serve as a means of upward social mobility for some working-class youth. By "striking it rich," an exceptional musical group might enjoy consumerist practices that their music deplored (albeit often different practices than those taken for granted by the middle classes). Indeed, it is possible to view the punk emphasis upon style as a variety of the "fetishism of the commodity," a brand of "aesthetic fetishism" (Rolf Meyersohn's term, personal communication, 1986)[14] different in form from that of the middle classes but not necessarily different in kind.

But not all British media research entailed fascination with the working-class youth rebellion or even resistance to the dominant media. Nor did all of it lead to empirical studies. In the late 1970s and early 1980s many articles by British sociologists of the media were programmatic essays about the best theoretical "problematic." Many devolved into excessively theoretical debates about the ideal sociological theory with which to analyze contemporary societies—what the British term "theoreticism." Much of the debate revolved around the work of Louis Althusser.[15] For, wishing to escape the influence of the American empiricism that they condemned, in the 1970s many British scholars turned toward France and steeped themselves in Althusser's writings.[16]

A rejection of Marxist theories of the economic determination of ideas, Althusser's work was heavily influenced "by that version of structuralism which derived from Saussurean linguistics" (Collins et al, 1986a). Suspicious of the possibility that one set of concrete practices could be related or reduced to another (as in the reduction of ideology to economic determinacy), it was concerned with "analysing the internal organization of discrete practices." Rather than discussing what the Americans had identified as effects, this Althusserian approach "argued that the condition for the effectiveness of ideology [including media] was a particular mental structure resulting from the mechanisms of psychic formation analyzed by Freud and . . . Lacan" (Collins et al., p. 4).

In Britain, this was interpreted to mean that (Marxist notions of) determination operated "in the last instance," that there was no rigorous causal relationship between base and superstructure, and that ideologies (namely, the media) were to be studied "within the framework provided by other practices, namely economic life." The media were to be viewed as a "social formation" with "relative autonomy."

Theoretical debate grew exceedingly complex.

Sometimes it even seemed as though the British were generating more theoretical debates about research programs than research. The two main positions are captured in the title of a 1979 essay, "Histories of Culture/Theories of Ideology: Notes on an Impasse" (Johnson, 1979). (Sometimes these positions were called, respectively, materialism and idealism.) In an essay influential in both Britain and the United States, Stuart Hall (1980/1986) discussed the two positions as complementary camps, the "culturalists" and the "structuralists" and called for a synthesis of the two positions. He explained that the culturalists "[relate] 'culture' to the sum of the available descriptions through which societies make sense of and reflect their common experience." In contrast, the structuralist position is "articulated" around the concept of ideology, especially developed by Althusser, Saussure, and their predecessor Levi-Strauss.

According to Hall (1986/1980), both positions entail contradictory assumptions. Consider the issue of "men" as actors in history, a central question in Marxist theory. The culturalists saw "men" as active agents in the making of their own history; the structuralists viewed them as "bearers of the structures that speak and place them." In his call for a synthesis, Hall suggested three potential rallying points for British cultural studies: (1) an emphasis upon signifying practices that recognizes the active agency of the speaker (author, media); (2) a return to the "more classical political economy of culture" and (3) a historically sophisticated structuralism that seeks to explore such issues as the correspondence between industrial capitalism and the bourgeoisie without falling into Marxian reductionism.

One reason that Hall could call for a synthesis is that both the structuralists and the culturalists hold some ideas in common. Foremost among these is the notion of *ideological hegemony* developed by Gramsci (1971) in his *Prison Notebooks* and mentioned earlier in this review essay as "ideological dominance." Gitlin (1980; see 1979) provides the most lucid discussion of the relevance of this concept to the study of the media. He starts by explaining Gramsci's concept this way:

> Hegemony is a ruling class's (or alliance's) domination of subordinate classes and groups through the elaboration and penetration of ideology (ideas and assumptions) into their common sense and everyday practice; it is the systematic (but not necessarily or even usually deliberate) engineering of mass consent to the established order. No

hard and fast line can be drawn between the mechanisms of hegemony and the mechanisms of coercion, the hold of hegemony rests on elements of coercion, just as the force of coercion over the dominated both presupposes and reinforces elements of hegemony. In any given society, hegemony and coercion are interwoven [1980, p. 253].

Gitlin continues by quoting Hall's (1977) elaboration:

> "hegemony" exists when a ruling class (or rather an alliance of ruling class fractions, a historical bloc) is able not only to coerce a subordinate class to conform to its interests, but exerts a "total social authority" over those classes and the social formation as a whole. "Hegemony" is in operation when the dominant class fractions not only dominate but *direct*—lead: when they not only possess the power to coerce but actively organize so as to command and win the consent of subordinated classes to their continuing sway. "Hegemony" thus depends upon a combination of force and consent. But—Gramsci argues—in the liberal-capitalist state, consent is normally in the lead, operating behind an "armor of coercion" [Hall quoted in Gitlin, 1980, p. 253].

Gitlin adds, "hegemony is, in the end, a process that is entered into by both dominators and dominated. Both rulers and ruled derive psychological and material rewards in the course of confirming and reconfirming their inequality" (p. 254). Moreover, "*the hegemonic sense of the world seeps into 'common sense' and gets reproduced there; it may even appear to be generated by that common sense*" (p. 254, emphasis added).

According to Gouldner (1976), ideological hegemony may be hidden, because in the modern liberal-capitalist state there is growing differentiation and autonomy among the economic, political, and bureaucratic orders. But even as the "relative autonomy of the different sectors legitimates the system as a whole," that very seeming autonomy of power and culture makes ideology essential as a "potentially cohesive force" (Gouldner, 1976, quoted in Gitlin, 1980, p. 255). To be sure, separated from the means of producing culture, the hegemonic elite may be displeased with it and prefer "other mechanisms of dominance and control more fully and routinely accessible to them" (ibid., p. 256). Their discomfort may actually reinforce the observation that a hegemony does not exist.

However, that hegemony maintains its force, because it entails and absorbs contradictions, including the tension between "the affirmation of patriarchal authority—currently enshrined in the national security State—and the [bourgeois] affirmation of individual worth and self-determination" (p. 256. As Gitlin stresses, *"the hegemonic ideology of bourgeois culture is extremely complex and absorptive; only by absorbing and domesticating conflicting values, definitions of reality, and demands on it, in fact, does it remain hegemonic"* (p. 256).

Because the notion of ideological hegemony is responsive to the interests of diverse class fractions, British scholars calling for a political economy of culture also stress it. For instance, Garnham (1983a) proposed that the proper study of media entails three questions excluded from both the ongoing debate about Althusser and traditional American discussions of media: (1) "the way by which the system of material production reproduces itself or *the question of crisis,"* (2) "the ways in which the resulting unequal distribution of the surplus product is legitimized or *the question of revolution,"* and (3) "the connection and the nature of the determinacy, if any, between the economic and ideological level" (p. 319, emphasis in the original.) The media are implicated in each of these questions; for each may be construed as a question about hegemony. As Garnham put it, research is best framed within the theory called "cultural materialism." Cultural materialism focuses upon

the irreducible material determinants of the social processes of symbolic exchange and upon the ways in which historically, within the general development of the capitalist mode of production, these processes have been brought within the sphere of commodity production and exchange and with what effects. In short, it [should] examine[] the process described by Enzensberger as "the industrialization of mind" [p. 321].[17]

In the midst of this theoretical debate, the British did produce some splendid research. Even studies accomplished prior to the debate anticipated some of its lines by addressing questions radically different from those raised by Americans in those years. Indeed, in their scope and theoretical sophistication, even research that seemed inspired by American studies went far beyond the earlier American efforts. One good example is *Demonstrations and Communications: A Case Study* by the team at the Leicester Centre for Mass Communications Research (Halloren, Elliot, and Murdock, 1969). It drew on Kurt Lang and Gladys Engel Lang's (1960/1953) classic study of television coverage of MacArthur Day in Chicago in 1951, but discussed hegemony. (General Douglas MacArthur, a hero in World War II, had just returned to the United States after President Harry Truman fired him as head of the American forces in Korea, because MacArthur had failed to carry out a presidential order.)

The Langs's study concerned the discrepancy between "actual events" and their televised coverage. With assistance from other graduate students, the Langs analyzed the news media's prior expectations about the day celebrating the general (he would receive a hero's welcome and Chicagoans would throng to pay tribute); television coverage (which seemed to show vast crowds); and through participant observation, the actual events (attended by sparse crowds). They emphasized how television news used the television technology, particularly the ability to include or exclude images from its broadcast pictures, to confirm its prophecy of tribute to a hero—even though the actual events did not involve a large and active crowd. Television's version of Chicago's MacArthur Day arose within a political context and had political implications, for it made it seem as though Chicagoans had massed to support the general in his conflict with the president.

As had the Lang and Lang article, the Leicester group's *Demonstrations and Communications* concerned an event of clear political importance: the October 27, 1968, demonstration against the Vietnam War held in front of London's American Embassy and coordinated with antiwar demonstrations elsewhere. The team analyzed the coverage of newspapers and electronic media before and after the march, as well as "live" television coverage. Additionally, some of them observed both the large march to Hyde Park and a much smaller group that broke off to demonstrate in front of the United States embassy, where some limited violence occurred.

Like Lang and Lang, the team found self-fulfilling prophecy. Before the march, coverage concentrated upon the possibility of violent clashes between the marchers and police in which foreign students would play a prominent role. This coverage did not discuss the ideas of the various protesting groups. After the march, coverage emphasized the violence incident in front of the embassy. Coverage also stressed that more violence had not occurred because the police were too organized for the "indecisive and ineptly led demonstrators" (p. 120).

In its most original contribution to media studies, the Leicester group pioneered a new way of studying effects by demonstrating that, by and large, those exposed to the news coverage accepted its definitions of events. Before the march, the team distributed a questionnaire to a nonrandom sample of police, students, and "neutrals." It included questions about what the respondents had heard about the demonstration, the sources of that information, and more general questions about politics and violence. This sample also received follow-up questionnaires after the march. Additionally, the team organized six "viewing groups," two of students, two of police, and two of "neutrals" and showed them television's late-evening news reports about the march. The researchers found some variation in responses to news coverage (the police were most likely to find it "fair," the students, least likely). But, by and large, reactions of this selected audience indicated that they "defined and interpreted the event from within the framework provided by the news coverage," not the framework offered by the marchers (Murdock, 1973, p. 172).

Several years after the Leicester study, Americans introduced a new concept to discuss the effect of the mass media: "agenda-setting" (McCombs and Shaw, 1972). It refers to the power of the media during election campaigns to set the topics people find politically important, as indicated by the correlation between topics covered in the news and citizens' identification of the most important public issues. But the British had gone beyond what Americans would term the innovative contribution represented by studies of agenda-setting; for they had inferred a possible *ideological impact* —what sociologists of the media in both countries were eventually to discuss as "hegemony."

Exploration of how ideology is built into media programs also was central to Elliott (1972) study of the production of a series of television documentaries. The larger study design included an examination of viewer responses to the seven programs about prejudice whose production Elliott examined. This study did not stress the media's ability to define an event, but rather an issue. Elliott carefully demonstrated how the very processes of gathering information transformed scholarly knowledge and set a political tone. For the logic inherent in those processes "directed" the staff's attention to the conventional wisdom about prejudice, a psychological phenomenon, rather than toward the then-

emerging body of scholarly work about a socioeconomic phenomenon, structural racism.

American Trends

Rather than exploring theories of culture or of ideology, in the late 1960s and early 1970s American sociologists turned toward the sociology of work. Some used theories of formal organization to set out what Peterson termed "the production of culture approach" (1976). Others used ideas central to the symbolic interactionist interpretation of the sociology of occupations and professions.[18] Drawing on ethnomethodology, a related variation explicitly explored the interstices of the sociology of knowledge and the sociology of work to incorporate phenomenological insights about the organization of knowledge in institutions.[19] However, implicitly or explicitly, all three variants shared a concern with the intersection of the sociology of work with the sociology of knowledge. Implicitly or explicitly, all three asked how, through their organization of "bundles of tasks" (Becker, 1982), the media operated as "consciousness industries."

Unlike British media sociology of those years, the earliest formal American statements of the new approach were naive about both culture and consciousness. The earliest formal statement, Peterson's introduction to his edited *The Production of Culture*, returned to nineteenth-century anthropology for an all-encompassing and imperialistic definition of culture (all symbol systems).[20] It did not delineate possible relationships between what Americans had traditionally termed levels of culture (such as high culture and popular culture), attitudes, and culture in the anthropological sense of the values and artifacts associated with daily life. Nor did this early statement broach the issue that so concerned the British: the historical relationship among political economy (especially the political economy of the media), social classes, and ideology.[21] Rather, Americans emphasized the media as organizational systems.

Many articles were quite sophisticated about organizational theory. One of the first articles to appear (Hirsch, 1972) posed the issue of the interaction between the organizations that produce "fads and fashions" and the organizations that distribute them. Noting the inability of "producers" to control "distributors," he wrote of the attempt by "producers" to control the permeable boundary between themselves and their environment. Powell's (1985) research on academic publishing houses again emphasized the question of environment. Powell noted how environments are "invasive," yet firms producing culture are capable of altering and managing them. Finally, explorations of culture-producing organizations led and DiMaggio and Powell (1983) to concentrate upon the forms of rationalization introduced by professionals working in organizations—how they make their organizations increasingly similar to one another as they try to change them.

Some of this research had clear, though undeveloped, implications for the political economy of media. Hirsch's unpublished doctoral dissertation (1973) provides a good example. Hirsch compared how pharmaceutical companies and record companies turned a profit after World War II. His discussion of the record industry turned on a series of homologies—developments flowing from the same cause (postwar transformations of American societies) but arising independently of each other.

Hirsch (1983) identified four postwar processes. (1) The market hegemony of the major record companies specializing in swing broke up. Their vertical integration disintegrated; their record stores disappeared; to increase sales, they began discounting in a market featuring noncompatible 45 rpm and 78 rpm records and record players. (2) In such locations as the new suburban malls, a new distribution system arose. A variety of stores, including supermarket chains, discounted a "new sound"—"race" and "country" music previously carried in specialty stores but now stocked for the chains by rack-jobbers. (3) Challenged by television, which initially broadcast what had been popular radio programs, radio searched for a new format. Returning to its earliest format—music—radio "invented" the top-40 station. (4) For a variety of reasons associated with postwar economic transformations, a youth culture arose. Its members had more disposable income to buy the now-cheaper records. Although Hirsch does not use such terms, I read Hirsch's account as a description of the impact of postwar capitalism on both the record industry and the middle-class adolescents who were transformed into a significant "market" (a topic explicitly discussed in Frith, 1981).

Peterson and Berger's (1975) work on successive styles of rock concentrated on monopolies. They argue that new styles emerged through challenges to the monopolies enjoyed by sets of four or five records companies, whose members changed from one stylistic period to the next. (The authors did not attempt to delineate theoretically what a sociologist might mean by style, but see Rosenblum, 1978). As the sales of a particular style waned, other sets of firms introduced "new" sounds.

This American work is more limited than the somewhat later British research on music (especially Frith, 1981). The British stress how rock became what Becker (1982) terms an "art world" and how that world is embedded in contemporary international socioeconomic systems. Thus Frith describes how such initial byproducts and eventual mainstays of record promotion as the concert tour helped to create a multifaceted industry. He analyzes the internal stratification of the industry-created market by age, class, gender, race, and ethnicity. By insistently placing music and the music industry in its historical context, British sociologists such as Frith demonstrate how an understanding of rock music enables a better analysis of British (and sometimes American) society.

Now and again, American scholars explicitly emphasized political economy. For instance, Powell (1985) described his study of academic publishing as an examination of the "local political economy—the set of relations both within the two [publishing] houses . . . studied and between them and a variety of external advisers and service-providers" (p. xviii). He related such issues as how a particular publisher expects to turn a profit to the strategies editors use to accept and to process manuscripts.

Nonetheless, even when not historically grounded, studies that are variants of the production of culture perspective and that Peterson (1982) identified with it did contribute to theoretical delineation of American media hegemony. These studies have tended to concern the production of news and of television entertainment. Among them are works by Tuchman (1978), Fishman (1980), Gans (1979), and Gitlin (1980, 1983), as well as Schudson's social history of news (1978). In sometimes very different ways, these works explore how professionals within organizations, which themselves exist within a larger socioeconomic context, act through seemingly inevitable processes to embed specific ideologies in the content of the media.

Schudson's work may be included under the rubric of the production of culture perspective, because it explores the development of journalistic professionalism within the context of the changing class and ethnic structure of American society. He highlights the emergence of journalistic "objectivity," including its supposed segregation of "facts" and "values." Starting in the 1830s, with the origin of the penny-press, Schudson identified journalism with the interests of the middle class in a democratic, market society. As the class structure changed, so did the media. By the 1920s information workers, including journalists and the emerging public relations industry, saw their task as providing under the rubric of a pseudoscientistic objectivity the information that they felt those less educated than they had to know. In an argument sometimes parallel to Freidson's (1971) work on medical ideology, Schudson argued journalists came to see themselves as professionals whose task is to "diagnose" objectively the ills of the political system, economy, and (sometimes) the social system by providing "facts." Supposedly, these "facts" lead news readers to understand the available remedies implied in those facts.

Based on participant observation, the Tuchman (1978) and Fishman (1980) works are both less historical and more critical of the news media. Starting with the premise that ideas develop in a historical context (that capitalism shaped news organizations, which in turn shaped journalistic professionalism), each study explores how the social organization of news gathering permits some occurrences to be identified and reported as news, but renders others invisible. Each argues that news is ideology, defined as a "means not to know" (Smith, 1984). Though each book emphasizes how the organization of news replicates (and draws on) the social organization of power, each follows a somewhat different path to that conclusion.

Tuchman (1978) emphasizes the dependence of news organizations on legitimated social institutions that claim to gather and to conserve centralized information. To do so, she traces the organization of the "news-net" through which reporters find occurrences to be transformed into stories; defines the "web of facticity" that accepts information from legitimated institutions as "facts," but rejects the facticity of information from other sources; and argues that news entails two simultaneous processes of "framing" (see Goffman, 1974; compare Bateson, 1955/1972).[22]

Both sorts of framing entail rules about how to cover a story. One set, identification of a story as "hard news" or "soft news," delineates how news workers expect occurrences to unfold temporally and spatially and so establishes the sorts of work reporters (and editors) expect to do in coming days, weeks, and months. Another set, topical frames, contains clues about how to gather "necessary" information. This emphasis upon framed "facts" means that the news concerns events (a demonstration) not issues (the United States's international military presence)

and leads to fragmentation of the interconnections among events and, necessarily, issues.

Fishman (1980) points out how reportorial rules may "hide" what's happening. To do so, he develops the notion of "bureaucratic phase structures," ideal-typical delineations of how occurrences unfold in the organizations with which reporters interact. These include notions of bureaucratic responsibility, including the assumption that politicians establish the policies that administrators carry out. So wed to the assumption that politicians' important function is to set policy, reporters tend not to listen when politicians debate administrative practices. They may not even notice that the politicians are setting new policies. Reportorial procedures and assumptions establish what reporters may perceive to be news.

Finally, as does Gans (1979), both stress that through their interdependence on legitimated institutions with centralized information, reporters come to accept official definitions of the situation. The police define the nature and seriousness of crimes; neither victims nor criminals do so. The Federal Aviation Authority determines whether the noise at airports is sufficient to interfere with the quality of life in homes near airports; residents of those homes do not do so. Welfare agencies, not welfare recipients, define what may be problematic in the welfare system. All these students of news argue that the content of news is embedded in the processes of its production. But Gans stresses that those processes incorporate significant elements of the political environment.[23]

Because the news media accept the ideologies of political institutions, the hegemonic impact of news may also be embedded in the processes of news production (Gitlin, 1980). Sociologists may not be able to prove that media effect individual attitudes (but see Lang and Lang, 1983, and Ball-Rokeach, Rokeach, and Grube, 1984, discussed below)[24]; but Gitlin (1980) clearly demonstrated that they have a powerful impact on social movements.[25] To do so, Gitlin analyzed *The New York Times* and CBS coverage of Students for a Democratic Society (SDS) and the anti-Vietnam War movement, while drawing on his scholarship about, and personal familiarity with, the antiwar movement. He argued that when initially SDS presented a multifaceted analysis of American society, reporters and editors were at a loss to "frame" stories about the group and so used the frame developed for "civil rights stories." As news organizations came to understand the depth of SDS's opposition to the war, they covered SDS's demonstrations as "crime stories." As had been true of British coverage of the antiwar demonstration studied by the Leicester group (Halloren, Elliott, and Murdock, 1969), they emphasized violence and arrests, not participants' ideas.

As Gitlin (1980) continues, this news coverage recruited new members to SDS. Most of them meant to join the organization the news portrayed and so they directed SDS toward the sorts of activities emphasized on TV news. Ultimately, when more members of the political and economic elite began to oppose the war, the news-portrait of both SDS's activities and its "long-haired" members enabled the news media to define student activity in antiwar presidential campaigns as the actions of responsible "clean-cut" youth. By this depiction, the media fostered legitimated political activity.

Gitlin's (1983) study of the production of prime-time television programming is also directed toward the general issue of hegemony. He presents it as a "thick description" of the activities of the small circle of network bureaucrats, employees of production companies, and freelancers, but it may be read as an expression of the production of culture perspective. Like Hirsch (1972) and Frith (1981), Gitlin emphasizes that in an industry where most offerings fail economically, participants cannot predict which "tastes" of the audience to foresee which of seemingly identical products will turn a profit. However, as in his analysis of hegemony, Gitlin's primary interest is in the responsiveness of the media to other legitimated institutions. In its ethnographic richness, Gitlin's story tells how powerful members of this industry "read the mood" of the Reagan years as indicative of a turn to the right; accordingly, after Reagan's election they offered "spin-offs, clones, and recombinant" programs stressing law and order.

Gitlin's work complements the earlier work on news: The various analyses of the production of news demonstrated how news workers may create controversies yet control them through framing techniques. Gitlin's discussion of prime-time television explains how programmers use a controversy to create a program that will draw an audience, but render it into a "personalized" conflict removed from its economic and political context so that the program does not challenge the authority of established social institutions.

Finally, in contradistinction to other American sociology of media, Gitlin (1983) sees the audience as having failed. He writes that since the class fractions contained in the mass audience have not organized themselves to demand "better" programming, they deserve what they have gotten. Some other American sociologists (e.g., Ball-Rokeach and Cantor 1986; Cantor, 1979) continue to emphasize that programming is implicitly pluralistic and that audience members indirectly influence program content.

That notion of an active audience runs throughout Ball-Rokeach and Cantor's (1986) recent compilation of American research. Their *Media, Audience and Social Structure* is so different from a recent British anthology, *Media, Culture and Society: A Critical Reader* (Collins et al., 1986b) that a student might wonder whether both books contribute to the same field.

The Contrast Between British and American Trends

Ideal texts, *Media, Audience and Social Structure* and *Media, Culture and Society: A Critical Reader*[26] address themselves to what has been happening in their respective countries. Earlier sections of this essay have drawn upon articles in both books. *Media, Culture and Society* contains Collins et al.'s lucid "culturalist" discussion of the history of British research since the 1960s and Hall's more "structuralist" call for a theoretical synthesis. *Media, Audience and Social Structure* includes Wright's historical essay and McCormack's critique of the treatment of power in American sociology.

Not only are the thrusts of these four essays very different, but the British text ignores traditional American materials, while Schudson's graceful essay (1986) in the American text subsumes the British work under the rubric "Neo-Marxist Approach: Hegemony and Ideology." Schudson also delineates two additional approaches: the "Neo-Weberian Approach: Organization, Profession, Production, and Market" (already presented as the production of culture perspective) and the "Neo-Durkheimian Approach: Ritual and Culture" (stress upon the media as providing people a sense of connection to the collective whole and upon genres as demonstrating how cultural forms constrain social action.)[27]

Schudson (1986) correctly stresses that internationally the best work (including his own) straddles several categories.[28] He notes, too, that despite the very different programmatic statements issued in Britain and the United States, research originating in each country finds a home in the other. Thus, explaining how they selected articles from the journal *Media, Culture and Society* for their anthology, its editors (Collins et al., 1986a) present an essay by the American Paul DiMaggio (1986), "Cultural entrepreneurship in nineteenth-century Boston," as "a good example" of the sort of "empirical historical inquiry into the material base of high culture," which advances the "culturalist" project (p. 5). Since *Media, Audience and Social Structure* was compiled from presentations at the 1984 meetings of the American Sociological Association, it does not contain British research (but does include a Danish contribution [Rosengren, 1986] on linking culture and other societal systems). However, British research on news (e.g., Chibnall, 1977; Schlesinger, 1978; Tunstall, 1971) sometimes anticipates and sometimes affirms American findings (compare Chibnall, 1981, and Fishman, 1981).[29]

Nonetheless, three aspects of these British and American texts make dramatic the very different orientations of British and American sociologists of the media. First, the British text ignores pre-1970 American research. It does not even mention the contribution of Paul Lazarsfeld. However, the editors' summation to the American text advises the following:

> This collection also demonstrates that the seminal work of Lazarsfeld and his colleagues continues to influence the direction of media research, although the scope has broadened considerably. No longer is the term "social" narrowly applied to mean simply demographic characteristics. The definition of "social" has been expanded to include history, industrial relations, culture, social structure, political economy, and social process. . . . The social scientist's effort to uncover the reciprocal relations between the media and social processes of change, conflict, integration, and control requires moving beyond demographics of audiences to questions of the structural position of the media in social life and its cumulative, as well as its more immediate, effects on belief, behavior, culture, and process [p. 350].

(Most British research would not use the term "reciprocal relations," but would instead discuss "the connection and the nature of the determinacy, if any, between the economic and ideological level" as done by Garnham and discussed above.)

Second, the arrangement of essays in each text indicates vastly different ways of conceiving the field. The shorter British text has three sections:

Approaches to Cultural Theory; Intellectuals and Cultural Production; and, British Broadcasting and the Public Sphere, which includes historical essays on broadcasting and unemployment, and the evolution of the style of radio talk, civic ritual, and historically situated essays on terrorism, the information society, and advertising. (The British text singles out intellectuals, because of their role in the maintenance of a "critical public sphere" [compare Elliott, 1986].) The five sections of the American text concern: sociological inquiry into the media and mass communications: historical and theoretical origins; media and social process; media organizations and their audiences; media and political conflict and change; and media content. Some, but not most, of these essays are historically oriented.

Third, each text has a different perspective on the audience. "Audience" has one of the largest listings in the index to the American text. The British text does not even include the term "audience" in its index; yet the British text does indeed discuss the audience. Like *Media, Audience and Social Structure*, it does so in an feminist essay on soap opera.[30] *Media, Audience and Social Structure* offers Muriel G. Cantor's and Joel Cantor's "Audience Composition and Television Content: The Mass Audience Revisited"; *Media, Culture and Society*, Michele Mattelart's "Women and the Cultural Industries." Each essay assumes that capitalism determines key characteristics of soap operas; each examines the genre historically. As announced by their respective titles, each conceives of the audience as "active," but cares about an "active" audience for different reasons.

Cantor and Cantor address their article to theories of mass society, which stress a large, undifferentiated, amorphous audience. They argue that any member of a production staff (or network) who is not (somehow) responsive to the audience would fail to attract an audience (and so be fired); for the media are capitalist enterprises. In Gitlin's (1983) terms, television exists to "rent the eyeballs" of viewers to advertisers. Cantor and Cantor argue: Although federal regulations and other organizational factors analyzed through the production of culture perspective determine the nature of programs, the audience matters, too. That audience is segmented by gender, age, and especially "taste segments" ("a cluster of people with both demographic and taste characteristics in common" [p. 217]).[31]

In the case of soap operas, Cantor and Cantor argue, both the target audiences (the audience that the programmers wish to attract in order to appeal to advertisers) and the actual audience change, as both the social structure and demographic structure change. Historically, to maintain and, preferably, to increase viewing by the target audience, programmers have altered the settings, characters, and topics broached in soap operas (Cantor and Pingree, 1983). Writing letters, reading fan magazines, attending "personal appearances" of soap-opera stars, and, more indirectly, through the ratings system, the actual audience has assisted them in this endeavor.

However, Cantor and Cantor stress, the soap opera audience, like the more general television audience, is also composed of distinct taste segments. Members of each segment tend to watch different shows. Furthermore, across and within historical periods, the content of soap operas has varied according to the image of the target audience held by members of the shows' staff.

In contrast, Mattelart's essay about soap opera "links the traditions of 'political economy' and discourse analysis . . . [Mattelart] argues that on one level . . . soap operas . . . are the result of producing commodities for an audience already segmented by capitalism's division of labour, especially the division between work outside the home and the domestic sphere. On another level, however, [Mattelart] argues that the only explanation for the pleasure women derive from such programmes must lie in the context of the relationship between their form and the deep structure of group unconsciousness" (Collins et al., 1986a, p. 8).

As do Cantor and Cantor, Mattelart stresses variations in the genre. For her, however, the key issue is "the manner in which the 'dominated' groups and individuals read and respond to [media messages], or oppose to them a specific manner of, precisely, *appropriation*, and resist them (if need be through a diversion of their original intention, implicit or explicit) in the name of some project of their own" (Mattelart, 1986, p. 71).

Because I have chosen to highlight the differences between American sociology of media and British cultural studies, I have made it seem as though these bodies of research are more disparate than they are. Many studies share questions, if not approaches. For instance, using theories other than those developed in France and debated in Britain, some American work addresses the question Mattelart asks: Why do audiences (especially women) get pleasure from the often shoddy media fare designed for them? Two of these studies (Long, 1986; Radway, 1984) concern readers and may be understood as a corrective to both the emphasis upon the individual implicit in uses and gratifications research and to the implication of a uniform response to media fare contained in some treatments of hegemony.

Without invoking the theoreticism of French structuralism, American studies of readers (Long, 1986; Radway, 1984) emphasize the power of distribution systems and the process of appropriation. By describing how (mainly women's) reading groups chose texts and by placing groups' discussions of these texts in the context of readers' everyday lives, Long (1986) does more than inquire as to what readers say they get out of books. Long argues that dependent upon availability in chain bookstores, groups' selection of texts is at the mercy of a hegemonic distribution system that ratifies elite definitions of what middle-class readers want, and should want, to read. By asking insistently how middle-class readers interpret both bestsellers and the literary canon and how these interpretations depart from the "preferred readings" tendered by literary critics, Long studies the process of appropriation.

American critic Janice Radway does not use such terms as *appropriation* in *Reading the Romance* (1984), a particularly astute book about why women derive pleasure from fare designed for their "market segment." Radway's question resembles that posed by Mattelart (1986), but her answer is empirically based; she draws on textual analyses of successful and failed romances, interviews with a group of readers in a midwestern city, and both feminist sociology and reader-response theory. *Reading the Romance* goes beyond uses and gratifications research, for Radway does not blithely accept her informants' assurances that they find these novels educational, entertaining, and relaxing. It also implies simultaneous acceptance of and resistance to hegemony: Radway shows how these mass-produced and promoted novels take advantage of women's subservience in patriarchal, capitalist society; how the act of reading protests the women's duty to nurture others without receiving nurturance themselves, and how the plots and characters satisfy readers by simultaneously criticizing and reproducing their lot as wives and mothers.

Another area of confluence occurs in the neo-Durkheimian emphasis on media as social cement holding together diverse and otherwise even antagonistic groups and classes. Both British (Chaney, 1986) and American work on media events (Lang and Lang, 1986) also emphasize how coverage of civic rituals has transformed political systems. In both countries, sociologists have analyzed discourse to illuminate how the media build social cohesion.

Although not based on data about the audience, Chaney's most recent work (1986) concerns the audience. Chaney (1986) argues that through the presentations of civic rituals, television creates and reproduces a shared social discourse and builds social cohesion. The media, he demonstrates, have transformed the civic rituals through which they accomplish these tasks. Covering in 1946 the state celebration of the end of World War II, television had access to those rituals. Televizing in 1953 the coronation of the Queen, it produced "a radical transformation of the ritual form to be more consistent with its social context . . . [Television created] new modes of civic ritual in which national festivals have become effectively media occasions rather than occasions to which the media has access" (p. 262). To use American examples, presenting as a shared political discourse such events as the televised funeral of John F. Kennedy, presidential inaugurations, and national political conventions transforms that discourse.

Although couched in different terms, Chaney's argument resonates with the work of Michael Schudson. Schudson's *Advertising: The Uneasy Persuasion* (1984) does not concern media events as delineated by Katz (1980a) and discussed by Chaney (1986). Media events (civic rituals) are exceptional; advertising is mundane. But Schudson brilliantly depicts the social meanings associated with a form of discourse that so permeates daily life as to be taken for granted.[32] Advertising, Schudson argues, is "capitalist realism." In style and execution, it fulfills all the dicta of how "socialist realism" should be "true to life." Ultimately, says Schudson, advertising is reminiscent of a marriage: The partners know they love one another, but nonetheless speak words of love as periodic affirmation of their bond. "Advertising," Schudson offers, "is capitalism saying 'I love you' to itself." It presupposes and reproduces acceptance of capitalism. It is ideological reaffirmation.

Unlike the emphasis on the text in Chaney (1986) and Schudson (1984), Lang and Lang's (1986) research on the effects of television on politics does not stress discourse. Nonetheless, like Chaney, they insist that television has transformed political life. By offering live coverage of presidential nominating conventions (a civic ritual), emphasizing party caucuses and primaries, and stressing personalities, television has contributed to the demise of the power of political parties. Their 1983 book on Watergate, discussed below, delineates how by following

everyday practices to cover extraordinary occurrences, the media—especially television—influence collective action.

Consensus and Dissensus

It seems appropriate that in a field intimately connected to politics and power, dispute and consensus revolves around issues involving the conceptualization of power, politics, and citizen's relationship to the state.

Scholarly Squabbles

Internationally, these issues are part of a fervid dispute between neo-Marxists and non-Marxists about the relationship of current research to previous work in the field and arguments about "empiricism," "empiricalism," and antiempiricism.

Especially in Europe, but also in both the United States and Great Britain, some young researchers tend to consider "American sociology" and "critical theory" to be antithetical terms. They tend to identify most American work with behaviorism (used as a derogatory epithet) and "empiricalism," the transformation of human experience into a "utilitarian cipher" through which experience becomes a "device of power" (Ewen, 1983, p. 222). Lang has argued that this characterization of American research is plainly wrong. Reviewing German and American research in the 1930s and 1940s, Lang (1979) argues that the "empirical tradition of communication research is as much a German as an American phenomenon" and that there is "no *inherent* incompatibility between the 'positivism' of administrative communications research and the critical approach associated with the Frankfurt School" (Lang, 1979, p. 83). Charging that neo-Marxist work is antiempirical (Open University, 1977), Blumler has himself been subjected to the countercharge that under the appearance of objectivity, his research hides a political agenda (see Garnham, 1979).

There are also criticisms of the neo-Weberian production of culture perspective. Some of these come from neo-Marxists. For instance, Williams (1977) implies this research is seriously flawed by its ahistoricity. Some come from neo-Durkheimians. For instance, Schudson (1984) criticizes the suggestion (Tuchman, 1978) that one can analyze the production of news much as one analyzes the production of bread. He correctly objects that news as symbol creates and carries social meanings in ways that bread cannot. From a neo-Marxist perspective, Wolff (1981; compare Rosenblum, 1978) levels a similar charge: The American production of cultural perspective does not sufficiently consider the content and style of the media. Still others (e.g., Ball-Rokeach and Cantor, 1986) object that although some neo-Weberians claim that the meaning and hence the effect of the media are embedded in the processes of production, they have not yet proved whether and how these embedded meanings have an affect on the audience (but see Gitlin, 1980, and Halloren et al., 1969).

There are additional disputes as well. For instance, reviewing Schudson (1984), Ewen (1985) argues that neo-Durkheimian work obscures the socioeconomic organization of the media. Long (1985) suggests that many discussions of hegemony have ignored the sometimes subtle and sometimes blatant differences among social classes and social periods. A variety of theorists continue to disagree about whether the notion of hegemony implies a passive audience (contrast Katz, 1980b, and Garnham and Williams, 1986/1980). And some researchers continue to find the concept of hegemony "metaphysical"; that is, not amenable to empirical verification.

Convergence

Despite conceptual disputes, including the tendency of British and American scholars to draw on divergent theories, researchers converge in their insistence that the media have a decided impact on both individuals and social institutions. The fervor of the British theoreticist debate obscures participants' shared devotion to elucidating how the media effect the conditions of social life under contemporary capitalism.[33] Although they are less likely to emphasize the capitalist context of media production, distribution, and appropriation, Americans do insist that the media have a political impact that ultimately reaffirms the "virtues" of their intertwined social, political, and economic systems.

Complementing each other and British research, the various American "schools" of media research have demonstrated that the media have an impact on social movements (Gitlin, 1980), political institutions (Lang and Lang, 1983, 1986) and the tenor of civic life (Alexander, 1986). Recent research on media events as civic rituals also complements what some of the sociologists engaged in those studies might condemn as "behaviorist" research. For

while the neo-Durkheimian approach delineates the shared discourse of political life, recent survey research documents how television has affected both attitudes and political behavior.

Two of these studies seem particularly important, because they address the topic that inspired both the British theoreticist debate and American and British research on news. That topic is power, especially the power to define political issues. The books are *The Battle for Public Opinion* (Lang and Lang, 1983) and *The Great American Values Test* (Ball-Rokeach, Rokeach, and Grube, 1984). Both are particularly interesting, because they use survey data in innovative ways to demonstrate the impact of the media.[34] Lang and Lang (1983) interweave the study of congressional and presidential politics, media coverage of rituals, and public opinion polls to explain Richard Nixon's forced resignation. Ball-Rokeach and colleagues demonstrate that one may use television to change individuals' values about politically relevant moral issues and so, with some misgivings about how their work may be used, they document how a demagogue may exploit television.

The Battle for Public Opinion

Examining the "Watergate events" in the context of comparable governmental crises, Lang and Lang (1983) develop two sets of findings about the effects of the media. One set addresses effects as traditionally construed; the other, long-range systemic impact.

Addressing the traditional behaviorist literature, Lang and Lang demonstrate the following: (1) Although news about any one event may have a minimal impact (as Klapper, 1960, claimed), it may nonetheless lay the groundwork for radical shifts in public opinion prompted by subsequent events. (2) Following "normal" rules of finding and presenting news, saturation coverage of the "Watergate events" did set citizens' political agenda (see McCombs and Shaw, 1972). (3) By defining political symbols, the media set the terms of public discourse and create a unifying (collective) experience.

Forging new ground, they interpret their historical research, content analyses, survey data, and interviews with government officials, to mean (1) "the ubiquitous presence of television most directly affects the political actors themselves. It forces them to be responsive to norms binding on other members of society" (p. 297). (2) Public debate of political controversies makes difficult their (historically customary) resolution by elites, because (3) "in widening the scope of a controversy, [the news media] modify the rules of the game, forcing politicians to justify themselves to an ever larger public'' (p. 305). (4) However, the public's "role in Watergate was [nonetheless that] of a bystander, whose opinions entered the calculations of political actors, sensitive to any murmuring among the multitude'' (p. 299). (5) Having appeared to respond to public opinion about Watergate, government could and did return to business as usual.

Finally, reconceptualizing "long range effects," Lang and Lang suggest the following: (1) "attitudes formed in response to critical events can be generalized to other political events or objects" (p. 238). Watergate contributed to, but did not cause the ongoing erosion of political trust. (2) "A generation whose attitudes are particularly marked by these events in time replaces an older generation of voters and leaders, whose political mentality was predominantly shaped by a different set of events" (p. 238). Children and adolescents had strong views on Watergate, though they do not seem marked by Watergate to the same degree that the (longer lasting and more structurally fundamental) depression and World War II are inscribed in the youth of those days. (3) "A controversy or complex of events comes to serve as a symbol that justifies or inhibits a broad range of politically relevant attitudes, actions, and policies" (p. 238). Although the outcome of Watergate was frequently in doubt, it is now interpreted as a symbol of how well the American political system works. The term *Watergate* now connotes affirmation that the news media guard citizens' interests and that Congress serves to check executive power. In sum, Lang and Lang demonstrate that, as waged by politicians in the media, the battle for public opinion during Watergate still remains consequential.

The Great American Values Test

Lang and Lang (1983) discuss long-range effects of the media without resorting to social psychology. Ball-Rokeach and colleagues (the Washington State University team) used innovative surveys and a natural experiment to address a social psychological issue: They demonstrated how "television induced long-range cognitive and behavioral effects in the daily lives of adults in the privacy of their homes" (p. 151).

The Washington State University team started from two theoretical premises, which they term "media system dependency theory" and "belief systems theory of stability and change."[35] "Media system dependency theory" emphasizes how members of an audience actively use media to understand themselves and social situations, to orient themselves toward action and social interaction, and to enjoy themselves when alone or with others. Individuals selectively expose themselves to programs they believe most likely to satisfy relevant needs. "[T]he greater the media dependency, the greater the level of attention during exposure, the greater the level of affect toward the message and its senders, and the greater the likelihood of postexposure communication about the message—and thus, the greater the probability of message effects, intended or unintended" (p. 13).

The belief systems theory of stability and change posits that a need of psychological consistency motivates individuals, as does a need to maintain and to enhance self-conceptions and self-presentations about their competence and morality. People may feel self-satisfaction or self-dissatisfaction if they become "consciously aware of, and knowledgeable about some specific and salient attribute of the self . . . perceived to have important positive or negative implications . . . for how [they] conceive of or present (themselves] as competent and moral" (p. 32). Rationally, people should be willing to change to fulfill these basic needs. Thus if an individual receives an unambiguous and credible message that forces self-confrontation about moral inconsistencies and enables psychological or social action, the individual may alter her or his beliefs.

Combining the two theories, the Washington State University team designed a half-hour television program to reveal to viewers some common American moral inconsistencies. Designed to permit "you" to understand "your values" and how "your values" compare with those of other Americans, *The Great American Values Test* was hosted by celebrities, simultaneously aired near prime-time on three network affiliates, hyped through radio, television, and newspaper ads, and listed in *TV Guide*. Using a sophisticated research design, the team randomly preselected respondents in both a control and an experimental city, gathered survey data on the values, attitudes, and media dependencies of half the sample through mailed questionnaires, determined who had watched *The Great American Values Test*, questioned some sample-members immediately after the program, administered a mailed questionnaire to the other half of the sample, and in three waves sent solicitations for organizations promoting the values and attitudes discussed on the program (race and gender equality and environmentalism) to sample members in each city.

Not many sample members watched the entire show, but the program changed the attitudes and behaviors of those who did. They were the group most likely to respond to solicitations mailed 13 weeks after the show had aired. The team reported some inconsistencies and not all analyses were statistically significant.[36] But in general, comparison of the preprogram and postprogram attitudes and behavior revealed that the program affected views in the predicted rank order: (1) uninterrupted viewers, (2) interrupted viewers, (3) nonviewers in Experimental City, and (4) nonviewers in Control City. The team was so convinced that their show had an impact and that other shows could also have a political impact, they concluded their book with a chapter on the ethical implications of their study.

Neither *The Battle for Public Opinion* nor *The Great American Values Test* directly addresses the issue of hegemony broached by recent research. Indeed, in its methodologically rigorous attention to the effect of television on individuals, *The Great American Values Test* may be attacked as behaviorism. Nonetheless, both books are valuable to those exploring new ways of conceptualizing the study of media, culture, and society. For, as do neo-Marxists, Lang and Lang affirm how elites may use the very citizens' attitudes that they create to justify political actions and to reaffirm their legitimacy. *The Great American Values Test* may be read as a text about the authoritarian potential of the media.

Other Trends

Recognizing the contradictions inherent in contemporary media, other social scientists are beginning to pose complementary questions about how people use media to make sense of the contradictions of their daily lives—or to resist the positions in which they find themselves. Some specific examples are these: What specifically do viewers get out of the news (Graber, 1984; compare Robinson et al., 1986, chap. 7), and how do middle-class suburban women make sense of American culture, including Hollywood versions of love (Swidler, in press)? Some of this research also considers the contradictory ways groups interpret the same message. Thus Katz and Liebes's (1986) discussion and examples of how Israelis of different national backgrounds retell and interpret the plot of an episode of *Dallas* leaves one wondering whether they all saw the same program. But it

affirms that audience members use interpretive schemes derived from cultural frameworks that they take for granted.[37]

Research on news also affirms the importance of interpretive schemes. In a series of papers, Gamson (1987) and Gamson and Modigliani (1986) propose a "constructionist model" to capture the relationship between media and public opinion. They explore both the construction of media discourse about political issues and the construction of people's opinions about those same topics. They use content analysis to analyze media discourse, but instead of merely sorting subject matter into categories, as most content analyses do, Gamson and Modigliani reveal the internal structures of media packages, including their frames and condensing symbols. Laying out the diversity of packages used to construct issues, they demonstrate that even on such a controversial topic as nuclear power, a package may express ambivalence. To understand the impact of media discourse, Gamson and Modigliani then use "peer conversations" to assess public opinion. (Held in the home of an informant, a peer conversation involves relatively unstructured talk among the researchers, the informant, and a few of his or her friends or relatives.) As others have, these researchers affirm that the media have a particularly powerful impact when they present information outside of the direct experience of a news reader or viewer. But, they add, by forcing respondents to choose between antithetical positions rather than permitting them to express ambivalence, public opinion polls hide the impact of the news media on citizens. Through peer conversations, Gamson and Modigliani hope to make visible the underlying "schemata" and even the thought processes hidden by public opinion polls.

Additionally, the American study of media is being increasingly integrated into "cultural sociology" (the American term for what the British call "cultural studies"). Gitlin (1983) compared mass media and French romanticism —albeit disparagingly; Clark (1978) explained how in France comparable social processes gave birth to newspapers and the popular nineteenth-century novel—a topic included in Williams (1965/1961; Tuchman (Tuchman with Fortin, in press) has turned to a study of how elite Victorian men appropriated the high-culture novel as their preserve.

In both countries, sociologists increasingly understand the term *culture* to include fads and fashions (Hirsch, 1972); furniture and foods; art (Becker, 1982; DiMaggio, 1986), photography (Becker, 1982; Rosenblum, 1978), music

(Faulkner, 1971; Gilmore, 1984), architecture (Blau, 1984), drama (Griswold, 1986), television (Cantor, 1979; Gitlin, 1983; Kellner, 1981; Newcomb, 1976; Tuchman, 1974), and the novel (Tuchman with Fortin, in press)—although no American has presented as theoretical sophisticated a justification for merging the study of popular culture, high culture, and everyday life as have Williams (1977) and Bourdieu (1984, 1986a, 1986b; compare Gans, 1974). In both countries, they have incorporated the ideas of Raymond Williams and, within the past decade, those of Pierre Bourdieu (1984) to understand the production of culture, the formation of the "tastes" of class fractions, and how in their daily lives members of different class fractions incorporate, interpret, reproduce, or resist cultural fare.[38] In both, sociologists are beginning to explore the social implications of new technologies (Mosco, 1983, and Melody, 1985). Much more of this research will be reported in the coming decade.

Alive with new paradigms and the revitalization of traditional behaviorism, cultural sociology—including the sociology of media institutions—is a thriving enterprise. Disputes between and among materialists, idealists, and behaviorists, neo-Marxists, neo-Weberians, and neo-Durkheimians continue—and sometimes generate rancor. They do so, however, in the midst of solid research.

NOTES

1. Among the most cited authors of the Frankfurt School are Theodor Adorno, Walter Benjamin, Jurgen Habermas, Max Horkheimer, and Herbert Marcuse. (See Jay, 1973.) Key figures in the Birmingham Center include its first director, Richard Hoggart, and Stuart Hall, who inspired many. Both were trained in literature.

2. For a critique of the conservative thrust of Giddings's work, see Gorelick (1981).

3. Works sympathetic to Lazarsfeld include: Coser (1984, pp. 110-120), Morrison (1976), Coleman (1980), and Sills (1979).

4. Many concepts in the communications literature have catchy names, which sometimes compare social to mechanical processes. See the review of the field in Robinson et al. (1986, pp. 29-54).

5. Some of these are explored in Gitlin (1987).

6. A useful compendium of articles using this approach is Katz and Blumler (1974). See Elliott (1974) for the best critique of uses and gratifications research.

7. *Personal Influence* may also be read as a structural description of the position of women in the early 1940s, when the data were gathered.

8. This is more generally discussed as the minimal effects theorem.

9. Psychological research on the effects of media is plentiful. One excellent review is Roberts and Bachen (1981). Much of the psychological literature criticizes the nonexperimental design of sociological work. (See Dorr, 1986; but see Phillips, 1983). Davis and Baran (1981) indicate how the communications literature handles the issue of effects. Robinson et al. (1986) provide a good example of how that literature discusses the impact of news, but see pp. 159-175. The most fascinating debate in the American effects literature (Hirsch, 1980, 1981a; 1981b, Gerbner et al., 1981a, 1981b) involves the notion of "cultivation theory" developed by Gerbner and his associates at the University of Pennsylvania's Annenberg School of Communications. Although behaviorist, "cultivation theory" shares with the concept of hegemony (discussed below) an emphasis on the impact of media on orientations toward everyday life. Four of the five articles in this debate are reprinted in Whitney, Wartella, with Windahl (1983).

10. Lang (1979) points out that in 1948 Lazarsfeld posited 16 types of effects, based on four "causal" influences and four different objects of influence. The "objects" included institutions.

11. See Wolff (1981) and the discussion in Tuchman (1983).

12. For examples of radical American theory, not discussed below, see Kellner (1981), Mosco (1983), and Mosco and Wasko (1983).

13. Both Williams and Hoggart were "scholarship boys." Williams is from the coal region in Wales; Hoggart, from Leeds.

14. Theories pertinent to such issues are also being developed in Germany. See Huyssen (1986). *Media, Culture and Society* (Garnham, 1983b) contains articles about contemporary work in Germany.

15. An attack on Althusser, whose devastating wit brings chuckles, is Thompson (1978).

16. The literature by and about Althusser is vast. One useful brief essay is Althusser (1971).

17. In studies about media and culture, the term "cultural materialism" refers to the research of Williams (1977) and those influenced by his theories. In anthropology, this term is associated with a radically different theory developed by Marvin Harris.

18. The best example is Becker (1982). See also the discussion in Elliott (1979).

19. See, especially, Molotch and Lester (1974, 1975). A less radical use of phenomenological sociology is Altheide (1976). On the sociology of news and the sociology of knowledge, see Tuchman (1980).

20. See Peterson (1976). Subsequently Peterson defined culture as norms, values, beliefs, and expressive symbols (Peterson, 1979), but still held to a linear and sequential model resembling that of Lasswell (1948). (See Tuchman, 1983).

21. Such matters are explicitly discussed in Wolff (1981).

22. For a different interpretation of framing, see Gamson (1984).

23. Gans (1979) stresses the interconnections among news media, the institutions with which they routinely interact, and the political system. He argues that the news favors well-known "personalities" and so, like Gitlin (1980), he sees similarities between the news media and media supposedly devoted to entertainment.

24. See note 10 above and the summary of sociological studies provided by McQuail (1979).

25. For earlier studies on the impact of media or institutions, see Cohen (1957) and Davison (1959).

26. Other British texts readily available in the United States include Curran, Gurevitch, and Woolacott (1979) and Cohen and Young (1981/1973).

27. Katz (1983) discusses studies of genre. Some examples are Newcomb (1976), Altheide and Snow (1979), Swidler (1980), Kapsis (1982), Cantor and Pingree (1983), Radway (1984) and feminist research on pornography (see Snitow, Stansell, and Thompson, 1983).

28. Thus Fine (1983) may be viewed as neo-Durkheimian, for it describes how a group shares fantasy. But, since it begins by noting the peculiarities of a fantasy designed and sold by a corporation, it also seems sympathetic to such neo-Marxist notions as the "industrialization of mind" (Enzensberger, 1974).

29. Burns (1977) and the Glasgow University Media Group (1980) do not seem as pertinent to this American work.

30. European and North American feminist sociologies have analyzed soap operas, daytime television, pornography, and the movies. Through literary criticism, aspects of structuralism have entered and found a home in feminist film criticism. Tuchman (1979) reviews some of the pertinent American sociology. In Britain, see the journal *Feminist Review* and working papers from the Centre for Contemporary Cultural Studies Woman's Working Group, including their *Women Take Issue* (1978). Other British works include Winship (1981), Ferguson (1983) and Root (1984). For an example of American Lacanian film criticism, see Kaplan (1983). Of course, non-feminists consider these genres, too.

31. Cantor derives the term *taste segments* by combining the concerns of Escarpit (1977) and Gans (1974). Recent American work responsive to European theories has been using the ideas of Bourdieu (1984, 1986a, 1986b), especially his discussion of taste as an element of the habitus of class fractions. Bourdieu (1984) shares Gans's (1974) devotion to eschew judgmental aesthetic comparisons. To do so, Gans develops the notion of "cultural relationism." Drawing on surveys intended to demonstrate rather than to prove his points, Bourdieu explicitly relates "taste" to the material conditions of the everyday lives of members of class fractions. Since 1980 Bourdieu's work has been particularly influential in Britain (see, for example, Garnham and Williams (1986/1980). The first discussion of Bourdieu's work by an American student in culture is probably DiMaggio (1979).

32. For a neo-Marxist criticism, see Ewen (1985).

33. Western sociologists are also beginning to discuss the media under socialism. One collection comparing the press under diverse political systems is Curry and Curry (1982).

34. David P. Phillips also makes innovative use of quantitative data to make (disputed) inferences about the effects of media on the behavior of individuals. See Phillips (1980, 1983); Bollen and Phillips (1982); compare Baron and Reiss (1985a, 1985b), Phillips and Bollen (1985).

35. These sets of ideas insist on the notion of an active audience. Some communications theorists seem to believe that if members of a (segmented) audience use the media for their own purposes, theories about hegemony must be wrong; for they mistakenly believe that the theory of hegemony presupposes a passive audience (see, for example, Katz, 1980b). However, the concept of appropriation used by neo-Marxists assumes an active audience. For instance, Garnham and Williams (1986/1980) note the necessary distinction between distribution and appropriation of media content. They point out that an individual may ingest some good, but not digest it. See also Bourdieu (1984, 1980a/1986a).

36. Gordon (1986) offers interesting interpretations of some of these seemingly discrepant findings.

37. By exploring how viewers reconstruct an episode of *Dallas*, Katz and Liebes (1986) go beyond other research in the uses and gratifications tradition. However, the authors hold in abeyance the question of whether the variations they found have any social or psychological significance. By exploring the meanings derived from this program, Katz and Liebes's (1986) treatment of uses and gratifications research begins to resemble some issues of effect posed by neo-Marxists.

38. Advocates of different theoretical approaches also offer divergent interpretations of how Bourdieu's work is relevant to the study of media. See Garnham and Williams (1986, 1980) cf. DiMaggio (1979).

REFERENCES

Alexander, J. 1986. "The Form of Substance: The Senate Watergate Hearings as Rituals." Pp. 243-251 in *Media, Audience and Social Structure*, edited by Sandra Ball-Rokeach and Muriel G. Cantor. Beverly Hills, CA: Sage.

Altheide, David. 1976. *Creating Reality*. Beverly Hills, CA: Sage.

Altheide, David and Robert Snow. 1979. *Media Logic*. Beverly Hills, CA: Sage.

Althusser, Louis. 1971. "Ideology and the ideological state apparatus." In *Lenin and Philosophy*. London: New Left Books.

Ball-Rokeach, Sandra J. and Muriel G. Cantor, eds. 1986. *Media, Audience and Social Structure*. Beverly Hills, CA: Sage.

Ball-Rokeach, Sandra J., Milton Rokeach, and Joel W. Grube. 1984. *The Great American Values*

Test: Influencing Behavior and Belief through Television. New York: Free Press.

Baron, James N. and Peter C. Reiss. 1985a. "Same Time, Next Year: Aggregate Analyses of the Mass Media and Violent Behavior." *American Sociological Review* 50:347-363.

———. 1985b. "Reply to Phillips and Bolen." *American Sociological Review* 50:372-376.

Bateson, Gregory. 1972. "A Theory of Play and Fantasy." Pp. 177-93 in *Steps to an Ecology of Mind*. New York: Ballantine Books. (Original work published 1955)

Becker, Howard. 1982. *Art Worlds*. Berkeley: University of California Press.

Berelson, Bernard. 1959. "The State of Communications Research." *Public Opinion Quarterly* 23: 1-6.

Centre for Contemporary Cultural Studies Women's Study Group. 1978. *Women Take Issue*. London: Hutchinson.

Blau, Judith. 1984. *Architects and Firms*. Cambridge, MA: MIT Press.

Bollen, Kenneth A. and David P. Phillips. 1982. "Imitative Suicides: A National Study of the Effects of Television News Stories." *American Sociological Review* 47:802-809.

Bourdieu, Pierre. 1984. *Distinction*, translated by Richard Nice. Cambridge, MA: Harvard University Press.

———. 1986a. "The Production of Belief." Pp. 131-163 in *Media, Culture and Society: A Critical Reader translated by Richard Nice*, edited by Richard Collins et al. Beverly Hills, CA: Sage. (Original work published 1980)

———. 1986b. "The Aristocracy of Culture." Pp. 164-193 in *Media, Culture and Society: A Critical Reader*, edited by Richard Collins et al., translated by Richard Nice. Beverly Hills, CA: Sage. (Original work published 1980)

Burns, Thomas. 1977. *The BBC: Public Institution and Private World*. London: Macmillan.

Cantor, Muriel G. 1979. *Prime-Time Television: Content and Control*. Beverly Hills, CA: Sage.

——— and Joel Cantor. 1986. "Audience Composition and Television Content: The Mass Audience Revisited." Pp. 214-225 in *Media, Audience and Social Structure*, edited by Sandra J. Ball-Rokeach and Muriel G. Cantor. Beverly Hills, CA: Sage.

Cantor, Muriel G. and Suzanne Pingree. 1983. *Soap Opera*. Beverly Hills, CA: Sage.

Carey, James W. 1979. "Mass Communications and Cultural Studies: An American View." Pp. 409-425 in *Mass Communications and Society*, edited by James Curran, Michael Gurevitch, and Janet Woollacott. Beverly Hills, CA: Sage.

———. 1983. "The Origins of the Radical Discourse on Cultural Studies in the United States." Pp. 311-313 in *Ferment in the Field*, vol. 33, special issue of *Journal of Communication*, edited by George Gerbner and Marsha Siefert.

Chaney, David. 1986. "The Symbolic Mirror of Our-

selves: Civic Ritual in Mass Society." Pp. 247-263 in *Media, Culture and Society: A Critical Reader*, edited by Richard Collins et al. Beverly Hills, CA: Sage.

Chibnall, Steve. 1977. *Law-and-Order News: Analysis of Crime Reporting in the British Press*. London: Tavistock.

———. 1981. "The Production of Knowledge by Crime Reporters." Pp. 75-97 in *The Manufacture of News: Deviance, Social Problems, and the Mass Media*, edited by Stanley Cohen and Jock Young. Beverly Hills, CA: Sage.

Clark, Priscilla. 1978. "The Beginnings of Mass Culture in France: Action and Reaction." *Social Research* 45:277-291.

Cohen, Bernard. 1957. *The Political Process and Foreign Policy*. Princeton, NJ: Princeton University Press.

Cohen, Stanley and Jock Young, eds. 1981. *The Manufacture of News: Deviance, Social Problems, and the Mass Media*. Beverly Hills, CA: Sage. (Original work published 1973).

Coleman, James. 1980. "Paul Lazarsfeld." In *Sociological Tradition from Generation to Generation*, edited by Robert K. Merton and Matilda White Riley. Norwood, NJ: Ablex.

Collins, Richard, James Curran, Nicholas Garnham, Paddy Scannell, Philip Schlesinger, and Colin Sparks, eds. 1986a. "Introduction." Pp. 1-6 in *Media, Culture and Society: A Critical Reader*. Beverly Hills, CA: Sage.

———, eds. 1986b *Media, Culture and Society: A Critical Reader*. Beverly Hills, CA: Sage.

Coser, Lewis A. 1984. *Refugee Scholars in America: Their Impact and Their Experiences*. New Haven, CT: Yale University Press.

Curran, James, Michael Gurevitch, and Janet Woollacott, eds. 1979. *Mass Communications and Society*. Beverly Hills, CA: Sage.

Curry, Jane Leftwich and Joan R. Curry, eds. 1982. *Press Control Around the World*. New York: Praeger.

Davis, Dennis K. and S. Baran. 1981. *Mass Communications and Everyday Life: a Perspective on Theory and Effects*. Belmont, CA: Wordsworth.

Davison, W. Phillips. 1958. *The Berlin Blockade: A Study in Cold-War Politics*. Princeton, NJ: Princeton University Press.

DiMaggio, Paul. 1979. "On Pierre Bourdieu" (Review Essay). *American Journal of Sociology* 84: 1460-1474.

———. 1986 [1983]. "Cultural Entrepreneurship in Nineteenth-century Boston." Pp. 194-211 in *Media, Culture and Society: A Critical Reader*, edited by Richard Collins et al. Beverly Hills, CA: Sage.

DiMaggio, Paul and Powell, Walter W. 1983. "The Iron Cage Revisited: Institutional Isomorphism and Collective Rationality in Organizational Fields." *American Sociological Review* 48:147-160.

Dorr, Aimee. 1986. *Television and Children: A*

Special Medium for a Special Audience. Beverly Hills, CA: Sage.

Elliott, Philip. 1972. *The Making of a Television Series*. London: Constable.

―――― 1974. "Uses and Gratifications Research: A Critique and a Sociological Alternative." Pp. 249-268 in *The Uses of Mass Communications: Current Perspectives on Gratifications Research*, edited by Jay Blumler and Elihu Katz. Beverly Hills, CA: Sage.

―――― 1979. "Media Occupations and Organizations: An Overview." Pp. 142-173. in *Mass Communications and Society*, edited by James Curran, Michael Gurevitch, and Janet Woollacott. Beverly Hills, CA: Sage.

―――― 1980. "Press Performance and Political Ritual." In *The Sociology of Journalism and the Press*, edited by H. Christian. Sociological Review Monograph 29. Keele: University of Keele.

―――― 1986. "Intellectuals, the 'Information Society,' and the Disappearance of the Public Sphere." Pp. 105-115 in *Media, Culture and Society: A Critical Reader*, edited by Richard Collins et al. Beverly Hills, CA: Sage.

Escarpit, Robert. 1977. "The Concept of 'Mass.' " *Journal of Communications* 27:44-47.

Ewen, Stuart. 1983. "The Implications of Empiricism." *Journal of Communications* 33 3:219-226.

―――― 1985. "Capitalist Realism" [book review of Schudson's *Advertising: The Uneasy Persuasion*]. *Journal of Communication* 35:192-196.

Enzensberger, Hans Magnus. 1974. *The Consciousness Industry*. New York: Seabury Press.

Faulkner, Robert R. 1971. *Hollywood Studio Musicians*. New York: Aldine-Atherton.

Ferguson, Marjorie. 1983. *Forever Feminine: Women's Magazines and the Cult of Femininity*. London: Heinemann.

Fine, Gary Alan. 1983. *Shared Fantasy: Role Playing Games as Social Worlds*. Chicago: University of Chicago Press.

Fishman, Mark. 1980. *Manufacturing the News*. Austin: University of Texas Press.

―――― 1981. "Crime Waves as Ideology." Pp. 98-117 in *The Manufacture of News: Deviance, Social Problems, and the Mass Media*, edited by Stanley Cohen and Jock Young. Beverly Hills, CA: Sage.

Freidson, Eliot. 1971. *Profession of Medicine*. New York: Dodd, Mead.

Frith, Simon. 1981. *Sound Effects*. New York: Pantheon.

Gamson, William. 1984. *What's News: A Game Simulation of News*. New York: Free Press.

―――― and Andre Modigliani. 1986. "Media Discourse and Public Opinion on Nuclear Power: A Constructionist Approach." *Working Paper #5*. Chestnut Hill, MA: Boston College Social Economy and Social Justice Program.

―――― 1987. "A Constructionist Approach to Mass Media & Public Opinion." *Working Paper #20*.

Chestnut Hill, MA: Boston College Social Economy and Social Justice Program.

Gans, Herbert. 1972 "The Famine in American Mass-Communications Research: Comments on Hirsch, Tuchman and Gecas." *American Journal of Sociology* 77:697-705.

―――― 1974. *Popular Culture and High Culture*. New York: Basic Books.

―――― 1979. *Deciding What's News*. New York: Pantheon.

Garnham, Nicholas. 1979. "Politics and the Mass Media in Britain." *Media, Culture and Society* 1:23-34.

―――― 1983a. "Toward a Theory of Cultural Materialism." *Journal of Communication* 33:314-329.

―――― , ed. 1983b. "After the Frankfurt School." *Media, Culture and Society* 5. (Entire issue)

―――― and Raymond Williams. 1986. "Pierre Bourdieu and the Sociology of Culture: An Introduction." Pp. 164-193 in *Media, Culture and Society: A Critical Reader*. Beverly Hills: Sage. (Original work published 1980).

Gerbner, George, Larry Gross, Michael Morgan, and Nancy Signorielli. 1981a. "A Curious Journey in the Scary World of Paul Hirsch." *Communications Research* 8:39-72.

―――― 1981b. "Final Reply to Hirsch." *Communications Research* 8:259-280.

Gerbner, George and Marsha Siefert, eds. 1983. *Ferment in the Field*, special issue of *Journal of Communication*, vol. 33.

Giddings, H. 1916. *The Principles of Sociology*. New York: Macmillan.

Gilmore, Samuel L. 1984. "Collaboration and Convention: A Comparison of Repertory, Academic and Avant Garde Concert Works." Ph.D. dissertation, Northwestern University.

Gitlin, Todd. 1978. "Media Sociology: The Dominant Paradigm." *Theory and Society* 6:205-253.

―――― 1979. "Prime-Time Ideology: the Hegemonic Process in Television Entertainment." *Social Problems* 26:251-266.

―――― 1980. *The Whole World Is Watching*. Berkeley: University of California Press.

―――― 1983. *Inside Prime-Time*. New York: Pantheon.

―――― , ed. 1987. *Watching Television*. New York: Pantheon.

Glascow University Media Group. 1980. *More Bad News*. London: Routledge & Kegan Paul.

Goffman, Erving. 1974. *Frame Analysis*. Philadephia: University of Pennsylvania Press.

Gordon, Margaret T. 1986. "A Countervalence in the Great Television Effects Debates." *Contemporary Sociology* 15:182-184.

Gorelick, Sherry. 1981. *City College and the Jewish Poor: Education in New York, 1880-1924*. New Brunswick, NJ: Rutgers University Press.

Gouldner, Alvin. 1976. *The Dialectic of Ideology and Technology*. New York: Seabury Press.

Graber, Doris. 1984. *Processing the News: How Peo-*

ple Tame the Information Tide. New York: Longmann.

Gramsci, Antonio. 1971. *Selections from the Prison Notebooks*, edited and translated by Quintin Hoare and Geoffrey Nowell Smith. New York: International Publishers.

Griswold, Wendy. 1986. *Renaissance Revivals: City Comedy and Revenge Tragedy in the London Theatre, 1576-1980.* Chicago: University of Chicago Press.

Hall, Stuart. 1979. "Culture, the Media, and the 'Ideological Effect.' " Pp. 315-348 in *Mass Communications and Society*, edited by James Curran, Michael Gurevitch, and Janet Woollacott. Beverly Hills, CA: Sage.

———. 1986. "Cultural Studies: Two Paradigms." Pp. 33-48 in *Media, Culture and Society: A Critical Reader*, edited by Richard Collins. Beverly Hills, CA: Sage. (Original work published 1980)

Halloren, James D., Philip Elliott, and Graham Murdock. 1969. *Demonstrations and Communication: A Case Study.* Harmondsworth: Penguin.

Hebdige, Dick. 1979. *Subculture: The Meaning of Style.* London: Methuen.

Himmelweit, Hilda, A. N. Oppenheim, and Pamela Vince. 1958. *Television and the Child.* London: Oxford University Press.

Hirsch, Paul. 1972. "Processing Fads and Fashions." *American Journal of Sociology* 77:639-659.

———. 1973. "The Organization of Consumption." Ph.D. dissertation, University of Michigan, Ann Arbor.

———. 1980. "The 'Scary World' of the Nonviewer and other Anomolies: A Reanalysis of Gerbner et al.'s Findings on Cultivation Analysis, Part 1." *Communications Research* 7:403-456.

———. 1981a. "On Not Learning from One's Own Mistakes: A Reanalysis of Gerbner et al.'s Findings on Cultivation Analysis, Part 2." *Communications Research*, 8:3-3.

———. 1981b. "Distinguishing Good Speculation from Bad Theory: Rejoinder to Gerbner et al." *Communications Research* 8:73-95.

Hoggart, Richard. 1958. *The Uses of Literacy.* Harmondsworth: Penguin. (Original work published 1957)

Horton, Donald and R. Richard Wohl. 1986. "Mass Communications and Para-social Interaction: Comments on Intimacy at a Distance." Pp. 185-206 in *Inter/Media: Interpersonal Communication in a Media World*, edited by Gary Gumpert and Robert Cathcart. New York: Oxford University Press. (Original work published 1956)

Hughes, Helen. 1940. *News and the Human Interest Story.* Chicago: University of Chicago Press.

Huyssen, Andreas. 1986. *After the Great Divide: Modernism, Mass Culture, and Post-Modernism.* Bloomington: Indiana University Press.

Jay, Martin. 1973. *The Dialectical Imagination: A History of the Frankfurt School and The Institute of Social Research 1923-1950.* Boston: Little, Brown.

Johnson, Richard. 1979. "Histories of Culture/ Theories of Ideology: Notes on an Impasse." Pp. 48-77 in *Ideology and Cultural Production*, edited by Michele Barrett et al. London: Croon Helm.

Kaplan, E. Ann. 1983. "Is the Gaze Male?" Pp. 309-327 in *Powers of Desire: The Politics of Sexuality*, edited by Ann Snitow, Christine Stansell, and Sharon Thompson. New York: Monthly Review Press.

Kapsis, Robert. 1982. "Dressed to Kill." *American Film* 7:52-56.

Katz, Elihu. 1980a. "Media Events: The Sense of Occasion." *Studies in Visual Anthropology* 6:84-89.

———. 1980b. "On Conceptualizing Media Effects." Pp. 119-142 in *Studies in Communications*, 1, edited by Thelma McCormack. Greenwich, CT: JAI Press.

———. 1983. "The Return of the Humanities and Sociology." *Journal of Communication* 33:51-52.

Katz, Elihu and Jay Blumler, eds. 1974. *The Uses of Mass Communications: Current Perspectives on Gratifications Research.* Beverly Hills, CA: Sage.

Katz, Elihu and D. Dayan. 1985. Media Events: "On the Experience of Not Being There." *Religion*, 15: 305-314.

Katz, Elihu and Paul F. Lazarsfeld. 1955. *Personal Influence.* Glencoe: Free Press.

Katz, Elihu and Tamar Liebes. 1986. "Decoding *Dallas*: Notes from a Cross-Cultural Study." Pp. 97-109 in *Inter/Media: Interpersonal Communication in a Media World*, edited by Gary Gumpert and Robert Cathcart. New York: Oxford University Press.

Kellner, Douglas. 1981. "Network Television and American Society." *Theory and Society* 10:31-62.

Klapper, Joseph. 1960. *The Effects of Mass Communications.* Glencoe, IL: Free Press.

Lang, Gladys Engel and Kurt Lang. 1983. *The Battle for Public Opinion: The President, the Press and the Polls During Watergate.* New York: Columbia University Press.

———. 1986. "Some Observations on the Long Range Effects of Television." Pp. 271-279 in *Media, Audience and Social Structure*, edited by Sandra J. Ball-Rokeach and Muriel G. Cantor. Beverly Hills, CA: Sage.

Lang, Kurt. 1979. "The Critical Functions of Empirical Communications Research: Observations on German-American Influences." *Media, Culture and Society* 1:83-96.

——— and Gladys Engel Lang. 1960. "The Unique Perspective of Television and Its Effects." Pp. 544-560 in *Mass Communications*, edited by Wilbur Schramm. Urbana: University of Illinois

Press. (Original work published 1953)

Lasswell, Harold. 1948. "The Structure and Function of Communication in Society." Pp. 37-51 in *The Communication of Ideas*, edited by Lyman Bryson. New York: Institute for Religious and Social Studies.

Lazarsfeld, Paul F., Marie Jahoda, and Hans Zeisel. 1971. *Marienthal: The Sociography of a Community*. Chicago: Aldine Atherton. (Original work published 1933)

Lazarsfeld, Paul F. and Robert K. Merton. 1948. "Mass Communication, Popular Taste, and Organized Social Action." Pp. 95-118 in *The Communication of Ideas*, edited by Lyman Bryson. New York: Institute for Religious and Social Studies.

Long, Elizabeth. 1985. *The American Dream and the Popular Novel*. Boston: Routledge & Kegan Paul.

_____ 1986. "Women, Reading, and Cultural Authority: Some Implications of the Audience Perspective in Cultural Studies." *American Quarterly* (Fall).

Lynd, Robert and Helen M. Lynd. 1922. *Middletown*. New York: Harcourt, Brace.

_____ 1939. *Middletown in Transition*. New York: Harcourt, Brace.

Mattelart, Michele. 1986. "Women and the Cultural Industries." Pp. 63-81 in *Media, Culture and Society: A Critical Reader*, edited by Richard Collins et al. Beverly Hills, CA: Sage.

McCombs, Maxwell and Donald Shaw. 1972. "The Agenda-Setting Function of Mass Media." *Public Opinion Quarterly* 36:176-187.

McCormack, Thelma. 1986. "Reflections on the Lost Vision of Communications Theory." Pp. 34-42 in *Media, Audience and Social Structure*, edited by Sandra J. Ball-Rokeach and Muriel G. Cantor. Beverly Hills, CA: Sage.

McQuail, Denis. 1979. "The Influence and Effects of Mass Media." Pp. 70-94 in *Mass Communications and Society*, edited by James Curran, Michael Gurevitch, and Janet Woollacott. Beverly Hills, CA: Sage.

Melody, William H., ed. 1985. "The Information Society." *Media, Culture and Society* 7. (Entire issue)

Merton, Robert K. 1949. "Patterns of Influence." In *Communications Research 1948-1949*, edited by Paul F. Lazarsfeld and Frank Stanton. New York: Harper.

Molotch, Harvey L. and Marilyn Lester. 1974. "News as Purposive Behavior." *American Sociological Review* 39:101-112.

_____ 1975. "Accidental News: The Great Oil Spill." *American Journal of Sociology* 81:235-260.

Morrison, David Edward. 1976. "Paul Lazarsfeld: The Biography of an Institutional Innovator." Ph.D. dissertation, Leicester University.

Mosco, Vincent. 1983. "Critical Research and the Role of Labor." *Journal of Communication* 33:237-248.

_____ and Janet Wasko, eds. 1983. *Labor, the Working Class and the Media*. Norwood, NJ: Ablex.

Mukerji, Chandra and Michael Schudson. 1986. "Popular Culture." Pp. 44-61 in *Annual Review of Sociology*.

Murdock, Graham. 1973. "Political Deviance: The Press Presentation of a Militant Mass Demonstration." Pp. 156-175 in *The Manufacture of News: Deviance, Social Problems and the Mass Media*, edited by Stanley Cohen and Jock Young. London: Constable.

_____ 1982. "Mass Communications and Social Violence: A Critical Review of Recent Research Trends." Pp. 62-90 in *Aggression and Violence*, edited by Peter Marsh and Anne Campbell. Oxford: Basil Blackwell.

Newcomb, Horace, ed. 1976. *Television: The Critical View*. Oxford, England: Oxford University Press.

Open University. 1977. *Mass Communication and Society. Unit Eight*. London: Author.

Park, Robert. 1922. *The Immigrant Press and Its Control*. Chicago: University of Chicago Press.

Peterson, Richard. 1976. "The Production of Culture." Pp. 7-22 in *The Production of Culture*. Beverly Hills, CA: Sage.

_____ 1979. "Revitalizing the Culture Concept." *Annual Review of Sociology* 5:137-166.

_____ 1982. "The Production and Consumption of Culture." Presented at the annual meetings of the American Sociological Association, San Francisco.

_____ and David Berger. 1975. "Cycles in Symbol Production: The Case of Popular Music." *American Sociological Review* 40:39-51.

Phillips, David. 1980. "Airplane Accidents, Murder, and the Mass Media: Towards a Theory of Imitations and Suggestion." Pp. 97-105 in *Mass Communication Review Yearbook* 3, edited by D. Charles Whitney and Ellen Wartella with Sven Windahl. Beverly Hills, CA: Sage.

_____ 1983. "The Impact of Media Violence on U.S. Homicides." *American Sociological Review* 48:560-568.

_____ and Kenneth A. Bollen. 1985. "Same Time, Last Year: Selective Data Dredging for Negative Findings." *American Sociological Review* 50:364-371.

Powell, Walter W. 1985. *Getting into Print: The Decision-Making Process in Scholarly Publishing*. Chicago: University of Chicago Press.

Putnis, Peter. 1986. "Communications Studies in Australia: Paradigms and Contexts." *Media, Culture and Society* 8:143-158.

Radway, Janice. 1984. *Reading the Romance: Women, Patriarchy, and Popular Literature*. Chapel Hill: University of North Carolina Press.

Roberts, Donald and Christine Bachen. 1981. "Mass Communications Effects." *Annual Review of*

Psychology 32:307-356.

Robinson, John P. and Mark R. Levy with Dennis K. Davis in association with W. Gill Woodall, Michael Gurevitch, and Haluk Sahin. 1986. *The Main Source: Learning from Television News*. Beverly Hills, CA: Sage.

Root, Jane. 1984. *Pictures of Women: Sexuality*. London: Pandora Press.

Rosenblum, Barbara. 1978. *Photographers at Work*. New York: Holmes and Meier.

Rosengren, Karl Erik. 1986. "Linking Culture and Other Societal Systems." Pp. 87-98 in *Media, Audience and Social Structure*, edited by Sandra J. Ball-Rokeach and Muriel G. Cantor. Beverly Hills, CA: Sage.

Schlesinger, Philip. 1978. *Putting Reality Together*. London: Constable.

Schramm, Wilbur. 1983. "The Unique Perspective of Communication: A Retrospective View." *Journal of Communication* 33:6-17.

Schudson, Michael. 1978. *Discovering the News*. New York: Basic Books.

———— 1986. "The Menu of Media Research." Pp. 43-48 in *Media, Audience, and Social Structure*, edited by Sandra J. Ball-Rokeach and Muriel G. Cantor. Beverly Hills, CA: Sage.

———— 1984. *Advertising: The Uneasy Persuasion*. New York: Basic Books.

Sills, David. 1979. "Lazarsfeld, Paul F." *Biographical Supplement to the International Encyclopedia to the Social Sciences*. New York: Macmillan.

Small, Albion W. and George C. Vincent. 1894. *An Introduction to the Study of Society*. New York: American Book Company.

Snitow, Ann, Christine Stansell, and Sharon Thompson, eds. 1983. *Powers of Desire: The Politics of Sexuality*. New York: Monthly Review Press.

Smith, Dorothy E. 1984. "Theorizing as Ideology." Pp. 41-44 in *Ethnomethodology*, edited by Roy Turner. Baltimore, MD: Penguin. (Excerpted from "The Ideological Practice of Sociology," manuscript originally written 1974)

Swidler, Ann. 1980. "Love and Adulthood in American Culture." Pp. 120-147 in *Themes of Work and Love in Adulthood*, edited by Neil Smelser and Erik H. Erikson. Cambridge, MA: Harvard University Press.

———— In press. *Talk of Love: How Americans Use Their Culture*. Chicago: University of Chicago Press.

Thompson, E. P. 1963. *The Making of the English Working-Class*. London: Gollancz.

———— 1978. *The Poverty of Theory*. London: Merlin Press.

Tuchman, Gaye, ed. 1974. *The TV Establishment: Programming for Power and Profit*. Englewood Cliffs: Prentice-Hall.

———— 1978. *Making News: A Study in the Construction of Reality*. New York: Free Press.

———— 1979. "The Depiction of Women in the Mass Media." *Signs: Journal of Women in Culture and Society* 4:528-542.

———— 1980. "Facts of the Moment: A Theory of News." *Social Interaction* 3:9-20.

———— 1983. "Consciousness Industries and the Production of Culture." *Journal of Communication* 33:330-341.

Tuchman, Gaye with Nina Fortin. In press. *Edging Women Out: Victorian Novelists, Publishers, and Professionalism*. New Haven, CT: Yale University Press.

Tunstall, Jeremy. 1971. *Journalists at Work*. London: Constable.

Whitney, D. Charles and Ellen Wartella with Sven Windahl, eds. 1983. *Mass Communications Review Yearbook* 3. Beverly Hills, CA: Sage.

Williams, Raymond. 1958. *Culture and Society: 1780-1950*. New York: Columbia University Press.

———— 1965. *The Long Revolution*. Harmondsworth: Penguin. (Original work published 1961)

———— 1975. *Television*. New York: Schoeken. (Original work published 1961)

———— 1976. *Keywords: A Vocabulary of Culture and Society*. New York: Oxford University Press.

———— 1977. *Marxism and Literature*. New York: Oxford University Press.

Winship, Janice. 1981. "Handling Sex." *Media, Culture and Society* 3:25-41.

Wolfenstein, Martha and Nathan Leites. 1960. "An Analysis of Themes and Plots in Motion Pictures." Pp. 380-391 in *Mass Communications*, edited by Wilbur Schramm. Urbana: University of Illinois Press. (Original work published 1947)

Wolff, Janet. 1981. *The Social Production of Art*. New York: St. Martin's. Press.

Wright, Charles. 1986. "Mass Communication Rediscovered." Pp. 22-33 in Sandra J. Ball-Rokeach and Muriel G. Cantor, editors. *Media, Audience and Social Structure*. Beverly Hills, CA: Sage.

Part IV

SOCIAL PROCESS AND CHANGE

19
Spatial Processes

W. PARKER FRISBIE
JOHN D. KASARDA

The centrality of spatial processes and relationships to social life manifests itself at numerous conceptual levels. At the most mundane, all behavior occurs in space. At a higher, but still quite basic level of abstraction, spatial processes and patterns serve as useful indicators of technological and organizational adaptations of human groups to their natural and social environments. In this chapter we emphasize both spatial patterns and the processes that give rise to particular patterns, but especially the latter, since spatial relationships are ever changing in response to cultural, economic, political, and technological forces (Berry and Kasarda, 1977, Castells, 1985; Gottdiener, 1985; Kasarda, 1980; Logan and Molotch, 1987).

We give particular emphasis to urban spatial processes because this is indeed an urban age in which few areas of our existence are untouched by urban influences (LaGory and Pipkin, 1981). That cities are the key arenas of capital accumulation and corporate influence is not debatable. Indeed, with large cities expanding their roles in the coordination and control of regional, national, and supranational space economies, many contemporary scholars now speak of world cities and of world systems of cities (Chase-Dunn, 1984; Hall, 1984; Meyer, 1986; Portes and Walton, 1981; Wallerstein, 1974, 1980). What may not be so well recognized is the historical evidence that supra-national economic systems have existed for centuries and that these systems have inexorably been coordinated and controlled through a dominant city or set of cities (Braudel, 1979, chap. 1). Accordingly, our discussion will maintain an urban focus while distinguishing spatial processes and patterns that extend beyond local communities.

Much of our effort draws conclusions based on evidence from the United States. Many, but not all, of these conclusions will be generalizable to conditions in other developed nations and somewhat fewer to Third World contexts. Hence, in later sections, it will be necessary to adopt a more comparative perspective. In each section, our primary aim is to explicate conceptual models of spatial patterns and processes and describe alternative perspectives that seek to interpret them.

Intraurban Spatial Processes

The number of intraurban spatial processes one might consider could vary indefinitely depending on one's conceptual point of departure and the degree of typological detail desired. Here, we focus on those that have inspired the greatest amount of interest across several generations of scholars: growth, expansion, and the distribution and redistribution of population and activities. These are broad categories, indeed, and each encompasses a wide range of interconnected spatial relationships. For example, while growth refers to the multiplication of population and organizations, expansion is defined as a progressive absorption and spatial integration of formerly unrelated populations and functions over a wider geographic area (Hawley, 1968; Kasarda, 1972). Under the expansion rubric is included the process of urban economic transformation and the spatial deconcentration of both population and industry, which, of course, involves mechanisms of distribution and redistribution. The latter are integral to any discussion of spatial processes, but other distribution/redistribution phenomena are important, including the separation (or segregation) of individuals and families according to attributes such as socioeconomic status, life-cycle stage, and race/ethnicity.

Also under the expansion rubric are interurban flows of products, information, and capital manifested in systems of cities, core-periphery relations, and metropolitan dominance. These will be focused upon in the latter half of this chapter. Yet, given the close connections between intra- and interurban processes and the forces that give them impetus, no effort is made to treat them in a completely discrete manner. To do so would seriously distort reality and obfuscate the very issues we wish to illuminate.

Urban Growth and Change

The most pervasive spatial process is the increase of population in urban places. From the earliest agglomerations of people in what might loosely be called cities (circa 4000 B.C., in southern Mesopotamia) until the nineteenth century, urban populations were small and compactly settled primarily because of the limits on food surpluses and the primitive nature of transportation. Although there is considerable variation in size estimates, it is unlikely that even the greatest of the preindustrial cities had populations of more than a few hundred thousand persons (Hawley, 1981, pp. 30-33).

Throughout most of the nineteenth century, urban settlement remained compact and cellular as the primitive state of intramural transportation made dense concentrations the only feasible alternative for ensuring regularity of social interaction and economic exchange (Hawley, 1981, pp. 86-88). However, with improvement of local transportation, first by use of horse-drawn conveyances, followed by the greater speed and efficiency of steam- and electrically powered transit, and finally by the spatial flexibility of automobile and truck, the dense, cellular patterns of urban areas began to break down (Hawley, 1981; LaGory and Pipkin, 1981; Tobin, 1976).

Such transformations frequently occurred over short intervals of time. For example, in 1890, 60% of urban transit was by animal power. By 1902 only about 1% of all intramural railway mileage was animal driven (Tobin, 1976). Indeed, we are just completing the one-hundredth anniversary of a brief but highly significant 12-year period of technological innovations that shaped cities as we know them today. Between 1877 and 1889, steel frame buildings, electric power lines, the light bulb, elevators, electric trolleys, the internal combustion automobile engine, subways, and telephones were introduced (Perlman, 1986). These advantages, together with the mechanization of agriculture, the rise of corporations, innovations in finance capitalism, and new mass-production manufacturing methods spurred the growth of cities during the ensuing three decades.

At the turn of the century 60% of the American population was rural, but by 1920 slightly over half of the population resided in urban areas, a figure that increased to two-thirds and then to three-quarters of the total by 1960 and 1970, respectively (Palen, 1981; U.S. Bureau of the Census, 1984). In the twentieth century, metropolitan areas have absorbed roughly 75% of all population growth, and by 1980 the 318 metropolitan areas (up from 169 in 1950) contained almost exactly 75% of all Americans (U.S. Bureau of the Census, 1984, table 18).

Among the more striking changes were the concentration of business activities in central business districts near the confluence of transportation lines and vastly increased competition for central locations that, coupled with the opportunity for persons to live at one location and work at another, gave impetus to the suburbanization of residences. It is important to recognize, however, that mass suburbanization in the United States commenced well before the widespread use of automobiles, zoning regulations, FHA-VHA mortgage subsidies, federal highway programs, and other government interventions that some argue were the primary causes of urban deconcentration. Indeed, when central city annexation of suburban territory is controlled, the suburban rings have been growing faster than the central cities during every decade at least as far back as 1900 (Jackson, 1985; Kasarda and Redfearn, 1975).

We do not wish to imply that the automobile and federal policies did not eventually play major roles in the suburbanization process. As automobile and truck use soared during the 1920s, urban deconcentration accelerated, only to slow dramatically during the Great Depression. Yet even during the 1930s, numerous public works programs were introduced that were instrumental in providing a peripheral infrastructure of water reservoirs, electric power and telephone lines, and paved roads that laid the foundation upon which many suburbs grew following World War II.

By the 1950s a well-developed suburban public infrastructure complemented by rising personal incomes and government-subsidized home mortgages resulted in the greatest period of suburbanization in American history (Hawley, 1981; Tobin, 1976). Outward movement from the cities continued apace during the 1960s as many metropolitan peripheral areas urbanized, capturing numerous retail and consumer service establishments that followed their traditional clientele to the suburbs. By the 1970s urban functions, activities, and consumption patterns had become so widespread throughout the suburbs, exurbs, and nonmetropolitan areas that the United States, for all intents and purposes, had become an urban society.

Before elaborating these space-transforming processes, let us briefly consider the "classical models" that sought to offer a description and explanation of the spatial and functional relationships observed in the great period of urban growth.

CLASSICAL MODELS OF
URBAN GROWTH AND FORM

One of the earliest and perhaps the best known model of urban growth is Burgess's *concentric zones* (1925). In this model, the central business district (CBD) formed the innermost zone at the convergence of transportation and communications lines. The CBD was occupied by functions capable of making highly intensive use of space which were therefore able to afford the higher costs associated with the accessibility offered by a strategic economic location. Surrounding the central business district was the Zone in Transition, an ephemeral area created by the encroachment of commercial and industrial interests on formerly residential areas. With CBD businesses pushing outward, residential use declined as the congestion, noise, and pollution associated with industry and the higher land costs associated with competition for space made the transition zone less desirable and

less affordable for residential use. Inhabitants unable to leave the area often resided in rooming houses and other multifamily dwellings in varying stages of dilapidation. Beyond the two inner zones were three primarily residential areas in which the socioeconomic status of occupants is described by an increasing gradient as distance from the core increased: working-class zone, middle-class zone, and commuters' zone.

Complementary to the Burgess zonal hypothesis was Hurd's earlier (1903) theory of *axiate growth*. Like Burgess, Hurd saw growth taking place outward in all directions from the center, but proceeding first, and most rapidly, along major transportation arteries. In addition, this axiate growth was viewed as continually being overtaken as the interstices between primary radial thoroughfares filled in when cross-cutting transportation lines developed. At any given point in time, the result would be more nearly a star-shaped spatial pattern as opposed to concentric circles.

Hoyt's perspective (1939) differs in emphasis from the above two models. Although, like Burgess and Hurd, Hoyt perceived urban expansion as being driven by competition for choice locations, the expectation was that once a particular type of land use was initiated near the center of the city, it tended to move in an encapsulated form toward the periphery, thereby producing a sectoral pattern. One salient example of this process at work over time began with wealthy urbanites outcompeting their less affluent counterparts for choice residential locations. Then, as population grew and settlement expanded outward, the relative status of the sector tended to be preserved, since the less affluent could not afford housing in higher-rent districts and the wealthy did not desire residence in the lower-socioeconomic-status sectors.

In contrast to the three models outlined above, Ullman and Harris propose that "in many cities the land-use pattern is built not around a single center but around discrete nuclei. . . . In some cities these nuclei have existed from the very origins of the city; in others they have developed as the growth of the city stimulated migration and specialization" (1970, p. 96). Ullman and Harris's theory of *multiple nuclei* reflects the reality of different locational needs, the fact that certain functions are ancillary and supportive of each other, while other activities are mutually detrimental, and the differential ability to pay the costs of location at desirable sites (Ullman and Harris, 1970, pp. 97-98; see also Harris and Ullman, 1945).

Somewhat similar to this formulation is Hawley's commentary on the hierarchical multinucleation of business districts. In particular, Hawley (1971, 1981) notes the tendency for secondary and tertiary business centers to develop at transportation intersections where business has the advantage of convergence of traffic from four directions. This arrangement is hierarchical in terms of both size and functional specialization as the large central business district provides all standard functions plus a wide range of specialized and expensive goods and services. The smallest business centers, on the other hand, primarily offer standard items, such as food and gasoline, which are in daily use (see also Berry and Kasarda, 1977, pp. 91-93).

In certain respects, Hawley's approach is more analogous to the Central Place Theory of interurban organization (described below) than it is to the Ullman and Harris model, which proposes what amounts to enclaves of differing land uses such as heavy and light manufacturing, wholesaling, commercial, and residential. Both are closer to the notion of the polynucleated city found in the more recent writings of a number of urban theorists (Gottdiener, 1983, 1985; Kasarda, 1980) than to the Burgess, Hurd, or Hoyt models. Although different in regard to the spatial patterns proposed, all of the classical theories of urban growth and form begin from the premise that the underlying process accounting for distributional patterns is "the interplay of socioeconomic forces of competition in the urban land market" (Schwirian, 1974, p. 5).

To this point, our discussion has dealt with theories pertaining to the spatial patterns and processes that characterize the city as a whole. Other models have been developed that attempt to describe and explicate the composition of subareas within cities. Among the earliest were the local community models of Robert Park and other members of the "Chicago School" of human ecology, which flourished during the first three decades of this century (Park, 1916; Park and Burgess, 1921, 1925). Park believed that considerable analytical leverage could be generated by conceptualizing local community organization along two dimensions, the biotic and the cultural. For Park, the term *biotic* was Darwinian in extraction, and was used to denote "subsocial" or unplanned spatial outcomes of competition, while cultural processes had to do with the norms, values, and the moral and political organization of human society. Although Park by no means argued that the latter were unimportant for understanding social and spatial organization, he did contend that the proper focus for human ecologists was at the biotic level.

Given their biotic perspectives, classical human ecologists viewed the urban community as a dynamic adaptive system in which competition served as the principal organizing force. This premise reflected the sociopolitical and economic milieu of late nineteenth- and early twentieth-century America, where the dynamics of privatism and laissez-faire enterprise prevailed. Relatively unfettered by public intervention, industries and commercial institutions competed for strategic locations, which, once established, provided them with economic advantages (externalities) through which they could maximize profits and exercise control (dominance) over the use of land in other parts of the community (McKenzie, 1933). The result was spatial differentiation and segregation of various industries, social classes, and activity patterns into relatively homogeneous subareas that were labeled "natural areas" because they evolved not through planning or design but primarily through competition in the marketplace (e.g., see Burgess, 1925; Park, 1916, 1936; Park and Burgess, 1925; Wirth, 1928; Zorbaugh, 1926).

Taking the work of urban ecologists, geographers, and economists as a point of departure, Shevky and his associates (Shevky and Bell, 1961; Shevky and Williams, 1949) moved beyond the concept of natural areas to consider what came to be known as *social areas*. Social area analysts viewed urban structure as a product of societal modernization, particularly as manifested by increases in the intensity of social relationships, in the degree of functional differentiation, and in the complexity of organizations. Embedded in these societal-level changes were three specific processes: "changes in the arrangement of occupations, changes in the ways of living, and redistribution of the population in space" (Shevky and Bell, 1961, p. 227). Moving down the ladder of abstraction, three structural reflections of change were identified for use in the study of urban social differentiation: (1) economic status (social rank), (2) family status (urbanization), and (3) ethnic status (segregation). These constructs were then adopted as a means of classifying and comparing subareas (often census tracts) in urban communities.

Social area analyses tended to focus on the questions of whether the tripartite classification was generalizable beyond the cities (Los Angeles and San Francisco) to which it was first applied and on whether distinct factors corresponding to the three dimensions could be isolated. In general, considerable evidence suggested that the answer to both of these questions was yes.

Studies of U.S. and Scandinavian cities (Sweetser, 1965; Van Arsdol et al., 1958) showed that economic, family, and ethnic status represent distinct and significant spatial reflections of urban social differentiation. Instances in which distinct factors representing the three dimensions failed to materialize were also uncovered. For example, socioeconomic status (measured in terms of standard indicators such as education, occupation, and/or income) and family status (measured by indicators such as fertility, family size, and female labor force participation) were found not to comprise distinct dimensions in Cairo (Abu-Lughod, 1968) and in a number of American cities (Van Arsdol et al., 1958). The nonorthogonality of factors defining social areas has generally been attributed either to lower levels of modernization (Schwirian, 1977) or to constraints imposed by problems of measurement (Berry and Kasarda, 1977).

Finally, it is interesting that the structural dimensions defined by Shevky and Bell sometimes appear as spatial configurations that conform to three classical models of growth and form. Specifically, socioeconomic differentiation has been found to be distributed according to a sectorlike pattern, with family status differences conforming roughly to the concentric zone model and ethnic status evidencing a multinucleated pattern in space (Anderson and Egeland, 1961; Berry and Kasarda, 1977).

The classical models of growth and form, as well as the more general theory of urban organization from which they emerged, were subjected to a rather stringent critique. For example, it was argued that ecological theory, as developed by Park and others of the Chicago School, depended on an overly simplistic biological analogy (Gettys, 1940; Gottdiener, 1985; Hatt, 1946), that it made no sense to separate the "community" (the biotic unit resulting from "subsocial" competition) from society in which organization depends on cultural controls (Alihan, 1938), and that certain spatial patterns predicted by the models (specifically, concentric zones) were not empirically observed (Davie, 1937; Hoyt, 1971). Further, Firey asserted that the ecological approach to urbanization overemphasized impersonal, cost-imposing variables to the neglect of cultural or "sentimental" factors such as those associated with the diseconomic preservation of Beacon Hill and the Boston Commons (Firey, 1945, 1947). Finally, anticipating by two decades the objections of political economists, Form contended that "the image of a free and unorganized market in which individuals compete impersonally for land must be abandoned" (1954, p. 317). Rather, one should recognize the influence of sociopolitical actors including realtors and developers, large consumers of land (business and industry), and agents of government.

Clearly, many of the theoretical and empirical criticisms of classical ecological models were well taken. Park's biological analogy, interpreted in a direct fashion, quite quickly breaks down. Without doubt, there are social, cultural, and political influences on spatial processes and patterns that must be taken into account. Moreover, those models assuming a monocentered metropolis are manifestly inaccurate given the emergence of a multinucleated spatial pattern of secondary and tertiary activity centers. Likewise, the assumption of equal ease of expansion in all directions from the city's core is untenable, if only because of topographical obstacles such as lakes, swamps, and mountains and constructed boundaries such as transportation lines.

On the other hand, many critics have failed to recognize the broader theoretical framework Park and his colleagues developed. For example, Park frequently stressed the pivotal role of nonbiotic factors, as evidenced by his conclusion "that in human society competition is limited by custom and culture. The cultural superstructure imposes itself *as an instrument of direction and control* upon the biotic substructure" (1936/1961, p. 29; emphasis added). Similarly, those who discounted Burgess's urban growth model failed to appreciate that, while concentric zones might not show up in urban spatial patterns, his conceptualization of spatial processes—notably the development of gradients, competition for space, and dominance of certain functional activities—remains highly pertinent in theories of land use (Haggerty, 1971; Hawley, 1971, pp. 102-103; LaGory and Pipkin, 1981). Although social area analysis (and certainly its computer-age descendant, factorial ecology) became more nearly a methodological paradigm than a conceptual model, these approaches demonstrate that the dimensions that stratify societies can be detected in specific spatial configurations.

More recently, other perspectives have emerged that although different in certain important respects, all derive directly or indirectly from Marxist theory (e.g., Castells, 1977, 1985; Gordon, 1977, 1984; Gottdiener, 1985; Lefebvre, 1979; Storper, 1985). These alternative explanations of the urban use of space have been referred to as "critical theories" in order to distinguish them from ecologically based "mainstream" or "conventional" theory (Gottdiener, 1983, 1985).

We will postpone a discussion of critical theory until later sections. However, it is worth mentioning here that, despite critiques such as those mentioned above, for over a half-century the ecological approach (with varying emphasis depending on whether the disciplinary base was sociology, economics, or geography) has remained the dominant (and, arguably, the only) general theory of urban form and process that has been generative of systematic, empirically verifiable models.

A THEORY OF LAND USE

In fact, urban ecology offers a theory of land use sufficiently close to reality that the spatial regularities incorporated in the theory have been adequately represented by simple mathematical expressions that are highly generalizable both temporally and geographically. The most basic regularity is captured in Clark's (1951) equation, which indicates that the density of settlement (the intensity of land use) declines exponentially with distance from the center of the city (see LaGory and Pipkin, 1981). Clark's equation may be given as follows:

$$d_x = d_o e^{-bx},$$

where d_x represents the density of population at some distance x from the center, d_o is the density at the center, e is the base of the natural logarithm, and b is some empirically determined density gradient. Alternatively, we have:

$$\ln d_x = \ln d_o - bx.$$

The most amazing feature of this formula is the consistency with which the negative exponent appears, wherever and whenever the equation has been applied. Its utility has been demonstrated with data stretching back some 150 years and for over 100 cities, including Budapest, Sydney, Colombo, Hyderabad, Manila, Singapore, and Tokyo, as well as in U.S. cities (Berry and Kasarda, 1977, pp. 94-95; see also Muth, 1969). The continued applicability of the negative exponential in describing population distribution in U.S. cities has recently been demonstrated in Edmonston and Guterbock's study (1984) of suburbanization from 1950 to 1975.

More important than the mathematical expressions, of course, are their fundamental conceptual underpinnings. "Sites within cities offer two goods—land and location (Alonso, 1960). Each urban activity derives utility from a site in accordance with the site's location" (Berry and Kasarda, 1977, p. 95). The benefit

that may be derived from any location is a function of the ability to bear the cost of land; that is, the price of the most desirable sites will be bid up. As cities begin the expansion process, "the most desirable locational property of urban sites is centrality (or maximum accessibility in the urban area, as transportation routes converge at the center); for any use, ability to pay is directly related to centrality (accessibility)" (Berry and Kasarda, 1977, p. 95).

At least four generalizations follow from the above: (1) Land costs decline with distance because less central locations offer less accessibility. (2) Since there is competition for the land, each site tends to be occupied by the function or land use best able to pay for the benefits. (3) The trade-off between distance and cost-benefit will be different for different functions, with those able to make the most intensive use of space being most capable of affording central locations. (4) Intensity of land use thus declines with distance from the center. Empirically verified regularities in spatial patterns of this sort, which appear regardless of time period, cultural setting, or political milieu, obviously constitute important evidence supporting the ecological theory of land use. However, as will be discussed, recent technological and organizational changes that have tended to attenuate the bond between centrality and accessibility may render such spatial models less susceptible to simple mathematical algorithms.

Urban Expansion and Metropolitan Change

Expansion represents a progressive increase in the territorial scope and influence of a system. Its widening radius of interdependence assumes greater centralization, that is, an increase in coordination and control functions at the system's core to ensure integration and administration of activities and relationships throughout an extended territorial complex (Kasarda, 1972). Expansion is predicated on (but not solely determined by) improvements in transportation and communication technology, which reduce the friction of space and increase the range and content of resource and information flows. Expansion also requires increased productivity (capital accumulation) by coordinating and controlling institutions linking dispersed activities and integrating them with what is being done in other parts of the system (Bidwell and Kasarda, 1985; Hawley, 1978, 1981, 1987). It is important to note that, just as expansion is not the same as growth, "centralization is not equivalent to concentration in space. Concentration has to do with density of settlement, while centralization refers to an increase in the volume and intensity of administrative and coordinative activities and their influence over a wider territory.

Suburbanization is a concrete manifestation of the more abstract concept of urban expansion. Although deconcentration of population has been more or less continuous during the twentieth century, there was a massive increase following World War II. By 1980 suburbs contained about 46% of the nation's population as compared to 29% and 25% for central cities and nonmetropolitan areas, respectively. In the same year, 61% of the metropolitan population resided in suburbs and 39% in central cities (U.S. Bureau of the Census, 1983, table 6). Since 1980 the process has continued, with the suburban rings of metropolitan areas increasing their demographic predominance over the growth rates of central cities and nonmetropolitan areas (U.S. Bureau of the Census, 1985).

Paralleling the process of population redistribution, the changing spatial arrangement of industry was partially the result of central-city firms shifting to the periphery and partly due to new businesses choosing fringe locations. One can easily get a sense of the changes that have transpired simply by noticing the buildup of industrial and business parks and retail concentrations in the suburban rings of most major U.S. cities. By 1978, over 15,000 shopping centers and malls had been built to serve the fringe population, and as early as 1975, these shopping centers and malls accounted for more than half the annual retail sales in the United States (Kasarda, 1985, p. 41; see also Muller, 1976).

Spatial deconcentration of economic activities to the suburbs and beyond continued during the 1980s. Retail, personal service, professional, financial, and entertainment establishments have relocated to open country and filled small-town shopping areas. Trucking firms and wholesale establishments have taken up sites along peripheral beltways and interstate routes. An increasing number of corporate office complexes have been moving to medium-sized cities, some in metropolitan, others in nonmetropolitan areas. Given today's advanced transportation and communication technologies, even newer, rapid growth industries—aerospace, microelectronics, pharmaceuticals, and research and development industries—enjoy a freedom of locational choice that enables them to be guided increasingly by environmental and local political conditions. The deconcentrating urban economic base has not only drawn many formerly

metropolitan residents into nonmetropolitan areas, but also has converted increasing shares of the rural labor force to urban-type occupations. As a consequence, agricultural employment (the historic occupation of rural residents) now constitutes less than 10% of the nonmetropolitan job base.

Underlying the urban expansion process were a number of factors, including (1) the spread of paved highways, electricity, water, and sewage disposal systems, and other public services throughout suburban and nonmetropolitan America; (2) the growing capital intensity of production technologies that reduced the need for manufacturing industries to be located near large population concentrations; (3) reduction in the bulk of material products and shifts from rail to truck transportation of these products; (4) the linkage of virtually all localities into nationwide and worldwide telecommunications networks; and (5) nearly universal ownership of motor vehicles, which allow workers and shoppers to exercise myriad options in a spatially extensive market. Market access is being further broadened in the 1980s by wire-communicated banking, shopping, credit, and other electronically transacted services conducted among homes and businesses, a point we return to later.

So extensive has been urban expansion and the territorial integration of our wired society that social scientists are finding it increasingly difficult to differentiate metropolitan and nonmetropolitan residents in terms of their occupations, consumer habits, lifestyles and degrees of sophistication. Indeed, the much publicized "rural renaissance" of the late 1970s turned out actually to be more of an urbanization of nonmetropolitan territory as traditionally urban industries, consumer goods and services, and lifestyles diffused to previously isolated rural communities (Kasarda, 1980).

The deconcentration of population and industry reflects a major territorial reorganization of the American spatial economy, which became especially manifest after 1970. Conventionally labeled as haphazard and inefficient "sprawl," deconcentrated development is far more organized and cost-effective than once believed (Haines, 1986; Muller, 1981). For those whose obsolete models still portray metropolitan areas as fried eggs (with single uniform cores surrounded by uniform suburban rings), this new form of polycentric urbanism looks like scrambled eggs, with little structure or internal organization. Yet, deconcentrated, polycentric urbanism reflects a highly reticulated computer-age territorial structure consisting of functionally integrated nodes, networks, and economic and social exchanges organized around advanced transportation and communications technologies on a time-cost (rather than a spatial distance) basis (Kasarda, 1980).

Within this new, more diffuse form of polycentric urbanization, networks of information flows are increasingly substituting for product and people flows. The traditional metropolitan central business district functions as the primary administrative, information, and financial nucleus of a multinodal system of activity centers extending as far as 100 miles from the metropolitan core. For our largest cities, their complex of administrative, financial, and information-based functions serve the entire nation (and, in some cases, the world).

Another way of conceptualizing the tremendous reorganization of urban space is to view the emerging polycentric pattern as an interconnected web of "urban villages," which in ideal form would enable the population "to live, work, shop, and play in the same geographic area—while retaining access to other urban village cores with specialized features that their own district lacks" (Leinberger and Lockwood, 1986, p. 52). The extent to which interdependence is developing in a far-flung urban periphery is seen in the commuting in 1982 of 27 million workers *between* suburbs, as contrasted with half that number making the commute from suburbs to downtown areas (Leinberger and Lockwood, 1986).

At first glance, such a pattern might be considered a return to scale that theories of nonproportional change suggest is an alternative when systems become too large to be effectively and efficiently coordinated by existing technology and organizational arrangements (Boulding, 1953). However, given the evidence of the interconnectedness of multiple urban nodes, it is more appropriate to conceive of the polycentric metropolitan field as a reasonably well-integrated unit that owes its functional integrity to interlocking expressways and recent advances in communications technology—organizational adaptations that couple spatial separation with functional accessibility (Kasarda, 1980).

Despite continuing deconcentration during the 1970s and 1980s, a number of countertrends occurred in central cities. Consistent with expansion theory, advertising agencies, brokerage houses, management consulting firms, financial institutions, legal, accounting, and other businesses engaged in coordination and control replaced many downtown department stores and other more traditional businesses unable to afford rapidly increasing rents in the central business districts. These central business districts

also experienced a remarkable growth of high-rise administrative office buildings. Even with major advances in telecommunications technologies, many headquarters office functions still require a complement of legal, financial, public relations, and other specialized business services that are most accessible at the city's core. Moreover, unlike manufacturing, wholesale trade and retail activities, which typically have large space-per-employee requirements and whose products cannot be moved efficiently in a vertical direction, most managerial, clerical, professional, and business functions are highly space intensive and their basic product (information) can be transferred as efficiently vertically as it can horizontally. Thus people who process information can be stacked, layer after layer, in downtown office towers with resulting proximity actually increasing the productivity of those whose activities require an extensive amount of nonroutine, face-to-face interaction.

The decline in manufacturing, retail, and wholesale activities in cities and corresponding rise in administrative activities resulted in a transformation of major cities from centers of goods processing to centers of information processing. Along with these changes has come increasing education and skill requirements for employment in transforming urban economies. The availability of entry-level and other lower-education requisite jobs that once attracted and socially upgraded millions of disadvantaged migrants has dropped precipitously in most larger cities while information-processing jobs requiring education beyond high school have rapidly expanded (Kasarda, 1985).

Cities that experienced the largest losses of jobs with low education requisites during the past two decades simultaneously experienced marked increases in minority populations. That many members of minority populations have limited educational qualifications precludes them from gaining employment in white-collar service industries that are beginning to dominate urban employment bases. As a result, unemployment rates, labor force dropout rates, and welfare dependency of urban minorities are substantially greater than the national averages and especially high among urban minorities with poor educations (for data, see Kasarda, 1985).

In summary, conflicting spatial processes are occurring in the demographic and employment bases of major cities. These processes include:

(1) suburbanization of middle- and upper-income residents and their partial replacement in the central cities by lower socioeconomic-

status minorities (see Kasarda, 1984; Long, 1981; Long and Dahman, 1980; Zimmer, 1975);

(2) deconcentration of manufacturing, retail, and wholesale establishments and increases in the central business districts of administrative, financial, and other coordinating and control activities (Kasarda, 1978, 1984; Noyelle and Stanback, 1983; Sternlieb and Hughes, 1975);

(3) corresponding declines in blue-collar and other lower-education requisite jobs in the central cities and growth in white-collar information-processing jobs requiring substantial education (Kasarda, 1983, 1985; Suttles, 1978; Wilson, 1983);

(4) a resulting widening gap between educational qualifications of minority groups residing in the central cities and educational requirements of new urban growth industries; and

(5) high rates of structural unemployment and welfare dependency among poorly educated minority residents as this gap widens (Kasarda, 1985).

These urban spatial processes and outcomes are not restricted to the United States. Similar processes and outcomes have been reported for Great Britain, West Germany, and other Western European nations (see Evans and Eversley, 1980; Friedrichs, 1982; Hall and Hays, 1981; Kasarda and Friedrichs, 1985; Metcalf and Richardson, 1976; Van den Berg et al., 1982).

Urban Expansion and Critical Theory

There is almost complete agreement among scholars concerning the intraurban spatial rearrangements that have taken place since the expansion of cities began in earnest. There is distinct disagreement between so-called main stream and critical theorists (Gottdiener, 1983, 1985) over how and why particular spatial processes have occurred, especially those involving the deconcentration of urban population and industry. The first group of scholars depends heavily, but certainly not entirely, on the paradigm of urban ecology, while the second relies mainly, but not exclusively, on Marxist theory.

For example, Castells (1985), in examining the effect of technology on spatial forms of capitalist development, observes that high-technology industries have given rise to a new spatial pattern of production in the United States. The traditional locational attractions of ports and depots have been replaced by pools

of technical and scientific laborers, centers of defense spending, sources of innovative venture capital, and strategic positions in a communication network. Castells echos the ecological view that changing technology has altered the locational behavior of industry and encouraged the growth of new areas. The new hierarchy of functions and power is structured by a "space of flows substituting a space of places" (p. 14).

Castells argues that it is mainly through the emergence of new economic structures within the United States that technology has modified the spatial pattern of production as well as our cities. The formation of new economic relations within the past decade is the result of three fundamental shifts: (1) the increased substitution of capital for labor in the production process, (2) a new role of government, and (3) an international division of labor. First, technological developments have led to the automation or abandonment of traditional factories, resulting in the decline of jobs and outmigration of people from older manufacturing cities (see also Bluestone and Harrison, 1982; Sawers and Tabb, 1984). There is a new dualism in the largest metropolitan areas as high-tech and white-collar service sectors grow rapidly and the traditional manufacturing processes continue to decline. Meanwhile, the state has changed its role from one of collective consumption and legitimation to a position of selective accumulation and domination. The government has increased its support of capital growth in the form of defense spending and reduced social expenditures, which in turn has resulted in further shifts of jobs and people away from traditional urban manufacturing areas while reducing state assistance to those left in areas of decline. Finally, the vast increase in communications capacity has stimulated a corporate strategy of interregional and international production regardless of the social and economic consequences for local areas. This new international form of production reduces the ability of cities and regions to control their destinies. Thus Castells contends that the major cause of recent spatial reorientation in the United States has been "the interconnected processes of economic restructuring and technological change" (1985, p. 32).

Critical theorists contend that urban ecology, geography, and economics have largely ignored the role of the state (allied with business interests) in urban development, have typically premised urban analyses on a form of technological reductionism, and have, in general, taken a too benign view of urbanization. To illustrate, Castells (1977, 1978) calls attention to state intervention in regard to reproduction of labor in an urban setting, and Feagin (1985) points to government aid in the form of subsidies for public works and protectionist legislation favoring the oil industry as crucial to the emergence of Houston as a major metropolis. Some authors discount the role of technological advance and tend to perceive deconcentration of industry and population as a capitalist effort to defuse labor unrest by isolating the labor force (Gordon, 1977). And Harvey (1975, 1976) apparently views governmental subsidization of homeownership as "a bribe by capitalists to the working class" (Gottdiener, 1983, p. 233).

On the other hand, Gottdiener, while rejecting what he regards as the technological determinism of urban ecology, also sharply criticizes urban political economists and Marxist theorists:

> Urban political economists . . . view the mechanization of urban growth as a capitalist plot perpetrated by a select group of individuals on the bulk of the residents, who are called the working class (whatever that means in today's society) [1985, p. 16].

And, more generally,

> In the main, American marxists perceive capitalism's influence in space as a monolithic corporate presence, because they fallaciously assume a direct link between capitalism's transformations and spatial forms [Gottdiener, 1985, p. 66].

Further, Gottdiener asserts that Castell's emphasis on collective consumption diverts attention from a theory of space and toward "a theory of urban problems," a focus that characterized the Chicago School of Robert Ezra Park (1985, p. 119). By contrast, Gottdiener stresses the relevance of the work of Lefebvre, who is the only Marxist who "sees the role of space as more than epiphenomenal" (1985, p. 145).

Because he makes space and spatial processes central to his theory of urban growth and expansion, let us consider Gottdiener's perspective in more detail. The essence of Gottdiener's perspective, as well as the core of his critique of the theories currently dominating urban studies, is that:

> In place of explanations for the production of space based upon the study of the actions of large numbers of economic actors making marginal decisions about transport and product costs, we need to closely observe the actions of the large firms and the combined private-public networks organized around the secondary circuit of space, which manipulate space in pursuit of profits and superprofits [1985, pp. 272-273].

In more specific terms, mainstream theory is criticized for focusing on transportation and communications technology as causes of urban expansion. In addition, demand forces are rejected, or at least heavily discounted, as explanations of the explosion of suburban development, in favor of emphasis on supply-side forces created by developers and real estate interests, aided and abetted by government.

Similarly, the maintenance and even increased concentration of financial and certain retail trade activities in central cities, facilitated by urban renewal policies, is viewed as the result of neither the advantages of proximity for certain higher-order functions nor of the need for greater centralization of coordinative activities in an expanding system, but rather of the willingness of the state to accede to the goal of real estate interests to profit from the turnover of land and/or to ameliorate a deteriorating situation when speculation in land creates a crisis of overinvestment and urban blight (Gottdiener, 1985, pp. 62-68, 192-193, 216-217, 252).

Somewhat similar perceptions of an alliance between government and land-based capital in promoting urban growth are, of course, found in the work of other critical theorists (e.g., Domhoff, 1983; Feagin, 1983, 1985; Logan and Motlotch, 1987; Molotch, 1976). Still others contend that to perceive the urban use of space as a product of manipulation and conspiracy perpetrated by the property development industry is to miss the point entirely, partly because landowners do not represent a separate class in American society and partly because the real culprit is not the profit motive of real estate interests, but rather the entire capitalist process of production and appropriation of surplus value (Roweis and Scott, 1981, p. 136).

Despite the fact that critical and mainstream urban scholars' premise their analyses on quite different conceptual frameworks, and although numerous differences regarding specific issues have been noted, the two approaches have a number of (often unrecognized) similarities in their interpretation of intraurban spatial processes. For example, Gottdiener cites "cheap land, lower taxes . . ., the presence of local boosters,. . . access to transportation routes such as interstate highways, and local government subsidies" as primary attractions leading to industrial growth at the periphery (1985, pp. 252-253). These are precisely the same factors that appear prominently in ecological explanations of the same phenomenon (Berry and Kasarda, 1977; Frisbie, 1980b; Hawley, 1981; Kasarda, 1980). If nothing else, the variety of factors taken into account should surely put to rest the notion that urban ecology tends toward technological reductionism. The obvious difference that exists here is that critical theorists emphasize class conflict, capitalist machinations, and the role of the state in creating conditions conducive to deconcentration, while ecologists focus more on proximate economic processes and technological requisites. To some extent, each perspective has taken the other's "explanations" as its "assumptions" and proceeds to analyze spatial processes in terms of the key constraints of its own perspective. Rather than denying the significance of the other perspective's explanatory factors, they treat them as "given."

Other similarities may be observed. For example, earlier sections dealt with the importance ecologists accord the concept of nodality; that is, the advantages (including external economies) of spatial contiguity for the efficient performance of certain functions. Likewise, in the context of his discussion of the informational city in which technological change has made concentration in space less necessary, Castells suggests the following:

> the new technologies also enhance, simultaneously, the importance of a few places as locations of those activities that cannot be easily transformed into flows and that still require spatial contiguity, thus reinforcing considerably the intraurban hierarchy. . . . Thus, high-level managerial functions, specialized leisure areas, key informational institutions, very specific production centers (such as high tech nests), and special-delivery activities . . . will still earmark the metropolitan space with their requirements for spatial contiguity and face-to-face interaction [1985, p. 18].

While we would in no way want to suggest that Castells completely accepts the ecological model of urban spatial processes, he comes remarkably close to the former approach when he points out that the recent transformation in spatial structure "appears to follow a logic that combines *spatial diffusion, territorial hierarchy (including an urban concentration of the highest level), and functional interconnectedness*" (1985, p. 32; emphasis in the original).

One very substantial difference that separates critical theorists from those working in the ecological tradition has to do with the degree of choice urban residents are assumed to retain over use of space. Gottdiener maintains that the massive suburbanization that transpired in the period since World War II would never have occurred in the absence of state subsidization of

home construction and tax deductions associated with property ownership (1985, p. 243). Although few would deny the significance of such incentives, an objection may well be raised to Gottdiener's conclusion that "the present form of metropolitan expansion represents less the desires of its many residents, as ecological theory would lead us to believe, than the uncoordinated activities of this leading edge of capital distinguished by the ideology of growth" (1985, p. 149). Other neo-Marxist theorists argue that tastes and preferences are mere epiphenomena created by the mode of production (e.g., Roweis and Scott, 1981, p. 134). While it may be true, as Gottdiener suggests, that the existence of suburbs "does not prove that free choice has been exercised" (1985, p. 249), it seems equally true that the fact that government has facilitated the ability of the population to own homes and that certain businesses have made a profit from housing development does not prove that urban residents were in any way forced to suburbanize. In any event, we reiterate that suburbanization of population had begun prior to the turn of the century and was rather far advanced by 1920, well before there were any government-provided incentives. Note that critical theorists do not contend that no suburbanization occurred prior to World War II, and we certainly do not deny that the State has played a significant role in urban deconcentration. However, one must be careful not to overemphasize state intervention as a root cause of deconcentration, for to do so comes perilously close to arguing that the effect was present before the cause.

A competing, but not contradictory, explanation is that the heavily built-up central cities simply lacked adequate space at prices capable of satisfying either developers attempting to make a profit or prospective homeowners trying to secure affordable housing and better physical and social environments. In other words, there is reason to assume that both demand- and supply-side factors were operating and that the models of critical and mainstream theorists alike contribute to our understanding of urban deconcentration.

It likewise seems reasonable to conclude this comparison of mainstream and critical interpretations of urban development by acknowledging that, while certain similarities between the two approaches may allow a useful dialogue, there is yet little sign of anything approaching synthesis. Critical theorists, especially in the Marxist tradition, may turn periodically to concepts central to mainstream urban theory. However, for the most part, these concepts are taken as representative of factors that exercise intermediate effects on urban form and growth, with the real causal explanation assumed to lie in the capitalist mode of production and the process of capital accumulation. Similarly, conventional theorists often incorporate capital accumulation into their analyses (e.g., by taking into account the profit motive of developers and industrialists), but do not share with Marxists the presumption that flaws or contradictions of capitalism underlie urban structure and process (Jaret, 1983).

Segregation

Sociological interest in residential segregation is at least as old as Park's contention that, because social relations are so inextricably intertwined with spatial relations, observation of physical separation serves as a useful indicator of social distance (Park, 1967, p. 68). Socioeconomic status, family life cycle, and race/ethnicity are all major dimensions along which populations have been "sifted and sorted" in space (Schnore, 1972), but the amount of scholarly attention devoted to each varies considerably. Relatively little attention has been given to segregation by socioeconomic status and age (or life cycle), and although there is a growing literature on ethnic segregation (especially of Hispanic groups), the vast majority of research has been limited to spatial separation of blacks and whites.

SOCIOECONOMIC STATUS

Findings regarding segregation by socioeconomic status can be fairly briefly summarized. Studies of this phenomenon have often relied on occupational distributions as a measure of socioeconomic status, and relatively low levels of separation have been observed. Some variability exists since segregation is greatest for groups near the extremes of the distribution and least for groups of intermediate status (Duncan and Duncan, 1955). From his survey of the literature, Frisbie (1980b, p. 206) comments that:

Residential dissimilarity by occupation may be somewhat greater in central cities than in suburbs (Fine, et al., 1971), socioeconomic segregation occurs among blacks as well as whites with rather small changes over time (Simkus, 1978), and only minor differences in socioeconomic segregation of residences exist across urbanized areas regardless of whether operationalization is in terms of occupation, income, or education (Farley, 1977).

A major reason for the existence of segregation by socioeconomic status resides in the inequalities that constitute the overall system of stratification. That is, greater affluence allows some persons to acquire housing in more desirable areas, leaving other locales for the less wealthy. However, income differences are apparently not the whole story. Because occupational origins (as indicated by father's occupation) are closely associated with residential segregation, it may be plausibly argued that childhood socialization results in differing residential preferences in the adult years. In turn, this implies that social status, in addition to social class, may exert a substantial influence on residential distributions (Duncan and Duncan, 1955). Further, the influence of class in the traditional Marxist sense has probably declined as moderately priced housing developments, in combination with governmental subsidies, have brought home ownership within the reach of middle and lower-income families, thereby creating a cleavage between owners and renters not based on work-related conditions (Gottdiener, 1985, pp. 166-170).

AGE/LIFE-CYCLE

Only a few investigations of segregation by age exist, and the results of these may be appropriately viewed as indications of spatial separation by stage in the family life cycle. Guest (1972, 1977) and Pampel and Choldin (1978) report only a modest degree of segregation of the elderly, and the patterns observed are consistent with conventional life-cycle theories regarding locational and accessibility needs. That is, there is a tendency for the elderly to be somewhat more concentrated near the center of cities in areas with multiunit dwellings, while the population in the prime childbearing and child-rearing years is somewhat overrepresented in peripheral areas that contain single-family dwellings. Nevertheless, with more multiunit dwellings being built in peripheral areas and with aging cohorts of residents who moved from the cities following World War II, many suburbs are developing concentrations of elderly ("grey ghettos") not unlike those in central cities.

RACE/ETHNICITY

All research demonstrates that residential segregation of blacks from whites is consistently high across metropolitan areas (Farley, 1977; Massey and Mullan, 1984; Taeuber and Taeuber, 1965; Van Valey, Roof, and Wilcox, 1977). Although there has been some diminution over time, and while there is some variation by age of metropolitan area (the date at which metropolitan status was achieved), there has been no major decline in the segregation of blacks. Analyses based on the most commonly used measure of segregation, the index of dissimilarity, typically conclude that about 90% of blacks (or whites) would have to change location in order to achieve a perfectly proportional distribution.

The situation with respect to ethnic segregation is considerably different. The segregation of ethnic populations is substantially less than that experienced by blacks and, unlike the case with blacks, segregation of ethnic groups declines with increases in socioeconomic status and over time (Guest and Weed, 1976, p. 1110; Lieberson, 1961, 1963; Massey, 1985).

Although levels of Hispanic-black segregation are high, Hispanic-Anglo segregation is relatively low—generally about half that recorded in black-white comparisons (Grebler, Moore, and Guzman, 1970; Massey, 1979a, 1979b, 1981). Finally, segregation of Hispanics (excepting Puerto Ricans) consistently diminishes as socioeconomic status increases (Massey, 1979b; Massey and Mullan, 1984).

THE PROCESS OF SEGREGATION

In ecological parlance, centrifugal and centripetal movements have always been active in the structuring of urban space. Centripetal movement, the concentration of population and functions, was most obvious in the early stages of urban development when pedestrian and fixed-route transit predominated (Hawley, 1971, 1981). However, centrifugal movement, the scattering of population and organizations over a wider area, which has always existed to some degree, gained considerable momentum in the first decades of the twentieth century and has resulted in the far-flung, polynucleated metropolitan areas described previously.

Ecological theories of expansion and differentiation account reasonably well for the spatial separation of many population subgroups. The conceptual premise of social area analysis holds that as societies develop, the degree of heterogeneity increases, the division of labor becomes more complex and ramified, and occupational niches become more specialized. The family loses many of its traditional productivity func-

tions and declines in importance as an economic unit while a greater variety of household and family types emerge (Shevky and Bell, 1955). If nothing else, social area analysis and factorial ecology have demonstrated that urban populations are distributed and redistributed according to socioeconomic status, family type, and race/ethnicity (Anderson and Egeland, 1961; Berry and Kasarda, 1977, pp. 131-134; Van Arsdol et al., 1958).

As just mentioned, segregation by socioeconomic characteristics can be largely explained by differentials in the ability to afford the locations most desirable in terms of housing, topography, proximity to amenities, and distance from nuisances (or dangers) of urban life. And different family types, within the constraints imposed by general socioeconomic conditions, personal preferences, and the availability of housing and financing, find residential space best suited to the size and composition of the family.

Ethnic (but not racial) segregation is also rather well accounted for in terms of ecological theory:

> The concentration of ethnic groups is rooted in the spatial differentiation of the urban economy, and reinforced by the nature of immigrants and immigration. Dispersion is driven by socioeconomic mobility and acculturation, and is based on the fact that a differentiated urban economy distributes resources and opportunities unevenly in space, encouraging immigrants to move in order to improve their position in society [Massey, 1985, p. 317].

The overall process is captured in invasion and succession models of Park, Burgess, and others of the Chicago School who observed waves of immigrants concentrating in and near the core of the city where entry-level jobs were to be found, only to move on (and outward) as they became culturally and structurally assimilated and were replaced by a new immigrant group. This pattern was most clearly evident when intramural transportation was poor and production was labor intensive. In general, residential segregation of particular ethnic groups broke down as the centrifugal forces of socioeconomic advancement and acculturation took hold (Massey, 1985). The consistent decline in the segregation of second-generation immigrants as compared to the first generation, and the strong inverse relationship between socioeconomic status and segregation constitutes "eloquent confirmation" of the ecological explanation of segregation/assimilation with respect to Hispanics as well as European ethnic groups (Massey, 1981, p. 647). Moreover, the same patterns delineated above appear to hold (with some variation) in a number of other countries including Canada, Britain, Australia, Israel, and nations of Western Europe (Massey, 1985).

However, ecological theory falls far short of explaining the continued high level of residential isolation of blacks. Not only are blacks the most highly segregated minority, but also the invasion-succession process does not appear to operate in the same fashion among blacks. Once blacks begin to penetrate white areas, complete succession or "consolidation" (LaGory and Pipkin, 1981, p. 159) often follows. By contrast, penetration by Hispanics is followed by loss of Anglo population less than 50% of the time (Massey and Mullan, 1984). Areas of Hispanic "invasion" tend to be those in which Anglos of high-socioeconomic status reside, and the latter are not particularly likely to leave such areas (Massey and Mullan, 1984, p. 848). An exception to the Hispanic pattern is in regard to Puerto Ricans, perhaps because a fairly large proportion of Puerto Ricans are of African ancestry and thus fall victim to the same prejudices associated with the avoidance by whites of black residential areas (Massey, 1985; Massey and Bitterman, 1985).

What then is the reason for the high degree of segregation of blacks from other groups? No doubt, the gap in socioeconomic resources between the black and white populations constitutes part of the explanation. But differences in income, occupation, and education leave a great deal unaccounted for. Upper-status blacks are more spatially separated from upper- (and lower-) status whites than they are from lower-status blacks (Farley, 1977). Further, based on economic differentials alone, the degree of black segregation would be only about 30% as high as that actually observed (Taeuber and Taeuber, 1965; see also LaGory and Pipkin, 1981, pp. 180-182). Other explanations include the historically more disadvantaged position of blacks, the timing of black migration to cities (Taeuber and Taeuber, 1965, pp. 16-17), and the greater degree of contemporary discrimination experienced by blacks (Massey and Mullan, 1984). As Massey and Mullan point out, "barriers to spatial mobility are barriers to social mobility" (1984, p. 838) because of the uneven distribution of opportunities over space and the constraints placed on returns to income spent on housing (1984, pp. 839-840). In other words, segregation of blacks must be viewed, at least in part, as a spatial manifestation of racism.

The massive dispersion of whites to suburban areas and continued concentration of blacks in central cities is the most obvious spatial representation of racial residential segregation. There is some evidence that whites frequently leave areas invaded by blacks based on their perception that housing values will fall (Berry and Kasarda, 1977, chap. 2; Laurenti, 1961). An alternative, but related, explanation is that whites have tended to flee central city areas occupied by a large and increasing black population because of the perception of economic and/or political threat (Marshall and Jiobu, 1975; see Blalock, 1967, for an elaboration on the general theoretical framework linking minority size to discrimination). While there is no doubt that suburbanward migration has been selective of whites, and therefore the center-periphery bifurcation more or less adequately describes the pattern of racial selectivity in space; the widespread reliance on a simple "white-flight" hypothesis runs aground on a considerable amount of contradictory evidence.

In the first place, blacks have also suburbanized to some extent, although the 1970-1980 decade apparently was the first time interval in which the number of black suburbanites increased in both relative and absolute terms (O'Hare et al., 1982). Second, Marshall's study (1979) of 112 metropolitan areas demonstrates that the relative size of the black population in central cities was only weakly and indirectly related to the movement of whites to the periphery. The most powerful explanatory factor of white suburbanization was the creation of new housing stock in suburbs (see also Marshall and Stahura, 1979). Of course, such findings do not mean that racial economic inequalities or prejudice should be discounted. Obviously, blacks have been less able than whites to afford new and higher-quality housing. It may be that what critical theorists, such as Gottdiener (1985, p. 240), refer to as "involuntary pressures . . . such as government policies, corporate restructuring, job relocations, and the like," constitute part of the explanation for the continuing sharply etched spatial pattern of largely white suburbs and increasingly black central cities. Critical theory does not appear to have developed a clear notion of how such a process might act directly to produce segregation of the sort that characterizes U.S. cities, but it is indisputable that the occupational skills and economic position of blacks, along with the redistribution of jobs and housing stock that has occurred since World War II, do not represent an optimal situation for black urban residents. Regardless of the validity of critical theory, changes in the residential and industrial use of urban space have, in some respects, trapped many blacks in central cities.

The outlook for central city minority populations may not be quite as bleak as the discussion thus far might seem to indicate. First, some authors, while emphasizing the continuing high degree of residential separation of blacks and whites in central cities and fringe areas, have adduced evidence that the patterns of the past may have changed in the direction of the greater spatial integration of the races in the interval since 1970 (Stahura, 1986). This view also "suggests a fundamental change in the intrametropolitan redistribution of blacks, indicating that they are now embarking on a suburbanization process that is reminiscent of white suburbanization several decades earlier" (Frey, 1985, p. 240). Recent research demonstrates that among whites, the post-1970 trend mirrors the earlier selective deconcentration, albeit at a reduced pace (Frey, 1985; Kasarda, 1980). In the case of blacks, however, suburbanization increased between 1975 and 1980, and the "selectivity patterns associated with this movement have come to resemble those of the white movement to suburbs in the immediate post-World War II period" (Frey, 1985, p. 240). Of particular importance are the findings that in the 1970s, black growth rates in upper-status suburbs exceeded those in lower-status suburbs and that the proportion of blacks in the population of suburbs was positively related to the growth of population and jobs (Stahura, 1986). On the other hand, the recency of this particular "turnaround" and the severity of the problem of central city minority unemployment cautions against the anticipation that any quick fix for the job-residence mismatch is in the offing.

Finally, it is interesting to note that residence in minority enclaves may be economically advantageous, if a semiseparate economy develops in which businesses owned and operated by minority group members provide jobs, as well as goods and services, for other members of the group. In other words, it is possible that external economies and other advantages tied to propinquity operate along racial or ethnic lines. Cubans appear to have achieved just such a successful ethnically based economy (Portes and Bach, 1985; Wilson and Portes, 1980). There is also some preliminary evidence that foreign-born Mexican Americans may experience positive increments in socioeconomic achievement from residence in ethnic enclaves (Tienda and Neidert, 1984), but there is as yet little indication of such a positive effect for blacks.

Interurban Spatial Processes

Systems of Cities: Theoretical Perspective

Cities in industrial (and postindustrial) nations are linked together in a larger spatial system based on a territorial division of labor, dominated by large urban centers, and sustained by interdependence and exchange. In these nations, a hierarchical system has emerged that has fundamentally reorganized the entire societal structure in such a way that no area, however remote, can be said to be untouched by urbanization (Hawley, 1971, chap. 10). On a global scale, so extensive has the influence of urban centers become that it is reasonable to refer to a world system involved in an international division of labor (Chase-Dunn, 1984; Meyer, 1986; Wallerstein, 1974, 1980; Walton, 1976). Within and across nations the "glue" binding systems of cities together may be found in the twin Durkheimian notions of functional differentiation and functional interdependence —though many world systems theorists would add force or coercion as an ingredient in the glue (Meyer, 1986).

Were we interested primarily in a comprehensive review of the literature, rather than in pursuing a discussion of spatial form and process, it would be necessary to catalog numerous analyses demonstrating the functional differentiation of city systems (Frisbie, 1980b; Meyer, 1986; Wanner, 1977). Suffice it to say that a voluminous sociological literature establishes that cities vary along a *horizontal* dimension according to specialization in various types of sustenance functions operationalized in terms of industrial activity (Alexandersson, 1956; Duncan et al., 1960; Hadden and Borgatta, 1965; Kass, 1973, among others). Many efforts along this line have relied on single-specialty typologies, but multifunctional classification schemes are also extant.

Research examining the *vertical* or hierarchical dimension is more interesting in that it inevitably brings into play the core ecological concepts of key function and dominance. By *key function* is meant the activity with the most direct and/or salient access to the environment (Hawley, 1968) and that therefore mediates the flow of sustenance among local units (Meyer, 1986, p. 555). In this context, *dominance* refers to the control and coordination exercised by a metropolitan center over other, usually smaller and less specialized urban communities. It should be noted that "Hawley (1968) coined the term key function to refer to those corporate units (or functionaries) that mediate the relations of a local population with its intermediate physical environment and social environment . . .'' (Wilson, 1984, p. 284). Thus when cites are said to exercise dominance, the reference is to the totality of corporate influences operational within a city and not to some amorphous and reified concept of metropolis.

More specifically, one may emphasize the dominance exercised by a city over its immediate hinterlands (Bogue, 1949; McKenzie, 1933) or of major metropolitan centers in an interurban hierarchy that may be regional, national, or international in scope (Eberstein and Frisbie, 1982; Pappenfort, 1959; Smith and Weller, 1977).

A theory of a system of cities must envision some degree of regularity of distribution of cities in space nested within a hierarchy defined in terms of size and functional complexity. This theory implies that cities in each larger size class will perform all the functions of the next smaller group of cities, plus other higher-order activities. The latter are often referred to as ''metropolitan functions'' and involve coordination and control activities that provide commercial and financial services over a wide territory and other services (e.g., wholesaling) that organize the market and channel exchange in an extra-local division of labor (Eberstein and Frisbie, 1982; Stern and Galle, 1978; Hawley, 1968; Vance and Sutker, 1954; Wanner, 1977).

When large metropolitan areas are compared according to industry specialization (horizontal dimension) and the degree of performance of higher-order coordinative functions (vertical dimension), a marked degree of similarity over time in the positioning of cities in this two-dimensional space has been observed (Duncan and Lieberson, 1970; Galle and Stern, 1981; South and Poston, 1980). This does not mean that no changes occur, however. Based on a region-specific analysis of factor loadings, South and Poston (1982) report that between 1950 and 1970, metropolitan areas of the northeastern United States became more service oriented, while maintaining their position with respect to financial and commercial dominance. In contrast, southern metropolitan areas sharply enhanced their position on the latter dimension. Finally, in the Midwest, metropolitan areas apparently became more manufacturing oriented and experienced some decline in dominance. These findings support the view that emergence of a service society and prominence of high-technology industries at the leading edge of economic growth may have altered historic

dominance-development relationships at the regional level (Eberstein, Wrigley, and Serow, 1985). The movement of population and growth industries toward the South and West has been well documented (Kasarda, 1980; Watkins and Perry, 1977). We return to this issue in a subsequent section, but it warrants mention at this juncture that recent variations in regional urban systems challenge perspectives that assume rigid stability of structure and indefinite advantages of an initial favorable position in the hierarchy (South and Poston, 1982, p. 202).

Systems of Cities: Spatial Patterns

In numerous societies and at numerous points in time, scholars have observed a regular distribution of cities by size of place. In general, the pattern is one involving many small cities, fewer places of intermediate size, and still fewer very large cities. Before discussing the social and economic implications of such regularities for society as a whole, it will be useful to consider efforts aimed at explaining why cities grow up in some locations and not in others.

One of the earliest attempts to account for the location of cities in a numerical and functional hierarchy is found in *central place theory* (Christaller, 1933; Losch, 1954). Christaller's formulation posits that cities supply a range of services to their hinterlands within constraints imposed by the size of the market and the distance consumers are willing to travel. Goods and services more infrequently consumed because of their costly and/or specialized nature ''are best provided in large central locations where the demand from smaller centers can be aggregated'' (Smith and Weller, 1977, p. 93). Other goods and services in more frequent use can therefore be profitably provided at locations with smaller populations. Thus the theory proposes a nested set of cities for which a hexagonal shape is assumed to be the most efficient spatial form (Losch, 1954).

> The effect of these conditions is to create a spatial distribution of service centers or central places that systematically vary in both the range of central goods provided and in the frequency with which centers of different sizes occur. . . . The highest order central place, of which there will be only one, will tend to be located at the center of the region [Smith and Weller, 1977, p. 93].

As Hawley (1971, p. 223) points out, the even scatter of urban places within regions anticipated by central place theory is most appropriate to less developed stages of societal organization. Another flaw is that the theory was built around the notion that cities function primarily to collect goods and distribute services. However, cities often develop around transformative activities that depend on proximity to raw materials and interregional transportation routes, and there is no reason to expect that either natural or created resources will inevitably be located in the geographic center of a region. Further, the high degree of symmetry proposed by central place theory cannot be realized except in rare locations where the topography is such as to allow equal access from all directions. Consequently, it is not at all unusual to find a region's major city or cities quite far removed from the geographic center.

A competing locational theory proposes that cities tend to grow up at transportation crossroads where goods are loaded and off-loaded for shipment in different directions. Hence, metropolises would be expected to develop at ports, rail junctions, and highway intersections where a *break-in-bulk* occurs (Cooley, 1894). More important than a physical shifting of goods from one carrier to another is a commercial break, because only in the latter instance will there be an impetus for the emergence of financial, brokerage, warehousing, accounting, and other ancillary services that spin off from change in ownership (Smith and Weller, 1977, pp. 90-91). Such activities are the essence of nodality. Nodes are places where multiple decisions are made regarding mixing of goods and changing the direction of flows and are central, not geographically, but in the sense that they are the loci of highly information-intensive processes (Stinchcombe, 1968, p. 280).

It can be plausibly argued that "although a symmetrical distribution of towns and cities is not evident within regions or sections, it may appear in a country or in a set of regions" (Hawley, 1971, p. 224). A particular distribution (consistent with a functional hierarchy as described above), detected in a large number of countries and over time has been referred to as *log-normal*, because when the logarithm of the cumulative percentage of cities in various size categories is plotted against the logarithm of city size, the resulting curve approximates a straight line. In contrast, some societies evidence a *primate* pattern in which there is one, or a small number, of extremely large cities and a virtual absence of cities of intermediate size, with the remainder of the "urban" population residing in small towns and villages.

The concept of urban hierarchy, when coupled with Zipf's principle of least effort

(1949), offers an explanation for processes that give rise to the log-normal pattern in space. In general, it is postulated that dependence on localized raw materials will lead to diversification—that is, to a wide dispersion of small communities so that the cost of transporting raw materials will be minimized. On the other hand, scale economies created by concentration of population in large cities tend to minimize the cost of distributing services and processed goods to the consuming population.

The mathematical formalization of Zipf's principle has come to be known as the rank-size rule. The original statement of the rank-size rule was by Auerbach (see Stephan, 1979), but as popularized by Zipf (1949), the rule is given as follows:

$$r = p^{-q}K \text{ or } r(p^q) = K$$

where r is the rank of a city, p is its population, and q and K are constants. The equation makes the point that rank of a city is a function of its size, with the further implication that there will be a regularity of patterning such that if there is one large city of $r = 1$, there will be three cities of $r = 2$ and $p = K/3$, nine cities of $r = 3$ and $p = K/9$, and so on.

In addition to the United States (Berry and Kasarda, 1977, p. 88), the rank-size rule has been found adequately to describe interurban patterning in Canada, Italy, Korea, Japan, and India, as well as in nineteenth-century northwestern Europe (Stephan, 1979, p. 815). A shortcoming of critical theory is that while it may shed light on the reasons particular cities grow (Feagin, 1985) and on how particular uses of space are affected by the process of capital accumulation (Gottdiener, 1985; Jaret, 1983), it offers no explanation for the indisputable regularities in spatial patterns, such as those embodied in the rank-size rule (or Clark's urban density gradient) that appear repeatedly in a wide range of economic, political, social, and temporal contexts. By contrast, ecological theory accounts for these regularities by reference to the need to reduce the cost of interaction across time and space of interdependent units embedded in a territorial division of labor. In this sense, spatial patterns and processes are important mainly (but not only) for what they can tell us about functional relationships.

Although a good deal of theoretical leverage has been purchased by focusing on reduction of strictly economic costs, the temporal aspect of organization must also be taken into account. This is so because "the territorial scope . . ., the number of individuals. . . [and] the distribution of units within the community varies with the time used in movement. A temporal pattern is implicit in each and every spatial pattern" (Hawley, 1950, p. 288). Put slightly differently, space is a time-cost variable.

Building on this principle, Stephan has derived the urban density gradient, the rank-size rule, and a version of the basic gravity model from the notion of time minimization. The density gradient formula follows rather directly from time minimization theory since the money cost of land use is typically "received in units of money per unit of time (e.g., dollars per hour of labor time, investment time, rental time, etc.)" (Stephan, 1979, p. 816). The rank-size rule follows from the observation that a hierarchical or log-normal system of cities allows a population to take simultaneous advantage of quick access to frequently used commodities (in numerous small cities) and of agglomeration economies (in a few larger cities). The gravity model as developed by Stewart (1948) and Zipf (1949) hypothesizes that the degree of interaction (e.g., migration, traffic, etc.) between two places will be directly proportional to population and size and inversely proportional to distance. In this instance, Stephan (1979) derives the traditional gravity model equation,

$$I_{ij} = kp_ip_j/D_{ij}$$

where I_{ij} refers to interaction, p_i and p_j to the populations of places i and j and D_{ij} is distance, by expressing the probability of movement from i to j as a function of travel time and the average velocity of the means of transportation.

Time minimization is a conceptual framework that helps to explain yet another spatial regularity, namely, the size-density law, which in logarithmic form holds that:

$$\log A = k + b(\log D)$$

where A is the area of territorial unit, D is the population density of the unit, k is the intercept, and b is the slope, which is expected to take on a value of approximately $-\frac{2}{3}$. The size-density hypothesis has been supported in research on political subdivisions of 98 countries (Stephan, 1972) and, generally, in other contexts (Stephan and McMullin, 1981; Stephan and Stephan, 1984).

Lest one become carried away by the observation that certain urban spatial patterns occur in a sufficiently consistent manner to allow mathematical formalization, one should remember that exceptions to any rule or model may always be found. Observed regularities are best treated as *indicators* of functional processes that are incompletely understood at best. Even the most quantitatively oriented scholars readily admit that all we as social scientists possess are imperfect indicators of underlying concepts. In fact, it is often the most quantitatively oriented among us who voice the strongest concern over the inability of our methods to capture reality in anything like its full complexity and over the tendency to focus on trivial issues simply because they can be more easily handled statistically (e.g., Blalock, 1980, pp. xiii-xv). In raising these caveats, we do not wish to imply that specification of spatial regularities is an idle exercise. Indeed, the goal of scientific inquiry is to produce theories generalizable to as many empirical findings as possible (Stephan, 1979, p. 821, citing Comte). However, it is well to resist any inclination toward reductionism by bearing in mind Rogers's warning that it is premature to conclude that we have at our disposal "unifying principles of great generality, analogous to those which have had such success in the physical sciences" (1971, p. 212).

Systems of Cities: Relationship to Economic Development

There seems to be little doubt that urbanization and economic development are interrelated. Correlations between the proportion of the population in cities and standard measures of development such as literacy rates, per capita income, and per capita energy consumption are consistently strong and positive (Schnore, 1969). Specifically, it has been argued that the log-normal city pattern not only tends to be associated with industrialization, but also that this spatial form aids economic development. The rationale for this expectation may be outlined as follows: First, a hierarchical system of cities spreads economic opportunities more widely and helps close the gap between urban and rural worlds. Second, a societywide network of cities brings markets for agricultural products closer to the producers. Third, it permits (but does not guarantee) a more equitable distribution of public services throughout a society. Fourth, it facilitates the conversion of an entire society into a market for industry because the hierarchical pattern presupposes wide-ranging transportation and communications services. Expansion of the latter allows a more extensive urban influence, which in turn makes for greater standardization and efficiency of exchange in the context of a highly developed territorial division of labor.

By contrast, the primate pattern may inhibit development if, as some scholars have argued, it indicates a lack of societal integration and contributes to a sharp duality between the ideas, values, and economic position of the population of large cities and the poorer, more traditional peasant population (Berry and Kasarda, 1977: chap. 19; Jefferson, 1939). The concentration of population and economic resources, in effect, means a relative absence of centralization. Such concentration, whether based on the disproportionate influence of an elite class, on structural immaturity of the urban system (or both), may be viewed as dysfunctional for overall societal development because of the monopolization of resources by primate cities (Roberts, 1986).

Although the rationale for expecting a lognormal spatial arrangement to be positively associated, and high primacy to be negatively associated, with economic development is logical enough in its derivation, it is the case that certain developed countries evidence a primate-like spatial pattern, while some less-developed nations have something approaching a log-normal distribution (Berry, 1961). There is apparently no consensus regarding the reasons for these inconsistencies, but several explanations may be suggested. First, one might quarrel with the schemes for classifying countries as developed or less developed, but this seems an unproductive quibble at best. Second, and more salient, national boundaries increasingly do not circumscribe a closed system. This may be an especially pertinent interpretation for the European countries identified by Berry as having a primate city size distribution, since many of these engage in regular exchange across national boundaries (Hawley, 1971, p. 279). The difficulty with this explanation is that it is not falsifiable because it can always be argued that the unit is too small and that a hierarchical pattern would be observed if only the proper unit of analysis could be examined. The latter problem does not necessarily invalidate the second explanation, but it does make it difficult to see how a conclusive test might be achieved. A third explanation is that for countries relatively small in population size and geographic area, one or two large cities may serve the coordinative and integrative needs of a society without the necessity of a full complement of intermediate-size cities. Regardless of whether exceptions can be perfectly accounted for, there is substantial agreement that a hierarchical system of cities is strongly, positively, and reciprocally related to economic development.

Systems of Cities: Unresolved Issues

Although there is agreement concerning the outline of the urban hierarchy, little empirical research has focused on the question of exactly what mechanisms serve to integrate metropolitan systems (Frisbie, 1980a). However, at least two different answers to this question have been proposed.

The first emerges from ecological theory, and its explication requires the restatement of some of the ideas discussed previously, in light of the proposition that trade flows constitute the basis of system integration. To begin with, it seems eminently reasonable to conclude that functional differentiation and interdependence necessitate exchange. In this context, it is also logical to posit that "the mechanisms underlying the differentiation of communities in mediating interarea trade are differences among areas in the functional significance of their sustenance activities for the greater national economy" (Eberstein and Frisbie, 1982, p. 678).

If these propositions have a solid basis in reality, then a disproportionate spatial concentration of coordinative and mediative activities, such as banking, finance, wholesaling, and transportation and communications should (1) serve as a means of identifying dominant metropolitan centers and (2) be positively and significantly related to measures of interdependence. Eberstein and Frisbie (1982) report just such relationships in their study of metropolitan regions. Taking what have been termed Daily Urban Systems, now more commonly referred to as Business Economic Areas (BEAs), as their units of analysis, these authors found rank in the metropolitan hierarchy (operationalized via indicators such as industrial development, service receipts, bank deposits, location of home offices of manufacturing firms, and transportation and communications establishments) to be closely associated with interdependence of metropolitan communities as measured by variety and volume of trade flows and number of trading partners (see also Meyer, 1984). More recent research demonstrates the relationship of trade linkages to community industrial profiles and interregional trade routes (Eberstein and Galle, 1984).

A second approach challenges the perspective that tends to rely heavily, if not exclusively, on the existence of trade flows as an explanation for the integration of systems of cities. Lincoln (1978) suggests that a primary mechanism of metropolitan dominance and interdependence is to be found in the territorial extension of the relationship between the headquarters of firms and their branch offices and plants. The alternative hypothesis is that "the control exercised by the home office over the operations of its plants becomes a channel through which the metropolis coordinates activities in its hinterland" (1978, p. 213). Since home offices tend to concentrate in the larger and more diversified cities, while branch plants are more likely to be located in small industrially homogeneous communities, the spatial patterning of this channel of control is essentially the same as that which ecologists have proposed and empirically observed. The point of contention is the relative importance for system integration of exchange based on functional specialization, on the one hand, and control arising out of the bureaucracy of formal organizations, on the other. A similar view holds that large "headquarters cities" are dominant less because they provide greater efficiencies for the firms who locate their home offices within them than because the agglomeration of coordinative and support services facilitates more rigid control by a firm over its own organization and other businesses (Molotch and Logan, 1985). This approach, like ecological theory, emphasizes the importance of agglomeration economies, but congruent with the work of Lincoln, it conceives the mechanism of control to be the bureaucracy of formal organizations.

As we have attempted to show with respect to other sets of competing theories, these perspectives on interurban integration are, in some ways complementary rather than contradictory. As Lincoln himself points out, ecological theory treats "organizations as the elementary units of community structure" and as the source of community integration (1979, p. 927). Second, even if exchange is accepted to be the single most effective means of integrating the system, it is obviously the case that trade does not emerge and flow randomly. Thus it might be argued that the work of Lincoln and others simply concentrates on the specific means by which order and efficiency of exchange are effected.

Changing Spatial Processes

An increasing number of scholars have called attention to certain alterations in sociospatial relationships that began after World War II and

gained momentum in the 1970s. In the most general terms, the observed changes involve an acceleration of the trend toward deconcentration and a growing "footlooseness" of population and industry. Among the more important specific manifestations of the general trend are (1) the declining significance of spatial proximity for maintenance of urban integration, with emergent implications for social relationships, (2) the revival of growth of nonmetropolitan areas, (3) rise of the Sunbelt, (4) the rapid growth of megacities in developing nations, and (5) emerging world divisions of labor and resulting international dependencies and interdependencies.

Although there is some debate over the primary causal mechanisms underlying these unprecedented variations in spatial patterns, most agree that technological advances, particularly with respect to the storage, retrieval, and rapid communication of information (and growth of high-technology industries that made these advances possible) have promoted sociospatial reorganization. In particular, spectacular strides in telecommunications and computer technology now permit the functioning of complex and highly interrelated organizations under much less densely settled conditions and over much of the world. As a result, since 1970 deconcentration has occurred at all levels of aggregation in the developed world, whether the units of analysis are cities, counties, metropolitan areas, or larger geographic divisions (Vining and Strauss, 1977). It remains to be seen if this sort of widespread dispersion can continue indefinitely (Heaton and Fuguitt, 1980); indeed, there is now evidence that the "nonmetropolitan turnaround" in the United States has slackened and perhaps been reversed (Fuguitt, 1985; Richter, 1985). Nevertheless, the changes have been of such magnitude, and represent such a substantial departure from previous trends, as to inspire an impressive new wave of urban and urban-related research.

*Declining Significance
of Spatial Proximity:
Polynucleation and Beyond*

Of course, the deconcentration of urban population and industry is not a new trend at all, but rather the continuation of the suburbanward movement that has long been a prominent feature of industrialized societies (Hall and Hays, 1980; Van den Berg et al., 1982). As was discussed in an earlier section, the vast movement of jobs and residences to the periphery makes it clear that agglomeration and mutual-scale economies are no longer tied to central locations. The obvious conclusion that a poly-nucleated form of urban organization has come to replace the monocentered city that constituted the analytical point of departure of many early conceptual models of urban form and growth requires no elaboration at this juncture. What does warrant attention is (1) that interurban deconcentration has continued apace even in the face of obstacles that many assumed would slow down the process and (2) the extent to which further deconcentration may be possible.

As Edmonston and Guterbock (1984) suggest, it was reasonable to expect a deceleration in the rate of deconcentration in the 1970s, since many of the causal forces assumed to produce suburbanization have recently been blunted. Presumably, extremely cheap energy and rapidly rising incomes facilitated the suburban boom into the 1960s. But in the 1970s energy costs soared and real income growth was dampened, while suburban housing costs rose. Certain demographic trends might also have been expected to slow movement to the periphery. In particular, overall metropolitan growth rates declined, as did average household size. Moreover, there was considerable excitement in some quarters over the "gentrification" or return-to-the-city movement (Laska and Spain, 1980). Despite these recent developments, Edmonston and Guterbock, after taking into account population size, age of city, and regional location, find no diminution in population deconcentration in the 1970s. The reasons, they suggest, are essentially the same as those that have, in the past, been given for population *concentration* at the core of the city.

> As expected theoretically, the response of households to increasing transportation costs, higher housing costs, lack of income growth, and changes in household form is to choose residential locations closer to important activities. But since the activities are dispersed, moving "closer to the action" does not necessarily mean movement toward the urban center [Edmonston and Guterbock, 1984, p. 923].

Indeed, in this case, it means movement toward the industrial parks, office complexes, and shopping malls that have been built at the periphery.

Perhaps more intriguing is the potential for an even greater degree of deconcentration as advances in automation and telecommunications have begun to create a space of flows instead of a space of places in an "informational city" (Castells, 1985, pp. 14-15). So great has this potential become that it is possible to conceive of urbanization without cities. Already, editors, stock brokers, bank clerks, and real estate brokers (among others) find it possible to conduct much of their business at home via micro-computers and advanced telecommunications. It is interesting, and a bit ironic, to observe that the industrial revolution that reorganized production in such a way as to remove work from the home has spawned computerization and related technologies that may now bring about a recoupling of work and place of residence (Calhoun, 1986).

Although the potential exists in a purely technological sense, anything like a complete recombination of place of residence with place of work seems remote. Even those most attuned to the possibilities of an "electronic city" point out that there are certain activities "that cannot be easily transformed into flows and that still require spatial contiguity" (Castells, 1985, p. 18). Among activities and facilities that appear most transformation resistant are "high-level managerial functions, specialized leisure areas, . . . and special service-delivery activities (from hospitals to high-class boutiques)" (Castells, 1985, p. 18). In any event, it is palpable that we are at a stage when the processes and patterns of the urban use of space are in transition. One view of the outcome is decidedly dark in that, in regard both to home and workplace, the telecommunications revolution allows the more powerful and affluent to isolate themselves in what Lefebvre and Gottdiener refer to as "privileged space" (see Gottdiener, 1985, p. 285). This could mean a discontinuity in space with the less well-off portion of the population left behind in "switched-off, wireless communities" (Castells, 1985, p. 19).

On the other hand, a brighter vision might be brought to realization since computers and telecommunications allow breathtaking reductions in the time that heretofore has had to be devoted to the secondary relationships required in making a living and acquiring necessary goods and services (Calhoun, 1986). The new technologies can vastly increase the amount of time we have available for engaging in primary relationships, such as participating in recreational and family activities. As with all tools, the potential for beneficial or deleterious consequences lies, not in the new technologies per se, but in our ability and will to use tools in ways that contribute to individual and societal well-being.

Apropos the above, technology is already having a revolutionary impact on the nature of social interactions, with traditional primary and secondary interactions increasingly being supplemented by more abstract interactions, giving rise to *tertiary relationships*. Tertiary relationships, which are mediated by new communications technologies, isolate individuals from one another, thus removing propinquity as a requisite for social exchange.

> If a primary relationship is one in which the individuals are known to each other in many role facets, and a secondary relationship implies a knowledge of the other individual only in a single formal role facet, then a tertiary relationship is one in which only the *roles* interact. Those performing the roles are interchangeable and, in fact, with the computerization of many interactions, are even dispensable, at least at the point of immediate contact. What are interacting are not individuals in one role capacity or another, but the functional roles themselves. Such tertiary relationships can be maintained only under conditions of *physical* isolation; once supplemented by physical contact, they tend to revert to the secondary [Berry and Kasarda, 1977, pp. 74-76].

The ability of persons to interact instantaneously over large distances, or conduct exchanges with impersonal machines, has immense social and spatial implications. Calhoun (1986) provides a rich discussion of a number of these.

Nonmetropolitan Revival

For nearly a century, redistribution of population followed a rural-to-urban direction, with ever greater concentration in metropolitan areas. However, in the mid-1970s, scholars called attention to what has become known as the "nonmetropolitan turnaround"—in which nonmetropolitan areas in the United States (and certain other developed nations) experienced a net migration gain at the expense of metropolitan areas (Beale, 1975). Although many observers were surprised by this historic reversal, hindsight reveals adumbrations of the new trend. The farm population peaked in the second decade of the twentieth century and has consistently declined since (albeit with some slackening in the rate of decline during the Great Depression). However, the rural non-farm population grew by over 12 million between 1950 and 1970, which should have been some advance indica-

tion of nonmetropolitan vitality. Furthermore, the number of nonmetropolitan counties recording net migration gains exceeded losing counties in all regions of the United States between 1960 and 1970. Positively associated with nonmetropolitan growth in this decade were industrial diversification (sustenance differentiation) and measures reflecting county-level specialization in land-intensive agriculture and the provision of retail and educational services (Frisbie and Poston, 1975, 1978).

The magnitude and suddenness of nonmetropolitan gains have been dramatic. Between 1965 and 1970, metropolitan areas gained over 350,000 net migrants, while between 1970 and 1975, metropolitan counties lost almost 1.6 million net migrants to nonmetropolitan counties (Tucker, 1976). The trend continued such that from 1970 to 1978, more than 2.7 million more people moved out of metropolitan areas than moved into them. Whereas one-sixth of all metropolitan areas lost population, three-fourths of all nonmetropolitan counties gained (Kasarda, 1980, p. 380). Moreover, the nonmetropolitan gains did not simply result from a spillover of urban population into adjacent hinterlands. More remote areas participated in the turnaround along with counties adjacent to metropolitan areas, although the latter experienced the most rapid growth (Fuguitt, 1985; McCarthy and Morrison, 1979). Comparative research involving urban and nonurban places (e.g., Lichter and Fuguitt, 1982), indicates that "the turnaround was almost entirely due to increased growth in nonurban locations" (Fuguitt, 1985, p. 262).

Several classes of explanations for the surge in nonmetropolitan growth have been offered. That the largest metropolitan areas experienced most of the declines in population (Wilson, 1984, pp. 292-93) and that the 15 largest SMSAs accounted for virtually all of the migration losses (Tucker, 1976, p. 442) might be taken as evidence in support of an *asymptotic explanation*. That is, constraints on urban growth might arise out of inherent limits to the efficiency of agglomeration (including certain diseconomies of scale), on the urban end of the spectrum, and to the certainty that the rural source population cannot decline forever. However, the generality of this interpretation is called into question because gains in nonurban regions have occurred in several countries of Northern and Western Europe, as well as in Japan. These countries are quite diverse in regard to size of the largest urban places and degree of urban concentration, and exhibit a high degree of variability in the relative size and rate of decline of the population engaged in agriculture and other extractive industry (Wardwell, 1980).

A more plausible explanation is that nonmetropolitan growth entails the spread of urban organization across the entire society. In other words, expansion of interstate highways, extension of public utilities (including electrical power, water, and telephone lines), telecommunications advances (especially television cable and satellite disks), and the society-wide availability of standardized goods and services means that no sector of society is without urban amenities and opportunities (Kasarda, 1980). Wilson terms this approach the *convergence model* since it derives more or less directly from the concept of isomorphism. From this perspective, societies that have reached a similar economic stage of development tend toward similarities in the adoption of technology and organizational structures (Hawley, 1968, 1971). Thus the nonmetropolitan turnaround can be seen as a more advanced form of urbanization in which the entire society is "integrated into one collective enterprise" (Wilson, 1984, p. 291).

Not the least of the urban opportunities that have been extended to nonmetropolitan areas is increased availability of employment. The same advances in transportation and communications that multiplied the number of locational options for population have also lifted territorial restrictions on industry. A growing body of research demonstrates that a wide variety of jobs have diffused to rural areas (Kasarda, 1980; see Fuguitt, 1985, for a useful summary). This trend includes deconcentration of some low-wage, labor-intensive jobs, but relocation of manufacturing activities demanding higher skills and paying higher wages occurred as well. Perhaps of greatest importance was the massive increase in service-sector employment, which added over 3.5 million jobs to nonmetropolitan economies during the 1970s, compared to an increase of 619,000 manufacturing jobs (Haren and Hollings, 1979). By 1980, nearly two-thirds of all nonmetropolitan workers were employed in the expanding service-performing sector and this trend shows no signs of abating (Kasarda, 1980, p. 381).

If the model proposing a convergence of metropolitan and nonmetropolitan differences is correct, then the nature of migration streams in both directions ought to be, or become, homogeneous. As Fuguitt (1985) points out, research taking into account socioeconomic (education, occupation, industry, and income) and demographic (age, sex, and family size) characteristics leads to the general conclusion that the migrant streams in both directions are rather similar (Wardwell, 1977; White, 1982; Zuiches and Fuguitt, 1978), although the streams may become more dissimilar over time (Lichter, Heaton, and Brown, 1979; see Fuguitt, 1985, pp. 269-79).

A third class of explanations rests on the premise that attitudes toward urban lifestyle partially account for the recent growth of nonmetropolitan areas. At the core of this approach is a dual emphasis. The first concentrates on socioeconomic and demographic characteristics of persons that may increase their propensity to consider a move from one place to another. Individuals and families who have enjoyed rising levels of real income and increased leisure time are assumed to be in a better position to indulge their preferences for less densely settled environments (Hawley and Mazie, 1980). Likewise, assuming adequate economic resources, older persons may choose to retire in rural settings that they hope will provide an escape from congestion, crime, pollution, and other problems of urban life. Further, it seems clear that natural amenities, such as a mild climate and presence of water resources suitable for recreational development, exercise a strong and persistent positive attraction for the elderly and nonelderly alike (Fuguitt, 1985; Heaton, Clifford, Fuguitt, 1980; Richter, 1985).

Moves need not be permanent in all cases in order for a positive effect on nonmetropolitan areas to accrue. Many urbanites have second residences or vacation homes in rural settings to which they retreat on a seasonal basis. Resort and leisure areas may grow and prosper by providing services to a large, temporary population of vacationers and seasonal residents.

The second emphasis has to do with attitudes and values that shape the destination choices of migrants once a decision to move has been made. For 50 years, public opinion surveys have reported that a large percentage of the population prefers small town or rural locations over residence in large cities, even while concentration in metropolises continued at high levels (Fuguitt and Zuiches, 1975). This paradox can be reduced to two issues: (1) Are residential preferences capable of exercising a significant influence on locational decisions, and (2) if they are, what has changed in recent years that now allows substantial numbers of persons to realize their long-standing desire for rural living? The literature is replete with findings that behavior does not regularly follow from attitudes. On the other hand, the reasons migrants give for moves to nonmetropolitan areas are different from those of migrants moving in the opposite direction or of those moving from one metropolitan area to another. In particular, migrants to non-metropolitan destinations are less likely to cite economic reasons and more apt to give quality-of-life reasons (both antiurban "pushes" and prorural "pulls") for their move (Williams and Sofranko, 1979). A recent summary of research on this topic concludes that preferences do affect migration behavior, that a different set of motivations underlies migration from metro-politan to nonmetropolitan areas, and that there has been a temporal increase in the preference for rural residence (Fuguitt, 1985, p. 274).

Without denying residential preferences a role in the explanatory framework applied to the nonmetropolitan turnaround, it seems unwise to place primary reliance on motivational and attitudinal variables in any effort to account for population redistribution. To reiterate, prorural and antiurban attitudes were prominent long before net migration shifted in favor of non-metropolitan locations. The answer to the second question would appear to be that more persons are able to act out their preferences for rural living because technoeconomic and structural changes have made it possible to reside in non-metropolitan settings while continuing to enjoy the economic opportunities and amenities that had previously been the more or less exclusive province of urban dwellers. In this light, it is not surprising, for instance, that migrants to nonmetropolitan destinations in the 1970s less often gave job-related reasons for their move, because they are much less likely than before to have to trade off employment ambitions for rural residence. In general, then, Hawley's maxim appears as salient now as when it was first enunciated:

> For an understanding of the general phenomenon it is important to know not why the migrant thinks he has moved but the conditions or characteristics common to all instances of migration and lacking in situations from which there is no migration [Hawley, 1950, p. 328].

This is not to imply that psychological variables are devoid of explanatory power. It does imply that their effects cannot be adequately interpreted apart from a consideration of technological and social organizational factors.

Finally, although the reality and significance of the revival of nonmetropolitan growth cannot be disputed, it is possible that the turnaround is coming to an end. Based on Census Bureau intercensal county population estimates, the growth of nonmetropolitan areas slowed in the latter part of the 1970s, and net inmigration diminished to the extent that natural increase once more became the most important source of growth (Richter, 1985, pp. 260-261). In contradistinction to the situation in the earlier years of the decade, the attractiveness of the more remote rural areas waned, and counties adjacent to SMSAs had higher rates of growth. Even more recent census estimates indicate that nonmetropolitan areas are now growing more slowly than metropolitan areas (Fuguitt, 1985, p. 275).

While the startling net migration advantage that nonmetropolitan areas enjoyed in the 1970s may have been lost, there seems to be no reason to expect that the alterations in sociospatial processes represented by the turnaround have been reversed. It has already been suggested, based on the assumption that the recent surge in non-metropolitan growth can be attributed to "convergence" (the spread of urban organization and amenities over the entire society), that one would expect migration streams to and from nonmetropolitan areas to become more similar (Fuguitt, 1985). The seminal work in this regard is Wardwell's (1977) hypothesis (which views the turnaround as partially a return to an equilibrium in which the streams of migration flowing in both directions between metropolitan and nonmetropolitan areas become roughly equal in volume and composition). The similarity of the two migration streams in regard to age structure and socioeconomic characteristics has already been noted, as has the overall tendency toward lower densities at all levels of geographic aggregation (Fuguitt, 1985; Heaton and Fuguitt, 1980). The most reasonable conclusion then would seem to be that we are now witnessing "a tendency towards balance in the interchange between metro and nonmetro areas," as part of the larger nationwide trend of population deconcentration (Richter, 1985, p. 262).

Rise of the Sunbelt

Prior to World War II, the Northeast and Midwest dominated America's financial markets and manufacturing base. In addition to their major cities being the nation's centers of capital availability and corporate headquarters' activities, the Northeast and Midwest contained myriad industrial locational advantages (e.g., excellent deep-water ports, extensive railroad and inland waterway systems, well-developed inter- and intrametropolitan highways, proximity to rich coal deposits, ubiquitous public utilities, a diverse and relatively better-educated labor force, and strong local markets). These externalities provided firms locating in the Northeast and Midwest with competitive cost and market advantages that allowed them to develop and expand much faster than in the relatively less developed, more agriculturally oriented West and South (Kasarda, 1980).

Since World War II, a number of economic, political, and technological forces have combined to accelerate industrial restructuring and shift the nation's employment growth pole—first to the West and then to the South. The rapid postwar growth of aerospace, defense, solid-state electronics, and other advanced technology industries together with expanding construction and services, spurred the economies of the far West, especially California (Biggar, 1979; Castells, 1985). With diversified economic expansion continuing in the West, the region's total employment doubled from 1960 to 1985. Nevertheless, the South emerged in the 1960s as the nation's leader in absolute employment gains. Between 1960 and 1985, the South added 17 million jobs to its economy, compared to a growth of just under 11 million in the West and 13 million in the Northeast and Midwest regions combined.

The South's more recent attractiveness as an industrial growth pole is a function of its improved accessibility to national and international markets via newer interstate highway systems and expanding airports, shifting energy sources, more modern physical plants, a benign climate, upgraded schools and universities, and relatively lower taxes and wage rates interacting with the changing structure of the national economy and negative externalities of many established northern industrial areas (e.g., congestion, strong unions, high land costs and taxes). To these technological and financial considerations were added healthy doses of progrowth attitudes and industrial boosterism on the part of southern states and their communities (Biggar, 1979; Cobb, 1982). Thus while manufacturing employment in the Frostbelt (Northeast and Midwest) actually declined between 1960 and 1985, manufacturing employment in the South increased by 2.5 million jobs. Nonetheless, employment growth in southern manufacturing was far overshadowed by remarkable increases in construction and services, which added more than 15 million jobs to the South's economy between 1960 and 1985 (Kasarda, Irwin, and Hughes, 1986).

The expanding economies of the West and South during the past three decades attracted major streams of migrants. Prior to 1970, the West was the net beneficiary of migration streams from all census regions. These streams were especially large in the 1950s. During the 1970s, more persons from the West began moving to the South than vice-versa, while net flows from the Northeast and Midwest to the South dramatically rose. Between 1970 and 1980, overall net migration to the South more than doubled that to the West. Led by a dramatic increase in net flows from the Midwest, net migration to the South nearly tripled that to the West between 1980 and 1985 (Kasarda, Irwin, and Hughes, 1986).

Another migration stream of growing importance to the Sunbelt is movers from abroad, especially Hispanics and Asians. Movers to the South from abroad increased from 505,000 between 1955 and 1960 to 1.2 million between 1980 and 1985. Today, the South and West absorb most of the immigration to the United States. Since 1975 over 2.8 million immigrants have settled in the West, 2.3 million in the South, 1.7 million in the Northeast, and 1 million in the Midwest. In fact, between 1980 and 1985, the West gained twice as many immigrants as it did movers from other regions of the nation (Kasarda, Irwin, and Hughes, 1986).

With increased numbers of immigrants supplementing substantial net interregional migration flows to the South and West, recent population growth in these regions has dwarfed that of the Northeast and Midwest. From 1980 to 1985, the South and the West accounted for more than 90% of the nation's 12.2 million population increase. Whether such regional disparities in population growth will continue into the 1990s is questionable. There are indications of substantial economic recovery in a number of northern states, especially those with major metropolitan areas that have successfully transformed from goods-producing to information-processing economic bases. As these areas build on their emerging service sector roles, they may be expected to be more competitive in attracting industry and population. Nevertheless, there is little evidence to suggest that future growth in the Frostbelt will surpass that of the Sunbelt.

Megaurbanization in the Third World

A striking international spatial process with immense social, economic, and environmental implications is the growth of massive urban agglomerations in developing nations. In 1950, 7 of the 10 largest metropolitan areas were in developed nations, with none exceeding 15 million residents. Within the next decade or two, 8 of the 10 largest metropolitan areas will be in developing nations and all are projected to exceed 15 million residents (United Nations, 1980). Indeed, the largest, Mexico City, may approach 30 million residents and the second largest, Sao Paulo, may approach 25 million residents.

Not only has the location and scope of megacity development shifted during recent decades, but so has its pace. The accelerating rate of urban agglomeration is illustrated by comparing the growth histories of New York and London (the world's largest metropolitan areas in 1950) with those of Mexico City and Sao Paulo. Whereas New York and London each took nearly 150 years to expand by 8 million residents, Mexico City and Sao Paulo are currently growing at a rate that will add 8 million to their population bases in fewer than 15 years.

Though not quite of the same scope, the rapid rate of urbanization represented by Mexico City and São Paulo is being echoed in developing nations around the world. The United Nations projects that by the year 2000 the number of cities in developing countries with one million or more residents will increase from 125 at present to nearly 300. Much of this urban growth is occurring in those developing regions whose national economic systems are least equipped to sustain megaurbanization. For example, in 1950 there were only two cities on the African continent with one million residents. By the end of this decade, there will be 37 such cities, containing nearly 40% of Africa's urban population (Rondinelli, 1988). A number of these large cities are experiencing annual growth rates approaching 6%, which implies doubling in size every 12 years.

The explosive growth of megacities in developing nations has resulted in a multitude of problems of seemingly unmanageable proportions, including insufficient housing, inadequate sanitation, overloaded transportation systems, pollution, and high rates of unemployment (Dogan and Kasarda, 1988a, 1988b).

Despite these problems, the flood of migrants to Third World megacities continues apace. Why? The answer lies in rapid rates of natural population increase, limited rural development, and the decision-making calculus of the migrants (Lattes, 1984). Declining mortality rates in many rural areas of developing nations have not been matched with corresponding declines in fertility. The resulting natural increase of population cannot be sustained by stagnating rural economies, which leads to growing demographic-employment opportunity imbalances in the countryside. With far more peo-ple being born and surviving in the rural areas than can be supported, migration becomes the only mechanism to relieve demographic pressures. Rural migrants flee to the cities, exacerbating the already overcrowded conditions in urban subareas. The age selectivity of rural migrants (largely adolescents and young adults) further contributes to city growth through new family formation and natural increase. What this all means, then, is that the primary cause of Third World overurbanization (more urban residents than the economies of cities can sustain) is increasingly severe overruralization (more rural residents than the economies of rural areas can sustain).

There is also mounting evidence that spatial bias in public policies toward investing government resources in metropolises (at the expense of rural areas and smaller towns) has accelerated inmigration from the countryside (Todaro, 1981). Not only are economic opportunities more abundant in the megacities (in both their formal and informal sectors), but these cities further afford migrants access to schools, health clinics, and other public facilities and services lacking in the countryside. In addition, there are numerous stimuli, consumption goods, and cultural attractions that urban agglomerations provide. Under such circumstances, the utility function of the individual migrant would logically be quite different from the utility function of the unit city to which he or she is migrating. Whereas additional numbers of migrants may bring more costs than benefits to the city, it improves the conditions of the migrants for whom the benefits of moving to the city substantially outweigh those of remaining in their rural communities.

Fiscal crises of many debt-ridden Third World nations further weaken their ability to cope with the rapid rates of urban growth—either in terms of providing sufficient job opportunities or public services. Unlike Europe, which adapted to its periodic demographic-employment opportunity imbalances during the nineteenth and early twentieth centuries by exporting surplus population to the Americas and other New World colonies, Third World nations do not have such demographic outlets. They have only inlets—their exploding metropolises—which simultaneously serve as demographic reservoirs and islands of hope for those seeking opportunity and a better life.

MODELS OF CHANGE

Although markedly different in current urban form, Third World cities may be in the early stages of sequential spatial processes that many large cities in developed nations have already experienced. These are: (1) urban growth-decline sequences; (2) changing residential distributions of social classes; and (3) economic base transformations.

Peter Hall (1984) presents an evolutionary model of urban population growth and decline. Briefly, Hall's model posits a population concentration-deconcentration continuum predicated on the degree of industrial development and transportation accessibility in national urban systems. In the initial stage, urban growth is concentrated in primate cities of large size and high density, with extensive rural-to-urban migration toward a single center of industrial activity. In the next stage, as regional transportation and communication networks expand, industrial and demographic growth filters to secondary cities. The third stage consists of a "spillover" effect; as urban cores mature, populations are redistributed to the urban periphery or "rings" for a variety of environmental, economic, social, and political reasons. During this stage, the urban rings and core grow apace. The fourth stage is marked by disinvestment and population decline in the urban core with continued growth and development of the periphery. Finally, at stage five, both urban core and periphery experience population decline, constituting the end of the urbanization course.

Klaassen and his associates (Klaassen and Scimeni, 1981; Van den Berg et al., 1982) propose a model analogous to Hall's. Their model consists of four stages of urban development: urbanization, suburbanization, desuburbanization, and reurbanization. Like the Hall model, *urbanization* is characterized by substantial immigration from rural to highly concentrated cities whose compact spatial configurations are determined largely by primitive short-distance transportation technologies. During this initial stage, industrialization and population growth outstrip urban infrastructure provision with housing construction and transit and water systems lagging behind. *Suburbanization* occurs as increased personal incomes combined with improved transportation technologies (especially autos and trucks) allow a deconcentration of population and industry to adjacent peripheral areas. Suburbanization is further facilitated by governments' subsidizing or providing infrastructure throughout the urban periphery. *Desuburbanization* occurs in two phases: (1) when growth of the periphery no longer compensates for large population declines in the core, and (2) when the entire functional urban region (FUR) loses a large segment of its popula-

tion to other areas. With population decline comes the concomitant patterns of declining economic and building activities and urban decay. This stage is marked by absolute deconcentration of populations and economic activities not only within the region but also intra- and internationally, suggesting that regional and global competition play important roles. The last stage, *reurbanization*, occurs when the urban core experiences renewed population growth and the disparity between this growth and that of other areas diminishes. Klaassen et al. argue that urban planning both on the part of the governments and industries is crucial if this hypothesized fourth stage is to occur.

The Klaassen et al. stage model differs from the Hall model in that it hypothesizes renewed central city growth following a period of extensive urban decline. There is emerging support for this hypothesis in the cases of London, Boston, and New York City, where total populations and jobs are again growing in the 1980s after decades of sharp declines.

Interwoven with both the Hall and Klaassen et al. models is another stage model that forms the basis of product-cycle theory (Vernon, 1960, 1966; Norton and Rees, 1979) and its neo-Marxian extension, profit-cycle theory (Markusen, 1985). New industries evolve at points where there are concentrations of skilled labor, venture capital, and other local agglomeration economies that provide a "seedbed" or "incubator" for product development (innovation stage). Successful new product industries expand, raising both local employment and income levels (expansion stage). The expansion process itself fosters local decentralization both by converting central-city land from residential to industrial use and by generating incomes sufficient for many to afford suburban residences. As the product matures, greater competition forces manufacturing process changes in which capital replaces labor and production becomes standardized and mechanized (maturation stage). Since standardization and mechanization reduce the need for skilled labor, firms relocate their production facilities from higher-skilled, high-wage core areas to peripheral regions offering an abundance of cheap labor. In the final stage (stagnation and decline), the product becomes obsolete and both sales and prices plummet. With marginal costs exceeding marginal revenues, factories close nationally and abroad, signifying the end of the product's life course.

If core areas are to stem decline, new products and services must be continuously developed there. Otherwise, their relatively high factor costs and competitive pressures will drain their employment bases, resulting in substantial job and populations losses.

Numerous other sequential models of urban growth and decline have been proposed (see, for example, Berry, 1979; Forrester, 1969; Jansen and Paelinck, 1981; Richardson, 1980). Most assume that intra- and interurban population changes constitute a single process and that population distribution is the prime indicator of urban evolution. In such models, one must, of course, be careful not to confuse demographic outcomes with their causes.

A second evolutionary sequence deals with the internal distribution of residential areas and social classes in cities. The Burgess concentric zonal model of urban growth in Western nations (which posits a positive association between income level and residential distance from the core) has been shown to be inappropriate to many Third World cities. Indeed, the residential distribution of classes has often been found to be opposite in cities in developing nations to that predicted by the Burgess model. However, research has shown that residential structures of Third World and Western cities are evolving in a predictable pattern (Hawley, 1971; Light, 1983; Schnore, 1965). In this evolutionary scheme, higher-income residents and better neighborhoods are located at the core of the metropolis during the initial stages of urban growth and the poorer population and neighborhoods at the outskirts of the city. These stages are typically characterized by low levels of industrial and commercial development in the city and limited means of transportation and communication. Under such conditions, a central location becomes prized because of its accessibility to work, shops, and cultural facilities and the relatively low amounts of core congestion, pollution, and noise.

As core city industrial development accelerates with corresponding increases in congestion and pollution, a central residential location becomes less desirable. With improvements in transportation and communication, those who can afford the cost of daily commuting gradually shift to suburbs some distance from the core. Many of the original residential structures of upper-income persons in turn become occupied (in much higher densities) by lower- income groups. The initial negative gradient between socioeconomic status and residential distance from the core eventually inverts as higher-income groups begin to predominate at the peripheries and lower-income groups in the core. Again, while this evolutionary sequence represents the historical pattern of Western in-

dustrial city residential change, there is evidence from Mexico City, Sao Paulo, Cairo, and Tokyo that similar sequences are commencing in non-Western cities (Dogan and Kasarda, 1988a, 1988b).

The third sequence of development follows economic stages from a handicraft and lower-order service structure, to a more formal commercial-industrial-based structure, eventually reaching an information processing, higher-order service structure. In the first stage, informal economic activities dominate with low costs of entry, family ownership of enterprises, and labor-intensive technologies. During this pre-industrial phase, urban economic activities are confined to traditional sectors such as crafts and the distribution of food by small family enterprises (Beavon and Rogerson, 1986). Urban employment consists primarily of artisans, petty trade, food venders, and other lower-order services.

In the second stage (where many major cities of the Third World are), economic activities are partially transformed from family enterprises to corporate production units, capital grows in importance relative to labor, and wage and salary employment expands. With technological development and capital accumulation, growth of an extended trading network and industrial concentration further stimulates urban growth, often creating a primate city (Golden, 1981). In this industrialization stage, cities specializing in manufacturing activities grow rapidly. The manufacturing sector as a powerful export-base industry has multiplier effects, creating new job opportunities and attracting waves of rural migrants seeking employment.

With mechanization of industrial production and a growing capital-to-labor ratio, a substantial increase in manufacturing output can be achieved with small increments in the manufacturing labor force. Because of the reduced labor absorption capacity of more capital-intensive manufacturing activities, the informal sector becomes increasingly important in providing employment opportunities. This sector often has advantages compared to the formal sector, including (1) a higher potential for absorbing migrant labor, (2) higher real wages for unskilled workers, (3) less sex discrimination, (4) better opportunities for upward mobility through entrepreneurship with limited capital, and (5) no involuntary unemployment (Beavon and Rogerson, 1986; Hackenberg, 1980; Tailhet-Waldorf and Waldorf, 1983).

As the national economy matures and transportation networks expand, competition from lower-cost outlying sites (à la product-cycle theory) reduces urban manufacturing employment. During this third stage, large-scale production units move to peripheral areas and smaller cities and are replaced by knowledge-intensive firms in the core employing well-educated, skilled persons. Higher-order, knowledge-based services are exported nationally and internationally as the functions of major cities gradually transform from goods-processing and lower-order consumer services to information processing and higher-order producer services. A hierarchy of urban places evolves based on function and size. In this hierarchy, impulses of development are transmitted from higher to lower centers, ultimately stimulating economic growth in even relatively remote peripheries (Berry and Kasarda, 1977, pp. 277-281). According to traditional regional growth theory, the end result should be a full integration of the space economy with corresponding reduction in income inequalities across localities and regions.

Dependency and Other Class-Based Theories of Uneven Development

A number of recent theoretical perspectives contend that sequences of urban evolution are generating more, rather than less, social and spatial inequality, and that current urban and development processes lock Third World nations into international systems of dependency (e.g., Castells, 1977; Portes and Walton, 1981; Wallerstein, 1974; Walton, 1976). Advocates of these perspectives contend that growth of Third World cities constitutes a unique pattern of urban development unparalleled in Western history. Overpopulation, poverty, ruling class hegemony, and dependency on economies of developed nations create huge primate cities that dominate Third World economies and discourage or prevent indigenous development of secondary cities (Misra and Dung, 1983). Although it is not possible here to detail the numerous ways in which these perspectives differ in specifics, they are unified by an emphasis on class relations, modes of production, exploitation, and capital accumulation.

Many, if not most, dependency theorists couch their arguments in terms of world economies and world systems of cities. According to Braudel, the pattern of development and underdevelopment arising out of an international division of labor represents "an ancient and no doubt incurable divide" (1979, p. 26). The matter is highly complex in that a series of world economies can be said to have existed for centuries with each earlier system giving way slowly to the next and with each being characterized by a hierarchy of individual economies organized around a core capitalist city or cities (Braudel, 1979, pp. 24-45).

Origins of dependency are usually traced to the dominance of a Western European core over countries of Southern Europe, Eastern Europe, and Latin America, which emerged in the fifteenth and sixteenth centuries in the wake of the expanding trade routes organized by merchant wholesalers based in cities such as Venice, London, and Amsterdam (Meyer, 1986; see also Braudel, 1979; Wallerstein, 1974). These trade relationships eventually evolved into an extensive colonial system in which the developed "metropolitan powers" exercised political and economic control over extraterritorial possessions. Colonialism connotes not only inequality of exchange, but also a suppression of the urban/industrial development of colonies that came to serve as a source of raw materials and a market for manufactured products of the mother country (Light, 1983, pp. 143-47).

Since the colonial import/export relationship was well served by one or a few large cities, one result was the growth of one or a few large cities (usually seaports) that served as collection and distribution nodes for the colonial import/export system, while the interior of the colonized society remained largely undeveloped and nonurbanized. In other words, the roots of the socioeconomic and spatial dualism commonly referred to as the primate city pattern may be traced to colonialism (Light, 1983, p. 144). With the passing of the colonial era, it is argued that developed Western nations have continued to exploit peripheral (less developed) countries. The basis is not so much political hegemony as it is the power of multinational corporations and financial institutions—power that derives from the access of multinationals to greater "specialized business information and larger capital resources than other businesses" (Meyer, 1986, p. 599) Thus, regardless of the historical era, dependency theorists conceptualize a system in which the major metropolises of the capitalist world control and siphon off resources from developing nations, thereby impeding their indigenous development. The driving engine behind this process is conceived to be the capitalist world's insatiable quest for new markets and accumulation of surplus value.

Building on the above perspectives, Armstrong and McGee (1985) provide an interesting appraisal of how multinational corporations in global centers of capitalism influence development strategies in Third World nations, from these nations' major cities on down to rural and small town areas. They treat cities at all levels as centers of wealth accumulation as well as diffusers of lifestyles and consumer habits of the capitalist world. These urban systems, according to Armstrong and McGee,

> act simultaneously as centres of operations for modern commerce, finance and industrial activity, and the providers of appropriate environments for capital's expansion and deepening. Cities are the arenas in which foreign and local capital markets advertise and sell the philosophy of modernization, efficiency and growth through imitative lifestyles and consumerism and, in so doing, undermine non-capitalist production systems and cultural values. In this sense, diffusion is a further means to enhance and promote the end of capital accumulation [pp. 41-42].

Armstrong and McGee see the simultaneous processes of centralization of wealth and diffusion of Western consumer habits as benefiting not only the multinational corporations at the capitalist core, but also strengthening the state-commercial ruling class of the Third World at the expense of the masses. The end result is growing poverty and widening social disparities within developing nations, which are trapped in an unequal exchange nexus with the developed nations and their own ruling elite.

Uneven spatial development is also seen as a fundamental outcome of capitalist development (Castells, 1977; Harvey, 1973; Hill, 1977; Jaret, 1983; Sawers and Tabb, 1984). Spatial disparities resulting from capital accumulation processes are treated as zero-sum situations where growth in one area is viewed as coming at the expense of another area (e.g., in the United States, suburbs versus central cities or Sunbelt versus Frostbelt). On both metropolitan and regional levels, uneven development is often argued to be a result of an alliance between business interests and government. Jaret's (1983) summarization of this perspective draws heavily on Hill's (1977) argument that cities operating in a monopoly corporate environment make large expenditures on two functions: (1) "investments in physical infrastructure to aid private enterprise and in human capital that raises worker productivity" and (2) spending on social welfare and other services in order to maintain social control in the face of "problems that result from the capital accumulation process" (Jaret, 1983, pp. 511, 512).

These class-based theories may be challenged on several grounds. First, the notion that the slow development of Third World nations is largely the result of exploitation by metropolitan powers of the developed world fails to take into account the demographic, political, and cultural obstacles to development that exist within Third World nations themselves (Light, 1983, pp. 146-147; see also Hermasi, 1978, and Horowitz, 1977). It also ignores the fact that certain Third World nations such as Taiwan and South Korea have been able to take rather dramatic strides toward development (Light, 1983, p. 146).

At the regional level, not all Marxist scholars believe that the process of capital accumulation must inevitably result in uneven spatial development (Jaret, 1983, p. 511, citing Markusen, 1980), and other urban scholars see a potential for a reduction of inequalities in that backward regions are eventually expected to profit from integration into the national space economy organized around a metropolitan hierarchy (Berry and Kasarda, 1977, pp. 280-281).

Finally, at the intrametropolitan level, Mollenkopf points out that market-based forces straining toward ever greater capital accumulation are often opposed by non-market community forces, and the former do not necessarily prevail over the latter (1975, 1981). As Jaret (1983, p. 515) suggests, Mollenkopf's formulation is useful in that it combines elements of both Marxist and mainstream urban analysis. The same may be said for Meyer's (1986) work in which he extends the ecological theory of metropolitan hierarchy to world systems and demonstrates that the core-periphery distinction may not be particularly useful apart from a consideration of rank on the vertical dimension of metropolitan dominance.

Conclusions

Our strategy in closing this discourse is to highlight major issues addressed herein. The first conclusion is that consideration of spatial processes is crucial for understanding social relationships. For example, it should be clear from investigations of suburbanization and segregation that spatial mobility is positively and reciprocally related to social mobility and that spatial distance is a useful indicator of social distance. On a more abstract level, the major axes of social differentiation, including socioeconomic status, life-cycle stage, and race/ethnicity are reflected in the sifting and sorting of population according to patterns described in the classical models of urban form and growth.

A still more general issue has to do with why there is an orderly spatial patterning (of whatever shape) of population and activities in the first place. Here we conclude that regularities in the spatial distribution of population and functions arises from the interdependence of human beings and the dependencies of functions on the characteristics of land. Although such elemental relationships constitute the basis for our understanding of the processes of concentration and deconcentration, they are not the whole story. Functional specialization, as embodied in a territorial division of labor, emphasizes the maintenance of accessibility for purposes of exchange. Thus the size, territorial scope, and distribution of units within a system varies with the time and cost consumed in movement. This being the case, technological and organizational innovations that reduce the friction of space are of immense significance. In particular, advances in transportation and communications have meant that accessibility is no longer inextricably linked to propinquity, that a greater flexibility of land use is obtained, and that the expansion of urban systems on a local, regional, and worldwide scale becomes possible.

Obviously, this perspective has direct implications for attempts to account for what has been referred to here and elsewhere as the growing "footlooseness" of population and industry, which in turn is important for understanding the emergence of polynucleated metropolises, the shifting migration streams between metropolitan and nonmetropolitan areas, and the major alterations in the territorial division of labor that have had such a strong impact on interregional and international economic development. Although the magnitude and rapidity of these and other changes witnessed in recent decades have been little short of breathtaking, we view this as evidence of a reorganization, not a disorganization, of sociospatial relationships. To argue otherwise would be to deny what seems to us to be undeniable: that space is a time-cost variable that human organizations have historically attempted to reduce. That an uneven distribution of economic opportunities develops at local, regional, or international levels may be unwelcome, but it is not a new phenomenon, and it is certainly not evidence that technological and market forces have diminished their capacity for organizing spatial interactions and exchange.

While market forces and advances in transportation and communication technologies are accorded central roles in this (ecological) line of reasoning, our conclusion is that these factors are necessary yet incomplete explanations of urban expansion and the reorganization of territorial relationships. Other factors must be added if we are to gain a more comprehensive understanding of spatial dynamics at the local, national, and global levels. One major contribution of critical theorists has been to point out the role of the state in providing incentives and disincentives for certain types of land use. Another is the demonstration of the ability of non-market forces to shape spatial processes and relations. Our final conclusion, then, is that although it may not be easy to synthesize the conceptual frameworks of human ecologists and critical theorists, there is certainly ample room for fruitful dialogue.

REFERENCES

Armstrong, Warwick and T. G. McGee. 1985. *Theaters of Accumulation: Studies in Asian and Latin American Urbanization*. London: Methuen.

Abu-Lughod, Janet L. 1968. "Testing the Theory of Social Area Analysis: The Ecology of Cairo, Egypt." *American Sociological Review* 34:198-212.

Alexandersson, Gunnar. 1956. *The Industrial Structure of American Cities: A Geographic Study of Urban Economics in the U.S.* Lincoln: University of Nebraska Press.

Anderson, Theodore R. and Lee L. Bean. 1961. "Spatial Aspects of Social Area Analysis." *American Sociological Review* 26:392-398.

Anderson, Theodore R. and Janice E. Egeland. 1961. "The Shevky-Bell Social Areas: Confirmation of Results and Reinterpretation." *Social Forces* 40:119-124.

Alihan, Milla. 1938. *Social Ecology: A Critical Analysis*, New York: Columbia University Press.

Alonso, William. 1960. "A Theory of the Urban Land Market." *Papers and Proceedings of the Regional Science Association* 6:149-158.

Beale, Calvin L. 1975 "The Revival of Population Growth in Nonmetropolitan America." Economic Development Division, Economic Research Service, U.S. Department of Agriculture (ERS605). Washington, DC: Government Printing Office.

Beavon, K.S.O. and C. M. Rogerson. 1986. "The Changing Role of Women in the Urban Informal Sector of Johannesburg." In *Urbanization in the Developing World*, edited by D. Drakakis-Smith. London: Croon-Helm.

Berry, Brian J.L. 1961. "City Size Distributions and Economic Development." *Economic Development and Cultural Change* 9:573-588.

_____, ed. 1979. *Urbanization and Counterurbanization*. Beverly Hills, CA: Sage.

_____ and John D. Kasarda. 1977. *Contemporary Urban Ecology*. New York: Macmillan.

Bidwell, Charles E. and John D. Kasarda. 1985. *The Organization and Its Ecosystem : A Theory of Structuring in Organizations*, Greenwich, CT: JAI Press, Inc.

Biggar, Jeanne C.. 1979 "The Sunning of America: Migration to the Sunbelt,". *Population Bulletin* 34, Washington, DC: Population Reference Bureau.

Blalock, Hubert M., Jr.. 1967. *Toward a Theory of Minority Group Relations*, New York, NY: Wiley.

_____ 1980 "Preface," pp . xiii-xv in Hubert M. Blalock, Jr. (ed .),. *Sociological Theory and Research: A Critical Approach*, New York, NY: The Free Press.

Bluestone, Barry and Bennett Harrison. 1982. *The Deindustrialization of America*. New York: Basic Books.

Bogue, Donald J.. 1949. *The Structure of the Metropolitan Community: A Study of Dominance and Subdominance*. Ann Arbor: University of Michigan Press.

Boulding, Kenneth E. 1953. "Toward a General Theory of Growth." *Canadian Journal of Economics and Political Science* 19:326-340.

Braudel, Fernand. 1979. *The Perspective of the World*. New York: Harper & Row.

Burgess, Ernest W. 1925. "The Growth of the City: An Introduction to a Research Project." Pp. 47-62 in *The City*, edited by Robert Park, Ernest Burgess, and Roderick D. McKenzie. Chicago: University of Chicago Press.

Calhoun, Craig J. 1986. "Computer Technology, Large Scale Social Integration and the Local Community." *Urban Affairs Quarterly* 8:204-228.

Castells, Manuel. 1977. *The Urban Question: A Marxist Approach*. Cambridge, MA: MIT Press.

_____ 1978. *City, Class and Power*, New York: Macmillan.

_____ 1985. "High Technology, Economic Restructuring and the Urban-Regional Process in the United States." Pp. 11-40 in *High Technology, Space, and Society*, edited by Manuel Castells. Beverly Hills, CA: Sage.

Chase-Dunn, C. K. 1984. "Urbanization in the World-System: New Directions for Research." In *Cities in Transformation*, edited by Michael P. Smith. *Urban Affairs Annual Review*, vol. 26. Beverly Hills, CA: Sage.

Christaller, Walter. 1933. *Die Zentralen Orte in Suddeutschland*. Jena: Gustav Fischer. (Translated by D. W. Baskin in *Central Places in Southern Germany*, Englewood Cliffs, NJ: Prentice-Hall, 1966)

Clark, Colin. 1951. "Urban Population Densities." *Journal of the Royal Statistical Society*, Series A, 114:490-496.

Cobb, James C. 1982. *The Selling of the South: The Southern Crusade for Industrial Development,* *1936-1980*. Baton Rouge: Louisiana State University Press.

Cooley, Charles H. 1894. "The Theory of Transportation." *Publications of the American Economics Association* 9:312-322.

Davie, Maurice R. 1937 "The Pattern of Urban Growth." Pp. 133-161 in *Studies in the Science of Society*, edited by George P. Murdock. New Haven, CT: Yale University Press.

Dogan, Mattei and John D. Kasarda, eds. 1988a. *The Metropolis Era, vol. I: A World of Giant Cities*. Beverly Hills. CA: Sage.

_____, eds. 1988b. *The Metropolis Era, vol. II: Mega-Cities*. Beverly Hills, CA: Sage.

Domhoff, William G. 1983. *Who Rules America Now?* Englewood Cliffs, NJ: Prentice-Hall.

Duncan, Beverly and Stanley Lieberson. 1970. *Metropolis and Region in Transition*. Beverly Hills, CA: Sage.

Duncan, Otis D. and Beverly Duncan. 1955. "Residential Distribution and Occupational Stratification." *American Journal of Sociology* 60:493-503.

Duncan, Otis D., W. R. Scott, Stanley Lieberson, Beverly Duncan, and Hal Winsborough. 1960. *Metropolis and Region*. Baltimore, MD: Johns Hopkins University Press.

Eberstein, Isaac W. and W. Parker Frisbie. 1982. "Metropolitan Function and Interdependence in the U.S. Urban System." *Social Forces* 60: 676-700.

Eberstein, Isaac W. and Omer R. Galle. 1984. "The Metropolitan System in the South: Functional Differentiation and Trade Patterns." *Social Forces* 62:926-940.

Eberstein, Isaac W., J. Michael Wrigley, and William J. Serow. 1985. "An Examination of the Utility of Ecological and Economic Base Approaches to Regional Structures." *Social Science Quarterly* 66:34-49.

Edmonston, Barry and Thomas M. Guterbock. 1984. "Is Suburbanization Slowing Down? Recent Trends in Population Deconcentration in U.S. Metropolitan Areas." *Social Forces* 62:905-925.

Evans, A. and D. Eversley, eds. 1980. *The Inner City, Employment and Industry*. London: Heinenmann.

Farley, Reynolds. 1977. "Residential Segregation in Urbanized Areas of the United States in 1970: An Analysis of Social Class and Racial Differences." *Demography* 14:497-518.

Feagin, Joe R. 1983. *The Urban Real Estate Game*. Englewood Cliffs, NJ: Prentice-Hall.

_____ 1985. "The Global Context of Metropolitan Growth: Houston and the Oil Industry." *American Journal of Sociology* 90:1204-1230.

Fine, John, Norval D. Glenn, and J. Kenneth Monts. 1971. "The Residential Segregation of Occupational Groups in Central Cities and Suburbs." *Demography* 8:91-102.

Firey, Walter. 1945. "Sentiment and Symbolism as Ecological Variables." *American Sociological*

Review 10:140-148.

———. 1947. *Land Use in Central Boston*. Cambridge, MA: Harvard University Press.

Form, William. 1954. "The Place of Social Structure in the Determination of Land Use: Some Implications for a Theory of Urban Ecology." *Social Forces* 32:317-323.

Forrester, Jay W. 1969. *Urban Dynamics*. Cambridge, MA: MIT Press.

Frey, William H. 1985. "Mover Destination Selectivity and the Changing Suburbanization of Metropolitan Whites and Blacks." *Demography* 22:223-243.

Friederichs, Jurgen, ed. 1982. "Suburbanization in the Hamburg Region." Pp. 31-44 in *Spatial Disparities and Social Behavior*. Hamburg: Christians Verlag.

Frisbie, W. Parker. 1980a. "Theory and Research in Urban Ecology: Persistent Problems and Current Progress." Pp. 203-219 in *Sociological Theory and Research: A Critical Approach*, edited by Hubert M. Blalock, Jr. New York: Free Press.

———. 1980b. "Urban Sociology in the United States." *American Behavioral Scientist* 24:177-214.

——— and Dudley L. Poston, Jr. 1975. "Components of Sustenance Organization and Nonmetropolitan Population Change." *American Sociological Review* 40:773-784.

———. 1978. *Sustenance Organization and Migration in Nonmetropolitan America*. Iowa City: Urban Community Resource Center.

Fuguitt, Glenn V. 1985. "The Nonmetropolitan Population Turnaround." *Annual Review of Sociology* 10:259-280.

——— and James J. Zuiches. 1975. "Residential Preferences and Population Distribution." *Demography* 12:491-504.

Galle, Omer R. and Robert N. Stern. 1981. "The Metropolitan System in the South: Continuity and Change." Pp. 155-174 in *The Population of the South*, edited by Dudley L. Poston, Jr. and Robert H. Weller. Austin: University of Texas Press.

Gettys, Warner E. 1940. "Human Ecology and Social Theory." *Social Forces* 18:469-476.

Golden, Hilda H. 1981. *Urbanization and Cities: Historical and Comparative Perspective on Our Urbanizing World*. Lexington, MA: D.C. Heath.

Gordon, David. 1977. "Class Struggle and the Stages of Urban Development." Pp. 55-82 in *The Rise of the Sunbelt Cities*, edited by D. Perry and A. Watkins. Beverly Hills, CA: Sage.

———. 1984. "Capitalist Development and the History of American Cities." Pp. 21-53 in *Marxism and the Metropolis*, edited by William K. Tabb and Larry Sawers. New York: Oxford University Press.

Gottdiener, M. 1983. "Understanding Metropolitan Deconcentration: A Clash of Paradigms." *Social Science Quarterly* 64:227-246.

———. 1985. *The Social Production of Urban Space*. Austin: University of Texas Press.

Grebler, Leo, Joan W. Moore, and Ralph C. Guzman. 1970. *The Mexican American People: The Nation's Second Largest Minority*. New York: Free Press.

Guest, Avery M. 1972. "Patterns of Family Location." *Demography* 9:159-171.

———. 1977. "Residential Segregation in Urban Areas." Pp. 268-336 in *Contemporary Topics in Urban Sociology*, edited by Kent P. Schwirian. Morristown, NJ: General Learning Press.

——— and James A. Weed. 1976. "Ethnic Residential Segregation: Patterns of Change." *American Journal of Sociology* 81:1088-1111.

Hackenberg, R. A. 1980. "New Patterns of Urbanization in Southeast Asia: An Assessment." *Population and Development Studies* 6.

Hadden, Jeffery K. and Edgar F. Borgatta. 1965. *American Cities: Their Social Characteristics*. Chicago: Rand McNally.

Haggerty, L. J. 1971. "Another Look at the Burgess Hypothesis: Time as an Important Variable." *American Journal of Sociology* 76:1084-1093.

Haines, Valerie A. 1986. "Energy and Urban Form: A Human Ecological Critique." *Urban Affairs Quarterly* 2:337-354.

Hall, Peter. 1984. *The World Cities*. London: Weidenfeld and Nicolson .

——— and Dennis Hays. 1980. *Growth Centers in the European Urban System*. Berkeley: University of California Press.

Haren, Claude C. and Ronald W. Hollings. 1979. "Industrial Development in Nonmetropolitan America: A Locational Perspective." In *Nonmetropolitan Industrialization*, edited by Richard E. Lonsdale and H. L. Seyler. New York: John Wiley.

Hatt, Paul. 1946. "The Concept of Natural Area." *American Sociological Review* 11:423-427.

Harris, Chauncey and Edward Ullman. 1945. "The Nature of Cities." *Annals of the American Academy of Political and Social Science* 242:7-17.

Harvey, David. 1973. *Social Justice and the City*. Baltimore, MD: Johns Hopkins Press.

———. 1975. "The Political Economy of Urbanization in Advanced Capitalist Societies." Pp. 119-163 in *The Social Economy of Cities*, edited by G. Gappert and H. Rose. Beverly Hills, CA: Sage.

———. 1976. "Labor, Capital, and Class Struggle Around the Built Environment." *Politics and Society* 6:265-295.

Hawley, Amos H. 1950. *Human Ecology: A Theory of Community Structure*. New York: Ronald.

———. 1968. "Human Ecology." Pp. 323-332 in *International Encyclopedia of the Social Sciences*, edited by David L. Sills. New York: Crowell, Collier and Macmillan.

———. 1971. *Urban Society: An Ecological Approach*. New York: Ronald.

_____ 1978. "Cumulative Change in Theory and in History." *American Sociological Review* 43: 787-796.

_____ 1981. *Urban Society: An Ecological Approach*. New York: John Wiley.

_____ and Sara H. Mazie. 1980. "Structural Changes in Nonmetropolitan America: An Overview." Presented to the Future for Rural America Advisory Group, Farmers Home Administration, Washington, DC.

Heaton, Tim B., W. B. Clifford, and Glenn V. Fuguitt. 1980. "Dimensions of Population Redistribution in the United States since 1950." *Social Science Quarterly* 61:508-523.

Hermasi, Elbaki. 1978. "Changing Patterns in Research on the Third World." *Annual Review of Sociology* 4:239-257.

Hill, Richard C. 1977. "Capital Accumulation and Urbanization in the United States." *Comparative Urban Research* 4:39-60.

Horowitz, Irving L. 1977. "Review Essay: Coming of Age of Urban Research in Latin America." *American Journal of Sociology* 83:761-765.

Hoyt, Homer. 1939. *The Structure and Growth of Residential Neighborhoods in American Cities*. Washington, DC: Government Printing Office.

_____ 1971. "Recent Distortions of the Classical Models of Urban Structure." Pp. 84-96 in *Internal Structure of the City: Readings on Space and Environment*, edited by Larry S. Bourne. New York: Oxford University Press.

Hurd, Richard M. 1903. *Principals of City Growth*. New York: The Record and Guide.

Jackson, Kenneth T. 1985. *Crabgrass Frontier: The Suburbanization of the United States*. New York: Oxford University Press.

Jansen, J. C. and J.H.P. Paelinck. 1981. "The Urbanization Phenomenon in the Process of Development: Some Statistical Evidence." In *Dynamics of Urban Development*, edited by L. H. Klaassen, W.T.M. Malle, and J.H.P. Paelinck. New York: St. Martin's Press.

Jaret, Charles. 1983. "Recent Neo-Marxist Urban Analysis." *Annual Review of Sociology* 9:499-525.

Jefferson, Mark. 1939. "The Law of the Primate City." *Geographical Review* 29:226-232.

Kasarda, John D. 1972. "The Theory of Ecological Expansion: An Empirical Test." *Social Forces* 51:165-175.

_____ 1978. "Urbanization, Community, and the Metropolitan Problem." Pp. 27-58 in *Handbook of Contemporary Urban Life*, edited by David Street and Associates. San Francisco: Jossey-Bass.

_____ 1980. "The Implications of Contemporary Redistribution Trends for National Urban Policy." *Social Science Quarterly* 61:373-400.

_____ 1983. "Entry-Level Jobs, Mobility, and Urban Minority Unemployment." *Urban Affairs Quarterly* 19:21-40.

_____ 1984. "Hispanics and City Change." *American Demographics* 6:25-29.

_____ 1985. "Urban Change and Minority Opportunities." Pp. 33-67 in *The New Urban Reality*, edited by Paul E. Peterson. Washington, DC: The Brookings Institution.

_____ and Jurgen Friederichs. 1985. "Comparative Demographic-Employment Mismatches in U.S. and West German Cities." Pp. 1-30 in *Research in the Sociology of Work*, vol. 3, edited by Richard L. Simpson and Ida Harper Simpson. Greenwich, CT: JAI Press.

Kasarda, John D., Michael D. Irwin, and Holly L. Hughes. 1986. "The South Is Still Rising." *American Demographics* 6:33-39.

Kasarda, John D. and George Redfearn. 1975. "Differential Patterns of City and Suburban Growth in the U.S." *Journal of Urban History* 2:43-66.

Kass, Roy. 1973. "A Functional Classification of Metropolitan Communities." *Demography* 10: 427-445.

Klaassen, L. H. and G. Scimeni. 1981. "Theoretical Issues in Urban Dynamics." In *Dynamics of Urban Development*, edited by L. H. Klaassen, W.T.M. Molle, and J.H.P. Paelinck. New York: St. Martin's Press.

LaGory, Mark and John Pipkin. 1981. *Urban Social Space*. Belmont, CA: Wadsworth.

Laska, Shirley Bradway and Daphne Spain, eds. 1980. *Back to the City: Issues in Neighborhood Renovation*. New York: Pergamon.

Lattes, Alfredo E. 1984. "Territorial Mobility and Redistribution of Population: Recent Developments." Pp. 74-106 in *Population Distribution, Migration and Development*, United Nations Department of International Economic and Social Affairs, International Conference on Population. New York: United Nations Press.

Laurenti, L. M. 1961. *Property Values and Race: Studies in Seven Cities*. Berkeley: University of California Press.

Lefebvre, Henri. 1979. "Space: Sociol Product and Use Value." Pp. 285-295 in *Critical Sociology: European Perspective*, edited by J. W. Freiberg. New York: Irvington.

Leinberger, Christopher B. and Charles Lockwood. 1986. "How Business is Shaping America." *The Atlantic Monthly* 10:43-52.

Lichter, Daniel T. and Glenn V. Fuguitt. 1982. "The Transition to Nonmetropolitan Population Deconcentration." *Demography* 19:211-221.

Lichter, Daniel T., Tim B. Heaton, and Glenn V. Fuguitt. 1979. "Trends in the Selectivity of Migration between Metropolitan and Nonmetropolitan Areas: 1955-1975." *Rural Sociology* 44:645-666.

Lieberson, Stanley. 1961. "The Impact of Residential Segregation on Ethnic Assimilation." *Social Forces* 40:52-57.

_____ 1963. *Ethnic Patterns in American Cities*. New York: Free Press.

Light, Ivan. 1983. *Cities in World Perspective*. New York: Macmillan.

Lincoln, James R. 1978. "The Urban Distribution of

Headquarters and Branch Plants in Manufacturing: Mechanisms of Metropolitan Dominance." *Demography* 15:213-222.

———. 1979. "Organizational Differentiation in Urban Communities: A Study in Organizational Ecology." *Social Forces* 57:15-930.

Logan, John R. and Harvey L. Molotch. 1987. *Urban Fortunes: The Political Economy of Place*. Berkeley: University of California Press.

Long, John F. 1981. *Population Deconcentration in the United States*. Washington, DC: U.S. Bureau of the Census.

Long, Larry H. and Donald C. Dahman. 1980. *The City-Suburb Income Gap*. Washington, DC: Government Printing Office.

Losch, August. 1954. *The Economics of Location*. New Haven, CT: Yale University Press.

Markusen, Ann R. 1980. "Regionalism and the Capitalist State." Pp. 31-52 in *Urban and Regional Planning in an Age of Austerity*, edited by P. Clavel, J. Forester, and W. W. Goldsmith. New York: Pergamon.

———. 1985. *Profit Cycles, Oligopoly, and Regional Development*. Cambridge: MIT Press.

Marshall, Harvey. 1979. "White Movement to the Suburbs: A Comparison of Explanations." *American Sociological Review* 44:975-994.

——— and Robert Jiobu. 1975. "Residential Segregation in United States Cities: A Causal Analysis." *Social Forces* 53:449-460.

Marshall, Harvey and John Stahura. 1979. "Black and White Population Growth in American Suburbs: Transition or Parallel Development." *Social Forces* 58:305-328.

Massey, Douglas S.. 1979a. "Effects of Socioeconomic Factors on the Residential Segregation of Blacks and Spanish Americans in U.S. Urbanized Areas." *American Sociological Review* 44: 1015-1022.

———. 1979b. "Residential Segregation of Spanish Americans in the United States Urbanized Areas." *Demography* 16:553-563.

———. 1981. "Social Class and Ethnic Segregation: A Reconsideration of Methods and Conclusions." *American Sociological Review* 46:641-650.

———. 1985. "Ethnic Residential Segregation: A Theoretical Synthesis and Empirical Review." *Sociology and Social Research* 69:315-350.

——— and Brooks Bitterman. 1985. "Explaining the Paradox of Puerto Rican Segregation." *Social Forces* 64:306-331.

Massey, Douglas S. and Brendan P. Mullan. 1984. "Processes of Hispanic and Black Spatial Assimilation." *American Journal of Sociology* 89:836-873.

McCarthy, K. F. and Peter A. Morrison. 1979. *The Changing Demographic and Economic Structure of Nonmetropolitan Areas in the 1970s*. Rand Paper Series P6062, Santa Monica, CA: Rand Corporation.

McKenzie, Roderick. 1933. *The Metropolitan Community*. New York: McGraw-Hill.

Metcalf, D. and R. Richardson. 1976. "Unemployment in London." In *Measurement of Unemployment*, edited by G.D.N. Worswick. London: Allen & Unwin.

Meyer, David R. 1984. "Control and Coordination Links in the Metropolitan System of Cities: The South as Case Study." *Social Forces* 63:349-362.

———. 1986. "The World System of Cities: Relations between International Financial Metropolises and South American Cities." *Social Forces* 64:553-581.

Misra, R. P. and Nguyen Tri Dung. 1983. "Large Cities: Growth Dynamics and Emerging Problems." *Habitat International* 7:47-65.

Mollenkopf, John. 1975. "The Postwar Politics of Urban Development." *Politics and Society* 5:247-296.

———. 1981. "Neighborhood Political Development and the Politics of Urban Growth: Boston and San Francisco, 1958-1978." *International Journal of Urban and Regional Research* 5:15-39.

Molotch, Harvey. 1976. "The City as a Growth Machine: Toward a Political Economy of Place." *American Journal of Sociology* 82:309-333.

——— and John R. Logan. 1985. "Urban Dependencies: New Forms of Use and Exchange in U.S. Cities." *Urban Affairs Quarterly* 21:143-169.

Muller, Peter. 1976. *The Outer City*. Resource Paper 75-2. Washington, DC: Association of American Geographers.

———. 1981. *Contemporary Suburban America*. Englewood Cliffs, NJ: Prentice-Hall.

Muth, Richard F. 1969. *Cities and Housing*. Chicago: University of Chicago Press.

Norton, R. D. and John Rees. 1979. "The Product Cycle and the Spatial Decentralization of American Manufacturing." *Regional Studies* 13: 141-151.

Noyelle, Thierry and Thomas Stanback. 1983. *The Economic Transformation of American Cities*. Totowa, NJ: Rowman & Allenheld.

O'Hare, W. P., Jane-Yu Li, R. Chatterjee, N. M. Schuker. 1982. *Blacks on the Move: A Decade of Demographic Change*. Washington, DC: Joint Center for Political Studies.

Palen, J. John. 1981. *The Urban World*. New York: McGraw-Hill.

Pampel, Fred C. and Harvey M. Choldin. 1978. "Urban Location and Segregation of the Aged: A Block-Level Analysis." *Social Forces* 56:1121-1139.

Pappenfort, Donnell M. 1959. "The Ecological Field and the Metropolitan Community." *American Journal of Sociology* 64:380-388.

Park, Robert E. 1916. "The City: Suggestions for the Investigation of Human Behavior in an Urban Environment." *American Journal of Sociology* 20:577-612.

———. 1936. "Human Ecology." *American Journal of Sociology* 42:1-15.

———. 1967. "The Urban Community as a Spatial

Pattern and a Moral Order.'' Pp. 55-68 in *Robert Park on Social Control and Collective Behavior*, edited by Ralph H. Turner. Chicago: University of Chicago Press.

———— and Ernest W. Burgess. 1921. *Introduction to the Science of Sociology*. Chicago: University of Chicago Press.

———— 1925. *The City*. Chicago: University of Chicago Press.

Perlman, Janice. 1986. "Mega-Cities and New Technologies." Presented at the XIth World Congress on Sociology, New Delhi, India.

Portes, Alejandro and Robert Bach. 1985. *Latin Journey: Cuban and Mexican Immigrants in the United States*. Berkeley: University of California Press.

Portes, Alejandro and John Walton. 1981. *Labor, Class and the International System*. New York: Academic Press.

Reckless, W. C. 1926. "The Distribution of Commercialized Vice in the City: A Sociological Analysis." *Publications of the American Sociological Society* 20:164-176.

Richardson, Harry W. 1980. "Polarization Reversal in Developing Countries." *Papers of the Regional Science Association* 45:67-85.

Richter, Kerry. 1985. "Nonmetropolitan Growth in the Late 1970s: The End of the Turnaround?" *Demography* 22:245-263.

Roberts, Bryan. 1986. "Centralization and the Urban System: The Case of Mexico." Mimeographed. University of Texas at Austin.

Rogers, Andrei. 1971. "Theories of Intra-Urban Spatial Structure: A Dissenting View." Pp. 210-215 in *Internal Structure of the City: Readings on Space and Environment*, edited by Larry S. Bourne. New York: Oxford University Press.

Rondinelli, Dennis. 1988. "Giant and Secondary City Development in Africa." In *The Metropolis Era: A World of Giant Cities*, edited by Mattei Dogan and John D. Kasarda. Beverly Hills, CA: Sage.

Roweis, Shoukry T. and Allen J. Scott. 1981. "The Urban Land Question." Pp. 123-157 in *Urbanization and Urban Planning in Capitalist Society*, edited by Michael Dear and Allen J. Scott. London: Methuen.

Sawers, Larry and William K. Tabb, eds. 1984. *Sunbelt/Snowbelt: Urban Development and Regional Restructuring*. New York: Oxford University Press.

Schnore, Leo F. 1965. "On the Spatial Structure of Cities in the Two Americas." Pp. 347-398 in *The Study of Urbanization*, edited by Philip Hauser and Leo F. Schnore. New York: John Wiley.

———— 1969. "The Statistical Measurement of Urbanization and Economic Development." Pp. 91-106 in *Comparative Perspectives on Industrial Society*, edited by W. A. Faunce and W. H. Form. Boston: Little, Brown.

———— 1972. *Class and Race in Cities and Suburbs*. Chicago: Markham.

Schwirian, Kent P., ed. 1974. "Some Recent Trends and Methodological Problems in Urban Ecological Research." Pp. 3-31 in *Comparative Urban Structure: Studies in the Ecology of Cities*. Lexington, MA: D. C. Heath.

————, ed. 1977. "Introduction: An Overview of Urban Sociology." Pp. 1-22 in *Contemporary Topics in Urban Sociology*. Morristown, NJ: General Learning Press.

Shevky, Eshref and Wendell Bell. 1955. *Social Area Analysis: Theory, Illustrative Application and Computational Procedures*. Stanford, CA: Stanford University Press.

———— 1961. "Social Area Analysis." Pp. 226-235 in *Studies in Human Ecology* edited by George A. Theodorson. New York: Harper & Row.

Shevky, Eshref and Marianne Williams. 1949. *The Social Areas of Los Angeles: Analysis and Typology*. Berkeley: University of California Press.

Simkus, A. A. 1978. "Residential Segregation by Occupation and Race in Ten Urbanized Areas, 1950-1970." *American Sociological Review* 43:81-93.

Smith, Richard A. and Robert H. Weller. 1977. "Growth and Structure of the Metropolitan Community." Pp. 76-149 in *Contemporary Topics in Urban Sociology* edited by Kent P. Schwirian. Morristown, NJ: General Learning Press.

South, Scott J. and Dudley L. Poston, Jr. 1980. "A Note on Stability in the U.S. Metropolitan System: 1950-1970." *Demography* 17:445-450.

———— 1982. "The U.S. Metropolitan South: Regional Change, 1950-1970." *Urban Affairs Quarterly* 18:187-206.

Stahura, John M. 1986. "Suburban Development, Black Suburbanization and the Civil Rights Movement Since World War II." *American Sociological Review* 51:131-144.

Stephan, G. Edward. 1972. "International Tests of the Size-Density Hypothesis." *American Sociological Review* 37:365-368.

———— 1979. "Derivation of Some Socio-Demographic Regularities from the Theory of Time-Minimization." *Social Forces* 57:812-823.

———— and Douglas R. McMullin. 1981. "The Historical Distribution of County Seats in the United States: A Review, Critique and Test of Time-Minimization Theory." *American Sociological Review* 46:907-17.

Stephan, G. Edward and Karen H. Stephan. 1984. "Population Redistribution and Changes in the Size-Density Slope." *Demography* 21:35-40.

Stern, Robert N. and Omer R. Galle. 1978. "Industrial Conflict and the Intermetropolitan Structure of Production." *Sociological Science Quarterly* 59:257-273.

Sternlieb, George and James W. Hughes, eds. 1975. *Post-Industrial America: Metropolitan Decline and Inter-Regional Job Shifts*. New Brunswick, NJ: Center for Urban Policy Research.

Stewart, J. Q. 1948. "Demographic Gravitation:

Evidence and Applications." *Sociometry* 11: 31-58.

Stinchcombe, Arthur L. 1968. *Constructing Social Theories*. New York: Harcourt, Brace and World.

Storper, Michael. 1985. "Technology and Spatial Production Relations: Disequilibrium, Interindustry Relationships, and Industrial Development." Pp. 265-283 in *High Technology, Space, and Society*, edited by Manuel Castells. Beverly Hills, CA: Sage.

Suttles, Gerlad. 1978. "Changing Priorities for the Urban Heartland." In *Handbook of Contemporary Urban Life*, edited by David Street and Associates. San Francisco: Jossey-Bass.

Sweetser, Frank L. 1965. "Factor Structure as Ecological Structure in Helsinki and Boston." *Acta Sociologica* 26:205-225.

Taeuber, Karl E. and Alma F. Taeuber. 1965. *Negroes in Cities: Residential Segregation and Neighborhood Change*. Chicago: Aldine.

Tailhet-Waldorf, S. and W. H. Waldorf. 1983. "Earnings of Self-Employed in an Informal Sector: A Case Study of Bangkok." *Economic Development and Cultural Change* 3: 587-607.

Tienda, Marta and Lisa J. Neidert. 1984. "Language, Education, and the Socioeconomic Achievement of Hispanic Origin Men." *Social Science Quarterly* 64:519-536.

Tobin, Gary A. 1976. "Suburbanization and the Development of Motor Transportation: Transportation Technology and the Suburbanization Process." Pp. 95-111 in *The Changing Face of the Suburbs*, edited by Barry Schwartz. Chicago: University of Chicago Press.

Todaro, Michael P. (with Jerry Stilkind). 1981. *City Bias and Rural Neglect: The Dilemma of Urban Development*. New York: The Population Council.

Tucker, C. Jack. 1976. "Changing Patterns of Migration between Metropolitan and Nonmetropolitan Areas in the United States: Recent Evidence." *Demography* 13:435-443.

Ullman, Edward and Chauncey Harris. 1970. "The Nature of Cities." Pp. 91-100 in *Urban Man and Society: A Reader in Urban Ecology*, edited by Albert N. Cousins and Hans Nagpaul. New York: Knopf.

United Nations. 1980. *Patterns of Urban and Rural Population Growth*. Department of International Economic and Social Affairs, Population Studies, No. 68 (ST/ESA/SER a/68). New York: United Nations Press.

U. S. Bureau of the Census. 1983. "Census of Population and Housing: 1980. Number of Inhabitants." In *United States Summary*. Washington, DC: Government Printing Office.

———— 1984. *Statistical Abstract of the United States, 1985*. Washington, DC: Government Printing Office.

———— 1985. "Patterns of Metropolitan Area and County Population Growth: 1980-1984." *Current Population Reports*. Series P25, No. 976. Washington, DC: Government Printing Office.

Van Arsdol, Maurice D., Jr., Santo F. Camilleri, and Calvin F. Schmid. 1958. "The Generality of Urban Social Area Analysis." *American Sociological Review* 23:277-284.

Van den Berg, Leo, Roy Drewett, Leo H. Klaassen, Angelo Rossi, and Cornelius H.T. Vijverberg. 1982. *Urban Europe: A Study of Growth and Decline*. New York: Pergamon Press.

Van Valey, Thomas L., Wade Clark Roof, and Jerome E. Wilcox. 1977. "Trends in Residential Segregation: 1960-1970." *American Journal of Sociology* 82:826-844.

Vance, Rupert B. and Sara Smith Sutker. 1954. "Metropolitan Dominance and Integration in the Urban South." Pp. 114-134 in *The Urban South*, edited by Rupert Vance and Nicholas J. Demerath. Chapel Hill: University of North Carolina Press.

Vernon, Raymond. 1960. *Metropolis 1985*. Cambridge, MA: Harvard University Press.

———— 1966. "International Investment and International Trade in the Product Cycle." *Quarterly Journal of Economics* 80:473-509.

Vining, Daniel R., Jr. and Anne Strauss. 1977. "A Demonstration that the Current Deconcentration of Population in the United States is a Clean Break with the Past." *Environment and Planning* 9:751-758.

Wallerstein, Immanuel. 1974. *The Modern World-System: Capitalist Agriculture and the Origins of the European World-Economy in the Sixteenth Century*. New York: Academic Press.

———— 1980. *The Modern World-System II: Mercantilism and the Consolidation of the European World-Economy, 1600-1750*. New York: Academic Press.

Walton, John. 1976. "Urban Hierarchies and Patterns of Dependence in Latin America: Theoretical Bases for a New Research Agenda." Pp. 43-70 in *Current Perspectives in Latin American Urban Research*, edited by Alejandro Portes and Harley L. Browning. Austin: Institute for Latin American Studies, University of Texas.

Wanner, Richard A. 1977. "The Dimensionality of the Urban Functional System." *Demography* 14: 519-537.

Wardwell, John W. 1977. "Equilibrium and Change in Nonmetropolitan Growth." *Rural Sociology* 42:156-179.

———— 1980. "Toward a Theory of Urban-Rural Migration in the Developed World." Pp. 71-114 in *New Directions in Urban-Rural Migration*, edited by David L. Brown and John M. Wardwell. New York: Academic Press.

Watkins, Alfred J. and David Perry, eds. 1977. "Regional Change and the Impact of Uneven Urban Development." Pp. 19-54 in *The Rise of the Sunbelt Cities*. Beverly Hills, CA: Sage.

Williams, James D. and Andrew J. Sofranko. 1979. "Motivations for the Immigration Component of Population Turnaround in Nonmetropolitan

Areas." *Demography* 16:239-255.

Wilson, Franklin D. 1984. "Urban Ecology: Urbanization and Systems of Cities." *Annual Review of Sociology* 10:283-307.

Wilson, Kenneth and Alejandro Portes. 1980. "Immigrant Enclaves: An Analysis of the Labor Market Experiences of Cubans in Miami." *American Journal of Sociology* 86:295-319.

Wilson, William J. 1983. "Inner-City Dislocations." *Society* 21:80-86.

Wirth, Louis. 1928. *The Ghetto*. Chicago: University of Chicago Press.

White, Ralph. 1982. "Family Size Composition Differentials between Central City-Suburb and Metropolitan-Nonmetropolitan Streams." *Demography* 19:29-36.

Zimmer, Basil. 1975. "The Urban Centrifugal Drift." Pp. 23-91 in *Metropolitan America in Contemporary Perspective*, edited by Amos H. Hawley and Vincent P. Rock. New York: Halsted Press.

Zipf, George. 1949. *Human Behavior and the Principle of Least Effort*. Reading, MA: Addison-Wesley.

Zorbaugh, Harvey W. 1926. "The Natural Areas of the City." *Publications of the American Sociological Society* 20:188-197.

Zuiches, James J. and Glenn V. Fuguitt. 1978. "The Changing Character of Nonmetropolitan Population, 1950-1975." Pp. 55-72 in *Rural U.S.A.: Persistence and Change*, edited by Thomas R. Ford. Ames: Iowa State University.

20

Deviance and Social Control

ANDREW T. SCULL

In what follows, I do not purport to provide a straightforward and "neutral" survey of the field of deviance and social control. Worthy and useful as such surveys can doubtless be, they run the risk of degenerating into a laundry list composed of potted summaries of "major contributions" to a given subspecialty, something of a chore to read and (I suspect) not much fun to write either. These dangers are compounded when one confronts and attempts to summarize an area as sprawling and heterogeneous as the sociology of deviance and social control. The vast literature devoted to the exploration of the troublesome and morally suspect (to say nothing of organized efforts to eliminate or keep such phenomena within bounds) makes even the process of cataloguing and analyzing the accumulation of empirical findings a task of formidable proportions. I shall make no such attempt here. Nor (except insofar as methodological concerns are necessarily linked to the larger theme I have chosen to emphasize) do I seek to focus upon the methodological problems and innovations that have marked the development of the field—the emergence, for example, of attempts to supplement and improve upon official criminal statistics through surveys of victims and self-report studies.

Instead, I have elected to provide a history of and interpretative commentary on the theoretical development of the study of deviance and social control, in an attempt to order a some-

what disparate and disorderly field through an analysis and critique of the major substantive perspectives that have characterized it over the past century or so. In what follows, I have striven to provide a balance between exposition and criticism, and (with the discreet aid of the book's editors) to rein in my more polemical impulses. Nevertheless, it must be emphasized that the account I have given is *a* version (more accurately *my* version) of the history and current status of the field; and that given the essentially contested nature of the terrain (and the fact that I am scarcely a neutral bystander but rather an active participant in current debates), my version can scarcely be expected to command universal assent. I trust, however, that I have at least provided a recognizable and defensible portrait of the field, perhaps even a somewhat provocative one, and that my own biases and preconceptions are sufficiently transparent to permit the reader to make allowances for my *parti-pris*.

Introduction

In the very earliest years of American sociology, the study of deviance and its linkages with efforts at social control occupied a central place, being seen as theoretically and empirically fundamental to the future development of the discipline. Threats to morality and the social order, and the institutionalized mechanisms for holding such tendencies in check, were seen as vital topics for sociological investigation, and during the heyday of the so-called Chicago School, few topics received more extended attention. But with the decline in the unquestioned preeminence of Chicago sociology in the 1930s and 1940s, work on deviance and social control also began to lose its respectability, to the point where it soon possessed an intellectual status scarcely more elevated or desirable than the moral status of the whores and addicts with which it concerned itself.

The "relevance" of its subject matter (which may even have contributed to its shunning by a generation fascinated by the grander theoretical projects of the European tradition) attracted a ready flow of funds to support research on such topics, but this constituted only dubious compensation for the academic marginalization of its practitioners. Leading sociologists of the forties and fifties—Talcott Parsons, Daniel Bell, Kingsley Davis, Robert Merton—all at one point or another were drawn to the discussion of deviance and/or social control. But all moved gingerly in this territory, and having trespassed on the turf of their lesser brethren, who spent their lives studying "nuts, sluts, and perverts," retreated rapidly to more elevated and edifying topics of sociological discourse.[1]

Nevertheless, with the partial exception of Edwin Sutherland's (Sutherland and Cressey, 1960) work on his theory of differential association as an explanation of crime and criminal careers, it was on the occasional pieces written by these mainstream figures that the sociology of deviance drew most heavily for its theoretical inspiration through the 1950s and into the 1960s—when, that is, "theory" became an issue at all. For in the postwar years, most work dealing with crime, delinquency, and related social problems continued to exhibit the "non-sociological or even anti-sociological" bias stigmatized by C. Wright Mills (1943) in his essay on "the social pathology of the social pathologists"; and in its concern for instant practicality and what Matza (1969) has termed its "correctionalism,"[2] this literature displayed only a passing concern with broader theoretical constructions. Within the traditional framework shared by those adopting this standard approach, deviance was viewed as merely a "given," and scant attention was generally paid to the processes of social control "precisely because control was interpreted as a natural response to behavior which was generally assumed to be problematic" (Spitzer, 1975, pp. 2-3).

Thus there was clearly something liberating and intellectually challenging about the emergence in the 1960s of a more skeptical viewpoint, one that began to question the assumption that the societal response to deviance represented no more than a benign and defensive response to the presence of individual pathology. Even in its early stages, before its perceptions and insights had hardened into a new orthodoxy, the "new" sociology of deviance brought together a number of theoretical traditions that coexisted uneasily under the same theoretical umbrella: a modified Durkheimianism (Erikson, 1966); more orthodox forms of symbolic interactionism (Davis, 1964; Scott, 1969; Wiseman 1969); the proponents of some form of phenomenology (Bittner, 1967; Phillipson and Roche, 1974; Sudnow, 1965; Warren, 1974); and ethnomethodological pioneers (Cicourel, 1968; Kitsuse and Cicourel, 1963). But the general intellectual gains that came with a pronounced shift away from a banal eclecticism about causality and an obsessive concern with the attributes of individual deviants; the growth of a concern for once more placing deviance and social control within a somewhat broader analytic framework, stressing their connections with larger social structures and processes; and the rupture with the traditional emphasis on "the static, insulated and immanent qualities of rule breaking" (Rock and MacIntosh, 1974, p. xi), all carried with them the promise of breaking down the isolation of the sociology of deviance and social control from the rest of the discipline. Increasingly, deviance was seen as analytically inseparable from the wider social context within which it occurred (though the "width" of the context considered was often no more than the immediate interactional frame), and was felt to be susceptible to analysis in terms of the conventional apparatus of sociological inquiry.

All of this marked a considerable gain in intellectual sophistication, and in the period between the late 1960s and the mid- to late 1970s, many began to see "the field of deviance . . . [as] one of the most creative fields of sociology . . . a field which . . . can properly be said to have been undergoing a revolution in theory and methods," and one whose emergent paradigm (to use a by now outmoded word) promised not just new insights into the phenomenon of deviance, but a new theoretical explanation or account of the social order more generally (Douglas, 1970, p. 368). Few would be as optimistic today, for the apparent unity provided by the so-called skeptical viewpoint has by now crumbled, and given way to a once fractious and now rather tired debate between competing factions, each more or less isolated from and critical of each other. Yet if the earlier sense of a shared intellectual outlook has vanished, the inseparably linked phenomena of deviance and social control continue to provide the occasion for a variety of first-rate sociological work, much of it embedded much more fully than was previously the case in an analytical program that takes seriously the need to grapple with their connections with the larger social and historical context.

At midcentury, the study of deviance and social control were arguably the most theoretically impoverished subfields of sociology. Such is no longer the case. Having long been considered topics of little intellectual moment, crime and its punishment, craziness and its treatment, deviance and its control, have all become issues of major scholarly concern. But it *is* fair to say, I think, that the best of recent work has tended to concentrate its attention far more on the control side of the equation, with deviance and the deviants themselves at times seeming to become almost a residual category in the analysis.

The Early Twentieth Century

In the very earliest years of American sociology, a vital interest in comprehending the basis of social control was perhaps the most abiding theoretical concern among those practicing the new discipline (see Borgatta and Meyer, 1959). In the dominant perspective on the subject, exemplified in Edward Ross's (1901) classic text (appropriately titled *Social Control: A Survey of the Foundations of Order*), and equally evident in the later work of Park and Burgess (1921)—indeed persisting as late as the mid-1960s in the work of people such as Albert Cohen (1966)—social control was defined as encompassing all those social practices and arrangements that contributed to the maintenance of social order and induced conformity amongst the members of any given social group or society. For these early theorists, social control was seen as those processes that operated to produce an emerging consensus on social goals, a "consensus" whose character and existence were presumed to emerge essentially "spontaneously" through mechanisms that remained almost wholly opaque and unscrutinized.

As Ross saw it—drawing much of his inspiration from the French sociologist Gabriel Tarde—the fundamental puzzle that required accounting for sociologically was how it was that people came to "live closely together and associate their efforts with that degree of harmony we see about us" (quoted in Janowitz, 1978, p. 35). In his work—as in that of Charles Horton Cooley and W. I. Thomas—social control, understood as the mechanisms by which society created and sustained this essential harmony, was thus the vital underpinning of organized social life. Just as the "invisible hand" of the marketplace acted to restore economic life to a state of equilibrium, so the forces of social control all but insensibly reinforced conformity and, wherever the social equilibrium was disturbed, acted to reassert it on a new and secure basis. Not that organized social life was never threatened by the forces of disorder: On the contrary, if an earlier, more primitive version of society had been characterized by a form of "natural order" deriving, in the final analysis, from an almost spontaneous accord of naturally sociable beings, possessed of both a sense of justice and a capacity for resentment, the rise of an urbanized, industrialized, and pluralistic social system, characterized by ever sharper pressures on smaller communities and the increased cultural heterogeneity that mass immigration brought in its train, threatened a breakdown of the moral order and a collapse of the constraints that held humanity's appetites and animal nature in check.

What accounted, then, for the reemergence of stability, cooperation, and harmony in the modern world? Not, on the most fundamental level, the mobilization of coercion and external discipline, though on occasion these no doubt entered the picture. Instead, all of the institutions of society were scrutinized to lay bare their contributions to the correction of temporary imbalances and the curbing of excesses that might threaten the social fabric. It was society's (or the social group's) capacity to regulate its own members' behavior *without recourse to forcible coercion* that fascinated these quintessentially Progressive intellectuals. In this sense, Morris Janowitz (1978, p. 3) is quite right to stress that "In its classical conception [and, he would argue, its continuing basic meaning]. . . .'social control' does not imply coercion or the repression of the individual by societal institutions. Social control is, rather, the obverse of coercive control. Social control refers to the capacity of a social group, including a whole society, to regulate itself. Self regulation must imply a set of 'higher moral principles' beyond those of self interest," and it is to these moral bonds that we must look to account for our ability to live together.

It was not, therefore, to the regulatory powers

of the state or the market that these analysts looked to discern the roots of social cohesion. Religion, the family, educational institutions, the whole apparatus of socialization, by fostering empathy and cooperation, corrected any temporary lapses from grace, reined in any tendency toward a Hobbesian war of all against all, and allowed people to complete their daily round within the confines of a mutually sustained and morally ordered universe. Reflecting on "the genesis of the self and social control," George Herbert Mead (1925), in an essay that characteristically "de-emphasized political institutions for an examination of what [he] believed to be the underlying, fundamental social processes of society" (Janowitz, 1978, p. 8), pronounced that in the final analysis, "social control depends, then, upon the degree to which the individuals in society are able to assume the attitudes of others who are involved with them in common endeavors."

In the not-so-long run, this anodyne portrait drew the boundaries of social control so broadly as to encompass almost all of organized social life within its net, a conception, as David Rothman (1983, p. 109) has noted, so "flabby" that "by the 1940s *social control* went out of style among sociologists. The textbooks might use the term, but serious researchers, with one or two exceptions did not pursue the issue in the Ross-Mead tradition."

In the short term, however, the reverse was clearly true. "Social control" was the organizing theme of the 1917 American Sociological Association meetings, and only a few years later, the bible of indigenous North American sociology pronounced solemnly that "all social problems turn out to be problems of social control" (Park and Burgess, 1921, p. 785). And if this were the case, then social control should certainly be "the central fact and the central problem of sociology" (Park and Burgess, 1921, p. 42).

Such views exercised great influence on the cohorts of students trained and molded by the Chicago department. In the process, the stress on the centrality of the notion of social control served to reinforce an even more long-standing disposition to view sociology as vitally concerned with the analysis and solution of "social problems." Understandably, it thereby contributed to a heightened interest in social deviance that had still other sources within the emerging intellectual consensus that constituted the Chicago School of sociology.

A concern with those who strayed from the precepts of conventional middle-class morality had, of course, been almost a defining feature of early American (and British) sociology. In both countries, strong intellectual and organizational ties linked sociology with the newly emerging profession of social work (Lubove, 1971) and with social reform (see Bernard, 1929; MacRae, 1962). Rarely pausing to "entertain the hypothesis that at least some forms of pathology might be useful or functional within the society in which they were found," these early social pathologists railed instead against "social abscesses or lesions within an otherwise healthy organism."

Allied with "practical philanthropists" and funded by such organizations as the Russell Sage Foundation, the first generation of university based sociologists adapted the nineteenth-century social survey to the task of locating and rooting out social pathology. Their work, dominated by a simplistic assumption that evil causes evil, contained few surprises. Deviance, for them, constituted an abdication of morality, a phenomenon produced by the disorganization of the slum, and concentrated among the socially marginal, where "poverty destroys the possibilities of normal development" (West Side Studies, 1914, p. 61; quoted in Matza, 1969, p. 20). The linkages between "anti-social behavior" and social environment were easily discerned: "When one is penniless and knows no moral code and see one's elders acknowledging none, the temptation to adopt the tactics of the thief and the thug becomes almost irresistible" (West Side Studies, 1914, p. 143, quoted in Matza 1969, p. 21). Consequently, those who sought to understand the genesis "of juvenile delinquency, of the race problem, of the social evil [prostitution], of liquor laws broken, of non-employment, and incapacity due to industrial causes" needed little more than a surface acquaintance with the rougher parts of the city, places that served as awful reminders of "how disintegrating forces assert themselves when progressive ones are shut off through civil lethargy and selfishness" (Lattimore, 1914, p. 124, quoted in Matza, 1969, p. 22).

As Edwin Lemert (1951, p. 1; see also Mills 1943) has noted,

> Generally speaking, these late nineteenth and early twentieth century sociologists grouped together under the heading of 'social pathology,' those human actions which ran counter to ideals of residential stability, property ownership, sobriety, thrift, habituation to work, small business enterprise, sexual discretion, family solidarity, neighborliness, and discipline of will. In effect, social problems were considered

to be any form of behavior violating the mores from which these ideals were projected. The mores behind the ideals, for the most part, were those of rural, small-town, and middle class America. . . .[not surprising when we consider] that many of the early writers on social pathology lived their more formative years in rural communities and small towns; often, too, they had theological training and experience, so that it was only natural that they should look upon many forms of behavior associated with urban life and industrial society as destructive of moral values they cherished as universally good and true.

The Chicago School of Sociology and the Study of Deviance

Crucially, however, the rise of the Chicago School of sociology marked a decisive break with this tradition of amateurish social meliorism. In place of a barely secularized moral pastoralism, the dominant figures at Chicago sought to institutionalize an aggressively professionalized "scientific" approach to the study of society, one that broke with the naive sentimentalism of social reformers masquerading as sociologists and, not so coincidentally, with the social survey as a dominant research methodology. Surveys were now disdained as a form of merely applied sociology, henceforth to be relegated to the lesser beings who populated the social work and social administration faculties, while the scientific core of the discipline would revolve around more rigorous "empirical" research, using life histories, ethnographic field studies, census data, and the like. (See the account offered in Bulmer, 1984.)

What was distinctive about Chicago sociology, and what marked its work off from earlier empirical research, were its possession of both an organizing theoretical framework, and its connections to a stable institutional base. Taken together, these prompted an emphasis on the training of new generations of researchers, and the establishment of a systematic and cumulative research tradition. With the entrenchment of a particular vision of the social universe, taking shape during the second and third decades of the present century and entailing a commitment to "rejecting all traditional answers and institutions that were allegedly the stabilizers of society" (Leonard Cottrell, quoted in Carey, 1975, p. 9), "the Department of Sociology at Chicago [became] . . . really the first big and

lasting one in the country; thus, also, the world" (Hughes, 1979, p. vii; on these developments, see also Dibble, 1975; Shils, 1970; and Rauschenbush, 1979).

It was primarily the second generation of Chicago sociologists, and especially Park, Burgess, and W. I. Thomas, who were responsible for this development. Their guiding vision was perhaps best encapsulated by Robert Park in his 1915 essay, "The City":

> Anthropology, the science of man, has, been mainly concerned up to the present with the study of primitive peoples. But civilized man is quite as interesting an object of investigation, and at the same time his life is more open to observation and study. Urban life and culture are more varied, subtle, and complicated, but the fundamental motives are in both instances the same. The same patient methods of observation which anthropologists like Boas and Lowie have expended on the study of the life and manners of the North American Indians might be even more fruitfully employed in the investigation of the customs, beliefs, social practices, and general conceptions of life prevalent in Little Italy on the Lower Side of Chicago, or in recording the more sophisticated folkways of the inhabitants of Greenwich Village and the neighborhood of Washington Square, New York [Park, 1915, p. 579].

A number of factors clearly contributed to the fascination Chicago sociologists exhibited with deviance and the demi-monde. Their focus on the urban world brought with it a concern to understand how cities expanded and grew through a process of internal differentiation. Convinced that there were "natural areas of the city," each with its own peculiar character, location, and functions, their urban sociology was perhaps most notable for its emphasis on the so-called zonal hypothesis, which pictured the city as made up of concentric layers of social life. Surrounding the central business district at the core of the city they noted the tendency for a "zone of transition" to develop, inhabited by the poor, the despised, the marginal. The problems this sector posed for the more "respectable" segments of urban society meant that sponsorship and funding were readily available for those who could promise to provide scientific understanding of its underlying dynamics. The incentives this provided for the study of the disaffected and morally disreputable, deriving in part from the concerns of voluntary organizations with the task of moralizing and Americanizing the new wave of immigrants, in turn were reinforced by perhaps the key reason for the extraordinary attention now focused on the deviant: the sheer availability of such people as grist for the sociologist's mill. The very nature of these deteriorated or deteriorating neighborhoods exposed their inhabitants to outside scrutiny in a far more thoroughgoing way than could be found elsewhere in the same society. Particularly for the graduate students the new department was bent on training, the problems of gaining access to the world of the poor and the powerless were trivial by comparison with those confronting anyone with the temerity to focus on less vulnerable segments of society.

Large portions of the new urban ethnography thus focused on the study of crime and other forms of social pathology. Studies of gangs (Thrasher, 1927), organized crime (Landesco, 1968), the hobo (Anderson, 1923) and the whore (Reckless, 1926) were accompanied by dissections of their characteristic environments: the taxi-dance hall (Cressey, 1932), the rooming house district (Zorbaugh, 1929), the neighborhoods populated by immigrants (Thomas and Znaniecki, 1927; Wirth, 1928) and blacks (Drake and Cayton, 1945). The concentration on the geography of urban scenes allowed the development and documentation of a central sociological theme, the emergence of characteristic modes of organization, of rules, roles, rewards, and behaviors attached not necessarily to the social group, but often to a particular environment or social setting. As Matza (1969, p. 30) has noted, nowhere was this more obvious than in Shaw and McKay's (1942) longitudinal study of juvenile delinquency in urban areas, which demonstrated how "a delinquent tradition is anchored in certain neighborhoods irrespective of the shifting ethnic groups inhabiting them."

The decision to treat the city as an extended sociological laboratory and the fascination with the minute documentation of evanescent and exotic social worlds were ultimately rooted in the larger meta-theoretical assumptions of the Chicago School, assumptions that exercised a decisive influence on the form and content of the knowledge its members produced. The emphasis on the primacy of direct observation was derived, in substantial measure, from the influence of the pragmatists, most notably Pierce, Dewey, and James, all of whom stressed the *processual* aspects of knowledge, viewing it as a transaction between the observer and the observed. "What," in William James's words, "does *thinking about* the experience of . . . persons come to, compared to directly and personally feeling it as they feel it?" (James, 1949, p. 30).

Loosed upon an urban environment of striking diversity and heterogeneity, Chicago sociologists behaved like social anthropologists bent on recovering and rendering, in often excruciating—even numbing—detail, the world of the raffish and the socially marginal.

Their work mirrored John Dewey's emphasis on the situated and local character of truth and bore the imprint of Robert Park's injunction to remember that "the real world [is] the experience of actual men and women and not the abbreviated and shorthand descriptions of it that we call knowledge" (quoted in Rauschenbush, 1979, p. 29). Perhaps the most striking manifestation of this almost obsessive concern with recovering "the subjective experiences and attitudes of . . . individuals" (Wirth, 1964, p. 240) were the "as-told-to" autobiographies of the jack-roller (Shaw, 1930) and the professional thief (Sutherland, 1956); but in a wider perspective, their concern with reconstructing the particularities and peculiarities of person and place is fundamental to the ethnographic tradition fostered at Chicago.

The stress on the importance of direct "personal experience" had, as its counterpart, a generalized distrust of "reification," of abstraction, and of systematic theorizing that was also to characterize later generations of deviancy theorists. Still, the question of explanation was not ignored, even if the approach adopted by the Chicagoans was, in subtle ways, undermined by their own empirical findings. Reflecting on the extraordinary apparent concentration of "pathological behavior" in the zone of transition, an impression reinforced by the data derived from official sources (court records, census data, and social surveys), sociologists sought to account for this epidemic of alcoholism, delinquency, mental disturbance, suicide, and crime in terms of the area's distinctive social features. Most visibly, this was an area of the city characterized by instability: immigrant groups moved in and out; the institutions of law, religion, the family, morality, those commonplace bastions and essential props of the social order, found their influence sharply attenuated; and in the absence of these social controls, a generalized lack of discipline produced a form of social existence that was certainly nasty and brutish, and often enough, short as well. "Common understandings" withered away, in an environment in which "contacts are extended, heterogeneous groups mingle, neighborhoods disappear, and people, deprived of local and family ties, are forced to live under . . . loose, transient and impersonal relations" (Wirth, 1964, p. 236).

Deviance was thus viewed as the product of social disorganization and fragmentation, in some sense as the loss of a common moral universe (Wirth, 1964). And yet the very detail of their own ethnographies tended to cast doubt on certain aspects of this formulation. In David Matza's (1969, p. 48) terms, "though the Chicagoans conceived disorganization, they described diversity." That is, the claim that deviance was simply a product of a lack of order tended to be undermined by their own evidence that deviant worlds possessed their own peculiar integrity and logic, and were in fact socially organized in varying degrees, albeit in ways that put them at odds with the larger, "conventional" society. Rather than disorganization, their ethnographies unmistakably pointed toward the existence of moral diversity, and alongside the emphasis on the pathological character of the zone of transition came a recognition that deviance (and delinquency was seen as a paradigmatic case in this regard) constituted an almost commonplace, taken-for-granted part of life in certain social settings and contexts. Taken a step further in Whyte's *Street Corner Society*, the view of deviance as "an unremarkable consequence of normal conditions" (Downes and Rock, 1982, p. 66) implicitly called into question the "commonsense" equation of deviance and personal pathology.

The Functionalist Approach to Deviance

If the ethnographic tradition thus produced a strain toward a less straightforward view of deviance, raising questions about the simple equation of rule-breaking with individual pathology and casting doubt upon the presumption that it was in any simple sense the product of the collapse of orderly social existence, its replacement as the dominant approach to this phenomenon, the various functional theories of deviance that began to achieve prominence in the 1930s, broke even more decisively with such presuppositions. Conventional views about the relationship of deviance and the social order were now virtually turned on their heads. Instead of being viewed as a purely negative phenomenon, deviance was increasingly portrayed as inescapable, even occupying a vital place in the maintenance of the social order.

Chicago's initial preeminence in American sociology had been built in part upon the absence of any effective challenge from competing departments in major universities. Some of the elite Eastern schools, such as Harvard and Princeton, elected not to allow the upstart discipline within their walls. Others, such as Yale, taught the subject to undergraduates but developed no effective research program in the discipline, or could trace their ineffectiveness in developing a substantial research program to the overpowering presence of a single dominant figure—for example, Franklin Giddings at Columbia (see Bulmer, 1984). During the 1930s this environment began to change, as first Harvard and then others began to develop major departments of their own. The Eastern schools, in particular, tended to look to Europe rather than to Chicago for theoretical inspiration, and to focus upon more elevated topics of sociological discourse than the mundane activities of nuts, sluts, and perverts. The study of deviance thus began to cede the central position it had earlier occupied in the field, acquiring some of the marginality of its subject matter. And to the extent that such topics *were* addressed, those who continued to theorize about them found the strong judgmental (and hence "nonscientific") elements so prominent in the earlier social pathology and social disorganization perspectives distinctly unpalatable.

Outside the United States, and particularly in continental Europe, sociology had developed in very different ways from those institutionalized at Chicago. One important strand in European sociology, building upon the work of Quetelet and other social statisticians (see Beirne, 1985), reflected the growing vogue, over the course of the nineteenth century, for the collection and collation of statistical information on domestic populations. This concern with counting and measuring quickly extended from the recording of vital statistics (births, deaths, marriages, etc.) to encompass a range of other social phenomena, including, quite prominently, data on the extent and social distribution of various forms of deviance (crime, divorce, suicide, mental illness, and so forth). Understandably, the very existence of these materials provided a recurrent source of temptation to those bent on building a new "social physics," inviting those concerned with establishing sociology's scientific credentials to take these "social facts" and use them as a basis for the systematic exploration of the social world. (Doubts and questions about the "facticity" of these bureaucratic records were not to receive sustained attention till more than half a century had passed.)

Durkheim's *Suicide* was only the most prominent and polemically successful study of this sort, though with his broader fascination with the sociology of morality and his ironical (and hence noncommonsensical) view of the positive place of deviance in the maintenance of social order, it should come as no surprise that it was his influence that was felt most profoundly among the new generation of American functionalists. Early on in his career, Durkheim saw crime in essentially conventional, negative terms: He sought to distinguish "the differentiation . . . which disintegrates (cancerous, microbic, criminal) . . . from that which concentrates vital forces (division of labor)" and saw the criminal as someone who seeks "to live at the expense of" society, and crime itself as "the very negation of solidarity." (Durkheim, 1964, p. 291) Within a few years, however, he had abandoned this stance, adopting what was at the time a highly controversial position that inverted "common sense" and argued that "crime is normal . . . a factor in public health, an integral part of all healthy societies." Crime, he now held, was "linked to the basic conditions of social life" and played "a useful part" in the "normal evolution of morality and law" (Durkheim, 1982, pp. 98, 101).[3] It provided the occasion, particularly in the ritual condemnation of the criminal, for the essential reaffirmation of our collective solidarity in the passionate denunciation of the deviant, and it was, besides, an inevitable feature of all organized social existence.[4] "Imagine," he urged, "a community of saints in an exemplary and perfect monastery. In it crime as such will be unknown, but faults which appear venial to the ordinary person will arouse the same scandal as does normal crime in ordinary consciences. If therefore that community has the power to judge and punish, it will term such acts criminal and deal with them as such" (Durkheim 1982, p. 100). Viewed through the appropriate sociological lens, therefore, and "contrary to current ideas, the criminal no longer appears as an utterly unsociable creature, a sort of parasitic element, a foreign, inassimilable body introduced into the bosom of society. He plays a normal role in social life." (Durkheim, 1982, p. 102) From the mid-1930s onwards, this ironical notion that crime "is a factor in public health, an integrative element in any healthy society" (Durkheim, 1982, p. 98) found many echoes in the attempts by American functionalists to account for the presence of social deviance. Central to functionalist theorizing was the contrast articulated by Robert Merton (1957) between manifest and latent functions, a distinction emphasizing that the central task for social analysts was to penetrate beneath the "obvious" surface realities to uncover the deeper structures and patterning of behavior that were the fundamental sources of the mundane social activities constituting the social order. Persistence being equated with functionality, the hunt was now on to demonstrate how the patently negative was the secretly positive glue holding the social order together.

Theorists like Daniel Bell, Kingsley Davis, and Merton himself prided themselves on breaking with what they saw as an earlier tendency to substitute "naive moral judgments for sociological analysis," taking particular pleasure in providing accounts of deviant phenomena that "[ran] counter to prevailing moral evaluations" (Merton, 1957, pp. 70-71). In gleeful pursuit of this project, urban political machines, the traditional whipping boys of high-minded Progressive-era reformers and symbols of the corruption of ethnic politics, were shown to be the product of a "structural context which makes it difficult, if not impossible, for morally approved structures to fill essential functions." So far from eating away at the fabric of organized social life, the machine and its boss, in Merton's portrait at least, essentially prevented the unraveling of an overly fragmented, legalistic, and bureaucratic operation—providing opportunities for social mobility to the otherwise excluded, assistance to the unsophisticated in navigating the shoals of bureaucratic officialdom, access to some of the perquisites of power for the otherwise powerless. (That such gains were purchased at a heavy price was, as David Matza, 1969, pp. 57-62, points out, subtly elided in Merton's account.) Crime, in Daniel Bell's vivid phrase, turned out to be nothing more or less than "an American way of life," and racketeering a natural response to the peculiar features of the New York dock land, performing "the function . . . which other agencies cannot do, of stabilizing a chaotic market and establishing an order and structure in the industry" (Bell, 1960, chap. 8 and 9). In like fashion, the virtue of maiden and matron and the moral sanctity of monogamous marriage rested, it now transpired, on the hidden foundation of the pimp and the whore. Prostitution obviated the need for a "mutual complementariness" of sexual desire throughout society; provided a social service to those otherwise deprived of sexual satisfaction (thus diminishing sexual aggression); and allowed the maintenance of a double standard that protected the "virtue" of the respectable woman and thereby the structure of the family. What would most likely happen were the moral crusades against the prostitute to succeed was suggested by Kinsey's finding "that what the male has lost in frequency of intercourse with prostitutes he has gained in frequency with non-prostitutes." The upright might rail against the whore, but in an irony that doubtless would have pleased the author of the *Fable of the Bees* (Mandeville, 1711), only her presence allowed society to "reduce the sexual irregularities of respectable women" and avoid a Hobbesian state of sexual promiscuity and licentiousness (Davis, 1971).

In a succession of essays, therefore, American functionalists gave new currency to the discomforting notion that the seemingly harmful, condemned and repressed by "cultural dopes" (to borrow one of Harold Garfinkel's more memorable phrases), secretly serves as one of the pillars of the social order, indeed constitutes a sine qua non of the moral cohesion and continuity of any organized community. Still, they represented occasional pieces by writers otherwise preoccupied with very different themes, and as such were of quite marginal importance in reorienting the focus of sociological studies of deviance. Talcott Parsons, by contrast, had made the issues of moral conformity and of the patterning and control of deviant behavior quite central to his ambitious attempts to construct a functionalist account of *The Structure of Social Action* (1937) and of *The Social System* (1951). But notwithstanding the respect most American sociologists felt for Parsons as their Grand Theorist, the huge gap between his abstractions and empirical reality limited the influence and appeal of his attempts to account for deviance among most of those concerned with this seemingly prosaic subject matter; a problem compounded by the patent inadequacies of an explanation that could do no better than to attribute deviance to defective childhood socialization and/or to the malintegration of the social system at its margins.

The same can scarcely be said of another essay written from within the functionalist tradition, Robert Merton's "Social Structure and Anomie" (Merton, 1938), which became probably the most frequently cited sociological paper ever written. The notion of anomie, or "normlessness," constituted yet another borrowing from Durkheim's work. In explaining the sociogenesis of suicide rates, Durkheim had given much prominence to the breakdown of moral regulation in modern societies. In the transition from "primitive" societies characterized by mechanical solidarity (social systems in which,

he contended, a single normative system held absolute sway) to the moral diversity of the "organically" solidary, the emergence of new forms of social regulation had a tendency to lag behind in the face of rapid social change. Cut loose from their formerly secure anchorage in the web of social relationships, "appetites have become freed of any limiting authority . . . from top to bottom of the ladder, greed is aroused without knowing where to find ultimate foothold [since "nothing appears in man's organic nor his psychological constitution which sets a limit to such tendencies"]. Nothing can calm it, since its goal is far beyond all it can attain" (Durkheim, 1951, p. 256) Purely economic regulation could not suffice, but must instead be accompanied by *moral* regulation imposed by the collectivity. Absent the latter, one inevitably finds the "passions being less disciplined, precisely when they need more discipline," a recipe for "perpetual unhappiness" and for a plethora of social pathology extending even to include an epidemic of self-destruction (Durkheim, 1951, pp. 248ff).

For Durkheim, then, moral deregulation led to the malady of infinite aspirations and hence posed a serious threat to the social order. Anomie was, however, an essentially temporary condition that could be expected to remit as newly emergent forms of social regulation (particularly "occupational associations") began to take hold. By contrast, Merton, while adopting Durkheim's terminology, radically transformed the essential meaning of the concept.

The central difference between the two usages is neatly captured by David Downes and Paul Rock (1982, p. 102), who note that for Durkheim, the basic idea was that "deregulation led to infinite aspirations; for Merton, infinite aspirations led to deregulation." In Merton's view, social norms lost their binding force, not because of a weakening of social networks or because of a mismatch between reward and talent, but because of a fundamental contradiction between a cultural structure that emphasized universal limitless aspiration and consumption and a social structure whose built-in inequalities sharply limited available opportunities for certain segments of the population. Anomie (and associated deviance) was not, therefore, the product of the weakening of social regulation, but rather the unintended consequence of the incessant inculcation of the virtues of mass consumption by American culture—an ingrained characteristic that necessarily created not just wants, but also profound dissatisfactions. In essence, as Merton himself put it, "The culture makes incompatible demands . . . a cardinal

American virtue—ambition—promotes a cardinal American vice—deviant behavior" (Merton, 1957, pp. 145-146). And anomie becomes a routine rather than an exceptional feature of the social world.

Faced with the strain produced by the disparities between aspirations and reality, Merton viewed a number of deviant outcomes as possible: One could accept culturally prescribed goals, but reject the proffered means for reaching them (what he referred to as innovation); reject the goals and rigidly adhere to the rules for reaching them (ritualism); reject both goals and means (retreatism); or substitute new goals and means for those one refused to abide by (rebellion). All of these responses were far less common than simple conformity, but given that discrepancies between goals and means increased as one moved toward the bottom of the social hierarchy, one should empirically expect to find that deviance was inversely related to social status.

In its newly Americanized form, anomie remained the most popular theoretical account of deviance for almost a quarter of a century. If nothing else, it appeared to make sense of an otherwise puzzling yet seemingly nearly universal phenomenon: persistently rising rates of crime and delinquency in the context of growing affluence and material abundance. The emergence of subcultural theory in the mid-1950s entailed some modification of Merton's basic approach, yet in essence served to enrich rather than break with its fundamental presuppositions.

In Albert Cohen's work on *Delinquent Boys*, for example (Cohen, 1955), delinquency is seen as a collective *solution*, rather than a problem, at least for those engaging in it. Delinquent subcultures emerge, in other words, among juveniles who find the weight of the system (particularly the educational system) stacked against them. Unable to succeed by following the conventional rules, they reject the legitimate world and invent their own. In Cohen's view, that is, "The crucial condition for the emergence of new cultural forms is the existence, in effective interaction with one another, of a number of actors with similar problems of adjustment" (Cohen, 1955, p. 59); and once viewed as a subcultural response to a perceived threat, apparently motiveless and meaningless behavior can be rescued and seen instead as a meaningful response to a difficult situation. The somewhat later work on the same subject by Richard Cloward and Lloyd Ohlin (1960) takes the argument a step further, accepting Merton's fundamental hypothesis about the genesis of the strain

toward deviance, but adding the notion of "illegitimate opportunity structures" to create a more complex portrait of the choice of delinquent "solution."

Subcultural theory may be seen as an attempt to cope with one of the most obvious deficiencies of Merton's approach, its tendency to provide a highly static, mechanistic, and (curiously enough for a sociological theory) individualistic account of the transition from conformity to deviance; or rather, to make the last point rather more precisely, to focus on "initial states and deviant outcomes rather than on processes whereby acts and complex structures of action are built, elaborated, and transformed." (Cohen 1965, p. 9) Yet the work of the leading subcultural theorists tended to remain abstract and formal, rather than providing detailed and convincing empirical accounts of the process of becoming deviant. Moreover, it left almost wholly unresolved (indeed it unfortunately shared) some more deep-seated if initially overlooked difficulties with anomie theory. Cumulatively, these deficiencies, and the criticisms to which they shortly gave rise, led to the exhaustion and virtual abandonment of both approaches.

Symptomatic of as well as contributing to this decline was the appearance of Marshall Clinard's (1964) edited volume, *Anomie and Deviant Behavior: A Discussion and Critique*. Here, both approaches were criticized for neglecting the complexities of the transition from conformity to deviance; for ignoring the often contingent nature of the latter, and the active role of social control operations in defining and even creating the deviant (the problem posed for sociological theory, for example, by the fact that most people steal, but only a minority are processed as thieves); and (particularly in Merton's case) for relying upon highly reified abstractions ("social structure," "cultural structure") whose concrete referents were all too often unclear. The use of culture as an explanatory variable also came in for harsh criticism, not just because some were inclined to doubt that American society was permeated by a single, homogeneous "value system," but also because "inescapable circularity lies in the use of 'culture' as a summary to describe modal tendencies in the behavior of human beings and, at the same time, as a term designating the causes of the modal tendencies" (Lemert, 1964, p. 60).

Perhaps most seriously of all, a problem traceable all the way back to Durkheim's *Suicide* itself, anomie theory and related work rested upon an unperceived, and hence unexamined, assumption about the "facticity" of official statistics. Durkheim's central methodological presuppositions were such as to preclude sustained attention to subjective meanings and actors' conceptions of reality as constitutive of the social order. Notwithstanding his concerns in his later work with "collective representations" and the cultural or ideational dimension of social reality, Durkheim remained committed to a vision of sociology within which knowledge is built up on the basis of hard data—"social facts" that in principle are supposedly identifiable wholly without reference to subjective or intersubjective meanings, and whose interrelationships are then subjected to causal analysis. Such a rigid, absolute conception of social reality necessarily and systematically obscures the essentially *meaningful* character of social interaction, and its limitations are present in an especially damaging form in *Suicide*. "A corpse," said Durkheim in a memorable phrase, "is a corpse." But is a suicide a suicide? Here was the nub of the issue, for the corpse had to be classified, and that process of classification necessarily involved the imputation of meaning and motive, often in highly ambiguous circumstances in which the verdict rendered was extremely socially consequential. The official statistics on which Durkheim (and Merton and the subcultural theorists) relied had all the appearance of "things," hard numbers that were independent of the messiness and ambiguity that questions of social meaning entail. But their "facticity" was spurious. On closer inspection, it turns out that official rates and indices—of suicide, of crime, delinquency, or other forms of deviance—cannot be constituted independently of social meanings, nor, indeed, of organizational practices and routines.

Official crime statistics, for example, appear amply to confirm the Mertonian assumption that deviance is essentially a lower-class phenomenon. But once the social processes attendant upon their production receive attention, certainty begins to dissolve. As Cicourel (1968) was to show, routine police practices tended to produce a focus on the lower class and a differential response to lower-class offenders; these in turn by producing a disproportionate number of working-class offenders, tend to confirm the "correctness" of the initial focus, and thus to reinforce the practices themselves, in a vicious circle of self-confirmation. Closer scrutiny of the activities of social control agencies (Kitsuse and Cicourel, 1963; Cicourel and Kitsuse, 1963; Sudnow, 1965; Douglas, 1970) as well as the results of self-report studies (Gold, 1966; Short and Nye, 1958; but see also Hindelgang, Herschi, and Weis, 1979) tended to expose still more starkly the fragility of the factual foundation of official portraits of deviance; and to render increasingly suspect those sociological theories that relied for their plausibility on the patterns traceable in official statistics. The increasing skepticism is neatly encapsulated in the scornful dismissal by R. D. Laing, that most unpsychiatric psychiatrist, of "those sociologists who think that they can find out what goes on by analysing medical records," a practice he likens to "trying to turn clinical sows' ears into statistical silk purses" (Laing and Esterson, 1968, p. 13).

Societal Reaction Theory

The dominance of any particular theoretical approach to the sociological explanation of deviance has never been total, and even during the heyday of functionalism in the 1940s and 1950s, subterranean traditions persisted that were at odds with its "metaphysical pathos" (Gouldner, 1962). Of particular importance in this regard is a loosely defined group of theorists whom David Matza refers to as "the neo-Chicagoans" —such people as Edwin Lemert, Howard S. Becker, and Erving Goffman, who kept alive the Chicago school's stress on direct observation and fieldwork and married it to an increasing concern with "the *process of becoming deviant* and the part played by the official registrars of deviation in that process" (Matza, 1969, p. 37; emphasis in the original). Ignored and marginalized in the early stages of their careers, they became steadily more celebrated and influential in the 1960s, as so-called labeling or societal reaction theory supplanted anomie and subcultures as the favored sociological explanation of nonconformity.

There can be little doubt that some of the attractions of the neo-Chicagoan approach came from a reaction among a significant minority of younger sociologists against the number-crunching "scientism" increasingly characteristic of the sociological mainstream.[5] Being deviant by definition carries associated risks of exclusion, moral disapproval, stigma, and punishment, making it inevitable that much deviance will be not merely hidden, but carefully and systematically screened from view. The subject matter itself, that is, calls into question the appropriateness of surveys, attitudinal research, and other techniques producing "data" that are lent to statistical manipulation, and the only alternative source of "hard" numbers—the extensive records produced by official agencies of social control—was, as we have seen, equally vulnerable to criticism. For those disenchanted (or never enchanted) with the quantification of social life, the new approach to the study of the deviant, with its stress on the study of the constitution and reconstitution of meaning, and on the contributions that the focus on deviance could make to the discovery of the nature of the ordering processes in a pluralistic society, had a number of obvious attractions.[6] Besides, the subject matter, with its built-in appeal to the prurient and its obvious contrast with the routine and the mundane, created a sizable audience for the sort of anthropological reports from the field at which the interactionists who now came to prominence specialized.

Central to the new approach was "a large turn away from older sociology which tended to rest heavily upon the idea that deviance leads to social control." Instead, the interactionists pursued the heretical notion that "social control leads to social deviance," seeing this as at least "equally tenable and the potentially richer premise for studying deviance in modern society. . . . social control must be taken as an independent variable rather than as a constant, or merely reciprocal, societal reaction to deviation" (Lemert, 1967, p. v). The logic of their arguments placed great weight on the attributions of meanings, and upon the effects this attributional process had on personal identity, both of which were seen as exercising very powerful influences upon subsequent behavior and social standing. Instead of the actions of the deviant, it was the responses of his or her audience that were now viewed as critical. In a more fully sociological perspective, it was now claimed, "the original 'causes' of . . . deviation give way to the central importance of the disapproving, degradational, and isolating reactions of society" (Lemert, 1964, p. 82).

Labeling theory thus attempted to make problematic what others had taken as a given, that certain forms of behavior were somehow deviant per se, independent of any social processes or definitions (Kitsuse, 1968). Deviance, these theorists argued, was a relative rather than an absolute concept, socially constructed and varying by time, place, and context. In a quite fundamental sense, nothing is really "there" until social definitions are applied.

If for the most part the intellectual ancestry of the labeling perspective lay in the ethnographic and symbolic interactionist traditions, support for this social relativism also tended to come from a rather different and, in some respects, more surprising direction: a sanitized, functionalized sociological history. Central to the societal reaction canon was Kai Erikson's

(1966) *Wayward Puritans*, a reconstruction of seventeenth-century New England history that borrows, in a wholly uncritical way, a number of Durkheimian notions—the conception of punishment as a symbolic reaffirmation of the community's moral values and beliefs, the idea that a certain level of crime is "normal" for a given society, and the realization that deviance is a social creation: "We should not say that an act offends the common consciousness because it is criminal, but that it is criminal because it offends that consciousness. We do not condemn it because it is a crime, but it is a crime because we condemn it." (Durkheim, 1984, p. 40) It was the last point that was critical, and which made Erikson's revival of these claims a central reference point for the societal reaction theorists. What better demonstration could there be of the socially contingent nature of deviant labels, and the crucial role of audience reactions in the manufacture of deviance and the constitution of deviant identity?

Durkheim's status as one of the "classical" sociological theorists lent added weight and legitimacy to this assertion, though the attempt to cloak labeling theory in the mantle of Durkheimian authority necessarily relied upon a kind of intellectual amnesia. For while Durkheim had indeed argued that criminality was not an intrinsic property of a particular class of actions but rather the outcome of a process of social definition, he had also insisted on the existence and importance of a set of universally accepted moral rules, which are absolute, clear, and obvious to all members of a society in all situations—a proposition that, if accepted, would have foreclosed most of the central problems societal reaction theorists were to attack. Durkheim's insistence that the nature of crime (and, by extension, the nature of other forms of deviance) does not lie in "the intrinsic importance of the acts" (Durkheim, 1982, p. 101) did not and could not lead him to explore the practical uses of social rules or the processes by which some rule violators and not others come to be defined as deviant. On the contrary, his most basic theoretical premises led him "to assume that the major social norms generally express the sentiments of the total society. He never seriously entertained the idea that they might only express the sentiments of a specific stratum within it." (Coser, 1960) The idea that moral meanings are to a high degree variable and uncertain, that they are not uniformly distributed through the social structure—indeed that it may not be possible to specify major social norms about which there is general agreement (all central assumptions of the societal reaction approach)—were notions radically incompatible with the Durkheimian vision of the ways in which societies are held together.[7]

Thus, in developing the new labeling perspective, the amount of borrowing from the dominant functionalist paradigm was necessarily limited, with the main axis of development occurring along quite different lines. Beginning in the late 1940s and early 1950s, Lemert began to delineate and develop a distinction between "primary" and "secondary" deviation, a distinction that "primary deviation . . . is polygenetic, arising out of a variety of social, cultural, psychological, and physiological factors, either in adventitious or recurring combinations." Although such deviance is quite common, it also has only very marginal implications for the individual and for society. Under some (rather vaguely specified) circumstances, however, there occurs some sort of more or less organized societal reaction to some of this primary deviation, a reaction usually involving elements of stigmatization, punishment, and actual or symbolic segregation of the offender. The general effect of these reactions is to produce marked changes in the social situation in which the person finds him or herself, and, in consequence,

> early or adult socialization is categorically affected. [The reactions] become central facts of experience for those experiencing them, altering psychic structure, producing specialized organization of social roles and self-regarding attitudes. . . . In effect, the original causes of the deviation recede and give way to the central importance of the disapproving, degradational, and labelling reactions of society [Lemert, 1967, pp. 63, 17].

Increasingly, these and related formulations provoked a shift in "the focus of theory and research from the forms of deviant behavior to the processes by which persons come to be defined as deviant by others" (Kitsuse, 1968, p. 19). Associated with this was an emphasis on the *contingency* of social control, and on the complexity of the exchanges between deviant and controller. In Howard Becker's (1963, p. 9) formulation,

> Social groups create deviance by making the rules whose infraction constitutes deviance, and by applying those rules to particular people and labeling them as outsiders. From this point of view, deviance is *not* a quality of the act the person commits, but rather a consequence of the application by others

of rules and sanctions to an "offender." The deviant is one to whom that label has been successfully applied; deviant behavior is behavior that people so label.

Much of the early work within the societal reaction perspective was concerned to analyze the process of becoming deviant on the social-psychological level, emphasizing the sequences of interaction through which deviant identities are built up and sustained. The social-psychological connotations of some of its central tools of analysis are almost all pervasive: stigma, degradation, mortification of self, discretion, and drift; typing and stereotyping, the reconstitution of self, and the retrospective reconstruction of identity; or again, perceptions, reputation, and the moral career. Attention was repeatedly focused on public degradation ceremonies (Garfinkel, 1956) and related socialization experiences that, by imposing a grossly stigmatizing "master status" (Becker, 1963) on their victims, served to usher the deviant firmly into his or her future role. In Goffman's (1961, p. 12) terms, control systems were now seen as "forcing houses for the change of persons," with the very process of being caught and labeled as deviant setting in motion a relentless, self-fulfilling prophecy. For, as the labeling theorists were quick to point out, once acquired, the deviant status was very difficult to relinquish, both because of the reluctance of the wider community to accept the deviant back in its midst, and because the experience of being singled out and publicly branded in this way usually culminates in a deviant world-view. In this way, the societal reaction allegedly produces a kind of role imprisonment, locking the deviant up within the confines of an all but impenetrable symbolic jail. Scheff's (1966) discussion of the making of a mental patient, one of the most influential and widely cited societal reaction texts, illustrates the basic approach quite well. Following Lemert, he argues that rule-breaking behavior (primary deviance) is a pervasive, if generally ignored or overlooked, feature of organized social life. It is only when rule breakers become the focus of public attention that they are transformed into full-fledged deviants. In most instances, the rules violated are relatively explicit and those on whom the whistle is blown are assigned, in a quite straightforward way, to the relevant deviant category: offenders against the criminal law to the ranks of the criminal and delinquent; drunks to the category of alcoholic or bum; those selling sexual services to the company of whores; and so forth. But certain "rules" governing interaction are so basic, taken for granted, or difficult to articulate, that no ready label is available for those "convicted" of violating them. These Scheff dubs "residual rules." (He cites such examples as failing to maintain proper eye contact with those with whom one is conversing, failing to remain at an appropriate physical distance from those with whom one is interacting, and the tendency to drift off or daydream in public settings.) The company of residual rule violators includes almost all of us at one time or another, and most such incidents are transient and provoke little or no public comment. Potentially, however, residual rule violation may trigger a very different and much more ominous public response, prompting, in our society, the invocation of the preexisting stereotype of "madness." At such moments,

> when the deviance of an individual becomes a public issue, the traditional stereotype of insanity becomes the guiding imagery for action, both for those reacting to the deviant and, at times, for the deviant himself. When societal agents and persons around the deviant react to him uniformly in terms of the traditional stereotypes of insanity, his amorphous and unstructured rule-breaking tends to crystallize in conformity to those expectations, thus becoming similar to the behavior of other deviants classified as mentally ill, and stable over time. The process . . . is completed when the traditional imagery becomes a part of the deviant's orientation for guiding his own behavior [Scheff, 1966, p. 82].

With deviance largely defined by the stigmatizing and punitive reactions of others, the boundaries of the field were significantly widened. Always marked by a degree of analytic vagueness, the relevant subject matter now expanded to encompass a whole range of populations: the socially devalued, the morally disreputable, the troublesome and disruptive; people who constituted, symbolically or actually, threats to the social order. Beyond such traditional deviants as the mad and the bad, labeling theorists reached out to include within their purview such diverse elements as the blind (Scott, 1969) and the disfigured (Davis, 1964; Goffman, 1963; stutterers (Lemert, 1967) and strippers (Skipper and McCaghy, 1970); prostitutes (Bryan, 1965, 1966; Heyl, 1979) and perverts (Plummer, 1975; Reiss, 1961); addicts (Ray, 1961) and alcoholics (Wiseman, 1969); the unwashed (Davis and Munoz, 1968); and the unwed (mothers, that is) (Rains, 1971). Whether it made sense to assimilate such an ex-

traordinarily varied assortment to the single category of the deviant was left essentially unexplored, an imprecision characteristic of, perhaps even welcomed by and courted by, those wedded to symbolic interactionism (see the discussion in Downes and Rock, 1982, pp. 159-162; and Rock, 1979b) Certainly, labeling theorists' emphasis on deviance as an ascribed rather than an achieved characteristic made the extension of the term to encompass statuses as well as behaviors more plausible than it might otherwise have been.

Robert Scott's *The Making of Blind Men* demonstrates that, used sensitively, the labeling perspective can provide considerable insight into the sociological dimensions of stigmatized and stigmatizing conditions. The social identity, the roles, and the behavior of the blind are, he insists, *socially constructed* through powerful socialization experiences, rather than somehow being *inherent in* the physical condition of being unable to see. So far from blindness being a purely physical condition, "The overwhelming majority of people who are classified as [legally] blind . . . can, in fact see" (Scott, 1969, p. 42). Yet the reactions of others to them, in part the product of our stereotyped notions of what it is to be blind, in part the outcome of the "uncertainty, awkwardness, and ambiguity" that attend contacts between the blind and the sighted, cut them off from normal interaction, "demoralizing and humiliating" them, and profoundly altering their public identities and sense of themselves.

Of still greater importance in "the making of blind men" is the impact of those agencies of social control whose primary task is the management and containment of blindness. Indeed, Scott (1969, p. 17) suggests that "it is difficult to exaggerate the important role such organizations play in the socialization of the blind" for it is here that "people who have difficulty seeing [learn] how to behave like blind people" (Scott, 1969, p. 71). Furthermore, "The strength of this socialization process is suggested by the fact that people who can see come to behave as though they cannot, and that from so heterogeneous a population such homogeneity is eventually created" (Scott, 1969, p. 43). Once moved from the ranks of those who have difficulty seeing to the ranks of the legally blind, an abrupt redefinition of the person's problems occurs. Great pressure is exerted to get him to conform to the "expert" view of his condition held by the agency on which he now comes to depend.

In theory, most blindness agencies endorse a restorative approach to the problem of blindness, seeking to prepare the blind for an independent and relatively normal existence. In practice, however, Scott's research documented a recurrent and pervasive tendency to encourage passivity and dependence, extending even to the physical environment and facilities provided to the blind, and tying the clientele every more inextricably to the agency's facilities. The discrepancy between ideology and practice has, he argues, multiple sources (the limited career options facing blindness workers and their consequent desire for security; competition for a handful of "socially attractive" clients in a mass of the aged, multiply handicapped, uneducable and unemployable; sensitivity to community pressures to segregate the blind and keep them out of sight; and the bureaucratic interests of the agency in a stable population of "clients" who provide vivid testimony to the value of its programs). And in perhaps an ultimate irony, to allow further fund raising to support the agency's activities, "the blind who have been victimized by this arrangement are ultimately required to give the public assurances that captivity is their genuine desire" (Scott, 1969, p. 97).

This sense of the deeper ironies of the social control process is central to the whole societal reaction tradition, and Scott's emphasis on the central role played by the blindness agencies finds many parallels elsewhere in the literature. As Kitsuse and Cicourel (1963) have noted, "in modern societies where bureaucratically organized agencies are increasingly invested with social control functions, the activities of such agencies are centrally important 'sources and contexts' which generate as well as maintain definitions of deviance and produce populations of deviants." Put somewhat differently, it is this aspect of the societal reaction, as expressed through the activities of these agencies, which produces a crystallization of the moral order, giving visible, concrete shape and form to the abstraction that is deviance. And it is in these contexts that "deviants come under the regulation of hierarchy, impersonality, specialization and systematic formal rules" (Rubington and Weinberg, 1968, p. 111).

Perhaps the single most influential account of the paradoxical effects of institutions of social control on those they purport to redeem or resocialize is Erving Goffman's classic series of essays, *Asylums* (Goffman, 1961). A quarter-century after its publication, it is apparent that *Asylums* adroitly made use of limited evidence of often dubious validity to advance some extremely general claims. Though the reader is hard put to recall the fact, Goffman's primary

data source is a relatively brief period of observation in a single mental hospital, St. Elizabeth's in Washington, DC. Instead of simply an ethnography of a particular institution, however (see Barrabee, 1951; Belknap, 1956; Dunham and Weinberg, 1960; Perrucci, 1974; Stanton and Schwartz, 1954), the outcome in this case is a general delineation of an organizational type to which *all* mental hospitals allegedly belong, along with prisons, monasteries, military schools, old age homes, and concentration camps. Replete with vivid "references to mortifications that disrupt, defile, assault, or contaminate the self" (McEwen, 1980, p. 147), Goffman's account of these "total institutions" provides a powerful indictment of such places as engines of degradation and oppression, a finely rendered "symbolic presentation of organizational tyranny and a closed universe symbolizing the thwarting of human possibilities" (Perry, 1974, p. 353). Total institutions serve as places "of residence and work where a large number of like-situated individuals, cut off from the wider society for an appreciable period of time, together lead an enclosed, formally administered round of life" (Goffman, 1961, p. xiii). Contrary to at least their *ostensible* purpose (and not unlike Dickens's Marshalsea)[8], these were places that manufactured chronic deviants, the very human materials that justify their existence. Goffman's central thrust, that is, was to examine the impact of life in such an environment on the structure of the self and to contend that the crucial factor in forming the mental patient, for example, was his institution rather than his illness. Modifications, reactions, and adjustments, pathological as they might seem to an outsider, were instead to be viewed as the product of the ill effects of his environment (with all its peculiar routines and deprivations) rather than the natural outcome of an unfolding intraindividual pathology. The total institution was a monolithic structure, and the key to understanding its operations, so it was alleged, was that it resorted to "the handling of many human needs by the bureaucratic organization of whole blocks of people" (Goffman, 1961, p. 6) in a context that isolated them both physically and symbolically from the larger society.

But, as I have already signaled, there were serious weaknesses in the evidentiary base on which these extraordinarily far-reaching claims rest. There is, for example, not even a token attempt in Goffman's work to confront the issue of what explains inmates' presence in the mental hospital in the first place. We are instead supposed to rest content with an unsubstantiated claim that they are the victims of "contingencies," somehow "betrayed" into the institution by their nearest and dearest (for reasons that remain entirely obscure). The "blame" for their situation, then, lies not at all in their own conduct or mental state, but rather in a conspiracy of others to secure their exclusion from society. Likewise, the questions of the social location of madness, and of the kinds of existence to which hospitalization is an alternative are simply passed over in silence. And perhaps most notably of all, there is not even a token attempt to generate valid and reliable evidence essential to any credible assessment of the respective contribution of intrapsychic and environmental influences on what Goffman calls "the moral career of the mental patient." As Craig McEwen puts it, "Goffman's analysis has persuaded readers as much by its literary power as by the weight of its evidence"; indeed, it relies for its persuasiveness on our willingness to take "literary metaphor as established fact" (McEwen, 1980, pp. 147-148). (One might add that over the long haul, and in the face of accumulating research evidence tending to undermine its central contentions—nicely reviewed in McEwen, 1980—even the most finely wrought literary persuasion has lost much of its charm.)

The looming presence of the formal social control apparatus in modern societies, coupled with labeling theory's analytic focus on the ways in which society unintentionally creates or aggravates deviance in the very process of attempting to control it, prompted many others to launch studies of control agencies. These, too, tended to concentrate primarily upon "the direct impact on the processed deviants of organizational settings and programs" (Schur, 1971, p. 98), and to focus their attention quite narrowly on the role of the agencies in selecting and processing the deviant population. Some of this work, particularly that undertaken by more phenomenologically inclined researchers, has provided quite detailed and valuable insights into "the processes by which persons come to be defined, classified, and recorded in the categories of the agency's statistics" (Cicourel and Kitsuse, 1963, p. 9). David Sudnow (1965), for example, has nicely documented the transformational process through which the courts and the plea bargaining process constitute "normal crimes"; and more recently, Hugh Mehan (1985) has illuminated the complicated bureaucratic processes through which children are labeled "handicapped" and then ushered into special educational programs.

The stress on the complex, negotiated character of deviant definitions is still more apparent in Aaron Cicourel's work on juvenile delinquency. As he notes, when we merely extract abstract information from official records so that structural comparisons are possible (e.g., broken home, low income, ethnicity, negative social character) the contingencies of unfolding interaction, the typifications (theories of "good" and "bad" juveniles, families, etc.) are excluded from our understanding of how legal or other rules were invoked to justify a particular interpretation and course of action [Cicourel, 1968, p. 121]. Yet his evidence suggests that "[t]he physical appearance of the juveniles, their facial expressions, affectual communication, and body motion are all integral features of the action scene" (Cicourel, 1968, p. 122), all with effects on the disposition of the case. Consider, for example, the contrast between clinical and criminal interpretations of juvenile conduct:

A juvenile who is "appealing and attractive" and who "wants very much to be liked and relates in a friendly manner to all around her," is a prime candidate for clinical interpretations as opposed to criminal imputations. Finding "problems" in the home is not difficult . . . [and] the transformation of the juvenile into a sick object permits all concerned to suspend the criminal interpretations of her acts, even though the penal code sections are quoted each time the police report theft or burglary. Having established the juvenile as "sick," the [probation officer] must sustain this depiction despite activities by the juvenile appearing to contradict this label. But having the label, it is easier to "explain" infractions by reference to aggravating conditions and the necessity of "more treatment" [Cicourel, 1968, p. 132].

Cicourel's work stresses a complexity that is missing from most labeling theory. Indeed, from a microsociological direction, he has been sharply critical of societal reaction theory for oversimplifying the "problems of objectification and verification" involved in studying "practical decision making" (Cicourel, 1968, p. 15, 332). More generally, however, and particularly among those more centrally committed to the societal reaction paradigm, the tendency has been, in Lorber's (1967, p. 309; see also Gouldner, 1968, p. 107) phrase, to see the deviant as "the put-upon victim, with the social control agents as the villain of the piece." Yet subsequent research, while providing *some* support for the notion that efforts at social control may, under *some* circumstances, act to amplify the existing deviance, has undercut the rather crude idea that there exists "a simple chain of events from primary deviation, through reaction, to secondary deviation . . . [and shows that] [f]ar from being passive receptors of deviant (and stigmatic) labels, individuals and groups display various and versatile responses to labeling" (Harris and Hill, 1982, p. 164).

A few of the more perceptive labeling theorists have themselves become somewhat uncomfortable with the romanticizing of the deviant implicit in studies that portray them as "more sinned against than sinning." Lemert (1972, p. 16; see also Becker, 1974), for example, has complained of his work being distorted so as to accent "the arbitrariness of official action, stereotyped decision-making in bureaucratic contexts, bias in the administration of law," and so on. He seems tempted to attribute these "distortions" to the vulgarization of labeling theory and its assimilation to popular causes, as well as to the reaction against "the preeminence and intrusion of large scale, bureaucratized organizations in the lives of the individuals" (Lemert, 1972, pp. 16-17). But in a deeper sense, as he himself begins to recognize elsewhere in the same essay, the crudeness was built into the approach from the outset, and has merely become more salient and noticeable with time, and as work within the perspective has sought to encompass concerns that were originally peripheral to it (such as the institutional arrangements that order political processes, or the nature of bureaucratic agencies of social control and their linkages to the larger social order, of which they are both a part and an essential support).

Labeling theory's deepest intellectual debts are to the symbolic interactionist view of society. Expressed in the dramaturgical metaphor, the central metatheoretical assumptions of this approach led to the overriding concern with deviant identity, as well as encouraging the crucial but only partially liberating insight that control could be an independent factor in shaping and producing deviance. But along with this undoubted advance came an adherence to a vision of social life as essentially episodic, and an analytical approach that largely confined itself to interpersonal transactions taking place in a resolutely ahistorical and noninstitutional context (see Gouldner, 1970, p. 391).

In keeping with this orientation to the world, the work of most societal reaction theorists "is chiefly distinguished by a phenomenalism and an emphasis on *Verstehen* [that is, by a stress on developing purely descriptive accounts of observable phenomena, and by an effort to put oneself in the place of the group being studied in order to describe the world from its subjec-

tive point of view; see Becker, 1967], which propel the analysis toward the study of small bounded settings. Both features engender an ingrained distrust of approaches which are thought to reify, systematize, or abstract" (Rock, 1974). To remove one's analysis from concrete, observable settings, it is argued, is to court the danger of falsifying and distorting the phenomena one seeks to describe and explain.

Hence the inseparable connection, which Howard Becker (1974, p. 52) celebrates, "between an interactionist theory of deviance and a reliance upon intensive field observation as a major method of data gathering." But the stress on ethnographic description and what David Matza (1969) terms *naturalistic faithfulness* also brought in its train the adoption of the Meadian view of society as process; an emphasis on "the vagueness, ambiguity and fluidity of everyday life" (Rock, 1974, p. 141); a perspective that envisions the larger social world as a structureless flux, within which "nothing is fixed or independent, everything is plastic and takes influence as well as gives it." (Cooley, 1918, pp. 44-45) The broader organizing contextual features of the interaction might be ritually acknowledged, but methodologically, conceptually, and even physically (because of the all but exclusive emphasis on participant observation of face-to-face interaction as a methodological tool), institutional and structural factors remained inaccessible to analysis.

In response to the first criticisms of this sort (e.g., Gouldner, 1968; Liazos, 1972; Spitzer, 1975; Thio, 1973), labeling theory's defenders tended to dismiss the objections as true but irrelevant, "basically unfair [attempts] to criticize a theory for what it does not set out to do." Invoking the truism that "no theory explains everything and the analyst is entitled to set his boundaries" (Plummer, 1979, pp. 103, 105), they claimed that it was "not the task of social psychology, whether symbolic interactionist or some other perspective, to account in great detail for the systematic and complex interrelationships among institutions, organizations, social classes, large-scale social change, and other 'structural' phenomena." (Hewitt, 1976, p. 148) But the earliest theoretical statements underpinning the societal reaction research agenda had emphasized the importance of the twin processes of rule creation and rule enforcement, and as empirical work increasingly moved to encompass these subjects, so the bracketing of the macrosociological realm became steadily less and less defensible.

In analyzing the social control apparatus, for example, societal reaction theorists opted all too frequently to confine their analysis to the immediate face-to-face encounters of deviants and front-line controllers, and to the shape of the resulting "moral careers," while systematically ignoring the organizations themselves, and the overarching social structural context within which any given agency of social control necessarily operates. Even in the hands of as skillful and sensitive an analyst as Erving Goffman, the outcome was "an explicitly conservative vision of societal process, founded . . . upon a total immobilism of micro-structures and a total indifference to macrostructures" (Sedgwick, 1982, p. 22).[9] Where efforts *were* made to examine the impact of the larger social and political order, the attempt to extend the face-to-face model of individual interaction to an examination of structural dynamics tended decisively to limit their value. David Matza's (1969) attempt to grapple with the importance of the state and political processes, perhaps exhibits these deficiencies in their starkest form, portraying the political system as a Leviathan whose operations remain wholly mysterious and whose "motives" entirely escape scrutiny. But an essentially personalistic approach to understanding political structures and processes is an enduring, if less explicit, feature of most interactionist forays into this level of analysis.

So we find an acknowledgement of the role of power in the social production of deviance that is formal rather than substantive, having little discernible effect on theory or analysis. (Certainly, the acknowledgement of the truism that those who label—or who construct and impose new labels—are more powerful than those who are labeled represents a dismal substitute for the analysis of power structures and their impact.)[10] One of the topics labeling theorists increasingly attended to was the question of *how* the rules that ascribe deviant status were first created. But within this body of work, "it is most difficult to discover . . . a description of legislation and rule-making which is more than anthropomorphic conspiracy theory." (Rock, 1974, p. 144) Representative here is the most widely cited study of the rule making process, Howard Becker's (1963, chaps. 7 and 8) analysis of the criminalization of marijuana use. Significantly, Becker concentrates on the role of "moral entrepreneurs" and "moral crusades," and essentially avoids any discussion of the social and political context within which the Marijuana Tax Act came to be passed. His distinction between crusading reformers and professional reformers is then attached to a simplistic portrait of their respective interests: the crusader pictures his mission as holy; the enforcer "may

not be interested in the content of the rule itself, but only in the fact that the existence of the rule provides him with a job, a profession, and a raison d'etre" (Becker, 1963, p. 156).[11] The final outcome, in Edwin Lemert's (1972, p. 19) apt and acid epigram, is no more than "a type of *reductio ad personam* theory."

During the 1970s powerful critiques of other aspects of societal reaction theory were voiced, compounding the growing dissatisfaction with labeling theorists' accounts of rule making and rule enforcement. Conceptually, the approach was criticized as too vague and unsystematic to warrant the status of a "theory," a charge that was difficult to dispute and one that most of the perspective's major advocates readily conceded was true. Labeling theory, it now appeared, "was never meant to be a formal theory" (Schur, 1980, p. 402; see also Becker, 1974; Kitsuse, 1980; Lemert, 1972, 1974), but was instead a new conception" (Gibbs, 1982) that at best deserved the status of "a sensitizing theory" (Scheff, 1974, p. 445). It offered a new set of heuristic questions, rather than a developed and testable theoretical analysis.

Much of the excitement aroused by the societal reaction perspective came from the new etiological account it appeared to offer of stable deviance, and the empirical accuracy of these assertions likewise came under increasing attack. Researchers of an empiricist bent, many of them trained in the distinctly different traditions characterizing mainstream criminology, presented persuasive evidence that so-called primary deviance was far more significant in accounting for deviant careers than almost all labeling theorists were willing to allow (see Gove, 1970, 1974, 1980; Hagan, 1974; Hirschi, 1973, 1980; Nettler, 1978, 1979; Wellford, 1975), and sharply questioned formulations that suggested deviance was largely an ascribed and arbitrary, rather than an achieved (and perhaps deserved) status. A few societal reaction theorists, notably Thomas Scheff (1974), tried valiantly to reinterpret the empirical evidence to show that control was indeed the primary etiological factor in the genesis of deviance; but most of their erstwhile allies chose to adopt a less exposed, if curiously lame, position: Claims that the societal reaction was the "cause" of deviance were now dismissed as a vulgarization of labeling theory, a mistaken attempt to assimilate the approach to a positivistic model of social process (Becker, 1974; Kitsuse, 1980; Lemert, 1972).

The unsatisfactory nature of this line of defense was compounded by the fact that labeling claims were simultaneously under attack from an even more staunchly antipositivist quarter, the ranks of the ethnomethodologists and their allies. Here the complaint was the rather different one—that the societal reaction approach had underestimated the situationally problematic nature of moral and member meanings, the "awesome indexicality of the social world" (Rock, 1979a, p. 15), and the crucial role of actors' subjective meanings and the constitutive rules of everyday praxis in the understanding of social action. Scheff's account of the construction of the category of "mental illness" came under particularly heavy criticism in these respects. His theoretical description of a category of socially unspecified rules was criticized for tending "to confuse normative rules with the evaluation of an actor's performance in relation to those rules" (Morgan, 1975, p. 273); and his claim that insanity differed from other forms of deviance because of the *category* of rule that had been broken was shown to be seriously misleading. The normative rules whose violation provokes the label of mad are often the very reverse of "residual," being both explicit and central to the structure of organized social life. Consider, for example, the occasions when a serious criminal charge is met by a plea of not guilty by reason of insanity. What is asserted here is *not* that a particular category of nonspecific rule has been violated, but rather that a highly specific rule has been violated in a way that renders the ascription of responsibility and blame socially inappropriate. To put it another way, "what is significant about insanity is not the category of rule that is broken, or the kind of behaviour involved, but how the *cognitive and moral relationship of a person to their acts* is socially perceived and explained" (Morgan, 1975, p. 273). Where common sense breaks down, and we are unable to account for deviance in terms of our conventional vocabulary of motives and goals, then insanity is likely to be attributed to the perpetrator (see also Coulter, 1973, 1979; Ingleby, 1982, 1983).

Although societal reaction theory was without question the conventional wisdom among sociologists of deviance in 1970, some 10 years later it had clearly lost its intellectual preeminence. But while conflict theorists (Turk, 1979, 1982), *soi-disant* Marxists (Greenberg, 1981; Hall et al., 1978; Quinney, 1977; Smart, 1977; Spitzer, 1975), ethnomethodologists (Cicourel, 1968; Coulter, 1973, 1979; Pollner, 1974, 1978), and proud, card-carrying positivists (Hirschi, 1980; Tittle, 1980) had actively and successfully plumbed its weaknesses and deficiencies, none of them had succeeded in establishing an alternative orientation to the field that commanded wide assent. The study of deviance is thus in a state of profound epistemological and theoretical confusion at present, with few signs that the intellectual crisis will soon be resolved.

The New Sociology of Social Control

If the bickering and disputes within the sociology of deviance are signs of the exhaustion of a once-dominant paradigm without the emergence of any satisfactory alternative, the raging debates among sociologists and historians engaged in studying the related phenomenon of social control have a very different flavor and import. Having ceased for some decades to be a topic of much intellectual moment in sociology, and having never enjoyed more than a marginally respectable status among academic historians, the study of the full panoply of efforts at social control—law and the forms of punishment, responses to madness, the mechanisms for the containment of poverty and disorder, and so forth—has suddenly acquired a new cachet in both disciplines. More remarkably still, there has been a striking convergence of interests and cross-fertilization of ideas and methods among sociologists and historians as they have approached this subject matter. If quarrels are fierce and consensus rare, this is accompanied by a sense of real intellectual progress and excitement.

Within sociology, societal reaction theory, whatever the deficiencies of its own studies of the phenomenon of social control, can clearly take a good deal of the credit for the revival of interest in this subject matter. Goffman's work on total institutions, for instance, was notable, among other things, for suggesting that what had hitherto been seen as disarticulated and disconnected in fact shared principles of coordination and coherence. Similarly, labeling theory's break with the traditional notion that the societal response to deviance represented no more than a benign and defensive response to the presence of individual pathology, and its emphasis on the active role the social control apparatus played in defining and identifying, shaping, and molding the deviant prompted a shift away from an obsessive concern with the attributes of individual deviants and toward a more wide-ranging interest in social process. And criticisms of the theory's blatant neglect of the impact of power, and of social and political structures, found their most obvious application in renewed attention to the interrelationships of state, society, and social control.

Nor can one discount the role of fashion. The intellectual prominence and influence of the French poststructuralist, Michel Foucault—however the Foucauldian cult is to be explained—obviously has played an almost equally important role in making the prison, the madhouse, and the leprosarium suitable topics for elevated intellectual discourse. (See, especially, Foucault, 1965, 1975; and, as samples of the Foucault industry, Dreyfus and Rabinow, 1982; Sheridan, 1980.) And the concern among historians with "history from below" has given to the history of riot, blackmail, poaching, smuggling, arson, wrecking, and madness (to say nothing of the police and the penitentiary, the psychiatrist and the madhouse, the social worker and his or her caseload), a wholly new significance (see Evans, 1982; Hay, Rule, and Thompson, 1975; Ignatieff, 1978; Perrot, 1980; Rothman, 1971, 1980; Thompson, 1975.)

However sizable their differences from one another, to a very large extent the new theorists of social control have shared some fundamental guiding assumptions:

> that a society's mechanisms of social control form a coherent whole; that the principles of that coherence change over time; and that examining the mechanisms of control, their principles of coherence, and the processes through which both change provides a window on larger matters . . . [most notably] the features and dynamics of social stability and change and the control functions of the state [Messinger and Greenspan, 1986, pp. 58-59].

The once dominant conception of social control as a linchpin of social order and the expression of fundamental shared social needs—a conception still taken seriously by some sociologists (e.g., Janowitz, 1975; Pitts, 1968)—has increasingly been replaced by a view that sees the relationships between "society" and "social control" as problematic and contingent over space and time (Black, 1984; Mayer, 1983; Meier, 1982). Instead of assuming that laws, regulations, and other socially organized sanctions are embedded in the immediate and informal arenas of "role taking" (Mead, 1925), the "complementarity of expectations" (Parsons, 1951), voluntary associations (Park and Burgess, 1925; Ross, 1901), or "community" (see Davis and Anderson, 1983, pp. 7-10), most recent accounts have moved the more coercive dimensions of social ordering to the fore. They have portrayed much of the social control apparatus

as consciously fashioned through the visible hand of definable organizations, groups, and classes, rather than being "naturally" produced by the invisible hand of society; and emphasized the significance of conflict, hierarchy, and ideology in the ordering and regulation of social life.

Most ambitiously, Donald Black and his associates (Black, 1976, 1984) have attempted to develop "a general theory of social control" (defined as "all of the processes by which people define and respond to deviant behavior"; Black, 1984, p. xi). Their approach sees social control as a "dependent variable, a 'thing' to be predicted and explained, a 'thing' of measurable quantity, a 'thing' that somehow varies with its own location and direction in space" (Cohen, 1985a, p. 715); and self-consciously focuses attention on forms of control that have little or nothing to do with the activities of the state: vengeance, gossip, ridicule, compensation, therapy, and the like. Black's project is somehow to transform the study of social control into a quantitative science, building upon his earlier work on "the behavior of law" (Black, 1976) to create a set of testable propositions linked to a consistent general theory.

Such an approach assumes that a concern with consciousness and meaning can be safely discarded in favor of a natural science model of social explanation. Understandably, this position has not commanded universal assent. Even those committed to the value of the attempt concede the deficiencies of the practice (Hagan, 1985); while for others, the whole enterprise is "improbable" if not misguided from the outset (Cohen, 1985a; Greenberg, 1983). In general, however, the inability of its supporters to advance much beyond programmatic calls for an articulated and testable theory, and their concentration upon "a peculiar landscape of social control [which proceeds] . . . as if the modern state does not exist" (Cohen, 1985a, p. 717) have distinctly limited the appeal of all such efforts.

The most influential recent studies of social control have begun instead with very different theoretical presuppositions and empirically have concentrated most of their attention on what Black terms "governmental social control." Politics and history have in the process been moved to center stage, as part of a serious effort to locate social control in historical, social, and even physical space. And such efforts have been marked by serious skepticism about the professed aims, beliefs, and intentions of those establishing and running the various parts of the social control apparatus; a concern with analyzing power and its effects; and curiosity about the relationships between intentions and consequences.

At the risk of some oversimplification, one can identify a number of problematic issues that have confronted those attempting to make sense of this terrain: (1) the impact of state, economy, and ideology on social control, particularly the ability of these forces to create, redefine, and reorganize our understandings of both the subjects and mechanisms of social control; (2) how and why certain actions, attributes, and actors become subject to social control under specific historical and cultural conditions; (3) the ways in which modern control systems (e.g., law, therapy, or welfare) and those who work within them (judges, lawyers, police, psychiatrists, social workers, and others) are both controlling of and controlled by the "deviants" they seek to manage; (4) the origins and effects of the professionalization of social control, and the interrelationships of power and knowledge; and (5), how one is to explain the puzzle of constancy *and* change in the locus, functions, and justification of control in modern states.

Many of the attempts to grapple with these issues have focused on the establishment of certain "master trends" (Cohen, 1985b) in the late eighteenth and early nineteenth centuries: the transformation of the law and of punitive strategies and tactics, including the decline of punishments visited upon the body, the rise of the penitentiary, and the not unconnected growth of bureaucratically organized public police forces (Foucault, 1977; Hay, Rule, and Thompson, 1975; Ignatieff, 1978; Miller, 1977; Rothman, 1971; Spitzer and Scull, 1977); the incarceration of the mad in state-supported asylums, and the emergence of the profession of psychiatry (Brown, 1983; Castel, 1976; Foucault, 1965; Ingleby, 1983; Scull, 1975, 1976, 1979). More recently, scholars have extended their analyses back into the seventeenth and eighteenth centuries (Haagen, 1983; Lenman and Parker, 1980; Ritchie, 1984; Rock, 1983) and forward into the twentieth (Fox, 1978; Liss and Schlossman, 1984; Rothman, 1980). At the extreme, this entails attempts to decipher the workings of the social control in the present (American Behavioral Scientist, 1981; Cohen, 1979, 1985a; Garland and Young, 1983; Jacobs, 1977; Lerman, 1982; Scull, 1984; Shearing and Stenning, 1981, 1983; South, 1984; Spitzer and Scull, 1977), long the central concern of most sociological treatises on social control. But even here the commitment to grounding the analysis in historical context and to addressing issues of power and ideology serve to distinguish contemporary analysts from their predecessors.

Deep divisions remain. Current work is marked by a much more sophisticated grasp of the nature of ideology, those images, beliefs, and systems of meaning that connect the interests and directives of the controllers with the perceptions and proclivities of the controlled. But debates remain fierce about the relative weight one should assign to ideology in producing and sustaining structures of social control (Cohen, 1983; Davis, 1980; Rothman, 1983; Schlossman, 1977; Scull, 1981, 1983). The role of professionals in the social control process has been central both to recent Anglo-American work in this area (Dowbiggin, 1985; Rothman, 1980; Scull, 1975, 1976; Smith, 1981; Treacher and Baruch, 1980; Zola, 1972) and to that inspired by Foucault's emphasis on the so-called "power-knowledge spiral" (Castel, 1976; Castel, Castel, and Lovel, 1982; Donzelot, 1980; Foucault, 1977, 1980). But where one group of analysts sees professionals as capturing a particular territory, the other stresses the role of professions in actively defining "the social"; where one distinguishes knowledge and power, the other assimilates them, stressing that "power produces; it produces reality; it produces domains of objects and rituals of truth" (Foucault, 1977); where one emphasizes the *delegation* of power to the professions by the state, the other views the experts' *savoir/pouvoir* as arising independent of the state and concentrates on the construction of "genealogies of power." Yet neither, as Ingleby (1983, 1985) points out, solves the question of "which values and interest groups will be supported by professional interventions." Analyses which point to economic structures and to the activities of the state as crucial explanatory variables (Cohen, 1985b; Hay, Rule, and Thompson, 1975; Ignatieff, 1978; Scull, 1979; Thompson, 1975) are countered by other work that explicitly rejects any analytic schema in which notions of central state power and the economic determination of action play any central role (Foucault, 1977); or by a no less thoroughgoing critique that attacks a fixation on the state and urges us to focus our attention on how "the powers of moral and punitive enforcement are distributed throughout civil society" (Ignatieff, 1983, p. 100, recanting his own earlier position; Black, 1984).

Such disputes, of course, reflect larger epistemological, meta-theoretical, and interpretive differences between the protagonists in these debates. Precisely because of this, they are unlikely to be resolved in the foreseeable future, or perhaps at all. But to note this degree of intellectual fragmentation and disagreement is to say little more than that the sociology of social control is no more (and no less) able to overcome certain profound intellectual and ideological perplexities than is the larger discipline of which it is a part. And it is precisely in its reconnection of the study of social control with the larger sociological agenda that recent work in the field has made its greatest contribution.[12]

NOTES

1. Compare Robert Merton's revealing acknowledgment, in the preface to his *Social Theory and Social Structure*, of his gratitude to Pitirim Sorokin for helping "me escape from . . . the slum-encouraged provincialism of thinking that the primary subject-matter of sociology was centered in such peripheral problems of social life as divorce and juvenile delinquency." (Merton, 1968, p. xiii)

2. As Matza (1969, p. 15) puts it, "the purpose of much research on deviation has been to assist established society ultimately to rid itself of such troublesome activities. . . . A basic difficulty with a correctional perspective is that it systematically interferes with the capacity to . . . comprehend the subject of inquiry."

3. For the contemporary debate, see the exchange between Durkheim and Tarde, translated and reprinted in Lukes and Scull (1983, pp. 76-101) and the discussion in Matza (1969, pp. 15-19).

4. George Herbert Mead's essay, "The Psychology of Punitive Justice" (Mead, 1918), provides an indigenous American version of these arguments.

5. No doubt Alvin Gouldner was also correct when he attributed some of the attractions of the subject matter to a narcissistic pleasure many academics seem to take in the tweaking of philistine bourgeois sensibilities.

6. Of course, this attachment to a deviant methodology, while helping to attract the disaffected, was not without its effects on the standing of the subdiscipline. The embrace of a variant of anthropological fieldwork and of a set of pretheoretical assumptions that did not lend themselves to the creation of systematic theory (indeed, that emerged, as I shall suggest, from a theoretical tradition actively hostile to systematization), added to the low status of its objects of observation to ensure that the appeal of even a revitalized sociology of deviance continued to be contained within strict limits.

7. For further discussion of the limitations of Durkheim's position on these issues, see Lukes and Scull (1983, pp. 20-24).

8. Foucault was to argue, a decade and a half later and with characteristics no reference to Goffman's work, that this was precisely their purpose and social role.

9. It is a striking testimony to the restrictiveness of this social vision that Goffman's description of total institutions as if they existed in a timeless Platonic realm, wholly insulated from history and from larger societal forces, was published just as evidence was accumulating that the demise of one the most important such institutions, the state mental hospital, might be imminent (see Scull, 1984). Similarly, his portrait of stigma (Goffman, 1963) is essentially a frozen one, viewing its imposition and management as bound by such "complex rules that it seemed impossible to think of violating or altering them. To be crippled or black was to be stigmatized, and no escape routes were open. Yet within a decade, black would become beautiful and the handicapped would mount successful campaigns for their rights" (Rothman 1983, p. 108)

10. When Howard Becker (1974) felt called upon to defend societal reaction theory against such charges, his defense instead revealed the essential accuracy of the criticism. Apparently, the fact that he and others had elsewhere insisted that upper-class white males were more likely to be successful entrepreneurs and to succeed in imposing their definitions on others was somehow supposed to count as an effective refutation of complaints that the role of power was ignored or inadequately handled within the labeling tradition. Similarly revealing are the examples he gives, later in the same paper, of what he has in mind when he speaks of "power relationships": "parents and children"; "welfare worker and client"; "teacher and student."

11. David Rothman's (1980) recent attempt to explain Progressive era "reforms" in the criminal justice, mental health, and juvenile justice realms rests upon essentially the same set of distinctions. For extended discussions of the resulting deficiencies of this type of analysis, see Davis (1980) and Scull (1981).

12. For assesments of the current "state of play" in the various subfields of the sociology of social control, see Cohen and Scull (1983), especially Part I.

REFERENCES

American Behavioral Scientist. 1981. New Forms of Social Control (July). (entire issue)

Anderson, N. 1923. *The Hobo*. Chicago: University of Chicago Press.

Barrabee, P. 1951. "A Study of a Mental Hospital: The Effect of Its Social Structure on Its Functions." Ph.D. dissertation, Harvard University.

Becker, H. S. 1963. *Outsiders: Studies in the Sociology of Deviance*. New York: Free Press.

_____ 1967. "Whose Side Are We On?" *Social Problems* 14:239-247.

_____ 1974. "Labelling Theory Reconsidered." Pp. 41-46 in *Deviance and Social Control*, edited by P. Rock and M. McIntosh. London: Tavistock.

Beirne, P. 1985. "Quetelet and Social Statistics." Unpublished manuscript, Sociology Department, University of Southern Maine.

Belknap, I. 1956. *Human Problems of a State Mental Hospital*. New York: McGraw-Hill.

Bell, Daniel. 1960. *The End of Ideology*. New York: Free Press.

Bernard, J. 1929. "The History and Prospects of Sociology in the United States." In *Trends in American Sociology*, edited by G. Lundberg, R. Bain, and N. Anderson. New York: Harper.

Bittner, E. 1967. "The Police on Skid Row: A Study of Peace Keeping." *American Sociological Review* 32:699-715.

Black, D. 1976. *The Behavior of Law*. New York: Academic Press.

_____, ed. 1984. *Toward a General Theory of Social Control*. Orlando, FL: Academic Press.

Borgatta, E. and H. J. Meyer. 1959. *Social Control and the Foundation of Sociology*. Boston: Beacon.

Brown, J. 1983. "Psychiatrists and the State in Tsarist Russia." In *Social Control and the State*, edited by S. Cohen and A. Scull. Oxford: Blackwell.

Bryan, J. H. 1965. "Apprenticeships in Prostitution." *Social Problems* 12:287-297.

_____ 1966. "Occupational Ideologies and Individual Attitudes of Call Girls." *Social Problems* 13:441-450.

Bulmer, M. 1984. *The Chicago School of Sociology*. Chicago: University of Chicago Press.

Carey, J. 1975. *Sociology and Public Affairs: The Chicago School*. Beverly Hills, CA: Sage.

Castel, R. 1976. *L'Ordre Psychiatrique: L'Age d'Or de l'Alienisme*. Paris: Minuit.

Castel, F, R. Castel, and A. Lovell. 1982. *The Psychiatric Society*. New York: Columbia University Press.

Cicourel, A. 1968. *The Social Organization of Juvenile Justice*. New York: John Wiley.

_____ and J. Kitsuse. 1963. *The Educational Decision Makers*. Indianapolis: Bobbs-Merrill.

Clinard, M., ed. 1964. *Anomie and Deviant Behavior: A Discussion and Critique*. New York: Free Press.

Cloward, R. and L. Ohlin. 1960. *Delinquency and Opportunity*. New York: Free Press.

Cohen, A. 1955. *Delinquent Boys*. New York: Free Press.

_____ 1965. "The Sociology of the Deviant Act: Anomie Theory and Beyond." *American Sociological Review* 30:5-14.

_____ 1966. *Deviance and Control*. Englewood Cliffs, NJ: Prentice-Hall.

Cohen, Stanley. 1979. "The Punitive City: Notes on the Future of Social Control." *Contemporary Crises* 3:339-363.

_____ 1983. "Social Control Talk: Telling Stories About Correctional Change." In *The Power to Punish*, edited by D. Garland and P. Young. London: Heinemann.

_____ 1985a. "Review Essay on Donald Black's *Toward a General Theory of Social Control*."

American Journal of Sociology 91:714-717.

_____ 1985b. *Visions of Social Control*. Cambridge: Polity Press.

_____ and A. Scull, eds. 1983. *Social Control and the State: Historical and Comparative Essays*. New York: St. Martin's.

Cooley, C. H. 1918. *The Social Process*. New York: Scribner's.

Coser, L. 1960. "Durkheim's Conservatism and Its Implications for His Sociological Theory." In *Essays on Sociology and Philosophy by Emile Durkheim et al.*, edited by K. Wolff. New York: Harper.

Coulter, J. 1973. *Approaches to Insanity*. London: Martin Robertson.

_____ 1979. *The Social Construction of Mind*. London: Macmillan.

Cressey, P. 1932. *The Taxi Dance Hall*. Chicago: University of Chicago Press.

Davis, D. B. 1980. "The Crime of Reform." *New York Review of Books* (June 26):14-17.

Davis, F. 1964. "Deviance Disavowal: The Management of Strained Interaction by the Visibly Handicapped." In *The Other Side*, edited by H. S. Becker. New York: Free Press.

_____ and L. Munoz. 1968. "Heads and Freaks: Patterns and Meanings of Drug Use Among Hippies." *Journal of Health and Social Behavior* 9:156-164.

Davis, K. 1971. "Prostitution." Pp. 313-360 in *Contemporary Social Problems*, edited by R. Merton and R. Nisbet. New York: Harcourt, Brace.

Davis, N. J. and B. Anderson. 1983. *Social Control: The Production of Deviance in the Modern State*. New York: Irvington.

Dibble, V. 1975. *The Legacy of Albion Small*. Chicago: University of Chicago Press.

Donzelot, J. 1980. *The Policing of Families*. New York: Pantheon.

Douglas, J. D. 1967. *The Social Meanings of Suicide*. Princeton, NJ: Princeton University Press.

_____ 1970. "Deviance and Order in a Pluralistic Society." In *Sociological Theory*, edited by E. A. Tiryakian and J. McKinney. New York: Appleton-Century-Crofts.

Dowbiggin, I. 1985. "French Psychiatry, Hereditarianism, and Professional Legitimacy: 1840-1900." Pp. 135-165 in *Research in Law, Deviance, and Social Control*, vol. 7, edited by S. Spitzer and A. Scull. Greenwich, CT: JAI Press.

Downes, D. and P. Rock. 1982. *Understanding Deviance*. Oxford: Oxford University Press.

Drake, S. and H. Cayton. 1945. *Black Metropolis*. New York: Harcourt Brace.

Dreyfus, H. L. and P. Rabinow. 1982. *Michel Foucault: Beyond Structuralism and Hermeneutics*. Chicago: University of Chicago Press.

Dunham, H. and S. K. Weinberg. 1960. *The Culture of the State Mental Hospital*. Detroit: Wayne State University Press.

Durkheim, E. 1951. *Suicide*. New York: Free Press.

_____ 1964. *The Division of Labor in Society*. New

York: Free Press.

———— 1966. *The Rules of Sociological Method*. New York: Free Press.

———— 1982. *The Rules of Sociological Method*. New York: Free Press.

———— 1984. *The Division of Labor in Society*. New York: Free Press.

Erikson, K. 1966. *Wayward Puritans*. New York: John Wiley.

Evans, R. 1982. *The Fabrication of Virtue: English Prison Architecture, 1750-1840*. Cambridge: Cambridge University Press.

Fox, Richard. 1978. *So Far Disordered in Mind*. Berkeley: University of California Press.

Foucault, M. 1965. *Madness and Civilization*. New York: Mentor Books.

———— 1975. *Surveiller et Punir*. Paris: Gallimard.

———— 1977. *Discipline and Punish*. New York: Pantheon.

———— 1980. *Power/Knowledge: Selected Interviews and Other Writings*. London: Harvester.

Garfinkel, H. 1956. "The Conditions of Successful Degradation Ceremonies." *American Journal of Sociology* 61:420-424.

Garland, D. and P. Young. 1983. *The Power to Punish*. London: Heinemann.

Gibbs, J. 1982. "Issues in Defining Deviant Behavior." In *Theoretical Perspectives on Deviance*, edited by R. A. Scott and J. D. Douglas. New York: Basic Books.

Goffman, E. 1961. *Asylums*. Garden City, NY: Doubleday.

———— 1963. *Stigma*. Harmondsworth: Penguin.

Gold, M. 1966. "Undetected Delinquent Behavior." *Journal of Research in Crime and Delinquency* 3:27-46.

Gouldner, A. 1962. "Anti-Minotaur: The Myth of a Value-Free Sociology." *Social Problems* 10.

———— 1968. "The Sociologist as Partisan: Sociology and the Welfare State." *American Sociologist* 3:103-116.

———— 1970. *The Coming Crisis of Western Sociology*. New York: Basic Books.

Gove, W. 1970. "Societal Reaction as an Explanation of Mental Illness: An Evaluation." *American Sociological Review* 35:873-884.

———— 1974. "Individual Resources and Mental Hospitalization: A Comparison and Evaluation of the Societal Reaction and Psychiatric Perspectives." *American Sociological Review* 39:36-100.

———— 1980. *The Labelling of Deviance: Evaluating a Perspective*. Beverly Hills, CA: Sage.

Greenberg, D. 1981. *Crime and Capitalism*. Palo Alto, CA: Mayfield.

———— 1983. "Donald Black's Sociology of Law: A Critique." *Law and Society Review* 17:337-368.

Haagen, P. 1983. "Eighteenth Century English Society and the Debt Law." Pp. 222-248 in *Social Control and the State*, edited by S. Cohen and A. Scull. Oxford: Blackwell.

Hagan, J. 1974. "Extra-Legal Attributes and Criminal Sentencing: An Assessment of a Sociological

Viewpoint." *Law and Society Review* 8:357-383.

———— 1985. "The Science of Social Control." *Contemporary Sociology* 14:667-670.

Hall, S., C. Critcher, T. Jefferson, J. Clarke, and B. Roberts. 1978. *Policing the Crisis*. London: Macmillan.

Harris, A. R. and G. D. Hill. 1982. "The Social Psychology of Deviance: Toward a Reconciliation with Social Structure." *Annual Review of Sociology* 8:161-186.

Hay, D., J. Rule, and E. P. Thompson, eds. 1975. *Albion's Fatal Tree*. New York: Pantheon.

Hewitt, J. 1976. *Self and Society*. London: Allyn and Bacon.

Heyl, B. 1979. *The Madam as Entrepreneur*. New Brunswick, NJ: Transaction Books.

Hindelgang, M., T. Hirschi, and J. Weis. 1979. "Correlates of Delinquency: The Illusion of Discrepancy Between Self-Report and Official Measures." *American Sociological Review* 44: 995-1014.

Hirschi, T. 1973. "Procedural Rules and the Study of Deviant Behavior." *Social Problems* 21:254-268.

———— 1980. "Labelling Theory and Juvenile Delinquency: An Assessment of the Evidence." In *The Labelling of Deviance*, edited by W. Gove. Beverly Hills, CA: Sage.

Hughes, E. C. 1979. "Preface." In *Robert Park*, edited by W. Rauschenbush. Durham, NC: Duke University Press.

Ignatieff, M. 1978. *A Just Measure of Pain: The Penitentiary and the Industrial Revolution*. New York: Pantheon.

———— 1983. "State, Civil Society and Total Institutions: A Critique of Recent Social Histories of Punishment." Pp. 75-105 in *Social Control and the State*, edited by S. Cohen and A. Scull eds. Oxford: Blackwell.

Ingleby, D. 1982. "The Social Construction of Mental Illness." In *The Problem of Medical Knowledge*, edited by A. Treacher and P. Wright. Edinburgh: Edinburgh University Press.

———— 1983. "Mental Health and Social Order." Pp. 141-190 in *Social Control and the State*, edited by S. Cohen and A. Scull. Oxford: Blackwell.

———— 1985. "Professionals as Socializers: The 'Psy' Complex." Pp. 79-110 in *Research in Law, Deviance, and Social Control*, vol. 7, edited by S. Spitzer and A. Scull. Greenwich, CT: JAI Press.

Jacobs, J. 1977. *Stateville: The Penitentiary and Mass Society*. Chicago: University of Chicago Press.

James, W. 1949. *Pragmatism*. New York.

Janowitz, M. 1975. "Sociological Theory and Social Control." *American Journal of Sociology* 81:82-108.

———— 1978. *The Last Half Century*. Chicago: University of Chicago Press.

Kitsuse, J. 1968. "Societal Reaction to Deviant Behavior." Pp. 15-24 in *Deviance: The Interactionist Perspective*, edited by E. Rubington and

M. Weinberg. New York: Macmillan.

———— 1980. "The 'New Conception of Deviance' and Its Critics." In *The Labelling of Deviance*, edited by W. Gove. Beverly Hills, CA: Sage.

———— and A. Cicourel. 1963. "A Note on the Use of Official Statistics." *Social Problems* 2: 131-139.

Laing, R. D. and A. Esterson. 1968. *Sanity, Madness, and the Family*. Baltimore, MD: Penguin Books.

Landesco, J. 1968. *Organized Crime in Chicago*. Chicago: University of Chicago Press.

Lattimore, F. 1914. "Three Studies in Housing and Responsibility." In *The Pittsburgh Survey*, edited by P. Kellog. New York: Russell Sage Foundation.

Lemert, E. 1951. *Social Pathology*. New York: McGraw-Hill.

———— 1964. "Social Structure, Social Control, and Deviation." Pp. 59-75 in *Anomie and Deviant Behavior*, edited by M. Clinard. New York: Free Press.

———— 1967. *Human Deviance, Social Problems, and Social Control*. Englewood Cliffs, NJ: Prentice-Hall.

———— 1972. *Human Deviance, Social Problems, and Social Control*. Englewood Cliffs, NJ: Prentice-Hall.

———— 1974. "Response to Critics: Feedback and Choice." In *The Uses of Controversy in Sociology*, edited by L. Coser and O. Larsen. New York: Macmillan.

Lenman, B. and G. Parker, G. 1980. "The State, the Community, and the Criminal Law in Early Modern Europe." In *Crime and the Law*, edited by V.A.C. Gatrell, B. Lenham, and G. Parker. London: Europa.

Lerman, P. 1982. *Deinstitutionalization and the Welfare State*. New Brunswick, NJ: Rutgers University Press.

Liazos, A. 1972. "The Poverty of the Sociology of Deviance: Nuts, Sluts, and Perverts." *Social Problems* 20:103-120.

Liss, Julia and Steven Schlossman. 1984. "The Contours of Crime Preventin in August Vollmer's Berkeley." Pp. 57-78 in *Research in Law, Deviance, and Social Control*. vol. 6, edited by S. Spitzer and A. Scull. Greenwich, CT: JAI Press.

Lorber, J. 1967. "Deviance as Performance: The Case of Illness." *Social Problems* 14:302-310.

Lubove, R. 1971. *The Professional Altruist*. New York: Atheneum.

Lukes, S. and A. Scull, eds. 1983. *Durkheim and the Law*. Oxford: Blackwell.

MacRae, D. 1962. *Ideology and Society*. New York: Free Press.

Mandeville, B. 1711. *The Fable of the Bees*. London.

Matza, D. 1969. *Becoming Deviant*. Englewood Cliffs, NJ: Prentice-Hall.

Mayer, J. 1983. "Notes Towards a Working Definition of Social Control in Historical Analysis." Pp. 17-38 in *Social Control and the State*, edited by S. Cohen and A. Scull. Oxford: Blackwell.

McEwen, C. 1980. "Continuities in the Study of Total and Non-Total Institutions." *Annual Review of Sociology*. Beverly Hills, CA: Sage.

Mead, G. H. 1918. "The Psychology of Punitive Justice." *American Journal of Sociology* 23:577-602.

———— 1925. "The Genesis of Self and Social Control." *International Journal of Ethics* 35:251-277.

Mehan, H. B. 1985. *Handicapping the Handicapped*. Palo Alto, CA: Stanford University Press.

Meier, R. 1982. "Perspectives on the Concept of Social Control." *Annual Review of Sociology* 8:35-55. Beverly Hills, CA: Sage.

Merton, R. K. 1938. "Social Structure and Anomie." *American Sociological Review* 3:673-682.

———— 1957. "Manifest and Latent Functions." In *Social Theory and Social Structure*. New York: Free Press.

———— 1968. *Social Theory and Social Structure*. New York: Free Press.

Messinger, S. and R. Greenspan. 1986. "Changes in Social Control." *Qualitative Sociology* 9:58-62.

Miller, W. 1977. *Cops and Bobbies*. Chicago: University of Chicago Press.

Mills, C. W. 1943. "The Professional Ideology of the Social Pathologists." *American Journal of Sociology* 49:165-180.

Morgan, D. 1975. "Explaining Mental Illness." *European Journal of Sociology* 16:262-280.

Nettler, G. 1978. *Explaining Crime*. New York: McGraw-Hill.

———— 1979. "Criminal Justice." Pp. 27-52 in *Annual Review of Sociology*, vol. 5. Beverly Hills, CA: Sage.

Park, R. 1915. "The City: Suggestions for the Investigation of Human Behavior in the City Environment." *American Journal of Sociology* 15:577-612.

———— and E. W. Burgess. 1921. *Introduction to the Science of Sociology*. Chicago: University of Chicago Press.

————, eds. 1925. *The City*. Chicago: University of Chicago Press.

———— 1937. *The Structure of Social Action*. New York: Free Press.

———— 1951. *The Social System*. New York: Free Press.

Perrot, M., ed. 1980. *L'Impossible Prison: Recherches sur le Systeme Penitentiare au XIXe Siecle*. Paris: Seuil.

Perrucci, R. 1974. *Circle of Madness*. Englewood Cliffs, NJ: Prentice-Hall.

Perry, N. 1974. "The Two Cultures and the Total Institution." *British Journal of Sociology* 25:345-355.

Phillipson, M. and M. Roche. 1974. "Phenomenology, Sociology, and the Study of Deviance." In *Deviance and Social Control*, edited by P. Rock and M. McIntosh. London: Tavistock.

Pitts, J. 1968. "Social Control: The Concept." P. 383 in *International Encyclopedia of the Social*

Sciences, edited by D. Sills. 14.

Plummer, K. 1975. *Sexual Stigma: An Interactionist Account*. London: Routledge & Kegan Paul.

———. 1979. "Misunderstanding Labelling Perspectives." In *Deviant Interpretations*, edited by D. Downes and P. Rock. Oxford: Martin Robertson.

Pollner, M. 1974. "Sociological and Commonsense Models of the Labelling Process." In *Ethnomethodology*, edited by R. Turner. London: Penguin.

———. 1978. "Constitutive and Mundane Versions of Labelling Theory." *Human Studies* Pp. 269-288.

Quinney, R. 1977. *Class, State and Crime*. New York: Longman.

Rains, P. 1971. *Becoming an Unwed Mother*. Chicago: Aldine.

Rauschenbush, W. 1979. *Robert Park: Biography of a Sociologist*. Durham, NC: Duke University Press.

Ray, M. 1961. "The Cycle of Abstinence and Relapse Among Heroin Addicts." *Social Problems* 9.

Reckless, W. C. 1926. "The Distribution of Commercialized Vice in the City." In *The Urban Community*, edited by E. W. Burgess. Chicago: University of Chicago Press.

Reiss, I. 1961. "The Social Integration of Queers and Peers." *Social Problems* 9.

Ritchie, R. C. 1984. "England and the Problem of Piracy." Pp. 3-18 in *Research in Law, Deviance, and Social Control*, vol. 6, edited by S. Spitzer and A. Scull. Greenwich, CT: JAI Press.

Rock, P. 1974. "The Sociology of Deviance and Conceptions of the Moral Order." *British Journal of Criminology* 14:139-149.

———. 1979a. "Has Deviance a Future?" Presented at the American Sociological Association annual meeting, Boston.

———. 1979b. *The Making of Symbolic Interactionism*. London: Macmillan.

———. 1983. "Law, Order, and Power in Late Seventeenth and Early Eighteenth Century England." Pp. 191-221 in *Social Control and the State*, edited by S. Cohen and A. Scull. Oxford: Blackwell.

——— and M. McIntosh, eds. 1974. *Deviance and Social Control*. London: Tavistock.

Ross, E. A. 1901. *Social Control: A Survey of the Foundations of Order*. New York: Macmillan.

Rothman, D. 1971. *The Discovery of the Asylum*. Boston: Little, Brown.

———. 1980. *Conscience and Convenience*. Boston: Little, Brown.

———. 1983. "Social Control: The Uses and Abuses of the Concept in the History of Incarceration." Pp. 106-117 in *Social Control and the State*, edited by S. Cohen and A. Scull. Oxford: Blackwell.

Rubington, E. and M. Weinberg, eds. 1968. *Deviance: The Interactionist Perspective*. New York: Macmillan.

Scheff, T. 1966. *Being Mentally Ill*. Chicago: Aldine.

———. 1974. "The Labelling Theory of Mental Illness." *American Sociological Review* 39:444-452.

Schlossman, S. 1977. *Love and the American Delinquent*. Chicago: University of Chicago Press.

Schur, E. 1971. *Labeling Deviant Behavior*. New York: Harper & Row.

———. 1980. "Comments." In *The Labelling of Deviance*, edited by W. Gove. Beverly Hills, CA: Sage.

Scott, R. A. 1969. *The Making of Blind Men*. New York: Russell Sage Foundation.

Scull, A. 1975. "From Madness to Mental Illness: Medical Men as Moral Entrepreneurs." *European Journal of Sociology* 16:219-261.

———. 1976. "Mad-Doctors and Magistrates: English Psychiatry's Struggle for Professional Autonomy in the Nineteenth Century." *European Journal of Sociology* 17:279-305.

———. 1979. *Museums of Madness: The Social Organization of Insanity in Nineteenth Century England*. London: Allen Lane.

———. 1981. "Progressive Dreams, Progressive Nightmares: Social Control in Twentieth Century America." *Stanford Law Review* 33:301-316.

———. 1983. "Community Corrections: Panacea, Progress, or Pretense?" Pp. 146-165 in *The Power to Punish*, edited by D. Garland and P. Young. London: Heinemann.

———. 1984. *Decarceration: Community Treatment and the Deviant. A Radical View*. New Brunswick, NJ: Rutgers University Press.

Sedgwick, P. 1982. *Psychopolitics*. London: Pluto Press.

Shaw, C. 1930. *The Jack Roller*. Chicago: University of Chicago Press.

——— and H. McKay 1942. *Juvenile Delinquency and Urban Areas*. Chicago: University of Chicago Press.

Shearing, C. and P. Stenning. 1981. "Modern Private Security: Its Growth and Implications." Pp. 193-245 in *Crime and Justice: An Annual Review of Research*, vol. 3, edited by M. Tonry and N. Morris. Chicago: University of Chicago Press.

———. 1983. "Private Security: Implications for Social Control." *Social Problems* 30:493-506.

Sheridan, A. 1980. *Michel Foucault: The Will to Truth*. London: Tavistock.

Shils, E. 1970. "Tradition, Ecology, and Institution in the History of Sociology." *Daedelus* 99:760-825.

Short, J. and I. M. Nye. 1958. "Extent of Unrecorded Deliquency: Tentative Conclusions." *Journal of Criminal Law, Criminology, and Police Science* 49:296-302.

Skipper, J. K. and C. H. McCaghy. 1970. "Stripteasers: The Anatomy and Career Contingencies of a Deviant Occupation." *Social Problems* 17:391-404.

Smart, C. 1977. *Women, Crime, and Criminology*.

London: Routledge & Kegan Paul.

Smith, R. 1981. *Trial by Medicine*. Edinburgh: Edinburgh University Press.

South, N. 1984. "Private Security, the Division of Policing Labor, and the Commercial Compromise of the State." Pp. 171-198 in *Research in Law, Deviance, and Social Control*, vol. 6, edited by S. Spitzer and A. Scull. Greenwich, CT: JAI Press.

Spitzer, S. 1975. "Toward a Marxian Theory of Deviance." *Social Problems* 22:638-651.

———— 1983. "Marxist Perspectives in the Sociology of Law." *Annual Review of Sociology* 9:103-124.

Spitzer, S. 1977. "Privatization and Capitalist Development: The Case of the Private Police." *Social Problems* 25:18-29.

———— and A. Scull 1977. "Social Control in Historical Perspective: From Private to Public Responses to Crime." In *Corrections and Punishment*, edited by D. Greenberg. Beverly Hills, CA: Sage.

Stanton, A. and M. S. Schwartz. 1954. *The Mental Hospital*. New York: Basic Books.

Sudnow, D. 1965. "Normal Crimes: Sociological Features of the Penal Code in the Public Defenders' Office." *Social Problems* 12:255-276.

Sutherland, E. 1924. *Principles of Criminology*. Philadelphia: Lippincott.

———— 1956. *The Professional Thief*. Chicago: University of Chicago Press.

———— and D. Cressey. 1960. *Principles of Criminology*. Philadelphia: Lippincott.

Thio, A. 1973. "Class Bias in the Sociology of Deviance." *American Sociologist* 8:1-12.

Thomas, W. I. and F. Znaniecki. 1927. *The Polish Peasant in Europe and America*. New York: Knopf.

Thompson, E. P. 1975. *Whigs and Hunters*. New York: Pantheon.

Thrasher, F. 1927. *The Gang: A Study of 1,313 Gangs in Chicago*. Chicago: University of Chicago Press.

Tittle, C. R. 1980. "Labelling and Crime: An Empirical Evaluation." In *The Labelling of Deviance*, edited by W. Gove. Beverly Hills, CA: Sage.

Treacher, A. and G. Baruch. 1980. "Toward a Critical History of the Psychiatric Profession." In *Critical Psychiatry*, edited by D. Ingleby. New York: Pantheon.

Turk, A. T. 1979. "Analysing Official Deviance: For Non-Partisan Conflict Analyses in Criminology." *Criminology* 16:516-526.

———— 1982. *Political Criminality: The Defiance and Defense of Authority*. Beverly Hills, CA: Sage.

Warren, C.A.B. 1974. *Identity and Community in the Gay World*. New York: John Wiley.

Wellford, C. 1975. "Labelling Theory and Criminology: An Assessment." *Social Problems* 22:332-345.

West Side Studies. 1914. New York: Russell Sage Foundation.

Whyte, W. F. 1943. *Street Corner Society*. Chicago: University of Chicago Press.

Wirth, L. 1928. *The Ghetto*. Chicago: University of Chicago Press.

———— 1964. *On Cities and Social Life*. Chicago: University of Chicago Press.

Wiseman, J. 1969. *Stations of the Lost*. Englewood Cliffs, NJ: Prentice-Hall.

Zola, I. K. 1972. "Medicine as an Institution of Social Control." *The Sociological Review* 20:487-504.

Zorbaugh, H. 1929. *The Gold Coast and the Slum*. Chicago: University of Chicago Press.

21

Social Movements

DOUG McADAM
JOHN D. McCARTHY
MAYER N. ZALD

The field of collective behavior and social movements has drawn the attention of sociologists from the earliest years of the discipline to the present time. Interest in the field, however, has hardly been constant, tending instead to wax and wane partly in response to the level of movement activity in society. In view of this relationship, it is hardly surprising that the field has experienced a renaissance in the last decade and a half. The political and social turbulence that shook the United States and many European countries after 1960 caught many in the sociological community off guard and triggered a new round of theorizing and research on social movements. In summarizing the current state of the field we will pay special attention to this new body of work.[1] In doing so, however, we will try to show how some of the newer work is continuous with earlier perspectives. Only by combining the broad conceptual foci of the newer and older approaches can we hope to produce a full understanding of movement dynamics.

Before turning to a brief discussion of the earlier perspectives, one other qualifying remark is in order. Review essays are, by their very nature, difficult to write. The breadth and diversity of topics in any field pose a challenge to those who would attempt to summarize the field in a single article. Our task is made all the more difficult by the range of phenomena lumped together under the heading of social movements. These include phenomenon as diverse as public interest lobbies (e.g., Common Cause, Sierra Club), full-scale revolutions (e.g., Nicaragua, China, etc.), and religious movements (e.g., People's Temple, Nichiren Shoshu). To simplify our task somewhat, we will not attempt to devote equal attention to the full range of movement types. Instead, consistent with our work, the text discussion will tend to focus on political reform movements, to the neglect of revolutions and religious movements. The topics we address, however, should be relevant to those who study all manner of social movements.

In writing various drafts of this chapter we have benefited from the helpful feedback of a number of our colleagues. In particular, we would like to thank Debra Friedman, Carol Mueller, Neil Smelser, Dave Snow, and Mark Wolfson for their comments on this and several earlier drafts of the manuscript. In addition, we would like to acknowledge the help of Barbara McIntosh and Sarah Sample in the preparation of this manuscript.

The Field in 1970

A student approaching the field of social movements in 1970 confronted a smorgasbord of theoretical perspectives and empirical foci. There was the *collective behavior* approach with its roots in the "Chicago School." Perhaps the most influential progenitor of this approach was Robert Park (1967; Park and Burgess, 1921), who had himself been heavily influenced by the French analyst of crowds, Gustave Le Bon (1960). However, it remained for one of Park's students, Herbert Blumer (1946, 1955), to systematize this perspective in a series of reviews that elaborated its substantive and empirical elements. With a heavy emphasis upon the emergent character of collective behavior and social movements, the perspective was in turn elaborated by a still later generation of theorists including Turner and Killian (1957, 1972, 1986) and Lang and Lang (1961). Though ostensibly in the same tradition, Neil Smelser's important book (1962) moved the field away from the emphasis on process so evident in earlier work and toward a social structural conception of movements as a response to strain.

The *mass society* approach emerged from debates about the rise of authoritarian and totalitarian regimes and was resonant with certain assumptions of the early "cold war" period. Though ostensibly macrosociological in its focus, some of the many variants of this approach stressed the theoretical importance of personal psychology or micro-social relations in understanding mass movements (Arendt, 1951; Hoffer, 1951; Selznick, 1952). On the other hand, Kornhauser (1959) based his version of this model on a macrosociological analysis of the relation of elites to masses. But the ultimate focus of his attention remained the atomized individual.

Relative deprivation represented a third perspective on social movements that received considerable support during this period. As formulated by its chief proponents (Aberle, 1966; Davies, 1963, 1969; Feieraband, Feieraband, and Nesvold, 1969; Geschwender, 1964; Gurr, 1970), relative deprivation theory attributed activism to the perception—often triggered by a shift in reference group—that "one's membership group is in a disadvantageous position, relative to some other group" (Gurney and Tierney, 1982, p. 34).[2] Relative deprivation was, of course, an advance over absolute deprivation theory, which saw grievances in isolation from a group's position in society.

Finally, there was the *institutional school* (Perrow, 1979), patterned after the earlier work of Max Weber and (Gerth and Mills, 1946) Roberto Michels (1959). Analysts in this tradition typically focused upon the evolution of a particular social movement organization. So

Gusfield (1955) analyzed the Women's Christian Temperance Union, Messinger (1955) the Townsend Movement, Selznick (1952) the American Communist Party, and Zald and his colleagues (Zald and Denton, 1963) the Young Men's Christian Association. Typically the structure and goals of a movement organization were seen as shifting over time in response to external environmental factors. Zald and Ash (1966) synthesized this tradition in an influential article that argued that movement organizations might develop in a variety of ways, undermining the heretofore dominant view emphasizing the inevitability of "oligarchization" in the evolution of movements and movement organizations.

Reflecting on the state of the field prior to 1970, one is struck by two points. First, there existed surprisingly little intellectual conflict between the proponents of the four major perspectives we have outlined.[3] Second, and perhaps accounting for the lack of conflict, except for the institutional school, the major perspectives shared two important emphases: They tended to stress micro-level over macro-level processes and to focus most of their attention on the question of movement emergence.[4]

Micro Focus of Analysis

Despite the many differences between the perspectives sketched above, the underlying focus of attention was similar in all but the institutional school. Ultimately, the impetus to collective action was to be found at the micro level with the individual as the appropriate unit of analysis. Disagreement arose only over the identification of those individual characteristics thought to be causally significant. Collective behavior theorists tended to emphasize the role of emergent norms and values in the generation of social movements. For mass society theorists it was the feelings of "alienation and anxiety" engendered by "social atomization" (Kornhauser, 1959, p. 32). Finally, relative deprivation theory took its name from the psychological state thought to trigger social protest. Ultimately, then, the origin of social movements tended to be explained by reference to the same dynamics that accounted for individual participation in movement activities.[5] Both phenomena had their origins in social psychological or normative processes operating at the microsociological or individual levels. Macropolitical and organizational dynamics were underplayed.

Focus on Movement Emergence

The other emphasis shared by most of the earlier perspectives was a preoccupation with the emergent phase of collective action. It was unusual, except among proponents of the institutional school, to find anything written by sociologists prior to 1970 on the development of a movement over time. Collective behavior theorists tended to debate the precise mix of factors that produced the social movement in the first place. Neil Smelser's (1962) "value-added" theory of collective behavior is but the most explicit of these schemes. However, on the dynamics of movement growth and decline, Smelser and the other collective behavior theorists were notably silent. So too were "classical" theorists (McAdam, 1982) in general. Like the collective behavior theorists, proponents of the mass society and relative deprivation models were less concerned with the movements themselves than those features of the pre-movement period that gave rise to the movement. For mass society theorists' interest centered on the massification of society and the feelings of alienation this produced.

In contrast, relative deprivation theorists focused their attention on a variety of economic dynamics—absolute gains, gains coupled with the failure to realize any progress relative to some reference group, and so forth—thought to produce the motivation to engage in collective action. Once again, however, none of the versions of the theory evidenced any interest in movements once they had emerged.

To a new generation of sociologists, the many popular and clearly political movements of the 1960s and 1970s seemed incompatible with and poorly explained by the traditional perspectives on social movements. In turn, this perceived lack of fit sparked a renaissance in the sociological study of social movements, triggered initially by a critical rethinking of the dominant theories in the field.

The theories were criticized on both theoretical and empirical grounds by many movement analysts (Aya, 1979; Gamson, 1975; Jenkins and Perrow, 1977; McAdam, 1982; McCarthy and Zald, 1973, 1977; Oberschall, 1973; Rule and Tilly, 1975; Schwartz, 1976; Shorter and Tilly, 1974; Tilly, 1978). The effect of these critiques was to shift the focus of movement analysis from microsocial-psychological to more macropolitical and structural accounts of movement dynamics.

The principal new theoretical perspectives to emerge from recent research and writing in the field are the resource mobilization and political process models. In contrast to earlier classical formulations, both perspectives attribute rationality to movement participants and posit a fundamental continuity between institutionalized and movement politics. The differences between the two models, then, are ones of emphasis and empirical focus. *Resource mobilization* theorists tend to emphasize the constancy of discontent and the variability of resources in accounting for the emergence and development of insurgency (see McCarthy and Zald, 1973, 1977; Oberschall, 1973). Accordingly, a principal goal of their work is understanding how emergent movement organizations seek to mobilize and routinize—frequently by tapping lucrative elite sources of support—the flow of resources, which ensures movement survival.

Though not incompatible with the resource mobilization perspective, the *political process* model represents a somewhat different approach to the study of movement dynamics. As formulated by its chief proponents (McAdam, 1982; Tilly, 1978), the approach emphasizes (a) the importance of indigenous organization, and (b) a favorable "structure of political opportunities" (Eisinger, 1973) far more than do resource mobilization theorists. Both are seen as necessary if a group is to be able to organize and sustain a successful social movement.

The effect of these new perspectives has been to shift the focus of movement scholarship away from the microdynamics of movement emergence to a broader macroanalysis of the processes that make for stability and change in the evolution of movements. While a positive development, this broadening of the frame for movement analysis has at times threatened to replace the conceptual orthodoxy of the classical perspectives with another tailored to the assumptions of the newer models. This would accomplish little. Rather, in our view, any complete account of social movements must do two things. First, it must take into account processes and variables operating at the *macro* and *micro* levels of analysis. Second, it must shed light on the dynamics that account for stability and change in mature movements as well as the processes that give rise to those movements in the first place. Combining these two foci produces the following two-by-two conceptualization of the field:

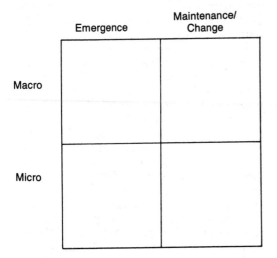

We will use this basic schema as the organizing framework for the paper. The advantage of doing so is that virtually all research and theorizing on social movements can be incorporated into one of the four cells of the table. By working our way through each of the four cells, then, we will review most of the major work in the field.

The problem with this conceptual frame is that it leaves the links between the macro and micro levels of analysis unexamined. This deficiency is shared by the field as a whole. Historically, researchers and theorists have tended to address one of the four topics shown in the table without regard to the links between the topics. We are particularly interested in developing conceptual bridges between movement dynamics that operate at the micro and macro levels. Reflecting a desire to redress what they see as the new macro bias in movement theory, several authors (Jenkins, 1983, p. 527; Klandermans, 1984, pp. 583-584) have recently voiced calls for the development of a new and viable social psychology of collective action. While we agree with their assessment of the current macro bias in the field, we are not persuaded that a reassertion of the social psychological is the best way to redress this imbalance. Such an assertion reifies the micro/macro distinction and reinforces the notion that the two constitute distinct levels of analysis. In our view, what is missing is not so much a viable social psychology of collective action—the broad contours of which already exists in the literature—but intermediate theoretical "bridges" that would allow us to join empirical work at both levels of analysis. With this in mind, we will structure the article

in the following way: After summarizing the literature on macro and micro emergence, we will discuss several promising conceptual bridges that might allow us to better understand the links between macroprocesses and individual actors during the period of movement emergence. We will then do the same for the later stages in a movement's development. The primary focus of this latter discussion will be on social movement organizations (SMOs) and their efforts to mediate between changing macroconditions and the ongoing micro challenges of member recruitment and resource mobilization.

Macro Theory and Research on Movement Emergence

The recent renaissance in movement scholarship has resulted in the accumulation of an impressive body of theory and research on the macrolevel correlates of collective action. Given the dominance of more micro-level conceptions of social movements in the various classical models, this development has been particularly welcome. But in proposing an explicitly macro conception of movement emergence, the newer scholarship has merely returned to a theoretical tradition with a long and rich history in European social thought. European social theorists have long sought to locate the roots of collective action in broad social, demographic, economic, and political processes. The prototypical version of this form of analysis is the Marxist one, which focuses upon the central importance of developing economic contradictions in industrial societies that create pools of discontented workers ripe for collective mobilization. But competing versions of this form of analysis focused, as well, upon the importance of urbanization, industrialization, and bureaucratization in creating the macro conditions necessary for collective action. In contrast, American scholarship prior to 1970 was far more micro in focus than its European forebears. Yet even this tradition was not totally devoid of consideration of macro conditions. For example, Davies's (1963) "J-curve" version of relative deprivation is argued at the macro level of analysis, purporting to meld the analyses of Marx and de Toqueville into a synthetic macro account of the emergence of revolutions. And while Neil Smelser's analysis emphasizes the social-psychological importance of "generalized beliefs," he also notes the role played by such macro conditions as "structural strain," and the absence of social control in the generation of collective action. Finally, while the work of the "mass society" theorists is intended to explicate the psychology of movement participation, much of its analytic focus remains pitched at the macro level.

So more recent work at the macro level is not discontinuous with American work of the recent past and the earlier European work upon which it draws. As a consequence some of the macro factors we shall discuss in passing have a long history of serious attention by movement analysts. Others, however, are of more recent origin as serious contenders for understanding the emergence of collective action and social movements. In the following section we will attempt to summarize what strikes us as the major empirical themes that run through this recent literature.

Macro Political Conditions

One of the major contributions of the recent paradigm shift in the field of social movements has been the reassertion of the political. In the United States, both the resource mobilization and political process perspectives locate social movements squarely within the realm of rational political action. So too does the European literature on "new social movements."[6] However, as Tilly and others have sought to remind us, this form of political action is itself historically specific. It is only against the backdrop of the modern centralized state that we begin to see the emergence of what Tilly has called the "national social movement." This is not to say that collective action was absent prior to the rise of the modern state, but that the form and focus of that action was very different. Specifically, collective action tended to be localized, reactive, and small in scale in feudal and semifeudal societies. But as the locus of power, privilege, and resources shifted to these large centralized states, the scope and focus of collective action expanded as well. As Bright and Harding (1984, p. 10) note, "A concept of state making involves not only state initiatives and the reaction of social groupings to them, but also social mobilizations which target the state and trigger responses by its governors." This observation places the contemporary analysis of collective behavior and social movements in a historical context and also highlights the continuities between institutionalized and movement politics. If most movements represent a form of political action, it is only logical that as the locus of power shifts to the centralized state, movements would also become larger and more national in scope. In our view, social movements are simply

"politics by other means," oftentimes the only means open to relatively powerless challenging groups. As such, social movements should be as responsive to the broad political trends and characteristics of the regions and countries in which they occur as are institutionalized political processes. Recent research in the field suggests as much.

STRUCTURE OF POLITICAL OPPORTUNITIES

Within the context of nation states considerable evidence now exists suggesting the crucial importance of changes in the "structure of political opportunities" (Eisinger, 1973) to the ebb and flow of movement activity. By structure of political opportunities we refer to the receptivity or vulnerability of the political system to organized protest by a given challenging group. Characteristically challengers are excluded from any real participation in institutionalized politics because of strong opposition on the part of most polity members. This unfavorable structure of political opportunities is hardly immutable, however. In so saying, our

> attention is directed away from systems characterizations presumably true for all times and places, which are basically of little value in understanding the social and political process. We are accustomed to describing communist political systems as "experiencing a thaw" or "going through a process of retrenchment." Should it not at least be an open question as to whether the American political system experiences such stages and fluctuations? Similarly, is it not sensible to assume that the system will be more or less open to specific groups at different times and at different places [Lipsky, 1970, p. 14]?

The answer to both of Lipsky's questions is yes. Challenging groups can count on the political systems they seek to influence being more or less vulnerable or receptive to challenge at different points in time. These variations in the structure of political opportunities may arise in either "bottom-up" or "top-down" fashion. In the first case, the political leverage available to a particular challenger is enhanced by broad political, economic, or demographic processes outside of the direct control of polity members. For example, Jenkins and Perrow (1977) attribute the success of the farm workers movement in the 1960s to "the altered political environment within which the challenge operated" (p. 263). The change, they contend, originated "in economic trends and political realignments that took place quite independent of any 'push' from insurgents" (p. 266). In similar fashion, McAdam (1982) has attributed the emergence of widespread black protest activity in the 1950s and 1960s in part to several broad political trends—expansion of the black vote, its shift to the Democratic Party, postwar competition for influence among emerging Third World nations—that served to enhance the bargaining position of civil rights forces. Improved political opportunities may also result from top-down efforts at political sponsorship by elite groups. In his analysis of the emergence of the contemporary environmental movement, Gale (1986, p. 208) notes the importance of the development of a "political system that included agencies already sympathetic to the movement." Indeed, with increased historical perspective has come the realization that the ascendant liberal-left coalition of the 1960s created a broad political context facilitating the emergence of a wide variety of leftist movements.

These last two examples illustrate the ways in which polity members may encourage activism through various forms of sponsorship. But, quite apart from the intention of elite groups, the very structure of a political system may encourage or discourage activism. For example, Nelkin and Pollack (1981) demonstrate that the cycle of protest against nuclear power in West Germany was quite different than the one in France even though the two movements looked very much alike in their early stages. The existence of manifold procedures of review nested in governmental agencies provided substantial opportunities for continuing protest in Germany that were far less available in France, where the movement quickly atrophied. Kitschelt (1986) expands this analysis to include Great Britain and the United States with similar conclusions.

REGIME CRISES AND CONTESTED POLITICAL ARENAS

Related to, yet distinct from, the expansion and contraction in political opportunities are regime crises and general contests for political dominance within a particular region or country. Both situations translate into a net gain in political opportunity for all organized challengers. In this sense the result is the same as in the cases discussed in the previous section. The difference stems from the conditions giving rise to the improved bargaining situation confronting the challenger. In the previous sec-

tion, we cited instances in which various processes increased the leverage of a particular challenger without affecting the systemwide distribution of political power. By contrast, regime crises or periods of generalized political instability improve the relative position of all challengers by undermining the hegemonic position of previously dominant groups or coalitions.

Despite this difference, both situations are expected to stimulate a rise in social movement activity. Certainly the literatures on regime crises and major contests for political dominance support this assumption. Shorter and Tilly (1974), for example, marshal data to show that peaks in French strike activity correspond to periods in which competition for national political power is unusually intense. They note that "factory and white-collar workers undertook in 1968 the longest, largest general strike in history as student unrest reopened the question of who were to be the constituent political groups of the Fifth Republic" (p. 344). Similarly, Schwartz (1976) argues that a period of political instability preceded the rise of the Populist Movement in the post-Civil War South. With the Southern planter aristocracy and emerging industrial interests deadlocked in a struggle for political control of the region, a unique opportunity for political gain was created for any group able to break the stalemate. To this list of well-researched examples one might also add the generalized political instability in Germany during the 1920s as the condition that made possible the Nazis' rise to power. Similar periods of political unrest also preceded the rise of totalitarian movements in Portugal (Schwartzman, in press) and Italy during the 1920s.

More generally, both Skocpol (1979) and Habermas (1973, 1976) have argued for a strong link between different types of regime crises and the generation and expansion of collective action. For Skocpol, the roots of revolution are to be found in major regime crises, typically set in motion by military losses and fiscal overextension. Habermas, on the other hand, locates the impetus to collective action in the chronic "legitimation crisis" confronting the modern capitalist state. He argues that the modern capitalist state is forced by the contradictions inherent in the system to engage in various forms of ideological socialization designed to legitimate the system in the eyes of the citizenry. One of the unintended consequences of these efforts is the generation of material expectations among many groups in society that the system will never be able to meet. Encoded in this failure to realize these expectations, then, is an ever greater likelihood of popular discontent and protest against the system.

ABSENCE OF REPRESSION

Another macro-political factor often associated with the rise of a social movement is the absence or relatively restrained use of repressive social control by movement opponents. Smelser (1962) was one of the first theorists to emphasize the importance of this factor. While analytically distinct from the previous two conditions, the absence of repression frequently occurs in conjunction with both of these factors.

In a situation where expanding political opportunities have significantly improved the bargaining position of a particular group, movement opponents are likely to exercise more restraint in dealing with the challenger. Unlike before, when the powerless status of the challenger made it a relatively "safe" target, its improved position now increases the risk of political reprisals against any who would seek to repress it. Thus repression is less likely to be attempted even in the face of an increased threat to the interests of other groups. This argument figures prominently in McAdam's (1982, pp. 87-90) account of the rise of the civil rights movement in the 1950s and 1960s. Using the annual number of lynchings as a crude measure of repression, he has documented a significant decline in lynching during the period (1930-1955) when black political fortunes were on the rise nationally. The suggestion is that the growing political power of blacks nationally increased the South's fear of federal intervention and thus restrained the use of extreme control measures. In turn, this restraint created a more favorable context in which blacks could mobilize.

Recourse to repressive measures is also likely to decline during regime crises as the coercive capacity of the state deteriorates. Skocpol (1979) places great stress on this dynamic in her analysis of revolution, arguing that it is the collapse of the state as a repressive agent that sets in motion widespread collective action. One need look no further than Iran under the Shah for a recent example of this. As the crisis in Iran deepened, the Shah's ability to utilize the repressive measures he had once used so successfully declined rapidly. When, at last, large segments of the armed forces abandoned the regime, the last restraints on mobilization were removed foreshadowing the Shah's ouster. A similar dynamic seems to have been played out in the Philippines in the month before Marcos's departure, as well as in Nicaragua in the period prior to the overthrow of the Somoza regime.[7]

WELFARE STATE EXPANSION AND THE RISE OF "NEW SOCIAL MOVEMENTS"

One final political factor that has been linked to the generation of social movements is the penetration of the state into previously private areas of life. This factor has primarily been stressed by proponents of the *new social movements* approach (see Klandermans, 1986; Melucci, 1980, 1981), and is often couched in terms of a broader Marxist view of the state. While there are nearly as many versions of new social movement theory as there are variations on the resource mobilization perspective, we can identify various themes that show up with great regularity in the writings of those working in this tradition.

Perhaps the most straightforward of those themes is simply that the new social movements —principally the women's, environmental, and peace movements—represent a reaction to certain modernization processes in late capitalist societies. Among the authors stressing this idea are Brand (1982), Melucci (1980) and Van der Loo, Snel, and Van Steenbergen (1984). Of the processes thought to be productive of these new movements, none would appear to have received as much attention as what has been termed the "politicization of private life." The argument here is straightforward. The contradictions inherent in postindustrial capitalist economies have forced the state to intervene in previously private areas of life. The state is required to do so both to underwrite the process of capital accumulation (O'Connor, 1973) as well as to satisfy needs no longer satisfactorily addressed by an ailing market economy. In turn, new social movements have emerged in response to this unprecedented state penetration into various private spheres of life. In this view, movements as diverse as the women's, environmental, and gay rights campaigns can be seen as efforts to regain control over decisions and areas of life increasingly subject to state control.

The rise of these movements has been accompanied, or in some formulations triggered, by the rise of new values (Inglehart, 1977). Born of popular discontent with the nature of postmodern society, these new values are seen as providing the ideological and motivational backdrop for the emergence of the new social movements. Among the new values thought to characterize the postmodern age are a desire for community, self-actualization, and personal, as opposed to occupational, satisfaction. Empirically, other value changes noted by researchers include a decline in the traditional work ethic, and an erosion of conventional middle-class values as regards work and family life (Brand, 1982; Oudijk, 1983).

All of the processes reviewed above have a kind of reactive quality to them. That is, the rise of postmodern values and the new movements thought to embody those values are typically described as reactions to the dissolution throughout Europe of more traditional ways of life following World War II. In this sense, it may be more accurate to classify the new social movements as "reactive" rather than new movements in any strict sense. There is, however, one final group of new social movement theorists who link the rise of these movements less to any collective reaction against modernization than to the frustration of new material and status aspirations that have accompanied the rise of the modern welfare state (see de Geest, 1984; Hirsch, 1980). As the state has come to penetrate more and more areas of life, it hasn't simply disrupted older ways of life, but also created new status groups who are dependent upon it for the satisfaction of a wide range of material and status needs. The failure to satisfy those needs has, in the view of these authors, contributed to the rise of these new social movements.

Macro Economic Conditions

Quite apart from the important influence of broad political processes, certain strictly economic characteristics of the larger society would seem to exert an independent influence on the likelihood of movement emergence.

PROSPERITY AS PRE-CONDITION OF SOCIAL MOVEMENT ACTIVITY

Much early theorizing about social movements centered on the relationship between collective action and economic conditions. Such theorizing was evident at both the micro and macro levels. At the micro level it was assumed that the most deprived individuals would be the most likely to participate in movements. Second, it was expected that massive growth in societal wealth would dampen the need for social movement activity. Both of these general assumptions appear to be contradicted by empirical evidence. The most deprived appear unlikely to sustain more than momentary insurgency, and, other things being equal, general societal prosperity seems often to be related to a rise in social movement activity. Several factors would seem to explain this latter relationship. First of all, wealthy societies tend to produce the general conditions that favor the emergence of newly organized collectivities. The growth of rapid communication, the expansion of the intellectual classes (Zald and McCarthy, 1977), and the development of new social technologies increase the level of grievance production in a society. Though such a state of affairs may not guarantee the success of social movement efforts, it can be expected to increase their relative frequency. So, indirectly, expanding wealth has led to expanding social movement activity (McCarthy and Zald, 1973). Prosperity may also encourage a rise in movement activity through two other, more direct, processes.

Wealthy societies may create the opportunities for entrepreneurs of grievances to attempt to develop new social movement products. This approach has been labeled the "entrepreneurial theory of social movements" (Jenkins, 1983). It has been shown useful in understanding the emergence of the "public interest movement" (Berry, 1977; McFarland, 1976, 1984), aspects of the "environmental movement" (Simcock, 1979; Wood, 1982), and the National Welfare Rights Organization (Bailis, 1974; West, 1981). Indeed, such an approach to understanding the generation of social movement activity has begun to be codified by theorists under the label of "social marketing." These analysts attempt to determine the most auspicious conditions under which the marketing of social causes may be successful (Fox and Kotler, 1980; Kotler and Zaltman, 1971).

In an ironic variation on Ronald Reagan's "trickle down" economics, general societal prosperity may also serve to promote collective action by raising the level of resources available to support such action. Those who provide such resources from outside of the aggrieved group have been called "conscience constituents" (McCarthy and Zald, 1973). Many movements in the recent period, such as animal rights and prolife, have been staffed and funded exclusively by conscience constituents. In addition, massive external resources have flowed into many movements ostensibly led by members of the deprived group. The civil rights movement, for instance, benefited by large flows of external resources, though assessments of the timing of such flows (McAdam, 1982) suggest that they followed the emergence and major growth of this movement rather than preceding and generating it. Jenkins and Eckert's (1986) analysis of the role of private foundations in the funding of civil rights groups supports this conclusion. In a wide variety of ways, then, wealth and the resources that accompany that wealth would seem to increase rather than dampen the prospects for successful collective action.

Macro Organizational Conditions

Another contribution of the recent scholarship on the macro-level dynamics of collective action is the accumulation of evidence attesting to the importance of broad organizational factors in the genesis of movements. Macro-political and economic processes may create the opportunity for successful collective action, but often it is the internal structure of the population in question that determines whether this opportunity will be realized.

ECOLOGICAL CONCENTRATION

One such characteristic is the degree of geographic concentration in the residential or occupational patterns of a group's everyday lives. Geographic concentration has the important effect of increasing the density of interaction between group members, thereby facilitating recruitment. This may help to explain the oft-noted relationship between urbanization/industrialization and collective action. Traditionally, movement theorists sought to explain this relationship on the basis of the presumed psychological tensions generated by rapid social change (see Kornhauser, 1959, pp. 143-58). It would seem more likely, however, that the impetus is more structural/organizational than psychological in nature. By creating ecologically dense concentrations of relatively homogeneous people, urbanization would seem to increase the structural potential for collective action. Several scholars (McAdam, 1982, pp. 94-98; Wilson, 1973, pp. 140-151) have advanced this argument with respect to the civil rights movement. In this view the rural to urban migration of blacks within the South greatly enhanced the prospects for collective action by transforming an impoverished, geographically dispersed mass into an increasingly well-organized urban population.

In his analysis of the "youth ghetto," John Lofland (1969) makes use of the same idea, arguing that large concentrations of young people around university campuses increases the likelihood of all manner of youth movements. Similarly, John D'Emillio (1983) has argued that the mass concentrations of servicemen during World War II had the effect of creating large homosexual populations in certain U.S. cities. In turn, these incipient gay communities were in the forefront of gay rights organizing in the late 1960s. Finally, Nielsen (1980) has noted the importance of ecological concentration in his account of the recent spate of ethnic separatist movements in Europe.

Other authors have attributed a similar effect to industrialization, arguing that the strike as the prototypical "modern" form of collective action was made possible by the ecological concentration of large numbers of economically homogeneous workers in large factories (see Foster, 1974; Lincoln, 1978; Lodhi and Tilly, 1973; Shorter and Tilly, 1974). As the Tillys explain, "urbanization and industrialization . . . are by no means irrelevant to collective violence. It is just that their effects do not work as . . . [traditional] theories say they should. Instead of a short-run generation of strain, followed by protest, we find a long-run transformation of the structures . . . of collective action" (Tilly, Tilly, and Tilly, 1975, p. 254).

LEVEL OF PRIOR ORGANIZATION

The level of prior organization in a given population is also expected to enhance the prospects for successful collective action. Certainly this is the important implication of a number of significant analyses of movement emergence. Oberschall (1973), for instance, has proposed a theory of mobilization in which he assigns paramount importance to the degree of organization in the aggrieved group. In her analysis of the emergence of the contemporary women's movement, Jo Freeman (1973) focuses special attention on several processes occurring in the early 1960s that left women with the stronger organizational "infrastructure" needed to generate and sustain collective action. Morris's analysis (1984) of the emergent phase of the civil rights movement stresses, above all else, the strength and breadth of indigenous organization as the crucial factor in the rapid spread of the movement. Consistent with Morris's analysis, McAdam (1982) has linked the emergence of the civil rights movement to a period of institution building in the black community that afforded blacks the indigenous organizations—black churches, black colleges, local NAACP chapters—out of which the movement grew and developed. Based on these studies, one would expect that the greater the density of social organization, the more likely that social movement activity will develop. This hypothesis can be used not only to predict variation in mobilization between groups within a society, but between societies as well.

Differences in the *types* of organizations active during particular eras is expected to correspond to shifts in the organizational locus of movement activity. Focusing only on the United States, it is clear that changes in the relative strength of various types of organizations is a common occurrence. So veterans' organizations form in waves, leaving some cohorts relatively unorganized. Burial societies have declined with the growth of the welfare state. PTAs grew commensurate with the growth of mass education. Finally, political parties have declined in the face of the broad substitution of mass-media political advertising for grass roots party organizing (Polsby, 1983).

Cross-national differences in type of organizations can also be linked to variation in the forms of collective action that predominate in various societies. For instance, union membership is much lower in the United States than in most Western European nations. This may help to explain why working class movements have historically—and especially since 1940—played less of a role in politics in this country than in most European nations.

On the other hand, the United States is especially dense in religiously based social organization compared with Western European nations and Japan, and this density has not lessened either with economic growth or other forms of secularization. Religious group membership is the most common form of associational membership in the United States. It is hardly surprising, then, that many mass movements have been organizationally rooted in churches. Such movements would include the abolition movement, the second Ku Klux Klan, the prohibition movement, the civil rights movement and the prolife movement (Zald and McCarthy, 1987), to say nothing of the countless religious movements to arise in the U.S.

ABSENCE OF CROSS-CUTTING SOLIDARITIES

It isn't simply the ecological concentration of groups or density of formal organizations that enhances the prospects for collective action. Just as important as the internal organization of the population in question, is the extent and strength of its ties to other groups in society. To the extent that these ties are strong and numerous, the likelihood of a social movement arising would seem to be diminished. This is an old idea that is embedded in pluralist and mass society (Kornhauser, 1959) perspectives, deriving in turn from de Tocqueville's analysis of the French Revolution. It deserves, however, to survive the decline of these two perspectives.

This factor may help account for the sizable opposition encountered by the women's movement among married women in the United States. The point is, women are not only geographically dispersed in society, but linked to men through a wide variety of social, political, and economic ties. These ties, then, give many women more of an interest in emphasizing the cooperative rather than the conflictual aspects of their relationships with men. This is all the more likely to be true when the net effect of those links is to make women financially dependent on men. Efforts to create groups or communities free from male influence, such as consciousness-raising groups or feminist communes, attest to the seriousness of the problem as well as the attempts of feminists to deal with it.

On the other hand, groups that are not well linked to other segments of society may find themselves at an advantage when it comes to organizing for collective action (Oberschall, 1973, pp. 118-124). The advantages of isolation are twofold. First, the absence of ties to other groups minimizes the effect that appeals to loyalty might have in the case of better integrated antagonists. Second, under conditions of real separation, the target group may lack the minimum ties required to threaten political or economic reprisals as a means of controlling the movement. The ability of southern blacks, farmworkers, students, and the untouchables in India to organize successful movements may owe in part to the benefits of this type of segregation.

Micro Theory and Research on Recruitment to Activism

Companion to the macro question of *movement emergence* is the micro question of *individual recruitment* to activism. Just as one might ask what broad political, economic, or organizational factors make a movement more likely in the first place, so too can one seek to identify those micro-level factors that lead an individual to get involved in collective action. Clearly, the two questions are closely related. Obviously no movement will take place unless individuals choose to become involved. At the same time, a lot of what prompts an individual to get involved is the sense of momentum that an already existing movement is able to communicate. Thus the two processes—movement emergence and individual recruitment—are expected to go hand in hand. It is important to keep in mind, though, that they remain two separate processes. Explaining why an individual comes to participate in collective action does not suffice as an account of why a particular movement emerged when it did. By the same token, knowing what processes produced a movement tells us little about the factors that encouraged particular individuals to affiliate with that movement. In this section we intend to stay focused on these latter factors. They can be grouped into two general categories. The traditional dominance of social psychological perspectives in the study of collective behavior and social movements has left us with an extensive empirical literature on the *individual* correlates of movement participation. At the same time, the recent popularity of the resource mobilization and other "rationalist" perspectives on social movements has served to stimulate a new body of research on the *micro-structural* dynamics of recruitment to action.

Individual Accounts of Activism

Among the topics that have most concerned researchers in the field of social movements is that of differential recruitment (Jenkins, 1983, p. 528; Zurcher and Snow, 1981, p. 449). What accounts for individual variation in movement participation? Why does one individual get involved while another remains inactive? Until recently, researchers have sought to answer these questions on the basis of individual characteristics of movement activists. The basic assumption underlying such accounts is simply that it is some attribute of the individual that either compels participation or, at the very least, renders them susceptible to movement recruiting appeals. This assumption has informed most individually based motivational accounts of participation in political or religious movements (see Block, Haan, and Smith, 1968; Braungart, 1971; Feuer, 1969; Glock, 1964; Klapp, 1969; Levine, 1980; Rothman and Lichter, 1978; Toch, 1965). Such accounts can be differentiated on the basis of those attributes of the individual that are held to be significant in producing activism. These would include psychological, attitudinal, and rational choice explanations of participation.

PSYCHOLOGICAL ACCOUNTS OF ACTIVISM

Many individual motivational accounts of activism identify a particular psychological state or characteristic as the root cause of participation. The emphasis is on character traits or stressful states of mind that dispose the individual toward participation.

But while the underlying model remains the same, the specific characteristics identified as significant by proponents of these approaches vary widely. As an example, the cluster of personality traits known as authoritarianism have been argued to serve as an important precipitant of involvement in social movements (Adorno and Frenkel-Brunswick, 1950; Hoffer, 1951; Lipset and Rabb, 1973). So too has the desire to achieve "cognitive consistency" in one's attitudes, values, or behavior. Drawing on theories of cognitive consistency (Rokeach, 1969), this account of individual activism is based on the idea that "when people become conscious of inconsistency, it is in their psychological self interest to change . . . members of a social movement represent a special case: they have recognized inconsistencies that other people do not acknowledge and that are institutionalized in society" (Carden, 1978). Another variation on this theme has movement participants being drawn disproportionately from among the marginal, alienated members of society (see Aberle, 1966; Klapp, 1969; Kornhauser, 1959). In this view it is the individual's desire to overcome his or her feelings of alienation and achieve the sense of community they lack in their life that prompts them to participate in collective action. In the same vein, Lewis Feuer (1969) sought to explain student activism on the basis of unresolved Oedipal conflicts between male activists and their fathers.

Of all the versions of this model, however, perhaps none has generated as much research attention as the theory of relative deprivation. The theory holds that it is an unfavorable gap between what a person feels he or she is entitled to and what, in fact, they are receiving that encourages activism. The underlying motivation for participation, however, is not so much the substantive desire to close the gap. Whether framed as an extension of the frustration-aggression hypothesis (Davies, 1963, 1969; Feieraband, Feieraband, and Nesvold, 1969; Gurr, 1970) or grounded in the literature on cognitive balance (Geschwender, 1968; Morrison, 1973), the theory assumes "an underlying state of individual psychological tension that is relieved by SM participation" (Gurney and Tierney, 1982, p. 36).

For all their apparent theoretical sophistication, empirical support for all of these individually based psychological accounts of participation has proved elusive. Summarizing his exhaustive survey of the literature on the relationship between activism and various psychological factors, Mueller (1980, p. 69) concludes that "psychological attributes of individuals, such as frustration and alienation, have minimal direct impact for explaining the occurrence of rebellion and revolution per se." Echoing this view, Wilson and Orum (1976, p. 189) offer a similar assessment of the empirical record. "We conclude," they say, "that the many analyses . . . of collective actions during the past decade, impress upon us the poverty of psychology; or, at the very least, the limitations of psychology" (p. 189).

ATTITUDINAL CORRELATES OF ACTIVISM

Similar to the logic of the psychological models reviewed above, attitudinal accounts of activism locate the roots of participation squarely within the individual actor. The claim is simple enough: Activism grows out of strong attitudinal support for the values and goals of the movement. Such accounts were especially popular as applied to student activism in the late 1960s and early 1970s. According to this view, the actions of student radicals were motivated by their desire to actualize the political values and attitudes of their parents (see Block, 1972; Flacks, 1967; Keniston, 1968).

To their credit, the advocates of this approach have rejected the somewhat mechanistic psychological models of activism sketched earlier. In their place, they have substituted a straightforward behavioral link between a person's political attitudes and participation in collective action. Unfortunately, this conceptual advance has not produced any corresponding improvement in predictive power at the empirical level. Based on his analysis of 215 studies of the relationship between individual attitudes and riot participation, McPhail (1971) concludes that "individual predispositions are, at best, insufficient to account" for participation in collective action.

In general, the discrepancy between attitudes and behavior has been borne out by countless studies conducted over the years. In summarizing the results of these studies, Wicker (1969) offered what remains the definitive word on the subject. Said Wicker, there exists "little evidence to support the postulated existence of stable, underlying attitudes within the individual which influence both his verbal expressions and his actions" (p. 75).

Does this mean that attitudes are totally irrelevant to the study of individual activism? Certainly not. Rather, their importance has been overstated in many accounts of movement participation. In our view, attitudes remain important insofar as they demarcate a "latitude of rejection" (Petty and Cacioppo, 1981) within

which individuals are highly unlikely to get involved in a given movement. That is, certain prior attitudes will virtually preclude a segment of the population from participating in even the mildest forms of activism. However, in the case of most movements the size of the pool of recruits—the "latitude of acceptance"—is still many times larger than the actual number of persons who take part in any given instance of activism. Klandermans and Oegema (1984) provide an interesting illustration of the size of these respective groups in their study of recruitment to a major peace demonstration in the Netherlands. Based on before-and-after interviews with a sample of 114 persons, the authors conclude that 26% of those interviewed fell within the "latitude of rejection" as regards the goals of the demonstration. That left nearly three-quarters of the sample as potentially available for recruitment. Yet only 4% actually attended the rally. It is precisely this disparity between attitudinal affinity and actual participation that, of course, requires explanation. One thing seems clear, however; given the size of this disparity, the role of individual attitudes (and the background factors from which they derive) in shaping activism must be regarded as fairly limited. If 96% of all those who are attitudinally available for activism choose, as they did in this case, not to participate, then clearly some other factor or set of factors is mediating the recruitment process.

SUDDENLY IMPOSED GRIEVANCES

A special set of circumstances that may encourage a larger number of people to act on their attitudinal dispositions follows from the imposition of what Edward Walsh (1981) has called "suddenly imposed grievances." The concept is intended to describe those dramatic, highly publicized, and often unexpected events—manmade disasters, major court decisions, official violence—that serve to dramatize and therefore increase public awareness of and opposition to particular grievances. As an example of this process, Walsh (1981) cites and analyzes the generation of antinuclear activity in the area of Three Mile Island following the accident there.

Nor is Walsh's the only example of this process. Bert Useem's (1980) analysis of the antibusing movement that developed in Boston during the mid-seventies leaves little doubt that the resistance was set in motion by a highly publicized court order mandating busing. Molotch (1970) documents a similar rise in protest activity among residents of Santa Barbara, California, in the wake of a major oil spill there. Even rising national opposition to the Vietnam War in the late 1960s can be interpreted within this framework. The war itself can be seen, as it was at the time, as a series of suddenly imposed grievances—higher draft quotas, the "secret" bombing of Cambodia, the killing of students at Kent State, the elimination of student deferments—each of which in turn fueled growing protest against the war.

RATIONAL CHOICE ACCOUNTS OF ACTIVISM

Many social movement theorists have posited the assumption that individuals are calculating actors who attempt, within the bounds of limited rationality, to judge the potential costs and benefits of various lines of action (see Friedman, 1983; Oberschall, 1973). As regards movement participation, the argument is straightforward. If the costs of participation are seen as extremely high, then many potential recruits are expected to choose another course of action. Alternatively, if the anticipated benefits of activism are high, then participation is the likely result.

It is this assumption that underlies the important work of Mancur Olson (1965). Olson's contention is that rational calculation would lead few actors to choose collective action as a means of obtaining public goods, since they could expect to obtain those goods whether they were active or not. He goes on to explore two conditions under which collective behavior can nevertheless be expected. These conditions involve the provision of selective incentives to increase the rewards of those engaging in collective action, and the sanctions on nonparticipants for their failure to participate. Others have explored additional factors that may alter the risk and reward matrices actors use to choose from among various courses of action, or undermine the salience of such narrowly economic cost-benefit calculations. The former include Oliver's work (1984) on the relationship between cost calculations and the numbers of people involved in actions or movements. An example of the latter would be Fireman and Gamson's work (1979) on the conditions under which group solidarity may be expected to override simple cost-benefit calculations. Another example would be Friedman's work (1988) on structural conditions—particularly contextual uncertainty—that serve to undermine the basis of rational calculus and thereby increase the likelihood of collective action. Finally, several large membership surveys suggest that solidary and purposive incentives are more important in explaining participation in a variety of voluntary associations (Knoke, 1986) and in the major national environmental groups (Mitchell, 1979) than are selective incentives. Mitchell argues further that the threat of "public bads" may be far more important in motivating some forms of activism than is the provision of "public goods," as conceived by rational choice theorists.

Micro-Structural Accounts of Activism

The increasing influence over the last decade of resource mobilization, political process, and other more political or structural perspectives on social movements has led to growing dissatisfaction with the individual accounts of activism. The argument is that people don't participate in movements so much because they are psychologically or attitudinally compelled to, but because their structural location in the world makes it easier for them to do so. It matters little if one is ideologically or psychologically disposed to participation if he or she lacks the structural vehicle that could "pull" them into protest activity.

Consistent with this line of argument, a number of recent studies have demonstrated the primacy of structural factors in accounting for activism (Fernandez and McAdam, 1987; McAdam, 1986; McCarthy, 1987; Orum, 1972; Rosenthal et al., 1985; Snow, Zurcher, and Ekland-Olson, 1980). Specifically, at least four structural factors have been linked to individual participation in movement activities.

PRIOR CONTACT WITH A MOVEMENT MEMBER

The factor that has been shown to bear the strongest relationship to activism is prior contact with another movement participant (Briet, Klandermans, and Kroon, 1984; Gerlach and Hine, 1970; Heirich, 1977; McAdam, 1986; Orum, 1972; Snow, Zurcher, and Ekland-Olson, 1980; Von Eschen, Kirk, and Pinard, 1971; Zurcher and Kirkpatrick, 1976). Bolton (1972, p. 558), for example, found that "most recruits" into the two peace groups he studied "were already associated with persons who belonged to or were organizing the peace group, and were recruited through these interpersonal channels." Similarly, Snow's (1976) analysis of the recruitment patterns of 330 members of the Nichiren Shoshu Buddhist movement in America revealed that 82% had been drawn into the movement by virtue of existing ties to other members. In a study of all applicants to the 1964 Mississippi Freedom Summer project, McAdam (1986) found twice as many participants to have "strong ties" to other volunteers than did applicants who withdrew in advance of the campaign. The fact that these "withdrawals" were indistinguishable from actual participants in their level of attitudinal support for the project only serves to underscore the relative importance of attitudinal versus micro-structural factors in recruitment to activism. These findings are very much in accord with those reported by Snow, Zurcher, and Ekland-Olson (1980) in their important survey of the empirical literature on movement recruitment. Of the nine empirical studies reviewed in their article, all but one identified prior interpersonal contact as the single richest source of movement recruits.[8]

MEMBERSHIP IN ORGANIZATIONS

Another micro-structural factor that has been linked to individual activism is the number of organizations the potential recruit belongs to. Belonging to a number of organizations may encourage activism in a variety of ways. In view of the well-documented association between organizational participation and feelings of personal efficacy (see Sayre, 1980; Neal and Seeman, 1964), it may simply be that those who are organizationally active are more likely to regard activism as potentially effective and therefore worth participating in. Or it may be that involvement in an organization increases a persons chances of learning about movement activity.Movement organizers have long appreciated how difficult it is to recruit single, isolated individuals and therefore expend most of their energies on mobilizing support within existing organizations. This tendency means that "joiners" are more likely to be aware and therefore "at risk" of being drawn into movement activities.

The final explanation for the link between organizational participation and activism represents a simple extension of the factor discussed in the previous section. To the extent that membership in organizations expands a person's range of interpersonal contacts, it also increases their susceptibility to the kind of personal recruiting appeals that have been shown to be so effective in drawing people into movements.

Regardless of the mix of factors accounting for the relationship, the empirical evidence for its existence is clear. Orum (1972, p. 50), for example, found a consistent positive relationship between involvement in the black student sit-in movement and number of campus organizations the student belonged to. McAdam's (1986) data on applicants to the Freedom Summer project showed participants to have higher

rates of organizational membership than non-participants. Several other studies report similar findings as well (see Barnes and Kaase, 1979; Von Eschen, Kirk, and Pinard, 1971; Walsh and Warland, 1983).

HISTORY OF PRIOR ACTIVISM

Though the relationship between activism at different points in time has not been studied much, the limited evidence that is available strongly supports the idea that a history of prior activism increases the likelihood of future activism. For instance, in their laboratory simulation of micro mobilization, Gamson, Freeman, and Rytina (1982) found that those individuals who had previously been involved in some form of collective action were more likely to be involved in "rebellious" groups. McAdam's follow-up study of the Freedom Summer applicants produced two pieces of evidence linking prior and subsequent activism. First, those who participated in the project had higher levels of prior civil rights activism than those who withdrew from the project (1986, pp. 81-82). Second, among the strongest predictors of current activism among the applicants was their level of activism between 1964 and 1970 (McAdam, 1988).

Three factors would seem to account for the positive relationship between prior and subsequent activism. The first is simply "know-how" or previous experience. To the extent that one is familiar with a particular form of social behavior, it makes sense that they would be more likely to engage in it. Some may gain this familiarity from sources other than direct experience, but experience is by far the most important teacher of such skills. Individuals who have engaged in collective action in the past can be expected to be more likely to possess the knowledge required to do so in the future.

A second explanation for the positive effect of movement participation on subsequent activism centers on role theory and the process by which we learn any new social role. The point is, "activist" is as much a social role as "college student," "sociologist," or any other role one could think of. Part of what happens in the course of movement activities, then, is that the new recruit is gradually socialized into this role (Lofland, 1977). The longer they stay in the movement, the greater the importance they are likely to ascribe to the role of "activist." As one accords any role greater importance, the desire to act out the role also increases, so that subsequent activism becomes a means of confirming or reinforcing an important part of one's identity.

A third way of accounting for the persistence of activism over time is to focus upon the "sunk social costs" that have been expended in any long-standing line of action. Becker (1963) uses this notion to understand such lines of action as behavioral "careers," whether deviant or legitimate. One can be thought to invest time, energy, relationships, as well as more tangible resources in pursuing activism. The costs of exit from such a line of action are thus substantial, thereby encouraging continued adherence to the role.

BIOGRAPHICAL AVAILABILITY

To this point we have emphasized the importance of various structural links between the potential recruit and movement in trying to account for individual activism. What this view omits is the biographical context in which this contact occurs. Quite apart from the "pull" exerted by these links, the biographical circumstances of a person's life may serve to encourage or constrain participation in important ways. The concept of "biographical availability" is intended to capture this impact and can be defined simply "as the absence of personal constraints that may increase the costs and risks of movement participation such as full-time employment, marriage, and family responsibilities" (McAdam, 1986, p. 70).

McCarthy and Zald (1973) appear to have been the first to note the effect of such constraints on the patterning of collective action. Their observations concerning the unusually high numbers of students and autonomous professionals who are active in movements reflected a clear understanding of the way biography constrains activism. Snow and Rochford (1983, p. 3) found that "a substantial majority of [Hare] Krishna recruits had few countervailing ties which might have served to constrain their participation in the movement." In his recent book on the Hare Krishna, Rochford (1985, pp. 76-84) provides additional data bearing on this issue. Finally, in his study of recruitment to the Freedom Summer project, McAdam (1986, p. 83) notes the degree to which his subjects were "remarkably free of personal constraints that might have inhibited participation."

Macro-Micro Bridges in Movement Emergence

How do we go about linking these two distinct literatures on movement emergence? That there must be a link between the two should be obvious. While broad political, economic, and organizational factors may combine to create a certain "macro potential" for collective action, that potential can only be realized through complex mobilization dynamics that unfold at either the micro or some intermediate institutional level. At the same time, these mobilization processes are clearly a collective, rather than an individual phenomena. That is, we are convinced that movements are not aggregations of discontented *individuals*. True to our designation, collective action is a profoundly *collective* phenomenon, not only once under way but in its genesis as well. Individual rebels did not take to the street and somehow come together on their way to the Boston Tea Party. Rather, we expect that the decision itself was framed and reached collectively. The point is, we can no more build social movements from the individual up than down from some broad societal process. We believe the real action takes place at a third level, intermediate between the individual and the broad macro contexts in which they are embedded. In the remainder of this section we will attempt to describe this intermediate level and account for its significance in the process of movement emergence. Just how does the assessment and translation of macro events into micro mobilization take place during the emergent phase of collective action?

Micro-Mobilization Contexts

The key concept linking macro- and microprocesses in movement emergence is that of the *micro-mobilization context*. A micro-mobilization context can be defined as any small group setting in which processes of collective attribution are combined with rudimentary forms of organization to produce mobilization for collective action. Several examples of such settings will help to clarify the concept. Perhaps the most obvious example is that of the extant political group. Unions, for instance, serve as the existing context in which grievances can be shared and translated into concrete forms of action. Nor is it only the entire union that can serve in this capacity. Subgroups within a union, organized informally on the basis of seniority or along task, racial, or even friendship lines may provide a basis for mobilization independent of the broader union context. This is often what happens in the case of wildcat strikes, or in instances where small, informally organized groups of workers become active in other movements. An example of the latter would be the "hardhat marches'' organized in the early 1970s by construction workers supporting the war in Vietnam.

This example of ''extracurricular'' mobilization can apply to *nonpolitical* groups as well. That is, groups organized for ostensibly *nonpolitical* purposes can serve as the settings within which attribution and organization come together to produce collective *political* action. Several authors have, for example, noted the importance of black churches as collective settings in which early civil rights organizing took place (see McAdam, 1982; Morris, 1984; Oberschall, 1973, pp. 126-127). Curtis and Zurcher (1973, p. 56) assign similar importance to a variety of ''nonpolitical'' organizations—but especially ''fraternal/service'' groups—in their analysis of the emergence of a local antipornography movement in Texas. Finally, Snow and Marshall (1984) document the important organizational role played by mosques in the early days of the Iranian Revolution.

Micro-mobilization may also take place in smaller, informal groups of people. For instance, friendship networks have been known to furnish the crucial context for micro mobilization. Perhaps the best-known example of this is the case of the four Greensboro A&T students who precipitated the 1960 black student sit-in movement with a demonstration that originated in informal ''bull sessions'' in one another's dorm rooms. Similarly, Sarah Evans (1980) locates the roots of the women's liberation movement in informal networks of women who had come to know one another in the context of civil rights and New Left organizing. Even participation in the urban riots of the 1960s has been seen as growing out of this type of informal group. Wilson and Orum (1976, p. 198) write: ''Many analysts have found themselves baffled by the riots of the 1960s; explanations presumed to work, such as those based on conventional psychological theories do not. On the basis of our limited experience with and observations of these events, it appears to us that social bonds alike, i.e. friendship networks, drew many people to become active participants.''

Despite these differences in the size and degree of formal organization of these various collective settings, all serve to encourage mobilization in at least three ways. First, they provide the context in which the all-important process of collective attribution can occur. We will discuss this process in greater detail later in this section. For now we need only note its significance in the generation of social insurgency. Broad macroprocesses only create a more or less favorable opportunity for collective ac-

tion. Mediating between opportunity and action are people and the subjective meanings they attach to their situations. As Edelman (1971, p. 133) has pointed out: ''Our explanations of mass political response have radically undervalued the ability of the human mind . . . to take a complex set of . . . cues into account [and] evolve a mutually acceptable form of response.'' This process must occur if an organized protest campaign is to take place. The important point for our purpose is that the potential for this process occurring is greatest in the type of contexts we have been discussing.

Second, these settings provide the rudiments of organization—leaders, whether formally designated or not, communication technologies, and so on—needed to translate attributions into concrete action. It is not enough that people define situations in new and potentially revolutionary ways; they must also act on these definitions to create a movement. These contexts provide the established roles and lines of interaction necessary for action to unfold.

Finally, in these collective settings are to be found the established structures of solidary incentives on which most social behavior depends. By ''structures of solidary incentives'' we refer to the myriad interpersonal rewards that attach to ongoing participation in any established group or informal association. It is expected that these incentive structures will solve or at least mitigate the effects of the ''free-rider'' problem (Fireman and Gamson, 1979).

First discussed by Mancur Olson (1965), the ''free-rider problem'' refers to the difficulties insurgents encounter in trying to convince participants to pursue goals whose benefits they would derive even if they did not participate in the movement. When viewed in the light of a narrow economic calculus, movement participation would indeed seem to be irrational. Even if we correct for Olson's overly rationalistic model of the individual, the ''free-rider'' mentality would still seem to pose a formidable barrier to movement recruitment. The solution to this problem is held to stem from the provision of selective incentives to induce the participation that individual calculation would alone seem to preclude (Gamson, 1975, pp. 66-71; Olson, 1965).

Within established groups, however, the need to provide selective incentives would appear to be substantially reduced. These groups already rest on a solid structure of solidary incentives that insurgents can attempt to appropriate by defining movement participation as synonymous with group membership. If this effect is successful, the myriad incentives that have heretofore served as the motive force for participation in the group will now be transferred to the movement. This spares insurgents the difficult task of inducing participation through the provision of new incentives of either a solidary or material nature.

For all these reasons then, informal groups or associational networks such as those discussed earlier are expected to serve as the basic building blocks of social movements. In effect, they constitute the "cell structure" of collective action. However, this still leaves the issue of micro-macro bridges unexamined. How *do* these mobilization contexts serve to link the macro and micro factors discussed earlier?

MACRO-DETERMINANTS OF
MICRO-MOBILIZATION CONTEXTS

What we have termed micro-mobilization contexts can be thought of as a dense network of intermediate-level groups and informal associations. The density of such networks, however, varies both between and within groups in society. Some groups appear as a veritable lattice work of such groupings, while others are handicapped by what McCarthy (1987) has termed "infrastructure deficits." In turn, the level of infrastructure in a given population is itself shaped by the type of macro factors discussed earlier. Broad macroprocesses, such as industrialization, urbanization, mass migration, and the like, largely determine the degree to which groups in society are organized and the structure of that organization. The extent and structure of that organization in turn imply very different potentials for collective action.

To illustrate the ways in which broad societal dynamics shape the level of social organization and therefore the potential for collective action of various groups, we have selected three examples for further discussion. In all three cases, the rise of new social movements has been linked by analysts to macro-level processes that left particular groups in a much stronger organizational position to launch collective action.

CHANGES IN THE STATUS OF WOMEN
AND THE EMERGENCE OF
THE WOMEN'S MOVEMENT

Feminist movements have emerged at various times in Western nations during the nineteenth and twentieth centuries. The most recent wave of feminist movements has attracted extensive attention and analysis by feminists and social movement scholars. Most of these accounts begin with a macroanalysis of the changing status of women in modern Western industrial nations. For instance, Jo Freeman writes, "The effects of women moving into paid employment —on women, the economy, the family, and a host of other institutions—have been a major source of strain to which the feminist movements of the nineteenth and twentieth centuries have been one response" (Freeman, 1975). Several authors have carried this theme a step further and analyzed the development of gender conflict in the workplace as a function of the clash of traditional and modern conceptions of the female role. Weinstein (1979), for example, shows how the massive movement of women into full-time employment has clashed with long-standing conceptions of "women's duties" to produce mini-feminist revolts in many offices and other work settings. In effect, the gender revolution in work has left women in a stronger organizational position to challenge traditional gender roles. Just as industrialization served to concentrate the urban proletariat in neighborhoods and factories from which they could launch collective action, the entrance of large numbers of women into paid employment has had a similar effect. Grouping women of considerable education and ambition together in gender-restrictive work settings has created a socially and politically volatile situation especially ripe for collective action. Pharr (in press) has noted the same dynamic in the Japanese workplace, where female workers have resisted pressure to be both modern employees and traditional women.

It is interesting that the same type of analysis has been used to account for the emergence of a variety of movements that have emerged in opposition to the feminist movement (i.e., Conover and Gray, 1983: Luker, 1984). Such reactionary movements include the anti-ERA and prolife movements. These movements are seen as emerging out of the pools of traditional women threatened by the lifestyles and politics of modern, employed, professional women. Like those who have studied the origins of modern feminism, analysts of these various countermovements have sought to understand their origins in relation to fundamental changes in the organization of women's lives.

MASS HIGHER EDUCATION AND THE
RISE OF THE "NEW CLASS"

Observers of changes in the class structure of modern societies have not ignored the massive growth in higher education and the political consequences thought to stem from it. The growth in numbers of young people enrolled in higher education is a worldwide phenomenon, and is led by trends in the United States where close to 50% of high school graduates go on to spend some time in college. Two lines of analysis have emerged from these observations that have important implications for an understanding of the emergence and development of contemporary social movements. These lines of analysis have focused on the formation of large ecological concentrations of students, and the rise of a large and increasingly homogeneous class of professional/technical workers. Both of these emergent groupings are seen as important in macro accounts of new collective action and social movements.

Large concentrations of physically mature students housed in institutions of higher education for longer and longer periods of time are seen as producing the organizational potential for chronic student movements. This potential is exacerbated by economic trends that impinge upon the future prospects of cohorts of students (Kriesi, 1985). Those American analysts who have sought to understand the origin of student movements here (i.e., Flacks, 1967) have generally produced quite similar macroanalyses as those Europeans who have focused upon the general rise of "new social movements" (Klandermans, 1986). Both accounts see macrosocial changes creating increasingly large, well-organized concentrations of students whose potential for collective action, even if it has presently waned, remains high.

In addition, these institutions of higher education produce trained "experts" who are coming to dominate employment in the service sector and professions of modern industry. Their training, it is alleged (i.e., Bruce-Briggs, 1979), creates progressive values and shared life circumstances that mark them as a "new class." Much debate has raged over the substantive sentiments of this group (see Brint, 1984) and their potential to be a progressive political force (see Gouldner, 1976). Some have argued that occupations within the "new class" can be productively conceived of as professional social movements whose goal is the creation, expansion, and defense of markets for their services (McAdam and McCarthy, 1982). Others have argued that this "new class" remains too diffuse and politically heterogeneous to constitute a serious source of new social movements. Both sides of the debate, however, betray the same logic in their analysis. Each seeks to understand the political potential of emerging work groups on the basis of macro-level changes in the structure of modern employment. In doing so, they are merely contributing to the oldest and richest research tradition in the study of movement emergence.

The nineteenth century was dominated by accounts of the rise and fall of social movements as a response to the massive social and economic upheavals occasioned by the Industrial Revolution (i.e., Marx, 1958). Indeed, the idea of a "general social movement" was derived from the rise of the movements of the working classes (Blumer, 1955; Tilly, 1984). To understand the rise of such a movement, one was led to analyze the shifts in the economic class structure of changing societies. So, too, do modern scholars seek the macro correlates of the rise of newer social movements in the changing social groupings that emerge from changes in the patterning of work and education in modern industrial society.

MASS MIGRATION AS AN IMPETUS TO MOVEMENT EMERGENCE

One final example of the link between broad macroprocesses and rise of social movements concerns the role of mass migration in creating new groups with the organizational potential for successful collective action. Two examples will serve to illustrate the relationship. The first concerns the effect of urbanization (and industrialization) on the locus and form of collective action in nineteenth-century Europe. As the Tillys have painstakingly documented in *The Rebellious Century* (1975), the rise of urban-based movements during this period was largely a response to migration processes that concentrated large numbers of the emerging working class into organizationally dense urban neighborhoods.

Blacks in the American South were party to a similar process. As long as blacks were subject to the extremely repressive system of social control on which Southern agriculture was founded, their concentration in the South and relative isolation from whites was never effectively translated into a strong network of intermediate association. Nor was it fear alone that produced this failure. More to the point, white planters, fearing "their" charges, forcibly discouraged the development of independent black institutions. Even the one exception to this rule, the black church, achieved independence only after an early history of "benevolent sponsorship" by white planters intent on civilizing the "natives."

The collapse of King Cotton, however, changed the situation drastically. Spurred by the collapse, the general pattern of rural-to-urban migration within the South freed blacks from the extreme forms of social control they had previously been subject to. In the relatively safe environs of the urban South, segregation and residential concentration served to produce a full flowering of independent black institutions—churches, colleges, political organizations—that would later play midwife to the civil rights movement (McAdam, 1982; Morris, 1984).

MICRO-DYNAMICS WITHIN MICRO-MOBILIZATION CONTEXTS

To this point our evaluation of the significance of micro-mobilization contexts has only focused attention on the macro side of the equation. That is, we have linked the presence and strength of these contexts to some of the macro-economic and organizational factors discussed earlier. But we have not yet explained their role in the generation of mobilization at the micro level. In our view, the significance of these contexts derives from the established organizational and interpersonal settings they afford insurgents. Within these settings, any number of processes crucial to micro mobilization take place. In the following pages we will identify three such processes.

FRAME ALIGNMENT AND THE PROCESS OF COLLECTIVE ATTRIBUTION

For all the recent emphasis on macro-political or other structural "determinants" of social movements, the immediate impetus to collective action remains a cognitive one. As Gamson, Fireman and Rytina's recent book (1982) makes abundantly clear, successful collective action precedes from a significant transformation in the collective consciousness of the actors involved. Analysts as diverse as Marx (1958), Edelman (1971), Smelser (1962), Turner and Killian (1972) and McAdam (1982) have noted the importance of this process while using a variety of concepts—"class consciousness," "generalized beliefs," "cognitive liberation" —to describe it. Recently, however, Snow and his colleagues (1986) have refined and extended our understanding of the cognitive basis of collective action by proposing a typology of "frame alignment processes" by which activists seek to construct legitimating accounts to support their own and others' activism. New movements always entail some break with established behavioral routines. In order to overcome people's natural reluctance to break with these routines, ideological rationales must be fashioned that legitimate the movement's behavioral proscriptions. Snow and his colleagues

distinguish four distinct frame alignment processes—frame bridging, frame amplification, frame extension, and frame transformation—by which these rationales are constructed.

It is important to recognize, however, that these processes "are overwhelmingly not based upon observation or empirical evidence available to participants, but rather upon cuings among groups of people who jointly create the meanings they will read into current and anticipated events" (Edelman, 1971, p. 32). The key phrase here is "groups of people." That is, the chances of frame alignment occurring are assumed to be greatest in precisely the kind of collective settings we've called micro-mobilization contexts. In the first place, groups—whether formal or informal—are the repositories for the existing frames that are often the raw materials for the various frame alignment processes. For example, established churches provide a rich and detailed "worldview" or frame that can be used to encourage activism by any movement that succeeds in appropriately this frame for its own uses. Accounting for the rapid spread of movements as diverse as the civil rights movement (McAdam, 1982, pp. 129-130), the Moral Majority (Snow et al., 1986, pp. 468) and the Iranian Revolution (Snow and Marshall, 1984) become fairly easy when one realizes how effectively the leaders of these movements tied the behavioral requirements of the new movement to the legitimating frame of an established religion.

Even in those rare instances where new frames are constructed from scratch—frame transformation, to use the term proposed by Snow and his coauthors—it is hard to see how the process could occur anywhere but in an established collective setting. Even in the unlikely event that a single person were to generate such a frame, his or her isolation would almost surely prevent its spread to the minimum number of people required to afford a reasonable basis for mounting successful collective action.More to the point, perhaps, is the suspicion that under such conditions, the process of frame transformation would never occur in the first place. The consistent finding linking feelings of efficacy to social integration supports this judgment (Neal and Seeman, 1964; Pinard, 1971; Sayre, 1980). In the absence of strong interpersonal links to others, people are likely to feel powerless to change their own lives, let alone the fundamental way they view the world.

To this finding one might add the educated supposition that what Ross (1977) calls the "fundamental attribution error"—the tendency of people to explain their situation as a function of individual rather than situational factors

—is more likely to occur under conditions of personal isolation than under those of integration. Lacking the information and perspective that others afford, isolated individuals would seem especially prone to explain their troubles on the basis of personal rather than "system attributions" (Ferree and Miller, 1985).

The practical significance of this distinction comes from the fact that only system attributions afford the necessary rationale for political movements. For analysts of such movements, then, the key question becomes what social circumstances are productive of "system attributions" or the construction of frames that attribute significance to political processes outside the individual? Following Ferree and Miller (1985, p. 46), the likely answer is that "without a homogeneous, intensely interacting group . . . people are unlikely to recognize that their private troubles are reflections of public issues rather than personal flaws." In our terms, the chances of any form of frame alignment occurring would seem greatest in the type of micro-mobilization context described earlier. These settings also provide a favorable context for a second important social psychological process.

VALUE EXPECTANCY AND THE AGGREGATION OF CHOICE

Should any frame legitimating activism come to be widely shared within a particular population, the chances of collective action occurring are substantially improved. This still tells us nothing about whether a given member of that population will take part in any resulting action. To better understand that process we need a model of individual decision making. Through his application of value expectancy theory to the phenomenon of individual activism, Klandermans (1984) has provided us with such a model. At the heart of his model is a view of the individual as a rational, calculating actor weighing the costs and benefits of activism. The key point, though, is that these anticipated costs and benefits are not independent of the individuals assessment of the likely actions of others. Instead, the perceived efficacy of participation for the individual will depend upon the following three sets of expectations they bring to the decision-making process:

(1) expectations about the number of participants;

(2) expectations about one's own contribution to the probability of success;

(3) expectations about the probability of success if many people participate (Klandermans, 1984, p. 585).

Individual activism, then, is most likely to occur in a situation where the individual has high expectations on all three of these counts.

As useful as Klandermans's application of value expectancy theory is, it nonetheless tends, as most choice theories do, to divorce the individual actor and the subjective utilities that shape his or her choices from the collective settings in which these utilities are derived. This is not to deny that the individual remains the ultimate locus of choice processes. At the same time the generation of expectancies on which choice depends remains a profoundly social process requiring attention to and information about other relevant actors. The significance of these micro-mobilization contexts, then, stems in part from the ready access to information they afford members. Imagine two students trying to decide whether or not to attend an anti-aparthied rally to be held on campus. Imagine further that one of the students lives in a dorm and is a member of several political groups on campus, while the other commutes to school and is not a member of any campus groups. Irrespective of their attitudes concerning the South African social and political situation, which of the two students is more likely to attend the rally? Probably the student who is more integrated into campus life. Why? There are several reasons, but among the most significant is the fact that our prospective activist is involved in several collective settings—the dorm and political groups—that favor the generation of high expectations concerning the prospects for successful group action. To the extent that others in either setting are giving indications that they are going to attend the rally, the likelihood that our potential recruit will go are increased as well.

But it isn't just that these collective settings encourage choices favoring participation. In addition, they serve as contexts within which these individual choices can be aggregated into a collective plan of action. It isn't enough that individual actors choose to participate in activism. Their choices must then be combined with those of others in such a way as to make group action possible. Micro-mobilization contexts provide the setting within which this aggregation process can occur.

RESOURCE MOBILIZATION

It isn't simply choices, however, that are aggregated in these micro-mobilization contexts.

The significance of these settings is as much organizational as social psychological. Micro-mobilization contexts serve as the organizational "staging ground" for the movement. It is within these contexts that a wide variety of resources essential to collective action are mobilized. Three resources in particular are worth noting.

I. MEMBERS

If there is anything approximating a consistent finding in the empirical literature, it is that movement participants are recruited along established lines of interaction. The explanation for this consistent finding would appear to be straightforward: The more integrated the person is into the aggrieved community, the more readily he or she can be mobilized for participation in protest activities. As Gerlach and Hine argue, "no matter how a typical participant describes his reasons for joining the movement, or what motives may be suggested by a social scientist on the basis of deprivation, disorganization, or deviancy models, it is clear that the original decision to join required some contact with the movement" (Gerlach and Hine, 1970, p. 79). The significance of micro-mobilization contexts stems from the fact that they render this type of facilitative contact more likely, thus promoting member recruitment.

II. COMMUNICATION NETWORK

Micro-mobilization contexts also constitute a communication network or infrastructure, the strength and breadth of which largely determine the pattern, speed, and extent of movement expansion. Both the failure of a new movement to take hold and the rapid spread of insurgent action have been credited to the presence or absence of such an infrastructure. Freeman has argued that it was the recent development of such a network that enabled women in the 1960s to create a successful feminist movement where they had earlier been unable to do so:

The development of the women's liberation movement highlights the salience of such a network precisely because the conditions for a movement existed *before* a network came into being, but the movement didn't exist until afterward. Socioeconomic strain did not change for women significantly during a 20-year period. It was as great in 1955 as in 1965. What changed was the organizational situation. It was not until a communications network developed among like-minded people beyond local boundaries that the movement could emerge and develop

past the point of occasional, spontaneous uprising [Freeman, 1973, p. 804].

Conversely, Jackson et al. (1960) document a case in which the absence of a readily cooptable communication network contributed to "The Failure of an Incipient Social Movement." The movement, an attempted property tax revolt in California, failed, according to the authors, because "there was no . . . preestablished network of communication which could be quickly employed to link the suburban residential property owners who constituted the principal base for the movement" (Jackson et al., 1960, p. 38).

These findings are consistent with the empirical thrust of studies of cultural diffusion, a body of literature that has unfortunately been largely overlooked by movement analysts despite its relevance to the topic. To our knowledge, only Maurice Pinard (1971, pp. 186-187) has explicitly applied the empirical insights of this literature to the study of social movements. He summarizes the central tenet of diffusion theory as follows: "The higher the degree of social integration of potential adopters, the more likely and the sooner they will become actual adopters . . . on the other hand, near-isolates tend to be the last to adopt an innovation" (1971, p. 187). The applicability of this idea to the study of social insurgency stems from recognition of the fact that a social movement is, after all, a new cultural item subject to the same pattern of diffusion or adoption as other innovations. Indeed, without acknowledging the theoretical basis of his insight, Oberschall has hypothesized for movements the identical pattern of diffusion noted earlier by Pinard: "The greater the number and variety of organizations in a collectivity, and the higher the participation of members in this network, the more rapidly and enduringly does mobilization into conflict groups occur" (Oberschall, 1973, p. 125).

Oberschall's statement has brought us full circle. Our brief foray into the diffusion literature only serves to amplify the basic argument by placing it in a theoretical context that helps explain the importance of micro-mobilization contexts in the generation of insurgency. The linkages characteristic of such groups facilitate movement emergence by providing the means of communication by which the movement, as a new cultural item, can be disseminated throughout the aggrieved population.

III. LEADERS

All manner of movement analysts have asserted the importance of leaders or organizers in the generation of social insurgency. To do so requires not so much a particular theoretical orientation as common sense.

The existence of established groups within the movement's mass base ensures the presence of recognized leaders who can be called upon to lend their prestige and organizing skills to the incipient movement. Indeed, given the pattern of diffusion discussed in the previous section, it may well be that established leaders are among the first to join a new movement by virtue of their central position within the community. There is in fact some empirical evidence to support this. To cite only one example, Lipset, in his study of the Socialist C.C.F. party, reports that "in Saskatchewan it was the local leaders of the Wheat Pool, of the trade-unions, who were the first to join the C.C.F." His interpretation of the finding is that "those who are most thoroughly integrated in the class through formal organizations are the first to change" (1950, p. 197). Regardless of the timing of their recruitment, the existence of recognized leaders is yet another resource whose availability is conditioned by the degree of organization within the aggrieved population.

Micro-mobilization contexts, then, are the primary source of resources facilitating movement emergence. These groups constitute the organizational context in which insurgency is expected to develop. As such, their presence is as crucial to the process of movement emergence as a conducive political environment. If one lacks the capacity to act, it hardly matters that one is afforded the chance to do so.

Movement Maintenance and Change

Although collective action is expected to develop within micro-mobilization contexts, rarely are movements able to rely on them for their survival. It must be remembered that in most cases these micro-mobilization contexts may be little more than informal friendship networks, ad hoc committees, or loosely structured coalitions of activists. Such groups may function as the organizational locus of early mobilizing efforts, but rarely as permanent movement organizations.

For the movement to survive, pioneering activists must be able to create a more enduring organizational structure. Efforts to do so normally entail the creation of formal social movement organizations (SMOs) to assume the centralized direction of the movement previously exercised by informal groups. Hereafter, the crucial task of mediating between the larger macro environment and the set of microdynamics on which the movement depends will fall to these SMOs. The challenge that confronts the SMO is not fundamentally different from the one that confronts any formal organization. At the macro level, the SMO must negotiate a niche for itself within the larger organizational environment in which it is embedded. This usually entails the negotiation and management of a complex set of relationships with other organizational actors representing the movement, the state, countermovements, the media, and the general public. How well the SMO manages the contradictory demands imposed by these groups will have a lot to do with the way the movement develops over time.

The movement and the SMOs that increasingly represent it face a challenge at the micro level as well. As organizations, SMOs must continue to mobilize the resources—members, money, and so on—they need to survive. Of necessity, this latter goal involves the SMO in a continuous process of micro mobilization. Converts must be sought, resources acquired, and the commitment of members maintained.

This micro challenge is no less important to the course of movement development than the macro challenge sketched earlier. One of the principal ways SMOs seek to mediate these twin challenges is through the selection of goals and tactics. As regards the larger macro environment, choices about either goals or tactics are likely to reflect calculations concerning the anticipated reactions of other organizational actors. At the same time, the internal resource needs of the SMO will also shape programmatic and tactical decisions. In effect, goals and tactics are the principal tools an SMO uses to shape its external environment while simultaneously attending to the ongoing demands of micro mobilization. In the remainder of this chapter, we will discuss all of these dynamics in more detail. Before we do so, however, we will want to know a good bit more about SMOs and the forms they typically take.

Social Movement Organizations

Movement organizations are usually the carriers of the mature movement. They serve to aggregate people and resources in the service of the "cause." While much movement activity may occur outside of SMOs by individuals and groups with little or no affiliation with the

SMOs, the formal movement groups attempt to remain the command posts of movements.

The acronym SMO entered the social movement literature through the analysis of Zald and Ash (1966). There it referred to the carrier organizations of social movement aims, and was seen to vary between inclusive and exclusive forms. This distinction captures the extent of involvement and commitment to the organization on the part of the typical member. Much research has focused on organized social movement forms since then, and a wide variety of dimensions of SMO structure have been explicated. The use of the denotation, however, remains vague. Let us here summarize the various organizational forms to which it has been applied.

John Lofland has developed a census of what he calls movement organization local forms. The types of SMO locals he identifies are: (1) associations sustained by volunteers, (2) bureaus employing staffers, (3) troups deploying soldiers, (4) communes composed of family members, (5) collectives consisting of cooperating workers, and (6) utopias populated by utopians. The array of forms is ordered in terms of increasing scope of involvement, and thus mirrors the Zald and Ash distinction between inclusive and exclusive SMO forms. There has been extensive analysis of these various forms. Some of the best-known analyses are those of Gamson (1975), Kanter (1972) and Curtis and Zurcher (1973). This array of forms appears to vary between the poles of intensity and extensity. Those forms that demand the most of members have the most difficulty gaining large numbers of members, and those forms that demand the least are capable of generating the widest support.[10] What constitutes the most local level of analysis here is a function of the focus of research. So Ronald Lawson (1983) described what he calls BOs (building organizations) and NOs (neighborhood organizations) in his account of the organizational stucture of the tenants' movement in New York City.

Movement locals may be disconnected organizations laboring in isolation toward their social change goals. Or they may be linked to other local organizations through a variety of organizational mechanisms. Or they may be linked to higher level organizations, or some combinations of these. The most general types of forms here are federation structure, chapter structure, and what Gerlach and Hine (1970) call reticulate, segmentary, decentralized structure. Snow (1986) provides an example of the latter type of structure in his analysis of the Nichiren Shoshu movement in the United States.

A quite modern form of the SMO is the professional social movement organization (PSMO) originally identified by McCarthy and Zald (1973):

Professional social movements are characterized by:

(1) A leadership that devotes full time to the movement
  (a) A large proportion of resources originating outside of the aggrieved group that the movement claims to represent.
(2) A very small or nonexistent membership base or a paper membership (membership implies little more than allowing name to be used upon membership rolls).
(3) Attempts to impart the image of 'speaking for a potential constituency.'
(4) Attempts to influence policy toward that same constituency. [p. 20].

Purely PSMOs communicate with adherents or members through the mails or the mass media. They link people together through very weak networks of communication (see McCarthy, 1987). But in fact there are few pure cases of this form, and many recent analyses of PSMOs have revised and extended the earlier statements about it. Common Cause, for instance, evolved into a mixed form with many vigorous local chapters, though its central still mirrors the PSMO form (McFarland, 1984). The Pennsylvanians for a Biblical Majority (Cable, 1984) shows a PSMO form at the state level, but through telephone trees, which link local congregational members whose churches support the PSMO, look more like a federation of the reticulate, segmentary, decentralized form.

Troyer and Markle (1983) describe ASH, an anti-smoking group, as a prototype of the PSMO form. Tierney (1982) describes the "battered women movement" at the local level as a professionalized movement, and views its vulnerability to cooptation as an important consequence of its lack of a beneficiary constituency that supports the movement. Johnston (1980) reviews the early history of Transcendental Meditation (TM) in the United States, and found elements of a PSMO, but other elements that lead him to term it a "marketed social movement."

Another interesting form of movement organization is what Morris (1984) has termed the "movement halfway house." "A movement halfway house is an established group or organization that is only partially integrated into the larger society because its participants are actively involved in efforts to bring about a desired change in society . . . What is distinctive about movement halfway houses is their relative isolation from the larger society and the absence of a mass base" (p. 139). Such institutions may serve as repositories of information about past movements, strategy and tactics, inspiration and leadership. They are especially important during lulls in social movement activity. Many of these halfway houses appear to be rooted in religious communities such as the Fellowship of Reconciliation (Robinson, 1981), The American Friends Service Committee (Jonas, 1971), and the Catholic Worker (Miller, 1974).

ORGANIZATIONAL TRAJECTORIES

An earlier literature emphasized the process of institutionalization as the inevitable outcome of movement development. What Zald and Ash (1966) labeled the Weber-Michels model of routinization and oligarchization was the dominant image of the trajectory of SMOs. Zald and Ash argued that the model was limited and that a more inclusive and dynamic model of organization-environment relations allowed one to expect a variety of other SMO trajectories, including demise, radicalization, schism, and movement organization becalmed. The Weber-Michels model suffered from the tyranny of the iron cage. As one adopts an organization-environment model for the study of ongoing movement development, it becomes apparent that SMOs exist in a larger macro environment that greatly constrains their actions. The net impact of these constraints is never so simple as to yield a single outcome—such as institutionalism—in the case of all SMOs. Rather, at the macro level, we are encouraged to analyze the process of movement development as turning on a complex process of interaction between SMOs and a variety of other organizational actors. The structural impact of this interaction process is expected to vary from SMO to SMO.

Macro Development: SMOs and the Larger Organizational Environment

At the macro level, the emergence of a social movement depends on informal collections of activists recognizing and exploiting the unique opportunity for collective action afforded them by shifting political, economic and demographic conditions. Once in place, however, the movement and the specific SMOs that are its carriers face a very different challenge. They now con-

front an established organizational environment aware of, and frequently hostile toward, the new movement. Just how successfully these SMOs negotiate this organizational environment will largely determine the ultimate fate of the movement. Among the specific actors SMOs are likely to confront in this process are competing SMOs, the state, countermovements, and the media.

MOVEMENT INDUSTRIES

Social movement industries (SMIs) comprise all SMOs pursuing relatively similar goals. Although SMOs in a given SMI may differ in tactics and may compete for resources and leadership, they may also cooperate. Under precisely what conditions we can expect competing SMOs to cooperate is an important question movement researchers have yet to answer.

A number of hypotheses about movement industries can, however, be stated. For instance, as demand for a movement expands, the number and size of SMOs should also increase. As an SMI expands, the member SMOs are likely to try to "product differentiate" their goals and tactics so as to ensure a distinctive niche for themselves within the movement. So far, no scholars have sought to test these hypotheses. Systematic studies of particular SMIs have also been rare. However, Conover and Gray (1983) present an excellent analysis of the movement/countermovement industries that have emerged around the issues of woman's rights and the family. Aldon Morris (1984) and Steve Barkan (1986) have addressed the interorganizational relationships and competition and cooperation of groups in the civil rights movement. Both examine the interplay of SCLC and the NAACP, and then, as the movement grew, the interplay of SNCC, CORE, and other groups. Finally, Staggenborg (1986), in a detailed analysis of the prochoice movement, has shown the importance of the prolife countermovement in shaping the interorganizational relations and growth of prochoice forces.

One especially promising topic in the study of SMIs is the analysis of what has been termed radical flank effects" (Haines, 1984). The concept is used to describe one effect that often follows from the presence of "extremist" SMOs within the same movement with other more "moderate" groups. As Haines (1984) shows in his analysis of changes in the funding of the major civil rights organizations, such a situation is likely to redound to the benefit of the moderate SMOs. In effect, the presence of "extremists" encourages funding support for the "moderates" as a way of undercutting the influence of the radicals. A similar dynamic may also characterize state/movement relations. Increasingly, the demands of movements are being adjudicated by representatives of the state. To respond to a movement, these representatives must focus on the movement leaders and organizations that seem to speak for the movement and yet who are reasonable coalition partners. In such a situation, the presence of "extremist" SMOs can actually help to legitimate and strengthen the bargaining hand of more moderate SMOs. Though not planned in most cases, these dynamics would appear to have important implications for the trajectory and success of the movement.

STATE/MOVEMENT RELATIONS

The central importance of the modern sate has made it a key target for most political movements. Therefore, any analysis of change or stability in political movements must couple efforts to study the ways in which movements seek to influence or overthrow states with an assessment of state efforts to control, channel, repress, or facilitate movements. The increasing volume of studies of this type has moved social movement analysis much closer to, or perhaps even made it a part of, political sociology, where Rudolph Heberle (1951) thought it should be nearly four decades ago. In the following three sections, we will attempt to delineate three topics that illustrate the increasingly close connection between much movement analysis and the field of political sociology.

THE STATE AS CONTROL AGENT

The control of social movements may, of course, involve persons other than state authorities. The employer who frowns upon, or dismisses, employees perceived to be overly active in social movement activity is part of the social control environment of a social movement, even if not a part of the state apparatus. Obviously, a movement's opponents will be implicated in efforts to control, or even destroy, the movement. The responses of friends and family to participation in social movements can also be seen as part of the micro context of social control. The individual activist's risk-reward calculus is expected to reflect this broad set of relations.

At the same time, however, the status of the modern state as the institutional embodiment of elite interests often puts state authorities in the position of having to defend those interests against the competing claims of challenging groups. This, coupled with the state's historic monopoly on the legitimate use of violence, often makes it the key actor in an analysis of the social control of political movements.

The efforts of authorities to control movements include general policies that apply to all movements as well as specific actions directed at particular movements or groups. In the former category are state policies regulating the forms of association, tax advantages, and tactics available (e.g., the legal status of boycotts, strikes, curfew regulations) to movements. The latter category includes activities by authorities to control or inhibit specific movements, their organizations, adherents, and leaders. FBI surveillance, denial of loans to student activists, attempts to deny nonprofit status to specific organizations, and application of restraint of trade legislation to the NAACP in Mississippi are examples of specific policies aimed at particular movements.

General state policies grow out of the specific histories of particular polities. The relative size of the social movement sector in any given society is at least in part a function of the types of general policies in place. Obviously, authoritarian, totalitarian, and pluralist democracies can be expected to differ greatly in the general policies that inhibit or facilitate SMO formation and tactics. All that seems clear. What is less clear are the conditions under which the specific attempts of authorities to control or facilitate a movement (a) are likely to occur and (b) be effective. The problem is, as Lipsky (1968) has so ably argued, that the analysis of protest as a political resource (and implicitly authority as a political response), cannot just examine the direct linkages and cost-benefit conditions imposed by movements on authorities, and authorities on movements. Instead, one must also examine the reaction and perceptions of bystander publics and reference elites. These perceptions and reactions are often filtered through the media. "Repression works," says Charles Tilly. To this must be added: under some conditions and not others. Indeed, attempts at repression may release "repression fallout" (Hancock, 1975). Systematic, sustained, unbridled repression works in the short run. But regimes—especially ostensibly democratic ones—can rarely buy social peace for long periods of time by recourse to repression. Even in the short run, the use of repression may trigger a positive response to the movement from previously neutral or only mildly sympathetic bystander publics (Turner, 1969).

By its own actions, the movement helps to condition the response of third parties and thus to encourage or discourage state repression. McAdam (1982) offers several examples of this dynamic in his analysis of the shifting fortunes of the civil rights movement between 1960 and 1970. In the early sixties, civil rights forces—especially Martin Luther King's Southern Christian Leadership Conference—were able to provoke violence on the part of Southern authorities, thus generating enormous sympathy and support for the movement among the media and general public. One effect of this support was to raise the costs of repression to prohibitive levels, thus reducing the level of official control efforts. In contrast, the rhetorical militance of various black power groups during the late sixties alarmed the general public, allowing state authorities to repress these groups with relative impunity.

In modern society, however, control over social movements is never a matter of repression alone. In addition, there are various forms of control embedded in the normal legal/bureaucratic routines of society. In this country, these include various rules and regulations whose enforcement is the responsibility of such agencies as the Internal Revenue Service, the U.S. Postal Service, and many state and local agencies set up to evaluate the "public-regardingness" of social movement organizations (Wolfson, 1987). For many SMOs, a particularly salient example of this type of bureaucratic control are the rules governing tax exempt status. The tax and fund-raising advantages of the designation "non-profit" are sufficiently attractive to many SMOs as to encourage them to modify their programs so as to attain this status (McCarthy and Britt, in press). The moderating effect of such efforts is obvious.

In addition, authorities often exercise covert surveillance in their attempts to control social movements. But the process of surveillance, too, has risks. Undercover agents may be coopted by the movement. They may even stimulate or contribute to movement activity. Gary Marx (1974, 1979) has done more than anyone else to show the dynamics of infiltration in modern American movements. But similar problems have also been documented, almost as an aside, in Victoria Bonnell's (1984) study of worker participation in revolutionary activity in Russia. She shows how the level of police infiltration facilitated movement activity in prerevolutionary Russia.

THE STATE AS FACILITATOR

We have already noted that in the attempt to control movements through surveillance,

government intrusion may actually facilitate movement activity. Beyond such indirect facilitation authorities may directly fund agencies and programs that are carriers of movement goals. Indeed, a major part of the Reagan agenda seems to have involved the "de-funding of the Left." For example, Himmelstein and Zald (1984) have shown that part of the Reagan Administration's attack on the social sciences was related to their perception that social scientists were part of the political "left." More generally, James T. Bennett and Thomas J. DeLorenzo (1985) have documented numerous case studies of government funding of liberal partisan politics.

There is, of course, an analytic and definitional issue here. When is government funding and agency activism part of the bureaucratic and routine operation of government, and when is it aimed at aiding social action? In practice the question may not have an either/or answer. Grants from the National Institute for Drug Abuse can fund organizations that offer routine services and promote social change activity. The National Highway Transportation Safety Agency can fund SMOs that work for social change on the drinking and driving issues. As social movement analysis intersects with political sociology, the distinction between social movements and pressure groups becomes less relevant (see Useem and Zald, 1982). Gamson (1975) has examined the process by which a challenging group gains standing in the polity. In this, he focuses both upon gaining access to government, and achieving substantive gains. In his empirical work, Gamson ends up treating access the same as gaining official recognition as a legitimate representative of the aggrieved group. But in his theoretical discussion, access is in fact a continuum along which the challenging groups achieves greater and greater penetration of government agencies. Movements do not end when their representatives take power; instead, they are transformed. Government officials may operate routinely to deliver substantive benefits to movement constituents or work with movement groups in and out of government to change official policy and procedures. Different agencies and branches of government may support specific social movement goals. Thus the social movement and countermovement activities may occur more or less within government itself. Richard Gale (1986) has documented the extent to which the environmental movement and its opposition were both represented in different agencies of the federal government.

DIVISIONS WITHIN THE STATE

As the Gale example illustrates, it would be a mistake to see the various components of the state as always acting in consort either to oppose or support a movement. More recent scholarship on state/movement relations has instead focused on divisions within the state and the movement's efforts to exploit these divisions. For example, scholars of the American civil rights movement (Barkan, 1985; Bloom, 1986; Garrow, 1978; McAdam, 1982, 1983) have demonstrated the necessity of examining the interplay of different branches and geographical units of government in accounting for the success or failure of movement campaigns. Southern sheriffs and voter registrars were restrained by federal laws and Justice Department suits. Governor Orville Faubus of Arkansas was constrained by President Eisenhower's calling out of the National Guard in the Little Rock school desegregation crisis. This is not to say that federal authorities were aggressive advocates of movement goals. On the contrary, federal support was forthcoming only on those occasions when movement forces were able to provoke Southern authorities into well- publicized and extreme violations of black civil rights. Nonetheless, as Garrow (1978), Hubbard (1968), and McAdam (1982, 1983) have shown, this characteristic response was enough to give movement forces the leverage they needed to achieve significant civil rights gains.

Similarly, different branches of government may be at odds with one another or may afford movements better or worse opportunities to pursue their goals. In a system of divided power, the legislative, executive, and judicial branches operate under different procedural and substantive norms and have different constituencies. Barkan (1985), Handler (1978), and Balbus (1973), have plowed new territory in showing how courts/juries and judges, and criminal and civil procedures may be used to facilitate or impede social movement goals. Barkan illuminates how juries may nullify formal law to impede authority, thus promoting social movements. Moreover, he shows how trials may be used as media events in order to publicize movement goals. Balbus shows how the courts may undercut police efforts to control participants during civil disorders. Rather than the courts aiding the control effort, judicial procedures and the political economy of courts may restrain their use as agents of repression. Handler illuminates the conditions under which SMOs may or may not be effective in seeking judicial redress of

their grievances. Courts are limited in the remedies they can impose. If the movement is seeking major substantive changes, courts are not especially useful. Moreover, SMOs must command legal resources for long periods of time, if they are to pursue legal remedies against well-organized, well-funded opponents.

COUNTERMOVEMENTS

By challenging existing institutional arrangements, social movements invite opposition. To the extent that opposition takes on an organized, relatively enduring character, we can say that a countermovement has developed. The composition of the countermovement will depend to a large degree on the nature and extent of the threat posed by the original movement. Revolutionary social movements attempt to drastically alter state policies or to overthrow regimes. In such cases, the state itself becomes the countermovement. But most social movements do not represent regime challenges; their goals are far more limited. They threaten some groups or classes and not others. The result is often a contest among groups for specific policy outcomes and generalized political influence. Should a countermovement arise in this situation, it is bound to be more limited in scope and membership than those that arise to challenge revolutionary movements.

Observers of the civil rights, antiwar, and feminist movements, among others, have sought to analyze the emergence of these more limited movements. More generally, Clarence Lo (1982) and Tahi Mottl (1980) have attempted to describe the typical features of the countermovement. Countermovements develop in segments of the population whose ways of life, status, and rewards are challenged by the movements. It has been traditional to see movements as progressive forces, and countermovements as reactionary. But such labeling serves little analytic purpose and may be contradicted in fact. What is most interesting about countermovements is that they attempt to capture the high ground from movements. Sometimes they succeed; sometimes they fail. Zald and Useem (1987) describe the interactive dance between movement and countermovement. They seek to explain why countermovements vary in the speed and strength of their mobilization, and to identify the types and range of conflicts between the movement and countermovement. Depending upon the timing of mobilization, countermovements may spend most of their time attempting to undo the effects of the movement without actually engaging the movement in battle. Such conflicts can be said to be "loosely coupled" in time and arena.

McAdam (1983) analyzed movement-countermovement interaction by demonstrating the succession of tactics that occurred in the civil rights movement. Using *New York Times* newspaper reports, McAdam shows how the pace of movement activity rose with the introduction of new tactical forms and then declined as the opposition developed effective tactical counters to defuse the impact of novel movement tactics. No doubt McAdam has understated the richness of the tactical repertoire of the civil rights movement during this period (Morris, 1984). Nonetheless, his represents a crude first attempt to map the chesslike interaction that characterizes movement-countermovement relations. As much as any other set of relations, it is these that shape the trajectory of the original movement.

THE MEDIA AND COMMUNICATIONS TECHNOLOGIES

While we have previously noted the importance of "frame alignment" and "collective attribution" as processes crucial to the generation of collective action, it is not true that the movement's cognitive challenge ends during its emergent phase. The creation of a revolutionary consciousness hardly ensures the survival of this consciousness over time. One need only point to the extinction of radical feminism in this country after the Civil War and again following the passage of the suffrage amendment to realize how tenuous political consciousness is. The cognitive challenge confronting insurgents only begins with the emergence of the movement. For the movement to succeed, it must be able to generate support among authorities, sympathy among bystanders and, most important, an ongoing sense of legitimacy and efficacy among movement cadre and members. Invariably, this requirement implicates the movement in an ongoing cognitive struggle with movement opponents over the meaning of various actions and events. Prochoice advocates seek to depict prolife activists as dangerous extremists threatening human life by their attacks on birth control clinics. In turn, prolifers, through "educational" materials, such as the controversial film, *The Silent Scream*, attempt to portray prochoice activists as insensitive murderers. What is at stake is nothing less than the popular perception of reality. This struggle presents one of the clearest examples of the ways in which the ongoing development of a movement turns on the ability of SMOs to successfully

translate macroprocesses into micro outcomes. The micro outcome in this case is public opinion formation and the reinforcement of member commitment through the manipulation/creation of meaning structures. We will turn to this process in the next section. Our concern here is with the macro companion to this process—namely, the systematic attempts of SMOs to exploit the media and existing communication technologies in an effort to bring their "message" to various audiences.

COMMUNICATION TECHNOLOGIES

Some means of communication are centrally important to generating collective action in settings that require linking individuals who do not typically find themselves in face-to-face interaction with each other. In modern society, most movements are of this variety. Increasingly, then, movements have come to depend upon and to be shaped by the means of communication available to them. The costs and accessibility of such technologies may influence the prospects for mobilization as well as the public's response to mobilization appeals. Let us review several of the more recent technological innovations in communication that have had important effects upon movement attempts to disseminate information as a way of influencing movement adherents and bystander publics.

The telephone has recently come into wide use by social movement activists. Telephone networks are widely used to inform SMO members and movement adherents about events and in organizing collective behavior among them. The low costs of telephone service and its wide accessibility mean that this technology is useful to all but those movements drawn from among the poorest groups in modern America. The significance of telephone technology for collective action may, however, be generally restricted to the United States. The fact that most nations, including many wealthy nations, do not possess phone systems as accessible as this one, has interesting comparative implications for understanding collective action in the United States and elsewhere. The ability to mobilize many adherents of a social movement in a very short period of time can depend upon it. The use of such telephone nets by antinuclear activists to block the so-called "White Trains" carrying nuclear warheads is an example of one use of this technology. Cable (1984) describes the heavy use of this technology by a state Moral Majority SMO. This technology allows for the relaying "instruction" to adherents concerning future collective actions, a process some collective behaviorists regard as critical to the understanding of those actions (McPhail and Wohlstein, 1983).

Direct mail technologies are also coming to be widely used by social movement activists. The use of these techniques is described in great detail by Sabato (1981). They have been used, in this context, primarily to generate resources for SMOs and to activate social movement adherents. A secondary benefit is that they may educate nonadherents on social movement issues. Thus far, the empirical literature on SMO use of direct-mail techniques would seem to support several conclusions. First, the technique is seen as especially useful in mobilizing resources and collective action among adherent pools that are not highly structured into preexisting infrastructures (McCarthy, 1987). Such techniques would also seem to be more useful in permanent organizations rather than temporary campaigns (Sabato, 1981). Finally, Hadden and Swan (1981) found the effectiveness of direct mail appeals to be enhanced when combined with television programming by evangelists.

MASS MEDIA

Television and newspapers constitute the central mass media in modern societies, and as such, play an important role in movement efforts to attract members, discredit opponents and influence the state and the general public. Typically, however, these media are more, or at least as, available to movement opponents as they are to the movement itself. This is especially true when the state itself opposes the aims of the movement. In most cases, then, movements cannot count on routine access to the media, nor editorial sympathy when coverage is forthcoming. Instead, they must exploit the "normal procedures" of these media in order to gain unpaid access as a means of relaying their message to a mass public. This has served to encourage attempts to understand what subset of potential events become "news." In turn, this has prompted researchers to move in two directions simultaneously. Some analysts have sought to understand the internal structure and logic of specific media organizations. Among the specific topics studied by researchers in this tradition are patterns of media ownership, the socialization of newspersons and routine decision making in media organizations. Gans (1979) provides a useful review of much of this research.

But the creation of news is clearly an interactive process. Recognition of this fact has prompted other researchers to study the various ways in which movements attempt to attract and then shape the editorial tone of media coverage (see Gitlin, 1980; Molotch, 1979; Molotch and Lester, 1974, 1975). As a general rule, these studies have tended to point up the difficulties inherent in courting the media. To cite one such difficulty, movements must prove "newsworthy" if they are to attract the attention of the media. This oftens puts a premium on illegal, violent, or otherwise extreme forms of action. At the same time, these forms of action are likely to frighten the public, antagonize authorities, and discourage supporters. As yet, however, little in the way of systematic analysis intended to tease out these dynamics has been undertaken.

The same can be said for efforts to study the complex and often contradictory patterns of interaction that develop between the movement and the full range of organizational actors touched on here. Suffice it to say that the contradictory demands inherent in the single media example noted above are multiplied many times over when all of the parties to the ongoing conflict are taken into account. One very challenging, and potentially valuable direction for future research, then, would entail the explication of the complex and changing relationships between these various actors over the life of specific movements.

Micro Processes in Movement Development

At the macro level, the task facing SMO's is managing the conflicting demands and interests of the groups that comprise the movement's organizational environment. But that is only half the story. To remain viable, these SMOs must also be able to retain the ideological loyalty and resource support of some constituency. To do so involves them in a series of important micro-level processes. One of these processes— the production and manipulation of meaning structures—has already been mentioned. But the production of meaning isn't the only ongoing problem SMOs must solve. They must also routinize the flow of resources and members into the movement if it is to remain a strong and viable force for social, political, or personal change.

The Ongoing Production and Maintenance of Meaning and Ideology

While a discussion of communication technologies highlights the ways in which movement activists seek to manipulate and shape the understanding of events, such a discussion leaves the microdynamics of this process unexamined. While a full-blown, dynamic theory of this process is beyond the scope of this chapter, we can review some of the more interesting recent conceptual and empirical work that has been done on the topic.

The new theories of social movements have been accused of deemphasizing the importance of meaning and ideology, or taking them for granted at any historical moment (i.e., Mueller, 1984). But historians, speech analysts, and some sociologists have continued to wrestle with ways of conceptualizing and empirically assessing the importance and relevance of meaning and ideology to social movements, social movement activists, social movement adherents, SMOs, and SMIs.

Of the four major theoretical perspectives on social movements and collective behavior available in the late 1960s, only that of collective behavior took meaning and ideology very seriously in attempting to understand social movement processes. Especially as developed and elaborated by Park (1967), this perspective attended to the centrality of the mass media and "publics" in understanding the development of social movements. The central insight underlying this view was that consensus could develop from the mediated process of information flow as well as from face-to-face interaction. Gouldner (1976) has summarized this perspective cogently:

> Historically speaking, then, a 'public' consists of persons who habitually acquire their news and orientation from impersonal mass media where they have available to them diverse information and orientation diffused by competing individual entrepreneurs or corporate organizations, and when this diversity increases *talk* among those sharing news but seeking consensus concerning its meaning. That is a bourgeois public [p. 96] . . . Ideologies serve to mobilize 'social movements' within publics through the mediation of newspapers and other media. Movements are sectors of the public committed to a common project and to a common social identity . . . News generates ideology centered social identities which, in turn, are now media constructed and defined. Thus social movements in the modern world are both ideology—and news constructed [p. 100].

Some analysts have focused upon the pre-existing structures of meaning in publics. It is widely noticed, for instance, that most individuals do not possess anything like a well-articulated "ideology," even among the most literate segments of a population. This has led to employing such concepts as "organic" or "popular" ideology for talking about collective meanings among mass publics (i.e., Rude, 1980). Public opinion polling has allowed for the extensive mapping of support for particular social movements, both at single points in time and over time as well. This allows the size of "adherent pools" available to various movements to be crudely estimated (see McCarthy, 1987; Mueller, 1983; Wood and Hughes, 1984). It leads, also, to attempts to understand the conceptual frames that characterize mass publics as they process the competing information bombarding them as regards any controversial social issues (i.e., Gamson, 1984).

Most recent analyses of the construction of meaning in social movements has been consistent with this approach, though some analysts have tended to emphasize more directly the competition and conflict between the purveyors of dominant understandings of social issues and those social movement activists presenting alternative understandings. In attempting to explain why so little collective action occurs, analysts of a variety of persuasions opt for the conclusion that meaning in publics is dominated by resource rich elites who exert control over the grammar and plot line of public discourse. Those operating from Marxist perspectives call such a state of affairs *ideological hegemony* (i.e., Garner, 1977), while pluralists label similar processes symbolic reassurance (i.e., Edelman, 1964, 1971, 1977).

Several processes, however, can be identified that tend to undercut elite interpretations of meaning. These processes involve the media and the intelligentsia as well as SMOs. Many analysts have noted how the mass media, and especially television, tend to focus upon disruption and violence in social life. This proclivity gives social movement activists the opportunity to gain some access to the media in their attempts to generate countermeanings in mass publics (Lipsky, 1968). Those who have been called "organizational intellectuals" (Zald and McCarthy, 1975) may also disseminate countermeanings through their positions in universities and other work settings. These intellectual workers have also been labeled the "new class" by analysts (i.e., Brint, 1984; Bruce-Briggs, 1979) who see them as central to the generation of counter-meanings in modern industrial settings.

But it is the activities of the social movement activists themselves that are especially crucial to an understanding of how new meanings and ideologies are developed, packaged, and disseminated. Sociologists are only now beginning to study how these processes work. Perhaps the most promising framework for analyzing these processes is one outlined by Snow and his colleagues (1986) and reviewed earlier in our discussion of "frame alignment." Borrowing the term "frame" from Erving Goffman (1974), the authors describe and elaborate a typology of "frame alignment processes" by which SMOs seek to bring the beliefs and attitudes of potential recruits into sync with the ideological frame of the movement. "The basic underlying premise is that frame alignment, of one variety or another, is a necessary condition of [movement] participation . . . and that it is typically an interactional and *ongoing* accomplishment" (p. 464; emphasis ours). The key word here is *ongoing*. For the later stages of collective action, the important thrust of this chapter is to alert movement scholars to the crucial microprocesses that SMOs must engage in if they are to retain the cognitive and ideological loyalties of movement members.

If sociologists are relative latecomers to the study of processes such as those described by Snow and his colleagues, speech communication analysts have made them a significant focus of research for some time. One especially productive area of scholarship has taken movement rhetoric as a topic for systematic analysis. Simons and his colleagues have exhaustively summarized this body of work (Simons, 1970, 1981). Utilizing a conceptual approach quite compatible with recent approaches in social movement analysis, which he calls the "requirement-problems-strategies approach," the various rhetorical tasks confronting movement activists are systematically explored. He says,

> Ideally, a full-blown theory of the rhetoric of social movement should specify the argument and appeals available to movement rhetoric for each of the tasks they characteristically confront. Likewise, a full *history* of movement rhetoric would identify time-specific, place specific, or even movement-specific repertoires. What we already know is that some argumentative patterns appear unchanging and, hence, are highly predictable [Simons, Mechling, and Schreier, 1985, p. 95].

The tasks that have been explored by these many rhetorical scholars are the rhetoric of mobilization, the rhetoric of external influence, and the rhetoric of counterinfluence. Each of these tasks are then broken down into more detailed rhetorical tasks for systematic analysis of meaning and its consequences.

So while some recent movement analysis has downplayed meaning in understanding social movement processes, the outlines of a micro-sociological literature on these topics has already begun to emerge. This literature should enable researchers increasingly to address systematically the dynamics and effects of meaning-making activity by social movement activists (i.e., Mueller, 1984).

Resource Maintenance

The challenge facing mature movements is not simply a cognitive or ideological one. Like all organizations, the SMOs that come to dominate a movement in its later stages must be able to establish routine flow of resources into the organization in order to survive. To solve the resource problem, the SMO can choose to emphasize either one of two problematic sources of support. Either it can seek to obtain most of its resources from among its grassroots base or from sources outside its natural "beneficiary constituency" (McCarthy and Zald, 1973). Either strategy represents a calculated gamble.

The downside of the grassroots strategy is straightforward. To the extent that the movement's natural constituency is poor and relatively powerless, any SMO that emphasizes grassroots support is likely to share in its supporters' poverty. Moreover, the meager resource base available to it is likely to make it necessary for the "grassroots SMO" to engage in a near continuous round of resource-generating activities just to survive. The implications of this pattern for program development are sobering.

Just as sobering are the potential dangers establishing primary resource linkages to groups outside the movement's mass base. The lure of such linkages should be obvious. In contrast to the all too often impoverished mass base, external groups—especially those of the elite variety—tend to be resource rich. At the same time, external groups do not share the same level of concern or self-interested commitment to the goals of the movement as the movement's beneficiary constituency. This means that external support is likely to prove more fleeting and more politically conditioned than grassroots support. The latter characterization highlights the very real dangers of cooptation and control inherent in the establishment of external support linkages. Such ties grant considerable control over movement affairs to the source from which the resources are obtained. Of course, the control embodied in these support linkages need not be exercised in any particular case. If the movement organization uses the resource(s) in a manner consistent with the interests of its sponsor(s), then support is likely to continue without interruption. The establishment of external support linkages threatens, then, to tame the movement by encouraging insurgents to pursue only those goals acceptable to external sponsors. The latter course of action may ensure the survival of the movement—or at least of its organizational offshoots—but only at the costs of reducing its programmatic effectiveness.

Sustaining Member Commitment

Besides mobilizing resources and attracting new recruits, movements must also strive to retain the energies and loyalties of old members. Failing this, the movement is likely to lack the continuity in personnel required to sustain an ongoing campaign of social and political change. This necessity highlights the efforts of SMOs in the same-meaning production processes discussed earlier. Obviously, if members come to feel that the goals of the SMO are no longer compatible with their own values, they are likely to defect. Thus the various "frame alignment processes" discussed by Snow et al. (1986) are as applicable to veteran activists as new recruits. Ongoing efforts to negotiate a reasonable fit between the attitudes of members and the official "party line" of the SMO is central to the process of sustaining commitment.

This process is not simply an ideological one, however. It is a tactical one as well. Presumably, most activists are attracted to a given SMO in part because they expect it to be an effective agent for social, political, or personal change. If, within a reasonable period of time, the organization fails to fulfill its implicit charge to action, it is likely to lose the support of a significant portion of its membership. This is especially true in the case of political movements. As Alinsky (1971) was keenly aware, nothing sustains the commitment of activists, nor draws others to a political movement, quite like victories. At least as regards collective action, the bandwagon effect is very real. The leaders of political SMOs must therefore be attuned to the ways in which strategy and tactics can be manipulated to reinforce the resolve of their troops.

Selection of Goals and Tactics

In the face of the severe macro pressures and micro challenges confronting movements, SMOs face an uphill battle to survive, let alone change existing social, political, or economic arrangements. At the same time, SMOs are not entirely powerless in the face of these twin sets of constraints. Perhaps the most powerful weapons they have at their disposal are the goals they choose to pursue and the tactics they utilize in this pursuit. Both may be used to attract new recruits, persuade authorities, neutralize opponents, and gain access to the media. In effect, an SMO uses its goals and tactics to mediate between macro-environmental pressures and the challenges of micro mobilization. Let us discuss each of these objectives in a bit more detail.

At the macro level, SMOs find themselves confronting a wide range of organizations with very different interests vis-a-vis the movement. Some, representing countermovements or segments of the elite, would like to see the movement destroyed or at least tamed. Other groups may be allies of the movement. Still others have yet to take a decisive stance either for or against the movement. The media are often among these "neutral third parties."

These groups play a decisive role in shaping the choices SMOs make regarding goals and tactics. In choosing between all tactical and programmatic options open to them, SMOs typically weigh the anticipated responses of these various groups and seek through their choices to balance the conflicting demands of the organizational environment in which they are embedded.

At the micro level, the strategic choices made by SMOs must serve still other functions. SMOs must balance the need to respond to macro-level pressures from other organizations with the micro-level need to maintain the strength and viability of the organization. It matters little if one has attracted media attention if, in the process, one has also antagonized support and jeopardized the flow of resources to the organization. This appears to have happened in the case of various Black Power groups in the late 1960s. While the rhetorical militance and radical goals of the groups assured them media attention, the message embodied in their actions frightened potential supporters and encouraged official repression. Any number of such strategic dilemmas confront SMOs as they seek both to adapt to and shape the ongoing macro- and microenvironments they confront.

This environment perspective on SMOs leaves the question of the efficacy of various goals or tactics unanswered. In point of fact, little systematic evidence on the question has yet been gathered by scholars. To our knowledge, only William Gamson (1975) has sought to assess the effect of goals and tactics on an SMO's long-range chances of success. His findings are interesting, if not entirely unexpected. As regards goals, Gamson found that single-issue SMOs had higher success rates than groups that pursue many goals (pp. 44-46). In addition, groups whose goals required the "displacement of antagonists" were less likely to be successful than those whose goals did not (pp. 41-44). The one counterintuitive finding concerned the apparent tactical advantage of employing force or violence in pursuit of movement goals. Those groups who did so had significantly higher success rates than those who refrained from using force or violence in pursuing their aims (chap. 6).

Our discussion of the efficacy of goals and tactics leads logically to yet another neglected topic in the study of social movements. Presumably, most movements set out to accomplish certain objectives. Rarely, however, have movement scholars sought to assess how effective movements are in achieving their ends. Nor have researchers been any better about studying the impact of collective action on society as a whole or on those who participated in the movement. We will close our chapter with a brief discussion of the neglected topic of movement outcomes.

The Outcome of Social Movements

The interest of many scholars in social movements stems from their belief that movements represent an important force for social change. Yet demonstrating the independent effect of collective action on social change is difficult. Snyder and Kelly (1979) attempt to lay out a systematic framework for the empirical evaluation of such effects, but their evidentiary requirements are generally beyond the means of most researchers in all but a few narrow instances.

Some work has been done trying to untangle the independent effects of collective action, however. Perhaps the most systematic attempt to isolate the effects of organized social movements is that of Gamson (1975). He shows that for a large sample of SMOs in the United States, winning acceptance by authorities was substantially more likely than achieving their stated goals, suggesting that in the American case, cooptation is the model response of authorities to the efforts of challenging groups. Murray Edelman argues this position directly (1964, 1977) when he attempts to demonstrate that the normal response to insurgent action is symbolic

reassurance, typically in the form of the establishment of a state agency responsible for tending the concerns of the insurgents through symbols rather than material rewards.

A number of researchers have attempted to trace the effects of several recent movements in the United States upon the creation of specific social policies. Among the movements studied have been the women's movement (Freeman, 1975), the civil rights movement (Burstein, 1985, Button, 1978) and the environmental movement (Mitchell, 1981). But collective action may also have the effect of stalling new public policy innovations. Nelkin and Pollack (1981) have shown such effects for the movement against nuclear power, and Turk and Zucker have shown the effects of organized minority efforts on attempts to reduce local welfare services (1984, 1985).

Another attempt to assess the effect of collective action on public policy has centered on the question of whether or not the general turbulence of the 1960s resulted in material gains through the welfare system. This literature was inspired by the work of Piven and Cloward (1971). The debate between various researchers seems to suggest that there was no direct local effect of the extent and seriousness of civil disorders upon relief levels, but that indirect effects worked through the federal level of authority in producing the possibility that states with many affected cities could more vigorously expand welfare services (Albritton, 1979; Issac and Kelly, 1981; Schram and Turbett, 1983).

The focus of research on social movement outcomes has tended to focus on changes in legislation or governmental policy. Of late, however, researchers have begun to shift attention toward other more indirect outcomes of movement action. Such outcomes include changes in the perceptions of mass publics, the creation of cohorts committed to activist careers, and the creation of countermovements.

The "social constructionists" have regularly pointed to the importance of collective action in producing shifts in public perception of social issues. For example, Troyer and Markle (1983) show how the efforts of the antitobacco social movement were important in changing public perspectives on this issue as well as directly affecting social policy at the federal level. Gusfield (1981) recounts the development of the idea of the "killer drunk" and its subsequent incorporation into the contemporary movement against drinking and driving. This movement in turn has altered public perceptions in such a way that with little political conflict, the legal age for drinking alcoholic beverages has, in many states, been raised to 21 years.

Carol Mueller (1984) demonstrates how the women's movement has had massive indirect effects upon the political behavior of women who have had little direct involvement in the movement themselves. These effects work through the shifting understandings of what women are capable of doing and also altering the opportunities for political action on the part of women. So the majority of the women now entering the formal political process have not been "organized by feminists" in the sense that they took part in activities organized by feminist SMOs, yet one can make the case that the movement has been important in providing the opportunity for them to enter the formal political process. Marx and Wood (1975) note that an important indirect effect of certain protest activities is the diffusion of tactical models so that new forms may be taken up by widely dispersed groups. Tilly (1979) discusses the general process of the diffusion of such "repertoires of contention" through time and space.

Another legacy of social movements is the ongoing patterns of activism they may inspire in their key activists. Some "survivors" may even remain active through long cycles of movement decline to nourish and support a new influx of activists in another day. This is the story that Rupp and Taylor (1987) tell about the feminist movement during the 1950s in the United States. Or activists may take up other causes. So the defectors from one movement may be the seedbed for the emergence of newer movements during the later cycles of collective action. McAdam (1988) demonstrates this pattern for many of the earliest white activists in the civil rights movement, many of whom went on to play pioneering roles in the women's, antiwar, and student movements. Or the leaders of such movements may utilize their organizational skills in other contexts when other political opportunities present themselves. For instance, many former civil rights activists have become political functionaries in a number of local political systems such as Atlanta and the District of Columbia. The penetration of the political system by former activists can be expected to have social policy consequences relevant to earlier movement goals.

Another frequent outcome of collective action is the mobilization of specific countermovements or generalized political resistance to the aims of the original movement. In some cases, the level of resistance may be great enough to set in motion a significant and prolonged shift in the direction of electoral and policy outcomes. The generalized "law and order" backlash nurtured by the Republican right in the late sixties

may well be an example of this phenomenon. The conditions under which these antagonistic and unintended consequences are likely to occur are as yet unclear and thus merit additional systematic study.

Conclusion

In the preceding pages we have tried both to review recent and earlier work on social movements and to sketch a comprehensive framework for organizing theory and research in the field. Specifically, we have argued that a complete understanding of social movements requires that researchers (a) distinguish between the emergent and later developmental phases of collective action, and (b) seek during both to link processses at the macro and micro levels by means of the intervening organizational bridges crucial during each. In our view a wide variety of informal, yet existing, associations of people provide the collective settings within which movements emerge. The significance of these *micro-mobilization contexts* derive from their potential for translating macro-structural opportunities for action into specific micro-mobilization dynamics.

The need for similar mediating structures hardly ends with the onset of collective action. Instead, formal social movement organizations (SMOs) are expected to develop to fill the ongoing need for an organizational bridge between the larger political and social environment and the specific constituencies the movement must mobilize if it is to succeed. How well SMOs are able to reconcile the pressures of their macroenvironment with the ongoing demands of micro mobilization will largely determine the movement's chances of success.

Besides shaping this view of collective action this review has also served to alert us to several underdeveloped areas of research and theorizing on the dynamics of collective action. We will conclude, then, by sketching what we see as three of the most glaring deficiencies in the literature and the research strategies that might address them.

The first concerns our relatively underdeveloped state of knowledge about the dynamics of collective action past the emergence of a movement. The sensitive reader was no doubt struck by the greater length and coherence of the section of the chapter dealing with the emergence of collective action. We simply have theorized more and amassed more empirical evidence concerning the early stage of a social movement. By comparison, we know comparatively little about the dynamics of collective action over time. Specifically, we see a need for the creation of more systematic theoretical frameworks for studying movements over time. While we have a number of specific theories of movement emergence, we lack for any comparable theory of movement development. Instead, what we have is a growing body of empirical studies on various aspects of movement growth. As yet, however, we do not have a broad theoretical frame to help organize and bring coherence to this collection of discrete studies. The development of such a theory or theories would contribute greatly to our understanding of the dynamics of social change as well as to movement theory.

A comparable situation confronts us in the study of individual activism. While there are several theoretical accounts of recruitment to collective action, we boast no real theory of the effect of movement participation on the individual. Theories of conversion or adult political socialization may afford us some useful models for constructing such a theory, but to date no one has taken the time to do so. Nor have there been many good longitudinal or follow-up studies of activists completed that might aid in the development of such a theory. If we want to better understand the ongoing dynamics of individual activism, such a theory and a body of systematic empirical studies to "test" it are a must.

Finally, we come away convinced that the real action in social movements takes place at some level intermediate between the macro and micro. It is there in the existing associational groups or networks of the aggrieved community that the first groping steps toward collective action are taken. It is there that the decision to embed the movement in more formal movement organizations is reached. And it is there, within the SMOs themselves, that the strategic decisions are made that shape the trajectory of the movement over time. Most of our research has missed this level of analysis. We have focused the lion's share of our research energies on the before and after of collective action. The "before" research has focused on the macro and micro factors that make movements and individual activism more likely. The "after" side of the research equation is composed of the few studies that focus on the outcomes of collective action. But we haven't devoted a lot of attention to the *ongoing accomplishment of collective action*. How do macro and micro propensities get translated into specific mobilization attempts? What are the actual dynamics by which movement activists reach decisions regarding goals and tactics? How concretely do SMOs seek to recruit new members? To answer these questions, what is needed is more systematic, qualitative fieldwork into the dynamics of collective action at the intermediate meso level. We remain convinced that it is *the* level at which most movement action occurs and of which we know the least.

NOTES

1. In recent years a number of useful surveys of the new scholarship on social movements have been produced. Among the best of these are those by Gusfield, 1978; Jenkins, 1983; Marx and Wood, 1975; Morris and Herring, in press; and Zurcher and Snow, 1981.

2. For critical reviews of this perspective, see Deutscher, 1973, and Gurney and Tierney, 1982.

3. Besides these four major perspectives, there were two others that also had some influence on the field. The first of these is the *natural history approach*, as represented by the works of scholars such as Crane Brinton (1968) and L. P. Edwards (1927). The central idea underlying work in the natural history tradition is that movements—and especially revolutions—betray a consistent pattern of development often involving a set number of stages through which they inevitably pass. In the past 20 years, movement scholars have overwhelming rejected this idea, viewing movements as less stagelike than highly variable in their patterns of development. The second perspective not discussed in the text was the psychoanalytic approach. In works such as those by Adorno et al. (1950), Freud (1955), Lowenthal and Guterman (1949), and Martin (1920), scholars tried to account for individual participation in episodes of collective behavior or social movements on the basis of various dynamics and factors embedded in classical psychoanalytic theory. Once again, this research tradition has not been carried forward by many scholars working in the field today.

4. The study of collective behavior and social movements up until this time was primarily a "textbook" enterprise. Some rich case studies, however, were available and some of the best are difficult to place within one or another of the traditions we have outlined here. These include S. M. Lipset's *Agrarian Socialism* (1950), C. Eric Lincoln's *Black Muslims in America* (1961), and Nathan Glazer's *The Social Bases of American Communism* (1961). See Gusfield (1978) for a review of the major empirical monographs on social movements up to this time.

5. A few of the earlier theorists did take issue with these micro-level explanations of movement emergence. In particular, Turner and Killian (1956, 1972, 1986) have long been critical of those who would explain movements on the basis of individual states of mind.

6. For an introduction to the "new social movements" literature, see Klandermans, 1986.

7. We must not forget, however, that there are conditions under which repression may in fact spur collective action rather than inhibit it. This seems to have been the case in a variety of peasant movements (Wolf, 1969; Womack, 1969), as well as of some of the collective action described by the Tillys (1975) during the "rebellious century."

8. In point of fact, subsequent research on the Hare Krishna movement, the one exception cited by Snow, Zurcher, and Ekland-Olson (1980), revealed that a sizable proportion of its membership was also recruited through existing networks, especially as the movement matured (Rochford, 1982).

9. A case can also be made for a special "life transition" version of the basic argument outlined above. The claim is that some combination of geographic, social (e.g., divorce), or occupational transition in a person's life may provide an especially fertile biographic context for activism. The problem with this view is that while such transitions may well reduce the pressure of biographical constraints, they also tend to rob a person of the kind of personal contacts that normally draw people into movements. However, where transitions are not accompanied by any consequent loss of personal contacts, the result may well be an increased likelihood of participation. For example, McAdam (1986) found that graduating seniors had higher rates of participation in the Freedom Summer project than any other group of applicants. In this case, the freedom that came with graduation, coupled with the rich interpersonal/organizational context of campus life, may well have made seniors uniquely available for participation.

10. For an interesting discussion and theoretical elaboration of this point, see Snow, Zurcher, and Ekland-Olson, 1980, pp. 796-798.

REFERENCES

Aberle, David. 1966. *The Peyote Religion Among the Navajo*. Chicago: Aldine.

Adorno, T. W., E. Frenkel-Brunswick, D. J. Levinson, and R. N. Sanford. 1950. *The Authoritarian Personality*. New York: Harper & Brothers.

Aguirre, B. E. 1984. "The Conventionalization of Collective Behavior in Cuba." *American Journal of Sociology* 90: 541-566.

Albritton, Robert B. 1979. "Social Amelioration through Mass Insurgency? A Re-examination of the Piven and Cloward Thesis." *American Political Science Review* 73:1003-1011.

Alinsky, Saul. 1971. *Rules for Radicals*. New York: Random House.

Arendt, Hannah. 1951. *The Origins of Totalitarianism*. New York: Harcourt, Brace.

Aya, Rod. 1979. "Theories of Revolution Reconsidered: Contrasting Models of Collective Violence." *Theory and Society* 8:39-99.

Bailis, Laurence. 1974. *Bread or Justice*. Lexington, MA: D. C. Heath.

Balbus, Isaac. 1973. *The Dialectics of Legal Repression*. New York: Russell Sage.

Barkan, Steven E. 1985. *Protesters on Trial: Criminal Justice in the Southern Civil Rights and Vietnam Antiwar Movements*. New Brunswick, NJ: Rutgers University Press.

———. 1986. "Interorganizational Conflict in the Southern Civil Rights Movement." *Sociological Inquiry* 56:190-209.

Barnes, Samuel H. and Max Kaase. 1979. *Political Action*. Beverly Hills, CA: Sage.

Becker, Howard S. 1963. *Outsiders*. New York: Free Press.

Bennett, James T. and Thomas J. DiLorenzo. 1985. *Destroying Democracy: How Government Funds Partisan Politics*. Washington, DC: Cato Institute.

Berry, Jeffery M. 1977. *Lobbying for the People*. Princeton, NJ: Princeton University Press.

Block, Jeanne H. 1972. "Generational Continuity and Discontinuity in the Understanding of Societal Rejection." *Journal of Personality and Social Psychology* 22:333-345.

———, N. Haan, and B. M. Smith. 1968. "Activism and Apathy in Contemporary Adolescents." In *Understanding Adolescence: Current Developments in Adolescent Psychology*, edited by James F. Adams. Boston: Allyn & Bacon.

Bloom, Jack. 1986. "Class, Race and the Civil Rights Movement: The Changing Political Economy of Racism." Unpublished manuscript, University of Indiana, Gary.

Blumer, Herbert. 1946. "Collective Behavior." Pp. 167-219 in *A New Outline of the Principles of Sociology*, edited by A. M. Lee. New York: Barnes and Noble.

———. 1955. "Social Movements." Pp. 99-220 in *Principles of Sociology*, edited by A. M. Lee. New York: Barnes and Noble.

———. 1969. "Collective Behavior." In *Principles of Sociology*, edited by A. M. Lee. New York: Barnes and Noble.

———. 1976. "Relative Deprivation, Rising Expectations, and Black Militancy." *Journal of Social Issues* 32:119-137.

Bolton, Charles D. 1972. "Alienation and Action: A Study of Peace Group Members." *American Journal of Sociology* 78:537-561.

Bonnell, Victoria E. 1984. *Roots of Rebellion: Workers' Politics and Organizations in St. Petersburg and Moscow, 1900-1914*. Berkeley, CA: University of California Press.

Brand, K. W. 1982. *Neue Soziale Bewegungen, Entstehung, Funktion und Perspektive neuer Protestpotentiale, eine Zwischenbilanz*. Opladen: Westdeutscher Verlag.

Braungart, Richard G. 1971. "Family Status, Socialization and Student Politics: A Multivariate Analysis." *American Journal of Sociology* 77: 108-129.

Briet, Martien, Bert Klandermans, and Frederike Kroon. 1984. "How Women Become Involved in the Feminist Movement." Presented at the annual meetings of the Society for the Study of Social Problems, San Antonio, Texas.

Bright, Charles and Susan Harding. 1984. *State Making and Social Movements*. Ann Arbor: University of Michigan Press.

Brint, Steven. 1984. " 'New Class' and Cumulative Trend Explanations of the Liberal Political Attitudes of Professionals." *American Journal of Sociology* 90:30-71.

Brinton, Crane. 1960. *The Anatomy of Revolution*. New York: W. W. Norton.

Bruce-Briggs, B., ed. 1979. *The New Class*. New York: McGraw-Hill.

Burstein, Paul. 1985. *Discrimination, Jobs and Politics*. Chicago: University of Chicago Press.

Button, James W. 1978. *Black Violence*. Princeton, NJ: Princeton University Press.

Cable, Sherry. 1984. "Professionalization in Social Movement Organizations: A Case Study of Pennsylvanians for Biblical Morality." *Sociological Forces* 7:287-304.

Carden, M. L. 1978. "The Proliferation of a Social Movement." *Research in Social Movements, Conflict, and Change* 1:179-196.

Conover, Pamela Johnston and Virginia Gray. 1983. *Feminism and the New Right: Conflict over the American Family*. New York: Praeger.

Curtis, Russell L. and Louise A. Zurcher, Jr. 1973. "Stable Resources of Protest Movement: The Multi-organizational Field." *Social Forces* 52: 53-60.

Davies, James C. 1963. *Human Nature in Politics: The Dynamics of Political Behavior*. New York: John Wiley.

———— 1969. "The J-curve of Rising and Declining Satisfaction as a Cause of Some Great Revolutions and a Contained Rebellion." In *Violence in America: Historical and Comparative Perspectives*. Washington, DC: Government Printing Office.

de Geest, A. 1984. "Nieuwe Sociale Bewegingen en de Verzorgingsstaat." *Tijdschrift Voor Sociologie* 5:239-267.

Deutscher, Irwin. 1973. *What We Say/What We Do*. Glenview, IL: Scott, Foresman.

D'Emillio, John. 1983. *Sexual Politics, Sexual Communities*. Chicago: University of Chicago Press.

Edelman, Murray. 1964. *The Symbolic Uses of Politics*. Urbana: University of Illinois Press.

———— 1971. *Politics as Symbolic Action*. New York: Academic Press.

———— 1977. *Political Language: Words that Succeed and Policies that Fail*. New York: Academic Press.

Edwards, L. P. 1927. *The Natural History of Revolution*. Chicago: University of Chicago Press.

Eisinger Peter K. 1973. "The Conditions of Protest Behavior in American Cities." *American Political Science Review* 67:11-28.

Evans, Sarah. 1980. *Personal Politics*. New York: Vintage Books.

Fainstein, Norman I. and Susan S. Fainstein. 1974. *Urban Political Movements: The Search for Power by Minority Groups in American Cities*. Englewood Cliffs, NJ: Prentice-Hall.

Feieraband, Ivo, Rosalind Feieraband, and Betty Nesvold. 1969. "Social Change and Political Violence: Cross National Patterns." Pp. 497-595 in *Violence in America: Historical and Comparative Perspectives*, edited by Hugh David Graham and Ted Robert Gurr. Washington, DC: Government Printing Office.

Ferree, Myra Marx and Frederick D. Miller. 1985. "Mobilization and Meaning: Toward an Integration of Social Movements." *Sociological Inquiry* 55:38-51.

Fernandez, Roberto and Doug McAdam. 1987. "Multiorganizational Fields and Recruitment to Social Movements." In *Organizing for Social Change: Social Movement Organizations Across Cultures*, edited by Bert Klandermans. Greenwich, CT: JAI Press.

Feuer, Lewis. 1969. *The Conflict of Generations: The Character and Significance of Student Movements*. New York: Basic Books.

Fireman, Bruce and William H. Gamson. 1979. "Utilitarian Logic in the Resource Mobilization Perspective." Pp. 8-45 in *The Dynamics of Social Movements*, edited by Mayer N. Zald and John D. McCarthy. Cambridge, MA: Winthrop.

Flacks, Richard. 1967. "The Liberated Generation: An Exploration of the Roots of Student Protest." *Journal of Social Issues* 23:52-75.

Foster, John. 1974. *Class Struggle and the Industrial Revolution: Early Industrial Capitalism in Three Towns*. London: Weidenfeld and Nicolson.

Fox, Karen F. and Phillip Kotler. 1980. "The Marketing of Social Causes: The First 10 Years." *Journal of Marketing* 44:22-33.

Freeman, Jo. 1973. "The Origins of the Women's Liberation Movement." *American Journal of Sociology* 78:792-811.

———— 1975. *The Politics of Women's Liberation*. New York: David McKay.

———— 1979. "The Women's Liberation Movement: Its Origins, Organization, Activities and Ideas." In *Women: A Feminist Perspective*, edited by Jo Freeman. Palo Alto, CA: Mayfield.

Freud, Sigmund. 1943. *The Standard Edition of the Complete Psychological Works of Sigmund Freud*, edited by J. Strachey et al. London: The Hogarth Press.

Friedman, Debra. 1983. "Why Workers Strike: Individual Decisions and Structural Constraints." Pp. 250-283 in *The Microfoundations of Macrosociology*, edited by Michael Hechter. Philadelphia: Temple University Press.

———— 1988. "Uncertainty as a Precondition for Strikes." Unpublished manuscript, University of Arizona.

Gale, Richard P. 1986. "Social Movements and the State: The Environmental Movement, Counter-

Movement, and Governmental Agencies." *Sociological Perspectives* 29:202-240.

Gamson, William. 1975. *The Strategy of Social Protest*. Homewood, IL: Dorsey.

_____. 1984. "Political Symbolism and Nuclear Arms Policy." Presented at the annual meeting of the American Sociological Association, San Antonio, Texas.

_____, Bruce Freeman, and Steven Rytina. 1982. *Encounters with Unjust Authority*. Homewood, IL: Dorsey.

Gans, Herbert. 1979. *Deciding What's News*. New York: Pantheon.

Garner, Roberta. 1977. *Social Movements in America*. Chicago: Rand-McNally.

Garrow, David J. 1978. *Protest at Selma*. New Haven, CT: Yale University Press.

Gerlach, Luther P. and Virginia H. Hine. 1970. *People, Power, and Change: Movements of Social Transformation*. Indianapolis: Bobbs-Merrill.

Gerth, Hans and C. Wright Mills. 1946. *From Max Weber: Essays in Sociology*. New York: Oxford University Press.

Geschwender, James. 1964. "Social Structure and the Negro Revolt: An Examination of Some Hypotheses." *Social Forces* 43:250-256.

_____ 1968. "Explorations in the Theory of Social Movements and Revolution." *Social Forces* 47:127-135.

Gitlin, Todd. 1980. *The Whole World is Watching*. Berkeley: University of California Press.

Glazer, Nathan. 1961. *The Social Bases of American Communism*. New York: Harcourt, Brace and World.

Glock, Charles Y. 1964. "The Role of Deprivation in the Origin and Evolution of Religious Groups." Pp. 24-36 in *Religion and Social Conflict*, edited by R. Lee and M. Marty. New York: Oxford University Press.

Godwin, R. Kenneth and Robert C. Mitchell. 1984. "The Implications of Direct Mail for Political Organizations." *Social Science Quarterly* 65: 829-839.

Goffman, Erving. 1974. *Frame Analysis*. Cambridge: Harvard University Press.

Gouldner, Alvin W. 1976. *The Dialectic of Ideology and Technology: The Origin, Grammar and Future of Ideology*. New York: Oxford University Press.

Gurney, J. N. and K. T. Tierney. 1982. "Relative Deprivation and Social Movements: A Critical Look at Twenty Years of Theory and Research." *Sociological Quarterly* 23:33-47.

Gurr, Ted. 1970. *Why Men Rebel*. Princeton, NJ: Princeton University Press.

Gusfield, Joseph. 1955. "Social Structure and Moral Reform: A Study of the Women's Christian Temperance Union." *American Journal of Sociology* 61:221-232.

_____ 1978. "Historical Problematics and Sociological Fields: American Liberalism and the Study of Social Movements." *Research in Sociology of Knowledge, Science and Art* 1: 121-149.

_____ 1981. *The Culture of Public Problems: Drinking and Driving and the Symbolic Order*. Chicago: University of Chicago Press.

Habermas, Jurgen. 1973. *Legitimation Crisis*. Boston: Beacon.

_____ 1976. *Communication and the Evolution of Society*. Boston: Beacon.

Hadden, Jeffrey K. and Charles E. Swann. 1981. *Prime Time Preachers: The Rising Power of Televangelism*. Reading, MA: Addison-Wesley.

Haines, Herbert H. 1984. "Black Radicalization and the Funding of Civil Rights: 1957-1970." *Social Problems* 32:31-43.

Hancock, Kelly. 1975. "From Innocence to Boredom: Revolution in the West." Ph.D. dissertation, Vanderbilt University, Nashville, Tennessee.

Handler, Joel. 1978. *Social Movements and the Legal System*. New York: Academic Press.

Heberle, Rudolph. 1951. *Social Movements: An Introduction to Political Sociology*. New York: Appleton-Century-Crofts.

Heirich, Max. 1977. "Changes of Heart: A Test of Some Widely Held Theories of Religious Conversion." *American Journal of Sociology* 83: 653-680.

Himmelstein, Jerome and Mayer N. Zald. 1984. "American Conservatism and the Funding of Art and Science." *Sociological Quarterly* 54: 171-187.

Hirsch, F. 1980. *Die Soziale Grenzen des Wachstums Ein Okenomische Analyse der Wachstumskrise*. Hamburg: Reinbek.

Hobsbawm, E. J. 1965. *Primitive Rebels*. New York: W. W. Norton.

Hoffer, Eric. 1951. *The True Believer: Thoughts on the Nature of Mass Movements*. New York: New American Library.

Hubbard, Howard. 1968. "Five Long Hot Summers and How They Grew." *Public Interest* 12:3-24.

Inglehart, R. 1977. *The Silent Revolution: Changing Values and Political Styles Among Western Publics*. Princeton, NJ: Princeton University Press.

Issac, Larry, and William R. Kelly. 1981. "Racial Insurgency, the State, and Welfare Expansion: Local and National Level Evidence from the Postwar United States." *American Journal of Sociology* 86:1348-1386.

Jackson, Maurice, Eleanora Peterson, James Bull, Sverre Monson, and Patricia Richmond. 1960. "The Failure of an Incipient Social Movement." *Pacific Sociological Review* 31:35-40.

Jenkins, J. Craig. 1983. Resource Mobilization Theory and the Study of Social Movements." *Annual Review of Sociology* 9:527-553.

_____ and Craig M. Eckert. 1986. "Channeling Black Insurgency: Elite Patronage and Professional Social Movement Organizations in the Development of the Black Movement." *American Sociological Review* 51:812-829.

Jenkins, J. Craig and Charles Perrow. 1977. "Insurgency of the Powerless: Farm Workers' Movements (1946-1972)." *American Sociological Review* 42:249-268.

Johnston, Hank. 1980. "The Marketed Social Movement: A Case Study of the Rapid Growth of TM." *Pacific Sociological Review* 23:333-354.

Jonas, Gerald. 1971. *On Doing Good: The Quaker Experiment*. New York: Schribner's.

Kaase, Max and Samuel H. Barnes. 1979. "In Conclusion: The Future of Political Protest in Western Democracies." Pp. 523-536 in *Political Action*, edited by Samuel H. Barnes and Max Kaase. Beverly Hills, CA: Sage.

Kanter, Rosebeth M. 1972. *Commitment and Community: Communes and Utopian Sociological Perspective*. Cambridge, MA: Harvard University Press.

Keniston, Kenneth. 1968. *Young Radicals*. New York: Harcourt, Brace and World.

Kitschelt, Herbert P. 1986. "Political Opportunity Structures and Political Protest." *British Journal of Political Science* 16:57-85.

Klandermans, Bert. 1984. "Mobilization and Participation: Social-Psychological Expansions of Resource Mobilization Theory." *American Sociological Review* 49:583-600.

———. 1986. "New Social Movements and Resource Mobilization: The European and the American Approach." *Journal of Mass Emergencies and Disasters* 4:13-37.

——— and Dirk Oegema. 1984. "Mobilizing for Peace: The 1983 Peace Demonstration in the Hague." Presented at the annual meetings of the American Sociological Association, San Antonio, Texas.

Klapp, Orrin. 1969. *Collective Search for Identity*. New York: Holt, Rinehart and Winston.

Knoke, David. 1986. "Incentives in Collective Action Organizations." Unpublished manuscript, Department of Sociology, University of Minnesota, Minneapolis.

Kornhauser, William. 1959. *The Politics of Mass Society*. Glencoe, IL: Free Press.

Kotler, Philip and Gerald Zaltman. 1971. "Social Marketing: An Approach to Planned Social Change." *Journal of Marketing* 35:3-12.

Kriesi, Hanspeter. 1985. *Bewegung in der Schweizer Politic Fallstudien zu Politischen Mobilierungsprozessen in der Schweiz*. Frankfurt/New York: Campus Verlag.

Lang, Kurt and Gladys Lang. 1961. *Collective Dynamics*. New York: Crowell.

Lawson, Ronald. 1983. "A Decentralized but Moving Pyramid: The Evolution and Consequences of the Structure of the Tenant Movement." Pp. 119-132 in *Social Movements of the Sixties and Seventies*, edited by Jo Freeman. New York: Longman.

Le Bon, Gustave. 1960. *The Crowd: A Study of the Popular Mind*. New York: Viking Press.

Levine, E. M. 1980. "Rural Communes and Religious Cults: Refugees for Middle-Class Youth." *Adolescent Psychiatry* 8:138-153.

Lincoln, C. Eric. 1961. *Black Muslims in America*. Boston: Beacon.

Lincoln, J. R. 1978. "Community Structure and Industrial Conflict." *American Sociological Review* 43:199-220.

Lipset, Seymour M. 1950. *Agrarian Socialism*. Berkeley: University of California Press.

———. 1960. *Political Man*. Garden City, NY: Doubleday.

——— and Earl Rabb. 1973. *The Politics of Unreason: Right-Wing Extremism in America, 1790-1970*. New York: Harper & Row.

Lipsky, Michael. 1968. "Protest as a Political Resource." *American Political Science Review* 62:1144-1158.

———. 1970. *Protest in City Politics*. Chicago: Rand McNally.

Lo, Clarence Y. H. 1982. "Counter-Movements and Conservative Movements in the Contemporary U.S." *Annual Review of Sociology* 8:107-134.

Lodhi, A. Q., and Charles Tilly. 1973. "Urbanization, Criminality and Collective Violence in Nineteenth Century France." *American Journal of Sociology* 79:296-318.

Lofland, John. 1969. *Deviance and Identity*. Englewood Cliffs, NJ: Prentice-Hall.

———. 1977. *Doomsdaycult*. New York: Irvington.

———. 1982. "Crowd Lobbying: An Emerging Tactic of Interest Group Influence in California." California Government Series II. Davis: Institute of Government Affairs, University of CA.

———. 1985. *Protest: Studies of Collective Behavior and Social Movements*. New Brunswick, NJ: Transaction Books.

——— and Michael Fink. 1982. *Symbolic Sit-ins: Protest Occupation at the California Capital*. Washington, DC: University Press of America.

Lowenthal, L. and N. Guterman. 1949. *Prophets of Deceit: A Study of the Techniques of the American Agitator*. New York: Harper & Brothers.

Luker, Kristin. 1984. *Abortion and the Politics of Motherhood*. Berkeley: University of California Press.

Marsh, Alan. 1977. *Protest and Political Consciousness*. Beverley Hills, CA: Sage.

——— and Max Kaase. 1979. "Measuring Political Action." In *Political Action*, edited by Samuel H. Barnes and Max Kaase. Beverly Hills, CA: Sage.

Martin, E. D. 1920. *The Behavior of Crowds*. New York: Harper & Brothers.

Marx, Gary. 1969. *Protest and Prejudice*. New York: Harper & Row.

———. 1974. "Thoughts on a Neglected Category of Social Movement Participant: The Agent Provocateur and the Informant." *American Journal of Sociology* 80:402-402.

———. 1979. "External Efforts to Damage or Facilitate Social Movements: Some Patterns, Explanations, Outcomes, and Complications." Pp. 94-125 in *The Dynamics of Social Movement*, edited by Mayer N. Zald and John D. McCarthy. Cambridge, MA: Winthrop.

――― and James Wood. 1975. "Strands of Theory and Research in Collective Behavior." *Annual Review of Sociology* 1:363-428.

Marx, Karl. 1958. "The Eighteenth Brumaire of Louis Bonaparte." In *Karl Marx and Frederich Engels, Selected Works*. Moscow: Foreign Language Publishing House.

McAdam, Doug. 1982. *Political Process and the Development of Black Insurgency, 1930-1970*. Chicago: University of Chicago Press.

――― 1983. "Tactical Innovation and the Pace of Insurgency." *American Sociological Review* 48: 735-754.

――― 1986. "Recruitment to High-Risk Activism: The Case of Freedom Summer." *American Journal of Sociology* 92:64-90.

――― 1988. *Freedom Summer. The Idealists Revisited*. New York: Oxford University Press.

――― and John McCarthy. 1982. "The Professional Project: The Invention of Work Through Collective Action." Presented at the annual meetings of the Society for the Study of Social Problems, San Francisco.

McCarthy, John D. 1987. "Pro-Life and Pro-Choice Mobilization: Infrastructure Deficits and New Technologies." Pp. 49-66 in *Social Movements in an Organizational Society*, edited by Mayer N. Zald and John D. McCarthy. New Brunswick, NJ: Transaction Books.

――― and David Britt. In press. "Adapting Social Movement Organizations to External Constraints in the Modern State: Tax Codes and Accreditation." In *Research in Social Movements, Conflict and Change*, edited by Louis Kriesberg. Greenwich, CT: JAI Press.

McCarthy, John D., Mark Wolfson, David P. Baker, and Elaine M. Mosakowski. In press. "The Founding of Social Movement Organizations: Local Citizens' Groups Opposing Drunken Driving." In *Ecological Models of Organization*, edited by Glenn R. Carroll. Cambridge, MA: Ballinger.

McCarthy, John D. and Mayer N. Zald. 1973. *The Trend of Social Movements in America: Professionalization and Resource Mobilization*. Morristown, NJ: General Learning Press.

――― 1974. "Tactical Consideration in Social Movement Organization." Presented at the annual meetings of the American Sociological Association, Totonto.

――― 1977. "Resource Mobilization and Social Movements: A Partial Theory." *American Journal of Sociology* 82:1212-1241.

McFarland, Andrew F. 1976. "The Complexity of Democratic Practice within Common Cause." Paper presented at the annual meetings of the American Political Science Association.

――― 1977. *Public Interest Lobbies*. Washington, DC: American Enterprise Institute.

――― 1984. *Common Cause: Lobbying in the Public Interest*. Chatham, NJ: Chatham House.

McPhail, Clark. 1971. "Civil Disorder Participation: A Critical Examination of Recent Research." *American Sociological Review* 36:1058-1073.

――― 1985. "The Social Organization of Demonstrations." Presented at the annual meetings of the American Sociological Association, Washington, DC.

――― and Ronald F. Wohlstein. 1983. "Individual and Collective Behaviors within Gatherings, Demonstrations and Riots." *Annual Review of Sociology* 9:579-600.

McQuail, Denis. 1985. "Sociology of Mass Communication." *Annual Review of Sociology* 11:93-111.

Melucci, Alberto. 1980. "The New Social Movements: A Theoretical Approach." *Social Science Information* 19:199-226.

――― 1981a. "New Movements, Terrorism and the Political System: Reflections on the Italian Case." *Socialist Review* 56:97-136.

――― 1981b. "Ten Hypotheses for the Analysis of New Movements." Pp. 173-194. in *Contemporary Italian Sociology*, edited by D. Pinto. Cambridge, MA: Cambridge University Press.

Messinger, Sheldon L. 1955. "Organizational Transformation: A Case Study of a Declining Social Movement." *American Sociological Review* 26: 3-10.

Michels, Robert. 1959. *Political Parties*. New York: Dover.

Miller, William D. 1974. *A Harsh and Dreadful Love: Dorothy Day and the Catholic Worker Movement*. Garden City, NY: Doubleday.

Mitchell, Robert C. 1979. "National Environmental Lobbies and the Apparent Illogic of Collective Action." Pp. 87-121 in *Collective Decision-Making Applications from Public Choice Theory*, edited by Clifford S. Russell. Baltimore: Johns Hopkins University Press.

――― 1981. "From Elite Quarrel to Mass Movement." *Society* 18:76-84.

Molotch, Harvey. 1970. "Oil in Santa Barbara and Power in America." *Sociological Inquiry* 40: 131-141.

――― 1979. "Media and Movements." Pp. 71-93 in *The Dynamics of Social Movements*, edited by Mayer N. Zald and John D. McCarthy. Cambridge, MA: Winthrop.

――― and Marylin Lester. 1974. "News as Purposive Behavior: On the Strategic Use of Routine Events, Accidents and Scandals." *American Sociological Review* 39:101-112.

――― 1975. "Accidental News: The Great Oil Spill as Local Occurrence and National Event." *American Journal of Sociology* 81:235-260.

Morris, Aldon. 1984. *The Origins of the Civil Rights Movement*. New York: Free Press.

――― 1986. "Birmingham Confrontation Reconsidered: An Analysis of Tactical Dynamics." Unpublished paper, Department of Sociology, University of Michigan, Ann Arbor.

_____ and Cedric Herring. In press. "Theory and Research in Social Movements: A Critical Review." In *Political Behavior Annual*, edited by Samuel Long. Boulder, CO: Westview Press.

Morrison, Denton. 1973. "Some Notes Toward Theory on Relative Deprivation, Social Movements, and Social Change." Pp. 103-116 in *Social Movements: A Reader and Source Book*, edited by R. R. Evans. Chicago: Rand McNally.

Mottl, Tahi L. 1980. "The Analysis of Counter-Movements." *Social Problems* 27:620-635.

Mueller, Carol. 1983. "In Search of a Constituency for the New Religious Right." *Public Opinion Quarterly* 47:213-229.

_____ 1984. "Women's Movement Success and the Success of Social Movement Theory." Presented at the annual meetings of the American Sociological Association, San Antonio, Texas.

Mueller, Edward N. 1980. "The Psychology of Political Protest and Violence." In *Handbook of Political Conflict*, edited by Ted Robert Gurr. New York: Free Press.

Neal, Arthur G. and Melvin Seeman. 1964. "Organization s and Powerlessness: A Test of the Mediation Hypothesis." *American Sociological Review* 29:216-226.

Nelkin, Dorothy and Michael Pollak. 1981. *The Atom Besieged*. Cambridge: MIT Press.

Nielsen, F. 1980. "The Flemish Movement in Belgium after World War II." *American Sociological Review* 45:76-94.

Oberschall, Anthony. 1973. *Social Conflict and Social Movements*. Englewood Cliffs, NJ: Prentice-Hall.

O'Connor, James. 1973. *The Fiscal Crisis of the State*. New York: St. Martin's.

Oliver, Pamela. 1984. "If You Don't Do It, Nobody Will. Active and Token Contributors to Local Collective Action." *American Sociological Review* 49:601-610.

Olson, Mancur, Jr. 1965. *The Logic of Collective Action*. Cambridge, MA: Harvard University Press.

Orum, Anthony M. 1972. *Black Students in Protest*. Washington, DC: American Sociological Association.

Oudijk, Corrine. 1983. *Sociale Atlas van de Vrouw. Sociale en Culturele Studies 3, Sociaal Culturele Planbureau*. Den Haag: Staatsuitgeverij.

Park, Robert E. 1967. *On Social Control and Collective Behavior*, edited by Ralph H. Turner. Chicago: University of Chicago Press.

_____ and Ernest W. Burgess. 1921. *Introduction to the Science of Society*. Chicago: University of Chicago Press.

Perrow, Charles. 1979. *Complex Organizations: A Critical Essay*. Glenview, IL: Scott, Foresman.

Persky, Stan. 1981. *At the Lenin Shipyard*. Vancouver, British Columbia: New Star Books.

Petty, R. E. and J. T. Cacioppo. 1981. *Attitudes and Attitude Change: The Social Judgement-Involvement Approach*. Dubuque, IA: W. C. Brown.

Pharr, Susan J. In press. *Status Politics in Japan*. Berkeley: University of California Press.

Pickvance, C. G. 1975. "On the Study of Urban Social Movements." *American Sociological Review* 23:29-49.

Pinard, Maurice. 1971. *The Rise of a Third Party: A Study in Crisis Politics*. Englewood Cliffs, NJ: Prentice-Hall.

Piven, Frances Fox and Richard A. Cloward. 1971. *Regulating the Poor*. New York: Pantheon.

Polsby, Nelson W. 1983. *Consequences of Party Reform*. New York: Oxford University Press.

Robinson, Jo Ann Ooiman. 1981. *Abraham Went Out: A Biography of A. J. Muste*. Philadelphia: Temple University Press.

Rochford, E. Burke. 1982. "Recruitment Strategies, Ideology, and Organization in the Hare Krishna Movement." *Social Problems* 29:399-410.

_____ 1985. *Hare Krishna in America*. New Brunswick, NJ: Rutgers University Press.

Rokeach, Milton. 1969. *Beliefs, Attitudes, and Values*. San Francisco: Jossey-Bass.

Rosenthal, Naomi, Meryl Fingrutd, Michele Ethier, Roberta Karant, and David McDonald. 1985. "Social Movements and Network Analysis: A Case Study of Nineteeth-Century Women's Reform in New York State." *American Journal of Sociology* 90:1022-1055.

Ross, Lee. 1977. "The Intuitive Psychologist and His Shortcomings: Distortions in the Attribution Process." In *Advances in Experimental Social Psychology*, vol. 10, edited by L. Berkowitz. New York: Academic Press.

Rothman, Stanley and S. Robert Lichter. 1978. "The Case of the Student Left." *Social Research* (Autumn):535-609.

Rude, George. 1980. *Ideology and Popular Protest*. New York: Pantheon Books.

Rule, James and Charles Tilly. 1975. "Political Process in Revolutionary France: 1830-1832." Pp. 41-85 in *1830 in France*, edited by John M. Merriman. New York: New Viewpoints.

Rupp, Leila and Verta Taylor. 1987. *Survival in the Doldrums: The American Women's Rights Movement, 1945 to 1960*. New York: Oxford University Press.

Sabato, Larry J. 1981. *The Rise of Political Consultants*. New York: Basic Books.

Sayre, Cynthia Woolever. 1980. "The Impact of Voluntary Association Involvement on Social-Psychological Attitudes." Presented at the annual meetings of the American Sociological Association, New York City.

Schneider, Joseph W. 1985. "The Constructionist View." *Annual Review of Sociology* 11:209-229.

Schram, Sanford F. and J. Patrick Turbett. 1983. "Civil Disorder and the Welfare Explosion: A Two-Step Process." *American Sociological Review* 48:408-414.

Schwartz, Michael. 1976. *Radical Protest and Social Structure*. New York: Academic Press.

Schwartzmann, Kathleen C. In press. *Coalitions in*

Crisis: Breakdown of the First Portuguese Republic. Lawrence: University of Kansas Press.

Selznick, Philip. 1952. *The Organizational Weapon.* New York: McGraw-Hill.

Shorter, Edward and Charles Tilly. 1974. *Strikes in France, 1830-1968.* London: Cambridge University Press.

Simcock, B. L. 1979. "Developmental Aspects of Antipollution Protest in Japan." *Research in Social Movements, Conflict and Change* 2:83-104.

Simons, Herbert W. 1970. "Requirements, Problems, and Strategies: A Theory of Persuasion for Social Movements." *Quarterly Journal of Speech* 56:1-11.

———— 1981. "The Rhetoric of Political Movements." Pp. 417-444 in *Handbook of Political Communication*, edited by Dan Nimmo and Keith Sanders. Beverly Hills: Sage.

————, E. W. Mechling, and H. Schreier. 1985. "Function of Communication in Mobilizing for Collective Action from the Bottom Up: The Rhetoric of Social Movements." In *Handbook of Rhetorical and Communication Theory*, edited by C. Arnold and J. Bowers. Boston: Allyn & Bacon.

Skocpol, Theda. 1979. *States and Social Revolutions.* New York: Cambridge University Press.

Smelser, Neil. 1962. *Theory of Collective Behavior.* New York: Free Press.

Snow, David A. 1976. "The Nichiren Shoshu Buddhist Movement in America: A Sociological Examination of its Value Orientation, Recruitment Effors, and Spread." Ann Arbor, Michigan: University Microfilms.

———— 1986. "Organization, Ideology and Mobilization: The Case of Nichiren Shoshu of America." In *The Future of New Religious Movements*, edited by D. G. Bromley and P. E. Hammond. Macon, GA: Mercer University Press.

———— and Susan Marshall. 1984. "Cultural Imperialism, Social Movements, and the Islamic Revival." Pp. 131-152 in *Social Movements, Conflicts and Change*, vol. 7, edited by Louis Kriesberg. Greenwich, CT: JAI Press.

Snow, David A. and E. Burke Rochford, Jr. 1983. "Structural Avialabilty, the Alignment Process and Movement Recruitment." Presented at the annual meetings of the American Sociological Association, Detroit.

Snow, David A., E. Burke Rochford, Jr., Steven K. Worden, and Robert D. Benford. 1986. "Frame Alignment Processes, Micromobilization, and Movement Participation." *American Sociological Review* 51:464-481.

Snow, David A., Louis A. Zurcher, Jr., and Sheldon Ekland-Olson. 1980. "Social Networks and Social Movements: A Microstructual Approach to Differential Recruitment." *American Sociological Review* 45:787-801.

Snyder, David and William R. Kelly. 1979. "Strategies for Investigating Violence and Social Change: Illustrations from Analyses of Racial

Disorders and Implications for Mobilization Research." Pp. 212-237 in *The Dynamics of Social Movements*, edited by Mayer N. Zald and John D. McCarthy. Cambridge, MA: Winthrop.

Staggenborg, Suzanne. 1986. "Coalition Work in the Pro-Choice Movement: Organizational and Environmental Opportunities and Obstacles." *Social Problems* 33:374-390.

Tarrow, Sidney. 1982. "Social Movements, Resource Mobilization and Reform during Cycles of Protest." *Western Studies Program Project, Social Protest and Policy Innovative Work*, Paper −1. Ithaca, NY: Cornell University.

Tierney, Kathleen J. 1982. "The Battered Women Movement and the Creation of the Wife Beating Problem." *Social Problems* 29:207-220.

Tilly, Charles, 1975. *The Formation of National States in Western Europe.* Princeton, NJ: Princeton University Press.

———— 1978. *From Mobilization to Revolution.* Reading, MA: Addison-Wesley.

———— 1979. "Repertories of Contention in America and Britain, 1750-1830." In *The Dynamics of Social Movements*, edited by Mayer N. Zald and John D. McCarthy. Cambridge, MA: Winthrop.

————, ed. 1984. "Social Movements and National Politics." In *Statemaking and Social Movements*, edited by Charles Bright and Susan Harding. Ann Arbor: University of Michigan Press.

————, Louis Tilly, and Richard Tilly. 1975. *The Rebellious Century, 1830-1930.* Cambridge, MA: Harvard University Press.

Toch, Hans. 1965. *The Social Psychology of Social Movements.* Indianapolis: Bobbs-Merrill.

Touraine, Alain. 1981. *The Voice and the Eye: An Analysis of Social Movements.* New York: Cambridge University Press.

Traugott, Mark. 1985. *Armies of the Poor.* Princeton, NJ: Princeton University Press.

Troyer, Ronald J. and Gerald E. Markle. 1983. *Cigarettes: The Battle over Smoking.* New Brunswick, NJ: Rutgers University.

Turk, Herman and Lynne G. Zucker. 1984. "Majority and Organized Opposition: On Effects of Social Movements." Pp. 249-269 in *Social Movements, Conflict and Change*, edited by Louis Kriesberg. Greenwich, CT: JAI Press.

———— 1985. "Structural Bases of Minority Effects on Majority-Supported Change." *Social Science Quarterly* 66:365-385.

Turner, Ralph. 1969. "The Public Perception of Protest." *American Sociological Review* 34:815-831.

———— and Lewis Killian. 1957. *Collective Behavior.* Englewood Cliffs, NJ: Prentice-Hall.

———— 1972. *Collective Behavior*, 2nd ed. Englewood Cliffs, NJ: Prentice-Hall.

———— 1986. *Collective Behavior*, 3rd ed. Englewood Cliffs, NJ: Prentice-Hall.

Useem, Bert. 1980. "Solidarity Model, Breakdown Model, and the Boston Anti-busing Movement." *American Sociological Review* 45:357-369.

_____ and Mayer Zald. 1982. "From Pressure Group to Social Movement: Efforts to Promote Use of Nuclear Power." *Social Problems* 30: 144-156.

Van der Loo, Hans, Erik Snel, and Bart Van Steenbergen. 1984. *Een Wenkend Perspectief? Nieuwe Social Bewegingen en Culturele Veranderingen.* Amersfoort: De Horstink.

Von Eschen, Donald, Jerome Kirk, and Maurice Pinard. 1971. "The Organizational Substructure of Disorderly Politics." *Social Forces* 49:529-544.

Walsh, Edward J. 1981. "Resource Mobilization and Citizen Protest in Communities Around Three Mile Island." *Social Problems* 29:1-21.

_____ and Rex H. Warland. 1983. "Social Movement Involvement in the Wake of a Nuclear Accident: Activists and Free Riders in the Three Mile Island Area." *American Sociological Review* 48:764-781.

Weinstein, Deena. 1979. *Bureaucratic Opposition.* New York: Pergamon.

West, Guida. 1981. *The National Welfare Rights Movement.* New York: Praeger.

Wicker, Allan. 1969. "Attitudes vs. Action: The Relationship of Verbal and Overt Behavioral Responses to Attitude Objects." *Journal of Social Issues* 25:41-78.

Wilson, Kenneth L. and Anthony M. Orum. 1976. "Mobilizing People for Collective Political Action." *Journal of Political and Military Sociology* 4:187-202.

Wilson, William J. 1973. *Power, Racism and Privilege.* New York: Free Press.

Wolf, Eric. 1969. *Peasant Wars of the Twentieth Century.* New York: Harper & Row.

Wolfson, Mark. 1987. "An Analysis of the Regulation of Social Movement Organizations and Industries." Presented at the annual meetings of the Eastern Sociological Association, Boston.

Womack, John, Jr. 1969. *Zapata and the Mexican Revolution.* New York: Knopf.

Wood, Michael and Michael Hughes. 1984. "The Moral Basis of Moral Reform: Status Discontent vs. Culture and Socialization as Explanations of Antipornography Social Movement Adherence." *American Sociological Review* 49:86-99.

Wood, P. 1982. "The Environmental Movement." Pp. 201-220 in *Social Movements*, edited by J. L. Wood and M. Jackson. Belmont, CA: Wadsworth.

Zald, Mayer N. and Roberta Ash. 1966. "Social Movement Organizations: Growth, Decay and Change." *Social Forces* 44:327-341.

Zald, Mayer N. and Patricia Denton. 1963. "From Evangelism to Social Service: The Transformation of the YMCA." *Administrative Science Quarterly* 8:214-234.

Zald, Mayer N. and John D. McCarthy. 1975. "Organizational Intellectuals and the Criticism of Society." *Social Service Review* 49:344-362.

_____ 1987. "Religious Groups as Crucibles of Social Movements." Pp. 67-96 in *Social Movements in an Organizational Society*, edited by Mayer N. Zald and John D. McCarthy. New Brunswick, NJ: Transaction Books.

Zald, Mayer N. and Bert Useem. 1987. "Movement and Countermovement Interaction: Mobilization, Tactics and State Involvement." Pp. 247-272 in *Social Movements in an Organizational Society*, edited by Mayer N. Zald and John D. McCarthy. New Brunswick, NJ: Transaction Books.

Zukier, Henri. 1982. "Situational Determinants of Behavior." *Social Research* 49:1073-1091.

Zurcher, Louis A. and R. George Kirkpatrick. 1976. *Citizens for Decency: Antipornography Crusades as Status Defense.* Austin: University of Texas Press.

Zurcher, Louis A. and David A. Snow. 1981. "Collective Behavior: Social Movements." In *Social Psychology: Sociological Perspectives*, edited by Morris Rosenberg and Ralph H. Turner. New York: Basic Books.

22

Development and the World Economy

PETER B. EVANS
JOHN D. STEPHENS

arochialism, long a hallmark of American social science, is on the decline. The rest of the world impinges increasingly on social, economic, and political life in the United States. The contradictions of building supposedly universal theories on the experience of a single country are harder to ignore. Theoretical perspectives on development have changed in response to the changing historical reality of the developmental process and of relations between developing and developed countries. They have also changed in response to the dialogue and debate among those engaged in theory building.

Chronicling the evolution of theoretical perspectives in the field is one of our principal aims, but it would be hubris to claim that this is a comprehensive review of contemporary work on development and the world economy. Instead we have tried to select several streams of work that converge in terms of both conceptual framework and substantive concerns, forming, we believe, a promising basis for future work.

This chapter was written in association with John W. Riley, Jr. We are deeply appreciative of editorial help on earlier versions of this chapter from Dale Dannefer, Beth B. Hess, David Kertzer, John Meyer, Bernice Neugarten, and Harris Schrank; of special suggestions from Kathleen Bond, Dennis Hogan, and Norman Ryder; and of invaluable assistance in manuscript preparation from Diane Zablotsky.

The emergence of "modernization theory" in the late fifties and early sixties set the stage for the contemporary synthesis. The body of literature built around the concept of modernization was the first substantial set of writings by mainstream sociologists and political scientists that focused on what was happening in the Third World. Interest in modernization clearly stemmed in part from America's new position of international hegemony, but it also grew out of a rediscovery of the central themes of classical nineteenth-century sociology.

The role of the modernization approach in stimulating and legitimating work on developing countries was fundamental, but dissatisfaction with the approach was as important as the lessons it offered. As interest in comparative and international issues grew, a series of critiques were raised. Explanations too often seemed "actorless"; urbanization, bureaucratization, and the other components of modernization appeared driven by inexorable impersonal forces rather than by the interests and actions of states, classes, and other social actors. The possibility that twentieth-century patterns of development might take forms that were distinctively different from earlier patterns was neglected as were questions of the impact of position in the international system on developmental possibilities.

Beginning in the mid-sixties, various alternatives to the modernization approach became increasingly important. These challenges involved recovering parts of the classic sociological traditions that had been neglected in the earlier reconstruction of modernization theorists, including Marx and the comparative historical side of Weber. They also involved a new emphasis on international factors. Dependency and world systems approaches turned the modernization theorists' emphasis on diffusion as a primary instrument of development on its head, arguing instead that ties to "core" countries were a principal impediment to development.

For more than a decade sharp conflicts dominated discourse in the field, but gradually a body of different studies began to grow up that embodied syntheses of a number of these conflicts. These new studies were diverse, covering a wide variety of substantive topics, but they share a number of characteristics that in combination serve to distinguish them from earlier work. These studies do not offer a theoretical paradigm in the strict sense of a set of axiomatic relationships that can be used to generate universalistic predictions of developmental outcomes. They do share some working hypotheses about the likely political and economic consequences of different patterns of interaction among states and classes. They also share common assumptions about what problems are most central to the study of development and what factors should be taken into account in order to understand outcomes in specific cases.

Like the classic tradition of political economy, the contemporary work on which we will focus begins with the conviction that economic and political development cannot fruitfully be examined in isolation from each other. It has absorbed the lessons that grew out of work on dependency and world system perspectives and is therefore much more sensitive to international factors than classic political economy, but it has rejected the idea that external factors determine the dynamics of domestic development. More generally, it rejects models that posit "necessary" outcomes, assuming instead that developmental paths are historically contingent. Consequently, comparative historical analysis is its hallmark. Multiple cases are preferred and when single cases are used they are set in a comparative framework, likewise quantitative and other cross-sectional data are located in the context of more historical evidence. Because it combines the classic concerns of nineteenth-century political economy with a comparative historical perspective that emphasizes the international context of national developmental trajectories, this work might be labeled "the new comparative historical political economy." We will refer to

it simply as new work in comparative political economy.

In order to illustrate the impact of this perspective, we have chosen four areas that most current practitioners of comparative political economy consider central to any general understanding of the developmental problems and prospects in an internationalized world. First, we examine the role of the state in the process of development. Next, we look at one issue in which state policy has been most obviously involved: the question of how the fruits of development should be distributed. Our third concern is with the consequences of economic change for political regimes. We focus on the relation between industrialization and political democracy. Finally, and perhaps most important, we examine current views on the relation between national development and the world political economy.

In all four of these areas, the new comparative political economy has drawn heavily on the critiques of modernization theory but has also succeeded in providing explanations for findings that seemed anomalous from Marxist or dependency points of view. In some instances the interpretations provided by this new work have managed to take findings that support the hypotheses of modernization theory and interpret them in the light of the perspectives of its critics in a way that provides a more satisfying synthesis that supersedes both earlier views. We will discuss several examples of this kind of advance, but before moving on to more specific substantive concerns, it makes sense to lay out the theoretical evolution that gave rise to the new comparative political economy in the first place.

Changing Theoretical Perspectives

Thomas Kuhn is responsible for the most dramatic model of how theoretical visions evolve. In his view, scientific paradigms always generate, along with evidence that confirms their validity, anomalies that they cannot explain. When the burden of the anomalies grows too great, a new paradigm eventually emerges, which views the same evidence in a new light, interprets it in different ways, and opens new avenues for amassing additional knowledge.

In social science the process is different, not just because the evidence is always more ambiguous and the social and political interests that affect its interpretation more direct, but also because history is always transforming the object of study. Nowhere is this more obvious than in the sociology of development. Copernicus and Ptolemy were at least studying roughly the same solar system; contemporary students of relations between the First and Third World are observing a very different system than their predecessors observed in 1950. Nevertheless, changes over the past 30 years in the way in which the process of development and the character of the world economy are described have not been due simply to changes in the reality observed. Changes in theoretical perspectives were equally important. In the fifties, and most of the sixties, modernization theory dominated the study of developing countries, but the comparative historical approach, which would later become very influential in the study of the Third World had already been extensively employed by Europeanists. Beginning in the late sixties the dependency approach and world system theory, which could legitimately be considered a rival paradigm, gradually gained ascendance.

By the eighties, however, the sequence looked rather un-Kuhnian. Comparative political economy combined the comparative historical method with certain of the insights of dependency and world system thinking. Even some of the hypotheses of the modernization approach had been recovered in altered form. The result looked more like a synthesis of past perspectives than a Kuhnian revolution.

The new work retained important elements that antedated the birth of the sociology of development as a subfield, elements from the original nineteenth-century confrontation of sociology and industrialization, but this was hardly surprising. A good deal of the conflict between the modernization theorists and their successors can be interpreted in terms of their different strategies for resuscitating the developmental concerns that had given birth to the discipline.

Rediscovering the "Sociology of Development"

With America's emergence as a world power and the simultaneous discovery of "The Appeal of Communism to the Underdeveloped Peoples" (Watnick, 1952), questions of industrialization and the sociopolitical changes accompanying it came to the fore of sociological discourse once again. There was, of course, one crucial difference from the concerns of the nineteenth-century founders. This time it was not the origins or consequences of "our" industrialization that was considered problematic, it was "their" industrialization, the progress or lack of progress of the people of the Third World. Our industrialization was taken as a model, both normatively and theoretically, and the principal issue was how the model might be extended to others with different histories, social structures, and cultural traditions.

A wide range of sociologists, political scientists, and economists attempted to investigate and theorize these concerns, but most theoretically influential was Talcott Parsons's elegant reconstruction of the classic nineteenth-century tradition. Originally designed to model American society, Parsonsian structural-functionalism became the underpinning for one important stream of what came to be known as "modernization theory." His reconstruction was both an exegesis of the nineteenth-century classics and an original model in its own right.

Weber's emphasis on "rationalization," on the key importance of being able to predict institutional responses and of calculability more generally, is the linchpin of the approach. Increased "rationality" is the definition of the movement toward modernity, or more crudely put, of progress. To this is added Weber's cultural analysis of the motivational underpinnings of capitalism, as exemplified positively in the Protestant ethic and the spirit of capitalism, and negatively in his studies of the other great world religions. For Parsons, Weber's work demonstrated above all the necessity of a certain pattern of values and norms if economic, social, and political progress were to be achieved. Normative patterns emphasizing "particularism" had to be replaced by those emphasizing universalism" in order for development to occur. Achievement has to replace ascription in order to motivate social actors to generate progressive change.

What was missing was Weber's preoccupation with classes, the state, and the historical evolution of the institutions of capitalism. In the Parsonsian reconstruction, bureaucracy became synonymous with rationality, whereas in the Weberian original, centralization of power and the domination of other social groups were equally central to the bureaucratic genie. What was missing was the "historical materialist" side of Weber.

To complement the cultural side of Weber, modernization theory drew very heavily on Durkheim. Durkheim's vision of increasing functional differentiation as the master process in the development of industrial society is as central to modernization theory as Weberian notions of rationality. Durkheimian anxieties over the disruptive, disequilibrating consequences of industrialization played an equally central role in the Parsonsian vision of modernization.

Preservation of the organic unity of society in the face of fundamental structural changes was the central problem facing European societies during the original process of industrialization. Modernization theorists saw the same problems in the Third World. As "modern" values and norms intruded into certain areas of social life, the traditional orientations that prevailed in other realms were threatened. More important, the normative consensus of the society as a whole was undermined.

The idealistic side of Weber and Durkheim's concept of social differentiation provided a road map of the sociocultural preconditions for development. Durkheim offered a diagnosis of the problems that were likely to occur enroute between traditional and modern social patterns. The resultant prescription for the citizens of the underdeveloped world and those who would assist them was to find ways of inculcating the attitudes purported to prevail in advanced capitalist countries without being overwhelmed by the tensions created by such drastic value change.

This basic message resonated across disciplinary boundaries and methodological approaches. Lerner (1958) investigated the connection between the movement from traditional to modern culture at the individual and societal levels. Banfield (1958) probed the ways in which the values and norms of the peasant family might impede economic modernization. David McClelland (1961) looked at "Need Achievement" as a psychological characteristic that depended on child rearing and early schooling but could be inculcated later if necessary. Inkeles and Smith (1974) examined the social structural circumstances conducive to the emergence of an entire complex of modern attitudes.

Just as the modernization perspective adapted easily to social-psychological analyses of the problems of development, it also fit well with neoclassical economic prescriptions. Need Achievement and entrepreneurship are easily conflated. Universalism is clearly one of the normative underpinnings of the market. Breaking the traditional bonds that prevent people from participating fully in market exchange is clearly a central component of modernization. Thus the institutional prerequisites of "takeoff" outlined in Rostow's classic (1960) *Stages of Economic Growth* jibe very nicely with those that would be prescribed by someone working in the Parsonsian frame.

The modernization paradigm was even more influential among those attempting to analyze political development.[1] In politics as in economics, use of the modernization perspective tended to carry in its wake the tendency to use an idealized version of contemporary society as the end point toward which development was (and, more implicitly, should be) aiming. As Leonard Binder put it (1986, p. 3), "Modernization theory is essentially an academic and pseudoscientific transfer of the dominant, and ideologically significant, paradigm employed in research on the American political system." Because of the "systems integration" assumptions built into structural-functional theorizing it was predicted that insofar as the Third World succeeded in replicating the economic success of the first, it would come to enjoy similarly structured political systems as well.

The modernization perspective did allow for, and under certain circumstances even predicted, conflict and tension during the process of development. It was assumed that as different institutions (e.g., the workplace and the family) modernized at different rates tensions would be created for the individuals whose lives spanned both institutions.[2] Or, one modernization process might proceed much more rapidly than others, creating social imbalances, as in Huntington's (1968) analysis of disorder created by political mobilization outstripping institutionalization. Resistance to new values on the part of the privileged traditional elites was also to be expected, but there was little in the way of analysis of conflicting interests among different groups and classes.[3] Given the strong presumption of correspondence between societal needs and the actual consequences of modernization, conflicts were likely to be seen as questions of adjustment rather than as involving long-term gains and losses. How the divergent interests of different groups might propel or deflect the process of development, and how the process of development might in turn benefit some groups at the expense of others remained largely unexplored questions.

The modernization approach also seemed to project a trajectory for all developing countries that replicated the experience of the advanced capitalist countries. Variations from this track were theorized as aberrations, deviations to be corrected. Here again the approach presented problems for those trying to explicate particular cases. It also created an impression of ethnocentrism. The distinctive cultures of Third World countries seemed only obstacles to be overcome and replaced by the value patterns of the industrial West.

Finally, there was little room in the modernization approach for dealing with the world political-economy. External influences were important. The diffusion of modern ideas and values from outside of the society is a principal means of breaking out of an internally consistent traditional social structure. What was missing was the idea that there might be real conflicts of interest between developing and developed countries. Also missing was the idea that the problems and possibilities of development are contingent on a country's position in a larger system of interrelations among nations. For small countries with recent colonial pasts, it was hard to accept this neglect as a convenient abstraction. It amounted to denial of the most salient features of their history and current problems.

Resuscitating Marx would have alleviated some of the problems of the modernization approach. A Marxist paradigm, however modified, requires social actors with conflicting interests. It also assumes that there is an international political-economy that has little respect for national borders and that must be understood as a whole. Nonetheless, the Marxist alternative as it existed at the time that modernization theory was being constructed was hardly a panacea.

Marx's description of how competition led to the concentration and centralization of capital often seems to have an automaticity that negates the possibility of diverse, historically contingent developmental outcomes. While in his own work, this abstract paradigm was balanced by a keen sense of the role of historically contingent political struggles, it was often possible to accuse his followers of arguing "that the significant characteristics of national economies and social formations can be 'read off' from the characteristics, especially the 'laws of motion' of the capitalist mode of production."[4]

When applied to the Third World this aspect of Marx's work produced a vision of unilinear evolution that was in some ways analogous to the vision of modernization theorists. In most general pronouncements on industrial development, it is clear that Marx expected that "the dynamism and capacity for expansion of the youthful capitalism of his period would be reproduced in any society which it penetrated" (Palma, 1978, p. 888). In one of his most famous passages from the *Communist Manifesto*, Marx waxes eloquent about the global role of the bourgeoisie saying:

> The bourgeoisie, by the rapid improvement of all instruments of production, by the immensely facilitated means of communica-

tion, draws all, even the most barbarian, nations into civilization. The cheap prices of its commodities are the heavy artillery with which it batters down all Chinese walls. . . . It compels all nations, on pain of extinction, to adopt the bourgeois mode of production [Marx and Engels, 1848, p. 11].

Some of his journalistic writings on India and the European periphery (Ireland, Poland) are more pessimistic, but in general Marx seemed to believe that "the country that is more developed industrially only shows, to the less developed, the image of its own future" (Marx, 1867, pp. 8-9).[5]

Constructing an alternative to modernization theory involved recovering the historically contingent Marx as well as recapturing the institutional side of Weber. Marxist ideas about the role of conflicting classes in the promotion of economic progress had to be used in a way that was sensitive to the distinctiveness of Third World capitalism and avoided the theoretical short-circuits created by the simplistic application of Eurocentric abstractions. Fortunately, a variety of work that spoke to these needs was already under way, even while the modernization approach was most thoroughly dominant.

Comparative Historical Approaches

While the modernization approach dominated work on Third World countries it did not, with a few exceptions (e.g., Smelser, 1959), play the same role in research on the historical development of advanced industrial countries. This role was filled by a series of comparative historical studies that began in the interwar period. Unlike practitioners of the modernization approach, the authors of these studies did not draw on a common theoretical paradigm. They did not even form a school of thought in the sense that different authors consistently address one another's work. Nonetheless, work in this tradition had a powerful influence on subsequent patterns of research and thinking in the field, not just among those who worked on Europe, but among students of the Third World as well.

Gerschenkron's (1962) studies of European historical development provided the earliest and most convincing arguments that, even within Europe, economic development took quite different paths depending on the timing of industrialization. Gerschenkron (1962, pp. 353-354) contended that late industrializers were more likely to experience industrialization in a sudden spurt, to emphasize large plants and enterprises, to stress producer rather than consumer goods, to put pressure on the levels of consumption of the population, to increase the supply of capital through centralized institutions (banks, and later, the state) and often through coercive methods and, finally, to rely on the domestic agrarian sector as a market for industrial goods. He added that the characteristics of later industrializers tend to favor authoritarian government as part of the effort to mobilize capital and repress wages.[6] Though it is not emphasized, the very logic of Gerschenkron's argument places economic relations between countries as a very important conditioning factor in a country's economic development, especially in the case of late developers.

International economic relations move to center stage in the work of Karl Polanyi (1944). In his analysis, Polanyi convincingly drives home the point that the development and eventual total dominance of market exchange in economic relationships on a world scale was the creation of individuals and groups, primarily but not entirely the bourgeoisie, pursuing their interest politically. While one may quarrel with his tendency to reify the market,[7] Polanyi's account of the economic development of the West and its political impact is remarkable in that it was perhaps the earliest attempt to integrate the interplay of classes within society and the interplay of states both in the world economy and in the world system of states in a single analysis. Moreover, Polanyi recognizes that the victims of the rise of market society, workers and peasants, were not simply on the receiving end of history.[8] On the contrary, they sought, sometimes with success, to protect themselves from the market through struggles to alter the rules of the game.

Among sociologists working in this tradition, Reinhard Bendix played a leading role. In a series of works of historical sociology (1956, 1964, 1978), he examined the transformation of authority relations, both private and public, that occurred in the development of contemporary industrial societies. Emphasizing the comparative historical side of the Weberian tradition,[9] Bendix attacked modernization theory for its ahistorical approach, its organic view of society and neglect of conflict, and its assumption of a single path of societal evolution. In his view, society was a product of historical group conflicts, which endure to shape present-day social structure and culture. In contrast, however, to purely materialist analyses, he contends that cultural ideas do have very important effects on societal development that cannot be reduced to material interest.

Perhaps the single most influential work in the comparative historical tradition is Barrington Moore's *The Social Origins of Dictatorship and Democracy*, which pioneered the use of the comparative historical method on a set of cases that spanned both First and Third Worlds. On the basis of historical case studies of six countries (England, France, the United States, Japan, India, and China) and extensive research on two more (Germany and Russia), Moore identifies three distinct sets of conditions that contribute to the development of communism, fascism, or parliamentary democracy.[10] While one may criticize Moore for his failure to integrate state capacity and an intersocietal perspective systematically in his analysis (see Skocpol, 1973), his work foreshadows subsequent work in comparative political economy more than any of the other early practitioners of the comparative historical approach. The central themes in Moore include the link between economic models and political forms, classes of varying strengths coming together in coalitions and compromises or opposing each other in struggle in given historical contexts, the historical specificity of economic development models due to the historical development of the world economic system, state strength as a variable, and the state/crown as an historical actor.

Though chronologically prior to the other authors discussed in this section, Otto Hintze's (1861-1940) impact in United States and British social science came last. Hintze's (1975) work served as a corrective to the reductionist views of the state being advanced in almost all other schools of thought. Changes in the state itself are an important element of his explanations. External pressure forces states to seek appropriate military organization, and this in turn modified its internal structure. Changes in the distribution of power within the state influence future policies and methods of government.

Hintze not only emphasized the state to a larger degree than other pioneers of the comparative historical approach, he also focused more on international factors. Hintze, like his predecessors in the Prussian historical school, began with the assumption that the interplay of states in the European state system had a central influence on the internal development of individual states. Hintze's analysis of the international political economy did not, however, focus on the economic aspects of relations between states. These became the central feature of another influential alternative to the modernization approach, one that grew out of work on the Third World rather than Europe.

DEPENDENCY AND THE WORLD SYSTEM

For a number of scholars working on Third World development during the sixties, myriad conflicts that pitted Third World countries against developed ones presented an anomaly that could not be accounted for within the modernization paradigm. In response they constructed a theoretical paradigm in which the effect of the international political economy took center stage. Struggles among local classes and interest groups were seen as shaped and conditioned by the local society's relation to the advanced industrial societies of the "core," "metropole," or "center." Foreign actors were viewed as inextricably involved in class struggles and alliances within the countries on the "periphery." Instead of assuming that increased contact between core and periphery would foster more rapid development as modernization theorists and traditional Marxists had, the "dependency school" made the opposite assumption.

The strongest statement of this position is found in the work of Andre Gunder Frank (1967), which argues for the "development of underdevelopment," that is, that increased external linkage actually produces retrogression on the periphery. While this assertion is almost impossible to sustain as initially put forward,[11] Frank's work, in combination with the earlier work of Paul Baran (1957), had a profound effect on the field. They reintroduced Marxist themes into the debate on development while at the same time focusing on the dynamics of change in the periphery. They also provided a clear-cut substantive antithesis to prevailing modernization views.

Ties with developed countries were the problem, not the solution. For precisely that reason, among others, the path followed by the developed countries could not be followed by currently developing countries. Having climbed the ladder of industrial development and built strong state apparatuses, the developed countries were now in a position to exploit other regions and prevent the ascension along a similar road of the developing countries. The principal obstacle to change at the local level was not irrational attachments to traditional values, it was the very rational attempts of local elites and their foreign allies to defend their own power and privilege.

Less obvious, but perhaps more influential in the long run than the substantive antithesis was the method of approach that Baran and Frank suggested by their example. Both works built their arguments around historical case studies that included an integrated examination of local and international actors. At both local and international levels, they emphasized interests rather than norms and values, economic and political structures rather than cultural patterns. Their materialism may have been overstated and their class analysis insufficiently sophisticated, but they helped move studies of the Third World in the direction that comparative historical studies of Europe had already taken. Baran, Frank, and those who followed them represented a reorientation of scholarship in the center. Even more fundamental to the influence of the dependency approach was the growing global role of Third World scholars, especially Latin Americans.[12] The principal direction of the diffusion of dependency theory was from South to North rather than the reverse.[13] Building on the work of Latin American historians and economists,[14] Fernando Henrique Cardoso and Enzo Faletto (1979) produced the essay that most would consider the founding statement of the dependency approach, *Dependence and Development in Latin America*.[15]

Cardoso and Faletto's approach was a "historical structural" one, that is, they tried to analyze the historical evolution of the major Latin American countries in ways that would reveal the central structural determinants of that evolution. Like Baran and Frank, Cardoso and Faletto focus on the interaction of local classes and social groups with externally based social actors. Concretely, they focus first on the class coalitions that enabled major Latin American countries to shift from export-oriented to more domestically oriented growth strategies and then on the growth of the alliance between foreign industrial capital and local elites in the post-World War II period. Cardoso and Faletto's approach is, in short, quite parallel to the comparative historical work being done on Europe.

While Cardoso and Faletto's model was primarily concerned with internal dynamics, other work in the dependency tradition was much more preoccupied with tracing the connections between the evolution of core countries and developmental sequences on the periphery. Perhaps most influential is the work of Immanuel Wallerstein (1974, 1979), which provides a vision in which the logic of capital accumulation dictates not just relations among classes but also those among states and geographically defined zones of production. The position of individual states and societies within the world system may shift, but the structure of the system as a whole defines the pattern of development both globally and within individual societies.

A second, less obtrusive aspect of Wallerstein's work is worth noting. It combined a theoretical structure that grew out of studies of the Third World with a heavily Eurocentric substantive content. His particular vision of the dependency argument required that he ground his arguments in an analysis of early modern European history. In doing so, he thrust an entire tradition of historical literature, European in origins as well as content, into the middle of American sociological discourse. Historical research that might have seemed marginal to sociological studies of development was given a new legitimacy by the prominence of Wallerstein's portrayal of the sixteenth century.

Wallerstein's "world-system" approach generated heated debate.[16] Those attracted by the approach ended up modifying or even rejecting the received framework as often as they worked within it. Like the controversies over dependency and the earlier clashes between Marxists and modernization theorists, the debate over the world-system approach was part of the humus that nurtured new work in comparative political economy.

The New Comparative Political Economy

Both the Europeanist tradition of comparative historical analysis and the "historical-structural" approach to the analysis of situations of dependency in the Third World produced a rich variety of descendants over the course of the seventies and eighties. Each approach was revised and modified. Researchers increasingly blended perspectives derived from the two, forming a new comparative political economy that dealt similarly and sometimes simultaneously with both First and Third World problems. This is not to say that work evolved smoothly. The literature was filled with critiques and counter-critiques and various kinds of internecine warfare, but by the mid-1980s there was a large body of work on development and the world economy that was both variegated but surprisingly coherent.

Methodologically this work has relied heavily on the analytical methods of comparative history in which nations are cases. The small number of cases, combined with concern with multiple paths leading to the same end point and conjunctural causation has meant reluctance to build interpretations on statistical evidence alone.[17] Statistical evidence has been used extensively to characterize social structures and processes within individual countries (see for

example Shorter and Tilly, 1974, or Zeitlin and Ratcliff, 1988). Quantitative research has also been fundamental in providing support for a number of key propositions cross-nationally (e.g., that foreign direct investment is related to inequality or that development enhances prospects for democracy), but the "black box" quality that would otherwise make such correlational findings unsatisfying is always mitigated by a complement of historical and theoretical arguments.

Substantively, recent work has not aimed at charting progress along a presumed unilinear path of societal development but rather with uncovering, interpreting, and trying to explain distinctive patterns of development. Why do different countries exhibit different patterns of distribution and accumulation over the course of their development? Why is industrialization associated with strikingly disparate political regimes in different periods and regions?[18] Associated with the concern about distinctiveness is the refusal to take for granted the relative strength of different classes or the character of the relations among them. The strength of dominant and subordinate classes, like the strength and autonomy of the state, is taken as a variable. Possibilities for conflict or compromise between classes is seen as arising out of domestic political histories but also as powerfully conditioned by international economic and political conjunctures.

Work on Europe has extended earlier analyses in two directions. First, they became much more concerned with the role of the state. In parallel critiques of Marxist explanations of history, Skocpol (1973, 1979) and Mann (1977, 1984, 1986, in press) have argued that the state—its structure, capacity, and strength vis-a-vis civil society—cannot be reduced to a reflection of class forces and must be brought back in as an independent force and actor in historical developments.[19] Skocpol demonstrates how state structures and international competition between states influenced the development and outcome of the three great social revolutions. In his more recent work, Mann (1986) argues that the social cohesion and organization of preindustrial societies was provided by overlapping networks of state power, military organization, and religious communities as well as by social class relations.

At the same time Tilly and his collaborators were "bringing the masses back in." In a number of interrelated works (Shorter and Tilly, 1974; Tilly, 1964, 1978; Tilly, Tilly, and Tilly, 1975), he shows that peasants, shopkeepers, and workers were not just the passive receivers of history, responding to social disorganization in their protests, but rather that the actions of these subordinate classes were efforts to shape the direction of events. Moreover, with the development of capitalism and the modern state through time, pure defensive action (e.g., riots and rebellions) gave way to efforts to transform society in a more desirable direction from the point of view of the subordinate groups (e.g., demonstrations and strikes).

Concern with the state and with the affect of subordinate groups on the course of development also came together in a number of studies of the development of advanced industrial societies in the twentieth century that substantially reoriented the dominant view of the welfare state. A number of Marxist authors began to argue that the expansion of the welfare state (Block, 1977; Gough, 1979; Przeworski, 1980, 1985) was at least in part due to working-class organization and struggle. Corporatism (Panitch, 1980) was seen as a strategy to contain that struggle and reintegrate the working class into the system. In a parallel but independently developed school of thought, a group of analysts whom we might term "Social democratic Marxists" developed what Weir and Skocpol (1985) call the "working class power approach" to the explanation of welfare state expansion. They argue that working-class political and economic power are the main determinants of cross-national differences in the political economies of the advanced capitalist societies and present empirical evidence that is strongly related to the level of welfare-state spending and its distributive impact, social control of the economy, level of employment and strike activity.[20] As is typical of comparative political economy, the argument is a historical and contingent one. It is not that industrialization produces the working class, which in turn produces the welfare state; rather, it is that the variable strength of working-class organizations, which is in turn dependent on other political, economic, and historical factors, is responsible for variations in the distributive impact and expenditure patterns of the welfare state.

Tentative explanations for differences in working-class organization and ideology among advanced capitalist countries have come from two sources. Stimulated by E. P. Thompson's *The Making of the English Working Class* (1963), historians and historical sociologists studied the development of the working class in various countries, resulting in a rich body of literature, which by the early eighties was ripe for the development of comparative generalizations about the causes of differences in working-

class formation, degree of organization, and political expression. In a recent edited book, Katznelson and Zolberg (1986) build on specific cases to construct historically bounded generalizations about the variations in working-class and labor movement formation. Zolberg's closing synthetic essay emphasizes two broad sets of factors accounting for these cross-national differences on the eve of World War I: variations in capitalist industrial structure (the pace and timing of industrialization and the structure of the economy) and the character of the political regime (legacies of absolutism and extent of political rights for the working class). His conclusions jibe nicely with recent work by working-class power theorists, which has concluded that differences in industrial structure and political regime (in this case, government by the Left) in addition to ethnic/linguistic diversity and shop-floor organization account for variations in the structure of labor movements (Ingham, 1974; Kjellberg, 1983; Miller, 1987; Stephens, 1979).[21]

Explaining variability and distinctive patterns of development was also a central concern to those who tried to build on the Cardoso-Faletto approach to dependency. Like their colleagues working on Europe, the dependencistas of the seventies and eighties found that they could not ignore the role of the state, but they arrived at their interest in the state first of all through a consideration of the role of external factors. The dependency perspective stimulated a plethora of analyses of the consequences of international ties, especially direct investment by multinational firms, on development.[22] The main thrust of this work was to reconfirm the suspicions of earlier dependencistas that there were real conflicts between the interest of capital organized on a global basis and the national development goals of Third World countries. Yet this left important instances of Third World industrialization unexplained. Explaining these cases required delving into the goals and capacity of Third World state apparatuses as well as understanding the global dynamics of international industries. For example, Evans (1979) found that Brazil's successful pursuit of dependent development was rooted in a complex alliance of the state, domestic, and foreign capital.[23]

At the same time, those working on situations of dependency focused on domestic class coalitions and the relations between domestic classes and the state in ways that paralleled the efforts of Europeanists working in the tradition of comparative political economy. Hamilton's (1983) analysis of the Mexican state, for example, while it is certainly mindful of international context, is primarily an analysis of how domestic class alliances worked in interaction with the state apparatus to produce a distinctive development strategy. Even more clearly, Zeitlin's (1984) historical reconstruction of political development in Chile argues that struggles within and between classes and the state determined Chile's position in the international political economy more than the reverse. Domestic factors also figure prominently in Collier and Collier's (in press) tight comparison of the impact of incorporation of organized labor on subsequent class alliances, party systems, and political dynamics in eight Latin American countries. They argue that these subsequent developments were largely determined by the degree of involvement of the state and political parties in the period of initial incorporation of the labor movement.

Similar convergence can be see in work on the agrarian sector. Just as Europeanists like Tilly (in his classic 1964 study of the Vendee), Moore (1966), and Brenner (1976) tried to explain different political and economic outcomes in Europe by looking at class relations in the rural sector, so Wolf (1969), Paige (1975, 1985), DeJanvry (1981), and others tried to do the same for Third World countries. Paige (1975), following a much earlier lead by Stinchcombe (1961), argues that unlike industrial class relations, agrarian class relations vary greatly depending on the property relations, marketing systems, and production organization. These differences in class relations give rise to differences in the typical political reactions of the peasantry. Given that the development of the world capitalist system created (or accelerated) specialization on a single or a few crops in peripheral countries, the characteristics of agrarian class relations in many peripheral countries have resulted in very different patterns of national politics in the respective countries. Thus the argument for comparative analysis is yet more compelling for agrarian societies.

Perhaps most exciting was the increase in the number of studies that combine reexamination of the European experience with explicit First World-Third World comparisons. One of the most provocative of these is Senghaas (1985), which includes a comprehensive comparative overview of industrialization in the "core" as well as a number of direct-pair comparisons with the peripheral countries (e.g., Uruguay and the Netherlands, Argentina and Australia) and concludes that the dynamics of peripheralization for late developers were more similar in the

European and Third World cases than previous work had suggested.

In the area of political development, explicit comparisons have become even more common. Linz and Stepan (1978) looked at the breakdown of democracies in Europe and Latin America. Mouzelis (1986) compares the problems of parliamentarism in the Balkans and Latin America. And, in a multivolume *tour de force* edited by O'Donnell, Schmitter, and Whitehead (1986) transitions to democracy in Southern Europe and Latin America are examined. What is important about these First World/Third World enterprises is that they are not attempts to project the future of the Third World based on the past of the First World. They are based instead on the assumption that processes in the two regions are sufficiently similar to make combined analysis essential to arriving at a valid theoretical understanding of what is going on in either.[24]

As this brief review makes clear, the new comparative political economy is a diverse and eclectic body of work, easier to convey in its richness than to summarize succinctly. In order to appreciate fully the extent to which this new work has built on earlier traditions and begun to move beyond them, it is necessary to turn to the examination a few of the debates in which new work has played a formative role.

Current Issues and Debates

All social institutions are transformed by development. New forces of production create new relations between gender and work that in turn restructure family roles. The intrusion of the market disrupts communities and stimulates new social movements. Technological advances in information processing alter both the content of cultural communication and the possibilities for political repression. The increasing intensity of interconnection between the international political economy and domestic social structures produces an equally wide range of effects. International migration restructures the labor markets of both sending and receiving countries while the growth of international capital markets creates new constraints on social welfare policies. Any selection of a few "issues and debates" out of myriad possibilities must be considered in some respects arbitrary.

We have selected only four topics: the role of the state in relation to the development of markets, the relation between economic development and democratization, the relation between the accumulation of capital and pursuit of a more egalitarian distribution of income and, finally, the consequences of insertion in the world political economy for national trajectories of development. The four are clearly neither a survey nor a representative sample. By restricting ourselves to four topics we have abdicated responsibility for dealing with a number of fundamental developmental issues, for example, the way in which racial, ethnic, and gender divisions shape and are shaped by the process of development.[25] Even within issue areas we have been forced to make difficult choices. For example, in choosing to focus our discussion on democracy and development, we have chosen not to deal with the issue of revolutionary political change, thus excluding an entire set of interesting debates (see Goldstone, 1982, 1986). Likewise, in our discussion of states and markets we were not able to deal with the rapidly growing literature on how this interaction plays itself out in state socialist societies.[26]

These and other major omissions were the price of generating a coherent and focused discussion that did some justice to the content of the debates rather than simply stringing together references. The four issues we have chosen do reflect preoccupations that have been central to the study of development since Marx, Weber, and Durkheim. They are nicely interconnected. Debates about accumulation and distribution are also debates about states and markets, while debates about whether growth promotes democracy lead naturally into questions of the political prerequisites of redistributive policies. Consideration of the effects of insertion into the world political economy intrudes into each of the other three discussions. Finally, all four serve well to explicate the method and perspective of comparative political economy.

States and Markets

Traditional readings of neoclassical economic theory suggested that the state's developmental role was best limited to ensuring property rights and eliminating obstacles to the emergence of efficient markets.[27] Modernization theory appeared to offer the same prescription. The state was the *locus classicus* of traditional rigidities and its power was a central reason for underdevelopment. Furthermore, state intervention in productive activities would represent retrogression toward a less differentiated social structure.[28] For both approaches, as for Marx, the market was the solvent that would break down traditional rigidities and allow development.

In direct contradiction were pessimistic versions of Marxist analysis, like that of Paul Baran, which argued that Third World market structures would never, on their own, produce dynamic capitalist development. In a similar vein, dependency theorists argued that reliance on markets domestically meant the eventual dominion of transnational capital and that the "unequal exchange" that occurred as a result of participation in international markets prejudiced the developmental prospects of the Third World. Both saw anemic states as part of the problem and stronger states built on the basis of political mobilization as central to the solution.

The binary opposition of administrative/ political allocation and market allocation has an undeniable theoretical elegance, whichever side of the dichotomy is chosen as positive. Its usefulness in the comparative analysis of industrialization is less clear. The effective operation of markets in the Third World is too often associated with the presence of strong, interventive states, while market failure is associated with states that lack autonomy and bureaucratic capacity. Assuming the simultaneous, and occasionally mutually reinforcing, importance of both states and markets is a more fruitful starting point and one that is increasingly common in new work on comparative political economy.

Gerschenkron's insightful analysis of the role of the state in the industrialization of European late developers offers an early version of such an approach. It assumes both that the degree of state intervention required to promote development will depend on historical circumstance and that higher levels of state entrepreneurship in no way preclude the future predominance of market relations. Not surprisingly, a good deal of the recent work in comparative political economy builds on the Gerschenkronian perspective.

Studies of extractive industries suggest that the initial situation of a Third World producer may in fact approximate the dependency vision in which linkage to external markets controlled by foreign corporations is both central to the overall operation of the economy and detrimental to the developmental prospects of the host. What is interesting about these situations, however, is that they so often generate increased state capacity to intervene. Beginning with relatively "easy" oversight and regulatory tasks they moved to entrepreneurial tasks demanding substantial technocratic expertise.

The nicest illustrations of this process come from studies of the evolution of the state's role in extractive industries, for example, copper mining in Chile and Peru. Moran (1974) shows how modest state attempts to gather information about the industry beginning in the fifties resulted in the construction of bureaucratic capacity and the training of technocrats within the state apparatus who were eventually able to run the mines as state-owned enterprises.

Becker's (1983) study of Peru illustrates the same process, but it goes further. Becker argues convincingly that the expansion of the state's role in Peruvian mining, while it represented an intervention of the state in what had previously been a private industry, cannot be represented simply as increased administrative dominance over the market. What Becker describes instead is a highly market-oriented group of professional managers operating within the state apparatus in an attempt to increase local output and value-added accruing from the industry. Becker considers this group to be part of a new corporate capitalist bourgeoisie, suggesting that their rise is fundamental to the further development of market-oriented industrialization.

A similar symbiosis prevails in cases of successful industrial development. In Korea, concerted and aggressive action by the state apparatus, helped to create the conglomerates (chaebol) that are now among the largest private economic actors in the Third World. In Brazil, an authoritarian military state fostered vertical integration of the country's economy by subsidizing local private capital goods firms, creating state-owned enterprises to produce intermediate goods and sponsoring the alliance of both types of firms with multinational corporations in technologically more difficult areas like petrochemicals (Evans, 1979). Economic rationality cannot be separated from political rationality in these economies. The prediction of future state policies is as important as predicting market reactions. They are, in Michael Barzelay's (1986) words, "politicized market economies."

If industrialization is the goal, then the performance of states like Korea and Brazil that have combined entrepreneurial state intervention and market orientation is clearly superior to that of regimes like those produced by the military in Chile and Argentina whose attempts at allowing the unfettered operation of the market produced deindustrialization (see Stepan, 1985; Foxley, 1983).[29] Nor is active state involvement in industrial development found together with market orientation only in the newly industrialized countries (NICs). Seng-haas's (1985) historical analysis of industrialization and Katzenstein's (1985) work on their contemporary industrial policy reveal a variant of this combination in the smaller European states. Historically these states protected their home markets until domestic industry developed. Having successfully industrialized, they turned to more open policies and depended on an active state role in promoting "flexible industrial adjustment." Equally central to their economic policies, according to Katzenstein, were policies of "domestic compensation," which entailed a high degree of state intervention in the form of welfare provisions and an active labor market policy. The vigorous postwar development of Japan and France also demonstrates the effectiveness of combining state intervention and market orientation (Johnson, 1982; Zysman, 1983), albeit with a very different class base and distributive outcome from the small European democracies.

If current research suggests that interventive state apparatuses are often associated with effective market-oriented policies, it suggests with at least equal force that states that lack autonomy from private elites and bureaucratic capacity are likely to subvert the market in developmentally detrimental ways. Bates's (1981) study of the role of state policies in African agriculture provides the best illustration.[30] Bates argues convincingly that state intervention, though ostensibly aimed at promoting development, derives primarily from the necessity of building political support among rural and urban elites and enhancing the economic position of state officials. Policies are aimed at maximizing rents that can be allocated by state officials either to allies or to themselves.[31] These states lack a solid institutional base and must "purchase" support directly rather than generating it through a long-term, universalistic program orientation. They lack the sort of cohesive, corporate bureaucratic structure that is able to suppress the tendencies of state officials to put a priority on individual aggrandizement and are unable to pursue anything that might be defined as the "national interest."[32]

The behavior of the Goumingdang state in its early years on Taiwan provides a useful contrast. Here also the state intervened powerfully in agriculture, overturning the structure of agrarian landholdings and "distorting" the prices of agricultural outputs and inputs. The policy was initiated for political even more than economic reasons, but not because the incumbents in this politically and bureaucratically cohesive state apparatus needed rents from the agrarian sector for distribution to political allies. Freed from the necessity of satisfying particularistic interests, the Goumingdang was able to construct an agrarian policy that was exemplary both in terms of its distributional and its developmental consequences (see Amsden, 1979; Gold, 1986).

The consequences of state intervention depend on the political character of the intervening state. Nor are the state's relevant political characteristics limited to questions of the economic interests of its political supporters. Economic initiatives are linked as intimately to questions of security and geopolitics as they are to domestic political agendas. In Brazil, for example, the military and their concerns were important to both the creation of the steel industry in the forties and the state-owned petroleum monopoly in the fifties. Later, in the seventies, military and security considerations were intimately involved in Brazil's decision to try to turn part of its computer market into a protected "infant industry" (Adler, 1986; Evans, 1986). In East Asia, the interconnections between geopolitical concerns and industrial development policies are even more pervasive. Park Chung Hee's commitment to heavy industrialization in Korea in the early seventies was security driven, motivated to a large degree by Nixon's decision to place clearer limits on U.S. military commitments in East Asia (Cumings, 1984; M. S. Kim, 1987). Taiwan's shift to a more liberal, export-oriented regime in the late fifties was also prompted by a shifting geopolitical environment, but went in the reverse direction, away from security driven self-sufficiency toward greater reliance on international markets. The examples are obvious, but the task of developing a systematic understanding of how, when, and in what directions security and geopolitical considerations influence the ways the industrializing states develop remains to be done. It should be one of the priorities of new work in comparative political economy.

The politics of states and markets do not, of course, move only in one direction. Political considerations shape state policies toward industrial development, but these policies in turn have consequences for the state's political foundations. Stepan's (1985) analysis of the political consequences of the economic policies pursued by the Chilean and Brazilian militaries is a good example. The Brazilian regime's successful pursuit of an industrialization strategy built on multinational subsidiaries using capital- intensive production had as one of its consequences the rapid expansion of a concentrated working-class community in the country's industrial heartland. The powerful metalworkers union

that grew out of this community in turn became an important actor in the movement to bring down the military regime. In Chile, on the other hand, the state's economic policy produced an absolute reduction in the size of the industrial working class, which had, of course, been a principal source of political opposition to the regime.

The Korean case provides an even more interesting example of the political consequences of industrial policy. In the sixties and early seventies it was suggested (Lim, 1985, p. 99) that it was "distinctive of Korea's dependent development that the state had the upper hand over both local capital and the multinationals" in part because of the historical weakness of the local bourgeoisie. Yet, one of the important effects of state industrial policy during the Park regime was to stimulate the growth of the chaebol (conglomerate economic groups). By the end of the seventies, these groups, which were at least in part products of state policy, were sufficiently central to the economy that they were in a position to successfully resist the guidance of state planners (see E. M. Kim, 1987; M. S. Kim, 1987). The state had, in short, undercut the basis of its own autonomy.

The major thrust of new work in comparative political economy has been to turn the analysis of states and markets away from the question of whether state decision making is more or less efficient than market allocation in the promotion of development. Instead, it is assumed that increasingly development is likely to be carried out by a combination of state direction and market orientation. The question then becomes how do political forces shape the policies that emerge from this combination and how are they in turn shaped by it. Within this larger question the issue of how economic motivations interact with security goals is a crucial subcomponent badly in need of further work.

Development and Democracy

Theorizing on the relation between economic development and democratization during the seventies was largely split between those associated with the modernization approach who saw a positive relation and documented it with cross-national statistical evidence and those who were more pessimistic, based on their interpretation of comparative historical evidence.

Cross-national statistical studies beginning with Lipset's (1959) essay have found economic development to be positively associated with democracy (e.g., see Cutright, 1963; Jackman, 1973). Lipset argued that there is a functional interdependence between various aspects of development and democracy: industrialization and urbanization are associated with increases in wealth, education, and literacy, mass communication, income equality, and the size of the middle class, and these in turn facilitate the development of political democracy. Later studies using cross-national quantitative methodology (e.g., Bollen, 1979, 1983; Bollen and Jackman, 1985) expanded the range of independent variables, but continued to find positive associations between developmental indicators and democracy.

Scholars using comparative historical case studies to attack the problem (see especially O'Donnell, 1973, 1978) rejected the results of cross-national statistical studies, arguing that the general prediction accounted for neither the timing of the emergence of democracy in Europe, the regression to authoritarian rule in major European powers in the interwar period, nor the fact that a number of major developing countries had shown an "elective affinity" for authoritarian rule rather than democracy as their economic development proceeded.

Rueschemeyer (1980) has suggested a synthesis of these two views. Accepting the results of cross-national studies as too persistent to be ignored, he then draws on the frame of reference of the comparative historical studies to explain them. The basic explanation, according to Rueschemeyer, lies in the fact that industrial capitalism creates conditions that facilitate the self-organization of the working class and the middle strata and in this and other ways increases these groups' political capacities, thus making it much more difficult for elites to politically exclude them.[33] Extending this "relative class power" argument to include closer consideration of class alliances that include the agrarian sector as well as analysis of some of the reasons for differential working-class strength offers an opportunity to demonstrate the heuristic value of such a synthesis. It also provides a good example of the way in which an argument may be constructed around the comparative analysis of the historical interaction of classes and the state. Finally, it demonstrates how material from the historical development of European countries can be combined with evidence from Third World cases. The discussion combines, in short, substantive exposition and an illustration of the approach.[34]

Between 1870 and 1920, continental Europe moved from a largely agrarian economy to an industrial one. At the same time, it was politic-

ally transformed. At the beginning of this period no country was democratic; by the end three-quarters were. As Therborn (1977) points out, in almost all of these countries, the organized working class and the socialist parties representing them played a key role in pressing for the breakthrough of democracy. The strength of the working class in itself does not, however, explain the emergence of democracy. Success in the struggle for democracy depended on the ability of the working class to find allies; failure was predicated on the emergence of an antidemocratic coalition with agrarian roots.

Agrarian class relations become then the key to the puzzle.[35] In all of the smaller European countries, there were too few large estates to support the development of a politically significant class of landholders. This prevented the development of the antidemocratic class alliance analyzed by Moore (1966): a strong coalition of large landholders engaged in labor repressive agriculture, the crown (the monarch, bureaucracy, and military, that is, the state), and a politically dependent bourgeoisie. Concentration of landholdings alone provides a powerful explanation for the survival or demise of democracy in the interwar period as well as its original emergence. Large landholdings dominated all of the countries in which authoritarian regimes were established.[36] Small landholdings prevailed in all the countries in which democracy survived the interwar period except England and the absence of "labor repressive" agriculture in England brings this case into line.[37]

In the small holding countries, most of whom became democratic before the outbreak of World War I, the working class found allies in sections of the urban middle classes (often represented by liberal parties) and/or sections of the rural population, especially small farmers, tenants, and rural wage workers. Indeed, in Norway and Switzerland, these groups played the leading role in the transition to democracy. Equally important, in no case did farmers emerge as outspoken and powerful opponents of democracy. The war and its outcome accelerated the transition to democracy because it changed the balance of power in society strengthening the working class and weakening the upper classes.[38] In the English case, it was divisions in the upper classes, originating in the pattern of economic and political development analyzed by Moore, which provided the opening for labor in the system.

In the remaining cases (Germany, Austria-Hungary, Italy, and Spain), no alliance strong enough to overcome the opposition of the coalition of the landed upper classes, the state, and the bourgeoisie could be constructed. It was only a temporary change in the balance of class power (caused in three of the cases by the war) that allowed for the democratic breakthrough. And, in the end, the working class and its allies (where it had any) were unable to maintain democracy when a new conjuncture and new alliance possibilities for the upper classes moved the bourgeoisie and the landlords from passive to active opposition to the democratic regime.[39] In these large states, extensive economic intervention, combined with geopolitical ambitions to produce strongly authoritarian tendencies. The military projects of the state tied the bourgeoisie, especially the coal and steel entrepreneurs, to the state (Kurth, 1979).[40] In the interwar period, the authoritarian tendencies internal to the state expressed themselves at critical points in support for the development of and/or seizure of power by authoritarian movements (Stephens, 1987).

The model seems to extend well outside of Western Europe. The British settler colonies fit this analysis. In the United States political dominance of the small-holding north and west ensured a democratic outcome (see Moore, 1966). Canada was predominantly small holding. Australia was dominated by large estates, but sheep raising made repressive forms of labor control unnecessary. The fragility of democracy in Eastern Europe also fits. Most of these countries were dominated by large estates with low levels of industrialization and thus weak working classes.

In the case of Latin America, closer attention to agrarian class relations, working-class strength, and the role of the state complements O'Donnell's industrial phases approach. Holding level of development constant, late, dependent development results in a smaller working class, a larger class of urban marginals, and greater internal stratification and fragmentation in the working class, all of which serve to limit working-class political strength (see Stephens and Stephens, 1980, in press; Mouzelis, 1985). Most Latin American countries did (and some still do) have a significant body of landlords engaged in labor-repressive agriculture. For example, in Chile, Zeitlin and Ratcliff (in press) have demonstrated that by the mid-1960s, a fused landlord-capitalist group had assumed political leadership of the upper class. Hence it is not surprising that when agrarian privilege was threatened by peasant mobilization the late sixties and early seventies, the upper class as a whole eventually supported an antidemocratic coup.

The relative class power model also helps elucidate aspects of redemocratization in contemporary Latin America that were inexplicable from the point of view of O'Donnell's original industrial phases approach. The dependent development experienced by Brazil in the sixties and seventies transformed the class structure of the country, increasing the power potential of the working and middle classes. In the Peruvian case, the land reform of the military government decisively weakened the old landed aristocracy, while political mobilization unintentionally ignited by the reform process greatly increased the strength of the lower classes (E. H. Stephens, 1983).[41]

As in the European cases, the relative class power model in Latin America must be complemented by an examination of the role of the state. Mouzelis (1985) sees the weakness of civil society relative to the state apparatus as a persistent source of antidemocractic tendencies in Latin America. He notes that the early development of an interventive state in combination with the relative weakness of the working class (due to the capital intensive nature of the dependent development pattern) allowed the state elites to co-opt and control working class mobilization. Thus, unlike Western Europe (even the late developers), the weakness of civil society relative to the state apparatus is a persistent source of antidemocratic tendencies.

The contrast between the English-speaking Caribbean and the rest of Latin America reinforces Mouzelis's point. Despite an agrarian past based on labor-repressive plantation agriculture, these societies have managed, for the most part, to maintain democratic regimes. The relative underdevelopment of the state apparatus, especially in its coercive aspects, under British colonial rule has unquestionably played a role in this outcome. The British left behind small armies, too small to effectively carry out a coup.[42] Intensive labor mobilization began in the thirties well before the expansion of the state's role in society, which began only after independence three decades later.

Shifting attention to the East Asian NICs further reinforces the importance of looking at the role of the state as well as class formations. Looking at the pattern of industrial and agricultural development in Taiwan and South Korea in the post-World War II period, which is strikingly similar to that of the small democracies of Europe at the time of their industrialization,[43] one would expect democratization to have occurred some time ago. Only when one takes into account the overwhelming dominance of the state apparatus vis-à-vis civil society does the persistence of authoritarian rule fit with the patterns observed in Europe and Latin America.

Moving from Europe to Latin America to Asia seems to vindicate the idea of extending the "relative class power" hypotheses. Combining a comparative historical analysis of the relative strength of different social classes and class fractions with an analysis of the relation between the state and civil society provides a powerful and parsimonious way of dealing with a wide range of cases, both over time and across regions.

Accumulation and Distribution

Trying to bring comparative evidence to bear on contending views of the relation between distribution and development is a central item on the agenda of the new comparative political economy. Those working within the modernization tradition tended to assume that development would naturally produce greater equality. Economic growth models have stressed the trade-off between savings and consumption, which if translated into a trade-off between growth and distribution is often taken to imply that inequality becomes necessary for growth. This idea parallels the classical Marxist vision of immiseration as inherent to capitalist accumulation and was not uncommon among those working with a dependency framework.

In the advanced industrial countries, investigation of the issue has focused on the origins and consequences of redistributive efforts associated with the welfare state. The literature on differential growth of the welfare states includes cross-national analyses using aggregate statistics,[44] as well as comparative historical and case study work.[45] These studies have concluded, first of all, that the growth of the welfare state is a consequence not simply of industrialization or demographic changes[46] but of political struggles.

On most measures of welfare state effort, the political composition of the government is the strongest predictor, with corporatist modes of interest group representation (tripartite bargaining on broad economic and social policy between government and centralized labor and employers' organizations), generally running second. Measures in which transfer payments weigh heavily (and thus are generally market conforming) are correlated with center-left governments, but those that tap the redistributive impact of public expenditure or include the direct provision of goods and services are most strongly correlated to left government. Since left government is related to union strength,[47] these

findings constitute an important example of the usefulness of "the working class power approach" as discussed earlier.[48]

As in the case of explanations for democracy, class arguments must be complemented by an analysis of state structures in order to explain the expansion of redistributive efforts. While variations in the structure of the state and the operation of the state bureaucracy are difficult to include in cross-national quantitative studies, features of the state, such as bureaucratic capacity and insulation from clientelistic pressures, have been found to be very important factors conditioning the early development of the welfare state in comparative historical case studies.[49] A good argument can also be made that the very modest postwar growth of public expenditure in the United States and Switzerland is due in part to very strong federalism plus other idiosyncratic aspects of the electoral systems that make it difficult to translate working-class organization into governmental influence.[50]

Relations with the international economy also play an important though indirect role in explaining welfare state expansion. The heavy reliance on trade of the small European democracies led to economic concentration and product specialization, which is causally related to politically strong, centralized union organizations (Ingham, 1974; Kjellberg, 1983; Stephens, 1979). Strong centralized unions are in turn associated, not only with the electoral success of left parties, but also with the existence of corporatist modes of interest group representation.[51]

Explanations of the expansion of welfare state expenditure that combine class alliances and state structure operating in the context of a particular set of trade relations is also relevant to arguments regarding the consequences of welfare state expansion for growth. "Consumption versus investment" reasoning suggests that welfare state expansion should be negatively associated with growth (e.g., see Bacon and Eltis, 1976; Lindbeck, 1981; Okun, 1975). Reflecting on the political pact that underlies the growth of the welfare state, however, suggests a possible positive association.

The corporatist bargain can be characterized as compromise between capital and a powerful labor movement in which labor restrains market wages in order to maintain international competitiveness and is compensated with expansion of the "social wage," that is, transfer payments and free or subsidized provision of public goods and services. An essential element of this compromise is that both sides agree on the desirability of rapid economic growth. A small, open economy gives the strong labor movement an incentive seriously to consider wage restraint as protectionism is not a viable option.

The evidence for the postwar period suggests that while corporatist capital/labor pacts have provided one route to growth, other models that do not involve redistribution have also been associated with high rates of accumulation. Analysis of cross-national statistical evidence shows no causal association between previous levels of welfare state spending and later growth.[52] Some of the high spenders perform well (Scandinavia and Austria) as do some low (Japan) and moderate (France) spenders. What unites high-growth countries, as we might expect from our earlier discussion of states and markets, is the existence of active state industrial policy. This may be associated either with corporatist flexible industrial adjustment (Katzenstein, 1985), or with Japanese-French style "concertation without labor" (Hicks, 1988; Lehmbruch, 1985; Zysman, 1983).

In the Third World, the focus has been on inequality rather than redistribution. The starting point for most arguments was the observation of very high levels of inequality among middle-level developing countries, especially in Latin America. This led to the hypothesis that dependent development was a particularly inegalitarian form of capitalist development, one in which the association between industrialization and eventual greater equality observed in the European context might be absent.

That late, dependent development should be inegalitarian relative to that produced by the original industrial revolution is plausible. The growth of population and labor force are much higher than they were during the original industrialization. Agriculture, especially if it is dominated by traditional latifundia/minifundia structures of land ownership cannot productively absorb the rapidly growing labor force. Industrialization based on center country technology and capital goods absorbs relatively little labor. Labor is therefore forced to choose between a marginal existence in the rural areas or marginal jobs in the urban service sector. In either case, labor is politically weakened and gets a very small return from the fruits of industrialization and is also unlikely to be able to organize in such a way as to be able to secure the kinds of benefits that the organized European working class was eventually able to achieve.

Cross-national analysis of aggregate statistical evidence supports this vision. Penetration by multinational corporations, which is likely to bring with it a pattern of industrialization that is more capital intensive and more dependent on foreign technology, has been consistently found to be associated with higher levels of inequality.[53] Rapid growth of service-sector employment has also been found to be associated with both heavy reliance on foreign corporations and high levels of inequality (Evans and Timberlake, 1980; Fiala, 1983; Kentor, 1981; Timberlake and Kentor, 1983).

These associations may be taken to suggest that late developers should try to escape from this pattern and develop less dependent, more labor-absorbing strategies of industrialization (see, for example, Knight, 1981). Alternatively, the evidence might be read to reinforce the idea that high levels of inequality were inescapable, confronting Third World countries with the "cruel dilemma" of choosing between high rates of growth accompanied by increasing inequality or relative stagnation (see, for example, Hewlett, 1980).

Brazil, which experienced both high rates of growth and dramatic increases in the level of inequality in the late sixties and early seventies was often used as an example by those arguing for an intrinsic relation between inequality and growth. Research at the end of the seventies undercut the latter view. The utilization of existing excess capacity, a boom in the consumption of consumer durables (Serra, 1979) and the unprecedented surge of international liquidity and international trade (Malan and Bonelli, 1977) explained higher growth rates, not an increase in the saving rate. In fact, declining real wages had had no discernable positive impact on the savings rate.

More fundamental to the destruction of the idea of an intrinsic relation between inegalitarian income distribution and increased rates of accumulation was the experience of the East Asian NICs. The ability of Taiwan, and to a lesser extent Korea, to grow rapidly with decreasing levels of inequality left the thesis of a trade-off between accumulation and distribution difficult to sustain (see Fei, Ranis, and Kuo, 1979; Gold, 1986; Koo, 1984). These cases also call into question the relation between late dependent development and inequality.

The relatively small role of transnational corporations in the historical shaping of East Asian industrialization fit nicely with the view of the dependency approach that direct foreign investment exacerbated inequality (see Evans, 1987). Nonetheless, these cases suggested that something beyond engagement with the international economy and reliance on foreign capital must be responsible for the extreme levels of inequality found in Latin American cases.[54] Since thoroughgoing land reform and the construction of a viable small-holder agriculture seems so critical in these East Asian cases (see Amsden, 1979, 1985), they draw attention to the legacy of agrarian class relations as a determinant of the degree of inequality that accompanies subsequent industrialization and suggest that those working within the dependency tradition should have paid more attention to agriculture.

The East Asian NICs are equally problematic from the point of view of the working-class power approach since they combine repressive labor regimes (see Deyo, 1986) with low levels of inequality. One possible explanation may be that the presence of an egalitarian agrarian structure when combined with a rapidly growing, labor-intensive manufacturing sector provides labor with sufficient intrinsic bargaining power to mitigate the negative consequences of lack of collective organization. Alternatively, the explanation may lie in the existence of a powerful state apparatus disconnected by historical circumstance from property holders as a class (at least temporarily). A third temptation would be, of course, to invoke a regional exemption based on unspecified cultural characteristics This temptation is, fortunately, mitigated by the case of Sri Lanka, which has a historically powerful labor movement and high levels of equality, despite the prevalence of large-scale landholdings (see Herring, 1986).

A parsimonious, regionally generalizable explanation of the historical interrelation between accumulation and distribution is still not within our grasp. Several simplistic hypotheses can be rejected. Neither inequality nor the absence of an extensive welfare state is necessary for growth.[55] There is no necessary relation either positive or negative between levels of industrialization and inequality, even in the case of late, dependent industrialization. But neither is it possible, in the face of extreme and persistent inequality in the Latin American NICs, to resuscitate the optimistic notion that development will somehow naturally produce more egalitarian patterns of distribution. The strongest positive finding is that the politically mediated power of working-class organization is a good predictor of redistribution in advanced industrial countries.

The eventual explanation of Third World inequality seems likely to require a "multiple path" model to equality in which the distribution of property rights in land, the presence of working class organizations and the role and orientation of the state will all figure, but the precise configuration of such an explanation remains obscure. Explanation of why alternate routes to growth among advanced industrial countries (either labor incorporating and redistributive or concertation without labor) are chosen and under what conditions each will succeed also remain to be constructed. In short, while the new comparative political economy has moved substantially beyond earlier understandings of growth and inequality, the work to be done is daunting.

The World Political Economy and National Development

Development has never taken place in isolated compartments defined by national borders but in the post-World War II period a confluence of secular technological trends and recurrent cyclical patterns has created an exceptionally "internationalized" world.[56] Flows and influences that cross national boundaries have become increasingly important relative to those that move within them, and the necessity of taking international influences into account when analyzing the development of domestic institutions has increased correspondingly. The consequences of international flows for domestic institutions are not, however, always what traditional theoretical perspectives would predict.

Work on labor markets offers a good example.[57] Recent research shows that international migration does more than insert a new set of workers into the existing production organization.[58] It changes the way in which the labor process itself is organized. In the advanced industrial countries, immigrants (especially illegal ones) are much less likely than domestic workers to be employed in large factories; instead they work in small highly mobile shops, at home under a piece-rate system, as sharecroppers in agriculture, or as itinerant wage laborers under the gang system (see, for example, Sassen-Koob, 1980, 1984; Waldinger, 1984; Wells, 1984). Old industries like garment and footwear production, and new ones like electronics have become increasingly "informalized" through their reliance on immigrant labor.[59]

Since both Marxist theory and the modernization approach have assumed a secular trend toward large-scale, bureaucratically organized production, this research suggests either that both theories are wrong or that the internationalization of labor has a regressive effect on the way in which work is organized in the advanced countries. Instead of being able to benefit from the more protective institutions that prevail in the labor markets they were entering, immigrants find themselves unable to escape the organizational form that prevailed in the labor markets they left behind.

The consequences of transnational capital flows for labor are also asymmetrical. Even in the NICs, which have received the largest influx of international capital, informal labor markets that allow labor little protection persist.[60] In addition, repressive institutional arrangements in these countries drastically curtail the extent to which the increased supply of capital improves labor's bargaining.[61] As a result, capital benefits differentially from internationalization. Because the modernization of productive capacity has not been accompanied by commensurate advances in local labor organization, Third World workers have not benefited to the degree that the modernization approach might have predicted. At the same time, the privileges of First World labor have proved more precarious than dependency theorists imagined. The combined effects of the internationalization of markets for labor, capital, and commodities increase the degree to which First World workers must compete with Third World workers while undercutting the historically constructed institutional arrangements that characterize advanced industrial countries.[62]

If we focus on national development more generally rather than on the consequences for the relative power of labor and capital, the argument becomes more complicated. Versions of the dependency perspective in which the interests of international capital are implacably opposed to Third World interests and cutting ties with the international economy is the best development strategy can no longer be sustained. This has not, however, led to a return to the position associated with the modernization approach, which sees links between developed and developing countries as simply channels for the infusion of modern cultural traits or opportunities to benefit from the workings of comparative advantage. The contemporary synthesis of these two positions views positive effects of international ties as possible but contingent on the ability of Third World states to renegotiate the nature of their links to the industrial north.

The idea that international ties must be negotiated is a central premise of the literature on states and markets that has already been discussed. State involvement in the mining industry in Chile and Peru was not just involvement in the domestic economy. Taking over the mines, like the simultaneous moves on the part of the OPEC states in the petroleum industry, were above all else an attempt to transform relations with the international economy. Studies of a wide range of manufacturing industries reinforce the view that north-south economic ties are not simply given in the structure of the international economy but also depend on the political will and skill of Third World states, which in turn depend on patterns of alliance and conflict among local classes and economic groups as well as on the nature of the state apparatus itself.[63]

Even if the character of ties to the international system is seen as contingent, the malleability of ties to the international system must not be exaggerated. As the shifting fortunes of Third World oil producers illustrate, the exigencies of international markets are not easy to escape. Numerous recent studies have made the point. In his original 1974 study, Moran was careful to point out the difficulties that state-owned copper companies would face given the structure of the international copper industry. His position is thoroughly vindicated by Shafer's (1983) subsequent review of the returns to African producers. Evelyne Stephen's (1987) work on the evolution of Jamaica's relations with the international aluminum industry illustrates both sides of the argument clearly. She shows how a more aggressive government policy was able to increase the benefits accruing to Jamaica significantly, but was unable to prevent these gains from being subsequently eroded by the evolution of the industry internationally. Gereffi's (1983) study of steroid hormones in Mexico is yet another example.

The thrust of current work is neither to decry the developmental costs of engagement in international commerce nor to extol the benefits of openness. The aim is rather to explicate the political and social structural factors that enable individual countries to transform ties to their benefit, while simultaneously analyzing the way in which the changing structures at the international level facilitate or limit possibilities for transformation. This interactive vision needs to be taken even further. As Gourevitch (1978) argues, the interaction of the world political economy and domestic development must be seen as recursive.

Third World countries attempt to construct more interventive state apparatuses in part precisely because of the dependent position in which they find themselves vis-a-vis the international economy. If they are able to develop such capacity, they are then better able to restructure their domestic economies and create new bases of comparative advantage in international trade. This in turn enables at least certain developing countries, most obviously the NICs, to "move up" in the international hierarchy of nation states. Conversely, countries that play a dominant role in the world political economy, especially major capital exporters, are more likely to be characterized by more passive policies toward domestic economic growth. As the British case illustrates nicely, such policies in turn are likely to have an effect on the future ability of these countries to maintain their hegemonic position.[64] Thus stimuli from the international political economy create changes in domestic institutions that in turn generate shifts in a country's relation to international system itself.[65]

Changes in domestic policies and capacities do not just influence the links between individual countries and the international system. When changes in several countries are mutually reinforcing or when the weight of a single national actor in the system is large, they may have the effect of restructuring the international system as a whole. Philip McMichael (1985) argues that nineteenth-century Britain "did not just lead the world for a time but fundamentally transformed it," constructing the international system of free trade it then dominated. McMichael rounds out his recursive vision by going on to argue that the British-engineered system generated in turn a variety of political responses on the part of other countries that undercut both the system as a whole and Britain's preeminence within it.

Stephen Krasner (1985) provides a useful contemporary illustration of how the international system reflects the constructive attempts of individual nations. He argues convincingly that in the postwar period the small poor nations of the south have consistently tended to support international regimes that authoritatively allocate resources and to benefit from the institution of such regimes, while the rich industrial nations of the north have favored regimes that give priority to market mechanisms and to dominate such regimes more easily.[66] By "regimes" Krasner means generally accepted principles, norms, laws, and procedures governing transnational flows or interactions. The differential benefits of authoritative and market regimes is evident in the area of transportation where an authoritative regime in civilian aviation has given Third World countries a much larger market share than the market-oriented regime that exists in shipping. His work raises anew the basic dependency contention that the construction of the world political economy is a conflictful process in which the interests of north and south are in opposition. At the same time, by emphasizing the political character of the international system, Krasner reminds us of

a serious lacuna in the traditional dependency analysis: its neglect of geopolitical concerns as independent factors in determining the character of ties between north and south.

Dependency and world-system theorists, following the lead of Marxist theories of imperialism tended to reduce geopolitical maneuvering to economic interests and motivations. Work done from a more "international relations" perspective like Schurmann's (1973) and Krasner's (1978) has raised serious general questions as to whether U.S. policy toward developing countries can be explained in strictly economic terms. Cross-regional comparisons have suggested that the "economistic" quality of previous writing on international influences on domestic development may represent a Latin Americanist bias (see Evans, 1987).

As Cumings (1984) points out, the entire regional political economy of Northeast Asia cannot be understood without reference to the unique combination of geopolitical and economic ties that unites Japan and the United States. U.S. policy toward Korea and Taiwan, which has been fundamental to the course of development in those countries, was clearly driven by a geopolitical vision of the world in which containment of Communism was the driving force. Possibilities for economic gain may well have been taken into consideration but they were not paramount. Evidence from other regions reinforces the point. Basu (1985), for example, points out that India's ability to define itself as "nonaligned" relative to the United States and the Soviet Union contributed significantly to enabling it to pursue an inward and public-sector-oriented strategy of development. Even in Latin America, Stephens and Stephens (1986) note that the U.S. pressure, which helped undermine the Manley government's development strategy, was stimulated less by the government's treatment of North American aluminum TNCs than by its friendly relations with Cuba. Finally, of course, current U.S. involvement in Central America, in contrast to pre-World War II interventions, is justified not by the protection of the interests of U.S. firms but by the projection of ideologically defined geopolitical struggles into the region.

Overall, recent work on the interaction of national development and the world political economy has four salient characteristics. First, it has attempted to examine the consequences of international flows for domestic institutions and how these are different in different regions of the world system. Second, it has moved toward a synthesis of the modernization and dependency positions on the consequences of international ties for developing countries, emphasizing the contingent character of these consequences. Third, it has moved toward a more recursive view in which the world political economy both shapes and is shaped by the historical trajectories of development within individual nation- states. Finally, it has brought geopolitics back into the traditionally economistic analysis of core-periphery relations.

Future Research Agendas

Recent progress in the analysis of development has been founded on the ability of the current generation of scholars selectively to combine elements from earlier theoretical traditions. The result is the synthesis that we have dubbed the "new comparative political economy." The studies that we have used to characterize this approach are solidly "structural." Their preferred explanations focus on the institutions and collectivities that shape historical processes of change: classes, state apparatuses, parties, and other groups whose interests can be defined in terms of social structural position.[67] They are also aggressively historical, preferring explanations that take into account the contingencies imposed by particular historical conjunctures, yet at the same time they have consistently sought explanatory frameworks that can be applied across regions and time periods. They assume that the strength, capacity, and coalitional preferences of dominant and subordinate classes are potentially variable, even holding the level of development constant. Equally, relations between domestic and international elites and between each of them and the state are seen as varying. In both cases, variation is related to structural differences such as the nature of agrarian production systems, the character of the industrial infrastructure, position in the world political economy, or the timing of development. Because of their interest in uncovering, interpreting, and explaining distinct paths of development and their concern with problems of conjunctural causation and multiple paths to the same point, researchers in this tradition are drawn to analytical comparisons of small numbers of cases, though this is often used in conjunction with statistical analysis of larger numbers of cases or intensive examination of single cases.

The components of the approach are hardly novel, but the approach as a whole must still be considered "new" when compared to the streams of work from which it is derived. It can be distinguished from preceding comparative historical work both in its greater preoccupation with relating its findings to more general theoretical frameworks, most prominently Marxist class analysis, and in the greater attention that it gives to international factors. It is distinct from dependency theory, even the historical structural variety, primarily in the greater attention that it gives to political variables, to the role of the state domestically, and to the role of geopolitics internationally.

Out of this work have come a number of new hypotheses that synthesize the positions of earlier schools. The assertion of a positive relation between democracy and development, first proposed by modernization theorists, is now explained using a framework drawn from comparative historical class analysis. The assertion of dependency theorists that Third World countries are prejudiced by their participation in the international economy is joined with the contrary assertion associated with the modernization school to produce the hypothesis that whether such participation produces positive results is contingent on the capacity of Third World states to negotiate the form their external linkages. Instead of accepting either the proposition that industrialization is intrinsically associated with higher degrees of equality or the counterassertion that dependent development inevitably brings increasing levels of inequality, the new comparative political economy sees the relation of accumulation and distribution as contingent on both the previous structure of agrarian property relations and the political character of the state apparatus.

The formulations associated with the new comparative political economy are more satisfying than their predecessors and do less violence to historical realities, but they are not a completed research agenda. They convey an invitation to further research rather than closure. The invitation takes two forms. First, it implies an extensive agenda. There is a clear need to reinforce the results already obtained with broader, more systematic cross-regional comparisons. Second, it suggests an "intensive agenda." There is a need to probe the relationships that have been proposed more deeply in order to better specify the mechanisms that are at work and clarify the nature of the contingencies involved.

Comparisons that cut across the First World/ Third World divide are one of the hallmark contributions of the new comparative political economy. Yet, research dealing in depth with cases from more than one region is still not common. Aside from studies based on generally available cross-national statistical data, case studies of single countries are still the modal fieldwork even though these are set in comparative focus by examining the literature on other single cases. Most comparisons involving more than one country are within regions. While, as we have noted, there has been considerable progress in the direction of comparisons between Europe and Latin America (e.g., Linz and Stepan; O'Donnell, Schmitter, and Whitehead; Mouzelis) and some embryonic efforts comparing Latin American and East Asian NICs (e.g., Deyo, 1987; Gereffi and Wyman, in press), careful comparative work that brings together cases from Africa and Latin America, or Asia and the Middle East, or any other more esoteric combination is still unusual.

As long as the range of cases being compared remains so restricted, claims to the establishment of general explanatory relations must be considered fragile. At the same time, the possibility of extending the range of cases raises an important methodological issue that needs to be addressed. Selection of cases for comparative analysis has so far been anything but systematic, dictated primarily by opportunities for fieldwork and the investigator's background. As the range of comparison is to be expanded, the necessity of more attention to Mills's classic criteria (similarity with regard to variables exogenous to the explanation, differences on explanatory variables, etc.) will be harder to escape.

Complementing the "extensive" agenda is an equally challenging "intensive" agenda. Most of the hypotheses that have been set out here still require additional specification. For example, in the discussion of states and markets it was pointed out that intervention by states with adequate levels of bureaucratic capacity has been developmentally effective, while states lacking sufficient autonomy and bureaucratic cohesion are likely to produce perverse results. Yet the crucial variable "bureaucratic capacity" is still very imperfectly specified. What is it about the bureaucratic structure of some states that makes them more "porous"? What are the attributes that enable a bureaucracy to pursue collective goals rather than disintegrating into a collection of rent-seekers? We have only the most rudimentary answers to these questions[68] and until they have been refined by further comparative research, the value of the proposition is limited by the imprecision of its central concept.

It is, of course, precisely the imprecisions and anomalies in the explanations offered by comparative political economy that provide the stimulus for new research, just as those of earlier approaches provoked the work that we have described here. Equally important in generating future agendas is the fact that the new comparative political economy is not a monolithic scholarly community. Instead of promoting an orthodoxy, the approach has stimulated continual dialogue among a range of "mini-orthodoxies" without becoming trapped in anyone of them. Its strength and vitality depends on advocates of the working-class power approach being able to debate advocates of more state-centric models without having the discussion degenerating into sectarian squabbles. Likewise, defenders of historical-structural dependency must be able to confront neo-Weberians with a shared sense that divergent theoretical predilections are less important than the common commitment to explanations that take serious account of the institutional contexts of other times and countries.

As long as such tolerant vitality can be maintained, the new comparative political economy will be a major force in shaping scholarship on development and the world economy. It will not, however, do so in a vacuum. The evolution of future research, like the evolution that we have described here, will be shaped by competition and dialogue among approaches built on different theoretical and methodological assumptions. Along with the new comparative political economy, there are at least two powerful competing tendencies that have not yet played a central role in shaping agendas in the study of development but are likely to do so in the future. First, there is a resurgence of interest in more cultural approaches to the study of social change. In so far as culturally oriented "grand theory" becomes generally more prominent in social science (see Skinner, 1985), the study of development will inevitably be affected. Second, there is the burgeoning body of work that attempts to use more rigorous models of rational individual behavior rather than comparative structural and institutional analysis as basis for understanding political and economic change. Both of these approaches offer challenges and useful possibilities for debate and dialogue.

If cultural approaches move in the direction of hermeneutics or return to the use of vague concepts like "national character," fruitful dialogue is unlikely, but as long as the social structural antecedents and consequences of cultural characteristics are specified, there is complementarity with the comparative political economy agenda. Even though the origins of the comparative political economy approach involved rejecting explanations that gave priority to cultural endowments and predispositions, it has often employed social structurally grounded explanations of value orientations and perceptions. Closer analysis of cultural factors could strengthen these explanations. For example, a careful linking of the ideology of the Junker/military/bureaucratic state-building coalition to the ideology of the German rural and urban middle classes in the interwar period could be a useful part of the further specification of our own argument on the breakdown of Weimar democracy.[69]

Fruitful incorporation of a more cultural approach can already be observed in the recent literature on dependency and world system. Imanuel Adler (1986), for example, blends a dependency analysis with a heavy emphasis on ideology and political culture in his analysis of attempts by Brazil and Argentina to move into high-technology industries. John Meyer and his collaborators have argued that societies actively reorganize around global cultural models as they enter the international system (see Meyer, 1980). For example, national constitutions prescribe remarkably similar rights and duties of citizens, with similarities increasing sharply in the mid-twentieth century (Boli-Bennett, 1979; Boli-Bennett and Meyer, 1978). Likewise, the expansion, structure, and content of educational systems reflect world models evolving over time as much as the economic or political situation of the individual country in which they are located (see, for example, Inkeles and Sirowy, 1983; Meyer et al., 1977; Ramirez and Boli, 1982).

The rational choice approach has also inspired work that is quite compatible with comparative political economy. Popkin's (1979) study of peasant political movements in Vietnam, for example, provides a vision of the interaction of the colonial state, peasant communities, and political reform movements that fits beautifully with Paige's comparative analysis of the same processes.[70] Likewise, the work of Bates (1981), which we have considered an example of comparative political economy, could also be taken as an application of a rational choice perspective.

There is an obvious complementarity between rational choice approaches and the work we have highlighted here. In the comparative political economy tradition, the problem of aggregating individual preferences to produce collective action is rarely at the center of the analysis. For rational choice explanations it almost always is. Rational choice models are wedded to "methodological individualism" and see "reductionism" not as a term of opprobrium but as a necessary virtue (Elster, 1985, p. 5). Debate

with rational choice theorists should have the salutary effect of forcing comparative political economy to consider more carefully the conditions under which shared social structural position is likely to produce a historically important political or economic actor. At the same time, however, defining developmental problems strictly in rational choice terms would undercut the most important contributions of the comparative political economy approach.

Faith in the explanatory power of universalistic models of rationality sets a priority on improving the rigor of the models themselves. Preoccupation with discovering whether it is in principle possible for individuals to pursue their interests jointly too often leads to projecting the same simplistic set of motives onto all individuals. The premium placed on rigor and elegance in the explanation of individual actions leaves little time or energy for analyzing the complexities of actual patterns of interaction among classes, state apparatuses, and other historical actors. Historical cases or those that require exotic fieldwork may be undertaken by rational choice theorists for serendipitous reasons or because of prior predilections, but the logic of the rational choice mode of inquiry is otherwise.

Dialogue with cultural or rational choice approaches can help push forward our understandings of development and the world economy, but the new comparative political economy should take care not to lose sight of its own agenda. This agenda respects the diversity and complexity of processes of historical change while continuing to aspire to generalizable explanations. It recaptures the scope of classic nineteenth-century sociological concerns but also addresses contemporary policy issues. It defines the sociology of development not as simply the study of poor countries but the study of long-term, large-scale socioeconomic and political change irrespective of the epoch or region in which it occurs. Such an agenda is not just essential to the survival of the sociology of development, it is central to the progress of any kind of macrosociological analysis and is the best insurance against a return to the parochialism of the past.

NOTES

1. The work of Almond, Coleman, Pye, and their collaborators (much of which was done under the auspices of the Comparative Politics Committee of

the Social Science Research Council) was central to the early growth of research on political development and drew heavily on the structural-functionalist perspective.

2. Neil Smelser's (1966) classic essay, "Towards a Theory of Modernization," provides a succinct statement of this idea while his *Social Change in the Industrial Revolution* (1959) applies it to a concrete historical case. For a more recent heterodox treatment of the problem of disjunctures among institutions in the process of modernization, see Rueschemeyer (1976).

3. In his essay on the "institutional framework of economic development," Parsons does mention that one would expect to find "a structure of vested interests operating as obstacles to change" (1960, p. 119), but the theme remains largely unelaborated in modernization research.

4. Quote is from Booth (1985, p. 773), who feels that this tendency has created a serious impasse for Marxists attempting to analyze development and that Marxism must be purged of its "functionalist" aspects.

5. Later Marxists have been generally pessimistic about the prospects for capitalist development on the periphery (see the discussion of dependency below), and a few even claim that Marx himself became pessimistic at the end of his life (see Booth, 1985, p. 764). Warren (1973) is the best example of a contemporary Marxist analysis that preserves the sense of capitalism as a universal agent of development.

6. Unlike Hirschman, who was directly influenced by Gerschenkron (Hirschman 1971, p. 95), and even more so the dependency school, Gerschenkron suggested late development was an economic advantage in that it could result in more rapid growth due to the borrowing of technology and so on (though it was often a political liability). Kurth (1979, pp. 322-323), however, points out that Gerschenkron's (1962, pp. 72-91) analysis of Italy shows many parallels to Latin American development, as the Italian spurt was less vigorous, the country emphasized light consumer goods to a much greater degree, and protection exhibited a more retarding effect. Gerschenkron's observations on the political effects of late development, industrial phases, and international economics have been developed both by Europeanists, such as Gourevitch (1978, 1984), but also by Latin Americanists, most notably O'Donnell (1973, 1978; also see Collier. 1979) via the work of Hirschman and the ECLA economists and later the dependency theorists. Kurth's essay crosses both bodies of literature.

7. For an interesting analysis of Polanyi's work see, Block and Somers (1984). They contend this charge of reification of the market is not accurate. This volume (Skocpol, 1984) also contains insightful discussions of the works of Bendix, Anderson, Tilly, Thompson, and Wallerstein.

8. The seminal contribution on the importance of the actions of subordinate classes is, of course, E. P. Thompson's (1963) work on the English working class.

9. As Rueschemeyer (1984) points out, Bendix is much less willing to generalize from historical materials than Weber was. Thematically Bendix's work is also influenced by Marshall (1950, 1964). Bendix's career was intertwined with two other leading comparative political sociologists of his generation, Rokkan and Lipset. Bendix and Rokkan coauthored the important essay on the extension of citizenship in Bendix (1964), a theme that Rokkan extended in later work (Rokkan, 1970). Bendix and Lipset (1959) coauthored the first systematic comparative study of social mobility. Lipset and Rokkan in turn coauthored several works, including the brilliant essay on the development of European party systems (Lipset and Rokkan, 1967). Two other "neo-Weberians" merit mentioning in this regard: Eisenstadt, whose concerns with political systems in preindustrial societies (Eisenstadt, 1969) in part overlaps that of Bendix, and Linz, whose work has focused on authoritarian regimes (e.g., Linz 1975, 1978), both of whom coauthored or coedited work with one or two of the aforementioned. Theoretically, these "neo-Weberians" are a heterogeneous lot, reflecting the ambiguity of Weber's legacy. Eisenstadt is a structural functionalist, whereas Bendix is a leading critic of that school. The first half of Lipset and Rokkan's party system essay is cast in Parsonsian terms, while the second half (on variations in nation-building alliances) bears a definite similarity to Moore's analysis in *Social Origins*, something Rokkan (1972) has remarked on. While only Eisenstadt could be classified as a consensus theorist, there is a definite tendency for the rest of these writers to see sharp political conflict as a characteristic of preindustrial Europe and developing countries, which is greatly attenuated if not disappearing altogether with the introduction of universal suffrage and the development of the welfare state.

10. See below for a brief summary of Moore's analysis.

11. The critiques of Frank and this particular hypothesis, most of which come from Marxists and neo-Marxists, form a literature in themselves. LeClau (1971), and Warren (1973, 1980) are among the best known. See also Oxaal, Barnett, and Booth (1975) and Booth (1986). As Binder (1986) puts it, Frank has "been treated by more sophisticate Marxist theories like some sort of country bumpkin who has marched into the living room without removing his muddy galoshes."

12. Palma (1978) provides one of the best reviews of the major theorists whose work may be loosely considered part of the dependency tradition. Third World contributors include, in addition to Latin Americans, scholars from the English-speaking Caribbean, such as Norman Girvan (1973, 1976), as well as scholars from other areas of the Third World with European training, most prominently Samir Amin and Arghiri Emmanuel.

13. Some Third World scholars had been involved in the development of the modernization approach, most notably Gino Germani, but their role was much less central. See Kahl (1976).

14. Most important among the latter were the members of the "ECLA" or CEPAL school, which grew out of the work of Raul Prebisch and later included a variety of "structuralist" economists such as Celso Furtado and Oswaldo Sunkel.

15. First written in the late sixties in Santiago and published in 1969 in Spanish, Cardoso and Faletto was not available to English readers until 1979. For a general review of Cardoso's work see Kahl (1976). For Cardoso's own critique of how his work has been interpreted in North America, see Cardoso (1977).

16. The Sage Publications series of *Political Economy of the World-system Annuals*, now in its ninth year, provides one means of keeping up with work in the world-system tradition. Ragin and Chirot (1984) provide a review of Wallerstein's work along with some bibliography. Among the more influential critiques of Wallerstein's approach are Brenner (1977), Skocpol (1977), Zolberg (1981), and Zeitlin (1984, chap. 5).

17. Ragin (1987) underlines these and other problems in statistical studies in his insightful discussion of the relative merits of using statistical and comparative historical evidence in comparative cross-national work. See also Ragin and Zaret (1983) and Skocpol and Somers (1980) on comparative methods.

18. It is this concern with distinctiveness and explanation of differences that separates work in the new political economy from the important comparative historical work of Perry Anderson (1974a, 1974b). As Fulbrook and Skocpol (1984, pp. 191-196) point out, Anderson does not employ the analytical comparative historical method as he is hostile to the attempts at causal generalization entailed in the approach. Rather, he uses comparison in order to distill pure types of the social formations under study.

19. The collection of articles in Tilly (1975) offers a similar perspective on the history of the European state.

20. For theoretical presentations of this view, see Martin (1975), Korpi (1978, 1982), Stephens (1979), Esping-Andersen (1978, 1985), Himmelstrand et al., 1981), and Esping-Andersen and Friedland (1982). For the empirical results referred to in the text, see the work on the welfare state reviewed below and Hicks, Friedland, and Johnson (1978), Friedland (1983), Esping-Andersen and Friedland (1982), Stephens and Stephens (1982), Hibbs (1977), and Korpi and Shalev (1979).

21. Wallerstein (1987) presents a contrasting theoretical interpretation, emphasizing size of the population per se rather than the industrial structure (which is partly dependent on the size of the domestic economy and thus on the size of the population), of essentially the same empirical results as presented in Kjellberg (1983) and Stephens (1979).

22. For reviews of this literature see Evans (1981) and Bornschier and Chase-Dunn (1985). It is worth pointing out that this was not simply a Latin American literature. In addition to a number of studies with worldwide samples, it included studies of all regions of the Third World, for example,

Biersteker (1978), McGowan and Smith (1978), and Bradshaw (1985) on Black Africa.

23. These studies were done from a variety of methodological approaches as well as regional foci, including quantitative cross-sectional studies (e.g., Delacroix and Ragin, 1981), country case studies (e.g., Evans, 1979; Gold, 1986), industry studies (e.g., Newfarmer, 1985), or a combination of industry and country approaches (e.g., Becker, 1983; Bennett and Sharpe, 1985; Gereffi, 1983; Grieco, 1984).

24. As Midgal (1983) points out, desire to understand political development in the Third World has served as an important stimulus to the reexamination of the historical experience of Europe.

25. See for example, Greenberg (1980) and Hintzen (in press) on race, Boserup (1970) on gender.

26. See Bunce (1985), Chirot (1976), Comisso (1986), and Stark (1985) on Eastern Europe; Walder (1986), Parish (1985) and Kelliher (1985) on China.

27. Assigning the state this "minimal" role does not, of course, make it an unimportant institution. Witness, for example, the crucial place of the state in Douglas North's "efficient property rights" theory of economic development (see, for example, North and Thomas, 1973).

28. Curiously, Parsons himself, though adamant in his assertions that structural differentiation was the key to economic progress, took a Gerschenkron-like position on the role of the state in developing countries arguing that in these countries "far from obstructing, it is likely strongly to facilitate the process" (1960, p. 116).

29. This is not, of course, to say that states like the Brazilian or Korean are always developmentally effective; see, for example, Bunker (1985).

30. While Bates offers the most elegant illustration of the perverse consequences of intervention by states that lack the capacity to do so effectively, this phenomenon is not limited to agriculture; analogous results obtain in mineral extraction. See, for example, Young and Turner (1985) or Shafer (1983) on Zaire and Hintzen (in press) on Guyana and Trinidad.

31. The negative consequences of rent seeking in countries dependent on agricultural exports may be exacerbated by the "urban bias" (see Lipton, 1977) of state elites. In the Ivory Coast, where export agriculture was more thoroughly entrenched in the state apparatus, state intervention has produced higher rates of growth (see Bates, 1981, p. 131-32; articles by Anyang' Nyong'o and Campbell in Lubeck, 1987).

32. The structural prerequisites of a bureaucracy that operates in a universalistic way are not obvious, as the particularism of the long- established Indian bureaucracy demonstrates (see Wade, 1985).

33. It should be noted here that there is a definite element of this class struggle view of the transition to democracy in some of the work that is generally associated with the modernization approach, for example, the work of Marshall (1950) and those who follow him (Bendix, 1964, Rokkan, 1970). Marshall (1950, p. 29) notes at one point that "in the twen-

tieth century, citizenship and the capitalist class system have been at war."

34. The argument presented here will be elaborated in Rueschemeyer, Stephens, and Stephens (in press). The section on Europe follows Stephens (1987).

35. In general those interested in development focus on industrialization at the expense of agrarian class relations only at their peril. Compare, for example, Paige (1975) for an excellent study using an analysis of agrarian class relations to explain the political outcomes of rural protest movements.

36. Austria-Hungary, Spain, Italy, and Germany.

37. Countries, other than England, in which democracy survived are Sweden, Denmark, Norway, Switzerland, Belgium, Netherlands, and France. On Finland, which is a more ambiguous case, see note 39.

38. The war discredited the ruling class. Labor was strengthened because its support was essential both on the front and in production in this first mass mobilization, mass conscription war. One indicator of this is the tripling of union membership in the antagonists in the war (Stephens, 1979, p. 115).

39. The Finnish case demonstrates the importance of landholding patterns for interwar events. Sections of the peasantry turned to the radical Right to the Lapua movement, which did manage to get the Communist Party suppressed (Alapuro and Allardt, 1978). But it never managed to effect the suspension of parliamentary politics. With no available allies in the bourgeoisie or a landed elite (which did not exist), its influence remained limited.

40. The association between world power/large-state status and landholding patterns is no accident: Tilly (1975, pp. 40-44) points out that military success was one factor that distinguished the successful state builders from the unsuccessful ones and success in war was greatly facilitated by "strong coalitions between the central power and major segments of the landed elite." Note that Spanish developments do not fit the Kurth thesis as well as developments in the other three countries.

41. The Argentine case (and the Chilean, were events to develop in that direction in the future) is quite different. There the regime change was brought on by the failure and disintegration of the authoritarian regime not by the strengthening of the political capacities of the lower classes, which were actually reduced by repression and economic decline.

42. See Stephens and Stephens (1987). Further exploration of this aspect of British colonialism in other regions might be a useful way of explaining Bollen and Jackman's (1985) finding of a strong relation between British rule and subsequent democracy.

43. This is evident if one compares Senghaas's (1985) account of development in the smaller European countries with Evans's (1987) interpretation of the development of the East Asian NICs.

44. The studies reviewed here are Wilensky (1976, 1981), Hewitt (1977), Cameron (1978), Stephens (1979), Bjorn (1976, 1979), Castles (1982), Korpi (1982), Hicks and Swank (1984a, 1984b), Myles (1984), Swank (1984), and Young (1986). For reviews

and insightful critiques of these and other similar studies, see Uusitalo (1984), Castles (1982) and Shalev (1983a, 1983b). Note that our summary assumes two coding decisions: following Lehmbruch (1985, also see Schmitter, 1979), we classify France and Italy as not corporatist; and we code the U.S. Democrats as a Center party rather than a Left party. Wilensky makes different decisions on these two accounts, which explains his somewhat different findings.

45. Castles (1978), Esping-Andersen (1985), Korpi (1978, 1982), Esping-Andersen and Korpi (1985), Martin (1973, 1975, 1979), Himmelstrand et al. (1981), and Headey (1978) present analyses generally consistent with the argument in the text emphasizing the importance of government by Left or Center-Left parties or coalitions for the welfare state expansion, equalization, and/or increased democratic control of the economy. For contrasting views, see Rimlinger (1971), Heidenheimer (1983), and the state centric views mentioned below.

46. It is, of course, the case that proportion of population over 65 explains some of the variation in pension spending and therefore of overall social security spending in which pensions are the largest part. Moreover, industrialization and its demographic consequences probably does account for some of the expansion of public expenditure that has occurred in all industrial societies but not for the great variation between them.

47. Cameron (1978, 1984), Kjellberg (1983), Korpi (1982), Lange and Garret (1985), Stephens (1979).

48. The effect of government ideology holding union strength constant is demonstrated by the case of Australia, where the union movement is strong but the Labour Party has been excluded from power most of the postwar period, having narrowly lost a number of elections. As expected, the country's market income distribution is relatively equal but the tax system effects virtually no redistribution of income (Sawyer, 1976, pp. 16, 17) and the welfare state is minimal.

49. See Skocpol (1980); Orloff and Skocpol (1984); and Weir and Skocpol (1985). Heclo goes so far as to argue for the irrelevance of parties and elections, but the evidence in his own chapter 5 would seem to contradict this assertion.

50. In the Swiss case, the idiosyncratic features are the referendum system and the requirement of a cantonal majority for approval, thus weighting the strength of the rural mountain cantons disproportionately. In the United States, the presidential system, single member districts, plurality elections, and primaries impede the development of disciplined parties.

51. Also see Wallerstein (1985), who contends that specialization in nonagricultural exports and openness are the distinguishing features of corporatist countries. In his study of the development of corporatism, Katzenstein (1985) emphasizes the role of economic openness along with a weak landed nobility, a moderate Left and various features of the political system. Cameron (1978) finds a direct relation between economic openness and the expansion of the welfare state.

52. This statement is based on the ambiguous and/or contradictory findings of the following studies for the pre-1973 period: Smith (1975), Cameron (1981), Katz, Mahler, and Franz (1983), Friedland and Sanders (1985), and Korpi (1985). Studies of the seventies and eighties by Cameron (1984), Lange and Garrett (1985), Scharpf (1984) and Korpi (1985) indicate, if anything, that the social democratic/corporatist countries outperformed other advanced capitalist democracies in this period, even though all countries had a much more difficult time sustaining the same level of growth.

53. See Chase-Dunn (1975), Kaufman, Chernotsky, and Geller (1975); Rubinson (1976); Bornschier and Chase-Dunn (1985). For an exception to this pattern of findings, see Dolan and Tomlin (1980).

54. The East Asian cases also undercut the idea that Latin American inequality might be explained by the baseline "industrialization effect," that is, the inverted "U" relation first pointed to by Kuznets (1955), who suggested that inequality would at first increase with industrialization because at extremely low levels of development, there is little urban-rural differentiation, little urban-rural inequality, and, more important, very little surplus that could be concentrated in higher-income groups. Observing the same empirical relationship, Lenski (1966) links the inverted "U" curve to changing power relationships between social strata in society.

55. In his review and analysis of the findings on the relationship between land inequality and growth of agricultural productivity in South Asia, Herring (1985) comes to a similar conclusion—namely, that there is no simple relationship.

56. The post-World War II period seems to combine the relatively liberal trade regime (and consequent growth of trade) that has been historically associated with stable hegemony with the upward phase of an economic long cycle of the Kondratieff type (see Chase-Dunn, 1986; Keohane, 1984). These cyclical features, which have occurred in earlier historical periods as well, are compounded by secular improvements in transportation and communication.

57. For some general discussions of the consequences of internationalization for labor and labor relations, see Portes and Walton (1981); Bergquist (1984); Deyo (1986); and Frobel, Heinrich, and Kreye (1981).

58. For a discussion of different types of immigration, see Piore (1979), Portes and Walton (1981), and Portes and Manning (1985). For a discussion of developmental consequences for sending communities see Portes (1982).

59. While this research is primarily based on U.S. data, there are intriguing parallels between the U.S. results and observation in at least certain areas of Europe, most notably the Emilia-Romagna area of Italy as reported by the joint U.S./Italian research project undertaken by MIT-Harvard and the Universities of Modena and Parma (see, for example, Sabel, 1982, and Brusco, 1982).

60. See, for example, Portes (1985).

61. See especially Deyo (1986) and Frobel, Heinrich, and Kreye (1981).

62. It has also been argued that there are differential effects by gender among both First and Third World workers. See Sassen-Koob (1985), Ward (1984), and Fernandez-Kelly (1983).

63. See, for example, Bennett and Sharpe (1985) and Kronish and Mericle (1984) on the auto industry, Evans (1986) and Adler (1986) on the computer industry, Gereffi (1983) on pharmaceuticals, and the studies in Newfarmer (1985).

64. See Evans (1985) for a more fully developed version of this argument.

65. Another important example of this kind of interaction is nicely explicated by Stallings (1987), who shows how, in the case of the United States, the transition to becoming a capital exporter was rooted in changes in domestic financial institutions and domestic class structures.

66. By "regimes" Krasner means generally accepted principles, norms, laws, and procedures governing transnational flows or interactions. The differential benefits of authoritative and market regimes are evident in the area of transportation where an authoritative regime in civilian aviation has given Third World countries a much larger market share than the market-oriented regime that exists in shipping.

67. Insofar as new research focuses on the organization of the state as an administrative apparatuses or on the organization of unions and political parties, it might be considered to exemplify what has been called "the new institutionalism" by March and Olsen (1984); overall, however, the "new institutionalist" label is misleading since it does not reflect comparative political economy's central concern with the underlying social structural bases of institutional forms.

68. See Rueschemeyer and Evans (1985) for some preliminary formulations. Also see Wade, note 30.

69. See Stephens (1987) and Gerschenkron (1943, pp. 53-55).

70. Popkin's dialog with Scott (1976) also offers a fascinating confrontation between a rational choice perspective and a culturally oriented explanation of political change in peasant communities. For an insightful analysis of the debate and its implication for the general question of the role of cultural values in the legitimation of inequality and exploitation and the occurrence of peasant revolts, see Herring (1984).

REFERENCES

Adler, Emanuel. 1986. "Ideological Guerrillas and the Quest for Technological Autonomy: Development of a Domestic Computer Industry in Brazil." *International Organization* 40(3).

Alapuro, Risto and Erik Allardt. 1978. "The Lapua Movement: The Threat of Rightist Takeover in

Finland.'' Pp. 122-141 in *The Breakdown of Democratic Regimes*, edited by Juan Linz and Alfred Stepan. Baltimore, MD: Johns Hopkins University Press.

Amsden, Alice. 1979. ''Taiwan's Economic History: A Case of Etatisme and a Challenge to Dependency Theory'' *Modern China* (July): 341-379.

———. 1985. ''The State and Taiwan's Economic Development.'' Pp. 78-106 in *Bringing the State Back In*, edited by Peter Evans et al. New York: Cambridge University Press.

Anderson, Perry. 1974a. *Lineages of the Absolutist State*. London: New Left Books.

———. 1974b. *Passages from Antiquity to Feudalism*. London: New Left Books.

Bacon, R. and W. Eltis. 1976. *Britain's Economic Problem: Too Few Producers*. London: Macmillan.

Banfield, Edward. 1958. *The Moral Basis of a Backward Society*. Glencoe, IL: Free Press.

Baran, Paul. 1957. *The Political Economy of Growth*. New York: Monthly Review Press.

Barzelay, Michael. 1986. *The Politicized Market Economy: Alcohol in Brazil's Energy Strategy*. Berkeley: University of California Press.

Basu, Sanjib. 1985. ''Nonalignment and Economic Development: Indian State Strategies, 1947-1962.'' Pp. 193-216 in *States versus Markets in the World System*, edited by Peter Evans et al. Beverly Hills, CA: Sage.

Bates, Robert H. 1981. *Markets and States in Tropical Africa*. Berkeley: University of California Press.

Becker, David. 1983. *The New Bourgeoisie and the Limits of Dependency: Mining, Class and Power in 'Revolutionary' Peru*. Princeton, NJ: Princeton University Press.

Bendix, Reinhard. 1956. *Work and Authority in Industry: Ideologies of Management in the Course of Industrialization*. New York: John Wiley.

———. 1964. *Nation-Building and Citizenship: Studies of Our Changing Social Order*. New York: John Wiley.

———. 1978. *Kings or People: Power and the Mandate to Rule*. Berkeley: University of California Press.

Bendix, Reinhard and Seymour Martin Lipset. 1959. *Social Mobility in Industrial Society*. Berkeley: University of California Press.

Bennett, Douglas and Kenneth Sharpe. 1985. *Transnational Corporations versus the State: The Political Economy of the Mexican Auto Industry*. Princeton, NJ: Princeton University Press.

Bergquist, Charles W., ed. 1984. *Labor in the World Capitalist Economy*. Beverly Hills, CA: Sage.

Biersteker, Tom. 1978. *Distortion or Development? Contending Perspectives on the Multinational Corporation*. Cambridge: MIT Press.

Binder, Leonard. 1986. ''The Natural History of Development Theory.'' *Comparative Studies in Society and History* 28:3-33.

Bjorn, Lars. 1976. ''Labor Parties and the Redistribution of Income in Capitalist Democracies.'' Ph.D. dissertation, University of North Carolina.

———. 1979. ''Labor Parties, Economic Growth, and the Redistribution of Income in Five Capitalist Democracies.'' *Comparative Studies in Sociology* 2.

Block, Fred. 1977. ''The Ruling Class Does Not Rule: Notes on the Marxist Theory of the State.'' *Socialist Revolution* 7:6-28.

——— and Margaret Sommers. 1984. ''Beyond the Economistic Fallacy: The Holistic Social Science of Karl Polanyi.'' Pp. 47-84 in *Vision and Method in Historical Sociology*, edited by Theda Skocpol. Cambridge: Cambridge University Press.

Boli-Bennett, John. 1979. ''The Ideology of Expanding State Authority in National Constitutions, 1870-1970.'' In *National Development and the World System*, edited by J. Meyer and M. Hannan. Chicago: University of Chicago Press.

——— and J. Meyer. 1978. ''The Ideology of Childhood and the State: Rules Distinguishing Children in National Constitutions, 1870-1970.'' *American Sociological Review* 43:797-812.

Bollen, Kenneth. 1979. ''Political Democracy and the Timing of Development.'' *American Sociological Review* 44:572-587.

———. 1983. ''World System Position, Dependency, and Democracy.'' *American Sociological Review* 48:468-479.

——— and Robert Jackman. 1985. ''Economic and Noneconomic Determinants of Political Democracy in the 1960s.'' In *Research in Political Sociology*, edited by Richard Braungart and Philo Washburn. Greenwich, CT: JAI Press.

Booth, David. 1985. ''Marxism and Development Sociology: Interpreting the Impasse.'' *World Development* 13:761-787.

Bornschier, Volker and Christopher Chase-Dunn. 1985. *Transnational Corporations and Underdevelopment*. New York: Praeger.

Boserup, Ester. 1970. *Women's Role in Economic Development*. New York: St. Martin's.

Bradshaw, York. 1985. ''Dependent Development in Black Africa: A Crossnational Study. *American Sociological Review* 50:195-206.

Brenner, Robert. 1976. ''Agrarian Class Structure and Economic Development in Pre-industrial Europe.'' *Past and Present* 70:30-75.

———. 1977. ''The Origins of Capitalist Development: A Critique of Neo-Smithian Marxism.'' *New Left Review* 104:24-92.

Brusco, Sebastiano. 1982. ''The Emilian Model: Productive Decentralization and Social Integration.'' *Cambridge Journal of Economic* 167-184.

Bunce, Valerie. 1985. ''The Empire Strikes Back: The Evolution of the Eastern Bloc from a Soviet Asset to a Soviet Liability.'' *International Organization* 39:1-46.

Bunker, Stephen. 1985. *Underdevelopment in the Amazon: Extraction, Unequal Exchange, and the Failure of the Modern State*. Urbana: University of Illinois Press.

Cameron, David. 1978. "The Expansion of the Public Economy: A Comparative Analysis." *The American Political Science Review* 72:1243-1261.

—————. 1981. "On the Limits of the Public Economy." *The Annals of the American Academy of Political and Social Science* 459:46-62.

—————. 1984. "Social Democracy, Corporatism, Labor Quiescence, and the Representation of Economic Interests in Advanced Capitalist Society." Pp. 143-178 in *Order and Conflict in Contemporary Capitalism*, edited by John Goldthorpe. Oxford: Oxford University Press.

Cardoso, F. H. 1977. "The Consumption of Dependency Theory in the United States." *Latin American Research Review* 12:7-25.

—————. and E. Faletto. 1979. *Dependency and Development in Latin America*. Berkeley: University of California Press.

Castles, Francis. 1978. *The Social Democratic Image of Society*. London: Routledge & Kegan Paul.

—————. 1982. *The Impact of Parties*. Beverly Hills, CA: Sage.

Chase-Dunn, Christopher. 1975. "The Effect of International Dependence on Development and Inequality: A Cross-National Study." *American Sociological Review* 40:720-738.

—————. 1986. "Cycles, Trends or Transformations?: The World System Since 1945." In *America's Changing Role in the World System*, edited by Terry Boswell and Albert Bergesen. London: Longmans.

Chirot, Daniel. 1976. *Social Change in a Peripheral Society: The Creation of a Balkan Colony*. New York: Academic Press.

Collier, David, ed. 1979. *The New Authoritarianism in Latin America*. Princeton, NJ: Princeton University Press.

Collier, Ruth Berins and David Collier. In press. *Shaping the Political Arena: Critical Junctures, Trade Unions, and the State in Latin America*.

Comisso, Ellen. 1986. "Introduction: State Structures, Political Processes, and Collective Choice in CMEA States." *International Organization* 40:195-238.

Cumings, Bruce. 1984. "The Origins of Development of the Northeast Asian Political Economy: Industrial Sectors, Product Cycles, and Political Consequences." *International Organization* 38:1-40.

Cutright, Phillips. 1963. "National Political Development." *American Sociological Review* 28:253-264.

DeJanvry, Alain. 1981. *The Agrarian Question and Reformism in Latin America*. Baltimore, MD: Johns Hopkins University Press.

Delacroix, Jacque and Charles Ragin. 1981. "Structural Blockage: A Crossnational Study of Economic Dependency, State Efficacy, and Underdevelopment." *American Journal of Sociology* 86:1311-1347.

Deyo, Fred. 1986. "Labor Movements in the East Asian NICs: Structural Demobilization and Preemptory Developmental Sequences." Unpublished manuscript.

—————. 1987, ed. *The Political Economy of the New Asian Industrialism*. Ithaca, NY: Cornell University Press.

Dolan, Michael B. and Brian Tomlin. 1980. "First World-Third World Linkages: External Relations and Economic Development." *International Organization* 34:41-63.

Eisenstadt, S. N. 1969. *The Political System of Empires*. New York: Free Press.

Elster, Jon. 1985. *Making Sense of Marx*. Cambridge: Cambridge University Press.

Esping-Anderson, Gosta. 1978. "Social Class, Social Democracy, and the State." *Comparative Politics* 11.

—————. 1985. *Politics against Markets: The Social Democratic Road to Power*. Princeton, NJ: Princeton University Press.

—————. and Roger Friedland. 1982. "Class Coalitions in the Making of West European Economies." *Political Power and Social Theory* 3:1-52.

Esping-Anderson, Gosta and Walter Korpi. 1985. "Social Policy as Class Politics in Post-War Capitalism: Scandinavia, Austria, and Germany." Pp. 179-208 in *Order and Conflict in Contemporary Capitalism*, edited by John Goldthorpe. Oxford: Oxford University Press.

Evans, P. B. 1979. *Dependent Development: The Alliance of Multinational, State and Local Capital in Brazil*. Princeton, NJ: Princeton University Press.

—————. 1981. "Recent Research on Multinational Corporations." *Annual Review of Sociology* 7:199-223.

—————. 1985. "Transnational Linkages and the Economic Role of the State: An Analysis of Developing and Industrialized Nations in the Post-World War II Period." Pp. 192-226 in *Bringing the State Back In*, edited by Peter Evans et al. New York: Cambridge University Press.

—————. 1986. "State, Capital and the Transformation of Dependence: The Brazilian Computer Case." *World Development* 14:791-808.

—————. 1987. "Class, State and Dependence in East Asia: Lessons for Latin Americanists." In *The Political Economy of the New Asian Industrialism*, edited by F. Deyo. Ithaca, NY: Cornell University Press.

—————. and Michael Timberlake. 1980. "Dependence, Inequality, and the Growth of the Tertiary: A Comparative Analysis of Less Developed Countries." *American Sociological Review* 45:531-551.

Fei, John C. H., Gustav Ranis, and Shirley W.Y. Kuo. 1979. *Growth with Equity: The Taiwan Case*. New York: Oxford University Press.

Fernandez-Kelly, M. Patricia. 1983. *For We Are Sold, I and My People: Women and Industry in Mexico's Frontier*. Albany: State University of New York Press.

Fiala, Robert. 1983. "Inequality and the Service Sector in Less Developed Countries: A Reanalysis and a Respecification.'' *American Sociological Review* 48:421-428.

Foxley, Alejandro. 1983. *Latin American Experiments in Neo-conservative Economics*. Berkeley: University of California Press.

Frank, Andre Gunder. 1967. *Capitalism and Underdevelopment in Latin America*. New York: Monthly Review Press.

Friedland, Roger. 1983. *Power and Crisis in the City: Corporations, Unions, and Urban Policy*. New York: Schocken.

———— and Jimy Sanders. 1985. ''The Public Economy and Economic Growth in Western Market Economies.'' *American Sociological Review* 50:421-437.

Frobel, Folker, Jurgen Heinrich, and Otto Kreye. 1981. *The New International Division of Labor: Structural Unemployment in Industrialized Countries and Industrialization in Developing Countries*. Cambridge: Cambridge University Press.

Fulbrook, Mary and Theda Skocpol. 1984. ''Destined Pathways: The Historical Sociology of Perry Anderson.'' Pp. 170-210 in *Vision and Method in Historical Sociology*, edited by Theda Skocpol. Cambridge: Cambridge University Press.

Gereffi, Gary. 1983. *The Pharmaceutical Industry and Dependency in the Third World*. Princeton, NJ: Princeton University Press.

———— and Don Wyman. In press. *Manufactured Miracles*. Princeton, NJ: Princeton University Press.

Gerschenkron, Alexander. 1962. *Economic Backwardness in Historical Prespective*. Cambridge: Harvard University Press.

Girvan, Norman. 1973. ''The Develoment of Dependency Economics in the Caribbean and Latin America: Review and Comparison.'' *Social and Economic Studies* 22:1-33.

———— 1976. *Corporate Imperialism: Conflict and Expropriation*. New York: Monthly Review Press.

Gold, Tom. 1986. *State and Society in the Taiwan Miracle*. Armonk, NY: M. E. Sharpe.

Goldstone, Jack. 1982. ''The Comparative and Historical Study of Revolutions.'' *Annual Review of Sociology* 8:187-207.

———— 1986. ''Revolutions.'' *Comparative Historical Sociology Newsletter*.

Gough, Ian. 1979. *The Political Economy of the Welfare State*. London: Macmillan.

Gourevitch, Peter. 1978. ''The Second Image Reversed: The International Sources of Domestic Politics.'' *International Organization* 32:881-911.

———— 1984. ''Breaking With Orthodoxy: The Politics of Economic Policy Responses to the Depression of the 1930s.'' *International Organization* 38:95-129.

Greenberg, Stanley. 1980. *Race and State in Capitalist Development*. New Haven, CT: Yale

University Press.

Grieco, Joseph. 1984. *Between Dependence and Autonomy: India's Experience with the International Computer Industry*. Berkeley: University of California Press.

Hamilton, Nora. 1983. *The Limits of State Autonomy: Post-Revolutionary Mexico*. Princeton, NJ: Princeton University Press.

Headey, Bruce. 1978. *Housing Policy in the Developed Economy: The United Kingdom, Sweden and the United States*. London: Croom Helm.

Heidenheimer, Arnold. 1983. ''Secularization Patterns and the Westward Spread of the Welfare State.'' *Comparative Social Research* 6.

Herring, Ronald. 1984. ''Some Methodological and Theoretical Problems in the Analysis of Agrarian Change: Structures and Legitimations.'' Presented at the International Conference on Symbolic and Material Dimensions of Agrarian Change, Sri Lanka.

———— 1985. ''Economic Consequences of Local Power Configurations in South Asia.'' Pp. 198-249 in *Agrarian Power and Agricultural Productivity in South Asia*, edited by Meghnad Desai et al. Berkeley: University of California Press.

———— 1986. ''Openness as Capacity and Vulnerability: Sri Lanka's Dependent Welfare State.'' Presented at the conference on Socialist Governments in Market Economies, Princeton, NJ.

Hewitt, Christopher. 1977. ''The Effect of Political Democracy and Social Democracy on Equality in Industrial Societies.'' *American Sociological Review* 42.

Hewlett, Sylvia. 1980. *The Cruel Dilemmas of Development: Twentieth Century Brazil*. New York: Basic Books.

Hibbs, Douglas. 1977. ''Political Parties and Macroeconomic Policies.'' *American Political Science Review* 71:467-487.

Hicks, Alexander. 1988. ''National Collective Action and Economic Performance.'' *International Studies Quarterly*.

————, Roger Friedland, and Edwin Johnson. 1978. ''Class Power and State Policy.'' *American Sociological Review* 43.

Hicks, Alexander and Dwane Swank. 1984a. ''Governmental Redistribution in Rich Capitalist Democracies.'' *Policy Studies Journal* 13:265-286.

———— 1984b. ''On the Political Economy of Welfare Expansion: A Comparative Analysis of 18 Advanced Capitalist Democracies, 1960-1971.'' *Comparative Political Studies* 17:81-118.

Himmelstrand, Ulf et al. 1981. *Beyond Welfare Capitalism: Issues, Actors, and Forces in Societal Change*. London: Heineman.

Hintze, Otto. 1975. *The Historical Essays of Otto Hintze*, edited by Felix Gilbert. New York: Oxford University Press.

Hintzen, Percy C. In press. *The Costs of Regime Survival: Racial Mobilization, Elite Domination and Control of the State in Guyana and Trinidad.* Cambridge: Cambridge University Press.

Hirschman, Albert. 1971. *A Bias for Hope: Essays on the Development of Latin America.* New Haven, CT: Yale University Press.

Huntington, Samuel. 1968. *Political Order in Changing Societies.* New Haven, CT: Yale University Press.

Ingham, Geoffery. 1974. *Strikes and Industrial Conflict: Britain and Scandinavia.* London: Macmillan.

Inkles, Alex and Larry Sirowy. 1983. "Convergent and Divergent Trends in National Education Systems." *Social Forces* 62:303-333.

Inkles, Alex and David Smith. 1974. *Becoming Modern: Individual Change in Six Developing Countries.* Cambridge, MA: Harvard University Press.

Jackman, Robert W. 1973. "On the Relation of Economic Development to Democratic Performance." *American Journal of Political Science* 17:611-621.

Johnson, Chalmers. 1982. *MITI and the Japanese Miracle.* Stanford, CA: Stanford University Press.

Kahl, Joseph. 1976. *Modernization, Exploitation and Dependency in Latin America.* New Brunswick, NJ: Transaction Books.

Katz, Claudio, Vincent Mahler, and Michael Franz. 1983. "The Impact of Taxes on Growth and Distribution in Developed Capitalist Countries: A Crossnational Study." *American Political Science Review* 77:871-886.

Katznelson, Ira and Aristide R. Zolberg, eds. 1986. *Working Class Formation: Nineteenth Century Patterns in Western Europe and the United States.* Princeton, NJ: Princeton University Press.

Katzenstein, Peter. 1985. *Small States in World Markets: Industrial Policy in Europe.* Ithaca, NY: Cornell University Press.

Kaufman, Robert, H. Chernotsky, and D. Geller. 1975. "A Preliminary Test of the Theory of Dependency." *Comparative Politics* 7:303-330.

Kelliher, Daniel. 1985. "State-Peasant Relations under China's Contemporary Reforms." Ph.D. dissertation, Yale University.

Kentor, Jeffery. 1981. "Structural Determinants of Peripheral Urbanization: The Effect of International Dependence." *American Sociological Review* 46:201-211.

Keohane, Robert. 1984. *After Hegemony: Cooperation and Discord in the World Political Economy.* Princeton, NJ: Princeton University Press.

Kim, Eun Mee. 1987. "From Dominance to Symbiosis: State and Chaebol in the Korean Economy. 1960-1985." Ph.D. dissertation, Brown University.

Kim, Myoung Soo. 1987. "The Making of Korean Society: The Role of the State in the Republic of Korea." Ph.D dissertation, Brown University.

Kjellberg, Anders. 1983. *Facklig Organisering i Tolv Lander.* Lund: Arkiv.

Knight, Peter. 1981. "Brazilian Socioeconomic Development: Issues for the Eighties." *World Development.*

Koo, Hagen. 1984. "The Political Economy of Income Distribution in South Korea: The Impact of the State's Industrialization Policies." *World Development* 12:1029-1037.

Korpi, Walter. 1978. *The Working Class in Welfare Capitalism.* London: Routledge & Kegan Paul.

———. 1982. *The Democratic Class Struggle.* London: Routledge & Kegan Paul.

———. 1985. "Economic Growth and the Welfare State: Leaky Bucket or Irrigation System?" *European Sociological Review* 1:97-118.

——— and Michael Shalev. 1979. "Industrial Relations and Class Conflict in Capitalist Societies." *British Journal of Sociology* 30:164-187.

Krasner, Stephen. 1978. *Defending the National Interest: Raw Materials Investments and U.S. Foreign Policy.* Princeton, NJ: Princeton University Press.

———. 1985. *Structural Conflict: The Third World Against Global Liberalism.* Berkeley: University of California Press.

Kronish, Richard and Ken Mericle. 1984. *The Political Economy of the Latin American Motor Vehicle Industry.* Cambridge: MIT Press.

Kurth, James. 1979. "Industrial Change and Political Change." Pp. 319-362 in *The New Authoritarianism in Latin America,* edited by D. Collier. Princeton, NJ: Princeton University Press.

Kuznets, Simon. 1955. "Economic Growth and Income Inequality." *American Economic Review* 45:1-26.

Lange, Peter and Geoff Garrett. 1985. "The Politics of Growth: Strategic Interaction and Economic Performance in the Advanced Industrial Democracies. 1974-1980." *Journal of Politics* 47:792-827.

LeClau, Ernesto. 1971. "Feudalism and Capitalism in Latin America." *New Left Review* 67.

Lehmbruch, Gerhard. 1985. "Concertation and the Structure of Corporatist Networks. Pp. 60-80 in *Order and Conflict in Contemporary Capitalism,* edited by John Goldthorpe. Oxford: Oxford University Press.

Lenski, Gerhard. 1966. *Power and Privilege: A Theory of Social Stratification.* New York: McGraw-Hill.

Lerner, Daniel. 1958. *The Passing of Traditional Society: Modernizing the Middle East.* New York: Free Press.

Lim, Hyun-chin. 1985. *Dependent Development in Korea, 1963-1979,* Korean Studies Series no. 8, Institute of Social Sciences, Seoul: Seoul National University Press.

Lindbeck, Assar. 1981. *Work Disincentives in the Welfare State.* Vienna: Manz.

Lipset, Seymour Martin. 1959. "Some Social Requites of Democracy." *American Political Science Review* 52:69-105.

———— and Stein Rokkan, eds. 1967. "Cleavage Structures, Party Systems, and Voter Alignments: An Introduction." Pp. 1-64 in *Party Systems and Voter Alignments*. New York: Free Press.

Lipton, Michael. 1977. *Why Poor People Stay Poor: Urban Bias in World Development*. London: Temple Smith.

Linz, Juan. 1975. "Totalitarian and Authoritarian Regimes." Pp. 175-411 in *Handbook of Political Science*, vol.3, edited by F. Greenstein and N. Polsby. Reading, MA: Addison-Wesley.

———— 1978. *The Breakdown of Democratic Regimes: Crisis, Breakdown, and Reequilibration*. Baltimore, MD: Johns Hopkins University Press.

———— and Alfred Stepan, eds. 1978. *The Breakdown of Democratic Regimes*. Baltimore, MD: Johns Hopkins University Press.

Lubeck, Paul, ed. 1987. *The African Bourgeoisie: Capitalist Development in Nigeria, Kenya and the Ivory Coast*. Boulder, CO: Lynne Rienner.

Malan, Pedro and Regis Bonelli. 1977. "The Brazilian Economy in the Seventies: Old and New Developments." *World Development*. 5:19-45.

Mann, Michael. 1977. "States, Ancient and Modern." *Archives Europeenes de Sociologie* 18:262-298.

———— 1984. "The Autonomous Power of the State: Its Origins, Mechanisms, and Results." *Archives Europeenes de Sociologie* 25:185-213.

———— 1986. *The Sources of Social Power, vol. I: A History of Power in Agrarian Societies*. New York: Cambridge University Press.

————. In press. *The Sources of Social Power, vol. II: A History of Power in Industrial Societies*. New York: Cambridge University Press.

March, James and Johan Olsen. 1984. "The New Institutionalism: Organizational Factors in Political Life." *American Political Science Review* 78: 734-749.

Martin, Andrew. 1973. *The Politics of Economic Policy in the United States*. Beverly Hills, CA: Sage.

———— 1975. "Is Democratic Control of Capitalism Possible? Some Notes Towards An Answer." Pp. 13-56 in *Stress and Contradiction in Modern Capitalism*, edited by Leon Lindberg et al. Lexington, MA: D. C. Heath.

———— 1979. "The Dynamics of Change in a Keynesian Political Economy: The Swedish Case and Its Implications." In *State and Economy in Contemporary Capitalism*, edited by Colin Crouch. London: Croom Helm.

Marshall, T. H. 1950. *Citizenship and Social Class*. Cambridge: Cambridge University Press.

———— 1964. *Class, Citizenship and Social Development*. Chicago: University of Chicago Press.

Marx, Karl. 1867. *Capital*, vol. 1. New York: International Publishers.

———— and Friedrich Engels. 1848. *The Manifesto of the Communist Party*. Pp.1-41 in *Marx and Engels: Basic Writings on Politics and Philosophy*, edited by Lewis Feuer. Garden City, NY: Anchor.

McClelland, David. 1961. *The Acheiving Society*. Princeton, NJ: Van Nostrand.

McGowan, Pat and Dale Smith. 1978. "Economic Dependency in Black Africa: A Causal Analysis of Competing Theories." *International Organization* 32:179-235.

McMichael, Philip. 1985. "Britain's Hegemony in the Nineteenth Century World-Economy." Pp. 117-150 in *States versus Markets in the World System*, edited by Peter Evans et al. Beverly Hills, CA: Sage.

Meyer, John. 1980. "The World Polity and the Authority of the Nation-State." In *Studies in the Modern World System*, edited by Albert Bergesen. New York: Academic Press.

————, Ramirez, F., R. Rubinson, and J. Boli-Bennett. 1977. "The World Educational Revolution, 1950-1970." *Sociology of Education* 50: 242-258.

Migdal, Joel S. 1983. "Studying the Politics of Development and Change: The State of the Art." Pp. 309-338 in *Political Science: The State of the Discipline*, edited by A. Finifter. Washington, DC: American Political Science Association.

Miller, R. Berkeley. 1987. "Industrial Structure, Political Power, and Unionization: The United States in Comparative Perspective." Ph. D. dissertation, Brown University.

Moran, T. H. 1974. *Multinational Corporations and the Politics of Dependence: Copper in Chile*. Princeton, NJ: Princeton University Press.

Moore, Barrington Jr. 1966. *The Social Origins of Dictatorship and Democracy*. Boston: Beacon Press.

Mouzelis, Nicos. 1986. *Politics in the Semi-Periphery: Early Parliamentarism and Late Industrialisation in the Balkans and Latin America*. London: Macmillan.

Myles, John. 1984. *Old Age in the Welfare State: The Political Economy of Public Pensions*. Boston: Little, Brown.

Newfarmer, Richard, ed. 1985. *Profits, Progress and Poverty: Case Studies of International Industries Latin America*. Notre Dame, IN: University of Notre Dame Press.

North, Douglas and Robert Thomas. 1973. *The Rise of the Western World: A New Economic History*. New York: Cambridge University Press.

O'Donnell, Guillermo A. 1973. *Modernization and Bureaucratic Authoritarianism*. Berkeley, CA: Institute of International Studies.

———— 1978. "Reflections on the Patterns of Change in the Bureaucratic Authoritarian State." *Latin American Research Review* 13:3-38.

————, Phillipe Schmitter, and Lawrence Whitehead, eds. 1986. *Transitions from Authoritarian Rule*. Baltimore, MD: Johns Hopkins University Press.

Okun, Arthur. 1975. *Equality and Efficiency: The*

Big Trade-Off. Washington, DC: Brookings Institute.

Orloff, Ann and Theda Skocpol. 1984. "Why Not Equal Protection? Explaining the Politics of Public Social Spending in Britain, 1900-1911 and the United States, 1890s-1920." *American Sociological Review* 49:726-750.

Oxaal, Ivar, Tony Barnett, and David Booth, ed. 1975. *Beyond the Sociology of Development: Economy and Society in Latin America and Africa.* London: Routledge & Kegan Paul.

Paige, Jeffery M. 1975. *Agrarian Revolution.* New York: Free Press.

———. 1985. "Cotton and Revolution in Nicaragua." Pp. 91-116 in *States versus Markets in the World System,* edited by Peter Evans et al. Beverly Hills, CA: Sage.

Palma, Gabriel. 1978. "Dependency: A Formal Theory of Underdevelopment or a Methodology for the Analysis of Concrete Situations of Underdevelopment." *World Development* 6:881-894.

Panitch, Leo. 1980. "Recent Theorizations of Corporatism: Reflections on a Growth Industry." *British Journal of Sociology* 31:159-187.

Parish, William, ed. 1985. *Chinese Rural Development: The Great Transformation.* Armonk, NY: M. E. Sharpe.

Parsons, Talcott, ed. 1960. "Some Reflections on the Institutional Framework of Economic Development" Pp. 98-131 in *Structure and Process in Modern Societies.* Glencoe, IL: Free Press.

Piore, Michael. 1979. *Birds of Passage: Migrant Labor and Industrial Societies.* New York: Cambridge University Press.

Polanyi, Karl. 1944. *The Great Transformation.* Boston: Beacon.

Popkin, Samuel. 1979. *The Rational Peasant.* Berkeley: University of California Press.

Portes, Alejandro. 1982. "International Labor Migration and National Development." Pp. 71-91 in *U.S. Immigration and Refugee Policy,* edited by M. M. Kritz. Lexington, MA: Lexington Books.

———. 1985. "Latin American Class Structures: Their Composition and Change During the Last Decades." *Latin American Research Review* 20:7-39.

———— and R. D. Manning. 1985. "The Immigrant Enclave: Theory and Empirical Examples." In *Ethnicity: Structure and Process,* edited by J. Nagel and S. Olzak. New York: Academic Press.

Portes, Alejandro and John Walton. 1981. *Labor, Class and the International System.* New York: Academic Press.

Przeworski, Adam. 1980. "Social Democracy as a Historical Phenomenon." *New Left Review* 122:27-58.

———. 1985. *Capitalism and Social Democracy.* Cambridge: Cambridge University Press.

Ragin, Charles. 1987. *Between Complexity and Generality: the Logic of Qualitative Comparison.* Berkeley: University of California Press.

———— and Daniel Chirot. 1985. "The World System of Immanuel Wallerstein: Sociology and Politics As History." Pp. 276-312 in *Vision and Method in Historical Sociology,* edited by Theda Skocpol. Cambridge: Cambridge University Press.

Ragin, Charles and David Zaret. 1983. "Theory and Method in Comparative Research: Two Strategies." *Social Forces* 61:731-754.

Ramirez, F. and J. Boli. 1982. "Global Patterns of Educational Institutionalization." In *Comparative Education,* edited by P. Albach et al. New York: MacMillan.

Rimlinger, Gaston. 1971. *Welfare Policy and Industrialization in Europe, America and Russia.* New York: John Wiley.

Roemer, John. 1982. *A General Theory of Class and Exploitation.* Cambridge, MA: Harvard University Press.

Rokkan, Stein. 1970. *Citizens, Elections, Parties.* Oslo: Universitets Forlaget.

———. 1972. "Models and Methods in the Comparative Study of Nation-Building." In *Imagination and Precision in the Social Sciences,* edited by T. J. Nossiter et al. London: Faber.

Rostow, W. W. 1960. *The Stages of Economic Growth: A Non-communist Manifesto.* Cambridge: Cambridge University Press.

Rubinson, Richard. 1976. "The World Economy and the Distribution of Income Within States." *American Sociological Review* 41:638-659.

Rueschemeyer, Dietrich. 1976. "Partial Modernization." Pp. 756-772 in *Explorations in General Theory in Social Science: Essays in Honor of Talcott Parsons,* edited by J. J. Loubser et al. New York: Free Press.

———. 1980. "Uber Sozialokonomische Entwicklung und Demokratie." Pp. 211-230 in *Weltgesellschaft und Sozialstruktur,* edited by G. Hirschier et al. Diessenhofen: Ruegger.

———. 1984. "Theoretical Generalization and Historical Particularity in the Comparative Sociology of Reinhard Bendix." Pp. 129-169 in *Vision and Method in Historical Sociology,* edited by Theda Skocpol. Cambridge: Cambridge University Press.

———— and Peter Evans. 1985. "The State and Economic Transformation: Toward an Analysis of the Conditions Underlying Effective Intervention." Pp. 107-163 in *Bringing the State Back In,* edited by Peter Evans et al. New York: Cambridge University Press.

Rueschemeyer, Dietrich, Evelyne Huber Stephens, and John D. Stephens. In press. *Capitalist Development and Democracy.* Cambridge, Polity Press.

Sabel, Charles. 1982. *Work and Politics.* New York: Cambridge University Press.

Sawyer, Malcolm. 1976. "Income Distribution in OECD Countries." *OECD Economic Outlook: Occassional Studies* (July).

Sassen-Koob, Saskia. 1980. "Immigrant and Minority

Workers in the Organization of the Labor Process." *Journal of Ethnic Studies* 8:1-34.

———. 1984. "The New Labor Demand in Global Cities." In *Cities in Transformation*, edited by M. D. Smith. Beverly Hills, CA: Sage.

———. 1985. "Capital Mobility and Labor Migration: Their Expression in Core Cities." Pp. 231-65 in *Urbanization in the World Economy*, edited by Michael Timberlake. Orlando, FL: Academic Press.

Scharpf, Fritz. 1984. "Economic and Institutional Constraints of Full-Employment Strategies: Sweden, Austria, and West Germany." Pp. 257-290 in *Order and Conflict in Contemporary Capitalism*, edited by John Goldthorpe. Oxford: Oxford University Press.

Schmitter, Philippe. 1979. "Still the Century of Corporatism?" In *Trends Toward Corporatist Intermediation*, edited by Philippe Schmitter and Gerhard Lehmbruch. Beverly Hills, CA: Sage.

Schurmann, Franz. 1973. *The Logic of World Power*. New York: Pantheon.

Scott, James. 1976. *The Moral Economy of the Peasant*. New Haven, CT: Yale University Press.

Senghaas, Dieter. 1985. *The European Experience: A Historical Critique of Development Theory*. Dover, NH: Berg.

Serra, Jose. 1979. "Three Mistaken Theses Regarding the Connection Between Industrialization and Authoritarian Regimes." Pp. 99-164 in *The New Authoritarianism in Latin America*, edited by David Collier. Princeton, NJ: Princeton University Press.

Shafer, Michael. 1983. "Capturing the Mineral Multinationals: Advantage or Disadvantage." *International Organization* 37:93-119.

Shalev, Michael. 1983a. "Class Politics and the Welfare State." Pp. 27-49 in *Evaluating the Welfare State: Social and Political Perspectives*, edited by Shimon E. Spiro and E. Yuchtman-Yaar. New York: Academic Press.

———. 1983b. "The Social Democratic Model and Beyond: Two Generations of Comparative Research on the Welfare State." *Comparative Social Research* 6.

Shorter, Edward and Charles Tilly. 1974. *Strikes in France 1830-1968*. Cambridge: Cambridge University Press.

Skinner, Quentin. 1985. *The Return of Grand Theory in the Human Sciences*. Cambridge: Cambridge University Press.

Skocpol, Theda. 1973. "A Critical Review of Barrington Moore's *Social Origins of Dictatorship and Democracy*." *Politics and Society* 4:1-34.

———. 1977. "Wallerstein's World Capitalist System: A Theoretical and Historical Critique." *American Journal of Sociology* 82:1075-1090.

———. 1979. *States and Social Revolutions*. Cambridge: Cambridge University Press.

———. 1980. "Political Response to Capitalist Crisis: Neo-Marxist Theories of the State and the Case of the New Deal." *Politics and Society* 10:155-201.

———. 1984. *Vision and Method in Historical Sociology*. Cambridge: Cambridge University Press.

——— and Margaret Somers. 1980. "The Uses of Comparative History in Macrosocial Inquiry." *Comparative Studies in Society and History* 22:174-197.

Smelser, Neil. 1959. *Social Change in the Industrial Revolution*. Chicago: University of Chicago Press.

———. 1966, ed. "Toward a Theory of Modernization" pp. 125-146 in *Essays in Sociological Explanation*. Englewood Cliffs, NJ: Prentice Hall.

Smith, D. 1975. "Public Consumption and Economic Performance." *National Westminster Bank Quarterly* (November).

Snidal, Duncan. 1985. "The Limits of Hegemonic Stability Theory." *International Organization* 39:580-614.

Stallings, Barbara. 1987. *Banker to the Third World: U.S. Portfolio Investment in Latin America, 1900-1986*. Berkeley: University of California Press.

Stark, David. 1985. "The Micropolitics of the Firm and the Macropolitics of Reform: New Forms of Workplace Bargaining in Hungarian Enterprises." Pp. 247-275 in *States versus Markets in the World System*, edited by Peter Evans et al. Beverly Hills, CA: Sage.

Stepan, Alfred, ed. 1973. "The New Professionalism of Internal Warfare and Military Role Expansion." Pp. 47-68 in *Authoritarian Brazil*. New Haven, CT: Yale University Press.

———. 1985. "State Power and the Strength of Civil Society in the Southern Cone of Latin America." Pp. 317-343 in *Bringing the State Back In*, edited by Peter Evans et al. New York: Cambridge University Press.

Stephens, Evelyne Huber. 1983. "The Peruvian Military Government, Labor Mobilization, and the Political Strength of the Left." *Latin American Research Review* 18:57-93.

———. 1987. "Mineral Strategies and Development: International Political Economy, State, Class and the Role of Bauxite/Aluminum and Copper Industries in Jamaica and Peru." *Studies in Comparative International Development*.

——— and John D. Stephens. 1980. "The 'Capitalist State' and the Parliamentary Road to Socialism: Lessons from Chile." Presented at the meetings of the Latin American Studies Association, Bloomington IN.

———. 1982. "The Labor Movement, Political Power, and Workers' Participation in Western Europe." *Political Power and Social Theory* 3:215-250.

———. 1986. *Democratic Socialism in Jamaica: The Political Movement and Social Transformation in Dependent Capitalism*. Princeton, NJ: Princeton University Press.

_____ 1987. "Democracy and Authoritarianism in the Caribbean Basin: Domestic and International Determinants." Presented at the meetings of the Caribbean Studies Association, Belize City, Belize.

_____. In press. "Jamaica: The PNP's Democratic Socialist Experiment." *World Politics.*

Stephens, John D. 1979. *The Transition from Capitalism to Socialism.* Urbana: University of Illinois Press.

_____ 1987. "The Breakdown of Democracy in Interwar Europe: A Test of the Moore Thesis." Presented at the meetings of the American Sociological Association, Chicago.

Stinchcombe, Arthur L. 1961. "Agricultural Enterprise and Rural Class Relations." *American Journal of Sociology* 67:165-176.

Swank, Duane. 1984. "The Political Economy of State Domestic Spending in Eighteen Advanced Capitalist Democracies, 1960-1980." Presented at the meetings of the American Political Science Association. Washington, DC.

Taylor, Michael, ed. In press. *Revolution and Rationality.* New York: Cambridge University Press.

Therborn, Goran. 1977. "The Rule of Capital and the Rise of Democracy." *New Left Review* 103.

Thompson, E. P. 1963. *The Making of the English Working Class.* New York: Vintage.

Tilly, Charles. 1964. *The Vendee.* Cambridge, MA: Harvard University Press.

_____ 1975. *The Formation of National States in Western Europe.* Princeton, NJ: Princeton University Press.

_____ 1978. *From Mobilization to Revolution.* Reading, MA: Addison-Wesley.

_____, Louise Tilly, and Richard Tilly. 1975. *The Rebellious Century, 1830-1930.* Cambridge, MA: Harvard University Press.

Timberlake, Michael and Jeffery Kentor. 1983. "Economic Dependence, Overurbanization, and Economic Growth: A Study of Less Developed Countries." *Sociological Quarterly* 24:489-507.

Uusitalo, Hannu. 1984. "Comparative Research on the Determinants of the Welfare State." *European Journal of Political Research* 12:403-422.

Wade, Robert. 1985. "The Market for Public Office: Why the Indian State is Not Better at Development." *World Development* 13:467-497.

Walder, Andrew. 1986. *Communist Neo-Traditionalism: Work and Authority in Chinese Industry.* Berkeley: University of California Press.

Waldinger, Roger. 1984. "The Garment Industry in New York City." In *Hispanics in the U. S. Economy*, edited by G. Borjas and M. Tienda. New York: Academic Press.

Wallerstein, Immanuel. 1974. *The Modern World-System I: Capitalist Agriculture and the Origins of the European World Economy.* New York: Academic Press.

_____ 1979. *The Capitalist World Economy.* Cambridge: Cambridge University Press.

Wallerstein, Michael. 1985. "The Micro-Foundations of Corporatism." Presented at the meetings of the American Political Science Association, New Orleans.

_____ 1987. "Union Growth from the Union's Perspective: Why Smaller Countries Are More Highly Organized." Presented at the meetings of the American Political Science Association, Chicago.

Ward, Katherine. 1984. *Women in the World System.* New York: Praeger.

Warren, Bill. 1973. "Imperialism and Capitalist Industrialization" *New Left Review* (September-October).

_____ 1980. *Imperialism: Pioneer of Capitalism.* London: New Left Books.

Watnick, Morris. 1952. "The Appeal of Communism to Underdeveloped Peoples." Pp. 152-172 in *The Progress of Underdeveloped Areas*, edited by Bert F. Hoselitz. Chicago: University of Chicago Press.

Weir, Margaret and Theda Skocpol. 1985. "State Structures and the Possibilities of 'Keynsian' Responses to the Great Depression in Sweden, Britain, and the United States." Pp. 107-163 in *Bringing the State Back In*, edited by P. Evans, D. Rueschemeyer and T. Skocpol. New York: Cambridge University Press.

Wells, Miriam. 1984. "The Resurgence of Sharecropping." *American Journal of Sociology* 90:1-19.

Wilensky, Harold. 1976. *The "New Corporatism," Centralization, and the Welfare State.* Beverly Hills, CA: Sage.

_____ 1981. "Leftism, Catholism, and Democratic Corporatism: The Role of Political Parties in Recent Welfare State Development." Pp. 345-382 in *The Development of Welfare States in Europe and America*, edited by Peter Flora and Arnold Heidenheimer. New Brunswick, NJ: Transaction Books.

Wolf, Eric R. 1969. *Peasant Wars of the Twentieth Century.* New York: Harper.

Young, Crawford and Thomas Turner. 1985. *The Rise and Decline of the Zairian State.* Madison: University of Wisconsin Press.

Young, Kathleen. 1986. "The Politics of Public Pensions: The Belgian Case in Comparative Perspective." Ph.D. dissertation, Brown University.

Zeitlin, Maurice. 1984. *The Civil Wars in Chile (or The Bourgeois Revolutions That Never Were).* Princeton, NJ: Princeton University Press.

_____ and Richard E. Ratcliff. 1988. *Landlords and Capitalists.* Princeton, NJ: Princeton University Press.

Zolberg, Aristide. 1981. "Origins of the Modern World System: A Missing Link." *World Politics* 33:253-281.

Zysman, John. 1983. *Governments, Markets, and Growth: Financial Systems and the Politics of Industrial Change.* Ithaca, NY: Cornell University Press.

Subject Index

A

Academic attainment 456
Action 53, 83
Active observation
  with social interaction 146–148
  without social interaction 148
Adaptation 110, 336
Administrative research 603
Administrative Science Quarterly 371
Adolescents 276
Adult children 277
Adultery 136
Affirmative action 304
Afghanistan 230
Africa 231, 233, 757
Afrikaanerdom 234
Afro–Americans 235
Age 243 ff.
  adolescents–parents relationships 276
  and family change 279–280
  and politics 274 ff.
  and the family 276 ff.
  as a process 243–244
  attitudes 274
  chronological 248
  conflict 275–276
  criteria 251
  division of labor 427–428
  elderly parents 277
  imbalance 280
  inequality 279 ff.
    by generations 279
  intergenerational relationships 276
  norms 266
  roles 247, 250–251
    and role sequences 251
  social movements and, 274–275
  sociology of 243
  strata 246 ff.
  stratification 244 ff.
    in work organizations 273–274
      age structure of 273

and seniority 273
and job satisfaction 273
organizational roles 273
  structure 268 ff.
    and old people 268, 272
    and social change 279
    and work 270 ff.
    change 270–271
    characteristics 268 ff.
    family life 273
    of people 269–270
    of roles 268
    participation 272–273
  transitions 254–255
  voting and, 274–275
Agenda setting 336, 610
Agentic orientation 309
Aggregation 118, 133–134
Aging 248 ff, 594
  and continuities 252
  and role sequences 250
  and role transition 252
  and status attainment 250
  and the social structure 244–245, 252–253
  asynchrony of, 245
Agriculture 182, 183 ff.
Alienation 394, 706
Alimony 305
America 89, 403, 410, 742
  society 412
  workers 182
American Association of University Professors 292
American Communist Party 696
American Economic Association 292
American Indian 186
American Journal of Sociology 363
American Medical Association 412, 592
American Sociological Association 13, 575, 581, 614, 670
American Telephone and Telegraph 301
Amish 481, 499
Amoskeag Mills 202
Amplification 57

Amsterdam   657
Anabaptism   479
Annexation   230
Anti-Semitism   233
Apprenticeship   179
Aristocracy   114
Armenianism   479
Artifacts   51–52
Artisans   182
Asia   231, 233, 755
Assimilation   234 ff.
Asynchrony   245
Atlanta   405
Atlas of Science   540
Attribution error   714
Audiences   141
Australia   753
Austria   412, 755
Authoritarianism   705
Authority   114, 121, 401–408
Authority relations   744
Automation   210 ff.
Automobile manufacturing   184
Axiate growth   631

B

Baby boom   428
Back–door analysis   123
Bargaining   194, 204
Beggar   182
Behavior   32, 37
   collective   695, 696
   sequences   145
Bereavement   483
Berlin   52
Biological analogy   107, 109
Biological decline   249
Biology   155
Biotic processes   632
   criticisms of   632
Blacks   193
Blindness   680–681
Bonus plans   207
Boston Tea Party   709
Boundaries, intergroup   226 ff.
Boundary maintenance   224 ff.
Bourgeoisie   744
Brazil   755
Break in bulk   645
Britain   77, 111, 185, 192, 550, 606, 615
British Sociological Association   575
Brittany   232
Budapest   634
Bureau of Applied Social Research   603
Bureau of the Census   139
Bureaucracy   121
Business Economic Areas   647
Business firms   140

C

Cairo   656
California   192–193, 199, 233, 383, 653
Calvinism   268, 479, 490
Cambria   203
Canada   231, 232, 753
Cape of South Africa   230
Capital   52, 182, 189
   accumulation   746
   fixed   182
   symbolic   68–69
Capitalism   109, 114, 115, 121, 177 ff.
Capitalists   179
Caribbean   231, 753
Catalonia   232
Catholic church   451
Pentacostalism   486
Catholics   427, 499
Causal parameters   163–164
Causality   156–157, 168
Census tract   139
Central cities   643
Central Europe   193, 479, 499
Central place theory   632, 644–645
Centrepital movements   641
Centrifugal movements   641
Ceremonies   493
Chaldeans   233
Chance   157–158
Change, organizational   367–368, 376–383
Chaos theory   169, 170
Chemistry   15
Chicago   577
Chicago School   9, 406, 632, 668, 671
   criticisms of   633
Child care   305
Children   435–441
   adult   277
   and divorce   433, 436
   and marital happiness   436
   and parental economic status   437
   and parental well–being   436
Chile   753, 757
China   231, 695
Chinese   196, 233
Christianity   474, 479
Church   140, 495–496
Circulation of elites   400
Citations   528–530
Cities   138
   central   643
   spatial patterns   644–657
   uneven development   652-657
City systems   643–644
   horizontal specialization   643
   metropolitan dominance   643–644
   vertical specialization   643
Civic culture   112
Civil religion   497–498
   social environment   497–498
   symbolism   497
Civil Rights Act of 1964   304

Civil rights movement 237
Civil society 114
Class and gender 299
  and physician utilization 582, 585
  differences in health 586
  struggle 394
Classification
  ordered 150
  unordered 150
Clerics 182
Coercion 107, 113, 114
Cognitive consistency 706
Cognitive exhaustiveness 27–28
Cognitive liberation 714
Cohort 244 ff.
  analysis 255, 256
  experience 266
    age norms 266
    and structural change 267
    norm-formation 266
  flow 244, 255 ff.
    and aging 256, 261
    and historical changes 261–262
    and longevity 263–264
    and structure 256, 263
    rate 265
    the future of, 267
  size 263 ff.
Collective action 190
Collective attribution 713
Collective behavior 695, 696
Collective effervescence 494
Collectivism 84–85, 90
Collectivities 37–38, 141–142
Colombo 640
Colonialization 230–231, 232
Columbia Broadcasting System 603, 613
Columbia School 602, 605–606
Commission on the Status of Women 291
Common Cause 695, 717
Communal orientation 309
Communes 717
Communication network 715
Communication technologies 722–723
Communicative rationality 117
Communism 396, 515, 744
Communist states 232
Community 138
Comparable worth 304
Comparative education 459, 466
Comparative historical approach 743
  to political economy 746
Concentration 649
Concentric zones 631
Conflict 10, 12, 105, 107, 176
Congress 14, 522
Conquest 230
Conscience 44
Consciousness of women 313–314
Consensus 107, 111, 126, 616 ff.
  in mass media research 616–617
Constructivist studies 553–556
Consumer advocates 412

Consumerism 587
Contest mobility 453
Contextuality 58–59
Contingency theory 373
Continuous product production 184
Continuous wage labor 177
Contraception 257
  and age strata 258
  and Catholic women 257
  and family size 258
Contradiction 395
Control of labor 201 ff.
  by size of workplace 204 ff.
  control hierarchies 204 ff.
Convergence 55
Cooperation 107
Core societies 745
Corporate craft production 177
Corporate pluralist systems 234 ff.
Corporations, multinational 237, 755–756
Counterfactuals 28
Countermovements 721–722, 728
Counterpart age transitions 253
Counties 138
Crackers 197
Craft industries 184
Craft production 184
Crafts 192
Craftsmen 184
Crime 672
  statistics 677
Criminology 12
Crisis 117
  economic 117
  legitimation 117
  rationality 117
  state-administrative 117
Critical school 112, 115, 116
Critical theory of urban growth 638
  differences with mainstream 638–639
  similarities with mainstream 639
Cross pressure 56
Crowds 141
Cultural division of labor 232 ff.
  and colonialization 232
  internal colonial theory 232
  middleman–minority theory 233–234
  split labor–market theory 232–233
Cultural entrepreneurship 614
Cultural studies 601, 619
Culturalism 91, 92
Culture 24, 225, 619–620
  of medicine 589–590
  of poverty 589
  production of 611
Curricula 457–458
Cybernetics 57–58

D

Daily Urban Systems 647
Dallas 619

Damping 57
Death 178, 482
Defense mechanisms 113
Degredation ceremonies 679
Democracy 116
 and development 751–754
Democratic Party 408, 700
Democrats 409, 410
Demographic effects 187
Demography 17, 146
 historical 426
Denominationalism 491–492
Department of Trade 378
Dependency theory 11, 740, 744–748
Deskilling 190 ff., 205, 210 ff., 334
Detroit 233
Development 176, 739 ff.
 and democracy 751–754
  correlated 751–752
  independent 752
  new classes 752
  class alliances 753–754
  civil society 754
 and the state 746–749
Deviance 12, 124, 520–526, 578, 667
 in science 520–526
  from cognitive norms 520–521
  from social norms 521–522
  incidence of 523–524
  social control of, 524–526
   replication 524–525
   codes of scientific conduct 525–526
  sources 522–523
  theories of, 522–523
 in urban sociology 671–673
  and crime 672
  and social disorganization 673
  and the socially marginal 672
  neighborhoods 672
  zonal hypothesis 671
  zone of transition 671
 functional approach 673–674
  and crime 675
  and social stability 674
  deviance as normal 673
  Durkheim's contribution 674
Diagnostic related groups 592
Dialectic 56
Dictionary of Occupational Titles 332, 351
Differentiation 106, 176, 492
Diffusion 743
 of innovation 337
Direct supervision 366
Disciplinary matrix 60–61
Discourse and text analysis 556–557
Discrimination 178, 196
 gender 306–307
Disintegration 58–59
Disinterestedness 515
Divergence 55
Division of labor
 cultural 232 ff.
 sexual 427–428

Divorce 136, 178, 305, 429–433
 age patterns 432
 and age at marriage 430
 and children 433
 and government payments 431
 and home ownership 431
 and investment in children 430
 and marital duration 431
 and market forces 431
 and marriage order 431
 and strains 430
 macrolevel theories of, 429–430
 marital dissolutions 432
 methodological problems, 430
 poverty and, 433
 quantitative evidence of, 430
 racial and ethnic differences in, 431–432
 trends in, 429
Doctor–patient relationship 111, 578
Doctors 191
Doctrine of minimal effects 605
Domestic service 177
Domination 107, 113, 115, 116, 402
Dramaturgy 89, 126
Dual labor market 301
Dualism 112–113
Durkheimian theory of education 451
Dutch East Indies Company 230
Dyadic social relationships 144–145

E

East Asia 753, 756
Eastern Europe 193, 204, 223, 657
Ecology 50–51
Economics 9, 10, 13, 118, 155
Education 428, 450 ff.
 and individual development 451
 and individual improvement 451
 and national identity 451
 and occupational attainment 454–455
 and social control 450–452
  American theories 451
  European theories 451–452
 and social mobility 452–453
 and social status 451–452
 and social stratification 452
 and status attainment 453–454
 comparative 459, 466
 Durkheimian theory 451
 gender equality 303 ff.
 higher 711–712
Educational attainment 455–456
Educational politics 466–467
 interest groups 467
 policy making 467
Educational qualifications for work 330, 332
 and evaluation 331–332
 and inefficiency of employment 331
 and screening 332
 credentialing 331
Educational transformations 187

Ego 112
Egypt 51
Elderly parents 277
Electronic city 649
Elite theorists 400
  and circulation 400
  and concentration 400
  oligarchy 400–401, 409
Elitism 405
Emancipatory approach 415
Embezzlement 205
Emergence 58–59
Empiricism 27, 79
Employers 202 ff.
  organizations 179
Employment 182
  of mothers 437
  statuses 178
Enculture 43
Encyclopedia of the Social Sciences 523
England 231, 498, 499, 744
Entrepreneurship 743
Environmental theorists 363
Epidemiology 256
Equal Employment Opportunities Commission 301
Equal Pay Act of 1963 304
Equality, gender 303 ff.
Equifinality 31–32, 36, 64 ?
Erasmianism 479
Ethnic boundaries 229 ff.
  and value consensus 238
  ideological basis for, 230
  rational basis for, 230
Ethnic groups 141
  formation 224 ff.
Ethnic mobilization 236 ff.
  and industrialization 236
  and institutional networks 237–238
  and mass communication 236–237
  and multinational corporations 237
  and supranational organizations 237
  and the state sector 237
  and urbanization 236
Ethnic movements 236–238
Ethnic politics 237–238
Ethnicity 224
  and affinity 225
  and human nature 225
  and interest 225
Ethnomethodology 11, 87, 89, 90, 122, 125, 126
Eurasia 427
Europe 127, 183, 253, 396, 397, 453, 481, 486, 576, 702, 703, 712, 752
  society 412
  workers 182
Evolution 311–312, 492–493, 743
Exchange theory 87, 90, 118, 126
Expectations 109
Experimentation 158–160
Explanation 38–40, 78
Expressive work 307
External space 309
Extracurricular memberships 463

F

Face-to-face encounters 683–684
Factory Act of 1833 188
False consciousness 116
Family 142, 257, 276 ff., 425 ff.
  and age 276 ff.
  and gender 302
  and residential segregation 640
  and subsistence 427–428
  change 279 280
  cycle 278, 640
  income 433
  policy 304–305
  size 258
  theories of 426
Family and Medical Leave Act 305
Fascism 744
Federal Aviation Authority 612
Feminine mystique 298
Feminism 292 ff., 313–314
Feminist theory 293
Fertility 263 ff.
  decline 428
Feudalism 109, 177
Fifth Republic 700
Firearms 52
First World 744
Fission 55–56
Fixed capital 182
Forced migration 230–231
Ford, Henry 202
Ford Motor Company 202
Formal organizations 140–141
Formalization 366
Frame alignment 713
France 77, 185, 209, 409, 410, 615, 700, 744, 755
Fraud 526
Free rider 494–495, 710
Freedom Summer Projects 708
French Canada 230
Frontier expansion 230–231
Frostbelt 651
Functional exigencies 110
Functionalism 10, 77, 103, 105, 106–111, 190, 194, 291, 582
Fundamentalism 483–484
  forms 483–484
  history 483
  worldview 484
Fusion 55–56, 70

G

Gender 294 ff., 328 ff.
  and evaluation of job content 330
  and family forms 302
  and housework 302
  and perception of work 328–329
  and physician utilization 582
  and social organization 294
  and the life course 310 ff.

and wage differences 185, 198–199
and women's work abilities 330
by class 299
by ethnicity 299
by race 299
cultural variation in, 298–299
discrimination 306–307
   boundary–maintaining processes 307
   by numbers 306–307
   devaluation of women 307
equality 303 ff.
   in education 303
in the workplace 300
in the household 300–301
organization 292 ff.
   in relation to scientific thought 292
   liberal feminist theory of, 293
   radical feminist theory of, 293
   socialist feminist theory of, 293
   traditional Marxist feminist theory of, 293
roles 294
societal variation in, 295 ff.
   and development 297
   societal complexity 295–296
stratification 293 ff., 315, 426
   and status attainment 293
   as determined by gender relations in
      reproduction 294
   as determined by gender relations in
      production 293
   as determined by larger society 293
   horizontal differentiation 294
Generalized belief 714
Generations 256, 273
Genius 544–545
Gentrification 649
Geographical units 139–140
Geopolitics 758
German Sociological Association 575
Germany 77, 536, 744
Goal–attainment 110
Golden Fleece award 14
Goodness–of–fit tests 164
Government 178, 180
Governmental agencies 140
Grand theory 759
Great Britain 232, 408, 453, 459, 466, 577, 585,
   586, 601, 637
Great Depression 183, 253, 267, 310, 452, 602, 631
Great Western Railway 188
Groups
   diagnostic related 592
   interest 412–413
   veto 404
Groups 105

H

Habituation 125
Habitus 68
Handbook of Modern Sociology 9, 10
Health 249, 314, 583–585
   and the life course 262–263
   and women's movement 314

class differences 586
maintenance organizations 592
male–female differences 583–585
management 587–588
   class differences in, 587
   and attitudes 588
   and lifestyle 588–589
Hermeneutics 78–79
Heteroskedasticity 170
Hicks–Marshall laws 201
Hierarchical multinucleation 631–632
Hierarchy fetishism 194
Hillbillies 197
Hill–Burton Act 372
Historical demography 426
Historicist causal imagery 415
Home ownership 430
Homosexuality 314, 435
   and women's movement 314
Horde 108
Horizontal specialization 643
House of Representatives Subcommittees 522
Household composition 178
Households 143, 179, 182, 185, 198
   and gender 300–301
Housework and gender 302
Houston 636
Human capital 191, 301, 330, 340, 455
Human documents 136–138
Human ecology 135
Human physical traces 135–136
Human Relations Area Files 425
Humanities 61
Hutterites 481
Hyderabad 634

I

Id 112
Ideal type 121
Ideological hegemony 608–609
Imperialism 232
Incentive systems 202
Income supports 305
Independence 133
Individualism 85, 112, 485–489
Individuals 143–144, 185
Indivisibility 132–133
Industrial capitalism 177 ff.
Industrial take–off 743
Industrialization 176–177, 236
Industries, craft 184
Inequality 18, 105, 172 ff., 177 ff., 185 ff.,
   195 ff., 207–209, 404, 528, 755
Infant mortality 428
Information city 655
Inner space 309
Innovations 336
   and agenda–setting 336
   and managerial practices 337–338
   and organizational adaptation 336
   and organizational matching 336
   and routinizing 336
   diffusion 337

Instinct 41, 113
Institute for Scientific Information 540
Institutional school 696
Institutionalization 125
Institutions 44, 225
Instrumentalism 84
Integration 58–59, 110, 114
Interaction 53–54, 74
  face-to-face 89
  two-way 56
Interest groups 412–413
  and political mobilization 412
  as lobbies 412
Intergenerational relationships 276
Intergroup boundaries 226 ff.
  learning theory226–227
  psychoanalytic theories 226
Intergroup contact 230 ff.
  annexation 230
  colonization 230–231
  conquest 230
  forced migration 231
  frontier expansion 230–231
  voluntary migration 231
Interlocking directorates 384
Intermittent wage labor 177
Internal conflict theory 232
Internalization 112
International migration 189
International Sociological Association 16
Internationalization of labor 758
Interpretative approach 58
Interurban spatial processes 629–630
Introjection 113
Invasion 641
Invisible colleges 536
Ireland 230, 231, 232, 743
Iron cage 718
Iron law of oligarchy 400–401, 409
Islam 83
Italians 193
Italy 193

J

Jamaica 757
Japan 459, 704, 744, 755
Japanese 197
Japanese-American 186
Jehovah's Witnesses 499
Jews 193
Job molding 338 ff.
  and job evolution 339
  and redesign 339
  as a negotiated process 338
  latitude of, 338
Job satisfaction 273
Jobs 178
Johnstown 203
Journal of Health and Social Behavior 581
Journal of Marriage and the Family 430
Journal of Mass Communication 601
Journal of the American Statistical Association 166
Judaism 474, 479, 483
Judgmental dope 123

K

King Cotton 712
Kinship groups 142–143
Kinship systems 426–427
Korea 233
Ku Klux Klan 704

L

Labeling theory 12, 124–125, 126, 582, 677–685
  critiques of, 582, 685
  and symbolic interactionism 678
Labor
  continuous wage 177
  control of 201 ff.
  force 182, 189
    participation 258 ff., 291, 428
      women's 258, 291, 300
      married women 428
      divorce and, 433
      cross-sectional data 258
      and aging 259
      and age structure 259
    U.S. 184
  intermittent wage 177
  internationalization of 758
  market 178, 191 ff.
    segregation 190
    external 191 ff.
    internal 194 ff.
    segmented 194, 301
    dual 301
  mobility 182
  processes 176–177, 184–185
  returns to 188
Language 137
Large batch producers 374
Late industrializers 744
Latent functions 69
Latent interests 115
Latent variable 155
Lateral pattern-maintenance and tension-
  management 110
Latin America 223, 299, 377, 497, 657, 753, 755
Leadership 710, 715–716
Learning opportunities 464–466
  and learning ability 464–465
  and tracking 465–466
Learning theory 226–227
Lebanese 233
Legitimization 125
Liberal feminist theory 293
Liberal Party 408
Liberal pluralist regimes 234 ff.
Life course 243, 251–252
  and gender 310 ff.
  and health 262–263
  duration 253
  institutionalization of, 268
  length 262
  ordering 253
  outcomes 253–254

timing 253
transitions 262
Life expectancy 583–584
Life sciences 15
Life world 117
Lifelong allocation 255
Lifelong socialization 254
Log normal distribution 645
London 654, 657
Longevity 261–262
Longitudinal analysis 255
Los Angeles 197
Love Canal episode 361
Loyalty 202
Lumpenproletariat 114, 116
Lutheranism 479, 498

M

MacFadden Publications 603
Macro–theory 87–93, 112, 119 ff.
Malaysia 231
Male–female differences 299 ff.
　in aggression 311–312
　in childhood 310–311
　in general orientation 299, 315
　in health 583–585
　in parenting 312
　instrumental–expressive 299
　public–private 300
Male–female interaction 307–308
　informal relations 307
　instrumental–expressive 307
　love and emotion 307–308
Management, health 587–588
Manhattan 577
Manifest functions 69
Manifest groups 115
Manifest interests 115
Manila 634
Manufacturing 181, 183, 184–185
Marginal productivity 194–195
Marginality 672
Marijuana Tax Act 684
Marital happiness 436
Marriage 430
　age 430
　Catholics and non–Catholics 434
Marxian image of state and society 395–397
　critiques of 395–396
　revisionist theories 396–397
Marxism 92
Marxist theory 179
Marxist–functionalism 190, 205
Mass communication 236
　and ethnic mobilization 236–237
　research 601–602
　　American trends 610–613
　　British trends 606–610
　　crisis in 601
　　differences between British and American 613–616
　　new models of 606–610

Mass media 601 ff., 723
Mass migration 712
　blacks 712
　urbanization 712
Mass production 184
Mass society 696
Massachusetts 494
Masters 182
Matching 191
Materialism 113–114, 746
Mathematics 15
Matthew effect 532
Measurement 61, 131, 149
　binary 149
　cardinal 151
　direct 151–152
　indirect 151–152
Medicaid 585, 592, 593
Medical sociology 575–581
　and applied research 576–578
　and public health 577–578
　theory in 595
Medicare 585, 592, 593
Medicine 576 ff.
Melanesia 190
Mental health 249, 585
Mental hospitals 681
Merchants 182
Mesopotamia 630
Metropolitan change 634–635
　by suburban rings 635
　central cities 642
　polycentric urbanization 642
　rural renaissance 635
Metropolitan dominance 643–644
Mexico 757
Mexico City 654, 656
Michigan 409
Michigan Study of Job Demands 346
Micro–dynamics of movements 713–714
　attribution error 714
　cognitive liberation 714
　collective attribution 713
　frame alignment 713
　generalized belief 714
　value expectancy 714
Micro–mobilization contexts 709–710
　communication 710
　existing political groups 709
　free–rider problem 710
　informal groups 710
　reward structure 710
Micro–theory 87–93, 106 ff., 112, 120
Middle East 497
Middleman minority theory 233–234
Midwest 652
Migration 192 ff., 196
　forced 230–231
　international 189
　mass 712
　voluntary 231
Militant society 106–107
Miracle 192–193
Mississippi 233

Mobilization, political 743
Modernity 176
Modernization 236
Modes of observation 145–149
Money 52
Monogamy 428
Monopolies 179
Moral community 476
Moral crusades 684
Moral density 108
Moral economy 479
Moral entrepreneurs 684
Moral obligation 487
Morbidity 584
Morrell Act 12
Mortality 263 ff., 584
Movements
  civil rights 237
  ethnic 236–238
  halfway house 717
  industries 718–719
  in mass higher education 711–712
    experts in, 712
    growth of 711–712
    new class 712
  maintenance 716
  micro–dynamics 713–714
  new social 106, 701–702
  racial 235
Multinational corporations 237, 755–756
Multiple discoveries 542–544
  frequency 543
  reasons for occurrence 545
  their existence 542–543
  types 543–544
Multiple nuclei 631

N

Narcissism 488
Natal 231
National Academy of Sciences 527
National Aeronautics and Space Administration 361
National character 759–760
National Council of Churches 500
National Health Service 587
National identiy 231
National Institute of Mental Health 576, 577
National Institutes of Health 576
National Longitudinal Survey 433
National Science Foundation 14
National Welfare Rights Organization 702
Nations 138
Native Americans 234
Natural history approach 729
Natural system theorists 363
Natural systems theory 363
Nature–nurture 315
Need achievement 743
Negotiation 338
Neighborhoods 672
Neo–corporatism 412
Network analysis 119–120

Networks 191, 193 ff., 203
New criminology 12
New Deal 13
New Haven 405, 406
New social movements 106, 701–702
  and welfare state 701
  and new values 701–702
New structuralism 252
New York 193, 409, 654
New York Times 613
Nicaragua 695
Niches 382–383
Nichiren Shoshu 695, 707
Nobel laureates 527, 530, 545
Non–traditional dyadic relations 434–435
  cohabitation 434–435
  gay relationships 435
  lesbian relationships 435
Norm formation 266
Norms 24, 109, 111
  scientific 514–515
North Africa 223
North America 127, 231, 305, 481
Northeast 652
Norway 294
Nuclear family 425
Nurses 191
Nurture 44–45
Nuts, sluts, and perverts 668

O

Observation active 146–148
  modes of 145–149
  passive 146–148
Observational studies 161
Occident 52
Occupational attainment 454–455
Occupational structure 332–336
  and autonomy 333
  and organizational scale 335
  and pricing of labor 335
  in office work 333–335
  over time 335–336
  profile 332
  skill and ability 333
  titles 332–333
Occupations 178
Offensive and defensive activities 106
Office of Budget and Management 14
Okies 197
Oligarchization 718
Opinion leaders 603
Organism 32, 37, 39, 64
Organization
  ideological conditions of 115
  gender 292 ff.
  political conditions of 115
  social conditions of 115
  technical conditions of 115
Organization for Economic Cooperation and Development 17
Organizational change 367–368, 376–383

adaptation 381
  by chance 367
  by necessity 367
  by population ecology 367
  by purposeful action 367
  by strategic choice 367
  creation rates 378
  dissolutions 381
  environmental conditions of 378
  formation 378
  foundings 377
  inertia 380
  mortality 381–382
  newness 382
  population processes 379–380, 382
  smallness 382
  transformations 379
Organizational diversity 367
Organizational effectiveness 368
Organizational environments 369 ff.
  capacity 370
  concentration of, 370
  coordination of, 370
  cultural components of, 371
  dependence on, 376
  heterogeneity of, 370, 375
  hostility 370
  instability of, 370
  levels of analysis 369–370
  munificence 370, 375
  temporal elements in, 371–372
  threat 370
  turbulence of, 371–372
Organizational fields 383–385
  density in societies 385
  interfirm relationships 384
  interlocking directorates 384
Organizational matching 336
Organizational roles 273
Organizational size 373–374
  and administrative costs 373
  and complexity 373
  and coordination 373
  and standardization 374
Organizational studies 363 ff.
Organizational theories 363 ff.
  natural system theory 363
  rational model 363
Organizational trajectories 718
  iron cage 718
  oligarchization 718
  routinization 718
Organizations 179, 361 ff.
  and collective activities 361
  and coordination 362
  and economic production 361
  and multiple goals 362
  and risk 361
  and technology 374
  and the life–cycle 362
  complexity 366, 373
  definitions of, 362
  formal 140–141
  health maintenance 592

inputs 366
  outputs 366–367
  religious 495–496
  size 363, 373–374
  supranational 237
  throughputs 366
  voluntary 140
Organized skepticism 515
Orient 52
Orientals 197
Overdetermination 81–82, 94
Oxford English Dictionary 104

P

Panel Survey of Income Dynamics 433
Paradigm 79
  of sociology 740–741
Parent Teachers Association 704
Parents 277, 435–441
  marital status 437
    teenage births 437
    and children's psychological well–being 437
  divorce and children 438
  family size 439
  father absence 437
  economic status 438
  of adult children 439–441
Paris 182
Parliamentary democracy 744
Parochialization 1
  in social science 739
Parsonian imagery of state and society 399–400
  system theory 399
  the polity 400
Parties 409–412
Partisanship 409–412
  changes in 410
  psychological roots of, 411–412
  social bases of, 411–412
  voting 410
Passive observation with social interaction 146–148
Path analysis 255
Pattern variables 41–42
Payment by results 202, 206–207
Peasantry 114
Peasants 182
Peer recognition 526–528
Peer review 525
Peers 461
Pennsylvanians for a Biblical Majority 717
People's Temple 695
Performance 177, 178
Periphery 745
Peru 757
Petty bourgeoisie 114
Phenomenology 11, 90, 116 ,120, 126
Philadelphia 198
Physician
  utilization 582
    and attitudes 586
    and ethnic groups 582
    and gender 582

and social class 582, 585
and the poor 585–586
women 590–591
Physics 15
Physiology 42–43
Piecework 206–207
Pietism 498
Plagiarism 522
Plasticity 248–250
and aging 248–249
and biological decline 249
and gender differences 249
and health 249
and mental health 249
Pluralism 231, 405–406
Poland 743
Political action committees 412
Political consciousness 416–417
Political economy 740
world 756–757
comparative historical approach 746
Political entities 138–139
Political imagery 414–416
Political machines 191
Political mobilization 743
Political participation 413–414
dimensions 413
social bases of, 413
psychological bases of, 414
Political parties 408–412
structure of, 408–409
branch 409
cell 409
Political sociology 393 ff.
its rise 393
future 393–394
Politics 274
and age 274 ff.
ethnic 237–238
of education 466–467
Polycentric urbanization 638, 642
Polygyny 428
Polynucleation 648–649
concentration 649
electronic city 649
gentrification 649
information city 649
Popular religion 481–483
informal social context 482
lack of structure 481–482
relation to the unanticipated 482
restricted codes 482
types 481
Population
ecology 111
size 46
Portugal 193
Positivism 10, 11, 15, 78
Post–capitalism 117
Postcolonial systems 236
Post–functionalism 83–84
Post–structuralism 92
Postulate of functional unity 108–109
Poverty and divorce 433

Power 401–408
and domination 402
and inequality 404
and veto groups 404
as arising from position 403–404
concentration of, 404
definition of, 402
in modern society 403
modern crisis in 404
public disenchantment in 405
Prediction 25 26, 39, 38 40, 62, 70
Prejudice 227 ff.
Presuppositions 84–85
Primary deviation 679
Privatism 488
Processes
labor 176–177, 184–185
social movement 723–727
spatial 629 ff.
Production craft 177, 184
mass 184
of culture 611
Productivity 195
Professional autonomy 583, 591–592
and business conglomerates 592–593
and government regulation 592
and self–interest 592
decline in, 591–592
Professional standards review organizations 592
Professions 190
Profit 203
Proletarianization 179, 181, 182, 185–187
Promotion 191, 195
Prostitution 675
Protestants 197, 233, 499
Psychical contagion 45–46, 68
Psychoanalysis 59, 116, 226
Psychology 9, 10, 13
Puberty 311
Public opinion 617–618
Pullman Company 200
Punks 607
Puritanism 485, 490, 498

Q

Quasi–experimental research designs 163
Quasi–groups 115
Quebec 232

R

Race
and divorce 431–432
and gender 299
and physician utilization 582
and residential segregation 634–635
and schooling 457
and wage differences 185
Race and ethnic relations 223 ff., 238–239, 640
descriptive approach to, 223–224
normative approach to, 223

quantitative studies 224
Racial movements 235
Racism 227 ff., 234 ff.
Radical feminist theory 293
Ranking 177 ff., 187 ff.
Rational choice 707, 760
Rational model theory 363
Rationalism 84–90
Rationality 397, 489
  its vagueness 489
Rationalization 742
Rebellion 676
Records 152–154
  first–order derived 152–153
  mixed character 153–154
  primitive 152
  reflective unit 153
  second–order derived 153
  unit 152
  zero–order 152
Recruitment 191
Redistribution 754–755
  and accumulation 755
  and international economy 754–755
  transfer payments 754
Reductionism 53, 96
Regression 113
Regularity 32, 33
Relations 105
Relationship
  doctor–patient 111, 578
  dyadic social 144–145
  intergenerational 276
non–traditional dyadic 434–435
Relative deprivation 696, 706
Relativism 79
Relativist studies 548–553
Religion 473 ff.
  and the state 496–498
  definitions of 473–474
  social environment of, 474–477
Religious individualism 485–489
  and classical thinker 485
  and moral obligation 487
  and religious responsibility 487
  and the market 488
  forms 485
  individuation of the individual 485–486
  lack of reform impulse 486
Religious movements 477–481, 495–496
  and relative deprivation 477–478
  and social resources 478
  and the moral order 478–479
Religious organizations 495–496
  and societal resources 495
  churches and sects 495–496
Religious rationality 489–493
  adaptability 491
  and denominationalism 491–492
  and heterogenous social environment 490
  and markets 491
  and modernity 489
  elaborate codes 490
  internal differentiation 492

its evolution 492–493
Religious symbols 475–476
Remarriage 433–434
  consequences of 434
  data problems 434–435
  rates and trends 434
Renaissance 85
Replacement rates 46
Replication 524–525
Reproductive behavior 314
Republicans 409, 410
Residential segregation 637–640
  by race and ethnicity 640–641
  by socioeconomic status 640
  by stage in family cycle 640
  centrepital movements 641
  centrifugal movements 641
  invasion 638, 641
  succession 638, 641
Residual rules 679
Resource mobilization 697, 714–716
  communication network 715
  leaders 715–716
  members 715
Retreatism 676
Returns to labor 188
Richmond 202
Right to life movement 142
Ritualism 676
Rituals 493–494
  and free–ridership 494–495
  and personal rewards 494
  and uncertainty 493–494
  defined 493
  examples 494
Rock music 611
Rocky Mountains 166
Role 24, 109
  expectations 44
  sick 578–579, 581
  theory 122
  work 338 ff.
Roman Catholicism 479
Rouen 182
Routinization 718
Routinizing 336
Ruling class 395, 403–404
Rural renaissance 635
Russell Sage Foundation 577
Russia 744

S

Sample survey 144
Sao Paolo 654, 656
Saskatchewan 716
Scandinavia 499, 755
Schooling
  and academic attainment 456
  and academic evaluation 463
  and curricula 457–458
  and educational attainment 455 ff.
  and educational resources 456

and educational tracks 456–457
and oppportunities to learn 464–466
and peers 461
and punishments and rewards 460
and race 457
and social labeling 461–462
and status origins 455
and students' tolerance for education 462–464
and teacher effects 457–458
Schools 456
Science 511 ff.
Science and Technology Committee 322
Scientific advancement 519–520
Scientific discovery, theories of 540–547
  constructivist studies 553–556
  discourse and text analysis 556–557
  relativist studies 548–553
  structural studies 541–547
Scientific ethos 514–520
Scientific norms 514–515
  communism 515
  disinterestedness 515
  organized skepticism 515
  universalism 515
Scientific conformity 517–519
Scientific specialties 535–541
  and scientific structure 539–540
  invisible colleges 536
  new specialties 536
  patterns of development 536–538
Scientific stratification 526–532
  concentration of rewards 530–531
  differential rewards 527–530
  peer recognition 526–528
Scientology 479
Scotland 232, 466
Seattle–Denver Negative Income Tax
  Experiments 315
Sect 495–496
Sectarianism 495–496
Secularization 475
Segmental society 108
Self 43–44
Self–fulfilling prophecy 609–610
Seniority 195, 273
Separation 178
Servants 198
Services 183
Sex composition 305 ff.
  in classrooms 305
  in families 306
  in play groups 306
  in the workplace 306
  in volunteer groups 305
Sex differentials 198 ff.
Sex ratio 46
Sex role attitudes 308–310
  about voting 309
  adult 310
  changes in, 310
  evaluation of, 311–312
  public–private 309
Sex roles 310 ff.
  and the life course 310

Sexual division of labor 427–428
Shah of Iran 700
Sick role 578–579, 581
  and deviance 578
  characteristics of, 578
  critiques of 578–579
  doctor–patient relationship 578
Sierra Club 695
Significance tests 163–164
Single–parent families 301
Skill 209–212
Slavery 177
Small batch producers 374
Small Business Administration 378
Smoking 583
Soap operas 614
Social areas 632–633
Social behaviorism 11, 118, 126
Social classes 185 ff., 397
Social control 124, 126, 667–669, 685–688
  and education 450–452
  and restoration of order 668
  and social consensus 667
  and social pathology 668
  decline of the concept 668
  general theory of, 686
  nuts, sluts and perverts 668
  relations to state, economy and ideology 687
Social facts 10, 33, 677
Social metabolism 256
Social movement organization 716–719
  associations 717
  bureaus 717
  collectives 717
  communes 717
  professional forms 717
  troops 717
Social movement processes 723–727
  goals and strategies 727–727
  maintenance of ideology 723–724
  member commitment 726
  resource maintenance 725–726
Social movements 274, 275, 695 ff.
  and age 274–275
  and social change 727–728
  and the state 719–721
  as political process 699
  emergence of 697
  micro explanations 704–709
    alienation 706
    authoritarianism 705
    individual recruitment 705
    individual motivation 705
    political attitudes 706
    cognitive consistency 706
    relative deprivation 706
    suddenly–imposed grievances 706
    biographical availability 708
    membership in organizations 708
    history of prior activism 708
    prior contact with movement member 707
  macro explanations 699–704
    regime crisis 699
    political opportunities 699

ecological concentration 702
economic prosperity 702
contested political arenas 700
absence of cross–cutting solidarities 704
level of prior organization 703–704
absence of repression 701
types 695
Social organization 33
Social phenomenon 24, 31–32, 66–67
macro 37, 66, 77
meso 37, 66
micro 37, 66, 77
Social philosophy 9
Social problems 9
Social psychology 17
Social relations of production 109
Social Science Research Council 17
Social structure 276
Social systems 65
Social theory 62, 85
Socialist C. C. F. Party 716
Socialist feminist theory 293
Socialization 112, 126, 254
Society
mass 696
militant 106–107
Sociobiology 42, 67
Socioeconomic groups 141
Sociological ideology 10
Sociological theory 77, 103
Sociologists for Women in Society 292
Sociology 9
American 78
as a natural science 23, 24, 28, 30, 79
as a science 13, 14, 59–60
as administration 117
as discourse 78–80, 94–95
as explanation 78–80
Durkheimian vision of 10
economic 16, 17
European 13
in medicine 581–583
international 15–17
national 15–17
North American 16
of age stratification 12
of art and literature 17
of development 739 ff.
of deviance 89, 667–669
of education 11, 449 ff.
of emotion 307
of environment 12
of family 425–426
of gender 11, 12, 291, 293 ff.
of knowledge 15
of law 17
of leisure 12
of medicine 575 ff.
of religion 473
of science 511–514
of work 327, 328
Socialist 16
the state 17
Third World 16

Western European 16
Sorbonne 451
Sorting 177, 187 ff.
South 193, 231, 651, 712
South Africa 234, 710
South Europe 204
South Korea 753
Southern Africa 223, 230, 231, 237
Southern Baptist Convention 500
Southern Christian Leadership Conference 142
Southern Europe 657
Soviet Union 230
Spatial patterns in cities 644–645
break in bulk 645
central place theory 644–645
log–normal distribution 645
Spatial processes 629 ff.
in cities 636–637
suburbanization 636
deconcentration 637
welfare dependency 637
structural unemployment 637
decline in blue-collar jobs 637
concentration of minority groups 637
interurban 629–630
Specialties in science 535–541
Species–being 394
Specification tests 164–165
Split labor market theory 232
Sponsored mobility 453
Sri Lanka 756
Stage of urban development 652–654
disurbanization 652
reurbanization 652
suburbanization 655
urbanization 655
Standard Metropolitan Statistical Areas 139
State 117, 138, 237, 395–399, 496–498
and development 746–749
intervention in markets 749
welfare state economy 749
agrarian class relations 750
extractive industries 750–751
military 750–751
and social movements 719–721
as control agent 719
state strategies 719
repression 719
bureaucratic control 720
surveillance 720
as facilitator 720
state divisions 721
and religion 496–498
and society, Marxian image 395–397
and society, Parsonian imagery 399–400
communist 232
structures 234 ff.
racist systems 234 ff.
assimilationist systems 234 ff.
liberal pluralist regimes 234 ff.
corporate pluralist systems 234 ff.
welfare 499, 701–702, 749
Status 24
and aging 250

and education 453–454
and gender 293
attainment 191, 250, 453–454
groups 397
Stepchildren 436
Stereotypes 226
Stigma 680
Stratification 111
age 244 ff.
and education 452
gender 293 ff., 315, 426
scientific 526–532
Stress 343–344
and emotional states 347
and mental health 334, 347–348, 594
and personality 346
and rewards 346
and sources of support 344
buffering of, 345
chronic sources of, 347
coping strategies 346
objective vs. perceived 344–345
Structural equations 155, 165, 255
Structural studies 541–547
Structural–functionalism 49–50, 109
objections to 111
Structuralism 89, 91
Structuration 92
Structure 83
age 268 ff.
anatomical 103
atomic 103
cultural 35, 46–50, 64
complementary 47–48
plural 48–49
consensus 47–48
ideas of 103
macroscopic 106 ff.
molecular 103
of the universe 103
occupational 332–336
social 17, 23, 35, 46–50, 64, 189, 229
unison 47
exchange 47–48
conflict 48
segregation 48–49
sociometric 104
Students for a Democratic Society 613
Subcultural theory 676–677
Suburban rings 635
Suburbanization 636
Suburbia 631
Succession 638–641
Sunbelt 652–653
migration into, 653
rise of the West and South 653
Superego 112
Superstructure 109, 114
Supervision 184
Supply and demand 190
Supranational organizations 237
Surveillance 202
Sustenance activities 106, 109
Symbolic capital 68–69

Symbolic interactionism 11, 12, 49–50, 87, 89, 121–122, 126, 582,678
Synanon 479
System 107
Systemic causal approach 415
Systems, city 643–644

T

Taiwan 753, 755
Tautology 32
Technology 192, 207 ff., 314, 336–338, 630
and culture 225
and inequality 207–209
and institutions 225
and organizations 374
and skill 209–212
and upgrading 212
and women's movement 314
and work structures 336–338
communication 722–723
indeterminacy of, for work 336
Tenants 182
Tension 56, 70
Theory
central place 632, 644–645
chaos 169, 170
contingency 373
dependency 11, 740, 744–748
elite 400
environmental 363
exchange 87, 90, 118, 126
feminist 293
grand 759
internal conflict 232
labeling 12, 124–125, 126, 582, 677–685
learning 226–227
macro 87–93, 112, 119 ff.
Marxist 179
micro 87–93, 106 ff., 112, 120
middle range 12
natural systems 363
of work 327–328
of family 426
organizational 363 ff.
social control 686
social 62, 85
sociological 77, 103
structural–functionalism 49–50, 109
subcultural 676–677
symbolic interactionism 11, 12, 49–50, 87, 89, 121–122, 126, 582, 678
Third Republic 451
Third World 481, 654, 656, 743, 744, 757
Tokyo 634, 656
Tolerance for education 462–464
and extracurricular memberships 463
and identification with school 463–464
and interpersonal ties 463
in relation to aspiration 462–463
Toronto 193
Total institutions 681–682
Towns 138

Townsend Movement 696
Tracking 456–457
Trade unions 179
Traditional cultures 743
Traditional Marxist feminist theory 293
Trancendental Meditation 717
Transportation 630
Two–step flow of communications 603
  critique of 604

U

Ulster 233
Underdetermination 81–82, 94
Unemployment 188, 253
Uneven development of cities 652–657
  dependency theory 652
  multinational corporations and, 652
United Farm Workers 192
United States 77, 111, 178, 186, 192, 199, 223,
    232, 237, 253,263, 291, 298, 364, 403, 408,
    412, 455, 459, 466, 467, 479, 575.576. 577,
    587, 588, 592, 593, 601, 603, 606, 630, 634,
    637, 704, 744, 753
  Air Force 337
  Bureau of the Census 267
  Commission on Civil Rights 329
  Department of Commerce 371
  Department of Justice 136
  Department of Labor 332
United States Census 139
Units of analysis 104, 135
Units of observation 131 ff.
Universalism 515
Upgrading 212
Urban development 652–654
Urban growth and change 630–631, 638
  and suburbia 631
  and technology 630
  and transportation 630
Urban power 405–408
  and city structure 406
  concentration of, 407
  critique of theories of, 406
  elitist theories of, 405
  mobilizing urban masses 407
  passivity of masses, 408
  pluralist theories of, 405–406
Urban villages 636
Urbanization 236
  and ethnic mobilization 236
Use values 188
Utility
  marginal 118
  maximization of 118

V

Vagabond 182
Validity 147
Value 24, 109, 111
  expectancy 714

proposition 119
  system 111
Value–added 55
Value–subtracted 55
Variables
  external 45–46, 51–52
  internal 40–42
  latent 155
  manipulation of 165–167
Venice 657
Verde 192–193
Verstehen 683
Vertical specialization 643
Veto groups 404
Vintage effects 534–535
Voluntarism 92, 107
Voluntary migration 231
Voluntary organizations 140
Voting 274–275, 410
  sex role attitudes 309

W

Wage differences 185, 195 ff.
  by gender 185, 198–199
  by other categories 185
  by race and ethnic group 185
Wages 182
War on Cancer 537
Washington 335
Watergate 617–618
Weber, Max
  imagery of state and society 397–399
    real and ideal interests 397
    rationality 397
    critiques of 398
  theory of education 451–452
Weimar Germany 233
Welfare state 499, 701–702, 749
West 651
West Africa 233
West Germany 580, 588, 637, 700
Western Europe 223, 305, 576, 577, 637, 657
    704, 753
Wheat Pool 716
White man's burden 231
White trash 197
Women 257–258
Women physicians 590–591
  and sexist attitudes 591
  in teaching and research 591
  increases in, 590–591
Women's Christian Temperance Union 696
Women's movement 313 ff., 711
  and health 314
  and homosexuality 314
  and reproductive behavior 314
  and technology 314
  and women's status 711
  consciousness 313–314
Work 270 ff., 327 ff.
  and age 273–274
  educational qualifications 330, 332

experience   340 ff.
  and expectancy theory   342
  and learning theory   341–342
  stress and coping theory 343–344
role   338 ff.
theoretical approaches to,   327–328
Workers   179 ff.
Workplace   327
  gender in the   300
World political economy   756–757
  and national development   757
World systems of cities   629
World systems theory   11, 232, 740, 744–748
World War I   179
World War II   200, 291, 576, 631, 640, 648, 652, 653, 702, 703, 753
Wurttemberg   498

Y

Young Men's Christian Association   696
Youth ghetto   703
Youth in science   533–535
  myth of   533–534
  vintage age effects   534–535

Z

Zen   479
Zonal hypothesis   671
Zone of transition   671

Name Index

A

ABBOTT, ANDREW 180, 190
ABELES, RONALD P. 253, 281
ABERBACH, JOEL D. 414
ABERLE, DAVID 49, 696, 705
ABRAHAM, KATHERINE 195
ABRAMS, M.H. 86
ABRAMSON, PAUL R. 410
ABU-LUGHOD, JANET L. 633
ACKER, JOAN 293, 329–330
ACOCK, ALAN 438
ADAM, HERBERT 234
ADAMS, JOHN 96
ADAY, LUANN 583
ADLER, EMANUEL 751, 765
ADORNO, THEODOR W. 226, 605, 620, 729
AGASSI, JUDITH B. 240
AGUIRRE, B.E. 431
AKERLOF, GEORGE 202
ALAPURO, RISTO 764
ALBA, RICHARD D. 226, 338
ALBERONI, FRANCESCO 92
ALBRECHT, GARY L. 594
ALBRECHT, JAMES W. 331
ALBRECHT, R. 254
ALBRITTON, ROBERT B. 727
ALDAG, RAMON 372
ALDERFER, CLAYTON P. 341, 342
ALDOUS, JOAN 426
ALDRICH, BRIAN C. 378
ALDRICH, HOWARD 111, 367, 368, 370, 374, 379
   380
ALEXANDER, JEFFREY 59, 67, 71, 78, 83, 84, 89, 90
   91, 93, 94–95, 96, 108, 127, 372, 617
ALEXANDER, K.L. 454, 455, 456, 457, 464
ALFORD, ROBERT R. 236, 408, 411, 413
ALIHAN, MILLA 633
ALINSKY, SAUL 408, 414, 726
ALLARDT, ERIK 764
ALLEN, HARRIS M. 228
ALLEN, MICHAEL PATRICK 404
ALLISON, PAUL D. 518, 530, 534, 561

ALLPORT, GORDON 226, 228
ALMOND, GABRIEL 112, 412, 461
ALONSO, WILLIAM 634
ALTBACH, P.G. 459
ALTHAUSER, ROBERT P. 88
ALTHEIDE, DAVID 620, 621
ALTHUSSER, LOUIS 90, 335, 395, 396, 406, 415,
   417, 607, 608, 620
ALWIN, DUANE F. 309, 439, 456, 462
AMBERT, ANNE-MARIE 436
AMBURGEY, TERRY 372
AMMERMAN, NANCY T. 484, 756
AMSDEN, ALICE 751
AMSTERDAMSKA, OLGA 562
ANDERSEN, KRISTI 410
ANDERSEN, MARGARET L. 293
ANDERSEN, RONALD 583, 585
ANDERSON, B. 686
ANDERSON, GREGORY 333
ANDERSON, J.G. 486
ANDERSON, N. 672
ANDERSON, ODIN W. 583, 585
ANDERSON, PERRY 92, 96, 762
ANDERSON, THEODORE R. 378, 396, 633, 641
ANSPACH, DONALD 440
ANTHONY, DICK 480, 501
ANTOUN, RICHARD 483
APOSTLE, RICHARD A. 486
APTER, DAVID 236
ARBER, SARA 309
ARCHER, MARGARET 91, 96
ARENDT, HANNAH 402, 696
ARGOTE, LINDA 375
ARIES, PHILIPPE 428, 501
ARISTOTLE 156
ARJOMAND, SAID AMIR 502
ARLUKE, ARNOLD 579, 588
ARMINGER, GEHARD 169
ARMSTRONG, WARWICK 658
ARNOVE, R.F. 459
ARONSON, NAOMI 541
ARROW, KENNETH J. 331
ARVEY, RICHARD 330, 351

ASCH, S. E. 47
ASH, ROBERTA 697, 717, 718
ASHBY, W. ROSS 65
ASHENFELTER, ORLEY 194
ASHTONE, NAN MARIE 253, 262
ASTLEY, W. GRAHAM 367, 380
ATCHLEY, ROBERT 439, 440
ATTEWELL, PAUL 212, 213, 333–334, 336
AULT, JAMES M. JR. 484, 494
AUSTER, ELLEN 382
AVOLIO, BRUCE J. 561
AYA, ROD 697

B

BABBAGE, CHARLES 521
BACH, ROBERT 643
BACHEN, CHRISTINE 620
BACHRACH, CHRISTINE 438
BACHRACH, PETER 406
BACHARACH, SAMUEL 372
BACKMAN, ELAINE 435
BACON, R. 754
BAHR, HOWARD M. 501, 524
BAHR, STEPHEN 430
BAILIS, LAURENCE 702
BAIN, R.K. 456
BAINBRIDGE, WILLIAM SIMS 477, 494, 501, 502
BAIROCH, PAUL 183
BAJ, JOHN 429, 434
BAKAN, DAVID 309
BALAZS, ETIENNE 361
BALBUS, ISAAC 721
BALDWIN, WENDY 437
BALES, ROBERT F. 57, 276, 281, 291, 299, 307, 309, 562
BALIBAR, ETIENNE 88, 396, 417
BALL-ROKEACH, SANDRA J. 612, 613, 617, 618
BALTES, PAUL P. 259, 250
BAMFORTH, K.W. 340
BANDURA, ALBERT 348
BANE, MARY JO 278
BANFIELD, EDWARD 406, 742
BANG, FREDERICK 43
BANKS, OLIVE 297
BANTON, MICHAEL 226, 228, 229
BARAN, PAUL 371, 402, 745, 749
BARAN, S. 620
BARATZ, MORTON 406
BARBER, BERNARD 512, 514, 515, 541, 555
BARBER, ELINOR 544, 545
BARBONI, EDWARD J. 539
BARDWICK, JUDITH M. 312
BARKAN, STEVEN E. 718, 721
BARKER, DEBORAH 438
BARKER, EILEEN 501
BARNARD, CHESTER I. 362
BARNES, BARRY 547, 557, 563
BARNES, S.B. 516, 517, 560
BARNES, SAMUEL H. 708
BARNETT, ROSALIND C. 293, 303, 310
BARNETT, TONY 762
BARNETT, VIC 164

BARON, JAMES N. 199–200, 252, 253, 301, 304, 314, 315, 329, 329–330, 335, 385, 621
BARON, REUBEN M. 348
BARR, R. 464
BARRABEE, P. 681
BARRETT, NANCY S. 300
BARRY, KATHLEEN 293
BART, PAULINE 581
BARTH, ERNEST A.T. 238
BARTH, FREDERICK 228
BARTHES, ROLAND 501
BARTOLKE, KLAUS 338–339
BARTON, MARGARET 201
BARUCH, G. 687
BARUCH, GRACE 293, 303, 310
BARZELAY, MICHAEL 750
BASU, SANJIB 758
BATES, ROBERT H. 750, 761, 763
BATESON, GREGORY 612
BATESON, MARY CATHERINE 299
BATSON, C. DANIEL 501
BATY, GORDON B. 384
BAUM, ANDREW S. 381
BAXTER, SANDRA 309
BAYER, ALAN E. 533
BAZERMAN, CHARLES 547, 556, 557
BEALE, CALVIN L. 652
BEARD, DONALD W. 370
BEAVER, DONALD 512
BEAVON, K.S.O. 656
BECHTEL, KENNETH H. JR. 559, 560
BECK, RUBYE 439, 440
BECK, SCOTT 439
BECKER, DAVID 750, 763
BECKER, GARY S. 331, 428, 430, 431, 432, 454
BECKER, HOWARD S. 49, 55, 89, 124–125, 579, 589, 590, 610, 611, 619, 620, 677, 679, 683, 684, 688, 709
BECKFORD, JAMES A. 478, 480, 501
BECKLEY, ROBERT E. 501
BEIRNE, P. 673
BELKNAP, I. 681
BELL, DANIEL 213, 234, 340, 489, 668, 674
BELL, WENDELL 632, 633, 641
BELLAH, ROBERT N. 417, 473, 474, 475, 478, 486, 488, 489, 492, 493, 497, 501, 502
BELLE, DEBORAH 310
BELLER, ANDREA 433, 434
BEM, SANDRA L. 310
BEN-DAVID, JOSEPH 459, 511, 513, 535, 536, 541, 548, 559, 560
BEN-YEHUDA, NACHMAN 494
BENDER, LAURETTA 483
BENDIX, REINHARD 393, 397, 402, 486, 744, 762, 763
BENEDICT, RUTH 299
BENGSTON, VERN L. 276, 438
BENIGER, JAMES R. 362, 490, 501
BENJAMIN, WALTER 620
BENNETT, DOUGLAS 763, 765
BENNETT, JAMES T. 720
BENSON, J. KENNETH 368
BENSON, PETER L. 502
BENSON-BABRI, KAREN 431, 432, 433

BENSTON, MARGARET 293
BERARDO, FELIX 426
BERELSON, BERNARD R. 56, 243, 255, 274, 275, 409, 601
BERENSON, EDWARD 95, 96
BERG, IVAR 331
BERG, MAXINE 182
BERGER, DAVID 611
BERGER, BRIGITTE 281
BERGER, JOSEPH 94, 329
BERGER, PETER L. 38, 42, 44, 55, 57, 66, 70, 125–126, 127, 281, 473, 474, 482
BERGESEN, ALBERT 37, 494, 501
BERGMANN, BARBARA R. 291, 303, 304
BERGQUIST, CHARLES W. 765
BERGUNDER, ANN 371
BERK, SARAH F. 302
BERK, RICHARD 147, 161, 164, 165, 166, 169
BERKANOVIC, EMIL 579, 589
BERKNER, LUTZ I. 278
BERLE, ADOLPH A. JR. 403, 404
BERNARD, JESSIE 291, 292, 299, 300, 301, 305, 314, 670
BERNARDI, BERNARDO 269
BERNERT, CHRISTOPHER 155
BERNSTEIN, BASIL 482, 490
BERRY, BRIAN J.L. 629, 632, 633, 634, 638, 641, 642, 645, 647, 650, 656, 657, 658
BERRY, JEFFREY M. 702
BERRY, MARY FRANCES 305
BERTRAM, H. 588
BEYHMER, CHARLES E. 533
BEZDEK, WILLIAM 307
BIANCHI, SUZANNE M. 300, 302, 303, 305, 309, 538
BIBBY, JOHN F. 410
BIBBY, R. 483
BICKHARD, MARK H. 348
BIDWELL, CHARLES E. 18, 375, 449, 461, 640
BIELBY, WILLIAM T. 155, 199–200, 252, 253, 301, 304, 314, 315, 329, 329–330, 335, 462, 530
BIERSTEKER, TOM 763
BIGGAR, JEANNE C. 653
BIGGART, NICHOLE W. 380, 385
BIGNER, JERRY 435
BILLIG, MICHAEL 225
BILLS, DAVID 331
BINDER, LEONARD 742, 762
BIRCH, D. 378, 382
BITTERMAN, BROOKS 642
BITTNER, EGON 668
BJORN, LARS 764
BLACK, BRUCE L. 362
BLACK, D. 686, 687
BLACK, H.C. 560
BLACKBURN, RICHARD T. 533
BLACKBURN, ROBIN M. 92
BLACKWELL, ELIZABETH 577
BLAKE, JUDITH 439
BLALOCK, ANN B. 157
BLALOCK, HUBERT M. JR. 31, 60–61, 70, 155, 157, 228–229, 260, 642, 646
BLAU, FRANCINE D. 301
BLAU, JUDITH R. 55, 620

BLAU, PETER M. 33, 46, 48, 49, 55, 58, 64, 66, 67, 70, 81, 82, 120, 126, 142, 144–145, 210, 228, 250, 373, 374, 375, 398, 454, 455, 463
BLAU, ZENA SMITH 254
BLAUNER, ROBERT 208, 209, 232, 336, 340
BLECKMAN, ELAINE 437
BLEIER, RUTH 553
BLISSET, MARLAN 517, 518
BLOCK, FRED 747, 762
BLOCK, JEANNE H. 310, 314, 315, 705, 706
BLOOD, MILTON R. 341
BLOOM, B.S. 462
BLOOM, JOAN R. 344
BLOOM, JACK 721
BLOOR, DAVID 513, 548, 549, 559
BLUESTONE, BARRY 186, 637
BLUM, TERRY 81
BLUMBERG, RAE LESSER 37, 43, 293, 295, 298, 306, 315, 427
BLUMER, HERBERT 11, 24, 45, 49, 57, 87, 89, 121–123, 236, 696, 712
BLUMLER, JAY 616, 620
BLUMSTEIN, PHILLIP 302, 435
BOBO, LAWRENCE 224
BODNAR, JOHN 193
BOECKMANN, MARGARET E. 518, 530
BOEKER, WARREN 380
BOGUE, DONALD J. 644
BOHANNAN, PAUL 434
BOHRNSTEDT, GEORGE 155, 164, 169
BOKEMEIER, JANET 426
BOLI-BENNETT, JOHN 449, 486, 761
BOLLARD, ALAN 378
BOLLEN, KENNETH A. 621, 752, 764
BOLOGH, ROSLYN WALLACH 299–300, 311
BOLTON, CHARLES D. 707
BONACICH, EDNA 233, 379
BOND, KATHLEEN 249, 272
BONELLI, REGIS 755
BONNELL, VICTORIA E. 720
BONNER, JOHN TYLER 42
BOOTH, ALAN 431, 432, 433, 436
BOOTH, DAVID 762
BORGATTA, EDGAR F. 643, 669
BORNSCHIER, VOLKER 763, 765
BOSERUP, ESTER 295, 296, 763
BOSK, CHARLES L. 581, 592
BOSSE, R. 253
BOSSERT, S.T. 461
BOSSY, JOHN 501
BOTTOMORE, TOM 400
BOUDON, RAYMOND 90, 453, 466
BOULDING, KENNETH E. 638
BOULDING, ELISE 298
BOURDIEU, PIERRE 15, 31, 32, 43, 46, 47, 48, 49, 53, 68–69, 92, 453, 458, 519, 539, 620, 621
BOURG, CARROLL J. 502
BOWEN, KURT 502
BOWEN, WILLIAM G. 300
BOWLES, SAMUEL 11, 455
BOWMAN, M.J. 454
BOX, GEORGE 163, 169
BOX, STEVEN 518
BOYD, MONICA 435

BOYLE, ROBERT 556
BRADSHAW, YORK 763
BRAITHWAITE, VALERIE 438
BRAND, K.W. 701, 702
BRANNIGAN, AUGUSTIN 544, 546, 563
BRASS, PAUL 235
BRAUDEL, FERNAND 628, 657
BRAUN, RACHEL E. 263
BRAUNGART, RICHARD G. 274, 705
BRAVERMAN, HARRY 11, 191, 205, 209, 211, 213, 333, 334
BREER, PAUL E. 342
BRENNER, ROBERT 748, 763
BRIET, MARTIEN 707
BRIGHT, CHARLES 699
BRIM, ORVILLE G. JR. 249, 253, 254, 341
BRINKERHOFF, DAVID 438
BRINKERHOFF, M. 483
BRINT, STEVEN 712, 725
BRINTON, CRANE 729
BRINTON, M.C. 459
BRITT, DAVID 720
BRITTAIN, JACK 378, 379
BROAD, WILLIAM 520, 523, 525, 559
BRODBECK, MAY 70
BRODERICK, CARLFRED 426
BRODY, ELAINE M. 305, 428, 439, 440
BRONTE, D. LYDIA 270
BROOM, LEONARD 292
BROWN, J. 687
BROWN, JUDITH 294, 313
BROWN, MICHAEL 361
BROWN, ROGER 307
BROWNE, RAY B. 501
BRUCE, STEVEN 478
BRUCE-BRIGGS, B. 712, 725
BRUCKNER, WOLFGANG 501
BRULIN, GORAN 328
BRUMMER, VINCENT 485
BRUNEAU, THOMAS C. 502
BRUNVAND, JAN 501
BRUSCO, SEBASTIANO 765
BRYAN, J.H. 680
BRYK, A.S. 457, 463
BUCHSBAUM, HELEN 438
BUCKLEY, WALTER 365
BUDD, SUSAN 501
BUDGE, IAN 233
BUECHLER, STEVEN M. 313
BULMER, M. 671, 673
BUMPASS, LARRY 257, 433, 434, 438
BUNCE, VALERIE 763
BUNGE, MARIO 157
BUNKER, STEPHEN 763
BURAWOY, MICHAEL 180, 205, 206, 210, 338, 339
BURCH, PHILLIP H. JR. 404
BURGESS, ERNEST W. 254, 280, 425, 631, 632, 633, 641, 656, 669, 670, 671, 686, 696
BURGUIERE, A. 501
BURNHAM, WALTER DEAN 405, 410
BURNS, JAMES MACGREGOR 404
BURNS, THOMAS 621
BURNS, TOM 367, 375
BURR, WESLEY 426

BURRIS, VAL 347
BURT, CYRIL 524
BURT, RON 119–120, 120, 337, 350, 370, 371, 376, 385
BYRNES, JOSEPH F. 501

C

CABLE, SHERRY 722
CACIOPPO, J.T. 706
CAIN, GLEN G. 300, 340
CAIN, LEONARD D. 243, 251, 266, 268
CAIN, MELINDA L. 314
CAIN, PAMELA S. 304, 332
CAIN, VIRGINIA 437
CALDERWOOD, ANN 300
CALDWELL, DAVID F. 344
CALDWELL, JOHN 428
CALHOUN, CRAIG J. 91, 652, 655
CALL, VAUGHAN R.A. 335
CAMBURN, DONALD 309
CAMERON, DAVID 764, 765
CAMERON, KIM S. 381, 383
CAMILLERI, SANTO F. 633, 635
CAMMANN, CORTLANDT 343, 351
CAMPBELL, ANGUS 224, 310, 409
CAMPBELL, BERNARD 42, 51, 69
CAMPBELL, DONALD T. 61, 65, 157, 158–159, 163, 540, 541, 555
CAMPBELL, E.Q. 457, 464
CAMPBELL, KAREN 192
CAMPBELL, RICHARD T. 250, 254, 261
CANCIAN, FRANCESCA M. 298, 308, 310
CANTOR, JOEL 613, 614, 615, 617
CANTOR, MURIEL G. 613, 614, 615, 617, 620, 621
CANTOR, NANCY 348, 349
CAPLAN, ROBERT D. 343, 346
CAPLOW, THEODORE 276, 501, 524
CARD, JOSEFINA 437
CARDELL, MONA 435
CARDEN, MAREN LOCKWOOD 293, 313, 705
CARDOSO, F.H. 745, 747, 763
CAREY, JAMES W. 606
CAREY, J. 671
CARMICHAEL, STOKLEY 48
CARNAP, RUDOLF 27, 28
CARNOY, MARTIN 404
CARO, ROBERT 408, 417
CARROLL, GLENN R. 369, 370, 373, 375, 378, 379, 380, 381, 382, 383, 385
CARROLL, MICHAEL P. 480, 483
CARROLL, STEPHEN J. 364
CASPARI, E. 560
CASPI, AVSHALOM 439
CASTEL, F. 687
CASTEL, R. 687
CASTELLS, MANUEL 406, 407, 408, 414, 629, 633, 636, 637, 639, 647, 651, 655, 658
CASTLES, FRANCIS 764
CAYTON, J. 672
CERULO, KAREN A. 501
CHADWICK, BRUCE A. 501
CHADWICK, W. 524

CHAFE, WILLIAM H.   309
CHAFETZ, JANET SALTZMAN   295, 315
CHALFANT, H. PAUL   501
CHAMBERS, WILLIAM NISBET   408
CHANDLER, ALFRED D.   361, 374, 377, 379
CHANEY, DAVID   615, 616
CHAPLIN, DAVID   198
CHASE-DUNN, CHRISTOPHER   139, 629, 643, 763, 765
CHATELAIN, ABEL   182
CHERLIN, ANDREW   253, 277, 278, 309, 429, 430, 431, 433, 434, 436, 438, 440
CHERNOTSKY, H.   765
CHIBNALL, STEVE   614
CHILD, JOHN   335, 367, 373
CHILMAN, CATHERINE   437
CHIROT, DANIEL   763
CHODOROW, NANCY   311, 314, 315
CHOLDIN, HARVEY M.   640
CHOQUETTE, DIANE   501
CHRISTALLER, WALTER   644
CHUBIN, DARYL E.   518, 530, 535, 559, 560
CICIRELLI, VICTOR   440, 441
CICOUREL, AARON V.   42, 68, 90, 457, 465, 517, 668, 677, 681, 682, 685
CITRIN, JACK   405
CLARK, BURTON R.   364, 449, 459, 467
CLARK, COLIN   634, 645
CLARK, PRISCILLA   619
CLARK, TERRY N.   407
CLARKE, ARTHUR C.   169
CLARKE, J.   685
CLAUS, LISABETH M.   575, 576, 577
CLAUSEN, JOHN   243, 251, 252, 254, 439
CLAUSEN, SUZANNE R.   439
CLAWSON, DAN   192, 205, 206, 210
CLAYTON, RICHARD   426
CLEARY, PAUL D.   585
CLIFFORD, W.B.   651
CLINARD, M.   676
CLIQUET, R.K.   253
CLOGG, CLIFFORD C.   331, 332
CLOWARD, RICHARD A.   402, 404, 413, 414, 676, 727
CLYNES, MANFRED   45–46
COBB, JAMES C.   653
COBERLY, SALLY   272
COCHRAN, WILLIAM G.   161
COCKERHAM, WILLIAM C.   18, 576, 578, 579, 581, 587, 588, 589
COHEN, A.   668, 676
COHEN, BERNARD S.   96, 621
COHEN, D.K.   459
COHEN, ELIZABETH G.   228
COHEN, G.A.   395
COHEN, ISAAC   210
COHEN, J.   457, 464
COHEN, MICHAEL E.   368
COHEN, MORRIS R.   156, 169
COHEN, ROBERT S.   524, 544, 549
COHEN, ROBERTA S.   412
COHEN, STANLEY   621, 686, 687, 688
COHEN, YINON   331
COHN, RICHARD   260

COHN, SAMUEL   188, 211, 333–334
COLE, JONATHAN R.   306–307, 511, 518, 519, 526, 527, 528, 529, 530, 531, 533, 534, 536, 537, 541, 560, 561
COLE, ROBERT   191
COLE, STEPHEN   255, 518, 526, 527, 528, 529, 530, 531, 534, 539, 540, 541, 561, 579, 588
COLEMAN, JAMES S.   58, 69, 67, 89, 90, 141, 271, 276, 281, 337, 364, 365, 378, 409, 449, 454, 457, 463, 620, 761
COLLIER, DAVID   748, 762
COLLIER, RUTH BERINS   748
COLLINGWOOD, CHARLES   79
COLLINS, HARRY M.   90, 511, 513, 525, 546, 547, 548, 549, 550, 557, 558, 559, 563
COLLINS, RANDALL   11–12, 44, 48, 59, 62, 66, 89, 92–93, 180, 188, 190, 191, 331, 397, 535, 536
COLLINS, RICHARD   607, 613, 614, 615
COLLINS, R.   454
COLLINS, SHARON   235
COLOMY, PAUL   90, 93, 96
COMAROFF, JEAN   479
COMBS, J.W. JR.   269, 270, 272, 280
COMISSO, ELLEN   763
COMMONS, JOHN R.   198
COMSTOCK, DONALD E.   374
COMTE, AUGUSTE   24, 25, 32–33, 52, 71, 473, 656
CONATY, JOSEPH   373
CONDON, E.U.   523
CONELL, CAROL   181, 201
CONK, MARGO A.   333
CONNOR, WALKER   235, 237
CONOVER, PAMELA JOHNSTON   305, 711, 718
CONVERSE, PHILIP E.   310, 409, 410
CONWAY, R.K.   158
COOK, JUDITH A.   501
COOK, KAREN S.   384
COOK, M.   454, 455, 456
COOK, STUART W.   228
COOK, THOMAS D.   157, 158–159, 163
COOK, TIMOTHY E.   412
COOKSON, P.W.   463
COOLEY, CHARLES H.   645, 669, 683
COOLEY, THOMAS F.   122, 165
COONEY, ROSEMARY   440
COOPER, JUDITH   438
COOPER, ROBERT   336
CORCORAN, MARY   178, 301
CORNELL, CLAIRE P.   276–277
CORNELL, STEVEN   225, 226
CORNING, P.A.   368
CORRMAN, JOHN M.   279
COSER, LEWIS A.   10–11, 48, 55, 89, 191, 275, 279, 603, 620, 678
COSER, ROSE LAUB   311, 314
COTGROVE, STEPHEN   518
COTT, NANCY F.   298
COTTER, CORNELIUS P.   410
COTTRELL, LEONARD S. JR.   243, 292, 425, 671
COULTER, J.   685
COURINGTON, SHEILA   346
COVERMAN, SHELLEY   306
COWGILL, DONALD O.   269, 270
COZZENS, SUSAN   541, 544, 563

CRAIG, STEPHEN C. 411
CRANE, DIANA 518, 530, 535, 537, 538, 541
CRENSON, MATHEW 406, 408
CRESSEY, DONALD 668, 672
CRITCHER, C. 685
CROUSE, D. 454, 455, 456
CROMPTON, ROSEMARY 334
CROSLAND, MAURICE P. 62
CROW, CHARLES L. 501
CROZIER, MICHEL 334, 338, 339, 402
CRUTCHFIELD, JAMES P 157–158, 169
CRYSTAL, STEPHEN 279
CUDDIHY, JOHN 486
CUMINGS, BRUCE 751, 758
CUMMING, ELAINE 254
CURELARU, M. 68, 95
CURRAN, JAMES 607, 613, 614, 615, 621
CURRY, JANE LEFTWICH 621
CURRY, JOAN R. 621
CURTIS, RUSSELL L. 710, 717
CUSICK, P.A. 459
CUTRIGHT, PHILLIPS 752
CZAJKA, JOHN L. 309

D

D'AQUILI, EUGENE G. 501
D'EMILIO, JOHN 314, 703
D'HOUTAUD, A. 588
DACHLER, H. PETER 338, 339, 351
DAHL, ROBERT A. 393, 403, 404, 405, 406, 407, 412
DAHMAN, DONALD C. 639
DAHRENDORF, RALF 11, 48, 49, 88, 112, 114–115, 402
DALTON, KATHLEEN M. 303, 307
DALTON, MELVILLE 195, 205, 210, 364
DANIELS, ARLENE KAPLAN 305
DANNEFER, DALE 250, 253, 260, 261, 274
DARITY, WILLIAM A. JR. 340
DARNTON, ROBERT 91, 96, 501
DARSEE, JOHN 522, 560
DARWIN, CHARLES 534, 545
DAUBER, ROSALYN 314
DAVIDSON, LAURIE 592
DAVIE, MAURICE R. 633
DAVIES, CELIA 333
DAVIES, JAMES C. 696, 698, 705
DAVIES, MARGERY W. 333, 334
DAVIES, MARK 438
DAVIES, PAUL 62, 157
DAVIS, D.B. 687, 688
DAVIS, DENNIS K. 619, 620
DAVIS, F. 668, 675, 680
DAVIS, FRED 582
DAVIS, J.S. 462
DAVIS, KINGSLEY 46, 50, 69, 190, 191, 204, 264, 269, 270, 277, 280, 429, 668, 674
DAVIS, N.J. 686
DAVIS, NATALIE ZEMON 96, 488
DAVIS-BLAKE, ALISON 329
DAVISON, W. PHILLIPS 621
DAWID, A.P. 166

DAWIS, RENE V. 340
DEAUX, KAY 294, 307, 308, 309, 310, 315
DE BEAUVOIR, SIMONE 295
DEGEEST, A. 702
DEJANVRY, ALAIN 748
DELACROIX, JACQUES 370, 378, 379, 382, 763
DELBECQ, ANDRE L. 373, 374
DELORENZO, THOMAS J. 720
DEMARIES, ALFRED 435
DEMO, D.H. 462
DEMOS, JOHN 270
DENNIS, JACK 411
DENTON, PATRICIA 364, 696
DERBER, CHARLES 339
DERYAGIN, BORIS 521
DESS, GREGORY C. 370
DEUTSCH, KARL 236
DEUTSCHER, IRWIN 729
DEVINEY, STANLEY 270
DEVRIES, D.L. 228
DEWEY, JOHN 450, 453, 672
DEYO, FRED 756, 765
DIAMOND, A.M. 529, 535, 561
DIBBLE, VERNON 671
DIBONA, PAMELA 435
DICKSON, WILLIAM J. 338, 340
DIETRICH, LORRAINE 541
DILL, WILLIAM R. 369, 372
DIMAGGIO, PAUL 91, 337, 350, 377, 384, 462, 611, 614, 619, 621
DIMOND, M.E. 431
DIPRETE, THOMAS A. 333, 334, 335
DIRAC, P.A.M. 533, 561
DITTMAN-KOHLI, FREYA 249
DITTON, JASON 205
DOBBELAERE, KAREL 501
DOBBIN, FRANK R. 329
DOGAN, MATTEI 654, 656
DOHRENWEND, BARBARA SNELL 482, 585
DOHRENWEND, BRUCE P. 482, 585
DOLAN, MICHAEL B. 765
DOLBY, R.G.A. 516, 517, 536
DOLLARD, JOHN 226, 341
DOMHOFF, G. WILLIAM 403, 404, 405, 406, 407, 638
DON-YEHIYA, ELIEZER 502
DONALD, CATHY 351
DONZELOT, J. 687
DORE, RONALD P. 331, 459
DORFMAN, D.D. 524
DORR, AIMEE 620
DOUGLAS, ANN 298
DOUGLAS, J.D. 677
DOUGLAS, J.W.B. 462
DOUGLAS, MARY 53, 91, 123, 473, 482, 487, 501
DOUVAN, ELIZABETH 310
DOVERSPIKE, DENNIS 330
DOWBIGGIN, I. 687
DOWD, JAMES 260, 273
DOWNES, DAVID 673, 675, 680
DOWNEY, GERALDINE 439
DOWNEY, H. KIRCK 372
DOWNS, ANTHONY 384, 412
DOWNTON, JAMES V. JR. 494

DRABEK, THOMAS E. 386
DRAKE, S. 672
DRAPER, N.R. 162
DRAPER, THOMAS 431
DRAZIN, ROBERT 376
DREEBEN, R. 461, 464, 465
DREWETT, ROY 637, 648, 655
DREYFUS, H.L. 686
DUBICK, MICHAEL 375
DUBOS, RENE 576
DUCHIN, FAYE 212
DUNCAN, BEVERLY 224, 311, 640, 643, 644
DUNCAN, GREG J. 176, 253, 301
DUNCAN, OTIS DUDLEY 142, 144–145, 152, 155,
    168, 224, 250, 255, 281, 311, 454, 455, 463,
    466, 640, 643
DUNG, NGUYEN TRI 657
DUNHAM, H. 681
DUNHAM, H. WARREN 577
DUNN, LESLIE 524
DUPEUX, GEORGES 410
DURKHEIM, EMILE 10, 13, 24, 25, 31, 33, 42, 45,
    47, 48, 52, 55,58, 64, 65, 66, 67, 84, 93, 95,
    103, 108, 268, 295, 327, 399, 412, 414, 449,
    450, 453, 461, 463, 473, 478, 485, 486, 488,
    494, 576, 578, 581, 674, 675, 676, 677, 678,
    688, 741, 749
DUSEL, ENRIQUE 502
DUTTON, DIANA B. 581, 585, 587
DUTTON, JEFFREY E. 533, 589
DUVERGER, MAURICE 409, 410
DYE, THOMAS R. 401, 403, 404
DYER, DAVIS 370

E

EASTERLIN, RICHARD A. 189, 261, 264, 265, 294,
    301, 314
EASTON, DAVID 400, 411
EBERSTEIN, ISAAC W. 644, 647
ECKERT, CRAIG M. 702
ECKLAND, BRUCE K. 41, 454, 455, 456
ECKSTROM, R.B. 458
EDELMAN, MURRAY 710, 713, 724, 727
EDER, D. 465
EDGE, DAVID 535, 536, 537, 538, 539, 560
EDMONSTON, BARRY 634, 649
EDWARDS, K.J. 228
EDWARDS, L.P. 729
EDWARDS, RICHARD 184, 190, 194–195, 205, 208,
    213, 214, 334, 335,366
EELLS, K. 454
EGELAND, JANICE E. 633, 641
EHRENBERG, WERNER 157
EHRENREICH, BARBARA 302, 581, 591
EINSTEIN, ALBERT 61, 293
EISENGER, PETER K. 697, 699
EISENSTADT, S.N. 59, 63, 64, 68, 91, 92, 95, 96,
    236, 243, 255, 268, 478, 762
EISENSTEIN, HESTER 299
EKEH, PETER K. 84, 90
EKERDT, D.J. 254
EKLAND-OLSON, SHELDON 707, 708, 730

ELAZAR, DANIEL J. 502
ELDER, GLENN H. JR. 243, 249, 253, 262, 281,
    310, 426, 431, 438, 439
ELDERSVELD, SAMUEL 409
ELINSON, JACK 586
ELKANA, YEHUDA 563
ELLIOTT, PHILIP 609, 610, 613, 614, 620
ELLWOOD, CHARLES 10
ELSHTAIN, JEAN BETHKE 300
ELSTER, JAN 92
ELSTER, JOHN 761
ELTIS, W. 754
EMBER, CAROL R. 311, 312
EMERY, F.E. 371
EMMANUEL, ARGHIRI 762
ENGELS, FRIEDRICH 24, 31, 32, 42, 44–45, 47, 48,
    52, 56, 58, 59, 66, 114, 292, 394, 395, 743
ENGELSING, ROLF 198
ENGERMAN, STANLEY 432
ENGLAND, PAULA 201
ENGLISH, DEIDRE 581, 592
ENZANSBERGER, HANS MAGNUS 607, 609, 621
EPSTEIN, CYNTHIA FUCHS 301
EPSTEIN, LEON 417
ERIKSON, ERIK H. 309, 310
ERIKSON, KAI 668, 678
ESCARPIT, ROBERT 621
ESPENSHADE, THOMAS J. 263, 432, 433, 437
ESPING-ANDERSON, GOSTA 763, 764
ESPOSITO, JOHN L. 502
ESTERSON, A. 677
ESTES, CARROLL 252, 280
ESTLER, SUZANNE, E. 339
ETAUGH, CLAIRE 438
ETKIN, WILLIAM 42
ETZIONI, AMITAI 333, 367
ETZKOWITZ, HENRY 520
EVAN, WILLIAM 256, 369, 384
EVANS, A. 637
EVANS, J.W. 588
EVANS, PETER B. 18, 126, 747, 750, 751, 755, 763,
    765
EVANS, SARAH, 710
EVERSLEY, D. 637
EWEN, STUART 616, 617, 621
EYERMAN, RON 92

F

FABER, HOMO 365
FAGEN, R.E. 56
FAGERLIND, I. 453, 466
FALETTO, E. 745, 747, 763
FALLERS, LLOYD 235
FALLOWS, JAMES 211
FANON, FRANTZ 48
FARBER, BERNARD 425
FARGE, ARLETTE 182
FARIS, ELLSWORTH 449
FARIS, ROBERT E. LEE 9, 292, 577
FARLEY, REYNOLDS 185, 195, 640, 641, 642
FARKAS, GEORGE 201
FARR, JAMES L. 330

FARRAR, E. 459
FAULKNER, ROBERT R. 191, 620
FEAGIN, JOE R. 407, 408, 638, 645
FEATHERMAN, DAVID L. 244, 246, 247, 249, 250, 262, 281, 310, 333, 454, 455, 456
FEDER, NED 522, 525, 560
FEDIGAN, LINDA MARIE 312
FEI, JOHN C.H. 755
FEIERABAND, IVO 696, 705
FEIERABAND, ROSALIND 696, 705
FEINBERG, STEPHEN E. 164
FELDBERG, ROSLYN 306
FELDMAN, DONALD C. 339
FELDMAN, JACOB J. 262, 586
FELMLEE, DIANE 532
FENNELL, MARY L. 329, 375
FENSTERMAKER, SARAH 155
FERBER, MARIANNE A. 306
FERGUSON, ADAM 112, 113, 114
FERGUSON, MARJORIE 621
FERGUSSON, D.M. 431
FERNANDEZ, ROBERTO 707
FERNANDEZ-KELLY, MARIA PATRICIA 298, 765
FERRAROTTI, FRANCO 112
FERREE, MYRA MARX 267, 313, 713
FESTINGER, LEON 341, 342
FETZER, JAMES H. 157
FEUER, LEWIS, S. 276, 705
FIALA, ROBERT 755
FIELD, G. LOWELL 400, 401
FIELD, MARK 588
FIENBERG, STEPHEN E. 260
FIGERT, ANNE E. 524
FINE, GARY ALAN 350, 368
FINE, JOHN 640
FINEGAN, T. ALDRICH 300
FINGARETTE, HERBERT 489
FINKEL, STEVEN E. 414
FINLAY, WILLIAM 335
FINN, STEPHEN 435
FIREMAN, BRUCE 707, 710, 713
FIREY, WALTER 633
FIRTH, RAYMOND 481
FISCHER, CLAUDE S. 345
FISCHER, MICHAEL M.J. 502
FISHER, CHARLES 562
FISHER, R.A. 524, 551
FISHER, SUE 581
FISHMAN, MARK 611, 612, 614
FISHMAN, PAMELA 306
FITZPATRICK, RAY 594
FLACKS, RICHARD 706, 712
FLECK, LUDWIK 548, 549, 563
FLEISHMAN, EDWIN A. 351
FLEMING, GRETCHEN V. 583
FLERON, FREDERIC JR. 411
FLETCHER, GARTH J.O. 330
FLIGSTEIN, NEIL 381
FLOGE, LILIANE 437
FLOUD, J.E. 453
FODOR, NANDOR 68
FOLBRE, NANCY 198
FOLKMAN, SUSAN 344
FONER, ANNE 18, 244, 247, 248, 249, 254, 255, 256, 258, 266, 269, 270, 271, 272, 273, 274, 275, 276, 277, 279, 280
FONER, NANCY 273
FORD, HENRY 189
FORD, REBECCA 307
FORD, THOMAS W. 307
FORM, WILLIAM 328, 333–334
FORMAN, PAUL 551
FORRESTER, JAY W. 656
FORTES, MEYER 268
FORTIN, NINA 619, 620
FORTMANN, LOUISE 298
FOSTER, JOHN 703
FOSTER, MICHAEL 336
FOUCAULT, MICHEL 80, 92, 168, 417, 485, 486, 686, 687
FOX, GREER LITTON 426, 437
FOX, JOHN 163
FOX, KAREN F. 703
FOX, MARY FRANK 303, 530
FOX, RENEE C. 575, 581, 583, 594
FOX, RICHARD 687
FOXLEY, ALEJANDRO 750
FRAKER, THOMAS 165
FRANK, ANDRE GUNDER 745, 762
FRANKEL, HENRY 550, 552
FRANKLIN, ALLAN 524, 525
FRANKLIN, CLYDE 313
FRANKS, FELIX 521
FRANZ, MICHAEL 765
FREDERICKSON, GEORGE M. 228
FREED, DORIS JONAS 433
FREEDMAN, ANNE 365
FREEDMAN, DAVID A. 155, 164
FREEDMAN, RONALD 295
FREEMAN, JO 703, 708, 711, 715, 727
FREEMAN, JOHN 111, 362, 364, 367, 368, 369, 370, 372, 373, 377, 380, 381, 382, 383, 492
FREEMAN, RICHARD 210
FREIDKIN, NOAH 18
FREIDSON, ELIOT 333, 579, 581, 582, 583, 587, 592, 594, 612
FREIFELD, MARY 210
FRENCH, JOHN R.P., JR. 343, 346
FRENCKEL-BRENSWICK, ELSE 705
FREUD, SIGMUND 24, 41, 43, 44, 52, 59, 68, 70, 86, 103, 112, 113, 118, 545, 578, 607, 729
FREY, WILLIAM H. 643
FRIED, ELLEN SHAPIRO 439
FRIEDAN, BETTY 293, 299
FRIEDBERG, ERHARD 339, 402
FRIEDERICHS, JURGEN 637
FRIEDL, ERNESTINE 296, 426, 427, 428
FRIEDLAND, ROGER 386, 413, 763, 765
FRIEDMAN, DEBRA 707
FRIEDMAN, GERALD 180, 181
FRIEDMAN, MILTON 204
FRIEDMAN, NORMAN L. 501
FRIEDMANN, HARRIET 183
FRIEDRICHS, ROBERT W. 29, 89, 94
FRISBIE, W. PARKER 18, 432, 638, 640, 643, 644, 647, 650
FRITH, SIMON 611, 613
FROBEL, FOLKER 765

FROMBY, THOMAS B. 165
FUGUITT, GLENN V. 648, 650, 651, 652
FULBROOK, MARY 498, 763
FURSTENBERG, FRANK F. JR. 249, 253, 262, 277, 303, 429, 433, 434, 438, 440
FURTADO, CELSO 763
FYE, W. BRUCE 535

G

GAGER, JOHN G. 480, 492
GAIL, M.H. 170
GALASKIEWICZ, JOSEPH 369, 371, 383, 384, 385
GALBRAITH, JOHN KENNETH 213, 404
GALE, RICHARD P. 700, 720, 721
GALLAGER, ERIC 502
GALLAGHER, EUGENE B. 579
GALLE, OMER R. 644, 647
GALLIE, DUNCAN 208, 209
GALLIGAN, RICHARD 430
GALLUP, GEORGE JR. 501
GAMORAN, A. 457, 465
GAMSON, TED 237
GAMSON, WILLIAM 409, 414, 619, 620, 697, 707, 708, 710, 711, 713, 717, 720, 724, 727
GANGULY, POM 378
GANS, HERBERT J. 59, 601, 605, 611, 612, 620, 621, 723
GARDEN, MAURICE 428
GARDNER, GILBERT 587, 589
GARFIELD, EUGENE 540, 560
GARFINKEL, HAROLD 11, 42, 43, 68, 87–88, 90, 122–123, 548, 564, 675, 679
GARLAND, D. 687
GARNER, ROBERTA 724
GARNHAM, NICHOLAS 602, 606, 607, 608, 609, 613, 614, 615, 616, 620, 621
GARNIER, MAURICE A. 458
GARNSEY, ELIZABETH 332
GARRETT, GEOFF 764, 765
GARRISON, HOWARD 429
GARROW, DAVID J. 721
GARSON, BARBARA 338
GASTON, JERRY 517, 518, 520, 523, 528, 529, 543, 559, 561
GAUDET, HAZEL 243, 255, 274
GAUNT, DAVID 253
GAY, DAVID A. 261
GAYNOR, FRANK 68
GEERTZ, CLIFFORD 65, 91, 96, 473, 474, 491, 501
GEHRIG, GAIL 502
GEIS, GILBERT 362
GELLER, D. 765
GELLES, RICHARD J. 276–277, 426
GENOVESE, EUGENE D. 501
GERAETS, THOMAS 489
GERARD, LEONORE E. 252
GERBNER, GEORGE 601, 620
GEREFFI, GARY 757, 763, 765
GERHARDT, UTA 578
GERLACH, LUTHER P. 478, 707, 715, 717
GERMANI, GINO 762

GERSCHENKRON, ALEXANDER 743, 744, 749, 762, 763, 765
GERSON, KATHLEEN 298
GERSTEIN, DEAN 66
GERTH, HANS 275, 696
GERWITZ, JACOB L. 342
GESCHWENDER, JAMES 696, 705
GETTYS, WARNER E. 633
GEWEKE, JOHN 167
GIBBS, JACK P. 62, 684
GIBSON, JAMES L. 348, 410
GIDDENS, ANTHONY 15, 26, 29, 32, 43, 56, 62, 63, 65, 69, 80, 89, 92, 93, 95, 96, 274, 295, 328, 350
GIDDINGS, FRANKLIN 602, 620, 673
GIELE, JANET Z. 18, 281, 295, 296, 297, 298, 299, 300, 304, 310, 313
GIERYN, THOMAS F. 534, 535, 562, 563
GIESEN, BERNHARD 38, 67, 93, 95
GILBERT, G. NIGEL 525, 537, 547, 557, 558, 559
GILFILLAN, S.C. 511
GILIOMEE, HERMANN 234
GILLIGAN, CAROL 311, 314
GILMORE, SAMUEL L. 620
GINGERICH, OWEN 524
GINGRAS, YVES 552
GINSBERG, CARLO 96
GINTIS, HERBERT 11, 455
GIRVAN, NORMAN 762
GITLIN, TODD 603, 608, 609, 611, 612, 613, 614, 617, 619, 620, 621, 723
GLADSTONE, JOSEPH 408
GLASER, BARNEY G. 253, 254, 582
GLASS, DAVID C. 62
GLAZER, NATHAN 729
GLAZER-MALVIN, NONA 302
GLENN, EVELYN 299, 306
GLENN, NORVAL D. 249, 254, 274, 410, 436, 438, 634
GLICK, PAUL C. 250, 254, 267, 278, 314, 429, 434
GLICK, WILLIAM 351
GLOCK, CHARLES Y. 474, 477, 484, 501, 523, 705
GLYMOUR, CLARK 154, 167
GODELIER, MAURICE 88
GOEL, M.L. 408, 413
GOETHALS, GREGOR T. 501
GOFFMAN, ERVING 41, 43, 49, 55, 87, 89, 124–125, 126, 307, 535, 579, 582, 612, 677, 679, 680, 681, 684, 685, 688, 725
GOLD, DAVID 396
GOLD, M. 677
GOLD, MARGARET 581
GOLD, TOM 751, 755, 763
GOLDEN, HILDA H. 656
GOLDIN, CLAUDE 206
GOLDMAN, NOREEN 434
GOLDSTONE, JACK 749
GOLDTHORPE, JOHN 89
GOODALL, JANE 32
GOODE, WILLIAM J. 44, 90, 296, 297, 425
GOODMAN, LEO 281
GOODY, JACK 426, 427, 428
GORDON, C.W. 449

GORDON, DAVID 633, 638
GORDON, DAVID M. 190, 213, 214
GORDON, GERALD 579
GORDON, LAURA KRAMER 592
GORDON, LINDA 314
GORDON, MARGARET T. 621
GORDON, MILTON 225, 232
GORELICK, SHERRY 620
GORSUCH, RICHARD L. 501
GOSLIN, DAVID A. 255
GOSNELL, HAROLD F. 148
GOTTDIENER, MARK 629, 632, 633, 638, 639, 640,
    642, 645, 649
GOTTFREDSON, MICHAEL 261
GOUGH, IAN 747
GOULD, MEREDITH 305, 312
GOULD, ROGER L. 310
GOULD, STEPHEN JAY 563
GOULDNER, ALVIN W. 48, 50, 53, 91, 364, 576,
    577, 608, 677, 682, 683, 688, 712, 724
GOUREVITCH, PETER A. 757, 762
GOVE, WALTER R. 312, 582, 584, 585, 684
GRABER, DORIS 619
GRAEBNER, WILLIAM 270
GRAEN, GEORGE 338
GRAHAM, JOHN 433, 434
GRAHAM, LOREN 519, 535
GRAMS, ROBERT 330, 378
GRAMSCI, ANTONIO 112, 396, 402, 608
GRANFORS, MARK 382
GRANGER, CLIVE 167, 168, 170
GRANOVETTER, MARK 18, 119–120, 182, 191, 192,
    194, 204, 205, 335, 365, 386
GRANT, LINDA 291, 292, 315
GRASMUCH, SHERRI 412
GRAY, AILSA 364
GRAY, VIRGINIA 305, 711
GREBLER, LEO 641
GREELEY, ANDREW M. 224, 501
GREEN, BERT F. 323
GREENBERG, D. 685, 687
GREENBERG, DAVID F. 261
GREENBERG, ELLEN 431, 438
GREENBERG, STANLEY 763
GREENE, PENELOPE 560
GREENE, WILLIAM 430
GREENSPAN, R. 686
GREENSTEIN, FRED 411
GREER, BLANCHE 590
GRIECO, JOSEPH 763
GRIFFIN, L.J. 454, 455, 456
GRIFFITH, BELVER C. 535, 537, 538
GRIFFITH, JANET D. 278, 434
GRIMES, MICHAEL 274
GRIMES, RONALD L. 501
GRISWOLD, WENDY 620
GROENEVELD, LYLE 305, 431
GROSS, LARRY 620
GROSS, N. 449
GRUBE, JOEL W. 612, 617
GUEST, AVERY M. 640, 641
GUILLEMIN, ROGER 564
GULLICKSON, GAY L. 182
GUREVITCH, MICHAEL 621

GURIN, PATRICIA 341
GURNEY, J.N. 696, 705, 729
GURR, TED 696, 705
GUSFIELD, JOSEPH R. 275, 313, 696, 727, 729
GUTEN, SHARON 587, 592
GUTERBOCK, THOMAS M. 634, 649
GUTERMAN, N. 729
GUTMAN, DAVID 310
GUTTENTAG, MARCIA 46
GUZMAN, RALPH C. 641

H

HAAGEN, P. 687
HAAN, N. 705
HAAS, J. EUGENE 367
HAAVIO-MANNILA, ELINA 297, 299
HABERMAS, JURGEN 11, 15, 79, 80, 92, 93, 94, 95,
    115, 116–117, 398, 400, 401, 402, 405, 415,
    488, 489, 492, 493, 620, 700
HACKENBERG, R.A. 656
HACKER, SALLY L. 301
HACKMAN, J. RICHARD 341, 351
HADDEN, JEFFREY K. 495, 501, 502, 643, 723
HADLEY, CHARLES D. 410
HAGAN, J. 684, 686
HAGESTAD, GUNHILD O. 250, 253, 260, 262, 266,
    276, 277, 432, 440
HAGGERTY, L.J. 633
HAGGSTROM, GUS 430, 433, 436
HAGSTROM, WARREN 514, 518, 520, 523, 526,
    530, 532, 537, 543, 559
HAHN, HARLAN 408
HAIGNERE, LOIS 330
HAINES, HERBERT H. 718
HAINES, VALERIN A. 635
HAJNAL, JOHN 427
HALBERSTAM, DAVID 404
HALL 92, 96
HALL, A.D. 56
HALL, DAVID E. 533
HALL, DONALD R. 412
HALL, PETER 629, 637, 648, 655
HALL, RICHARD H. 366, 367
HALL, ROBERT 191
HALL, ROBERTA 307
HALL, S. 685
HALL, STUART 608, 613, 620
HALLE, DAVID 208–209, 211, 212
HALLIDAY, TERRENCE 382
HALLINAN, M. 464, 465, 467
HALLOREN, JAMES D. 609, 613, 617
HALSEY, A.H. 453
HAMILTON, CHARLES V. 48
HAMILTON, MYKOL 435
HAMILTON, NORA 747
HAMMERSLOUGH, CHARLES 434
HAMMOND, JUDITH 591
HAMMOND, PHILLIP E. 484, 501, 502
HAMPE, GARY 440
HAMPTON, ROBERT 431, 432
HANADA, MITSUYO 385

HANCOCK, KELLY 719
HANDEL J. 90
HANDL, JOHANN 262
HANDLER, JOEL 721
HANDLER, PHILIP 522
HANNAN, MICHAEL 111, 281, 305, 364, 367, 368,
    369, 370, 372, 373, 377, 379, 380, 381, 382,
    383, 431, 492
HANSON, SANDRA 438
HANUSHEK, ERIC A. 169
HARDING, SANDRA 292
HARDING, SUSAN 699
HAREVEN, TAMARA 202, 260, 262, 278, 426
HARGENS, LOWELL 530, 532, 539, 561
HARMON, L.R. 535
HARPER, DAVID 378
HARRE, R. 227
HARRIS, A.R. 683
HARRIS, CHAUNCEY 631, 632, 637
HARRIS, DANIEL M. 587, 592
HARRIS, J. 194
HARRIS, MARVIN 620
HARRISON, BENNETT 186
HARRY, JOSEPH 435
HART, HORNELL 55
HARTMANN, HEIDI 11, 199, 304, 329
HARVEY, A.C. 163–164, 170
HARVEY, BILL 549
HARVEY, DAVID 406, 407, 638, 658
HARVEY, EDWARD 336
HATT, PAUL 633
HAUG, MARIE 589
HAUSER, PHILIP M. 280
HAUSER, ROBERT M. 250, 333, 439, 454, 455, 456,
    464
HAVIGHURST, R.J. 254, 454
HAWLEY, AMOS 50, 365, 382, 407, 630, 631, 632,
    633, 634, 638, 641, 643, 644, 645, 651, 652,
    646, 647
HAY, D. 687, 688
HAYS, DENNIS 637, 648
HEADEY, BRUCE 764
HEARNSHAW, L.S. 524
HEARST, NORMAN 169
HEATON, TIM B. 648, 651, 652
HEBDIGE, DICK 607
HEBERLE, RUDOLPH 719
HECHT, PAMELA K. 532, 539
HECHTER, MICHAEL 229, 230, 232, 237
HEDBERG, BO 350
HEDGES, LARRY V. 163
HEDIGER, HEINZ P. 42
HEER, DAVID 439
HEGEL, G.W.F. 57, 86, 394, 395, 396
HEGLAND, MARY 483
HEIDENHEIMER, ARNOLD 464
HEINRICH, JURGEN 765
HEINZ, DONALD 480
HEIRICH, MAX 707
HEISENBERG 62, 157
HELLRIEGEL, DON 372
HELMREICH, ROBERT L. 294, 307, 308, 309, 310,
    315, 533
HELSING, 253

HEMPEL, CARL G. 38, 64, 66
HENLEY, NANCY 305, 307, 314
HENRETTA, JOHN C. 249, 250, 253
HENRY, WILLIAM F. 254
HERACLITUS 69
HERMASSI, ELBAKI 658
HERNANDEZ, DONALD 433
HERRICK, NEAL Q. 340
HERRING, CEDRIC 729
HERRING, RONALD 756, 765
HERSHBERG, THEODORE 262
HERTZ, ROSANNA 298, 303, 306
HERZBERG, FREDERICK 341
HESS, BETH B. 262, 267, 277, 279, 313, 439, 440
HESS, ROBERT 411, 412
HESSE, MARY 548, 550
HESSE-BIBER, SHARLENE 303
HEWITT, CHRISTOPHER 764
HEWITT, J. 683
HEWLETT, SYLVIA 298, 304, 755
HEYL, B. 680
HEYNS, BARBARA 457, 465
HIBBS, DOUGLAS 763
HICKS, ALEXANDER 755, 763, 764
HICKS, J.R. 201
HICKSON, DAVID J. 336, 367, 371, 373, 374
HIGLEY, JOHN 400, 401
HILKE, JOHN C. 494
HILL, CHARLES 435
HILL, G.D. 683
HILL, MARTHA S. 178, 431, 436
HILL, R. CATER 165
HILL, REUBEN 276, 426
HILL, RICHARD C. 658
HILLER, DANA 429
HILTON, T.L. 459
HIMMELSTEIN, JEROME 720
HIMMELSTRAND, ULF 328, 763, 764
HIMMELWEIT, HILDA 606
HINDELANG, M. 677
HINE, VIRGINIA H. 478, 707, 715, 717
HININGS, C.R. 367, 373
HINTIKKA, MERRILL B. 292
HINTON, JOHN 594
HINTZE, OTTO 744
HINTZEN, PERCY C. 763
HIRSCH, F. 702
HIRSCH, HERBERT 411
HIRSCH, JERRY 41
HIRSCH, PAUL M. 362, 376, 610, 611, 613, 619,
    620
HIRSCH, SUSAN 200
HIRSCHI, TRAVIS 261, 677, 684, 685
HIRSCHMAN, ALBERT O. 60, 95, 762
HIRSCHMAN, CHARLES 186
HIRSCHORN, BARBARA 279
HITCHENS, DONNA 435
HOBBES, THOMAS 85, 103, 112–113, 118, 401, 402
HOBSBAWM, ERIC J. 210
HOCHSCHILD, ARLIE R. 254, 307–308, 501
HOCKEY, BARBARA 364
HODGE, R.D. 454, 455
HODGE, ROBERT W. 560
HODGES, WILLIAM 438

HODSON, RANDY   335
HOFFER, ERIC   696, 705
HOFFER, T.   463
HOFFERTH, SANDRA LYNN   437, 438, 439
HOFFMAN, SAUL D.   178, 433
HOFLAND, BRIAN   435
HOGAN, DENNIS P.   253, 262, 310
HOGE, DEAN R.   260
HOGE, JANN L.   260
HOGGART, RICHARD   606, 607, 620
HOLLAND, JOHN L.   340
HOLLAND, PAUL   155, 159–161, 166, 167, 168, 170
HOLLINGSHEAD, AUGUST B.   454, 577
HOLLINGSWORTH, J. ROGERS   585, 586
HOLLIS, M.   501
HOLMAN, JACQUELINE   538
HOLMAN, THOMAS   426
HOLMSTROM, LYNDA LYTLE   301
HOLTER, HARRIET   293–294
HOLTON, GERALD   179, 524, 536, 538, 562
HOMANS, GEORGE   11, 32, 33–34, 36, 41, 48, 53,
    67, 68, 70, 87, 90, 95, 118–119, 122, 228
HOOD, RALPH W. JR.   501
HOPE, K.   454, 466
HOPPER, KIM   585, 586
HORKHEIMER, MAX   620
HORNER, KAREN L.   533
HOROBIN, GORDON   577, 581
HOROWITZ, AMY   305
HOROWITZ, DONALD   227, 233, 234, 235
HORWITZ, IRVING L.   658
HORSFIELD, PETER G.   495
HORTON, DONALD   604
HORWITZ, ALLAN V.   273
HORWOOD, L.J.   431
HOSTETLER, JOHN A.   501
HOUSE, JAMES S.   250, 344, 345, 346, 347, 348, 351
HOUSE, ROBERT J.   380, 382
HOUSEKNECHT, SHARON   430
HOVLAND, CARL   602
HOWELL, MARY C.   581, 591
HOYT, HOMER   631, 632, 633
HREBINIAK, LAWRENCE G.   381
HUBBARD, HOWARD   720
HUBER, JOAN   18, 294, 298, 306, 209, 432, 436
HUCKSHORN, ROBERT J.   410
HUDSON, PAT   182
HUGHES, E. C.   579, 590, 671
HUGHES, H. STUART   95
HUGHES, HELEN   603
HUGHES, HOLLY L.   653
HUGHES, JAMES W.   637
HUGHES, MICHAEL   584, 585, 724
HULIN, CHARLES L.   341
HULL, DAVID   515, 535
HUME, DAVID   156
HUMPHRIES, LAUD   314
HUNT, H. ALLAN   336
HUNT, JAMES G.   376
HUNT, LYNN   91
HUNT, TIMOTHY L.   336
HUNTER, FLOYD   405, 406
HUNTER, J. STUART   169
HUNTER, JAMES DAVISON   483, 484, 486, 498, 502

HUNTER, WILLIAM G.   169
HUNTINGTON, GERTRUDE ENDERS   501
HUNTINGTON, SAMUEL   742
HUO, YANCHUNG PAUL   378, 382, 383
HURD, RICHARD M.   631, 632
HUSAINI, BAQAR A.   346
HUSSERL   86
HUSTON, ALETHA C.   308
HUYSSEN, ANDREAS   620
HYLTON, LYDIA   371
HYMAN, HERBERT H.   253, 408, 411, 455, 602

I

IGNATIEFF, M.   686, 687
INAZU, JUDITH   437
INGHAM, GEOFFERY   747, 754
INGLEBY, D.   685, 687
INGLEHART, R.   701
INKELES, ALEX   55, 742, 761
INVERARITY, JAMES M.   494
IRELAND, R. DUANE   372
IRVINE, J.   528
IRWIN, MICHAEL E.   653
ISAACS, HAROLD   225
ISAAC, LARRY   727

J

JACKLIN, CAROL N.   41, 310, 314
JACKMAN, ROBERT   752, 764
JACKSON, JACQUELYNE J.   279
JACKSON, JOHN   169
JACKSON, KENNETH T.   630
JACKSON, MAURICE   715
JACKSON, ROBERT MAX   179, 192
JACOBS, J.   687
JACOBSEN, BROOKE   435
JACOBY, SANFORD M.   340, 381
JAFFE, STEVEN   483
JAGGER, ALISON, M.   293
JAHODA, MARIE   138, 602, 603
JAMES, LAWRENCE R.   345
JAMES, W.   672
JANOWITZ, MORRIS   238–239, 436, 669, 670, 686
JANSEN, J.C.   646
JARET, CHARLES   634, 645, 658
JAROS, DEAN   411
JARVIE, I.C.   491
JASTROW, ROBERT   70
JEANNERET, PAUL R.   341, 351
JEFFERSON, GAIL   88
JEFFERSON, MARK   657
JENCKS, CHRISTOPHER   340, 454, 455, 456
JENKINS, C. DAVID   585
JENKINS, G. DOUGLAS JR.   351
JENKINS, J. CRAIG   275, 697, 698. 699, 702, 705,
    729
JENNINGS, M. KENT   411, 455
JENNINGS, P. DEVEREAUX   329
JENSEN, ARTHUR R.   41
JENSEN, M.S.   435

JENSEN, RODERICK V. 158
JIOBU, ROBERT 642
JOHNSON, BENTON 576
JOHNSON, CHALMERS 750
JOHNSON, DAVID 431, 433
JOHNSON, EDWIN 763
JOHNSON, ELIZABETH 440
JOHNSON, JAMES H. 346
JOHNSON, MALCOLM 576
JOHNSON, MARILYN 244, 255, 258, 266, 276, 281
JOHNSON, MIRIAM 294
JOHNSON, NORMAN J. 367
JOHNSON, PAUL E. 479
JOHNSON, RICHARD 608
JOHNSON, STANLEY R. 165
JOHNSON, WILLIAM 430, 433
JOHNSTON, HANK 717
JONAS, GERALD 718
JONES, ALLAN P. 345
JONES, BRYN 209–210, 211
JONES, GARETH 334
JONES, J.D. 457
JONES, JACQUELINE 299
JONES, REBECCA 348
JONES, S.R.H. 205
JORASVSKY, DAVID 519, 522
JORESKOG, KARL G. 155, 164
JOYCE, WILLIAM F. 381
JUSENIUS, CAROL L. 301

K

KAASE, MAX 708
KADANE, JOSEPH 169, 170
KADUSHIN, CHARLES 90, 191
KAEBLE, HARTMUT 185
KAGAN, JEROME 249
KAHL, JOSEPH 762, 763
KAHN, ALFRED J. 305
KAHN, ROBERT L. 365
KAHN, STEPHEN 341
KAHOE, RICHARD D. 501
KALLEBERG, ARNE L. 252, 253, 261, 273, 335, 343, 346
KAMERMAN, SHEILA B. 305
KANDEL, D.B. 457
KANDEL, DENISE 438
KANE, ROBERT 252
KANOUSE, DAVID 433
KANTER, ROSABETH MOSS 293, 304, 306, 315, 330, 717
KAPLAN, ABRAHAM 70, 157
KAPLAN, E. ANN 621
KAPLAN, FRANCES BAGLEY 291
KAPSIS, ROBERT 621
KARWEIT, NANCY 255
KASARDA, JOHN D. 18, 375, 629, 630, 632, 633, 634, 635, 636, 637, 638, 641, 642, 643, 644, 645, 647, 650, 651, 654, 656, 657, 658
KASH, DON E. 527
KASS, ROY 643
KATZ, CLAUDIO 765
KATZ, DANIEL 365, 381

KATZ, ELIHU 337, 602, 603, 604, 616, 617, 619, 620, 621
KATZ, MICHAEL B. 333
KATZ, RALPH 338, 339
KATZENSTEIN, PETER 750, 755, 764
KATZNELSON, IRA 233, 747
KAUFMAN, HERBERT 405
KAUFMAN, ROBERT H. 765
KAUFMAN, ROBERT L. 270
KAVCIC, BOGDAN 338–339
KEDDIE, NIKKI R. 502
KEITH, JENNIE 281
KELLER, EVELYN FOX 292, 520
KELLEY, JONATHAN 411
KELLIHER, DANIEL 763
KELLNER, DOUGLAS 620
KELLY, J. 437
KELLY, DEAN M. 483
KELLY, G.P. 459
KELLY, WILLIAM R. 432, 727
KENISTON, KENNETH 706
KENNEY, JOHN 616
KENNEDY, DONALD 523
KENNEDY, LOUANNE 579, 588
KENTOR, JEFFERY 755
KEOHANE, ROBERT 765
KERBO, HAROLD 365
KERCKHOFF, A.C. 453, 458, 464
KERR, CLARK 213
KERR, HOWARD 501
KERTZER, DAVID I. 246, 248, 254, 255, 266, 269, 281, 502
KESSLER, RONALD C. 343, 344, 345, 346, 579, 588
KESSLER-HARRIS, ALICE 309, 315
KEY, V.O. JR. 410
KEYES, CHARLES 235
KEYSSAR, ALEXANDER 182
KICK, EDWARD L. 539
KIESLER, SARA B. 281
KILBOURNE, BROCK K. 501
KILBOURNE, M.T. 559
KILGORE, SALLY 463
KILLIAN, LEWIS 696, 713
KIM EUN MEE 751
KIM, MYOUNG SOO 751
KIM, YONG-HAK 362, 384
KIMBERLY, JOHN M. 337, 373
KINGSON, ERIC R. 279
KIRK, JEROME 707, 708
KIRKPATRICK, R. GEORGE 707
KITSCHELT, HERBERT 700
KITSON, GAYE 431, 432, 433
KITSUSE, J.I. 457, 465, 668, 677, 678, 679, 681, 684
KJELLBERG, ANDERS 747, 754, 763, 764
KLAASSEN, LEO H. 637, 648, 655
KLANDERMANS, BERT 106, 698, 701, 706, 707, 712, 714, 729
KLAPP, ORRIN 705
KLAPPER, JOSEPH T. 523, 605, 617
KLECK, GARY 54
KLEIN, SUSAN S. 303, 306
KLUEGEL, CHARLES 228
KNIGHT, PETER 755

KNOKE, DAVID 365, 383, 384, 411, 707
KNORR-CETINA, KAREN 90, 519, 525, 527, 539, 546, 547, 548, 553, 554, 555, 556, 557, 559, 561, 564
KNOX, WILLIAM E. 345, 351
KOBASA, SUZANNE C. 346
KOBRIN, SOLOMON 438
KOCHAN, THOMAS 381
KOCKA, JURGEN 334
KOENIG, RICHARD JR. 373, 374
KOESTER, DAVID 541
KOHLER, ROBERT E. 535
KOHLI, MARTIN 260, 263, 267, 268
KOHN, ALEXANDER 521, 524
KOHN, MELVIN 251, 339, 342, 345, 349, 351, 454, 457
KOLATA, GINA 158
KOMAROVSKY, MIRRA 294, 299, 425
KONDA, SURESH 195
KONNER, MELVIN J. 312
KOO, HAGEN 755
KOO, HELEN 434, 436
KOOPMAN, PAUL L. 339
KOOS, EARL 582, 585, 586, 589
KORNHABER, ARTHUR 279
KORNHAUSER, ARTHUR 340
KORNHAUSER, WILLIAM 412, 469, 703, 704, 705
KORPI, WALTER 181, 763, 764, 765
KOSHLAND, DANIEL 521, 523
KOTLER, PHILLIP 702
KRAFT, PHILIP 333, 334, 336
KRAMARAE, CHERIS 307
KRAMER, B.M. 226
KRAMER, KATHY 438
KRARUP, HELEN 501
KRASNER, STEPHEN 758, 765
KRAUSE, ELLIOT A. 595
KRAUZE, TADCUSZ 540, 561
KRAVITS, JOANNA 583
KREPS, GARY 93
KREPS, JUANITA M. 258, 259
KREYE, OTTO 465
KRIEDTE, PETER 182
KRIESI, HANSPETER 712
KROEBER, ALFRED L. 65, 544, 563
KROHN, ROGER G. 518, 537
KROLL-SMITH, J. STEPHEN 494
KRONISH, RICHARD 765
KROON, FREDERIKE 707
KRUSE, ANDREA 276
KUHN, THOMAS S. 43–44, 61, 70, 79, 93, 95, 512, 514, 516, 520, 537, 541, 542, 543, 544, 547, 548, 549, 559, 562, 563, 740
KULKA, RICHARD A. 310
KUMKA, DONALD S. 345, 351
KUO, SHIRLEY W.Y. 755
KUPER, LEO 48
KURTH, JAMES 753, 762, 764
KURTZ, LESTER R. 494
KUSSMALL, ANN 198
KUSTERER, KEN 210
KUZNETS, SIMON 185, 204, 765
KWAN, KIAN M. 238

L

LADD, EVERETT CARL 405, 410, 411
LAGORY, MARK 629, 630, 633, 634, 642
LAING, R.D. 677
LAKATOS, IMRE 535, 541, 544, 562, 562
LALONDE, ROBERT J. 165
LAMMERS, CORNELIUS 371
LAMPHERE, LOUISE 295, 296
LANDES, ELISABETH 430, 431, 432
LANDESCO, J. 672
LANDY, FRANK J. 330
LANE, ROBERT E. 413
LANG, ABIGAIL 440
LANG, GLADYS ENGEL 609, 612, 615, 616, 617, 618, 696
LANG, KURT 609, 612, 615, 616, 617, 618, 620, 696
LANGE, PETER 765
LANGLIE, JEAN K. 589
LANSING, MARJORIE 309
LAPLACE, PIERRE 157
LAROCCO, JAMES M. 345, 346
LARSON, JUDITH K. 379
LARSON, MAGALI SARFATTI 180, 333
LASCH, CHRISTOPHER 488
LASH, SCOTT 92, 96
LASKA, SHIRLEY BRADWAY 649
LASKI, M. 483
LASLETT, BARBARA 425
LASLETT, PETER 278, 425
LASSWELL, HAROLD 602, 605, 606, 620
LATOUR, BRUNO 519, 527, 547, 553, 554, 555, 556, 560, 564
LATTES, ALFREDO E. 654
LATTIMORE, F. 670
LAUDERDALE, PAT 494
LAUGHLIN, CHARLES D. JR. 501
LAUMANN, EDWARD O. 58, 369, 383, 384, 385
LAURENTI, L.M. 642
LAURIE, BRUCE 198
LAVIN, BEBE 589
LAW, JOHN 536
LAWLER, EDWARD E. III 341, 342, 372
LAWRENCE, BARBARA S. 273
LAWRENCE, PAUL R. 336, 340, 341, 365, 367, 369, 370, 375
LAWSON, RONALD 717
LAZARSFELD, PAUL F. 56, 138, 243, 255, 274, 275, 602, 603, 604, 605, 606, 607, 614, 620
LAZARUS, RICHARD S. 344
LE BON, GUSTAVE 45, 55, 696
LEACH, E.R. 501
LEAMER, EDWARD E. 155, 164, 165
LEAPER, R. JOHN 258, 259
LEAVIS, F.R. 606
LEBLEBICI, HUSEYIN 376
LECLAU ERNESTO 762
LEDERBERG, JOSHUA 541, 558, 563
LEE, DAVID 213
LEE, EUGENE 408
LEE, GARY 426
LEE, RICHARD 406

LEE, V.E. 458
LEFCOURT, HERBERT M. 345
LEFEBVRE, HENRI 633
LEFTON, MARK 594
LEGOFF, JACQUES 490, 491
LEHMAN, HARVEY C. 533
LEHMBRUCH, GERHARD 412, 755, 764
LEIB, JEFFREY 207
LEIBNIZ, G.W. 49, 69, 542, 543
LEIBOWITZ, LILA 312
LEINBERGER, CHRISTOPHER B. 636
LEINHARDT, SAMUEL 120
LEITES, NATHAN 605
LEJEUNE, ROBERT 579, 588
LEMAINE, GERARD 535
LEMERT, EDWIN M. 124–125, 670, 676, 678, 679, 680, 683, 684
LENIHAN, KENNETH 147
LENIN, V.I. 396
LENMAN, B. 687
LENSKI, GERHARD 58, 185, 243, 279, 295, 296, 426, 427, 765
LEONTIEF, WASSILY 212
LEPENIES, WOLF 535
LERMAN, P. 687
LERNER, DANIEL 742
LERNER, RICHARD M. 244, 246, 249, 281
LERNER, ROBERT E. 501
LEROY LADURIE, EMMANUEL 165, 428, 501
LESLIE, GERALD R. 435
LESTER, MARILYN 620, 723
LESTHAEGHE, RON 428
LEVER, JANET 306
LEVI, MARGARET 237
LEVI-STRAUSS, CLAUDE 309, 608
LEVIN, SHARON G. 534
LEVINE, ADELINE 361
LEVINE, DANIEL H. 502
LEVINE, DONALD N. 61–62
LEVINE, E.M. 705
LEVINE, SOL 383, 384, 586
LEVINGER, GEORGE 429, 430, 433
LEVINSON, DANIEL J. 250, 261, 310
LEVITSKY, DAVID A. 45
LEVY, JUDITH A. 594
LEVY, MARION J. JR. 49, 425
LEVY, MARK R. 619, 620
LEWIN, KURT 602
LEWIS, J. DAVID 84, 90, 95
LEWIS, RICHARD 538
LEWIS, ROBERT 436
LIAZOS, A. 683
LICHTER, DANIEL T. 651
LICHTER, S. ROBERT 705
LIEBERSON, STANLEY 81, 82, 88, 155, 169, 193–194, 197, 224, 231, 641, 643, 644
LIEBES, TAMAR 604, 619, 621
LIEBMAN, CHARLES S. 496
LIEBMAN, ROBERT C. 502
LIEBOW, ELLIOTT 205
LIGHT, IVAN 233, 379, 656, 657, 658
LIGHTFOOT, SARAH LAWRENCE 305
LIKER, JEFFREY K. 249

LIM, HYUN-CHIN 751
LIM, LINDA Y.C. 298
LINCOLN, C. ERIC 703, 729
LINCOLN, JAMES R. 345, 384, 385
LINDBECK, ASSAR 754
LINDEN, EUGENE 32
LINDENBERG, SIEGWART 67
LINDENBERG, ZIEGFRIED 90
LINDERT, PETER H. 186
LINDSAY, PAUL 345, 351
LINDSEY, MICHAEL L. 383
LINDZEY, GARDNER 43
LINTON, RALPH 279, 295
LINZ, JUAN 748, 760
LIPMAN-BLUMEN, JEANN 291, 300, 305
LIPSET, SEYMOUR 236, 274, 275, 364, 393, 398, 400, 405, 409, 705,716, 729, 751, 752, 762
LIPSITT, L. 250
LIPSKY, MICHAEL 408, 699
LIPTON, MICHAEL 763
LISS, JULIA 687
LITTLER, CRAIG 192, 205, 207, 210
LITWAK, EUGENE 251, 341
LIU, KORBIN 260, 267–268
LIVINGSTON, ERIC 548, 564
LO, CLARENCE Y.H. 396, 721
LOCKE, EDWIN A. 342
LOCKE, JOHN 85
LOCKHEED, MARLAINE 306
LOCKWOOD, CHARLES 19, 636
LOCKWOOD, DAVID 333, 334
LODHI, A.W. 703
LOEB, M.B. 454
LOEWEN, JAMES W. 233
LOFLAND, JOHN 703, 708, 717
LOFQUIST, LLOYD H. 340
LOGAN, JOHN R. 629, 638, 648
LONG, ELIZABETH 615
LONG, J. SCOTT 518, 530, 561
LONG, JOHN F. 637
LONG, LARRY H. 637
LONG, RICHARD J. 338–339
LONG, THEODORE E. 501
LONGFELLOW, CYNTHIA 437
LOPATA, HELENA Z. 294, 440
LORBER, JUDITH 299, 315, 591, 682
LORENCE, JON 252, 335, 345, 351
LORENZ, KONRAD 42
LORSCH, JAY W. 336, 365, 367, 369, 375
LORTIE, D.C. 449
LOSCH, AUGUST 644
LOSCOCCO, KARYN 261
LOTKA, ALFRED J. 528, 560
LOTT, ALBERT J. 342
LOTT, BERNICE 342
LOUGHLIN, JULIA 547
LOUNSBERG, JOHN W. 330, 351
LOVELL, A. 687
LOWE, JOHN C. 254
LOWE, MARIAN 312
LOWENTHAL, LEO 729
LUBECK, PAUL 763
LUBOVE, R. 670

LUCKMANN, THOMAS 31, 38, 42, 44, 57, 66, 70, 125–126, 127, 473, 474, 489
LUDTE, ALF 205
LUESCHEN, GUENTHER 587
LUHMANN, NIKLAS 15, 65, 96, 473, 476
LUKACS, GEORGE 402, 415
LUKER, KRISTIN 309, 313, 481, 711
LUKES, STEVEN 400, 403, 406, 501
LURIA, SALVADOR 521
LYNCH, MICHAEL 88, 90, 541, 564
LYND, HELEN M. 136, 602, 603
LYND, ROBERT S. 10, 136, 602, 603
LYOTARD, JEAN-FRANCOIS 92

M

MACCOBY, ELEANOR E. 41, 310, 314
MACE, WILLIAM 348
MACHALEK, RICHARD 501
MACHIAVELLI, NICCOLO 85, 401, 402
MACIVER, R.M. 157
MACKE, ANN STATHAM 438
MACKENZIE, DONALD A. 551, 552, 557
MACKLIN, E.D. 435
MACRAE, DUNCAN 670
MACROBERTS, BARBARA R. 561
MACROBERTS, MICHAEL H. 561
MADDEN, JANICE F. 199
MADDEN, N.A. 228
MADDI, SAVATORE R. 346
MADDOX, GEORGE L. 249, 254, 260
MAHLER, VINCENT 765
MAINES, DAVID 90
MALAN, PEDRO 755
MALINOWSKI, BRONISLAW 49, 109
MALLET, SERGE 208, 209
MANDEVILLE, B. 675
MANN, MICHAEL 92, 96, 746
MANNARI, HIROSHI 373, 374
MANNHEIM, KARL 24, 26, 56, 62, 243, 255, 256, 264, 266, 275, 292
MANNING, ROBERT D. 765
MANSBRIDGE, JANE J. 305
MANSFIELD, ROBERT 373
MANTON, KENNETH 249, 260, 262, 267, 267–268
MARACEK, JEANNE 435
MARCH, JAMES G. 364, 368, 765
MARCUSE, HERBERT 115–116, 117, 398, 401, 620
MARGER, MARTIN N. 401
MARGLIN, STEPHEN 205
MARINI, MARGARET, M. 251, 253
MARKIDES, KYRIADOS S. 279
MARKLE, GERALD E. 717, 727
MARKUS, HAZEL 348
MARKUSEN, ANN R. 655
MARRETT, CORA BAGLEY 379
MARSDEN, DAVID 191
MARSDEN, GEORGE 484
MARSDEN, PETER 111, 369, 384, 385
MARSH, ROBERT M. 373, 374
MARSHALL, HARVEY 642
MARSHALL, SUSAN 710, 713
MARSHALL, T.H. 762, 763

MARTIN, ANDREW 763, 764
MARTIN, B.R. 428
MARTIN, E.D. 729
MARTIN, F.M. 453
MARTIN, M. KAY 296
MARVEL, HOWARD P. 188
MARX, GARY T. 224, 712, 720, 728, 729
MARX, KARL 24, 31, 32, 41, 42, 44–45, 47, 48, 52, 53, 56, 58, 59, 64, 66, 70, 83, 93, 103, 105, 109, 112, 113–115, 116, 125, 176, 270, 292, 327, 394, 395, 396, 397, 398, 399, 400, 401, 405, 411, 414, 415, 416, 473, 485, 486, 698, 743, 749, 762
MASLOW, A.H. 342
MASNICK, GEORGE 278
MASON, KAREN OPPENHEIM 309
MASON, W.S. 449
MASON, WILLIAM M. 260
MASSEY, DOUGLAS S. 641, 642
MATARAZZO, JOSEPH 281
MATHIS, ARTHUR 431
MATRAS, J. 458
MATTELART, MICHELE 614, 615
MATTHEWS, KAREN A. 62
MATTHEWS, SARAH 440
MATZA, DAVID 668, 670, 672, 673, 674, 677, 683, 684, 688
MAUKSCH, HANS 590
MAYER, J. 686
MAYER, KARL U. 268
MAYNARD, REBECCA 165
MAZIE, SARA H. 651
MAZRUI, ALI A. 225
MCADAM, DOUG 18, 237, 394, 697, 700, 701, 702, 703, 707, 708, 709, 710, 712, 713, 720, 721, 722, 728, 730
MCALLISTER, IAN 411
MCARTHUR, LESLIE Z. 330, 348, 351
MCBRIDE, KERRY 384, 385
MCCAGHY, C.H. 680
MCCANN, H. 534
MCCARL, ROBERT S. JR. 501
MCCARTHY, JAMES 432, 434, 438
MCCARTHY, JOHN D. 18, 362, 394, 697, 704, 707, 711, 712, 717, 720, 723, 724, 725
MCCARTHY, K.F. 650
MCCLELLAND, DAVID C. 309, 311, 396, 742
MCCLINTOCK, BARBARA 520, 559, 560
MCCOMBS, MAXWELL 610, 617
MCCONAHY, J.G. 228
MCCORMACK, ERNEST J. 341, 351
MCCORMACK, THELMA 605, 613
MCCULLOUGH, M. R. 273
MCDILL, E.L. 454, 455, 456
MCDONALD, JOHN 429
MCEACHERN, A.W. 449
MCEWEN, C. 681, 682
MCFARLAND, ANDREW F. 702, 717
MCGEE, JEANNE 267
MCGEE, T.G. 657, 658
MCGINNIS, ROBERT 518, 530
MCGOWAN, PAT 763
MCGUIRE, MEREDITH B. 486, 494, 501
MCINTOSH, M. 668

McCay, H.　672
McKelvey, Bill　367, 372
McKenzie, Roderick　632, 644
McKeown, Thomas　586
McKinley, John B.　586
McKinley, Sonja M.　586
McKinley, William　373
McLanahan, Sara S.　254, 436, 438
McLeod, Jane D.　345, 346
McManus, John　501
McMichael, Philip　758
McMullin, Douglas R.　646
McNamara, Patrick　501
McPhail, Clark　706, 723
McPhee, William N.　56, 274, 275
McPherson, J. Miller　309, 365, 379, 386
McQuail, Denis　621
McQueen, David V.　594
Mead, George Herbert　24, 41, 42, 43, 50, 51, 61, 64, 70, 90, 122, 670, 686, 688
Mead, Margaret　291, 299, 417
Meadow, Mary Jo　501
Meadows, Paul　423
Meadows, Peter　423
Means, Gardiner C.　403, 404
Mecham, Robert C.　341, 351
Mechanic, David　45, 249, 585
Mechling, Jay　502
Mechling, E.W.　725
Medawar, Peter　521, 555, 559
Medick, Hans　182
Medoff, James　195, 210
Meeker, B.F.　329
Meeker, M.　454
Mehan, H.B.　682
Mehrtens, Herbert　519
Meier, R.　686
Meiers, Mary L.　560
Melbin, Murray　69
Melody, William H.　420
Melucci, Alberto　701
Menaghen, Elizabeth G.　344, 346, 347
Menken, Jane L.　262, 263, 264
Menzel, Herbert　337
Mercy, James　439
Mericle, Ken　765
Merino, Barbara D.　334
Merkle, Judith　299
Merton, Robert K.　26, 27, 29, 31, 33, 49, 50, 55, 56, 57, 65–66, 69, 70, 94, 104, 108, 111, 255, 260, 263, 264, 281, 292, 294, 340, 417, 490, 511, 512, 513, 514, 515, 516, 518, 519, 520, 521, 522, 526, 529, 531, 532, 533, 534, 535, 536, 538, 541, 542, 543, 544, 545, 555, 556, 559, 561, 562, 564, 579, 581, 602, 604, 668, 674, 675, 676, 677, 688
Merves, Esther S.　344, 346, 347
Messeri, Peter　535, 541
Messinger, Sheldon L.　686
Metcalf, D.　637, 643
Metzner, Helen L.　250
Meyer, David R.　629, 657, 658
Meyer, H.J.　669
Meyer, John W.　91, 96, 251–252, 268, 364, 371, 373, 374, 377, 384, 449, 454, 463, 486, 493, 761
Meyer, Marshall W.　398
Meyersohn, Rolf　601
Michael, Robert　431, 432
Michaelson, William　199
Michels, Robert　400, 401, 402, 409, 413, 696, 718
Migdal, Joel S.　763
Milbrath, Lester W.　408, 413
Miles, Robert H.　381, 383
Miliband, Ralph　396, 403, 404
Milic, V.　559
Milkman, Ruth　350
Miller, Ann R.　332, 351
Miller, Arthur H.　274, 405
Miller, Brian　314, 435
Miller, Delbert C.　328
Miller, Frederick D.　714
Miller, George A.　373
Miller, Joanne　18, 251, 365, 429
Miller, Jon　345
Miller, Judith　435
Miller, K.A.　454, 457
Miller, Neal E.　341
Miller, R. Berkeley　747
Miller, Sheila　439, 440
Miller, W.　687
Miller, Warren E.　274
Miller, William D.　718
Millett, Kate　295
Millikan, R.A.　524
Millman, Marcia　581, 592
Mill, John Stuart　156, 157, 169, 399, 401, 403, 404, 405, 668, 696
Mills, C. Wright　11, 275, 334
Mincer, Jacob　300, 331, 454
Mindlin, Sergio　370
Miner, Anne S.　339
Minsky, Marvin　70
Mintz, Beth　384
Mintzberg, Henry　366, 374, 376, 380
Mirande, Alfredo　432
Mirowsky, John　585, 588
Misra, R.P.　647
Mitchell, Robert C.　707, 727
Mitchell, Terrence R.　344
Mitroff, Ian　517, 518, 519, 559
Mittermeir, Roland　561
Mizruchi, Mark　385, 386
Moberg, David O.　501
Model, Suzanne　193
Modell, John　233, 262, 267, 278
Modigliani, Andre　619
Mollenkopf, John　396, 407, 658
Molotch, Harvey L.　90, 406, 620, 629, 638, 648, 706, 723
Monahan, Thomas　430, 436
Monroe, Robert L.　313
Montgomery, David　211, 333
Monts, J. Kenneth　640
Moodie, T. Dunbar　502
Moore, Barrington Jr.　88, 90–91, 744, 748, 753, 762

MOORE, GWEN 404
MOORE, JOAN W. 254, 635
MOORE, KRISTIN 430, 431, 432, 437
MOORE, R.I. 501
MOORE, MARY E. 41, 43, 276
MOORE, SYLVIA 431, 432, 434
MOORE, WILBERT E. 31, 70, 175–176, 190, 191, 204
MOORMAN, JEANNE E. 302
MORAN, T.H. 750, 757
MORAVEC, HANS P. 70
MORAWSKA, EWA 203–204
MORE, CHARLES 210
MORGAN, D. 685
MORGAN, JAMES N. 178, 253, 281
MORGAN, MICHAEL 620
MORGAN, PHILIP 430, 431, 432
MORGAN, WILLIAM 438
MORONEY, ROBERT 305
MORRIS, ALDON 703, 710, 713, 717, 718, 722, 729
MORRIS, NAOMI M. 249
MORRIS, RICHARD 274
MORRISON, DAVID EDWARD 620
MORRISON, DENTON 705
MORRISON, PETER A. 650
MORRISSEY, JOSEPH P. 383
MORTIMER, JEYLAN T. 252, 254, 340, 345, 351
MOSCA, GAETANO 400, 401, 402
MOSCO, VINCENT 620
MOSSEL, P.A. 455
MOTT, FRANK 431, 432, 434
MOTTEZ, BERNARD 206
MOTTL, TAHI L. 721
MOUZELIS, NICOS 748, 753, 760
MOYNIHAN, DANIEL PATRICK 305, 364
MUELLER, CAROL 724, 725, 727
MUELLER, CHARLES W. 434, 438
MUELLER, EDWARD N. 705
MUELLER, WALTER 268
MUESER, P. 454, 455, 456
MUGHAM, ANTHONY 411
MULKAY, MICHAEL 26, 90, 511, 516, 517, 519, 520, 524, 525, 529, 535, 536, 537, 538, 539, 546, 547, 548, 557, 558, 559, 560
MULLAN, BRENDAN P. 641, 642
MULLER, PETER 635
MULLINS, NICHOLAS C. 529, 535, 536, 537, 538, 539, 541
MUNCH, RICHARD 65, 66, 70, 71, 96, 578
MUNOZ, L. 680
MURDOCK, GRAHAM 605, 609, 610, 613
MURPHY, RAYMOND J. 274
MURRAY, STEPHEN O. 541
MUTH, RICHARD F. 634
MUTRAN, ELIZABETH 277, 436
MYERHOFF, BARBARA 227
MYERS, DAVID 432
MYERS, GEORGE C. 278
MYLES, JOHN 270, 764
MYRDAL, GUNNAR 26

N

NADEL, EDWARD 541, 552

NAGATA, JUDITH 235
NAGEL, ERNST 27–28, 155, 157, 169
NAGEL, JOAN 236, 237
NAIRN, TOM 236
NAKANO, HIDEICHIRO 26, 56
NASH, JUNE 298
NATHANSON, CONSTANCE A. 584
NAVARRO, VICENTE 595
NAY, ORBERT 431, 438
NEAL, ARTHUR G. 708, 713
NEIDERT, LISA J. 643
NELKIN, DOROTHY 700, 727
NELSON, DANIEL 192
NELSON, EDWARD E. 255
NESVOLD, BETTY 696
NETTLER, G. 684
NEUGARTEN, BERNICE L. 243, 250, 253, 254, 260, 266, 279
NEUGARTEN, DAIL A. 279
NEUGEBAUER, OTTO 524
NEUHAUS, RICHARD JOHN 489, 501
NEUSTADT, RICHARD E. 404
NEWBOLD, PAUL 167
NEWCOMB, HOWARD 620, 621
NEWCOMB, PAUL 435
NEWFARMER, RICHARD 763, 765
NEWMAN, STANTON 594
NEWPORT, FRANK 484
NEWTON, ISAAC 64, 524, 533, 542, 543, 544
NICHOLSON, MICHAEL 29
NICHOLSON, NIGEL 339
NIE, NORMAN H. 408, 410, 413, 414
NIELSEN, F. 703
NIEMI, RICHARD G. 411
NISBET, ROBERT A. 327
NOBLE, DAVID 210, 211, 337
NOEL, DONALD L. 227–228, 238
NORD, CHRISTINE 433, 438
NORTH, DOUGLAS 763
NORTON, ARTHUR 254, 302
NORTON, MARY BETH 295, 297
NORTON, R.D. 655
NOVAK, MICHAEL 499
NOWAK, PHILIP 376
NOYELLE, THIERRY 637
NRIAGU, JEROME E. 45
NYE, IVAN 426, 677
NYONGO, ANYANG 763

O

O'CONNOR, JAMES 88, 402, 404
O'DEA, JANET 501
O'DEA, THOMAS 501
O'DONNELL, GUILLERMO A. 748, 753, 760, 762
O'HARE, W.P. 642
O'LEARY, CORNELIUS 233
O'RAND, ANGELA M. 249, 253
O'REILLY, CHARLES A. III 344
OBERSCHALL, ANTHONY 697, 703, 704, 707, 710, 715
OBRANT, SARAH W. 330, 351
OEGEMA, DIRK 706
OFFE, CLAUS 88, 404, 405

OGBURN, WILLIAM F.　10, 52, 55, 70, 425, 545, 563
OKIN, SUSAN MOLLER　300
OKUN, ARTHUR　754
OLDHAM, GREG R.　351
OLIVER, DOUGLAS　191
OLIVER, PAMELA　707
OLKIN, INGRAM　163
OLLMAN, BERTEL　397
OLNECK, J.　455
OLSEN, JOHAN P.　364, 368, 765
OLSEN, MARVIN E.　403, 414
OLSON, JON　345
OLSON, MANCUR　180, 228, 494, 707, 710
OLZAK, SUSAN　236, 237
ONG, WALTER J.　52
OPPENHEIM, A.M.　606
OPPENHEIMER, VALERIE　264, 281, 300, 301, 314
OPTIZ, WOLFGANG　431
ORFIELD, G.　457, 465
ORLOFF, ANN SHOLA　361
ORNTER, SHERRY B.　309, 314, 315
ORUM, ANTHONY M.　18, 394, 402, 407, 414, 417,
　　706, 707, 708, 710
OSBORN, RICHARD N.　376
OSTROGORSKI, M.　408
OTTO, LUTHER B.　335, 345, 351, 426, 462
OUCHI, WILLIAM G.　377, 385
OUDIJK, CORRINE　702
OWENS, VIRGINIA STEM　501
OXAAL, IVAR　762

P

PADESKY, CHRISTINE　435
PADGETT, JOHN　368
PAELINCK, J.H.P.　656
PAGELS, HEINZ R.　38, 63, 66
PAHL, RAYMOND　406, 407
PAIGE, JEFFERY M.　313, 501, 748, 761, 764
PAIGE, KAREN ERICKSEN　313, 501
PALEN, J. JOHN　630
PALLAS, A.M.　457
PALMA, GABRIEL　743, 762
PALMER, C. EDDIE　501
PALMER, DAVID　386
PALOUTZIAN, RAYMOND F.　501
PAMPEL, FRED C.　265, 269, 270, 640
PANITCH, LEO　747
PANNENBERG, WOLFHART　474
PAPANEK, HANNA　298
PAPPENFORT, DONNELL M.　644
PAPPI, FRANZ U.　58
PARENTI, MICHAEL　401, 403
PARETO, VILFREDO　400, 401, 402, 405
PARISH, WILLIAM　763
PARK, ROBERT E.　68, 406, 602, 632, 633, 638, 640,
　　641, 669, 670, 671, 672, 686, 696, 724
PARK, SOOKJA　265
PARKE, ROBERT JR.　278
PARKER, G.　687
PARLETTE, NICHOLAS　344
PARR, W.C.　431
PARSONS, TALCOTT　9-10, 12, 30, 34, 35, 41-42,
　　47, 49-50, 50, 56, 57-58, 64, 65, 66, 68, 69,

70, 83, 87, 93, 94, 96, 108, 109-112, 114,
　123-125, 127-128, 243, 263, 276, 280, 281,
　291, 294, 295, 299, 307, 309, 328, 342, 367,
　371, 394, 389, 399, 400, 401, 402, 406, 415,
　416, 425, 457, 473, 501, 516, 578, 579, 580,
　581, 582, 588, 590, 594, 668, 675, 741, 762, 763
PASSERON, JEAN-CLAUDE　31, 47, 69, 453, 458
PASSINO, EMILY M.　330, 351
PATCHEN, M.　228
PATEMAN, CAROLE　413
PATINKIN, DON　562
PATTERSON, ORLANDO　226, 239, 431
PAUL, CAROLYN S.　272
PAUL, F.　457, 465
PEARLIN, LEONARD I.　343, 344, 345, 346, 347
PEARSON, WILLIE JR.　560
PENCAVEL, JOHN　206
PENN, ROGER　210
PENNINGS, JOHANNES　376, 378, 379
PEPLAU, LETITIA ANNE　435
PERLMAN, JANICE　630
PERMAN, LAURI　340
PERROT, M.　686
PERROW, CHARLES　336, 361, 364, 365, 366, 367,
　　368, 696, 697, 699
PERRY, DAVID　644
PERRUCCI, R.　681
PERRY, N.　681
PERSELL, C.H.　463
PETERS, VICTOR　501
PETERSDORF, ROBERT G.　521, 523
PETERSON, JAMES L.　433, 438
PETERSON, RICHARD　620
PETROCIK, JOHN　410
PETTY, R.E.　706
PEUKERT, HELMUT　474
PFEFFER, JEFFREY　208, 273, 331, 344, 350, 368,
　　376, 378
PFEFFER, LEO　502
PFLANZ, MANFRED　580, 581
PHARR, SUSAN J.　297
PHEYSEY, DIANA C.　336, 374
PHILLIBER, WILLIAM　429
PHILLIPS, ALMARIN　384
PHILLIPS, DAVID P.　620, 621
PHILLIPSON, M.　668
PIAGET, JEAN　541
PIANTODOSI, S.　170
PICKERING, ANDREW　549, 550, 551, 552
PICOU, J. STEVEN　68
PIFER, ALAN　270
PINARD, MAURICE　707, 708, 713, 715
PINCH, TREVOR　549, 550, 559, 563
PINCH, T.J.　90
PINDYCK, ROBERT S.　161, 162, 165, 169
PINGREE, SUZANNE　615, 621
PIORE, MICHAEL　765
PIPES, DANIEL　502
PIPKIN, JOHN　629, 630, 633, 634, 642
PISCATORI, JAMES P.　502
PISTRANG, NANCY　436
PITTS, J.　686
PIVEN, FRANCES FOX　402, 404, 413, 414, 727
PLANCK, MAX　533, 538
PLATT, GERALD M.　262

PLECK, ELIZABETH   309
PLECK, JOSEPH H.   298, 302, 303, 309, 313, 314
PLUMMER, K.   680, 683
PLUTCHIK, ROBERT   46
POLANYI, KARL   744
POLANYI, MICHAEL   519, 559, 762
POLLAK, MICHAEL   700, 727
POLLNER, M.   685
POLSBY, NELSON W.   404, 405, 704
POMIAN-SRZEDNICKI, MACIEJ   502
PONZA, MICHAEL   301
POPE, HALLOWELL   434, 438
POPENOE, CRIS   495
POPENOE, OLIVER   495
POPKIN, SAMUEL   761, 765
POPPER, KARL R.   62–63, 66, 395, 417, 513, 541, 562
PORTER, ALAN L.   518, 530
PORTER, MICHAEL E.   367
PORTER, THEODORE M.   551
PORTES, ALEJANDRO   629, 643, 657, 765
POSTMAN, NEIL   53
POSTON, DUDLEY L. JR.   644, 650
POTTER, JONATHAN   557
POTTER, WILLIAM GREY   560
POULANTZAS, NICO   88, 396, 403, 404, 416, 417
POWELL, A.G.   459
POWELL, BRIAN   438
POWELL, G. BINGHAM JR.   412
POWELL, WALTER W.   191, 337, 350, 377, 384, 610, 611
POWERS, MICHAEL T.   43
PRAGER, JEFFREY   91
PRATT, J.W.   166, 167
PREVISCH, RAUL   763
PRESSER, HARRIET   249, 277, 437
PRESTHUS, ROBERT   377, 406, 417
PRESTON, SAMUEL H.   189, 263, 279, 429, 431, 439
PREVITS, GARY J.   334
PRICE, DEREK J. DE S.   511, 528, 535, 544, 558, 562
PRICE, RICHARD H.   343
PRITCHARD, LINDA   488
PRZEWORSKI, ADAM   185–186, 747
PUGH, DEREK S.   336, 364, 367, 373, 374, 376
PUGLIESI, KAREN   345
PUTNAM, ROBERT D.   401
PUTNIS, PETER   601

Q

QUADAGNO, JILL   269, 275
QUAINTANCE, MARILYN K.   351
QUESTER, ALINE   430
QUINN, ROBERT A.   273
QUINN, ROBERT P.   338, 340
QUINNEY, R.   685

R

RABB, EARL   705
RABB, THEODORE K.   96

RABINOW, P.   686
RADCLIFFE-BROWN, A.R.   49, 105, 108–109
RADWAY, JANICE   615
RAGIN, CHARLES   763
RAINS, P.   680
RAINWATER, LEE   340
RAJCHMAN, JOHN   94
RAMBO, LEWIS R.   501
RAMIREZ, F.O.   449, 761
RANIS, GUSTAV   755
RAPOPORT, RHONA   298, 301
RAPOPORT, ROBERT   298, 301
RATCLIFF, RICHARD E.   746, 753
RATNER, RONNIE STEINBERG   304
RAUMA   169
RAUSCHENBUSH, W.   671
RAY, M.   680
RECKLESS, W.C.   672
REDER, MELVIN   212, 213
REDFEARN, G.   630
REDFIELD, ROBERT   481
REDLICH, FREDERICK C.   577
REED, EDWARD   348
REED, J.S.   455
REEDER, LEO G.   587, 589
REES, JOHN   655
REESE, H.   250
REHBERG, R.A.   456, 458
REICH, MICHAEL   190, 213, 214
REID, IVAN   587
REINHARZ, SHULAMIT   292
REISS, ALBERT   145
REISS, IRA   426, 680
REITZ, JEFFREY G.   193
REITZES, DONALD C.   277, 436
REMPEL, JUDITH   436
RESKIN, BARBARA F.   303, 304, 330, 518, 530, 531, 533
RESTIVO, SAL   547, 564
REX, JOHN   88, 90, 228, 229, 230, 235
RHETT, H.   459
RIBEIRO DE OLIVEIRA, PEDOR A.   491
RICHARDSON, HARRY W.   656
RICHARDSON, JAMES T.   478, 501
RICHARDSON, R.   637
RICHIE, D. MICHAEL   348
RICHTER, KERRY   652, 648
RICKLES, PATRICIA K.   501
RIESMAN, DAVID   403
RILEY, JOHN W. JR.   249, 253, 262, 276, 280, 331
RILEY, MATILDA WHITE   41, 244, 245, 246, 247, 248, 249, 250, 252, 253, 254, 255, 258, 262, 263, 266, 270, 272, 276, 278, 279, 280, 281
RIMLINGER, GASTON   764
RINDFUSS, RONALD   430, 431, 432, 433
RISMAN, BARBARA   435
RITZER, GEORGE   80, 89
RIZZO, JOHN R.   364
ROACH, MARY JOAN   431, 432, 433
ROBBINS, CYNTHIA   250
ROBBINS, THOMAS   480, 499, 501
ROBERTS, B.   685
ROBERTS, BRYAN   647
ROBERTS, DONALD   620

ROBERTS, KARLENE H. 251
ROBERTS, KEITH A. 501
ROBERTSON, JOAN F. 276
ROBERTSON, ROLAND 502
ROBINS, JAMES A. 386
ROBINSON, A. 543
ROBINSON, JO ANN OOIMAN 718
ROBINSON, JOHN B. 619, 620
ROBINSON, PAULINE K. 272
ROBINSON, R.V. 458
ROCHE, M. 668
ROCHFORD, E. BURKE 709, 730
ROCK, P. 668, 673, 675, 680, 683, 684, 685, 687
ROCKWELL, R.C. 262
RODGERS, WILLARD L. 260, 310
ROETHLISBERGER, F.J. 120, 338, 340
ROGERS, DAVID L. 383, 384
ROGERS, EVERETT M. 336, 337, 379
ROGERS, MARIAN 228
ROGERSON, C.M. 656
ROGLER, LLOYD 440
ROGOSA, DAVID 164, 166, 170
ROHLEN, T.P. 459
ROKEACH, MILTON 612, 617, 705
ROKKAN, STEIN 236, 400, 762, 763
ROLLHANSEN, NILS 550
ROLLINS, JUDITH 303
ROMANELLI, ELAINE 380
RONDINELLI, DENNIS 654
RONIGER, LOUIS 478
ROOF, WADE CLARK 484, 501, 641
ROOS, LESLIE 338
ROOS, PATRICIA 199, 298, 301, 303, 304, 330
ROOT, JANE 621
RORTY, RICHARD 93–94, 95
ROSALDO, M.Z. 295
ROSE, STEPHEN 371
ROSEN, SHERWIN 204
ROSENBAUM, J.E. 454, 457, 461
ROSENBAUM, JAMES E. 195, 338
ROSENBAUM, PAUL R. 161, 166, 169
ROSENBERG, M.I. 462, 464, 465
ROSENBERG, MORRIS 17
ROSENBLATT, DANIEL 588
ROSENBLUM, BARBARA 611, 617, 619
ROSENFELD, RACHEL 192, 429
ROSENGREN, KARL ERIK 614
ROSENHOLTZ, SUSAN J. 329
ROSENTHAL, E.R. 456, 458
ROSENTHAL, NAOMI 707
ROSOW, IRVING 251, 252, 255, 264, 280
ROSS, CATHERINE 436, 587, 588, 589
ROSS, EDWARD ALSWORTH 602, 669, 686
ROSS, HEATHER 431
ROSS, LEE 713
ROSS, MICHAEL 330
ROSSI, ALICE S. 42–43, 249, 253, 267, 276, 291, 299, 301, 308, 311–312, 314, 315
ROSSI, ANGELO 637, 648, 655
ROSSI, PETER H. 41, 60, 140, 147, 559, 560
ROSSITER, MARGARET 530
ROSTOW, W.W. 742
ROTBERG, ROBERT I. 96
ROTELLA, ELYCE J. 334

ROTHENBERG, STUART 484
ROTHERMEL, TERRY W. 384
ROTHMAN, DAVID 670, 686, 687, 688
ROTHMAN, ROBERT 333
ROTHMAN, STANLEY 705
ROTHSCHILD, JOSEPH 235
ROTHSCHILD, NANCY 277
ROTHSCHILD-WHITT, JOYCE 381
ROTONDO, E. ANTHONY 313
ROWAN, BRIAN 369, 371, 493
ROWBOTHAM, SHEILA 295
ROWEIS, SHOUKRY T. 638, 639
ROY, DONALD 338
ROYKO, MIKE 408
RUBIN, BARNETT R. 185–186
RUBIN, DONALD B. 159–161, 166, 168, 169, 170
RUBIN, GAYLE 293
RUBIN, LEONARD 518
RUBIN, LILLIAN 299, 309
RUBIN, ZICK 435
RUBINFELD, DANIEL L. 161, 162, 165, 167, 169
RUBINSON, R. 449, 467, 765
RUBINTON, E. 681
RUCHLIN, HIRSCH S. 331
RUDE, GEORGE 724
RUDERMAN, FLORENCE 575, 579
RUDWICK, MARTIN J. 552, 563
RUESCHMEYER, DIETRICH 752, 762, 764, 765
RULE, JAMES 336, 686, 687, 697
RUNDALL, THOMAS G. 581, 585, 587, 589
RUPP, LEILA 728
RUSHTON, J. PHILLIPE 533
RUSSELL, RAYMOND 339
RUTTER, M. 466
RYAN, MARY P. 297
RYDER, NORMAN B. 243, 246, 256, 257, 260, 261, 264
RYFF, CAROL D. 253
RYTINA, STEPHEN 708, 713

S

SABATO, LARRY J. 723
SABEL, CHARLES 176, 182, 205, 208, 209, 210, 211, 212, 379, 765
SACKS, HARVEY 42, 88
SACKS, KAREN 296
SAFILIO-ROTHSCHILD, CONSTANTINA 300
SALAFF, JANET 299
SALAMAN, GRAEME 210, 365
SALANCIK, GERALD R. 344, 368, 376
SAN GIOVANI, LUCINDA 251, 254
SANDAY, PEGGY R. 296
SANDER, LEONARD 158
SANDERS, JIMY 765
SANDLER, BERNICE 301, 304, 307
SANYAL, B.C. 449
SARASON, IRWIN G. 346
SARTON, GEORGE 537
SARTORI, GIOVANNI 411
SASSEN-KOOB, SASKIA 756, 765
SAVIN-WILLIAMS, R.C. 462
SAWERS, LARRY 637, 658

SAWHILL, ISABEL 431
SAWYER, MALCOLM 764
SAYLES, LEONARD 205
SAYRE, CYNTHIA WOOLEVER 708, 713
SAYRE, WALLACE S. 405
SCANZONI, JOHN H. 299, 426
SCHAFER, WOLF 537
SCHAIE, K. WARNER 249, 260
SCHARPF, FRITZ 765
SCHEFF, THOMAS J. 582, 679, 680, 684
SCHEGLOFF, EMANUEL 47–48, 66, 88, 90, 123
SCHERMERHORN, R.A. 224, 230, 238
SCHLAIFER, ROBERT 166, 167
SCHLESIGNER, PHILIP 614
SCHLOSSMAN, S. 687
SCHLUCHTER, WOLFGANG 490
SCHLUMBOHM, JURGEN 182
SCHMAUS, WARREN 559
SCHMID, CALVIN F. 633
SCHMIECHEN, JAMES A. 192
SCHMITTER, PHILIPPE 412, 748, 760, 764
SCHMOOKLET, JACOB 562
SCHNEIDER, BETH E. 306
SCHNEIDER, EDWARD J. 274
SCHNEIDER, WILLIAM 398, 405
SCHNELLE, THOMAS 549
SCHNORE, LEO F. 640, 646, 656
SCHOEN, ROBERT 429, 434
SCHOENHERR, RICHARD A. 335, 367, 373, 374
SCHOOLER, CARMI 249, 251, 339, 342, 343, 344,
    345, 349, 351, 454, 457
SCHOONHOVEN, CLAUDIA BIRD 376
SCHRAM, SANFORD F. 727
SCHRAMM, WILBUR 602
SCHRANK, HARRIS T. 255, 260, 266, 273, 280
SCHREIER, H. 725
SCHRODINGER, ERWIN 66
SCHUDSON, MICHAEL 611, 612, 613, 616, 617, 620
SCHUKER, N.M. 642
SCHULTZ, T.W. 454
SCHUMAN, HOWARD 224
SCHUR, E. 684
SCHURMANN, FRANZ 492, 758
SCHWAB, DONALD P. 330
SCHWAB, KAREN 270, 271, 272, 273, 280
SCHWAGER, SALLY 306
SCHWALBE, MICHAEL L. 348
SCHWARTZ, GARY 477
SCHWARTZ, JOSEPH E. 81
SCHWARTZ, M.S. 681
SCHWARTZ, MICHAEL 384, 697, 700
SCHWARTZ, PEPPER 302, 435
SCHWARTZ, WILLIAM 339
SCHWEBER, SILVAN S. 552
SCHWIRIAN, KENT P. 632, 633
SCIEMNI, G. 655
SCOTT, ALLEN J. 638, 639
SCOTT, HILDA 293
SCOTT, JAMES C. 478, 479, 481, 484, 493, 765
SCOTT, JOAN W. 429
SCOTT, JOHN FINLEY 44
SCOTT, R.A. 680, 681
SCOTT, W. RICHARD 33, 91, 362, 363, 365, 367,
    368, 369, 370, 371, 372, 373, 374, 376, 377, 384

SCRAMBLER, GRAHAM 594
SCULL, ANDREW 18, 687, 688
SCULLY, DIANE 581, 591
SEARLE, JOHN R. 485
SEARS, DAVID O. 228
SEASHORE, STANLEY E. 369
SEAVER, PAUL S. 485
SECCOMBE, WALLY 198
SECORD, PAUL F. 46
SEE, KATHERINE O'SULLIVAN 18, 229, 230, 236,
    237
SEELBACH, WAYNE 440
SEEMAN, MELVIN 340, 588, 708, 713
SEEMAN, TERESA E. 588
SEGALL, ALEXANDER 578
SEIDENFELD, TEDDY 169, 170
SEIDMAN, STEVEN 82, 91
SEIFER, NANCY 299
SELTZER, JUDITH 438
SELVIN, HANNAN C. 364
SELZNICK, PHILIP 362, 364, 371, 696
SEN, AMARTYA 198
SENGHAAS, DIETER 748, 750, 764
SENNETT, RICHARD 488
SEROW, WILLIAM J. 644
SERRA, JOSE 755
SERRIN, WILLIAM 339
SEWELL, WILLIAM 91, 94, 96, 250, 439, 454, 455,
    456, 464
SHAFER, MICHAEL 757, 763
SHAIKEN, HARLEY 210, 211, 212
SHALEV, MICHAEL 270, 763, 764
SHANAS, ETHEL 249, 276, 277, 278
SHAPIN, STEVEN 512, 547, 551, 556, 563
SHAPIRO-PERL, NINA 338
SHARLIN, ALLAN 333
SHARP, KIMBERLY 587, 589
SHARPE, KENNETH 763, 765
SHAW, C. 672
SHAW, DONALD 610, 617
SHAW, JAMES B. 344
SHAW, ROBERT 348
SHEARING, C. 687
SHEATSLEY, PAUL S. 224
SHELDON, ELEANOR BERNERT 314
SHEPARD, LINDA J. 340
SHEPELA, SHARON T. 329
SHEPPARD, HAROLD L. 340
SHERIDAN, A. 686
SHERIF, CAROLYN W. 228
SHERIF, MUZAFER 58, 228
SHERMAN, LAWRENCE W. 166
SHERROD, L.R. 281
SHEVKY, ESHREF 632, 633, 641
SHIBUTANI, TAMOTSO 238
SHILS, EDWARD A. 41, 47, 64, 66, 68, 671
SHOCKEY, JAMES W. 331, 332
SHORT, JAMES F. JR. 677
SHORTER, EDWARD 697, 700, 703
SHOWERS, CAROLINE 348, 349
SHRUM, WESLEY 362
SICA, ALAN 94
SIEFERT, MARSHA 601
SIEGEL, JACOB S. 278, 279

SIEGEL, PAUL 560
SIEGRIST, JOHANNES 588, 594
SIGNORIELLI, NANCY 620
SILLS, DAVID 620
SIMCOCK, B.L. 702
SIMKUS, ALBERT A. 261, 640
SIMMEL, GEORG 25, 27, 31, 33, 37–38, 41, 42, 43, 44, 45, 46, 52, 53, 54, 56, 57, 58, 66, 327, 473, 581
SIMMONS, L. 577
SIMMONS, R. 462
SIMMONS, ROBERTA G. 254, 312, 340
SIMON, GARY A. 529, 561
SIMON, HERBERT 30
SIMON, ROGER 193
SIMONS, HERBERT W. 725
SIMONTON, DEAN K. 544, 545, 561, 563
SIMPSON, RICHARD 333
SINGER, BURTON 267
SINGER, JEROME E. 62
SINGH, JITENDRA 374, 382, 386
SIROWY, LARRY 761
SKINNER, BURRHUS F. 341, 342
SKINNER, JONATHAN 430, 433
SKINNER, QUENTIN 760
SKIPPER, J.K. 680
SKOCPOL, THEDA 82–83, 88, 90, 91, 94, 361, 700, 701, 744, 746, 747, 762, 763, 764
SLATER, PHILIP E. 295
SLAVIN, R.E. 228
SLOCUM, JOHN W. JR. 372
SLOMCZYNSKI, KAZIMIERZ M. 251
SMALL, ALBION W. 449, 453, 458, 602
SMALL, HENRY G. 535, 538, 539, 540
SMART, C. 685
SMELSER, NEIL J. 44, 49–50, 53, 55, 57, 65, 66, 68, 70, 71, 81–82, 94, 110, 121, 236, 260, 266, 270, 295, 297, 328, 425, 696, 697, 713, 762
SMITH, A. WADE 227
SMITH, ADAM 103, 180
SMITH, BRIAN H. 502
SMITH, CONSTANCE 365
SMITH, D. RANDALL 335
SMITH, DALE 763
SMITH, DAVID 765
SMITH, DONALD EUGENE 502
SMITH, DOROTHY E. 90, 292, 612
SMITH, EDWARD J. 249
SMITH, ELIOT R. 228
SMITH, H. 162
SMITH, JAMES P. 437, 441
SMITH, R. 687
SMITH, RALPH E. 291, 300
SMITH, RICHARD A. 644, 645
SMITH, RICHARD L. 84, 90, 95
SMITH-LOVIN, LYNN 305, 365, 379
SMOCK, A.C. 297, 299
SMYER, MICHAEL 431, 439, 440
SNEL, ERIK 701
SNITOW, ANN 621
SNOW, DAVID A. 501, 707, 708, 709, 710, 713, 726, 730
SNOW, ROBERT 621
SNYDER, DAVID 727

SOBEL, MICHAEL 155, 164
SODERBERG, JOHAN 185
SORBOM, DAG 155
SOFRANKO, ANDREW J. 652
SOKOLOFF, NATALIE J. 293
SOLOMON, BARBARA MILLER 297, 306
SOLOMON, SUSAN 519
SOLT, MICHAEL 378, 380
SOMERS, MARGARET 762, 763
SONENSCHER, MICHAEL 182
SORAUF, FRANK J. 502
SORENSEN, AAGE B. 250, 252, 254, 273, 281, 464, 465, 467
SORENSEN, ELAINE 304
SORENSON, ANNEMETTE 262, 310
SOROKIN, PITIRIM A. 243, 267, 279, 280, 452, 453, 454, 455, 458, 466, 541, 688
SOUTH, N. 687
SOUTH, SCOTT J. 429, 431, 432, 644
SPADE, J.Z. 457
SPAIN, DAPHNE 300, 302, 303, 305, 309, 655
SPANIER, GRAHAM B. 250, 277, 278, 429, 430, 433, 434, 435, 436, 440
SPENCE, JANET T. 294, 307, 308, 309, 310, 315, 533
SPENCE, MICHAEL 331
SPENCER, HERBERT 54, 106–108, 109, 127–128, 295, 473
SPENGLER, OSWALD 267
SPENNER, KENNETH I. 210, 335, 336, 340, 345, 351, 456
SPICER, JERRY 440
SPIEGELBERG, H. 86
SPIELGEL-ROSING, INA 558
SPILERMAN, SEYMOUR 251, 270
SPILKA, BERNARD 501
SPINOZA, BERNARD 88
SPIRO, MELFORD 474
SPITZE, GLENNA 306, 309, 431, 432
SPITZER, S. 668, 683, 685, 687
SPREY, JETSE 440
SPROULL, LEE 338
SPUHLER, JAMES 43
SRINIVASAN, MANGALAM 298
STABER, UDO 383
STACEY, JUDITH 293, 315
STAFFORD, REBECCA 435
STAGGENBORG, SUZANNE 719
STAHL, SIDNEY M. 487, 489
STAHURA, JOHN 642, 643
STAINES, GRAHAM L. 273, 302, 338
STALKER, GEORGE M. 336, 367, 375
STALLINGS, BARBARA 765
STAMM, LISA 296
STANBACK, THOMAS 637
STANLEY, JULIAN 163
STANSELL, CHRISTINE 192, 621
STANTON, A. 681
STANTON, FRANK 603
STAPLES, ROBERT 431
STARBUCK, WILLIAM 380
STARK, DAVID 763
STARK, RODNEY 474, 477, 484, 501, 502
STARKE, FREDERICK A. 338

STARR, PAUL 180, 188, 190, 191, 592, 593
STATHAM, ANNE 350
STAW, BARRY M. 375
STEARNS, LINDA BREWSTER 386
STEELE, CHARLOTTE 224
STEEL, L. 253
STEELMAN, LALA CARR 438, 439
STEFFENS, LINCOLN 408
STEINBERG, RONNIE J. 329, 330
STEINER, GILBERT 434
STEINMETZ, SUZANNE 426
STEMBER, C.H. 455
STENNING, P. 687
STENT, GUNTHER 541
STEPAN, ALFRED 748, 750, 751, 760
STEPHAN, G. EDWARD 645, 646
STEPHAN, KAREN H. 646
STEPHEN, PAULA E. 534
STEPHENS, EVELYNE HUBER 753, 757, 758, 763, 764, 765
STEPHENS, JOHN D. 126, 747, 753, 754, 758, 763, 764
STERLING, THEODORE 524
STERN, BERNARD F. 577
STERN, MARC J. 210
STERN, NANCY 533
STERN, ROBERT N. 644
STERNLIEB, GEORGE 637
STETSON, DOROTHY 429
STEVENS, GILLIAN 438
STEVENS, JOHN 18
STEVENS, ROSEMARY 592
STEWART, J.W. 646
STEWART, JOHN A. 518, 534, 552, 561
STEWART, WALTER 522, 525, 560
STEWMAN, SHELBY 195, 213, 339
STIGLER, GEORGE 524, 551, 560
STIGLITZ, JOSEPH E. 331
STINCHCOMBE, ARTHUR L. 31, 57, 69, 70, 80–81, 184, 208, 336, 364, 372, 377, 378, 380, 382, 417, 462, 645, 748
STINGLE, KAREN G. 342
STOCKARD, JEAN 294
STOKES, ANSON PHELPS 502
STOKES, KENNETH E. 482
STOLLER, ELEANOR PALO 440
STONE, KATHERINE 333
STORER, NORMAN 514, 559
STOREY, RONALD 372
STORPER, MICHAEL 633
STOUFFER, SAMUEL A. 260, 455
STRACHEY, RICHARD 113
STRAITS, BRUCE C. 407
STRAUS, MURRAY 276–277
STRAUS, ROBERT 579, 581
STRAUSS, ANNE 654
STRAUSS, ANSELM 90, 243, 245, 253, 254, 338, 582, 586
STRAUSS, GEORGE 339
STREIB, GORDON F. 253, 260 ,279, 439, 440
STRODTBECK, FRED L. 307
STROM, SHARON H. 334
STROUP, HERBERT 502
STRYKER, SHELDON 43, 49, 90, 350

STUPP, BARBARA J. 45
STYLE, CAROLYN BRIGGS 585
SUCHINDRAN, CHIRAYATH M. 434
SUCHMAN, EDWARD A. 45, 577, 582, 586, 588
SUDNOW, D. 668, 677
SULLIVAN, DANIEL 518, 523
SULLIVAN, TERESA 517
SUNKEL, OSWALD 763
SUPPES, PATRICK 158, 169
SUSSER, MERVYN 256, 258, 585, 586, 587
SUSSMAN, GEORGE 428
SUSSMAN, MARVIN 32, 276, 425
SUTHERLAND, E. 668, 672
SUTKER, SARA SMITH 644
SUTTLES, GERALD 637
SUTTMEIER, RICHARD 559
SUTTON, R. JR. 266
SUZMAN, RICHARD 263, 267
SWAMY, P.A.V.B. 158
SWAN, CHARLES E. 495, 723
SWAN, JAMES H. 252
SWANK, DWANE 764
SWANSON, GUY E. 483, 489
SWEDBERG, RICHARD 328
SWEET, JAMES A. 258, 264
SWEET, LEONARD I. 498
SWEETSER, FRANK L. 633
SWEEZY, PAUL 371, 402, 403
SWIDLER, ANN 43, 65, 68, 308, 350, 619, 621
SZELENYI, IVAN 180
SZTOMPKA, PIOTR 92
SZWAJKOWSKI, EUGENE 375

T

TABB, WILLIAM K. 637, 658
TAEUBER, ALMA F. 224, 641, 642
TAEUBER, CYNTHIA M. 272, 278, 279
TAEUBER, KARL E. 224, 258, 264, 641, 642
TAI, HUE-TAM HO 480
TAILHET-WALDORF, S. 646
TAJFEL, HERNI 224, 225
TALVITIE, KATHY GORDON 438
TANNENBAUM, ARNOLD S. 338–339
TANNER, NANCY 312
TAUSIG, MARK 383
TAYLOR, CHARLES 26, 29–30, 62, 63, 86
TAYLOR, DAVID GARTH 224
TAYLOR, FREDERICK W. 327, 362
TAYLOR, HOWARD F. 41
TAYLOR, I. 11
TAYLOR, MARK C. 485
TEACHMAN, JAY 430, 431
TEICHLER, U. 449
TEITELBAUM, MICHAEL S. 281
TERKEL, STUDS 338
TESSNER, P.D. 535
THACKRAY, ARNOLD 535, 563
THERBORN, GORAN 752
THIO, A. 683
THOITS, PEGGY A. 345, 482
THOMAS, DOROTHY S. 544, 545, 562, 563
THOMAS, GEORGE 488, 502

THOMAS, J.A. 460, 464
THOMAS, KAUSAR 439
THOMAS, KEITH 501
THOMAS, ROBERT H. 192–193, 763
THOMAS, WILLIAM I. 138, 243, 265, 281, 669, 671, 672
THOMPSON, DENNIS F. 410
THOMPSON, E.P. 91–92, 96, 415, 416, 607, 620, 686, 687, 747, 762
THOMPSON, JAMES D. 367, 370
THOMPSON, LINDA 433
THOMPSON, SHARON 621
THOMSON, ELIZABETH 439
THORNE, BARRIE 294, 306, 307, 315
THORNTON, ARLAND 309, 429, 430, 431, 432, 436, 439
THRASHER, F. 672
THUROW, LESTER 210, 301
TIAO 163
TICKAMYER, ANN R. 291
TIEFER, LENORE 553
TIENDA, MARTA 643
TIERNEY, CAROL 438
TIERNEY, KATHLEEN J. 696, 705, 717, 729
TIGER, LIONEL 41
TILLICH, PAUL 474
TILLY, CHARLES 18, 91, 182, 365, 697, 700, 703, 712, 719, 730, 746, 748, 762, 763, 764
TILLY, CHRIS 186
TILLY, LOUISE 429, 703, 712, 730, 746, 748
TILLY, RICHARD 703, 712, 730, 746, 748
TIMBERLAKE, MICHAEL 755
TINKER, IRENE 298
TIPTON, STEVEN M. 478, 489
TITTLE, C.R. 685
TOBIN, GARY A. 630, 631
TOCH, HANS 705
TOCQUEVILLE, ALEXIS DE 112, 327, 413, 487, 698, 704
TODARA, MICHAEL P. 654
TOENNIES, FERDINAND 295
TOLBERT, PAMELA S. 371, 381
TOMLIN, BRIAN 765
TOREN, NINA 516, 518
TORGENSON, WARREN F. 152
TORNER, JUDITH 412
TOSI, HENRY 364, 372
TOULMIN, STEPHEN 562
TOURRAINE, ALAIN 15, 92, 106
TOWLER, ROBERT 501
TRACHTENBERG, JOSHUA 501
TREAS, JUDITH 439, 440
TREIMAN, DONALD 88, 199, 304, 329, 329–330, 332, 350, 351
TREVOR-ROPER, H.R. 81
TRIMBERGER, ROSEMARY 447
TRIST, ERIC L. 336, 340, 371
TROCHIM, WILLIAM M.K. 168, 169
TROELTSCH, ERNST 488, 495
TROLL, LILLIAN 439, 440
TROW, MARTIN A. 364, 409, 449
TROYER, RONALD J. 717, 727
TRUMAN, DAVID 403, 412
TUCH, STEVEN 438

TUCHMAN, GAYE 18, 611, 612, 616, 619, 620
TUCKER, C. JACK 652
TUCKER, DAVID J. 380, 382
TUDOR, JEANNETTE F. 585
TULLER, N.R. 435
TUMA, NANCY B. 281, 305, 383, 431
TUNSTALL, JEREMY 614
TURBETT, J. PATRICK 727
TURK, A.T. 685
TURK, HERMAN 384, 727
TURKLE, SHERRY 313
TURNER, ARTHUR N. 340, 341
TURNER, BRYAN S. 487, 488, 501
TURNER, JONATHAN 80, 94
TURNER, RALPH H. 17, 24, 262, 453, 696, 713, 719, 729
TURNER, THOMAS 763
TURNER, VICTOR 91, 482
TURVEY, M.T. 348
TWADDLE, ANDREW C. 578

U

UDRY, J. RICHARD 249, 253, 433, 439
UDY, STANLEY H. JR. 23, 386
UHLENBERG, PETER 260, 262, 264, 267, 314, 432
ULLMAN, EDWARD 631
UNDERHILL, ERNEST 185–186
URRY, JOHN 92
URTON, WILLIAM 429
USEEM, BURT 706, 720, 721
USEEM, MICHAEL 365, 384, 404
UUSITALO, HANNU 764

V

VAILLANT, GEORGE E. 250
VALLIER, IVAN 502
VAN ARSDOL, MAURICE D. JR. 633, 641
VAN BAAREN, TH. P. 481
VAN BERTALANFFY, LUDWIG 30, 56
VAN DE VEN, ANDREW H. 367, 368, 373, 374, 376, 380
VAN DEN BERG, AXEL 86
VAN DEN BERG, ELO 637, 648, 655
VAN DEN BERG, JAN HENDRICH 590
VAN DEN BERGHE, PIERRE 225, 227, 229, 239
VAN DEN DAELE, BOHME 537
VAN DUSEN, ROXANN 314
VAN GENNEP, ARNOLD 254
VAN HARRISON, R. 343, 346
VAN STEENBERGEN, BART 701
VAN VALEY, THOMAS L. 641
VANCE, RUPERT B. 644
VANDERLOO, HANS 701
VANFOSSEN, B.E. 457
VAUGHAN, DIANE 362
VENTIS, W. LARRY 501
VERBA, SIDNEY 112, 408, 410, 413, 414
VERBRUGGE, LOIS M. 249, 262, 583, 584
VERNON, RAYMOND 655
VEROFF, JOSEPH 310

VIJVERBERG, CORNELIUS H.T.   637, 648, 655
VINCE, PAMELA   606
VINCENT, GEORGE C.   602
VINING, DANIEL R. JR.   648
VINOVSKIS, MARIS A.   260, 261
VIVIANO, ANN T.   329
VOELLER, B.   435
VOGEL, LISE   293
VOLL, JOHN OBERT   502
VON ESCHEN, DONALD   707, 708
VON ZUR MUEHLEN, P.   158
VOORHIES, BARBARA   296
VRIJHOF, PIETER HENDRIK   481
VROOM, VICTOR H.   342

W

WAARDENBERG, JACQUES   481
WACHTER, M.   194
WACKER, GRANT   498
WADE, NICHOLAS   520, 523, 525
WADE, ROBERT   763, 765
WAGNER, DAVID G.   79, 94, 307
WAITE, LINDA   430, 431, 432, 433, 436, 437
WAITZKIN, HOWARD   595
WALBY, SYLVIA   94
WALDELL, MARK L.   94
WALDER, ANDREW G.   180, 763
WALDINGER, ROBERT D.   193
WALDINGER, ROGER   756
WALDORF, W.H.   656
WALDRON, INGRID   584
WALKER, HENRY A.   329
WALKER, TIMOTHY   433
WALLACE, ANTHONY F.C.   183
WALLACE, WALTER L.   17, 26, 32, 43, 62, 63, 64,
    65, 66, 67, 79, 80, 94, 449
WALLAIS, ROY   501
WALLER, WILLARD   425, 452, 453, 461
WALLERSTEIN, IMMANUEL   37, 54, 62, 629, 643,
    657, 745, 746, 762, 763
WALLERSTEIN, J.   437
WALLERSTEIN, MICHAEL   764
WALLIS, ROY   480
WALSH, EDWARD J.   706, 708
WALTERS, JAMES   435, 437
WALTERS, LINDA   435, 437
WALTERS, PAMELA B.   309
WALTON, JOHN   407, 629, 643, 657, 765
WALZER, MICHAEL   92, 94
WANNER, RICHARD A.   544, 643, 644
WANOUS, JOHN P.   338
WARBASSE, JAMES   577
WARD, KATHERINE   765
WARD, KATHRYN B.   291, 292, 315
WARD, L.F.   449, 450, 453
WARD, MICHAEL   437, 441
WARDWELL, JOHN W.   651, 652
WARDWELL, WALTER I.   581
WARE, JOHN E. JR.   351
WARING, JOAN   18, 46, 253, 260, 262, 264, 266,
    273, 277, 280, 439, 440
WARLAND, REX H.   708

WARNER, W.L.   454
WARR, MARK   494
WARREN, BILL   762
WARREN, ROLLAND L.   364, 371
WARRINER, CHARLES K.   23
WARTELLA, ELLEN   620
WASSERMAN, STANLEY   385
WATKINS, ALFRED J.   644
WATKINS, J.W.N.   41
WATNICK, MORRIS   741
WATSON, JAMES D.   543
WATSON, WILLIAM   585, 586, 587
WEAVER, CHARLES   436
WEBB, EUGENE   136
WEBER, EUGENE   95–96
WEBER, MAX   24, 25, 26, 27, 28, 31, 33, 35, 38,
    40–41, 43, 45, 47, 51, 52, 53, 56, 59–60, 61, 63,
    64, 65, 66, 67, 68, 70, 71, 81, 83, 86, 93, 103,
    120–121, 122, 196, 205, 275, 327, 362, 371,
    394, 397, 398, 399, 400, 402, 405, 410, 415,
    416, 449, 450, 451, 452, 453, 473, 487, 489,
    490, 492, 494 578, 581, 696, 740, 742, 762
WEBER, MICHAEL P.   193
WEED, JAMES A.   641
WEICK, KARL E.   338, 372
WEIDNER, GERDI   62
WEINBERG, I.   463
WEINBERG, M.   681
WEINBERG, S.K.   681
WEINERT, F.E.   281
WEINGART, PETER   535
WEINRICH, PETER   227
WEINSTEIN, ALEXANDER   522, 559
WEINSTEIN, DEENA   711
WEIR, MARGARET   747, 764
WEIS, J.   677
WEISS, FRED C.   270
WEISS, HOWARD M.   344
WEISS, ROBERT   433
WEITZEL-O'NEILL, P.A.   329
WEITZMAN, LENORE   305, 433
WEITZMAN, MARTIN   207
WELLER, ROBERT H.   644, 645
WELLFORD, C.   684
WELLS, KATHLEEN   267
WELLS, MIRIAM   756
WELLS, RICHARD H.   68
WELTER, BARBARA   298
WEST, CANDACE   591
WEST, S.S.   514, 517, 518
WESTHUES, KENNETH   28–29
WESTLEY, FRANCES   489, 501
WESTOFF, CHARLES F.   257, 434
WESTRUM, RON   559
WEXLER, P.   450
WHEATON, BLAIR   345, 346, 349, 351, 588, 594,
    595
WHEELER, JOHN R.C.   581, 585, 587, 588
WHEELER, STANTON   254
WHELPTON, PASCAL K.   256
WHETTEN, DAVID A.   383, 384
WHICKER, MARICA LYNN   304
WHITE, HARRISON C.   195, 213
WHITE, LYNN   431, 432, 433, 436

WHITE, PAUL E. 383, 384
WHITE, O.K. JR. 499
WHITE, RALPH 651
WHITE, SAM E. 344
WHITE, WINSTON 280
WHITEHEAD, HARRIET 309, 315
WHITEHEAD, LAWRENCE 748, 760
WHITING, JOHN W.M. 313
WHITLEY, RICHARD 539, 540, 541
WHITNEY, D. CHARLES 620
WHYTE, MARTIN KING 296
WHYTE, WILLIAM F. 136, 206, 207, 339
WICKER, ALLAN 706
WICKES, THOMAS H. 200
WIEAND, S. 170
WIENER, NORBERT 57
WILCOX, JEROME E. 641
WILENSKY, HAROLD 489, 764
WILENTZ, SEAN 96
WILEY, NORBERT 59
WILKEN, PAUL I. 229
WILKINSON, R. 463
WILLET, JOHN B. 164, 166
WILLIAMS, BERNARD 94
WILLIAMS, DOROTHY L. 502
WILLIAMS, MARIANNE 632, 652
WILLIAMS, PETER W. 481, 482
WILLIAMS, RAYMOND 606, 607, 616, 617, 619, 620, 621
WILLIAMS, ROBIN W. 226
WILLIAMSON, JEFFREY 185, 186
WILLIAMSON, JOHN B. 270
WILLIAMSON, MARGARET HOLMES 501
WILLIAMSON, OLIVER 194, 204–205, 339, 364, 368, 376
WILLIS, SHERRY L. 249
WILLMOTT, PETER 301
WILPERT, BERNHARD 338, 339, 351
WILSON, BRYAN R. 473, 489, 501
WILSON, E.O. 11
WILSON, FRANKLIN D. 644, 650, 651
WILSON, GRAHAM K. 412
WILSON, JOHN F. 478, 502
WILSON, KENNETH L. 643, 706, 710
WILSON, WILLIAM J. 18, 186, 196, 227, 228, 229, 231, 233, 235, 236, 237–239, 637, 703
WIMBERLEY, DALE W. 501
WINCH, PETER 28–29, 62
WINDAHL, SVEN 620
WINSBOROUGH, HALLIMAN H. 250, 253, 262, 266
WINSHIP, JANICE 621
WIPPLER, REINHARD 67, 90
WIRTH, LOUIS 632, 672, 673
WISE, L.L. 253
WISMAN, J. 668
WISTER, ANDREW 439
WOHL, R. RICHARD 604
WOHLSTEIN, RONALD F. 723
WOLF, ERIC R. 730, 748
WOLF, FRED ALAN 157
WOLFE, ALAN 405
WOLFENSTEIN, MARTHA 605
WOLFF, JANET 617, 620
WOLFSON, MARK 720

WOLINSKY, FREDERIC D. 579, 580, 588
WOLINSKY, SALLY R. 579, 580, 588
WOLPIN, KENNETH I. 331
WOMACK, JOHN JR. 730
WONG, MORRISON G. 186
WOOD, JAMES R. 496, 501, 729, 730
WOOD, MICHAEL 724
WOOD, P. 702
WOOD, STEPHEN 210
WOODROW, KAREN 429, 434
WOODWARD, JOAN 208, 210, 336, 365, 367, 374
WOOLF, PATRICIA K. 523, 524, 559
WOOLGAR, STEVEN 519, 553, 554, 555, 556, 560
WOOLLACOTT, JANET 621
WORRALL, STANLEY 502
WORTMAN, CAMILLE B. 343
WRIGHT, C.R. 455
WRIGHT, CHARLES 602, 605, 613
WRIGHT, ERIC OLIN 88, 188, 252, 396
WRIGHT, GERALD 429
WRIGHT, JAMES D. 139, 140
WRONG, DENNIS H. 11, 350
WUTHNOW, ROBERT 18, 35–36, 65, 91, 362, 474, 475, 477, 479, 486, 488, 489, 492, 496, 498, 499, 500, 501, 502
WYNNE, BRIAN 520, 550

Y

YANKELOVICH, DANIEL 489
YEARLEY, STEVEN 557
YELLEN, JANET 202
YOUNG, CRAWFORD 235, 763, 764
YOUNG, MICHAEL 301
YOUSSEF, NADIA HAGGAG 298, 299, 315
YUCHTMAN, EPHRAIM 369

Z

ZABLOCKI, BENJAMIN 494
ZAJONC, R.B. 346, 439
ZALD, MAYER N. 18, 362, 394, 478, 697, 704, 709, 717, 718, 720, 721, 724, 725
ZALTMAN, GERALD 702
ZARET, DAVID 485, 763
ZBOROWSKI, MARK 579, 582
ZEISEL, HANS 138, 602, 603
ZEITLIN, JONATHAN 176, 182
ZEITLIN, MAURICE 404, 746, 748, 753, 763
ZELDITCH, MORRIS 127, 329, 425, 440
ZELIZER, VIVIANA 91
ZENZEN, MICHAEL 564
ZIHLMAN, ADRIENNE 312
ZILL, NICHOLAS 433, 438
ZIMAN, JOHN 518, 528, 539
ZIMBALIST, ANDREW 336
ZIMMER, BASIL 639
ZIMMER, CATHERINE 378
ZINDER, NORTON 524
ZINNSER, HANS 51
ZIPF, GEORGE 645, 646
ZLOCZOWER, AWRAHAM 635

ZNANIECKI, FLORIAN   138, 243, 265, 672
ZOLA, IRVING K.   579, 582, 586, 594
ZOLBERG, ARISTIDE R.   763
ZORBAUGH, HARVEY W.   672
ZUCKER, LYNNE G.   91, 328, 371, 381
ZUCKERMAN, HARRIET   18, 27, 255, 260, 264, 511,
     518, 521, 529, 530, 531, 533, 534, 535, 536,
     537, 538, 541, 545, 556, 558, 559, 560, 561,
     563, 564
ZUNZ, OLIVIER   202
ZURCHER, LOUIS Λ. JR.   707, 708, 710, 717, 729,
     730
ZYSMAN, JOHN   755

About the Authors

HOWARD E. ALDRICH (Ph.D., University of Michigan) is Professor of Sociology and Chairman of the Curriculum in Industrial Relations at the University of North Carolina at Chapel Hill. His book, *Organizations and Environments*, was one of the first major statements in organizational ecology. His book *Population Perspectives on Organizations* brings together his writings on entrepreneurship, the origins of new organizational forms, a population perspective on business strategy, and the history of American trade associations. With Peter Marsden and Arne Kalleberg, he is investigating the relative merits of five methods of creating a sampling frame for studying organizational populations.

JEFFREY C. ALEXANDER is Professor and Director of Graduate Studies in the Sociology Department at UCLA. He has written the four-volume *Theoretical Logic in Sociology; Twenty Lectures: Sociological Theory Since World War Two; Action and Its Environments: Towards a New Synthesis*; and *Structure and Meaning: Relinking Classical Sociology* (forthcoming); and has edited a number of other works, including *Neofunctionalism* and *Durkheimian Sociology: Cultural Studies*. Past Chair of the Theory Section of the American Sociological Association, he has been the recipient of a Guggenheim Fellowship and a member of the School of Social Science at the Princeton Institute for Advanced Studies.

RICHARD A. BERK (Ph.D., Johns Hopkins University) is Professor of Sociology and a member of the Social Statistics Program at UCLA. He currently serves as Chair of the Methodology Section of the American Sociological Association and is Vice Chair of the board of directors of the Social

Science Research Council. He is on the editorial boards of many social science journals and is a founding editor of *Evaluation Quarterly*. Professor Berk's research interests in applied social research touch on a large number of substantive areas: law, criminology, natural resource conservation, and others. Among his most recent projects is a study of the social consequences of AIDS, three field experiments on police responses to incidents of wife battery, and an evaluation of the impact of the Vietnam draft on subsequent criminal behavior.

CHARLES E. BIDWELL (Ph.D., University of Chicago) is William Claude Reavis Professor of Education and Sociology, Chair of the Department of Sociology, and Director of the Ogburn-Stouffer Center for the Study of Population and Social Organization at the University of Chicago. Author of numerous articles on the sociology of education and the sociology of organizations, his recent publications include *Structuring in Organizations* and *The Organization and Its Ecosystem: A Theory of Structuring in Organizations* (with John D. Kasarda). From 1973 to 1978 he served as Editor of the *American Journal of Sociology*.

WILLIAM C. COCKERHAM (Ph.D., University of California, Berkeley) is Associate Professor of Sociology and College of Medicine in the Department of Psychiatry and Program in Medical Humanities and Social Sciences at the University of Illinois at Urbana-Champaign. He was a senior Fulbright Scholar in West Germany in 1985 and has recently completed a cross-national research project comparing Americans and West Germans with respect to health attitudes, lifestyles, psychological distress, and utilization of medical services. He is author of *Medical*

Sociology and *Sociology of Mental Disorder* and has published numerous articles on medical sociology.

PETER B. EVANS has worked primarily on the development of Third World countries and is the author of *Dependent Development: The Alliance of State, Multinational and Local Capital in Brazil* and coeditor of *Bringing the State Back In*. His current professorial affiliations include the Department of Sociology and Graduate School of International Relations and Pacific Studies at the University of California at San Diego as well as the Department of Sociology and the Latin American Institute at the University of New Mexico. His current research interests include comparing the role of the state in the development of the computer industry in Latin American and East Asian NICs (new industrialized countries).

ANNE FONER (Ph.D., New York University) is Professor and Vice Chair for Graduate Studies in Sociology at Rutgers University. She has served as Chair, Section on Aging of the American Sociology Association and on the editorial boards of the *American Sociological Review*, the *Journal of Gerontology*, and *Journal of Family Issues*. Her publications include *Aging and Society. Volume 1: An Inventory of Research Findings* (with Matilda White Riley) and *Volume 3: A Sociology of Aging Stratification* (with M. W. Riley and Marilyn Johnson); *Aging and Old Age: New Perspectives; Aging and Retirement* (with Karen Schwab); and numerous articles on age and society.

NOAH E. FRIEDKIN (Ph.D., University of Chicago) is Associate Professor of Education and Sociology at the University of California, Santa Barbara. He was a Spencer Fellow of the National Academy of Education from 1980 to 1983. His articles on organizations and social networks have appeared in *Administrative Science Quarterly, American Journal of Sociology*, and *Social Forces*. Currently, he is examining the accuracy and applications of a formal theory on how networks of interpersonal power and influence enter into the formation of opinions and agreements.

W. PARKER FRISBIE (Ph.D., University of North Carolina—Chapel Hill) is Professor in the Department of Sociology and Research Associate in the Population Research Center at the University of Texas—Austin. His research interests are in the areas of ecology, household and family demography, and the demography of racial and ethnic groups. His publications include numerous journal articles and book chapters, 16 of which deal with issues in human and urban ecology. He is author of *Sustenance Organization and Migration in Nonmetropolitan America* (with Dudley L. Poston, Jr.) and coeditor (with Frank D. Bean) of *The Demography of Racial and Ethnic Groups*.

JANET Z. GIELE (Ph.D., Harvard University) is Associate Professor and Codirector of the Program on Families and Children at the Heller Graduate School of Social Welfare, Brandeis University. With a 1987 award from the Rockefeller Foundation for Research on Gender Roles, she continues her research on the changing life patterns of women in a sample of alumnae from three colleges and in the National Longitudinal Surveys. Her books include *Women and the Future, Women: Roles and Status in Eight Countries*, and *Women in the Middle Years*. Her research interests also concern aging and social movements, and she is currently at work on a comparison of the nineteenth century women's suffrage and temperance movements.

MARK GRANOVETTER (Ph.D., Harvard University) is Professor of Sociology, State University of New York at Stony Brook. In 1986-1987 he was Distinguished Visiting Professor of Research at the Graduate School of Business, Stanford University. He is author of *Getting a Job: A Study of Contacts and Careers* (Harvard University Press, 1974) and received the Theory Section Prize of the American Sociological Association in 1985 for his article "Economic action and social structure: The problem of embeddedness." He is currently at work on a book tentatively titled *Society and Economy: The Social Construction of Economic Institutions*.

JOAN HUBER taught at the University of Notre Dame and at the University of Illinois at Urbana-Champaign after receiving a Ph.D. from Michigan State University in 1967. She is currently Dean of the College of Social and Behavioral Sciences at the Ohio State University and President-Elect of the American Sociological Association. Her major research interest is in gender stratification, work, and family.

JOHN D. KASARDA is Kenan Professor and Chairman of the Department of Sociology at the University of North Carolina—Chapel Hill. He is coauthor of *Contemporary Urban Ecology, The Metropolis Era*, and numerous scholarly articles on the spatial redistribution of people and jobs.

PETER V. MARSDEN is Professor of Sociology at Harvard University. He is interested in social network analysis, organization studies, and stratification. At present he is working on a comparison of organizational sampling frames, with Howard Aldrich and Arne Kalleberg, and on methods for the collection and analysis of survey network data.

DOUG McADAM is currently an Associate Professor of Sociology at the University of Arizona. He is the author of two books specifically concerned with the historical dynamics of collective action: *Political Process and the Development of Black Insurgency, 1930-1970* (University of Chicago Press, 1982) and *Yours in Freedom: The Societal and Personal Impact of the 1964 Mississippi Summer Project* (Oxford University Press, 1988). He was the recipient of a 1985 Guggenheim Fellowship in support of the research on which this latter book is based. In addition to these books, McAdam has published articles on social movements and political sociology in numerous scholarly journals including the *American Sociological Review* and the *American Journal of Sociology*.

JOHN D. McCARTHY (Ph.D., University of Oregon) is Professor and Chair, Department of Sociology, and member of the Center for the Study of Youth Development at the Catholic University of America. He has written widely on social movements and is coeditor (with Mayer N. Zald) of two volumes, *The Dynamics of Social Movements in an Organizational Society* and *Social Movements in an Organizational Society*. He currently heads the Project on the Citizens' Movement Against Drunk Driving, has just completed an extensive assessment of local community organizing projects funded by the Campaign for Human Development, and continues (with Doug McAdam) to research the political mobilization of modern professional groups.

JOANNE MILLER (Ph.D., University of Wisconsin—Madison) is Associate Professor of Sociology at the City University of New York, Queens College and the Graduate School. She is Director of the M.A. Program in Applied Social Science Research and serves as Associate Director of the Graduate Center for Social Research. She is former Program Director for Sociology at the National Science Foundation and was a Research Sociologist in the Laboratory of Socioenvironmental Studies at the National Institute of Mental Health. Her research focuses on the social stratification of the workplace and its effects on workers. Relevant publications appear in the *American Journal of Sociology*, *American Sociological Review*, *Work and Occupations*, and *Social Psychology Quarterly*. She is currently investigating authority relationships in bureaucratic organizations and is a principal investigator of the CUNY, New York City Study on labor in the postindustrial age.

ANTHONY M. ORUM is Professor of Sociology and Head of the Department of Sociology at the University of Illinois—Chicago. A lifelong student of politics, he has written articles on the politics of black Americans, the origins of the civil rights movement in America, and city politics, among others. He is author of *Introduction to Political Sociology*, which currently is going into its third edition and has just recently been translated into Chinese, as well as the Arnold and Caroline Rose Monograph, *Black Students in Protest*. His most recent book is *Power, Money, and the People: The Making of Modern Austin*, a history of Austin, Texas, and it is intended to be the first of a projected series of books on the politics of expanding and declining cities.

MATILDA WHITE RILEY is Associate Director for Behavioral and Social Research (National Institutes of Health), and Emeritus Professor of Sociology at Rutgers University and Bowdoin College. She is a member of the American Academy of Arts and Sciences and the Institute of Medicine (National Academy of Sciences). She has received an honorary LHD from Rutgers and the Commonwealth Award in Sociology. Her publications include *Sociological Research* (3 volumes), *Aging and Society* (3 volumes), *Aging from Birth to Death* (2 volumes), *Sociological Studies in Scale Analysis*, and numerous articles on mass communications, socialization, intergenerational relationships, research methods, and other topics.

PETER H. ROSSI (Ph.D., Columbia, 1951) is currently Stuart A. Rice Professor of Sociology at the University of Massachusetts. He is the author of numerous articles, monographs, and textbooks. Recent publications include *The Handbook of Survey Research*, *Evaluation: A Systematic Approach*, and *Money, Work and Crime*. He has taught at Harvard, Chicago, and Johns Hopkins and has served as Director of NORC and the Social and Demographic Research Institute. He is Past President of the American Sociological Association.

ANDREW T. SCULL is Professor and Chairman of the Department of Sociology at the University of California, San Diego. He is author of *Museums of Madness: The Social Organization of Insanity in Nineteenth Century England* and of *Decarceration: Community Treatment* and the Deviant, a Radical View, and has edited or coedited Madhouses, Mad-Doctors, and Madmen; Social Control and the State; Durkheim and the Law; and Research in Law, Deviance, and Social Control, Vols. 6-9. His articles have appeared in leading journals in sociology, history, psychiatry, and law. In 1976-1977 he held a fellowship from the American Council of Learned Societies at the University of London. He was a fellow of the Shelby Cullom Davis Center for Historical Studies at Princeton University during 1978-1979, and a Guggenheim Fellow in 1981-1982.

KATHERINE O'SULLIVAN SEE (Ph.D., University of Chicago) is Associate Professor at James Madison College, Michigan State University. She is the author of several articles on comparative race and ethnic relations and First World Nationalisms: Class and Ethnic Politics in Northern Ireland and Quebec (Chicago: University of Chicago Press). A former Rockefeller Fellow in Human Rights at Columbia University and Past Executive Secretary of the Research Committee on Ethnic, Race and Minority Relations of the International Sociological Association, her current research focuses on racial conflicts and policies in Britain and the United States.

NEIL J. SMELSER is University Professor of Sociology at the University of California, Berkeley. He is the author of numerous books and articles, including Economy and Society, Social Change in the Industrial Revolution, Theory of Collective Behavior, Comparative Methods in the Official Sciences, and The Changing Academic Market. He has served as Editor of the American Sociological Review and as Vice President of the American Sociological Association. He is a Fellow of the American Academy of Arts and Sciences and a member of the American Philosophical Society.

GLENNA SPITZE (Ph.D., University of Illinois) is Associate Professor of Sociology and Women's Studies at the State University of New York at Albany. She coauthored (with Joan Huber) Sex Stratification: Children, Housework, and Jobs (1983) and coedited (with Christine Bose) Ingredients for Women's Employment Policy (1987). She has served on the editorial boards of Gender and Society, Journal of Marriage and the Family, and Social Science Quarterly, and was Book Review Editor of Work and Occupations. She has published a number of articles on women's employment-family linkages and on divorce, and is currently conducting research on adult intergenerational relations.

JOHN D. STEPHENS (Ph.D., Yale University) is Associate Professor of Political Science and Sociology at Northwestern University. He is the author of The Transition from Capitalism to Socialism (University of Illinois Press) and coauthor with Evelyne Huber Stephens of Democratic Socialism in Jamaica: The Political Movement and Social Transformation in Dependent Capitalism (Princeton University Press). With Dietrich Rueschemeyer and Evelyne Stephens, he is currently working on theoretical and comparative historical study of the emergence and breakdown of democracy tentatively titled Economic Development and Democracy, to be published by Polity Press.

CHARLES TILLY is Distinguished Professor of Sociology and History and Director of the Center for Studies of Social Change at the New School for Social Research. His work centers on conflict, collective action, the development and dynamics of capitalism, the formation and transformation of national states, and the social organization of demographic processes. His most recent books are Big Structures, Large Processes, Huge Comparisons and The Contentious French.

GAYE TUCHMAN (Ph.D., Brandeis University) is Professor of Sociology at Queens College and the Graduate School and University Center of City University of New York. Her books include Edging Women Out: Victorian Novelists, Publishers, and Social Change, Making News: A Study in the Construction of Reality, and Hearth and Home: Images of Women in the Mass Media. Tuchman has served as Vice President of both the Eastern Sociological Society and Sociologists for Women in Society, as well as a member of the Council of the American Sociological Association.

WALTER L. WALLACE (Ph.D., University of Chicago) is Professor of Sociology at Princeton University. Author of Student Culture: Social Structure and Continuity in a Liberal Arts College, The Logic of Science in Sociology, and Principles of Scientific Sociology, coauthor of Black Elected Officials, and author-editor of Sociological Theory: An Introduction, he has taught at Spelman College, Atlanta University, Northwestern University, and Columbia University. He has been a visiting scholar at the Russell Sage Foundation, and a fellow of the Center for Advanced Study in the Behavioral Sciences. He has served on the staff of the Russell Sage Foundation, the Council of the American Sociological Association, the Executive Committee of the Assembly of Behavioral and Social Sciences of the National Research Council, the Editorial Board of *Social Forces*, and the Social Sciences Advisory Committee of *World Book*.

JOAN WARING is Director, Corporate Research, of the Equitable Assurance Society of the United States. A member of the age stratification study group at Rutgers University, where she did her graduate work, she has been the author or coauthor of several articles in the area of aging. She has been Program Development Officer for the Program on Age and Aging at the Russell Sage Foundation, and she has taught at Rutgers University and Fairleigh Dickinson University —Madison. Current research interests are work organizations and white-collar workers.

WILLIAM J. WILSON (Ph.D., Washington State University) is the Lucy Flower Distinguished Service Professor of Sociology at the University of Chicago. He was a Fellow (1981-1982) at the Center for the Advanced Study in the Behavioral Sciences at Stanford University. He was named a MacArthur Prize Fellow in June 1987. His publications include *Power, Racism, and Privilege: Race Relations in Theoretical and Sociohistorical Perspectives; Through Different Eyes: Black and White Perspectives on American Race Relations* (with Peter I. Rose and Stanley Rothman); *The Declining Significance of Race: Blacks and Changing American Institutions*; and *The Truly Disadvantaged: The Inner City, the Underclass, and Public Policy*. Wilson is currently directing a larger research project on poverty, joblessness, and family structure in the inner city.

ROBERT J. WUTHNOW is Professor of Sociology at Princeton University. He is the author of numerous books and articles on sociology of religion, cultural sociology, and sociological theory. His most recent books are *Meaning and Moral Order: Explorations in Cultural Analysis* (University of California, 1987), and the *Restructuring of American Religion: Society and Faith Since World War II* (Princeton University Press, 1988). He is currently writing a book about the articulation of ideology and social structure based on comparisons of the Protestant Reformation, the Enlightenment, and the rise of Marxist socialism.

MAYER N. ZALD is Professor of Sociology and Social Work at the University of Michigan. He has published widely on complex organizations, social welfare, and political sociology. Recently (with John D. McCarthy) he edited *Social Movements in an Organizational Society: Collected Essays* (Transaction Books). Aside from essays on social movements, he is currently engaged in studies of the intersection of organizational theory and history. In 1986-1987 he was Vice President of the American Sociological Association.

HARRIET ZUCKERMAN (Ph.D., Columbia University) is Professor of Sociology at Columbia University and chaired the department there from 1978-1982. The author of *Scientific Elite: Nobel Laureates in the United States* and coeditor of *Toward a Metric of Science and Science Indicators: Implications for Research and Policy*, she is now working on two studies. One compares the research careers of American men and women scientists and the other examines forms of discontinuity in the development of scientific knowledge. She has served on the boards of directors of the American Association for the Advancement of Science and the Social Science Research Council, on the council of the American Sociological Association, and is now a Trustee of the Center for Advanced Study in the Behavioral Sciences. She is also a Fellow of the American Academy of Arts and Sciences.